DIGITAL DESIGN

Principles and Practices

DIGITAL DESIGN
Principles and Practices

Fourth Edition

John F. Wakerly

Cisco Systems, Inc.
Stanford University

Upper Saddle River, New Jersey 07458

Wakerly, John F.
    Digital design: principles and practices/ John F. Wakerly.--4th ed.
    p. cm.
    Includes index
    ISBN 0-13-186389-4
    1. Digital integrated circuits--Design and construction. I. Title
TK7874.65,W34 2005
621.39'5-dc22

                                    2005048710

Vice President and Editorial Director, ECS: *Marcia Horton*
Editorial Assistant: *Richard Virginia*
Executive Managing Editor: *Vince O'Brien*
Managing Editor: *David A. George*
Production Editor: *Scott Disanno*
Director of Creative Services: *Paul Belfanti*
Art Director: *Kenny Beck*
Cover Designer: *Bruce Kenselaar*
Art Editor: *Xiaohong Zhu*
Manufacturing Manager: *Alexis Heydt-Long*
Manufacturing Buyer: *Lisa McDowell*
Senior Marketing Manager: *Holly Stark*
About the Cover: Original cover artwork © 2001 Ken Bakeman, www.kennyzen.com

© 2006, 2000, 1994, 1990 by Pearson Education, Inc.
Pearson Prentice Hall
Pearson Education Inc.
Upper Saddle River, NJ 07458

ISBN 0-13-186389-4

10 9 8 7 6

Pearson Education Ltd., London
Pearson Education Australia Pty., Ltd., Sydney
Pearson Education Singapore, Pte. Ltd.
Pearson Education North Asia Ltd., Hong Kong
Pearson Education Canada, Inc., Toronto
Pearson Educación de Mexico, S.A. de C.V.
Pearson Education—Japan, Tokyo
Pearson Education Malaysia, Pte. Ltd.
Pearson Education, Inc., Upper Saddle River, New Jersey

To Joanne

CONTENTS

PREFACE

This book is for everyone who wants to design and build real digital circuits. It is based on the idea that, in order to do this, you have to grasp the fundamentals, but at the same time you need to understand how things work in the real world. Hence, the "principles and practices" theme.

The practice of digital design has undergone a major transformation during the past 30 years, a direct result of the stunning increases in integrated-circuit speed and density over the same time period. In the past, when digital designers were building systems with thousands or at most tens of thousands of gates and flip-flops, academic courses emphasized minimization and efficient use of chip and board-level resources.

Today, a single chip can contain tens of millions of transistors and can be programmed to create a system-on-a-chip that, using the technology of the past, would have required hundreds of discrete chips containing millions of individual gates and flip-flops. Successful product development nowadays is limited more by the design team's ability to correctly and completely specify the product's detailed functions, than by the team's ability to cram all the needed circuits into a single board or chip. Thus, a modern academic program must necessarily emphasize design methodologies and software tools, including hardware description languages (HDLs), that allow very large, hierarchical designs to be accomplished by teams of designers.

On one hand, with HDLs, we see the level of abstraction for typical designs moving higher, above the level of individual gates and flip-flops. But at the same time, the increased speed and density of digital circuits at both the chip and board level is forcing many digital designers to be more competent at a lower, electrical circuit level.

The most employable and ultimately successful digital designers are skilled, or at least conversant, at both levels of abstraction. This book gives you the opportunity to learn the basics at the high level (HDLs), at the low level (electrical circuits), and throughout the "vast middle" (gates, flip-flops, and somewhat higher-level digital-design building blocks).

Target Audience

introductory courses

electronics concepts

DDPPonline

The material in this book is appropriate for introductory courses on digital logic design in electrical or computer engineering or computer science curricula. Computer science students who are unfamiliar with basic electronics concepts or who just aren't interested in the electrical behavior of digital devices may wish to skip Chapter 3; the rest of the book is written to be independent of this material as much as possible. On the other hand, *anyone* with a basic electronics background who wants to get up to speed on digital electronics can do so by reading Chapter 3. In addition, students with *no* electronics background can get the basics by reading a 20-page electronics tutorial, Section Elec at DDPPonline (DDPPonline is my shorthand for this book's web-based supplemental material; more about this later).

optional sections

Although this book's level is introductory, it contains much more material than can be taught in a typical introductory course. Once I started writing, I found that I had many important things to say that wouldn't fit into a one-quarter course at Stanford or in a 400-page book. Therefore, I have followed my usual practice of including *everything* that I think is at least moderately important, and leaving it up to the instructor or reader to decide what is most important in a particular environment. To help these decisions along, though, I've marked the headings of *optional sections* with an asterisk. In general, these sections can be skipped without any loss of continuity in the non-optional sections that follow. Even more optional material can be found at DDPPonline.

advanced courses
laboratory courses
fun stuff

Undoubtedly, some people will use this book in advanced courses and in laboratory courses. Advanced students will want to skip the basics and get right into the fun stuff. Once you know the basics, the most important and fun stuff in this book is in the sections on hardware description languages ABEL, VHDL, and Verilog, where you'll discover that your programming courses actually helped prepare you to design hardware.

working digital designers

Another use of this book is as a self-study reference for a working digital designer, who may be one of either of two kinds:

Novice If you're just getting started as a working digital designer, and you took a very "theoretical" logic design course in school, you should concentrate on Chapter 3, one of the HDLs in Chapter 5 and Sections 7.11–7.13, and Chapters 6, 8, and 9 to get prepared for the real world.

Old pro If you're experienced, you may not need all of the "practices" material in this book, but the principles in Chapters 2, 4, and 7 can help you organize your thinking, and the discussions there of what's important and what's not might relieve the guilt you feel for not having used a Karnaugh map in 10 years. The examples in Chapters 6 and 8 should give you additional insights into and appreciation for a variety of design methods. Finally, the ABEL, VHDL, and Verilog language descriptions and examples sprinkled throughout Chapters 5 through 8 may serve as your first organized introduction to HDL-based design.

All readers should make good use of the comprehensive index and of the *marginal notes* throughout the text that call attention to definitions and impor-   *marginal notes*
tant topics. Maybe the highlighted topics in *this* section were more marginal than   *marginal pun*
important, but I just wanted to show off my text formatting system.

A FEW WORDS TO REVIEWERS AND OTHERS

Over the years, several computer-science students and others have written reviews complaining about various aspects of what was covered and how it was presented in previous editions of this book. As for the presentation, I can only apologize for my own inability to do a better job. But as for the choice of topics, and what I emphasize as important, this is *exactly* the material that I would expect a potential digital-design employee to know. Since I've hired a lot of them, you really shouldn't complain, unless you're reading this book for some reason other than getting or keeping a job.

I'm not deprecating CS students or Computer Science. I love CS and I have a lot of CS education and experience myself—I can analyze algorithms, understand the inner workings of compilers and operating systems, and write code in LISP and a couple dozen other languages along with the best of them. But the most common complaint I hear from digital-design managers today is about new grads who know how to sling code in Verilog or VHDL but have no idea of what produces a good hardware result—or even what metrics define "good"!

Digital design is not just about writing HDL code—at least, not yet. One chip-design manager tells me that the first question he asks to a job applicant who claims to know how to do HDL-based hardware design is, "How many flip-flops are in a 16-bit counter?" This isn't even a trick question, but you'd be surprised at how many applicants can't answer it!

So, if you are using this book merely to satisfy a requirement for a CS or other degree, then I apologize in advance if you should find the book to be complex, confusing, too formal, too dry, or full of jargon, or if you think that the included software is a Frisbee. All are real comments about the previous edition made by CS and other non-EE/CE reviewers!

On the other hand, if you think you may someday be working as a digital designer at any level from circuits to systems, then please do your best to learn all of the non-optional topics in this book, including either Verilog or VHDL. It shouldn't be that difficult, since the many reviewers who liked the previous edition called it precise, logical, crystal clear, easy to understand, deep but very straightforward, practical, complete, very good, very nice, enjoyable, rockin', humorous, and, I agree, a little silly or corny at times (like now, maybe). And oh, by the way, even one CS reviewer said, "I love this book."

NOT AS LONG AS IT SEEMS
A few reviewers complained about the length of the previous edition of this book. The present, printed edition is a little shorter, but when you include the material at DDPPonline, it's actually a bit longer. (That's right, the page count of the previous edition could be written in 10 bits, but the page count of this edition plus the material at DDPPonline requires 11 bits.) But please keep in mind:

- You don't have to read everything. The headings of sections and subsections that are optional for most readers are marked with an asterisk.

- You don't have to study all of the HDLs. The HDL sections are written to be independent of each other, and non-HDL sections and subsections are written to be independent of the HDL sections. So you can ignore any or all of the HDLs. But I still recommend that you learn either Verilog or VHDL.

- I asked the publisher to print this book in a larger font (11 point) than is typical for technical texts (10 point). This is easier on your eyes and mine, and it also allowed me to put in more figures and tables while still keeping most of them on the same facing pages as the referring text. (I do the page layout myself and pay a lot of attention to this.)

- Stuff written in these "boxed comments" (a.k.a. sidebars) is usually optional too.

Chapter Descriptions

What follows is a list of short descriptions of this book's nine chapters. This may remind you of the section in typical software guides, "For People Who Hate Reading Manuals." If you read this list, then maybe you don't have to read the rest of the book.

- Chapter 1 gives a few basic definitions and lays down the ground rules for what we think is and is not important in this book.

- Chapter 2 is an introduction to binary number systems and codes. Readers who are already familiar with binary number systems from a software course should still read Sections 2.10–2.13 to get an idea of how binary codes are used by hardware. Advanced students can get a nice introduction to error-detecting codes by reading Sections 2.14 and 2.15. The material in Section 2.16.1 should be read by everyone; it is used in a lot of modern systems.

- Chapter 3 describes digital circuit operation, placing primary emphasis on the external electrical characteristics of logic devices. The starting point is a basic electronics background including voltage, current, and Ohm's law; readers unfamiliar with these concepts may wish to consult Section Elec at DDPPonline. This chapter may be omitted by readers who aren't interested in how to make real circuits work, or who have the luxury of having someone else to do the dirty work.

- Chapter 4 teaches combinational logic design principles, including switching algebra and combinational-circuit analysis, synthesis, and minimization.

- Chapter 5 gives a general introduction to HDL-based design, and then has tutorials on three HDLs—ABEL, VHDL, and Verilog. You need learn only one of these languages, typically the one used in a digital-design lab that you may work in.

- Chapter 6 begins with a discussion of digital-system documentation standards, probably the most important practice for aspiring designers to start practicing. Next, this chapter introduces programmable logic devices (PLDs), focusing on their capability to realize combinational logic functions. The rest of the chapter describes commonly used combinational logic functions and applications. For each function, it describes standard MSI building blocks, ABEL programs for PLD realizations, and VHDL- and Verilog-based designs.

- Chapter 7 teaches sequential logic design principles, starting with latches and flip-flops. The main emphasis in this chapter is on the analysis and design of clocked synchronous state machines. However, for the brave and daring, the chapter includes an introduction to fundamental-mode circuits and the analysis and design of feedback sequential circuits. The chapter ends with sections on ABEL, VHDL, and Verilog features and coding styles for sequential-circuit design.

- Chapter 8 is all about the practical design of synchronous sequential circuits. This chapter focuses on commonly used functions and gives examples using MSI building blocks, ABEL and PLDs, and VHDL and Verilog. Sections 8.8 and 8.9 discuss the inevitable impediments to the ideal of fully synchronous design and address the important problem of how to live synchronously in an asynchronous world.

- Chapter 9 is an introduction to memory devices, CPLDs, and FPGAs. Memory coverage includes read-only memory and static and dynamic read/write memories from the points of view of both internal circuitry and functional behavior. The last two sections introduce CPLD and FPGA architecture.

Most of the chapters contain references, drill problems, and exercises. Drill problems are typically short-answer or turn-the-crank questions that can be answered directly based on the text material, while exercises typically require a little more thinking. The drill problems in Chapter 3 are particularly extensive and are designed to allow non-EE types to ease into this material.

Quite a lot of additional material, including just about everything that has been deleted since the third edition of this book, is available at DDPPonline. We'll have more to say about that shortly.

Digital-Design Software Tools

Two leading suppliers have kindly allowed us to package their digital-design software tools on CD-ROMs in the domestic and some international printings of this book.

Xilinx, Inc. (www.xilinx.com) has provided the student edition of their ISE (Integrated Software Environment), version 6.3 or later. This tool suite includes an ABEL compiler, VHDL and Verilog language processors, a schematic drawing package, and a fitter to target HDL-based designs to Xilinx CPLDs and FPGAs. This package does not include a simulator, however.

Additional tools have been provided by Aldec, Inc. (www.aldec.com) in the student edition of their popular Active-HDL™ tool suite, version 6.3 or later. This package includes VHDL and Verilog language processors and a simulator and waveform viewer that allows you to test your HDL-based designs.

These tools were very useful to me as an author. Using them, I was able to write and test all of the example programs in the text. I trust that the tools will be even more useful to the students who use the text. They will allow you to write and test your own hardware designs and download them into Xilinx CPLDs and FPGAs in a digital lab environment.

Though not included with this book, Lattice Semiconductor's ispLEVER tool suite is another nice set of tools that is used at some universities. It includes basic tools for targeting ABEL-based designs to simple PLDs, as well as VHDL, Verilog, and simulator support as in the combination of the Xilinx and Aldec packages.

Even if you're not ready to do your own original designs, you can use the included Xilinx and Aldec tools to try out and modify any of the examples in the text, since the source code for all of them is available at the book's web site, discussed next.

www.ddpp.com, OneKey, and DDPPonline

Abundant support materials for this book are available on the web. These include free materials, such as selected exercise solutions and the latest errata, and protected materials, such as supplemental sections and additional exercises and solutions. The free materials are accessible by everyone, at *www.ddpp.com*, this book's traditional web site.

www.ddpp.com

OneKey

The protected materials are accessible to registered users using *OneKey*, Prentice Hall's exclusive new online resource for instructors and students, at www.prenhall.com/OneKey. A unique OneKey access code is included with each new copy of *Digital Design Principles and Practices*. For students who buy used books, access codes are also available for purchase separately. To obtain and use your access code, please follow the instructions that are shrink-wrapped with your new text or included in your separate OneKey purchase.

Throughout this book, we use *DDPPonline* as an alias for the publisher's OneKey site, which you access at `www.prenhall.com/OneKey`. You must use your access code to register at this site, and then log in each time you use the site. If the URL `www.prenhall.com/OneKey` is too difficult for you to remember, you can also access OneKey via a prominent link at `www.ddpp.com` or its alias `www.DDPPonline.com`.

Among other things, DDPPonline contains the following resources for students:

- Over 300 pages of additional supplemental material and design examples, organized as over two dozen sections of a few to 30 pages each. Some of these sections contain additional exercises.

- Additional exercise solutions, if your instructor also subscribes to OneKey. He or she can choose which additional solutions to make available to you. Please be aware that I haven't written a solution for every problem, so don't blame your instructor if he or she is unable to publish some solutions.

- Source files for all of the example C, ABEL, VHDL, and Verilog programs in the printed book and in the supplemental sections.

At the time of this book's publication in autumn 2005, the DDPPonline site included the following supplemental sections (names and topics):

ABEL   Miscellaneous ABEL topics.

BiPLD   Bipolar PLDs.

BJT   Bipolar junction transistors.

CAD   Computer-aided design tools.

Cntr   Counter design topics.

Dec   Decoder design topics.

DFT   Design for testability.

Diode   Diodes and diode logic.

ECL   Emitter-coupled logic.

Elec   Electrical circuits review, by Bruce M. Fleischer.

Enc   Encoder design topics.

IEEE   IEEE standard symbols.

JKSM   Analysis and synthesis of state machines using J-K flip-flops.

Min   Additional topics in combinational minimization.

Mux   Multiplexer design topics.

Pin   SSI, MSI, PLD, and ROM/RAM pinouts.

Pmin   Programmed combinational-minimization topics.

Rel   Reliability estimation.

<u>Sreg</u>	Shift-register design topics.
<u>TTL</u>	Additional topics on TTL logic.
<u>XCabl</u>	Examples of combinational logic design using ABEL.
<u>XCbb</u>	Examples of combinational logic design using MSI blocks.
<u>XCver</u>	Examples of combinational logic design using Verilog.
<u>XCvhd</u>	Examples of combinational logic design using VHDL.
<u>XPLD</u>	X-series PLDs.
<u>XSabl</u>	Examples of sequential logic design using ABEL.
<u>XSbb</u>	Examples of sequential logic design using MSI blocks.
<u>XSver</u>	Examples of sequential logic design using Verilog.
<u>XSvhd</u>	Examples of sequential logic design using VHDL.
<u>Zo</u>	Transmission lines and reflections.

Throughout this book, we refer to the above material using the underlined, color section name, sometimes adding a subsection number (e.g., <u>Dec.1</u>).

For Instructors

The <u>DDPPonline</u> web site has additional materials for instructors only; these materials are accessible by registered instructors through the OneKey system. To register or to learn more about OneKey, visit `www.prenhall.com/OneKey` or contact your Prentice Hall representative.

The instructors' site includes files with all of the figures and tables in the book. You can use these files to make presentation slides directly, or you can insert selected materials into your own customized presentations.

The site also contains answers to selected exercises—more than half of the exercises in the book, equivalent to over 200 printed pages. Using the OneKey course management system, you can choose a subset of these solutions and make them visible to your OneKey-registered students. Note that some solutions (basically, all of the third-edition *student* solutions) are available to students at `www.ddpp.com`, whether or not you make them visible on OneKey. The site tells you which ones these are, and also contains a cross-reference from third-edition to fourth-edition exercises.

Other resources for instructors include the Xilinx University Program (`www.xilinx.com/univ`) and Aldec's Educational Program (`www.aldec.com/education/university`). The Xilinx site offers a variety of product materials, course materials, and discounts on chips and boards that you can use in digital-design lab courses. Aldec's site offers both Aldec's own software packages and third-party compatible tools and prototyping systems.

www.prenhall.com/
wakerlyinfo

The publisher's marketing information about this book and many accompanying resources, as well as the latest ordering information, can be found at *www.prenhall.com/wakerlyinfo*.

Errors

Warning: This book may contain errors. The author and the publisher assume no liability for any damage—incidental, brain, or otherwise—caused by errors.

There, that should make the lawyers happy. Now, to make *you* happy, let me assure you that a great deal of care has gone into the preparation of this book to make it as error free as possible. I am anxious to learn of the remaining errors so that they may be fixed in future printings, editions, and spin-offs. Therefore I will pay $5 via PayPal to the first finder of each undiscovered error—technical, typographical, or otherwise—in the printed book. Reports of errors in the web-based materials are also appreciated, but I don't pay for those. Please email your comments to me by using the appropriate link at `www.ddpp.com`.

An up-to-date list of discovered errors can always be obtained using the appropriate link at `www.ddpp.com`. It will be a very short file transfer, I hope.

Acknowledgements

Many people helped make this book possible. Most of them helped with the first three editions and are acknowledged there. Preparation of the fourth edition has been a very lonely task, but it was made easier by my friends Prem Jain and Mike Volpi at Cisco Systems. They and the company made it possible for me to cut back my commitment at Cisco to less than half time for the ten months that it took to prepare this revised edition.

For the ideas on the "principles" side of this book, I still owe great thanks to my teacher, research advisor, and friend Ed McCluskey. On the "practices" side, Dave Raaum, one of the leading members of my "Digital Designers Hall of Fame," reviewed the new Verilog material and provided many suggestions.

Since the third edition was published, I have received many helpful comments from readers. In addition to suggesting or otherwise motivating many improvements, readers have spotted dozens of typographical and technical errors whose fixes are incorporated in this fourth edition.

My sponsoring editor at Prentice Hall, Tom Robbins, deserves thanks for shepherding this project over the past years. He's the third or fourth editor who has changed jobs after (almost) completing one of my book projects, leading me to wonder whether working with me inevitably leads to burnout or success or both (and if so, then in which order?). Special thanks go to Tom's boss, Marcia Horton, who took over after his departure. If you're reading this, then she did a terrific job of pulling this one out of the fire!

Copy editor and proofreader Jennie Kaufman did a marvelous job of ensuring consistency and catching typos, including several that had been overlooked by me and everyone else since the second or third edition. Production editor Scott Disanno also deserves credit for providing a very smooth interface with the production side of the house and for inspiring me with his very quick response times during the final "crunch" stage of the project.

Thanks go to artist Ken Bakeman, whose work I discovered a couple of years ago while doing a Google search for "wakerly." His original all-electronic "painting" appears on the back cover, and the front cover is adapted from it. The circular pattern that appears in both, as well as in the chapter openings, is based on a crop circle that sources say was discovered in June 2001 near Wakerly Woods in Barrowden, Northamptonshire, England. Now, "Wakerly Woods" appears to be a misspelling of "Wakerley Woods," but I'm not complaining. I used to live on Waverley Street and people always got the spellings confused. Anyway, Ken agreed to provide his art for this edition's cover, and I think it's very striking and appropriate.

At this point in a preface, I usually thank my wife Kate for putting up with me during the arduous months of book writing or revision. I am very sad to say that after living through seven book projects and almost 34 years of marriage, Kate passed away in early 2004 after a long battle with breast cancer. So you see, when I said that preparation of this edition has been a very lonely task, I wasn't exaggerating. Still, for me, for our children, and for all of our family, friends, and community, Kate will always be in our hearts.

Sigh. As they say, life goes on. Closing thanks go to my old and new friend, fellow author and, by the time this is published, fiancée Joanne Jacobs, for her loving support and encouragement during the final preparation of this edition.

John F. Wakerly
Oakbrook Terrace, Illinois

DIGITAL DESIGN
Principles and Practices

chapter 1

Introduction

Welcome to the world of digital design. Perhaps you're a computer science student who knows all about computer software and programming, but you're still trying to figure out how all that fancy hardware could possibly work. Or perhaps you're an electrical engineering student who already knows something about analog electronics and circuit design, but you wouldn't know a bit if it bit you. No matter. Starting from a fairly basic level, this book will show you how to design digital circuits and subsystems.

We'll give you the basic principles that you need to figure things out, and we'll give you lots of examples. Along with principles, we'll try to convey the flavor of real-world digital design by discussing current, practical considerations whenever possible. And I, the author, will often refer to myself as "we" in the hope that you'll be drawn in and feel that we're walking through the learning process together.

1.1 About Digital Design

Some people call it "logic design." That's OK, but ultimately the goal of design is to build systems. To that end, we'll cover a whole lot more in this text than logic equations and theorems.

This book claims to be about principles and practices. Most of the principles that we present will continue to be important years from now;

some may be applied in ways that have not even been discovered yet. As for practices, they may be a little different from what's presented here by the time you start working in the field, and they will certainly continue to change throughout your career. So you should treat the "practices" material in this book as a way to reinforce principles, and as a way to learn design methods by example.

One of the book's goals is to present enough about basic principles for you to know what's happening when you use software tools to "turn the crank" for you. The same basic principles can help you get to the root of problems when the tools happen to get in your way.

Listed in the box on this page are several key points that you should learn through your studies with this text. Most of these items probably make no sense to you right now, but you should come back and review them later.

Digital design is engineering, and engineering means "problem solving." My experience is that only 5%–10% of digital design is "the fun stuff"—the creative part of design, the flash of insight, the invention of a new approach. Much of the rest is just "turning the crank." To be sure, turning the crank is much easier now than it was 25 or even 10 years ago, but you still can't spend 100% or even 50% of your time on the fun stuff.

IMPORTANT THEMES IN DIGITAL DESIGN

- Good tools do not guarantee good design, but they help a lot by taking the pain out of doing things right.
- Digital circuits have analog characteristics.
- Know when to worry and when not to worry about the analog aspects of digital design.
- Always document your designs to make them understandable to yourself and to others.
- Use consistent coding, organizational, and documentation styles in your HDL-based designs, following your company's guidelines.
- Understand and use standard functional building blocks.
- State-machine design is like programming; approach it that way.
- Design for minimum cost at the system level, including your own engineering effort as part of the cost.
- Design for testability and manufacturability.
- Use programmable logic to simplify designs, reduce cost, and accommodate last-minute modifications.
- Avoid asynchronous design. Practice synchronous design until a better methodology comes along (if ever).
- Pinpoint the unavoidable asynchronous interfaces between different subsystems and the outside world, and provide reliable synchronizers.

Besides the fun stuff and turning the crank, there are many other areas in which a successful digital designer must be competent, including the following:

- *Debugging.* It's next to impossible to be a good designer without being a good troubleshooter. Successful debugging takes planning, a systematic approach, patience, and logic: if you can't discover where a problem *is*, find out where it *is not*!

- *Business requirements and practices.* A digital designer's work is affected by a lot of nonengineering factors, including documentation standards, component availability, feature definitions, target specifications, task scheduling, office politics, and going to lunch with vendors.

- *Risk-taking.* When you begin a design project you must carefully balance risks against potential rewards and consequences, in areas ranging from component selection (will it be available when I'm ready to build the first prototype?) to schedule commitments (will I still have a job if I'm late?).

- *Communication.* Eventually, you'll hand off your successful designs to other engineers, other departments, and customers. Without good communication skills, you'll never complete this step successfully. Keep in mind that communication includes not just transmitting but also receiving; learn to be a good listener!

In the rest of this chapter, and throughout the text, I'll continue to state some opinions about what's important and what is not. I think I'm entitled to do so as a moderately successful practitioner of digital design.

Additional materials related to this book, such as supplemental chapter sections, selected exercise solutions, and downloadable source code for all programs, can be found at DDPPonline (via www.ddpp.com; see the Preface).

1.2 Analog versus Digital

Analog devices and systems process time-varying signals that can take on any value across a continuous range of voltage, current, or other metric. So do *digital* circuits and systems; the difference is that we can pretend that they don't! A digital signal is modeled as taking on, at any time, only one of two discrete values, which we call *0* and *1* (or LOW and HIGH, FALSE and TRUE, negated and asserted, Frank and Teri, or whatever).

analog
digital

0
1

Digital computers have been around since the 1940s and have been in widespread commercial use since the 1960s. Yet only in the past 10 to 20 years has the "digital revolution" spread to many other aspects of life. Examples of once-analog systems that have now "gone digital" include the following:

- *Still pictures.* Ten years ago, the majority of cameras still used silver-halide film to record images. Today, inexpensive digital cameras record a picture as a 1024×768 or larger array of pixels, where each pixel stores the intensities of its red, green, and blue color components as 8 or more bits each. This data, over 18 million bits in this example, is processed and compressed in JPEG format down to as few as 5% of the original number of bits. So, digital cameras rely on both digital storage and digital processing.

- *Video recordings*. A digital versatile disc (DVD) stores video in a highly compressed digital format called MPEG-2. This standard encodes a small fraction of the individual video frames in a compressed format similar to JPEG, and encodes each other frame as the difference between it and the previous one. The capacity of a single-layer, single-sided DVD is about 35 billion bits, sufficient for about 2 hours of high-quality video, and a two-layer, double-sided disc has four times that capacity.

- *Audio recordings*. Once made exclusively by impressing analog wave-forms onto vinyl or magnetic tape, audio recordings now commonly use digital compact discs (CDs). A CD stores music as a sequence of 16-bit numbers corresponding to samples of the original analog waveform, one sample per stereo channel every 22.7 microseconds. A full-length CD recording (73 minutes) contains over 6 billion bits of information.

- *Automobile carburetors*. Once controlled strictly by mechanical linkages (including clever "analog" mechanical devices that sensed temperature, pressure, etc.), automobile engines are now controlled by embedded microprocessors. Various electronic and electromechanical sensors convert engine conditions into numbers that the microprocessor can examine to determine how to control the flow of fuel and oxygen to the engine. The microprocessor's output is a time-varying sequence of numbers that operate electromechanical actuators which, in turn, control the engine.

- *The telephone system*. It started out over a hundred years ago with analog microphones and receivers connected to the ends of a pair of copper wires (or was it string?). Even today, most homes still use analog telephones, which transmit analog signals to the phone company's central office (CO). However, in the majority of COs, these analog signals are converted into a digital format before they are routed to their destinations, be they in the same CO or across the world. For many years the private branch exchanges (PBXs) used by businesses have carried the digital format all the way to the desktop. Now many businesses, COs, and traditional telephony service providers are converting to integrated systems that combine digital voice with data traffic over a single IP (Internet Protocol) network.

- *Traffic lights*. Stop lights used to be controlled by electromechanical timers that would give the green light to each direction for a predetermined amount of time. Later, relays were used in controllers that could activate the lights according to the pattern of traffic detected by sensors embedded in the pavement. Today's controllers use microprocessors and can control the lights in ways that maximize vehicle throughput or, in Sunnyvale, California, frustrate drivers with all kinds of perverse behavior.

- *Movie effects.* Special effects used to be created exclusively with miniature clay models, stop action, trick photography, and numerous overlays of film on a frame-by-frame basis. Today, spaceships, bugs, otherworldly scenes, and even babies from hell (in Pixar's animated short *Tin Toy*) are synthesized entirely using digital computers. Might the stunt man or woman someday no longer be needed, either?

The electronics revolution has been going on for quite some time now, and the "solid-state" revolution began with analog devices and applications like transistors and transistor radios. So why has there now been a *digital* revolution? There are in fact many reasons to favor digital circuits over analog ones:

- *Reproducibility of results.* Given the same set of inputs (in both value and time sequence), a properly designed digital circuit always produces exactly the same results. The outputs of an analog circuit vary with temperature, power-supply voltage, component aging, and other factors.

- *Ease of design.* Digital design, often called "logic design," is logical. No special math skills are needed, and the behavior of small logic circuits can be visualized mentally without any special insights about the operation of capacitors, transistors, or other devices that require calculus to model.

- *Flexibility and functionality.* Once a problem has been reduced to digital form, it can be solved using a set of logical steps in space and time. For example, you can design a digital circuit that scrambles your recorded voice so that it is absolutely indecipherable by anyone who does not have your "key" (password), but it can be heard virtually undistorted by anyone who does. Try doing that with an analog circuit.

- *Programmability.* You're probably already quite familiar with digital computers and the ease with which you can design, write, and debug programs for them. Well, guess what? Much of digital design is carried out today by writing programs, too, in *hardware description languages (HDLs)*. These languages allow both structure and function of a digital circuit to be specified or *modeled*. Besides a compiler, a typical HDL also comes with simulation and synthesis programs. These software tools are used to test the hardware model's behavior before any real hardware is built, and then to synthesize the model into a circuit in a particular component technology.

  hardware description language (HDL)

  hardware model

- *Speed.* Today's digital devices are very fast. Individual transistors in the fastest integrated circuits can switch in less than 10 picoseconds, and a complete, complex device built from these transistors can examine its inputs and produce an output in less than a nanosecond. This means that such a device can produce a billion or more results per second.

SHORT TIMES   A *millisecond (ms)* is 10^{-3} second, and a *microsecond (µs)* is 10^{-6} second. A *nanosecond (ns)* is just 10^{-9} second, and a *picosecond (ps)* is 10^{-12} second. In a vacuum, light travels about a foot in a nanosecond, and an inch in 85 picoseconds. With individual transistors in the fastest integrated circuits now switching in less than 10 picoseconds, the speed-of-light delay between these transistors across a half-inch-square silicon chip has become a limiting factor in circuit design.

- *Economy.* Digital circuits can provide a lot of functionality in a small space. Circuits that are used repetitively can be "integrated" into a single "chip" and mass-produced at very low cost, making possible throw-away items like calculators, digital watches, and singing birthday cards. (You may ask, "Is this such a good thing?" Never mind!)

- *Steadily advancing technology.* When you design a digital system, you almost always know that there will be a faster, cheaper, or otherwise better technology for it in a few years. Clever designers can accommodate these expected advances during the initial design of a system, to forestall system obsolescence and to add value for customers. For example, desktop computers often have "expansion sockets" to accommodate faster processors or larger memories than are available at the time of the computer's introduction.

So, that's enough of a sales pitch on digital design. The rest of this chapter will give you a bit more technical background to prepare you for the rest of the book.

1.3 Digital Devices

gate

The most basic digital devices are called *gates*, and no, they were not named after the founder of a large software company. Gates originally got their name from their function of allowing or retarding ("gating") the flow of digital information. In general, a gate has one or more inputs and produces an output that is a function of the current input value(s). While the inputs and outputs may be analog conditions such as voltage, current, even hydraulic pressure, they are modeled as taking on just two discrete values, 0 and 1.

AND gate

Figure 1-1 shows symbols for the three most important kinds of gates. A 2-input *AND gate*, shown in (a), produces a 1 output if both of its inputs are 1; otherwise it produces a 0 output. The figure shows the same gate four times, with the four possible combinations of inputs that may be applied to it and the resulting outputs. A gate is called a *combinational circuit* because its output depends only on the current combination of input values (called an *input combination*).

combinational circuit
input combination
OR gate

A 2-input *OR gate*, shown in (b), produces a 1 output if one or both of its inputs are 1; it produces a 0 output only if both inputs are 0. Once again, there are four possible input combinations, resulting in the outputs shown in the figure.

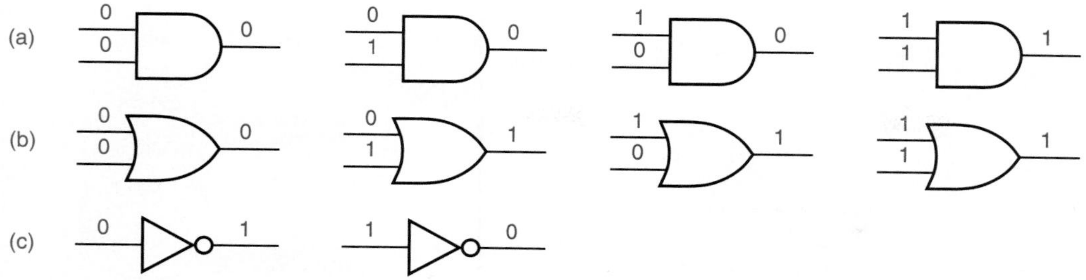

Figure 1-1 Digital devices: (a) AND gate; (b) OR gate; (c) NOT gate or inverter.

A *NOT gate*, more commonly called an *inverter*, produces an output value   *NOT gate*
that is the opposite of the input value, as shown in (c).   *inverter*

We called these three gates the most important for good reason. Any digital
function can be realized using just these three kinds of gates. In Chapter 3 we'll
show how gates are realized using transistor circuits. You should know, however,
that gates have been built or proposed using other technologies, such as relays,
vacuum tubes, hydraulic devices, and molecular structures.

A *flip-flop* is a device that stores either a 0 or 1. The *state* of a flip-flop is   *flip-flop*
the value that it currently stores. The stored value can be changed only at certain   *state*
times determined by a "clock" input, and the new value may further depend on
the flip-flop's current state and its "control" inputs. A flip-flop can be built from
a collection of gates hooked up in a clever way, as we'll show in Section 7.2.

A digital circuit that contains flip-flops is called a *sequential circuit*,   *sequential circuit*
because its output at any time depends not only on its current input but also on
the past sequence of inputs that have been applied to it. In other words, a sequential circuit has *memory* of past events.   *memory*

1.4 Electronic Aspects of Digital Design

Digital circuits are not exactly a binary version of alphabet soup—with all due
respect to Figure 1-1, they don't have little 0s and 1s floating around in them. As
we'll see in Chapter 3, digital circuits deal with analog voltages and currents and
are built with analog components. The "digital abstraction" allows analog
behavior to be ignored in most cases, so circuits can be modeled as if they really
did process 0s and 1s.

One important aspect of the digital abstraction is to associate a *range* of
analog values with each logic value (0 or 1). As shown in Figure 1-2 on the next
page, a typical gate is not guaranteed to have a precise voltage level for a logic 0
output. Rather, it may produce a voltage somewhere in a range that is a *subset* of
the range guaranteed to be recognized as a 0 by other gate inputs. The difference
between the range boundaries is called *noise margin*—in a real circuit, a gate's   *noise margin*
output can be corrupted by this much noise and still be correctly interpreted at
the inputs of other gates.

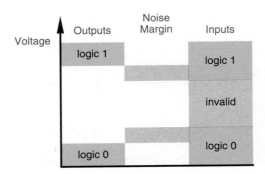

Figure 1-2
Logic values and
noise margins.

Behavior for logic 1 outputs is similar. Note in the figure that there is an "invalid" region between the input ranges for logic 0 and logic 1. Although any given digital device operating at a particular voltage and temperature will have a fairly well defined boundary (or threshold) between the two ranges, different devices may have different boundaries. Still, all properly operating devices have their boundary *somewhere* in the "invalid" range. Therefore, any signal that is within the defined ranges for 0 and 1 will be interpreted identically by different devices. This characteristic is essential for reproducibility of results.

It is the job of an *electronic* circuit designer to ensure that logic gates produce and recognize logic signals that are within the appropriate ranges. This is an analog circuit-design problem; we touch upon some of its aspects in Chapter 3. It's not possible to design a circuit that has the desired behavior under every possible condition of power-supply voltage, temperature, loading, and other factors. Instead, the electronic circuit designer or device manufacturer provides *specifications* (also known as *specs*) that define the conditions under which correct behavior is guaranteed.

specifications (specs)

As a *digital* designer, then, you need not delve into the detailed analog behavior of a digital device to ensure its correct operation. Rather, you need only study enough about the device's operating environment to determine that it is operating within its published specifications. Granted, some analog knowledge is needed to perform this study, but not nearly what you'd need to design a digital device starting from scratch. In Chapter 3 we'll give you just what you need.

1.5 Software Aspects of Digital Design

Digital design need not involve any software tools. For example, Figure 1-3 shows the primary tool of the "old school" of digital design—a plastic template for drawing logic symbols in schematic diagrams by hand (the designer's name was engraved into the plastic with a soldering iron).

Today, however, software tools are an essential part of digital design. Indeed, the availability and practicality of hardware description languages (HDLs) and accompanying circuit simulation and synthesis tools have changed

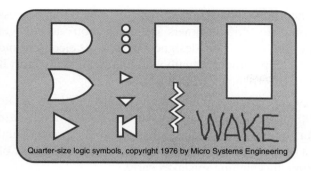

Quarter-size logic symbols, copyright 1976 by Micro Systems Engineering

Figure 1-3
A logic-design
template.

the entire landscape of digital design over the past several years. We'll make extensive use of HDLs throughout this book.

In *computer-aided design* (also called *computer-aided engineering*, *CAE*), various software tools improve the designer's productivity and help to improve the correctness and quality of designs. In a competitive world, the use of software tools is mandatory to obtain high-quality results on aggressive schedules. Important examples of software tools for digital design are listed below:

computer-aided design (CAD)

computer-aided engineering (CAE)

- *Schematic entry.* This is the digital designer's equivalent of a word processor. It allows schematic diagrams to be drawn "on-line," instead of with paper and pencil. The more advanced schematic-entry programs also check for common, easy-to-spot errors, such as shorted outputs, signals that don't go anywhere, and so on. Such programs are discussed in greater detail in Section CAD.2 at DDPPonline.

- *HDLs.* Hardware description languages, originally developed for circuit modeling, are now being used extensively for hardware *design.* They can be used to design anything from individual function modules to large, multichip digital systems. We'll introduce three commonly used HDLs, ABEL, VHDL, and Verilog, in Chapter 5, and we'll provide examples in later chapters. (Don't worry, you needn't learn all three languages!)

- *HDL text editors, compilers, and synthesizers.* A typical HDL software package has many components. The designer uses a text editor to write an HDL "program," and an HDL compiler checks it for syntax and related errors. The designer then can give the program to a synthesizer that creates a corresponding circuit realization that is targeted to a particular hardware technology. Most often, though, before synthesis, the designer runs the HDL program on a "simulator" to verify the behavior of the design.

- *Simulators.* The design cycle for a customized, single-chip digital integrated circuit is long and expensive. Once the first chip is built, it's very difficult, often impossible, to debug it by probing internal connections (they are really tiny), or to change the gates and interconnections. Usually, changes must be made in the original design database and a new chip must be manufactured to incorporate the required changes. Since this process can take months to complete, chip designers are highly motivated to "get it right" on the first try. Simulators help designers predict the electrical and functional behavior of a chip without actually building it, allowing most if not all bugs to be found before the chip is fabricated.

- Simulators are also used in the overall design of systems that incorporate many individual components. They are somewhat less critical in this case because it's easier for the designer to make changes in components and interconnections on a printed-circuit board. However, even a little bit of simulation can save time by catching mistakes early.

- *Test benches.* HDL-based digital designs are simulated and tested in software environments called "test benches." The idea is to build a set of programs around the HDL programs to automatically exercise them, checking both their functional and timing behavior. This is especially handy when small design changes are made—the test bench can be run to ensure that bug fixes or "improvements" in one area do not break something else. Test-bench programs may be written in the same HDL as the design itself, in C or C++, or in a combination of languages including scripting languages like Perl.

- *Timing analyzers and verifiers.* The time dimension is very important in digital design. All digital circuits take time to produce a new output value in response to an input change, and much of a designer's effort is spent ensuring that such output changes occur quickly enough (or, in some cases, not too quickly). Specialized programs can automate the tedious task of drawing timing diagrams and specifying and verifying the timing relationships between different signals in a complex system.

- *Word processors.* HDL-specific text editors are useful for writing source code, but word processors supporting fancy fonts and pretty graphics also have an important use in every design—to create documentation!

In addition to using the tools above, designers may sometimes write specialized programs in high-level languages like C or C++, or scripts in languages like Perl, to solve particular design problems. For example, Section 9.1.6 gives a couple of examples of C programs that generate the "truth tables" for complex combinational logic functions.

Although CAD tools are important, they don't make or break a digital designer. To take an analogy from another field, you couldn't consider yourself to be a great writer just because you're a fast typist or very handy with a word processor. During your study of digital design, be sure to learn and use all the tools that are available to you, such as schematic-entry programs, simulators, and HDL compilers. But remember that learning to use tools is no guarantee that you'll be able to produce good results. Please pay attention to what you're producing with them!

**PROGRAMMABLE
LOGIC DEVICES
VERSUS
SIMULATION**

Later in this book you'll learn how programmable logic devices (PLDs) and field-programmable gate arrays (FPGAs) allow you to design a circuit or subsystem by writing a sort of program. PLDs and FPGAs are now available with up to tens of millions of gates, and the capabilities of these technologies are ever increasing. If a PLD- or FPGA-based design doesn't work the first time, you can often fix it by changing the program and physically reprogramming the device, without changing any components or interconnections at the system level. The ease of prototyping and modifying PLD- and FPGA-based systems can eliminate the need for simulation in board-level design; simulation is required only for chip-level designs.

The most widely held view in industry trends says that as chip technology advances, more and more design will be done at the chip level, rather than the board level. Therefore, the ability to perform complete and accurate simulation will become increasingly important to the typical digital designer.

However, another view is possible. The past decade has seen the emergence of programmable devices that include not only gates and flip-flops as building blocks, but also higher-level functions such as microprocessors, memories, and input/output controllers. Using these devices, the digital designer is relieved of the need to design the most complex and critical on-chip components and interconnections—they have already been designed and tested by the device manufacturer.

In this view, it is still possible to misapply high-level programmable functions, but it is also possible to fix mistakes simply by changing a program; detailed simulation of a design before simply "trying it out" could be a waste of time. Another, compatible view is that the PLD or FPGA is merely a full-speed simulator for the program, and this full-speed simulator is what gets shipped in the product!

Does this extreme view have any validity? To guess the answer, ask yourself the following question. How many software programmers do you know who debug a new program by "simulating" its operation rather than just trying it out?

In any case, modern digital systems are much too complex for a designer to have any chance of testing every possible input condition, with or without simulation. As with software, correct operation of digital systems is best accomplished through practices that ensure that the systems are "correct by design." It is a goal of this text to encourage such practices.

1.6 Integrated Circuits

A collection of one or more gates fabricated on a single silicon chip is called an *integrated circuit (IC)*. Large ICs with tens of millions of transistors may be half an inch or more on a side, while small ICs may be less than one-tenth of an inch on a side.

integrated circuit (IC)

Regardless of its size, an IC is initially part of a much larger, circular *wafer*, up to ten inches in diameter, containing dozens to hundreds of replicas of the same IC. All of the IC chips on the wafer are fabricated at the same time, like pizzas that are eventually sold by the slice, except in this case, each piece (IC

wafer

die
pad

chip) is called a *die*. Each die has *pads* around its periphery—electrical contact points that are much larger than other chip features, so wires can be connected later. After the wafer is fabricated, the dice are tested in place on the wafer using tiny, probing pins that temporarily contact the pads, and defective dice are marked. Then the wafer is sliced up to produce the individual dice, and the marked ones are discarded. (Compare with the pizza-maker who sells all the pieces, even the ones without enough pepperoni!) Each "good" die is mounted in a package, its pads are wired to the package pins, the packaged IC is subjected to a final test, and it is shipped to a customer.

Some people use the term "IC" to refer to a silicon die. Some use "chip" to refer to the same thing. Still others use "IC" or "chip" to refer to the combination of a silicon die and its package. Digital designers tend to use the two terms interchangeably, and they really don't care what they're talking about. They don't require a precise definition, since they're only looking at the functional and electrical behavior of these things. In the balance of this text, we'll use the term *IC* to refer to a packaged die.

IC

In the early days of integrated circuits, ICs were classified by size—small, medium, or large—according to how many gates they contained. The simplest type of commercially available ICs are still called *small-scale integration (SSI)* and contain the equivalent of 1 to 20 gates. SSI ICs typically contain a handful of gates or flip-flops, the basic building blocks of digital design.

small-scale integration (SSI)

The SSI ICs that you might encounter in an educational lab come in a 14-pin *dual inline-pin (DIP)* package. As shown in Figure 1-4(a), the spacing between pins in a column is 0.1 inch and the spacing between columns is 0.3 inch. Larger DIP packages accommodate functions with more pins, as shown in (b) and (c). A *pin diagram* shows the assignment of device signals to package pins, or *pinout*. Figure 1-5 shows the pin diagrams for a few common SSI ICs. Such diagrams are used only for mechanical reference, when a designer needs to determine the pin numbers for a particular IC. In the schematic diagram for a digital circuit, pin diagrams are not used. Instead, the various gates are grouped functionally, as we'll show in Section 6.1.

dual inline-pin (DIP) package

pin diagram
pinout

NOT A DICEY DECISION   A reader of a previous edition wrote to me to collect a $5 reward for pointing out my "glaring" misuse of "dice" as the plural of "die." According to the dictionary, she said, the plural form of "die" is "dice" *only* when describing those little cubes with dots on each side; otherwise it's "dies," and she produced the references to prove it.

Being stubborn, I recently did some searching using Google. It reported 259 web pages with the term "integrated-circuit dice" and only 113 with "integrated-circuit dies." None of the 259 pages appeared to be about a game-of-chance-on-a-chip, while at least one of the 113 was actually talking about chip failures. ("Sometimes it happens that an integrated circuit dies, and its soul transforms into a ghost that haunts the device.") So, I'm sticking with "dice"!

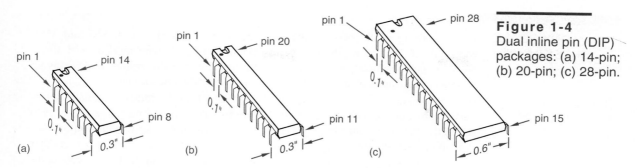

Figure 1-4
Dual inline pin (DIP)
packages: (a) 14-pin;
(b) 20-pin; (c) 28-pin.

Although SSI ICs are still sometimes used as "glue" to tie together larger-scale elements in complex systems, they have been largely supplanted by programmable logic devices (PLDs), which we'll study in Sections 6.3 and 8.3.

The next larger commercially available ICs are called *medium-scale integration (MSI)* and contain the equivalent of about 20 to 200 gates. An MSI IC typically contains a functional building block, such as a decoder, register, or counter. In Chapters 6 and 8 we'll place a strong emphasis on these building blocks. Even though the use of discrete MSI ICs has declined, the equivalent building blocks are used extensively in the design of larger ICs.

Large-scale integration (LSI) ICs are bigger still, containing the equivalent of 200 to 1,000,000 gates or more. LSI parts include small memories, microprocessors, programmable logic devices, and customized devices.

The dividing line between LSI and *very large-scale integration (VLSI)* is fuzzy and tends to be stated in terms of transistor count rather than gate count. Any IC with over a few million transistors is definitely VLSI, and that includes

medium-scale integration (MSI)

large-scale integration (LSI)

very large-scale integration (VLSI)

Figure 1-5 Pin diagrams for a few 7400-series SSI ICs.

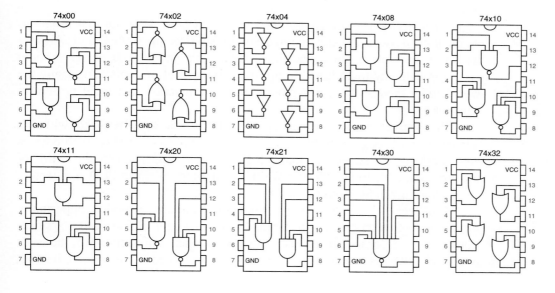

TINY-SCALE INTEGRATION In the coming years, perhaps the most popular remaining use of SSI and MSI, especially in DIP packages, will be in educational labs. These devices will afford students the opportunity to "get their hands dirty" by "breadboarding" and wiring up simple circuits in the same way that their professors did decades ago.

However, much to my surprise, a segment of the IC industry actually introduced parts that went *down*scale from SSI during the past ten years. The idea was to sell individual logic gates in very small packages. These devices handle simple functions that are sometimes needed to match larger-scale components to a particular design, or in some cases they are used to work around bugs in the larger-scale components or their interfaces.

An example of such an IC was Motorola's 74VHC1G08. This chip was a single 2-input AND gate housed in a 5-pin package (power, ground, two inputs, and one output). The entire package, including pins, measured only 0.08 inches on a side and was only 0.04 inches high! Now that's what I would call "tiny-scale integration"!

most microprocessors and memories nowadays, as well as larger programmable logic devices and customized devices. In 2005, VLSI ICs with over 100 million transistors were available.

1.7 Programmable Logic Devices

There are a wide variety of ICs that can have their logic function "programmed" into them after they are manufactured. Most of these devices use technology that also allows the function to be *re*programmed, which means that if you find a bug in your design, you may be able to fix it without physically replacing or rewiring the device. In this book, we give a lot of attention to the design methods for such devices.

programmable logic array (PLA)

Historically, *programmable logic arrays (PLAs)* were the first programmable logic devices. PLAs contained a two-level structure of AND and OR gates with user-programmable connections. Using this structure, a designer could accommodate any logic function up to a certain level of complexity using the well-known theory of logic synthesis and minimization that we'll present in Chapter 4.

programmable array logic (PAL) device
programmable logic device (PLD)

PLA structure was enhanced and PLA costs were reduced with the introduction of *programmable array logic (PAL) devices*. Today, such devices are generically called programmable logic devices (PLDs) and are the "MSI" of the programmable logic industry. We'll have a lot to say about PLD architecture and technology in Sections 6.3 and 8.3.

The ever-increasing capacity of integrated circuits created an opportunity for IC manufacturers to design larger PLDs for larger digital-design applications. However, for technical reasons that we'll discuss in Section 9.5, the basic two-level AND-OR structure of PLDs could not be scaled to larger sizes. Instead,

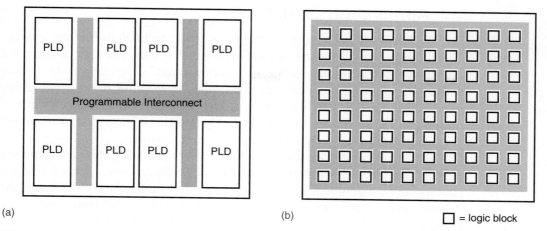

Figure 1-6 Large programmable-logic-device scaling approaches: (a) CPLD; (b) FPGA.

IC manufacturers devised *complex PLD (CPLD)* architectures to achieve the required scale. A typical CPLD is merely a collection of multiple PLDs and an interconnection structure, all on the same chip. In addition to the individual PLDs, the on-chip interconnection structure is also programmable, providing a rich variety of design possibilities. CPLDs can be scaled to larger sizes by increasing the number of individual PLDs and the richness of the interconnection structure on the CPLD chip.

complex PLD (CPLD)

At about the same time that CPLDs were being invented, other IC manufacturers took a different approach to scaling the size of programmable logic chips. Compared to a CPLD, a field-programmable gate array (FPGA) contains a much larger number of smaller individual logic blocks and provides a large, distributed interconnection structure that dominates the entire chip. Figure 1-6 illustrates the difference between the two chip-design approaches.

field-programmable gate array (FPGA)

Proponents of one approach or the other used to get into "religious" arguments over which way was better, but several leading manufacturers of large programmable logic devices acknowledge that there is a place for both approaches, and they manufacture both types of devices. What's more important than chip architecture is that both approaches support a style of design in which products can be moved from design concept to prototype and production in a very short time.

Also important in achieving short "time to market" for all kinds of PLD-based products is the use of HDLs in their design. HDLs like ABEL, Verilog, and VHDL, and their accompanying software tools, enable a design to be compiled, synthesized, and downloaded into a PLD, CPLD, or FPGA in minutes. Highly structured, hierarchical languages like VHDL and Verilog are especially powerful in helping designers to utilize the millions of gates provided in the largest CPLDs and FPGAs.

1.8 Application-Specific ICs

Perhaps the most interesting development in IC technology for the average digital designer is not the ever-increasing number of transistors per chip, but the ever-increasing opportunity to "design your own chip." Chips designed for a particular, limited product or application are called *semicustom ICs* or *application-specific ICs (ASICs)*. ASICs generally reduce the total component and manufacturing cost of a product by reducing chip count, physical size, and power consumption, and they often provide higher performance.

semicustom IC
application-specific IC (ASIC)

The *nonrecurring engineering (NRE) cost* for an ASIC design can exceed the cost of a discrete design by $10,000 to $500,000 or more. NRE charges are paid to the IC manufacturer and others who are responsible for designing the internal structure of the chip, creating tooling such as the metal masks for manufacturing the chips, developing tests for the manufactured chips, and actually making the first few sample chips. So, an ASIC design normally makes sense only if NRE cost is offset by the per-unit savings over the expected sales volume of the product.

nonrecurring engineering (NRE) cost

There are a few approaches to ASIC design, differing in their capabilities and cost. The NRE cost to design a *custom LSI* chip—a chip whose functions, internal architecture, and detailed transistor-level design is tailored for a specific customer—is very high, $500,000 or more. Thus, full custom LSI design is done only for chips that have general commercial application (e.g., microprocessors) or that will enjoy very high sales volume in a specific application (e.g., a digital watch chip, a network interface, or a bus-interface circuit for a PC).

custom LSI

To reduce NRE charges, IC manufacturers have developed libraries of *standard cells* including commonly used MSI functions such as decoders, registers, and counters and commonly used LSI functions such as memories, programmable logic arrays, and microprocessors. In a *standard-cell design*, the logic designer interconnects functions in much the same way as in a multichip MSI/LSI design. Custom cells are created (at added cost, of course) only if absolutely necessary. All of the cells are then laid out on the chip, optimizing the layout to reduce propagation delays and minimize the size of the chip. Minimizing the chip size reduces the per-unit cost of the chip, since it increases the number of chips that can be fabricated on a single wafer. The NRE cost for a standard-cell design is typically on the order of $250,000 or more.

standard cells

standard-cell design

Well, $250,000 is still a lot of money for most folks, so IC manufacturers have gone one step further to bring ASIC design capability to the masses. A *gate array* is an IC whose internal structure is an array of gates whose interconnections are initially unspecified. The logic designer specifies the gate types and interconnections. Even though the chip design is ultimately specified at this very low level, the designer typically works with "macrocells," the same high-level functions used in multichip MSI/LSI and standard-cell designs; software expands the high-level design into a low-level one.

gate array

The main difference between standard-cell and gate-array design is that the macrocells and the chip layout of a gate array are not as highly optimized as those in a standard-cell design, so the chip may be 25% or more larger and therefore may cost more. Also, there is no opportunity to create custom cells in the gate-array approach. On the other hand, a gate-array design can be finished faster and at lower NRE cost, ranging from about $10,000 (what you're told initially) to $100,000 (what you find you've spent when you're all done).

The basic digital design methods that you'll study throughout this book apply very well to the functional design of ASICs. However, there are additional opportunities, constraints, and steps in ASIC design, which usually depend on the particular ASIC vendor and design environment.

1.9 Printed-Circuit Boards

An IC is normally mounted on a *printed-circuit board (PCB)* [or *printed-wiring board (PWB)*] that connects it to other ICs in a system. The multilayer PCBs used in typical digital systems have copper wiring etched on multiple, thin layers of fiberglass that are laminated into a single board usually about 1/16 inch thick.

printed-circuit board (PCB)

printed-wiring board (PWB)

Individual wire connections, or *PCB traces*, are usually quite narrow, 10 to 25 mils in typical PCBs. (A *mil* is one-thousandth of an inch.) In *fine-line* PCB technology, the traces are extremely narrow, as little as 3 mils wide with 3-mil spacing between adjacent traces. Thus, up to 166 connections may be routed in a one-inch-wide band on a single layer of the PCB. If higher connection density is needed, then more layers are used.

PCB traces
mil
fine-line

Most of the components in modern PCBs use *surface-mount technology (SMT)*. Instead of having the long pins of DIP packages that poke through the board and are soldered to the underside, the leads of SMT IC packages are bent to make flat contact with the top surface of the PCB. Before such components are mounted on the PCB, a special "solder paste" is applied to contact pads on the PCB using a stencil whose hole pattern matches the contact pads to be soldered. Then the SMT components are placed (by hand or by machine) on the pads, where they are held in place by the solder paste (or in some cases, by glue). Finally, the entire assembly is passed through an oven to melt the solder paste, which then solidifies when cooled.

surface-mount technology (SMT)

Surface-mount technology, coupled with fine-line PCB technology, allows extremely dense packing of integrated circuits and other components on a PCB. This dense packing does more than save space. For very high-speed circuits, dense packing helps to minimize certain adverse analog phenomena, such as transmission-line effects and speed-of-light limitations.

To satisfy the most stringent requirements for speed and density, *multichip modules (MCMs)* have been developed. In this technology, IC dice are not mounted in individual plastic or ceramic packages. Instead, the IC dice for a high-speed subsystem (say, a processor and its cache memory) are bonded

multichip module (MCM)

directly to a substrate that contains the required interconnections on multiple layers. The MCM is hermetically sealed and has its own external pins for power, ground, and just those signals that are required by the system that contains it.

1.10 Digital-Design Levels

Digital design can be carried out at several different levels of representation and abstraction. Although you may learn and practice design at a particular level, from time to time you'll need to go up or down a level or two to get the job done. Also, the industry itself and most designers have been steadily moving to higher levels of abstraction as circuit density and functionality have increased.

The lowest level of digital design is device physics and IC manufacturing processes. This is the level that is primarily responsible for the breathtaking advances in IC speed and density that have occurred over the past decades. The effects of these advances are summarized in *Moore's Law*, first stated by Intel founder Gordon Moore in 1965: that the number of transistors per square inch in the newest ICs will double every year. In recent years, the rate of advance has slowed down to doubling about every 24 months, but it is important to note that with each doubling of density has also come a significant increase in speed.

Moore's Law

This book does not reach down to the level of device physics and IC processes, but you need to recognize the importance of that level. Being aware of likely technology advances and other changes is important in system and product planning. For example, decreases in chip geometries have recently forced a move to lower logic-power-supply voltages, causing major changes in the way designers plan and specify modular systems and upgrades.

In this book, we jump into digital design at the transistor level and go all the way up to the level of logic design using HDLs. We stop short of the next level, which includes computer design and overall system design. The "center" of our discussion is at the level of functional building blocks.

To get a preview of the levels of design that we'll cover, consider a simple design example. Suppose you are to build a "multiplexer" with two data input bits, A and B, a control input bit S, and an output bit Z. Depending on the value of S, 0 or 1, the circuit is to transfer the value of either A or B to the output Z. This idea is illustrated in the "switch model" of Figure 1-7. Let us consider the design of this function at several different levels.

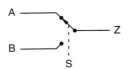

Figure 1-7
Switch model for multiplexer function.

Although logic design is usually carried out at a higher level, for some functions it is advantageous to optimize them by designing at the transistor level. The multiplexer is such a function. Figure 1-8 shows how the multiplexer can be designed in "CMOS" technology using specialized transistor circuit structures called "transmission gates," discussed in Section 3.7.1. Using this approach, the multiplexer can be built with just six transistors. Any of the other approaches that we describe requires at least 14 transistors.

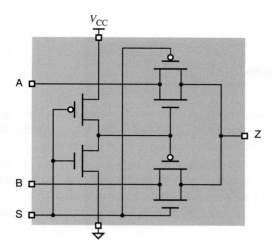

Figure 1-8
Multiplexer design using
CMOS transmission gates.

In the traditional study of logic design, we would use a "truth table" to describe the multiplexer's logic function. A truth table lists all possible combinations of input values and the corresponding output values for the function. Since the multiplexer has three inputs, it has 2^3 or 8 possible input combinations, as shown in the truth table in Table 1-1.

Once we have a truth table, traditional logic design methods, described in Section 4.3, use Boolean algebra and well-understood minimization algorithms to derive an "optimal" two-level AND-OR equation from the truth table. For the multiplexer truth table, we would derive the following equation:

$$Z = S' \cdot A + S \cdot B$$

This equation is read "Z equals not S and A, or S and B." Going one step further, we can convert the equation into a set of logic gates that perform the specified logic function, as shown in Figure 1-9 on the next page. This circuit requires 14 transistors if we use standard CMOS technology for the four gates shown.

S	A	B	Z
0	0	0	0
0	0	1	0
0	1	0	1
0	1	1	1
1	0	0	0
1	0	1	1
1	1	0	0
1	1	1	1

Table 1-1
Truth table for the
multiplexer function.

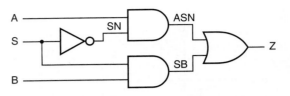

Figure 1-9
Gate-level logic diagram
for multiplexer function.

A multiplexer is a very commonly used function, and most digital logic technologies provide predefined multiplexer building blocks. For example, the 74x157 is an MSI chip that performs multiplexing on two 4-bit inputs simultaneously. Figure 1-10 is a logic diagram that shows how we can hook up just one bit of this 4-bit building block to solve the problem at hand. The numbers in color are pin numbers of a 16-pin DIP package containing the device.

We can also realize the multiplexer function as part of a programmable logic device. HDLs like ABEL allow us to specify logic functions using Boolean equations similar to the one on the previous page, but an HDL's "higher-level" language elements can create a more readable program. For example, Table 1-2 is an ABEL program for the multiplexer function. The first three lines define the name of the program module and specify the type of PLD in which the function will be realized. The next two lines specify the device pin numbers for inputs and output. The "when" statement specifies the actual logic function in a way that's very easy to understand, even though we haven't covered ABEL yet.

Two even higher-level languages, VHDL and Verilog, can be used to specify the multiplexer function in a way that is very flexible and hierarchical. Table 1-3 is an example VHDL program for the multiplexer. The first two lines specify a standard library and set of definitions to use in the design. The next four lines specify only the inputs and outputs of the function, purposely hiding any details about the way the function is realized internally. The "architecture" section of the program is a behavioral specification of the multiplexer's function. VHDL syntax takes a little getting used to, but the single "when" statement says basically the same thing that the ABEL version did. A synthesizer can use this behavioral description to produce a circuit that has this behavior in a specified target digital-logic technology, such as a PLD or ASIC.

Figure 1-10
Logic diagram for a
multiplexer using an
MSI building block.

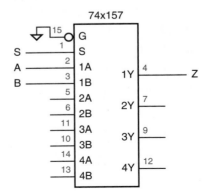

```
module chap1mux
title 'Two-input multiplexer example'
CHAP1MUX device 'P16V8'

A, B, S       pin 1, 2, 3;
Z             pin 13 istype 'com';

equations

when S == 0 then Z = A;   else Z = B;

end chap1mux
```

Table 1-2
ABEL program for
the multiplexer.

```
library IEEE;
use IEEE.std_logic_1164.all;

entity Vchap1mux is
    port ( A, B, S: in  STD_LOGIC;
           Z:       out STD_LOGIC );
end Vchap1mux;

architecture Vchap1mux_arch of Vchap1mux is
begin
  Z <= A when S = '0' else B;
end Vchap1mux_arch;
```

Table 1-3
VHDL program for
the multiplexer.

By explicitly enforcing a separation of input/output definitions ("entity") and internal realization ("architecture"), VHDL makes it easy for designers to define alternate realizations of functions without having to make changes elsewhere in the design hierarchy. For example, a designer could specify an alternate, structural architecture for the multiplexer as shown in Table 1-4. This architecture is basically a text equivalent of the logic diagram in Figure 1-9.

Going one step further, VHDL is powerful enough that we could actually define operations that model functional behavior at the transistor level (though we won't explore such capabilities in this book). Thus, we could come full circle by writing a VHDL program that specifies a transistor-level realization of the multiplexer equivalent to Figure 1-8.

```
architecture Vchap1mux_gate_arch of Vchap1mux is
signal SN, ASN, SB: STD_LOGIC;
    -- required component declarations have been omitted
    --    for brevity in this example.
begin
  U1: port map INV (S, SN);
  U2: port map AND2 (A, SN, ASN);
  U3: port map AND2 (S, B, SB);
  U4: port map OR2 (ASN, SB, Z);
end Vchap1mux_gate_arch;
```

Table 1-4
"Structural" VHDL
program for the
multiplexer.

```
module Vrchap1mux(A, B, S, Z);
  input A, B, S;
  output Z;

  assign Z = (S==0) ? A : B;
endmodule
```

Table 1-5
Verilog program for
the multiplexer.

Table 1-5 is a Verilog program for the same multiplexer function. Verilog syntax is somewhat C-like; see, for example, the conditional expression that tests the value of S so that either A or B is assigned to Z depending on the test's outcome. Like C, Verilog is less picky about variable and type definitions—for example, in Table 1-5 all of the variables default to being 1-bit "wires." Unlike VHDL, Verilog does not require separate definitions of entity and architecture—it's all together in one "module." But Verilog also provides a means for defining functions structurally as in the VHDL example of Table 1-4.

1.11 The Name of the Game

board-level design

Given the functional and performance requirements for a digital system, the name of the game in practical digital design is to minimize cost. For *board-level designs*—systems that are packaged on a single PCB—this usually means minimizing the number of IC packages. If too many ICs are required, they won't all fit on the PCB. "Well, just use a bigger PCB," you say. Unfortunately, PCB sizes are usually constrained by factors such as preexisting standards (e.g., add-in boards for PCs), packaging constraints (e.g., it has to fit in your pocket), or edicts from above (e.g., in order to get the project approved three months ago, you foolishly told your manager that it would all fit on a 3×5 inch PCB, and now you've got to deliver!). In each of these cases, the cost of using a larger PCB or multiple PCBs may be unacceptable.

Minimizing the number of ICs is usually the rule even though individual IC costs vary. For example, a typical SSI or MSI IC may cost 20 cents, while a small PLD may cost a dollar. It may be possible to perform a particular function with three SSI and MSI ICs (60 cents) or one PLD (a dollar). In many situations, the more expensive PLD solution is used, not because the designer owns stock in the PLD company, but because the PLD solution uses less PCB area and is also a lot easier to change if it's not right the first time.

ASIC design

In *ASIC design*, the name of the game is a little different, but the importance of structured, functional design techniques is the same. Although it's easy to burn hours and weeks creating custom macrocells and minimizing the total gate count of an ASIC, only rarely is this advisable. The per-unit cost reduction achieved by having a 10% smaller chip is negligible except in high-volume applications. In applications with low to medium volume (the majority), two other factors are more important: design time and NRE cost.

A shorter design time allows a product to reach the market sooner, increasing revenues over the lifetime of the product. A lower NRE cost also flows right to the "bottom line" and in small companies may be the only way the project can be completed before the company runs out of money (believe me, I've been there!). If the product is successful, it's always possible and profitable to "tweak" the design later to reduce per-unit costs. The need to minimize design time and NRE cost argues in favor of a structured, as opposed to highly optimized, approach to ASIC design, using standard building blocks provided in the ASIC manufacturer's library.

The considerations in PLD, CPLD, and FPGA design are a combination of the above. The choice of a particular PLD technology and device size is usually made fairly early in the design cycle. Later, as long as the design "fits" in the selected device, there's no point in trying to optimize gate count or board area—the device has already been committed. However, if new functions or bug fixes push the design beyond the capacity of the selected device, that's when you must work very hard to modify the design to make it fit.

1.12 Going Forward

This concludes the introductory chapter. As you continue reading this book, keep in mind two things. First, the ultimate goal of digital design is to build systems that solve problems for people. While this book will give you the basic tools for design, it's still your job to keep "the big picture" in the back of your mind. Second, cost is an important factor in every design decision; and you must consider not only the cost of digital components, but also the cost of the design activity itself.

Finally, as you get deeper into the text, if you encounter something that you think you've seen before but don't remember where, please consult the index. I've tried to make it as helpful and complete as possible.

Drill Problems

1.1   Suggest some better-looking chapter-opening artwork to put on page 1 of the next edition of this book.

1.2   Give three different definitions for the word "bit" as used in this chapter.

1.3   Define the following acronyms: ASIC, CAD, CD, CO, CPLD, DIP, DVD, FPGA, HDL, IC, IP, LSI, MCM, MSI, NRE, PBX, PCB, PLD, PWB, SMT, SSI, VHDL, VLSI.

1.4   Research the definitions of the following acronyms: ABEL, CMOS, DDPP, JPEG, MPEG, OK, PERL. (Is OK really an acronym?)

1.5   Excluding the topics in Section 1.2, list three once-analog systems that have "gone digital" since you were born.

1.6   Draw a digital circuit consisting of a 2-input **AND** gate and three inverters, where an inverter is connected to each of the **AND** gate's inputs and its output. For each of the four possible combinations of inputs applied to the two primary inputs of this circuit, determine the value produced at the primary output. Is there a simpler circuit that gives the same input/output behavior?

1.7   When should you use the pin diagrams of Figure 1-5 in the schematic diagram of a circuit?

1.8   What is the relationship between "die" and "dice"?

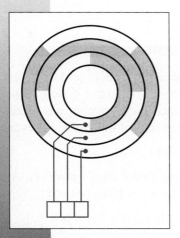

c h a p t e r 

Number Systems and Codes

D igital systems are built from circuits that process binary digits—
0s and 1s—yet very few real-life problems are based on binary
numbers or any numbers at all. As a result, a digital system
designer must establish some correspondence between the
binary digits processed by digital circuits and real-life numbers,
events, and conditions. The purpose of this chapter is to show you how
familiar numeric quantities can be represented and manipulated in a digital
system, and how nonnumeric data, events, and conditions also can be
represented.

The first nine sections describe binary number systems and show how
addition, subtraction, multiplication, and division are performed in these
systems. Sections 2.10–2.13 show how other things, such as decimal
numbers, text characters, mechanical positions, and arbitrary conditions,
can be encoded using strings of binary digits.

Section 2.14 introduces "*n*-cubes," which provide a way to visualize
the relationship between different bit strings. The *n*-cubes are especially
useful in the study of error-detecting codes in Section 2.15. We conclude the
chapter with an introduction to codes for transmitting and storing data one
bit at a time.

2.1 Positional Number Systems

positional number system

The traditional number system that we learned in school and use every day in business is called a *positional number system*. In such a system, a number is represented by a string of digits, where each digit position has an associated *weight*. The value of a number is a weighted sum of the digits, for example:

weight

$$1734 = 1 \cdot 1000 + 7 \cdot 100 + 3 \cdot 10 + 4 \cdot 1$$

Each weight is a power of 10 corresponding to the digit's position. A decimal point allows negative as well as positive powers of 10 to be used:

$$5185.68 = 5 \cdot 1000 + 1 \cdot 100 + 8 \cdot 10 + 5 \cdot 1 + 6 \cdot 0.1 + 8 \cdot 0.01$$

In general, a number D of the form $d_1 d_0 . d_{-1} d_{-2}$ has the value

$$D = d_1 \cdot 10^1 + d_0 \cdot 10^0 + d_{-1} \cdot 10^{-1} + d_{-2} \cdot 10^{-2}$$

base
radix

Here, 10 is called the *base* or *radix* of the number system. In a general positional number system, the radix may be any integer $r \geq 2$, and a digit in position i has weight r^i. The general form of a number in such a system is

$$d_{p-1} d_{p-2} \cdots d_1 d_0 . d_{-1} d_{-2} \cdots d_{-n}$$

radix point

where there are p digits to the left of the point and n digits to the right of the point, called the *radix point*. If the radix point is missing, it is assumed to be to the right of the rightmost digit. The value of the number is the sum of each digit multiplied by the corresponding power of the radix:

$$D = \sum_{i=-n}^{p-1} d_i \cdot r^i$$

high-order digit
most significant digit
low-order digit
least significant digit

Except for possible leading and trailing zeroes, the representation of a number in a positional number system is unique. (Obviously, 0185.6300 equals 185.63, and so on.) The leftmost digit in such a number is called the *high-order* or *most significant digit*; the rightmost is the *low-order* or *least significant digit*.

binary digit
bit
binary radix

As we'll learn in Chapter 3, digital circuits have signals that are normally in one of only two conditions—low or high, charged or discharged, off or on. The signals in these circuits are interpreted to represent *binary digits* (or *bits*) that have one of two values, 0 and 1. Thus, the *binary radix* is normally used to represent numbers in a digital system. The general form of a binary number is

$$b_{p-1} b_{p-2} \cdots b_1 b_0 . b_{-1} b_{-2} \cdots b_{-n}$$

and its value is

$$B = \sum_{i=-n}^{p-1} b_i \cdot 2^i$$

In a binary number, the radix point is called the *binary point*. When dealing with binary and other nondecimal numbers, we use a subscript to indicate the radix of each number, unless the radix is clear from the context. Examples of binary numbers and their decimal equivalents are given below.

binary point

$$10011_2 = 1 \cdot 16 + 0 \cdot 8 + 0 \cdot 4 + 1 \cdot 2 + 1 \cdot 1 = 19_{10}$$
$$100010_2 = 1 \cdot 32 + 0 \cdot 16 + 0 \cdot 8 + 0 \cdot 4 + 1 \cdot 2 + 0 \cdot 1 = 34_{10}$$
$$101.001_2 = 1 \cdot 4 + 0 \cdot 2 + 1 \cdot 1 + 0 \cdot 0.5 + 0 \cdot 0.25 + 1 \cdot 0.125 = 5.125_{10}$$

The leftmost bit of a binary number is called the *high-order* or *most significant bit (MSB)*; the rightmost is the *low-order* or *least significant bit (LSB)*.

MSB
LSB

2.2 Octal and Hexadecimal Numbers

Radix 10 is important because we use it in everyday business, and radix 2 is important because binary numbers can be processed directly by digital circuits. Numbers in other radices are not often processed directly but may be important for documentation or other purposes. In particular, the radices 8 and 16 provide convenient shorthand representations for multibit numbers in a digital system.

The *octal number system* uses radix 8, while the *hexadecimal number system* uses radix 16. Table 2-1 shows the binary integers from 0 to 1111 and their octal, decimal, and hexadecimal equivalents. The octal system needs 8 digits, so it uses digits 0–7 of the decimal system. The hexadecimal system needs 16 digits, so it supplements decimal digits 0–9 with the letters *A–F*.

octal number system
hexadecimal number system

hexadecimal digits A–F

The octal and hexadecimal number systems are useful for representing multibit numbers because their radices are powers of 2. Since a string of three bits can take on eight different combinations, it follows that each 3-bit string can be uniquely represented by one octal digit, according to the third and fourth columns of Table 2-1. Likewise, a 4-bit string can be represented by one hexadecimal digit according to the fifth and sixth columns of the table.

Thus, it is very easy to convert a binary number to octal. Starting at the binary point and working left, we simply separate the bits into groups of three and replace each group with the corresponding octal digit:

binary-to-octal conversion

$$100011001110_2 = 100\ 011\ 001\ 110_2 = 4316_8$$
$$11101101110101001_2 = 011\ 101\ 101\ 110\ 101\ 001_2 = 355651_8$$

The procedure for binary-to-hexadecimal conversion is similar, except we use groups of four bits:

binary-to-hexadecimal conversion

$$100011001110_2 = 1000\ 1100\ 1110_2 = 8CE_{16}$$
$$11101101110101001_2 = 0001\ 1101\ 1011\ 1010\ 1001_2 = 1DBA9_{16}$$

In these examples we have freely added zeroes on the left to make the total number of bits a multiple of 3 or 4 as required.

Table 2-1
Binary, decimal, octal, and hexadecimal numbers.

Binary	Decimal	Octal	3-Bit String	Hexadecimal	4-Bit String
0	0	0	000	0	0000
1	1	1	001	1	0001
10	2	2	010	2	0010
11	3	3	011	3	0011
100	4	4	100	4	0100
101	5	5	101	5	0101
110	6	6	110	6	0110
111	7	7	111	7	0111
1000	8	10	—	8	1000
1001	9	11	—	9	1001
1010	10	12	—	A	1010
1011	11	13	—	B	1011
1100	12	14	—	C	1100
1101	13	15	—	D	1101
1110	14	16	—	E	1110
1111	15	17	—	F	1111

If a binary number contains digits to the right of the binary point, we can convert them to octal or hexadecimal by starting at the binary point and working right. Both the lefthand and righthand sides can be padded with zeroes to get multiples of three or four bits, as shown in the example below:

$$10.1011001011_2 = 010 . 101 \ 100 \ 101 \ 100_2 = 2.5454_8$$
$$= 0010 . 1011 \ 0010 \ 1100_2 = 2.B2C_{16}$$

octal- or hexadecimal-to-binary conversion

Converting in the reverse direction, from octal or hexadecimal to binary, is very easy. We simply replace each octal or hexadecimal digit with the corresponding 3- or 4-bit string, as shown below:

$$1357_8 = 001 \ 011 \ 101 \ 111_2$$
$$2046.17_8 = 010 \ 000 \ 100 \ 110 . 001 \ 111_2$$
$$BEAD_{16} = 1011 \ 1110 \ 1010 \ 1101_2$$
$$9F.46C_{16} = 1001 \ 1111 . 0100 \ 0110 \ 1100_2$$

The octal number system was quite popular 30 years ago because of certain minicomputers that had their front-panel lights and switches arranged in groups of three. However, the octal number system is not used much today, because of the preponderance of machines that process 8-bit *bytes*. It is difficult to extract individual byte values in multibyte quantities in the octal representation; for

byte

WHEN I'M 64	As you grow older, you'll find that the hexadecimal number system is useful for more than just computers. When I turned 40, I told friends that I had just turned 28_{16}. The "$_{16}$" was whispered under my breath, of course. At age 50, I was only 32_{16}.
	People get all excited about decennial birthdays like 20, 30, 40, 50, ..., but you should be able to convince your friends that the decimal system is of no fundamental significance. More significant life changes occur around birthdays 2, 4, 8, 16, 32, and 64, when you add a most significant bit to your age. Why do you think the Beatles sang "When I'm sixty-*four*"?

example, what are the octal values of the four 8-bit bytes in the 32-bit number with octal representation 12345670123_8?

In the hexadecimal system, two digits represent an 8-bit byte, and $2n$ digits represent an n-byte word; each pair of digits constitutes exactly one byte. For example, the 32-bit hexadecimal number $5678ABCD_{16}$ consists of four bytes with values 56_{16}, 78_{16}, AB_{16}, and CD_{16}. In this context, a 4-bit hexadecimal digit is sometimes called a *nibble*; a 32-bit (4-byte) number has eight nibbles. Hexa- *nibble* decimal numbers are often used to describe a computer's memory address space. For example, a computer with 16-bit addresses might be described as having read/write memory installed at addresses $0–EFFF_{16}$, and read-only memory at addresses $F000–FFFF_{16}$. Many computer programming languages use the prefix "0x" to denote a hexadecimal number, for example, 0xBFC0000. *0x prefix*

2.3 General Positional-Number-System Conversions

In general, conversion between two radices cannot be done by simple substitutions; arithmetic operations are required. In this section, we show how to convert a number in any radix to radix 10 and vice versa, using radix-10 arithmetic.

In Section 2.1, we indicated that the value of a number in any radix is given *radix-r-to-decimal* by the formula *conversion*

$$D = \sum_{i=-n}^{p-1} d_i \cdot r^i$$

where r is the radix of the number and there are p digits to the left of the radix point and n to the right. Thus, the value of the number can be found by converting each digit of the number to its radix-10 equivalent and expanding the formula using radix-10 arithmetic. Some examples are given below:

$$1CE8_{16} = 1 \cdot 16^3 + 12 \cdot 16^2 + 14 \cdot 16^1 + 8 \cdot 16^0 = 7400_{10}$$
$$F1A3_{16} = 15 \cdot 16^3 + 1 \cdot 16^2 + 10 \cdot 16^1 + 3 \cdot 16^0 = 61859_{10}$$
$$436.5_8 = 4 \cdot 8^2 + 3 \cdot 8^1 + 6 \cdot 8^0 + 5 \cdot 8^{-1} = 286.625_{10}$$
$$132.3_4 = 1 \cdot 4^2 + 3 \cdot 4^1 + 2 \cdot 4^0 + 3 \cdot 4^{-1} = 30.75_{10}$$

nested expansion formula

A shortcut for converting whole numbers to radix 10 can be obtained by rewriting the expansion formula in a nested fashion:

$$D = ((\cdots((d_{p-1})\cdot r + d_{p-2})\cdot r + \cdots)\cdot r + d_1)\cdot r + d_0$$

That is, we start with a sum of 0; beginning with the leftmost digit, we multiply the sum by r and add the next digit to the sum, repeating until all digits have been processed. For example, we can write

$$\text{F1AC}_{16} = (((15)\cdot 16 + 1)\cdot 16 + 10)\cdot 16 + 12$$

decimal-to-radix-r conversion

This formula is used in iterative, programmed conversion algorithms (such as Table 5-25 on page 268). It is also the basis of a very convenient method of converting a decimal number D to a radix r. Consider what happens if we divide the formula by r. Since the parenthesized part of the formula is evenly divisible by r, the quotient will be

$$Q = (\cdots((d_{p-1})\cdot r + d_{p-2})\cdot r + \cdots)\cdot r + d_1$$

and the remainder will be d_0. Thus, d_0 can be computed as the remainder of the long division of D by r. Furthermore, the quotient Q has the same form as the original formula. Therefore, successive divisions by r yield successive digits of D from right to left, until all the digits of D have been derived. Examples are given below:

$$179 \div 2 = 89 \text{ remainder } 1 \quad \text{(LSB)}$$
$$\div 2 = 44 \text{ remainder } 1$$
$$\div 2 = 22 \text{ remainder } 0$$
$$\div 2 = 11 \text{ remainder } 0$$
$$\div 2 = 5 \text{ remainder } 1$$
$$\div 2 = 2 \text{ remainder } 1$$
$$\div 2 = 1 \text{ remainder } 0$$
$$\div 2 = 0 \text{ remainder } 1 \quad \text{(MSB)}$$
$$179_{10} = 10110011_2$$

$$467 \div 8 = 58 \text{ remainder } 3 \quad \text{(least significant digit)}$$
$$\div 8 = 7 \text{ remainder } 2$$
$$\div 8 = 0 \text{ remainder } 7 \quad \text{(most significant digit)}$$
$$467_{10} = 723_8$$

$$3417 \div 16 = 213 \text{ remainder } 9 \quad \text{(least significant digit)}$$
$$\div 16 = 13 \text{ remainder } 5$$
$$\div 16 = 0 \text{ remainder } 13 \quad \text{(most significant digit)}$$
$$3417_{10} = \text{D59}_{16}$$

Table 2-2 summarizes methods for converting among the most common radices.

Table 2-2 Conversion methods for common radices.

Conversion	Method	Example
Binary to		
Octal	Substitution	$10111011001_2 = 10\ 111\ 011\ 001_2 = 2731_8$
Hexadecimal	Substitution	$10111011001_2 = 101\ 1101\ 1001_2 = 5D9_{16}$
Decimal	Summation	$10111011001_2 = 1 \cdot 1024 + 0 \cdot 512 + 1 \cdot 256 + 1 \cdot 128 + 1 \cdot 64$ $+ 0 \cdot 32 + 1 \cdot 16 + 1 \cdot 8 + 0 \cdot 4 + 0 \cdot 2 + 1 \cdot 1 = 1497_{10}$
Octal to		
Binary	Substitution	$1234_8 = 001\ 010\ 011\ 100_2$
Hexadecimal	Substitution	$1234_8 = 001\ 010\ 011\ 100_2 = 0010\ 1001\ 1100_2 = 29C_{16}$
Decimal	Summation	$1234_8 = 1 \cdot 512 + 2 \cdot 64 + 3 \cdot 8 + 4 \cdot 1 = 668_{10}$
Hexadecimal to		
Binary	Substitution	$C0DE_{16} = 1100\ 0000\ 1101\ 1110_2$
Octal	Substitution	$C0DE_{16} = 1100\ 0000\ 1101\ 1110_2 = 1\ 100\ 000\ 011\ 011\ 110_2 = 140336_8$
Decimal	Summation	$C0DE_{16} = 12 \cdot 4096 + 0 \cdot 256 + 13 \cdot 16 + 14 \cdot 1 = 49374_{10}$
Decimal to		
Binary	Division	$108_{10} \div 2 = 54$ remainder 0 (LSB) $\div 2 = 27$ remainder 0 $\div 2 = 13$ remainder 1 $\div 2 = 6$ remainder 1 $\div 2 = 3$ remainder 0 $\div 2 = 1$ remainder 1 $\div 2 = 0$ remainder 1 (MSB) $108_{10} = 1101100_2$
Octal	Division	$108_{10} \div 8 = 13$ remainder 4 (least significant digit) $\div 8 = 1$ remainder 5 $\div 8 = 0$ remainder 1 (most significant digit) $108_{10} = 154_8$
Hexadecimal	Division	$108_{10} \div 16 = 6$ remainder 12 (least significant digit) $\div 16 = 0$ remainder 6 (most significant digit) $108_{10} = 6C_{16}$

Table 2-3
Binary addition and
subtraction table.

c_{in} **or** b_{in}	x	y	c_{out}	s	b_{out}	d
0	0	0	0	0	0	0
0	0	1	0	1	1	1
0	1	0	0	1	0	1
0	1	1	1	0	0	0
1	0	0	0	1	1	1
1	0	1	1	0	1	0
1	1	0	1	0	0	0
1	1	1	1	1	1	1

2.4 Addition and Subtraction of Nondecimal Numbers

Addition and subtraction of nondecimal numbers by hand uses the same technique that we learned in grammar school for decimal numbers; the only catch is that the addition and subtraction tables are different.

binary addition

Table 2-3 is the addition and subtraction table for binary digits. To add two binary numbers X and Y, we add together the least significant bits with an initial carry (c_{in}) of 0, producing carry (c_{out}) and sum (s) bits according to the table. We continue processing bits from right to left, adding the carry out of each column into the next column's sum.

Two examples of decimal additions and the corresponding binary additions are shown in Figure 2-1, using a colored arrow to indicate a carry of 1. The same examples are repeated below along with two more, with the carries shown as a bit string C:

$$
\begin{array}{rr}
C & 101111000 \\
X \quad 190 & 10111110 \\
Y \quad +141 & + \quad 10001101 \\
\hline
X+Y \quad 331 & 101001011
\end{array}
\qquad
\begin{array}{rr}
C & 001011000 \\
X \quad 173 & 10101101 \\
Y \quad + \ 44 & + \ 00101100 \\
\hline
X+Y \quad 217 & 11011001
\end{array}
$$

$$
\begin{array}{rr}
C & 011111110 \\
X \quad 127 & 01111111 \\
Y \quad + \ 63 & + \ 00111111 \\
\hline
X+Y \quad 190 & 10111110
\end{array}
\qquad
\begin{array}{rr}
C & 000000000 \\
X \quad 170 & 10101010 \\
Y \quad + \ 85 & + \ 01010101 \\
\hline
X+Y \quad 255 & 11111111
\end{array}
$$

binary subtraction

minuend
subtrahend

difference

Binary subtraction is performed similarly, using borrows (b_{in} and b_{out}) instead of carries between steps, and producing a difference bit d. Two examples of decimal subtractions and the corresponding binary subtractions (*minuend* minus *subtrahend* yields *difference*) are shown in Figure 2-2. As in decimal subtraction, the binary minuend values in the columns are modified when borrows occur, as shown by the colored arrows and bits. The examples from the figure are

```
                   1 1 1 1                                     1     1 1
X       190    1 0 1 1 1 1 1 0        X       173    1 0 1 0 1 1 1 0 1
Y     + 141  + 1 0 0 0 1 1 0 1        Y      + 44  + 0 0 1 0 1 1 1 0 0
X + Y   331    1 0 1 0 0 1 0 1 1      X + Y   217    1 1 0 1 1 0 0 1
```

Figure 2-1   Examples of decimal and corresponding binary additions.

repeated below along with two more, this time showing the borrows as a bit string B:

```
B                   001111100          B                   011011010
X       229         11100101           X       210         11010010
Y      - 46       - 00101110           Y     -109        - 01101101
X - Y   183         10110111           X - Y   101         01100101


B                   010101010          B                   000000000
X       170         10101010           X       221         11011101
Y      - 85       - 01010101           Y      - 76       - 01001100
X - Y    85         01010101           X - Y   145         10010001
```

A very common use of subtraction in computers is to compare two numbers. For example, if the operation $X - Y$ produces a borrow out of the most significant bit position, then X is less than Y; otherwise, X is greater than or equal to Y. The relationship between carries and borrows in adders and subtractors will be explored in Section 6.10.

comparing numbers

Addition and subtraction tables can be developed for octal and hexadecimal digits, or any other desired radix. However, few computer engineers bother to memorize these tables. If you rarely need to manipulate nondecimal numbers,

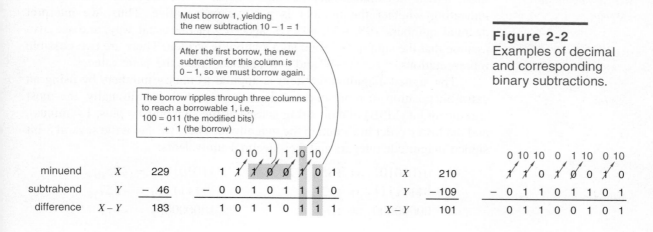

Must borrow 1, yielding the new subtraction 10 − 1 = 1

After the first borrow, the new subtraction for this column is 0 − 1, so we must borrow again.

The borrow ripples through three columns to reach a borrowable 1, i.e., 100 = 011 (the modified bits) + 1 (the borrow)

Figure 2-2
Examples of decimal and corresponding binary subtractions.

```
                       0 10  1  1 10 10
minuend      X   229   1 1 1 0 0 1 0 1           X   210
subtrahend   Y  - 46 - 0 0 1 0 1 1 1 0           Y  -109
difference  X - Y 183   1 0 1 1 0 1 1 1          X - Y 101
```

then it's easy enough on those occasions to convert them to decimal, calculate results, and convert back. On the other hand, if you must perform calculations in binary, octal, or hexadecimal frequently, then you should ask Santa for a programmer's "hex calculator" from Texas Instruments or Casio.

If the calculator's battery wears out, some mental shortcuts can be used to facilitate nondecimal arithmetic. In general, each column addition (or subtraction) can be done by converting the column digits to decimal, adding in decimal, and converting the result to corresponding sum and carry digits in the nondecimal radix. (A carry is produced whenever the column sum equals or exceeds the radix.) Since the addition is done in decimal, we rely on our knowledge of the decimal addition table; the only new thing that we need to learn is the conversion from decimal to nondecimal digits and vice versa. The sequence of steps for mentally adding two hexadecimal numbers is shown below:

hexadecimal addition

C	1	1	0	0	1	1	0	0
X	1	9	B	9_{16}	1	9	11	9
Y	+ C	7	E	6_{16}	+12	7	14	6
$X+Y$	E	1	9	F_{16}	14	17	25	15
					14	16+1	16+9	15
					E	1	9	F

2.5 Representation of Negative Numbers

So far, we have dealt only with positive numbers, but there are many ways to represent negative numbers. In everyday business we use the signed-magnitude system, discussed next. However, most computers use one of the complement number systems that we introduce later.

2.5.1 Signed-Magnitude Representation

signed-magnitude system

In the *signed-magnitude system*, a number consists of a magnitude and a symbol indicating whether the number is positive or negative. Thus, we interpret decimal numbers +98, −57, +123.5, and −13 in the usual way, and we also assume that the sign is "+" if no sign symbol is written. There are two possible representations of zero, "+0" and "−0", but both have the same value.

sign bit

The signed-magnitude system is applied to binary numbers by using an extra bit position to represent the sign (the *sign bit*). Traditionally, the most significant bit (MSB) of a bit string is used as the sign bit (0 = plus, 1 = minus), and the lower-order bits contain the magnitude. Thus, we can write several 8-bit signed-magnitude integers and their decimal equivalents:

$$01010101_2 = +85_{10} \qquad 11010101_2 = -85_{10}$$
$$01111111_2 = +127_{10} \qquad 11111111_2 = -127_{10}$$
$$00000000_2 = +0_{10} \qquad 10000000_2 = -0_{10}$$

The signed-magnitude system has an equal number of positive and negative integers. An n-bit signed-magnitude integer lies within the range $-(2^{n-1}-1)$ through $+(2^{n-1}-1)$, and there are two possible representations of zero.

Now suppose that we wanted to build a digital logic circuit that adds signed-magnitude numbers. The circuit must examine the signs of the addends *signed-magnitude* to determine what to do with the magnitudes. If the signs are the same, it must *adder* add the magnitudes and give the result the same sign. If the signs are different, it must compare the magnitudes, subtract the smaller from the larger, and give the result the sign of the larger. All of these "ifs," "adds," "subtracts," and "compares" translate into a lot of logic-circuit complexity. Adders for complement number systems are much simpler, as we'll show next. Perhaps the one redeeming feature of a signed-magnitude system is that, once we know how to build a signed-magnitude adder, a signed-magnitude subtractor is almost trivial to *signed-magnitude* build—it need only change the sign of the subtrahend and pass it along with the *subtractor* minuend to an adder.

2.5.2 Complement Number Systems

While the signed-magnitude system negates a number by changing its sign, a *complement number system* negates a number by taking its complement as *complement number* defined by the system. Taking the complement is more difficult than changing *system* the sign, but two numbers in a complement number system can be added or subtracted directly without the sign and magnitude checks required by the signed-magnitude system. We shall describe two complement number systems, called the "radix complement" and the "diminished radix-complement."

In any complement number system, we normally deal with a fixed number of digits, say n. (However, we can increase the number of digits by "sign extension" as shown in Exercise 2.25, and decrease the number by truncating high-order digits as shown in Exercise 2.26.) We further assume that the radix is r, and that numbers have the form

$$D = d_{n-1}d_{n-2}\cdots d_1 d_0.$$

The radix point is on the right and so the number is an integer. If an operation produces a result that requires more than n digits, we throw away the extra high-order digit(s). If a number D is complemented twice, the result is D.

2.5.3 Radix-Complement Representation

In a *radix-complement system*, the complement of an n-digit number is obtained *radix-complement* by subtracting it from r^n. In the decimal number system, the radix complement *system* is called the *10's complement*. Some examples using 4-digit decimal numbers *10's complement* (and subtraction from 10,000) are shown in Table 2-4.

By definition, the radix complement of an n-digit number D is obtained by subtracting it from r^n. If D is between 1 and $r^n - 1$, this subtraction produces another number between 1 and $r^n - 1$. If D is 0, the result of the subtraction is r^n,

Table 2-4
Examples of 10's and
9s' complements.

Number	10's Complement	9s' Complement
1849	8151	8150
2067	7933	7932
100	9900	9899
7	9993	9992
8151	1849	1848
0	10000 (= 0)	9999

which has the form $100 \cdots 00$, where there are a total of $n + 1$ digits. We throw away the extra high-order digit and get the result 0. Thus, there is only one representation of zero in a radix-complement system.

It seems from the definition that a subtraction operation is needed to compute the radix complement of D. However, this subtraction can be avoided by rewriting r^n as $(r^n - 1) + 1$ and $r^n - D$ as $((r^n - 1) - D) + 1$. The number $r^n - 1$ has the form $mm \cdots mm$, where $m = r - 1$ and there are n m's. For example, 10,000 equals 9,999 + 1. If we define the complement of a digit d to be $r - 1 - d$, then $(r^n - 1) - D$ is obtained by complementing the digits of D. Therefore, the radix complement of a number D is obtained by complementing the individual

computing the radix complement

Table 2-5
Digit complements.

	Complement			
Digit	Binary	Octal	Decimal	Hexadecimal
0	1	7	9	F
1	0	6	8	E
2	–	5	7	D
3	–	4	6	C
4	–	3	5	B
5	–	2	4	A
6	–	1	3	9
7	–	0	2	8
8	–	–	1	7
9	–	–	0	6
A	–	–	–	5
B	–	–	–	4
C	–	–	–	3
D	–	–	–	2
E	–	–	–	1
F	–	–	–	0

digits of D and adding 1. For example, the 10's complement of 1849 is $8150 + 1$, or 8151. You should confirm that this trick also works for the other 10's-complement examples above. Table 2-5 lists the digit complements for binary, octal, decimal, and hexadecimal numbers.

2.5.4 Two's-Complement Representation

For binary numbers, the radix complement is called the *two's complement*. The MSB of a number in this system serves as the sign bit; a number is negative if and only if its MSB is 1. The decimal equivalent for a two's-complement binary number is computed the same way as for an unsigned number, except that the weight of the MSB is -2^{n-1} instead of $+2^{n-1}$. The range of representable numbers is $-(2^{n-1})$ through $+(2^{n-1}-1)$. Some 8-bit examples are shown below:

two's complement

weight of MSB

$$
\begin{array}{ll}
17_{10} = & 00010001_2 \\
& \Downarrow \quad \text{complement bits} \\
& 11101110 \\
& \underline{+1} \\
& 11101111_2 \ = -17_{10}
\end{array}
\qquad
\begin{array}{ll}
-99_{10} = & 10011101_2 \\
& \Downarrow \quad \text{complement bits} \\
& 01100010 \\
& \underline{+1} \\
& 01100011_2 \ = 99_{10}
\end{array}
$$

$$
\begin{array}{ll}
119_{10} = & 01110111_2 \\
& \Downarrow \quad \text{complement bits} \\
& 10001000^2 \\
& \underline{+1} \\
& 10001001_2 \ = -119_{10}
\end{array}
\qquad
\begin{array}{ll}
-127_{10} = & 10000001_2 \\
& \Downarrow \quad \text{complement bits} \\
& 01111110^2 \\
& \underline{+1} \\
& 01111111_2 \ = 127_{10}
\end{array}
$$

$$
\begin{array}{ll}
0_{10} = & 00000000_2 \\
& \Downarrow \quad \text{complement bits} \\
& 11111111 \\
& \underline{+1} \\
& 1\ 00000000_2 \ = 0_{10}
\end{array}
\qquad
\begin{array}{ll}
-128_{10} = & 10000000_2 \\
& \Downarrow \quad \text{complement bits} \\
& 01111111 \\
& \underline{+1} \\
& 10000000_2 \ = -128_{10}
\end{array}
$$

A carry out of the MSB position occurs in one case, as shown in color above. As in all two's-complement operations, this bit is ignored and only the low-order n bits of the result are used.

In the two's-complement number system, zero is considered positive because its sign bit is 0. Since two's complement has only one representation of zero, we end up with one extra negative number, -2^{n-1}, that doesn't have a positive counterpart.

extra negative number

We can convert an n-bit two's-complement number X into an m-bit one, but some care is needed. If $m > n$, we must append $m - n$ copies of X's sign bit to the left of X (see Exercise 2.25). That is, we pad a positive number with 0s and a negative one with 1s; this is called *sign extension*. If $m < n$, we discard X's $n - m$

sign extension

leftmost bits; however, the result is valid only if all of the discarded bits are the same as the sign bit of the result (see Exercise 2.26).

Most computers and other digital systems use the two's-complement system to represent negative numbers. However, for completeness, we'll also describe the diminished radix-complement and ones'-complement systems.

*2.5.5 Diminished Radix-Complement Representation

diminished radix-complement system

9s' complement

In a *diminished radix-complement system*, the complement of an n-digit number D is obtained by subtracting it from $r^n - 1$. This can be accomplished by complementing the individual digits of D, *without* adding 1 as in the radix-complement system. In decimal, this is called the *9s' complement*; some examples are given in the last column of Table 2-4 on page 36.

*2.5.6 Ones'-Complement Representation

ones' complement

The diminished radix-complement system for binary numbers is called the *ones' complement*. As in two's complement, the most significant bit is the sign, 0 if positive and 1 if negative. Thus there are two representations of zero, positive zero $(00 \cdots 00)$ and negative zero $(11 \cdots 11)$. Positive-number representations are the same for both ones' and two's complements. However, negative-number representations differ by 1. A weight of $-(2^{n-1} - 1)$, rather than -2^{n-1}, is given to the most significant bit when computing the decimal equivalent of a ones'-complement number. The range of representable numbers is $-(2^{n-1} - 1)$ through $+(2^{n-1} - 1)$. Some 8-bit numbers and their ones' complements are shown below:

$$17_{10} = 00010001_2 \qquad\qquad -99_{10} = 10011100_2$$
$$\Downarrow \qquad\qquad\qquad\qquad\qquad \Downarrow$$
$$11101110_2 = -17_{10} \qquad\qquad 01100011_2 = 99_{10}$$

$$119_{10} = 01110111_2 \qquad\qquad -127_{10} = 10000000_2$$
$$\Downarrow \qquad\qquad\qquad\qquad\qquad \Downarrow$$
$$10001000_2 = -119_{10} \qquad\qquad 01111111_2 = 127_{10}$$

$$0_{10} = 00000000_2 \text{ (positive zero)}$$
$$\Downarrow$$
$$11111111_2 = 0_{10} \text{ (negative zero)}$$

The main advantages of the ones'-complement system are its symmetry and the ease of complementation. However, the adder design for ones'-complement numbers is somewhat trickier than a two's-complement adder (see

---

* Throughout this book, *optional sections* are marked with an asterisk.

Exercise 7.73). Also, zero-detecting circuits in a ones'-complement system either must check for both representations of zero, or must always convert $11 \cdots 11$ to $00 \cdots 00$.

*2.5.7 Excess Representations

Yes, the number of different systems for representing negative numbers *is* excessive, but there's just one more for us to cover. In *excess-B representation*, an *m*-bit string whose unsigned integer value is M ($0 \leq M < 2^m$) represents the signed integer $M - B$, where B is called the *bias* of the number system.

      For example, an *excess-2^{m-1} system* represents any number X in the range -2^{m-1} through $+2^{m-1} - 1$ by the *m*-bit binary representation of $X + 2^{m-1}$ (which is always nonnegative and less than 2^m). The range of this representation is exactly the same as that of *m*-bit two's-complement numbers. In fact, the representations of any number in the two systems are identical except for the sign bits, which are always opposite. (Note that this is true only when the bias is 2^{m-1}.)

      The most common use of excess representations is in floating-point number systems (see References).

excess-B representation

bias

excess-2^{m-1} system

2.6 Two's-Complement Addition and Subtraction

2.6.1 Addition Rules

A table of decimal numbers and their equivalents in different number systems, Table 2-6, reveals why the two's complement is preferred for arithmetic operations. If we start with 1000_2 (-8_{10}) and count up, we see that each successive two's-complement number all the way to 0111_2 ($+7_{10}$) can be obtained by adding 1 to the previous one, ignoring any carries beyond the fourth bit position. The same cannot be said of signed-magnitude and ones'-complement numbers. Because ordinary addition is just an extension of counting, two's-complement numbers can thus be added by ordinary binary addition, ignoring any carries beyond the MSB. The result will always be the correct sum as long as the range of the number system is not exceeded. Some examples of decimal addition and the corresponding 4-bit two's-complement additions confirm this:

two's-complement addition

$$
\begin{array}{rl}
+3 & 0011 \\
+\ +4 & +\ 0100 \\
\hline
+7 & 0111
\end{array}
\qquad
\begin{array}{rl}
-2 & 1110 \\
+\ -6 & +\ 1010 \\
\hline
-8 & 1\,1000
\end{array}
$$

$$
\begin{array}{rl}
+6 & 0110 \\
+\ -3 & +\ 1101 \\
\hline
+3 & 1\,0011
\end{array}
\qquad
\begin{array}{rl}
+4 & 0100 \\
+\ -7 & +\ 1001 \\
\hline
-3 & 1101
\end{array}
$$

Table 2-6 Decimal and 4-bit numbers.

Decimal	Two's Complement	Ones' Complement	Signed Magnitude	Excess 2^{m-1}
−8	1000	—	—	0000
−7	1001	1000	1111	0001
−6	1010	1001	1110	0010
−5	1011	1010	1101	0011
−4	1100	1011	1100	0100
−3	1101	1100	1011	0101
−2	1110	1101	1010	0110
−1	1111	1110	1001	0111
0	0000	1111 or 0000	1000 or 0000	1000
1	0001	0001	0001	1001
2	0010	0010	0010	1010
3	0011	0011	0011	1011
4	0100	0100	0100	1100
5	0101	0101	0101	1101
6	0110	0110	0110	1110
7	0111	0111	0111	1111

2.6.2 A Graphical View

Another way to view the two's-complement system uses the 4-bit "counter" shown in Figure 2-3. Here we have shown the numbers in a circular or "modular" representation. The operation of this counter very closely mimics that of a real 4-bit up/down counter circuit, which we'll encounter in Section 8.4.3.

Figure 2-3
A modular counting representation of 4-bit two's-complement numbers.

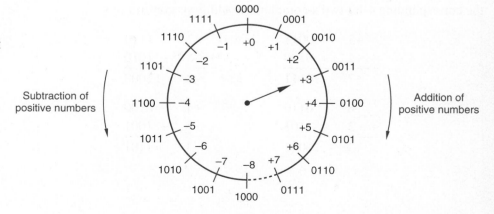

Subtraction of positive numbers

Addition of positive numbers

Starting with the arrow pointing to any number, we can add $+n$ to that number by counting up n times, that is, by moving the arrow n positions clockwise. It is also evident that we can subtract n from a number by counting down n times, that is, by moving the arrow n positions counterclockwise. Of course, these operations give correct results only if n is small enough that we don't cross the discontinuity between -8 and $+7$.

What is most interesting is that we can also subtract n (or add $-n$) by moving the arrow $16 - n$ positions clockwise. Notice that the quantity $16 - n$ is what we defined to be the 4-bit two's complement of n, that is, the two's-complement representation of $-n$. This graphically supports our earlier claim that a negative number in two's-complement representation may be added to another number simply by adding the 4-bit representations using ordinary binary addition. In Figure 2-3, adding a number is equivalent to moving the arrow a corresponding number of positions clockwise.

2.6.3 Overflow

If an addition operation produces a result that exceeds the range of the number system, *overflow* is said to occur. In the modular counting representation of Figure 2-3, overflow occurs during addition of positive numbers when we count past $+7$. Addition of two numbers with different signs can never produce overflow, but addition of two numbers of like sign can, as shown by the following examples:

overflow

$$
\begin{array}{rl}
-3 & 1101 \\
+\ -6 & +\ 1010 \\
\hline
-9 & 1\,0111 = +7
\end{array}
\qquad
\begin{array}{rl}
+5 & 0101 \\
+\ +6 & +\ 0110 \\
\hline
+11 & 1011 = -5
\end{array}
$$

$$
\begin{array}{rl}
-8 & 1000 \\
+\ -8 & +\ 1000 \\
\hline
-16 & 1\,0000 = +0
\end{array}
\qquad
\begin{array}{rl}
+7 & 0111 \\
+\ +7 & +\ 0111 \\
\hline
+14 & 1110 = -2
\end{array}
$$

Fortunately, there is a simple rule for detecting overflow in addition: An addition overflows if the addends' signs are the same but the sum's sign is different from the addends'. The overflow rule is sometimes stated in terms of carries generated during the addition operation: An addition overflows if the carry bits c_{in} into and c_{out} out of the sign position are different. Close examination of Table 2-3 on page 32 shows that the two rules are equivalent—there are only two cases where $c_{in} \neq c_{out}$, and these are the only two cases where $x = y$ and the sum bit is different.

overflow rules

2.6.4 Subtraction Rules

Two's-complement numbers may be subtracted as if they were ordinary unsigned binary numbers, and appropriate rules for detecting overflow may be formulated. However, most subtraction circuits for two's-complement numbers

two's-complement subtraction

do not perform subtraction directly. Rather, they negate the subtrahend by taking its two's complement, and then add it to the minuend using the normal rules for addition.

Negating the subtrahend and adding the minuend can be accomplished with only one addition operation as follows: Perform a bit-by-bit complement of the subtrahend and add the complemented subtrahend to the minuend with an initial carry (c_{in}) of 1 instead of 0. Examples are given below:

$$
\begin{array}{rr} & 1 \longleftarrow c_{in} \\ +4 \quad\quad 0100 & 0100 \\ -\ +3 \quad -\ 0011 & +\ 1100 \\ \hline +1 & 1\,0001 \end{array}
\qquad
\begin{array}{rr} & 1 \longleftarrow c_{in} \\ +3 \quad\quad 0011 & 0011 \\ -\ +4 \quad -\ 0100 & +\ 1011 \\ \hline -1 & 1111 \end{array}
$$

$$
\begin{array}{rr} & 1 \longleftarrow c_{in} \\ +3 \quad\quad 0011 & 0011 \\ -\ -4 \quad -\ 1100 & +\ 0011 \\ \hline +7 & 0111 \end{array}
\qquad
\begin{array}{rr} & 1 \longleftarrow c_{in} \\ -3 \quad\quad 1101 & 1101 \\ -\ -4 \quad -\ 1100 & +\ 0011 \\ \hline +1 & 1\,0001 \end{array}
$$

Overflow in subtraction can be detected by examining the signs of the minuend and the *complemented* subtrahend, using the same rule as in addition. Or, using the technique in the preceding examples, the carries into and out of the sign position can be observed and overflow detected irrespective of the signs of inputs and output, again using the same rule as in addition.

An attempt to negate the "extra" negative number results in overflow according to the rules above, when we add 1 in the complementation process:

$$
-(-8) = -1000 = \quad
\begin{array}{r} 0111 \\ +\ 0001 \\ \hline 1000 \ = \ -8 \end{array}
$$

However, this number can still be used in additions and subtractions as long as the final result does not exceed the number range:

$$
\begin{array}{rr} +4 \quad\quad 0100 \\ +\ -8 \quad +\ 1000 \\ \hline -4 \quad\quad 1100 \end{array}
\qquad
\begin{array}{rr} & 1 \longleftarrow c_{in} \\ -3 \quad\quad 1101 & 1101 \\ -\ -8 \quad -\ 1000 & +\ 0111 \\ \hline +5 & 1\,0101 \end{array}
$$

2.6.5 Two's-Complement and Unsigned Binary Numbers

Since two's-complement numbers are added and subtracted by the same basic binary addition and subtraction algorithms as unsigned numbers of the same length, a computer or other digital system can use the same adder circuit to deal with numbers of both types. However, the results must be interpreted differently, depending on whether the system is dealing with signed numbers (e.g., −8 through +7) or unsigned numbers (e.g., 0 through 15).

signed vs. unsigned numbers

We introduced a graphical representation of the 4-bit two's-complement system in Figure 2-3. We can relabel this figure as shown in Figure 2-4 to obtain a representation of the 4-bit unsigned numbers. The binary combinations occupy the same positions on the wheel, and a number is still added by moving the arrow a corresponding number of positions clockwise, and subtracted by moving the arrow counterclockwise.

An addition operation can be seen to exceed the range of the 4-bit unsigned-number system in Figure 2-4 if the arrow moves clockwise through the discontinuity between 0 and 15. In this case a *carry* out of the most significant bit position is said to occur.

carry

Likewise a subtraction operation exceeds the range of the number system if the arrow moves counterclockwise through the discontinuity. In this case a *borrow* out of the most significant bit position is said to occur.

borrow

From Figure 2-4 it is also evident that we may subtract an unsigned number n by counting *clockwise* $16 − n$ positions. This is equivalent to *adding* the 4-bit two's-complement of n. The subtraction produces a borrow if the corresponding addition of the two's complement *does not* produce a carry.

In summary, in unsigned addition the carry or borrow in the most significant bit position indicates an out-of-range result. In signed, two's-complement addition the overflow condition defined earlier indicates an out-of-range result. The carry from the most significant bit position is irrelevant in signed addition in the sense that overflow may or may not occur independently of whether or not a carry occurs.

Figure 2-4 A modular counting representation of 4-bit unsigned numbers.

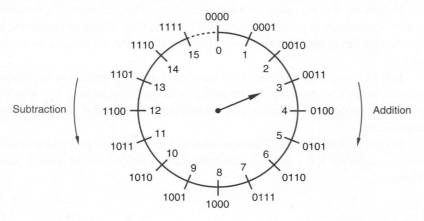

*2.7 Ones'-Complement Addition and Subtraction

Another look at Table 2-6 helps to explain the rule for adding ones'-complement numbers. If we start at 1000_2 (-7_{10}) and count up, we obtain each successive ones'-complement number by adding 1 to the previous one, *except* at the transition from 1111_2 (negative 0) to 0001_2 ($+1_{10}$). To maintain the proper count, we must add 2 instead of 1 whenever we count past 1111_2. This suggests a technique for adding ones'-complement numbers: Perform a standard binary addition, but add an extra 1 whenever we count past 1111_2.

ones'-complement addition

Counting past 1111_2 during an addition can be detected by observing the carry out of the sign position. Thus, the rule for adding ones'-complement numbers can be stated quite simply:

- Perform a standard binary addition; if there is a carry out of the sign position, add 1 to the result.

end-around carry

This rule is often called *end-around carry*. Examples of ones'-complement addition are given below; the last three include an end-around carry:

$$
\begin{array}{rr}
+3 & 0011 \\
+ \ +4 & + \ 0100 \\
\hline
+7 & 0111 \\
\end{array}
\qquad
\begin{array}{rr}
+4 & 0100 \\
+ \ -7 & + \ 1000 \\
\hline
-3 & 1100 \\
\end{array}
\qquad
\begin{array}{rr}
+5 & 0101 \\
+ \ -5 & + \ 1010 \\
\hline
-0 & 1111 \\
\end{array}
$$

$$
\begin{array}{rr}
-2 & 1101 \\
+ \ -5 & + \ 1010 \\
\hline
-7 & 10111 \\
& + \quad 1 \\
\hline
& 1000 \\
\end{array}
\qquad
\begin{array}{rr}
+6 & 0110 \\
+ \ -3 & + \ 1100 \\
\hline
+3 & 10010 \\
& + \quad 1 \\
\hline
& 0011 \\
\end{array}
\qquad
\begin{array}{rr}
-0 & 1111 \\
+ \ -0 & + \ 1111 \\
\hline
-0 & 11110 \\
& + \quad 1 \\
\hline
& 1111 \\
\end{array}
$$

Following the two-step addition rule above, the addition of a number and its ones' complement produces negative 0. In fact, an addition operation using this rule can never produce positive 0 unless both addends are positive 0 (think about it!).

ones'-complement subtraction

Just like two's-complement subtraction, ones'-complement subtraction is easiest to do by complementing the subtrahend and then adding. Overflow rules for ones'-complement addition and subtraction are also the same as for two's complement.

In conclusion, Table 2-7 summarizes the rules that we presented in this and previous sections for negation, addition, and subtraction in binary number systems.

Table 2-7 Summary of addition and subtraction rules for binary numbers.

Number System	Addition Rules	Negation Rules	Subtraction Rules
Unsigned	Add the numbers. Result is out of range if a carry out of the MSB occurs.	Not applicable	Subtract the subtrahend from the minuend. Result is out of range if a borrow out of the MSB occurs.
Signed magnitude	(same sign) Add the magnitudes; overflow occurs if a carry out of the MSB occurs; result has the same sign. (opposite sign) Subtract the smaller magnitude from the larger; overflow is impossible; result has the sign of the larger.	Change the number's sign bit.	Change the sign bit of the subtrahend and proceed as in addition.
Two's complement	Add, ignoring any carry out of the MSB. Overflow occurs if the carries into and out of the MSB are different.	Complement all bits of the number; add 1 to the result.	Complement all bits of the subtrahend and add to the minuend with an initial carry of 1.
Ones' complement	Add; if there is a carry out of the MSB, add 1 to result. Overflow occurs if carries into and out of the MSB are different.	Complement all bits of the number.	Complement all bits of the subtrahend and proceed as in addition.

*2.8 Binary Multiplication

In grammar school we learned to multiply by adding a list of shifted multiplicands computed according to the digits of the multiplier. The same method can be used to obtain the product of two unsigned binary numbers. Forming the shifted multiplicands is trivial in binary multiplication, since the only possible values of the multiplier digits are 0 and 1. An example is shown below:

shift-and-add multiplication

unsigned binary multiplication

```
      11              1011    multiplicand
    × 13          ×   1101    multiplier
    ─────         ────────
      33              1011
      11              0000
    ─────                     shifted multiplicands
     143              1011
                      1011
                  ────────
                  10001111    product
```

partial product

Instead of listing all the shifted multiplicands and then adding, in a digital system it is more convenient to add each shifted multiplicand as it is created to a *partial product*. Applying this technique to the previous example, four additions and partial products are used to multiply 4-bit numbers:

$$
\begin{array}{rl}
11 & \\
\times\ 13 & \\
\end{array}
\qquad
\begin{array}{rl}
1011 & \text{multiplicand} \\
\times\quad 1101 & \text{multiplier} \\
\hline
0000 & \text{partial product} \\
1011 & \text{shifted multiplicand} \\
\hline
01011 & \text{partial product} \\
0000\downarrow & \text{shifted multiplicand} \\
\hline
001011 & \text{partial product} \\
1011\downarrow\downarrow & \text{shifted multiplicand} \\
\hline
0110111 & \text{partial product} \\
1011\downarrow\downarrow\downarrow & \text{shifted multiplicand} \\
\hline
10001111 & \text{product} \\
\end{array}
$$

In general, when we multiply an *n*-bit number by an *m*-bit number, the resulting product requires at most $n + m$ bits to express. The shift-and-add algorithm requires *m* partial products and additions to obtain the result, but the first addition is trivial, since the first partial product is zero. Although the first partial product has only *n* significant bits, after each addition step the partial product gains one more significant bit, since each addition may produce a carry. At the same time, each step yields one more partial product bit, starting with the rightmost and working toward the left, that does not change. The shift-and-add algorithm can be performed by a digital circuit that includes a shift register, an adder, and control logic, as shown in <u>Section XSbb.3</u> at <u>DDPPonline</u>.

signed multiplication

Multiplication of signed numbers can be accomplished using unsigned multiplication and the usual grammar-school rules: Perform an unsigned multiplication of the magnitudes and make the product positive if the operands had the same sign, negative if they had different signs. This is very convenient in signed-magnitude systems, since the sign and magnitude are separate.

two's-complement multiplication

In the two's-complement system, obtaining the magnitude of a negative number and negating the unsigned product are nontrivial operations. This leads us to seek a more efficient way of performing two's-complement multiplication, described next.

Conceptually, unsigned multiplication is accomplished by a sequence of unsigned additions of the shifted multiplicands; at each step, the shift of the multiplicand corresponds to the weight of the multiplier bit. The bits in a two's-complement number have the same weights as in an unsigned number, except for the MSB, which has a negative weight (see Section 2.5.4). Thus, we can perform two's-complement multiplication by a sequence of two's-complement additions of shifted multiplicands, except for the last step, in which the shifted multiplicand corresponding to the MSB of the multiplier must be negated before it is added to the partial product. Our previous example is repeated below, this time interpreting the multiplier and multiplicand as two's-complement numbers:

−5	1011	multiplicand
× −3	× 1101	multiplier
	00000	partial product
	11011	shifted multiplicand
	111011	partial product
	00000↓	shifted multiplicand
	1111011	partial product
	11011↓↓	shifted multiplicand
	11100111	partial product
	00101↓↓↓	shifted and negated multiplicand
	00001111	product

Handling the MSBs is a little tricky because we gain one significant bit at each step and we are working with signed numbers. Therefore, before adding each shifted multiplicand and k-bit partial product, we change them to $k + 1$ significant bits by sign extension, as shown in color above. Each resulting sum has $k + 1$ bits; any carry out of the MSB of the $k + 1$-bit sum is ignored.

*2.9 Binary Division

The simplest binary division algorithm is based on the shift-and-subtract method that we learned in grammar school. Table 2-8 gives examples of this method for unsigned decimal and binary numbers. In both cases, we mentally compare the reduced dividend with multiples of the divisor to determine which multiple of

shift-and-subtract division

unsigned division

19	10011	quotient
11)217	1011)11011001	dividend
11	1011	shifted divisor
107	0101	reduced dividend
99	0000	shifted divisor
8	1010	reduced dividend
	0000	shifted divisor
	10100	reduced dividend
	1011	shifted divisor
	10011	reduced dividend
	1011	shifted divisor
	1000	remainder

Table 2-8
Example of long division.

the shifted divisor to subtract. In the decimal case, we first pick 11 as the greatest multiple of 11 less than 21, and then pick 99 as the greatest multiple less than 107. In the binary case, the choice is somewhat simpler, since the only two choices are zero and the divisor itself.

Division methods for binary numbers are somewhat complementary to binary multiplication methods. A typical division algorithm takes an $(n + m)$-bit dividend and an n-bit divisor, and produces an m-bit quotient and an n-bit remainder. A division *overflows* if the divisor is zero or the quotient would take more than m bits to express. In most computer division circuits, $n = m$.

division overflow

signed division

Division of signed numbers can be accomplished using unsigned division and the usual grammar school rules: Perform an unsigned division of the magnitudes and make the quotient positive if the operands had the same sign, negative if they had different signs. The remainder should be given the same sign as the dividend. As in multiplication, there are special techniques for performing division directly on two's-complement numbers; these techniques are often implemented in computer division circuits (see References).

2.10 Binary Codes for Decimal Numbers

Even though binary numbers are the most appropriate for the internal computations of a digital system, most people still prefer to deal with decimal numbers. As a result, the external interfaces of a digital system may read or display decimal numbers, and some digital devices actually process decimal numbers directly.

The human need to represent decimal numbers doesn't change the basic nature of digital electronic circuits—they still process signals that take on one of only two states that we call 0 and 1. Therefore, a decimal number is represented in a digital system by a string of bits, where different combinations of bit values in the string represent different decimal numbers. For example, if we use a 4-bit string to represent a decimal number, we might assign bit combination 0000 to decimal digit 0, 0001 to 1, 0010 to 2, and so on.

code
code word

A set of n-bit strings in which different bit strings represent different numbers or other things is called a *code*. A particular combination of n bit-values is called a *code word*. As we'll see in the examples of decimal codes in this section, there may or may not be an arithmetic relationship between the bit values in a code word and the thing that it represents. Furthermore, a code that uses n-bit strings need not contain 2^n valid code words.

At least four bits are needed to represent the ten decimal digits. There are billions and billions of different ways to choose ten 4-bit code words, but some of the more common decimal codes are listed in Table 2-9.

binary-coded decimal (BCD)

Perhaps the most "natural" decimal code is *binary-coded decimal (BCD)*, which encodes the digits 0 through 9 by their 4-bit unsigned binary representations, 0000 through 1001. The code words 1010 through 1111 are not used.

Table 2-9 Decimal codes.

Decimal digit	BCD (8421)	2421	Excess-3	Biquinary	1-out-of-10
0	0000	0000	0011	0100001	1000000000
1	0001	0001	0100	0100010	0100000000
2	0010	0010	0101	0100100	0010000000
3	0011	0011	0110	0101000	0001000000
4	0100	0100	0111	0110000	0000100000
5	0101	1011	1000	1000001	0000010000
6	0110	1100	1001	1000010	0000001000
7	0111	1101	1010	1000100	0000000100
8	1000	1110	1011	1001000	0000000010
9	1001	1111	1100	1010000	0000000001
Unused code words					
	1010	0101	0000	0000000	0000000000
	1011	0110	0001	0000001	0000000011
	1100	0111	0010	0000010	0000000101
	1101	1000	1101	0000011	0000000110
	1110	1001	1110	0000101	0000000111
	1111	1010	1111	. . .	. . .

Conversions between BCD and decimal representations are trivial, a direct substitution of four bits for each decimal digit. Some computer programs place two BCD digits in one 8-bit byte in *packed-BCD representation*; thus, one byte may represent the values from 0 to 99 as opposed to 0 to 255 for a normal unsigned 8-bit binary number. BCD numbers with any desired number of digits may be obtained by using one byte for each two digits.

packed-BCD representation

As with binary numbers, there are many possible representations of negative BCD numbers. Signed BCD numbers have one extra digit position for

BINOMIAL COEFFICIENTS   The number of different ways to choose m items from a set of n items is given by a *binomial coefficient*, denoted $\binom{n}{m}$, whose value is $\dfrac{n!}{m! \cdot (n-m)!}$. For a 4-bit decimal code, there are $\binom{16}{10}$ different ways to choose 10 out of 16 4-bit code words, and 10! ways to assign each different choice to the 10 digits. So there are $\dfrac{16!}{10! \cdot 6!} \cdot 10!$ or 29,059,430,400 different 4-bit decimal codes.

the sign. Both the signed-magnitude and 10's-complement representations are popular. In signed-magnitude BCD, the encoding of the sign bit string is arbitrary; in 10's-complement, 0000 indicates plus and 1001 indicates minus.

BCD addition
Addition of BCD digits is similar to adding 4-bit unsigned binary numbers, except that a correction must be made if a result exceeds 1001. The result is corrected by adding 6; examples are shown below:

$$
\begin{array}{rl}
5 & 0101 \\
+\ 9 & +\ 1001 \\
\hline
14 & 1110 \\
 & +\ 0110 \quad\text{— correction} \\
\hline
10+4 & 1\ 0100
\end{array}
\qquad
\begin{array}{rl}
4 & 0100 \\
+\ 5 & +\ 0101 \\
\hline
9 & 1001
\end{array}
$$

$$
\begin{array}{rl}
8 & 1000 \\
+\ 8 & +\ 1000 \\
\hline
16 & 1\ 0000 \\
 & +\ 0110 \quad\text{— correction} \\
\hline
10+6 & 1\ 0110
\end{array}
\qquad
\begin{array}{rl}
9 & 1001 \\
+\ 9 & +\ 1001 \\
\hline
18 & 1\ 0010 \\
 & +\ 0110 \quad\text{— correction} \\
\hline
10+8 & 1\ 1000
\end{array}
$$

Notice that the addition of two BCD digits produces a carry into the next digit position if either the initial binary addition or the correction-factor addition produces a carry. Many computers perform packed-BCD arithmetic using special instructions that handle the carry correction automatically.

weighted code
Binary-coded decimal is a *weighted code* because each decimal digit can be obtained from its code word by assigning a fixed weight to each code-word bit. The weights for the BCD bits are 8, 4, 2, and 1, and for this reason the code

8421 code
2421 code
self-complementing code
is sometimes called the *8421 code*. Another set of weights results in the *2421 code* shown in Table 2-9. This code has the advantage that it is *self-complementing*, that is, the code word for the 9s' complement of any digit may be obtained by complementing the individual bits of the digit's code word.

excess-3 code
Another self-complementing code shown in Table 2-9 is the *excess-3 code*. Although this code is not weighted, it has an arithmetic relationship with the BCD code—the code word for each decimal digit is the corresponding BCD code word plus 0011_2. Because the code words follow a standard binary counting sequence, standard binary counters can easily be made to count in excess-3 code, as we show at DDPPonline in Section Cntr.

biquinary code
Decimal codes can have more than four bits; for example, the *biquinary code* in Table 2-9 uses seven. The first two bits in a code word indicate whether the number is in the range 0–4 or 5–9, and the last five bits indicate which of the five numbers in the selected range is represented.

One potential advantage of using more than the minimum number of bits in a code is an error-detecting property. In the biquinary code, if any one bit in a code word is accidentally changed to the opposite value, the resulting code word does not represent a decimal digit and can therefore be flagged as an error. Out of 128 possible 7-bit code words, only 10 are valid and recognized as decimal digits; the rest can be flagged as errors if they appear.

A *1-out-of-10 code*, such as the one shown in the last column of Table 2-9, is the sparsest encoding for decimal digits, using 10 out of 1024 possible 10-bit code words.

1-out-of-10 code

2.11 Gray Code

In electromechanical applications of digital systems—such as machine tools, automotive braking systems, and copiers—it is sometimes necessary for an input sensor to produce a digital value that indicates a mechanical position. For example, Figure 2-5 is a conceptual sketch of an encoding disk and a set of contacts that produce one of eight 3-bit binary-coded values depending on the rotational position of the disk. The dark areas of the disk are connected to a signal source corresponding to logic 1, and the light areas are unconnected, which the contacts interpret as logic 0.

The encoder in Figure 2-5 has a problem when the disk is positioned at certain boundaries between the regions. For example, consider the boundary between the 001 and 010 regions of the disk; two of the encoded bits change here. What value will the encoder produce if the disk is positioned right on the theoretical boundary? Since we're on the border, both 001 and 010 are acceptable. However, because the mechanical assembly is not perfect, the two righthand contacts may both touch a "1" region, giving an incorrect reading of 011. Likewise, a reading of 000 is possible. In general, this sort of problem can occur at any boundary where more than one bit changes. The worst problems occur when all three bits are changing, as at the 000–111 and 011–100 boundaries.

The encoding-disk problem can be solved by devising a digital code in which only one bit changes between each pair of successive code words. Such a code is called a *Gray code*; a 3-bit Gray code is listed in Table 2-10. We've

Gray code

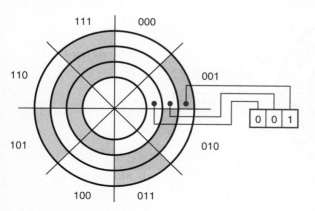

Figure 2-5
A mechanical encoding disk using a 3-bit binary code.

Table 2-10
A comparison of 3-bit binary code and Gray code.

Decimal Number	Binary Code	Gray Code
0	000	000
1	001	001
2	010	011
3	011	010
4	100	110
5	101	111
6	110	101
7	111	100

redesigned the encoding disk using this code as shown in Figure 2-6. Only one bit of the new disk changes at each border, so borderline readings give us a value on one side or the other of the border.

There are two convenient ways to construct a Gray code with any desired number of bits. The first method is based on the fact that Gray code is a *reflected code*; it can be defined (and constructed) recursively using the following rules:

reflected code

1. A 1-bit Gray code has two code words, 0 and 1.

2. The first 2^n code words of an $(n+1)$-bit Gray code equal the code words of an n-bit Gray code, written in order with a leading 0 appended.

3. The last 2^n code words of an $(n+1)$-bit Gray code equal the code words of an n-bit Gray code, but written in reverse order with a leading 1 appended.

If we draw a line between rows 3 and 4 of Table 2-10, we can see that rules 2 and 3 are true for the 3-bit Gray code. Of course, to construct an n-bit Gray code for an arbitrary value of n with this method, we must also construct a Gray code of each length smaller than n.

Figure 2-6
A mechanical encoding disk using a 3-bit Gray code.

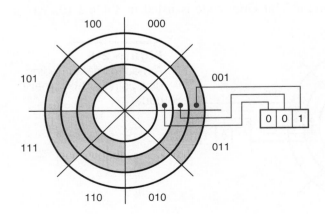

The second method allows us to derive an *n*-bit Gray-code code word directly from the corresponding *n*-bit binary code word:

1. The bits of an *n*-bit binary or Gray-code code word are numbered from right to left, from 0 to $n - 1$.

2. Bit *i* of a Gray-code code word is 0 if bits *i* and $i + 1$ of the corresponding binary code word are the same, else bit *i* is 1. (When $i + 1 = n$, bit *n* of the binary code word is considered to be 0.)

Again, inspection of Table 2-10 shows that this is true for the 3-bit Gray code.

*2.12 Character Codes

As we showed in the preceding section, a string of bits need not represent a number, and in fact most of the information processed by computers is nonnumeric. The most common type of nonnumeric data is *text*, strings of characters from some character set. Each character is represented in the computer by a bit string according to an established convention.

text

The most commonly used character code is *ASCII* (pronounced *ASS key*), the American Standard Code for Information Interchange. ASCII represents each character with a 7-bit string, yielding a total of 128 different characters shown in Table 2-11. The code contains the uppercase and lowercase alphabet, numerals, punctuation, and various nonprinting control characters. Thus, the text string "Yeccch!" is represented by a rather innocuous-looking list of seven 7-bit numbers:

ASCII

1011001   1100101   1100011   1100011   1100011   1101000   0100001

2.13 Codes for Actions, Conditions, and States

The codes that we've described so far are generally used to represent things that we would probably consider to be "data"—things like numbers, positions, and characters. Programmers know that dozens of different data types can be used in a single computer program.

In digital system design, we often encounter nondata applications where a string of bits must be used to control an action, to flag a condition, or to represent the current state of the hardware. Probably the most commonly used type of code for such an application is a simple binary code. If there are *n* different actions, conditions, or states, we can represent them with a *b*-bit binary code with $b = \lceil \log_2 n \rceil$ bits. (The brackets $\lceil \ \rceil$ denote the *ceiling function*—the smallest integer greater than or equal to the bracketed quantity. Thus, *b* is the smallest integer such that $2^b \geq n$.)

$\lceil \ \rceil$

ceiling function

For example, consider a simple traffic-light controller. The signals at the intersection of a north-south (N-S) and an east-west (E-W) street might be in any

Table 2-11 American Standard Code for Information Interchange (ASCII), Standard No. X3.4-1968 of the American National Standards Institute.

$b_3b_2b_1b_0$	Row (hex)	000 0	001 1	010 2	011 3	100 4	101 5	110 6	111 7
0000	0	NUL	DLE	SP	0	@	P	`	p
0001	1	SOH	DC1	!	1	A	Q	a	q
0010	2	STX	DC2	"	2	B	R	b	r
0011	3	ETX	DC3	#	3	C	S	c	s
0100	4	EOT	DC4	$	4	D	T	d	t
0101	5	ENQ	NAK	%	5	E	U	e	u
0110	6	ACK	SYN	&	6	F	V	f	v
0111	7	BEL	ETB	'	7	G	W	g	w
1000	8	BS	CAN	(	8	H	X	h	x
1001	9	HT	EM	)	9	I	Y	i	y
1010	A	LF	SUB	*	:	J	Z	j	z
1011	B	VT	ESC	+	;	K	[	k	{
1100	C	FF	FS	,	<	L	\	l	|
1101	D	CR	GS	–	=	M	]	m	}
1110	E	SO	RS	.	>	N	^	n	~
1111	F	SI	US	/	?	O	_	o	DEL

$b_6b_5b_4$ (column)

Control codes

NUL	Null	DLE	Data link escape
SOH	Start of heading	DC1	Device control 1
STX	Start of text	DC2	Device control 2
ETX	End of text	DC3	Device control 3
EOT	End of transmission	DC4	Device control 4
ENQ	Enquiry	NAK	Negative acknowledge
ACK	Acknowledge	SYN	Synchronize
BEL	Bell	ETB	End transmitted block
BS	Backspace	CAN	Cancel
HT	Horizontal tab	EM	End of medium
LF	Line feed	SUB	Substitute
VT	Vertical tab	ESC	Escape
FF	Form feed	FS	File separator
CR	Carriage return	GS	Group separator
SO	Shift out	RS	Record separator
SI	Shift in	US	Unit separator
SP	Space	DEL	Delete or rubout

Table 2-12 States in a traffic-light controller.

State	Lights						Code Word
	N-S Green	N-S Yellow	N-S Red	E-W Green	E-W Yellow	E-W Red	
N-S go	ON	off	off	off	off	ON	000
N-S wait	off	ON	off	off	off	ON	001
N-S delay	off	off	ON	off	off	ON	010
E-W go	off	off	ON	ON	off	off	100
E-W wait	off	off	ON	off	ON	off	101
E-W delay	off	off	ON	off	off	ON	110

of the six states listed in Table 2-12. These states can be encoded in three bits, as shown in the last column of the table. Only six of the eight possible 3-bit code words are used, and the assignment of the six chosen code words to states is arbitrary, so many other encodings are possible. An experienced digital designer chooses a particular encoding to minimize circuit cost or to optimize some other parameter (like design time—there's no need to try billions and billions of possible encodings).

Another application of a binary code is illustrated in Figure 2-7(a) on the next page. Here, we have a system with n devices, each of which can perform a certain action. The characteristics of the devices are such that they may be enabled to operate only one at a time. The control unit produces a binary-coded "device-select" word with $\lceil \log_2 n \rceil$ bits to indicate which device is enabled at any time. The "device-select" code word is applied to each device, which compares it with its own "device ID" to determine whether it is enabled.

Although a binary code has the smallest code words (fewest bits), it isn't always the best choice for encoding actions, conditions, or states. Figure 2-7(b) shows how to control n devices with a *1-out-of-n code*, an n-bit code in which valid code words have one bit equal to 1 and the rest of the bits equal to 0. Each bit of the 1-out-of-n code word is connected directly to the enable input of a corresponding device. This simplifies the design of the devices, since they no longer have device IDs; they need only a single "enable" input bit.

1-out-of-n code

The code words of a 1-out-of-10 code were listed in Table 2-9. Sometimes an all-0s word may also be included in a 1-out-of-n code, to indicate that no device is selected. Another common code is an *inverted 1-out-of-n code*, in which valid code words have one 0 bit and the rest of the bits equal to 1.

inverted 1-out-of-n code

In complex systems, a combination of coding techniques may be used. For example, consider a system similar to Figure 2-7(b), in which each of the n devices contains up to s subdevices. The control unit could produce a device-

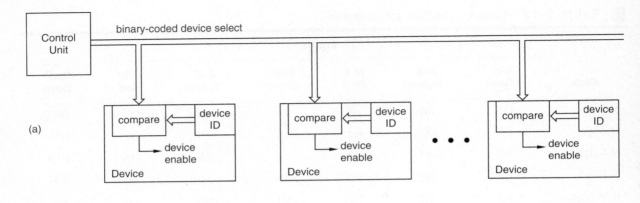

(a)

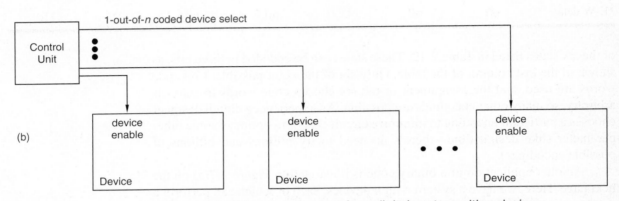

(b)

Figure 2-7 Control structure for a digital system with *n* devices:
(a) using a binary code; (b) using a 1-out-of-*n* code.

select code word with a 1-out-of-*n* coded field to select a device, and a $\lceil \log_2 s \rceil$-bit binary-coded field to select one of the *s* subdevices of the selected device.

m-out-of-n code

An *m-out-of-n code* is a generalization of the 1-out-of-*n* code in which valid code words have *m* bits equal to 1 and the rest of the bits equal to 0. An *m*-out-of-*n* code word can be detected with an *m*-input **AND** gate, which produces a 1 output if all of its inputs are 1. This is fairly simple and inexpensive to do, yet for most values of *m*, an *m*-out-of-*n* code typically has far more valid code words than a 1-out-of-*n* code. The total number of code words is given by the binomial coefficient $\binom{n}{m}$, which has the value $\frac{n!}{m! \cdot (n-m)!}$. Thus, a 2-out-of-4 code has 6 valid code words, and a 3-out-of-10 code has 120.

8B10B code

An important variation of an *m*-out-of-*n* code is the *8B10B code* used in the 802.3z Gigabit Ethernet standard. This code uses 10 bits to represent 256 valid code words, or 8 bits worth of data. Most code words use a 5-out-of-10 coding. However, since $\binom{10}{5}$ is only 252, some 4- and 6-out-of-10 words are also used to complete the code in a very interesting way; more on this in Section 2.16.2.

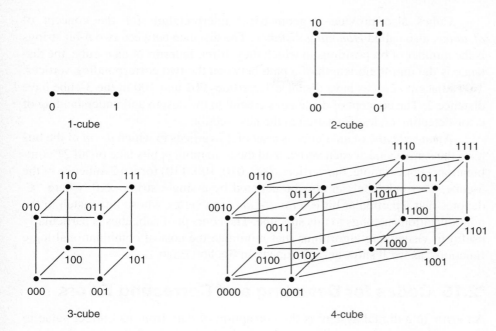

Figure 2-8
n-cubes for $n = 1, 2,$
3, and 4.

*2.14 *n*-Cubes and Distance

An *n*-bit string can be visualized geometrically, as a vertex of an object called an   *n-cube*
n-cube. Figure 2-8 shows *n*-cubes for $n = 1, 2, 3, 4$. An *n*-cube has 2^n vertices,
each of which is labeled with an *n*-bit string. Edges are drawn so that each vertex
is adjacent to *n* other vertices whose labels differ from the given vertex in only
one bit. Beyond $n = 4$, *n*-cubes are really tough to draw.

For small values of *n*, *n*-cubes make it easy to visualize certain coding and
logic-minimization problems. For example, the problem of designing an *n*-bit
Gray code is equivalent to finding a path along the edges of an *n*-cube, a path that
visits each vertex exactly once. The paths for 3- and 4-bit Gray codes are shown
in Figure 2-9.

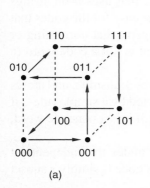

(a)

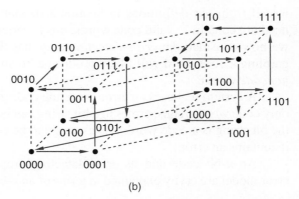

(b)

Figure 2-9
Traversing *n*-cubes
in Gray-code order:
(a) 3-cube;
(b) 4-cube.

distance
Hamming distance

Cubes also provide a geometrical interpretation for the concept of *distance*, also called *Hamming distance*. The distance between two n-bit strings is the number of bit positions in which they differ. In terms of an n-cube, the distance is the minimum length of a path between the two corresponding vertices. Two adjacent vertices have distance 1; vertices 001 and 100 in the 3-cube have distance 2. The concept of distance is crucial in the design and understanding of error-detecting codes, discussed in the next section.

m-subcube

An *m-subcube* of an n-cube is a set of 2^m vertices in which $n - m$ of the bits have the same value at each vertex, and the remaining m bits take on all 2^m combinations. For example, the vertices (000, 010, 100, 110) form a 2-subcube of the 3-cube. This subcube can also be denoted by a single string, xx0, where "x"

don't-care

denotes that a particular bit is a *don't-care*; any vertex whose bits match in the non-x positions belongs to this subcube. The concept of subcubes is particularly useful in visualizing algorithms that minimize the cost of combinational logic functions, as we'll show at <u>DDPPonline</u> in <u>Section Pmin.1</u>.

*2.15 Codes for Detecting and Correcting Errors

error
failure
temporary failure
permanent failure

An *error* in a digital system is the corruption of data from its correct value to some other value. An error is caused by a physical *failure*. Failures can be either temporary or permanent. For example, a cosmic ray or alpha particle can cause a temporary failure of a memory circuit, changing the value of a bit stored in it. Letting a circuit get too hot or zapping it with static electricity can cause a permanent failure, so that it never works correctly again.

error model
*independent error
  model*
single error
multiple error

The effects of failures on data are predicted by *error models*. The simplest error model, which we consider here, is called the *independent error model*. In this model, a single physical failure is assumed to affect only a single bit of data; the corrupted data is said to contain a *single error*. Multiple failures may cause *multiple errors*—two or more bits in error—but multiple errors are normally assumed to be less likely than single errors.

2.15.1 Error-Detecting Codes

Recall from our definitions in Section 2.10 that a code that uses n-bit strings need not contain 2^n valid code words; this is certainly the case for the codes that we now consider. An *error-detecting code* has the property that corrupting or garbling a code word will likely produce a bit string that is *not* a code word (a

error-detecting code

noncode word

noncode word).

A system that uses an error-detecting code generates, transmits, and stores only code words. Thus, errors in a bit string can be detected by a simple rule—if the bit string is a code word, it is assumed to be correct; if it is a noncode word, it contains an error.

An n-bit code and its error-detecting properties under the independent error model are easily explained in terms of an n-cube. A code is simply a subset

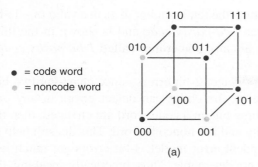

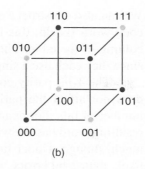

● = code word
● = noncode word

(a)

(b)

Figure 2-10
Code words in two
different 3-bit codes:
(a) minimum distance
= 1, does not detect
all single errors;
(b) minimum distance
= 2, detects all single
errors.

of the vertices of the n-cube. In order for the code to detect all single errors, no code-word vertex can be immediately adjacent to another code-word vertex.

For example, Figure 2-10(a) shows a 3-bit code with five code words. Code word 111 is immediately adjacent to code words 110, 011, and 101. Since a single failure could change 111 to 110, 011, or 101, this code does not detect all single errors. If we make 111 a noncode word, we obtain a code that does have the single-error-detecting property, as shown in (b). No single error can change one code word into another.

The ability of a code to detect single errors can be stated in terms of the concept of distance introduced in the preceding section:

- A code detects all single errors if the *minimum distance* between all possible pairs of code words is 2.

minimum distance

In general, we need $n + 1$ bits to construct a single-error-detecting code with 2^n code words. The first n bits of a code word, called *information bits*, may be any of the 2^n n-bit strings. To obtain a minimum-distance-2 code, we add one more bit, called a *parity bit*, that is set to 0 if there are an even number of 1s among the information bits, and to 1 otherwise. This is illustrated in the first two columns of Table 2-13 for a code with three information bits. A valid $(n + 1)$-bit code word has an even number of 1s, and this code is called an *even-parity code*.

information bit

parity bit

even-parity code

Information Bits	Even-parity Code	Odd-parity Code
000	000 0	000 1
001	001 1	001 0
010	010 1	010 0
011	011 0	011 1
100	100 1	100 0
101	101 0	101 1
110	110 0	110 1
111	111 1	111 0

Table 2-13
Distance-2 codes with
three information bits.

We can also construct a code in which the total number of 1s in a valid $(n + 1)$-bit code word is odd; this is called an *odd-parity code* and is shown in the third column of the table. These codes are also sometimes called *1-bit parity codes*, since they each use a single parity bit.

The 1-bit parity codes do not detect 2-bit errors, since changing two bits does not affect the parity. However, the codes can detect errors in any *odd* number of bits. For example, if three bits in a code word are changed, then the resulting word has the wrong parity and is a noncode word. This doesn't help us much, though. Under the independent error model, 3-bit errors are much less likely than 2-bit errors, which are not detectable. Thus, practically speaking, the 1-bit parity codes' error-detection capability stops after 1-bit errors. Other codes, with minimum distance greater than 2, can be used to detect multiple errors.

2.15.2 Error-Correcting and Multiple-Error-Detecting Codes

check bits

By using more than one parity bit, or *check bits*, according to some well-chosen rules, we can create a code whose minimum distance is greater than 2. Before showing how this can be done, let's look at how such a code can be used to correct single errors or detect multiple errors.

Suppose that a code has a minimum distance of 3. Figure 2-11 shows a fragment of the *n*-cube for such a code. As shown, there are at least two noncode words between each pair of code words. Now suppose we transmit code words

Figure 2-11
Some code words and noncode words in a 7-bit, distance-3 code.

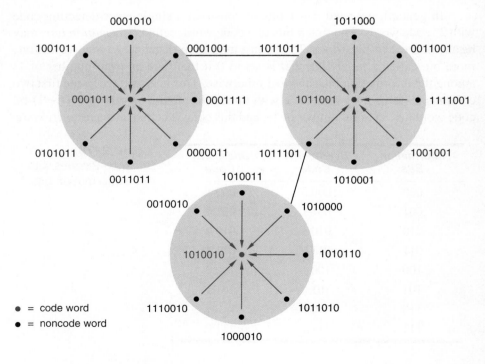

● = code word
● = noncode word

and assume that failures affect at most one bit of each received code word. Then a received noncode word with a 1-bit error will be closer to the originally transmitted code word than to any other code word. Therefore, when we receive a noncode word, we can *correct* the error by changing the received noncode word to the nearest code word, as indicated by the arrows in the figure. Deciding which code word was originally transmitted to produce a received word is called *decoding*, and the hardware that does this is an error-correcting *decoder*.

error correction

decoding
decoder

A code that is used to correct errors is called an *error-correcting code*. In general, if a code has minimum distance $2c + 1$, it can be used to correct errors that affect up to c bits ($c = 1$ in the preceding example). If a code's minimum distance is $2c + d + 1$, it can be used to correct errors in up to c bits and to detect errors in up to d additional bits.

error-correcting code

For example, Figure 2-12(a) on the next page shows a fragment of the n-cube for a code with minimum distance 4 ($c = 1$, $d = 1$). Single-bit errors that produce noncode words 00101010 and 11010011 can be corrected. However, an error that produces 10100011 cannot be corrected, because no single-bit error can produce this noncode word, and either of two 2-bit errors could have produced it. So the code can detect a 2-bit error, but it cannot correct it.

When a noncode word is received, we don't know which code word was originally transmitted; we only know which code word is closest to what we've received. Thus, as shown in Figure 2-12(b), a 3-bit error may be "corrected" to the wrong value. The possibility of making this kind of mistake may be acceptable if 3-bit errors are very unlikely to occur. On the other hand, if we are concerned about 3-bit errors, we can change the decoding policy for the code. Instead of trying to correct errors, we just flag all noncode words as uncorrectable errors. Thus, as shown in (c), we can use the same distance-4 code to detect up to 3-bit errors but correct no errors ($c = 0$, $d = 3$).

2.15.3 Hamming Codes

In 1950, R. W. Hamming described a general method for constructing codes with a minimum distance of 3, now called *Hamming codes*. For any value of i, his method yields a $(2^i - 1)$-bit code with i check bits and $2^i - 1 - i$ information bits. Distance-3 codes with a smaller number of information bits are obtained by deleting information bits from a Hamming code with a larger number of bits.

Hamming code

The bit positions in a Hamming code word can be numbered from 1 through $2^i - 1$. In this case, any position whose number is a power of 2 is a check bit, and the remaining positions are information bits. Each check bit is grouped with a subset of the information bits, as specified by a *parity-check matrix*. As

parity-check matrix

DECISIONS,
DECISIONS   The names *decoding* and *decoder* make sense, since they are just distance-1 perturbations of *deciding* and *decider*.

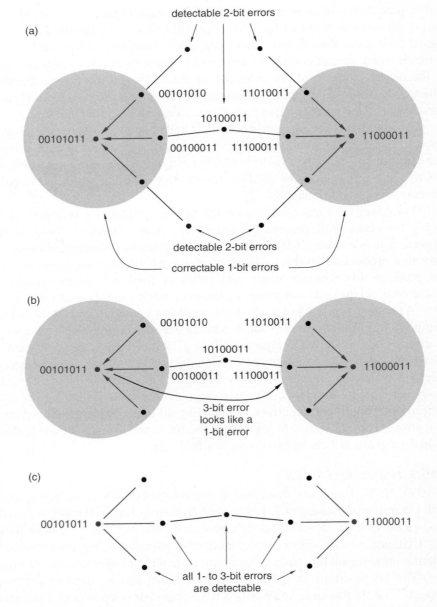

Figure 2-12
Some code words and
noncode words in an 8-bit,
distance-4 code:
(a) correcting 1-bit and
detecting 2-bit errors;
(b) incorrectly "correcting"
a 3-bit error;
(c) correcting no errors but
detecting up to 3-bit errors.

shown in Figure 2-13(a), each check bit is grouped with the information positions whose numbers have a 1 in the same bit when expressed in binary. For
example, check bit 2 (010) is grouped with information bits 3 (011), 6 (110), and
7 (111). For a given combination of information-bit values, each check bit is
chosen to produce even parity, that is, so the total number of 1s in its group
is even.

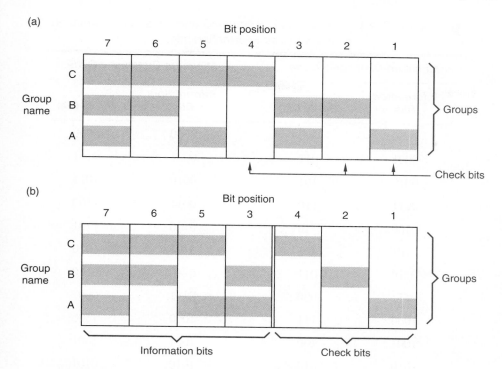

Figure 2-13
Parity-check
matrices for 7-bit
Hamming codes:
(a) with bit positions
in numerical order;
(b) with check bits
and information bits
separated.

Traditionally, the bit positions of a parity-check matrix and the resulting code words are rearranged so that all of the check bits are on the right, as in Figure 2-13(b). The first two columns of Table 2-14 list the resulting code words.

We can prove that the minimum distance of a Hamming code is 3 by proving that at least a 3-bit change must be made to a code word to obtain another code word. That is, we'll prove that a 1-bit or 2-bit change in a code word yields a noncode word.

If we change one bit of a code word, in position j, then we change the parity of every group that contains position j. Since every information bit is contained in at least one group, at least one group has incorrect parity, and the result is a noncode word.

What happens if we change two bits, in positions j and k? Parity groups that contain both positions j and k will still have correct parity, since parity is not affected when an even number of bits are changed. However, since j and k are different, their binary representations differ in at least one bit, corresponding to one of the parity groups. This group has only one bit changed, resulting in incorrect parity and a noncode word.

If you understand this proof, you should also understand how the position-numbering rules for constructing a Hamming code are a simple consequence of the proof. For the first part of the proof (1-bit errors), we required that the position numbers be nonzero. And for the second part (2-bit errors), we required

Table 2-14 Code words in distance-3 and distance-4 Hamming codes with four information bits.

Minimum-Distance-3 Code		Minimum-Distance-4 Code	
Information Bits	Parity Bits	Information Bits	Parity Bits
0000	000	0000	0000
0001	011	0001	0111
0010	101	0010	1011
0011	110	0011	1100
0100	110	0100	1101
0101	101	0101	1010
0110	011	0110	0110
0111	000	0111	0001
1000	111	1000	1110
1001	100	1001	1001
1010	010	1010	0101
1011	001	1011	0010
1100	001	1100	0011
1101	010	1101	0100
1110	100	1110	1000
1111	111	1111	1111

that no two positions have the same number. Thus, with an i-bit position number, you can construct a Hamming code with up to $2^i - 1$ bit positions.

error-correcting decoder

syndrome

The proof also suggests how we can design an *error-correcting decoder* for a received Hamming code word. First, we check all of the parity groups; if all have even parity, then the received word is assumed to be correct. If one or more groups have odd parity, then a single error is assumed to have occurred. The pattern of groups that have odd parity (called the *syndrome*) must match one of the columns in the parity-check matrix; the corresponding bit position is assumed to contain the wrong value and is complemented. For example, using the code defined by Figure 2-13(b), suppose we receive the word 0101011. Groups B and C have odd parity, corresponding to position 6 of the parity-check matrix (the syndrome is 110, or 6). By complementing the bit in position 6 of the received word, we determine that the correct word is 0001011.

A distance-3 Hamming code can easily be extended to increase its minimum distance to 4. We simply add one more check bit, chosen so that the parity of all the bits, including the new one, is even. As in the 1-bit even-parity code, this bit ensures that all errors affecting an odd number of bits are detectable. In particular, any 3-bit error is detectable. We already showed that 1- and 2-bit errors are detected by the other parity bits, so the minimum distance of the extended code must be 4.

extended Hamming code

Distance-3 and distance-4 extended Hamming codes are commonly used to detect and correct errors in computer memory systems, especially in large servers where memory circuits account for the bulk of the system's electronics and hence failures. These codes are especially attractive for very wide memory words, since the required number of parity bits grows slowly with the width of the memory word, as shown in Table 2-15.

Table 2-15 Word sizes of distance-3 and distance-4 extended Hamming codes.

Information Bits	Minimum-Distance-3 Codes		Minimum-Distance-4 Codes	
	Parity Bits	Total Bits	Parity Bits	Total Bits
1	2	3	3	4
≤ 4	3	≤ 7	4	≤ 8
≤ 11	4	≤ 15	5	≤ 16
≤ 26	5	≤ 31	6	≤ 32
≤ 57	6	≤ 63	7	≤ 64
≤ 120	7	≤ 127	8	≤ 128

2.15.4 CRC Codes

Beyond Hamming codes, many other error-detecting and -correcting codes have been developed. The most important codes, which happen to include Hamming codes, are the *cyclic-redundancy-check (CRC) codes*. A rich theory has been developed for these codes, focused both on their error-detecting and correcting properties and on the design of inexpensive encoders and decoders for them (see References).

cyclic-redundancy-check (CRC) code

Two important applications of CRC codes are in disk drives and in data networks. In a disk drive, each block of data (typically 512 bytes) is protected by a CRC code, so that errors within a block can be detected and sometimes corrected. In a data network, each packet of data ends with check bits in a CRC code. The CRC codes for both applications were selected because of their burst-error detecting properties. In addition to single-bit errors, they can detect multibit errors that are clustered together within the disk block or packet. Such errors are more likely than errors of randomly distributed bits, because of the likely physical causes of errors in the two applications—surface defects in disk drives and noise bursts in communication links.

2.15.5 Two-Dimensional Codes

two-dimensional code

Another way to obtain a code with large minimum distance is to construct a *two-dimensional code*, as illustrated in Figure 2-14(a). The information bits are conceptually arranged in a two-dimensional array, and parity bits are provided to check both the rows and the columns. A code C_{row} with minimum distance d_{row} is used for the rows, and a possibly different code C_{col} with minimum distance d_{col} is used for the columns. That is, the row-parity bits are selected so that each row is a code word in C_{row} and the column-parity bits are selected so that each column is a code word in C_{col}. (The "corner" parity bits can be chosen according to either code.) The minimum distance of the two-dimensional code is the product of d_{row}

product code

and d_{col}; in fact, two-dimensional codes are sometimes called *product codes*.

As shown in Figure 2-14(b), the simplest two-dimensional code uses 1-bit even-parity codes for the rows and columns and has a minimum distance of $2 \cdot 2$,

Figure 2-14
Two-dimensional codes:
(a) general structure;
(b) using even parity for both the row and column codes to obtain minimum distance 4;
(c) typical pattern of an undetectable error.

(a)

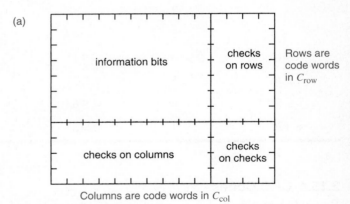

(b)

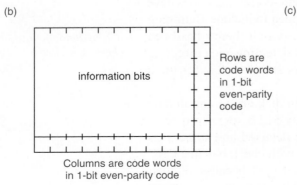

(c)

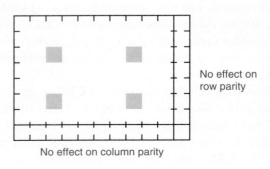

or 4. You can easily prove that the minimum distance is 4 by convincing yourself that any pattern of one, two, or three bits in error causes incorrect parity of a row or a column or both. In order to obtain an undetectable error, at least four bits must be changed in a rectangular pattern as in (c).

The error-detecting and correcting procedures for this code are straightforward. Assume we are reading information one row at a time. As we read each row, we check its row code. If an error is detected in a row, we can't tell which bit is wrong from the row check alone. However, assuming only one row is bad, we can reconstruct it by forming the bit-by-bit Exclusive OR of the columns, omitting the bad row, but including the column-check row.

To obtain an even larger minimum distance, a distance-3 or -4 Hamming code can be used for the row or column code or both. It is also possible to construct a code in three or more dimensions, with minimum distance equal to the product of the minimum distances in each dimension.

An important application of two-dimensional codes is in RAID storage systems. *RAID* stands for "redundant array of inexpensive disks." In this scheme, $n + 1$ identical disk drives are used to store n disks worth of data. For example, eight 200-gigabyte drives could be used to store 1.6 terabytes of non-redundant data, and a ninth 200-gigabyte drive would be used to store checking information. With such a setup, you could store about 400 movies in MPEG-2 format, and never have to worry about losing one to a (single) hard-drive crash!

Figure 2-15 shows the general scheme of a two-dimensional code for a RAID system; each disk drive is considered to be a row in the code. Each drive stores m blocks of data, where a block typically contains 512 bytes. For example, a 200-gigabyte drive would store about 4 billion blocks. As shown in the figure, each block includes its own check bits in a CRC code, to detect and possibly correct errors within that block. The first n drives store the nonredundant data. Each block in drive $n + 1$ stores parity bits for the corresponding blocks in the first n

RAID

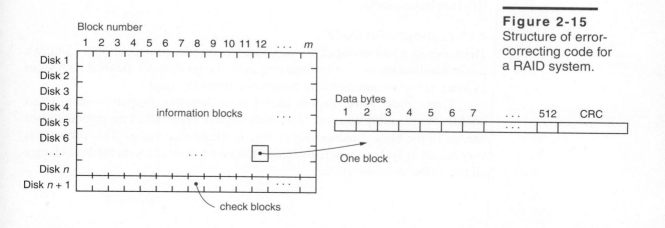

Figure 2-15
Structure of error-correcting code for a RAID system.

drives. That is, each bit i in drive $n+1$, block b, is chosen so that there are an even number of 1s in block b, bit position i, across all the drives.

In operation, errors in the information blocks are detected by the CRC code. Whenever an error is detected on one of the drives and cannot be corrected using the local CRC code, the block's original contents can still be reconstructed by computing the parity of the corresponding blocks in all the other drives, including drive $n+1$. This method still works even if you lose *all* of the data on a single drive.

Although RAID correction operations require n extra disk reads plus some computation, it's better than losing your data! Write operations also have extra disk accesses, to update the corresponding check block when an information block is written (see Exercise 2.50). Since disk writes are much less frequent than reads in typical applications, this overhead usually is not a problem.

2.15.6 Checksum Codes

The parity-checking operation that we've used in the previous subsections is essentially modulo-2 addition of bits—the sum modulo 2 of a group of bits is 0 if the number of 1s in the group is even, and 1 if it is odd. This approach of modular addition can be extended to other bases besides 2 to form check digits.

For example, a computer stores information as a set of 8-bit bytes. Each byte may be considered to have a decimal value from 0 to 255. Therefore, we can use modulo-256 addition to check the bytes. We form a single check byte, called *checksum*
checksum code a *checksum*, that is the sum modulo 256 of all the information bytes. The resulting *checksum code* can detect any single *byte* error, since such an error will cause a recomputed sum of bytes to disagree with the checksum.

Checksum codes can also use a different modulus of addition. In particular, *ones'-complement* checksum codes using modulo-255, ones'-complement addition are important
checksum code because of their special computational and error-detecting properties, and because they are used to check packet headers in the ubiquitous Internet Protocol (IP) (see References).

2.15.7 *m*-out-of-*n* Codes

The 1-out-of-n and m-out-of-n codes that we introduced in Section 2.13 have a minimum distance of 2, since changing only one bit changes the total number of 1s in a code word and therefore produces a noncode word.

These codes have another useful error-detecting property—they detect *unidirectional error* unidirectional multiple errors. In a *unidirectional error*, all of the erroneous bits change in the same direction (0s change to 1s, or vice versa). This property is very useful in systems where the predominant error mechanism tends to change all bits in the same direction.

2.16 Codes for Serial Data Transmission and Storage

2.16.1 Parallel and Serial Data

Most computers and other digital systems transmit and store data in a *parallel* format. In parallel data transmission, a separate signal line is provided for each bit of a data word. In parallel data storage, all of the bits of a data word can be written or read simultaneously.

parallel data

    Parallel formats are not cost effective for some applications. For example, parallel transmission of data bytes over the telephone network would require eight phone lines, and parallel storage of data bytes on a magnetic disk would require a disk drive with eight separate read/write heads. *Serial* formats allow data to be transmitted or stored one bit at a time. Even in board-level design and in computer-peripheral interfacing, serial formats can reduce cost and simplify certain system-design problems; for example, PCI Express uses a serial format.

serial data

    Figure 2-16 illustrates some of the basic ideas in serial data transmission. A repetitive clock signal, named CLOCK in the figure, defines the rate at which bits are transmitted, one bit per clock cycle. Thus, the *bit rate* in bits per second (bps) numerically equals the clock frequency in cycles per second (hertz, or Hz).

bit rate, bps

    The reciprocal of the bit rate is called the *bit time* and numerically equals the clock period in seconds (s). This amount of time is reserved on the serial data line (named SERDATA in the figure) for each bit that is transmitted. The time occupied by each bit is sometimes called a *bit cell*. The format of the actual signal that appears on the line during each bit cell depends on the *line code*. In the simplest line code, called *Non-Return-to-Zero (NRZ)*, a 1 is transmitted by placing a 1 on the line for the entire bit cell, and a 0 is transmitted as a 0. More complex line codes have other rules, as discussed in the next subsection.

bit time

bit cell
line code
Non-Return-to-Zero (NRZ)

Figure 2-16 Basic concepts for serial data transmission.

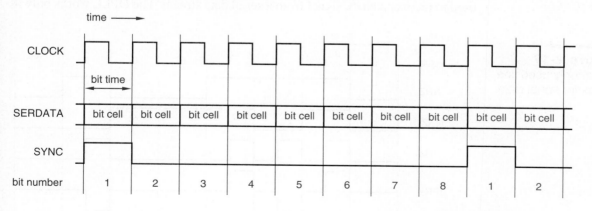

synchronization signal

Regardless of the line code, a serial data-transmission or storage system needs some way of identifying the significance of each bit in the serial stream. For example, suppose that 8-bit bytes are transmitted serially. How can we tell which bit is the first bit of each byte? A *synchronization signal*, named SYNC in Figure 2-16, provides the necessary information; it is 1 for the first bit of each byte.

Evidently, we need a minimum of three signals to recover a serial data stream: a clock to define the bit cells, a synchronization signal to define the word boundaries, and the serial data itself. In some applications, like the interconnection of modules in a computer or telecommunications system, a separate wire is used for each of these signals, since reducing the number of wires per connection from *n* to three is savings enough. We give an example of a 3-wire serial data system in Section XSbb.1 at DDPPonline.

But in many applications, the cost of having three separate signals is still too high (e.g., three phone lines, three read/write heads). Such systems typically combine all three signals into a single serial data stream and use sophisticated analog and digital circuits to recover the clock and synchronization information from the data stream, as discussed in the next subsection.

*2.16.2 Serial Line Codes

The most commonly used line codes for serial data are illustrated in Figure 2-17. In the NRZ code, each bit value is sent on the line for the entire bit cell. This is the simplest and most reliable coding scheme for short-distance transmission. However, it generally requires a clock signal to be sent along with the data to define the bit cells. Otherwise, it is not possible for the receiver to determine how many 0s or 1s are represented by a continuous 0 or 1 level. For example, without a clock signal to define the bit cells, the NRZ waveform in Figure 2-17 might be erroneously interpreted as 01010.

digital phase-locked loop (DPLL)

A *digital phase-locked loop (DPLL)* is an analog/digital circuit that can be used to recover a clock signal from a serial data stream. The DPLL works only if

Figure 2-17
Commonly used line codes for serial data.

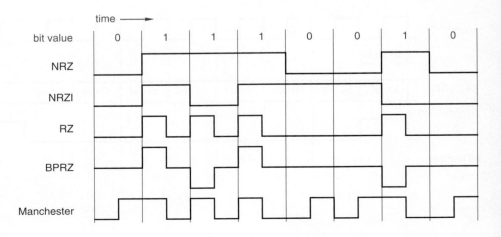

the serial data stream contains enough 0-to-1 and 1-to-0 transitions to give the DPLL "hints" about when the original clock transitions took place. With NRZ-coded data, the DPLL works only if the data does not contain any long, continuous streams of 1s or 0s.

Some serial transmission and storage media are *transition sensitive*; they cannot transmit or store absolute 0 or 1 levels, only transitions between two discrete levels. For example, a magnetic disk or tape stores information by changing the polarity of the medium's magnetization in regions corresponding to the stored bits. When the information is recovered, it is not feasible to determine the absolute magnetization polarity of a region, only that the polarity changes between one region and the next.

transition-sensitive media

Data stored in NRZ format on transition-sensitive media cannot be recovered unambiguously; the data in Figure 2-17 might be interpreted as 01110010 or 10001101. The *Non-Return-to-Zero Invert-on-1s (NRZI)* code overcomes this limitation by sending a 1 as the opposite of the level that was sent during the previous bit cell, and a 0 as the same level. A DPLL can recover the clock from NRZI-coded data as long as the data does not contain any long, continuous streams of 0s.

Non-Return-to-Zero Invert-on-1s (NRZI)

The Return-to-Zero (RZ) code is similar to NRZ except that, for a 1 bit, the 1 level is transmitted only for a fraction of the bit time, usually 1/2. With this code, data patterns that contain a lot of 1s create lots of transitions for a DPLL to use to recover the clock. However, as in the other line codes, a string of 0s has no transitions, and a long string of 0s makes clock recovery impossible.

Return-to-Zero (RZ)

Another requirement of some transmission media, such as high-speed fiber-optic links, is that the serial data stream be *DC balanced*. That is, it must have an equal number of 1s and 0s; any long-term DC component in the stream (created by having a lot more 1s than 0s or vice versa) creates a bias at the receiver that reduces its ability to distinguish reliably between 1s and 0s.

DC balance

Ordinarily, NRZ, NRZI or RZ data has no guarantee of DC balance; there's nothing to prevent a user data stream from having a long string of words with more than 1s than 0s or vice versa. However, DC balance can still be achieved by using a few extra bits to code the user data in a *balanced code*, in which each code word has an equal number of 1s and 0s, and then sending these code words in NRZ format.

balanced code

For example, in Section 2.13 we introduced the 8B10B code, which codes 8 bits of user data into 10 bits in a mostly 5-out-of-10 code. Recall that there are only 252 5-out-of-10 code words, but there are another $\binom{10}{4} = 210$ 4-out-of-10 code words and an equal number of 6-out-of-10 code words. Of course, these code words aren't quite DC balanced. The 8B10B code solves this problem by associating with each 8-bit value to be encoded a *pair* of unbalanced code words, one 4-out-of-10 ("light") and the other 6-out-of-10 ("heavy"). The coder also keeps track of the *running disparity*, a single bit of information indicating

running disparity

KILO-, MEGA-,
GIGA-, TERA-

The prefixes k(kilo-), M (mega-), G (giga-), and T (tera-) mean 10^3, 10^6, 10^9, and 10^{12}, respectively, when referring to bps, hertz, ohms, watts, and most other engineering quantities. However, when referring to memory sizes, the prefixes mean 2^{10}, 2^{20}, 2^{30}, and 2^{40}. Historically, the prefixes were co-opted for this purpose because memory sizes are normally powers of 2, and 2^{10} (1024) is very close to 1000.

Now, when somebody offers you 60 kilobucks a year for your first engineering job, it's up to you to negotiate what the prefix means!

---

whether the last unbalanced code word that it transmitted was heavy or light. When it comes time to transmit another unbalanced code word, the coder selects the one of the pair with the opposite weight. This simple trick makes available $252 + 210 = 462$ code words for the 8B10B to encode 8 bits of user data. Some of the "extra" code words are used to conveniently encode nondata conditions on the serial line, such as IDLE, SYNC, and ERROR. Not all the unbalanced code words are used. Also, some of the balanced code words, such as 0000011111, are not used either, in favor of unbalanced pairs that contain more transitions.

A DPLL can recover a clock signal, but not byte synchronization. Still, byte synchronization can be achieved in various clever ways by embedding special patterns into the long-term serial data stream, recognizing them digitally, and then "locking" onto them. For example, suppose that the IDLE code word in a 10-bit code is 1011011000, and IDLE is sent continuously at system startup. Then the beginning of the code word can be easily recognized as the bit after three 0s in a row. Successive code words, even if not IDLE, can be expected to begin at every tenth bit time thereafter. Of course, additional work is needed to recognize loss of synchronization due to noise, and to get the transmitter to send IDLE again, and this is an area of much cleverness and variety.

All of the preceding codes transmit or store only two signal levels. The *Bipolar Return-to-Zero (BPRZ)* code transmits three signal levels: +1, 0, and −1. The code is like RZ except that 1s are alternately transmitted as +1 and −1; for this reason, the code is also known as *Alternate Mark Inversion (AMI)*.

Bipolar Return-to-Zero (BPRZ)

Alternate Mark Inversion (AMI)

The big advantage of BPRZ over RZ is that it's DC balanced. This makes it possible to send BPRZ streams over transmission media that cannot tolerate a DC component, such as transformer-coupled phone lines. In fact, the BPRZ code has been used in T1 digital telephone links for decades, where analog speech signals are carried as streams of 8000 8-bit digital samples per second that are transmitted in BPRZ format on 64-Kbps serial channels.

As with RZ, it is possible to recover a clock signal from a BPRZ stream as long as there aren't too many 0s in a row. Although TPC (The Phone Company) has no control over what you say (at least, not yet), they still have a simple way of limiting runs of 0s. If one of the 8-bit bytes that results from sampling your analog speech pattern is all 0s, they simply change second-least significant bit

> **ABOUT TPC**   Watch the 1967 James Coburn movie, *The President's Analyst*, for an amusing view of TPC. With the growing pervasiveness of digital technology and cheap wireless communications, the concept of universal, *personal* connectivity to the network as presented in the movie's conclusion has become much less far-fetched.

to 1! This is called *zero-code suppression* and I'll bet you never noticed it. And this is also why, in many data applications of T1 links, you get only 56 Kbps of usable data per 64-Kbps channel; the LSB of each byte is always set to 1 to prevent zero-code suppression from changing the other bits.

zero-code suppression

The last code in Figure 2-17 is called *Manchester* or *diphase* code. The major strength of this code is that, regardless of the transmitted data pattern, it provides at least one transition per bit cell, making it very easy to recover the clock. As shown in the figure, a 0 is encoded as a 0-to-1 transition in the middle of the bit cell, and a 1 is encoded as a 1-to-0 transition. The Manchester code's major strength is also its major weakness. Since it has more transitions per bit cell than other codes, it also requires more media bandwidth to transmit a given bit rate. Bandwidth is not a problem in coaxial cable, however, which was used in the original Ethernet local area networks to carry serial data at the rate of 10 Mbps (megabits per second) in a Manchester-like code (it swaps 0 and 1).

Manchester
diphase

References

The presentation in the first nine sections of this chapter is based on Chapter 4 of *Microcomputer Architecture and Programming*, by John F. Wakerly (Wiley, 1981). Precise, thorough, and entertaining discussions of these topics can also be found in Donald E. Knuth's *Seminumerical Algorithms*, third edition (Addison-Wesley, 1997). Mathematically inclined readers will find Knuth's analysis of the properties of number systems and arithmetic to be excellent, and all readers should enjoy the insights and history sprinkled throughout the text.

Descriptions of algorithms for arithmetic operations appear in *Digital Arithmetic* by Miloš Ercegovac and Tomas Láng (Morgan Kaufmann, 2003). *Decimal Computation* by Hermann Schmid (Wiley, 1974) contains a thorough description of techniques for BCD arithmetic.

An introduction to algorithms for binary multiplication and division and to floating-point arithmetic appears in *Microcomputer Architecture and Programming: The 68000 Family* by John F. Wakerly (Wiley, 1989). A more thorough discussion of arithmetic techniques and floating-point number systems can be found in *Introduction to Arithmetic for Digital Systems Designers* by Shlomo Waser and Michael J. Flynn (Holt, Rinehart and Winston, 1982).

CRC codes are based on the theory of *finite fields,* which was developed by French mathematician Évariste Galois (1811–1832) shortly before he was killed

finite fields

in a duel with a political opponent. The classic book on error-detecting and error-correcting codes is *Error-Correcting Codes* by W. W. Peterson and E. J. Weldon, Jr. (MIT Press, 1972, second edition); however, this book is recommended only for mathematically sophisticated readers. A more accessible introduction to coding can be found in *Error Correcting Codes: A Mathematical Introduction* by John Baylis (Chapman & Hall/CRC, 1997), despite its use of the word "mathematical" in the title. The latest treatise on coding is *Error Control Coding* by S. Lin and D. J. Costello, Jr. (Prentice Hall, 2004, second edition).

A communication-oriented introduction to coding theory can be found in *Error-Control Techniques for Digital Communication* by A. M. Michelson and A. H. Levesque (Wiley-Interscience, 1985). Hardware applications of codes in computer systems are discussed in *Error-Detecting Codes, Self-Checking Circuits, and Applications* by John F. Wakerly (Elsevier/North-Holland, 1978).

As shown in the above reference by Wakerly, ones'-complement checksum codes have the ability to detect long bursts of unidirectional errors; this is useful in communication channels where errors all tend to be in the same direction. The special computational properties of these codes also make them quite amenable to efficient checksum calculation by software programs, important for their use in the Internet Protocol; see RFC-1071 and RFC-1141. RFCs (Requests for Comments) are archived in many places on the Web; just search for "RFC".

Speaking of the Web, an introduction to coding techniques for serial data transmission, as well as useful coverage of the higher layers of communication and networking, appears in *Data and Computer Communications* by William Stallings (Prentice Hall, 2003, seventh edition).

The structure of the 8B10B code and the rationale behind it is explained nicely in the original IBM patent by Peter Franaszek and Albert Widmer, U.S. patent number 4,486,739 (1984). This and all U.S. patents issued after 1971 can be found on the Web at www.uspto.gov.

Drill Problems

2.1   Perform the following number system conversions:

(a) $1101011_2 = ?_{16}$ (b) $174003_8 = ?_2$

(c) $10110111_2 = ?_{16}$ (d) $67.24_8 = ?_2$

(e) $10100.1101_2 = ?_{16}$ (f) $F3A5_{16} = ?_2$

(g) $11011001_2 = ?_8$ (h) $AB3D_{16} = ?_2$

(i) $101111.0111_2 = ?_8$ (j) $15C.38_{16} = ?_2$

2.2   Convert the following octal numbers into binary and hexadecimal:

(a) $1234_8 = ?_2 = ?_{16}$ (b) $174637_8 = ?_2 = ?_{16}$

(c) $365517_8 = ?_2 = ?_{16}$ (d) $2535321_8 = ?_2 = ?_{16}$

(e) $7436.11_8 = ?_2 = ?_{16}$ (f) $45316.7414_8 = ?_2 = ?_{16}$

2.3 Convert the following hexadecimal numbers into binary and octal:

(a) $1023_{16} = ?_2 = ?_8$ (b) $7E6A_{16} = ?_2 = ?_8$

(c) $ABCD_{16} = ?_2 = ?_8$ (d) $C350_{16} = ?_2 = ?_8$

(e) $9E36.7A_{16} = ?_2 = ?_8$ (f) $DEAD.BEEF_{16} = ?_2 = ?_8$

2.4 What are the octal values of the four 8-bit bytes in the 32-bit number with octal representation 32107654321_8?

2.5 Convert the following numbers into decimal:

(a) $1101011_2 = ?_{10}$ (b) $174003_8 = ?_{10}$

(c) $10110111_2 = ?_{10}$ (d) $67.24_8 = ?_{10}$

(e) $10100.1101_2 = ?_{10}$ (f) $F3A5_{16} = ?_{10}$

(g) $12010_3 = ?_{10}$ (h) $AB3D_{16} = ?_{10}$

(i) $7156_8 = ?_{10}$ (j) $15C.38_{16} = ?_{10}$

2.6 Perform the following number-system conversions:

(a) $125_{10} = ?_2$ (b) $3489_{10} = ?_8$

(c) $209_{10} = ?_2$ (d) $9714_{10} = ?_8$

(e) $132_{10} = ?_2$ (f) $23851_{10} = ?_{16}$

(g) $727_{10} = ?_5$ (h) $57190_{10} = ?_{16}$

(i) $1435_{10} = ?_8$ (j) $65113_{10} = ?_{16}$

2.7 Add the following pairs of binary numbers, showing all carries:

(a)	110011	(b)	100111	(c)	11100011	(d)	1100110
+	11010	+	101010	+	1011101	+	1111001

2.8 Repeat Drill 2.7 using subtraction instead of addition, and showing borrows instead of carries.

2.9 Add the following pairs of octal numbers:

(a)	1776	(b)	57734	(c)	252757	(d)	511042
+	1432	+	1066	+	465521	+	57647

2.10 Add the following pairs of hexadecimal numbers:

(a)	1776	(b)	4F1A5	(c)	F35B	(d)	1B90F
+	1432	+	B8D5	+	27E6	+	C44E

2.11 Write the 8-bit signed-magnitude, two's-complement, and ones'-complement representations for each decimal number: +25, +120, +82, −42, −6, −111.

2.12 Indicate whether or not overflow occurs when adding the following 8-bit two's-complement numbers:

(a)	11010100	(b)	10111111	(c)	01011101	(d)	01100001
+	11101011	+	11011111	+	00110001	+	00011111

2.13   How many errors can be detected by a code with minimum distance $d+1$?

2.14   What is the minimum number of parity bits required to obtain a distance-4, two-dimensional code with n information bits?

2.15   Sometimes the terms Dec, Oct and Hex are placed in front of numbers to indicate their base. However, for some digital engineers, this creates confusion at holiday time. What two U.S. holidays might a digital engineer get confused on Oct 31?

Exercises

2.16   Here's a problem to help keep you awake at night. What is the hexadecimal equivalent of 12648430_{10}?

2.17   Find an 8-bit binary number that has the same negative value when interpreted as either a decimal or a two's-complement number. Can you find another one?

2.18   Each of the following arithmetic operations is correct in at least one number system. Determine possible radices of the numbers in each operation.

    (a) $1234 + 5432 = 6666$ (b) $41 / 3 = 13$

    (c) $33/3 = 11$ (d) $23 + 44 + 14 + 32 = 223$

    (e) $302/20 = 12.1$ (f) $\sqrt{41} = 5$

2.19   The first expedition to Mars found only the ruins of a civilization. From the artifacts and pictures, the explorers deduced that the creatures who produced this civilization were four-legged beings with a tentacle that branched out at the end with a number of grasping "fingers." After much study, the explorers were able to translate Martian mathematics. They found the following equation:

$$5x^2 - 50x + 125 = 0$$

with the indicated solutions $x = 5$ and $x = 8$. The value $x = 5$ seemed legitimate enough, but $x = 8$ required some explanation. Then the explorers reflected on the way in which Earth's number system developed, and found evidence that the Martian system had a similar history. How many fingers would you say the Martians had? (From *The Bent of Tau Beta Pi*, February 1956.)

2.20   Suppose a $4n$-bit number B is represented by an n-digit hexadecimal number H. Prove that the two's complement of B is represented by the 16's complement of H. Make and prove true a similar statement for octal representation.

2.21   Repeat Exercise 2.20 using the ones' complement of B and the 15s' complement of H.

2.22   Given an integer x in the range $-2^{n-1} \leq x \leq 2^{n-1} - 1$, we define $[x]$ to be the two's-complement representation of x, expressed as a positive number: $[x] = x$ if $x \geq 0$ and $[x] = 2^n - |x|$ if $x < 0$, where $|x|$ is the absolute value of x. Let y be another integer in the same range as x. Prove that the two's-complement addition rules given in Section 2.6 are correct by proving that the following equation is always true:

$$[x + y] = [x] + [y] \text{ modulo } 2^n$$

(*Hints:* Consider four cases based on the signs of x and y. Without loss of generality, you may assume that $|x| \geq |y|$.)

2.23 Repeat Exercise 2.22, this time using appropriate expressions and rules for ones'-complement addition.

2.24 State an overflow rule for addition of two's-complement numbers in terms of counting operations in the modular representation of Figure 2-3.

2.25 Show that a two's-complement number can be converted to a representation with more bits by *sign extension*. That is, given an n-bit two's-complement number X, show that the m-bit two's-complement representation of X, where $m > n$, can be obtained by appending $m - n$ copies of X's sign bit to the left of the n-bit representation of X.

2.26 Show that a two's-complement number can be converted to a representation with fewer bits by removing higher-order bits. That is, given an n-bit two's-complement number X, show that the m-bit two's-complement number Y obtained by discarding the d leftmost bits of X represents the same number as X if and only if the discarded bits all equal the sign bit of Y.

2.27 Why is the punctuation of "two's complement" and "ones' complement" inconsistent? (See the first two citations in the References.)

2.28 A n-bit binary adder can be used to perform an n-bit unsigned subtraction operation $X - Y$, by performing the operation $X + \overline{Y} + 1$, where X and Y are n-bit unsigned numbers and $\overline{Y}$ represents the bit-by-bit complement of Y. Demonstrate this fact as follows. First, prove that $(X - Y) = (X + \overline{Y} + 1) - 2^n$. Second, prove that the carry out of the n-bit adder is the opposite of the borrow from the n-bit subtraction. That is, show that the operation $X - Y$ produces a borrow out of the MSB position if and only if the operation $X + \overline{Y} + 1$ *does not* produce a carry out of the MSB position.

2.29 In most cases, the product of two n-bit two's-complement numbers requires fewer than $2n$ bits to represent it. In fact, there is only one case in which $2n$ bits are needed—find it.

2.30 Prove that a two's-complement number can be multiplied by 2 by shifting it one bit position to the left, with a carry of 0 into the least significant bit position and disregarding any carry out of the most significant bit position, assuming no overflow. State the rule for detecting overflow.

2.31 State and prove correct a technique similar to the one described in Exercise 2.30, for multiplying a ones'-complement number by 2.

2.32 Show how to subtract BCD numbers, by stating the rules for generating borrows and applying a correction factor. Show how your rules apply to each of the following subtractions: $8 - 3, 4 - 8, 5 - 9, 2 - 7$.

2.33 How many different 3-bit binary state encodings are possible in a controller with 5 states? How many are possible with 7 states? How many are possible with 8 states?

2.34 Your pointy-haired boss says every code word has to contain at least one "zero", because it "saves power." So how many different 3-bit binary state encodings are now possible for the traffic-light controller of Table 2-12?

2.35   List all of the "bad" boundaries in the mechanical encoding disk of Figure 2-5, where an incorrect position may be sensed.

2.36   As a function of n, how many "bad" boundaries are there in a mechanical encoding disk that uses an n-bit binary code?

2.37   A manufacturer of mechanical encoders discovers the 2-bit Gray code and manufactures encoders with the decimal sequence 0, 1, 3, 2. Generalizing to n-bit encoders, they decide all they need to do is to reverse every other pair of values in the decimal sequence, resulting in a sequence of 0, 1, 3, 2, 4, 5, 7, 6, 8, 9, etc. But this proves to be less than perfect. As a function of n, how many "bad" boundaries are there? How much better is their code than an n-bit binary code?

2.38   On-board altitude transponders on commercial and private aircraft use Gray code to encode the altitude readings that are transmitted to air traffic controllers. Why?

2.39   An incandescent light bulb is stressed every time it is turned on, so in some applications the lifetime of the bulb is limited by the number of on/off cycles rather than the total time it is illuminated. Use your knowledge of codes to suggest a way to double the lifetime of 3-way bulbs in such applications.

2.40   As a function of n, how many different distinct subcubes of an n-cube are there?

2.41   Find a way to draw a 3-cube on a sheet of paper (or other two-dimensional object) so that none of the lines cross, or prove that it's impossible.

2.42   Repeat Exercise 2.41 for a 4-cube.

2.43   Write a formula that gives the number of m-subcubes of an n-cube for a specific value of m. (Your answer should be a function of n and m.)

2.44   Define parity groups for a distance-3 Hamming code with 11 information bits.

2.45   Write the code words of a Hamming code with one information bit.

2.46   Exhibit the pattern for a 3-bit error that is not detected if the "corner" parity bits are not included in the two-dimensional codes of Figure 2-14.

2.47   The *rate of a code* is the ratio of the number of information bits to the total number of bits in a code word. High rates, approaching 1, are desirable for efficient transmission of information. Construct a graph comparing the rates of distance-2 parity codes and distance-3 and -4 Hamming codes for up to 100 information bits.

2.48   Which type of distance-4 code has a higher rate—a two-dimensional code or a Hamming code? Support your answer with a table in the style of Table 2-15, including the rate as well as the number of parity and information bits of each code for up to 100 information bits.

2.49   Show how to construct a distance-6 code with four information bits. Write a list of its code words.

2.50   Describe the operations that must be performed in a RAID system to write new data into information block b in drive d, so the data can be recovered in the event of an error in block b in any drive. Minimize the number of disk accesses required.

2.51   In the style of Figure 2-17, draw the waveforms for the bit pattern 10101110 when sent serially using the NRZ, NRZI, RZ, BPRZ, and Manchester codes, assuming that the bits are transmitted in order from left to right.

chapter 3

Digital Circuits

Marketing hype notwithstanding, we live in an analog world, not a digital one. Voltages, currents, and other physical quantities in real circuits take on values that are infinitely variable, depending on properties of the real devices that comprise the circuits. Because real values are continuously variable, we could use a physical quantity such as a signal voltage in a circuit to represent a real number (e.g., 3.14159265358979 volts represents the mathematical constant *pi* to 14 decimal digits of precision).

However, stability and accuracy in physical quantities are difficult to obtain in real circuits. They can be affected by manufacturing variations, temperature, power-supply voltage, cosmic rays, and noise created by other circuits, among other things. If we used an analog voltage to represent *pi*, we might find that instead of being an absolute mathematical constant, *pi* varied over a range of 10% or more.

Also, many mathematical and logical operations can be difficult or impossible to perform with analog quantities. While it is possible with some cleverness to build an analog circuit whose output voltage is the square root of its input voltage, no one has ever built a 100-input, 100-output analog circuit whose outputs are a set of voltages identical to the set of input voltages, but sorted arithmetically.

The purpose of this chapter is to give you a solid working knowledge of the electrical aspects of digital circuits, enough for you to understand and build real circuits and systems. We'll see in later chapters that with modern software tools, it's possible to "build" circuits in the abstract, using hardware design languages to specify their design and simulators to test their operation. But to build real, production-quality circuits, either at the board level or the chip level, you'll need to understand most of the material in this chapter. If you're really anxious to start designing and simulating abstract circuits, you can just read the first section of this chapter and come back to the rest of it later, after you've discovered that you really need it.

3.1 Logic Signals and Gates

digital logic

logic values

Digital logic hides the pitfalls of the analog world by mapping the infinite set of real values for a physical quantity into two subsets corresponding to just two possible numbers or *logic values*—0 and 1. Thus, digital logic circuits can be analyzed and designed functionally, using switching algebra, tables, and other abstract means to describe the operation of well-behaved 0s and 1s in a circuit.

binary digit
bit

A logic value, 0 or 1, is often called a *binary digit*, or *bit*. If an application requires more than two discrete values, additional bits may be used, with a set of n bits representing 2^n different values.

Examples of the physical phenomena used to represent bits in some modern (and not-so-modern) digital technologies are given in Table 3-1. With most phenomena, there is an undefined region between the 0 and 1 states (e.g., voltage = 1.8 V, dim light, capacitor slightly charged, etc.). This undefined region is needed so that the 0 and 1 states can be unambiguously defined and reliably detected. Noise can more easily corrupt results if the boundaries separating the 0 and 1 states are too close.

LOW
HIGH

When discussing electronic logic circuits such as CMOS and TTL, digital designers often use the words "LOW" and "HIGH" in place of "0" and "1" to remind them that they are dealing with real circuits, not abstract quantities:

LOW A signal in the range of algebraically lower voltages, which is interpreted as a logic 0.

HIGH A signal in the range of algebraically higher voltages, which is interpreted as a logic 1.

Note that the assignments of 0 and 1 to LOW and HIGH are somewhat arbitrary. Still, assigning 0 to LOW and 1 to HIGH seems natural and is called *positive logic*. The opposite assignment, 1 to LOW and 0 to HIGH, is not often used and is called *negative logic*.

positive logic
negative logic

buffer

Because a wide range of physical values represent the same binary value, digital logic is highly immune to component and power-supply variations and noise. Furthermore, *buffer* circuits can be used to regenerate (or amplify) "weak" values into "strong" ones, so that digital signals can be transmitted over arbitrary distances without loss of information. For example, a buffer for CMOS logic converts any HIGH input voltage into an output very close to 5.0 V, and any LOW input voltage into an output very close to 0.0 V.

Table 3-1 Physical states representing bits in different logic and memory technologies.

Technology	State Representing Bit	
	0	1
Pneumatic logic	Fluid at low pressure	Fluid at high pressure
Relay logic	Circuit open	Circuit closed
Complementary metal-oxide semiconductor (CMOS) logic	0–1.5 V	3.5–5.0 V
Transistor-transistor logic (TTL)	0–0.8 V	2.0–5.0 V
Dynamic memory	Capacitor discharged	Capacitor charged
Nonvolatile, erasable memory	Electrons trapped	Electrons released
Microprocessor on-chip serial number	Fuse blown	Fuse intact
Polymer memory	Molecule in state A	Molecule in state B
Fiber optics	Light off	Light on
Magnetic disk or tape	Flux direction "north"	Flux direction "south"
Compact disc (CD)	No pit	Pit
Writeable compact disc (CD-R)	Dye in crystalline state	Dye in noncrystalline state

A logic circuit can be represented with a minimum amount of detail simply as a "black box" with a certain number of inputs and outputs. For example, Figure 3-1 shows a logic circuit with three inputs and one output. However, this representation does not describe how the circuit responds to input signals.

From the point of view of electronic circuit design, it takes a lot of information to describe the precise electrical behavior of a circuit. However, since the inputs of a digital logic circuit can be viewed as taking on only discrete 0 and 1 values, the circuit's "logical" operation can be described with a table that ignores electrical behavior and lists only discrete 0 and 1 values.

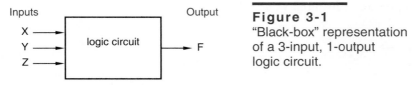

Figure 3-1
"Black-box" representation of a 3-input, 1-output logic circuit.

STATE TRANSITIONS The last four technologies in Table 3-1 don't actually use absolute states to represent bit values. Rather, they use transitions (or absence of transitions) between states to represent 0s and 1s using a code such as the Manchester code described on page 73.

combinational circuit

truth table

A logic circuit whose outputs depend only on its current inputs is called a *combinational circuit*. Its operation is fully described by a *truth table* that lists all combinations of input values and the output value(s) produced by each one. Table 3-2 is the truth table for a logic circuit with three inputs X, Y, and Z and a single output F. This truth table lists all eight possible combinations of values of X, Y, and Z and the circuit's output value F for each combination.

Table 3-2
Truth table for a combinational logic circuit.

X	Y	Z	F
0	0	0	0
0	0	1	1
0	1	0	0
0	1	1	0
1	0	0	0
1	0	1	0
1	1	0	1
1	1	1	1

sequential circuit

state table

A circuit with memory, whose outputs depend on the current input *and* the sequence of past inputs, is called a *sequential circuit*. Its behavior may be described by a *state table* that specifies its output and next state as functions of its current state and input. Sequential circuits are introduced in Chapter 7.

As we'll show in Section 4.1, just three basic logic functions, AND, OR, and NOT, can be used to build any combinational digital logic circuit. Figure 3-2 shows the truth tables and symbols for logic "gates" that perform these functions. The symbols and truth tables for AND and OR may be extended to gates with any number of inputs. The gates' functions are easily defined in words:

AND gate

OR gate

NOT gate

inverter

- An *AND gate* produces a 1 output if and only if all of its inputs are 1.

- An *OR gate* produces a 1 if and only if one or more of its inputs are 1.

- A *NOT gate,* usually called an *inverter*, produces an output value that is the opposite of its input value.

Figure 3-2
Basic logic elements:
(a) AND; (b) OR;
(c) NOT (inverter).

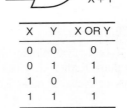

(a)

X	Y	X AND Y
0	0	0
0	1	0
1	0	0
1	1	1

(b)

X	Y	X OR Y
0	0	0
0	1	1
1	0	1
1	1	1

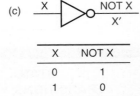

(c)

X	NOT X
0	1
1	0

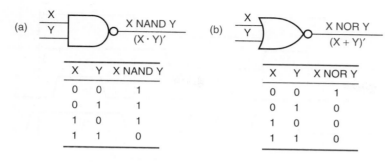

X	Y	X NAND Y
0	0	1
0	1	1
1	0	1
1	1	0

X	Y	X NOR Y
0	0	1
0	1	0
1	0	0
1	1	0

Figure 3-3
Inverting gates:
(a) NAND; (b) NOR.

Notice that in the definitions of AND and OR functions, we only had to state the input conditions for which the output is 1, because there is only one possibility when the output is not 1—it must be 0.

The circle on the inverter symbol's output is called an *inversion bubble* and is used in this and other gate symbols to denote "inverting" behavior. For example, two more logic functions are obtained by combining inversion with an AND or OR function in a single gate. Figure 3-3 shows the truth tables and symbols for these gates. Their functions are also easily described in words:

inversion bubble

- A *NAND gate* produces the opposite of an AND gate's output, a 0 if and only if all of its inputs are 1.

  NAND gate

- A *NOR gate* produces the opposite of an OR gate's output, a 0 if and only if one or more of its inputs are 1.

  NOR gate

As with AND and OR gates, the symbols and truth tables for NAND and NOR may be extended to gates with any number of inputs.

Figure 3-4 is a logic circuit using AND, OR, and NOT gates that functions according to the truth table of Table 3-2. In Chapter 4 you'll learn how to go from a truth table to a logic circuit, and vice versa, and you'll also learn about the switching-algebra notation (in color) used in Figures 3-2 through 3-4.

Real logic circuits function in another very important analog dimension— time. For example, Figure 3-5 on the next page is a *timing diagram* that shows how the circuit of Figure 3-4 might respond to a time-varying pattern of input signals. The timing diagram shows that the logic signals do not change between the analog values corresponding to 0 and 1 instantaneously, and also that there is a lag between an input change and the corresponding output change. Later in this

timing diagram

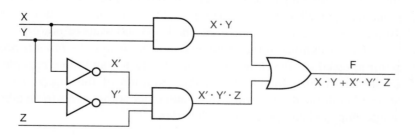

Figure 3-4
Logic circuit with the truth table of Table 3-2.

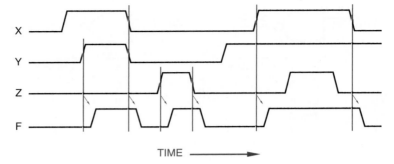

Figure 3-5
Timing diagram for a
logic circuit.

chapter you'll learn some of the reasons for this timing behavior, and how it is specified and handled in real circuits. And you'll be happy to learn in a later chapter how this analog timing behavior can be generally ignored in most sequential circuits, and how instead the circuit can be viewed as moving between discrete states at precise intervals defined by a clock signal.

Thus, even if you know nothing about analog electronics, you should be able to understand the logical behavior of digital circuits. However, there comes a time in design and debugging when every digital logic designer must throw out "the digital abstraction" temporarily and consider the analog phenomena that limit or disrupt digital performance. The rest of this chapter prepares you for that day by discussing the electrical characteristics of digital logic circuits.

THERE'S HOPE FOR NON-EE'S   If all of this electrical "stuff" bothers you, don't worry, at least for now. The rest of this book is written to be as independent of this stuff as possible. But you'll need it later, if you ever have to design and build digital systems in the real world.

3.2 Logic Families

There are many, many ways to design an electronic logic circuit. The first electrically controlled logic circuits, developed at Bell Laboratories in the 1930s, were based on relays. In the mid-1940s, the first electronic digital computer, the Eniac, used logic circuits based on vacuum tubes. The Eniac had about 18,000 tubes and a similar number of logic gates, not a lot by today's standards of microprocessor chips with tens of millions of transistors. However, the Eniac could hurt you a lot more than a chip could if it fell on you—it was 100 feet long, 10 feet high, 3 feet deep, and consumed 140,000 watts of power!

semiconductor diode
bipolar junction
*   transistor*

integrated circuit (IC)

The inventions of the *semiconductor diode* and the *bipolar junction transistor* allowed the development of smaller, faster, and more capable computers in the late 1950s. In the 1960s, the invention of the *integrated circuit (IC)* allowed multiple diodes, transistors, and other components to be fabricated on a single chip, and computers got still better.

The 1960s also saw the introduction of the first integrated-circuit logic families. A *logic family* is a collection of different integrated-circuit chips that have similar input, output, and internal circuit characteristics, but that perform different logic functions. Chips from the same family can be interconnected to perform any desired logic function. Chips from different families may not be compatible; they may use different power-supply voltages or may use different input and output conditions to represent logic values.

logic family

The most successful *bipolar logic family* (one based on bipolar junction transistors) was *transistor-transistor logic (TTL)*. First introduced in the 1960s, TTL evolved into a family of logic families that were compatible with each other but differed in speed, power consumption, and cost. Digital systems could mix components from several different TTL families, according to design goals and constraints in different parts of the system.

bipolar logic family
transistor-transistor logic (TTL)

Ten years *before* the bipolar junction transistor was invented, the principles of operation were patented for another type of transistor, called the *metal-oxide semiconductor field-effect transistor (MOSFET)*, or simply *MOS transistor.* However, MOS transistors were difficult to fabricate in the early days, and it wasn't until the 1960s that a wave of developments made MOS-based logic and memory circuits practical. Even then, MOS circuits lagged bipolar circuits considerably in speed. They were attractive only in a few applications because of their lower power consumption and higher levels of integration.

metal-oxide semiconductor field-effect transistor (MOSFET)

MOS transistor

Beginning in the mid-1980s, advances in the design of MOS circuits, in particular *complementary MOS (CMOS)* circuits, tremendously increased their performance and popularity. Almost all new large-scale integrated circuits, such as microprocessors and memories, use CMOS. Likewise, small- to medium-scale applications, for which TTL was once the logic family of choice, are now much more likely to use CMOS devices with equivalent functionality or better, and higher speed and lower power consumption. CMOS circuits now account for the vast majority of the worldwide integrated-circuit market.

complementary MOS (CMOS)

CMOS logic is both the most capable and the easiest to understand commercial digital logic technology. Beginning in the next section, we describe the basic structure of CMOS logic circuits and introduce the most commonly used commercial CMOS logic families.

A LITTLE BIT OF TTL   Although TTL was largely replaced by CMOS in the 1990s, you still may encounter TTL components in your academic labs; therefore, basic TTL concepts are covered in Sections 3.10.3 through 3.10.7.

As a consequence of the industry's transition from TTL to CMOS over a long period of time, many CMOS families were designed to be somewhat compatible with TTL. Section 3.10.8 describes how TTL and CMOS families can be mixed within a single system.

3.3 CMOS Logic

The functional behavior of a CMOS logic circuit is fairly easy to understand, even if your knowledge of analog electronics is not particularly deep. The basic (and typically only) building blocks in CMOS logic circuits are MOS transistors, described shortly. But before getting into that, we need to talk about logic levels.

3.3.1 CMOS Logic Levels

Abstract logic elements process binary digits, 0 and 1. However, real logic circuits process electrical signals such as voltage levels. In any logic circuit, there is a range of voltages (or other circuit conditions) that is interpreted as a logic 0, and another, nonoverlapping range that is interpreted as a logic 1.

A typical CMOS logic circuit operates from a 5-volt power supply. Such a circuit may interpret any voltage in the range 0–1.5 V as a logic 0, and in the range 3.5–5.0 V as a logic 1. Thus, the definitions of LOW and HIGH for 5-volt CMOS logic are as shown in Figure 3-6. Voltages in the intermediate range (1.5–3.5 V) are not expected to occur except during signal transitions, and yield undefined logic values (i.e., a circuit may interpret them as either 0 or 1). CMOS circuits using other power-supply voltages, such as 3.3 or 2.7 volts, partition the voltage range similarly.

Figure 3-6
Logic levels for typical
CMOS logic circuits.

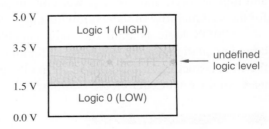

3.3.2 MOS Transistors

A MOS transistor can be modeled as a 3-terminal device that acts like a voltage-controlled resistance. As suggested by Figure 3-7, an input voltage applied to one terminal controls the resistance between the remaining two terminals. In digital logic applications, a MOS transistor is operated so its resistance is always either very high (and the transistor is "off") or very low (and the transistor is "on").

"off" transistor
"on" transistor

V_{IN}

Figure 3-7
The MOS transistor as a voltage-controlled resistance.

There are two types of MOS transistors, *n*-channel and *p*-channel; the names refer to the type of semiconductor material used for the resistance-controlled terminals. The circuit symbol for an *n-channel MOS (NMOS) transistor* is shown in Figure 3-8. The terminals are called *gate, source,* and *drain.* (Note that the "gate" of a MOS transistor has nothing to do with a "logic gate.") As you might guess from the orientation of the circuit symbol, the drain is normally at a higher voltage than the source.

n-channel MOS
 (NMOS) transistor
gate
source
drain

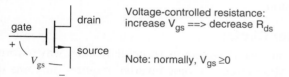

gate

+

V_{gs} —

drain

source

Voltage-controlled resistance:
increase V_{gs} ==> decrease R_{ds}

Note: normally, $V_{gs} \geq 0$

Figure 3-8
Circuit symbol for an n-channel MOS (NMOS) transistor.

The voltage from gate to source (V_{gs}) in an NMOS transistor is normally zero or positive. If $V_{gs} = 0$, then the resistance from drain to source (R_{ds}) is very high, at least a megohm (10^6 ohms) or more. As we increase V_{gs} (i.e., increase the voltage on the gate), R_{ds} decreases to a very low value, 10 ohms or less in some devices.

The circuit symbol for a *p-channel MOS (PMOS) transistor* is shown in Figure 3-9. Operation is analogous to that of an NMOS transistor, except that the source is normally at a higher voltage than the drain, and V_{gs} is normally zero or negative. If V_{gs} is zero, then the resistance from source to drain (R_{ds}) is very high. As we algebraically decrease V_{gs} (i.e., *decrease* the voltage on the gate), R_{ds} decreases to a very low value.

p-channel MOS
 (PMOS) transistor

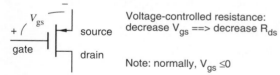

V_{gs}

+

gate

source

drain

Voltage-controlled resistance:
decrease V_{gs} ==> decrease R_{ds}

Note: normally, $V_{gs} \leq 0$

Figure 3-9
Circuit symbol for a p-channel MOS (PMOS) transistor.

IMPEDANCE VS. RESISTANCE	Technically, there's a difference between the words "impedance" and "resistance," but electrical engineers often use the terms interchangeably. So do we in this text.

The gate of a MOS transistor has a very high impedance. That is, the gate is separated from the source and the drain by an insulating material with a very high resistance. However, the gate voltage creates an electric field that enhances or retards the flow of current between source and drain. This is the "field effect" in the "MOSFET" name.

Regardless of gate voltage, almost no current flows from the gate to source, or from the gate to drain for that matter. The resistance between the gate and the other terminals of the device is extremely high, well over a megohm. The small amount of current that flows across this resistance is very small, typically less than one *microampere* (μA, 10^{-6} A), and is called a *leakage current*.

leakage current
microampere, μA

The MOS transistor symbol itself reminds us that there is no connection between the gate and the other two terminals of the device. However, the gate of a MOS transistor is capacitively coupled to the source and drain, as the symbol might suggest. In high-speed circuits, the power needed to charge and discharge this capacitance on each input-signal transition accounts for a nontrivial portion of a circuit's power consumption.

3.3.3 Basic CMOS Inverter Circuit

CMOS logic

NMOS and PMOS transistors are used together in a complementary way to form *CMOS logic*. The simplest CMOS circuit, a logic inverter, requires only one of each type of transistor, connected as shown in Figure 3-10(a). The power-supply voltage, V_{DD}, typically may be in the range 1–6 V and is often set at 5.0 V for compatibility with the older TTL family.

Figure 3-10
CMOS inverter:
(a) circuit diagram;
(b) functional behavior;
(c) logic symbol.

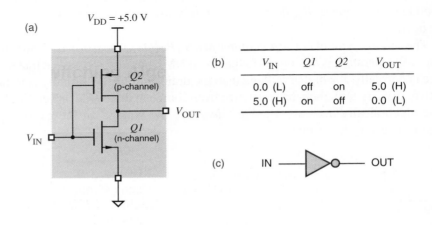

V_{IN}	$Q1$	$Q2$	V_{OUT}
0.0 (L)	off	on	5.0 (H)
5.0 (H)	on	off	0.0 (L)

WHAT'S IN A NAME?   The "DD" in the name "V_{DD}" refers to the *drain* terminals of MOS transistors. This may seem strange, since in the CMOS inverter V_{DD} is actually connected to the *source* terminal of a PMOS transistor. However, CMOS logic circuits evolved from NMOS logic circuits, where the supply *was* connected to the drain of an NMOS transistor through a load resistor, and the name "V_{DD}" stuck.

Also note that ground is sometimes referred to as "V_{SS}" in CMOS and NMOS circuits. Some authors and most circuit manufacturers use "V_{CC}" as the symbol for the CMOS supply voltage, since this name is used in TTL circuits, which historically preceded CMOS. To get you used to both, we'll start using "V_{CC}" in Section 3.4.

Ideally, the functional behavior of the CMOS inverter circuit can be characterized by just two cases tabulated in Figure 3-10(b):

1. V_{IN} is 0.0 V. In this case, the bottom, *n*-channel transistor $Q1$ is off, since its V_{gs} is 0, but the top, *p*-channel transistor $Q2$ is on, since its V_{gs} is a large negative value (−5.0 V). Therefore, $Q2$ presents only a small resistance between the power-supply terminal (V_{DD}, +5.0 V) and the output terminal (V_{OUT}), and the output voltage is 5.0 V.

2. V_{IN} is 5.0 V. Here, $Q1$ is on, since its V_{gs} is a large positive value (+5.0 V), but $Q2$ is off, since its V_{gs} is 0. Thus, $Q1$ presents a small resistance between the output terminal and ground, and the output voltage is 0 V.

With the foregoing functional behavior, the circuit clearly behaves as a logical inverter, since a 0-volt input produces a 5-volt output, and vice versa.

Another way to visualize CMOS operation uses switches. As shown in Figure 3-11(a), the *n*-channel (bottom) transistor is modeled by a normally-open switch, and the *p*-channel (top) transistor by a normally-closed switch. Applying a HIGH voltage "pushes" each switch to the opposite of its normal state, as shown in (b).

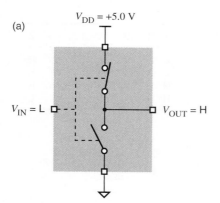

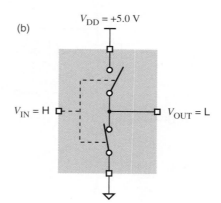

Figure 3-11
Switch model for CMOS inverter: (a) LOW input; (b) HIGH input.

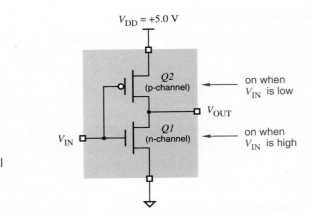

Figure 3-12
CMOS inverter logical
operation.

The switch model gives rise to a way of drawing CMOS circuits that makes their logical behavior more readily apparent. As shown in Figure 3-12, different symbols are used for the *p*- and *n*-channel transistors to reflect their logical behavior. The *n*-channel transistor ($Q1$) is switched "on," and current flows between source and drain, when a HIGH voltage is applied to its gate; this seems natural enough. The *p*-channel transistor ($Q2$) has the opposite behavior. It is "on" when a LOW voltage is applied; the inversion bubble on its gate indicates this inverting behavior.

3.3.4 CMOS NAND and NOR Gates

Both NAND and NOR gates can be constructed using CMOS. A *k*-input gate uses *k* *p*-channel and *k* *n*-channel transistors.

Figure 3-13 shows a 2-input CMOS NAND gate. If either input is LOW, the output Z has a low-impedance connection to V_{DD} through the corresponding "on" *p*-channel transistor, and the path to ground is blocked by the correspond-

Figure 3-13
CMOS 2-input
NAND gate:
(a) circuit diagram;
(b) function table;
(c) logic symbol.

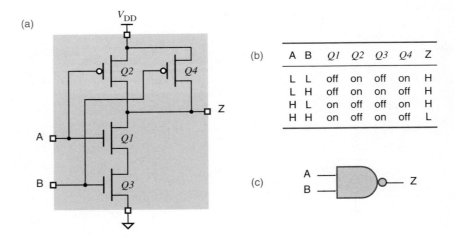

A	B	$Q1$	$Q2$	$Q3$	$Q4$	Z
L	L	off	on	off	on	H
L	H	off	on	on	off	H
H	L	on	off	off	on	H
H	H	on	off	on	off	L

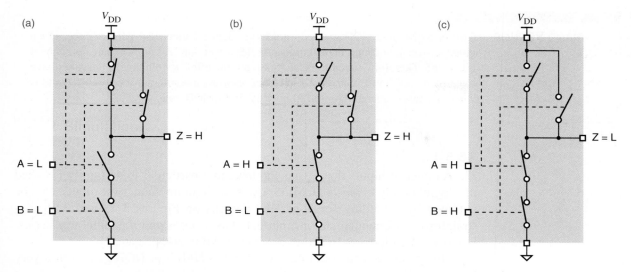

Figure 3-14 Switch model for CMOS 2-input NAND gate: (a) both inputs LOW; (b) one input HIGH; (c) both inputs HIGH.

ing "off" *n*-channel transistor. If both inputs are HIGH, the path to V_{DD} is blocked, and Z has a low-impedance connection to ground. Figure 3-14 shows the switch model for the NAND gate's operation.

Figure 3-15 shows a CMOS NOR gate. If both inputs are LOW, then the output Z has a low-impedance connection to V_{DD} through the "on" *p*-channel transistors, and the path to ground is blocked by the "off" *n*-channel transistors. If either input is HIGH, the path to V_{DD} is blocked, and Z has a low-impedance connection to ground.

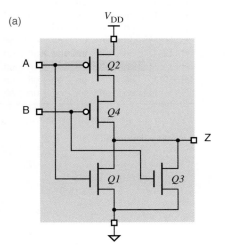

(b)

A	B	Q1	Q2	Q3	Q4	Z
L	L	off	on	off	on	H
L	H	off	on	on	off	L
H	L	on	off	off	on	L
H	H	on	off	on	off	L

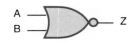

Figure 3-15
CMOS 2-input
NOR gate:
(a) circuit diagram;
(b) function table;
(c) logic symbol.

NAND VS. NOR   CMOS NAND and NOR gates do not have identical electrical performance. For a given silicon area, an n-channel transistor has lower "on" resistance than a p-channel transistor. Therefore, when transistors are put in series, k n-channel transistors have lower "on" resistance than do k p-channel ones. As a result, a k-input NAND gate is generally faster than and preferred over a k-input NOR gate.

3.3.5 Fan-In

fan-in

The number of inputs that a gate can have in a particular logic family is called the logic family's *fan-in*. CMOS gates with more than two inputs can be obtained by extending series-parallel designs on Figures 3-13 and 3-15 in a straightforward manner. An n-input gate has n series and n parallel transistors. For example, Figure 3-16 shows a 3-input CMOS NAND gate.

In principle, you could design a CMOS NAND or NOR gate with a very large number of inputs. In practice, however, the additive "on" resistance of series transistors limits the fan-in of CMOS gates, typically to 4 for NOR gates and 6 for NAND gates.

As the number of inputs is increased, designers of CMOS gate circuits may compensate by increasing the size of the series transistors to reduce their

Figure 3-16 CMOS 3-input NAND gate: (a) circuit diagram; (b) function table; (c) logic symbol.

(a)

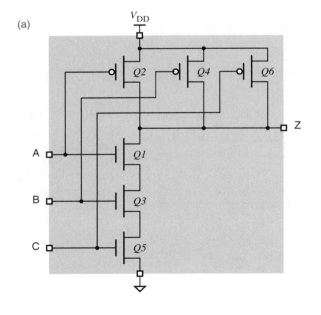

(b)

A	B	C	$Q1$	$Q2$	$Q3$	$Q4$	$Q5$	$Q6$	Z
L	L	L	off	on	off	on	off	on	H
L	L	H	off	on	off	on	on	off	H
L	H	L	off	on	on	off	off	on	H
L	H	H	off	on	on	off	on	off	H
H	L	L	on	off	off	on	off	on	H
H	L	H	on	off	off	on	on	off	H
H	H	L	on	off	on	off	off	on	H
H	H	H	on	off	on	off	on	off	L

(c)

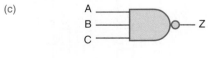

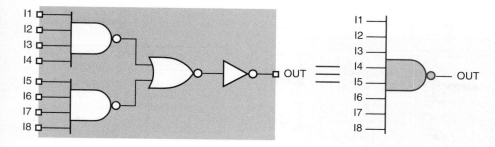

Figure 3-17 Logic diagram equivalent to the internal structure of an 8-input CMOS NAND gate.

resistance and the corresponding switching delay. However, at some point this becomes inefficient or impractical. Gates with a large number of inputs can be made faster and smaller by cascading gates with fewer inputs. For example, Figure 3-17 shows the logical structure of an 8-input CMOS NAND gate. The total delay through a 4-input NAND, a 2-input NOR, and an inverter is typically less than the delay of a one-level 8-input NAND circuit.

3.3.6 Noninverting Gates

In CMOS, and in most other logic families, the simplest gates are inverters, and the next simplest are NAND gates and NOR gates. A logical inversion comes "for free," and it typically is not possible to design a noninverting gate with a smaller number of transistors than an inverting one.

CMOS noninverting buffers and AND and OR gates are obtained by connecting an inverter to the output of the corresponding inverting gate. For example, Figure 3-18 shows a noninverting buffer and Figure 3-19 shows an AND gate. Combining Figure 3-15(a) with an inverter yields an OR gate.

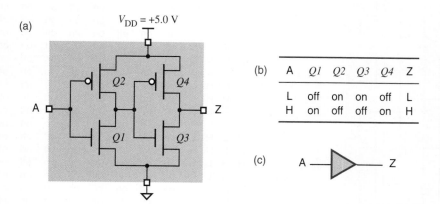

(b)

A	Q1	Q2	Q3	Q4	Z
L	off	on	on	off	L
H	on	off	off	on	H

Figure 3-18
CMOS noninverting buffer:
(a) circuit diagram;
(b) function table;
(c) logic symbol.

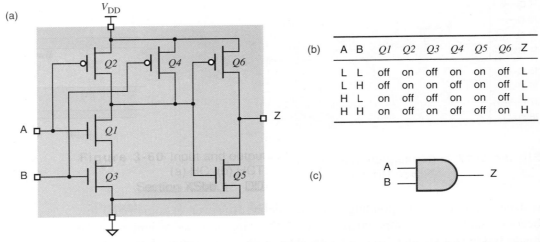

A	B	Q1	Q2	Q3	Q4	Q5	Q6	Z
L	L	off	on	off	on	on	off	L
L	H	off	on	on	off	on	off	L
H	L	on	off	off	on	on	off	L
H	H	on	off	on	off	off	on	H

(c)

Figure 3-19 CMOS 2-input AND gate: (a) circuit diagram; (b) function table; (c) logic symbol.

3.3.7 CMOS AND-OR-INVERT and OR-AND-INVERT Gates

AND-OR-INVERT (AOI) gate

CMOS circuits can perform two levels of logic with just a single "level" of transistors. For example, the circuit in Figure 3-20(a) is a 2-wide, 2-input CMOS *AND-OR-INVERT (AOI) gate*. The function table for this circuit is shown in (b) and a logic diagram for this function using AND and NOR gates is shown in

Figure 3-20 CMOS AND-OR-INVERT gate: (a) circuit diagram; (b) function table.

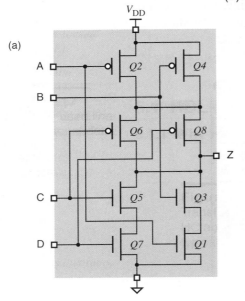

A	B	C	D	Q1	Q2	Q3	Q4	Q5	Q6	Q7	Q8	Z
L	L	L	L	off	on	off	on	off	on	off	on	H
L	L	L	H	off	on	off	on	off	on	on	off	H
L	L	H	L	off	on	off	on	on	off	off	on	H
L	L	H	H	off	on	off	on	on	off	on	off	L
L	H	L	L	off	on	on	off	off	on	off	on	H
L	H	L	H	off	on	on	off	off	on	on	off	H
L	H	H	L	off	on	on	off	on	off	off	on	H
L	H	H	H	off	on	on	off	on	off	on	off	L
H	L	L	L	on	off	off	on	off	on	off	on	H
H	L	L	H	on	off	off	on	off	on	on	off	H
H	L	H	L	on	off	off	on	on	off	off	on	H
H	L	H	H	on	off	off	on	on	off	on	off	L
H	H	L	L	on	off	on	off	off	on	off	on	L
H	H	L	H	on	off	on	off	off	on	on	off	L
H	H	H	L	on	off	on	off	on	off	off	on	L
H	H	H	H	on	off	on	off	on	off	on	off	L

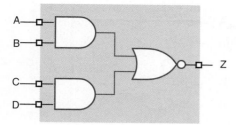

Figure 3-21
Logic diagram for CMOS
AND-OR-INVERT gate.

Figure 3-21. Transistors can be added to or removed from this circuit to obtain an AOI function with a different number of ANDs or a different number of inputs per AND.

The contents of each of the *Q1–Q8* columns in Figure 3-20(b) depends only on the input signal connected to the corresponding transistor's gate. The last column is constructed by examining each input combination and determining whether Z is connected to V_{DD} or to ground by "on" transistors for that input combination. Note that Z is never connected to *both* V_{DD} and ground for any input combination; in such a case the output would be a nonlogic value somewhere between LOW and HIGH, and the output structure would consume excessive power due to the low-impedance connection between V_{DD} and ground.

A circuit can also be designed to perform an OR-AND-INVERT function. For example, Figure 3-22(a) shows a 2-wide, 2-input CMOS *OR-AND-INVERT (OAI) gate*. The function table for this circuit is shown in (b); the values in each

OR-AND-INVERT (OAI) gate

Figure 3-22 CMOS OR-AND-INVERT gate: (a) circuit diagram; (b) function table.

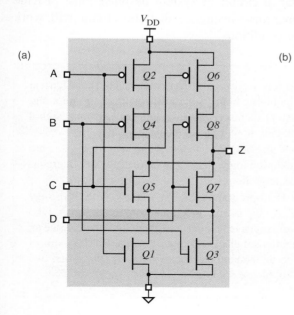

(a)

(b)

A	B	C	D	*Q1*	*Q2*	*Q3*	*Q4*	*Q5*	*Q6*	*Q7*	*Q8*	Z
L	L	L	L	off	on	off	on	off	on	off	on	H
L	L	L	H	off	on	off	on	off	on	on	off	H
L	L	H	L	off	on	off	on	on	off	off	on	H
L	L	H	H	off	on	off	on	on	off	on	off	H
L	H	L	L	off	on	on	off	off	on	off	on	H
L	H	L	H	off	on	on	off	off	on	on	off	L
L	H	H	L	off	on	on	off	on	off	off	on	L
L	H	H	H	off	on	on	off	on	off	on	off	L
H	L	L	L	on	off	off	on	off	on	off	on	H
H	L	L	H	on	off	off	on	off	on	on	off	L
H	L	H	L	on	off	off	on	on	off	off	on	L
H	L	H	H	on	off	off	on	on	off	on	off	L
H	H	L	L	on	off	on	off	off	on	off	on	H
H	H	L	H	on	off	on	off	off	on	on	off	L
H	H	H	L	on	off	on	off	on	off	off	on	L
H	H	H	H	on	off	on	off	on	off	on	off	L

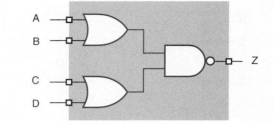

Figure 3-23
Logic diagram for CMOS
OR-AND-INVERT gate.

column are determined just as we did for the CMOS AOI gate. A logic diagram for the OAI function using OR and NAND gates is shown in Figure 3-23.

The speed and other electrical characteristics of a CMOS AOI or OAI gate are quite comparable to those of a single CMOS NAND or NOR gate. As a result, these gates are very appealing because they can perform two levels of logic (AND-OR or OR-AND) with just one level of delay. Most digital designers don't bother to use AOI gates in their discrete designs. However, CMOS VLSI devices often use these gates internally, since many HDL synthesis tools can automatically convert AND/OR logic into AOI gates when appropriate.

3.4 Electrical Behavior of CMOS Circuits

The next three sections discuss electrical, not logical, aspects of CMOS circuit operation. It's important to understand this material when you design real circuits using CMOS or other logic families. Most of this material is aimed at providing a framework for ensuring that the "digital abstraction" is really valid for a given circuit. In particular, a circuit or system designer must provide adequate engineering design margins—insurance that the circuit will work properly even under the worst of conditions.

engineering design margins

IS ALL THIS REALLY NECESSARY?

The behaviors described in the next few sections are a consequence of the electrical design of the CMOS logic gates, including both their transistor-level structure and the analog properties of the transistors themselves. Since you may never design a logic gate yourself, you might think that these topics are unimportant.

However, these behaviors are also a consequence of the way that gates are selected and interconnected to form digital logic circuits, and creating such interconnections is exactly what a digital designer does.

Some technologies, such as field-programmable gate arrays (FPGAs), may hide the electrical consequences of on-chip interconnections from the designer, who can specify the design in a high-level language and use a software tool to generate an internal connection pattern that satisfies all electrical requirements. But it is almost *always* necessary for the designer to understand electrical characteristics when two or more chips are interconnected. So, please read on.

3.4.1 Overview

The topics that we examine in Sections 3.5–3.7 pertain to both the static and the dynamic behavior of CMOS devices and circuits:

- *Static behaviors.* These topics cover situations where a circuit's input and output signals are not changing. They include things like power consumption, the match-up and tolerances between input and output logic levels, and noise immunity.

- *Dynamic behaviors.* These topics cover situations where a circuit's input and output signals are changing. They include things like the extra power that is consumed as signals change, and the timing from an input-signal change to the resulting output-signal change.

When analyzing or designing a digital circuit, the designer must consider both static and dynamic behaviors. Most of the topics that we discuss in Sections 3.5–3.7 have both static and dynamic aspects. The topics include the following:

- *Logic voltage levels.* CMOS devices operating under normal conditions are guaranteed to produce output voltage levels within well-defined LOW and HIGH ranges. And they recognize LOW and HIGH input voltage levels over somewhat wider ranges. CMOS manufacturers specify these ranges and operating conditions very carefully to ensure compatibility among different devices in the same family and to provide a degree of interoperability (if you're careful) among devices in different families.

- *DC noise margins.* Positive DC noise margins ensure that the highest LOW voltage produced by an output is always lower than the highest voltage that an input can reliably interpret as LOW; and that the lowest HIGH voltage produced by an output is always higher than the lowest voltage that an input can reliably interpret as HIGH. A good understanding of noise margins is especially important in circuits that use devices from a number of different families.

- *Fanout.* This refers to the number and type of device inputs and other loads that are connected to a given output. If too many loads are connected to an output, the DC noise margins of the circuit may be inadequate. Fanout may also affect the speed at which the output changes from one state to another.

- *Speed.* The time that it takes a CMOS output to change from the LOW state to the HIGH state, or vice versa, depends on both the internal structure of the device and the characteristics of the other devices that it drives, even to the extent of being affected by the wire or printed-circuit-board traces connected to the output. We'll look at two separate components of "speed"— transition time and propagation delay.

- *Power consumption.* The power consumed by a CMOS device depends on a number of factors, including not only its internal structure, but also the input signals that it receives, the other devices that it drives, and how often its output changes between LOW and HIGH.

- *Noise.* The main reason for providing engineering design margins is to ensure proper circuit operation in the presence of noise. Noise can be generated by a number of sources; several of them are listed below, from the least likely to the (perhaps surprisingly) most likely:

  - Cosmic rays.
  - Power-supply disturbances.
  - Magnetic fields from nearby equipment.
  - The switching action of the logic circuits themselves.

- *Electrostatic discharge.* Would you believe that you can destroy a CMOS device just by touching it? Ordinary "static electricity" can have a voltage potential of a thousand volts or more, enough to puncture and damage the thin insulating material between a MOS transistor's gate and its source and drain.

- *Open-drain outputs.* Some CMOS outputs omit the usual *p*-channel pull-up transistors. In the HIGH state, such an output behaves essentially like a "no-connection," which is useful in some applications.

- *Three-state outputs.* Some CMOS devices have an extra "output enable" control input that can be used to disable both the *p*-channel pull-up transistors and the *n*-channel pull-down transistors. Many such device outputs can be tied together to create a multisource bus, as long as the control logic is arranged so that at most one output is enabled at a time.

Among these topics, timing is probably the most important, since it's an area where designers typically must spend the most time, even if they're otherwise working at a strictly "logical" level. So, we'll keep coming back to timing in later chapters, even after we've dismissed the other electrical topics discussed here.

3.4.2 Data Sheets and Specifications

data sheet

The manufacturers of real-world devices provide *data sheets* that specify the devices' logical and electrical characteristics. The electrical specifications portion of a minimal data sheet for a simple CMOS device, the 54/74HC00 quadruple NAND gate, is shown in Table 3-3. ("Quadruple" means there are four gates in the same chip and package.) Different manufacturers typically specify additional parameters, and they may vary in how they specify even the "standard" parameters shown in the table. For example, they usually also show the test circuits and waveforms that they use to define various parameters, as in Figure 3-24. Note that this figure contains information for some additional parameters beyond those used with the 54/74HC00.

Table 3-3 Manufacturer's data sheet for a typical CMOS device, a 54/74HC00 quad NAND gate.

DC ELECTRICAL CHARACTERISTICS OVER OPERATING RANGE

The following conditions apply unless otherwise specified:

Commercial: $T_A = -40°C$ to $+85°C$, $V_{CC} = 5.0$ V $\pm5\%$;   Military: $T_A = -55°C$ to $+125°C$, $V_{CC} = 5.0$ V $\pm10\%$

Sym.	Parameter	Test Conditions[1]		Min.	Typ.[2]	Max.	Unit
V_{IH}	Input HIGH level	Guaranteed logic HIGH level		3.15	—	—	V
V_{IL}	Input LOW level	Guaranteed logic LOW level		—	—	1.35	V
I_{IH}	Input HIGH current	$V_{CC} = $ Max., $V_I = V_{CC}$		—	—	1	μA
I_{IL}	Input LOW current	$V_{CC} = $ Max., $V_I = 0$ V		—	—	-1	μA
V_{IK}	Clamp diode voltage	$V_{CC} = $ Min., $I_N = -18$ mA		—	-0.7	-1.2	V
I_{IOS}	Short-circuit current	$V_{CC} = $ Max.,[3] $V_O = $ GND		—	—	-35	mA
V_{OH}	Output HIGH voltage	$V_{CC} = $ Min., $V_{IN} = V_{IL}$	$I_{OH} = -20$ μA	4.4	4.499	—	V
			$I_{OH} = -4$ mA	3.84	4.3	—	V
V_{OL}	Output LOW voltage	$V_{CC} = $ Min., $V_{IN} = V_{IH}$	$I_{OL} = 20$ μA	—	.001	0.1	V
			$I_{OL} = 4$ mA		0.17	0.33	V
I_{CC}	Quiescent power supply current	$V_{CC} = $ Max. $V_{IN} = $ GND or V_{CC}, $I_O = 0$		—	2	10	μA

SWITCHING CHARACTERISTICS OVER OPERATING RANGE, $C_L = 50$ pF

Sym.	Parameter[4]	Test Conditions	Min.	Typ.	Max.	Unit
t_{PD}	Propagation delay	A or B to Y	—	9	19	ns
C_I	Input capacitance	$V_{IN} = 0$ V	—	3	10	pF
C_{pd}	Power dissipation capacitance per gate	No load	—	22	—	pF

NOTES:

1. For conditions shown as Max. or Min., use appropriate value specified under Electrical Characteristics.

2. Typical values are at $V_{CC} = 5.0$ V, $+25$ °C ambient.

3. Not more than one output should be shorted at a time. Duration of short-circuit test should not exceed one second.

4. This parameter is guaranteed but not tested.

WHAT'S IN A NUMBER?   Two different prefixes, "74" and "54," are used in the part numbers of CMOS and TTL devices. These prefixes simply distinguish between commercial and military versions. A 74HC00 is the commercial part and the 54HC00 is the military version.

TEST CIRCUIT FOR ALL OUTPUTS

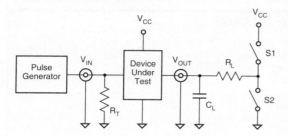

LOADING

Parameter		R_L	C_L	S1	S2
t_{en}	t_{pZH}	1 KΩ	50 pF or 150 pF	Open	Closed
	t_{pZL}			Closed	Open
t_{dis}	t_{pHZ}	1 KΩ	50 pF or 150 pF	Open	Closed
	t_{pLZ}			Closed	Open
t_{pd}		—	50 pF or 150 pF	Open	Open

DEFINITIONS:
C_L = Load capacitance, includes jig and probe capacitance.
R_T = Termination resistance, should equal Z_{OUT} of the Pulse Generator.

SETUP, HOLD, AND RELEASE TIMES

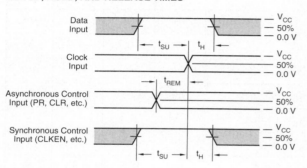

PULSE WIDTH

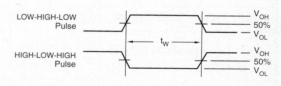

PROPAGATION DELAY

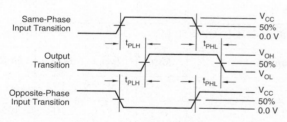

THREE-STATE ENABLE AND DISABLE TIMES

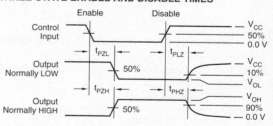

Figure 3-24 Test circuits and waveforms for HC-series logic.

Most of the terms in the data sheet and the waveforms in the figure are probably meaningless to you at this point. However, after reading the next three sections you should know enough about the electrical characteristics of CMOS circuits that you'll be able to understand the salient points of this or any other data sheet. As a digital designer, you'll need this knowledge to create reliable and robust real-world circuits and systems.

DON'T BE AFRAID   Computer science students and other non-EE readers should not have undue fear of the material in the next three sections. Only a basic understanding of electronics, at about the level of Ohm's law, is required.

3.5 CMOS Static Electrical Behavior

This section discusses the "DC" or static behavior of CMOS circuits, that is, the circuits' behavior when inputs and outputs are not changing. Electrical engineers also call this "steady-state" behavior, because the electrical state of the inputs is not changing.

3.5.1 Logic Levels and Noise Margins

The table in Figure 3-10(b) on page 88 defined the CMOS inverter's behavior only at two discrete input voltages; other input voltages may yield different output voltages. The complete input-output transfer characteristic of a particular inverter can be described by a graph such as Figure 3-25. In this graph, the input voltage is varied from 0 to 5 V, as shown on the X axis; and the Y axis plots the output voltage.

   If we believed the curve in Figure 3-25, we could define a CMOS LOW input level as any voltage under 2.4 V, and a HIGH input level as anything over 2.6 V. Only when the input is between 2.4 and 2.6 V does the inverter produce a nonlogic output voltage under this definition.

   Unfortunately, the typical transfer characteristic shown in Figure 3-25 is just that—typical, but not guaranteed. It varies greatly under different conditions such as power-supply voltage, temperature, and output loading. For example, the transition in the middle of the curve may become more or less steep, and it may shift to the left or the right. The transfer characteristic may even vary depending on when the device was fabricated. For example, after months of trying to figure out why gates made on some days were good and on other days were bad, legend has it that one manufacturer discovered that the bad gates were victims of airborne contamination by a particularly noxious perfume worn by one of its production-line workers!

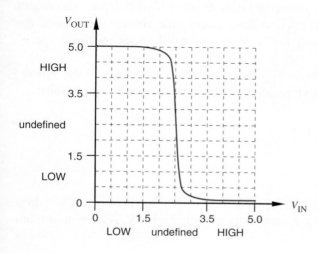

Figure 3-25
Typical input-output transfer characteristic of a CMOS inverter.

Figure 3-26
Logic levels and
noise margins
for the HC-series
CMOS logic family.

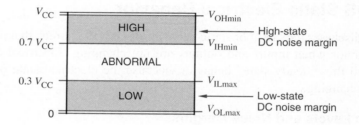

Sound engineering practice dictates that we use specifications (or "specs") for LOW and HIGH that are more conservative. Conservative logic-level specs for a typical CMOS logic family (HC-series) are depicted in Figure 3-26. These parameters are specified by CMOS device manufacturers in data sheets like Table 3-3 on page 99, and are defined as follows:

V_{OHmin} The minimum output voltage produced in the HIGH state.

V_{IHmin} The minimum input voltage guaranteed to be recognized as a HIGH.

V_{ILmax} The maximum input voltage guaranteed to be recognized as a LOW.

V_{OLmax} The maximum output voltage produced in the LOW state.

The input voltages are determined mainly by switching thresholds of the two transistors, while the output voltages are determined mainly by the "on" resistance of the transistors.

All of the parameters in Figure 3-26 are guaranteed by CMOS manufacturers over a range of temperature and output loading. Parameters are also guaranteed over a range of power-supply voltage V_{CC}, typically 5.0 V±10%.

The data sheet in Table 3-3 specifies values for each of these parameters for HC-series CMOS. Notice that there are two values specified for V_{OHmin} and V_{OLmax}, depending on whether the output current (I_{OH} or I_{OL}) is large or small. When the device outputs are connected only to other CMOS inputs, the output current is low (e.g., $I_{OL} \leq 20\ \mu A$), so there's very little voltage drop across the output transistors. In the next few subsections we'll focus on these "pure" CMOS applications.

power-supply rails

The power-supply voltage V_{CC} and ground are often called the *power-supply rails*. CMOS levels are typically a function of the power-supply rails:

V_{OHmin} $V_{CC} - 0.1$ V

V_{IHmin} 70% of V_{CC}

V_{ILmax} 30% of V_{CC}

V_{OLmax} ground + 0.1 V

Notice in Table 3-3 that V_{OHmin} is specified as 4.4 V. This is only a 0.1-V drop from V_{CC}, since the worst-case number is specified with V_{CC} at its minimum value of 5.0 − 10% = 4.5 V.

DC noise margin is a measure of how much noise it takes to corrupt a   *DC noise margin*
worst-case output voltage into a value that may not be recognized properly by an
input. For example, with HC-series CMOS in the LOW state, V_{ILmax} (1.35 V)
exceeds V_{OLmax} (0.1 V) by 1.25 V, so the LOW-state DC noise margin is 1.25 V.
With HC-series CMOS in the HIGH state, V_{IHmin} (3.15 V) is 1.25 V lower than
V_{OHmin} (4.4 V), so there is 1.25 V of HIGH-state DC noise margin as well. In
general, CMOS outputs have excellent DC noise margins when driving other
CMOS inputs.

Regardless of the voltage applied to the input of a CMOS inverter, the input
consumes very little current, only the leakage current of the two transistors'
gates. The maximum amount of leakage current that can flow is specified by the
device manufacturer:

I_{IH} The maximum current that flows into the input in the HIGH state.

I_{IL} The maximum current that flows into the input in the LOW state.

The input current shown in Table 3-3 for the 'HC00 is only ±1 μA. Thus, it takes
very little power to maintain a CMOS input in one state or the other. This is in
sharp contrast to older bipolar logic circuits like TTL and ECL, whose inputs
may consume significant current (and power) in one or both states.

3.5.2 Circuit Behavior with Resistive Loads

As mentioned previously, CMOS gate inputs have very high impedance and
consume very little current from the circuits that drive them. There are other
devices, however, which require nontrivial amounts of current to operate. When
such a device is connected to a CMOS output, we call it a *resistive load* or a *DC*   *resistive load*
load. Here are some examples of resistive loads: *DC load*

- Discrete resistors may be included to provide transmission-line termination, discussed in <u>Section Zo</u> at <u>DDPPonline</u>.

- Discrete resistors may not really be present in the circuit, but the load
  presented by one or more TTL or other non-CMOS inputs may be modeled
  by a simple resistor network.

- The resistors may be part of or may model a current-consuming device
  such as a light-emitting diode (LED) or a relay coil.

When the output of a CMOS circuit is connected to a resistive load, the
output behavior is not nearly as ideal as we described previously. In either logic
state, the CMOS output transistor that is "on" has a nonzero resistance, and a
load connected to the output terminal will cause a voltage drop across this
resistance. Thus, in the LOW state, the output voltage may be somewhat higher
than 0.1 V, and in the HIGH state it may be lower than 4.4 V. The easiest way to
see how this happens is look at a resistive model of the CMOS circuit and its
load.

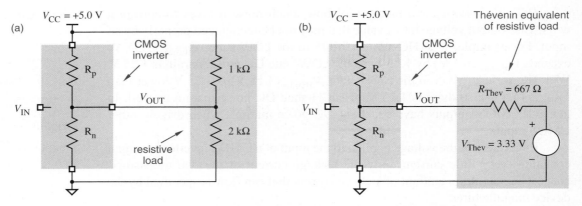

Figure 3-27 Resistive model of a CMOS inverter with a resistive load:
(a) showing actual load circuit; (b) using Thévenin equivalent
of load.

Figure 3-27(a) shows the resistive model. The p-channel and n-channel transistors have resistances R_p and R_n, respectively. In normal operation, one resistance is high (> 1 MΩ) and the other is low (perhaps 100 Ω), depending on whether the input voltage is HIGH or LOW. The load in this circuit consists of two resistors attached to the supply rails; a real circuit may have any resistor values, or an even more complex resistive network. In any case, a resistive load, consisting only of resistors and voltage sources, can always be modeled by a Thévenin equivalent network, such as the one shown in Figure 3-27(b).

When the CMOS inverter has a HIGH input, the output should be LOW; the actual output voltage can be predicted using the resistive model shown in Figure 3-28. The p-channel transistor is "off" and has a very high resistance,

**REMEMBERING
THÉVENIN**

Any two-terminal circuit consisting of only voltage sources and resistors can be modeled by a *Thévenin equivalent* consisting of a single voltage source in series with a single resistor. The *Thévenin voltage* is the open-circuit voltage of the original circuit, and the *Thévenin resistance* is the Thévenin voltage divided by the short-circuit current of the original circuit.

In the example of Figure 3-27, the Thévenin voltage of the resistive load, including its connection to V_{CC}, is established by the 1-kΩ and 2-kΩ resistors, which form a voltage divider:

$$V_{Thev} = \frac{2 \text{ k}\Omega}{2 \text{ k}\Omega + 1 \text{k}\Omega} \cdot 5.0 \text{ V} = 3.33 \text{ V}$$

The short-circuit current is $(5.0 \text{ V})/(1 \text{ k}\Omega) = 5$ mA, so the Thévenin resistance is $(3.33 \text{ V})/(5 \text{ mA}) = 667 \Omega$. Readers who are electrical engineers may recognize this as the parallel resistance of the 1-kΩ and 2-kΩ resistors.

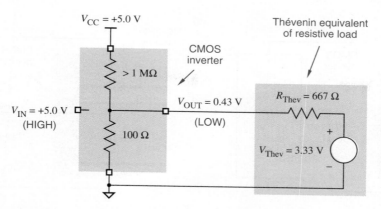

Figure 3-28
Resistive model for CMOS LOW output with resistive load.

high enough to be negligible in the calculations that follow. The *n*-channel transistor is "on" and has a low resistance, which we assume to be 100 Ω. (The actual "on" resistance depends on the CMOS family and other characteristics such as operating temperature and whether or not the device was manufactured on a good day.) The "on" transistor and the Thévenin-equivalent resistor R_{Thev} in Figure 3-28 form a simple voltage divider. The resulting output voltage can be calculated as follows:

$$V_{OUT} = 3.33 \text{ V} \cdot [100/(100 + 667)]$$

$$= 0.43 \text{ V}$$

Similarly, when the inverter has a LOW input, the output should be HIGH, and the actual output voltage can be predicted with the model in Figure 3-29. We'll assume that the *p*-channel transistor's "on" resistance is 200 Ω. Once again, the "on" transistor and the Thévenin-equivalent resistor R_{Thev} in the figure form a simple voltage divider, and the resulting output voltage can be calculated as follows:

$$V_{OUT} = 3.33 \text{ V} + (5 \text{ V} - 3.33 \text{ V}) \cdot [667/(200 + 667)]$$

$$= 4.61 \text{ V}$$

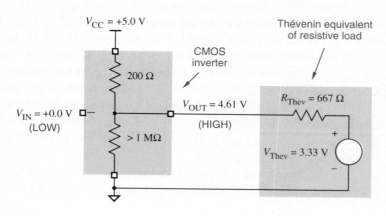

Figure 3-29
Resistive model for CMOS HIGH output with resistive load.

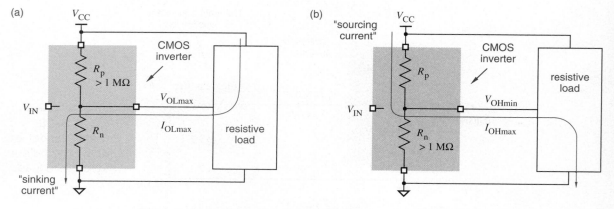

Figure 3-30 Circuit definitions of (a) I_{OLmax}; (b) I_{OHmax}.

In practice, it's seldom necessary to calculate output voltages as in the preceding examples. In fact, IC manufacturers usually don't specify the equivalent resistances of the "on" transistors, so you wouldn't have the necessary information to make the calculation anyway. Instead, IC manufacturers specify a maximum load for the output in each state (HIGH or LOW), and guarantee a worst-case output voltage for that load. The load is specified in terms of current:

I_{OLmax} The maximum current that the output can sink in the LOW state while still maintaining an output voltage no greater than V_{OLmax}.

I_{OHmax} The maximum current that the output can source in the HIGH state while still maintaining an output voltage no less than V_{OHmin}.

sinking current

sourcing current

These definitions are illustrated in Figure 3-30. A device output is said to *sink current* when current flows from the power supply, through the load, and through the device output to ground as in (a). The output is said to *source current* when current flows from the power supply, out of the device output, and through the load to ground as in (b).

Most CMOS devices have two sets of loading specifications. One set is for "CMOS loads," where the device output is connected to other CMOS inputs, which consume very little current. The other set is for "TTL loads," where the output is connected to resistive loads such as TTL inputs or other devices that consume significant current. For example, the specifications for HC-series CMOS outputs were shown in Table 3-3 and are repeated in Table 3-4.

current flow

Notice in Table 3-4 that the output current in the HIGH state is shown as a negative number. By convention, the *current flow* measured at a device terminal is positive if positive current flows *into* the device; in the HIGH state, current flows *out* of the output terminal.

As the table shows, with CMOS loads, the CMOS gate's output voltage is maintained within 0.1 V of the power-supply rail. With TTL loads, the output

Table 3-4 Output loading specifications for HC-series CMOS with a 5V±10% supply.

Parameter	CMOS Load		TTL Load	
	Name	Value	Name	Value
Maximum LOW-state output current (mA)	I_{OLmaxC}	0.02	I_{OLmaxT}	4.0
Maximum LOW-state output voltage (V)	V_{OLmaxC}	0.1	V_{OLmaxT}	0.33
Maximum HIGH-state output current (mA)	I_{OHmaxC}	-0.02	I_{OHmaxT}	-4.0
Minimum HIGH-state output voltage (V)	V_{OHminC}	4.4	V_{OHminT}	3.84

voltage may degrade quite a bit. Also notice that for the same output current (±4 mA) the maximum voltage drop with respect to the power-supply rail is twice as much in the HIGH state (0.66 V) as in the LOW state (0.33 V). This suggests that the *p*-channel transistors in HC-series CMOS have a higher "on" resistance than the *n*-channel transistors do. This is natural, since in any CMOS circuit, a *p*-channel transistor has over twice the "on" resistance of an *n*-channel transistor with the same area. Equal voltage drops in both states could be obtained by making the *p*-channel transistors much larger than the *n*-channel transistors, but for various reasons this was not done.

Ohm's law can be used to determine how much current an output sources or sinks in a given situation. In Figure 3-28 on page 105, the "on" *n*-channel transistor modeled by a 100-Ω resistor has a 0.43-V drop across it; therefore it sinks (0.43 V)/(100 Ω) = 4.3 mA of current. Similarly, the "on" *p*-channel transistor in Figure 3-29 sources (0.39 V)/(200 Ω) = 1.95 mA.

The actual "on" resistances of CMOS output transistors usually aren't published, so it's generally not possible to use the exact models of the previous paragraphs. However, you can estimate "on" resistances using the following equations, which rely on specifications that are always published:

$$R_{p(on)} \approx \frac{V_{DD} - V_{OHminT}}{|I_{OHmaxT}|}$$

$$R_{n(on)} \approx \frac{V_{OLmaxT}}{I_{OLmaxT}}$$

These equations use Ohm's law to compute the "on" resistance as the voltage drop across the "on" transistor divided by the current through it with a worst-case resistive load. Using the numbers given for HC-series CMOS in Table 3-4, we can calculate $R_{p(on)} \approx$ 165 Ω and $R_{n(on)} \approx$ 82.5 Ω Note that $V_{DD} = 4.5$ V (the minimum value) for this calculation.

Very good *worst-case* estimates of output current can be made by assuming that there is *no* voltage drop across the "on" transistor. This assumption simpli-

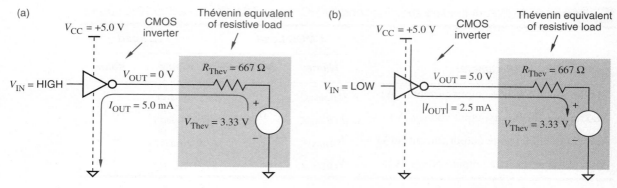

Figure 3-31 Estimating sink and source current: (a) output LOW; (b) output HIGH.

fies the analysis, and yields a conservative result that is almost always good enough for practical purposes. For example, Figure 3-31 shows a CMOS inverter driving the same Thévenin-equivalent load that we've used in previous examples. The resistive model of the output structure is not shown, because it is no longer needed; we assume that there is no voltage drop across the "on" CMOS transistor. In (a), with the output LOW, the entire 3.33-V Thévenin-equivalent voltage source appears across R_{Thev}, and the estimated sink current is $(3.33 \text{ V})/(667 \text{ }\Omega) = 5.0 \text{ mA}$. In (b), with the output HIGH and assuming a 5.0-V supply, the voltage drop across R_{Thev} is 1.67 V, and the estimated source current is $(1.67 \text{ V})/(667 \text{ }\Omega) = 2.5 \text{ mA}$.

An important feature of the CMOS inverter (or any CMOS circuit) is that the output structure by itself consumes very little current in either state, HIGH or LOW. In either state, one of the transistors is in the high-impedance "off" state. All of the current flow that we've been talking about occurs when a resistive load is connected to the CMOS output. If there's no load, then there's no current flow, and the power consumption is zero. With a load, however, current flows through both the load and the "on" transistor, and power is consumed in both.

3.5.3 Circuit Behavior with Nonideal Inputs

So far, we have assumed that the HIGH and LOW inputs to a CMOS circuit are ideal voltages, very close to the power-supply rails. However, the behavior of a real CMOS inverter circuit depends on the input voltage as well as on the characteristics of the load. If the input voltage is not close to the power-supply rail, then the "on" transistor may not be fully "on" and its resistance may increase. Likewise, the "off" transistor may not be fully "off" and its resistance may be quite a bit less than one megohm. These two effects combine to move the output voltage away from the power-supply rail.

For example, Figure 3-32(a) shows a CMOS inverter's possible behavior with a 1.5-V input. The *p*-channel transistor's resistance has doubled at this point, and the *n*-channel transistor is beginning to turn on. (These values are just assumed for the purposes of illustration; the actual values depend on the detailed characteristics of the transistors.)

In the figure, the output at 4.31 V is still well within the valid range for a HIGH signal, but not quite the ideal of 5.0 V. Similarly, with a 3.5-V input in (b), the LOW output is 0.24 V, not 0 V. The slight degradation of output voltage is generally tolerable; what's worse is that the output structure is now consuming a nontrivial amount of power. The current flow with the 1.5-V input is

$$I_{wasted} = 5.0 \text{ V}/(400 \text{ }\Omega + 2.5 \text{ k}\Omega) = 1.72 \text{ mA}$$

and the power consumption is

$$P_{wasted} = 5.0 \text{ V} \cdot I_{wasted} = 8.62 \text{ mW}$$

Figure 3-32 CMOS inverter with nonideal input voltages: (a) equivalent circuit with 1.5-V input; (b) equivalent circuit with 3.5-V input.

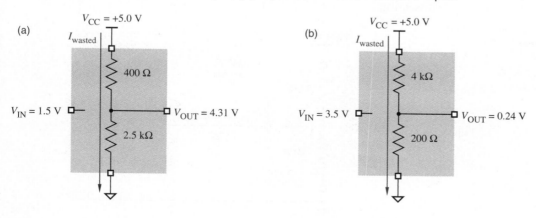

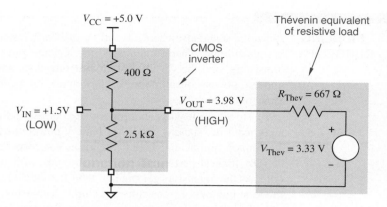

Figure 3-33
CMOS inverter with
load and nonideal
1.5-V input.

The output voltage of a CMOS inverter deteriorates further with a resistive load. Such a load may exist for any of a variety of reasons discussed previously. Figure 3-33 shows the CMOS inverter's possible behavior with a resistive load. With a 1.5-V input, the output at 3.98 V is still within the valid range for a HIGH signal, but it is still farther from the ideal of 5.0 V. Similarly, with a 3.5-V input as shown in Figure 3-34, the LOW output is 0.93 V, not 0 V.

In "pure" CMOS systems, all of the logic devices in a circuit are CMOS. Since CMOS inputs have a very high impedance, they present very little resistive load to the CMOS outputs that drive them. Therefore, the CMOS output levels all remain very close to the power-supply rails (0 V and 5 V), and none of the devices waste power in their output structures. In "non-pure" CMOS systems, additional power can be consumed in two ways:

- If TTL outputs or other nonideal logic signals are connected to CMOS inputs, then the CMOS outputs use power in the way depicted in this subsection; this is formalized in the box on page 145.

- If TTL inputs or other resistive loads are connected to CMOS outputs, then the CMOS outputs use power in the way depicted in the preceding subsection.

Figure 3-34
CMOS inverter with
load and nonideal
3.5-V input.

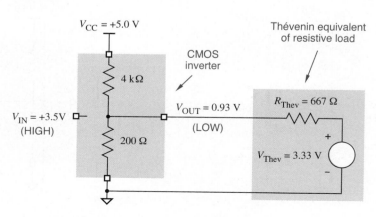

3.5.4 Fanout

The *fanout* of a logic gate is the number of inputs that the gate can drive without exceeding its worst-case loading specifications. The fanout depends not only on the characteristics of the output, but also on the inputs that it is driving. Fanout must be examined for both possible output states, HIGH and LOW.

fanout

For example, we showed in Table 3-4 on page 107 that the maximum LOW-state output current I_{OLmaxC} for an HC-series CMOS gate driving CMOS inputs is 0.02 mA (20 μA). We also stated previously that the maximum input current I_{Imax} for an HC-series CMOS input in any state is ± 1 μA. Therefore, the *LOW-state fanout* for an HC-series output driving HC-series inputs is 20. Table 3-4 also showed that the maximum HIGH-state output current I_{OHmaxC} is -0.02 mA (-20 μA) Therefore, the *HIGH-state fanout* for an HC-series output driving HC-series inputs is also 20.

LOW-state fanout

HIGH-state fanout

Note that the HIGH-state and LOW-state fanouts of a gate aren't necessarily equal. In general, the *overall fanout* of a gate is the minimum of its HIGH-state and LOW-state fanouts, 20 in the foregoing example.

overall fanout

In the fanout example that we just completed, we assumed that we needed to maintain the gate's output at CMOS levels, that is, within 0.1 V of the power-supply rails. If we were willing to live with somewhat degraded, TTL output levels, then we could use I_{OLmaxT} and I_{OHmaxT} in the fanout calculation. Table 3-4 shows that these specifications are 4.0 mA and -4.0 mA, respectively. Therefore, the fanout of an HC-series output driving HC-series inputs at TTL levels is 4000—for practical purposes, virtually unlimited, apparently.

Well, not quite. The calculations that we've just carried out give the *DC fanout,* defined as the number of inputs that an output can drive *with the output in a constant state* (HIGH or LOW). Even if the DC fanout specification is met, a CMOS output driving a large number of inputs may not behave satisfactorily on transitions, LOW-to-HIGH or vice versa.

DC fanout

During transitions, the CMOS output must charge or discharge the stray capacitance associated with the inputs that it drives. If this capacitance is too large, the transition from LOW to HIGH (or vice versa) may be too slow, causing improper system operation.

The ability of an output to charge and discharge stray capacitance is sometimes called *AC fanout*, though it is seldom calculated as precisely as DC fanout. As you'll see in Section 3.6.1, it's more a matter of deciding how much speed degradation you're willing to live with.

AC fanout

3.5.5 Effects of Loading

Loading an output beyond its rated fanout has several effects:

- In the LOW state, the output voltage (V_{OL}) may increase beyond V_{OLmax}.
- In the HIGH state, the output voltage (V_{OH}) may fall below V_{OHmin}.
- Propagation delay to the output may increase beyond specifications.

- Output rise and fall times may increase beyond their specifications.
- The operating temperature of the device may increase, thereby reducing the reliability of the device and eventually causing device failure.

The first four effects reduce the DC noise margins and timing margins of the circuit. Thus, a slightly overloaded circuit may work properly in ideal conditions, but experience says that it will fail once it's out of the friendly environment of the engineering lab.

3.5.6 Unused Inputs

Sometimes not all of the inputs of a logic gate are used. In a real design problem, you may need an n-input gate but have only an $(n + 1)$-input gate available. Tying together two inputs of the $(n + 1)$-input gate gives it the functionality of an n-input gate. You can convince yourself of this fact intuitively now, or use switching algebra to prove it after you've studied Section 4.1. Figure 3-35(a) shows a NAND gate with its inputs tied together.

You can also tie unused inputs to a constant logic value. An unused AND or NAND input should be tied to logic 1, as in (b), and an unused OR or NOR input should be tied to logic 0, as in (c). In high-speed circuit design, it's usually better to use method (b) or (c) rather than (a), which increases the capacitive load on the driving signal and may slow things down. In (b) and (c), a resistor value in the range 1–10 kΩ is typically used, and a single pull-up or pull-down resistor can serve multiple unused inputs. It is also possible to tie unused inputs directly to the appropriate power-supply rail.

floating input

Unused CMOS inputs should never be left unconnected (or *floating*). On one hand, such an input will behave as if it had a LOW signal applied to it and will normally show a value of 0 V when probed with an oscilloscope or voltmeter. So you might think that an unused OR or NOR input can be left floating, because it will act as if a logic 0 is applied and will not affect the gate's output. However, since CMOS inputs have such high impedance, it takes only a small amount of circuit noise to temporarily make a floating input look HIGH, creating some very nasty intermittent circuit failures.

Figure 3-35 Unused inputs: (a) tied to another input; (b) NAND pulled up; (c) NOR pulled down.

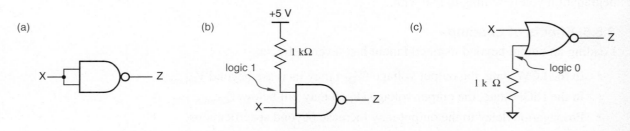

SUBTLE BUGS Floating CMOS inputs are often the cause of mysterious circuit behavior, as an unused input erratically changes its effective state based on noise and conditions elsewhere in the circuit. When you're trying to debug such a problem, the extra capacitance of an oscilloscope probe touched to the floating input is often enough to damp out the noise and make the problem go away. This can be especially baffling if you don't realize that the input is floating!

3.5.7 How to Destroy a CMOS Device

Hit it with a sledgehammer. Or simply walk across a carpet and then touch an input pin with your finger. Because CMOS device inputs have such high impedance, they are subject to damage from *electrostatic discharge (ESD)*.

electrostatic discharge (ESD)

ESD occurs when a buildup of charge ("static electricity") on one surface arcs through a dielectric to another surface with the opposite charge. In the case of a CMOS input, the dielectric is the insulation between an input transistor's gate and its source and drain. ESD may damage this insulation, causing a short-circuit between the device's input and its output.

Ordinary activities of people, such as walking on a carpet, can create static electricity with surprisingly high voltage potentials—1000 V or more. The input structures of modern CMOS devices use various measures to reduce their susceptibility to ESD damage, but no device is completely immune. Therefore, to protect CMOS devices from ESD damage during shipment and handling, manufacturers normally package their devices in conductive bags, tubes, or foam. To prevent ESD damage when handling loose CMOS devices, circuit assemblers and technicians usually wear conductive wrist straps that are connected by a coil cord to earth ground; this prevents a static charge from building up on their bodies as they move around the factory or lab.

Ordinary operation of some equipment, such as repeated or continuous movement of mechanical components like doors or fans, can also create static electricity. For that reason, printed-circuit boards containing CMOS circuits are carefully designed with ESD protection in mind. Typically, this means grounding connector housings, the edges of the board, and any other points where static might be encountered because of proximity to people or equipment. This "encourages" ESD to take a safe, metallic path to ground, rather than through the pins of CMOS chips mounted on the board.

Once a CMOS device is installed in a system, another possible source of damage is *latch-up*. The physical input structure of just about any CMOS device contains parasitic bipolar transistors between V_{CC} and ground configured as a "silicon-controlled rectifier (SCR)." In normal operation, this "parasitic SCR" has no effect on device operation. However, an input voltage that is less than ground or more than V_{CC} can "trigger" the SCR, creating a virtual short-circuit between V_{CC} and ground. Once the SCR is triggered, the only way to turn it off

latch-up

ELIMINATE RUDE, SHOCKING BEHAVIOR!

Some design engineers consider themselves above such inconveniences, but to be safe you should follow several ESD precautions in the lab:

- Before handling a CMOS device, touch the grounded metal case of a plugged-in instrument or another source of earth ground.

- Before transporting a CMOS device, insert it in conductive foam.

- When carrying a circuit board containing CMOS devices, handle the board by the edges, and touch a ground terminal on the board to earth ground before poking around with it.

- When handing over a CMOS device to a partner, especially on a dry winter day, touch the partner first. He or she will thank you for it.

is to turn off the power supply. Before you have a chance to do this, enough power may be dissipated to destroy the device (i.e., you may see smoke).

One possible trigger for latch-up is "undershoot" on high-speed HIGH-to-LOW signal transitions, discussed in Section Zo at DDPPonline. In this situation, the input signal may go several volts below ground for several nanoseconds before settling in the normal LOW range. However, modern CMOS logic circuits are fabricated with special structures that prevent latch-up in this transient case.

Latch-up can also occur when CMOS inputs are driven by the outputs of another system or subsystem with a separate power supply. If a HIGH input is applied to a CMOS gate before power is present, the gate may come up in the "latched-up" state when power is applied. Again, modern CMOS logic circuits are fabricated with special structures that prevent this in most cases. However, if the driving output is capable of sourcing lots of current (e.g., tens of milliamperes), latch-up is still possible. One solution to this problem is to apply power before hooking up input cables.

3.6 CMOS Dynamic Electrical Behavior

Both the speed and the power consumption of a CMOS device depend to a large extent on "AC" or dynamic characteristics of the device and its load, that is, what happens when the output changes between states. As part of the internal design of CMOS ASICs, digital designers must carefully examine the effects of output loading, and resize or redesign circuits where the load is too high. Even in board-level design, the effects of loading must be considered for clocks, buses, and other signals that have high fanout or long interconnections.

Speed depends on two characteristics, transition time and propagation delay, discussed in the next two subsections. Power dissipation is discussed in the third subsection, and a few nasty real-world effects are discussed in the last three subsections.

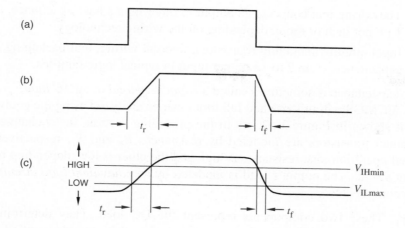

Figure 3-36
Transition times:
(a) ideal case of
zero-time switching;
(b) a more realistic
approximation;
(c) actual timing,
showing rise and fall
times.

3.6.1 Transition Time

The amount of time that the output of a logic circuit takes to change from one state to another is called the *transition time*. Figure 3-36(a) shows how we might like outputs to change state—in zero time. However, real outputs cannot change instantaneously, because they need time to charge the stray capacitance of the wires and other components that they drive. A more realistic view of a circuit's output is shown in (b). An output takes a certain time, called the *rise time* (t_r), to change from LOW to HIGH, and a possibly different time, called the *fall time* (t_f), to change from HIGH to LOW.

transition time

rise time (t_r)
fall time (t_f)

Even Figure 3-36(b) is not quite accurate, because the rate of change of the output voltage does not change instantaneously, either. Instead, the beginning and the end of a transition are smooth, as shown in (c). To avoid difficulties in defining the endpoints, rise and fall times are normally measured at the boundaries of the valid logic levels as indicated in the figure.

With the convention in (c), the rise and fall times indicate how long an output voltage takes to pass through the "undefined" region between LOW and HIGH. The initial part of a transition is not included in the rise- or fall-time number. Instead, the initial part of a transition contributes to the "propagation delay" number discussed in the next subsection.

The rise and fall times of a CMOS output depend mainly on two factors, the "on" transistor resistance and the load capacitance. A large capacitance increases transition times; since this is undesirable, it is very rare for a digital designer to purposely connect a capacitor to a logic circuit's output. However, *stray capacitance* is present in every circuit; it comes from at least three sources:

stray capacitance

1. Output circuits, including a gate's output transistors, internal wiring, and packaging, have some capacitance associated with them, in the range of 2–10 picofarads (pF) in typical logic families, including CMOS.

2. The wiring that connects an output to other inputs has capacitance, about 1 pF per inch or more, depending on the wiring technology.

3. Input circuits, including transistors, internal wiring, and packaging, have capacitance, from 2 to 15 pF per input in typical logic families.

capacitive load
AC load

Stray capacitance is sometimes called a *capacitive load* or an *AC load*.

A CMOS output's rise and fall times can be analyzed using the equivalent circuit shown in Figure 3-37. As in the preceding section, the *p*-channel and *n*-channel transistors are modeled by resistances R_p and R_n, respectively. In normal operation, one resistance is high and the other is low, depending on the

equivalent load circuit

output's state. The output's load is modeled by an *equivalent load circuit* with three components:

R_L, V_L These two components represent the DC load. They determine the voltages and currents that are present when the output has settled into a stable HIGH or LOW state. The DC load doesn't have too much effect on transition times when the output changes state.

C_L This capacitance represents the AC load. It determines the voltages and currents that are present while the output is changing, and how long it takes to change from one state to the other.

When a CMOS output drives only CMOS inputs, the DC load is negligible. To simplify matters, we'll analyze only this case, with $R_L = \infty$ and $V_L = 0$, in the remainder of this subsection. The presence of a nonnegligible DC load would affect the results, but not dramatically (see Exercise 3.68).

We can now analyze the transition times of a CMOS output. For the purpose of this analysis, we'll assume $C_L = 100$ pF, a moderate capacitive load. Also, we'll assume that the "on" resistances of the *p*-channel and *n*-channel transistors are 200 Ω and 100 Ω, respectively, as in the preceding subsection. The rise and fall times depend on how long it takes to charge or discharge the capacitive load C_L.

Figure 3-37
Equivalent circuit for
analyzing transition
times of a CMOS output.

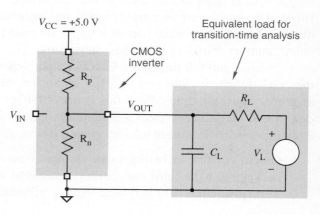

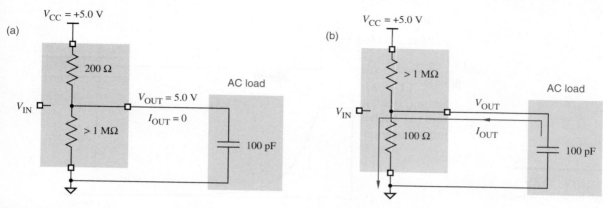

Figure 3-38 Model of a CMOS HIGH-to-LOW transition: (a) in the HIGH state; (b) after *p*-channel transistor turns off and *n*-channel transistor turns on.

First, we'll look at fall time. Figure 3-38(a) shows the electrical conditions in the circuit when the output is in a steady HIGH state. (R_L and V_L are not drawn; they have no effect, since we assume $R_L = \infty$.) For the purposes of our analysis, we'll assume that when CMOS transistors change between "on" and "off," they do so instantaneously. We'll assume that at time $t = 0$ the CMOS output changes to the LOW state, resulting in the situation depicted in (b).

At time $t = 0$, V_{OUT} is still 5.0 V. (A useful electrical engineering maxim is that the voltage across a capacitor cannot change instantaneously.) At time $t = \infty$, the capacitor must be fully discharged and V_{OUT} will be 0 V. In between, the value of V_{OUT} is governed by an exponential law:

$$V_{OUT} = V_{DD} \cdot e^{-t/(R_n C_L)}$$

$$= 5.0 \cdot e^{-t/(100 \cdot 100 \cdot 10^{-12})} \text{ V}$$

$$= 5.0 \cdot e^{-t/(10 \cdot 10^{-9})} \text{ V}$$

The factor $R_n C_L$ has units of seconds and is called an *RC time constant*.   *RC time constant*
The preceding calculation shows that the *RC* time constant for HIGH-to-LOW transitions is 10 nanoseconds (ns).

Figure 3-39 plots V_{OUT} as a function of time. To calculate fall time, recall that 1.5 V and 3.5 V are the defined boundaries for LOW and HIGH levels for CMOS inputs being driven by the CMOS output. To obtain the fall time, we must solve the preceding equation for $V_{OUT} = 3.5$ and $V_{OUT} = 1.5$, yielding:

$$t = -R_n C_L \cdot \ln \frac{V_{OUT}}{V_{DD}} = -10 \cdot 10^{-9} \cdot \ln \frac{V_{OUT}}{5.0}$$

$$t_{3.5} = 3.57 \text{ ns}$$

$$t_{1.5} = 12.04 \text{ ns}$$

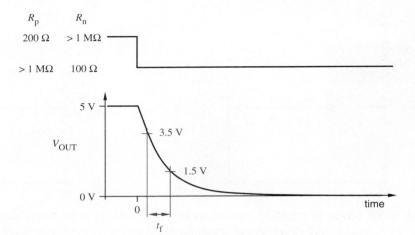

Figure 3-39
Fall time for a HIGH-to-LOW transition of a CMOS output.

The fall time t_f is the difference between these two numbers, or about 8.5 ns.

Rise time can be calculated in a similar manner. Figure 3-40(a) shows the conditions in the circuit when the output is in a steady LOW state. If at time $t = 0$ the CMOS output changes to the HIGH state, the situation depicted in (b) results. Once again, V_{OUT} cannot change instantly, but at time $t = \infty$, the capacitor will be fully charged and V_{OUT} will be 5.0 V. Once again, the value of V_{OUT} in between is governed by an exponential law:

$$
\begin{aligned}
V_{OUT} &= V_{DD} \cdot (1 - e^{-t/(R_p C_L)}) \\
&= 5.0 \cdot (1 - e^{-t/(200 \cdot 100 \cdot 10^{-12})}) \text{ V} \\
&= 5.0 \cdot (1 - e^{-t/(20 \cdot 10^{-9})}) \text{ V}
\end{aligned}
$$

Figure 3-40 Model of a CMOS LOW-to-HIGH transition: (a) in the LOW state; (b) after n-channel transistor turns off and p-channel transistor turns on.

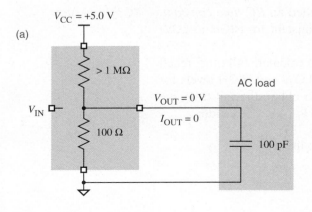

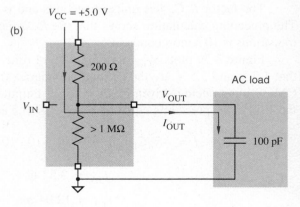

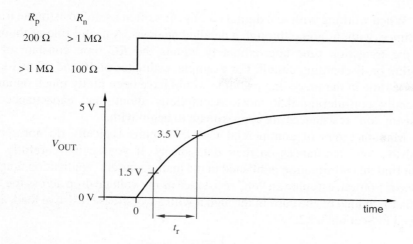

Figure 3-41
Rise time for a LOW-to-HIGH transition of a CMOS output.

The RC time constant in this case is 20 ns. Figure 3-41 plots V_{OUT} as a function of time. To obtain the rise time, we must solve the preceding equation for $V_{OUT} = 1.5$ and $V_{OUT} = 3.5$, yielding

$$t = -RC \cdot \ln \frac{V_{DD} - V_{OUT}}{V_{DD}}$$

$$= -20 \cdot 10^{-9} \cdot \ln \frac{5.0 - V_{OUT}}{5.0}$$

$$t_{1.5} = 7.13 \text{ ns}$$

$$t_{3.5} = 24.08 \text{ ns}$$

The rise time t_r is the difference between these two numbers, or about 17 ns.

The foregoing example assumes that the p-channel transistor has twice the resistance of the n-channel one, and as a result the rise time is twice as long as the fall time. It takes longer for the "weak" p-channel transistor to pull the output up than it does for the "strong" n-channel transistor to pull it down; the output's drive capability is "asymmetric." High-speed CMOS devices are sometimes fabricated with larger p-channel transistors to make the transition times more nearly equal and output drive more symmetric.

Regardless of the transistors' characteristics, an increase in load capacitance causes an increase in the RC time constant and a corresponding increase in the transition times of the output. Thus, it is a goal of high-speed circuit designers to minimize load capacitance, especially on the most timing-critical signals. This can be done by minimizing the number of inputs driven by the signal, by creating multiple copies of the signal, and by careful physical layout of the circuit.

When working with real digital circuits, it's often useful to estimate transition times, without going through a detailed analysis. A useful rule of thumb is that the transition time approximately equals the RC time constant of the charging or discharging circuit. For example, estimates of 10 and 20 ns for fall and rise time in the preceding example would have been pretty much on target, especially considering that most assumptions about load capacitance and transistor "on" resistances are approximate to begin with.

Manufacturers of commercial CMOS circuits typically do not specify transistor "on" resistances on their data sheets. If you search carefully, you might find this information published in the manufacturers' application notes. In any case, you can estimate an "on" resistance as the voltage drop across the "on" transistor divided by the current through it with a worst-case resistive load, as we showed in Section 3.5.2:

$$R_{p(on)} \approx \frac{V_{DD} - V_{OHminT}}{|I_{OHmaxT}|}$$

$$R_{n(on)} \approx \frac{V_{OLmaxT}}{I_{OLmaxT}}$$

THERE'S A CATCH!   Calculated transition times are actually quite sensitive to the choice of logic levels. In the examples in this subsection, if we used 2.0 V and 3.0 V instead of 1.5 V and 3.5 V as the thresholds for LOW and HIGH, we would calculate shorter transition times. On the other hand, if we used 0.0 and 5.0 V, the calculated transition times would be infinity! You should also be aware that in some logic families (most notably TTL), the thresholds are not symmetric around the voltage midpoint. Still, it is the author's experience that the "time-constant-equals-transition-time" rule of thumb usually works for practical circuits.

3.6.2 Propagation Delay

Rise and fall times only partially describe the dynamic behavior of a logic element; we need additional parameters to relate output timing to input timing. *signal path*   A *signal path* is the electrical path from a particular input signal to a particular *propagation delay t_p*   output signal of a logic element. The *propagation delay t_p* of a signal path is the amount of time that it takes for a change in the input signal to produce a change in the output signal.

A complex logic element with multiple inputs and outputs may specify a different value of t_p for each different signal path. Also, different values may be specified for a particular signal path, depending on the direction of the output change. Assuming zero rise and fall times for simplicity, Figure 3-42(a) shows

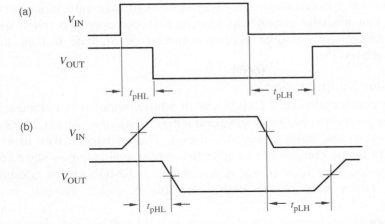

Figure 3-42
Propagation delays
for a CMOS inverter:
(a) ignoring rise and
fall times; (b) measured at
midpoints of transitions.

two different propagation delays for the input-to-output signal path of a CMOS inverter, depending on the direction of the output change:

t_{pHL} The time between an input change and the corresponding output change when the output is changing from HIGH to LOW. t_{pHL}

t_{pLH} The time between an input change and the corresponding output change when the output is changing from LOW to HIGH. t_{pLH}

Several factors lead to nonzero propagation delays. In a CMOS device, the rate at which transistors change state is influenced both by the semiconductor physics of the device and by the circuit environment, including input-signal transition rate, input capacitance, and output loading. Multistage devices such as noninverting gates or more complex logic functions may require several internal transistors to change state before the output can change state. And even when the output begins to change state, with nonzero rise and fall times it takes quite some time to cross the region between states, as we showed in the preceding subsection. All of these factors are included in propagation delay.

To factor out the effect of rise and fall times, manufacturers usually specify propagation delays at the midpoints of input and output transitions, as shown in Figure 3-42(b). However, sometimes the delays are specified at the logic-level boundary points, especially if the device's operation may be adversely affected by slow rise and fall times. For example, Figure 3-43 shows how the minimum input pulse width for an S-R latch (discussed in Section 7.2.1) might be specified.

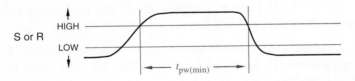

Figure 3-43
Worst-case timing
specified using logic-
level boundary points.

In addition, a manufacturer may specify absolute maximum input rise and fall times that must be satisfied to guarantee proper operation. High-speed CMOS circuits may consume excessive current or oscillate if their input transitions are too slow.

3.6.3 Power Consumption

The power consumption of a CMOS circuit whose output is not changing is called *static power dissipation* or *quiescent power dissipation*. Most CMOS circuits have very low static power dissipation. This is what makes them so attractive for laptop computers and other low-power applications—when computation pauses, very little power is consumed. A CMOS circuit consumes significant power only during transitions; this is called *dynamic power dissipation*.

static power dissipation

quiescent power dissipation

dynamic power dissipation

One source of dynamic power dissipation is the partial short-circuiting of the CMOS output structure. When the input voltage is not close to one of the power supply rails (0 V or V_{CC}), both the *p*-channel and *n*-channel output transistors may be partially "on," creating a series resistance of 600 Ω or less. In this case, current flows through the transistors from V_{CC} to ground. The amount of power consumed in this way depends on both the value of V_{CC} and the rate at which output transitions occur, according to the formula

$$P_T = C_{PD} \cdot V_{CC}^2 \cdot f$$

The following variables are used in the formula:

P_T The circuit's internal power dissipation due to output transitions.

V_{CC} The power-supply voltage. As all electrical engineers know, power dissipation across a resistive load (the partially-on transistors) is proportional to the *square* of the voltage.

transition frequency

f The *transition frequency* of the output signal. This implies the number of power-consuming output transitions per second. (But note that the number of transitions per second is the transition frequency times 2.)

power-dissipation capacitance

C_{PD} The *power-dissipation capacitance*. This constant, normally specified by the device manufacturer, completes the formula. C_{PD} turns out to have units of capacitance, but does not represent an actual output capacitance. Rather, it embodies the dynamics of current flow through the changing output-transistor resistances during a single pair of output transitions, HIGH-to-LOW and LOW-to-HIGH. For example, C_{PD} for HC-series CMOS gates is typically 20–24 pF, even though the actual output capacitance is much less.

The P_T formula is valid only if input transitions are fast enough, leading to fast output transitions. If the input transitions are too slow, then the output transistors stay partially on for a longer time, and power consumption increases.

Device manufacturers usually recommend a maximum input rise and fall time, below which the value specified for C_{PD} is valid.

A second, and often more significant, source of CMOS power consumption is the capacitive load (C_L) on the output. During a LOW-to-HIGH transition, current flows through a *p*-channel transistor to charge C_L. Likewise, during a HIGH-to-LOW transition, current flows through an *n*-channel transistor to discharge C_L. In each case, power is dissipated in the "on" resistance of the transistor. We'll use P_L to denote the total amount of power dissipated by charging and discharging C_L.

C_L

P_L

The units of P_L are power, or energy usage per unit time. The energy for one transition could be determined by calculating the current through the charging transistor as a function of time (using the *RC* time constant as in Section 3.6.1), squaring this function, multiplying by the "on" resistance of the charging transistor, and integrating over time. An easier way is described below.

During a transition, the voltage across the C_L changes by $\pm V_{CC}$. According to the definition of capacitance, the total amount of charge that must flow to make a voltage change of V_{CC} across C_L is $C_L \cdot V_{CC}$. The total amount of energy used in one transition is charge times the average voltage change. The first little bit of charge makes a voltage change of V_{CC}, while the last bit of charge makes a vanishingly small voltage change; hence the average change is $V_{CC}/2$. The total energy per transition is therefore $C_L \cdot V_{CC}^2 /2$. If there are $2f$ transitions per second, the total power dissipated due to the capacitive load is

$$P_L = C_L \cdot (V_{CC}^2 /2) \cdot 2f$$
$$= C_L \cdot V_{CC}^2 \cdot f$$

The total dynamic power dissipation of a CMOS circuit is the sum of P_T and P_L:

$$P_D = P_T + P_L$$
$$= C_{PD} \cdot V_{CC}^2 \cdot f + C_L \cdot V_{CC}^2 \cdot f$$
$$= (C_{PD} + C_L) \cdot V_{CC}^2 \cdot f$$

Based on this formula, dynamic power dissipation is often called CV^2f *power*. In most applications of CMOS circuits, CV^2f power is by far the major contributor

CV^2f *power*

to total power dissipation. Note that CV^2f power is also consumed by bipolar logic circuits like TTL and ECL, but at low to moderate frequencies it is insignificant compared to the static (DC or quiescent) power dissipation of bipolar circuits.

3.6.4 Current Spikes and Decoupling Capacitors

current spikes

When a CMOS output switches between LOW and HIGH, current flows from V_{CC} to ground through the partially-on *p*- and *n*-channel transistors. These currents, often called *current spikes* because of their brief duration, may show up as noise on the power-supply and ground connections in a CMOS circuit, especially when multiple outputs are switched simultaneously.

decoupling capacitors

For this reason, systems that use CMOS circuits require *decoupling capacitors* between V_{CC} and ground. These capacitors must be distributed throughout the printed-circuit board, at least one within an inch or so of each

filtering capacitors

chip, to supply current during transitions. The large *filtering capacitors* typically found in the power supply itself don't satisfy this requirement, because stray wiring inductance prevents them from supplying the current fast enough, hence the need for a *physically distributed* system of decoupling capacitors.

3.6.5 Inductive Effects

Digital logic circuits rarely contain any discrete inductors but, just like stray

stray inductance

capacitance, *stray inductance* arises in circuit wiring, even in straight wires. (Electrical engineers know that discrete inductors are usually formed by a coil of wire.)

When the amount of current flowing through an inductor changes, a voltage is developed across that inductor according to the formula

$$V = L \cdot \frac{dI}{dt}$$

henries
nanohenries

where L is the inductance in henries and dI/dt is the current's rate of change in amperes per second. Stray inductance can be on the order of 10 nanohenries (nH, 10^{-9} H) per inch of wire on a printed circuit board.

With such tiny stray inductances, it may not seem possible that significant voltages could be developed across them, and that inductive effects could be safely ignored. This was the case with most digital circuits until the late 1990s.

However, two factors have combined to make inductance a significant factor and sometimes an obstacle in high-speed CMOS design, especially at the printed-circuit-board level. First, the output transistors in modern CMOS circuits are able to switch on or off in extremely short times—on the order of tens of picoseconds or less in the fastest circuits. Changing so quickly from a no-current condition to one in which even just a few milliamperes of current is flowing results in a *rate of change* (dI/dt) that is very high. Second, CMOS circuits' power-supply voltage (V_{CC}) has been steadily declining from 5 V to 1.2 V or less in the densest ASICs. This has resulted in smaller noise margins between logic levels, exacerbating the error-inducing effects of any voltage disturbances.

Under reasonable assumptions (see references), the maximum value of dI/dt when driving a resistive load can be approximated by the formula

$$\left(\frac{dI}{dt}\right)_{\text{Max-resistor}} = \frac{\Delta V}{T_t} \cdot \frac{1}{R}$$

where R is the load resistance, and ΔV is the voltage change and T_t is the rise or fall time for the transition. So, let's consider the voltage that could be developed across a 1-inch PCB trace driving a 2-kΩ load, for a couple of different CMOS logic families. A 5-V 74HC output can have transition times as low as 5 ns. Based on the preceding formula,

$$\left(\frac{dI}{dt}\right)_{\text{Max-resistor}} = \frac{5 \text{ V}}{5 \text{ ns}} \cdot \frac{1}{2000 \ \Omega} = 5 \cdot 10^5 \text{ A/s}$$

Wow, 500,000 amps per second! Of course, the current doesn't continue to ramp up or down for anywhere near a second, but the rate of change during the 5-ns output transition really is that high. Now, we can plug that number into the voltage formula to see how much voltage is developed across our 1-inch, 10-nH PCB trace:

$$V = 10 \cdot 10^{-9} \cdot 5 \cdot 10^5 = 5 \text{ mV}$$

When all's said and done, the voltage change across the PCB trace is only 5 mV (plus or minus, depending on the direction of current change). This is nothing to worry about in a logic family that has 1.35 V of DC noise margin in either state.

Now let's consider the case for a more advanced technology, 74AC, which can source or sink six times as much current as 74HC and do so with transition times as short as 1 ns. The maximum current-change rate for 74AC driving a 1-kΩ load is

$$\left(\frac{dI}{dt}\right)_{\text{Max-resistor}} = \frac{5 \text{ V}}{1 \text{ ns}} \cdot \frac{1}{1000 \ \Omega} = 5 \cdot 10^6 \text{ A/s}$$

or 10 times higher than the previous case. So the voltage change across a 1-inch, 10-nH PCB trace is also 10 times higher, or 50 mV. That's still not quite enough to worry about, but wait, there's more!

So far we've considered only resistive loads. As discussed in Section 3.6.1, gate inputs and wiring have stray capacitance, and current must flow to charge or discharge this capacitance. Under reasonable assumptions (once again, see references), the maximum value of dI/dt when driving a capacitive load C can be approximated by the formula

$$\left(\frac{dI}{dt}\right)_{\text{Max-capacitor}} = \frac{1.52 \Delta V}{T_t^2} \cdot C$$

On a good day, our 74AC output can drive a 50-pF load at the end of a 1-inch PCB trace and deliver a transition time of about 5 ns. Based on the preceding formula,

$$\left(\frac{dI}{dt}\right)_{\text{Max-capacitor}} = \frac{1.52 \cdot 5 \text{ V}}{(25 \cdot 10^{-18}) \text{ ns}^2} \cdot 50 \cdot 10^{-12} \text{ F} = 1.52 \cdot 10^7 \text{ A/s}$$

Plugging that into the voltage formula, the voltage developed across our 1-inch, 10-nH PCB trace is

$$V = 10 \cdot 10^{-9} \cdot 1.52 \cdot 10^7 = 152 \text{ mV}$$

Although this case eats into the noise margin even more than the last example, it's probably not enough to cause an incorrect logic value to be produced. The real problem occurs when the inductive effects of several changing outputs are concentrated on a single wire, as discussed in the next subsection.

HAND WAVING   In this subsection, we assumed some transition times for 74HC and 74AC outputs driving certain resistive and capacitive loads. Where did these numbers come from? Minimum transition times, especially as a function of loading, are seldom if ever specified in manufacturers' data sheets. Actually, these numbers came from the author's experience in the lab.

You might also be wondering, what if we had a 10-inch instead of a 1-inch PCB trace and a 500-pF load instead of a 50-pF load? Could there be 15.2 V across that trace during a transition? No, of course not. Experience shows that the transition time would be much longer, and dI/dt would be much less. How can that be? The answer is that the actual electrical model of the circuit output, the PCB trace, and the load is much more complicated than we've shown, with each element having resistive, capacitive, and inductive components.

The approximations in this subsection are intended only to give you a rough feel for inductive effects. A more detailed study, typically using a circuit analysis tool such as SPICE, is needed to predict the dynamic effects of output transitions more accurately. Most IC manufacturers provide SPICE models (or equivalent) for their high-speed output circuits to aid electrical engineers who need to analyze such dynamic effects.

3.6.6 Simultaneous Switching and Ground Bounce

The current that flows through a gate's output pin has to come from or go to somewhere—from the device's V_{CC} pin when an output is sourcing current, and to the ground pin when it's sinking current. Now let's consider what happens when multiple gates use the same ground pin.

Figure 3-44 shows the situation when eight inverters are fabricated on a single chip with one ground and one V_{CC} pin. The connection from the chip's

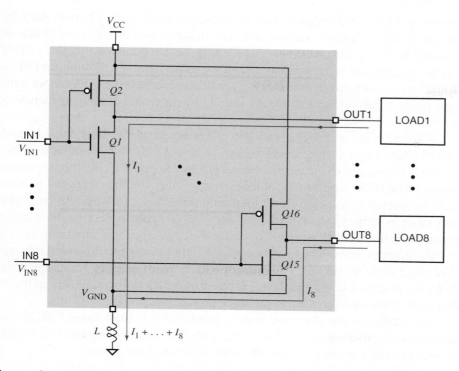

Figure 3-44
Ground bounce in an
IC with eight inverters
and one ground pin.

internal ground has stray inductance due to the chip and package substrates, the bonding wire between the chip and its package, and the wiring between the package and the PCB's ground plane. In the figure, this is shown as a lumped inductance L between the chip's ground pin and the actual ground on the PCB. The amount of stray inductance varies greatly with different packaging technologies, but in a 20-pin plastic DIP package with the ground pin in the corner, L is on the order of 10 nH.

Now consider the situation when all eight inputs are LOW, so all eight outputs are HIGH, and all eight inputs are simultaneously changed to HIGH. This kind of event is often called *simultaneous switching*. At that moment, all of the outputs change to LOW, and the single ground pin must sink the current from all eight loads. Assuming these are 74AC outputs each driving a 50 pF load as in the previous subsection, maximum value of dI/dt for each output is $1.52 \cdot 10^7$ A/s. With simultaneously switching outputs, the current change across the stray inductance L will be eight times this amount, and the voltage drop across L will be

simultaneous switching

$$V_{\text{GND}} = L \cdot \left(8 \cdot \frac{dI}{dt} \right) = 10 \cdot 10^{-9} \cdot 8 \cdot 1.52 \cdot 10^7 \text{ A/s} = 1.216 \text{ V}$$

This change in the chip's internal ground voltage compared to the PCB and system ground is called ground bounce, and its effects can be significant. A chip

ground bounce

has many inputs and outputs, and at any given time some of them may be changing while others are supposed to remain static. But consider the effects of a ground-bounce event on outputs that are supposed to remain static. Since LOW output voltages are referenced to a chip's internal ground (through an ON *n*-channel transistor), any increase in V_{GND} will also increase the LOW output voltages, possibly raising them above the valid LOW range and causing misbehavior elsewhere.

Ground bounce on a chip can also affect *inputs* on the same chip. A valid CMOS HIGH input voltage could be as low as 3.15 V. Keep in mind that this voltage is referenced to the chip's internal ground. Suppose a chip input receives a static, valid HIGH signal of 3.2 V from another chip. But then a ground-bounce event temporarily raises the chip's internal ground V_{GND} to 1.2 V. As far as the chip input is concerned, it now sees only 2.0 V with respect to its internal ground, and this is well into the "undefined" region for logic inputs. In fact, a slightly larger event could cause the apparent input voltage to drop well into the valid range for LOW signals. Thus, the ground bounce created by simultaneously switching outputs can change the logic value seen on totally unrelated inputs, as long as they are all referenced to the same ground pin.

A certain amount of ground bounce is inevitable in high-speed CMOS circuit design, but there are several ways that chip and system designers can reduce it enough to mask it safely within the noise margins of the circuit:

- Create or use a logic family whose output circuits are explicitly designed to have slower transition times, such as 74FCT versus 74AC/ACT.

- Place the ground pins on the IC package so that the lead lengths to the chip will be shorter and hence inductance will be lower. For example, many high-speed circuits packaged in DIPs now have V_{CC} and ground pins in the middle of each row of pins instead of on the corners.

- Use an IC package with lower inductance, such as a square PLCC versus a long rectangular DIP.

- Use multiple ground pins to split the current demand across multiple paths and thereby reduce the voltage drop across any one path. This is one reason that high-pin-count ICs are designed with lots and lots of ground pins.

At this point, you might be wondering, what about "V_{CC} bounce"? After all, V_{CC} wiring paths have stray inductance similar to ground paths, and they suffer voltage drops when multiple outputs switch from LOW to HIGH. However, logic levels are referenced to ground, not V_{CC}, and CMOS inputs are more sensitive to an input's voltage relative to ground than to V_{CC}. Thus, "V_{CC} bounce" is seldom a problem. Still, most high-pin-count ICs are designed with lots of V_{CC} pins to handle dynamic as well as static current demands with little voltage drop. A typical VLSI chip has at least half as many V_{CC} pins as ground pins and, quite often, just as many.

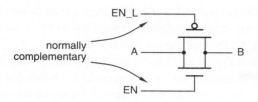

Figure 3-45
CMOS transmission gate.

3.7 Other CMOS Input and Output Structures

Circuit designers have modified the basic CMOS circuit in many ways to produce gates that are tailored for specific applications. This section describes some of the more common variations in CMOS input and output structures.

3.7.1 Transmission Gates

A *p*-channel and *n*-channel transistor pair can be connected together to form a logic-controlled switch. Shown in Figure 3-45, this circuit is called a CMOS *transmission gate*.

transmission gate

A transmission gate is operated so that its input signals EN and EN_L are always at opposite levels. When EN is HIGH and EN_L is LOW, there is a low-impedance connection (as low as 2–5 Ω) between points A and B. When EN is LOW and EN_L is HIGH, points A and B are disconnected.

Once a transmission gate is enabled, the propagation delay from A to B (or vice versa) is very short. Because of their short delays and conceptual simplicity, transmission gates are often used internally in larger-scale CMOS devices such as multiplexers and flip-flops. For example, Figure 3-46 shows how transmission gates can be used to create a "2-input multiplexer." When S is LOW, the X "input" is connected to the Z "output"; when S is HIGH, Y is connected to Z.

At least one manufacturer (Integrated Device Technology [IDT]) makes a variety of logic functions based on transmission gates. In their multiplexer devices, it takes several nanoseconds for a change in the "select" inputs (such as

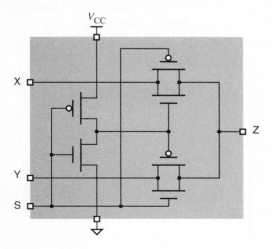

Figure 3-46
Two-input multiplexer using CMOS transmission gates.

in Figure 3-46) to affect the input-output path (X or Y to Z). Once a path is set up, however, the propagation delay from input to output is specified to be at most 0.25 ns; this is the fastest discrete CMOS multiplexer you can buy.

The *p*-channel (top) transistor in Figure 3-45 has a low impedance when its gate (EN_L) is LOW. The *n*-channel transistor has a low impedance when EN is HIGH. Two transistors are used because a typical "on" *p*-channel transistor can't conduct a LOW voltage between points A and B very well, and a typical "on" *n*-channel transistor can't conduct a HIGH voltage very well, but the parallel transistors cover the entire voltage range just fine. Some manufacturers, such as IDT, have improved their *n*-channel transistors enough to omit the *p*-channel transistor. Besides saving a transistor, this approach also eliminates a parasitic diode to V_{CC} that would otherwise result from the chip's physical structure.

3.7.2 Schmitt-Trigger Inputs

Schmitt-trigger input

The input-output transfer characteristic for a typical CMOS gate was shown in Figure 3-25 on page 101. The corresponding transfer characteristic for a gate with *Schmitt-trigger inputs* is shown in Figure 3-47(a). A Schmitt trigger is a special circuit that uses feedback internally to shift the switching threshold depending on whether the input is changing from LOW to HIGH or from HIGH to LOW.

For example, suppose the input of a Schmitt-trigger inverter is initially at 0 V, a solid LOW. Then the output is HIGH, close to 5.0 V. If the input voltage is increased, the output will not go LOW until the input voltage reaches about 2.9 V. However, once the output is LOW, it will not go HIGH again until the input is decreased to about 2.1 V. Thus, the switching threshold for positive-going input changes, denoted V_{T+}, is about 2.9 V, and for negative-going input changes, denoted V_{T-}, is about 2.1 V. The difference between the two thresholds is called

hysteresis

hysteresis. The Schmitt-trigger inverter provides about 0.8 V of hysteresis.

To demonstrate the usefulness of hysteresis, Figure 3-48(a) shows an input signal with long rise and fall times and about 0.5 V of noise on it. An ordinary inverter, without hysteresis, has the same switching threshold for both positive-going and negative-going transitions, $V_T \approx 2.5$ V. Thus, the ordinary inverter

Figure 3-47
A Schmitt-trigger inverter: (a) input-output transfer characteristic; (b) logic symbol.

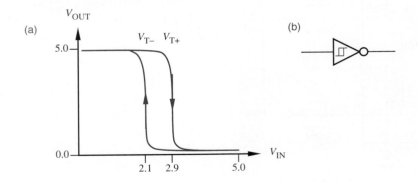

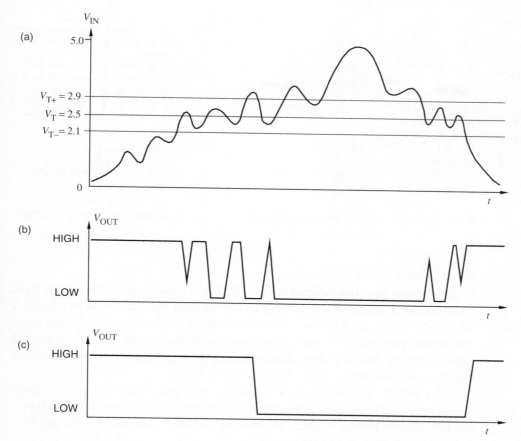

Figure 3-48 Device operation with slowly changing inputs: (a) a noisy, slowly changing input; (b) output produced by an ordinary inverter; (c) output produced by an inverter with 0.8 V of hysteresis.

responds to the noise as shown in (b), producing multiple output changes each time the noisy input voltage crosses the switching threshold. However, as shown in (c), a Schmitt-trigger inverter does not respond to the noise, because its hysteresis is greater than the noise amplitude.

FIXING YOUR TRANSMISSION   Schmitt-trigger inputs have better noise immunity than ordinary gate inputs for signals with transmission-line reflections, discussed at <u>DDPPonline</u> in <u>Section Zo</u>, or long rise and fall times. Such signals typically occur in physically long connections, such as input-output buses and computer interface cables. Noise immunity is important in these applications, since long signal lines are more likely to have reflections or to pick up noise from adjacent signal lines, circuits, and appliances.

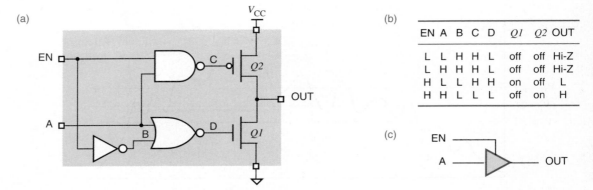

Figure 3-49 CMOS three-state buffer: (a) circuit diagram; (b) function table; (c) logic symbol.

3.7.3 Three-State Outputs

high-impedance state
Hi-Z state
floating state

Logic outputs have two normal states, LOW and HIGH, corresponding to logic values 0 and 1. However, some outputs have a third electrical state that is not a logic state at all, called the *high-impedance, Hi-Z,* or *floating state*. In this state, the output behaves as if it isn't even connected to the circuit, except for a small leakage current that may flow into or out of the output pin. Thus, an output can have one of three states—logic 0, logic 1, and Hi-Z.

three-state output
tri-state output

An output with three possible states is called (surprise!) a *three-state output* or, sometimes, a *tri-state output*. Three-state devices have an extra input, usually called "output enable" or "output disable," for placing the device's output(s) in the high-impedance state.

three-state bus

A *three-state bus* is created by wiring several three-state outputs together. Control circuitry for the "output enables" must ensure that at most one output is enabled (not in its Hi-Z state) at any time. The single enabled device can transmit logic levels (HIGH and LOW) on the bus. Examples of three-state bus design are given in Section 6.6.

three-state buffer

A circuit diagram for a CMOS *three-state buffer* is shown in Figure 3-49(a). To simplify the diagram, the internal NAND, NOR, and inverter functions are shown in functional rather than transistor form; they actually use a total of 10 transistors (see Exercise 3.82). As shown in the function table (b), when the enable (EN) input is LOW, both output transistors are off, and the output is in the Hi-Z state. Otherwise, the output is HIGH or LOW as controlled by the "data" input A. Logic symbols for three-state buffers and gates are normally drawn with the enable input coming into the top, as shown in (c).

In practice, the three-state control circuit may be different from what we have shown, in order to provide proper dynamic behavior of the output transistors during transitions to and from the Hi-Z state. In particular, devices with three-state outputs are normally designed so that the output-enable delay (Hi-Z to LOW or HIGH) is somewhat longer than the output-disable delay (LOW or HIGH to Hi-Z). Thus, if a control circuit activates one device's output-enable input and simultaneously deactivates a second's, the second device is guaranteed to enter the Hi-Z state before the first places a HIGH or LOW level on the bus.

If two three-state outputs on the same bus are enabled at the same time and try to maintain opposite states, the situation is similar to tying standard active-pull-up outputs together as in Figure 3-57 on page 139—a nonlogic voltage is produced on the bus. If fighting is only momentary, the devices probably will not be damaged, but the large current drain through the tied outputs can produce noise pulses that affect circuit behavior elsewhere in the system.

There is a leakage current of up to 10 μA associated with a CMOS three-state output in its Hi-Z state. This current, as well as the input currents of receiving gates, must be taken into account when calculating the maximum number of devices that can be placed on a three-state bus. That is, in the LOW or HIGH state, an enabled three-state output must be capable of sinking or sourcing up to 10 μA of leakage current for every other three-state output on the bus, as well as handling the current required by every input on the bus. As with standard CMOS logic, separate LOW-state and HIGH-state calculations must be made to ensure that the fanout requirements of a particular circuit configuration are met.

*3.7.4 Open-Drain Outputs[1]

The *p*-channel transistors in CMOS output structures are said to provide *active pull-up*, since they actively pull up the output voltage on a LOW-to-HIGH transition. These transistors are omitted in gates with *open-drain outputs*, such as the NAND gate in Figure 3-50(a). The drain of the topmost *n*-channel transistor is left unconnected internally, so if the output is not LOW it is "open," as indicated in (b). The underscored diamond in the symbol in (c) is sometimes used to indicate an open-drain output. A similar structure, called an "open-collector output," is provided in TTL logic families as described at DDPPonline in Section TTL.

active pull-up
open-drain output

An open-drain output requires an external *pull-up resistor* to provide *passive pull-up* to the HIGH level. For example, Figure 3-51 shows an open-drain CMOS NAND gate, with its pull-up resistor, driving a load.

pull-up resistor
passive pull-up

For the highest possible speed, an open-drain output's pull-up resistor should be as small as possible; this minimizes the *RC* time constant for LOW-to-

---

1[*]Throughout this book, optional sections are marked with an asterisk.

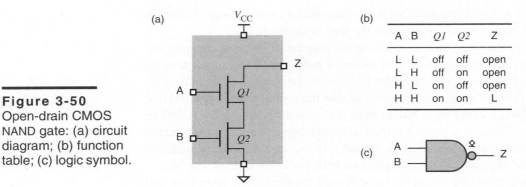

Figure 3-50
Open-drain CMOS
NAND gate: (a) circuit
diagram; (b) function
table; (c) logic symbol.

HIGH transitions (rise time). However, the pull-up resistance cannot be arbitrarily small; the minimum resistance is determined by the open-drain output's maximum sink current, I_{OLmax}. For example, in HC- and HCT-series CMOS, I_{OLmax} is 4 mA, and the pull-up resistor can be no less than 5.0 V/4 mA, or 1.25 kΩ. Since this is an order of magnitude greater than the "on" resistance of the p-channel transistors in a standard CMOS gate, the LOW-to-HIGH output transitions are much slower for an open-drain gate than for standard gate with active pull-up.

As an example, let us assume that the open-drain gate in Figure 3-51 is HC-series CMOS, the pull-up resistance is 1.5 kΩ, and the load capacitance is 100 pF. We showed in Section 3.5.2 that the "on" resistance of an HC-series CMOS output in the LOW state is about 80 Ω. Thus, the RC time constant for a HIGH-to-LOW transition is about 80 Ω · 100 pF = 8 ns, and the output's fall time is about 8 ns. However, the RC time constant for a LOW-to-HIGH transition is about 1.5 kΩ · 100 pF = 150 ns, and the rise time is about 150 ns. This relatively slow rise time is contrasted with the much faster fall time in Figure 3-52. A friend of the author calls such slow rising transitions *ooze*.

ooze

Figure 3-51
Open-drain CMOS
NAND gate driving
a load.

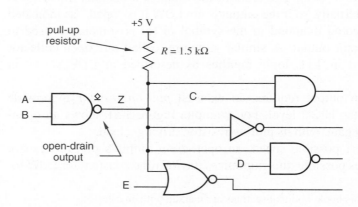

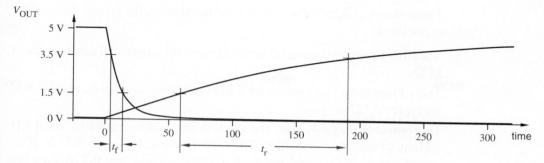

Figure 3-52 Rising and falling transitions of an open-drain CMOS output.

So why use open-drain outputs? Despite slow rise times, they can be useful in three applications discussed next: driving light-emitting diodes (LEDs) and other devices; driving multisource buses; and performing wired logic.

*3.7.5 Driving LEDs

An open-drain output can drive an LED as shown in Figure 3-53. If either input A or B is LOW, the corresponding n-channel transistor is off and the LED is off. When A and B are both HIGH, both transistors are on, the output Z is LOW, and the LED is on. The value of the pull-up resistor R is chosen so that the proper amount of current flows through the LED in the "on" state.

Typical LEDs require 10 mA for normal brightness. HC- and HCT-series CMOS outputs are only specified to sink or source 4 mA and are not normally used to drive LEDs. However, the outputs in advanced CMOS families such as 74ACT and 74FCT can sink 24 mA or more and can be used quite effectively to drive LEDs.

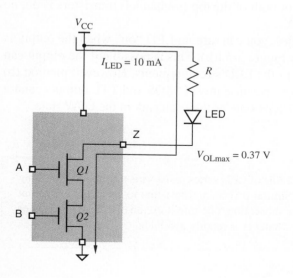

Figure 3-53
Driving an LED with an open-drain output.

Three pieces of information are needed to calculate the proper value of the pull-up resistor R:

1. The LED current I_{LED} needed for the desired brightness, 10 mA for typical LEDs.

2. The voltage drop V_{LED} across the LED in the "on" condition, about 1.6 V for typical LEDs.

3. The output voltage V_{OL} of the open-drain output that sinks the LED current. In the 74AC and 74ACT CMOS families, V_{OLmax} is 0.37 V. If an output can sink I_{LED} and maintain a lower voltage, say 0.2 V, then the calculation below yields a resistor value that is a little too low, but normally with no harm done. A little more current than I_{LED} will flow and the LED will be just a little brighter than expected.

Using the above information, we can write the following equation:

$$V_{OL} + V_{LED} + (I_{LED} \cdot R) = V_{CC}$$

Assuming $V_{CC} = 5.0$ V and the other typical values above, we can solve for the required value of R:

$$R = \frac{V_{CC} - V_{OL} - V_{LED}}{I_{LED}}$$

$$= (5.0 - 0.37 - 1.6) \text{ V}/10 \text{ mA} = 303 \text{ } \Omega$$

Note that you don't have to use an open-drain output to drive an LED. Figure 3-54(a) shows an LED driven by an ordinary CMOS NAND-gate output with active pull-up. If both inputs are HIGH, the bottom (n-channel) transistors pull the output LOW as in the open-drain version. If either input is LOW, the output is HIGH; although one or both of the top (p-channel) transistors is on, no current flows through the LED.

With some CMOS families, you can turn an LED "on" when the output is in the HIGH state, as shown in Figure 3-54(b). This is possible if the output can source enough current to satisfy the LED's requirements. However, method (b) isn't used as often as method (a), because most CMOS and TTL outputs cannot source as much current in the HIGH state as they can sink in the LOW state.

RESISTOR VALUES   In most applications, the precise value of LED series resistors is unimportant, as long as groups of nearby LEDs have similar drivers and resistors to give equal apparent brightness. In the example in this subsection, one might use an off-the-shelf resistor value of 270, 300, or 330 ohms, whatever is readily available.

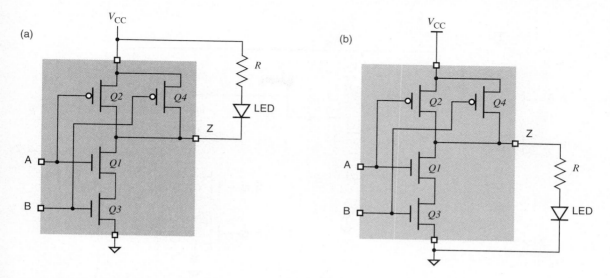

Figure 3-54 Driving an LED with an ordinary CMOS output: (a) sinking current, "on" in the LOW state; (b) sourcing current, "on" in the HIGH state.

*3.7.6 Multisource Buses

Open-drain outputs can be tied together to allow several devices, one at a time,   *open-drain bus*
to put information on a common bus. At any time all but one of the outputs on
the bus are in their HIGH (open) state. The remaining output either stays in the
HIGH state or pulls the bus LOW, depending on whether it wants to transmit a
logical 1 or a logical 0 on the bus. Control circuitry selects the particular device
that is allowed to drive the bus at any time.

For example, in Figure 3-55, eight 2-input open-drain NAND-gate outputs
drive a common bus. The top input of each NAND gate is a data bit, and the

Figure 3-55 Eight open-drain outputs driving a bus.

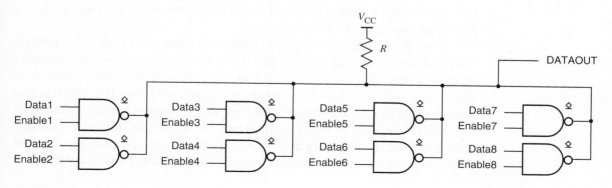

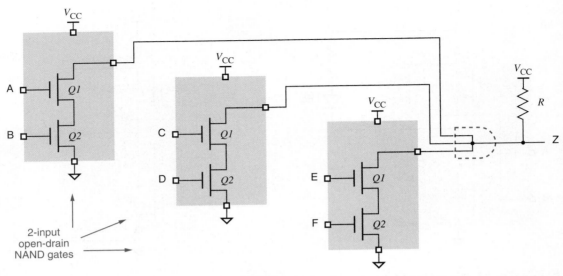

Figure 3-56 Wired-AND function on three open-drain NAND-gate outputs.

bottom input of each is a control bit. At most one control bit is HIGH at any time, enabling the corresponding data bit to be passed through to the bus. (Actually, the complement of the data bit is placed on the bus.) The other gate outputs are HIGH, that is, "open," so the data input of the enabled gate determines the value on the bus.

*3.7.7 Wired Logic

wired logic

wired AND

fighting

If the outputs of several open-drain gates are tied together with a single pull-up resistor, then *wired logic* is performed. (That's *wired*, not *weird*!) An AND function is obtained, since the wired output is HIGH if and only if all of the individual gate outputs are HIGH (actually, open); any output going LOW is sufficient to pull the wired output LOW. For example, a 3-input *wired AND* function is shown in Figure 3-56. If any of the individual 2-input NAND gates has both inputs HIGH, it pulls the wired output LOW; otherwise, the pull-up resistor *R* pulls the wired output HIGH.

Note that wired logic cannot be performed using gates with active pull-up. Two such outputs wired together and trying to maintain opposite logic values result in a very high current flow and an abnormal output voltage. Figure 3-57 shows this situation, which is sometimes called *fighting*. The exact output voltage depends on the relative "strengths" of the fighting transistors, but with 5-V CMOS devices it is typically about 1–2 V, almost always a nonlogic voltage. Worse, if outputs fight continuously for more than a few seconds, the chips can get hot enough to sustain internal damage *and* to burn your fingers!

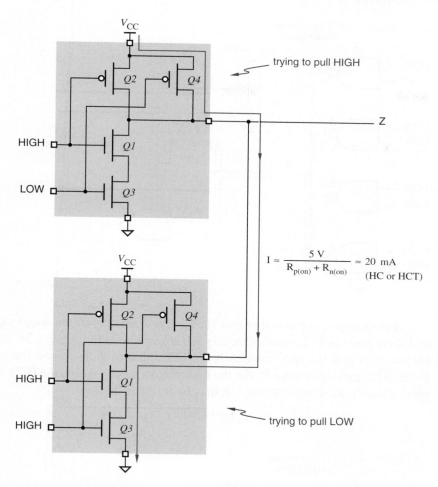

$$I \approx \frac{5 \text{ V}}{R_{p(on)} + R_{n(on)}} \approx 20 \text{ mA}$$
(HC or HCT)

Figure 3-57
Two CMOS outputs
trying to maintain
opposite logic values
on the same line.

*3.7.8 Pull-Up Resistors

A proper choice of value for the pull-up resistor R must be made in open-drain *pull-up-resistor* applications. Two calculations are made to bracket the allowable values of R: *calculation*

Minimum The sum of the current through R in the LOW state and the LOW-state input currents of the gates driven by the wired outputs must not exceed the LOW-state driving capability of the active output, for example, 4 mA for HC/HCT and 8 mA for AHC/AHCT devices.

Maximum The voltage drop across R in the HIGH state must not reduce the output voltage below 2.4 V, which is V_{IHmin} for typical driven gates plus a 400-mV noise margin. This drop is produced by the HIGH-state output leakage current of the wired outputs and the HIGH-state input currents of the driven gates.

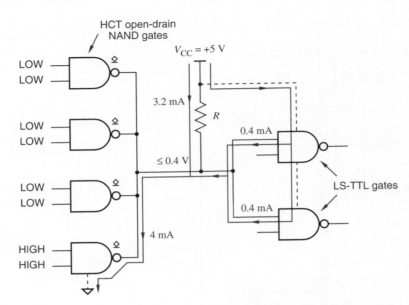

Figure 3-58
Four open-drain
outputs driving two
inputs in the LOW
state.

For example, suppose that four HCT open-drain outputs are wired together and drive two LS-TTL inputs (Section 3.10.6) as shown in Figure 3-58. A LOW output must sink 0.4 mA from each LS-TTL input as well as sink the current through the pull-up resistor R. For the total current to stay within the HCT I_{OLmax} spec of 4 mA, the current through R may be no more than

$$I_{R(max)} = 4 - (2 \cdot 0.4) = 3.2 \text{ mA}$$

Figure 3-59
Four open-drain
outputs driving two
inputs in the HIGH
state.

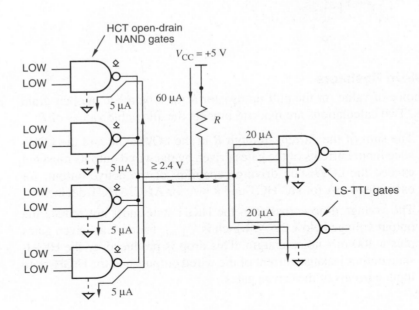

Assuming that V_{OL} of the open-drain output is 0.0 V, the minimum value of R is

$$R_{min} = (5.0 - 0.0)/I_{R(max)} = 1562.5 \ \Omega$$

In the HIGH state, typical open-drain outputs have a maximum leakage current of 5 μA, and typical LS-TTL inputs require 20 μA of source current. Hence, the HIGH-state current requirement as shown in Figure 3-59 is

$$I_{R(leak)} = (4 \cdot 5) + (2 \cdot 20) = 60 \ \mu A$$

This current produces a voltage drop across R, and must not lower the output voltage below $V_{OHmin} = 2.4$ V; thus the maximum value of R is

$$R_{max} = (5.0 - 2.4)/I_{R(leak)} = 43.3 \ k\Omega$$

Hence, any value of R between 1562.5 Ω and 43.3 kΩ may be used. Higher values reduce power consumption and improve the LOW-state noise margin, while lower values increase power consumption but improve both the HIGH-state noise margin and the speed of LOW-to-HIGH output transitions.

OPEN-DRAIN ASSUMPTION   In our open-drain resistor calculations, we assume that the output voltage can be as low as 0.0 V rather than 0.4 V (V_{OLmax}) in order to obtain a worst-case result. That is, even if the open-drain output is so strong that it can pull the output voltage all the way down to 0.0 V (it's only required to pull down to 0.4 V), we'll never allow it to sink more than 4 mA, so it doesn't get overstressed. Some designers prefer to use 0.4 V in this calculation, figuring that if the output is so good that it can pull lower than 0.4 V, a little bit of excess sink current beyond 4 mA won't hurt it.

3.8 CMOS Logic Families

The first commercially successful CMOS family was *4000-series CMOS*. Although 4000-series circuits offered the benefit of low power dissipation, they were fairly slow and were not easy to interface with the most popular logic family of the time, bipolar TTL. Thus, the 4000 series was supplanted in most applications by the more capable CMOS families discussed in this section.   *4000-series CMOS*

   All of the CMOS devices that we discuss have part numbers of the form "74FAM*nn*," where "FAM" is an alphabetic family mnemonic and *nn* is a numeric function designator. Devices in different families with the same value of *nn* perform the same function. For example, the 74HC30, 74HCT30, 74AC30, 74ACT30, 74AHC30, and 74AHCT30 are all 8-input NAND gates.

   The prefix "74" is simply a number that was used by an early, popular supplier of TTL devices, Texas Instruments. The prefix "54" is used for identical parts that are specified for operation over a wider range of temperature and power-supply voltage, for use in military applications. Such parts are usually

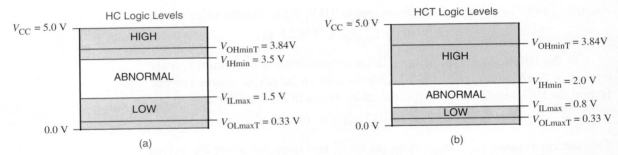

Figure 3-60 Input and output levels for CMOS devices using a 5-V supply: (a) HC; (b) HCT.

fabricated in the same way as their 74-series counterparts, except that they are tested, screened, and marked differently, a lot of extra paperwork is generated, and a higher price is charged, of course.

3.8.1 HC and HCT

HC (High-speed CMOS)

HCT (High-speed CMOS, TTL compatible)

The first two 74-series CMOS families are *HC (High-speed CMOS)* and *HCT (High-speed CMOS, TTL compatible)*. Compared with the original 4000 family, HC and HCT both have higher speed and better current sinking and sourcing capability. The HCT family uses a power-supply voltage V_{CC} of 5 V and can be intermixed with TTL devices, which also use a 5-V supply.

The HC family is optimized for use in systems that use CMOS logic exclusively, and can use any power-supply voltage between 2 and 6 V. A higher voltage is used for higher speed, and a lower voltage for lower power dissipation. Lowering the supply voltage is especially effective, since most CMOS power dissipation is proportional to the square of the voltage (CV^2f power).

Even when used with a 5-V supply, HC devices are not quite compatible with TTL. In particular, HC circuits are designed to recognize CMOS input levels. Assuming a supply voltage of 5.0 V, Figure 3-60(a) shows the input and output levels of HC devices. The output levels produced by TTL devices do not quite match this range, so HCT devices use the different input levels shown in (b). These levels are established in the fabrication process by making transistors with different switching thresholds, producing the different transfer characteristics shown in Figure 3-61.

Figure 3-61
Transfer characteristics of HC and HCT circuits under typical conditions.

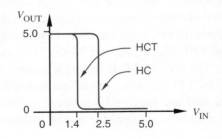

We'll say more about CMOS/TTL interfacing in Section 3.10.8. For now, it is useful to note that HC and HCT have essentially identical output specs. Only their input levels differ, with the "T" suffix denoting TTL compatibility.

3.8.2 AHC and AHCT

Several new CMOS families were introduced in the 1980s and the 1990s. Two of the most recent and probably the most versatile are *AHC (Advanced High-speed CMOS)* and *AHCT (Advanced High-speed CMOS, TTL compatible)*. These families are two to three times as fast as HC/HCT while maintaining backward compatibility with their predecessors. Like HC and HCT, the AHC and AHCT families differ from each other only in the input levels that they recognize; their output characteristics are the same.

AHC (Advanced High-speed CMOS)

AHCT (Advanced High-speed CMOS, TTL compatible)

Also like HC/HCT, AHC/AHCT outputs have *symmetric output drive.* That is, an output can sink or source equal amounts of current; the output is just as "strong" in both states. Other logic families, including the FCT and TTL families introduced later, have *asymmetric output drive;* they can sink much more current in the LOW state than they can source in the HIGH state.

symmetric output drive

asymmetric output drive

3.8.3 HC, HCT, AHC, and AHCT Electrical Characteristics

Electrical characteristics of the HC, HCT, AHC, and AHCT families are summarized in this subsection. The specifications assume that the devices are used with a nominal 5-V power supply, although (derated) operation is possible with any supply voltage in the range 2–5.5 V (up to 6 V for HC/HCT). We'll take a closer look at low-voltage and mixed-voltage operation in Section 3.9.

Commercial (74-series) parts are intended to be operated at temperatures between 0°C and 70°C, while military (54-series) parts are characterized for operation between −55°C and 125°C. The specs in Table 3-5 assume an operating temperature of 25°C. A full manufacturer's data sheet provides additional specifications for device operation over the entire temperature range.

Most devices within a given logic family have the same electrical specifications for inputs and outputs, typically differing only in power consumption and propagation delay. Table 3-5 includes specifications for a 74x00 2-input NAND gate and a 74x138 3-to-8 decoder in the HC, HCT, AHC, and AHCT families. The '00 NAND gate is included as the smallest logic-design building block in each family, while the '138 is a "medium-scale" part containing the equivalent of about 15 NAND gates. (The '138 spec is included to allow

---

VERY = ADVANCED, SORT OF   The AHC and AHCT logic families are manufactured by several companies, including Texas Instruments and Philips. Compatible families with similar but not identical specifications are manufactured by STMicro, Fairchild, and Toshiba; they are called VHC and VHCT, where the "V" stands for "Very."

Table 3-5 Speed and power characteristics of CMOS families operating at 5 V.

Description	Part	Symbol	Condition	Family HC	HCT	AHC	AHCT
Typical propagation delay (ns)	'00	t_{PD}		9	10	3.7	5
	'138			18	20	5.7	7.6
Quiescent power-supply current (μA)	'00	I_{CC}	$V_{in} = 0$ or V_{CC}	2.5	2.5	5.0	5.0
	'138		$V_{in} = 0$ or V_{CC}	40	40	40	40
Quiescent power dissipation (mW)	'00		$V_{in} = 0$ or V_{CC}	0.0125	0.0125	0.025	0.025
	'138		$V_{in} = 0$ or V_{CC}	0.2	0.2	0.2	0.2
Power-dissipation capacitance (pF)	'00	C_{PD}		22	15	2.4	2.6
	'138	C_{PD}		55	51	13	14
Dynamic power dissipation (mW/MHz)	'00			0.55	0.38	0.06	0.065
	'138			1.38	1.28	0.33	0.35
Total power dissipation (mW)	'00		$f = 100$ kHz	0.068	0.050	0.031	0.032
	'00		$f = 1$ MHz	0.56	0.39	0.085	0.09
	'00		$f = 10$ MHz	5.5	3.8	0.63	0.68
	'138		$f = 100$ kHz	0.338	0.328	0.23	0.24
	'138		$f = 1$ MHz	1.58	1.48	0.53	0.55
	'138		$f = 10$ MHz	14.0	13.0	3.45	3.7
Speed-power product (pJ)	'00		$f = 100$ kHz	0.61	0.50	0.11	0.16
	'00		$f = 1$ MHz	5.1	3.9	0.31	0.45
	'00		$f = 10$ MHz	50	38	2.3	3.38
	'138		$f = 100$ kHz	6.08	6.55	1.33	1.79
	'138		$f = 1$ MHz	28.4	29.5	2.99	4.2
	'138		$f = 10$ MHz	251	259	19.7	28.1

comparison with the faster FCT family in Section 3.8.5; '00 gates are not manufactured in the FCT family.)

The first row of Table 3-5 specifies propagation delay. As discussed in Section 3.6.2, two numbers, t_{pHL} and t_{pLH}, may be used to specify delay; the number in the table is the worst case of the two. Skipping ahead to Table 3-10 on page 167, you can see that HC and HCT are about the same speed as LS TTL, and that AHC and AHCT about the same as ALS TTL. The propagation delay

---

NOTE ON NOTATION   The "x" in the notation"74x00" takes the place of a family designator such as HC, HCT, AHC, AHCT, FCT, LS, ALS, AS, or F. We may also refer to such a generic part simply as a " '00" and leave off the "74x."

QUIETLY GETTING MORE DISS'ED

HCT and AHCT circuits can also be driven by TTL devices, which may produce HIGH output levels as low as 2.4 V. As we explained in Section 3.5.3, a CMOS output may draw additional current from the power supply if any of the inputs are nonideal. In the case of an HCT or AHCT inverter with a HIGH input of 2.4 V, the bottom, *n*-channel output transistor is fully "on." However, the top, *p*-channel transistor is also partially "on." This allows the additional quiescent current flow, specified as ΔI_{CC} or I_{CCT} in the data sheet, which can be as much as 2–3 mA per nonideal input in HCT and AHCT devices.

for the '138 is somewhat longer than for the '00, since signals must travel through three or four levels of gates internally.

The second and third rows of the table show that the quiescent power dissipation of these CMOS devices is practically nil, well under a milliwatt (mW) if the inputs have CMOS levels—0 V for LOW and V_{CC} for HIGH. (Note that in the table, the quiescent power dissipation numbers given for the '00 are per gate, while for the '138 they apply to the entire MSI device.)

As we discussed in Section 3.6.3, the dynamic power dissipation of a CMOS gate depends on the voltage swing of the output (usually V_{CC}), the output transition frequency (f), and the capacitance that is being charged and discharged on transitions, according to the formula

$$P_D = (C_L + C_{PD}) \cdot V_{DD}^2 \cdot f$$

Here, C_{PD} is the power-dissipation capacitance of the device and C_L is the capacitance of the load attached to the CMOS output in a given application. The table lists both C_{PD} and an equivalent dynamic power-dissipation factor in units of milliwatts per megahertz, assuming that $C_L = 0$. Using this factor, the total power dissipation is computed at various frequencies as the sum of the dynamic power dissipation at that frequency and the quiescent power dissipation.

speed-power product

Shown next in the table, the *speed-power product* is simply the product of the propagation delay and power consumption of a typical gate; the result is measured in picojoules (pJ). Recall from physics that the joule is a unit of energy, so the speed-power product measures a sort of efficiency—how much energy a logic gate uses to switch its output. In this day and age, it's obvious that the lower the energy usage, the better.

SAVING ENERGY

There are practical as well as geopolitical reasons for saving energy in digital systems. Lower energy consumption means lower cost of power supplies and cooling systems. Also, a digital system's reliability is improved more by running it cooler than by any other single reliability improvement strategy.

Table 3-6 Input specifications for CMOS families with V_{CC} between 4.5 and 5.5 V.

Description	Symbol	Condition	Family			
			HC	HCT	AHC	AHCT
Input leakage current (μA)	I_{Imax}	V_{in} = any	±1	±1	±1	±1
Maximum input capacitance (pF)	C_{INmax}		10	10	10	10
LOW-level input voltage (V)	V_{ILmax}		1.35	0.8	1.35	0.8
HIGH-level input voltage (V)	V_{IHmin}		3.85	2.0	3.85	2.0

Table 3-6 gives the input specs of typical CMOS devices in each of the families. Some of the specs assume that the 5-V supply has a ±10% margin; that is, V_{CC} can be anywhere between 4.5 and 5.5 V. These parameters were discussed in previous sections, but for reference purposes their meanings are summarized here:

I_{Imax} The maximum input current for any value of input voltage. This spec states that the current flowing into or out of a CMOS input is 1 μA or less for any value of input voltage. In other words, CMOS inputs create almost no DC load on the circuits that drive them.

C_{INmax} The maximum capacitance of an input. This number can be used when figuring the AC load on an output that drives this and other inputs. Most manufacturers also specify a lower, typical input capacitance of 2 to 5 pF, which gives a good estimate of AC load if you're not unlucky.

V_{ILmax} The maximum voltage that an input is guaranteed to recognize as LOW. Note that the values are different for HC/AHC versus HCT/AHCT. The "CMOS" value, 1.35 V, is 30% of the minimum power-supply voltage, while the "TTL" value is 0.8 V for compatibility with TTL families.

CMOS VS. TTL POWER DISSIPATION

At high transition frequencies (f), CMOS families actually use more power than TTL. For example, compare HCT CMOS in Table 3-5 at f = 10 MHz with LS TTL in Table 3-10; a CMOS gate uses three times as much power as a TTL gate at this frequency. Both HCT and LS may be used in systems with maximum "clock" frequencies of up to about 20 MHz, so you might think that CMOS is not so good for high-speed systems. However, the transition frequencies of most outputs in typical systems are much less than the maximum frequency present in the system (e.g., see Exercise 3.79). Thus, typical CMOS systems have a lower total power dissipation than they would have if they were built with TTL.

Table 3-7 Output specifications for CMOS families operating with V_{CC} between 4.5 and 5.5 V.

Description	Symbol	Condition	Family HC	HCT	AHC	AHCT
LOW-level output current (mA)	I_{OLmaxC}	CMOS load	0.02	0.02	0.05	0.05
	I_{OLmaxT}	TTL load	4.0	4.0	8.0	8.0
LOW-level output voltage (V)	V_{OLmaxC}	$I_{out} \le I_{OLmaxC}$	0.1	0.1	0.1	0.1
	V_{OLmaxT}	$I_{out} \le I_{OLmaxT}$	0.33	0.33	0.44	0.44
HIGH-level output current (mA)	I_{OHmaxC}	CMOS load	−0.02	−0.02	−0.05	−0.05
	I_{OHmaxT}	TTL load	−4.0	−4.0	−8.0	−8.0
HIGH-level output voltage (V)	V_{OHminC}	$|I_{out}| \le |I_{OHmaxC}|$	4.4	4.4	4.4	4.4
	V_{OHminT}	$|I_{out}| \le |I_{OHmaxT}|$	3.84	3.84	3.80	3.80

V_{IHmin} The minimum voltage that an input is guaranteed to recognize as HIGH. The "CMOS" value, 3.85 V, is 70% of the maximum power-supply voltage, while the "TTL" value is 2.0 V for compatibility with TTL families. (Unlike CMOS levels, TTL input levels are not symmetric with respect to the power-supply rails.)

The specifications for TTL-compatible CMOS outputs usually have two sets of output parameters; one set or the other is used depending on how an output is loaded. A *CMOS load* is one that requires the output to sink and source very little DC current, 20 μA for HC/HCT and 50 μA for AHC/AHCT. This is, of course, the case when the CMOS outputs drive only CMOS inputs. With CMOS loads, CMOS outputs maintain an output voltage within 0.1 V of the supply rails, 0 and V_{CC}. (A worst-case $V_{CC} = 4.5$ V is used for the table entries; hence, $V_{OHminC} = 4.4$ V.)

CMOS load

A *TTL load* can consume much more sink and source current, up to 4 mA from an HC/HCT output and 8 mA from an AHC/AHCT output. In this case, a higher voltage drop occurs across the "on" transistors in the output circuit, but the output voltage is still guaranteed to be within the normal range of TTL output levels.

TTL load

Table 3-7 lists CMOS output specifications for both CMOS and TTL loads. These parameters have the following meanings:

I_{OLmaxC} The maximum current that an output can supply in the LOW state while driving a CMOS load. Since this is a positive value, current flows *into* the output pin.

I_{OLmaxT} The maximum current that an output can supply in the LOW state while driving a TTL load.

V_{OLmaxC} The maximum voltage that a LOW output is guaranteed to produce while driving a CMOS load, that is, as long as I_{OLmaxC} is not exceeded.

V_{OLmaxT} The maximum voltage that a LOW output is guaranteed to produce while driving a TTL load, that is, as long as I_{OLmaxT} is not exceeded.

I_{OHmaxC} The maximum current that an output can supply in the HIGH state while driving a CMOS load. Since this is a negative value, positive current flows out of the output pin.

I_{OHmaxT} The maximum current that an output can supply in the HIGH state while driving a TTL load.

V_{OHminC} The minimum voltage that a HIGH output is guaranteed to produce while driving a CMOS load, that is, as long as I_{OHmaxC} is not exceeded.

V_{OHminT} The minimum voltage that a HIGH output is guaranteed to produce while driving a TTL load, that is, as long as I_{OHmaxT} is not exceeded.

The voltage parameters above determine DC noise margins. The LOW-state DC noise margin is the difference between V_{OLmax} and V_{ILmax}. This depends on the characteristics of both the driving output and the driven inputs. For example, the LOW-state DC noise margin of HCT driving a few HCT inputs (a CMOS load) is $0.8 - 0.1 = 0.7$ V. With a TTL load, the noise margin for the HCT inputs drops to $0.8 - 0.33 = 0.47$ V. Similarly, the HIGH-state DC noise margin is the difference between V_{OHmin} and V_{IHmin}. In general, when different families are interconnected, you have to compare the appropriate V_{OLmax} and V_{OHmin} of the driving gate with V_{ILmax} and V_{IHmin} of all the driven gates to determine the worst-case noise margins.

The I_{OLmax} and I_{OHmax} parameters in the table determine fanout capability and are especially important when an output drives inputs in one or more different families. Two calculations must be performed to determine whether an output is operating within its rated fanout capability:

HIGH-state fanout   The I_{IHmax} values for all of the driven inputs are added. The sum must not exceed I_{OHmax} of the driving output.

LOW-state fanout   The I_{ILmax} values for all of the driven inputs are added. The sum must not exceed I_{OLmax} of the driving output

Note that the input and output characteristics of specific components may vary from the representative values given in Table 3-7, so you must always consult the manufacturers' data sheets when analyzing a real design.

*3.8.4 AC and ACT

AC (Advanced CMOS)
ACT (Advanced CMOS, TTL compatible)

Introduced in the mid-1980s, a pair of more advanced CMOS families are aptly named— *AC (Advanced CMOS)* and *ACT (Advanced CMOS, TTL compatible)*. These families are very fast, and they can source or sink a lot of current, up to

24 mA in either state. Like HC and HCT, and AHC and AHCT, the AC and ACT families differ only in the input levels that they recognize; their output characteristics are the same. Also like the other CMOS families, AC/ACT outputs have symmetric output drive.

Devices in the AC and especially ACT families were popular because of their ability to drive heavy DC loads, including TTL devices. Their outputs also have very fast rise and fall times, which contributes to faster overall system operation, but at a price. The rise and fall times are so fast that they are often a major source of "analog" problems, including switching noise and ground bounce. As a result, the families in the next subsection were developed, and they gradually supplanted the ACT family in most applications requiring TTL compatibility.

*3.8.5 FCT and FCT-T

In the early 1990s, yet another CMOS family was launched. The key benefit of the *FCT (Fast CMOS, TTL compatible)* family was its ability to meet or exceed the speed and the output drive capability of the best TTL families while reducing power consumption and maintaining full compatibility with TTL. FCT output circuits are specifically designed with rise and fall times that are more controlled as compared to those of AC/ACT outputs, so FCT outputs do not create quite the same magnitude of "analog" problems.

FCT (Fast CMOS, TTL compatible)

Still, the original FCT family had the drawback of producing a full 5-V CMOS V_{OH}, creating enormous CV^2f power dissipation and circuit noise as its outputs swung from 0 V to almost 5 V in high-speed (25 MHz+) applications. A variation of the family, *FCT-T (Fast CMOS, TTL compatible with TTL V_{OH})*, was quickly introduced with circuit innovations to reduce the HIGH-level output voltage, thereby reducing both power consumption and switching noise while maintaining the same high operating speed as the original FCT. A suffix of "T" is used on part numbers to denote the FCT-T output structure, for example, 74FCT138T versus 74FCT138.

FCT-T (Fast CMOS, TTL compatible with TTL V_{OH})

The FCT-T family remains very popular today. A key application of FCT-T is driving buses and other heavy loads. To reduce transmission-line reflections (Section Zo at DDPPonline), another high-speed design worry, some FCT-T outputs have built-in 25-Ω series resistors. Compared with other CMOS families, FCT can source or sink gobs of current, up to 64 mA in the LOW state.

*3.8.6 FCT-T Electrical Characteristics

Electrical characteristics of the 5-V FCT-T family are summarized in Table 3-8. The family is specifically designed to be intermixed with TTL devices, so its operation is only specified with a nominal 5-V supply and TTL logic levels.

Individual logic gates are not manufactured in the FCT family. Perhaps the simplest FCT logic element is a 74FCT138T decoder, which has six inputs, eight outputs, and contains the equivalent of about a dozen 4-input gates internally.

Table 3-8 Specifications for a 74FCT138T decoder in the FCT-T logic family.

Description	Symbol	Condition	Value
Maximum propagation delay (ns)	t_{PD}		5.8
Quiescent power-supply current (μA)	I_{CC}	$V_{in} = 0$ or V_{CC}	200
Quiescent power dissipation (mW)		$V_{in} = 0$ or V_{CC}	1.0
Dynamic power-supply current (mA/MHz)	I_{CCD}	Outputs open, one input changing	0.12
Quiescent power-supply current per TTL input (mA)	ΔI_{CC}	$V_{in} = 3.4$ V	2.0
Total power dissipation (mW)		$f = 100$ kHz	0.60
		$f = 1$ MHz	1.06
		$f = 10$ MHz	1.6
Speed-power product (pJ)		$f = 100$ kHz	6.15
		$f = 1$ MHz	9.3
		$f = 10$ MHz	41
Input leakage current (μA)	I_{Imax}	$V_{in} = $ any	± 5
Typical input capacitance (pF)	C_{INtyp}		5
LOW-level input voltage (V)	V_{ILmax}		0.8
HIGH-level input voltage (V)	V_{IHmin}		2.0
LOW-level output current (mA)	I_{OLmax}		64
LOW-level output voltage (V)	V_{OLmax}	$I_{out} \leq I_{OLmax}$	0.55
HIGH-level output current (mA)	I_{OHmax}		-15
HIGH-level output voltage (V)	V_{OHmin}	$|I_{out}| \leq |I_{OHmax}|$	2.4
	V_{OHtyp}	$|I_{out}| \leq |I_{OHmax}|$	3.3

(This function is described later, in Section 6.4.3.) Comparing its propagation delay and power consumption in Table 3-8 with the corresponding HCT and AHCT numbers in Table 3-5 on page 144, you can see that the FCT-T family is superior in both speed and power dissipation. When comparing, note that FCT-T manufacturers specify only maximum, not typical propagation delays.

Unlike other CMOS families, FCT-T does not have a C_{PD} specification. Instead, it has an I_{CCD} specification:

I_{CCD} Dynamic power-supply current, in units of mA/MHz. This is the amount of additional power-supply current that flows when one input is changing at the rate of 1 MHz.

The I_{CCD} specification gives the same information as C_{PD}, but in a different way. The circuit's internal power dissipation due to transitions at a given frequency f can be calculated by the formula

$$P_T = V_{CC} \cdot I_{CCD} \cdot f$$

Thus, I_{CCD}/V_{CC} is algebraically equivalent to the C_{PD} specification of other CMOS families (see Exercise 3.85). FCT-T also has a ΔI_{CC} specification for the extra quiescent current that is consumed with nonideal HIGH inputs (see box at the top of page 145).

*3.9 Low-Voltage CMOS Logic and Interfacing

Two important factors have led the IC industry to move toward lower power-supply voltages in CMOS devices:

- In most applications, CMOS output voltages swing from rail to rail, so the V in the CV^2f equation is the power-supply voltage. Cutting power-supply voltage reduces dynamic power dissipation more than proportionally.

- As the industry moves toward ever-smaller transistor geometries, the oxide insulation between a CMOS transistor's gate and its source and drain is getting ever thinner, and thus incapable of insulating voltage potentials as "high" as 5 V.

As a result, JEDEC, an IC industry standards group, selected $3.3\,V \pm 0.3V$, $2.5\,V \pm 0.2V$, $1.8\,V \pm 0.15V$, $1.5\,V \pm 0.1V$, and $1.2\,V \pm 0.1V$ as the next "standard" logic power-supply voltages. JEDEC standards specify the input and output logic voltage levels for devices operating with these power-supply voltages.

The migration to lower voltages has occurred in stages and will continue to do so. For discrete logic families, the trend has been to produce parts that operate and produce outputs at the lower voltage but can also tolerate inputs at the higher voltage. This approach has allowed 3.3-V CMOS families to operate with 5-V CMOS and TTL families, as we'll see in the next section.

MORE POWER (SUPPLIES) TO YOU   Many microprocessors and ASICs use a simple approach to accommodate different internal and external logic levels—they have two power-supply voltages. A low voltage, such as 1.8 V, is supplied to operate the chip's internal gates, or *core logic*. A higher voltage, such as 3.3 V, is supplied to operate the external input and output circuits, or *pad ring*, for compatibility with older-generation devices in the system. Special buffer circuits are used internally to translate safely and quickly between the core-logic and the pad-ring logic voltages. With microprocessors, the internal voltage may even be varied dynamically depending on the application's needs—a lower voltage for lower power, and a higher voltage for higher speed.

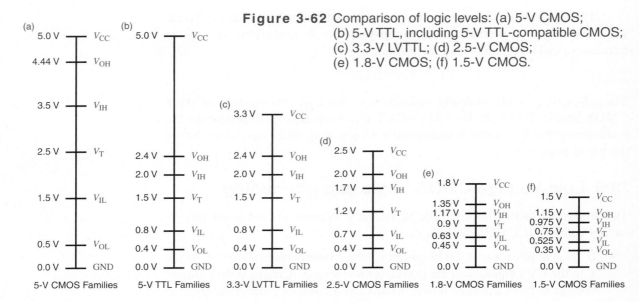

Figure 3-62 Comparison of logic levels: (a) 5-V CMOS;
(b) 5-V TTL, including 5-V TTL-compatible CMOS;
(c) 3.3-V LVTTL; (d) 2.5-V CMOS;
(e) 1.8-V CMOS; (f) 1.5-V CMOS.

*3.9.1 3.3-V LVTTL and LVCMOS Logic

The relationships among signal levels for standard TTL and low-voltage CMOS devices operating at their nominal power-supply voltages are illustrated nicely in Figure 3-62, adapted from a Texas Instruments application note. The original, symmetric signal levels for pure 5-V CMOS families such as HC and AHC are shown in (a). TTL-compatible CMOS families such as HCT, AHCT, and FCT shift the voltage levels downward for compatibility with TTL as shown in (b).

The first step in the progression of lower CMOS power-supply voltages was 3.3 V. The JEDEC standards for 3.3-V logic actually define two sets of

LVCMOS (low-voltage CMOS)

LVTTL (low-voltage TTL)

levels. *LVCMOS (low-voltage CMOS)* levels are used in pure CMOS applications where outputs have light DC loads (less than 100 μA), so V_{OL} and V_{OH} are maintained within 0.2 V of the power-supply rails. *LVTTL (low-voltage TTL)* levels, shown in (c), are used in applications where outputs have significant DC loads, so V_{OL} can be as high as 0.4 V and V_{OH} can be as low as 2.4 V.

The positioning of TTL's logic levels at the low end of the 5-V range was really quite fortuitous. As shown in Figure 3-62(b) and (c), it was possible to define the LVTTL levels to match up with TTL levels exactly. Thus, an LVTTL output can drive a TTL input with no problem, as long as its output current specifications (I_{OLmax}, I_{OHmax}) are respected. Similarly, a TTL output can drive an LVTTL input, except for the problem of driving it beyond LVTTL's 3.3-V V_{CC}, as discussed in the next subsection.

Notice the narrowing of the ranges of valid logic levels and the DC noise margins in the even lower-voltage standards in (d) through (f). This narrowing further drives the importance of minimizing analog effects such as switching noise and ground bounce in modern high-speed designs.

*3.9.2 5-V Tolerant Inputs

The inputs of a gate won't necessarily tolerate voltages greater than V_{CC}. This is a problem when two different logic voltage ranges are used in a system. For example, 5-V CMOS devices easily produce 4.9-V outputs when lightly loaded, and both CMOS and TTL devices routinely produce 4.0-V outputs even when moderately loaded. The inputs of 3.3-V devices may not like these high voltages.

The maximum voltage V_{Imax} that an input can tolerate is listed in the "absolute maximum ratings" section of the manufacturer's data sheet. For HC devices, V_{Imax} equals V_{CC}. Thus, if an HC device is powered by a 3.3-V supply, its inputs cannot be driven by any 5-V CMOS or TTL outputs without damage. For AHC devices, on the other hand, V_{Imax} is 5.5 V; thus, AHC devices with a 3.3-V power supply may be used to convert 5-V outputs to 3.3-V levels for use with 3.3-V microprocessors, memories, and other devices in a pure 3.3-V subsystem.

Figure 3-63 explains why some inputs are 5-V tolerant and others are not. As shown in (a), the HC and HCT input structure actually contains two reverse-biased *clamp diodes*, which we haven't shown before, between each input signal *clamp diode* and V_{CC} and ground. The purpose of these diodes is specifically to shunt any transient input signal voltage less than 0 through *D1* or greater than V_{CC} through *D2* to the corresponding power-supply rail. Such transients can occur as a result of transmission-line reflections, as described in <u>Section Zo</u> at <u>DDPPonline</u>. Shunting the so-called "undershoot" or "overshoot" to ground or V_{CC} reduces the magnitude and duration of reflections.

Of course, diode *D2* can't distinguish between transient overshoot and a persistent input voltage greater than V_{CC}. Hence, if a 5-V output is connected to one of these inputs, it will not see the very high impedance normally associated with a CMOS input. Instead, it will see a relatively low impedance path to V_{CC} through the now forward-biased diode *D2*, and excessive current will flow.

Figure 3-63(b) shows a 5-V tolerant CMOS input. This input structure simply omits *D2*; diode *D1* is still provided to clamp undershoot. The AHC family uses this input structure.

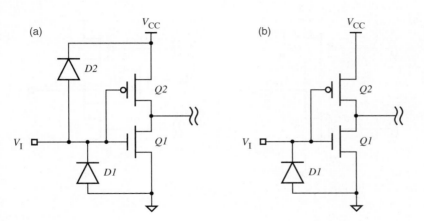

Figure 3-63
CMOS input structures:
(a) non-5-V tolerant HC;
(b) 5-V tolerant AHC.

The kind of input structure shown in Figure 3-63(b) is necessary but not sufficient to create 5-V tolerant inputs. The transistors in a device's particular fabrication process must also be able to withstand voltage potentials higher than V_{CC}. On this basis, V_{Imax} in the AHC family is limited to 5.5 V. In many 3.3-V ASIC processes, it's not possible to get 5-V tolerant inputs, even if you're willing to give up the transmission-line benefits of diode $D2$.

*3.9.3 5-V Tolerant Outputs

Five-volt tolerance must also be considered for outputs, in particular, when both 3.3-V and 5-V three-state outputs are connected to a bus. When the 3.3-V output is in the disabled, Hi-Z state, a 5-V device may be driving the bus, and a 5-V signal may appear on the 3.3-V device's *output*.

In this situation, Figure 3-64 explains why some outputs are 5-V tolerant and others are not. As shown in (a), the standard CMOS three-state output has an *n*-channel transistor $Q1$ to ground and a *p*-channel transistor $Q2$ to V_{CC}. When the output is disabled, circuitry (not shown) holds the gate of $Q1$ near 0 V, and the gate of $Q2$ near V_{CC}, so both transistors are off and Y is Hi-Z.

Now consider what happens if V_{CC} is 3.3 V and a different device applies a 5-V signal to the output pin Y in (a). Then the drain of $Q2$ (Y) is at 5 V while the gate (V_2) is still at only 3.3 V. With the gate at a lower potential than the drain, $Q2$ will begin to conduct and provide a relatively low-impedance path from Y to V_{CC}, and excessive current will flow. Both HC and AHC three-state outputs have this structure and therefore are not 5-V tolerant.

Figure 3-64(b) shows a 5-V tolerant output structure. An extra *p*-channel transistor $Q3$ is used to prevent $Q2$ from turning on when it shouldn't. When V_{OUT} is greater than V_{CC}, $Q3$ turns on. This forms a relatively low impedance path from Y to the gate of $Q2$, which now stays off because its gate voltage V_2 can no longer be below the drain voltage. This output structure is used in Texas Instruments' LVC (Low-Voltage CMOS) family.

Figure 3-64
CMOS three-state output structures:
(a) non-5-V tolerant HC and AHC;
(b) 5-V tolerant LVC.

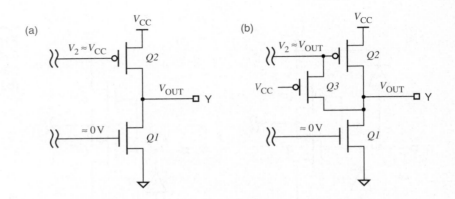

*3.9.4 TTL/LVTTL Interfacing Summary

Based on the information in the preceding subsections, TTL (5-V) and LVTTL (3.3-V) devices can be mixed in the same system subject to just three rules:

1. LVTTL outputs can drive TTL inputs directly, subject to the usual constraints on output current (I_{OLmax}, I_{OHmax}) of the driving devices.
2. TTL outputs can drive LVTTL inputs if the inputs are 5-V tolerant.
3. TTL and LVTTL three-state outputs can drive the same bus if the LVTTL outputs are 5-V tolerant.

*3.9.5 Logic Levels Less Than 3.3 V

The transition from 3.3-V to 2.5-V logic is not so easy. It is true that 3.3-V outputs can drive 2.5-V inputs as long as the inputs are 3.3-V tolerant. However, a quick look at Figure 3-62(c) and (d) on page 152 shows that V_{OH} of a 2.5-V output equals V_{IH} of a 3.3-V input. In other words, there is zero HIGH-state DC noise margin when a 2.5-V output drives a 3.3-V input—not a good situation, but it could be worse.

Comparing the logic levels for 2.5-V and 1.8-V logic, you can see that the minimum HIGH output voltage for 1.8-V logic is quite a bit higher than what can be recognized as HIGH by a 2.5-V input. A smaller mismatch occurs between 1.8-V and 1.5-V logic, but it still cannot be ignored.

The solution to this problem is to use a *level shifter* (or *level translator*), a device which is powered by both supply voltages and which internally boosts the lower logic levels to the higher ones. For example, the 74ALVC164245 level shifter can connect two 16-bit buses with different logic levels on each side. One side could use 5.0-V or 3.3-V power and logic levels, while the other side uses 2.5-V or 1.8-V power and logic levels.

level translator
level shifter

Many of today's ASICs and microprocessors contain level translators internally. This allows them to operate, for example, with a 1.8-V or lower core and a 3.3-V pad ring, as we discussed in the box on page 151.

*3.10 Bipolar Logic

Bipolar logic families use semiconductor diodes and bipolar junction transistors as the basic building blocks of logic circuits. The simplest bipolar logic elements use diodes and resistors to perform logic operations; this is called *diode logic*. The original *transistor-transistor logic (TTL)* families used transistors both to perform logic functions and to boost output drive capability. Many newer TTL families use diode logic internally and use transistors only to boost their output drive capability. *Emitter-coupled logic (ECL)* families use transistors as current switches to achieve very high speed. *BiCMOS logic* uses both bipolar and MOS transistors—input and logic circuits are CMOS for low power consumption, while outputs use bipolar transistors to achieve higher driving capability.

diode logic
transistor-transistor logic (TTL)
emitter-coupled logic (ECL)
BiCMOS logic

As you already know, bipolar logic families have been largely supplanted by the CMOS families that we studied in previous sections. Still, it is useful to study basic TTL operation for the occasional application that requires TTL/CMOS interfacing, discussed in Section 3.10.8. Also, an understanding of TTL may give you insight into the fortuitous similarity of logic levels that allowed the industry to migrate smoothly from TTL to 5-V CMOS logic, and later to lower-voltage, higher-performance 3.3-V CMOS logic.

This section covers the basic operation of bipolar logic circuits at the "black box" level. More details can be found at <u>DDPPonline</u>, as noted as we go along in the sections below.

*3.10.1 Diode Logic

diode

anode

cathode

diode action

The schematic symbol for a *diode* is shown in Figure 3-65(a). The physical properties of a diode are such that positive current can easily flow only in the direction shown by the arrow in the figure, from *anode* to *cathode*; current flow in the other direction is blocked. This is called *diode action*.

The transfer characteristic of an ideal diode, shown in Figure 3-65(b), further illustrates this principle. If the anode-to-cathode voltage, V, is negative,

reverse-biased diode

forward-biased diode

the diode is said to be *reverse biased* and the current I through the diode is zero. If V is nonnegative, the diode is said to be *forward biased* and I can be an arbitrarily large positive value. In fact, V can never get larger than zero, because an ideal diode acts like a zero-resistance short circuit when forward biased.

Stated another way, an ideal diode acts like a short circuit as long as the voltage across the anode-to-cathode junction is nonnegative. If the anode-to-cathode voltage is negative, the diode acts like an open circuit and no current flows.

leakage current

Real diodes do not behave as ideally as this, of course. When a real diode is reverse biased, it's not quite an open circuit; a small *leakage current* flows. When the diode is forward biased, it acts like a small resistance, R_f, in series with

forward resistance

diode-drop

V_d, a small voltage source. R_f is called the *forward resistance* of the diode, and V_d is called a *diode-drop*, about 0.6 V for typical silicon diodes. For more information, see <u>Section Diode.1</u> at <u>DDPPonline</u>.

Figure 3-65
Diodes: (a) schematic symbol; (b) transfer characteristic of an ideal diode.

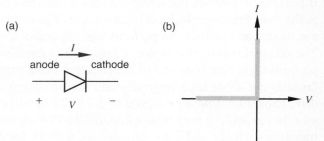

Signal Level	Designation	Binary Logic Value
0–2 volts	LOW	0
2–3 volts	noise margin	undefined
3–5 volts	HIGH	1

Table 3-9
Logic levels in a simple diode logic system.

Diode action can be exploited to perform logical operations. Consider a logic system with a 5-V power supply and the definitions shown in Table 3-9. Within the 5-volt range, signal voltages are partitioned into two ranges, LOW and HIGH, with a 1-volt noise margin between. A voltage in the LOW range is considered to be a logic 0, and a voltage in the HIGH range is a logic 1.

LOW

HIGH

With these definitions, a *diode AND gate* can be constructed as shown in Figure 3-66(a). In this circuit, suppose that both inputs X and Y are connected to HIGH voltage sources, say 4 V, so that V_X and V_Y are both 4 V as in (b). Then both diodes are forward biased, and the output voltage V_Z is one diode-drop above 4 V, or about 4.6 V. A small amount of current, determined by the value of R, flows from the 5-V supply through the two diodes and into the 4-V sources. The colored arrows in the figure show the path of this current flow.

diode AND gate

Figure 3-66 Diode AND gate: (a) electrical circuit; (b) both inputs HIGH; (c) one input HIGH, one LOW; (d) function table; (e) truth table.

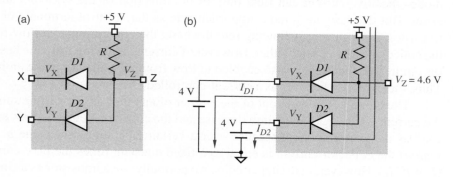

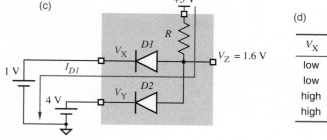

V_X	V_Y	V_Z
low	low	low
low	high	low
high	low	low
high	high	high

X	Y	Z
0	0	0
0	1	0
1	0	0
1	1	1

When diode logic gates are cascaded, the voltage levels of the logic signals move away from the power-supply rails and toward the undefined region, as a result of the voltage drops across the diodes and resistors. For an example, see Section Diode.2 at DDPPonline. Thus, in practice, a diode AND gate normally must be followed by a transistor amplifier to restore the logic levels; this is the scheme used in TTL NAND gates, described in Section 3.10.3. Still, board-level digital designers are occasionally tempted to use discrete diodes to perform logic under special circumstances; for example, see Exercise 3.86.

*3.10.2 Bipolar Junction Transistors

bipolar junction transistor

A *bipolar junction transistor* is a three-terminal device that, in most logic circuits, acts like a current-controlled switch. There are two basic types of bipolar junction transistors, with schematic symbols shown in Figure 3-67. If we put a small current into one of the terminals, called the *base*, then the switch is "on"—current may flow between the other two terminals, called the *emitter* and the *collector*. If no current is put into the base, then the switch is "off"—no current flows between the emitter and the collector.

base

emitter

collector

The schematic symbol of an *npn transistor* is shown in (a). The symbol for a *pnp transistor* is shown in (b); however, *pnp* transistors are seldom used in digital circuits, so we won't discuss them any further.

npn transistor

pnp transistor

The base-to-emitter junction of an *npn* transistor acts somewhat like a diode—positive current can flow only in the direction of the symbol's subtle arrow. But the base has a more important role as the "control terminal" of the transistor. If no current is flowing into the base, then no current can flow from the collector to the emitter either. However, if current is flowing from the base to the emitter, then current is also enabled to flow from the collector to the emitter. Thus, the transistor behaves as a current-controlled switch.

amplifier

active region

The current I_e flowing out of the emitter of an *npn* transistor is the sum of the currents I_b and I_c flowing into the base and the collector. A transistor is often used as a signal *amplifier*, because over a certain operating range (the *active region*) the collector current is equal to a fixed constant times the base current ($I_c = \beta \cdot I_b$). However, in digital circuits, we normally use a transistor as a simple switch that's always fully "on" or fully "off," as explained next.

Figure 3-67
Bipolar transistor symbols:
(a) *npn* transistor;
(b) *pnp* transistor.

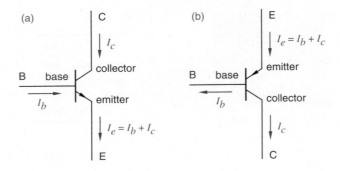

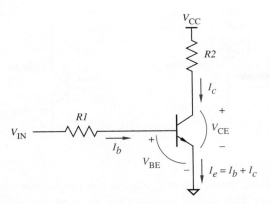

Figure 3-68
Common-emitter
configuration of an
npn transistor.

Figure 3-68 shows the *common-emitter configuration* of an *npn* transistor,   *common-emitter*
which is most often used in digital switching applications. This configuration   *configuration*
uses two discrete resistors, *R1* and *R2*, in addition to a single *npn* transistor. In
this circuit, if V_{IN} is 0 or negative, then the base-to-emitter diode junction is
reverse biased, and no base current (I_b) can flow. If no base current flows, then
no collector current (I_c) can flow, and the transistor is said to be *cut off (OFF)*. In   *cut off (OFF)*
this state, there is no current through and hence no voltage drop across *R2*, so
$V_{CE} = V_{CC}$.

When base current is flowing, a certain amount of current may flow from
the collector to the emitter, directly proportional to the base current. This current
creates a voltage drop across *R2* and lowers V_{CE}. However, V_{CE} can never drop
lower than $V_{CE(sat)}$, a transistor parameter that is typically about 0.2 V. When the
base current is great enough to drop V_{CE} to $V_{CE(sat)}$, the transistor is said to be
saturated (ON). In digital logic applications, most transistors are operated so   *saturated (ON)*
that they are always either saturated or cut off.

Figure 3-69 shows that we can make a logic inverter from an *npn* transistor
in the common-emitter configuration. When the input voltage is LOW, the output
voltage is HIGH, and vice versa.

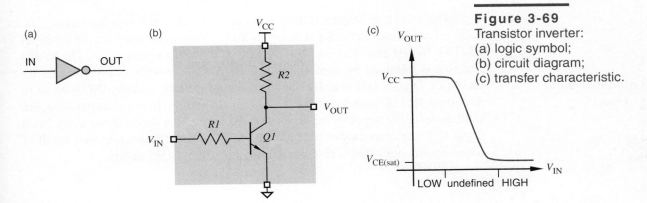

Figure 3-69
Transistor inverter:
(a) logic symbol;
(b) circuit diagram;
(c) transfer characteristic.

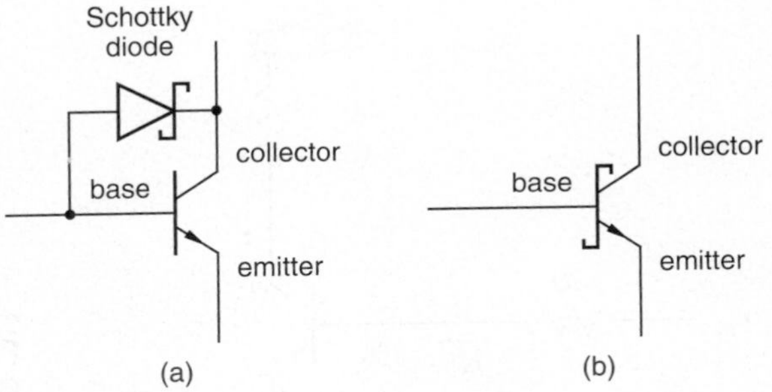

Figure 3-70
Schottky-clamped
transistor: (a) circuit;
(b) symbol.

storage time

When the input of a saturated transistor is changed, the output does not change immediately; it takes extra time, called *storage time*, to come out of saturation. In fact, storage time accounts for a significant portion of the propagation delay in the original TTL logic family.

Schottky diode
Schottky-clamped transistor
Schottky transistor

Storage time can be eliminated and propagation delay can be reduced by ensuring that transistors do not saturate in normal operation. Contemporary TTL logic families do this by placing a *Schottky diode* between the base and collector of each transistor that might saturate, as shown in Figure 3-70. The resulting transistors, which do not saturate, are called *Schottky-clamped transistors* or *Schottky transistors* for short.

Additional information about bipolar transistors, transistor inverters, and Schottky transistors can be found at DDPPonline in Section BJT.

*3.10.3 Transistor-Transistor Logic

There are many different TTL families, with a range of speed, power consumption, and other characteristics. These families use basically the same logic levels as the TTL-compatible CMOS families in previous sections. We'll use the following definitions of LOW and HIGH in our discussions of TTL circuit behavior:

LOW   0–0.8 volts.

HIGH   2.0–5.0 volts.

diode AND gate
clamp diode

The circuit examples in this section are based on a representative TTL family, Low-power Schottky (LS, or LS-TTL). The circuit diagram for a 2-input LS-TTL NAND gate, part number 74LS00, is shown in Figure 3-71 . The NAND function is obtained by combining a diode AND gate with an inverting buffer amplifier. Diodes $D1X$ and $D1Y$ and resistor $R1$ in form a *diode AND gate,* as in Section 3.10.1. *Clamp diodes* $D2X$ and $D2Y$ do nothing in normal operation, but limit undesirable negative excursions on the inputs to a single diode-drop. Such negative excursions may occur on HIGH-to-LOW input transitions as a result of transmission-line effects, discussed in Section Zo at DDPPonline.

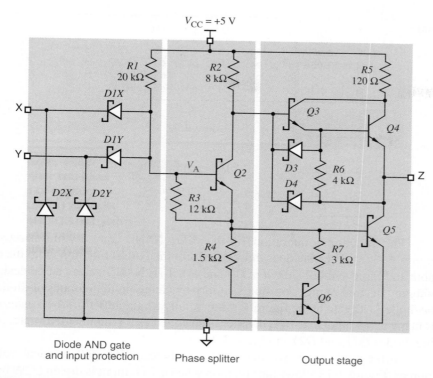

Figure 3-71
Circuit diagram of
2-input LS-TTL
NAND gate.

Transistor *Q2* and the surrounding resistors form a *phase splitter* that *phase splitter* controls the output stage. Depending on whether the diode AND gate produces a "low" or a "high" voltage at V_A, *Q2* is either cut off or turned on.

The *output stage* has two transistors, *Q4* and *Q5*, only one of which is on at any time. The TTL output stage is sometimes called a *totem-pole* or *push-pull output*. Similar to the *p*-channel and *n*-channel transistors in CMOS, *Q4* and *Q5* provide active pull-up and pull-down to the HIGH and LOW states, respectively. Additional details of TTL circuit operation can be found at <u>DDPPonline</u> in Section <u>TTL</u>.

output stage
totem-pole output
push-pull output

WHERE IN THE WORLD IS *Q1*? Notice that there is no transistor *Q1* in Figure 3-71, but the other transistors are named in a way that's traditional; some TTL devices do in fact have a transistor named *Q1*. Instead of diodes like *D1X* and *D1Y*, these devices use a multiple-emitter transistor *Q1* to perform logic. This transistor has one emitter per logic input, as shown in the figure to the right. Pulling any one of the emitters LOW is sufficient to turn the transistor ON and thus pull V_A LOW.

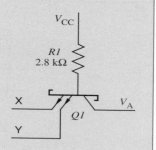

Figure 3-72
Functional operation
of a TTL 2-input
NAND gate:
(a) function table;
(b) truth table;
(c) logic symbol.

(a)

X	Y	V_A	Q2	Q3	Q4	Q5	Q6	V_Z	Z
L	L	1.05	off	on	on	off	off	2.7	H
L	H	≤1.05	off	on	on	off	off	2.7	H
H	L	≤1.05	off	on	on	off	off	2.7	H
H	H	1.2	on	off	off	on	on	≤0.35	L

(b)

X	Y	Z
0	0	1
0	1	1
1	0	1
1	1	0

(c)

The functional operation of the TTL NAND gate is summarized in Figure 3-72(a). The gate does indeed perform the NAND function, with the truth table and logic symbol shown in (b) and (c). TTL NAND gates can be designed with any desired number of inputs simply by changing the number of diodes in the diode AND gate in the figure. Commercially available TTL NAND gates have as many as 13 inputs. A TTL inverter is designed as a 1-input NAND gate, omitting diodes *D1Y* and *D2Y* in Figure 3-71.

So far we have shown the input signals to a TTL gate as ideal voltage sources. Figure 3-73 shows the situation when a TTL input is driven LOW by the output of another TTL gate. Transistor *Q5A* in the driving gate is ON, and thereby provides a path to ground for the current flowing out of the diode *D1XB* in the driven gate. When current flows *into* a TTL output in the LOW state, as in this case, the output is said to be *sinking current*.

sinking current

Figure 3-74 shows the same circuit with a HIGH output. In this case, *Q4A* in the driving gate is turned on enough to supply the small amount of leakage current flowing through reverse-biased diodes *D1XB* and *D2XB* in the driven gate. When current flows out of a TTL output in the HIGH state, the output is said to be *sourcing current*.

sourcing current

*3.10.4 TTL Logic Levels and Noise Margins

At the beginning of this section, we indicated that we would consider TTL signals between 0 and 0.8 V to be LOW, and signals between 2.0 and 5.0 V to be HIGH. Actually, we can be more precise by defining TTL input and output levels in the same way as we did for CMOS:

V_{OHmin} The minimum output voltage in the HIGH state, 2.7 V for most TTL families.

V_{IHmin} The minimum input voltage guaranteed to be recognized as a HIGH, 2.0 V for all TTL families.

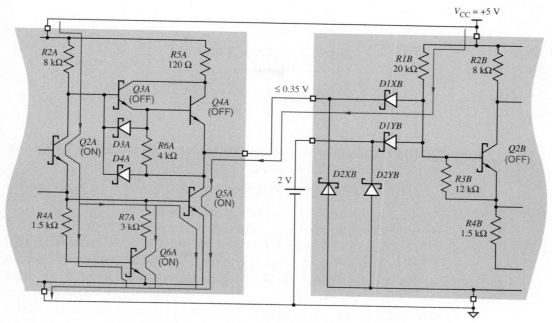

Figure 3-73 A TTL output driving a TTL input LOW.

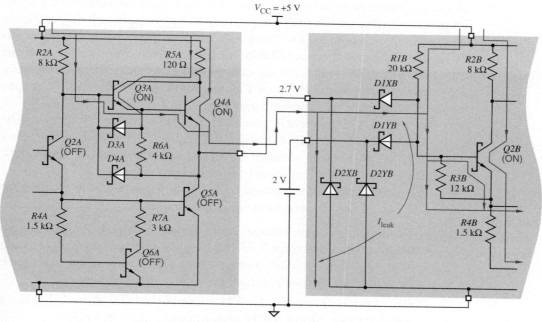

Figure 3-74 A TTL output driving a TTL input HIGH.

Figure 3-75
Noise margins for
popular TTL logic
families (74LS, 74S,
74ALS, 74AS, 74F).

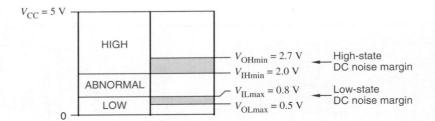

V_{ILmax} The maximum input voltage guaranteed to be recognized as a LOW, 0.8 V for most TTL families.

V_{OLmax} The maximum output voltage in the LOW state, 0.5 V for most families.

These noise margins are illustrated in Figure 3-75.

DC noise margin

In the HIGH state, the V_{OHmin} specification of most TTL families exceeds V_{IHmin} by 0.7 V, so TTL has a *DC noise margin* of 0.7 V in the HIGH state. That is, it takes at least 0.7 V of noise to corrupt a worst-case HIGH output into a voltage that is not guaranteed to be recognizable as a HIGH input. In the LOW state, however, V_{ILmax} exceeds V_{OLmax} by only 0.3 V, so the DC noise margin in the LOW state is only 0.3 V. In general, TTL and TTL-compatible circuits tend to be more sensitive to noise in the LOW state than in the HIGH state.

*3.10.5 TTL Fanout

fanout

As we defined it previously in Section 3.5.4, *fanout* is a measure of the number of gate inputs that are connected to (and driven by) a single gate output. As we showed in that section, the DC fanout of CMOS outputs driving CMOS inputs is virtually unlimited, because CMOS inputs require almost no current in either state, HIGH or LOW. This is not the case with TTL inputs. As a result, there are very definite limits on the fanout of TTL or CMOS outputs driving TTL inputs, as you'll learn in the paragraphs that follow.

current flow

As in CMOS, the *current flow* in a TTL input or output lead is defined to be positive if the current actually flows *into* the lead, and negative if current flows *out* of the lead. As a result, when an output is connected to one or more inputs, the algebraic sum of all the input and output currents is 0.

The amount of current required by a TTL input depends on whether the input is HIGH or LOW, and is specified by two parameters:

I_{ILmax} The maximum current that an input requires to pull it LOW. Recall from the discussion of Figure 3-73 that positive current is actually flowing from V_{CC}, through $R1B$, through diode $D1XB$, out of the input lead, through the driving output transistor $Q5A$, and into ground.

Since current flows out of a TTL input in the LOW state, I_{ILmax} has a negative value. Most LS-TTL inputs have $I_{ILmax} = -0.4$ mA.

I_{IHmax} The maximum current that an input requires to pull it HIGH. As shown in Figure 3-74 on page 163, positive current flows from V_{CC}, through *R5A* and *Q4A* of the driving gate, and *into* the driven input, where it leaks to ground through reverse-biased diodes *D1XB* and *D2XB*.

Since current flows *into* a TTL input in the HIGH state, I_{IHmax} has a positive value. Most LS-TTL inputs have $I_{IHmax} = 20\ \mu A$.

Like CMOS outputs, TTL outputs can source or sink a certain amount of current depending on the state, HIGH or LOW:

I_{OLmax} The maximum current an output can sink in the LOW state while maintaining an output voltage no more than V_{OLmax}. Since current flows into the output, I_{OLmax} has a positive value, 8 mA for most LS-TTL outputs.

I_{OHmax} The maximum current an output can source in the HIGH state while maintaining an output voltage no less than V_{OHmin}. Since current flows out of the output, I_{OHmax} has a negative value, $-400\ \mu A$ for most LS-TTL outputs.

Notice that the value of I_{OLmax} for typical LS-TTL outputs is exactly 20 times the absolute value of I_{ILmax}. As a result, LS-TTL is said to have a *LOW-state fanout* of 20, because an output can drive up to 20 inputs in the LOW state. Similarly, the absolute value of I_{OHmax} is exactly 20 times I_{IHmax}, so LS-TTL is said to have a *HIGH-state fanout* of 20 also. The *overall fanout* is the lesser of the LOW- and HIGH-state fanouts.

LOW-state fanout

HIGH-state fanout
overall fanout

Loading a TTL output with more than its rated fanout has the same deleterious effects that were described for CMOS devices in Section 3.5.5 on page 111. That is, DC noise margins may be reduced or eliminated, transition times and delays may increase, and the device may overheat.

In general, two calculations must be carried out to confirm that an output is not being overloaded:

HIGH state   The I_{IHmax} values for all of the driven inputs are added. This sum must be less than or equal to the absolute value of I_{OHmax} for the driving output.

LOW state   The I_{ILmax} values for all of the driven inputs are added. The absolute value of this sum must be less than or equal to I_{OLmax} for the driving output.

For example, suppose you designed a system in which a certain LS-TTL output drives ten LS-TTL and three S-TTL gate inputs. In the HIGH state, a total of $10 \cdot 20 + 3 \cdot 50\ \mu A = 350\ \mu A$ is required. This is within an LS-TTL output's HIGH-state current-sourcing capability of 400 μA. But in the LOW state, a total of $10 \cdot 0.4 + 3 \cdot 2.0\ mA = 10.0\ mA$ is required. This is more than an LS-TTL output's LOW-state current-sinking capability of 8 mA, so the output is overloaded.

BURNED FINGERS   If a TTL or CMOS output is forced to sink a lot more than I_{OLmax}, the device may be damaged, especially if high current is allowed to flow for more than a second or so. For example, suppose that a TTL output in the LOW state is short-circuited directly to the 5 V supply. The ON resistance, $R_{CE(sat)}$, of the saturated $Q5$ transistor in a typical TTL output stage is less than 10 Ω. Thus, $Q5$ must dissipate about $5^2/10$ or 2.5 watts. Don't try this yourself unless you're prepared to deal with the consequences! That's enough heat to destroy the device (and burn your finger) in a very short time.

*3.10.6 TTL Families

TTL families have evolved over the years in response to the demands of digital designers for better performance. As a result, several TTL families have come and gone, and today there are just a few surviving TTL families. Instead, TTL-compatible CMOS families are generally preferred for new designs. Some of the history of TTL is described in <u>DDPPonline</u> in <u>Section TTL</u>. All of these TTL families are compatible in that they use the same 5-V power-supply voltage and logic levels, but each family has its own advantages in terms of speed, power consumption, and cost.

74S (Schottky TTL)

74LS (Low-power Schottky TTL)

74AS (Advanced Schottky TTL)

74ALS (Advanced Low-power Schottky TTL)

74F (Fast TTL)

All current TTL families use Schottky transistors to improve their speed. The oldest of these are *74S (Schottky TTL)* and *74LS (Low-power Schottky TTL)*. Subsequent IC processing and circuit innovations led to three more Schottky logic families. The *74AS (Advanced Schottky TTL)* family offers speeds about twice as fast as 74S with about the same power consumption. The *74ALS (Advanced Low-power Schottky TTL)* family offers both lower power and higher speeds than 74LS. The *74F (Fast TTL)* family is positioned between 74AS and 74ALS in the speed/power tradeoff, and is probably the most popular choice for high-speed requirements in new TTL designs.

The important characteristics of these TTL families are summarized in Table 3-10. The first two rows of the table list the propagation delay (in nanoseconds) and the power consumption (in milliwatts) of a typical 2-input NAND gate in each family. The third row lists the corresponding speed-power product.

The remaining rows in Table 3-10 describe the input and output parameters of typical TTL gates in each of the families. Using this information, you can analyze the external behavior of TTL gates without knowing the details of the internal TTL circuit design. The input and output characteristics of specific components may vary from the representative values given in Table 3-10, so you must always consult the manufacturer's data book when analyzing a real design.

*3.10.7 A TTL Data Sheet

Table 3-11 shows part of a typical manufacturer's data sheet for the 74LS00. The 54LS00 listed in the data sheet is identical to the 74LS00, except that it is

Table 3-10 Characteristics of gates in TTL families.

Description	Symbol	Family				
		74S	**74LS**	**74AS**	**74ALS**	**74F**
Maximum propagation delay (ns)		3	9	1.7	4	3
Power consumption per gate (mW)		19	2	8	1.2	4
Speed-power product (pJ)		57	18	13.6	4.8	12
LOW-level input voltage (V)	V_{ILmax}	0.8	0.8	0.8	0.8	0.8
LOW-level output voltage (V)	V_{OLmax}	0.5	0.5	0.5	0.5	0.5
HIGH-level input voltage (V)	V_{IHmin}	2.0	2.0	2.0	2.0	2.0
HIGH-level output voltage (V)	V_{OHmin}	2.7	2.7	2.7	2.7	2.7
LOW-level input current (mA)	I_{ILmax}	−2.0	−0.4	−0.5	−0.2	−0.6
LOW-level output current (mA)	I_{OLmax}	20	8	20	8	20
HIGH-level input current (μA)	I_{IHmax}	50	20	20	20	20
HIGH-level output current (μA)	I_{OHmax}	−1000	−400	−2000	−400	−1000

specified to operate over the full "military" temperature and voltage range, and it costs more. Most TTL parts have corresponding 54-series (military) versions. Three sections of the data sheet are shown in the table:

- *Recommended operating conditions* specify power-supply voltage, input-voltage ranges, DC output loading, and temperature values under which the device is normally operated. *recommended operating conditions*

- *Electrical characteristics* specify additional DC voltages and currents that are observed at the device inputs and output when it is operated under the recommended conditions: *electrical characteristics*

    I_I Maximum input current for a very high HIGH input voltage.

    I_{OS} Output current with HIGH output shorted to ground.

    I_{CCH} Power-supply current when all outputs (on four NAND gates) are HIGH. (The number given is for the entire package, which contains four NAND gates, so the current per gate is one-fourth of the specified amount.)

    I_{CCL} Power-supply current when all outputs (on four NAND gates) are LOW.

Table 3-11 Typical manufacturer's data sheet for the 74LS00.

RECOMMENDED OPERATING CONDITIONS

Parameter	Description	SN54LS00			SN74LS00			Unit
		Min.	Nom.	Max.	Min.	Nom.	Max.	
V_{CC}	Supply voltage	4.5	5.0	5.5	4.75	5.0	5.25	V
V_{IH}	High-level input voltage	2.0			2.0			V
V_{IL}	Low-level input voltage			0.7			0.8	V
I_{OH}	High-level output current			−0.4			−0.4	mA
I_{OL}	Low-level output current			4			8	mA
T_A	Operating free-air temperature	−55		125	0		70	°C

ELECTRICAL CHARACTERISTICS OVER RECOMMENDED FREE-AIR TEMPERATURE RANGE

Parameter	Test Conditions[1]	SN54LS00			SN74LS00			Unit
		Min.	Typ.[2]	Max.	Min.	Typ.[2]	Max.	
V_{IK}	V_{CC} = Min., I_N = −18 mA			−1.5			−1.5	V
V_{OH}	V_{CC} = Min., V_{IL} = Max., I_{OH} = −0.4 mA	2.5	3.4		2.7	3.4		V
V_{OL}	V_{CC} = Min., V_{IH} = 2.0 V, I_{OL} = 4 mA		0.25	0.4		0.25	0.4	V
	V_{CC} = Min., V_{IH} = 2.0 V, I_{OL} = 8 mA					0.35	0.5	V
I_I	V_{CC} = Max., V_I = 7.0 V			0.1			0.1	mA
I_{IH}	V_{CC} = Max., V_I = 2.7 V			20			20	μA
I_{IL}	V_{CC} = Max., V_I = 0.4 V			−0.4			−0.4	mA
I_{OS}[3]	V_{CC} = Max.	−20		−100	−20		−100	mA
I_{CCH}	V_{CC} = Max., V_I = 0 V		0.8	1.6		0.8	1.6	mA
I_{CCL}	V_{CC} = Max., V_I = 4.5 V		2.4	4.4		2.4	4.4	mA

SWITCHING CHARACTERISTICS, V_{CC} = 5.0 V, T_A = 25°C

Parameter	From (Input)	To (Output)	Test Conditions	Min.	Typ.	Max.	Unit
t_{PLH}	A or B	Y	R_L = 2 kΩ, C_L = 15 pF		9	15	ns
t_{PHL}					10	15	ns

NOTES:

1. For conditions shown as Max. or Min., use appropriate value specified under Recommended Operating Conditions.

2. All typical values are at V_{CC} = 5.0 V, T_A = 25 °C.

3. Not more than one output should be shorted at a time; duration of short-circuit should not exceed one second.

- *Switching characteristics* give maximum and typical propagation delays under "typical" operating conditions of $V_{CC} = 5$ V and $T_A = 25°C$. A conservative designer must increase these delays by 5%–10% to account for different power-supply voltages and temperatures, and even more under heavy loading conditions.

A fourth section is also included in the manufacturer's data book:

- *Absolute maximum ratings* indicate the worst-case conditions for operating or storing the device without damage.

A complete data book also shows test circuits that are used to measure the parameters when the device is manufactured, and graphs that show how the typical parameters vary with operating conditions such as power-supply voltage (V_{CC}), ambient temperature (T_A), and load (R_L, C_L).

*3.10.8 CMOS/TTL Interfacing

A digital designer selects a "default" logic family to use in a system, based on general requirements of speed, power, cost, and so on. However, the designer may select devices from other families in some cases because of availability or other special requirements. (For example, not all 74LS part numbers are available in 74HCT, and vice versa.) Thus, it's important for a designer to understand the implications of connecting TTL outputs to CMOS inputs, and vice versa.

There are several factors to consider in TTL/CMOS interfacing, and the first is noise margin. The LOW-state DC noise margin depends on V_{OLmax} of the driving output and V_{ILmax} of the driven input, and equals $V_{ILmax} - V_{OLmax}$. Similarly, the HIGH-state DC noise margin equals $V_{OHmin} - V_{IHmin}$. Figure 3-76 shows the relevant numbers for TTL and CMOS families.

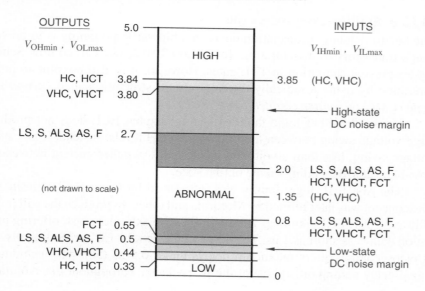

Figure 3-76
Output and input levels for interfacing TTL and CMOS families. (Note that HC and VHC inputs are not TTL compatible.)

For example, the LOW-state DC noise margin of HC or HCT driving TTL is 0.8 − 0.33 = 0.47 V, and the HIGH-state is 3.84 − 2.0 =1.84 V. On the other hand, the HIGH-state margin of TTL driving HC or VHC is 2.7 − 3.85 = −1.15 V. In other words, TTL driving HC or AC doesn't work, unless the TTL HIGH output happens to be higher and the CMOS HIGH input threshold happens to be lower by a total of 1.15 V compared to their worst-case specs. To drive CMOS inputs properly from TTL outputs, the CMOS devices should be HCT, VHCT, or FCT rather than HC or VHC.

The next factor to consider is fanout. As with pure TTL (Section 3.10.5), a designer must sum the input current requirements of devices driven by an output and compare with the output's capabilities in both states. Fanout is not a problem when TTL drives CMOS, since CMOS inputs require almost no current in either state. On the other hand, TTL inputs, especially in the LOW state, require substantial current, especially compared to HC and HCT output capabilities. For example, an HC or HCT output can drive ten LS or only two S-TTL inputs.

The last factor is capacitive loading. We've seen that load capacitance increases both the delay and the power dissipation of logic circuits. Increases in delay are especially noticeable with HC and HCT outputs, whose transition times increase about 1 ns for each 5 pF of load capacitance. The transistors in FCT outputs have very low "on" resistances, so their transition times increase only about 0.1 ns for each 5 pF of load capacitance.

For a given load capacitance, power-supply voltage, and application, all of the CMOS families have similar dynamic power dissipation, since each variable in the CV^2f equation is the same. On the other hand, TTL outputs have somewhat lower dynamic power dissipation, since the voltage swing between TTL HIGH and LOW levels is smaller.

*3.10.9 Emitter-Coupled Logic

The key to reducing propagation delay in a bipolar logic family is to prevent a gate's transistors from saturating. In Section 3.10.2, we learned how Schottky diodes prevent saturation in TTL gates. However, it is also possible to prevent saturation by using a radically different circuit structure, called *current-mode logic (CML)* or *emitter-coupled logic (ECL)*.

current-mode logic (CML)

emitter-coupled logic (ECL)

Unlike the other logic families in this chapter, ECL does not produce a large voltage swing between the LOW and HIGH levels. Instead, it has a small voltage swing, less than a volt, and it internally switches current between two possible paths, depending on the output state.

The first ECL logic family was introduced by General Electric in 1961. The concept was later refined by Motorola and others to produce the still popular 10K and 100K ECL families. These families are extremely fast, offering propagation delays as short as 1 ns. The newest ECL family, ECLinPS (literally, ECL in picoseconds), offers maximum delays under 0.5 ns (500 ps), including the signal delay getting on and off of the IC package. Throughout the evolution of digital circuit technology, some type of ECL has always been the fastest technology for discrete, packaged logic components.

Still, commercial ECL families aren't nearly as popular as CMOS and TTL, mainly because they consume much more power. In fact, high power consumption made the design of ECL supercomputers, such as the Cray-1 and Cray-2, as much of a challenge in cooling technology as in digital design. Also, ECL has a poor speed-power product, does not provide a high level of integration, has fast edge rates requiring design for transmission-line effects in most applications, and is not directly compatible with TTL and CMOS. Nevertheless, ECL still finds its place as a logic and interface technology in very high-speed communications gear, including fiber-optic transceiver interfaces for gigabit Ethernet and Asynchronous Transfer Mode (ATM) networks.

The basic idea of current-mode logic is illustrated by the inverter/buffer circuit in Figure 3-77. This circuit has both an inverting output (OUT1) and a noninverting output (OUT2). Two transistors are connected as a *differential amplifier* with a common emitter resistor. The supply voltages for this example are $V_{CC} = 5.0$, $V_{BB} = 4.0$, and $V_{EE} = 0$ V, and the input LOW and HIGH levels are defined to be 3.6 and 4.4 V. This circuit actually produces output LOW and HIGH levels that are 0.6 V higher (4.2 and 5.0 V), but this is corrected in real ECL circuits.

differential amplifier

When V_{IN} is HIGH, as shown in the figure, transistor $Q1$ is on, but not saturated, and transistor $Q2$ is OFF. This is true because of a careful choice of resistor values and voltage levels. Thus, V_{OUT2} is pulled to 5.0 V (HIGH) through $R2$, and it can be shown that the voltage drop across $R1$ is about 0.8 V, so that V_{OUT1} is about 4.2 V (LOW).

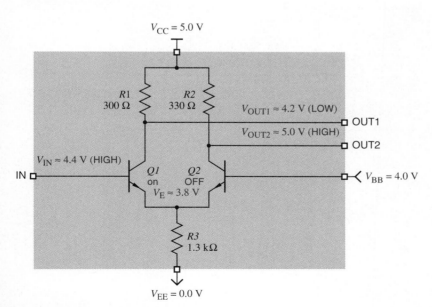

Figure 3-77
Basic ECL inverter/buffer circuit with input HIGH.

When V_{IN} is LOW, as shown in Figure 3-78, transistor $Q2$ is on, but not saturated, and transistor $Q1$ is OFF. Thus, V_{OUT1} is pulled to 5.0 V through $R1$, and it can be shown that V_{OUT2} is about 4.2 V.

differential outputs

The outputs of this inverter are called *differential outputs* because they are always complementary, and it is possible to determine the output state by looking at the difference between the output voltages ($V_{OUT1} - V_{OUT2}$) rather than their absolute values. That is, the output is 1 if ($V_{OUT1} - V_{OUT2}$) > 0, and it is 0 if ($V_{OUT1} - V_{OUT2}$) < 0. It is possible to build input circuits with two wires per logical input that define the logical signal value in this way; these are called

differential inputs

differential inputs.

Differential signals are used in most ECL "interfacing" and "clock distribution" applications because of their low skew and high noise immunity. They are "low skew" because the timing of a 0-to-1 or 1-to-0 transition does not depend critically on voltage thresholds, which may change with temperature or between devices. Instead, the timing depends only on when the voltages cross over relative to each other. Similarly, the "relative" definition of 0 and 1 provides outstanding noise immunity, since noise created in the power supply distribution

common-mode signal

or coupled from external sources tends to be a *common-mode signal* that affects both differential signals similarly, leaving the difference value unchanged.

single-ended input

It is also possible, of course, to determine the logic value by sensing the absolute voltage level of one input signal, called a *single-ended input.* Single-ended signals are used in most ECL "logic" applications to avoid the obvious

Figure 3-78
Basic ECL inverter/buffer
circuit with input LOW.

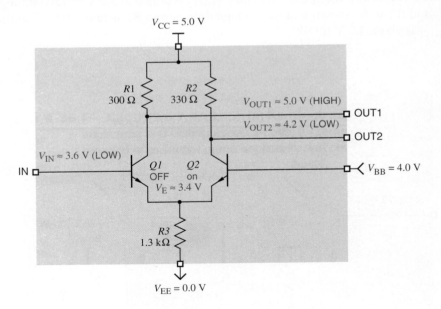

expense of doubling the number of signal lines. The basic CML inverter in Figure 3-77 and 3-78 has a single-ended input. It always has both "outputs" available internally; the circuit is actually either an inverter or a noninverting buffer, depending on whether we use OUT1 or OUT2.

To perform logic with the basic circuit of Figure 3-78, we place additional transistors in parallel with $Q1$. For example, Figure 3-79 shows a 2-input ECL OR/NOR gate. If any input is HIGH, the corresponding input transistor is active, and V_{OUT1} is LOW (NOR output). At the same time, $Q3$ is OFF, and V_{OUT2} is HIGH (OR output).

Additional information on ECL circuits can be found at DDPPonline in Section ECL. This includes a discussion of the common ECL families—10K and 100K—as well as positive ECL (PECL) operation.

Figure 3-79 ECL 2-input OR/NOR gate: (a) circuit diagram; (b) function table; (c) logic symbol; (d) truth table.

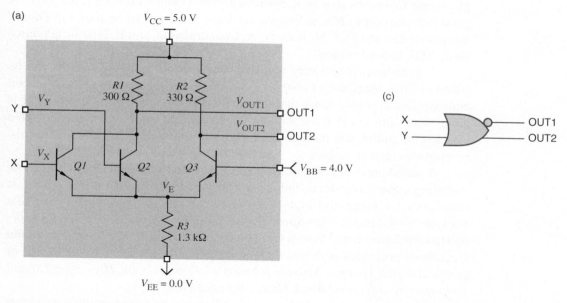

(b)

X	Y	V_X	V_Y	$Q1$	$Q2$	$Q3$	V_E	V_{OUT1}	V_{OUT2}	OUT1	OUT2
L	L	3.6	3.6	OFF	OFF	on	3.4	5.0	4.2	H	L
L	H	3.6	4.4	OFF	on	OFF	3.8	4.2	5.0	L	H
H	L	4.4	3.6	on	OFF	OFF	3.8	4.2	5.0	L	H
H	H	4.4	4.4	on	on	OFF	3.8	4.2	5.0	L	H

(d)

X	Y	OUT1	OUT2
0	0	1	0
0	1	0	1
1	0	0	1
1	1	0	1

References

Students who need to study the basics may wish to consult "Electrical Circuits Review" by Bruce M. Fleischer. This 20-page tutorial covers all of the basic circuit concepts that are used in this chapter. It appears both as an appendix in this book's first edition and as a .pdf file in <u>Section Elec</u> at <u>DDPPonline</u>.

After seeing the results of last few decades' amazing pace of development in digital electronics, it's easy to forget that logic circuits had an important place in technologies that came before the transistor. In Chapter 5 of *Introduction to the Methodology of Switching Circuits* (Van Nostrand, 1972), George J. Klir shows how logic can be (and has been) performed by a variety of physical devices, including relays, vacuum tubes, and pneumatic systems.

For another perspective on the electronics material in this chapter, you can consult almost any modern electronics text. Many contain a much more analytical discussion of digital circuit operation; for example, see *Introduction to Electronic Circuit Design* by R. Spencer and M. Ghausi (Prentice Hall, 2003). A good introduction to ICs and important logic families can be found in *Digital Integrated Circuits* by J. M. Rabaey, A. Chandrakasan, and B. Nikolic (Prentice Hall, 2003, second edition).

A light-hearted and very readable introduction to digital circuits can be found in Clive Maxfield's *Bebop to the Boolean Boogie* (Newnes, 2002, second edition). Some people think that the seafood gumbo recipe in Appendix H is alone worth the price! Even without the recipe, the book is a well-illustrated classic that guides you through the basics of digital electronics fundamentals, components, and processes.

A sound understanding of the electrical aspects of digital circuit operation, including capacitive effects, inductive effects, and transmission-line effects, is mandatory for successful high-speed circuit design. Unquestionably the best book on this subject is *High-Speed Digital Design: A Handbook of Black Magic*, by Howard Johnson and Martin Graham (Prentice Hall, 1993). It combines solid electronics principles with tremendous insight and experience in the design of practical digital systems. Also see Johnson's follow-on book, *High-Speed Signal Propagation: Advanced Black Magic* (Prentice Hall, 2003).

Characteristics of today's logic families can be found in the data sheets published by the device manufacturers. Old-time digital designers are proud of their collections of thick databooks published by the device manufacturers, but nowadays all of the latest specs can be found on the Web. Among the better sites for logic-family data sheets and design application notes are www.ti.com (Texas Instruments), www.philips.com, and www.fairchildsemi.com.

The JEDEC (Joint Electron Device Engineering Council) standards for digital logic levels can be found on JEDEC's web site, www.jedec.org. The JEDEC standards for 3.3-V, 2.5-V, 1.8-V, and 1.5-V logic were published in 1994, 1995, 1997, and 2001, respectively.

Drill Problems

3.1   The Stub Series Terminated low Voltage Logic (SSTV) family, used for SDRAM modules, defines a LOW signal to be in the range 0.0–0.7 V and a HIGH signal to be in the range 1.7–2.5 V. Under a positive-logic convention, indicate the logic value associated with each of the following signal levels:

   (a)   0.0 V   (b)   0.7 V   (c)   1.7 V   (d)   −0.6 V
   (e)   1.6 V   (f)   −2.0 V   (g)   2.5 V   (h)   3.3 V

3.2   Repeat Drill 3.1 using a negative-logic convention.

3.3   Discuss how a logic buffer amplifier is different from an audio amplifier.

3.4   Is a buffer amplifier equivalent to a 1-input AND gate or a 1-input OR gate?

3.5   True or false: For a given set of input values, a NAND gate produces the opposite output as an OR gate with inverted inputs.

3.6   Write two completely different definitions of "gate" used in this chapter.

3.7   How many transistors are used in a 2-input CMOS NAND gate? How many of each type are used?

3.8   (Hobbyists only.) Draw an equivalent circuit for a CMOS NAND gate using two single-pole, double-throw relays.

3.9   For a given silicon area, which is likely to be faster, a CMOS NAND gate or a CMOS NOR?

3.10   Define "fan-in" and "fanout." Which one are you likely to have to calculate?

3.11   The circuit in Figure X3.11(a) is a type of CMOS AND-OR-INVERT gate. Write a function table for this circuit in the style of Figure 3-15(b), and a corresponding logic diagram using AND and OR gates and inverters.

3.12   The circuit in Figure X3.11(b) is a type of CMOS OR-AND-INVERT gate. Write a function table for this circuit in the style of Figure 3-15(b), and a corresponding logic diagram using AND and OR gates and inverters.

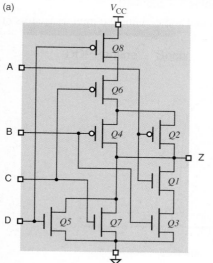

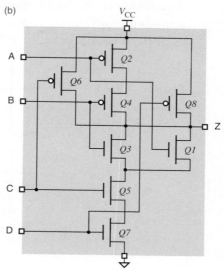

Figure X3.11

3.13   Draw the circuit diagram, function table, and logic symbol for a 3-input CMOS NOR gate in the style of Figure 3-16.

3.14   Draw switch models in the style of Figure 3-14 for a 2-input CMOS NOR gate for all four input combinations.

3.15   Draw a circuit diagram, function table, and logic symbol for a CMOS OR gate in the style of Figure 3-19.

3.16   Which has fewer transistors, a CMOS inverting gate or a noninverting gate?

3.17   Name and draw the logic symbols of four different 3-input CMOS gates that each use six transistors.

3.18   Which 8-input CMOS gate would you expect to be faster, NAND or AND? Why?

3.19   How is it that perfume can be bad for digital designers?

3.20   Using the data sheet in Table 3-3, determine the worst-case LOW-state and HIGH-state DC noise margins of the 74HC00. State any assumptions required by your answer.

3.21   How much high-state DC noise margin is available in an inverter whose transfer characteristic under worst-case conditions is shown in Figure X3.21? How much low-state DC noise margin is available? (Assume 1.5-V and 3.5-V thresholds for LOW and HIGH.)

3.22   Section 3.5 defines seven different electrical parameters for CMOS circuits. Using the data sheet in Table 3-3, determine the worst-case value of each of these for the 74HC00. State any assumptions required by your answer.

3.23   Based on the conventions and definitions in Section 3.4, if the current at a device output is specified as a negative number, is the output sourcing current or sinking current?

3.24   Across the range of valid HIGH input levels, 3.15–5.0 V, at what input level would you expect the 74HC00 (Table 3-3) to consume the most power?

3.25   Determine the LOW-state and HIGH-state DC fanout of the 74HC00 when it drives 74ALS00-like inputs. (Refer to Tables 3-3 and 3-10.)

3.26   Estimate the "on" resistances of the p-channel and n-channel output transistors of the 74HC00 using information in Table 3-3.

Figure X3.21

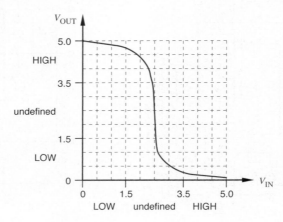

3.27 For each of the following resistive loads, determine whether the output drive specifications of the 74HC00 over the commercial operating range are exceeded. Refer to Table 3-3, and use $V_{OLmax} = 0.33$ V, $V_{OHmin} = 3.84$ V, and $V_{CC} = 5.0$ V. You may not exceed I_{OLmax} or I_{OHmax} in any state.

(a)	120 Ω to V_{CC}	(b)	270 Ω to V_{CC} and 330 Ω to GND
(c)	820 Ω to GND	(d)	470 Ω to V_{CC} and 470 Ω to GND
(e)	1 kΩ to V_{CC}	(f)	1.2 kΩ to V_{CC} and 820 Ω to GND
(g)	4.7 kΩ to V_{CC}	(h)	1.2 kΩ to V_{CC} and 1 kΩ to GND

3.28 Under what circumstances is it safe to allow an unused CMOS input to float?

3.29 Explain "latch up" and the circumstances under which it occurs.

3.30 Explain why replacing small decoupling capacitors to larger ones with larger capacitance may not be a good idea.

3.31 When is it important to hold hands with a friend?

3.32 Name the two components of CMOS logic gate's delay. How are either or both affected by the direction of the output transition?

3.33 Determine the RC time constant for each of the following resistor-capacitor combinations:

(a)	$R = 100$ Ω, $C = 50$ pF	(b)	$R = 4.7$ kΩ, $C = 150$ pF
(c)	$R = 47$ Ω, $C = 47$ pF	(d)	$R = 1$ kΩ, $C = 100$ pF

3.34 Which would you expect to have a bigger effect on the power consumption of a CMOS circuit, a 5% increase in power-supply voltage or a 5% increase in internal and load capacitance?

3.35 Explain why the number of CMOS inputs connected to the output of a CMOS gate generally is not limited by DC fanout considerations.

3.36 It is possible to operate 74VHC CMOS devices with a 2.5-volt power supply. How much power does this typically save, compared to 5-volt operation?

3.37 A particular Schmitt-trigger inverter has $V_{ILmax} = 0.8$ V, $V_{IHmin} = 2.0$ V, $V_{T+} = 1.7$ V, and $V_{T-} = 1.2$ V. How much hysteresis does it have?

3.38 What would happen if three-state outputs turned on faster than they turned off?

3.39 Discuss the pros and cons of larger vs. smaller pull-up resistors for open-drain CMOS outputs.

3.40 A particular LED has a voltage drop of about 2.0 V in the "on" state and requires about 5 mA of current for normal brightness. Determine an appropriate value for the pull-up resistor when the LED is connected to a 74AC00 NAND gate as shown in Figure 3-54(a).

3.41 How does the answer for Drill 3.40 change if the LED only requires 2 mA and is connected to a 74HC00 as shown in Figure 3-54(b)?

3.42 A wired-AND function is obtained simply by tying two open-drain or open-collector outputs together, without going through another level of transistor circuitry. How is it, then, that a wired-AND function can actually be slower than a discrete AND gate?

3.43   Which CMOS or TTL logic family in this chapter has the strongest output driving capability?

3.44   Concisely summarize the difference between HC and ACT logic families.

3.45   Why don't the specifications for FCT devices include parameters like V_{OLmaxC} that apply to CMOS loads, as HCT and ACT specifications do?

3.46   How do FCT-T devices reduce power consumption compared to FCT devices?

3.47   How many diodes are required for an n-input diode AND gate?

3.48   Are TTL outputs more capable of sinking current or sourcing current?

3.49   Compute the maximum fanout for each of the following cases of a TTL output driving multiple TTL inputs. Also indicate how much "excess" driving capability is available in the LOW or HIGH state for each case.

    (a)   74LS driving 74AS   (b)   74LS driving 74F

    (c)   74F driving 74LS   (d)   74F driving 74AS

    (e)   74AS driving 74S   (f)   74S driving 74ALS

    (g)   74ALS driving 74S   (h)   74F driving 74F

3.50   Which resistor dissipates more power, the pull-down for an unused LS-TTL NOR-gate input, or the pull-up for an unused LS-TTL NAND-gate input? Use the maximum allowable resistor value in each case.

3.51   Which would you expect to be faster, a CMOS AND gate or a CMOS AND-OR-INVERT gate, assuming all transistors switch at the same speed? Why?

3.52   Describe the key benefit of Schottky transistors in TTL.

3.53   Using the data sheet from the Texas Instruments (www.ti.com), determine the worst-case LOW-state and HIGH-state DC noise margins of the 74ALS00.

3.54   Sections 3.10.4 and 3.10.5 define eight different electrical parameters for TTL circuits. Using the data sheet from Texas Instruments (www.ti.com), determine the worst-case value of each of these for the 74ALS00.

3.55   For each of the following resistive loads, determine whether the output drive specifications of the 74LS00 over the commercial operating range are exceeded. (Refer to Table 3-11, and use $V_{OLmax} = 0.5$ V and $V_{CC} = 5.0$ V.)

    (a)   470 Ω to V_{CC} (b)   330 Ω to V_{CC} and 470 Ω to GND

    (c)   6.8 kΩ to GND   (d)   910 Ω to V_{CC} and 1200 Ω to GND

    (e)   620 Ω to V_{CC} (f)   510 Ω to V_{CC} and 470 Ω to GND

    (g)   5.1 kΩ to GND   (h)   464 Ω to V_{CC} and 510 Ω to GND

3.56   Compute the LOW-state and HIGH-state DC noise margins for each of the following cases of a TTL output driving a TTL-compatible CMOS input, or vice versa.

    (a)   74HCT driving 74LS   (b)   74ALS driving 74HCT

    (c)   74AS driving 74VHCT   (d)   74VHCT driving 74F

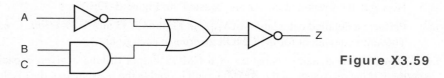

Figure X3.59

3.57 Compute the maximum fanout for each of the following cases of a TTL-compatible CMOS output driving multiple inputs in a TTL logic family. Also indicate how much "excess" driving capability is available in the LOW or HIGH state for each case.

(a) 74HCT driving 74LS   (b) 74VHCT driving 74S

(c) 74VHCT driving 74ALS (d) 74HCT driving 74AS

3.58 For a given load capacitance and transition rate, which logic family in this chapter has the highest dynamic power dissipation? How does it compare to the family with the lowest dynamic power dissipation?

Exercises

3.59 Design a CMOS circuit that has the functional behavior shown in Figure X3.59. (*Hint:* Only eight transistors are required.)

3.60 Design a CMOS circuit that has the functional behavior shown in Figure X3.60. (*Hint:* Only eight transistors are required.)

3.61 Draw a circuit diagram, function table, and logic symbol in the style of Figure 3-19 for a CMOS gate with two inputs A and B and an output Z, where Z=1 if A=0 and B=1, and Z=0 otherwise. (*Hint:* Only six transistors are needed.)

3.62 Draw a circuit diagram, function table, and logic symbol in the style of Figure 3-19 for a CMOS gate with two inputs A and B and an output Z, where Z=0 if A=1 and B=0, and Z=1 otherwise. (*Hint:* Only six transistors are needed.)

3.63 Draw a figure showing the logical structure of an 8-input CMOS NAND gate, assuming that at most 4-input NAND and 2-input NOR gate circuits are practical. Using your general knowledge of CMOS characteristics, select a circuit structure that minimizes the NAND gate's propagation delay for a given silicon area, and explain why this is so.

3.64 The circuit designers of TTL-compatible CMOS families presumably could have made the voltage drop across the "on" transistor under load in the HIGH state as little as it is in the LOW state, simply by making the *p*-channel transistors bigger. Why do you suppose they didn't bother to do this?

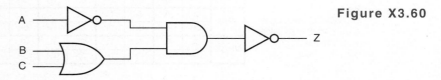

Figure X3.60

3.65   How much current and power are "wasted" in Figure 3-32(b)?

3.66   Perform a detailed calculation of V_{OUT} in Figures 3-33 and 3-34. (*Hint:* Create a Thévenin equivalent for the CMOS inverter in each figure.)

3.67   Consider the dynamic behavior of a CMOS output driving a given capacitive load. If the resistance of the charging path is double the resistance of the discharging path, is the rise time exactly twice the fall time? If not, what other factors affect the transition times?

3.68   Analyze the fall time of the CMOS inverter output of Figure 3-37 with $R_L = 900\,\Omega$ and $V_L = 2.0$ V. Compare your result with the result in Section 3.6.1 and explain.

3.69   Repeat Exercise 3.68 for rise time.

3.70   Assuming that the transistors in an FCT CMOS three-state buffer are perfect zero-delay on-off devices that switch at an input threshold of 1.5 V, determine the value of t_{PLZ} for the test circuit and waveforms in Figure 3-24. (*Hint:* You have to determine the time using an RC time constant.)

3.71   Repeat Exercise 3.70 for t_{PHZ}.

3.72   Using the specifications in Table 3-7, estimate the "on" resistances of the p-channel and n-channel transistors in 74HCT-series CMOS logic.

3.73   Create a $4 \times 4 \times 2 \times 2$ matrix of worst-case DC noise margins for the following CMOS interfacing situations: an (HC, HCT, VHC, or VHCT) output driving an (HC, HCT, VHC, or VHCT) input with a (CMOS, TTL) load in the (LOW, HIGH) state; Figure X3.73 illustrates. (*Hints:* There are 64 different combinations, but many give identical results. Some combinations yield negative margins.)

3.74   The 74LVC00 is capable of being driven by up to 5.5 V, even when it is operating at only 1.8 V. Using Figure 3-62, determine the DC noise margins when a 74LVC00 is driven by a) 3.3-V CMOS, and b) 2.5-V CMOS.

3.75   Using Figure 3-62, determine the DC noise margins for 5-V-tolerant, 3.3-V CMOS driving 5-V CMOS logic with TTL input levels, and vice versa.

3.76   Using Figure 3-62, determine the DC noise margins for 3.3-V-tolerant, 2.5-V CMOS driving 3.3-V CMOS, and vice versa.

3.77   Using Figure 3-62, determine the DC noise margins for a) 2.5-V CMOS driving itself, and b) 1.8-V CMOS driving itself.

Figure X3.73

Key:
CL = CMOS load, LOW
CH = CMOS load, HIGH
TL = TTL load, LOW
TH = TTL load, HIGH

Output

		Input							
		HC		HCT		VHC		VHCT	
HC		CL	TL	CL	TL	CL	TL	CL	TL
		CH	TH	CH	TH	CH	TH	CH	TH
HCT		CL	TL	CL	TL	CL	TL	CL	TL
		CH	TH	CH	TH	CH	TH	CH	TH
VHC		CL	TL	CL	TL	CL	TL	CL	TL
		CH	TH	CH	TH	CH	TH	CH	TH
VHCT		CL	TL	CL	TL	CL	TL	CL	TL
		CH	TH	CH	TH	CH	TH	CH	TH

3.78   In the LED example in Section 3.7.5, a designer chose a resistor value of 390 Ω and found that the open-drain gate was able to maintain its output at 0.3 V while driving the LED. How much current flows through the LED, and how much power is dissipated by the pull-up resistor in this case?

3.79   Consider a CMOS 8-bit binary counter (Section 8.4) clocked at 16 MHz. For the purpose of computing the counter's dynamic power dissipation, what is the transition frequency of the least significant bit? Of the most significant bit? For the purpose of determining the dynamic power dissipation of the eight output bits, what frequency should be used?

3.80   Using only AND and NOR gates, draw a logic diagram for the logic function performed by the circuit in Figure 3-56.

3.81   Calculate the approximate output voltage at Z in Figure 3-57, assuming that the gates are HCT-series CMOS.

3.82   Redraw the circuit diagram of a CMOS 3-state buffer in Figure 3-49 using actual transistors instead of NAND, NOR, and inverter symbols. Can you find a circuit for the same function that requires a smaller total number of transistors? If so, draw it.

3.83   Modify the CMOS 3-state buffer circuit in Figure 3-49 so that the output is in the High-Z state when the enable input is HIGH. The modified circuit should require no more transistors than the original.

3.84   Using information in Table 3-3, estimate how much current can flow through each output pin if the outputs of two different 74HC00s are fighting.

3.85   Show that at a given power-supply voltage, an FCT-type I_{CCD} specification can be derived from an HCT/ACT-type C_{PD} specification, and vice versa.

3.86   A digital designer found a problem in a certain circuit's function after the circuit had been released to production and 1000 copies of it built. A portion of the circuit is shown in Figure X3.86 in black; all of the gates are 74HCT00 NAND gates. The digital designer fixed the problem by adding the two diodes shown in color. What do the diodes do? Describe both the logical effects of this change on the circuit's function and the electrical effects on the circuit's noise margins.

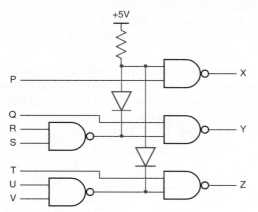

Figure X3.86

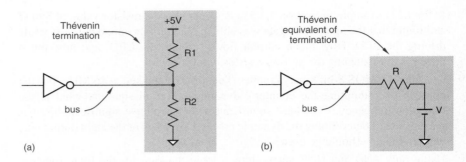

Figure X3.87   (a)   (b)

3.87 A *Thévenin termination* for an open-collector or three-state bus has the structure shown in Figure X3.87(a). The idea is that, with appropriate values of *R1* and *R2*, this circuit is equivalent to the termination in (b) for any desired values of *V* and *R*. The value of *V* determines the voltage on the bus when no device is driving it, and the value of *R* is selected to match the characteristic impedance of the bus for transmission-line purposes (<u>Section Zo</u> at <u>DDPPonline</u>). For each of the following pairs of *V* and *R*, determine the required values of *R1* and *R2*.

(a) $V = 3.0, R = 120$ (b) $V = 2.7, R = 179$

(c) $V = 2.4, R = 150$ (d) $V = 1.5, R = 50$

3.88 For each of the *R1* and *R2* pairs in Exercise 3.87, determine whether the termination can be properly driven by a three-state output in each of the following logic families: 74LS, 74S, 74FCT-T. For proper operation, the family's I_{OL} and I_{OH} specs must not be exceeded when $V_{OL} = V_{OLmax}$ and $V_{OH} = V_{OHmin}$, respectively.

3.89 Determine the total power dissipation of the circuit in Figure X3.89 as function of transition frequency *f* for two realizations: (a) using 74LS gates; (b) using 74HC gates. Assume that input capacitance is 3 pF for a TTL gate and 7 pF for a CMOS gate, that a 74LS gate has an internal power-dissipation capacitance of 20 pF, and that there is an additional 20 pF of stray wiring capacitance in the circuit. Also assume that the X, Y, and Z inputs are always HIGH, and that input C is driven with a CMOS-level square wave with frequency *f*. Other information that you need for this problem can be found in Tables 3-5 and 3-10. State any other assumptions that you make. At what frequency does the TTL circuit dissipate less power than the CMOS circuit?

3.90 Find a commercially available 74-series device with a very long part number, based on the logic family and the device number, but excluding the package type, temperature range, and so on. You should be able to beat 74ALVCH16244.

Figure X3.89

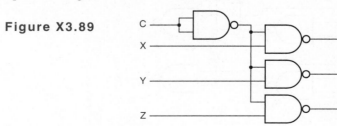

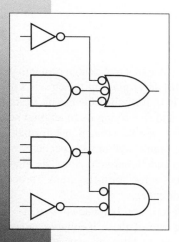

chapter 4

Combinational
Logic Design Principles

L ogic circuits are classified into two types, "combinational" and "sequential." A *combinational logic circuit* is one whose outputs depend only on its current inputs. The rotary channel selector knob on an old-fashioned television is like a combinational circuit—its "output" selects a channel based only on the current position of the knob ("input").

The outputs of a *sequential logic circuit* depend not only on the current inputs but also on the past sequence of inputs, possibly arbitrarily far back in time. The channel selector controlled by the up and down pushbuttons on a TV remote control is a sequential circuit—the channel selection depends on the past sequence of up/down pushes, at least since when you started viewing 10 hours before, and perhaps as far back as when you first powered up the device. Sequential circuits are discussed in Chapters 7 and 8.

A combinational circuit may contain an arbitrary number of logic gates and inverters but no feedback loops. A *feedback loop* is a signal path of a circuit that allows the output of a gate to propagate back to the input of that same gate; such a loop generally creates sequential circuit behavior.

In combinational circuit *analysis* we start with a logic diagram and proceed to a formal description of the function performed by that circuit, such as a truth table or a logic expression. In *synthesis* we do the reverse, starting with a formal description and proceeding to a logic diagram.

SYNTHESIS VS. DESIGN

Logic circuit design is a superset of synthesis, since in a real design problem we usually start out with an informal (word or thought) description of the circuit. Often the most challenging and creative part of design is to formalize the circuit description, defining the circuit's input and output signals and specifying its functional behavior by means of truth tables and equations. Once we've created the formal circuit description, we can usually follow a "turn-the-crank" synthesis procedure to obtain a logic diagram for a circuit with the required functional behavior. The material in the first four sections of this chapter is the basis for "turn-the-crank" procedures, whether the crank is turned by hand or by a computer.

The next chapter describes hardware description languages—ABEL, VHDL and Verilog. When we create a design using one of these languages, a computer program can perform the synthesis steps for us. In later chapters we'll encounter many examples of the real design process.

Combinational circuits may have one or more outputs. In this chapter, we'll discuss methods that apply to single-output circuits. Most analysis and synthesis techniques can be extended in an obvious way from single-output to multiple-output circuits (e.g., "Repeat these steps for each output"). Some techniques can be extended in a not-so-obvious way for improved effectiveness in the multiple-output case.

The purpose of this chapter is to give you a solid theoretical foundation for the analysis and synthesis of combinational logic circuits, a foundation that will be doubly important later when we move on to sequential circuits. Although most of the analysis and synthesis procedures in this chapter are automated nowadays by computer-aided design tools, you need a basic understanding of the fundamentals to use the tools and to figure out what's wrong when you get unexpected or undesirable results.

Before launching into a discussion of combinational logic circuits, we must introduce switching algebra, the fundamental mathematical tool for analyzing and synthesizing logic circuits of all types.

4.1 Switching Algebra

Boolean algebra

Formal analysis techniques for digital circuits have their roots in the work of an English mathematician, George Boole. In 1854, he invented a two-valued algebraic system, now called *Boolean algebra*, to "give expression ... to the fundamental laws of reasoning in the symbolic language of a Calculus." Using this system, a philosopher, logician, or inhabitant of the planet Vulcan can formulate propositions that are true or false, combine them to make new propositions, and determine the truth or falsehood of the new propositions. For example, if we agree that "People who haven't studied this material are either failures or not nerds," and "No computer designer is a failure," then we can answer questions like "If you're a nerdy computer designer, then have you already studied this?"

Long after Boole, in 1938, Bell Labs researcher Claude E. Shannon showed how to adapt Boolean algebra to analyze and describe the behavior of circuits built from relays, the most commonly used digital logic elements of that time. In Shannon's *switching algebra*, the condition of a relay contact, open or closed, is represented by a variable X that can have one of two possible values, 0 or 1. In today's logic technologies, these values correspond to a wide variety of physical conditions—voltage HIGH or LOW, light off or on, capacitor discharged or charged, fuse blown or intact, and so on—as we detailed in Table 3-1 on page 81.

switching algebra

In the remainder of this section we develop the switching algebra directly, using "first principles" and what we already know about the behavior of logic elements (gates and inverters). For more historical and/or mathematical treatments of this material, consult the References section of this chapter.

4.1.1 Axioms

In switching algebra we use a symbolic variable, such as X, to represent the condition of a logic signal. A logic signal is in one of two possible conditions— low or high, off or on, and so on, depending on the technology. We say that X has the value "0" for one of these conditions and "1" for the other.

For example, with the CMOS and TTL logic circuits in Chapter 3, the *positive-logic convention* dictates that we associate the value "0" with a LOW voltage and "1" with a HIGH voltage. The *negative-logic convention* makes the opposite association: 0 = HIGH and 1 = LOW. However, the choice of positive or negative logic has no effect on our ability to develop a consistent algebraic description of circuit behavior; it only affects details of the physical-to-algebraic abstraction, as we'll explain later in our discussion of "duality." For the moment, we may ignore the physical realities of logic circuits and pretend that they operate directly on the logic symbols 0 and 1.

positive-logic convention

negative-logic convention

The *axioms* (or *postulates*) of a mathematical system are a minimal set of basic definitions that we assume to be true, from which all other information about the system can be derived. The first two axioms of switching algebra embody the "digital abstraction" by formally stating that a variable X can take on only one of two values:

axiom

postulate

$$\text{(A1)} \quad X = 0 \quad \text{if } X \neq 1 \qquad \text{(A1}') \quad X = 1 \quad \text{if } X \neq 0$$

Notice that we stated these axioms as a pair, the only difference between A1 and A1' being the interchange of the symbols 0 and 1. This is a characteristic of all the axioms of switching algebra and is the basis of the "duality" principle that we'll study later.

complement
prime (')

In Section 3.3.3 we showed the design of an inverter, a logic circuit whose output signal level is the opposite (or *complement*) of its input signal level. We use a *prime (')* to denote an inverter's function. That is, if a variable X denotes an inverter's input signal, then X′ denotes the value of a signal on the inverter's output. This notation is formally specified in the second pair of axioms:

(A2)   If X = 0, then X′ = 1   (A2′)   If X = 1, then X′ = 0

algebraic operator
expression
NOT operation

As shown in Figure 4-1, the output of an inverter with input signal X may have an arbitrary signal name, say Y. Algebraically, however, we write Y = X′ to say "signal Y always has the opposite value as signal X." The prime (′) is an *algebraic operator*, and X′ is an *expression*, which you can read as "X prime" or "NOT X." This usage is analogous to what you've learned in programming languages, where if J is an integer variable, then −J is an expression whose value is 0 − J. Although this may seem like a small point, you'll learn that the distinction between signal names (X, Y), expressions (X′), and equations (Y = X′) is very important when we study documentation standards and software tools for logic design. In the logic diagrams in this book we maintain this distinction by writing signal names in black and expressions in color.

Figure 4-1
Signal naming and algebraic
notation for an inverter.

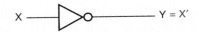

In Section 3.3.6 we showed how to build a 2-input CMOS AND gate, a circuit whose output is 1 if both of its inputs are 1. The function of a 2-input AND gate is sometimes called *logical multiplication* and is symbolized algebraically by a *multiplication dot (·)*. That is, an AND gate with inputs X and Y has an output signal whose value is X · Y, as shown in Figure 4-2(a). Some authors, especially mathematicians and logicians, denote logical multiplication with a wedge (X ∧ Y). We follow standard engineering practice by using the dot (X · Y).

logical multiplication
multiplication dot (·)

**NOTE ON
NOTATION**
The notations X̄, ~X, and ¬X are also used by some authors to denote the complement of X. The overbar notation (X̄) is probably the most widely used and the best looking typographically. However, we use the prime notation to get you used to writing logic expressions on a single text line without the more graphical overbar, and to force you to parenthesize complex complemented subexpressions—because that's what you'll have to do when you use HDLs and other tools.

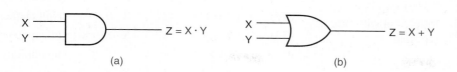

Figure 4-2
Signal naming and
algebraic notation:
(a) AND gate;
(b) OR gate.

Among hardware description languages (HDLs), Verilog uses an ampersand (&) to denote the same thing, while VHDL forces you to write out "and".

We also described in Section 3.3.6 how to build a 2-input CMOS OR gate, a circuit whose output is 1 if either of its inputs is 1. The function of a 2-input OR gate is sometimes called *logical addition* and is symbolized algebraically by a plus sign (+). An OR gate with inputs X and Y has an output signal whose value is $X + Y$, as shown in Figure 4-2(b). Some authors denote logical addition with a vee ($X \vee Y$), but we follow the typical engineering practice of using the plus sign ($X + Y$). Once again, other notations may be used in HDLs, such as "|" in Verilog and "or" in VHDL. By convention, in a logic expression involving both multiplication and addition, multiplication has *precedence*, just as in integer expressions in conventional programming languages. That is, the expression $W \cdot X + Y \cdot Z$ is equivalent to $(W \cdot X) + (Y \cdot Z)$.

logical addition

precedence

The last three pairs of axioms state the formal definitions of the AND and OR operations by listing the output produced by each gate for each possible input combination:

AND operation
OR operation

(A3)	$0 \cdot 0 = 0$	(A3′)	$1 + 1 = 1$
(A4)	$1 \cdot 1 = 1$	(A4′)	$0 + 0 = 0$
(A5)	$0 \cdot 1 = 1 \cdot 0 = 0$	(A5′)	$1 + 0 = 0 + 1 = 1$

The five pairs of axioms, A1–A5 and A1′–A5′, completely define switching algebra. All other facts about the system can be proved using these axioms as a starting point.

JUXT A MINUTE...   Older texts use simple *juxtaposition* (XY) to denote logical multiplication, but we don't. In general, juxtaposition is a clear notation only when signal names are limited to a single character. Otherwise, is XY a logical product or a two-character signal name? One-character variable names are common in algebra, but in real digital design problems we prefer to use multicharacter signal names that mean something. Thus, we need a separator between names, and the separator might just as well be a multiplication dot rather than a space. The HDL equivalent of the multiplication dot (such as "&" and " and " in Verilog and VHDL, respectively) is absolutely required when logic formulas are written in a hardware-description language.

Table 4-1
Switching-algebra theorems with one variable.

(T1)	$X + 0 = X$	(T1′)	$X \cdot 1 = X$	(Identities)
(T2)	$X + 1 = 1$	(T2′)	$X \cdot 0 = 0$	(Null elements)
(T3)	$X + X = X$	(T3′)	$X \cdot X = X$	(Idempotency)
(T4)	$(X')' = X$			(Involution)
(T5)	$X + X' = 1$	(T5′)	$X \cdot X' = 0$	(Complements)

4.1.2 Single-Variable Theorems

During the analysis or synthesis of logic circuits, we often write algebraic expressions that characterize a circuit's actual or desired behavior. Switching-algebra *theorems* are statements, known to be always true, that allow us to manipulate algebraic expressions to allow simpler analysis or more efficient synthesis of the corresponding circuits. For example, the theorem $X + 0 = X$ allows us to substitute every occurrence of $X + 0$ in an expression with X.

theorem

Table 4-1 lists switching-algebra theorems involving a single variable X. How do we know that these theorems are true? We can either prove them ourselves or take the word of someone who has. OK, we're in college now, let's learn how to prove them.

perfect induction

Most theorems in switching algebra are exceedingly simple to prove using a technique called *perfect induction*. Axiom A1 is the key to this technique—since a switching variable can take on only two different values, 0 and 1, we can prove a theorem involving a single variable X by proving that it is true for both $X = 0$ and $X = 1$. For example, to prove theorem T1, we make two substitutions:

$$[X = 0] \quad 0 + 0 = 0 \quad \text{true, according to axiom A4′}$$
$$[X = 1] \quad 1 + 0 = 1 \quad \text{true, according to axiom A5′}$$

All of the theorems in Table 4-1 can be proved using perfect induction, as you're asked to do in the Drills 4.2 and 4.3.

4.1.3 Two- and Three-Variable Theorems

Switching-algebra theorems with two or three variables are listed in Table 4-2. Each of these theorems is easily proved by perfect induction, by evaluating the theorem statement for the four possible combinations of X and Y, or the eight possible combinations of X, Y, and Z.

The first two theorem pairs concern commutativity and associativity of logical addition and multiplication and are identical to the commutative and associative laws for addition and multiplication of integers and reals. Taken together, they indicate that the parenthesization or order of terms in a logical sum or logical product is irrelevant. For example, from a strictly algebraic point of view, an expression such as $W \cdot X \cdot Y \cdot Z$ is ambiguous; it should be written as $(W \cdot (X \cdot (Y \cdot Z)))$ or $(((W \cdot X) \cdot Y) \cdot Z)$ or $(W \cdot X) \cdot (Y \cdot Z)$ (see Exercise 4.26).

Table 4-2 Switching-algebra theorems with two or three variables.

(T6)	$X + Y = Y + X$	(T6')	$X \cdot Y = Y \cdot X$	(Commutativity)
(T7)	$(X + Y) + Z = X + (Y + Z)$	(T7')	$(X \cdot Y) \cdot Z = X \cdot (Y \cdot Z)$	(Associativity)
(T8)	$X \cdot Y + X \cdot Z = X \cdot (Y + Z)$	(T8')	$(X + Y) \cdot (X + Z) = X + Y \cdot Z$	(Distributivity)
(T9)	$X + X \cdot Y = X$	(T9')	$X \cdot (X + Y) = X$	(Covering)
(T10)	$X \cdot Y + X \cdot Y' = X$	(T10')	$(X + Y) \cdot (X + Y') = X$	(Combining)
(T11)	$X \cdot Y + X' \cdot Z + Y \cdot Z = X \cdot Y + X' \cdot Z$			(Consensus)
(T11')	$(X + Y) \cdot (X' + Z) \cdot (Y + Z) = (X + Y) \cdot (X' + Z)$			

But the theorems tell us that the ambiguous form of the expression is OK because we get the same results in any case. We even could have rearranged the order of the variables (e.g., $X \cdot Z \cdot Y \cdot W$) and gotten the same results.

As trivial as this discussion may seem, it is very important, because it forms the theoretical basis for using logic gates with more than two inputs. We defined $\cdot$ and $+$ as *binary operators*—operators that combine *two* variables. Yet we use 3-input, 4-input, and larger AND and OR gates in practice. The theorems tell us we can connect gate inputs in any order; in fact, many printed-circuit-board and ASIC layout programs take advantage of this to optimize wiring. We can use either one n-input gate or $(n-1)$ 2-input gates interchangeably, though propagation delay and cost are likely to be higher with multiple 2-input gates.

binary operator

Theorem T8 is identical to the distributive law for integers and reals—that is, logical multiplication distributes over logical addition. Hence, we can "multiply out" an expression to obtain a sum-of-products form, as in the example below:

$$V \cdot (W + X) \cdot (Y + Z) = V \cdot W \cdot Y + V \cdot W \cdot Z + V \cdot X \cdot Y + V \cdot X \cdot Z$$

However, switching algebra also has the unfamiliar property that the reverse is true—logical addition distributes over logical multiplication—as demonstrated by theorem T8'. Thus, we can also "add out" an expression to obtain a product-of-sums form:

$$(V \cdot W \cdot X) + (Y \cdot Z) = (V + Y) \cdot (V + Z) \cdot (W + Y) \cdot (W + Z) \cdot (X + Y) \cdot (X + Z)$$

Theorems T9 and T10 are used extensively in the minimization of logic functions. For example, if the subexpression $X + X \cdot Y$ appears in a logic expression, the *covering theorem* T9 says that we need only include X in the expression; X is said to *cover* $X \cdot Y$. The *combining theorem* T10 says that if the subexpression $X \cdot Y + X \cdot Y'$ appears in an expression, we can replace it with X. Since Y must be 0 or 1, either way the original subexpression is 1 if and only if X is 1.

covering theorem
cover
combining theorem

Although we could easily prove T9 by perfect induction, the truth of T9 is more obvious if we prove it using the other theorems that we've proved so far:

$$
\begin{aligned}
X + X \cdot Y &= X \cdot 1 + X \cdot Y \quad &&\text{(according to T1')}\\
&= X \cdot (1 + Y) \quad &&\text{(according to T8)}\\
&= X \cdot 1 \quad &&\text{(according to T2)}\\
&= X \quad &&\text{(according to T1')}
\end{aligned}
$$

Likewise, the other theorems can be used to prove T10, where the key step is to use T8 to rewrite the lefthand side as $X \cdot (Y + Y')$.

consensus theorem

consensus

Theorem T11 is known as the *consensus theorem*. The $Y \cdot Z$ term is called the *consensus* of $X \cdot Y$ and $X' \cdot Z$. The idea is that if $Y \cdot Z$ is 1, then either $X \cdot Y$ or $X' \cdot Z$ must also be 1, since Y and Z are both 1 and either X or X' must be 1. Thus, the $Y \cdot Z$ term is redundant and may be dropped from the righthand side of T11. The consensus theorem has two important applications. It can be used to eliminate certain timing hazards in combinational logic circuits, as we'll see in Section 4.4. And it also forms the basis of the iterative-consensus method of finding prime implicants (see Section ProgMin at DDPPonline).

In all of the theorems, it is possible to replace each variable with an arbitrary logic expression. A simple replacement is to complement one or more variables:

$$(X + Y') + Z' = X + (Y' + Z') \quad \text{(based on T7)}$$

But more complex expressions may be substituted as well:

$$(V' + X) \cdot (W \cdot (Y' + Z)) + (V' + X) \cdot (W \cdot (Y' + Z))' = V' + X \quad \text{(based on T10)}$$

4.1.4 *n*-Variable Theorems

Several important theorems, listed in Table 4-3, are true for an arbitrary number of variables, n. Most of these theorems can be proved using a two-step method called *finite induction*—first proving that the theorem is true for $n = 2$ (the *basis step*) and then proving that if the theorem is true for $n = i$, then it is also true for $n = i + 1$ (the *induction step*). For example, consider the generalized idempotency theorem T12. For $n = 2$, T12 is equivalent to T3 and is therefore true. If it is true for a logical sum of i X's, then it is also true for a sum of $i + 1$ X's, according to the following reasoning:

finite induction

basis step

induction step

$$
\begin{aligned}
X + X + X + \cdots + X &= X + (X + X + \cdots + X) \quad &&(i + 1 \text{ X's on either side})\\
&= X + (X) \quad &&(\text{if T12 is true for } n = i)\\
&= X \quad &&(\text{according to T3})
\end{aligned}
$$

Thus, the theorem is true for all finite values of n.

DeMorgan's theorems

DeMorgan's theorems (T13 and T13') are probably the most commonly used of all the theorems of switching algebra. Theorem T13 says that an n-input

Table 4-3 Switching-algebra theorems with n variables.

(T12)	$X + X + \cdots + X = X$	(Generalized idempotency)
(T12′)	$X \cdot X \cdot \ \cdots \ \cdot X = X$	
(T13)	$(X_1 \cdot X_2 \cdot \ \cdots \ \cdot X_n)' = X_1' + X_2' + \cdots + X_n'$	(DeMorgan's theorems)
(T13′)	$(X_1 + X_2 + \cdots + X_n)' = X_1' \cdot X_2' \cdot \ \cdots \ \cdot X_n'$	
(T14)	$[F(X_1, X_2, \ldots, X_n, +, \cdot)]' = F(X_1', X_2', \ldots, X_n', \cdot, +)$	(Generalized DeMorgan's theorem)
(T15)	$F(X_1, X_2, \ldots, X_n) = X_1 \cdot F(1, X_2, \ldots, X_n) + X_1' \cdot F(0, X_2, \ldots, X_n)$	(Shannon's expansion theorems)
(T15′)	$F(X_1, X_2, \ldots, X_n) = [X_1 + F(0, X_2, \ldots, X_n)] \cdot [X_1' + F(1, X_2, \ldots, X_n)]$	

AND gate whose output is complemented is equivalent to an n-input OR gate whose inputs are complemented. That is, the circuits of Figure 4-3(a) and (b) are equivalent.

In Section 3.3.4 we showed how to build a CMOS NAND gate. The output of a NAND gate for any set of inputs is the complement of an AND gate's output for the same inputs, so a NAND gate can have the logic symbol in Figure 4-3(c). However, the CMOS NAND circuit is not designed as an AND gate followed by a transistor inverter (NOT gate); it's just a collection of transistors that happens to perform the AND-NOT function. In fact, theorem T13 tells us that the logic symbol in (d) denotes the same logic function (bubbles on the OR-gate inputs indicate logical inversion). That is, a NAND gate may be viewed as performing a NOT-OR function.

By observing the inputs and output of a NAND gate, it is impossible to determine whether it has been built internally as an AND gate followed by an inverter, as inverters followed by an OR gate, or as a direct CMOS realization, because all NAND circuits perform precisely the same logic function. Although the choice of symbol has no bearing on the functionality of a circuit, we'll show in Section 6.1 that the proper choice can make the circuit's function much easier to understand.

Figure 4-3 Equivalent circuits according to DeMorgan's theorem T13:
(a) AND-NOT; (b) NOT-OR; (c) logic symbol for a NAND gate;
(d) equivalent symbol for a NAND gate.

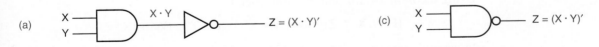

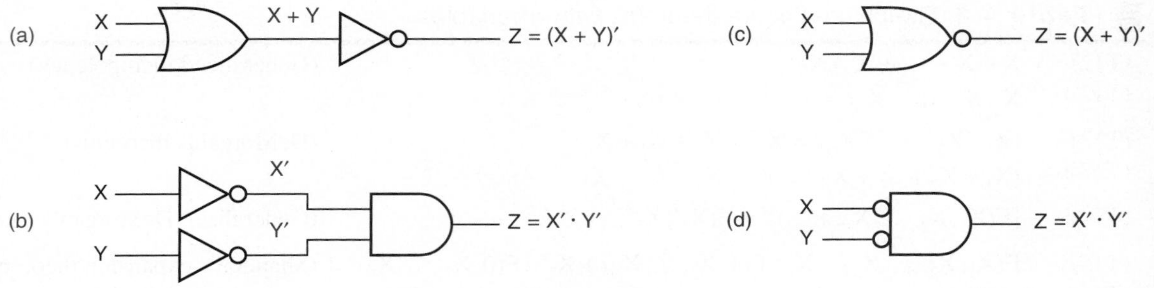

Figure 4-4 Equivalent circuits according to DeMorgan's theorem T13′:
(a) OR-NOT; (b) NOT-AND; (c) logic symbol for a NOR gate;
(d) equivalent symbol for a NOR gate.

A similar symbolic equivalence can be inferred from theorem T13′. As shown in Figure 4-4, a NOR gate may be realized as an OR gate followed by an inverter, or as inverters followed by an AND gate.

generalized DeMorgan's theorem

complement of a logic expression

Theorems T13 and T13′ are just special cases of a *generalized DeMorgan's theorem*, T14, that applies to an arbitrary logic expression F. By definition, the *complement of a logic expression*, denoted (F)′, is an expression whose value is the opposite of F's for every possible input combination. Theorem T14 is very important because it gives us a way to manipulate and simplify the complement of an expression.

Theorem T14 states that, given any *n*-variable logic expression, its complement can be obtained by swapping + and · and complementing all variables. For example, suppose that we have

$$F(W, X, Y, Z) = (W' \cdot X) + (X \cdot Y) + (W \cdot (X' + Z'))$$
$$= ((W)' \cdot X) + (X \cdot Y) + (W \cdot ((X)' + (Z)'))$$

In the second line we have enclosed complemented variables in parentheses to remind you that the ′ is an operator, not part of the variable name. By applying theorem T14, we obtain

$$[F(W, X, Y, Z)]' = ((W')' + X') \cdot (X' + Y') \cdot (W' + ((X')' \cdot (Z')'))$$

Using theorem T4, this can be simplified to

$$[F(W, X, Y, Z)]' = (W + X') \cdot (X' + Y') \cdot (W' + (X \cdot Z))$$

In general, we can use theorem T14 to complement a parenthesized expression by swapping + and ·, complementing all uncomplemented variables, and uncomplementing all complemented ones.

The generalized DeMorgan's theorem T14 can be proved by showing that all logic functions can be written as either a sum or a product of subfunctions, and then applying T13 and T13′ recursively. However, a much more enlightening and satisfying proof can be based on the principle of duality, explained next.

4.1.5 Duality

We stated all of the axioms of switching algebra in pairs. The primed version of each axiom (e.g., A5′) is obtained from the unprimed version (e.g., A5) by simply swapping 0 and 1 and, if present, · and +. As a result, we can state the following metatheorem (a *metatheorem* is a theorem about theorems):

metatheorem

Principle of Duality   Any theorem or identity in switching algebra remains true if 0 and 1 are swapped and · and + are swapped throughout.

The metatheorem is true because the duals of all the axioms are true, so duals of all switching-algebra theorems can be proved using duals of the axioms.

    After all, what's in a name, or in a symbol for that matter? If the software that was used to typeset this book had a bug, one that swapped 0 ↔ 1 and · ↔ + throughout this chapter, you still would have learned exactly the same switching algebra; only the nomenclature would have been a little weird, using words like "product" to describe an operation that uses the symbol "+".

    Duality is important because it doubles the usefulness of everything that you learn about switching algebra and manipulation of switching functions. Stated more practically, from a student's point of view, it halves the amount that you have to learn! For example, once you learn how to synthesize two-stage AND-OR logic circuits from sum-of-products expressions, you automatically know a dual technique to synthesize OR-AND circuits from product-of-sums expressions.

    There is just one convention in switching algebra where we did not treat · and + identically, so duality does not necessarily hold true—can you figure out what it is before reading the answer below? Consider the following statement of theorem T9 and its clearly absurd "dual":

$$X + X \cdot Y = X \qquad \text{(theorem T9)}$$
$$X \cdot X + Y = X \qquad \text{(after applying the principle of duality)}$$
$$X + Y = X \qquad \text{(after applying theorem T3′)}$$

Obviously the last line above is false—where did we go wrong? The problem is in operator precedence. We were able to write the lefthand side of the first line without parentheses because of our convention that · has precedence. However, once we applied the principle of duality, we should have given precedence to + instead, or written the second line as $X \cdot (X + Y) = X$. The best way to avoid problems like this is to parenthesize an expression fully before taking its dual.

    Let us formally define the notion of the *dual of a logic expression*. If $F(X_1, X_2, ..., X_n, +, \cdot, ')$ is a fully parenthesized logic expression involving the

dual of a logic expression

(a)

X	Y	Z
LOW	LOW	LOW
LOW	HIGH	LOW
HIGH	LOW	LOW
HIGH	HIGH	HIGH

(b) Z = X · Y

X	Y	Z
0	0	0
0	1	0
1	0	0
1	1	1

(c) Z = X + Y

X	Y	Z
1	1	1
1	0	1
0	1	1
0	0	0

Figure 4-5 A "type-1" logic gate: (a) electrical function table; (b) logic function table and symbol with positive logic; (c) logic function table and symbol with negative logic.

variables $X_1, X_2, ..., X_n$ and the operators $+$, $\cdot$, and $'$, then the dual of F, written F^D, is the same expression with $+$ and $\cdot$ swapped:

$$F^D(X_1, X_2, ..., X_n, +, \cdot, ') = F(X_1, X_2, ..., X_n, \cdot, +, ')$$

You already knew this, of course, but we wrote the definition in this way just to highlight the similarity between duality and the generalized DeMorgan's theorem T14, which may now be restated as follows:

$$[F(X_1, X_2, ..., X_n)]' = F^D(X_1', X_2', ..., X_n')$$

Let's examine this statement in terms of a physical network.

Figure 4-5(a) shows the electrical function table for a logic element that we'll simply call a "type-1" gate. Under the positive-logic convention ($LOW = 0$ and $HIGH = 1$), this is an AND gate, but under the negative-logic convention ($LOW = 1$ and $HIGH = 0$), it is an OR gate, as shown in (b) and (c). We can also imagine a "type-2" gate, shown in Figure 4-6, that is a positive-logic OR or a negative-logic AND. Similar tables can be developed for gates with more than two inputs.

Figure 4-6 A "type-2" logic gate: (a) electrical function table; (b) logic function table and symbol with positive logic; (c) logic function table and symbol with negative logic.

(a)

X	Y	Z
LOW	LOW	LOW
LOW	HIGH	HIGH
HIGH	LOW	HIGH
HIGH	HIGH	HIGH

(b) Z = X + Y

X	Y	Z
0	0	0
0	1	1
1	0	1
1	1	1

(c) Z = X · Y

X	Y	Z
1	1	1
1	0	0
0	1	0
0	0	0

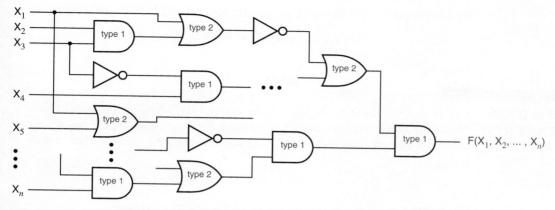

Figure 4-7 Circuit for a logic function using inverters and type-1 and type-2 gates under a positive-logic convention.

Suppose that we are given an arbitrary logic expression, $F(X_1, X_2, ..., X_n)$. Following the positive-logic convention, we can build a circuit corresponding to this expression using inverters for NOT operations, type-1 gates for AND, and type-2 gates for OR, as shown in Figure 4-7. Now suppose that, without changing this circuit, we simply change the logic convention from positive to negative. Then we should redraw the circuit as shown in Figure 4-8. Clearly, for every possible combination of input voltages (HIGH and LOW), the circuit still produces the same output voltage. However, from the point of view of switching algebra, the output value—0 or 1—is the opposite of what it was under the positive-logic convention. Likewise, each input value is the opposite of what it was. Therefore, for each possible input combination to the circuit in Figure 4-7, the output is the opposite of that produced by the opposite input combination applied to the circuit in Figure 4-8:

$$F(X_1, X_2, ..., X_n) = [F^D(X_1', X_2', ..., X_n')]'$$

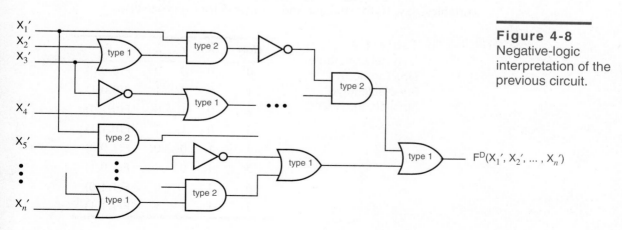

Figure 4-8
Negative-logic interpretation of the previous circuit.

By complementing both sides, we get the generalized DeMorgan's theorem:

$$[F(X_1, X_2, ..., X_n)]' = F^D(X_1', X_2', ..., X_n')$$

Amazing!

DUALITY IS GOOD FOR STUDENTS AND AUTHORS	You've seen that duality is the basis for the generalized DeMorgan's theorem. Going forward, it will halve the number of methods you must learn to manipulate and simplify logic functions. It also halved the amount of original material I had to write in these sections!

4.1.6 Standard Representations of Logic Functions

Before moving on to analysis and synthesis of combinational logic functions we'll introduce some necessary nomenclature and notation.

truth table

The most basic representation of a logic function is the *truth table*. Similar in philosophy to the perfect-induction proof method, this brute-force representation simply lists the output of the circuit for every possible input combination. Traditionally, the input combinations are arranged in rows in ascending binary counting order, and the corresponding output values are written in a column next to the rows. The general structure of a 3-variable truth table is shown below in Table 4-4.

The rows are numbered 0–7, corresponding to the binary input combinations, but this numbering is not an essential part of the truth table. The truth table for a particular 3-variable logic function is shown in Table 4-5. Each distinct pattern of eight 0s and 1s in the output column yields a different logic function; there are 2^8 such patterns. Thus, the logic function in Table 4-5 is one of 2^8 different logic functions of three variables.

The truth table for an n-variable logic function has 2^n rows. Obviously, truth tables are practical to write only for logic functions with a small number of variables, say, 10 for students and about 4–5 for everyone else.

Table 4-4
General truth table structure for a 3-variable logic function, F(X, Y, Z).

Row	X	Y	Z	F
0	0	0	0	F(0,0,0)
1	0	0	1	F(0,0,1)
2	0	1	0	F(0,1,0)
3	0	1	1	F(0,1,1)
4	1	0	0	F(1,0,0)
5	1	0	1	F(1,0,1)
6	1	1	0	F(1,1,0)
7	1	1	1	F(1,1,1)

Row	X	Y	Z	F
0	0	0	0	1
1	0	0	1	0
2	0	1	0	0
3	0	1	1	1
4	1	0	0	1
5	1	0	1	0
6	1	1	0	1
7	1	1	1	1

Table 4-5
Truth table for a particular 3-variable logic function, F(X, Y, Z).

The information contained in a truth table can also be conveyed algebraically. To do so, we first need some definitions:

- A *literal* is a variable or the complement of a variable. Examples: X, Y, X′, Y′. *literal*

- A *product term* is a single literal or a logical product of two or more literals. Examples: Z′, W · X · Y, X · Y′ · Z, W′ · Y′ · Z. *product term*

- A *sum-of-products expression* is a logical sum of product terms. Example: Z′ + W · X · Y + X · Y′ · Z + W′ · Y′ · Z. *sum-of-products expression*

- A *sum term* is a single literal or a logical sum of two or more literals. Examples: Z′, W + X + Y, X + Y′ + Z, W′ + Y′ + Z. *sum term*

- A *product-of-sums expression* is a logical product of sum terms. Example: Z′ · (W + X + Y) · (X + Y′ + Z) · (W′ + Y′ + Z). *product-of-sums expression*

- A *normal term* is a product or sum term in which no variable appears more than once. A nonnormal term can always be simplified to a constant or a normal term using one of theorems T3, T3′, T5, or T5′. Examples of nonnormal terms: W · X · X · Y′, W + W + X′ + Y, X · X′ · Y. Examples of normal terms: W · X · Y′, W + X′ + Y. *normal term*

- An *n-variable minterm* is a normal product term with *n* literals. There are 2^n such product terms. Some examples of 4-variable minterms: W′ · X′ · Y′ · Z′, W · X · Y′ · Z, W′ · X′ · Y · Z′. *minterm*

- An *n-variable maxterm* is a normal sum term with *n* literals. There are 2^n such sum terms. Examples of 4-variable maxterms: W′ + X′ + Y′ + Z′, W + X′ + Y′ + Z, W′ + X′ + Y + Z′. *maxterm*

There is a close correspondence between the truth table and minterms and maxterms. A minterm can be defined as a product term that is 1 in exactly one row of the truth table. Similarly, a maxterm can be defined as a sum term that is 0 in exactly one row of the truth table. Table 4-6 shows this correspondence for a 3-variable truth table.

Table 4-6
Minterms and maxterms for a 3-variable logic function, F(X, Y, Z).

Row	X	Y	Z	F	Minterm	Maxterm
0	0	0	0	F(0,0,0)	$X' \cdot Y' \cdot Z'$	$X + Y + Z$
1	0	0	1	F(0,0,1)	$X' \cdot Y' \cdot Z$	$X + Y + Z'$
2	0	1	0	F(0,1,0)	$X' \cdot Y \cdot Z'$	$X + Y' + Z$
3	0	1	1	F(0,1,1)	$X' \cdot Y \cdot Z$	$X + Y' + Z'$
4	1	0	0	F(1,0,0)	$X \cdot Y' \cdot Z'$	$X' + Y + Z$
5	1	0	1	F(1,0,1)	$X \cdot Y' \cdot Z$	$X' + Y + Z'$
6	1	1	0	F(1,1,0)	$X \cdot Y \cdot Z'$	$X' + Y' + Z$
7	1	1	1	F(1,1,1)	$X \cdot Y \cdot Z$	$X' + Y' + Z'$

minterm number
minterm i

An n-variable minterm can be represented by an n-bit integer, the *minterm number*. We'll use the name *minterm i* to denote the minterm corresponding to row i of the truth table. In minterm i, a particular variable appears complemented if the corresponding bit in the binary representation of i is 0; otherwise, it is uncomplemented. For example, row 5 has binary representation 101 and the corresponding minterm is $X \cdot Y' \cdot Z$. As you might expect, the correspondence

maxterm i

for maxterms is just the opposite: in *maxterm i*, a variable is complemented if the corresponding bit in the binary representation of i is 1. Thus, maxterm 5 (101) is $X' + Y + Z'$. Note that all of this makes sense only if we know the number of variables in the truth table, three in the examples.

Based on the correspondence between the truth table and minterms, we can easily create an algebraic representation of a logic function from its truth table.

canonical sum

The *canonical sum* of a logic function is a sum of the minterms corresponding to truth-table rows (input combinations) for which the function produces a 1 output. For example, the canonical sum for the logic function in Table 4-5 on page 197 is

$$F = \Sigma_{X,Y,Z}(0, 3, 4, 6, 7)$$
$$= X' \cdot Y' \cdot Z' + X' \cdot Y \cdot Z + X \cdot Y' \cdot Z' + X \cdot Y \cdot Z' + X \cdot Y \cdot Z$$

minterm list

Here, the notation $\Sigma_{X,Y,Z}(0, 3, 4, 6, 7)$ is a *minterm list* and means "the sum of minterms 0, 3, 4, 6, and 7 with variables X, Y, and Z." The minterm list is also

on-set

known as the *on-set* for the logic function. You can visualize that each minterm "turns on" the output for exactly one input combination. Any logic function can be written as a canonical sum.

canonical product

The *canonical product* of a logic function is a product of the maxterms corresponding to input combinations for which the function produces a 0 output. For example, the canonical product for the logic function in Table 4-5 is

$$F = \Pi_{X,Y,Z}(1, 2, 5)$$
$$= (X + Y + Z') \cdot (X + Y' + Z) \cdot (X' + Y + Z')$$

Here, the notation $\prod_{X,Y,Z}(1,2,5)$ is a *maxterm list* and means "the product of *maxterm list* maxterms 1, 2, and 5 with variables X, Y, and Z." The maxterm list is also known as the *off-set* for the logic function. You can visualize that each maxterm "turns *off-set* off" the output for exactly one input combination. Any logic function can be written as a canonical product.

It's easy to convert between a minterm list and a maxterm list. For a function of n variables, the possible minterm and maxterm numbers are in the set $\{0, 1, \ldots, 2^n - 1\}$; a minterm or maxterm list contains a subset of these numbers. To switch between list types, take the set complement, for example,

$$\Sigma_{A,B,C}(0,1,2,3) = \prod_{A,B,C}(4,5,6,7)$$

$$\Sigma_{X,Y}(1) = \prod_{X,Y}(0,2,3)$$

$$\Sigma_{W,X,Y,Z}(0,1,2,3,5,7,11,13) = \prod_{W,X,Y,Z}(4,6,8,9,10,12,14,15)$$

We have now learned five possible representations for a combinational logic function:

1. A truth table.
2. An algebraic sum of minterms, the canonical sum.
3. A minterm list using the Σ notation.
4. An algebraic product of maxterms, the canonical product.
5. A maxterm list using the $\prod$ notation.

Each one of these representations specifies exactly the same information; given any one of them, we can derive the other four using a simple mechanical process.

4.2 Combinational-Circuit Analysis

We analyze a combinational logic circuit by obtaining a formal description of its logic function. Once we have a description of the logic function, a number of other operations are possible:

- We can determine the behavior of the logic circuit for various input combinations.

- We can manipulate an algebraic description to suggest different circuit structures for the logic function.

- We can transform an algebraic description into a standard form corresponding to an available circuit structure. For example, a sum-of-products expression corresponds directly to the circuit structure used in PLAs (programmable logic arrays), and a truth table corresponds to the lookup memory used in most FPGAs (field programmable gate arrays).

- We can use an algebraic description of the circuit's functional behavior in the analysis of a larger system that includes the circuit.

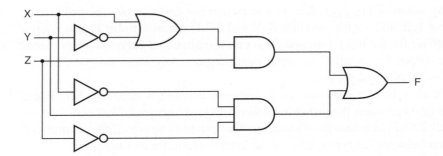

Figure 4-9
A 3-input,1-output
logic circuit.

Given a logic diagram for a combinational circuit, such as Figure 4-9, there are a number of ways to obtain a formal description of the circuit's function. The most basic functional description is the truth table.

Using only the basic axioms of switching algebra, we can obtain the truth table of an n-input circuit by working our way through all 2^n input combinations. For each input combination, we determine all of the gate outputs produced by that input, propagating information from the circuit inputs to the circuit outputs. Figure 4-10 applies this "exhaustive" technique to our example circuit. Written on each signal line in the circuit is a sequence of eight logic values, the values present on that line when the circuit inputs XYZ are 000, 001, ..., 111. The truth table can be written by transcribing the output sequence of the final OR gate, as

Figure 4-10 Gate outputs created by all input combinations.

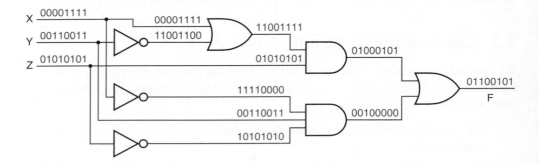

A LESS
EXHAUSTING
WAY TO GO
You can easily obtain the results in Figure 4-10 with typical logic design tools that include a logic simulator. First, you draw the schematic. Then, you apply the outputs of a 3-bit binary counter to the X, Y, and Z inputs. (Most simulators have such counter outputs built in for just this sort of exercise.) The counter repeatedly cycles through the eight possible input combinations, in the same order that we've shown in the figure. The simulator allows you to graph the resulting signal values at any point in the schematic, including the intermediate points as well as the output.

Row	X	Y	Z	F
0	0	0	0	0
1	0	0	1	1
2	0	1	0	1
3	0	1	1	0
4	1	0	0	0
5	1	0	1	1
6	1	1	0	0
7	1	1	1	1

Table 4-7
Truth table for the
logic circuit of
Figure 4-9.

shown in Table 4-7. Once we have the truth table for the circuit, we can also directly write a logic expression—the canonical sum or product—if we wish.

The number of input combinations of a logic circuit grows exponentially with the number of inputs, so the exhaustive approach can quickly become exhausting. Instead, we normally use an algebraic approach whose complexity is more linearly proportional to the size of the circuit. The method is simple—we build up a parenthesized logic expression corresponding to the logic operators and structure of the circuit. We start at the circuit inputs and propagate expressions through gates toward the output. Using the theorems of switching algebra, we may simplify the expressions as we go, or we may defer all algebraic manipulations until an output expression is obtained.

Figure 4-11 applies the algebraic technique to our example circuit. The output function is given on the output of the final OR gate:

$$F = ((X+Y') \cdot Z) + (X' \cdot Y \cdot Z')$$

No switching-algebra theorems were used to obtain this expression. However, we can use theorems to transform this expression into another form. For example, a sum of products can be obtained by "multiplying out":

$$F = X \cdot Z + Y' \cdot Z + X' \cdot Y \cdot Z'$$

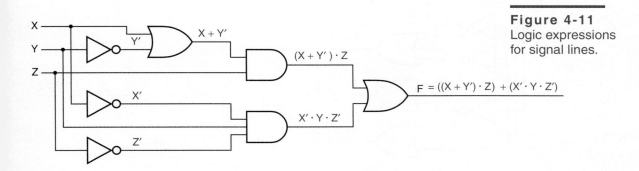

Figure 4-11
Logic expressions
for signal lines.

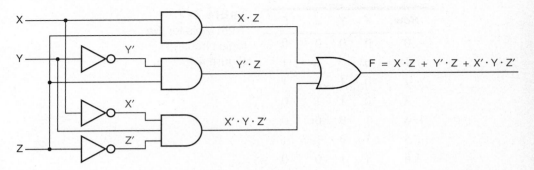

Figure 4-12 Two-level AND-OR circuit.

The new expression corresponds to a different circuit for the same logic function, as shown in Figure 4-12.

Similarly, we can "add out" the original expression to obtain a product of sums:

$$
\begin{aligned}
F &= ((X + Y') \cdot Z) + (X' \cdot Y \cdot Z') \\
&= (X + Y' + X') \cdot (X + Y' + Y) \cdot (X + Y' + Z') \cdot (Z + X') \cdot (Z + Y) \cdot (Z + Z') \\
&= 1 \cdot 1 \cdot (X + Y' + Z') \cdot (X' + Z) \cdot (Y + Z) \cdot 1 \\
&= (X + Y' + Z') \cdot (X' + Z) \cdot (Y + Z)
\end{aligned}
$$

The corresponding logic circuit is shown in Figure 4-13.

Our next example of algebraic analysis uses a circuit with NAND and NOR gates, shown in Figure 4-14. This analysis is a little messier than the previous example, because each gate produces a complemented subexpression, not just a simple sum or product. However, the output expression can be simplified by repeated application of the generalized DeMorgan's theorem:

Figure 4-13 Two-level OR-AND circuit.

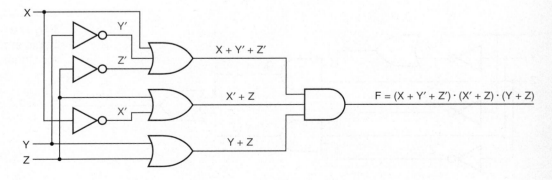

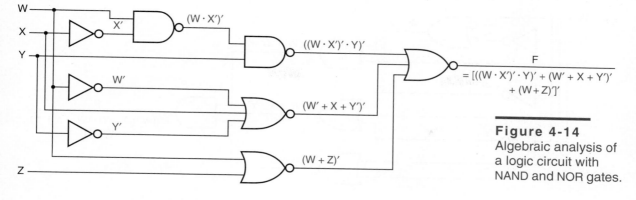

Figure 4-14
Algebraic analysis of
a logic circuit with
NAND and NOR gates.

$$F = [((W \cdot X')' \cdot Y)' + (W' + X + Y')' + (W + Z)']'$$
$$= ((W' + X)' + Y')' \cdot (W \cdot X' \cdot Y)' \cdot (W' \cdot Z')'$$
$$= ((W \cdot X')' \cdot Y) \cdot (W' + X + Y') \cdot (W + Z)$$
$$= ((W' + X) \cdot Y) \cdot (W' + X + Y') \cdot (W + Z)$$

Quite often, DeMorgan's theorem can be applied *graphically* to simplify algebraic analysis. Recall from Figures 4-3 and 4-4 that NAND and NOR gates each have two equivalent symbols. By judiciously redrawing Figure 4-14, we make it possible to cancel out some of the inversions during the analysis by using theorem T4 [$(X')' = X$], as shown in Figure 4-15. This manipulation leads us to a simplified output expression directly:

$$F = ((W' + X) \cdot Y) \cdot (W' + X + Y') \cdot (W + Z)$$

Figures 4-14 and 4-15 were just two different ways of drawing the same physical logic circuit. However, when we simplify a logic expression using the theorems of switching algebra, we get an expression corresponding to a different physical circuit. For example, the simplified expression above corresponds to the circuit of Figure 4-16, which is physically different from the one in the previous two figures. Furthermore, we could multiply out and add out the

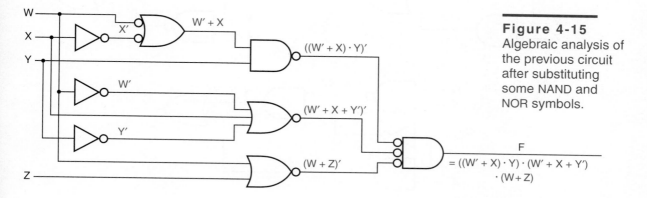

Figure 4-15
Algebraic analysis of
the previous circuit
after substituting
some NAND and
NOR symbols.

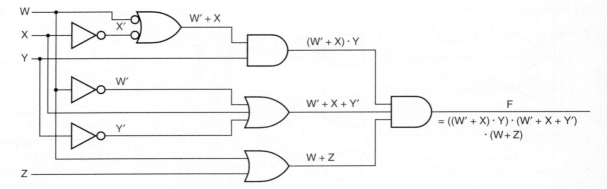

Figure 4-16 A different circuit for same logic function.

expression to obtain sum-of-products and product-of-sums expressions corresponding to two more physically different circuits for the same logic function.

Although we used logic expressions above to convey information about the physical structure of a circuit, we don't always do this. For example, we might use the expression $G(W, X, Y, Z) = W \cdot X \cdot Y + Y \cdot Z$ to describe any one of the circuits in Figure 4-17. Normally, the only sure way to determine a circuit's structure is to look at its schematic drawing. However, for certain restricted classes of circuits, structural information can be inferred from logic expressions. For example, the circuit in (a) could be described without reference to the drawing as "a two-level AND-OR circuit for $W \cdot X \cdot Y + Y \cdot Z$," while the circuit in (b) could be described as "a two-level NAND-NAND circuit for $W \cdot X \cdot Y + Y \cdot Z$."

Figure 4-17 Three circuits for $G(W, X, Y, Z) = W \cdot X \cdot Y + Y \cdot Z$: (a) two-level AND-OR; (b) two-level NAND-NAND; (c) with 2-input gates only.

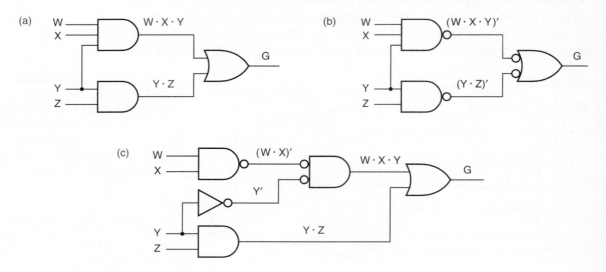

4.3 Combinational-Circuit Synthesis

What is the starting point for designing combinational logic circuits? Usually, we are given a word description of a problem or we develop one ourselves. In modern digital-design environments, we can translate that word description into a program in a hardware description language (HDL), and the HDL tools can synthesize a circuit structure for that program, targeting a selected device or technology (such as an FPGA or an ASIC cell library). In such a case, the designer never gets involved in synthesis at all. However, even in modern environments, there are still many situations where the designer should be capable of synthesizing combinational circuits "by hand," and this section introduces the basic skills needed to perform such synthesis.

4.3.1 Circuit Descriptions and Designs

Occasionally, a logic circuit description is just a list of input combinations for which a signal should be on or off, the verbal equivalent of a truth table or the Σ or Π notation introduced previously. For example, the description of a 4-bit prime-number detector might be, "Given a 4-bit input combination $N = N_3N_2N_1N_0$, produce a 1 output for $N = 1, 2, 3, 5, 7, 11, 13$, and 0 otherwise." A logic function described in this way can be designed directly from the canonical sum or product expression. For the prime-number detector, we have

$$F = \Sigma_{N_3,N_2,N_1,N_0}(1, 2, 3, 5, 7, 11, 13)$$
$$= N_3' \cdot N_2' \cdot N_1' \cdot N_0 + N_3' \cdot N_2' \cdot N_1 \cdot N_0' + N_3' \cdot N_2' \cdot N_1 \cdot N_0 + N_3' \cdot N_2 \cdot N_1' \cdot N_0$$
$$+ N_3' \cdot N_2 \cdot N_1 \cdot N_0 + N_3 \cdot N_2' \cdot N_1 \cdot N_0 + N_3 \cdot N_2 \cdot N_1' \cdot N_0$$

ROLLING YOUR OWN There are sometimes cases when an HDL or an appropriate synthesizer is not available, or the synthesizer's results just aren't good enough. The last case is especially common when a designer needs to optimize the speed, power consumption, or size of a critical circuit. For example, in a microprocessor system-on-a-chip with millions of gates, an HDL-based approach is essential for the "routine" parts of the design to achieve a reasonable time to market. Yet, it is still very common for critical data paths, such as adders, multipliers, multiplexers, and specialized high-speed control structures to be synthesized "by hand," with no synthesis tool, and the HDL being used at most to specify the desired interconnection between individual gates and larger hand-designed logic modules (e.g., adders, multiplexers, and decoders).

There are also cases where the synthesizer may "run amok," creating a circuit that is much less efficient (in speed, size, or some other metric) than what is expected and required. In these cases, it is important for the designer to have a good feel for what *could* be achieved, and either synthesize the circuit by hand or try a different style of HDL coding to try to cajole the synthesizer into creating a result that is closer to what is desired.

PRIME TIME   Mathematicians will tell you that "1" is not really a prime number. But our prime-number detector example is not nearly as interesting, from a logic-design point of view, if "1" is not prime. So, please go do Drill 4.11 if you want to be a mathematical purist.

The corresponding circuit is shown in Figure 4-18.

More often, we describe a logic function using the English-language connectives "and," "or," and "not." For example, we might describe an alarm circuit by saying, "The ALARM output is 1 if the PANIC input is 1, or if the ENABLE input is 1, the EXITING input is 0, and the house is not secure; the house is secure if the WINDOW, DOOR, and GARAGE inputs are all 1." Such a description can be translated directly into algebraic expressions:

$$\text{ALARM} = \text{PANIC} + \text{ENABLE} \cdot \text{EXITING}' \cdot \text{SECURE}'$$
$$\text{SECURE} = \text{WINDOW} \cdot \text{DOOR} \cdot \text{GARAGE}$$
$$\text{ALARM} = \text{PANIC} + \text{ENABLE} \cdot \text{EXITING}' \cdot (\text{WINDOW} \cdot \text{DOOR} \cdot \text{GARAGE})'$$

Notice that we used the same method in switching algebra as in ordinary algebra to formulate a complicated expression—we defined an auxiliary variable SECURE to simplify the first equation, developed an expression for SECURE, and used substitution to get the final expression. We can easily draw a circuit

Figure 4-18 Canonical-sum design for 4-bit prime-number detector.

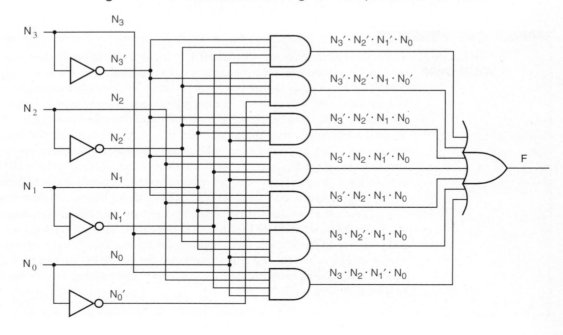

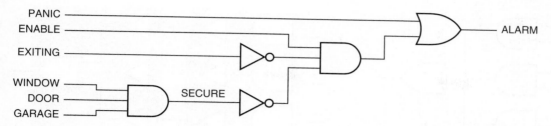

Figure 4-19 Alarm circuit derived from logic expression.

using AND, OR, and NOT gates that realizes the final expression, as shown in Figure 4-19. A circuit *realizes* ["makes real"] an expression if its output function equals that expression, and the circuit is called a *realization* of the function.

realize
realization

Once we have an expression, any expression, for a logic function, we can do other things besides building a circuit directly from the expression. We can manipulate the expression to get different circuits. For example, the ALARM expression above can be multiplied out to get the sum-of-products circuit in Figure 4-20. Or, if the number of variables is not too large, we can construct the truth table for the expression and use any of the synthesis methods that apply to truth tables, including the canonical sum or product method described earlier and the minimization methods described later.

In general, it's easier to describe a circuit in words using logical connectives and to write the corresponding logic expressions than it is to write a complete truth table, especially if the number of variables is large. However, sometimes we have to work with imprecise word descriptions of logic functions, for example, "The ERROR output should be 1 if the GEARUP, GEARDOWN, and GEARCHECK inputs are inconsistent." In this situation, the truth-table approach is best because it allows us to determine the output required for every input combination, based on our knowledge and understanding of the problem environment (e.g., the brakes cannot be applied unless the gear is down).

Figure 4-20 Sum-of-products version of alarm circuit.

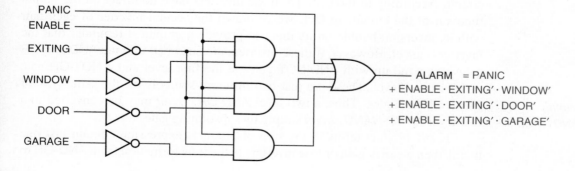

ALARM = PANIC
+ ENABLE · EXITING′ · WINDOW′
+ ENABLE · EXITING′ · DOOR′
+ ENABLE · EXITING′ · GARAGE′

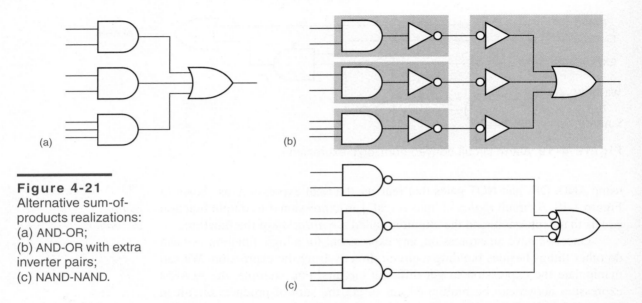

Figure 4-21
Alternative sum-of-products realizations:
(a) AND-OR;
(b) AND-OR with extra inverter pairs;
(c) NAND-NAND.

4.3.2 Circuit Manipulations

The design methods that we've described so far use AND, OR, and NOT gates. We might like to use NAND and NOR gates, too—they're faster than ANDs and ORs in most technologies. However, most people don't develop logical propositions in terms of NAND and NOR connectives. That is, you probably wouldn't say, "I won't date you if you're not clean or not wealthy and also you're not smart or not friendly." It would be more natural for you to say, "I'll date you if you're clean and wealthy, or if you're smart and friendly." So, given a "natural" logic expression, we need ways to translate it into other forms.

We can translate any logic expression into an equivalent sum-of-products expression, simply by multiplying it out. As shown in Figure 4-21(a), such an expression may be realized directly with AND and OR gates. The inverters required for complemented inputs are not shown.

As shown in Figure 4-21(b), we may insert a pair of inverters between each AND-gate output and the corresponding OR-gate input in a two-level AND-OR circuit. According to theorem T4, these inverters have no effect on the output function of the circuit. In fact, we've drawn the second inverter of each pair with its inversion bubble on its input to provide a graphical reminder that the inverters cancel. However, if these inverters are absorbed into the AND and OR gates, we wind up with AND-NOT gates at the first level and a NOT-OR gate at the second level. These are just two different symbols for the same type of gate—a NAND gate. Thus, a two-level *AND-OR* circuit may be converted to a two-level *NAND-NAND* circuit simply by substituting gates.

If any product terms in the sum-of-products expression contain just one literal, then we may gain or lose inverters in the transformation from AND-OR to

AND-OR circuit
NAND-NAND circuit

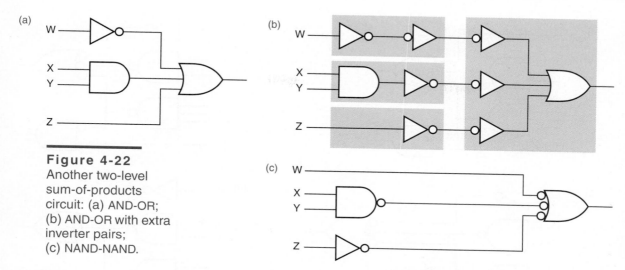

Figure 4-22
Another two-level
sum-of-products
circuit: (a) AND-OR;
(b) AND-OR with extra
inverter pairs;
(c) NAND-NAND.

NAND-NAND. For example, Figure 4-22 is an example where an inverter on the W input is no longer needed, but an inverter must be added to the Z input.

We have shown that any sum-of-products expression can be realized in either of two ways—as an AND-OR circuit or as a NAND-NAND circuit. The dual of this statement is also true: any product-of-sums expression can be realized as an *OR-AND circuit* or as a *NOR-NOR circuit*. Figure 4-23 shows an example. Any logic expression can be translated into an equivalent product-of-sums expression by adding it out, and hence has both OR-AND and NOR-NOR circuit realizations.

OR-AND circuit
NOR-NOR circuit

Figure 4-23
Realizations of a
product-of-sums
expression:
(a) OR-AND;
(b) OR-AND with extra
inverter pairs;
(c) NOR-NOR.

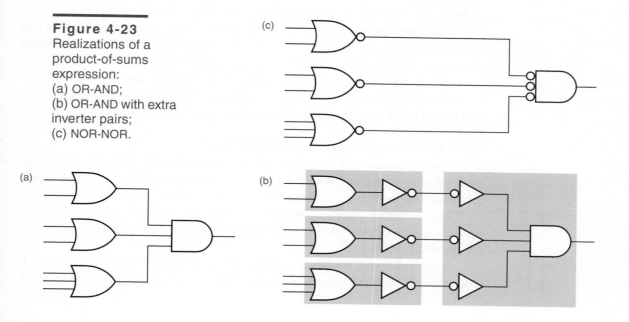

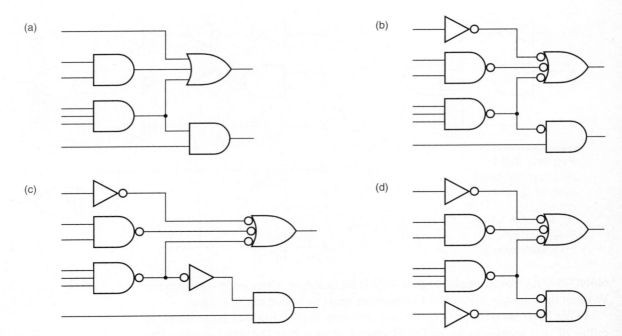

Figure 4-24 Logic-symbol manipulations: (a) original circuit;
(b) transformation with a nonstandard gate; (c) inverter used to
eliminate nonstandard gate; (d) preferred inverter placement.

The same kind of manipulations can be applied to arbitrary logic circuits. For example, Figure 4-24(a) shows a circuit built from AND and OR gates. After adding pairs of inverters, we obtain the circuit in (b). However, one of the gates, a 2-input AND gate with a single inverted input, is not a standard type. We can use a discrete inverter as shown in (c) to obtain a circuit that uses only standard gate types—NAND, AND, and inverters. Actually, a better way to use the inverter is shown in (d); one level of gate delay is eliminated, and the bottom gate becomes a NOR instead of AND. In most logic technologies, inverting gates like NAND and NOR are faster than noninverting gates like AND and OR.

4.3.3 Combinational-Circuit Minimization

It's often uneconomical to realize a logic circuit directly from the first logic expression that pops into your head. Canonical sum and product expressions are especially expensive because the number of possible minterms or maxterms (and hence gates) grows exponentially with the number of variables. We *minimize* a combinational circuit by reducing the number and size of gates that are needed to build it.

minimize

The traditional combinational-circuit-minimization methods that we'll study have as their starting point a truth table or, equivalently, a minterm list or

WHY MINIMIZE? Minimization is an important step in both ASIC design and in PLD-based design. Extra gates and gate inputs require more area in an ASIC chip and thereby increase cost. The number of gates in a PLD is fixed, so you might think that extra gates are free—and they are, until you run out of them and have to upgrade to a bigger, slower, more expensive PLD. Fortunately, most software tools for both ASIC and PLD design have a minimization program built in. The purpose of Sections 4.3.3 through 4.3.7 is to give you a feel for how minimization works.

maxterm list. If we are given a logic function that is not expressed in this form, then we must convert it to an appropriate form before using these methods. For example, if we are given an arbitrary logic expression, then we can evaluate it for every input combination to construct the truth table. The minimization methods reduce the cost of a two-level AND-OR, OR-AND, NAND-NAND, or NOR-NOR circuit in three ways:

1. By minimizing the number of first-level gates.
2. By minimizing the number of inputs on each first-level gate.
3. By minimizing the number of inputs on the second-level gate. This is actually a side effect of the first reduction.

However, the minimization methods do not consider the cost of input inverters; they assume that both true and complemented versions of all input variables are available. While this is not always the case in gate-level or ASIC design, it's very appropriate for PLD-based design; PLDs have both true and complemented versions of all input variables available "for free."

Most minimization methods are based on a generalization of the combining theorems, T10 and T10′:

$$\text{given product term} \cdot Y + \text{given product term} \cdot Y' = \text{given product term}$$

$$(\text{given sum term} + Y) \cdot (\text{given sum term} + Y') = \text{given sum term}$$

That is, if two product or sum terms differ only in the complementing or not of one variable, we can combine them into a single term with one less variable. So we eliminate one gate and the remaining gate has one fewer input.

We can apply this algebraic method repeatedly to combine minterms 1, 3, 5, and 7 of the prime-number detector shown in Figure 4-18 on page 206:

$$
\begin{aligned}
F &= \Sigma_{N_3,N_2,N_1,N_0}(1, 3, 5, 7, 2, 11, 13) \\
&= N_3' \cdot N_2' \cdot N_1' \cdot N_0 + N_3' \cdot N_2' \cdot N_1 \cdot N_0 + N_3' \cdot N_2 \cdot N_1' \cdot N_0 + N_3' \cdot N_2 \cdot N_1 \cdot N_0 + \ldots \\
&= (N_3' \cdot N_2' \cdot N_1' \cdot N_0 + N_3' \cdot N_2' \cdot N_1 \cdot N_0) + (\cdot N_3' \cdot N_2 \cdot N_1' \cdot N_0 + N_3' \cdot N_2 \cdot N_1 \cdot N_0) + \ldots \\
&= N_3' \cdot N_2' \cdot N_0 + N_3' \cdot N_2 \cdot N_0 + \ldots \\
&= N_3' \cdot N_0 + \ldots
\end{aligned}
$$

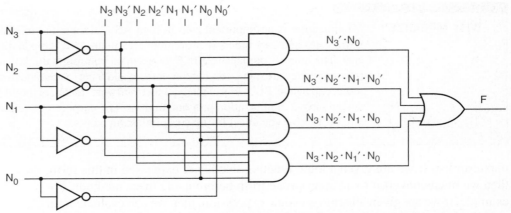

Figure 4-25 Simplified sum-of-products realization for 4-bit prime-number detector.

The resulting circuit is shown in Figure 4-25; it has three fewer gates, and one of the remaining gates has two fewer inputs.

   If we had worked a little harder on the preceding expression, we could have saved a couple more first-level gate inputs, though not any more gates. But it's difficult to find terms that can be combined in a jumble of algebraic symbols. In the next subsection we'll begin to explore a minimization method that is more fit for human consumption. Our starting point will be the graphical equivalent of a truth table.

4.3.4 Karnaugh Maps

Karnaugh map

A *Karnaugh map* is a graphical representation of a logic function's truth table. Figure 4-26 shows Karnaugh maps for logic functions of two, three, and four variables. The map for an n-input logic function is an array with 2^n cells, one for each possible input combination or minterm.

Figure 4-26 Karnaugh maps: (a) 2-variable; (b) 3-variable; (c) 4-variable.

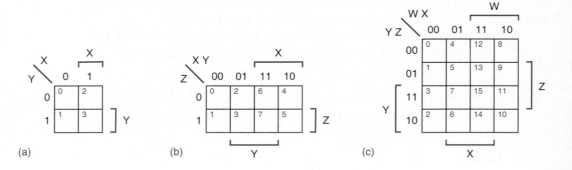

The rows and columns of a Karnaugh map are labeled so that the input combination for any cell is easily determined from the row and column headings for that cell. The small number inside each cell is the corresponding minterm number in the truth table, assuming that the truth-table inputs are labeled alphabetically from left to right (e.g., X, Y, Z) and the rows are numbered in binary counting order, like all the examples in this text. For example, cell 13 in the 4-variable map corresponds to the truth-table row in which W X Y Z = 1101.

When we draw the Karnaugh map for a given function, each cell of the map contains the information from the like-numbered row of the function's truth table—a 0 if the function is 0 for that input combination, a 1 otherwise.

In this text we use two redundant labelings for map rows and columns. For example, consider the 4-variable map in Figure 4-26(c). The columns are labeled with the four possible combinations of W and X, W X = 00, 01, 11, and 10. Similarly, the rows are labeled with the Y Z combinations. These labels give us all the information we need. However, we also use brackets to associate four regions of the map with the four variables. Each bracketed region is the part of the map in which the indicated variable is 1. Obviously, the brackets convey the same information that is given by the row and column labels.

When we draw a map by hand, it is much easier to draw the brackets than to write out all of the labels. However, we retain the labels in the text's Karnaugh maps as an additional aid to understanding. In any case, you must be sure to label the rows and columns in the proper order to preserve the correspondence between map cells and truth-table row numbers shown in Figure 4-26.

To represent a logic function on a Karnaugh map, we simply copy 1s and 0s from the truth table or equivalent to the corresponding cells of the map. Figure 4-27(a–c) shows Karnaugh maps for $F = \Sigma_{X,Y}(3)$ (a 2-input AND gate), $F = \Sigma_{X,Y,Z}(0, 3, 4, 6, 7)$ (truth table 4-5 on page 197), and $F = \Sigma_{W,X,Y,Z}(1, 2, 3, 5, 7, 11, 13)$ (our 4-bit prime-number detector).

Figure 4-27 Karnaugh map for logic functions: (a) $F = \Sigma_{X,Y}(3)$; (b) $F = \Sigma_{X,Y,Z}(0,3,4,6,7)$; (c) $F = \Sigma_{W,X,Y,Z}(1,2,3,5,7,11,13)$.

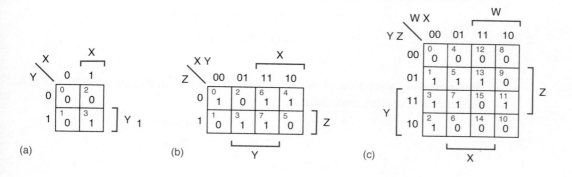

X	Y	Z	F
0	0	0	0
0	0	1	1
0	1	0	1
0	1	1	0
1	0	0	0
1	0	1	1
1	1	0	0
1	1	1	1

(a)　　　(b)　　　(c)

Figure 4-28 $F = \Sigma_{X,Y,Z}(1,2,5,7)$: (a) truth table; (b) Karnaugh map; (c) combining adjacent 1-cells.

Figures 4-28(a) and (b) show the truth table and Karnaugh map for a logic function that we analyzed (beat to death?) in Section 4.2. From now on, we'll reduce the clutter in maps by copying only the 1s or the 0s, not both, as in (c).

4.3.5 Minimizing Sums of Products

By now you must be wondering about the "strange" ordering of the row and column numbers in a Karnaugh map. There is a very important reason for this ordering—each cell corresponds to an input combination that differs from each of its immediately adjacent neighbors in only one variable. For example, cells 5 and 13 in the 4-variable map differ only in the value of W. In the 3- and 4-variable maps, corresponding cells on the left/right or top/bottom borders are less obvious neighbors; for example, cells 12 and 14 in the 4-variable map are "adjacent" because they differ only in the value of Y.

Each input combination with a "1" in the truth table corresponds to a minterm in the logic function's canonical sum. Since pairs of adjacent "1" cells in the Karnaugh map have minterms that differ in only one variable, the minterm pairs can be combined into a single product term using the generalization of theorem T10, term $\cdot$ Y + term $\cdot$ Y' = term. Thus, we can use a Karnaugh map to simplify the canonical sum of a logic function.

For example, consider cells 5 and 7 in Figure 4-28(b) and their contribution to the canonical sum for this function:

$$F = \cdots + X \cdot Y' \cdot Z + X \cdot Y \cdot Z$$
$$= \cdots + (X \cdot Z) \cdot Y' + (X \cdot Z) \cdot Y$$
$$= \cdots + X \cdot Z$$

Remembering wraparound, we see that cells 1 and 5 in Figure 4-28(b) are also adjacent and can be combined:

$$F = X' \cdot Y' \cdot Z + X \cdot Y' \cdot Z + \cdots$$
$$= X' \cdot (Y' \cdot Z) + X \cdot (Y' \cdot Z) + \cdots$$
$$= Y' \cdot Z + \cdots$$

In general, we can simplify a logic function by first combining pairs of adjacent 1-cells (minterms) wherever possible and then selecting a set of product terms that covers all of the 1-cells and summing them. Figure 4-28(c) shows the result for our example logic function. We circle a pair of 1s to indicate that the corresponding minterms are combined into a single product term. The corresponding AND-OR circuit is shown in Figure 4-29.

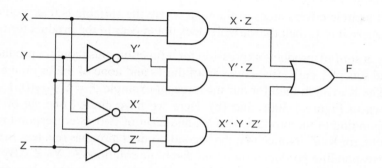

Figure 4-29
Minimized AND-OR circuit.

In many logic functions the cell-combining procedure can be extended to combine more than two 1-cells into a single product term. The number of cells combined will always be a power of 2. For example, consider the canonical sum for the logic function $F = \Sigma_{X,Y,Z}(0, 1, 4, 5, 6)$. We can use the algebraic manipulations of the previous examples iteratively to combine four minterms:

$$
\begin{aligned}
F &= X' \cdot Y' \cdot Z' + X' \cdot Y' \cdot Z + X \cdot Y' \cdot Z' + X \cdot Y' \cdot Z + X \cdot Y \cdot Z' \\
&= [(X' \cdot Y') \cdot Z' + (X' \cdot Y') \cdot Z] + [(X \cdot Y') \cdot Z' + (X \cdot Y') \cdot Z] + X \cdot Y \cdot Z' \\
&= X' \cdot Y' + X \cdot Y' + X \cdot Y \cdot Z' \\
&= [X' \cdot (Y') + X \cdot (Y')] + X \cdot Y \cdot Z' \\
&= Y' + X \cdot Y \cdot Z'
\end{aligned}
$$

In general, 2^i 1-cells may be combined to form a product term containing $n - i$ literals, where n is the number of variables in the function.

A precise mathematical rule determines how 1-cells may be combined and the form of the corresponding product term:

- A set of 2^i 1-cells may be combined if there are i variables of the logic function that take on all 2^i possible combinations within that set, while the remaining $n - i$ variables have the same value throughout that set. The corresponding product term has $n - i$ literals, where a variable is complemented if it appears as 0 in all of the 1-cells, and uncomplemented if it appears as 1.

Graphically, this rule means that we can circle *rectangular* sets of 2^i 1s, literally as well as figuratively stretching the definition of rectangular to account for wraparound at the edges of the map. We can determine the literals of the

rectangular sets of 1s

corresponding product terms directly from the map; for each variable we make the following determination:

- If a circle covers only areas of the map where the variable is 0, then the variable is complemented in the product term.

- If a circle covers only areas of the map where the variable is 1, then the variable is uncomplemented in the product term.

- If a circle covers areas of the map where the variable is 0 as well as areas where it is 1, then the variable does not appear in the product term.

Finally, a sum-of-products expression for a function must contain product terms (circled sets of 1-cells) that cover all of the 1s and none of the 0s on the map.

The Karnaugh map for our most recent example, $F = \Sigma_{X,Y,Z}(0, 1, 4, 5, 6)$, is shown in Figure 4-30(a) and (b). Here we have circled one set of four 1s, corresponding to the product term Y', and a set of two 1s corresponding to the product term $X \cdot Z'$. Notice that the second product term has one less literal than the corresponding product term in our algebraic solution ($X \cdot Y \cdot Z'$). By circling the largest possible set of 1s containing cell 6, we have found a less expensive realization of the logic function, since a 2-input AND gate should cost less than a 3-input one. The fact that two different product terms now cover the same 1-cell (4) does not affect the logic function, since for logical addition $1 + 1 = 1$, not 2! The corresponding two-level AND/OR circuit is shown in (c).

As another example, the prime-number detector circuit that we introduced in Figure 4-18 on page 206 can be minimized as shown in Figure 4-31.

At this point, we need some more definitions to clarify what we're doing:

minimal sum

- A *minimal sum* of a logic function $F(X_1,...,X_n)$ is a sum-of-products expression for F such that no sum-of-products expression for F has fewer product terms, and any sum-of-products expression with the same number of product terms has at least as many literals.

Figure 4-30
$F = \Sigma_{X,Y,Z}(0,1,4,5,6)$:
(a) initial Karnaugh map; (b) Karnaugh map with circled product terms;
(c) AND/OR circuit.

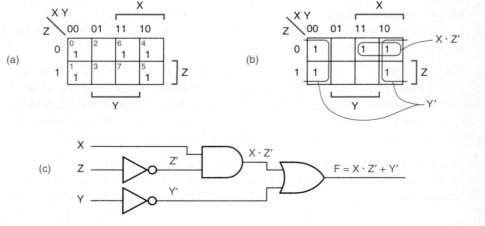

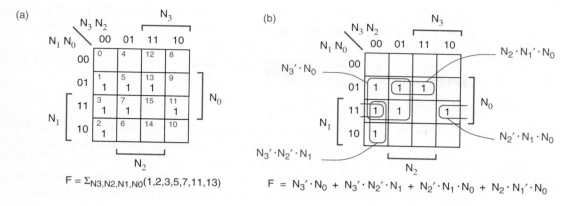

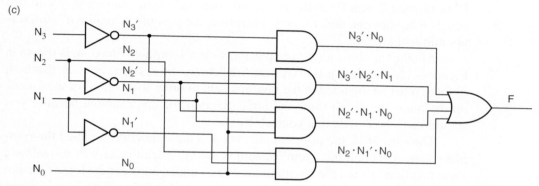

Figure 4-31 Prime-number detector: (a) initial Karnaugh map; (b) circled product terms; (c) minimized circuit.

That is, the minimal sum has the fewest possible product terms (first-level gates and second-level gate inputs) and, within that constraint, the fewest possible literals (first-level gate inputs). Thus, among our three prime-number detector circuits, only the one in Figure 4-31 realizes a minimal sum.

The next definition says precisely what the word "imply" means when we talk about logic functions:

- A logic function $P(X_1,...,X_n)$ *implies* a logic function $F(X_1,...,X_n)$ if for every input combination such that $P = 1$, then $F = 1$ also.

imply

That is, if P implies F, then F is 1 for every input combination that P is 1, and maybe some more. We may write the shorthand $P \Rightarrow F$. We may also say that "F *includes* P," or that "F *covers* P."

includes
covers
prime implicant

- A *prime implicant* of a logic function $F(X_1,...,X_n)$ is a normal product term $P(X_1,...,X_n)$ that implies F, such that if any variable is removed from P, then the resulting product term does not imply F.

In terms of a Karnaugh map, a prime implicant of F is a circled set of 1-cells satisfying our combining rule, such that if we try to make it larger (covering twice as many cells), it covers one or more 0s.

Now comes the most important part, a theorem that limits how much work we must do to find a minimal sum for a logic function:

Prime-Implicant Theorem   A minimal sum is a sum of prime implicants.

That is, to find a minimal sum, we need not consider any product terms that are not prime implicants. This theorem is easily proved by contradiction. Suppose that a product term P in a "minimal" sum is *not* a prime implicant. Then according to the definition of prime implicant, if P is not one, it is possible to remove some literal from P to obtain a new product term P* that still implies F. If we replace P with P* in the presumed "minimal" sum, the resulting sum still equals F but has one fewer literal. Therefore, the presumed "minimal" sum was not minimal after all.

Another minimization example, this time a 4-variable function, is shown in Figure 4-32. There are just two prime implicants, and it's quite obvious that both of them must be included in the minimal sum in order to cover all of the 1-cells on the map. We didn't draw the logic diagram for this example because you should know how to do that yourself by now.

complete sum   The sum of all the prime implicants of a logic function is called the *complete sum*. Although the complete sum is always a legitimate way to realize a logic function, it's not always minimal. For example, consider the logic function shown in Figure 4-33. It has five prime implicants, but the minimal sum includes only three of them. So, how can we systematically determine which prime implicants to include and which to leave out? Two more definitions are needed:

distinguished 1-cell   • A *distinguished 1-cell* of a logic function is an input combination that is covered by only one prime implicant.

Figure 4-32 $F = \Sigma_{W,X,Y,Z}(5,7,12,13,14,15)$: (a) Karnaugh map; (b) prime implicants.

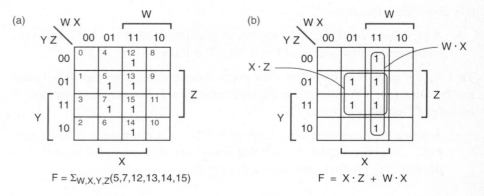

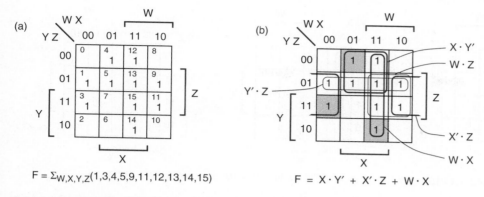

$F = \Sigma_{W,X,Y,Z}(1,3,4,5,9,11,12,13,14,15)$

$F = X \cdot Y' + X' \cdot Z + W \cdot X$

Figure 4-33 $F = \Sigma_{W,X,Y,Z}(1,3,4,5,9,11,12,13,14,15)$: (a) Karnaugh map; (b) prime implicants and distinguished 1-cells.

- An *essential prime implicant* of a logic function is a prime implicant that covers one or more distinguished 1-cells.

essential prime implicant

Since an essential prime implicant is the *only* prime implicant that covers some 1-cell, it *must* be included in every minimal sum for the logic function. So, the first step in the prime-implicant selection process is simple—we identify distinguished 1-cells and the corresponding prime implicants, and we include the essential prime implicants in the minimal sum. Then we need only determine how to cover the 1-cells, if any, that are not covered by the essential prime implicants. In the example of Figure 4-33, the three distinguished 1-cells are shaded, and the corresponding essential prime implicants are circled with heavier lines. All of the 1-cells in this example are covered by essential prime implicants, so we need go no further. Likewise, Figure 4-34 shows an example where all of the prime implicants are essential, and so all are included in the minimal sum.

Figure 4-34 $F = \Sigma_{W,X,Y,Z}(2,3,4,5,6,7,11,13,15)$: (a) Karnaugh map; (b) prime implicants and distinguished 1-cells.

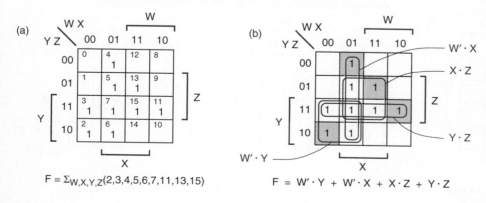

$F = \Sigma_{W,X,Y,Z}(2,3,4,5,6,7,11,13,15)$

$F = W' \cdot Y + W' \cdot X + X \cdot Z + Y \cdot Z$

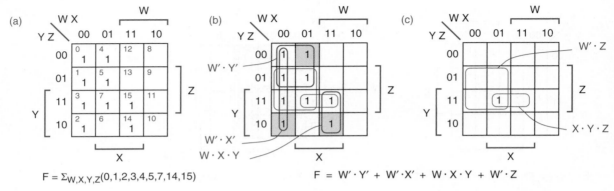

$F = \Sigma_{W,X,Y,Z}(0,1,2,3,4,5,7,14,15)$

$F = W' \cdot Y' + W' \cdot X' + W \cdot X \cdot Y + W' \cdot Z$

Figure 4-35 $F = \Sigma_{W,X,Y,Z}(0,1,2,3,4,5,7,14,15)$: (a) Karnaugh map; (b) prime implicants and distinguished 1-cells; (c) reduced map after removal of essential prime implicants and covered 1-cells.

A logic function in which not all the 1-cells are covered by essential prime implicants is shown in Figure 4-35. By removing the essential prime implicants and the 1-cells they cover, we obtain a reduced map with only a single 1-cell and two prime implicants that cover it. The choice in this case is simple—we use the $W' \cdot Z$ product term because it has fewer inputs and therefore lower cost.

For more complex cases, we need yet another definition:

eclipse

- Given two prime implicants P and Q in a reduced map, P is said to eclipse Q (written $P \supseteq Q$) if P covers at least all the 1-cells covered by Q.

If P costs no more than Q and eclipses Q, then removing Q from consideration cannot prevent us from finding a minimal sum; that is, P is at least as good as Q.

An example of eclipsing is shown in Figure 4-36. After removing essential prime implicants, we are left with two 1-cells, each of which is covered by two

Figure 4-36 $F = \Sigma_{W,X,Y,Z}(2,6,7,9,13,15)$: (a) Karnaugh map; (b) prime implicants and distinguished 1-cells; (c) reduced map after removal of essential prime implicants and covered 1-cells.

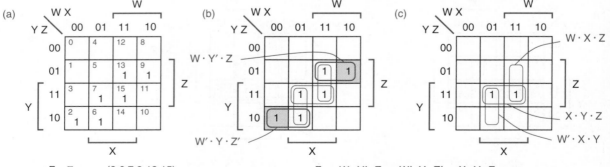

$F = \Sigma_{W,X,Y,Z}(2,6,7,9,13,15)$

$F = W \cdot Y' \cdot Z + W' \cdot Y \cdot Z' + X \cdot Y \cdot Z$

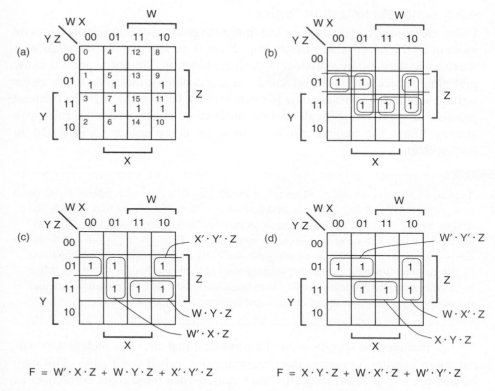

Figure 4-37 $F = \Sigma_{W,X,Y,Z}(1,5,7,9,11,15)$: (a) Karnaugh map; (b) prime implicants; (c) a minimal sum; (d) another minimal sum.

prime implicants. However, $X \cdot Y \cdot Z$ eclipses the other two prime implicants, which therefore may be removed from consideration. The two 1-cells are then covered only by $X \cdot Y \cdot Z$, which is a *secondary essential prime implicant* that must be included in the minimal sum.

secondary essential prime implicant

Figure 4-37 shows a more difficult case—a logic function with no essential prime implicants. By trial and error we can find two different minimal sums for this function.

We can also approach the problem systematically using the *branching method*. Starting with any 1-cell, we arbitrarily select one of the prime implicants that covers it, and we include it as if it were essential. This simplifies the remaining problem, which we can complete in the usual way to find a tentative minimal sum. We repeat this process starting with all other prime implicants that cover the starting 1-cell, generating a different tentative minimal sum from each starting point. We may get stuck along the way and have to apply the branching method recursively. Finally, we compare the costs of all of the tentative minimal sums that we generated in this way and select one that is truly minimal.

branching method

4.3.6 Other Minimization Topics

product-of-sums minimization

Using the principle of duality, we can minimize product-of-sums expressions by looking at the 0s on a Karnaugh map. Each 0 on the map corresponds to a maxterm in the canonical product of the logic function. The entire process in the preceding subsection can be reformulated in a dual way, including the rules for writing sum terms corresponding to circled sets of 0s, in order to find a *minimal product*. It's not too difficult to find minimal products using the rules you already know for finding minimal sums, as described at DDPPonline in Section Min.1.

minimal product

PLD MINIMIZATION

Typical PLDs have an AND-OR array corresponding to a sum-of-products form, so you might think that only the minimal sum-of-products is relevant to a PLD-based design. However, most PLDs also have an inverter/buffer at the output of the AND-OR array, which can be programmed to invert or not. Thus, the PLD can utilize the equivalent of the minimal sum by using the AND-OR array to realize the complement of the desired function and then programming the inverter/buffer to invert. Most logic-minimization programs for PLDs automatically find both the minimal sum and the minimal product and select the one that requires fewer terms.

---

don't-care

Sometimes the specification of a combinational circuit is such that its output doesn't matter for certain input combinations, called *don't-cares*. This may be true because the outputs really don't matter when these input combinations occur, or because these input combinations never occur in normal operation. It's possible to adapt the minimization method of the preceding subsection to allow either a 0 or a 1 output—whichever results in a lower-cost circuit—for each don't-care input combination. Such *don't-care minimization* is described at DDPPonline in Section Min.2.

don't-care minimization

Most practical combinational logic circuits require more than one output. We can always handle a circuit with n outputs as n independent single-output design problems. However, in doing so, we may miss some opportunities for optimization. For example, consider the following three logic functions:

$$F = \Sigma_{X,Y,Z}(1,4)$$
$$G = \Sigma_{X,Y,Z}(1,7)$$
$$H = \Sigma_{X,Y,Z}(4,7)$$

Each function could be realized as a sum of products using two 3-input AND gates—one for each minterm—and one 2-input OR gate, for a total of six AND gates and three OR gates. But it's obvious that each AND gate's output can be used in two of the functions, and only three unique AND gates are required after this sharing. A formal method for finding such sharing opportunities to perform *multiple-output minimization* using Karnaugh maps is described at DDPPonline in Section Min.3.

multiple-output minimization

4.3.7 Programmed Minimization Methods

Obviously, logic minimization can be a very involved process. In real logic-design applications you are likely to encounter only two kinds of minimization problems: functions of a few variables that you can "eyeball" using the methods of the previous subsections, and more complex, multiple-output functions that are hopeless without the use of a minimization program.

We know that minimization can be performed visually for functions of a few variables using the Karnaugh-map method. The same operations can be performed for functions of an arbitrarily large number of variables (at least in principle) using a tabular method called the *Quine-McCluskey algorithm*. Like the map method, the algorithm has two steps: (a) finding all prime implicants of the function, and (b) selecting a minimal set of prime implicants that covers the function.

Quine-McCluskey algorithm

The Quine-McCluskey algorithm was originally developed as a paper-and-pencil tabular procedure, but like all algorithms, it can be translated into a computer program. Section Pmin at DDPPonline details the operation of such a program. As discussed there, both the program's data structures and its execution time can become quite large for functions, growing exponentially with the number of inputs. So, even with very fast computers with gigabytes of main memory, this program is practical only for logic functions with a relatively small number of inputs (a dozen or so).

The computational complexity of another minimization algorithm, called *iterative consensus*, grows with the number of product terms rather than the number of inputs. Compared to the Quine-McCluskey algorithm, this behavior is more desirable for realizing functions for a PLD, which may have a lot of inputs (16 or more) but is naturally limited anyway in the number of product terms in its internal AND-gate array. Like Quine-McCluskey, the iterative consensus algorithm has two steps, finding all prime implicants and selecting a minimal set that covers the function. It uses the consensus theorem (T11) as the basis for both steps. This algorithm and a corresponding program are discussed in detail at DDPPonline in Section Pmin.

iterative consensus

Spurred on by the ever-increasing density of VLSI chips, many researchers have discovered more effective ways to minimize combinational logic functions. Their results fall roughly into three categories:

1. *Computational improvements.* Improved algorithms typically use clever data structures or rearrange the order of the steps to reduce the memory requirements and execution time of the classical Quine-McCluskey and iterative consensus algorithms.

2. *Heuristic methods.* Some minimization problems are just too big to be solved using an "exact" algorithm. These problems can be attacked using shortcuts and well-educated guesses to reduce memory size and execution time to a fraction of what an "exact" algorithm would require. However,

rather than finding a provably minimal expression for a logic function, heuristic methods attempt to find an "almost minimal" one.

Even for problems that can be solved by an "exact" method, a heuristic method typically finds a good solution ten times faster. The most successful heuristic program, Espresso-II, does in fact produce minimal or near-minimal results for the majority of problems (within one or two product terms), including problems with dozens of inputs and hundreds of product terms.

3. *Looking at things differently.* Multiple-output minimization can be handled by straightforward, fairly mechanical modifications to single-output minimization methods. However, by looking at multiple-output minimization using multivalued (nonbinary) logic, the designers of the Espresso-MV algorithm were able to make substantial performance improvements over Espresso-II.

More information on these methods can be found in the References.

*4.4 Timing Hazards

steady-state behavior

The analysis methods that we developed in Section 4.2 ignore circuit delay and predict only the *steady-state behavior* of combinational logic circuits. That is, they predict a circuit's output as a function of its inputs under the assumption that the inputs have been stable for a long time, relative to the delays in the circuit's electronics. However, we showed in Section 3.6 that the actual delay from an input change to the corresponding output change in a real logic circuit is nonzero and depends on many factors.

transient behavior

glitch
hazard

Because of circuit delays, the *transient behavior* of a combinational logic circuit may differ from what is predicted by a steady-state analysis. In particular, a circuit's output may produce a short pulse, often called a *glitch*, at a time when steady-state analysis predicts that the output should not change. A *hazard* is said to exist when a circuit has the possibility of producing such a glitch. Whether or not the glitch actually occurs depends on the exact delays and other electrical characteristics of the circuit. Since such parameters are difficult to control in production circuits, a logic designer must be prepared to eliminate hazards (the *possibility* of a glitch) even though a glitch may occur only under a worst-case combination of logical and electrical conditions.

Depending on how the circuit's output is used, a system's operation may or may not be adversely affected by a glitch. When we discuss sequential circuits in Chapters 7 and 8, you'll see situations where such glitches may be harmful, and hazards must be eliminated. This section will give you the tools to predict and eliminate hazards, allowing you to design glitch-free circuits when required.

*4.4.1 Static Hazards

A *static-1 hazard* is the possibility of a circuit's output producing a 0 glitch when   *static-1 hazard*
we would expect the output to remain at a nice steady 1 based on a static analysis
of the circuit function. A formal definition is given as follows.

Definition: A static-1 hazard is a pair of input combinations that: (a) differ in
only one input variable and (b) both give a 1 output; such that it is
possible for a momentary 0 output to occur during a transition in
the differing input variable.

For example, consider the logic circuit in Figure 4-38(a). Suppose that X
and Y are both 1 and that Z is changing from 1 to 0. Then (b) shows the timing
diagram, assuming that the propagation delay through each gate or inverter is
one unit time. Even though "static" analysis predicts that the output is 1 for both
input combinations X,Y,Z = 111 and X,Y,Z = 110, the timing diagram shows that
F goes to 0 for one unit time during a 1-0 transition on Z, because of the delay in
the inverter that generates Z'.

A *static-0 hazard* is the possibility of a 1 glitch when we expect the circuit   *static-0 hazard*
to have a steady 0 output:

Definition: A static-0 hazard is a pair of input combinations that: (a) differ in
only one input variable and (b) both give a 0 output; such that it is
possible for a momentary 1 output to occur during a transition in
the differing input variable.

Since a static-0 hazard is just the dual of a static-1 hazard, an OR-AND circuit
that is the dual of Figure 4-38(a) would have a static-0 hazard.

An OR-AND circuit with four static-0 hazards is shown in Figure 4-39(a).
One of the hazards occurs when W,X,Y = 000 and Z is changed, as shown in (b).
You should be able to find the other three hazards and eliminate all of them after
studying the next subsection.

Figure 4-38 Circuit with a static-1 hazard: (a) logic diagram; (b) timing diagram.

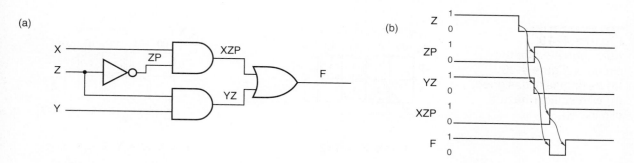

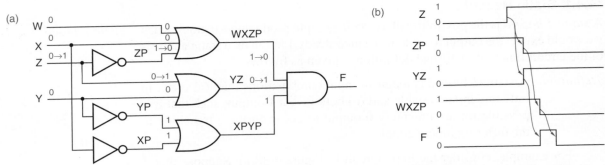

Figure 4-39 Circuit with static-0 hazards: (a) logic diagram; (b) timing diagram.

*4.4.2 Finding Static Hazards Using Maps

A Karnaugh map can be used to detect static hazards in a two-level sum-of-products or product-of-sums circuit. The existence or nonexistence of static hazards depends on the circuit design for a logic function.

A properly designed two-level sum-of-products (AND-OR) circuit has no static-0 hazards. A static-0 hazard would exist in such a circuit only if both a variable and its complement were connected to the same AND gate, which would usually be silly. However, the circuit *may* have static-1 hazards. Their existence can be predicted from a Karnaugh map where the product terms corresponding to the AND gates in the circuit are circled.

Figure 4-40(a) shows the Karnaugh map for the circuit of Figure 4-38. It is clear from the map that there is no single product term that covers both input combinations $X,Y,Z = 111$ and $X,Y,Z = 110$. Thus, intuitively, it is possible for the output to "glitch" momentarily to 0 if the AND gate output that covers one of the combinations goes to 0 before the AND gate output covering the other input combination goes to 1. The way to eliminate the hazard is also quite apparent: Simply include an extra product term (AND gate) to cover the hazardous input pair, as shown in Figure 4-40(b). The extra product term, it turns out, is the *consensus* of the two original terms; in general, we must add consensus terms to

consensus

Figure 4-40
Karnaugh map for the circuit of Figure 4-38: (a) as originally designed; (b) with static-1 hazard eliminated.

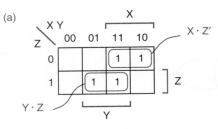

$$F = X \cdot Z' + Y \cdot Z$$

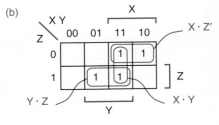

$$F = X \cdot Z' + Y \cdot Z + X \cdot Y$$

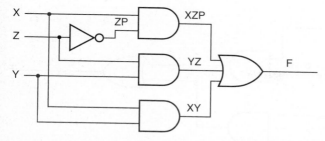

Figure 4-41 Circuit with static-1 hazard eliminated.

eliminate hazards. The corresponding hazard-free circuit is shown in Figure 4-41.

Another example is shown in Figure 4-42. In this example, three product terms must be added to eliminate the static-1 hazards.

A properly designed two-level product-of-sums (OR-AND) circuit has no static-1 hazards. It *may* have static-0 hazards, however. These hazards can be detected and eliminated by studying the adjacent 0s in the Karnaugh map, in a manner dual to the foregoing.

*4.4.3 Dynamic Hazards

A *dynamic hazard* is the possibility of an output changing more than once as the result of a single input transition. Multiple output transitions can occur if there are multiple paths with different delays from the changing input to the changing output.

dynamic hazard

Figure 4-42 Karnaugh map for another sum-of-products circuit: (a) as originally designed; (b) with extra product terms to cover static-1 hazards.

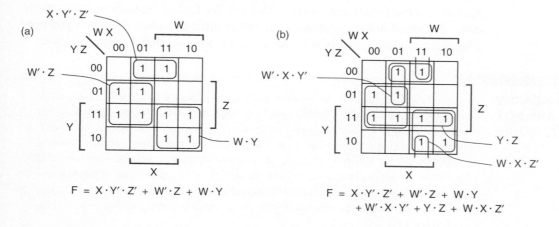

$$F = X \cdot Y' \cdot Z' + W' \cdot Z + W \cdot Y$$

$$F = X \cdot Y' \cdot Z' + W' \cdot Z + W \cdot Y$$
$$+ W' \cdot X \cdot Y' + Y \cdot Z + W \cdot X \cdot Z'$$

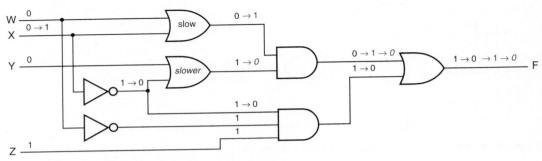

Figure 4-43 Circuit with a dynamic hazard.

For example, consider the circuit in Figure 4-43; it has three different paths from input X to the output F. One of the paths goes through a slow OR gate, and another goes through an OR gate that is even slower. If the input to the circuit is W, X, Y, Z = 0, 0, 0, 1, then the output will be 1, as shown. Now suppose we change the X input to 1. Assuming that all of the gates except the two marked "slow" and "slower" are very fast, the transitions shown in black occur next, and the output goes to 0. Eventually, the output of the "slow" OR gate changes, creating the transitions shown in nonitalic color, and the output goes to 1. Finally, the output of the "slower" OR gate changes, creating the transitions shown in italic color, and the output goes to its final state of 0.

Dynamic hazards do not occur in a properly designed two-level AND-OR or OR-AND circuit, that is, one in which no variable and its complement are connected to the same first-level gate. In multilevel circuits, dynamic hazards can be discovered using a method described in the References.

*4.4.4 Designing Hazard-Free Circuits

Only a few situations, such as the design of feedback sequential circuits, require hazard-free combinational circuits. Methods for finding hazards in arbitrary circuits, described in the References, are rather difficult to use. So, when you need a hazard-free design, it's best to use a circuit structure that's easy to analyze.

MOST HAZARDS ARE NOT HAZARDOUS!	Any combinational circuit can be analyzed for the presence of hazards. However, a well-designed, *synchronous* digital system is structured so that hazard analysis is not needed for most of its circuits. In a synchronous system, all of the inputs to a combinational circuit are changed at a particular time, and the outputs are not "looked at" until they have had time to settle to a steady-state value. Hazard analysis and elimination are typically needed only in the design of asynchronous sequential circuits, such as the feedback sequential circuits discussed in Section 7.9. You'll rarely need to design such a circuit, but if you do, an understanding of hazards will be essential for a reliable result.

In particular, we have indicated that a properly designed two-level AND-OR circuit has no static-0 or dynamic hazards. Static-1 hazards may exist in such a circuit, but they can be found and eliminated using the map method described earlier. If cost is not a problem, then a brute-force method of obtaining a hazard-free realization is to use the complete sum—the sum of all of the prime implicants of the logic function (see Exercise 4.62). In a dual manner, a hazard-free two-level OR-AND circuit can be designed for any logic function. Finally, note that everything we've said about AND-OR circuits naturally applies to the corresponding NAND-NAND designs, and about OR-AND applies to NOR-NOR.

References

A historical description of Boole's development of "the science of Logic" appears in *The Computer from Pascal to von Neumann* by Herman H. Goldstine (Princeton University Press, 1972). Claude E. Shannon showed how Boole's work could be applied to logic circuits in "A Symbolic Analysis of Relay and Switching Circuits" (*Trans. AIEE,* Vol. 57, 1938, pp. 713–723).

Although the two-valued Boolean algebra is the basis for switching algebra, a Boolean algebra need not have only two values. Boolean algebras with 2^n values exist for every integer n; for example, see *Discrete Mathematical Structures and Their Applications* by Harold S. Stone (SRA, 1973). Such algebras may be formally defined using the so-called *Huntington postulates* devised by E. V. Huntington in 1907; for example, see *Digital Design* by M. Morris Mano (Prentice Hall, 2002, third edition). Our engineering-style, "direct" development of switching algebra follows that of Edward J. McCluskey in his *Introduction to the Theory of Switching Circuits* (McGraw-Hill, 1965) and *Logic Design Principles* (Prentice Hall, 1986).

Huntington postulates

The prime-implicant theorem was proved by W. V. Quine in "The Problem of Simplifying Truth Functions" (*Am. Math. Monthly*, Vol. 59, No. 8, 1952, pp. 521–531). It's also possible to prove a more general theorem showing that there exists at least one minimal sum that is a sum of prime implicants even without the constraint on the number of literals in the definition of "minimal."

A graphical method for simplifying Boolean functions was proposed by E. W. Veitch in "A Chart Method for Simplifying Boolean Functions" (*Proc. ACM*, May 1952, pp. 127–133). His *Veitch diagram*, shown in Figure 4-44,

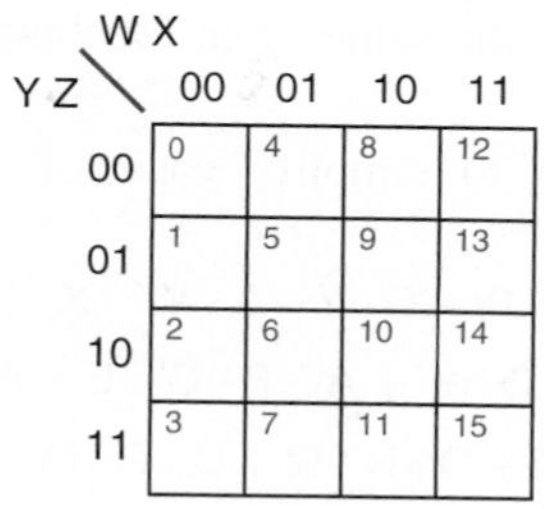

Figure 4-44
A 4-variable Veitch diagram or Marquand chart.

actually reinvented a chart proposed by an English archaeologist, A. Marquand ("On Logical Diagrams for *n* Terms," *Philosophical Magazine* XII, 1881, pp. 266–270). The Veitch diagram or Marquand chart uses "natural" binary counting order for its rows and columns, with the result that some adjacent rows and columns differ in more than one value, and product terms do not always cover adjacent cells. M. Karnaugh, an engineer, showed how to fix the problem in "A Map Method for Synthesis of Combinational Logic Circuits" (*Trans. AIEE, Comm. and Electron.*, Vol. 72, Part I, November 1953, pp. 593–599).

0-set
1-set
P-set
S-set

In this chapter we described a map method for finding static hazards in two-level AND-OR and OR-AND circuits, but any combinational circuit can be analyzed for hazards. In both his 1965 and 1986 books, McCluskey defines the *0-set* and *1-sets* of a circuit and shows how they can be used to find static hazards. He also defines *P-sets* and *S-sets* and shows how they can be used to find dynamic hazards.

Many deeper and varied aspects of switching theory have been omitted from this book but have been beaten to death in other books and literature. A good starting point for an academic study of classical switching theory is Zvi Kohavi's book, *Switching and Finite Automata Theory*, second edition (McGraw-Hill, 1978), which includes material on set theory, symmetric networks, functional decomposition, threshold logic, fault detection, and path sensitization. Another area of great academic interest (but little commercial

multiple-valued logic

activity) is nonbinary *multiple-valued logic*, in which each signal line can take on more than two values. In his 1986 book, McCluskey gives a good introduction to multiple-valued logic, explaining its pros and cons and why it has seen little commercial development.

Drill Problems

4.1   Using variables NERD, DESIGNER, FAILURE, and STUDIED, write a Boolean expression that is 1 for successful designers who never studied and for nerds who studied all the time.

4.2   Prove theorems T2–T5 using perfect induction.

4.3   Prove theorems T1′–T3′ and T5′ using perfect induction.

4.4   Prove theorems T6–T9 using perfect induction.

4.5   According to DeMorgan's theorem, the complement of $W \cdot X + Y \cdot Z$ is $W' + X' \cdot Y' + Z'$. Yet both functions are 1 for WXYZ = 1110. How can both a function and its complement be 1 for the same input combination? What's wrong here?

4.6   Use switching-algebra theorems to simplify each of the following logic functions:

(a) $F = W \cdot X \cdot Y \cdot Z \cdot (W \cdot X \cdot Y \cdot Z' + W \cdot X' \cdot Y \cdot Z + W' \cdot X \cdot Y \cdot Z + W \cdot X \cdot Y' \cdot Z)$

(b) $F = A \cdot B + A \cdot B \cdot C' \cdot D + A \cdot B \cdot D \cdot E' + A' \cdot B \cdot C' \cdot E + A' \cdot B' \cdot C' \cdot E$

(c) $F = M \cdot R \cdot P + Q \cdot O' \cdot R' + M \cdot N + O \cdot N \cdot M + Q \cdot P \cdot M \cdot O'$

4.7   Write the truth table for each of the following logic functions:

(a) $F = X' \cdot Y + X' \cdot Y' \cdot Z$ (b) $F = W' \cdot X + Y' \cdot Z' + X' \cdot Z$

(c) $F = W' \cdot X + W \cdot (Y' + Z)$ (d) $F = A \cdot B' + B' \cdot C + C \cdot D' + C \cdot A'$

(e) $F = V \cdot W' + X \cdot Y' \cdot Z$ (f) $F = (A' + B' \cdot C \cdot D) \cdot (B' + C' + D \cdot E')$

(g) $F = (W \cdot Z)' \cdot (X' + Y')'$ (h) $F = (((A + B')' + C)' + D)'$

(i) $F = (A' + B + C') \cdot (A' + B' + D) \cdot (B + C + D') \cdot (A + B + C + D)$

4.8   Write the truth table for each of the following logic functions:

(a) $F = X' \cdot Y' \cdot Z' + X \cdot Y \cdot Z + X \cdot Y' \cdot Z$ (b) $F = M' \cdot N' + M \cdot P + N' \cdot P$

(c) $F = A \cdot B + A \cdot B' \cdot C' + A' \cdot B \cdot C$ (d) $F = A' \cdot B \cdot (C \cdot B \cdot A' + B \cdot C')$

(e) $F = X \cdot Y \cdot (X' \cdot Y \cdot Z + X \cdot Y' \cdot Z + X \cdot Y \cdot Z' + X' \cdot Y' \cdot Z)$ (f) $F = M \cdot N + M' \cdot N' \cdot P'$

(g) $F = (A + A') \cdot B + B \cdot A \cdot C' + C \cdot (A + B') \cdot (A' + B)$ (h) $F = X \cdot Y' + Y \cdot Z + Z' \cdot X$

4.9   Write the canonical sum and product for each of the following logic functions:

(a) $F = \Sigma_{X,Y}(1,2)$ (b) $F = \Pi_{A,B}(0,1,2)$

(c) $F = \Sigma_{A,B,C}(1,2,4,6)$ (d) $F = \Pi_{W,X,Y}(0,2,3,6,7)$

(e) $F = X' + Y \cdot Z$ (f) $F = V + (W \cdot X')'$

4.10 Write the canonical sum and product for each of the following logic functions:

(a) $F = \Sigma_{X,Y,Z}(0,3)$ (b) $F = \Pi_{A,B,C}(1,2,4)$

(c) $F = \Sigma_{A,B,C,D}(1,2,5,6)$ (d) $F = \Pi_{M,N,P}(0,1,3,6,7)$

(e) $F = X' + Y \cdot Z' + Y \cdot Z'$ (f) $F = A'B + B'C + A$

4.11 Mathematicians will tell you that "1" is not really a prime number. Rewrite the minterm list and the canonical sum and redraw the logic diagram of the prime-number-detector example on page 205, assuming that "1" is not prime.

4.12 If the canonical sum for an *n*-input logic function is also a minimal sum, how many literals are in each product term of the sum? Might there be any other minimal sums in this case?

4.13 Give two reasons why the cost of inverters is not included in the definition of "minimal" for logic minimization.

4.14 Using Karnaugh maps, find a minimal sum-of-products expression for each of the following logic functions. Indicate the distinguished 1-cells in each map.

(a) $F = \Sigma_{X,Y,Z}(1,3,5,6,7)$ (b) $F = \Sigma_{W,X,Y,Z}(1,4,5,6,7,9,14,15)$

(c) $F = \Pi_{W,X,Y}(1,4,5,6,7)$ (d) $F = \Sigma_{W,X,Y,Z}(0,1,6,7,8,9,14,15)$

(e) $F = \Pi_{A,B,C,D}(4,5,6,13,15)$ (f) $F = \Sigma_{A,B,C,D}(4,5,6,11,13,14,15)$

4.15 Using Karnaugh maps, find a minimal sum-of-products expression for each of the following logic functions. Indicate the distinguished 1-cells in each map.

(a) $F = \Sigma_{A,B,C}(0,1,2,4)$ (b) $F = \Sigma_{W,X,Y,Z}(1,4,5,6,11,12,13,14)$

(c) $F = \Pi_{A,B,C}(1,2,6,7)$ (d) $F = \Sigma_{W,X,Y,Z}(0,1,2,3,7,8,10,11,15)$

(e) $F = \Sigma_{W,X,Y,Z}(1,2,4,7,8,11,13,14)$ (f) $F = \Pi_{A,B,C,D}(1,3,4,5,6,7,9,12,13,14)$

4.16   Re-do the prime-number-detector minimization example of Figure 4-31, assuming that "1" is not a prime number.

4.17   Find the complete sum for the logic functions in Drill 4.15(d) and (e).

4.18   Using Karnaugh maps, find a minimal sum-of-products expression for each of the following logic functions. Indicate the distinguished 1-cells in each map.

(a) $F = \Sigma_{W,X,Y,Z}(0,1,3,5,14) + d(8,15)$ (b) $F = \Sigma_{W,X,Y,Z}(0,1,2,8,11) + d(3,9,15)$

(c) $F = \Sigma_{A,B,C,D}(4,6,7,9,13) + d(12)$ (d) $F = \Sigma_{A,B,C,D}(1,5,12,13,14,15) + d(7,9)$

(e) $F = \Sigma_{W,X,Y,Z}(4,5,9,13,15) + d(0,1,7,11,12)$

4.19   For each of the following logic expressions, find all of the static hazards in the corresponding two-level AND-OR or OR-AND circuit, and design a hazard-free circuit that realizes the same logic function.

(a) $F = W \cdot X + W' \cdot Y'$ (b) $F = W \cdot X' \cdot Y' + X \cdot Y' \cdot Z + X \cdot Y$

(c) $F = W \cdot Y + W' \cdot Z' + X \cdot Y' \cdot Z$ (d) $F = W' \cdot X' + Y' \cdot Z + W' \cdot X \cdot Y \cdot Z + W \cdot X \cdot Y \cdot Z'$

(e) $F = (W' + X + Y') \cdot (X' + Z)$ (f) $F = (W + Y' + Z') \cdot (W' + X' + Z') \cdot (X' + Y + Z)$

(g) $F = (W + Y + Z') \cdot (W + X' + Y + Z) \cdot (X' + Y') \cdot (X + Z)$

Exercises

4.20   Design a non-trivial-looking logic circuit that contains a feedback loop but has an output that depends only on its current input.

4.21   Prove the combining theorem T10 without using perfect induction, but assuming that theorems T1–T9 and T1'–T9' are true.

4.22   Show that the combining theorem T10 is just a special case of consensus (T11) used with covering (T9).

4.23   Prove that $(X + Y') \cdot Y = X \cdot Y$ *without* using perfect induction. You may assume that theorems T1–T11 and T1'–T11' are true.

4.24   Prove that $(X + Y) \cdot (X' + Z) = X \cdot Z + X' \cdot Y$ *without* using perfect induction. You may assume that theorems T1–T11 and T1'–T11' are true.

4.25   Show that an n-input OR gate can be replaced by $(n-1)$ 2-input OR gates. Can the same statement be made for NOR gates? Justify your answer.

4.26   How many physically different ways are there to realize $V \cdot W \cdot X \cdot Y \cdot Z$ using four 2-input AND gates (4/4 of a 74x08)? Justify your answer.

4.27   Use switching algebra to prove that tying together two inputs of an $(n+1)$-input AND or OR gate gives it the functionality of an n-input gate.

4.28   Prove DeMorgan's theorems (T13 and T13') using finite induction.

4.29   Which logic symbol more closely approximates the internal realization of a TTL NOR gate, Figure 4-4(c) or (d)? Why?

4.30   Use the theorems of switching algebra to rewrite the following expression using as few inversions as possible (complemented parentheses are allowed):

$B' \cdot C + A \cdot C \cdot D' + A' \cdot C + E \cdot B' + E \cdot (A + C) \cdot (A' + D')$

4.31   Prove Shannon's expansion theorems. (*Hint:* Don't get carried away; it's easy.)

4.32   The *generalized Shannon expansion theorems* "pull out" not just one but i variables so that a logic function can be expressed as a sum or product of 2^i terms. Figure out and state the generalized Shannon expansion theorems.

generalized Shannon-expansion theorems

4.33   Show how the generalized Shannon expansion theorems lead to the canonical sum and canonical product representations of logic functions.

4.34   Prove or disprove the following propositions:

(a) Let A and B be switching-algebra *variables*. Then $A \cdot B = 0$ and $A + B = 1$ implies that $A = B'$.

(b) Let X and Y be switching-algebra *expressions*. Then $X \cdot Y = 0$ and $X + Y = 1$ implies that $X = Y'$.

4.35   An *Exclusive OR (XOR) gate* is a 2-input gate whose output is 1 if and only if exactly one of its inputs is 1. Write a truth table, sum-of-products expression, and corresponding AND-OR circuit for the Exclusive OR function.

Exclusive OR (XOR) gate

4.36   An *Exclusive NOR (XNOR) gate* is a 2-input gate whose output is 1 if and only if both of its inputs are equal. Write a truth table, sum-of-products expression, and corresponding AND-OR circuit for the Exclusive NOR function.

Exclusive NOR (XNOR) gate

4.37   From the point of view of switching algebra, what is the function of a 2-input XNOR gate whose inputs are tied together? How might the output behavior of a real XNOR gate differ?

4.38   After completing the design and fabrication of an SSI-based digital system, a designer finds that one more inverter is required. However, the only spare gates in the system are a 2-input OR, a 3-input AND, and a 2-input XNOR. How should the designer realize the inverter function without adding another IC?

4.39   Any set of logic-gate types that can realize any logic function is called a *complete set* of logic gates. For example, 2-input AND gates, 2-input OR gates, and inverters are a complete set, because any logic function can be expressed as a sum of products of variables and their complements, and AND and OR gates with any number of inputs can be made from 2-input gates. Do 2-input NAND gates form a complete set of logic gates? Prove your answer.

complete set

4.40   Do 2-input AND gates which have one input inverted form a complete set of logic gates? Prove your answer. Why might this type of gate be called an "inhibit" gate? Does this mean that a standard AND gate could be called "uninhibited"?

4.41   Do 2-input XNOR gates form a complete set of logic gates? Prove your answer.

4.42   Some people think that there are *four* basic logic functions, AND, OR, NOT, and *BUT*. Figure X4.42 is a possible symbol for a 4-input, 2-output *BUT gate*. Invent a useful, nontrivial function for the BUT gate to perform. The function should have something to do with the name (BUT). Keep in mind that, due to the symmetry of the symbol, the function should be symmetric with respect to the A and B inputs of each section and with respect to sections 1 and 2. Describe your BUT's function and write its truth table.

BUT
BUT gate

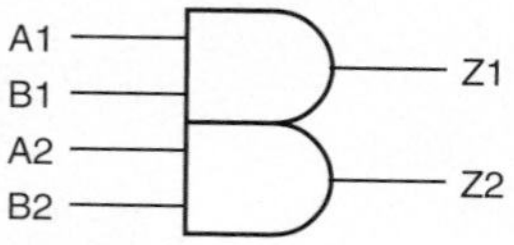

Figure X4.42

4.43   Write logic expressions for the Z1 and Z2 outputs of the BUT gate you designed in the preceding exercise, and draw a corresponding logic diagram using AND gates, OR gates, and inverters.

4.44   How many different nontrivial logic functions are there of n variables? Here, "nontrivial" means that all of the variables affect the output.

4.45   A digital system that includes three signals, X, Y, and Z, has been designed so that at all times, at least two of these three signals are 1. In this system, how many different 3-variable logic functions F(X,Y,Z) are there? Functions are considered to be different only if their outputs differ for at least one of the normally occurring input combinations. Write a simplified algebraic expression for each function.

4.46   Most students have no problem using theorem T8 to "multiply out" logic expressions, but many develop a mental block if they try to use theorem T8′ to "add out" a logic expression. How can duality be used to overcome this problem?

self-dual logic function
$\oplus$

4.47   A *self-dual logic function* is a function F such that $F = F^D$. Which of the following functions are self-dual? (Here, $\oplus$ denotes the Exclusive OR (XOR) operation.)

(a) $F = X$

(b) $F = \Sigma_{X,Y,Z}(1,2,5,7)$

(c) $F = X' \cdot Y \cdot Z' + X \cdot Y' \cdot Z' + X \cdot Y$

(d) $F = W \cdot (X \oplus Y \oplus Z \oplus W') + (X \oplus Y \oplus Z)$

(e) A function F of 6 variables such that $F = 1$ if and only if 3 or more of the variables are 1

(f) A function F of 9 variables such that $F = 1$ if and only if 5 or more of the variables are 1

4.48   How many self-dual logic functions of n input variables are there? (*Hint:* Consider the structure of the truth table of a self-dual function.)

4.49   Prove that any n-input logic function $F(X_1,\dots,X_n)$ that can be written in the form $F = X_1 \cdot G(X_2,\dots,X_n) + X_1' \cdot G^D(X_2,\dots,X_n)$ is self-dual.

4.50   Assuming that an inverting gate has a propagation delay of 5 ns, and that a non-inverting gate has a propagation delay of 8 ns, compare the speeds of the circuits in Figure 4-24(a), (c), and (d).

4.51   Prove that the rule for combining 2^i 1-cells in a Karnaugh map is true, using the axioms and theorems of switching algebra.

irredundant sum

4.52   An *irredundant sum* for a logic function F is a sum of prime implicants for F such that if any prime implicant is deleted, the sum no longer equals F. This sounds a lot like a minimal sum, but an irredundant sum is not necessarily minimal. For example, the minimal sum of the function in Figure 4-36 has only three product terms, but there is an irredundant sum with four product terms. Find the irredundant sum and draw a map of the function, circling only the prime implicants in the irredundant sum.

4.53   Find another logic function in Section 4.3 that has one or more nonminimal irredundant sums, and draw its map, circling only the prime implicants in the irredundant sum.

4.54   Draw a Karnaugh map and assign variables to the inputs of the OR-XOR circuit in Figure X4.54 so that its output is $F = \Sigma_{W,X,Y,Z}(2,3,8,9)$. What is the solution if the OR gates are changed to NOR gates? Note that the output gate is a 2-input XOR rather than an AND or OR.

Figure X4.54

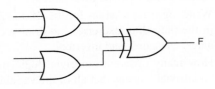

F

4.55 A 3-bit "comparator" circuit receives two 3-bit numbers, $P = P_2P_1P_0$ and $Q = Q_2Q_1Q_0$. Design a minimal sum-of-products circuit that produces a 1 output if and only if $P < Q$.

4.56 Find minimal multiple-output sum-of-products expressions for $F = \Sigma_{X,Y,Z}(0,1,2)$, $G = \Sigma_{X,Y,Z}(1,4,6)$, and $H = \Sigma_{X,Y,Z}(0,1,2,4,6)$.

4.57 Prove whether or not the following expression is a minimal sum. Do it the easiest way possible, not using maps.

$$F = S' \cdot T \cdot U \cdot V \cdot W + S' \cdot T \cdot U' \cdot W \cdot Y + S' \cdot T \cdot V \cdot W \cdot X' \cdot Y$$

4.58 The text states that a truth table or equivalent is the starting point for traditional combinational minimization methods. A Karnaugh map itself contains the same information as a truth table. Given a sum-of-products expression, it is possible to write the 1s corresponding to each product term directly on the map without developing an explicit truth table or minterm list, and then proceed with the map-minimization procedure. In this way, find a minimal sum-of-products expression for each of the following logic functions:

(a) $F = X' \cdot Z + X \cdot Y + X \cdot Y' \cdot Z$

(b) $F = A' \cdot C' \cdot D + B' \cdot C \cdot D + A \cdot C' \cdot D + B \cdot C \cdot D$

(c) $F = W' \cdot X \cdot Z' + W \cdot X \cdot Y \cdot Z + W' \cdot Z$

(d) $F = (W + Z') \cdot (W' + Y' + Z') \cdot (X + Y' + Z)$

(e) $F = A' \cdot B' \cdot C' \cdot D' + A' \cdot C' \cdot D + B \cdot C' \cdot D' + A \cdot B \cdot D + A \cdot B' \cdot C'$

4.59 A *5-variable Karnaugh map* can be drawn for a 5-variable function as shown in Figure X4.59. In such a map, cells that occupy the same relative position in the $V = 0$ and $V = 1$ submaps are considered to be adjacent. (Many worked examples of 5-variable Karnaugh maps appear in Section 7.4.4 and in Section JKSM.2 at DDPPonline.) Find a minimal sum-of-products expression for each of the following functions using a 5-variable map:

5-variable Karnaugh map

(a) $F = \Sigma_{V,W,X,Y,Z}(5,7,13,15,16,20,25,27,29,31)$

(b) $F = \Sigma_{V,W,X,Y,Z}(0,7,8,9,12,13,15,16,22,23,30,31)$

(c) $F = \Sigma_{V,W,X,Y,Z}(0,1,2,3,4,5,10,11,14,20,21,24,25,26,27,28,29,30)$

(d) $F = \Sigma_{V,W,X,Y,Z}(0,2,4,6,7,8,10,11,12,13,14,16,18,19,29,30)$

(e) $F = \Pi_{V,W,X,Y,Z}(4,5,10,12,13,16,17,21,25,26,27,29)$

(f) $F = \Sigma_{V,W,X,Y,Z}(4,6,7,9,11,12,13,14,15,20,22,25,27,28,30) + d(1,5,29,31)$

Figure X4.59

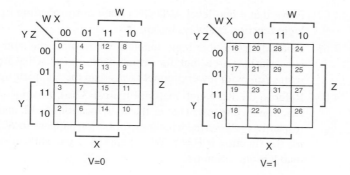

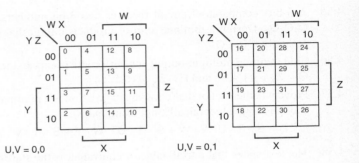

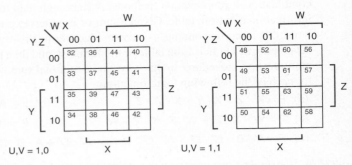

Figure X4.60

6-variable Karnaugh map

4.60   A Karnaugh map for a 6-variable function can be drawn as shown in Figure X4.60. In such a map, cells that occupy the same relative position in adjacent submaps are considered to be adjacent. Minimize the following functions using 6-variable maps:

(a) $F = \Sigma_{U,V,W,X,Y,Z}(1,5,9,13,21,23,29,31,37,45,53,61)$

(b) $F = \Sigma_{U,V,W,X,Y,Z}(0,4,8,16,24,32,34,36,37,39,40,48,50,56)$

(c) $F = \Sigma_{U,V,W,X,Y,Z}(2,4,5,6,12\text{--}21,28\text{--}31,34,38,50,51,60\text{--}63)$

4.61   (*Hamlet circuit.*) Complete the timing diagram and explain the function of the circuit in Figure X4.61. Where does the circuit get its name?

Figure X4.61

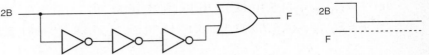

4.62   Prove that a two-level AND-OR circuit corresponding to the complete sum of a logic function is always hazard free.

4.63   Find a four-variable logic function whose minimal sum-of-products realization is not hazard free, but for which there exists a hazard-free sum-of-products realization with fewer product terms than the complete sum.

4.64   Refer to the Karnaugh map in Figure 4-32(a). Imagine sliding all the 1s in that function up one row. That is, the 1s in locations 5, 12, and 13 go to 4, 12, and 14, respectively. Describe what transformation happens to W, X, Y, and Z. *Hint:* Imagine the function is $F = Y$. What happens if you shift the contents of a Karnaugh map left one column?

```
module ButGate
  (A, B, C, D, Y, Z);
input A, B, C, D;
output Y, Z;
reg Y, Z;

always @ (A, B, C, D)
  begin
    if ((A==B)&&(C!=D))
      Y = 1;
    else Y = 0;
    if ((C==D)&&(A!=B))
      Z = 1;
    else Z = 0;
  end
endmodule
```

chapter 5

Hardware Description Languages

Thirty years ago, the primary tools of a digital designer included a logic-drawing template, such as in Figure 1-3 on page 9, a ruler, and a pencil, all for drawing schematic diagrams. In the 1980s, schematics were still the primary means of describing digital circuits and systems, but at least schematic creation and maintenance had been simplified by the introduction of schematic editor tools. That decade also saw limited use of hardware description languages (HDLs), mainly to describe logic equations to be realized in programmable logic devices (PLDs).

In the 1990s, HDL usage by digital system designers accelerated as PLDs, CPLDs, and FPGAs became inexpensive and commonplace. At the same time, as ASIC densities continued to increase, it became increasingly more difficult to describe large circuits using schematics alone, and many ASIC designers turned to HDLs as a means to design individual modules within a system-on-a-chip. Today, HDLs are by far the most common way to describe both the top-level and the detailed module-level design of a PLD, CPLD, FPGA, or ASIC. Schematics are often used only to specify the board-level interconnections among these devices and other components such as memories, microprocessors, and SSI/MSI "glue" logic.

The first HDL to enjoy widespread commercial use was PALASM (PAL Assembler) from Monolithic Memories, Inc., the inventors of the PAL device. Introduced in the early 1980s, it was used to specify logic equations for realization in PAL devices. In terms of computer programming languages, the first version of PALASM was like assembly language—it provided a text-based means to specify the information to be programmed (in PALASM's case, logic equations), but little else. Subsequent developments in PALASM and in competing languages, like CUPL (Compiler Universal for Programmable Logic) and ABEL (Advanced Boolean Equation Language), yielded more capabilities. These included logic minimization, "high-level" statement constructs like "if-then-else" and "case", and the ability to derive logic equations from high-level constructs. We'll describe ABEL in Section 5.2.

The next important innovations in HDLs occurred in the mid-1980s, and were the developments of VHDL and Verilog, described in Sections 5.3 and 5.4. Both languages support modular, hierarchical coding (like C and other high-level computer programming languages) and support a rich variety of high-level constructs, including arrays, procedure and function calls, and conditional and iterative statements.

Both VHDL and Verilog started out as *simulation* languages, allowing a digital system's hardware to be described and then its operations to be simulated on a computer. Thus, many of these languages' features have roots in their original simulation-only application. However, later developments in the language tools allowed actual hardware designs, based on real components, to be synthesized from the language-based descriptions. You might even think of the "D" in "HDL" changing its meaning from "Description" to "Design." ABEL, on the other hand, started as a synthesizable design language, specifically targeted to PAL devices, and simulation capability was added later.

The practices and examples chapters in the rest of this book give examples in three languages—ABEL, VHDL, and Verilog. But there are separate sections for each language and the rest of this text is written so that you only have to read about and learn just one of them (or none of them, if you want to stay in the dark ages!). In any case, before reading one or more of the language tutorials in Sections 5.2 through 5.4, you should read the section below to get some general information.

5.1 HDL-Based Digital Design

5.1.1 Why HDLs?

In previous decades, most logic design was performed graphically, using block diagrams and schematics. However, the rise of synthesizable HDLs coupled with programmable logic devices and very-large-scale ASIC technology in the 1990s has radically changed the way that typical digital designs are done.

In traditional software design, high-level programming languages like C, C++, and Java have raised the level of abstraction so that programmers can design larger, more complex systems with some sacrifice in performance compared to hand-tuned assembly-language programs. The situation for hardware design is similar. The circuit produced by a VHDL or Verilog synthesis tool may not be as small or fast as one designed and tweaked by hand by an experienced designer, but in the right hands these tools can support much larger system designs. This is, of course, a requirement if we're ever to take advantage of the millions of gates offered by the most advanced CPLD, FPGA, and ASIC technologies.

REGISTER-TRANSFER LANGUAGE (RTL)	The use of HDLs has taken off with the availability of synthesis tools, but non-synthesizable hardware description languages have been around for a while. Most prominent are *register-transfer languages*, which have been used for decades to describe the operation of synchronous systems. Such a language combines the control-flow notation of a state-machine description language with a means for defining and operating on multibit registers. Register-transfer languages have been especially useful in computer design, where individual machine-language instructions are defined as a sequence of more primitive steps involving loading, storing, combining, and testing registers.

5.1.2 HDL Tool Suites

Typically, a single integrated tool suite handles several different aspects of an HDL's use. We might informally call this "the HDL compiler," but an HDL tool suite really has several different tools with their own names and purposes:

- A *text editor* allows you to write, edit, and save an HDL program. Since the editor is coupled to the rest of the HDL development system, it often contains HDL-specific features, such as recognizing specific filename extensions associated with the HDL, and recognizing HDL reserved words and comments and displaying them in different colors.   *text editor*

- The *compiler* is responsible for parsing the HDL program, finding syntax errors, and figuring out what the program really "says." A typical HDL compiler creates a file in an intermediate, technology-neutral digital-design description language that is an unambiguous description of the interconnections and logic operations, both combinational and sequential, implied by the HDL program. However, this is still not quite a hardware realization.   *compiler*

- A *synthesizer* (or *synthesis tool*) targets the design to a specific hardware technology, such as a PLD, CPLD, FPGA, or ASIC. In doing so, it refers to one or more *libraries* having specifics on the targeted technology, such as features and limitations of PLD macrocells, or the kinds of gates and flip-flops available as basic building blocks in an ASIC. Libraries may also contain larger-scale components, such as multibit adders, registers, and counters. By analyzing the intermediate design description, a sophisticated synthesizer can "infer" the opportunity to map portions of the design into these larger-scale library components.   *synthesizer*
    synthesis tool
    libraries

simulator

test bench

waveform editor

- The inputs to a *simulator* are the HDL program and a timed sequence of inputs for the hardware that it describes. The input sequence can be contained in another HDL program, called a *test bench*, written in the same language, or it can be described graphically, using another tool called a *waveform editor*. The simulator "runs" the specified input sequence on the described hardware and determines the values of the hardware's internal signals and its outputs over a specified period of time. The outputs of the simulator can include waveforms to be viewed using the waveform editor, text files that list signal values over simulated time, and error and warning messages that highlight unusual conditions or deviations of signal values from what's expected.

Several other useful programs and utilities may be found in a typical HDL integrated tool suite:

template generator

- A *template generator* creates a text file with the outline of a commonly used program structure, so the designer can "fill in the blanks" to create source code for a particular purpose. Examples include program input and output declarations, logic structures like decoders, adders, and registers, and test benches.

schematic viewer

- A *schematic viewer* may create a schematic diagram corresponding to an HDL program, based on the intermediate-language output of the compiler. The depicted circuit is an accurate representation of the *function* performed by the final, synthesized circuit, but beware. The compiler output has not yet been targeted to a particular technology and optimized, so the depicted circuit structure may be quite different from the final, synthesized result.

translator

fitter
chip viewer

- A *translator* targets the compiler's intermediate-language output to a real device, such as a PLD, FPGA, or ASIC. There may also be an associated *fitter*, which fits the translated realization into the available resources on the real device, and a *chip viewer,* which lets the designer see how the design has been laid out on the chip. This is important for devices, like FPGAs, where layout can profoundly affect the electrical and timing performance of the final chip.

timing analyzer

- A *timing analyzer* calculates the delays through some or all of the signal paths in the final chip, and produces a report showing the worst-case paths and their delays.

back annotator

- A *back annotator* inserts delay clauses or statements in the original HDL source program, corresponding to the delays calculated by the timing analyzer. This allows subsequent simulations to include timing, whether the source program is simulated by itself or as part of a larger system.

The best way to learn about all these kinds of tools, and more, is to get some hands-on experience with an actual HDL tool suite, such as the one packaged with some printings of this book.

5.1.3 HDL-Based Design Flow

It's useful to understand the overall HDL design environment before jumping into any of the languages themselves. There are several steps in an HDL-based design process, often called the *design flow*. These steps are applicable to any HDL-based design process and are outlined in Figure 5-1.

design flow

The so-called "front end" begins with figuring out the basic approach and building blocks at the block-diagram level. Large logic designs, like software programs, are hierarchical, and VHDL and Verilog give you a good framework for defining modules and their interfaces and filling in the details later.

block diagram and hierarchy

The next step is the actual writing of HDL code for modules, their interfaces, and their internal details. Although you can use any text editor for this step, the editor included in the HDL's tool suite can make the job a little easier. HDL editor features may include highlighting of keywords, automatic indenting, templates for frequently used program structures, built-in syntax checking, and one-click access to the compiler.

coding

Once you've written some code, you will want to compile it, of course. The HDL compiler analyzes your code for syntax errors and also checks it for compatibility with other modules on which it relies. It also creates the internal information that is needed for the simulator to process your design later. As in other programming endeavors, you probably shouldn't wait until the very end of coding to compile all of your code. Doing a piece at a time can prevent you from proliferating syntax errors, inconsistent names, and so on, and can certainly give you a much-needed sense of progress when the project end is far from sight!

compilation

Perhaps the most satisfying step comes next—*simulation*. The HDL simulator allows you to define and apply inputs to your design, and to observe its outputs, without ever having to build the physical circuit. In small projects, the kind you might do as homework in a digital-design class, you would probably generate inputs and observe outputs manually. But for larger projects, HDL tool suites gives you the ability to create "test benches" that automatically apply inputs and compare them with expected outputs.

simulation

Actually, simulation is just one piece of a larger step called *verification*. Sure, it is satisfying to watch your simulated circuit produce simulated outputs,

verification

Figure 5-1 Steps in an HDL-based design flow.

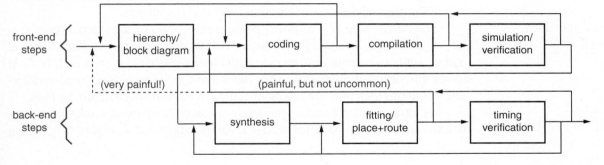

but the purpose of simulation is larger—it is to *verify* that the circuit works as desired. In a typical large project, a substantial amount of effort is expended both during and after the coding stage to define test cases that exercise the circuit over a wide range of logical operating conditions. Finding design bugs at this stage has a high value; if bugs are not found until later, all of the so-called "back-end" steps must typically be repeated.

functional verification

Note that there are at least two dimensions to verification. In *functional verification*, we study the circuit's logical operation independent of timing considerations; gate delays and other timing parameters are considered to be zero. In *timing verification*, we study the circuit's operation including estimated delays, and we verify that the setup, hold, and other timing requirements for sequential devices like flip-flops are met. It is customary to perform thorough *functional* verification before starting the back-end steps. However, our ability to do *timing* verification at this stage is often limited, since timing may be heavily dependent on the results of synthesis and fitting. We may do preliminary timing verification to gain some comfort with the overall design approach, but detailed timing verification must wait until the end.

timing verification

back end

After verification, we are ready to move into the *back-end* stage. The nature of and tools for this stage vary somewhat, depending on the target technology for the design, but there are three basic steps. The first is *synthesis*, converting the HDL description into a set of primitives or components that can be assembled in the target technology. For example, with PLDs or CPLDs, the synthesis tool may generate two-level sum-of-products equations. With ASICs, it may generate a list of gates and a *netlist* that specifies how they should be interconnected. The designer may "help" the synthesis tool by specifying certain technology-specific *constraints*, such as the maximum number of logic levels or the strength of logic buffers to use.

synthesis

netlist

constraints

fitting

In the *fitting* step, a fitter maps the synthesized primitives or components onto available device resources. For a PLD or CPLD, this may mean assigning equations to available AND-OR elements. For an FPGA or ASIC, it may mean selecting macrocells or laying down individual gates in a pattern and finding ways to connect them within the physical constraints of the FPGA or ASIC die; this is called the *place-and-route* process. The designer can usually specify additional constraints at this stage, such as the placement of modules within a chip or the pin assignments of external input and output pins.

place and route

post-fitting timing verification

The "final" step is *post-fitting timing verification* of the fitted circuit. It is only at this stage that the actual circuit delays due to wire lengths, electrical loading, and other factors can be calculated with reasonable precision. It is usual during this step to apply the same test cases that were used in functional verification, but in this step they are run against the circuit as it will actually be built.

As in any other creative process, you may occasionally take two steps forward and one step back (or worse!). As we suggested in Figure 5-1, during

IT WORKS!?   As a long-time logic designer and system builder, I always thought I knew what it means when a circuit designer says, "It works!" It means you can go into the lab, power-up a prototype without seeing smoke, and push a reset button and use an oscilloscope or logic analyzer to watch the prototype go through its paces.

But over the years, the meaning of "It works" has changed. When I took a new job in the late 1990s, I was very pleased to hear that several key ASICs for an important new product were all "working." But later (just a short time later) I figured out that the ASICs were working only in simulation, and that the design team and I still had to endure many arduous months of synthesis, fitting, timing verification, and repeating, before they could order any prototypes. "It works!"—sure. Just like my kids' homework—"It's done!"

coding you may encounter problems that force you to go back and rethink your hierarchy, and you will almost certainly have compilation and simulation errors that force you to rewrite parts of the code.

The most painful problems are the ones that you encounter in the back end of the design flow. For example, if the synthesized design doesn't fit into an available FPGA or doesn't meet timing requirements, you may have to go back as far as rethinking your whole design approach. That's worth remembering—excellent tools are still no substitute for careful thought at the outset of a design.

5.2 The ABEL Hardware Description Language

The ABEL hardware description language was invented to allow designers to specify logic functions for realization in PLDs. An ABEL program is a text file containing several elements:

- Documentation, including program name and comments.
- Declarations that identify the inputs and outputs of the logic functions to be performed.
- Statements that specify the logic functions to be performed.
- Usually, a declaration of the type of PLD or other targeted device in which the specified logic functions are to be performed.
- Usually, "test vectors" that specify the logic functions' expected outputs for certain inputs.

LEGAL NOTICE   ABEL (Advanced Boolean Equation Language) is a trademark of the Data I/O Corporation (www.dataio.com).

<table>
<tr><td>*ABEL language processor*
ABEL compiler</td><td>ABEL is supported by an *ABEL language processor*, which we'll simply call an *ABEL compiler*. The compiler's job is to translate the ABEL text file into a "fuse pattern" that can be downloaded into a physical PLD. Even though most PLDs can be physically programmed only with patterns corresponding to sum-of-products expressions, ABEL allows PLD functions to be expressed with truth tables or nested "IF" statements as well as in algebraic expression format. The compiler manipulates these formats and minimizes the resulting equations to fit, if possible, into a specified PLD.

We'll talk about PLD structures, fuse patterns, and related topics later, in Section 6.3, and we'll show how to target ABEL programs to specific PLDs. In the meantime, we'll show how ABEL can be used to specify combinational logic functions without necessarily having to declare the targeted device type. Later, in Section 7.11, we'll do the same for sequential logic functions.</td></tr>
</table>

5.2.1 ABEL Program Structure

Table 5-1 shows the typical structure of an ABEL program, including the following language features:

identifier

- *Identifiers* must begin with a letter or underscore, may contain up to 31 letters, digits, and underscores, and are case sensitive.

module statement

- A program file begins with a *module* statement, which associates an identifier (Alarm_Circuit) with the program module. Large programs can have multiple modules, each with its own local title, declarations, and equations. Note that keywords such as "module" are not case sensitive, and they are shown in color in ABEL programs in this book.

title statement

- The *title* statement specifies a title string that will be inserted into the documentation files that are created by the compiler.

string

- A *string* is a series of characters enclosed by single quotes.

device declaration

- The optional *device* declaration includes a device identifier (ALARMCKT) and a string that denotes the device type ('P16V8C' for a GAL16V8). The compiler uses the device identifier in the names of documentation files that it generates, and it uses the device type to determine whether the device can really perform the logic functions specified in the program.

comment

- *Comments* begin with a double quote and end with another double quote or the end of the line, whichever comes first.

pin declarations

- *Pin declarations* tell the compiler about symbolic names associated with the device's external pins. If the signal name is preceded with the NOT prefix (!), then the complement of the named signal will appear on the pin. Pin declarations may or may not include pin numbers; if none are given, the compiler assigns them based on the capabilities of the targeted device.

istype keyword
com keyword

- The *istype* keyword precedes a list of one or more properties, separated by commas. This tells the compiler the type of output signal. The "com"

module *module name*
title *string*
deviceID device *deviceType* ;
pin declarations
other declarations
equations
equations
test_vectors
test vectors
end *module name*

Table 5-1
Typical structure of
an ABEL program.

keyword indicates a combinational output. If no istype keyword is given, the compiler generally assumes that the signal is an input unless it appears on the lefthand side of an equation, in which case it tries to figure out the output's properties from the context. For your own protection, it's best just to use the istype keyword for all outputs!

- *Other declarations* allow the designer to define constants and expressions to improve program readability and to simplify logic design. *other declarations*

- The *equations* statement indicates that logic equations defining output signals as functions of input signals will follow. *equations statement*

- *Equations* are written like assignment statements in a conventional programming language. Each equation is terminated by a semicolon. ABEL uses the following symbols for logical operations: *equations*

    & AND. *& (AND)*
    # OR. *# (OR)*
    ! NOT (used as a prefix). *! (NOT)*
    $ XOR. *$ (XOR)*
    !$ XNOR. *!$ (XNOR)*

As in conventional programming languages, AND (&) has precedence over OR (#) in expressions. The *@ALTERNATE* directive makes the compiler recognize an alternate set of symbols for these operations: *, +, /, :+:, and :*:, respectively. This book uses the default symbols throughout. *@ALTERNATE*

- The optional *test_vectors* statement indicates that test vectors follow. *test_vectors statement*

- *Test vectors* associate input combinations with expected output values; they are used for simulation and testing as explained in Section 5.2.6. *test vectors*

- The compiler recognizes several special constants, including .X., a single bit whose value is "don't-care." *.X.*

- The *end* statement marks the end of the module. *end statement*

Table 5-2 on the next page shows an actual ABEL program that exhibits the features above.

Table 5-2 An ABEL program for the alarm circuit of Figure 4-19.

```
module Alarm_Circuit
title 'Alarm Circuit Example
J. Wakerly, Micro Systems Engineering'
ALARMCKT device 'P16V8C';

" Input pins
PANIC, ENABLEA, EXITING        pin 1, 2, 3;
WINDOW, DOOR, GARAGE           pin 4, 5, 6;
" Output pins
ALARM                          pin 11 istype 'com';

" Constant definition
X = .X.;

" Intermediate equation
SECURE = WINDOW & DOOR & GARAGE;

equations
ALARM = PANIC # ENABLEA & !EXITING & !SECURE;

test_vectors
([PANIC,ENABLEA,EXITING,WINDOW,DOOR,GARAGE] -> [ALARM])
[    1,    .X.,    .X.,    .X., .X.,    .X.] -> [    1];
[    0,     0,     .X.,    .X., .X.,    .X.] -> [    0];
[    0,     1,      1,     .X., .X.,    .X.] -> [    0];
[    0,     1,      0,      0, .X.,    .X.] -> [    1];
[    0,     1,      0,     .X.,  0,    .X.] -> [    1];
[    0,     1,      0,     .X., .X.,     0] -> [    1];
[    0,     1,      0,      1,   1,     1] -> [    0];

end Alarm_Circuit
```

unclocked assignment operator, =

Equations for combinational outputs use the *unclocked assignment operator*, =. The lefthand side of an equation normally contains a signal name. The righthand side is a logic expression, not necessarily in sum-of-products form. The signal name on the lefthand side of an equation may be optionally preceded by the NOT operator !; this is equivalent to complementing the righthand side. The compiler's job is to generate a fuse pattern such that the signal named on the lefthand side realizes the logic expression on the righthand side.

5.2.2 ABEL Compiler Operation

The program in Table 5-2 realizes the alarm function that we described on page 206. The signal named ENABLE has been coded as ENABLEA because ENABLE is a reserved word in ABEL.

Table 5-3 Synthesized equations file produced by ABEL for Table 5-2.

```
ABEL 6.30
Design alarmckt created Wed Mar 30 2005

Title: Alarm Circuit Example
Title: J. Wakerly, Micro Systems Engineering

P-Terms   Fan-in  Fan-out  Type  Name (attributes)
---------  ------  -------  ----  -----------------
   4/3       6        1     Pin   ALARM
=========
   4/3                 Best P-Term Total: 3
                            Total Pins: 7
                           Total Nodes: 0
                Average P-Term/Output: 3

Equations:

ALARM = (ENABLEA & !EXITING & !DOOR
    # ENABLEA & !EXITING & !WINDOW
    # ENABLEA & !EXITING & !GARAGE
    # PANIC);

Reverse-Polarity Equations:

!ALARM = (!PANIC & WINDOW & DOOR & GARAGE
    # !PANIC & EXITING
    # !PANIC & !ENABLEA);
```

Notice that not all of the equations appear under the equations statement. An intermediate equation for an identifier SECURE appears earlier. This equation is merely a definition that associates an expression with the identifier SECURE. The ABEL compiler substitutes this expression for the identifier SECURE in every place that SECURE appears after its definition.

intermediate equation

In Figure 4-19 on page 207 we realized the alarm circuit directly from the SECURE and ALARM expressions, using multiple levels of logic. The ABEL compiler doesn't use expressions to interconnect gates in this way. Rather, it manipulates the expressions to obtain a minimal two-level sum-of-products result appropriate for realization in a PLD. Thus, when compiled, Table 5-2 should yield a result equivalent to the AND-OR circuit that we showed in Figure 4-20 on page 207, which happens to be minimal.

In fact, it does. Table 5-3 shows the synthesized equations file created by the ABEL compiler. Notice that the compiler creates equations only for the ALARM signal, the only output. The SECURE signal does not appear anywhere.

The compiler finds a minimal sum-of-products expression for both ALARM and its complement, !ALARM. As mentioned previously, many PLDs have the ability selectively to invert or not to invert their AND-OR output. The "reverse-polarity equation" in Table 5-3 is a sum-of-products realization of !ALARM and would be used if output inversion were selected.

In this example, the reverse-polarity equation has one less product term than the normal-polarity equation for ALARM, so the compiler will select this equation if the targeted device has selectable output inversion. A user can also force the compiler to use either normal or reverse polarity for a signal by including the keyword "buffer" or "invert", respectively, in the signal's istype property list. (With some ABEL compilers, keywords "pos" and "neg" can be used for this purpose.)

5.2.3 WHEN Statements and Equation Blocks

when statement

In addition to equations, ABEL provides the *when statement* as another means to specify combinational logic functions in the *equations* section of an ABEL program. Table 5-4 shows the general structure of a when statement, similar to an IF statement in a conventional programming language. The else clause is optional. Here *LogicExpression* is an expression which results in a value of true (1) or false (0). Either *TrueEquation* or *FalseEquation* is "executed" depending on the value of *LogicExpression*. But we need to be a little more precise about what we mean by "executed," as discussed below.

In the simplest case, *TrueEquation* and the optional *FalseEquation* are assignment statements, as in the first two when statements in Table 5-5 (for X1 and X2). In this case, *LogicExpression* is logically ANDed with the righthand side of *TrueEquation*, and the complement of *LogicExpression* is ANDed with the righthand side of *FalseEquation*. Thus, the equations for X1A and X2A produce the same results as the corresponding when statements but do not use when.

Notice in the first example that X1 appears in the *TrueEquation*, but there is no *FalseEquation*. So, what happens to X1 when *LogicExpression* (!A#B) is false? You might think that X1's value should be don't-care for these input combinations, but it's not, as explained below.

Formally, the unclocked assignment operator, =, specifies input combinations that should be added to the on-set for the output signal appearing on the lefthand side of the equation. An output's on-set starts out empty and is augmented each time that the output appears on the lefthand side of an equation. That is, the righthand sides of all equations for the same (uncomplemented) output are ORed together. (If the output appears complemented on the lefthand

Table 5-4
Structure of an ABEL
when statement.

```
when LogicExpression then
    TrueEquation;
else
    FalseEquation;
```

Table 5-5 Examples of when statements.

```
module WhenEx
title 'WHEN Statement Examples'

" Input pins
A, B, C, D, E, F                      pin;

" Output pins
X1, X1A, X2, X2A, X3, X3A, X4      pin istype 'com';
X5, X6, X7, X8, X9, X10           pin istype 'com';

equations

when (!A # B) then X1 = C & !D;

X1A = (!A # B) & (C & !D);

when (A & B) then X2 = C # D;
else X2 = E # F;

X2A = (A & B) & (C # D)
    # !(A & B) & (E # F);

when (A) then X3 = D;
else when (B) then X3 = E;
else when (C) then X3 = F;

X3A = (A) & (D)
    # !(A) & (B) & (E)
    # !(A) & !(B) & (C) & (F);

when (A) then
  {when (B) then X4 = D;}
else X4 = E;

when (A & B) then X5 = D;
else when (A # !C) then X6 = E;
else when (B # C) then X7 = F;

when (A) then {
    X8 = D & E & F;
    when (B) then X8 = 1; else {X9 = D; X10 = E;}
  } else {
    X8 = !D # !E;
    when (D) then X9 = 1;
    {X10 = C & D;}
  }

end WhenEx
```

side, the righthand side is complemented before being ORed.) Thus, the value of
X1 is 1 only for the input combinations for which *LogicExpression* (!A#B) is
true and the righthand side of *TrueEquation* (C&!D) is also true.

In the second example, X2 appears on the lefthand side of two equations, so the equivalent equation shown for X2A is obtained by ORing two righthand sides after ANDing each with the appropriate condition.

The *TrueEquation* and the optional *FalseEquation* in a when statement can be any equation. In addition, when statements can be "nested" by using another when statement as the *FalseEquation*. When statements are nested, all of the conditions leading to an "executed" statement are ANDed. The equation for X3 and its when-less counterpart for X3A in Table 5-5 illustrate the concept.

The *TrueEquation* can be another when statement if it's enclosed in braces, as shown in the X4 example in the table. This is just one instance of the general use of braces described shortly.

Although all of our when examples have assigned values to the same output within each part of a given when statement, this does not have to be the case. The second-to-last when statement in Table 5-5 is such an example.

equation block
{}

It's often useful to make more than one assignment in *TrueEquation* or *FalseEquation* or both. For this purpose, ABEL supports equation blocks anywhere that it supports a single equation. An *equation block* is just a sequence of statements enclosed in braces *{}*, as shown in the last when statement in the table. The individual statements in the sequence may be simple assignment statements, or they may be when statements or nested equation blocks. A semicolon is not used after a block's closing brace.

5.2.4 Truth Tables

truth table
truth_table keyword
input-list
output-list

unclocked truth-table operator, ->

ABEL provides one more way to specify combinational logic functions—the *truth table*, with the general format shown in Table 5-6. The keyword `truth_table` introduces a truth table. The *input-list* and *output-list* give the names of the input signals and the outputs that they affect. Each of these lists is either a single signal name or a *set*; sets are described fully in Section 5.2.5. Following the truth-table introduction are a series of statements, each of which specifies an input value and a required output value using the "->" operator. For example, the truth table for an inverter is shown below:

```
truth_table (X -> NOTX)
            0 -> 1;
            1 -> 0;
```

The list of input values does not need to be complete; only the on-set of the function needs to be specified unless don't-care processing is enabled (as shown in <u>Section ABEL.2</u> at <u>DDPPonline</u>). Table 5-7 shows how the prime-number-

Table 5-6
Structure of an ABEL
truth table.

```
truth_table  (input-list -> output-list)
             input-value -> output-value;
             . . .
             input-value -> output-value;
```

Table 5-7 An ABEL program for the prime-number detector.

```
module PrimeDet
title '4-Bit Prime Number Detector'

" Input and output pins
N0, N1, N2, N3                        pin;
F                                     pin istype 'com';

" Definition
NUM = [N3,N2,N1,N0];

truth_table (NUM -> F)
               1 -> 1;
               2 -> 1;
               3 -> 1;
               5 -> 1;
               7 -> 1;
              11 -> 1;
              13 -> 1;
end PrimeDet
```

detector function that was described on page 205 can be specified using an ABEL program. For convenience, the identifier NUM is defined as a synonym for the set of four input bits [N3,N2,N1,N0], allowing a 4-bit input value to be written as a decimal integer.

Both truth tables and equations can be used within the same ABEL program. The equations keyword introduces a sequence of equations, while the truth_table keyword introduces a single truth table.

Some versions of the ABEL compiler have a limited ability to handle don't-care entries in truth tables. Again, see Section ABEL.2 at DDPPonline.

5.2.5 Ranges, Sets, and Relations

Most digital systems include buses, registers, and other circuits that handle a group of two or more signals in an identical fashion. ABEL provides several shortcuts for conveniently defining and using such signals.

The first shortcut is for naming similar, numbered signals. As shown in the pin definitions in Table 5-8 on the next page, a *range* of signal names can be defined by stating the first and last names in the range, separated by "..". For example, writing "N3..N0" is the same as writing "N3,N2,N1,N0." Notice in the table that the range can be ascending or descending.

range

Next, we need a facility for writing equations more compactly when a group of signals are all handled identically, in order to reduce the chance of errors and inconsistencies. An ABEL *set* is simply a defined collection of signals that is handled as a unit. When a logical operation such as AND, OR, or assignment is applied to a set, it is applied to each element of the set.

set

Table 5-8 Examples of ABEL ranges, sets, and relations.

```
module SetOps
title 'Set Operation Examples'

" Input and output pins
N3..N0, M3..M0, SEL                               pin;
Y1..Y4, Z0..Z3, EQ, GE, GTR, LTH, UNLUCKY        pin istype 'com';

" Definitions
N    = [N3,N2,N1,N0];
M    = [M3,M2,M1,M0];
YOUT = [Y1..Y4];
ZOUT = [Z3..Z0];

COMP = [EQ,GE];
GT   = [ 0, 1];
LT   = [ 0, 0];

equations

YOUT = N & M;
ZOUT = (SEL & N) # (!SEL & M);
EQ = (N == M);
GE = (N >= M);
GTR = (COMP == GT);
LTH = (COMP == LT);
UNLUCKY = (N == 13) # (M == ^hD) # ((N + M) == ^b1101);

end SetOps
```

Each set is defined at the beginning of the program by associating a set name with a bracketed list of the set elements (e.g., N=[N3,N2,N1,N0] in Table 5-8). The set element list may use shortcut notation (YOUT=[Y1..Y4]), but the element names need not be similar or have any correspondence with the set name (COMP=[EQ,GE]). Set elements can also be constants (GT=[0,1]). In any case, the number and order of elements in a set are significant, as we'll see.

Most of ABEL's operators can be applied to sets. When an operation is applied to two or more sets, all of the sets must have the same number of elements, and the operation is applied individually to set elements in like positions, regardless of their names or numbers. Thus, the equation "YOUT = N & M" is equivalent to four equations:

```
Y1 = N3 & M3;
Y2 = N2 & M2;
Y3 = N1 & M1;
Y4 = N0 & M0;
```

Symbol	Relation
==	equality
!=	inequality
<	less than
<=	less than or equal
>	greater than
>=	greater than or equal

Table 5-9
Relational operators
in ABEL.

When an operation includes both set and nonset variables, the nonset variables are combined individually with set elements in each position. Thus, the equation "ZOUT = (SEL & N) # (!SEL & M)" is equivalent to four equations of the form "Zi = (SEL & Ni) # (!SEL & Mi)" for i equal 0 to 3.

Another important feature is ABEL's ability to convert "relations" into logic expressions. A *relation* is a pair of operands combined with one of the *relational operators* listed in Table 5-9. The compiler converts a relation into a logic expression that is 1 if and only if the relation is true.

relation
relational operator

The operands in a relation are treated as unsigned integers, and either operand may be an integer or a set. If the operand is a set, it is treated as an unsigned binary integer with the leftmost variable representing the most significant bit. *Addition* and *subtraction* operators + and − are supported (for example, see Section 8.4.5). By default, numbers in ABEL programs are assumed to be base-10. Hexadecimal and binary numbers are denoted by a prefix of "^h" or "^b", respectively, as shown in the last equation in Table 5-8.

addition operator, +
subtracttion operator, −
^h hexadecimal prefix
^b binary prefix

Using ABEL sets and relations, just a few lines of code can express a lot of functionality that requires lots of gates. For example, the equations in Table 5-8 yield a total of 69 product terms when compiled and minimized. So, be careful.

5.2.6 Test Vectors

ABEL programs may contain optional test vectors, as we showed in Table 5-2 on page 246. The general format of test vectors is very similar to a truth table and is shown in Table 5-10. The keyword *test_vectors* introduces a truth table. The *input-list* and *output-list* give the names of the input signals and the outputs that they affect. Each of these lists is either a single signal name or a set. Following the test-vector introduction are a series of statements, each of which specifies an input value and an expected output value using the "->" operator.

test_vectors
 keyword

input-list
output-list
->

```
test_vectors (input-list -> output-list)
             input-value -> output-value;
             . . .
             input-value -> output-value;
```

Table 5-10
Structure of ABEL
test vectors.

Table 5-11
Test vectors for the
alarm circuit program
in Table 5-2.

```
test_vectors
([PANIC,ENABLEA,EXITING,WINDOW,DOOR,GARAGE] -> [ALARM])
[     1,      X,      X,      X,    X,      X] -> [    1];  "1
[     0,      0,      X,      X,    X,      X] -> [    0];  "2
[     0,      1,      1,      X,    X,      X] -> [    0];  "3
[     0,      1,      0,      0,    X,      X] -> [    1];  "4
[     0,      1,      0,      X,    0,      X] -> [    1];  "5
[     0,      1,      0,      X,    X,      0] -> [    1];  "6
[     0,      1,      0,      1,    1,      1] -> [    0];  "7
```

ABEL test vectors have two main uses and purposes:

1. After the ABEL compiler translates the program into "fuse pattern" for a particular device, it simulates the operation of the final programmed device by applying the test-vector inputs to a software model of the device and comparing its outputs with the corresponding test-vector outputs. The designer may specify a series of test vectors in order to double-check that the device will behave as expected for some or all input combinations.

2. After a PLD is physically programmed, the programming unit applies the test-vector inputs to the physical device and compares the device outputs with the corresponding test-vector outputs. This is done to check for correct device programming and operation.

Unfortunately, ABEL test vectors seldom do a very good job at either one of these tasks, as we'll explain.

The test vectors from Table 5-2 are repeated in Table 5-11, except that for readability we've used the identifier X which was equated to the don't-care constant .X., and we've added comments to number the test vectors.

Table 5-11 actually appears to be a pretty good set of test vectors. From the designer's point of view, these vectors fully cover the expected operation of the alarm circuit, as itemized vector-by-vector below:

1. If PANIC is 1, then the alarm output (F) should be on regardless of the other input values. The remaining vectors cover cases where PANIC is 0.

2. If the alarm is not enabled, then the output should be off.

3. If the alarm is enabled but we're exiting, then the output should be off.

4-6. If the alarm is enabled and we're not exiting, then the output should be on if any of the sensor signals WINDOW, DOOR, or GARAGE is 0.

7. If the alarm is enabled, we're not exiting, and all of the sensor signals are 1, then the output should be off.

The problem is that ABEL doesn't handle don't-cares in test-vector inputs the way that it should. For example, by all rights, test vector 1 should test 32 distinct input combinations corresponding to all 32 possible combinations of don't-care inputs ENABLEA, EXITING, WINDOW, DOOR, and GARAGE. But it doesn't.

```
test_vectors
([PANIC,ENABLEA,EXITING,WINDOW,DOOR,GARAGE]  -> [ALARM])
[     1,      0,      1,      1,    1,     1] -> [    1]; "1
[     0,      1,      0,      0,    1,     1] -> [    1]; "2
[     0,      1,      0,      1,    0,     1] -> [    1]; "3
[     0,      1,      0,      1,    1,     0] -> [    1]; "4
[     0,      0,      0,      0,    0,     0] -> [    0]; "5
[     0,      1,      1,      0,    0,     0] -> [    0]; "6
[     0,      1,      0,      1,    1,     1] -> [    0]; "7
```

Table 5-12
Single stuck-at fault test vectors for the minimal sum-of-products realization of the alarm circuit.

In this situation, the ABEL compiler interprets "don't care" as "the user doesn't care what input value I use," and it just assigns 0 to all don't-care inputs in a test vector. In this example, you could have incorrectly written the output equation as "F = PANIC & !ENABLEA # ENABLEA & . . ."; the test vectors would still pass, even though the panic button would work only when the system is disabled.

The second use of test vectors is in physical device testing. Most physical defects in logic devices can be detected using the *single stuck-at fault model*, which assumes that any physical defect is equivalent to having a single gate input or output stuck at a logic 0 or 1 value. Just putting together a set of test vectors that seems to exercise a circuit's functional specifications, as we did in Table 5-11, doesn't guarantee that all single stuck-at faults can be detected. The test vectors have to be chosen so that every possible stuck-at fault causes an incorrect value at the circuit output for some test-vector input combination.

single stuck-at fault model

Table 5-12 shows a complete set of test vectors for the alarm circuit when it is realized as a two-level sum-of-products circuit. The first four vectors check for stuck-at-1 faults on the OR gate, and the last three check for stuck-at-0 faults on the AND gates; it turns out that this is sufficient to detect all single stuck-at faults. If you know something about fault testing you can generate test vectors for small circuits by hand (as I did in this example), but most designers use automated third-party tools to create high-quality test vectors for their PLD designs.

5.2.7 Additional ABEL Features

ABEL has several more features, mostly for sequential logic design, which are introduced later in this book. For reference purposes, we list them here:

- *Attribute suffixes*, used to identify a particular signal associated with a PLD pin (pages 424, 612, and 617).

- *@CARRY directive*, used when synthesizing adders (page 488).

- *Registered outputs* and *clocked assignments* (Section 7.11.1 starting on page 612).

- *State_diagram* syntax and semantics, used to specify clocked synchronous state machines (Sections 7.11.2 through 7.11.5, starting on page 613).

- *.C.* constant, used to specify clock edges in sequential test vectors (Section 7.11.6 starting on page 622).

5.3 The VHDL Hardware Description Language

VHDL

In the mid-1980s, the U.S. Department of Defense (DoD) and the IEEE sponsored the development of a highly capable hardware-description language called *VHDL*. The language started out with and still has the following features:

- Designs may be decomposed hierarchically.
- Each design element has both a well-defined interface (for connecting it to other elements) and a precise functional specification (for simulating it).
- Functional specifications can use either a behavioral algorithm or an actual hardware structure to define an element's operation. For example, an element can be defined initially by an algorithm, to allow design verification of higher-level elements that use it; later, the algorithmic definition can be replaced by a preferred hardware structure.
- Concurrency, timing, and clocking can all be modeled. VHDL handles asynchronous as well as synchronous sequential-circuit structures.
- The logical operation and timing behavior of a design can be simulated.

Thus, VHDL started out as a documentation and modeling language, allowing the behavior of digital-system designs to be precisely specified and simulated.

VHDL synthesis tools

While the VHDL language and simulation environment were important innovations by themselves, VHDL's utility and popularity took a quantum leap with the commercial development of *VHDL synthesis tools*. These programs can create logic-circuit structures directly from VHDL behavioral descriptions. Using VHDL, you can design, simulate, and synthesize anything from a simple combinational circuit to a complete microprocessor system on a chip.

VHDL-1987
VHDL-1993
VHDL-2002

VHDL was standardized by the IEEE in 1987 (*VHDL-1987*) and extended in 1993 (*VHDL-1993*) and again in 2002 (*VHDL-2002*). In this book we'll use a subset of language features that are legal in all versions. We'll show additional features for sequential logic design in Section 7.12.

5.3.1 Program Structure

entity

VHDL was designed with principles of structured programming in mind, borrowing ideas from the Pascal and Ada software programming languages. A key idea is to define the interface of a hardware module while hiding its internal details. Thus, a VHDL *entity* is simply a declaration of a module's inputs and

---

THE MEANING OF VHDL

"VHDL" stands for "VHSIC Hardware Description Language." VHSIC, in turn, stands for "Very High Speed Integrated Circuit," which was a U.S. Department of Defense program to encourage research on high-performance IC technology (using Very Healthy Sums of Instant Cash!).

outputs, while a VHDL *architecture* is a detailed description of the module's internal behavior or structure.

architecture

Figure 5-2(a) illustrates the concept. Many designers like to think of a VHDL entity declaration as a "wrapper" for the architecture, hiding the details of what's inside while providing the "hooks" for other modules to use it. This forms the basis for hierarchical system design—the architecture of a top-level entity may use, or *instantiate,* other entities, while hiding the architectural details of lower-level entities from the higher-level ones. As shown in (b), a higher-level architecture may use a lower-level entity multiple times, and multiple top-level architectures may use the same lower-level one. In the figure, architectures B, E, and F stand alone; they do not use any other entities.

instantiate

In the text file of a VHDL program, the *entity declaration* and *architecture definition* are separated, as shown in Figure 5-3 on the next page. For example, Table 5-13 is a very simple VHDL program for a 2-input "inhibit" gate. In large projects, entities and architectures are sometimes defined in separate files, which the compiler matches up according to their declared names.

entity declaration
architecture definition

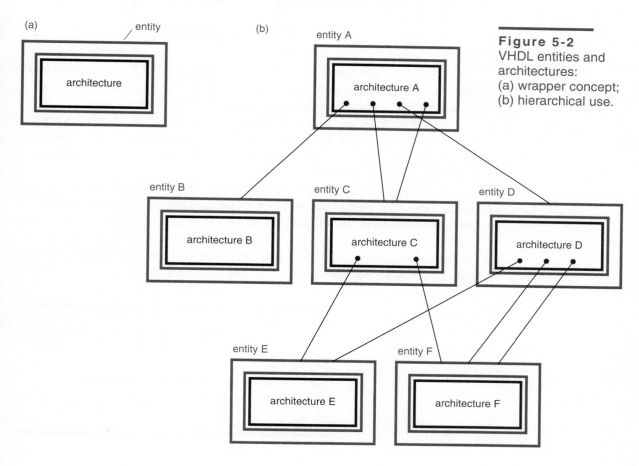

Figure 5-2
VHDL entities and architectures:
(a) wrapper concept;
(b) hierarchical use.

GO CONFIGURE!   VHDL actually allows you to define multiple architectures for a single entity, and it provides a configuration management facility that allows you to specify which one to use during a particular compilation or synthesis run. This lets you try out a different architectural approach without throwing away or hiding your other efforts. However, we won't use or further discuss this facility in this text.

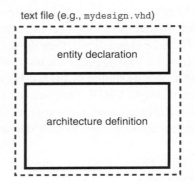

Figure 5-3
VHDL program file
structure.

Like other high-level programming languages, VHDL generally ignores spaces and line breaks, and these may be provided as desired for readability. *comments*
reserved words
keywords

Comments begin with two hyphens (--) and end at the end of a line.

VHDL defines many special character strings, called *reserved words* or *keywords*. Our example includes several—entity, port, is, in, out, end, architecture, begin, when, else, and not. We use color for keywords in VHDL programs in this book.

identifiers

User-defined *identifiers* begin with a letter and contain letters, digits, and underscores. (An underscore may not follow another underscore or be the last character in an identifier.) Identifiers in the example are Inhibit, X, Y, BIT, Z, and Inhibit_arch. "BIT" is a built-in identifier for a predefined type; it's not considered a reserved word because it can be redefined. VHDL's reserved words and identifiers are not case sensitive, unlike ABEL's and Verilog's.

Table 5-13
VHDL program for
an "inhibit" gate.

```
entity Inhibit is     -- also known as 'BUT-NOT'
  port (X,Y: in BIT;    -- as in 'X but not Y'
        Z:   out BIT);  -- (see [Klir, 1972])
end Inhibit;

architecture Inhibit_arch of Inhibit is
begin
  Z <= '1' when X='1' and Y='0' else '0';
end Inhibit_arch;
```

```
entity entity-name is
    port (signal-names : mode signal-type;
          signal-names : mode signal-type;
          ...

          signal-names : mode signal-type);
end entity-name;
```

Table 5-14
Syntax of a VHDL
entity declaration.

A basic entity declaration has the syntax shown in Table 5-14. Besides naming the entity, the purpose of the entity declaration is to define its external interface signals or *ports* in its *port declaration* part. In addition to the keywords entity, is, port, and end, an entity declaration has the following elements:

port
port declaration

entity-name   A user-selected identifier to name the entity.

signal-names   A comma-separated list of one or more user-selected identifiers to name external-interface signals.

mode   One of four reserved words, specifying the signal direction:

in   The signal is an input to the entity.

out   The signal is an output of the entity. Note that the value of such a signal cannot be "read" inside the entity's architecture, only by other entities that use it.

buffer   The signal is an output of the entity, and its value can also be read inside the entity's architecture.

inout   The signal can be used as an input or an output of the entity. This mode is typically used for three-state input/output pins on PLDs.

signal-type   A built-in or user-defined signal type. We'll have a lot to say about types in the next subsection.

Note that there is no semicolon after the final *signal-type*; swapping the closing parenthesis with the semicolon after it is a common syntax error for beginning VHDL programmers.

An entity's ports and their modes and types are all that is seen by other modules that use the entity. The entity's internal operation is specified in its *architecture definition*, whose general syntax is shown in Table 5-15 on the next page. The *entity-name* in this definition must be the same as the one given previously in the entity declaration. The *architecture-name* is a user-selected identifier, usually related to the entity name; it can be the same as the entity name if desired.

architecture definition

An architecture's external interface signals (ports) are inherited from the port-declaration part of its corresponding entity declaration. An architecture may also include signals and other declarations that are local to that architecture,

Table 5-15
Syntax of a VHDL
architecture definition.

```
architecture architecture-name of entity-name is
    type declarations
    signal declarations
    constant declarations
    function definitions
    procedure definitions
    component declarations
begin
    concurrent-statement
    . . .
    concurrent-statement
end architecture-name;
```

similar to other high-level languages. Declarations common to multiple entities can be made in a separate "package" used by all entities, as discussed later.

The declarations in Table 5-15 can appear in any order. In due course we'll discuss many different kinds of declarations and statements that can appear in *signal declaration* the architecture definition, but the easiest to start with is the *signal declaration*. It gives the same information about a signal as in a port declaration, except that no mode is specified:

> signal *signal-names* : *signal-type*;

Zero or more signals can be defined within an architecture, and they roughly correspond to named wires in a logic diagram. They can be read or written within the architecture definition and, like other local objects, can be referenced only within the encompassing architecture definition.

variable   VHDL *variables* are similar to signals, except that they usually don't have physical significance in a circuit. In fact, notice that Table 5-15 has no provision for "variable declarations" in an architecture definition. Rather, variables are used in VHDL functions, procedures, and processes, each of which we'll discuss *variable declaration* later. Within these program elements, the syntax of a *variable declaration* is just like that of a signal declaration, except that the variable keyword is used:

> variable *variable-names* : *variable-type*;

5.3.2 Types, Constants, and Arrays

Every signal, variable, and constant in a VHDL program must have an associ-
type   ated "type." The *type* specifies the set or range of values that the object can take on, and there is also typically a set of operators (such as add, AND, and so on) associated with a given type.

predefined types   VHDL has just a few *predefined types*, listed in Table 5-16. In the rest of this book, the only predefined types that we'll use are integer, character, and boolean. You would think that types with names "bit" and "bit_vector" would be essential in digital design, but in VHDL it turns out that user-defined versions of these types are more useful, as discussed shortly.

bit	character	severity_level
bit_vector	integer	string
boolean	real	time

Table 5-16
VHDL predefined types.

integer Operators		*boolean* Operators	
+	addition	and	AND
−	subtraction	or	OR
*	multiplication	nand	NAND
/	division	nor	NOR
mod	modulo division	xor	Exclusive OR
rem	modulo remainder	xnor	Exclusive NOR
abs	absolute value	not	complementation
**	exponentiation		

Table 5-17
Predefined operators for VHDL's integer and boolean types.

Type *integer* is defined as the range of integers including at least the range −2,147,483,647 through +2,147,483,647 ($-2^{31}+1$ through $+2^{31}-1$); VHDL implementations may extend this range. Type *boolean* has two values, *true* and *false*. The *character* type contains all of the characters in the ISO 8-bit character set; the first 128 are the ASCII characters. Built-in operators for the integer and boolean types are listed in Table 5-17.

integer

boolean
true, false
character

The most commonly used types in typical VHDL programs are *user-defined types*, and the most common of these are *enumerated types*, which are defined by listing their values. Predefined types boolean and character are enumerated types. A type declaration for an enumerated type has the format shown in the first line of Table 5-18. Here, *value-list* is a comma-separated list (enumeration) of all possible values of the type. The values may be user-defined identifiers or characters (where a "character" is any ISO character enclosed in single quotes). The first style is used most often to define cases or states for a state machine, for example,

user-defined type
enumerated type

```
type traffic_light_state is (reset, stop, wait, go);
```

The second style is used in the very important, standard, user-defined logic type *std_logic*, shown in Table 5-19 on the next page and part of the IEEE 1164 standard package, discussed in Section 5.3.4. This type includes not only '0' and '1', but seven other values that have been found useful in simulating logic signals (bits) in real logic circuits, as explained in detail in Section 6.6.4.

std_logic

```
type type-name is (value-list);

subtype subtype-name is type-name start to end;
subtype subtype-name is type-name start downto end;

constant constant-name: type-name := value;
```

Table 5-18
Syntax of VHDL type and constant declarations.

Table 5-19
Definition of VHDL
std_logic type
(see Section 6.6.4
for discussion of
"resolved").

```
type STD_ULOGIC is ( 'U',   -- Uninitialized
                     'X',   -- Forcing  Unknown
                     '0',   -- Forcing  0
                     '1',   -- Forcing  1
                     'Z',   -- High Impedance
                     'W',   -- Weak     Unknown
                     'L',   -- Weak     0
                     'H',   -- Weak     1
                     '-'    -- Don't care
                   );
subtype STD_LOGIC is resolved STD_ULOGIC;
```

subtypes

VHDL also allows users to create *subtypes* of a type, using the syntax shown in Table 5-18. The values in the subtype must be a contiguous range of values of the base type, from *start* to *end*. For an enumerated type, "contiguous" refers to positions in the original, defining *value-list*. Some examples of subtype definitions are shown below:

```
subtype twoval_logic is std_logic range '0' to '1';
subtype fourval_logic is std_logic range 'X' to 'Z';
subtype negint is integer range -2147483647 to -1;
subtype bitnum is integer range 31 downto 0;
```

UNNATURAL ACTS	Although VHDL defines the subtype "natural" as being nonnegative integers starting with 0, most mathematicians consider and define the natural numbers to begin with 1. After all, in early history people began counting with 1, and the concept of "0" arrived much later. Still, there is some discussion and perhaps controversy on the subject, especially as the computer age has led more of us to think with 0 as a starting number. For the latest thinking on this fascinating subject, search the Web for "natural numbers."

Notice that the order of a range may be specified in ascending or descending order, depending on whether *to* or *downto* is used. There are certain attributes of subtypes for which this distinction is significant, but we don't use them in this book and we won't discuss this further.

to
downto

VHDL has two predefined `integer` subtypes, defined below:

```
subtype natural is integer range 0 to highest-integer;
subtype positive is integer range 1 to highest-integer;
```

Constants contribute to the readability, maintainability, and portability of programs in any language. The syntax of a *constant declaration* in VHDL is shown in the last line of Table 5-18; examples are shown below:

constants
constant declaration

```
constant BUS_SIZE: integer := 32;      -- width of component
constant MSB: integer := BUS_SIZE-1; -- bit number of MSB
constant Z: character := 'Z';          -- synonym for Hi-Z value
```

Notice that the value of a constant can be a simple expression. Constants can be used anywhere the corresponding value can be used, and they can be put to especially good use in type definitions, as we'll soon show.

Another very important category of user-defined types are *array types*. Like other languages, VHDL defines an *array* as an ordered set of elements of the same type, where each element is selected by an *array index*. Table 5-20 shows several versions of the syntax for declaring an array in VHDL. In the first two versions, *start* and *end* are integers that define the possible range of the array index and hence the total number of array elements. In the last three versions, all or a subset of the values of an existing type (*range-type*) are the range of the array index.

array types
array
array index

```
type type-name is array (start to end) of element-type;

type type-name is array (start downto end) of element-type;

type type-name is array (range-type) of element-type;

type type-name is array (range-type range start to end) of element-type;

type type-name is array (range-type range start downto end) of element-type;
```

Table 5-20
Syntax of VHDL
array declarations.

Table 5-21
Examples of VHDL
array declarations.

```
type monthly_count is array (1 to 12) of integer;
type byte is array (7 downto 0) of STD_LOGIC;

constant WORD_LEN: integer := 32;
type word is array (WORD_LEN-1 downto 0) of STD_LOGIC;

constant NUM_REGS: integer := 8;
type reg_file is array (1 to NUM_REGS) of word;

type statecount is array (traffic_light_state) of integer;
```

Examples of array declarations are given in Table 5-21. The first pair of examples are very ordinary and show both ascending and descending ranges. The next example shows how a constant, WORD_LEN, can be used with an array declaration, showing also that a range value can be a simple expression. The third example shows that an array element may itself be an array, thus creating a two-dimensional array. The last example shows that an enumerated type (or a subtype) may be specified as the array element range; the array in this example has four elements, based on our previous definition of traffic_light_state.

Array elements are considered to be ordered from left to right, in the same direction as index range. Thus, the leftmost elements of arrays of types monthly_count, byte, word, reg_file, and statecount have indices 1, 7, 31, 1, and reset, respectively.

Within VHDL program statements, individual array elements are accessed using the array name and the element's index in parentheses. For example, if M, B, W, R, and S are signals or variables of the five array types defined in Table 5-21, then M(11), B(5), W(WORD_LEN-5), R(1,0), R(0), and S(reset) are all valid elements.

array literal   *Array literals* can be specified by listing the element values in parentheses. For example, the byte variable B could be set to all ones by the statement

```
B := ('1','1','1','1','1','1','1','1');
```

VHDL also has a shorthand notation that allows you to specify values by index. For example, to set word variable W to all ones except for zeroes in the LSB of each byte, you can write

others   `W := (0=>'0',8=>'0',16=>'0',24=>'0',others=>'1');`

The methods just described work for arrays with any *element-type*, but the easiest way to write a literal of a STD_LOGIC array type is to use a "string." A
string   VHDL *string* is a sequence of ISO characters enclosed in double quotes, such as "Hi there". A string is just an array of characters; as a result, a STD_LOGIC array of a given length can be assigned the value of a string of the same length, as long as the characters in the string are taken from the set of nine characters

defined as the possible values of the STD_LOGIC elements—'0', '1', 'U', and so on. Thus, the previous two examples can be rewritten as follows:

```
B := "11111111";
W := "111111101111111011111111011111110";
```

It is also possible to refer to a contiguous subset or *slice* of an array by specifying the starting and ending indices of the subset, for example, M(6 to 9), B(3 downto 0), W(15 downto 8), R(1,7 downto 0), R(1 to 2), S(stop to go). Notice that the slice's direction must be the same as the original array's.

array slice

Finally, you can combine arrays or array elements using the *concatenation operator &*, which joins arrays and elements in the order written, from left to right. For example, '0'&'1'&"1Z" is equivalent to "011Z", and the expression B(6 downto 0) & B(7) yields a 1-bit left circular shift of the 8-bit array B.

&, concatenation operator

The most important array type in typical VHDL programs is the IEEE 1164 standard user-defined logic type *std_logic_vector*, which defines an ordered set of std_logic bits. The definition of this type is:

std_logic_vector

```
type STD_LOGIC_VECTOR is array ( natural range <> ) of STD_LOGIC;
```

This is an example of an *unconstrained array type*—the range of the array is unspecified, except that it must be a subrange of a defined type, in this case, natural. This VHDL feature allows us to develop architectures, functions, and other program elements in a more general way, somewhat independent of the array size or its range of index values. An actual range is specified when a signal or variable is assigned this type. We'll see examples in the next subsection.

unconstrained array type

5.3.3 Functions and Procedures

Like a function in a high-level programming language, a VHDL *function* accepts a number of *arguments* and returns a *result*. Each of the arguments and the result in a VHDL function definition or function call have a predetermined type.

function
arguments
result

The syntax of a *function definition* is shown in Table 5-22 on the next page. After giving the name of the function, it lists zero or more *formal parameters* which are used within the function body. When the function is *called*, the *actual parameters* in the function call are substituted for the formal parameters. In accordance with VHDL's strong-typing philosophy, the actual parameters must be the same type or a subtype of the formal parameters. When the function is called from within an architecture, a value of the type *return-type* is returned in place of the function call.

function definition
formal parameters

actual parameters

As shown in the table, a function may define its own local types, constants, variables, and nested functions and procedures. The keywords begin and end enclose a series of "sequential statements" that are executed when the function is called. We'll take a closer look at different kinds of sequential statements and their syntax in Section 5.3.7, but you should be able to understand the examples here based on your previous programming experience.

Table 5-22
Syntax of a VHDL
function definition.

```
function function-name (
        signal-names : signal-type;
        signal-names : signal-type;
        . . .
        signal-names : signal-type
) return return-type is
    type declarations
    constant declarations
    variable declarations
    function definitions
    procedure definitions
begin
    sequential-statement
    . . .
    sequential-statement
end function-name;
```

The VHDL "inhibit-gate" architecture of Table 5-13 on page 258 is modified in Table 5-23 to use a function. Within the function definition, the keyword *return* indicates when the function should return to the caller, and it is followed by an expression with the value to be returned to the caller. The type resulting from this expression must match the *return-type* in the function declaration.

return

The IEEE 1164 standard logic package defines many functions that operate on the standard types std_logic and std_logic_vector. Besides specifying a number of user-defined types, the package also defines the basic logic operations on these types such as and and or. This takes advantage of VHDL's ability to *overload* operators. This facility allows the user to specify a function that is invoked whenever a built-in operator symbol (and, or, +, etc.) is used with a matching set of operand types. There may be several definitions for a given operator symbol; the compiler automatically picks the definition that matches the operand types in each use of the operator.

operator overloading

Table 5-23
VHDL program for
an "inhibit" function.

```
architecture Inhibit_archf of Inhibit is

function ButNot (A, B: bit) return bit is
begin
  if B = '0' then return A;
  else return '0';
  end if;
end ButNot;

begin
  Z <= ButNot(X,Y);
end Inhibit_archf;
```

```
SUBTYPE UX01 IS RESOLVED std_ulogic RANGE 'U' TO '1';
                                        -- ('U','X','0','1')
TYPE stdlogic_table IS ARRAY(std_ulogic, std_ulogic) OF std_ulogic;

-- truth table for "and" function
CONSTANT and_table : stdlogic_table := (
--       ------------------------------------------------------
--       |  U    X    0    1    Z    W    L    H    -         |   |
--       ------------------------------------------------------
       ( 'U', 'U', '0', 'U', 'U', 'U', '0', 'U', 'U' ),  -- | U |
       ( 'U', 'X', '0', 'X', 'X', 'X', '0', 'X', 'X' ),  -- | X |
       ( '0', '0', '0', '0', '0', '0', '0', '0', '0' ),  -- | 0 |
       ( 'U', 'X', '0', '1', 'X', 'X', '0', '1', 'X' ),  -- | 1 |
       ( 'U', 'X', '0', 'X', 'X', 'X', '0', 'X', 'X' ),  -- | Z |
       ( 'U', 'X', '0', 'X', 'X', 'X', '0', 'X', 'X' ),  -- | W |
       ( '0', '0', '0', '0', '0', '0', '0', '0', '0' ),  -- | L |
       ( 'U', 'X', '0', '1', 'X', 'X', '0', '1', 'X' ),  -- | H |
       ( 'U', 'X', '0', 'X', 'X', 'X', '0', 'X', 'X' )   -- | - |
);
FUNCTION "and" ( L : std_ulogic; R : std_ulogic ) RETURN UX01 IS
BEGIN
    RETURN (and_table(L, R));
END "and";
```

Table 5-24
Definitions relating to the "and" operation on STD_LOGIC values in IEEE 1164.

For example, Table 5-24 contains code, taken from the IEEE package, that shows how the "and" operation is defined for std_logic operands. This code may look complicated, but we've already introduced all of the basic language elements that it uses (except for "resolved", which we describe in connection with three-state logic in Section 6.6.4).

The inputs to the function may be of type std_ulogic or its subtype std_logic. Another subtype UX01 is defined to be used as the function's return type; even if one of the "and" inputs is a nonlogic value ('Z', 'W', etc.), the function will return one of only four possible values. Type stdlogic_table defines a two-dimensional, 9×9 array indexed by a pair of std_ulogic values. For the and_table, the table entries are arranged so that if either index is '0' or 'L' (a weak '0'), the entry is '0'. A '1' entry is found only if both inputs are '1' or 'H' (a weak '1'). Otherwise, a 'U' or 'X' entry appears.

In the function definition itself, double quotes around the function name indicate operator overloading. The "executable" part of the function is just a single statement that returns the table element indexed by the two inputs, L and R, of the "and" function.

Because of VHDL's strong typing requirements, it's often necessary to convert a signal from one type to another, and the IEEE 1164 package contains several conversion functions—for example, from BIT to STD_LOGIC or vice

Table 5-25
VHDL function
for converting
STD_LOGIC_VECTOR
to INTEGER.

```
function CONV_INTEGER (X: STD_LOGIC_VECTOR) return INTEGER is
  variable RESULT: INTEGER;
begin
  RESULT := 0;
  for i in X'range loop
    RESULT := RESULT * 2;
    case X(i) is
      when '0' | 'L'  => null;
      when '1' | 'H'  => RESULT := RESULT + 1;
      when others     => null;
    end case;
  end loop;
  return RESULT;
end CONV_INTEGER;
```

versa. A commonly needed conversion is from STD_LOGIC_VECTOR into a corresponding integer value. IEEE 1164 does not include such a conversion function, because different designs may need to use different number interpretations—for example, signed versus unsigned. However, we can write our own conversion function as shown in Table 5-25.

The CONV_INTEGER function uses a simple iterative algorithm equivalent to the nested expansion formula on page 30. We won't be describing the for, case, and when statements that it uses until Section 5.3.7, but you should get the idea. The *null statement* is easy—it means "do nothing." The range of the for loop is specified by "X'range", where the single quote after a signal name means "attribute," and *range* is a built-in attribute identifier that applies only to arrays and means "range of this array's index, from left to right."

In the other direction, we can convert an integer to a STD_LOGIC_VECTOR as shown in Table 5-26. Here we must specify not only the integer value to be converted (ARG), but also the number of bits in the desired result (SIZE). Notice

null statement

range attribute

Table 5-26
VHDL function
for converting
INTEGER to
STD_LOGIC_VECTOR.

```
function CONV_STD_LOGIC_VECTOR(ARG: INTEGER; SIZE: INTEGER)
    return STD_LOGIC_VECTOR is
  variable result: STD_LOGIC_VECTOR (SIZE-1 downto 0);
  variable temp: integer;
begin
  temp := ARG;
  for i in 0 to SIZE-1 loop
    if (temp mod 2) = 1 then result(i) := '1';
    else result(i) := '0';
    end if;
    temp := temp / 2;
  end loop;
  return result;
end;
```

that the function declares a local variable "result", a STD_LOGIC_VECTOR whose index range is dependent on SIZE. For this reason, SIZE must be a constant or other value that is known when CONV_STD_LOGIC_VECTOR is compiled. To perform the conversion, the function uses the successive-division algorithm that was described on page 30.

A VHDL *procedure* is similar to a function, except it does not return a result. While a function call can be used in the place of an expression, a *procedure call* can be used in the place of a statement. VHDL procedures allow their arguments to be specified with type out or inout, so it is actually possible for a procedure to "return" a result. However, we don't use VHDL procedures in the rest of this book, so we won't discuss them further.

procedure

procedure call

5.3.4 Libraries and Packages

A VHDL *library* is a place where the VHDL compiler stores information about a particular design project, including intermediate files used in the analysis, simulation, and synthesis of the design. The location of the library within a host computer's file system is implementation dependent. For a given VHDL design, the compiler automatically creates and uses a library named "work".

library

A complete VHDL design usually has multiple files, each containing different design units including entities and architectures. When the VHDL compiler analyzes each file in the design, it places the results in the "work" library, and it also searches this library for needed definitions, such as other entities. Because of this feature, a large design can be broken up into multiple files, yet the compiler will find external references as needed.

Not all of the information needed in a design may be in the "work" library. For example, a designer may rely on common definitions or functional modules across a family of different projects. Each project has its own "work" library (typically a subdirectory within that project's overall directory), but it must also refer to a common library containing the shared definitions. Even small projects may use a standard library such as the one containing IEEE standard definitions. The designer can specify the name of such a library using a *library clause* at the beginning of the design file. For example, we can specify the IEEE library:

library clause

```
library ieee;
```

The clause "library work;" is included implicitly at the beginning of every VHDL design file.

Specifying a library name in a design gives it access to any previously analyzed entities and architectures stored in the library, but it does not give access to type definitions and the like. This is the function of "packages" and "use clauses," described next.

A VHDL *package* is a file containing definitions of objects that can be used in other programs. The kind of objects that can be put into a package include signal, type, constant, function, procedure, and component declarations.

package

Signals that are defined in a package are "global" signals, available to any VHDL entity that uses the package. Types and constants defined in a package are known in any file that uses the package. Likewise, functions and procedures defined in a package can be called in files that use the package, and components (described in the next subsection) can be instantiated in architectures that use the package.

use clause

A design can "use" a package by including a *use clause* at the beginning of the design file. For example, to use all of the definitions in the IEEE standard 1164 package, we would write

```
use ieee.std_logic_1164.all;
```

Here, "ieee" is the name of a library which has been previously given in a library clause. Within this library, the file named "std_logic_1164" contains the desired definitions. The suffix "all" tells the compiler to use all of the definitions in this file. Instead of "all", you can write the name of a particular object to use just its definition, for example,

```
use ieee.std_logic_1164.std_ulogic
```

This clause would make available just the definition of the std_ulogic type in Table 5-19 on page 262, without all of the related types and functions. However, multiple "use" clauses can be written to use additional definitions.

"STANDARD" VHDL PACKAGES

VHDL has excellent capabilities for extending its data types and functions. This is important, because the language's built-in BIT and BIT_VECTOR actually are quite inadequate for modeling real circuits that also handle three-state, unknown, don't-care, and varying-strength signals.

As a result, soon after the language was formalized as IEEE standard 1076, commercial vendors began to introduce their own built-in data types to deal with logic values other than 0 and 1. Of course, each vendor had different definitions for these extended types, creating a potential "Tower of Babel." To avoid this situation, the IEEE developed the 1164 standard logic package (std_logic_1164) with a nine-valued logic system that satisfies most designers' needs.

Meanwhile, synthesis supplier Synopsys created several packages with standard types and operations for vectors of STD_LOGIC components that are interpreted as signed or unsigned integers, including std_logic_arith, std_logic_signed, and std_logic_unsigned. While these packages aren't IEEE standards, Synopsys placed them into their IEEE library, and we discuss and use them later in this book.

Around the same time, other vendors produced their own incompatible versions of std_logic_arith and also put them in their IEEE libraries, and the IEEE 1076.3 committee introduced its own standard arithmetic package, numeric_std.

The result of all this is that you must be extremely careful in selecting and applying "standard" packages. As cynical designers say, "Standards are great because there are so many to choose from!"

```
package package-name is
    type declarations
    signal declarations
    constant declarations
    component declarations
    function declarations
    procedure declarations
end package-name;
package body package-name is
    type declarations
    constant declarations
    function definitions
    procedure definitions
end package-name;
```

Table 5-27
Syntax of a VHDL
package definition.

Defining packages is not limited to standards bodies. Anyone can write a package, using the syntax shown in Table 5-27. All of the objects declared between "package" and the first "end" statement are visible in any design file that uses the package; objects following the "package body" keyword are local. In particular, notice that the first part includes "function declarations," not definitions. A *function declaration* lists only the function name, arguments, and type, up to but not including the "is" keyword in Table 5-22 on page 266. The complete function definition is given in the package body and is not visible to function users.

function declaration

5.3.5 Structural Design Elements

We're finally ready to look at the guts of a VHDL design, the "executable" portion of an architecture. Recall from Table 5-15 on page 260 that the body of an architecture is a series of concurrent statements. In VHDL, each *concurrent statement* executes simultaneously with the other concurrent statements in the same architecture body.

concurrent statement

This behavior is markedly different from that of statements in conventional software programming languages, where statements execute sequentially. Concurrent statements are necessary to simulate the behavior of hardware, where connected elements affect each other continuously, not just at particular, ordered time steps. Thus, in a VHDL architecture body, if the last statement updates a signal that is used by the first statement, then the simulator will go back to that first statement and update its results according to the signal that just changed. In fact, the simulator will keep propagating changes and updating results until the simulated circuit stabilizes; we'll discuss this in more detail in Section 5.3.8.

VHDL has several different concurrent statements, as well as a mechanism for bundling a set of sequential statements to operate as a single concurrent statement. Used in different ways, these statements give rise to three somewhat distinct styles of circuit design and description, which we cover in this and the next two subsections.

Table 5-28 Syntax of a VHDL component statement.

label: *component-name* port map(*signal1*, *signal2*, ..., *signaln*);

label: *component-name* port map(*port1=>signal1*, *port2=>signal2*, ..., *portn=>signaln*);

Table 5-29
Syntax of a
VHDL component
declaration.

```
component component-name
  port (signal-names : mode signal-type;
        signal-names : mode signal-type;
        ...
        signal-names : mode signal-type);
end component;
```

The most basic of VHDL's concurrent statements is the *component statement*, whose basic syntax is shown in Table 5-28. Here, *component-name* is the name of a previously defined entity that is to be used, or *instantiated*, within the current architecture body. One instance of the named entity is created for each component statement that invokes its name, and each instance must be named by a unique *label*.

instantiate

The *port map* keywords introduce a list that associates ports of the named entity with signals in the current architecture. The list may be written in either of two different styles. The first is a positional style; as in conventional programming languages, the signals in the list are associated with the entity's ports in the same order in which they appear in the entity's definition. The second is an explicit style; each of the entity's ports is connected to a signal using the "=>" operator, and these associations may be listed in any order.

port map

Before being instantiated in an architecture, a component must be declared in a *component declaration* in the architecture's definition (see Table 5-15 on page 260). As shown in Table 5-29, a component declaration is essentially the same as the port-declaration part of the corresponding entity declaration—it lists the name, mode, and type of each of its ports.

component declaration
component keyword

The components used in an architecture may be ones that were previously defined as part of a design, or they may be part of a library. Table 5-30 is an example of a VHDL entity and its architecture that uses components, a "prime-number detector" that is structurally identical to the gate-level circuit in Figure 4-31(c) on page 217. The entity declaration names the inputs and the output of the circuit. The declarations section of the architecture defines all of the signal names and the components that are used internally. The components, INV, AND2, AND3, and OR4, are predefined in the design environment in which this example was created and compiled (Xilinx ISE 6.x unisims library).

Note that component statements in Table 5-30 execute *concurrently*. Even if the statements were listed in a different order, the same circuit would be synthesized, and the simulated circuit operation would be the same.

Table 5-30 Structural VHDL program for a prime-number detector.

```
library IEEE;
use IEEE.std_logic_1164.all;
library unisim;
use unisim.vcomponents.all;

entity prime is
    port ( N: in STD_LOGIC_VECTOR (3 downto 0);
           F: out STD_LOGIC );
end prime;

architecture prime1_arch of prime is
signal N3_L, N2_L, N1_L: STD_LOGIC;
signal N3L_N0, N3L_N2L_N1, N2L_N1_N0, N2_N1L_N0: STD_LOGIC;
component INV port (I: in STD_LOGIC; O: out STD_LOGIC); end component;
component AND2 port (I0,I1: in STD_LOGIC; O: out STD_LOGIC); end component;
component AND3 port (I0,I1,I2: in STD_LOGIC; O: out STD_LOGIC); end component;
component OR4 port (I0,I1,I2,I3: in STD_LOGIC; O: out STD_LOGIC); end component;
begin
  U1: INV port map (N(3), N3_L);
  U2: INV port map (N(2), N2_L);
  U3: INV port map (N(1), N1_L);
  U4: AND2 port map (N3_L, N(0), N3L_N0);
  U5: AND3 port map (N3_L, N2_L, N(1), N3L_N2L_N1);
  U6: AND3 port map (N2_L, N(1), N(0), N2L_N1_N0);
  U7: AND3 port map (N(2), N1_L, N(0), N2_N1L_N0);
  U8: OR4 port map (N3L_N0, N3L_N2L_N1, N2L_N1_N0, N2_N1L_N0, F);
end prime1_arch;
```

A VHDL architecture that uses components is often called a *structural description* or *structural design*, because it defines the precise interconnection structure of signals and entities that realize the entity. In this regard, a pure structural description is equivalent to a schematic or a net list for the circuit.

structural description
structural design

In some applications it is necessary to create multiple copies of a particular structure within an architecture. For example, we'll see in Section 6.10.2 that an *n*-bit "ripple adder" can be created by cascading *n* "full adders." VHDL includes a *generate statement* that allows you to create such repetitive structures using a kind of "for loop," without having to write out all of the component instantiations individually.

generate statement

The syntax of a simple iterative generate loop is shown in Table 5-31. The *identifier* is implicitly declared as a variable with type compatible with the *range*. The *concurrent statement* is executed once for each possible value of the

```
label: for identifier in range generate
          concurrent-statement
       end generate;
```

Table 5-31
Syntax of a VHDL
for-generate loop.

Table 5-32
VHDL entity and
architecture for an
8-bit inverter.

```
library IEEE;
use IEEE.std_logic_1164.all;

entity inv8 is
    port ( X: in STD_LOGIC_VECTOR (1 to 8);
            Y: out STD_LOGIC_VECTOR (1 to 8) );
end inv8;

architecture inv8_arch of inv8 is
component INV port (I: in STD_LOGIC; O: out STD_LOGIC); end component;
begin
  g1: for b in 1 to 8 generate
        U1: INV port map (X(b), Y(b));
      end generate;
end inv8_arch;
```

identifier within the range, and *identifier* may be used within the concurrent statement. For example, Table 5-32 shows how an 8-bit inverter can be created.

The value of a constant must be known at the time that a VHDL program is compiled. In many applications it is useful to design and compile an entity and its architecture while leaving some of its parameters, such as bus width, unspecified. VHDL's "generic" facility lets you do this.

generic constant
generic declaration

One or more *generic constants* can be defined in an entity declaration with a *generic declaration* before the port declaration, using the syntax shown in Table 5-33. Each of the named constants can be used within the architecture definition for the entity, and the value of the constant is deferred until the entity is instantiated using a component statement within another architecture. Within that component statement, values are assigned to the generic constants using a

generic map

`generic map` clause in the same style as the port map clause. Table 5-34 is an example that combines `generic` and `generate` statements to define a "bus inverter" with a user-specifiable width. Multiple copies of this inverter, each with a different width, are instantiated in the program in Table 5-35.

Table 5-33
Syntax of a VHDL
generic declaration
within an entity
declaration.

```
entity entity-name is
  generic (constant-names : constant-type;
            constant-names : constant-type;
                    . . .
            constant-names : constant-type);
  port (signal-names : mode signal-type;
         signal-names : mode signal-type;
                 . . .
         signal-names : mode signal-type);
end entity-name;
```

```
library IEEE;
use IEEE.std_logic_1164.all;

entity businv is
    generic (WIDTH: positive);
    port ( X: in STD_LOGIC_VECTOR (WIDTH-1 downto 0);
           Y: out STD_LOGIC_VECTOR (WIDTH-1 downto 0) );
end businv;

architecture businv_arch of businv is
component INV port (I: in STD_LOGIC; O: out STD_LOGIC); end component;
begin
  g1: for b in WIDTH-1 downto 0 generate
        U1: INV port map (X(b), Y(b));
      end generate;
end businv_arch;
```

Table 5-34
VHDL entity and architecture for an arbitrary-width bus inverter.

```
library IEEE;
use IEEE.std_logic_1164.all;

entity businv_example is
    port ( IN8: in STD_LOGIC_VECTOR (7 downto 0);
           OUT8: out STD_LOGIC_VECTOR (7 downto 0);
           IN16: in STD_LOGIC_VECTOR (15 downto 0);
           OUT16: out STD_LOGIC_VECTOR (15 downto 0);
           IN32: in STD_LOGIC_VECTOR (31 downto 0);
           OUT32: out STD_LOGIC_VECTOR (31 downto 0) );
end businv_example;

architecture businv_ex_arch of businv_example is
component businv
    generic (WIDTH: positive);
    port ( X: in STD_LOGIC_VECTOR (WIDTH-1 downto 0);
           Y: out STD_LOGIC_VECTOR (WIDTH-1 downto 0) );
end component;
begin
U1: businv generic map (WIDTH=>8) port map (IN8, OUT8);
U2: businv generic map (WIDTH=>16) port map (IN16, OUT16);
U3: businv generic map (WIDTH=>32) port map (IN32, OUT32);
end businv_ex_arch;
```

Table 5-35
VHDL entity and architecture that use the arbitrary-width bus inverter.

5.3.6 Dataflow Design Elements

If component statements were its only concurrent statements, then VHDL would be little more than a strongly typed, hierarchical net-list description language. Several additional concurrent statements allow VHDL to describe a circuit in terms of the flow of data and operations on it within the circuit. This style is called a *dataflow description* or *dataflow design*.

dataflow description
dataflow design

Table 5-36
Syntax of VHDL
concurrent signal-
assignment statements.

signal-name <= *expression*;

signal-name <= *expression* when *boolean-expression* else
                expression when *boolean-expression* else
                . . .
                expression when *boolean-expression* else
                expression;

concurrent signal-
assignment statement

Two additional concurrent statements used in dataflow designs are shown in Table 5-36. The first of these is the most often used and is called a *concurrent signal-assignment statement*. You should read this as "*signal-name* gets *expression*." Because of VHDL's strong typing, the type of *expression* must be compatible with that of *signal-name*. In general, this means that either the types must be identical or *expression*'s type is a subtype of *signal-name*'s. In the case of arrays, both the element type and the length must match; however, the index range and direction need not match.

Table 5-37 shows an architecture for the prime-number detector entity (Table 5-30 on page 273) written in dataflow style. In this style we don't show the explicit gates and their connections; rather, we use VHDL's built-in and, or, and not operators. (Actually, these operators are not built in for signals of type STD_LOGIC, but they are defined and overloaded by the IEEE 1164 package.) Note that the not operator has the highest precedence, so no parentheses are required around subexpressions like "not N(3)" to get the intended result.

conditional signal-
assignment statement

when

else

relational operators

=, /=, >, >=, <, <=

We can also use the second, *conditional* form of the concurrent signal-assignment statement, using the keywords *when* and *else* as shown in Table 5-36. Here, a *boolean-expression* combines individual boolean terms using VHDL's built-in boolean operators such as and, or, and not. Boolean terms are typically boolean variables or results of comparisons using *relational operators* =, /= (inequality), >, >=, <, and <=.

Table 5-38 is an example using conditional concurrent assignment statements. Each of the comparisons of an individual STD_LOGIC bit such as N(3) is made against a character literal '1' or '0' and returns a value of type boolean.

Table 5-37
Dataflow VHDL
architecture for the
prime-number
detector.

```
architecture prime2_arch of prime is
signal N3L_N0, N3L_N2L_N1, N2L_N1_N0, N2_N1L_N0: STD_LOGIC;
begin
  N3L_N0      <= not N(3)                           and N(0);
  N3L_N2L_N1 <= not N(3) and not N(2) and     N(1)        ;
  N2L_N1_N0  <=                 not N(2) and     N(1) and N(0);
  N2_N1L_N0  <=                          N(2) and not N(1) and N(0);
  F <= N3L_N0 or N3L_N2L_N1 or N2L_N1_N0 or N2_N1L_N0;
end prime2_arch;
```

```
architecture prime3_arch of prime is
signal N3L_N0, N3L_N2L_N1, N2L_N1_N0, N2_N1L_N0: STD_LOGIC;
begin
   N3L_N0      <= '1' when N(3)='0' and N(0)='1' else '0';
   N3L_N2L_N1 <= '1' when N(3)='0' and N(2)='0' and N(1)='1' else '0';
   N2L_N1_N0  <= '1' when N(2)='0' and N(1)='1' and N(0)='1' else '0';
   N2_N1L_N0  <= '1' when N(2)='1' and N(1)='0' and N(0)='1' else '0';
   F <= N3L_N0 or N3L_N2L_N1 or N2L_N1_N0 or N2_N1L_N0;
end prime3_arch;
```

Table 5-38
Prime-number-detector architecture using conditional assignments.

These comparison results are combined in the boolean expression between the when and else keywords in each statement. The else clauses are generally required; the combined set of conditions in a single statement should cover all possible input combinations.

Another kind of concurrent assignment statement is the *selected signal assignment*, whose syntax is shown in Table 5-39. This statement evaluates the given *expression*, and when the value matches one of the *choices*, it assigns the corresponding *signal-value* to *signal-name*. The *choices* in each when clause may be a single value of *expression* or a list of values separated by vertical bars (|). The *choices* for the entire statement must be mutually exclusive and all-inclusive. The keyword *others* can be used in the last when clause to denote all values of *expression* that have not yet been covered.

selected signal-assignment statement

others

Table 5-40 is an architecture for the prime-number detector that uses a selected signal-assignment statement. All of the *choices* for which F is '1' could have been written in a single when clause, but multiple clauses are shown just for instructional purposes. In this example, the selected signal-assignment statement reads somewhat like a listing of the on-set of the function F.

```
with expression select
   signal-name <= signal-value when choices,
                  signal-value when choices,
                  . . .
                  signal-value when choices;
```

Table 5-39
Syntax of VHDL selected signal-assignment statement.

```
architecture prime4_arch of prime is
begin
   with N select
     F <= '1' when "0001",
          '1' when "0010",
          '1' when "0011" | "0101" | "0111",
          '1' when "1011" | "1101",
          '0' when others;
end prime4_arch;
```

Table 5-40
Prime-number-detector architecture using selected signal assignment.

Table 5-41
A more behavioral
description of the
prime-number
detector.

```
architecture prime5_arch of prime is
begin
  with CONV_INTEGER(N) select
    F <= '1' when 1 | 2 | 3 | 5 | 7 | 11 | 13,
         '0' when others;
end prime5_arch;
```

We can modify the previous architecture slightly to take advantage of the numeric interpretation of N in the function definition. Using the CONV_INTEGER function that we defined previously, Table 5-41 writes the *choices* in terms of integers, which we can readily see are prime as required. We can think of this version of the architecture as a "behavioral" description, because it describes the desired function in such a way that its behavior is quite evident.

COVERING ALL THE CASES

Conditional and selected signal assignments require all possible conditions to be covered. In a conditional signal assignment, the final "else *expression*" covers missing conditions. In a selected signal assignment, "others" can be used in the final when clause to pick up the remaining conditions.

In Table 5-40, you might think that instead of writing "others" in the final when clause, we could have written the nine remaining 4-bit combinations, "0000", "0100", and so on. But that's not true! Remember that STD_LOGIC is a nine-valued system, so a 4-bit STD_LOGIC_VECTOR actually has 9^4 possible values. So "others" in this example is really covering 6,554 cases!

5.3.7 Behavioral Design Elements

As we saw in the last example, it is sometimes possible to directly describe a desired logic-circuit behavior using a concurrent statement. This is a good thing, as the ability to create a *behavioral design* or *behavioral description* is one of

behavioral design
behavioral description

the key benefits of hardware-description languages in general and VHDL in particular. However, for most behavioral descriptions, we need to employ some additional language elements described in this subsection.

process
sequential statement

VHDL's key behavioral element is the "process." A *process* is a collection of *sequential statements* (described shortly) that executes in parallel with other concurrent statements and other processes. Using a process, you can specify a complex interaction of signals and events in a way that executes in essentially zero simulated time during simulation and that gives rise to a synthesized combinational or sequential circuit that performs the modeled operation directly.

process statement
process

A VHDL *process statement* can be used anywhere that a concurrent statement can be used. A process statement is introduced by the keyword *process* and has the syntax shown in Table 5-42. Since a process statement is written within the scope of an enclosing architecture, it has visibility of the types,

```
process (signal-name, signal-name, ..., signal-name)
    type declarations
    variable declarations
    constant declarations
    function definitions
    procedure definitions
begin
    sequential-statement
    ...
    sequential-statement
end process;
```

Table 5-42
Syntax of a VHDL
process statement.

signals, constants, functions, and procedures that are declared or are otherwise visible in the enclosing architecture. However, you can also define types, variables, constants, functions, and procedures that are local to the process.

Note that a process may not declare signals, only "variables." A VHDL *variable* keeps track of the state within a process and is not visible outside of the process. Depending on its use, it may or may not give rise to a corresponding signal in a physical realization of the modeled circuit. The syntax for defining a variable within a process is similar to the syntax for a signal declaration within an architecture, except that the keyword `variable` is used:

variable

variable

`variable` *variable-names* : *variable-type*;

A VHDL process is always either *running* or *suspended*. The list of signals in the process definition, called the *sensitivity list*, determines when the process runs. A process initially is suspended; when any signal in its sensitivity list changes value, the process resumes execution, starting with its first sequential statement and continuing until the end. If any signal in the sensitivity list changes value as a result of running the process, it runs again. This continues until the process runs without any of these signals changing value. In simulation, all of this happens in zero simulated time.

running process
suspended process
sensitivity list

Upon resumption, a properly written process will suspend after one or a few runs. However, it is possible to write an incorrect process that never suspends. For example, consider a process with just one sequential statement, "X <= not X" and a sensitivity list of "(X)". Since X changes on every pass, the process will run forever in zero simulated time—not very useful! In practice, simulators have safeguards that normally can detect such unwanted behavior, terminating the misbehaving process after a thousand or so passes.

The sensitivity list is optional; a process without a sensitivity list starts running at time zero in simulation. One application of such a process is to generate input waveforms in a test bench, as in Table 5-52 on page 285.

VHDL has several kinds of sequential statements. The first is a *sequential signal-assignment statement*; this has the same syntax as the concurrent version

*sequential signal-
assignment statement*

WEIRD BEHAVIOR   Remember that the statements within a process are executed *sequentially*. Suppose that for some reason we moved the last statement in Table 5-43 (the signal assignment to F) to be the first statement. Then we would see rather weird behavior from this process.

The first time the process was run, the simulator would complain that the variables were uninitialized—that they were being read before any value had been assigned to them. On subsequent resumptions, a value would be assigned to F based on the *previous* values of the variables, which are remembered while the process is suspended. New values would then be assigned to the variables and remembered until the next resumption. So the circuit's output value would always be one input-change behind.

variable-assignment statement

:=

(*signal-name* <= *expression*;), but it occurs within the body of a process rather than an architecture. An analogous statement for variables is the *variable-assignment statement*, which has the syntax "*variable-name* := *expression*;". Notice that a different assignment operator, :=, is used for variables.

For instructional purposes, the dataflow architecture of the prime-number detector in Table 5-37 is rewritten as a process in Table 5-43. Notice that we're still working off the same original entity declaration of prime that appeared in Table 5-30. Within the new architecture (prime6_arch), we have just one concurrent statement, which is a process. The process sensitivity list contains just N, the primary inputs of the desired combinational logic function. The AND-gate outputs must be defined as variables rather than signals, since signal definitions are not allowed within a process. Otherwise, the body of the process is very similar to that of the original architecture. In fact, a typical synthesis tool would probably create the same circuit from either description.

if statement

Other sequential statements, beyond simple assignment, can give us more creative control in expressing circuit behavior. The *if statement*, with the syntax shown in Table 5-44, is probably the most familiar of these. In the first and

Table 5-43
Process-based dataflow VHDL architecture for the prime-number detector.

```
architecture prime6_arch of prime is
begin
  process(N)
    variable N3L_N0, N3L_N2L_N1, N2L_N1_N0, N2_N1L_N0: STD_LOGIC;
  begin
    N3L_N0      := not N(3)                          and N(0);
    N3L_N2L_N1 := not N(3) and not N(2) and     N(1)          ;
    N2L_N1_N0  :=                 not N(2) and     N(1) and N(0);
    N2_N1L_N0  :=                         N(2) and not N(1) and N(0);
    F <= N3L_N0 or N3L_N2L_N1 or N2L_N1_N0 or N2_N1L_N0;
  end process;
end prime6_arch;
```

```
if boolean-expression then sequential-statements
end if;

if boolean-expression then sequential-statements
else sequential-statements
end if;

if boolean-expression then sequential-statements
elsif boolean-expression then sequential-statements
. . .
elsif boolean-expression then sequential-statements
end if;

if boolean-expression then sequential-statements
elsif boolean-expression then sequential-statements
. . .
elsif boolean-expression then sequential-statements
else sequential-statements
end if;
```

Table 5-44
Syntax of a VHDL
if statement.

simplest form of the statement, a *boolean-expression* is tested, and a list of one
or more *sequential-statements* are executed if the expression's value is true. In
the second form, we've added an "*else*" keyword followed by another list of
sequential-statements that are executed if the expression's value is false.

else

To create nested if-then-else statements, VHDL uses a special keyword
elsif, which introduces the "middle" clauses. An elsif clause's *sequential-
statements* are executed if its *boolean-expression* is true and all the preceding
boolean-expressions were false. The optional final else-clause's *sequential-
statements* are executed if all the preceding *boolean-expressions* were false.

elsif

Table 5-45 is a version of the prime-number-detector architecture that uses
an if statement. A local variable NI is used to hold a converted, integer version
of the input N, so that the comparisons in the if statement can be written using
integer values instead of constants of type STD_LOGIC VECTOR.

```
architecture prime7_arch of prime is
begin
  process(N)
    variable NI: INTEGER;
  begin
    NI := CONV_INTEGER(N);
    if NI=1 or NI=2 then F <= '1';
    elsif NI=3 or NI=5 or NI=7 or NI=11 or NI=13 then F <= '1';
    else F <= '0';
    end if;
  end process;
end prime7_arch;
```

Table 5-45
Prime-detector
architecture using
an if statement.

Table 5-46
Syntax of a VHDL
case statement.

```
case expression is
  when choices => sequential-statements
  ...
  when choices => sequential-statements
end case;
```

The boolean expressions in Table 5-45 are nonoverlapping; that is, only one of them is true at a time. For this application we really didn't need the full power of nested if statements. In fact, a synthesis tool might create a circuit that evaluates the boolean expressions in series, with slower operation than might otherwise be possible. When we need to select among multiple alternatives based on the value of just one signal or expression, a *case statement* is usually more readable and may yield a better synthesized circuit.

case statement

Table 5-46 shows the syntax of a case statement. This statement evaluates the given *expression*, finds a matching value in one of the *choices*, and executes the corresponding *sequential-statements*. Note that one or more sequential statements can be written for each set of *choices*. The *choices* may take the form of a single value or of multiple values separated by vertical bars (|). The *choices* must be mutually exclusive and include all possible values of *expression*'s type; the keyword others can be used as the last *choices* to denote all values that have not yet been covered.

Table 5-47 is yet another architecture for the prime-number detector, this time coded with a case statement. Like the concurrent version, the select statement in Table 5-41 on page 278, the case statement makes it very easy to see the desired functional behavior.

loop statement

Another important class of sequential statements are the *loop statements*. The simplest of these has the syntax shown in Table 5-48 and creates an infinite loop. Although infinite loops are undesirable in conventional software programming languages, we'll show in Section 7.12.1 how such a loop can be used in simulation to create a free-running clock signal.

for loop

A more familiar loop, one that we've seen before, is the *for loop*, with the syntax shown in Table 5-49. Note that the loop variable, *identifier*, is declared

Table 5-47
Prime-detector
architecture using a
case statement.

```
architecture prime8_arch of prime is
begin
  process(N)
  begin
    case CONV_INTEGER(N) is
      when 1 => F <= '1';
      when 2 => F <= '1';
      when 3 | 5 | 7 | 11 | 13 => F <= '1';
      when others => F <= '0';
    end case;
  end process;
end prime8_arch;
```

```
loop
    sequential-statement
    . . .
    sequential-statement
end loop;
```

Table 5-48
Syntax of a basic
VHDL `loop`
statement.

```
for identifier in range loop
    sequential-statement
    . . .
    sequential-statement
end loop;
```

Table 5-49
Syntax of a VHDL
`for` loop.

implicitly by its appearance in the `for` loop and has the same type as *range*. This variable may be used within the loop's sequential statements, and it steps through all of the values in *range*, from left to right, one per iteration.

Two more useful sequential statements that can be executed within a loop are "*exit*" and "*next*". When executed, *exit* transfers control to the statement immediately following the loop end. On the other hand, *next* causes any remaining statements in the loop to be bypassed and begins the next iteration of the loop.

exit statement
next statement

Our good old prime-number detector is coded one more time in Table 5-50, this time using a `for` loop. The striking thing about this example is that it is truly a behavioral description—we have actually used VHDL to compute whether the

Table 5-50
Prime-number-detec-
tor architecture using
a `for` statement.

```
entity prime9 is
    port ( N: in STD_LOGIC_VECTOR (15 downto 0);
           F: out STD_LOGIC );
end prime9;

architecture prime9_arch of prime9 is
begin
  process(N)
  variable NI: INTEGER;
  variable prime: boolean;
  begin
    NI := CONV_INTEGER(N);
    prime := true;
    if NI=1 or NI=2 then null; -- take care of boundary cases
    else for i in 2 to 253 loop
            if (NI mod i = 0) and (NI /= i) then
                prime := false; exit;
            end if;
          end loop;
    end if;
    if prime then F <= '1'; else F <= '0'; end if;
  end process;
end prime9_arch;
```

BAD DESIGN   Table 5-50 has a good example of a `for` loop, but it's a bad example of how to design a circuit. Although VHDL is a powerful programming language, design descriptions that use its full power may be inefficient or unsynthesizable.

The culprit in Table 5-50 is the `mod` operator. This operation requires an integer division, and most VHDL tools are unable to synthesize division circuits except for special cases, such as division by a power of two (realized as a shift).

Even if the tools could synthesize a divider, you wouldn't want to specify a prime-number detector in this way. The description in Table 5-50 implies a combinational circuit, and the poor synthesizer would have to create 252 combinational dividers and comparators, one for each value of `i`, to "unroll" the `for` loop and realize the circuit! This would be an extremely expensive solution.

Table 5-51
Syntax of a VHDL
`while` loop.

```
while boolean-expression loop
    sequential-statement
    ...
    sequential-statement
end loop;
```

input `N` is a prime number. We've also increased the size of `N` to 16 bits, just to emphasize the fact that we were able to create a compact model for the circuit without having to explicitly list hundreds of primes.

while loop

The last kind of `loop` statement is the *while loop*, with the syntax shown in Table 5-51. In this form, *boolean-expression* is tested before each iteration of the loop, and the loop is executed only if the value of the expression is `true`.

We can use processes to write behavioral descriptions of both combinational and sequential circuits. Many more examples of combinational-circuit descriptions appear in the VHDL subsections of Chapter 6.

5.3.8 The Time Dimension

None of the examples that we've dealt with so far models the time dimension of circuit operation—everything happens in zero simulated time. However, VHDL has very good facilities for modeling time, and it is indeed another significant dimension of the language. In this book we won't go into detail on this subject, but we'll introduce just a few ideas here.

after keyword

VHDL allows you to specify a time delay using the keyword *after* in any signal-assignment statement, including sequential, concurrent, conditional, and selected assignments. For example, in the inhibit-gate architecture of Table 5-13 on page 258 you could write

```
Z <= '1' after 4 ns when X='1' and Y='0' else '0' after 3 ns;
```

This allows you to model an inhibit gate that has 4 ns of delay on a 0-to-1 output transition and only 3 ns on a 1-to-0 transition. In typical ASIC design environ-

```
entity InhibitTestBench is
end InhibitTestBench;

architecture InhibitTB_arch of InhibitTestBench is
component Inhibit port (X,Y: in BIT; Z: out BIT); end component;
signal XT, YT, ZT: BIT;
begin
  U1: Inhibit port map (XT, YT, ZT);
  process
  begin
    XT <= '0'; YT <= '0';
    wait for 10 ns;
    XT <= '0'; YT <= '1';
    wait for 10 ns;
    XT <= '1'; YT <= '0';
    wait for 10 ns;
    XT <= '1'; YT <= '1';
    wait; -- this suspends the process indefinitely
  end process;
end InhibitTB_arch;
```

Table 5-52
Using the VHDL `wait` statement to generate input waveforms in a test-bench program.

ments, the VHDL models for all of the low-level components in the component library include such delay parameters. Using these estimates, a VHDL simulator can predict the approximate timing behavior of a larger circuit that uses these components.

Another way to invoke the time dimension is with *wait*, a sequential statement. This statement can be used to suspend a process for a specified time period. Table 5-52 is an example program that uses `wait` to create simulated input waveforms to test the operation of the inhibit gate for four different input combinations at 10-ns time steps.

wait statement

5.3.9 Simulation

Once you have a VHDL program whose syntax and semantics are correct, you can use a simulator to observe its operation. Although we won't go into great detail, it's useful to have a basic understanding of how such a simulator works.

Simulator operation begins at *simulation time* of zero. At this time, the simulator initializes all signals to a default value (which you shouldn't depend on!). It also initializes any signals or variables for which initial values have been declared explicitly (we haven't shown you yet how to do this). Next, the simulator begins the execution of all the processes and concurrent statements in the design.

simulation time

Of course, the simulator can't really simulate all of the processes and other concurrent statements simultaneously, but it can pretend that it does, using a time-based *event list* and a *signal-sensitivity matrix* based on the signal-sensitivity lists of all the processes. Note that each component instantiation or

event list
signal-sensitivity matrix

concurrent assignment statement implies one process. Any signals that are used as inputs in a component instantiation or that appear on the righthand side of a concurrent assignment are automatically included in the sensitivity list of the implied process.

At simulation time zero, all of the processes are scheduled for execution, and one of these is selected. All of its sequential statements are executed, including any looping behavior that is specified. When the execution of this process is completed, another one is selected, and so on, until all of the processes have been executed. This completes one *simulation cycle*.

simulation cycle

During its execution, a process may assign new values to signals. The new values are not assigned immediately; rather, they are placed on the event list and scheduled to become effective at a certain time. If the assignment has an explicit simulation time associated with it (for example, after a delay specified by an `after` clause), then it is scheduled on the event list to occur at that time. Otherwise, it is supposed to occur "immediately"; however, it is actually scheduled to occur at the current simulation time plus one "delta delay." The *delta delay* is an infinitesimally short time, such that the current simulation time plus any number of delta delays still equals the current simulation time. This concept allows processes to execute multiple times if necessary in zero simulated time.

delta delay

After a simulation cycle completes, the event list is scanned for the signal or signals that change at the next earliest time on the list. This may be as little as one delta delay later, or it may be a real circuit delay later, in which case the simulation time is advanced to this time. In any case, the scheduled signal changes are made. Some processes may be sensitive to the changing signals, as indicated by their signal-sensitivity lists. The signal-sensitivity matrix indicates, for each signal, which processes have that signal in their sensitivity list. All of the processes that are sensitive to a signal that just changed are scheduled for execution in the next simulation cycle, which now begins.

The simulator's two-phase operation of a simulation cycle followed by scanning the event list and making the next scheduled signal assignments goes on indefinitely, until the event list is empty. At this point the simulation is complete.

The event-list mechanism makes it possible to simulate the operation of concurrent processes even though the simulator runs on a single computer with a single thread of execution. And the delta-delay mechanism ensures correct operation even though a process or set of processes may require multiple executions, spanning several delta delays, before changing signals settle down to a stable value. This mechanism is also used to detect runaway processes (such as "X <= not X"); if a thousand simulation cycles occur over a thousand delta delays without advancing simulation time by any "real" amount, it's most likely that something's amiss.

**SIGNALS VERSUS
VARIABLES**

What's the difference? At one level it's simple—*signals* typically correspond to wires within a circuit realization, while *variables* are ephemeral. They exist only during each execution of a process, and in typical uses they do not give rise to corresponding physical signals. But at another level, the difference is subtle yet very important.

Within a process, assignments to variables are made *immediately*. Assignments to signals are scheduled but not made until *after* the the simulator completes execution of the current process. This makes coding with signals in a process different from what you're used to in computer-programming languages.

For example, suppose X and Y are variables in a C program. To swap X and Y, you would write "`temp = X; X = Y; Y = temp;`". But if X and Y are signals in a VHDL program, you would simply write "`X <= Y; Y <= X;`".

You may think "OK, this is convenient," but it can lead to bugs as well. For example, you may write "`X <= Y`" and then several lines later in the same process write "`if X=1 then ...`". But the value of X that is tested is the *old* value; the new value is not there until the next time that this (or any other) process runs.

Finally, consider the VHDL version of our original swapping code. If temp is a variable (`temp := X; X <= Y; Y <= temp;`), the code is more verbose than needed, but it works. If temp is a signal (`temp <= X; X <= Y; Y <= temp;`), the code fails to work as intended.

5.3.10 Test Benches

A *test bench* specifies a sequence of inputs to be applied by the simulator to an HDL-based design, such as a VHDL entity. The entity being tested is often called the *unit under test (UUT)*, in accordance with traditional parlance in the hardware testing field, even though the UUT in this case is not a device, but a program that specifies the behavior of one.

test bench

unit under test (UUT)

Using just VHDL features that we've introduced so far, Table 5-52 on page 285 showed a very simple test bench for the "inhibit gate" that we specified in Table 5-13 on page 258. It's simple, but it illustrates most of the basic parts of a VHDL test-bench program:

- Like all VHDL programs, there is an entity declaration, but notice that it has no inputs or outputs. The inputs to the UUT are created within the test bench, and the outputs are observed on the simulator.

- The architecture definition makes a component declaration for the UUT, and the UUT is instantiated using local signals for its inputs and outputs.

- A process with no sensitivity list starts at simulation time 0, and applies new input combinations to the UUT at specified times (every 10 ns in this example).

Table 5-53
Syntax of VHDL
assert and report
statements.

```
assert boolean-expression
   report string-expression severity severity-expression;

report string-expression severity severity-expression;
```

This particular test bench doesn't do a lot—all you can do is run it on the simulator, and use the waveform viewer to see if it produces the expected output sequence of 0, 0, 1, 0. But by using a few more VHDL features, described below, you can write test benches that do more. In particular, you can specify the expected values of signals, and instruct the simulator to print an error message when a signal is different from its expected value, as discussed below.

assert statement

The VHDL *assert statement* tests the value of a boolean expression, and if it evaluates to false, it prints the designated string and severity level on the simulator console, as well as the name of the entity that executed the assert statement and the current simulated time. In order of increasing severity, the pre-defined severity levels are note, warning, error, and failure. The VHDL

report statement

report statement is similar, except that it omits the boolean expression—it *always* prints the designated string and severity level.

Table 5-54 is an improved version of the inhibit-gate test bench. It uses report statements to announce the beginning and end of the test-bench run, and it uses assert statements at each step to compare the output of the UUT with the expected value.

Table 5-54
VHDL test bench
using assert and
report.

```
entity InhibTBc is
end InhibTBc;

architecture InhibitTBc_arch of InhibTBc is
component Inhibit port (X,Y: in BIT; Z: out BIT); end component;
signal XT, YT, ZT: BIT;
begin
  U1: Inhibit port map (XT, YT, ZT);
  process
  begin
    report "Beginning test bench for Inbibit" severity NOTE;
    XT <= '0'; YT <= '0'; wait for 10 ns;
    assert (ZT = '0') report "Failed -- 0,0" severity ERROR;
    XT <= '0'; YT <= '1'; wait for 10 ns;
    assert (ZT = '0') report "Failed -- 0,1" severity ERROR;
    XT <= '1'; YT <= '0'; wait for 10 ns;
    assert (ZT = '1') report "Failed -- 1,0" severity ERROR;
    XT <= '1'; YT <= '1'; wait for 10 ns;
    assert (ZT = '0') report "Failed -- 1,1" severity ERROR;
    report "Ending test bench for Inbibit" severity NOTE;
    wait; -- all done
  end process;
end InhibitTBc_arch;
```

It is also possible to construct test benches that compare the outputs of two or more architectures for the same entity, for example, a "golden" behavioral architecture and a structural architectural that is thought by the designer to satisfy the behavioral requirements. With appropriate design of the test bench, a specified, a random, or an exhaustive set of inputs can be applied.

In complex test benches, VHDL's looping statements, procedures, and functions can come in handy. VHDL also provides formatted text and file input and output facilities. Thus, test vectors can be taken from a file, and output messages can be written to another file. These advanced test-benching facilities are beyond the scope of this book.

5.3.11 VHDL Features for Sequential Logic Design

A few additional language features are needed to describe sequential circuits; for reference purposes, we list them here:

- The *event attribute* can be attached to a signal name to create edge-triggered behavior in a process, giving us a way to simulate edge-triggered flip-flops (Section 7.12.1).

- Unlike ABEL, VHDL has no specific syntax for creating *state machines*, and in fact provides many ways to do so. However, it's important to use a consistent coding style for state machines, and we show and use such a style throughout Section 7.12.

5.3.12 Synthesis

As we mentioned at the beginning of this section, VHDL was originally invented as a logic circuit description and simulation language and was later adapted to synthesis. The language has many features and constructs that cannot be synthesized. However, the subset of the language and the style of programs that we've presented in this section are generally synthesizable by most tools.

Still, the code that you write can have a big effect on the quality of the synthesized circuits that you get. A few examples are listed below:

- "Serial" control structures like `if-elsif-elsif-else` can result in a corresponding serial chain of logic gates to test conditions. It's better to use a `case` or `select` statement if the conditions are mutually exclusive.

- Loops in processes are generally "unwound" to create multiple copies of combinational logic to execute the statements in the loop. If you want to use just one copy of the combinational logic in a sequence of steps, then you have to design a sequential circuit, as discussed in later chapters.

- When using conditional statements in a process, failing to state an outcome for some input combination will cause the synthesizer to create a "latch" to hold the old value of a signal that might otherwise change. Such latches are generally not intended.

In addition, some language features and constructs may just be unsynthesizable, depending on the tool. Naturally, you have to consult the documentation to find out what's disallowed, allowed, and recommended for a particular tool.

For the foreseeable future, digital designers who use synthesis tools will need to pay reasonably close attention to their coding style in order to obtain good results. And for the moment, the definition of "good coding style" depends somewhat on both the synthesis tool and the target technology. The examples in the rest of this book, while syntactically and semantically correct, hardly scratch the surface of coding methods for large HDL-based designs. The art and practice of large HDL-based hardware design is still very much evolving.

5.4 The Verilog Hardware Description Language

At about the same time that VHDL was being developed, a different hardware design language appeared on the scene. *Verilog HDL*, or simply *Verilog*, was introduced by Gateway Design Automation in 1984 as a proprietary hardware description and simulation language. The introduction of Verilog-based synthesis tools in 1988 by then-fledgling Synopsys and the 1989 acquisition of Gateway by Cadence Design Systems were important events that led to widespread use of the language.

Verilog synthesis tools

Verilog synthesis tools can create logic-circuit structures directly from Verilog behavioral descriptions, and target them to a selected technology for realization. Using Verilog, you can design, simulate, and synthesize anything from a simple combinational circuit to a complete microprocessor system on a chip.

VERILOG AND VHDL

Today, VHDL and Verilog both enjoy widespread use and share the logic synthesis market roughly 50/50. Verilog has its syntactic roots in C and is in some respects an easier language to learn and use, while VHDL is more like Ada (a DoD-sponsored software programming language). Verilog initially had fewer features than VHDL to support large project development, but with new features added in 2002, it has pretty much caught up.

Comparing the pros and cons of starting out with one language versus the other, David Pellerin and Douglas Taylor probably put it best in their book, *VHDL Made Easy!* (Prentice Hall, 1997):

> Both languages are easy to learn and hard to master. And once you have learned one of these languages, you will have no trouble transitioning to the other.

While writing this book, I found their advice to be generally true. But it *is* hard to go back and forth between the two on a daily or even weekly basis. So my advice is to learn one well and, only if necessary, tackle the other later.

One thing led to another, and in 1993 the IEEE was asked to formally standardize the language as it was being used at that time. So, the IEEE created a standards working group which created IEEE 1364, the official Verilog standard published in 1995 (*Verilog-1995*). By 1997, the Verilog community, including users and both simulator and synthesizer suppliers, wanted to make several enhancements to the language, and an IEEE standards group was reconvened. The result was an enhanced standard published in 2001 (*Verilog-2001*).

Verilog-1995

Verilog-2001

Verilog started out with and still has the following features:

- Designs may be decomposed hierarchically.

- Each design element has both a well-defined interface (for connecting it to other elements) and a precise functional specification (for simulating it).

- Functional specifications can use either a behavioral algorithm or an actual hardware structure to define an element's operation. For example, an element can be defined initially by an algorithm, to allow design verification of higher-level elements that use it; later, the algorithmic definition can be replaced by a preferred hardware structure.

- Concurrency, timing, and clocking can all be modeled. Verilog handles asynchronous as well as synchronous sequential-circuit structures.

- The logical operation and timing behavior of a design can be simulated.

Thus, like VHDL, Verilog started out as a documentation and modeling language, allowing the behavior of digital-system designs to be precisely specified and simulated. But as with VHDL, synthesis tools are what led to widespread use of Verilog.

In this book we'll use a subset of Verilog's features that are legal in both Verilog-1995 and Verilog-2001. In this section, we focus on general language structure and combinational logic design, but we'll discuss additional features for sequential logic design in Section 7.13.

5.4.1 Program Structure

The basic unit of design and programming in Verilog is a *module*—a text file containing declarations and statements, as shown in Figure 5-4(a) on the next page. A typical Verilog module corresponds to a single piece of hardware, in much the same sense as a "module" in traditional hardware design. A Verilog module has *declarations* that describe the names and types of the module's

module

declarations

ONE MODULE PER FILE, PLEASE   The Verilog language specification allows multiple modules to be stored in a single text file. However, most designers like to put just one module in each file, with the filename based on the module name, for example, `adder.v` for module `adder`. This just makes it easier to keep track of things.

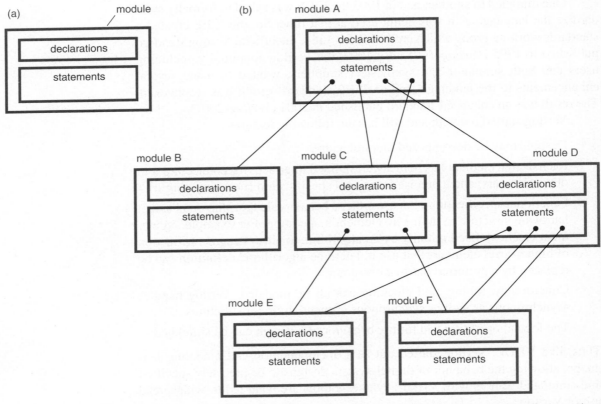

Figure 5-4 Verilog modules: (a) one module; (b) modules instantiating other modules hierarchically.

inputs and outputs, as well as local signals, variables, constants, and functions that are used strictly internally to the module, and are not visible outside. The rest of the module contains *statements* that specify the operation of the module's outputs and internal signals.

statements

behavioral specification   Verilog statements can specify a module's operation *behaviorally*, for example, by making assignments of new values to signals based on tests of logical conditions, using familiar constructs like if and case. They can also specify

structural specification   the module's operation *structurally*. In this case, the statements instantiate other modules and individual components (such as gates and flip-flops) and specify their interconnections.

Verilog modules can use a mix of behavioral and structural specifications, and may do so hierarchically, as shown in Figure 5-4(b). Just as procedures and functions in a high-level software programming language can "call" others, Verilog modules can "instantiate" other modules. A higher-level module may use a lower-level module multiple times, and multiple top-level modules may use the same lower-level one. In the figure, modules B, E, and F stand alone; they

CONFIGURATION MANAGEMENT

When one Verilog module instantiates another, the compiler finds the other by searching the current workspace, as well as predefined libraries, for a module with the instantiated name. Thus, when using Verilog-1995, there should be only one definition of each module, usually in a file with the same name as the module.

However, Verilog-2001 actually allows you to define multiple versions of each module, and it provides a separate configuration management facility that allows you to specify which one to use for each different instantiation during a particular compilation or synthesis run. This lets you try out different approaches without throwing away or renaming your other efforts. Still, we won't use or further discuss this facility in this text.

do not instantiate any others. In Verilog, the scope of signal, constant, and other definitions remains local to each module; values can be passed between modules only by using declared input and output signals.

scope

Verilog's modular approach provides a great deal of flexibility in designing large systems, especially when multiple designers and design phases are involved. For example, a given module can be specified with a rough behavioral model during the initial phase of system design, so that overall system operation can be checked. Later, it can be replaced with a more accurate behavioral model for synthesis, or perhaps with a hand-tuned structural design that achieves higher performance than a synthesized realization.

Now we're ready to talk about some of the details of Verilog syntax and program structure. A simple example module is shown in Table 5-55. Like other high-level languages, Verilog mostly ignores spaces and line breaks, which may be used as desired for readability. Single-line *comments* begin with two slashes (//) and end at the end of a line. Verilog also allows C-style, multi-line long comments that begin anywhere with /* and end anywhere with */.

comments

Verilog defines many special character strings, called *reserved words* or *keywords*. Our example includes a few—module, input, output, assign, and endmodule. Following the practice of most Verilog text-editor programs, we use color for keywords in Verilog programs in this book.

reserved words
keywords

User-defined *identifiers* begin with a letter or underscore and can contain letters, digits, underscores (_), and dollar signs ($). (Identifiers that start with a dollar sign refer to built-in system functions.) Identifiers in the example are VrInhibit, X, Y, and Z. Unlike VHDL, Verilog is sensitive to case for both

identifiers

```
module VrInhibit( X, Y, Z ); // also known as 'BUT-NOT'
  input X, Y;                 // as in 'X but not Y'
  output Z;                   // (see [Klir, 1972])

  assign Z = X & ~Y;
endmodule
```

Table 5-55
Verilog program for an "inhibit" gate.

Table 5-56
Syntax of a Verilog
module declaration.

```
module module-name (port-name, port-name, ..., port-name);
    input declarations
    output declarations
    inout declarations
    net declarations
    variable declarations
    parameter declarations
    function declarations
    task declarations

    concurrent statements
endmodule
```

keywords (lowercase only) and identifiers (XY, xy, and Xy are all different). Case
sensitivity can create problems in projects containing modules in both languages, when the same identifier must be used in both Verilog and VHDL, but
most compilers provide renaming facilities to deal with it in large projects. Still,
it's best not to rely on case alone to distinguish two different identifiers.

module declaration
module keyword
input and output ports

The basic syntax for a Verilog *module declaration* is shown in Table 5-56.
It begins with the keyword *module*, followed by an identifier for the module's
name and a list of identifiers for the module's *input and output ports*. The input
and output ports are signals by which the module communicates with other modules. Think of them as wires, since that's what they usually are in the module's
realization.

Next comes a set of optional declarations that we describe in this and later
subsections. These declarations can be made in any order. Besides the ones
shown in Table 5-56, there are a few more that we don't use in this book and
have therefore omitted. Concurrent statements, introduced in Section 5.4.7,

endmodule keyword

follow the declarations, and a module ends with the *endmodule* keyword.

Table 5-57
Syntax of Verilog
input/output
declarations.

```
input   identifier, identifier, ..., identifier;
output  identifier, identifier, ..., identifier;
inout   identifier, identifier, ..., identifier;

input   [msb:lsb] identifier, identifier, ..., identifier;
output  [msb:lsb] identifier, identifier, ..., identifier;
inout   [msb:lsb] identifier, identifier, ..., identifier;
```

OPTIONAL?   We said that the declarations in Table 5-56 are optional, and that's true even for
input, output, and inout declarations if the module does not have the corresponding
port types. For example, most modules do not have inout ports. A module that
generates a clock signal would have an output port but might have no inputs. And a
test-bench module, discussed later, has no inputs or outputs.

Each port that is named at the beginning of the module, in the input/output list, must have a corresponding *input*, *output*, or *inout declaration*. The simplest form of these declarations is shown in the first three lines of Table 5-57. The keyword `input`, `output`, or `inout` is followed by a comma-separated list of the identifiers for signals (ports) of the corresponding type. The keyword specifies the signal direction as follows:

input, output, and inout declarations

`input` The signal is an input to the module.

input keyword

`output` The signal is an output of the module. Note that the value of such a signal cannot necessarily be "read" inside the module architecture, only by other modules that use it. A "reg" declaration, shown in the next subsection, is needed to make it readable.

output keyword

`inout` The signal can be used as a module input or output. This mode is typically used for three-state input/output pins on PLDs.

inout keyword

An input/output signal declared as described above is one bit wide. Multi-bit or "vector" signals can be declared by including a *range specification*, [*msb*:*lsb*], in the declaration as in the last three lines of Table 5-57. Here, *msb* and *lsb* are integers that indicate the starting and ending indexes of the individual bits within a *vector* of signals. The signals in a vector are ordered from left to right, with *msb* giving the index of the leftmost signal. A range can be ascending or descending; that is, [7:0], [0:7], and [13:20] are all valid 8-bit ranges. We'll have more to say about vectors in Section 5.4.3.

range specification

vector

5.4.2 Logic System, Nets, Variables, and Constants

Verilog uses a simple, four-valued logic system. A 1-bit signal can take on one of only four possible values:

0 Logical 0, or false

1 Logical 1, or true

x An unknown logical value

z High impedance, as in three-state logic (Section 3.7.3)

Verilog has built-in *bitwise boolean operators*, shown in Table 5-58 on the next page. The AND, OR, and XOR operators combine a pair of 1-bit signals and

bitwise boolean operators

SIMPLE BUT EFFECTIVE Verilog's logic system is a lot simpler than the nine-valued system provided in typical VHDL environments, but it's all that's normally used anyway. Because Verilog was targeted to digital logic design and only that, it does not have anything like VHDL's mechanisms for creating user-defined types and operators. On the other hand, you can usually count on Verilog to have just the operators you need and to do just what you would expect it to do in logic applications, without forcing you to struggle with type matching and type conversions.

Table 5-58
Bitwise boolean operators in Verilog's logic system.

Operator	Operation
&	AND
|	OR
^	Exclusive OR (XOR)
~^, ^~	Exclusive NOR (XNOR)
~	NOT

produce the expected result, and the NOT operator complements a single bit. The XNOR operation can be viewed as either the complement of XOR, or as XOR with the second signal complemented, corresponding to the two different symbols for XNOR shown in the table.

In Verilog's boolean operations, if one or both of the input signals is x or z, then the output is x unless another input dominates. That is, if at least one input of an OR operation is 1, then the output is always 1; if at least one input of an AND operation is 0, then the output is always 0. Verilog's boolean operations can also be applied to vector signals, as discussed in Section 5.4.3.

net

Up until now, we've used the word "signal" somewhat loosely. Verilog actually has two classes of signals—nets and variables. A *net* corresponds roughly to a wire in a physical circuit, and provides connectivity between modules and other elements in a Verilog structural model. The signals in a Verilog module's input/output port list are often nets.

wire keyword

Verilog provides several kinds of nets, which can be specified by type name in net declarations. The default net type is *wire*—any signal name that appears in a module's input/output port list but not in a net declaration is assumed to be type wire. A wire net provides basic connectivity, but no other functionality is implied.

Verilog also provides several other net types, shown in Table 5-59. The supply0 and supply1 net types are considered to be permanently wired to the corresponding power-supply rail, and provide a source of constant logic-0 and logic-1 signals. The remaining types allow modeling of three-state and wired-logic connections in a board-level system. They are seldom used inside a CPLD, FPGA, or ASIC design, except for modeling external-pin connections to other three-state devices. Note that the net types are all reserved words.

net declaration

The syntax of Verilog *net declarations* is similar to an input/output declaration, as shown in Table 5-60 for wire and tri net types. A list of identifiers follows the keyword for the desired net type. For vector nets, a range specification precedes the list of identifiers.

Table 5-59
Verilog net types.

wire	trior	trireg	supply0
tri	tri0	wand	supply1
triand	tri1	wor	

`wire` *identifier, identifier, ..., identifier;* `wire [msb:lsb]` *identifier, identifier, ..., identifier;* `tri` *identifier, identifier, ..., identifier;* `tri [msb:lsb]` *identifier, identifier, ..., identifier;*	**Table 5-60** Syntax of Verilog `wire` and `tri` net declarations.

`reg` *identifier, identifier, ..., identifier;* `reg [msb:lsb]` *identifier, identifier, ..., identifier;* `integer` *identifier, identifier, ..., identifier;*	**Table 5-61** Syntax of Verilog `reg` and `integer` variable declarations.

Keep in mind that net declarations have two uses: to specify the net type of a module's input/output ports, if not `wire`; and to declare signals (nets) that will be used to establish connectivity in structural descriptions inside a module. We'll see many examples of the latter in Sections 5.4.7 and 5.4.8.

Verilog *variables* store values during a Verilog program's execution, and they need not have physical significance in a circuit. They are used only in "procedural code," discussed in Section 5.4.9. A variable's value can be used in an expression and can be combined with and assigned to other variables, as in conventional software programming languages. The most commonly used Verilog variable types are `reg` and `integer`.

variable

A *reg* variable is a single bit or a vector of bits, declared as shown in the first two lines of Table 5-61. The value of a 1-bit `reg` variable is always 0, 1, x, or z. The main use of `reg` variables is to store values in Verilog procedural code. An *integer* variable is declared as shown in the last line of Table 5-61. Its value is a 32-bit or larger integer, depending on the word length used by the simulator. An `integer` variable is typically used to control a repetitive statement, such as a `for` loop, in Verilog procedural code. Integers in an actual circuit are normally modeled using multibit vector signals, as discussed in Section 5.4.3.

variable declaration
reg keyword

integer keyword

The difference between Verilog's nets and variables is subtle. A variable's value can be changed only within procedural code within a module; it cannot be changed from outside the module. Thus, input and inout ports cannot have a variable type; they must have a net type such as `wire`. Output ports, on the other hand, can have either a net or a `reg` type, and can drive the input and inout ports

A `reg` IS NOT **A FLIP-FLOP**	The variable-type name "reg" in Verilog has nothing to do with flip-flops and registers in sequential circuits. When the language designers came up with this name, they were thinking in terms of storage registers, or *variables*, that are used during the simulator's program execution to keep track of modeled values. So, `reg` variables can be used for sequential *or* combinational circuit outputs. Sequential-circuit flip-flops and registers are defined in Verilog by an entirely different mechanism, introduced in Section 7.13.

LESS ANTSY DEFINITIONS   In Verilog-1995, the order of ports in a module is defined by the list of identifiers following the module name, and the ports' direction, size, and type are defined by declarations that follow. The identifiers used in both places must match up, of course, and this can be a source of errors, besides requiring extra typing.

Verilog-2001 supports a second style for input/output port declarations, similar to the function definition style used in ANSI C. Here, the parenthesized port list also includes the ports' direction, size, and type, defining everything in one place. For example, the first three lines in Table 5-55 on page 293 become:

```
module VrInhibit( input X, Y,
                  output Z   );
```

Instead of requiring extra declarations to specify net and variable types for ports, Verilog-2001 can include these in the declarations, as in the example below:

```
module Vr3to8deca( input wire G1, G2, G3,
                   input wire [2:0] A,
                   output reg [0:7] Y );
```

of other modules. Another important difference, as we'll see later, is that procedural code can assign values only to variables.

The result of all this is that if you want to write procedural Verilog code to specify the value of a module output, you have basically two ways to do it:

1. Declare the output port to have type `reg`, and use procedural code to assign values to it directly.

2. If for any reason the port must be declared as a net type (such as `wire`), define an internal "output" `reg` variable and specify its value procedurally. Then assign the value of the internal `reg` variable to the module output net. This situation occurs, for example, in Table 6-41 on page 432.

literals   Verilog has its own particular syntax for writing numeric *literals*, tailored to its use in describing digital logic circuits. Literals that are written as a sequence of decimal digits, with no other frills, are interpreted as decimal numbers, as you would expect. Verilog also gives you the ability to write numeric literals in a specific base and with a specific number of bits, using the format *n'Bdd...d*, where:

- *n* is a decimal number that gives the size of the literal in bits. This is the number of bits represented, not the number of digits *dd...d*.

- *B* is a single letter specifying the base, one of the following: b (binary), o (octal), h (hexadecimal), or d (decimal, and the default).

- *dd...d* is a string of one or more digits in the specified base.

parameter *identifier* = *value*;
parameter *identifier* = *value*,
         identifier = *value*,
         ...
         identifier = *value*;
	Table 5-62
	Syntax of Verilog
	parameter declarations.

Sized literals are automatically interpreted as multibit vectors as required, as shown in examples in the next subsection. Literals written without a size indicator default to 32 bits or the word width used by the simulator program; this may cause errors or ambiguity, so you have to be careful with unsized literals.

Verilog provides a facility for defining named constants within a module, to improve the readability and maintainability of code. A *parameter declaration* has the syntax shown in Table 5-62. An identifier is assigned a constant value that will be used in place of the identifier throughout the current module. Multiple constants can be defined in a single parameter declaration using a comma-separated list of assignments. Some examples are shown below:

parameter declaration
parameter keyword

```
parameter BUS_SIZE = 32,             // width of bus
          MSB = BUS_SIZE-1, LSB = 0; // range of indices
parameter ESC = 7'b0011011;          // ASCII escape character
```

The *value* in a parameter declaration can be a simple constant, or it can be a *constant expression*—an expression involving multiple operators and constants, including other parameters, that yields a constant result at compile time. Note that the scope of a parameter is limited to the module in which it is defined.

constant expression

NOTHING TO DECLARE?   Verilog allows you to use nets that have not been declared. In structural code, you can use an undeclared identifier in a context where the compiler would allow a net to be used. In such a case, the compiler will define the identifier to be a `wire`, local to the module in which it appears.

But to experienced programmers, using undeclared identifiers seems like a bad idea. In a large module, declaring all the identifiers in one place gives you a greater opportunity to document and ensure consistency among names. Whether or not you declare all identifiers, if you mistype an identifier, the compiler will usually notice and warn you that the accidental wire (or, in some cases, the intended wire) is not being driven by anything.

5.4.3 Vectors and Operators

As shown earlier, Verilog allows individual 1-bit signals to be grouped together in a *vector*. Nets, variables, and constants can all be vectors. Verilog provides a number of operations and conventions related to vectors. In general, Verilog does "the right thing" with vectors, but it's important to know the details.

vector

Table 5-63	`reg [7:0] byte1, byte2, byte3;`
Examples of Verilog	`reg [15:0] word1, word2;`
vectors.	`reg [1:16] Zbus;`

Table 5-63 gives some example definitions of vectors for this subsection. In a vector definition, you should think of the first (left) index in the definition as corresponding to the bit on the left end of the vector, and the second (right) index as corresponding to the bit on the right. Thus, the rightmost bit in `byte1` has index 0, and the leftmost bit in `Zbus` has index 1. As shown in the examples, index numbers can be ascending or descending from left to right.

bit select

Verilog provides a natural *bit-select* syntax to select an individual bit in a vector, using square brackets and a constant (or constant expression). Thus, `byte1[7]` is the leftmost bit of `byte1`, and `Zbus[16]` is the rightmost bit of `Zbus`. The *part-select* syntax is also natural, using the same range-specification syntax that is used in declarations. Thus, `Zbus[1:8]` and `Zbus[9:16]` are the left and right bytes of `Zbus`, and `byte1[5:2]` is the middle four bits of `byte1`. Note that the indices in a part select should be in the same order as the range specification in the original definition.

part select

Just as bits and parts can be extracted from vectors, so can bits and parts be combined to create larger vectors. *Concatenation* uses curly brackets `{}` to combine two or more bits or vectors into a single vector. Thus, `{2'b00,2'b11}` is equivalent to `4'b0011`, and `{byte1,byte1,byte2,byte2}` is a 32-bit vector with two copies of `byte1` on the left, and two copies of `byte2` on the right. Verilog also has a *replication operator n{}* that can be used within a concatenation to replicate a bit or vector *n* times. Thus, `{2{byte1},2{byte2}}` is the same 32-bit vector that we defined two sentences ago.

{}, concatenation operator

n{}, replication operator

The bitwise boolean operators that we listed in Table 5-58 also work on vectors. For example, the expression `byte1 & byte2` yields an 8-bit vector where each bit is the logical **AND** of the bits in the corresponding position of `byte1` and `byte2`; the value of `4'b0011 & 4'b0101` is `4'b0001`; and the value of `~2'b01` is `2'b10`.

padding

Vectors of different sizes can be combined by the bitwise boolean operators. The vectors are aligned on their rightmost bits, and the shorter vector is padded on the left with 0s. Thus, the value of `2'b11 & 4'b0101` is `4'b0001`.

Zero-padding also applies in general to constants. Thus, `16'b0` is a 16-bit constant in which all the bits are zero. However, if the leftmost specified bit is x or z, then the vector is padded with x or z. Thus, `8'bx` is an 8-bit vector of all x's, and `8'bz00` is equivalent to `8'bzzzzzz00`.

Later, we'll see assignment statements where the value of an expression is assigned to a net or a variable. If the expression's result size is smaller than the size of the net or variable, then it is padded on the left with 0s. If the result size is wider than the net or variable, then its rightmost bits are used.

Operator	Operation
+	Addition
–	Subtraction
*	Multiplication
/	Division
%	Modulus (remainder)
<<	Shift left
>>	Shift right

Table 5-64
Arithmetic and shift operators in Verilog.

Verilog has built-in *arithmetic operators*, shown in Table 5-64, that treat vectors as unsigned integers. An integer value is associated with a vector in the "natural" way. The rightmost bit has a weight of 1, and bits to the left have weights of successive powers of two. This is true regardless of the index range of the vector. Thus, if the constant 4'b0101 is assigned to the Zbus[1:16] variable that we defined earlier, the integer value of Zbus is 5.

arithmetic operators

Addition and subtraction are the most often used arithmetic operators, and Verilog synthesis tools know how to synthesize adders and subtractors; for example, see Section 6.10.10. Unary plus and minus are also allowed. Multiplication is also handled by most synthesis tools, although the multiplier's size and speed may not be as good as what you would get from a hand-tuned design (see Section 6.11.4). Division and modulus typically cannot be synthesized unless the divisor is a power of two. In that case, the operation is equivalent to shifting the dividend to the right (division) or selecting the rightmost bits of the dividend (modulus).

Verilog also has explicit *shift operators*, for vectors, shown in the last two rows of Table 5-64. As in C, the first operand is shifted by a number of positions indicated by the second operand, and vacated positions are filled with 0s. Thus, the value of 8'b11010011<<3 is 8'b10011000.

shift operators

SIGNED ARITHMETIC   Verilog-2001 provides for signed as well as unsigned arithmetic. A reg variable, a net, or a function output can be declared as signed by including the keyword signed in the declaration, for example, "reg signed [15:0] A". Likewise, a module's ports may be declared as signed, for example, "output signed [15:0] A". A numeric literal is signed if the letter "s" is included after the base, for example, 8'bs11111111 is an 8-bit two's-complement number, −1.

Operations and comparisons on signed variables and nets follow the rules for two's-complement arithmetic, in both simulation and synthesis. However, for signed arithmetic to be simulated and synthesized, all operands in an expression must be signed.

boolean reduction
operators

Besides its frequently used bitwise boolean operators, Verilog also has infrequently used *boolean reduction operators*. These operations use the same operator symbols as in the first four rows of Table 5-58 on page 296, but they take a single vector operand. They combine all of the bits in the vector using the corresponding operation, and return a 1-bit result. Thus, the value of &Zbus is 1'b1 if all the bits of Zbus are 1, else it's 1'b0. Similarly, the value of ^byte1 is 1'b1 if byte1 has an odd number of 1s, else it's 1'b0. (Well, OK, the results are actually 1'bx if any of the operand bits are z or x.)

5.4.4 Arrays

array
array index

Verilog-1995 has a limited capability to define and use one-dimensional arrays of reg and integer variables. An *array* is an ordered set of variables of the same type, where each element is selected by an *array index*. The array declaration format is shown in Table 5-65; the reg or integer identifier is followed by an array-index range in square brackets. Here, *start* and *end* are integer constants or constant expressions that define the possible range of the array index and hence the total number of array elements.

As shown in the table, array elements can be bits, vectors, or integers. Multiple variables of the same type and size, including arrays of different sizes, can be defined in a single declaration, for example,

```
reg [7:0] byte1, recent[1:5], mem1[0:255], mem2[0:511];
```

Here, byte1 is an 8-bit vector, and the other variables are arrays containing 5, 256, and 512 8-bit vectors, respectively.

Table 5-65
Syntax of Verilog
array declarations.

reg *identifier* [*start*:*end*];
reg [*msb*:*lsb*] *identifier* [*start*:*end*];

integer *identifier* [*start*:*end*];

VERILOG-2001 ARRAYS

The Verilog-2001 standard provides several enhancements for array definition and use. In Verilog-2001, you can define arrays of net-type signals such as wire, as well as reg and integer types. With vector array elements, it is now possible to use a bit or part select to access an individual bit or part of the array. For example, you can use mem1[117][5] to access byte 117, bit 5 of the mem1 array. However, it is still not possible to select multiple elements or subarrays of an array as you can in VHDL.

Verilog-2001 also supports multidimensional arrays. In the declaration, a [*start*:*end*] index range is provided for each additional dimension, and to access an element, an index is needed for each dimension. Thus, you could declare a two-dimensional array of bytes, "reg [7:0] mem3 [1:10] [0:255]" and access the lower nibble of the byte in row 5, column 7 as mem3[5][7][3:0].

Individual array elements are accessed using the array name followed by the index of the desired element, enclosed in square brackets. For example, recent[1] is the first 8-bit-vector element in the recent array, and recent[i] is the *i*th element, assuming that i is an integer variable and its value is in the range 1 to 5. Verilog-1995 does not provide a means to directly access individual bits of a vector array element; you must first copy the array element to a like-size reg variable or net, and then access the desired bit(s) using a bit or part select. For example, to read bit 5 of mem1[117], you could copy mem1[117] to byte1, and then access byte1[5].

EXPRESSIONS & OPERATOR PRECEDENCE (OR, ALWAYS OBEY YOUR PARENS!)

So far, we've introduced a bunch of Verilog net and variable types, and operators that combine them; and there are a few more to come. All of these can be combined in *expressions* that yield a value.

As in other programming languages, each Verilog operator has a certain *precedence* that determines the order in which operators are applied in a non-parenthesized expression. For example, the NOT operator ~ has higher precedence than AND and OR (& and |), so ~X&Y is the same as (~X)&Y. Also, & has higher precedence than | (but see the potential trap discussed in Section 4.1.5 on page 193). Therefore, W&X|Y&Z is the same as (W&X)|(Y&Z). But W|X & Y|Z does not mean what you might think from the spacing—it's the same as W|(X&Y)|Z.

Verilog reference manuals can show you the detailed pecking order that is defined for operator precedence. However, it's not a good idea to rely on this. It's not that the manuals aren't correct—they usually are. It's that *you* can easily slip up, especially if you move frequently among different programming languages with different operators and precedence orders. Even if you always get it right, others who read your code may interpret your expressions incorrectly. So, although W|X&Y|Z is the same as W|(X&Y)|Z, if that's what you want, you should write it the second way.

Thus, the best policy is always to parenthesize expressions fully, except for the very common case of negating a single variable, and perhaps for the case of ANDing two variables. With parentheses, there can be no confusion.

5.4.5 Logical Operators and Expressions

Verilog has several operators and statements that rely on the concept of true/false values. In Verilog, a 1-bit value of 1'b1 is considered to be *true*, and 1'b0 is *true* considered to be *false*. With multibit values, any nonzero value is considered *false* true, and only a zero value is considered false; thus, 4'b0100 is just as true as 4'b1111; among possible 4-bit values, only 4'b0000 is false.

True and false values can be combined and created by the *logical* *logical operators* *operators*, shown in Table 5-66 on the next page. A logical operation yields a value of 1'b1 or 1'b0, depending on whether the result is true or false. If such a value is assigned to a wider variable or net, it is extended on the left with 0s.

Table 5-66
Verilog logical
operators.

Operator	Operation
&&	logical AND
||	logical OR
!	logical NOT
==	logical equality
!=	logical inequality
>	greater than
>=	greater than or equal
<	less than
<=	less than or equal

Keep in mind that in the first three logical operations, the truth or falsehood of each operand is evaluated before the operands are logically combined. For example, the expression 4'b0100 && 4'b1011 evaluates as "true && true" and yields the value true in a logical expression. But the corresponding bitwise boolean operation 4'b0100 & 4'b1011 has the value 4'b0000, which would be considered false in a logical expression.

The logical equality and inequality operators do a bit-by-bit comparison of their operands, and consider them equal only if corresponding bits are equal. The magnitude comparisons in the last four rows of Table 5-66 consider their operands to be unsigned numbers. In all six of the comparison operations, if the operand sizes are unequal, the shorter operand is extended on the left with 0s before the comparison is made. Thus, the expression 2'b11 < 4'b0100 is true, 8'h08 < 4'b1001 is false, and 8'h05==4'b0101 is true.

In synthesis, the last six logical operators lead to the creation of comparators, which can be expensive. We'll have more to say about this in the box on page 319 and in Section 6.9.8.

LOGICAL VS. BOOLEAN

It is very important to understand the difference between logical operations and the corresponding bitwise boolean operations and to use whichever one is appropriate according to the circumstances. Logical operations normally should be used only when the result is used as a condition with a conditional operator or in a conditional statement (both introduced later), while bitwise boolean operations should be used to combine bits and vectors to produce a value as in combinational logic.

Because of the way that true and false are defined, it turns out that logical operators have the same effect as the corresponding bitwise boolean operators when the operands are one bit wide. Especially in the case of NOT, you sometimes see example programs that mix ! with & and |, when what is really meant is ~. Although this may seem "OK" to C programmers, it's a bad idea, because the ! operation will produce unintended results if those 1-bit operands are ever changed to multibit vectors.

```
logical-expression ? true-expression : false-expression

X ? Y : Z

(A>B) ? A : B;

(sel==1) ? op1 : (
  (sel==2) ? op2 : (
    (sel==3) ? op3 : (
      (sel==4) ? op4 : 8'bx )))
```

Table 5-67
Syntax and examples of the Verilog conditional operator.

Verilog's *conditional operator ?:* selects one of two alternate expressions depending on the value of a logical expression. Its syntax and a few examples are given in Table 5-67. In the first example, the value of the expression is Y if X is true, else it's Z. The second example selects the maximum of two vector operands, A and B. The last example shows how conditional operations can be nested. For complex conditional operations, parenthesization is recommended for both readability and correctness. Also see page 311 for a design example.

?:, conditional operator

5.4.6 Compiler Directives

A Verilog compiler provides several directives for controlling compilation; we'll introduce two of them here. All compiler directives begin with an accent grave (`` ` ``). First is the `` `include `` compiler directive, with the syntax below:

`` `include `` *filename*

`` `include ``

The named file is read immediately and processed as if its contents were part of the current file. This facility is typically used to read in definitions that are common to multiple modules in a project. Nesting is allowed; that is, an include'd file can contain `` `include `` directives of its own.

Next is the `` `define `` compiler directive, with the syntax below:

`` `define ``

`` `define `` *identifier text*

Notice that there is no ending semicolon. The compiler textually replaces each appearance of *identifier* in subsequent code with *text*. Remember, this is a *textual* substitution; no expression evaluation or other processing takes place. Also, it is important to know that the definition is in effect not only in the current file, but in subsequent files that are processed during a given compiler run (for example, in files that are include'd by this one).

A `` `timescale `` compiler directive is described in Section 5.4.11.

`` `define `` VS. parameter   Although `` `define `` can be used to define constants, such as bus sizes and range starting and ending indexes, in general it's better to use parameter declarations for such definitions, unless the constant is truly a global one. With `` `define ``, you run the risk that unbeknownst to you, another module or include'd file will change the constant's definition. Parameter definitions are local to a module.

5.4.7 Structural Design Elements

concurrent statement

We're finally ready to look at the guts of a Verilog design, the part that actually specifies digital-logic operation, and from which a realization is synthesized. This is the series of *concurrent statements* shown in the module declaration in Table 5-56 on page 294. The most important concurrent-statement types, covered in this text, are instance statements, continuous-assignment statements, and `always` blocks. They give rise to three somewhat distinct styles of circuit design and description, which we cover in this and the next two subsections.

Statements of these different types, and the corresponding design styles, can be freely intermixed within a Verilog module declaration. In Section 5.4.13 we'll cover one more statement type, `initial`, which is typically used in test benches.

Each concurrent statement in a Verilog module "executes" simultaneously with the other statements in the same module declaration. This behavior is markedly different from that of statements in conventional software programming languages, which execute sequentially. Concurrent operation is necessary to simulate the behavior of hardware, where connected elements affect each other continuously, not just at particular, ordered time steps.

Thus, in a Verilog module, if the last statement updates a signal that is used by the first statement, then the simulator will go back to that first statement and update its results according to the signal that just changed. In fact, the simulator will keep propagating changes and updating results until the simulated circuit stabilizes; we'll discuss this in more detail in Section 5.4.12.

structural design
structural description

In the *structural* style of circuit description or design, individual gates and other components are instantiated and connected to each other using nets. This is a language-based equivalent of a logic diagram, schematic, or net list.

built-in gate types

Verilog has several *built-in gate types*, shown in Table 5-68. The names of these gates are reserved words. The `and`, `or`, and `xor` gates and their complements may have any number of inputs. A `buf` gate is a 1-input noninverting buffer, and a `not` gate is an inverter.

The remaining four gates are 1-input buffers and inverters with three-state outputs. They drive the output with the data input (or its complement) if the enable input is 0 or 1, as in the gate's name; else the output is z. For example, `bufif0` drives its output with its data input if the control input is 0.

A typical design environment has libraries that provide many other predefined components such as AND-OR-INVERT gates, flip-flops, and higher-

Table 5-68
Verilog built-in gates.

and	xor	bufif0
nand	xnor	bufif1
or	buf	notif0
nor	not	notif1

```
component-name instance-identifier ( expr, expr, ..., expr );

component-name instance-identifier ( .port-name(expr),
                                     .port-name(expr),
                                     ...
                                     .port-name(expr) );
```

Table 5-69
Syntax of Verilog
instance statements.

complexity functions such as decoders and multiplexers. Each of these components has a corresponding module declaration in a library.

Gates and other components are instantiated in an *instance statement* with the syntax shown in Table 5-69. The statement gives the name of the component, such as **and**, followed by an identifier for this particular instance, followed by a parenthesized list that associates component ports (inputs and outputs) with an expression (*expr*). In the case of an inout or output port, the associated *expr* must be simply the name of a local net to which the port connects. In the case of an input port, the *expr* can be a net name or any expression which evaluates to a value compatible with the input-port type.

instance statement

Note that instance identifiers must be unique within a module, but may be reused in different modules. The compiler creates a longer, globally unique identifier for each instance based on its position in the overall design hierarchy. Using this identifier, a given instance can be tracked in system-level simulation and synthesis.

As shown in Table 5-69, two different formats are allowed for the port-association list. The first format depends on the order in which port names appear in the original component definition. The local expressions are listed in the same order as the ports to which they're supposed to connect. For the built-in multi-input gates, the defined port-name order is (output, input, input, ...), and the order among the multiple inputs doesn't matter. For the built-in three-state buffers and inverters, the defined order is (output, data-input, enable-input). The built-in gates can be instantiated only using the first format.

Using the first format, Table 5-70 shows a module that uses structural code and built-in gates to define an "inhibit" gate—basically an AND gate with one inverted input. Table 5-71 on the next page defines a module with the same inputs, output, and function as the logic diagram in Figure 4-19 on page 207.

```
module VrInh( in, invin, out );    // also known as 'BUT-NOT'
  input in, invin;                 // as in 'in but not invin'
  output out;                      // (see [Klir, 1972])
  wire notinvin;

  not U1 (notinvin, invin);
  and U2 (out, in, notinvin);
endmodule
```

Table 5-70
Structural Verilog
program for an
"inhibit" gate.

Table 5-71
Structural Verilog
program for an
alarm circuit.

```
module VrAlarmCkt(panic, enable, exiting, window, door, garage, alarm);
  input panic, enable, exiting, window, door, garage;
  output alarm;
  wire secure, notsecure, notexiting, otheralarm;

  or U1 (alarm, panic, otheralarm);
  and U2 (otheralarm, enable, notexiting, notsecure);
  not U3 (notexiting, exiting);
  not U4 (notsecure, secure);
  and U5 (secure, window, door, garage);
endmodule
```

Library components and user-defined modules can be instantiated with either the first or the second format, although the best coding practices use the second format only. In the second format, each item in the port-association list gives the port name preceded by a period and followed by a parenthesized expression. Here, port associations can be listed in any order. For example, Table 5-72 instantiates two inverters and three copies of the inhibit-gate module of Table 5-70 to create a 2-input XOR gate, albeit in a very roundabout way. A corresponding logic diagram is shown in Figure 5-5.

Remember that the instance statements in the example modules, Tables 5-70 through 5-72, execute *concurrently*. In each module, even if the statements were listed in a different order, the same circuit would be synthesized, and the simulated circuit operation would be the same.

Table 5-72
Structural Verilog
program for an XOR
function.

```
module VrSillyXOR(in1, in2, out);
  input in1, in2;
  output out;
  wire inh1, inh2, notinh2, notout;

  VrInh U1 ( .out(inh1), .in(in1), .invin(in2) );
  VrInh U2 ( .out(inh2), .in(in2), .invin(in1) );
  not U3 ( notinh2, inh2 );
  VrInh U4 ( .out(notout), .in(notinh2), .invin(inh1) );
  not U5 ( out, notout );
endmodule
```

Figure 5-5
Logic diagram
corresponding to the
VrSillyXOR module.

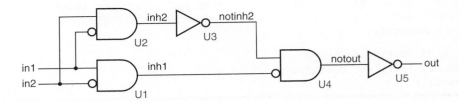

SERIOUS SYNTHESIS A competent synthesizer can analyze the `VrSillyXOR` and `VrInh` modules together and reduce the circuit realization down to a single 2-input XOR gate. Such a synthesizer typically also has an option to turn off global optimization and force synthesis of each module individually.

Parameters, introduced at the end of Section 5.4.2, can be put to good use to *parameterize* structural modules that can handle inputs and outputs of any width. For example, consider a 3-input *majority function*, which produces a 1 output if at least two of its inputs are 1. That is, $OUT = I0 \cdot I1 + I1 \cdot I2 + I0 \cdot I2$. A module that performs the majority function on input vectors of any width can be defined as shown in Table 5-73.

parameterized module

majority function

When the `Maj` module is instantiated using the syntax in the previous examples, the parameter `WID` takes on its default value of 1, and the module works on 1-bit vectors (bits). However, instance-statement syntax has an option that allows the instantiated module's parameter definitions to be overridden. In the instance statement, the component name is followed by `#` and a parenthesized list of values that are substituted for the parameter values used in the module definition. These values appear in the same order that the parameters are defined in the module. Thus, if `W`, `X`, `Y`, and `Z` are all 8-bit vectors, the following instance statement creates an 8-bit majority function for `X`, `Y`, and `Z`:

parameter substitution
#

```
Maj #(8) U1 ( .OUT(W), .I0(X), .I1(Y), .I2(Z) );
```

We create both 1-bit and 8-bit instances of `Maj` in a structural design example in Table 6-85 on page 506.

Note that parameters can be *defined* in modules that are coded in any style—dataflow and procedural as well as structural. But parameters can be *substituted* as shown above only when a module is instantiated. (Verilog provides another parameter definition and substitution mechanism, using the `defparam` keyword, but this mechanism is not supported by all compilers and its use is not generally recommended.) Although module instantiations are structural by definition, they can of course be mixed with the dataflow and procedural coding styles discussed in the next two subsections.

defparam keyword

```
module Maj(OUT, I0, I1, I2);
  parameter WID = 1;
  input [WID-1:0] I0, I1, I2;
  output [WID-1:0] OUT;

  assign OUT = I0 & I1 | I0 & I2 | I1 & I2 ;
endmodule
```

Table 5-73
Parameterized Verilog module for a 3-input majority function.

VERILOG'S GENERATE

In some applications it is necessary to create multiple copies of a particular structure within an architecture. VHDL addresses this need with its generate statement, and Verilog-2001 provides a similar facility.

New keywords generate and endgenerate begin and end a "generate block." Within a generate block, certain "behavioral" statements introduced later (if, case, and for) can be used to control whether or not instance and dataflow-style statements are executed. Instances can be generated in iterative loops (for), but the loop must be controlled by a new variable type (genvar).

As in VHDL, the Verilog compiler takes care of generating unique component identifiers and, if necessary, net names for all instances and nets that are created within a for loop in a generate block, so they can be tracked during simulation and synthesis.

Table 6-85 on page 506 is a detailed design example with generate blocks.

5.4.8 Dataflow Design Elements

If Verilog had only instance statements, then it would be nothing more than a hierarchical net-list description language. "Continuous-assignment statements" allow Verilog to describe a combinational circuit in terms of the flow of data and operations on the circuit. This style is called a *dataflow design* or *description*.

dataflow design
dataflow description
continuous-assignment statement

assign keyword

The basic syntax of a *continuous-assignment statement* is shown in the first line of Table 5-74. The keyword *assign* is followed by the name of a net, then an = sign, and finally an expression giving the value to be assigned. As shown in the remaining lines of the table, the statement may also specify a bit or part of a net vector, or a concatenation using standard concatenation syntax. The syntax also has options that allow a drive strength and a delay value to be specified, but they aren't often used in design for synthesis, and we don't discuss or use them in this book.

A continuous-assignment statement evaluates the value of its righthand side and assigns it to the lefthand side, well, continuously. In simulation, the assignment occurs in zero simulated time.

As with instance statements, the order of continuous assignment statements in a module doesn't matter. If the last statement changes a net value used by the first statement, then the simulator will go back to that first statement and update its results according to the net that just changed, as mentioned previously and discussed in more detail in Section 5.4.12. So, if a module contains two statements, "assign X = Y" and "assign Y = ~X", then a simulation of it will

Table 5-74
Syntax of Verilog continuous-assignment statements.

```
assign net-name = expression;
assign net-name[bit-index] = expression;
assign net-name[msb:lsb] = expression;
assign net-concatenation = expression;
```

```
module Vrprimed (N, F);
input [3:0] N;
output F;
wire N3L_N0, N3L_N2L_N1, N2L_N1_N0, N2_N1L_N0;

  assign N3L_N0      = ~N[3]                    & N[0];
  assign N3L_N2L_N1 = ~N[3] & ~N[2] &  N[1]          ;
  assign N2L_N1_N0   =        ~N[2] &  N[1] & N[0];
  assign N2_N1L_N0   =         N[2] & ~N[1] & N[0];
  assign F = N3L_N0 | N3L_N2L_N1 | N2L_N1_N0 | N2_N1L_N0;
endmodule
```

Table 5-75
Dataflow Verilog code for a prime-number detector.

loop "forever" (until the simulator times out) and the corresponding synthesized circuit would be an inverter with its input connected to its output.

Table 5-75 shows a Verilog module for a prime-number detector circuit (Figure 4-31(c) on page 217) written in dataflow style. In this style we don't show the explicit gates and their connections; rather, we use Verilog's bitwise-boolean operators to write the logic equations directly.

Verilog's continuous-assignment statement is unconditional, but different values can be assigned if the righthand side uses the conditional operator (?:). For example, Table 5-76 codes the same prime-number detection function using a completely different approach involving a conditional operator. This operator corresponds very naturally to a 2-input multiplexer (introduced in Section 1.10 on page 18), a device that selects one of two possible data inputs based on the value of a select input. Thus, in an ASIC design, a synthesizer would typically realize the assignment in Table 5-76 using the circuit structure in Figure 5-6.

```
module Vrprimec (N, F);
input [3:0] N;
output F;

assign F = N[3] ? (N[0] & (N[1]^N[2])) : (N[0] | (~N[2]&N[1]) ) ;
endmodule
```

Table 5-76
Prime-number-detector code using a conditional operator.

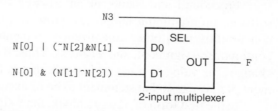

2-input multiplexer

Figure 5-6
Logic circuit corresponding to a conditional operator.

HOW DID HE COME UP WITH THAT? You're probably wondering how I came up with the conditional expression in Table 5-76. Don't worry about it. It's based on an old theory of logic function decomposition as applied to multiplexers in the first two editions of this book.

Table 5-77
Verilog module for
selecting an input
byte.

```
module Vrbytesel (A, B, C, selA, selB, selC, Z);
input [7:0] A, B, C;
input selA, selB, selC;
output [7:0] Z;

   assign Z = selA ? A : (
              selB ? B : (
              selC ? C : 8'b0 )) ;

endmodule
```

A dataflow-style example in which the conditional operator's use is more natural and intuitive is shown in Table 5-77. This module transfers one of three input bytes to its output depending on which of three corresponding select inputs is asserted. The order of the nested conditional operations determines which byte is transferred if multiple select inputs are asserted—input A has the highest priority, and C has the lowest. If no select input is asserted, the output is 0.

5.4.9 Behavioral Design Elements (Procedural Code)

behavioral design
behavioral description

As we saw in the last example, it is sometimes possible to describe a desired logic-circuit behavior directly using a continuous-assignment statement and a conditional operator. This is a good thing, because the ability to create a *behavioral design* or *description* is one of the key benefits of hardware-description languages in general and of Verilog in particular. However, for most behavioral designs, we need to use some additional language elements that allow us to write "procedural code," as described in this subsection.

always block
always keyword

The key element of Verilog behavioral design is the *always block*, with syntax shown in Table 5-78. An always block contains one or more "procedural statements," introduced shortly. The syntax in the table shows only one procedural statement. But as we'll show later, one type of procedural statement is a "begin-end block" that encloses a list of other procedural statements. That's what's used in all but the simplest always blocks, and that's why we call it an always *block*.

Procedural statements in an always block execute sequentially, as in software programming languages. However, the always block itself executes concurrently with other concurrent statements in the same module (instance, continuous-assignment, and always). Thus, if one of the procedural statements changes the value of a net or variable that is used in another concurrent statement, it may cause that statement to be re-executed (more on this below).

sensitivity list
or keyword

In the first form of always block, the @ sign and parenthesized list of signal names separated by the keyword or is called a *sensitivity list*. These signals (nets or variables) determine when the always block executes, as discussed below.

executing statement
suspended statement

A Verilog concurrent statement such as an always block is always either *executing* or *suspended*. A concurrent statement initially is suspended; when any signal in its sensitivity list changes value, it resumes execution, starting with its

Table 5-78
Syntax of Verilog
`always` blocks.

```
always @ (signal-name or signal-name or ... or signal-name)
    procedural-statement

always procedural-statement
```

first procedural statement and continuing until the end. If any signal in the sensitivity list changes value as a result of executing the concurrent statement, it executes again. This continues until the statement executes without any of these signals changing value at the current time. In simulation, all of this happens in zero simulated time.

An instance or continuous-assignment statement also has a sensitivity list, an implicit one. All of the input signals in an instantiated component or module are on the instance statement's implicit sensitivity list. Likewise, all of the signals on the righthand side of a continuous-assignment statement are on its implicit sensitivity list.

Upon resumption, a properly written concurrent statement will suspend after one or a few executions. However, it is possible to write a statement that never suspends. For example, consider the continuous-assignment statement "assign X = ~X". Since X changes on every pass, the statement will execute forever in zero simulated time—not very useful! In practice, simulators have safeguards that normally can detect such unwanted behavior, terminating the misbehaving statement after a thousand or so passes.

As shown in the second part of Table 5-78, the sensitivity list in an `always` block is optional. An `always` block without a sensitivity list starts running at time zero in simulation and keeps looping forever. This is not a good thing in synthesis, but such an `always` block can be useful in a test bench. By coding explicit delays within the `always` block, you can generate a repetitive waveform such as a clock signal. See, for example, Table 7-68 on page 661.

Verilog has several different *procedural statements* that are used within an `always` block. Procedural statements are written in a style similar to software programming languages like C. They assume that every value assigned to a variable is preserved until it is changed by a subsequent execution of the `always` block. This behavior is natural in software programming languages, but it can cause problems and confusion in Verilog code if you stray from recommended coding guidelines as discussed in the next three paragraphs.

Consider an `always` block which is intended to create combinational logic and assigns a value to a variable X. As we'll soon see, besides unconditional

procedural statement

A POOR CHOICE **OF WORDS**	The "or" in a Verilog sensitivity list has nothing to do with a logical OR. But then VHDL's language designers made some poor choices too, like using the symbol "&" to denote concatenation, and spelling out the logical operators like "or", thereby making logical expressions less readable and much more tedious to type.

assignments, Verilog has conditional procedural statements such as `if` and `case` that can control whether other statements, including assignments, are executed. So, X might appear on the lefthand side of several different assignments, and in a given pass through the `always` block, zero, one, or more of them might actually be executed, depending on current condition values.

There's no problem if one or even if multiple values are assigned to X during a given pass through the `always` block. Since the block executes in zero simulated time, the last value assigned dominates. But suppose that *no* value is assigned to X. Since this is procedural code, the simulator "infers" that you don't want the value of X to be changed from the value it had during the previous pass through this `always` block. And so the synthesizer *infers a latch*—it creates a storage element to retain the previous value of X if conditions are such that no new value is assigned. This is rarely the designer's intent.

latch inference

The solution to this problem is to ensure that a value is assigned to X (and to every other variable on the lefthand side of an assignment statement) in every possible execution path through an `always` block. Although nothing is fool-proof, we'll show a pretty reliable way to do this in the box on page 323.

DON'T BE SO SENSITIVE!

The problem of inferred latches is just one problem that can occur in improperly coded `always` blocks. Another pitfall is related to the sensitivity list.

By definition, a Verilog simulator executes the procedural statements within an `always` block only when one or more of the signals in its sensitivity list changes. It is very easy to inadvertently write a "combinational" `always` block with an incomplete sensitivity list—one in which not all of the signals that affect the outcomes of the procedural statements are listed. For example, you might forget to include one or more signals that appear on the righthand side of an assignment statement.

Faced with such an error, the simulator still follows the definition and does not execute the `always` block until one of the *listed* signals changes. Thus, the block's behavior will be partially sequential, rather than combinational as intended. A synthesizer, on the other hand, does not attempt to create logic with this weird behavior. Instead, it ignores your error and synthesizes your intended combinational logic.

No problem then, right? Wrong. Now the behaviors of the simulator and the synthesized logic don't match. The "incorrect" simulated behavior may mask other errors give you the intended and expected results at the system level, while the synthesized circuit may not work properly in all cases.

One solution to this problem is always to pay close attention to warning messages from the synthesizer—most will flag this condition.

Verilog-2001 offers another solution. Instead of using a parenthesized sensitivity list, an `always` block can simply put the character "`*`" after the @ sign. In this case, the simulator creates an implicit sensitivity list with all of the signals that might affect the procedural statements' outcomes.

By the way, Verilog-2001 also allows a parenthesized sensitivity list to use a comma instead of "`or `" as the separator.

variable-name = *expression* ; `// blocking assignment`	**Table 5-79** Procedural assign- ment statements.
variable-name <= *expression* ; `// nonblocking assignment`	

Now we're finally ready to talk about the different types of *procedural statements* that can appear within an `always` block. They are blocking assignment, nonblocking assignment, begin-end blocks, `if`, `case`, `while`, and `repeat`. There are a few other seldom-used types, but they are not synthesizable, so we don't cover them in this book.

procedural statement

The first two are *blocking* and *nonblocking assignment statements*, with the syntax shown in Table 5-79. The lefthand side of a procedural assignment statement must be a variable, but the righthand side can be any expression that produces a compatible value and can include both nets and variables.

blocking assignment statement, =

nonblocking assignment statement, <=

A blocking assignment looks and acts like an assignment statement in any other procedural language, such as C. A nonblocking assignment looks and acts a little different—it evaluates its righthand side immediately, but it does not assign the resulting value to the lefthand side until an infinitesimal delay *after*

WHY "BLOCKING"?

Blocking assignments get their name because they block the execution of subsequent procedural statements in the same `always` block until the assignment has actually been made. Well, duh, that's what you'd expect in any procedural programming language, like C, right?

What you don't know is that Verilog also allows a procedural assignment statement to specify a delay. Since such delays are not synthesizable, we don't describe or use them in this book. But if you did specify such a delay, it would block the execution of the rest of the `always` block until the delay had passed.

Probably a better name for blocking assignment, at least for designers who are using Verilog for synthesis, would be "immediate assignment."

AND WHY "NONBLOCKING"?

Nonblocking assignments, whether a delay is specified or not, allow execution of the `always` block to continue. But they're still not the same as assignments in typical procedural programming languages like C.

As noted in the main text above, a nonblocking-assignment statement evaluates its righthand side immediately, but it does not assign this value to the lefthand side until an infinitesimal delay after the entire `always` block has completed execution.

Perhaps a more accurate name for nonblocking assignment would be "nonblocking and slightly deferred assignment." And a more concise one for design-for-synthesis would be "late assignment."

<table>
<tr><td>

LEARN THE RULES, YOU BLOCKHEAD!

</td><td>

The two rules below are so important, it's the only place that you'll find boldface roman font used in this book:

- Always use **blocking** assignments (=) in `always` blocks intended to create **combinational** logic.

- Always use **nonblocking** assignments (<=) in `always` blocks intended to create **sequential** logic. (See Section 7.13.1.)

- Do not mix blocking and nonblocking assignments in the same `always` block.

- Do not make assignments to the same variable in two different `always` blocks.

Once you've learned these rules, the only thing left is for you to remember is which assignment operator symbol is which. But that's easy, too. The < sign in the non-blocking assignment operator is a mirror image of the dynamic-input indicator (>) used in an edge-triggered flip-flop's logic symbol, on the clock input. So, be sure to use it in `always` blocks that are intended to create sequential logic.

</td></tr>
</table>

the entire `always` block has been executed. Thus, the "old" value of the lefthand side continues to be available for the rest of the `always` block. You can read a nonblocking assignment as "*variable-name* eventually gets *expression*."

If you think too hard about the subtle differences between the two types of assignment statements, your head may hurt or you may get confused. But fortunately, if you follow a basic, consistent coding style for synthesis as practiced in this book, it's easy to know which one to use—just follow the simple rules at the top of this page. Still, we'll give some examples in this section and in Section 7.13 that shed some more light on the reasons for the rules.

For instructional purposes, we've rewritten the dataflow Verilog code for a prime-number detector in Table 5-75 on page 311 using an `always` statement, in Table 5-80. There are several things to notice about this code:

- The output signal F must be declared as a `reg` variable, since it appears on the lefthand side of an assignment statement in an `always` block.

- The vector input N appears in the sensitivity list.

- The assignment statement is a blocking one, as recommended by our coding guidelines.

- We combined the AND and OR operations from the original version into a single expression, so we could use a single assignment statement and no intermediate signals.

We could have used multiple assignments to intermediate signals as in the original code, but to do that, we need "begin-end" blocks.

```
module Vrprimea (N, F);
input [3:0] N;
output F;
reg F;

  always @ (N)
    F = ~N[3] & N[0] | ~N[3] & ~N[2] &  N[1]
       | ~N[2] &  N[1] & N[0] | N[2] & ~N[1] & N[0] ;
endmodule
```

Table 5-80
Prime-number
detector using an
always block.

The first part of Table 5-81 shows the basic syntax of a *begin-end block*, simply a list of one or more procedural statements enclosed by the keywords *begin* and *end*. As shown in the second part of the table, a begin-end block can have its own local parameters or variables (typically `integer` or `reg`). In this case, the block must be named, so that these items can be tracked during simulation and synthesis. Also, a begin-end block can be named even if it has no local parameters or variables.

begin-end block
begin keyword
end keyword

Note that the procedural statements within a begin-end block execute sequentially, not concurrently like the instance, continuous-assignment, and

```
begin
    procedural-statement
    . . .
    procedural-statement
end

begin  :  block-name
    variable declarations
    parameter declarations

    procedural-statement
    . . .
    procedural-statement
end
```

Table 5-81
Syntax of Verilog
begin-end blocks.

**WHEN TO USE A
SEMICOLON**   You might think of a begin-end block as being a list of procedural statements separated by semicolons, but that's not quite right; the syntax is just as we show it above. A semicolon is already included in an assignment statement as defined in Table 5-79. And the "end" in a begin-end block has the semicolon "built-in." The same is true of the "endcase" in a `case` statement, introduced later.

Still, Verilog defines a semicolon all by itself to be a null statement, so it usually doesn't hurt to put in extras.

Table 5-82
Prime-number
detector using
multiple statements in
an `always` block.

```
module Vrprimeb (N, F);
input [3:0] N;
output F;
reg F;

  always @ (N)
    begin : Fcomp
    reg N3L_N0, N3L_N2L_N1, N2L_N1_N0, N2_N1L_N0;
      N3L_N0      = ~N[3]                      & N[0] ;
      N3L_N2L_N1 = ~N[3] & ~N[2] &  N[1]             ;
      N2L_N1_N0  =          ~N[2] &  N[1] & N[0] ;
      N2_N1L_N0  =           N[2] & ~N[1] & N[0] ;
      F = N3L_N0 | N3L_N2L_N1 | N2L_N1_N0 | N2_N1L_N0;
    end
endmodule
```

other `always` statements at the top level of a module. Of course, sequential execution is what you'd expect in procedural code.

Our prime-number detector is coded in an `always` block once again in Table 5-82, this time illustrating the use of a `begin-end` block and intermediate signals. At a glance, this code has a lot of textual similarity to the dataflow code in Table 5-75 on page 311, but it actually has a few important differences:

- This code uses an `always` block.
- The intermediate signals are declared as `reg` variables, local to the `begin`-`end` block.
- Since variables are declared, the block is named.

There are a couple of other important things to notice:

- The output F must still be declared as a `reg` variable, for the same reason as before.
- The local `reg` variables are *not* included in the sensitivity list. If you did include them, you'd get an error message, since they're undefined outside the scope of the `begin-end` block.

if statement
if keyword
condition

else keyword

Other procedural statements, beyond assignment and `begin-end` blocks, give designers more powerful ways to express circuit behavior. An *if statement*, with the syntax shown in Table 5-83, is probably the most familiar of these. In the first and simplest form of the statement, a *condition* (a logical expression) is tested, and a procedural statement is executed if the condition is true. In the second form, we've added an "*else*" clause with another procedural statement that's executed if the condition is false.

As in other languages, `if` statements can be nested—any of the procedural statements in Table 5-83 can be `if` statements. Also as in other languages, an `if` statement that is nested immediately after the condition in an `if-else` should be

```
if ( condition ) procedural-statement

if ( condition ) procedural-statement
else procedural-statement
```

Table 5-83
Syntax of Verilog
if statements.

enclosed in a begin-end block to eliminate any ambiguity about which "if" the "else" goes with. Even if your mind works as perfectly as a Verilog parser, someone else who reads your code might make the association incorrectly.

Table 5-84 is a version of the prime-number-detector module that uses a nested if statement. It defines a parameter that you can change depending on whether you believe that 1 is prime. The first if clause handles this special case, and the second one separates the remaining cases into even and odd. Notice the use of begin-end around the if statement that is nested immediately after the condition in its parent.

```
module Vrprimei (N, F);
input [3:0] N;
output F;
reg F;
parameter OneIsPrime = 1; // Change this to 0 if you
                          // don't consider 1 to be prime.
  always @ (N)
    if (N == 1) F = OneIsPrime;
    else if ( (N % 2) == 0 )
      begin if (N == 2) F = 1; else F = 0; end
    else if (N <= 7) F = 1;
    else if ( (N==11) || (N==13) ) F = 1;
    else F = 0;
endmodule
```

Table 5-84
Prime-detector
module using an
if statement.

EXPENSIVE,
MAYBE

In synthesis, the Verilog code in Table 5-84 can lead to the creation of five comparators. Depending on the optimization capabilities of the synthesis tool, the final circuit may or may not have a lot more gates than necessary.

One operand of each comparator is a constant, providing opportunities for simplification. For n-bit equality or inequality checking with a constant, the operation can be done with a single n-input AND or NAND gate. Magnitude comparisons such as <= can also be simplified, though usually not as much.

When Verilog code is targeted to a CPLD or an FPGA, the compiler may use comparators in an intermediate representation of the logic function, and it may show comparators in an automatically generated logic diagram. But eventually, the synthesizer converts the comparators into equivalent boolean equations and feeds them in a logic minimizer. Thus, all versions of the same prime-number-detector function in this subsection yield the same synthesized result.

Notice in Table 5-84 that a value is assigned to F in every possible execution path through the always block. Suppose that we inadvertently left out the first "else F = 0" clause. Then, for the reasons discussed on page 314, the synthesizer would infer a latch to hold the previous value of F whenever N is even but not 2. One way to avoid latch inference is to ensure that every if statement has an else clause, and that every variable that is assigned a value in one if or else clause is also assigned a value in every other clause. Another method is discussed in the box on page 323.

When two or more different variables must be tested to determine different outcomes, a nested series of if statements is usually the right coding approach. However, if all of the if statements would be testing the same variable, as in Table 5-84, it is often better to use a case statement, described below. When we use a long series of nested if statements, as in Table 5-84, the synthesizer might create a circuit that evaluates the boolean expressions in series, with slower operation than might otherwise be possible. A case statement may yield a faster synthesized circuit, based on "multiplexers," and is usually more readable.

Table 5-85
"Improved" prime-detector module.

```
module Vrprimel (N, F, special);
input [3:0] N;
output F, special;
reg F, special;

  always @ (N)
    if (N == 1) begin F = 1; special = 1; end
    else if ( (N % 2) == 0 )
      begin if (N == 2) F = 1; else F = 0; end
    else if (N <= 7) F = 1;
    else if ( (N==11) || (N==13) ) F = 1;
    else F = 0;
endmodule
```

THIS IS AN IMPROVEMENT?

A picky mathematician called me to complain about my incorrect treatment of "1" as a prime number in examples such as Table 5-84. So, to accommodate him, I quickly wrote a new version, Table 5-85. I added a "special" output just for him, to indicate that the input value is getting special treatment. The problem is, this program doesn't work as intended.

In my haste, I forgot that every variable has to be assigned a value in every possible execution path through an always statement. So, when my new module was synthesized, a latch was inferred for special. Then, adding insult to injury, the optimizer determined that special is always 1, got rid of the latch, and tied special to V_{cc}! To fix this, I first thought I would have to change every other assignment to F into a begin-end block that also assigns 0 to special. What a pain! But there's an easier way, discussed in the box on page 323.

Table 5-86
Syntax of a Verilog
case statement.

```
case ( selection-expression )
    choice , ... , choice : procedural-statement
    ...
    choice , ... , choice : procedural-statement
    default : procedural-statement
endcase
```

Table 5-86 shows the syntax of a Verilog *case statement*. This statement begins with the keyword *case* and a parenthesized "selection expression," usually one that evaluates to an integer or to a bit-vector value of a certain width. Next comes a series of case items, each of which has a comma-separated list of "choices" and a corresponding procedural statement. (If there is only one choice in a particular case item, then the comma is omitted.) A single "default" case item may be included as discussed shortly. The statement ends with the *endcase* keyword.

    The operation of case statement is simple—it evaluates the selection expression, finds the first one of the choices that matches the expression's value, and executes the corresponding procedural statement.

    Although each choice in a case statement is usually just a constant value compatible with the selection expression, it can also be a more complex expression. This leads to the possibility that some of the choices may overlap; that is, some values of the selection expression may match multiple choices. When the choices do not overlap, they are said to be "mutually exclusive." Sometimes this is called a *parallel case*. The best Verilog coding practices avoid nonparallel case statements.

    Quite often the listed choices in a case statement are not "all-inclusive." That is, they may not include all possible values of the selection expression. The keyword *default* can be used in the last case item to denote all expression values that have not yet been covered. (The colon after "default" is optional, syntactically.) Even if you're sure that your listed choices are all-inclusive, it's a good practice to include a default choice in your case statements.

case statement

case keyword

endcase keyword

parallel case

default keyword

NONPARALLEL case STATEMENTS

When the choices in a case statement are not mutually exclusive (nonparallel case), only the first matching choice has its corresponding procedural statement executed. To ensure this, a synthesizer must infer expensive "priority-encoder" logic to guarantee proper operation.

    However, if the synthesizer can determine that the choices are mutually exclusive, it can use faster and less expensive "multiplexer" logic. So, you should generally avoid writing nonparallel case statements. If you need a priority encoder, you should write one explicitly, either using nested if statements or as shown in Section 6.5.5, for example.

Table 5-87
Prime-detector
module using a
case statement.

```
module Vrprimecs (N, F);
input [3:0] N;
output F;
reg F;

    always @ (N)
      case (N)
        1, 2, 3, 5, 7, 11, 13 : F = 1;
        default : F = 0;
      endcase
endmodule
```

full case

A case statement in which the listed choices are all-inclusive is sometimes called a *full case*. In a nonfull case, the synthesizer will infer a latch to retain the previous values of outputs for any cases that are not covered. This is usually not desired, so the best Verilog coding practices use full case statements only.

Table 5-87 is yet another version of the prime-number detector, this time coded with a case statement. In this very simple example, the case statement has, in effect, written out the truth table for the output function F.

A slightly more complex use of case is shown in Table 5-88. This module transfers one of three 8-bit inputs to its output depending on the value of a 2-bit select code, sel. If sel is 3, the 8-bit output is placed in the high-impedance state. A couple of aspects of this code are worth noting:

- A default choice is coded, even though the choices that precede it are all-inclusive. This is a good coding practice, especially for simulation. It ensures that if sel contains any x or z bits, then x's will be propagated to the output. You can also put a Verilog $display command (discussed in Section 5.4.10) here to flag this case in simulation if you wish.

- The choices are coded as 2-bit-wide vectors. With most Verilog compilers, we could have gotten away simply with "0, 1, 2, 3," but see the box below.

MIXING INTEGERS AND VECTORS IN case CHOICES

Note in Table 5-87 that the parenthesized expression in the case statement yields a 4-bit vector value, while the choices are integers, which are 32 bits or more depending on the Verilog compiler. You would expect the Verilog compiler to figure out that you're only interested in the low-order four bits of the integers, and usually it does. However, in more complex situations where the vector widths don't match, some compilers may produce unexpected results. Therefore, their suppliers recommend that integer choices be written with explicit widths. In Table 5-87, you would write:

```
4'd1, 4'd2, 4'd3, 4'd5, 4'd7, 4'd11, 4'd13 : F = 1;
```

```
module Vrbytecase (A, B, C, sel, Z);
input [7:0] A, B, C;
input [1:0] sel;
output [7:0] Z;
reg [7:0] Z;

  always @ (A or B or C or sel)
    case (sel)
      2'd0 : Z = A;
      2'd1 : Z = B;
      2'd2 : Z = C;
      2'd3 : Z = 8'bz;
      default : Z = 8'bx;
    endcase
endmodule
```

Table 5-88
Bus-selector module
using a case
statement.

Verilog has two other case statements, identical in syntax to the one we just covered, except introduced by the keywords *casex* and *casez*. The *casez statement* allows z or ? to be used in one or more bit positions in a binary choice constant in, for example, 4'b10??. These characters are interpreted as "don't cares" when the choice constant is matched with the selection expression. Both characters mean the same thing, but ? is preferred so as not to be confused with the high-impedance state. The *casex statement* allows x also to be used as a "don't care," but it is not recommended, since in simulation it can hide the existence of unknown (x) values generated upstream. Even casez is tricky to use, and should be avoided when possible (as in the rest of this book!)

casex keyword
casez keyword
casez statement

casex statement

AVOIDING INFERRED LATCHES

By now you know that to avoid inferring unwanted latches, you must assign a value to a variable in every possible execution path through an always block. The easiest way to do this is to unconditionally assign default values to variables at the beginning of the always block. This approach works with the if and case statements that we've covered so far, as well as with the looping statements that are yet to come.

In some cases the appropriate default assignment will be to a value of "x" (unknown). This is good if you intend your subsequent code to cover all cases, but you'd like to catch inadvertent omissions in simulation. In other cases, you'd like the default to assign the most commonly needed result, so an assignment need not be repeated in all the subsequent cases. Table 5-89 on the next page shows an example of each.

You may say, "But, the signals F and special now may have values assigned to them twice. Can't this cause glitches in the realized circuit?" No. These statements execute in zero simulated time, and the last assignment prevails. And the synthesizer uses the last assigned value, too.

Table 5-89
Prime-detector
module with default
assignments.

```
module Vrprimef (N, F, special);
input [3:0] N;
output F, special;
reg F, special;

  always @ (N) begin
    F = 1'bx; special = 1'b0; // defaults
    if (N == 1) begin F = 1; special = 1; end
    else if ( (N % 2) == 0 )
      begin if (N == 2) F = 1; else F = 0; end
    else if (N <= 7) F = 1;
    else if ( (N==11) || (N==13) ) F = 1;
    else F = 0;
  end
endmodule
```

looping statement
for statement
for loop
for keyword

Another important class of procedural statements are *looping statements*. The most commonly used of these is the *for statement* or *for loop*, with the syntax in Table 5-90. Here the *loop-index* is a register variable, typically an integer or a bit vector that's being used like one, and *first-expr* is an expression giving a value that is assigned to *loop-index* when the for loop begins execution.

After initializing the *loop-index*, a for loop executes *procedural-statement* for a certain number of iterations. At the beginning of each iteration, it evaluates *logical-expression*. If the value is false, the for loop stops execution. If the value is true, it executes *procedural-statement* and at the end of the iteration it assigns *next-expr* to *loop-index*. Iterations continue until *logical-expression* is false.

For synthesis, the kinds of expressions that can be used for iteration control are limited. Typically, *first-expr* must be a constant expression, it must be possible to determine the value of *logical-expression* at compile time, and *next-expr* may be limited to simple incrementing and decrementing. Thus, the last two lines of Table 5-90 show a typical syntax of a for loop as it is used for synthesis.

The single procedural statement in a for loop is often a begin-end block, so that a series of other procedural statements may be executed in each iteration.

Our good old prime-number detector is coded one more time in Table 5-91, this time using a for loop. The interesting thing about this example is that it is truly a behavioral description—we have actually used Verilog to compute whether the input N is a prime number, by dividing it by all prime numbers (as well as a lot of odd nonprimes) that are less than its square root. We've also increased the size of N to 16 bits, just for fun.

Table 5-90
Syntax of a Verilog
for statement.

for (*loop-index* = *first-expr* ; *logical-expression* ; *loop-index* = *next-expr*)
    procedural-statement

for (*loop-index* = *first*; *loop-index* <= *last*; *loop-index* = *loop-index* + 1;)
    procedural-statement

```
module Vrprimebv (N, F);
input [15:0] N;
output F;
reg F, prime;
integer i;

  always @ (N) begin
    prime = 1;   // initial values
    if ( (N==1) || (N==2) ) prime = 1; // Special cases
    else if ((N % 2) ==0) prime = 0;    // Even, not prime
    else for ( i = 3 ; i <= 255 ; i = i+2 )
      if ( ((N % i) == 0) && (N != i) )
        prime = 0;    // Set to 0 if N is divisible by any i
    if (prime==1) F = 1; else F = 0;
  end
endmodule
```

Table 5-91
Prime-number
detector using a
for statement.

The bad thing about this design is that it's not synthesizable. The for loop is OK, but the modulo operation (%) is synthesizable only if its divisor is a power of two. We're actually lucky that modulo is *not* synthesizable; if it were, the resulting synthesized circuit would be horrible for the kind of reasons discussed in the box on page 284. We'll see much better, in-context examples of Verilog for statements in Chapter 6, as well as in test benches in Section 5.4.13.

The other Verilog looping statements are repeat, while, and forever, with the syntax shown in Table 5-92. A *repeat statement* repeats a procedural statement a number of times determined by *integer-expression*. A *while statement* repeats a procedural statement until *logical-expression* is false. A *forever statement* repeats a procedural statement "forever."

repeat statement
while statement
forever statement

As in a for statement, the procedural statement is usually a begin-end block containing a series of other procedural statements. Any of these looping statements can be temporarily suspended by certain timing control statements that can appear in such a begin-end block.

```
repeat ( integer-expression )
    procedural-statement

while ( logical-expression )
    procedural-statement

forever
    procedural-statement
```

Table 5-92
Syntax of Verilog
repeat, while, and
forever statements.

AYE, AYE, SIR!   Some designers like to use variable names like ii, jj, and kk for loop control, rather than the more traditional i, j, and k. The former are easier find in text searches during code rewrites and debugging.

Table 5-93
An 8-bit comparator
module using `for`
and `disable`.

```
module Vrcompdis (X, Y, gt);
input [7:0] X, Y;
output gt;        // Should be 1 if X > Y
reg gt;
integer i;

  always @ (X or Y) begin : COMP
    gt = 0; // default is 'not greater'
    for ( i = 7 ; i >=0 ; i = i-1 )
      if ( X[i] > Y[i] )
        begin gt = 1; disable COMP; end
      else if ( X[i] < Y[i] )
        begin gt = 0; disable COMP; end
  end
endmodule
```

The `repeat`, `while`, and `forever` statements cannot be used to synthesize combinational logic, only sequential logic, and then only if the procedural statement is a `begin-end` block that includes timing control that waits for a signal edge. This is not covered here, since the most predominant Verilog coding practices consistently use other mechanisms, discussed in Sections 7.13.1 and 7.13.9, to create sequential-circuit behavior. These statements can also find use in advanced test-bench code, but that's also not covered in this text.

disable statement
disable keyword

One more statement is sometimes used in conjunction with Verilog looping statements. The *disable statement* can be used anywhere within a named `begin-end` block. It consists of the *disable* keyword, followed by the name of the block, followed by a semicolon. When executed, it immediately terminates execution of the block; subsequent statements in the block are not executed. For example, Table 5-93 shows how to specify an 8-bit comparator, using a `for` loop enclosed by a named block, and `disable` statements. Although this module creates combinational logic, it is not synthesizable by all tools.

5.4.10 Functions and Tasks

function

Like a function in a high-level programming language, a Verilog *function* accepts a number of inputs and returns a single result. The inputs may be bits or bit vectors, and they may be any variable type, including `integer` and `reg` variables and a few types that we don't cover in the book.

function definition
function keyword

The syntax of a Verilog *function definition* is shown in Table 5-94. It begins with the keyword *function*, followed by an optional specification of the result type—`integer`, a bit-vector [*msb:lsb*], or blank for a single-bit result, the default. Next comes the function name and a semicolon.

```
function result-type function-name ;
    input declarations
    variable declarations
    parameter declarations

    procedural-statement
endfunction
```

Table 5-94
Syntax of a Verilog
function definition.

The inputs of a function are listed in order next in input declarations. These are declared using the `input` keyword, similar to input declarations in a module declaration, and are single bits or bit vectors. A function may not have any `output` or `inout` declarations. However, as shown in the table, a function may declare its own local variables and parameters. But it may not declare any nets or nested functions and tasks.

The "executable" part of a function is a single procedural statement. Usually this is a `begin-end` block containing a series of procedural statements. The function name is implicitly defined to be a local `reg` variable of the declared result type, and somewhere in the function, a value must be assigned to this variable. This value is returned to the function's caller.

A function is invoked or *called* by writing the function name followed by a parenthesized list of expressions. The expressions are evaluated and assigned to the function's inputs in the order that they appear in the function definition. A function name can be used in an expression, and thus the function can be called, anywhere that a signal of the same type could be used—in `always` blocks, in continuous assignments, and in other functions in the same module.

function call

A function executes in zero simulated time, and therefore cannot contain any delay or other timing-related statements. Also, the values of any local variables are lost from one function call to the next. So, a function is primarily used as a way to code a commonly used operation in one place to reduce typing and thinking, minimize inconsistency, and improve the readability, modularity, and maintainability of Verilog programs.

The Verilog module in Table 5-95 on the next page is a behavioral version of the `SillyXOR` module (Table 5-72 on page 308). It defines function `Inhibit`

**MULTIPLE-
OUTPUT
FUNCTIONS**   A function can have only one output. But a simple trick lets you to create a function with multiple outputs—you just concatenate the needed outputs before assigning to the function name, and then use part selects in the caller to pull out the individual values. If you use this trick, you must be extremely careful—the size and order of the concatenated signals in the function and in the caller must match perfectly.

Table 5-95
Verilog program for
an XOR gate using
an "inhibit" function.

```verilog
module VrSillierXOR(in1, in2, out);
  input in1, in2;
  output out;
  reg out;

  function Inhibit ;
    input In, invIn;
    Inhibit = In & ~invIn;
  endfunction

always @ (in1 or in2) begin : IB
    reg inh1, inh2;
    inh1 = Inhibit(in1,in2);
    inh2 = Inhibit(in2,in1);
    out = ~Inhibit(~inh2,inh1);
  end
endmodule
```

**RECURSIVE
FUNCTION CALLS**

Theoretically, you could replace the `always` block in Table 5-95 with a single continuous-assignment statement:

```verilog
assign out = ~Inhibit(~Inhibit(in2,in1), Inhibit(in1,in2));
```

However, most Verilog tools do not support recursive function calls; that is, they do not let a function call itself. In practice, the utility of this sort of program construction is quite limited anyway, and should be avoided even if the tools do support it.

that acts like a 2-input inhibit gate, and calls `Inhibit` three times within an `always` block to perform the module's specified function (a rather roundabout XOR operation). The names of the local variables and the structure of the function calls match the logic diagram in Figure 5-5 on page 308 exactly.

task
task definition
task keyword

A Verilog *task* is similar to a function, except it does not return a result. Table 5-96 shows the syntax of a *task definition*. It begins with the keyword *task*, followed by the task name. Unlike functions, tasks can have inout and output arguments, which are declared in the same way as input arguments, but using the keywords `inout` and `output`.

task call
task enable

While a function call can be used in the place of an expression, a *task call* (sometimes called a *task enable*) can be used in the place of a statement. Like a function, a task is called using its name and a parenthesized list of expressions. These expressions are associated in the order written with the input, inout, and output declarations in the task definition. Expressions corresponding to inputs are evaluated when the task is called and their values are assigned to the corresponding input arguments of the task. When task execution completes, its local inout and output variables are copied to the corresponding "expressions" in the calling code, which must be individual signal names or concatenations.

```
task task-name ;
    input declarations
    inout declarations
    output declarations
    variable declarations
    parameter declarations

    procedural-statement
endtask
```

Table 5-96
Syntax of a Verilog
task definition.

Although delays can be specified within tasks, they are not synthesizable; a task is synthesized as combinational logic. Verilog synthesizers can't handle tasks at all. When supported, user-defined tasks can be useful in structuring larger module designs, but we won't discuss them further in this book.

Verilog has many built-in system tasks and functions that are used in test benches and simulation, including the following:

- $display. This task is used to print formatted signal values and text to the "standard output," the system console in simple simulation environments. The arguments to this task are a formatting string, similar to what's used in C's printf function, and a list of signals to be printed. This task and other tasks can be called anywhere in a module, and it immediately prints the list of signals in the specified format, followed by a newline character.

- $write. This task is used the same as $display, except that it does not automatically append a newline character at the end.

- $monitor. This task is similar to $display, except that it remains active continuously, and prints the listed signals whenever any one of them changes. Although multiple $monitor calls may be made within a simulation, only one can be active at a time; calling $monitor cancels the monitoring specified by any previous call.

- $monitoroff and $monitoron. These tasks turn off and on the monitoring specified by the most recent $monitor call.

- $time. This function has no arguments, and simply returns the value of the current simulated time.

- $stop. This task suspends simulation and returns control to the user. If called with the argument "(1)", it prints the simulated time and location.

We'll see example uses of some of these tasks and functions in test benches in Sections 5.4.13 and 7.13.8. For more details on these functions, consult a Verilog reference manual. There you can also find information on many other built-in tasks and functions. These include file input/output tasks that are very useful in large test benches, allowing expected inputs to be read from a file, and output results to be written to another file.

5.4.11 The Time Dimension

None of the examples that we've dealt with so far models the time dimension of circuit operation—everything happens in zero simulated time. However, Verilog has very good facilities for modeling time, and it is indeed another significant dimension of the language. In this book we won't go into great detail on this subject, but we'll introduce just a few ideas here.

 # (delay specifier)

Verilog allows you to specify a time delay in a continuous assignment by following the keyword `assign` with a pound sign (#) and a real number, which may include a decimal point. This number indicates the delay in units of the *time*

time scale

`timescale

scale then in effect. The default time scale is 1 ps (picosecond), but this can be changed using the `timescale` compiler directive, with the syntax below:

`timescale *time-unit* / *time-precision*

Here the "time-unit" indicates the new default units that will be associated with any delay numbers, as well as with time values used by `$time` and other system functions and tasks. Although you could specify "100 ps", typically single units like "1 ps" and "1 ns" are specified to avoid confusion. The "time-precision," on the other hand, is often given in less round numbers. It specifies the time granularity with which the simulator will operate.

time keyword

The smallest time unit or precision that can be specified is 1 femtosecond (fs)—or 10^{-15} s. Chips aren't fast enough to require that yet. But even with nanosecond time units (10^{-9} s), a 32-bit timer would "roll over" in about four seconds of simulated time (2^{32} ps). Therefore, time is maintained in Verilog as a 64-bit integer, and 64-bit variables can be declared using the keyword *time*. Such variables can be useful in simulation. Recall that the width of `integer` variables is compiler-dependent, and may be as small as 32 bits.

Table 5-97 is a Verilog module using delays. It specifies a time unit of 1 ns and a time precision of 100 ps. This module's code is identical to the dataflow code for a prime-number detector in Table 5-75 on page 311, except that its continuous-assignment statements specify a delay of 2 ns for AND operations and 3.5 ns for the OR operation. In synthesis, these delays are ignored, but in simulation, the outputs will be produced only after the specified delays.

Table 5-97
Dataflow Verilog code for a prime-number detector.

```
`timescale 1 ns / 100 ps
module Vrprimedly (N, F);
input [3:0] N;
output F;
wire N3L_N0, N3L_N2L_N1, N2L_N1_N0, N2_N1L_N0;

  assign #2 N3L_N0      = ~N[3]                    & N[0];
  assign #2 N3L_N2L_N1 = ~N[3] & ~N[2] &  N[1]          ;
  assign #2 N2L_N1_N0  =           ~N[2] &  N[1] & N[0];
  assign #2 N2_N1L_N0  =            N[2] & ~N[1] & N[0];
  assign #3.5 F = N3L_N0 | N3L_N2L_N1 | N2L_N1_N0 | N2_N1L_N0;
endmodule
```

In procedural assignments, delays can be specified by writing # sign and a delay number after the = or <= symbol. Yet another way to invoke the time dimension within a block of procedural code is with a *delay statement*, simply a # sign and a delay number. A following semicolon is optional. This statement can be used to suspend the procedural block for the specified time period. In Section 5.4.13, we'll see how delay statements are used in Verilog test benches.

delay statement

5.4.12 Simulation

Once you have a Verilog program whose syntax and semantics are correct, you can use a simulator to observe its operation. Although we won't go into great detail, it's useful to have a basic understanding of how such a simulator works.

Simulator operation begins at *simulation time* of zero. At this time, the simulator initializes all signals to a default value of "x". It also initializes any signals or variables for which initial values have been declared explicitly (we haven't shown you yet how to do this). Next, the simulator begins the execution of all the concurrent statements in the design.

simulation time

Of course, the simulator can't really simulate all of the concurrent statements simultaneously, but it can pretend that it does, using a time-based *event list* and a *sensitivity matrix* based on all of their individual sensitivity lists. Each concurrent statement—continuous assignment, instance, always, or initial—gives rise to at least one software *process* in the simulator. Module instantiations may give rise to additional processes, depending on the module's definition (e.g., a module containing five continuous assignment statements, such as in Table 5-97, gives rise to five software processes).

event list
sensitivity matrix

process

At simulation time zero, all of the software processes are scheduled for execution, and one of them is selected. If it corresponds to an always or initial block, all of its procedural statements are executed, unless and until a delay specification or statement is encountered, in which case the process is suspended. Procedural statement execution includes any looping behavior that is specified. When the execution of the selected process is either completed or suspended, another one is selected, and so on, until all of the processes have been executed. This completes one *simulation cycle*.

simulation cycle

During its execution, a process may assign new values to nets and variables. In blocking assignments with no delay specification, the new values are assigned immediately. If a blocking or nonblocking assignment has a delay specification, then a new entry is scheduled on the event list to make the assignment effective after the specified delay.

A nonblocking assignment with no delay specification is supposed to take place in zero simulated time, but it is actually scheduled to occur at the current simulation time plus one "delta delay." The *delta delay* is an infinitesimally short time, such that the current simulation time plus any number of delta delays still equals the current simulation time. This concept allows software processes to execute multiple times if necessary, in zero simulated time.

delta delay

After a simulation cycle completes, the event list is scanned for the signal or signals that change at the next earliest time on the list. This may be as little as one delta delay later, or it may be a real circuit delay later, in which case the simulation time is advanced to this time. In any case, the scheduled signal changes are made. Some processes may be sensitive to the changing signals, as indicated by their sensitivity lists. The sensitivity matrix indicates, for each signal, which processes have that signal in their sensitivity list. All of the processes that are sensitive to a signal that just changed are scheduled for execution in the next simulation cycle, which now begins.

The simulator's two-phase operation of a simulation cycle followed by scanning the event list and making the next scheduled assignments goes on indefinitely, until the event list is empty. At this point the simulation is complete.

The event-list mechanism makes it possible to simulate the operation of concurrent processes even though the simulator runs on a single computer with a single thread of execution. And the delta-delay mechanism ensures correct operation even though a process or set of processes may require multiple executions, spanning several delta delays, before changing signals settle down to a stable value. This mechanism is also used to detect runaway processes (such as implied by "assign X = ~X"); if a thousand simulation cycles occur over a thousand delta delays without advancing simulation time by any "real" amount, it's most likely that something's amiss.

5.4.13 Test Benches

A test bench specifies a sequence of inputs to be applied by the simulator to an HDL-based design, such as a Verilog module. The entity being tested is often called the *unit under test (UUT)*, in accordance with traditional parlance in the hardware testing field, even though the UUT in this case is not a device, but a program that specifies the behavior of one.

unit under test (UUT)

A while ago, we promised to introduce one more kind of Verilog concurrent statement, which is typically used in test benches. An *initial block* has the syntax shown in Table 5-98. Like an always block, it contains one or more procedural statements, but it does not have a sensitivity list. An initial block executes just once, beginning at simulated time zero. As in an always block, the begin-end block can be named and can have its own variable and parameter declarations.

initial block
initial keyword

Table 5-98
Syntax of Verilog initial blocks.

```
initial
    procedural-statement

initial begin
    procedural-statement
    . . .
    procedural-statement
end
```

```
`timescale 1 ns / 100 ps
module Vrprime_tb () ;
reg [3:0] Num;
wire Prime;

Vrprimedly UUT ( .N(Num), .F(Prime) );

initial begin : TB
  integer i;
  for (i = 0; i <=15; i = i+1 ) begin
    Num = i;
    #10    // Wait 10 ns per iteration
    $write ("Time: %d  Number: %d  Prime? ", $time, Num);
    if (Prime) $display ("Yes");
    else $display("No");
  end
end
endmodule
```

Table 5-99
Verilog test bench for a prime-number-detector circuit.

Table 5-99 is a test bench for our prime-number-detector modules. Like all test benches, this module has no inputs or outputs. It begins by declaring local signals Num and Prime, which are used to apply stimuli and observe the outputs of the UUT. Next, it instantiates the UUT (module Vrprimedly in Table 5-97 on page 330). By changing just the module name in the instance statement, this test bench could instantiate any of this section's prime-number detectors, except for the one in Table 5-89, which has an extra output.

The test bench uses an initial block and delay statements within a for loop to apply all 16 possible input combinations to the UUT. It calls the $write and $display tasks to print the result for each iteration. It's up to the interactive user to look at these outputs and decide if they're right.

Another approach to the test bench is shown in Table 5-100 on the next page. Here we use a case statement within the for loop to enumerate the expected value of the UUT's output for each input combination. And we define a task, Check, to print an error message if the UUT's output is different from what we expect. This test bench has the same compile-time option as some of our prime-detector modules—the value of parameter OneIsPrime should match the assumption made in the UUT.

SUV ROLLOVER ACCIDENTS   Notice in Table 5-100 that we use an integer variable i to control the for loop, and then assign (the lower four bits of) this integer to Num inside the loop. You may ask, "Why not just use Num to control the loop directly?" You'd have a subtle, unexpected problem if you did this. Since reg variable Num is only four bits wide, when it's 15 and you add 1 to it, it rolls over to 0 and the for loop keeps going forever.

Table 5-100
Verilog test bench that compares expected and actual outputs of a prime-number detector.

```verilog
`timescale 1 ns / 100 ps
module Vrprime_tbc () ;
reg [3:0] Num;
wire Prime;

task Check;
input expect;
  if (Prime != expect)
    $display ("Error: N = %b, expect %b, got %b", Num,expect,Prime);
endtask

Vrprimedly UUT ( .N(Num), .F(Prime) );

initial begin : TB
  integer i;
  parameter OneIsPrime = 1; // Change to 0 if 1 is not prime.

  for (i = 0; i <= 15; i = i+1) begin
    Num = i;
    #10
    case (Num)
      4'd1 : Check(OneIsPrime);
      4'd2, 4'd3, 4'd5, 4'd7, 4'd11, 4'd13 : Check(1);
      default Check(0);
    endcase
  end
end
endmodule
```

5.4.14 Verilog Features for Sequential Logic Design

Only one more language feature is needed to describe sequential circuits in Verilog; for reference purposes, we discuss it here.

Most Verilog-based digital design is directed to clocked, synchronous systems that use edge-triggered flip-flops. Like combinational behavior, edge-triggered behavior in Verilog is specified using always blocks. The difference between combinational and edge-triggered behavior is in the sensitivity list of the always block. The keyword posedge or negedge is placed in front of a signal name to indicate that the block should be executed only at the positive (rising) or negative (falling) edge of the named signal. We'll see many examples of this in Section 7.13 and throughout Chapter 8.

posedge keyword
negedge keyword

Unlike ABEL, Verilog has no specific syntax for creating state machines, and in fact provides several ways to do so. However, it's important to use a consistent coding style for state machines, as we show in Section 7.13.2.

5.4.15 Synthesis

As we mentioned at the beginning of this section, Verilog was originally designed as a logic circuit description and simulation language and was only later adapted to synthesis. Thus, the language has several features and constructs that cannot be synthesized. However, the subset of the language and the style of programs that we've presented in this section are generally synthesizable by most tools.

Still, the code that you write can have a big effect on the quality of the synthesized circuits that you get. A few examples are listed below:

- "Serial" control structures like if, else if, else if, ... else can result in a corresponding serial chain of logic gates to test conditions. It's often better to use a case statement, especially if the conditions are mutually exclusive.
- Loops in procedural code are generally "unwound" to create multiple copies of combinational logic to execute the statements in the loop. If you want to use just one copy of the combinational logic in a sequence of steps, then you have to design a sequential circuit, as discussed in later chapters.
- When using conditional statements in procedural code, failing to code an outcome for some input combination will cause the synthesizer to create an inferred latch to hold the old value of a signal that might otherwise change. Such latches are generally not intended.

In addition, some language features and constructs may just be unsynthesizable, depending on the tool. Naturally, you have to consult the documentation to find out what's disallowed, allowed, and recommended for a particular tool.

For the foreseeable future, digital designers who use synthesis tools will need to pay reasonably close attention to their coding style in order to obtain good results. And for the moment, the definition of "good coding style" depends somewhat on both the synthesis tool and the target technology. The examples in the rest of this book, while syntactically and semantically correct, hardly scratch the surface of coding methods for large HDL-based designs. The art and practice of large HDL-based hardware design is still very much evolving.

References

ABEL, VHDL, and Verilog are used every day by thousands of digital designers, and their associated compilers and other tools are well supported by many different suppliers. Nowadays, VHDL and Verilog have especially active user communities, and there are frequent workshops and conferences devoted to applications and enhancements of the languages and tools. Because of all this activity, you can easily find up-to-date HDL references, examples, and tutorials on the Web. For example, searching for "Verilog tutorial" yields dozens of good hits.

Still, there are some good print references out there too, which are described here. The most readily accessible and definitive reference on the ABEL language that I've found is Appendix A of *Digital Design Using ABEL*, by David Pellerin and Michael Holley (Prentice Hall, 1994). It makes sense that this would be the definitive work—Pellerin and Holley invented the language and wrote the original compiler code! Pellerin also wrote, with co-author Douglas Taylor, a nice stand-alone introduction to VHDL, titled *VHDL Made Easy!* (Prentice Hall, 1997).

VHDL is a "Very Huge Design Language," and we cover only a subset of its features and capabilities in this book. There are many language options (such as statement labels) that we don't use, but these are covered in dedicated VHDL tutorial and reference books. One of the best is *The Designer's Guide to VHDL* by Peter J. Ashenden (Morgan Kaufmann, 2002, second edition). Though it's big (700 pages), it covers the whole language quite systematically, including features of VHDL-1987, -1993, and -2002.

A somewhat shorter VHDL introduction, but still with lots of examples, is *Circuit Design with VHDL* by Volnei A. Pedroni (MIT Press, 2004). This book is recommended for its nice emphasis on practical design issues including synthesis and test benches. Another practical book is *VHDL for Programmable Logic*, by Kevin Skahill of Cypress Semiconductor (Addison-Wesley, 1996).

The IEEE standard VHDL packages are important elements of any VHDL design environment. A listing of their type and function definitions is included as an appendix in some VHDL texts, but if you're really curious about them, you can find the complete source files in the library directory of any VHDL design system, including the Xilinx ISE software that is packaged with some editions of this book.

A comprehensive treatment of Verilog for design and synthesis can be found in *Verilog HDL* by Samir Palnitkar (Prentice Hall, 2003, second edition). One thing this book has going for it is that a reviewer who hated my previous edition thought that Palnitkar's was the best Verilog book for beginners—so it's definitely worth a try if you're struggling with my very concise introduction to Verilog. On the other hand, if you're looking for "concise but not as insanely concise as Wakerly," try *Starter's Guide to Verilog 2001* by Michael D. Ciletti (Prentice Hall, 2003).

As mentioned previously, there's a lot of good HDL reference material on the Web. But the practical and insightful articles by Clifford E. Cummings on Verilog features, usage, and coding styles are particularly worth reading (go to `www.sunburst-design.com` or search for "Cummings Verilog"). For example, our discussion of the rules for blocking versus nonblocking assignments on page 316 is based on one of his articles.

All of the ABEL, VHDL, and Verilog examples in this chapter and throughout this book were compiled and in most cases simulated using one of the following HDL software packages: Xilinx ISE 6.x Student Edition (Xilinx, Inc., San Jose, CA 95124, www.xilinx.com), Aldec Active-HDL 6.x Student Edition (Aldec, Inc., Henderson, NV 89074, www.aldec.com), or Lattice ispLEVER 4.x (Lattice Semiconductor, Hillsboro, OR 97124, www.latticesemi.com).

All three packages have VHDL and Verilog compilers and a schematic editor; the Xilinx and Lattice packages support ABEL as well. The Aldec and Lattice packages include a simulator and waveform viewer for the supported HDLs, and the Xilinx package has synthesis tools for targeting Xilinx CPLDs and FPGAs, as well as for checking and tweaking the final fitted results. The Xilinx and/or Aldec packages are included in some editions of this book.

Source-code files for all the examples in this chapter and throughout this book are available at DDPPonline. Each filename corresponds to the example's module or entity name, and has the suffix .abl, .vhd, or .v for ABEL, VHDL, or Verilog, respectively.

Drill Problems

5.1   Write an ABEL program for the combinational circuit in Figure 6-32.

5.2   Write a set of ABEL test vectors for prime-number detector in Table 5-7.

5.3   Write a structural VHDL program (entity and architecture) for the alarm circuit in Figure 4-19.

5.4   Repeat Drill 5.3, using the dataflow style of description.

5.5   Repeat Drill 5.3, using a process and a behavioral description style.

5.6   Write a structural VHDL program (entity and architecture) for the logic circuit in Figure 4-9.

5.7   Repeat Drill 5.6, using the dataflow style of description.

5.8   Repeat Drill 5.6, using a process and a behavioral description style.

5.9   Write a VHDL test bench that instantiates the circuit from one of the previous three drills, and applies all eight possible input combinations to it, at 10 ns per step. Your test bench need not look at the output values. Instead, use the simulator to run the test bench and observe the circuit's output sequence, and compare with the values shown in Figure 4-10.

5.10   Write a structural VHDL program corresponding to the NAND-gate based logic circuit in Figure 6-17.

5.11   Which assignment operator should you use in Verilog always blocks intended to synthesize combinational logic, = or <=?

5.12   If multiple values are assigned to the same signal in a Verilog combinational always block, what is the signal's value when the always block completes execution: (a) the AND of all values assigned; (b) the OR of all values; (c) the last value assigned; or (d) it depends?

5.13   Write a structural Verilog module for the logic circuit in Figure 4-9.

5.14   Repeat Drill 5.13, using the dataflow style of description.

5.15   Repeat Drill 5.13, using an `always` block and a behavioral description style.

5.16   Write a Verilog test bench that instantiates the circuit from one the previous three drills, and applies all eight possible input combinations to it, at 10 ns per step. Your test bench need not look at the output values. Instead, use the simulator to run the test bench and observe the circuit's output sequence, and compare with the values shown in Figure 4-10.

5.17   Write a structural Verilog program corresponding to the NAND-gate based logic circuit in Figure 6-17.

5.18   Synthesize the `VrSillyXOR` Verilog module in Table 5-72, targeting your favorite PLD, CPLD, or FPGA. Determine whether the synthesizer is smart enough to realize the module using a single XOR gate.

Exercises

5.19   Write an ABEL program for a combinational logic function with six input bits N5–N0 representing an integer between 0 and 63, and two outputs M3 and M5 that indicate whether the number is a multiple of 3 or 5, respectively. Compile the program and determine the number of product terms needed for each output.

5.20   After completing the preceding exercise, write a set of ABEL test vectors that checks the outputs of your circuit for all multiples of 7.

5.21   Starting with the ABEL program in Table 5-5, write equivalent, parenthesized logic equations for variables X4 through X10 in the program *without* using `when` statements. Run both your equations and the original `when` statements through an ABEL compiler and make sure they produce the same results.

5.22   Draw a circuit diagram corresponding to the minimal two-level sum-of-products equations for the alarm circuit, as given in Table 5-3. On each inverter, AND gate, and OR gate input and output, write a pair of numbers ($t0, t1$), where $t0$ is the test number from Table 5-12 that detects a stuck-at-0 fault on that line, and $t1$ is the test number that detects a stuck-at-1 fault.

5.23   Rewrite the VHDL prime-number-detector architecture of Table 5-50 using a `while` statement.

5.24   Write a VHDL program (entity and architecture) for a combinational logic function with six input bits N5–N0 representing an integer between 0 and 63, and two outputs M3 and M5 that indicate whether the integer is a multiple of 3 or 5, respectively. Target your design to an available PLD, CPD, or FPGA and determine how many resources are used by the realization.

5.25   After completing the preceding exercise, write a VHDL test bench that compares the outputs of your circuit for all possible input combinations against results computed by the simulator using its own arithmetic. The test bench should stop and display an error message if there is a mismatch. Test your test bench by putting a bug in your original VHDL program and running the test bench. Extra credit (in your own mind only) if you already had an unknown bug in the original program!

5.26   Write a VHDL test bench that applies all 16 possible input combinations to the VHDL `prime` entity of Table 5-30 and displays the output value for each input combination.

5.27   Write a VHDL test bench that applies all 16 possible input combinations to the VHDL `prime` entity of Table 5-30, compares each output value with the expected result, and prints an error message for any unexpected results.

5.28   Write a dataflow-style VHDL program (entity and architecture) corresponding to the full-adder circuit in Figure 6-83.

5.29   Instantiating multiple copies of the module that you designed in Exercise 5.28, write a structural VHDL program for a 4-bit ripple adder using the structure of Figure 6-84.

5.30   After doing Exercise 5.29, write a VHDL test bench that tests the adder for all possible pairs of 4-bit addends, and displays any incorrect results.

5.31   Using the entity that you defined in Exercise 5.28, write a structural VHDL program for a 16-bit ripple adder along the lines of Figure 6-84. Use a `generate` statement to create the 16 full adders and their signal connections.

5.32   After doing Exercise 5.31, write a VHDL test bench that tests the adder for a subset of the 2^{32} possible pairs of 16-bit addends, and displays any incorrect results. Try to come up with a strategy for generating the input pairs that catches likely coding errors while using less than a million input combinations.

5.33   An experienced digital designer who reviewed the Verilog code in this book commented that the logical expression `S[2] == 0` in Table 6-41 on page 432 could be written much more concisely (in only five characters). He was correct—what was his alternate formulation that yields the same result? Comment on the pros and cons of his formulation versus the original expression.

5.34   Write a Verilog module for a combinational logic function with six inputs N5–N0 representing an integer between 0 and 63, and two outputs M3 and M5 indicating whether the integer is a multiple of 3 or 5, respectively. Target your design to an available PLD, CPD, or FPGA and determine how many resources are used by the realization.

5.35   After completing the preceding exercise, write a Verilog test bench that compares the outputs of your circuit for all possible input combinations against results computed by the simulator using its own arithmetic. The test bench should stop and display the actual and computed outputs if there is a mismatch. Test your test bench by putting a bug in your original Verilog program and running the test bench. Extra credit (in your own mind only) if you already had an unknown bug in the original program!

5.36   Modify the `Vrprimebv` module in Table 5-91 to find 8-bit primes. Then use this module in a test bench to print all the primes between 0 and 255.

5.37   Write a dataflow-style Verilog module corresponding to the full-adder circuit in Figure 6-83.

5.38   Instantiating multiple copies of the module that you designed in Exercise 5.37, write a structural Verilog program for a 4-bit ripple adder using the structure of Figure 6-84.

5.39   After doing Exercise 5.38, write a Verilog test bench that tests the adder for all possible pairs of 4-bit addends. The test bench should stop and display the actual and expected outputs if there is any mismatch.

5.40   Using the entity that you defined in Exercise 5.37, write a structural Verilog program for a 16-bit ripple adder along the lines of Figure 6-84. Use a `generate` statement to create the 16 full adders and their signal connection.

5.41   After doing Exercise 5.40, write a Verilog test bench that tests the adder for a subset of the 2^{32} possible pairs of 16-bit addends. The test bench should stop and display the actual and expected outputs if there is any mismatch. Try to come up with a strategy for generating the input pairs that catches likely coding errors while using less than a million input combinations.

5.42   Look in a Verilog reference manual, and determine how Verilog handles "ambiguous" logical values and expressions that may be either true or false, such as `4'bxx00`. Write a small test bench program that demonstrates that they are handled as you say they are.

5.43   Look in a Verilog reference manual, and read about Verilog file I/O. Then write a test bench that checks the output of one of the `prime` modules (such as Table 5-75, 5-76, or 5-80) for all possible inputs, reading the expected output value from a file.

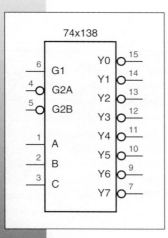

74x138

6	G1	Y0 15
4	G2A	Y1 14
5	G2B	Y2 13
		Y3 12
1	A	Y4 11
2	B	Y5 10
3	C	Y6 9
		Y7 7

chapter 6

Combinational Logic Design Practices

T
he theoretical principles used in combinational logic design were described previously in Chapter 4. Now we'll build on that foundation and describe many of the devices, structures, and methods used by engineers to solve practical digital design problems. We'll give examples using individual gates and drawing logic diagrams as we did in Chapter 4, and we'll also give examples using the hardware description languages ABEL, VHDL, and Verilog from Chapter 5. This book is written and organized so that your study of these languages is optional. However, if you're contemplating a career in digital design, it's recommended that you study the examples at least for Verilog or VHDL.

A practical combinational circuit may have dozens of inputs and outputs and could require hundreds, thousands, even millions of terms to describe as a sum of products, and *billions and billions* of rows to describe in a truth table. Thus, most real combinational logic design problems are too large to solve by "brute-force" application of theoretical techniques.

But wait, you say, how could any human being conceive of such a complex logic circuit in the first place? The key is structured thinking. A complex circuit or system is conceived as a collection of smaller subsystems, each of which has a much simpler description.

In combinational logic design, there are several straightforward structures—decoders, multiplexers, comparators, and the like—that turn up quite regularly as building blocks in larger systems. The most important of

---

THE IMPORTANCE OF 74-SERIES LOGIC

Later in this chapter we'll look at commonly used 74-series ICs that perform well-structured logic functions. These parts are important building blocks in a digital designer's toolbox, because their level of functionality often matches a designer's level of thinking when partitioning a large problem into smaller chunks.

Even when you design for PLDs, FPGAs, or ASICs, understanding 74-series MSI functions is important. In PLD-based design, standard MSI functions can be used as a starting point for developing logic equations for more specialized functions. And in FPGA and ASIC design, some of the basic building blocks (or "standard cells" or "macros") provided by the FPGA or ASIC manufacturer may actually have the same definitions as corresponding 74-series MSI functions, even to the extent of having similar descriptive numbers.

---

these structures are described in this chapter. We describe each structure generally at the gate level and then we give examples and applications using both 74-series components and ABEL, VHDL, and Verilog.

Before launching into these combinational building blocks, we need to discuss several important topics. The first topic is documentation standards that are used by digital designers to ensure that their designs are correct, manufacturable, and maintainable. Next we discuss circuit timing, a crucial element for successful digital design. Third, we describe the internal structure of combinational PLDs. These devices correspond directly to the sum-of-products logic representation that we studied in Chapter 4, so we can use them later as "universal" building blocks.

6.1 Documentation Standards

Good documentation is essential for correct design and efficient maintenance of digital systems. In addition to being accurate and complete, documentation must be somewhat instructive, so that a test engineer, maintenance technician, or even the original design engineer (six months after designing the circuit) can figure out how the system works just by reading the documentation.

Although the type of documentation depends on system complexity and the engineering and manufacturing environments, a documentation package should generally contain at least the following six items:

circuit specification

1. A *specification* describes exactly what the circuit or system is supposed to do, including a description of all inputs and outputs ("interfaces") and the functions that are to be performed. Note that the "spec" doesn't have to specify *how* the system achieves its results, just *what* the results are supposed to be. However, in many companies it is common practice also to incorporate one or more of the documents below into the spec to describe how the system works at the same time.

DOCUMENTS ON-LINE Professional engineering documentation nowadays is carefully maintained on corporate intranets, so it's very useful to include pointers, such as URLs, in circuit specifications and descriptions so that references can be easily located. Of course, URLs sometimes change as a result of network and server reconfiguration, so documents might be referenced instead by a permanent number assigned by the company's document-control system.

On-line documentation is so important and authoritative in one company that the footer on every page of every specification contains the warning that "A printed version of this document is an uncontrolled copy." That is, a printed copy could very well be obsolete.

2. A *block diagram* is an informal pictorial description of the system's major functional modules and their basic interconnections.

block diagram

3. A *schematic diagram* is a formal specification of the electrical components of the system, their interconnections, and all of the details needed to build the system, including IC types, reference designators, and pin numbers. We've been using the term *logic diagram* for an informal drawing that does not have quite this level of detail. Most schematic-drawing programs have the ability to generate a *bill of materials (BOM)* from the schematic; this tells the purchasing department what electronic components they have to order to build the system.

schematic diagram

logic diagram

bill of materials (BOM)

4. A *timing diagram* shows the values of various logic signals as a function of time, including the cause-and-effect delays between critical signals.

timing diagram

5. A *structured logic device description* describes the internal function of a programmable logic device (PLD), field-programmable gate array (FPGA), or application-specific integrated circuit (ASIC). It is normally written in an HDL such as ABEL, Verilog, or VHDL, but it may be in the form of logic equations, state tables, or state diagrams. In some cases, a conventional programming language such as C may be used to model the operation of a circuit or to specify its behavior.

structured logic device description

6. A *circuit description* is a narrative text document that, in conjunction with the other documentation, explains how the circuit works internally. The circuit description should list any assumptions and potential pitfalls in the circuit's design and operation, and point out the use of any nonobvious design "tricks." A good circuit description also contains definitions of acronyms and other specialized terms and has references to related documents.

circuit description

You've probably already seen block diagrams in many contexts. We present a few rules for drawing them in the next subsection, and then in the rest of this section we concentrate on schematics for combinational logic circuits. Section 6.2.1 introduces timing diagrams. Structured logic descriptions in the form of ABEL, VHDL, and Verilog programs were covered in Sections 5.2, 5.3, and 5.4, respectively. In Section 9.1.6 we'll show how a C program can be used to generate the contents of a read-only memory.

The last area of documentation, the circuit description, is very important in practice. Just as an experienced programmer creates a program design document before beginning to write code, an experienced logic designer starts writing the circuit description before drawing the schematic or writing the HDL code. Sadly, the circuit description is sometimes the last document to be created, and sometimes it's never written at all. A circuit without a description is difficult to debug, manufacture, test, maintain, modify, and enhance.

DON'T FORGET TO WRITE!   In order to create great products, logic designers must develop their language and writing skills, especially in the area of *logical* outlining and organization. The most successful logic designers (and later, project leaders, system architects, and entrepreneurs) are the ones who communicate their ideas, proposals, and decisions effectively to others. Even though it's a lot of fun to tinker in the digital design lab, don't use that as an excuse to shortchange your writing and communications courses and projects!

6.1.1 Block Diagrams

block diagram

A *block diagram* shows the inputs, outputs, functional modules, internal data paths, and important control signals of a system. In general, it should not be so detailed that it occupies more than one page, yet it must not be too vague. A small block diagram may have three to six blocks, while a large one may have 10 to 15, depending on system complexity. In any case, the block diagram must show the most important system elements and how they work together. Large systems may require additional block diagrams of individual subsystems, but there should always be a "top-level" diagram showing the entire system.

Figure 6-1 shows a sample block diagram. Each block is labeled with the function of the block, not the individual chips that comprise it. As another example, Figure 6-2(a) shows the block-diagram symbol for a 32-bit register. If the register is to be built using four 74AHC377 8-bit registers, and this information is important to someone reading the diagram (e.g., for cost reasons), then it can be conveyed as shown in (b). However, splitting the block to show individual chips as in (c) is incorrect.

bus

A *bus* is a collection of two or more related signal lines. In a block diagram, buses are drawn with a double or heavy line. A slash and a number may indicate how many individual signal lines are contained in a bus. Alternatively, size may be denoted in the bus name (e.g., INBUS[31..0] or INBUS[31:0]). Active levels

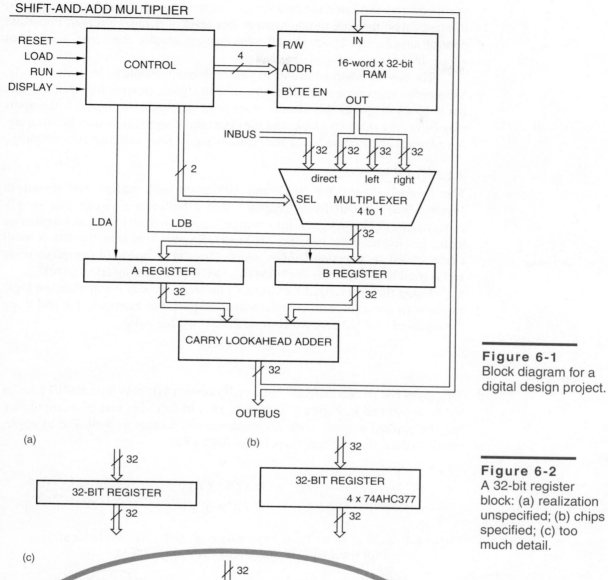

Figure 6-1
Block diagram for a digital design project.

Figure 6-2
A 32-bit register block: (a) realization unspecified; (b) chips specified; (c) too much detail.

(defined later) and inversion bubbles may or may not appear in block diagrams; in most cases, they are unimportant at this level of detail. However, important control signals and buses should have names, usually the same names that appear in the more detailed schematic.

The flow of control and data in a block diagram should be indicated clearly. Schematic diagrams are generally drawn with signals flowing from left to right, but in block diagrams this ideal is more difficult to achieve. Inputs and outputs may be on any side of a block, and the direction of signal flow may be arbitrary. Arrowheads are used on buses and ordinary signal lines to eliminate ambiguity.

6.1.2 Gate Symbols

The symbol shapes for AND and OR gates and buffers are shown in Figure 6-3(a). (Recall from Chapter 3 that a buffer is a circuit that simply converts "weak" logic signals into "strong" ones.) To draw logic gates with more than a few inputs, we expand the AND and OR symbols as shown in (b). A small *inversion bubble* circle, called an *inversion bubble*, denotes logical inversion or complementing and is used in the symbols for NAND and NOR gates and inverters in (c).

Using the generalized DeMorgan's theorem, we can manipulate the logic expressions for gates with complemented outputs. For example, if X and Y are the inputs of a NAND gate with output Z, then we can write

$$Z = (X \cdot Y)'$$
$$= X' + Y'$$

This gives rise to two different but equally correct symbols for a NAND gate, as we demonstrated in Figure 4-3 on page 191. In fact, this sort of manipulation may be applied to gates with uncomplemented outputs as well. For example, consider the following equations for an AND gate:

$$Z = X \cdot Y$$
$$= ((X \cdot Y)')'$$
$$= (X' + Y')'$$

Figure 6-3 Shapes for basic logic gates: (a) AND, OR, and buffers; (b) expansion of inputs; (c) inversion bubbles.

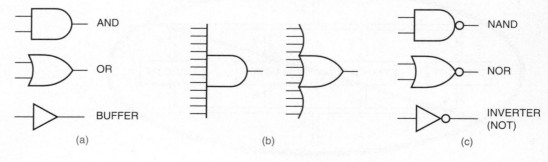

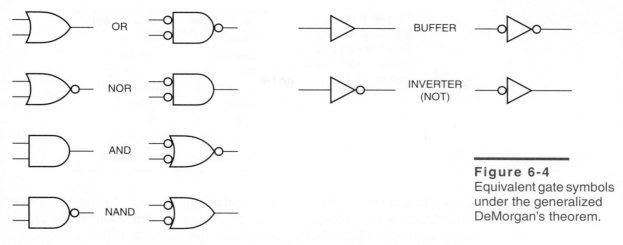

Figure 6-4
Equivalent gate symbols under the generalized DeMorgan's theorem.

Thus, an AND gate may be symbolized as an OR gate with inversion bubbles on its inputs and output.

Equivalent symbols for standard gates that can be obtained by these manipulations are summarized in Figure 6-4. Even though both symbols in a pair represent the same logic function, the choice of one symbol or the other in a logic diagram is not arbitrary, at least not if we are adhering to good documentation standards. As we'll show in the next three subsections, proper choices of gate symbols can make logic diagrams much easier to use and understand. In addition, corresponding choices of signal names can make both logic diagrams and HDL programs more understandable.

IEEE STANDARD LOGIC SYMBOLS   Together with the American National Standards Institute (ANSI), the Institute of Electrical and Electronics Engineers (IEEE) has developed a standard set of logic symbols. The most recent revision of the standard is ANSI/IEEE Std 91-1984, *IEEE Standard Graphic Symbols for Logic Functions*, and it allows both rectangular- and distinctive-shape symbols for logic gates. We have been using and will continue to use the distinctive-shape symbols in this book, but the rectangular-shape symbols are described in a guide to IEEE symbols on the Web at <u>DDPPonline</u>.

6.1.3 Signal Names and Active Levels

Each input and output signal in a logic circuit should have a descriptive alphanumeric label, the signal's name. Most computer-aided design systems for drawing logic circuits also allow certain special characters, such as *, _, and !, to be included in signal names. In the analysis and synthesis examples in Chapter 4, we used mostly single-character signal names (X, Y, etc.) because the circuits didn't do much. However, in a real system, well-chosen signal names

Table 6-1
Each line shows a different naming convention for active levels.

Active Low	Active High
READY–	READY+
ERROR.L	ERROR.H
ADDR15(L)	ADDR15(H)
RESET*	RESET
ENABLE~	ENABLE
~GO	GO
/RECEIVE	RECEIVE
TRANSMIT_L	TRANSMIT

convey information to someone reading the logic diagram the same way that variable names in a software program do. A signal's name indicates an action that is controlled (GO, PAUSE), a condition that it detects (READY, ERROR), or data that it carries (INBUS[31:0]).

active level
active high

active low
assert
negate
deassert

active-level naming convention

Each signal name should have an *active level* associated with it. A signal is *active high* if it performs the named action or denotes the named condition when it is HIGH or 1. (Under the positive-logic convention, which we use throughout this book, "HIGH" and "1" are equivalent.) A signal is *active low* if it performs the named action or denotes the named condition when it is LOW or 0. A signal is said to be *asserted* when it is at its active level. A signal is said to be *negated* (or, sometimes, *deasserted*) when it is not at its active level.

The active level of each signal in a circuit is normally specified as part of its name, according to some convention. Examples of several different *active-level naming conventions* are shown in Table 6-1. The choice of one of these or other signal-naming conventions is sometimes just a matter of personal preference, but more often it is constrained by the engineering environment. Since the active-level designation is part of the signal name, the naming convention must be compatible with the input requirements of any computer-aided design tools that will process the signal names, such as schematic editors, HDL compilers, and simulators. In this text, we'll use the last convention in the table: An active-low signal name has a suffix of _L, and an active-high signal has no suffix. The _L suffix may be read as if it were a prefix "not."

_L suffix

signal name
logic expression

logic equation

It's extremely important for you to understand the difference between signal names, expressions, and equations. A *signal name* is just a name—an alphanumeric label. A *logic expression* combines signal names using the operators of switching algebra—AND, OR, and NOT—as we explained and used throughout Chapter 4. A *logic equation* is an assignment of a logic expression to a signal name—it describes one signal's function in terms of other signals.

The distinction between signal names and logic expressions can be related to a concept used in computer programming languages: The lefthand side of an assignment statement contains a variable *name*, and the righthand side contains an *expression* whose value will be given to the named variable (e.g., Z = - (X+Y) in C). In a programming language, you can't put an expression on the lefthand side of an assignment statement. In logic design, you can't use a logic expression as a signal name.

Logic signals may have names like X, READY, and GO_L. The "_L" in GO_L is just part of the signal's name, like an underscore in a variable name in a C program. There is *no* signal whose name is READY'—this is an expression, since ' is an operator. However, there may be two signals named READY and READY_L such that READY_L = READY' during normal operation of the circuit.

We are very careful in this book to distinguish between signal names, which are always printed in black, and logic expressions, which are always printed in color when they are written near the corresponding signal lines.

6.1.4 Active Levels for Pins

When we draw the outline of an AND or OR symbol, or a rectangle representing a larger-scale logic element, we think of the given logic function as occurring *inside* that symbolic outline. In Figure 6-5(a), we show the logic symbols for an AND and an OR gate and for a larger-scale element with an ENABLE input. The AND and OR gates have active-high inputs—they require 1s on the input to assert their outputs.

Likewise, the larger-scale element has an active-high ENABLE input, which must be 1 to enable the element to do its thing. In (b), we show the same logic elements with active-low input and output pins. Exactly the same logic functions are performed *inside* the symbolic outlines, but the inversion bubbles indicate that 0s must now be applied to the input pins to activate the logic functions, and that the outputs are 0 when they are "doing their thing."

Thus, active levels may be associated with the input and output pins of gates and larger-scale logic elements. We use an inversion bubble to indicate an active-low pin and the absence of a bubble to indicate an active-high pin. For

Figure 6-5 Logic symbols: (a) AND, OR, and a larger-scale logic element; (b) the same elements with active-low inputs and outputs.

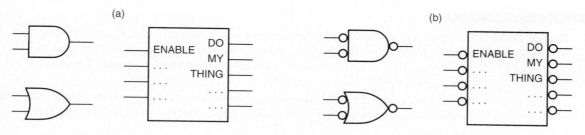

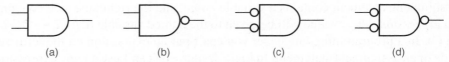

Figure 6-6 Four ways of obtaining an AND function: (a) AND gate;
(b) NAND gate; (c) NOR gate; (d) OR gate.

example, the AND gate in Figure 6-6(a) performs the logical AND of two active-high inputs and produces an active-high output: if both inputs are asserted (1), the output is asserted (1). The NAND gate in (b) also performs the AND function, but it produces an active-low output. Even a NOR or OR gate can be construed to perform the AND function using active-low inputs and outputs, as shown in (c) and (d). All four gates in the figure can be said to perform the same function: the output of each gate is asserted if both of its inputs are asserted.

Figure 6-7 shows the same idea for the OR function: The output of each gate is asserted if either of its inputs is asserted.

Figure 6-7 Four ways of obtaining an OR function: (a) OR gate;
(b) NOR gate; (c) NAND gate; (d) AND gate.

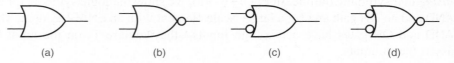

Sometimes a noninverting buffer is used simply to boost the fanout of a logic signal without changing its function. Figure 6-8 shows the possible logic symbols for both inverters and noninverting buffers. In terms of active levels, all of the symbols perform exactly the same function: Each asserts its output signal if and only if its input is asserted.

Figure 6-8 Alternate symbols: (a, b) inverters; (c, d) noninverting buffers.

NAME THAT SIGNAL!   Although it is absolutely necessary to name only a circuit's main inputs and outputs, most logic designers find it useful to name internal signals as well. During circuit debugging, it's nice to have a name to use when pointing to an internal signal that's behaving strangely.

Most computer-aided design systems automatically generate labels for unnamed signals, but a user-chosen name is preferable to a computer-generated one like XSIG1057.

6.1.5 Bubble-to-Bubble Logic Design

Experienced logic circuit designers formulate their circuits in terms of the logic functions performed *inside* the symbolic outlines. Whether you're designing with discrete gates or in an HDL, it's easiest to think of logic signals and their interactions using active-high names. However, once you're ready to realize your circuit, you may have to deal with active-low signals due to the requirements of the environment.

When you design with discrete gates, either at board or ASIC level, a key requirement is often speed. As we showed in Section 3.3.6, inverting gates are typically faster than noninverting ones, so there's often a significant performance payoff in carrying some signals in active-low form.

When you design with larger-scale elements, many of them may be off-the-shelf chips or other existing components that already have some inputs and outputs fixed in active-low form. The reasons that they use active-low signals may range from performance improvement to years of tradition, but in any case, you still have to deal with it.

Bubble-to-bubble logic design is the practice of choosing logic symbols and signal names, including active-level designators, that make the function of a logic circuit easier to understand. Usually, this means choosing signal names and gate types and symbols so that most of the inversion bubbles "cancel out" and the design can be analyzed as if all of the signals were active high.

bubble-to-bubble logic design

For example, suppose we need to produce a signal that tells a device to "GO" when we are "READY" and we get a "REQUEST." Clearly from the problem statement, an AND function is required; in switching algebra, we would write GO = READY · REQUEST. However, we can use different gates to perform the AND function, depending on the active level required for the GO signal and the active levels of the available input signals.

Figure 6-9(a) shows the simplest case, where GO must be active-high and the available input signals are also active-high; we use an AND gate. If, on the other hand, the device that we're controlling requires an active-low GO_L signal, we can use a NAND gate as shown in (b). If the available input signals are active-low, we can use a NOR or OR gate as shown in (c) and (d).

Figure 6-9 Many ways to GO: (a) active-high inputs and output;
(b) active-high inputs, active-low output; (c) active-low
inputs, active-high output; (d) active-low inputs and output.

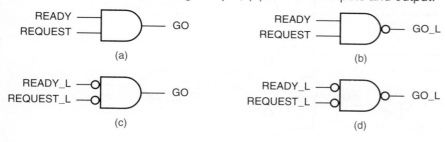

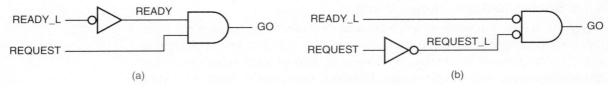

Figure 6-10 Two more ways to GO, with mixed input levels: (a) with an AND gate; (b) with a NOR gate.

The active levels of available signals don't always match the active levels of available gates. For example, suppose we are given input signals READY_L (active-low) and REQUEST (active-high). Figure 6-10 shows two different ways to generate GO using an inverter to generate the active level needed for the AND function. The second way is generally preferred, since inverting gates like NOR are generally faster than noninverting ones like AND. We drew the inverter differently in each case to make the output's active level match its signal name.

To understand the benefits of bubble-to-bubble logic design, consider the circuit in Figure 6-11(a). What does it do? In Section 4.2 we showed several ways to analyze such a circuit, and we could certainly obtain a logic expression for the DATA output using these techniques. However, when the circuit is redrawn in Figure 6-11(b), the output function can be read directly from the logic diagram, as follows. The DATA output is asserted when either ADATA_L or BDATA_L is asserted. If ASEL is asserted, then ADATA_L is asserted if and only if A is asserted; that is, ADATA_L is a copy of A. If ASEL is negated, BSEL is asserted and BDATA_L is a copy of B. In other words, DATA is a copy of A if ASEL is asserted, and DATA is a copy of B if ASEL is negated. Even though there are five inversion bubbles in the logic diagram, we mentally had to perform only one negation to understand the circuit—that BSEL is asserted if ASEL is not.

Figure 6-11 A 2-input multiplexer (you're not expected to know what that is yet): (a) cryptic logic diagram; (b) proper logic diagram using active-level designators and alternate logic symbols.

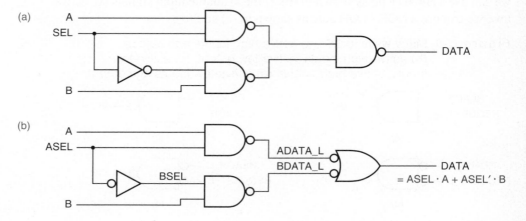

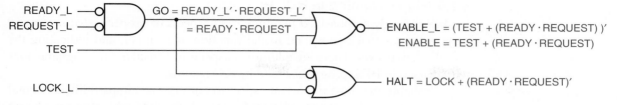

Figure 6-12 Another properly drawn logic diagram.

If we wish, we can write an algebraic expression for the DATA output. We use the technique of Section 4.2, simply propagating expressions through gates toward the output. In doing so, we can ignore pairs of inversion bubbles that cancel, and directly write the expression shown in color in the figure.

Another example is shown in Figure 6-12. Reading directly from the logic diagram, we see that ENABLE_L is asserted if READY_L and REQUEST_L are asserted or if TEST is asserted. The HALT output is asserted if READY_L and REQUEST_L are not both asserted or if LOCK_L is asserted. Once again, this example has only one place where a gate input's active level does not match the input signal level, and this is reflected in the verbal description of the circuit.

We can, if we wish, write algebraic equations for the ENABLE_L and HALT outputs. As we propagate expressions through gates toward the output, we obtain expressions like READY_L′ · REQUEST_L′. However, we can use our active-level naming convention to simplify terms like READY_L′. The circuit contains no signal with the name READY; but if it did, it would satisfy the relationship READY = READY_L′ according to the naming convention. This allows us to write the ENABLE_L and HALT equations as shown. Complementing both sides of the ENABLE_L equation, we obtain an equation that describes a hypothetical active-high ENABLE output in terms of hypothetical active-high inputs.

We'll see more examples of bubble-to-bubble logic design in this and later chapters, especially as we begin to use larger-scale logic elements.

BUBBLE-TO-BUBBLE LOGIC DESIGN RULES	The following rules are useful for performing bubble-to-bubble logic design:

The following rules are useful for performing bubble-to-bubble logic design:

- The signal name on a device's output should have the same active level as the device's output pin—that is, active-low if the device symbol has an inversion bubble on the output pin, active-high if not.
- If the active level of an input signal is the same as that of the input pin to which it is connected, then the logic function inside the symbolic outline is activated when the signal is asserted. This is the most common case in a logic diagram.
- If the active level of an input signal is the opposite of the input pin's, then the logic function inside the symbolic outline is activated when the signal is negated. This case should be avoided if possible because it forces us to keep track mentally of a logical negation to understand the circuit.

6.1.6 Signal Naming in HDL Programs

We have already emphasized two important aspects of proper signal naming—picking names that correspond to the function of a signal, and indicating the signal's active level. There are additional aspects to consider when signal names will be used in HDL programs and other CAD tools.

Probably the most important aspect to consider is compatibility of signal names among a collection of different CAD tools. Each tool has its own rules on what it accepts as legal identifiers, and what other characters it might interpret as giving special commands or information to the tool, such as macros, compiler directives, and so on. Therefore, it's important to construct your signal names only from a restricted, "least-common-denominator" set of characters, accepted by *all* tools. The safest such set is usually letters, digits, and the underscore "_", and that's what we use in this book.

Tools may also differ in what characters may be used to begin an identifier; for example, some may allow a leading digit, and others may not. Thus, it's also best to begin each signal name with a letter. Some or perhaps even all of the tools you use may also allow a leading underscore. But such signal names may, by convention, have special meaning or significance in some environments; for example, they may be used for signal names that are made up by the compiler or synthesizer. So, it is still best to begin your own signal names with letters.

There is also the issue of case for letters—upper or lower. In some HDLs (ABEL and Verilog), case is significant—`sig`, `Sig`, and `SIG` are three different signals. In others (VHDL), it is not. So, it's best not to define multiple signal names that differ only in case; the distinction may be lost on some designers.

There's another aspect to the use of case, as it affects the readability of programs. Historically, software programming languages have used several different case conventions to distinguish different language elements. The most popular convention in HDL programming is to use UPPERCASE for constants and other definitions, `lowercase` for signal names, and `color` for reserved words. The use of color is easy because typical modern, programming-language aware text editors automatically recognize reserved words and put them in color. In fact, they typically also recognize the syntax for comments and put them into a different color.

JUST IN CASE   We use a couple of case conventions in this book, just to keep you flexible. In program listings, we use `lowercase color` for reserved words. We normally give signal names in UPPERCASE in small examples typically with accompanying logic equations or schematics that also have signal names in UPPERCASE. Later in the book, we'll have some larger HDL examples that have signal names in `lowercase`—as is typical in industry for Verilog and VHDL programs—and we may define constant names in UPPERCASE.

We've shown many examples of using the suffix "_L" to denote an active-low signal. But now if you consider the use of lowercase signal names, this suffix loses a bit of its appeal because the need either to shift when typing the suffix or to suffer eyestrain to distinguish between "_l" and "_1". So, some design environments may use a different suffix, such as "_n", to denote an active-low signal.

Some design environments may have conventions for additional suffixes, before or after the active-level suffix, to convey additional information. For example, suffixes "_1", "_2", and so on, might be used to name multiple copies of a signal that has been replicated for fanout purposes.

Signal names that are used in an HDL program have limited "scope," just like variables in a software programming language. So, it's possible for the same signal name to be reused in multiple modules, and for it to denote completely independent signals. Just as in software programs, though, one must be careful.

In large projects with multiple hardware designers, it's difficult to ensure that designers use unique names for commonly needed functions. For example, each module may have a reset input signal named "reset". So, large projects may adopt a convention to guarantee signal-name uniqueness. Each high-level module is assigned a short, two- or three-letter designator corresponding to the module name (e.g., "sam" for "ShiftAddMultiplier"). All signals connected to the module use its designator as a prefix (e.g., "sam_reset").

CHOOSING CONVENTIONS The bottom line for all this is that there are many good signal-naming conventions, and you should follow the particular ones that have been established in your current environment, so that your designs will be maintainable by you and by others in the long term.

6.1.7 Drawing Layout

Logic diagrams and schematics should be drawn with gates in their "normal" orientation with inputs on the left and outputs on the right. The logic symbols for larger-scale logic elements are also normally drawn with inputs on the left and outputs on the right.

A complete schematic page should be drawn with system inputs on the left and outputs on the right, and the general flow of signals should be from left to right. If an input or output appears in the middle of a page, it should be extended to the left or right edge, respectively. In this way, a reader can find all inputs and outputs by looking at the edges of the page only. All signal paths on the page should be connected when possible; paths may be broken if the drawing gets crowded, but breaks should be flagged in both directions, as described later.

Sometimes block diagrams are drawn without crossing lines for a neater appearance, but this is never done in logic diagrams. Instead, lines are allowed to cross and connections are indicated clearly with a dot. Still, some computer-

Figure 6-13
Line crossings and
connections.

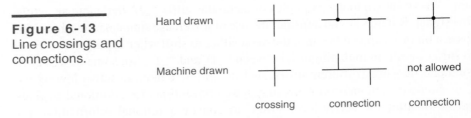

aided design systems (and some designers) can't draw legible connection dots. To distinguish between crossing lines and connected lines, they adopt the convention that only "T"-type connections are allowed, as shown in Figure 6-13. This is a good convention to follow in any case.

Schematics that fit on a single page are the easiest to work with. The largest practical paper size for a schematic might be E-size (34"×44"). Although its drawing capacity is great, such a large paper size is unwieldy to work with. The best compromise of drawing capacity and practicality is B-size (11"×17"). It can be easily folded for storage and quick reference in standard 3-ring notebooks, and it can be copied on most office copiers. Regardless of paper size, schematics come out best when the page is used in landscape format, that is, with its long dimension oriented from left to right, the direction of most signal flow.

Schematics that don't fit on a single page should be broken up into individual pages in a way that minimizes the connections (and confusion) between pages. They may also use a coordinate system, like that of a road map, to flag the sources and destinations of signals that travel from one page to another. An out-

signal flags

Figure 6-14 Flat schematic structure.

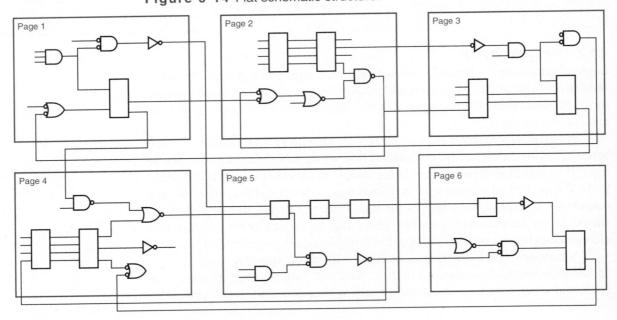

going signal should have flags referring to all of the destinations of that signal, while an incoming signal should have a flag referring to the source only. That is, an incoming signal should be flagged to the place where it is generated, not to a place somewhere in the middle of a chain of destinations that use the signal.

A multiple-page schematic usually has a "flat" structure. As shown in Figure 6-14, each page is carved out from the complete schematic and can connect to any other page as if all the pages were on one large sheet.

flat schematic structure

Much like programs, schematics can also be constructed hierarchically, as illustrated in Figure 6-15. In this approach, the "top-level" schematic is just a single page that may take the place of a block diagram. Typically, the top-level schematic contains no gates or other logic elements; it only shows blocks corresponding to the major subsystems, and their interconnections. The blocks or subsystems are in turn defined on lower-level pages, which may contain ordinary gate-level descriptions, or which may themselves use blocks defined in lower-level hierarchies. If a particular lower-level hierarchy needs to be used more than once, it may be reused (instantiated, or "called" in the programming sense) multiple times by the higher-level pages.

hierarchical schematic structure

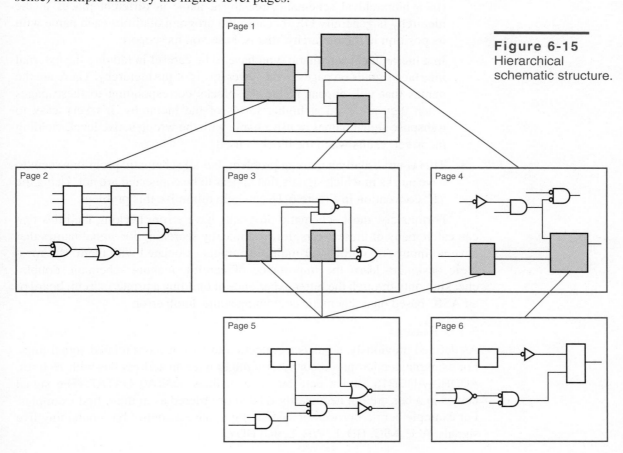

Figure 6-15
Hierarchical schematic structure.

HDLs such as Verilog and VHDL also support hierarchical design; for example, a module can instantiate another module. In a hierarchical design, it's possible for some modules (or "hierarchical schematic pages") to be specified by gate-level logic diagrams, while others are specified by HDL programs. In such a "mixed" environment, a given schematic page may contain gates, other MSI and LSI hardware components, and blocks that represent HDL modules or other schematic pages.

Most computer-aided logic design environments support both flat and hierarchical schematics. As in HDLs, proper signal naming is very important in both styles, since there are a number of common errors that can occur:

- Like any other program, a schematic-entry program does what you say, not what you mean. If you use slightly different names for what you intend to be the same signal on different pages, they won't be connected.

- Conversely, if you inadvertently use the same name for different signals on different pages of a flat schematic, many programs will dutifully connect them together, even if you haven't connected them with an off-page flag. (In a hierarchical schematic, reusing a name at different places in the hierarchy is generally OK, because the program qualifies each name with its position in the hierarchy, that is, based on its scope.)

- In a hierarchical schematic, you have to be careful in naming the external interface signals on pages in the lower levels of the hierarchy. These are the names that will appear inside the blocks corresponding to these pages when they are used at higher levels of the hierarchy. It's very easy to transpose signal names or use a name with the wrong active level, yielding incorrect results when the block is used.

- This is not usually a naming problem, but all schematic programs seem to have quirks in which signals that appear to be connected are not. Using the "T" convention in Figure 6-13 can help minimize this problem.

Fortunately, most schematic programs have error-checking facilities that can catch many of these errors, for example, by searching for signal names that have no inputs, no outputs, or multiple outputs associated with them. But most logic designers learn the importance of careful, manual schematic double-checking only through the bitter experience of building a printed-circuit board or an ASIC based on a schematic containing some dumb error.

6.1.8 Buses

As defined previously, a bus is a collection of two or more related signal lines. For example, a microprocessor system might have an address bus with 16 lines, ADDR0–ADDR15, and a data bus with 8 lines, DATA0–DATA7. The signal names in a bus are not necessarily related or ordered as in these first examples. For example, a microprocessor system might have a control bus containing five signals, ALE, MIO, RD_L, WR_L, and RDY.

Logic diagrams use special notation for buses to reduce the amount of drawing and to improve readability. As shown in Figure 6-16, a bus has its own descriptive name, such as ADDR[15:0], DATA[7:0], or CONTROL. A bus name might use brackets and a colon to denote a range. Buses may be drawn with different or thicker lines than ordinary signals. Individual signals are put into or pulled out of the bus by connecting an ordinary signal line to the bus and writing the signal name. Often a special connection dot is also used, as in the example. Different environments may use different conventions.

A computer-aided design system keeps track of the individual signals in a bus. When it actually comes time to build a circuit from the schematic, signal lines in a bus are treated just as though they had all been drawn individually.

The symbols at the righthand edge of Figure 6-16 are interpage signal flags. They indicate that LA goes out to page 2, DB is bidirectional and connects to page 2, and CONTROL is bidirectional and connects to pages 2 and 3.

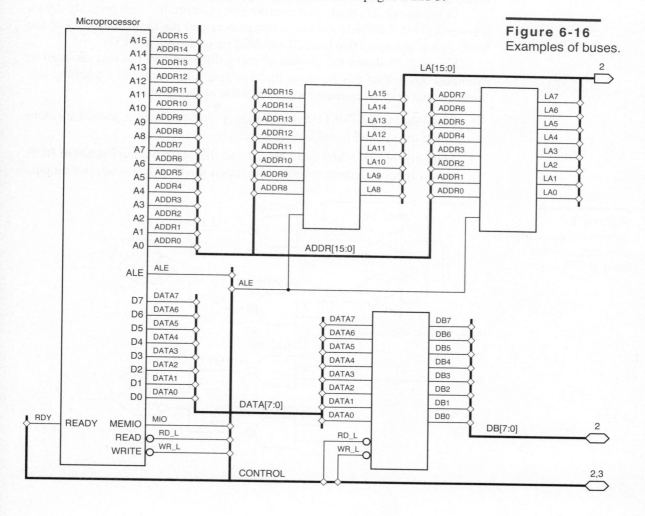

Figure 6-16
Examples of buses.

6.1.9 Additional Schematic Information

IC type

Complete schematic diagrams indicate IC types, reference designators, and pin numbers, as in Figure 6-17. The *IC type* is a part number identifying the integrated circuit that performs a given logic function. For example, a 2-input NAND gate might be identified as a 74HCT00 or a 74LS00. In addition to the logic function, the IC type identifies the device's logic family and speed.

reference designator

The *reference designator* for an IC identifies a particular instance of that IC type installed in the system. In conjunction with the system's mechanical documentation, the reference designator allows a particular IC to be located during assembly, test, and maintenance of the system. Traditionally, reference designators for ICs begin with the letter U (for "unit").

pin number

Once a particular IC is located, *pin numbers* are used to locate individual logic signals on its pins. The pin numbers are written near the corresponding inputs and outputs of the standard logic symbol, as shown in Figure 6-17.

In the rest of this book, just to make you comfortable with properly drawn schematics, we'll include reference designators and pin numbers for all of the logic-circuit examples that use SSI and MSI parts, as well as PLDs.

Figure 6-18 shows the pinouts of many different SSI ICs that are used in examples throughout this book, or that you might encounter in a teaching lab. Some special graphic elements appear in a few of the symbols:

- Symbols for the 74x14 Schmitt-trigger inverter have a special element inside the symbol to indicate hysteresis.

- Symbols for the 74x03 quad NAND and the 74x266 quad Exclusive NOR have a special element to indicate an open-drain or open-collector output.

Figure 6-17
Schematic diagram for a circuit using several SSI parts.

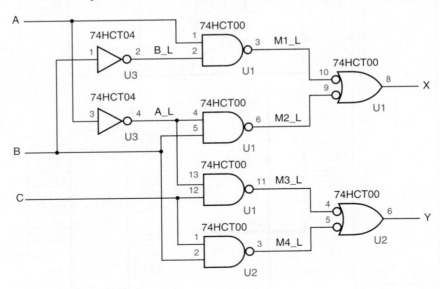

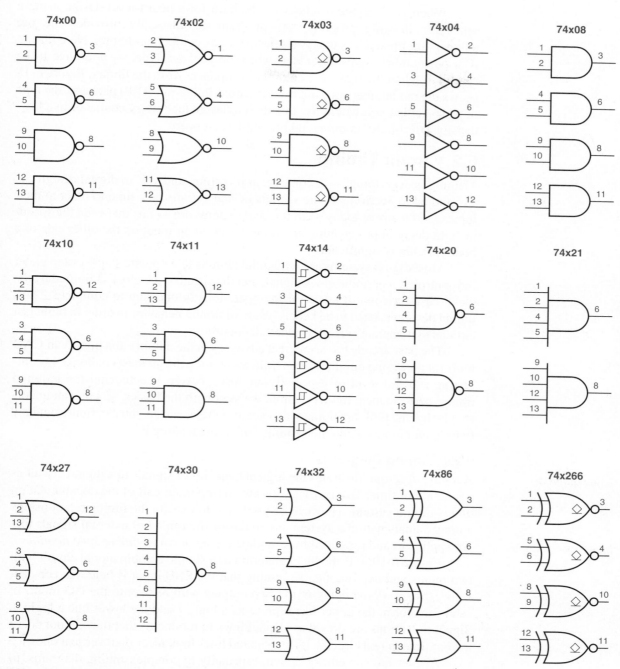

Figure 6-18 Pinouts for SSI ICs in standard dual-inline packages.

When you prepare a schematic diagram for a board-level design using a schematic drawing program, the program automatically provides the pin numbers for the devices that you select from its component library. Note that an IC's pin numbers may differ depending on package type, so you have to be careful to select the right version of the component from the library. Figure 6-18 shows the pin numbers that are used in a dual-inline-pin (DIP) package, the type of package that you would use in a digital design laboratory course or in a low-density, "thru-hole" commercial printed-circuit board.

6.2 Circuit Timing

"Timing is everything"—in comedy, in investing, and yes, in digital design. As we studied in Section 3.6, the outputs of real circuits take time to react to their inputs, and many of today's circuits and systems are so fast that even the speed-of-light delay in propagating an output signal to an input on the other side of a board or chip is significant.

Most digital systems are sequential circuits that operate step-by-step under the control of a periodic clock signal, and the speed of the clock is limited by the worst-case time that it takes for the operations in one step to complete. Thus, digital designers need to be keenly aware of timing behavior in order to build fast circuits that operate correctly under all conditions.

The past decade has seen great advances in the number and quality of CAD tools for analyzing circuit timing. Still, quite often the greatest challenge in completing a board-level or especially an ASIC design is achieving the required timing performance. In this section, we start with the basics, so you can understand what the tools are doing when you use them, and so you can figure out how to fix your circuits when their timing isn't quite making it.

6.2.1 Timing Diagrams

timing diagram

A *timing diagram* illustrates the logical behavior of signals in a digital circuit as a function of time. Timing diagrams are an important part of the documentation of any digital system. They can be used both to explain the timing relationships among signals within a system and to define the timing of external signals that

timing specifications

are applied to and produced by a module (also known as *timing specifications*).

Figure 6-19(a) is the block diagram of a simple combinational circuit with two inputs and two outputs. Assuming that the ENB input is held at a constant value, (b) shows the delay of the two outputs with respect to the GO input. In each waveform, the upper line represents a logic 1 and the lower line a logic 0. Signal transitions are drawn as slanted lines to remind us that they do not occur in zero time in real circuits. (Also, slanted lines look nicer than vertical ones.)

causality

Arrows are sometimes drawn, especially in complex timing diagrams, to show *causality*—which input transitions cause which output transitions. In any case, the most important information provided by a timing diagram is a

delay

specification of the *delay* between transitions.

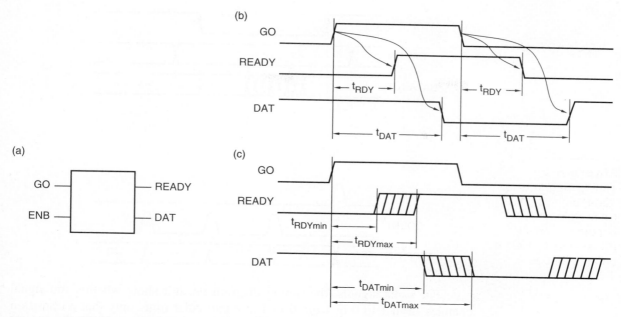

Figure 6-19 Timing diagrams for a combinational circuit: (a) block diagram of circuit; (b) causality and propagation delay; (c) minimum and maximum delays.

Different paths through a circuit may have different delays. For example, Figure 6-19(b) shows that the delay from GO to READY is shorter than the delay from GO to DAT. Similarly, the delays from the ENB input to the outputs may vary, and could be shown in another timing diagram. And, as we'll discuss later, the delay through any given path may vary depending on whether the output is changing from LOW to HIGH or from HIGH to LOW (this phenomenon is not shown in the figure).

Delay in a real circuit is normally measured between the centerpoints of transitions, so the delays in a timing diagram are marked this way. A single timing diagram may contain many different delay specifications. Each different delay is marked with a different identifier, such as t_{RDY} and t_{DAT} in the figure. In large timing diagrams, the delay identifiers are usually numbered for easier reference (e.g., $t_1, t_2, \ldots, t_{42}$). In either case, the timing diagram is normally accompanied by a *timing table* that specifies each delay amount and the conditions under which it applies.

timing table

Since the delays of real digital components can vary depending on voltage, temperature, and manufacturing parameters, delay is seldom specified as a single number. Instead, a timing table may specify a range of values by giving *minimum*, *typical*, and *maximum* values for each delay. The idea of a range of delays is sometimes carried over into the timing diagram itself by showing the transitions to occur at uncertain times, as in Figure 6-19(c).

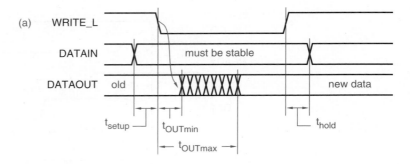

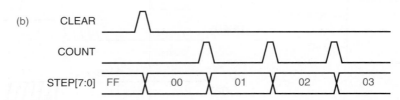

Figure 6-20
Timing diagrams for
"data" signals:
(a) certain and
uncertain transitions;
(b) sequence of values
on an 8-bit bus.

For some signals, the timing diagram needn't show whether the signal changes from 1 to 0 or from 0 to 1 at a particular time, only that a transition occurs then. Any signal that carries a bit of "data" has this characteristic—the actual value of the data bit varies according to circumstances but, regardless of value, the bit is transferred, stored, or processed at a particular time relative to "control" signals in the system. Figure 6-20(a) is a timing diagram that illustrates this concept. The "data" signal is normally at a steady 0 or 1 value, and transitions occur only at the times indicated. The idea of an uncertain delay time can also be used with "data" signals, as shown for the DATAOUT signal.

Quite often in digital systems, a group of data signals in a bus is processed by identical circuits. In this case, all signals in the bus have the same timing, and they can be represented by a single line in the timing diagram and corresponding specifications in the timing table. If the bus bits are known to take on a particular combination at a particular time, this is sometimes shown in the timing diagram using binary, octal, or hexadecimal numbers, as in Figure 6-20(b).

6.2.2 Propagation Delay

propagation delay

In Section 3.6.2 we formally defined the *propagation delay* of a signal path as the time that it takes for a change at the input of the path to produce a change at the output of the path. A combinational circuit with many inputs and outputs has many different paths, and each one may have a different propagation delay. Also, the propagation delay when the output changes from LOW to HIGH (t_{pLH}) may be different from the delay when it changes from HIGH to LOW (t_{pHL}).

The manufacturer of a combinational-logic IC normally specifies all of these different propagation delays, or at least the delays that would be of interest in typical applications. A logic designer who combines ICs in a larger circuit uses the individual device specifications to analyze the overall circuit timing. The delay of a path through the overall circuit is the sum of the delays through subpaths in the individual devices.

6.2.3 Timing Specifications

The timing specification for a device may give minimum, typical, and maximum values for each propagation-delay path and transition direction:

- *Maximum.* This specification is the one that is most often used by experi- *maximum delay*
  enced designers, since a path "never" has a propagation delay longer than
  the maximum. However, the definition of "never" varies among logic
  families and manufacturers. For example, "maximum" propagation delays
  of 74LS and 74S TTL devices are specified with $V_{CC} = 5$ V, $T_A = 25°C$, and
  almost no capacitive load. If the voltage or temperature is different, or if
  the capacitive load is more than 15 pF, the delay may be longer. On the
  other hand, a "maximum" propagation delay is specified for 74AC and
  74ACT devices over the full operating voltage and temperature range and
  with a heavier capacitive load of 50 pF.

- *Typical.* This specification is the one most often used by designers who *typical delay*
  don't expect to be around when their product leaves the friendly environment of the engineering lab and is shipped to customers. The "typical"
  delay is what you see from a device that was manufactured on a good day
  and is operating under near-ideal conditions.

- *Minimum.* This is the smallest propagation delay that a path will ever *minimum delay*
  exhibit. Most well-designed circuits don't depend on this number; that is,
  they will work properly even if the delay is zero. That's good, because
  manufacturers don't specify minimum delay in most moderate-speed logic
  families, including 74LS and 74S TTL. However, in high-speed families,
  including ECL and 74AC and 74ACT CMOS, a nonzero minimum delay
  is specified to help the designer ensure that hold-time requirements of
  latches and flip-flops, discussed in Section 7.2, are met.

Table 6-2 lists the typical and maximum delays of several 74-series CMOS and TTL gates. Table 6-3 does the same thing for most of the CMOS and TTL MSI parts that are introduced later in this chapter.

HOW TYPICAL IS TYPICAL?	Most ICs, perhaps 99%, really are manufactured on "good" days and exhibit delays near the "typical" specifications. However, if you design a system that works only if all of its 100 ICs meet the "typical" timing specs, probability theory suggests that 63% $(1 - .99^{100})$ of the systems won't work. But see the next box ….

Table 6-2 Propagation delay in nanoseconds of selected 5-V CMOS and TTL SSI parts.

Part Number	74HCT Typical t_{pLH}, t_{pHL}	74HCT Maximum t_{pLH}, t_{pHL}	74AHCT Typical t_{pLH}	74AHCT Typical t_{pHL}	74AHCT Maximum t_{pLH}	74AHCT Maximum t_{pHL}	74LS Typical t_{pLH}	74LS Typical t_{pHL}	74LS Maximum t_{pLH}	74LS Maximum t_{pHL}
'00, '10	11	35	5.5	5.5	9.0	9.0	9	10	15	15
'02	9	29	3.4	4.5	8.5	8.5	10	10	15	15
'04	11	35	5.5	5.5	8.5	8.5	9	10	15	15
'08, '11	11	35	5.5	5.5	9.0	9.0	8	10	15	20
'14	16	48	5.5	5.5	9.0	9.0	15	15	22	22
'20	11	35					9	10	15	15
'21	11	35					8	10	15	20
'27	9	29	5.6	5.6	9.0	9.0	10	10	15	15
'30	11	35					8	13	15	20
'32	9	30	5.3	5.3	8.5	8.5	14	14	22	22
'86 (2 levels)	13	40	5.5	5.5	10	10	12	10	23	17
'86 (3 levels)	13	40	5.5	5.5	10	10	20	13	30	22

A COROLLARY OF MURPHY'S LAW

Murphy's law states, "If something can go wrong, it will." A corollary to this is, "If you want something to go wrong, it won't."

In the boxed example on the previous page, you might think that you have a 63% chance of detecting the potential timing problems in the engineering lab. The problems aren't spread out evenly, though, since all ICs from a given batch tend to behave about the same. Murphy's corollary says that *all* of the engineering prototypes will be built with ICs from the same, "good" batches. Therefore, everything works fine for a while, just long enough for the system to get into volume production and for everyone to become complacent and self-congratulatory.

Then, unbeknownst to the manufacturing department, a "slow" batch of some IC type arrives from a supplier and gets used in every system that is built, so that *nothing* works. The manufacturing engineers scurry around trying to analyze the problem (not easy, because the designer is long gone and didn't bother to write a circuit description), and in the meantime the company loses big bucks because it is unable to ship its product.

Table 6-3 Propagation delay in nanoseconds of selected CMOS and TTL MSI parts.

Part	From	To	74HCT Typ. t_{pLH}, t_{pHL}	74HCT Max. t_{pLH}, t_{pHL}	74AHCT Typ. t_{pLH}, t_{pHL}	74AHCT Max. t_{pLH}, t_{pHL}	74FCT Typ. t_{pLH}, t_{pHL}	74FCT Max. t_{pLH}, t_{pHL}	74LS Typ. t_{pLH}	74LS Typ. t_{pHL}	74LS Max. t_{pLH}	74LS Max. t_{pHL}
'138	any select	output (2)	23	45	8.1	13	5	9	11	18	20	41
	any select	output (3)	23	45	8.1	13	5	9	21	20	27	39
	$\overline{G2A}, \overline{G2B}$	output	22	42	7.5	12	4	8	12	20	18	32
	G1	output	22	42	7.1	11.5	4	8	14	13	26	38
'139	any select	output (2)	14	43	6.5	10.5	5	9	13	22	20	33
	any select	output (3)	14	43	6.5	10.5	5	9	18	25	29	38
	enable	output	11	43	5.9	9.5	5	9	16	21	24	32
'151	any select	Y	17	51			5	9	27	18	43	30
	any select	$\overline{Y}$	18	54			5	9	14	20	23	32
	any data	Y	16	48			4	7	20	16	32	26
	any data	$\overline{Y}$	15	45			4	7	13	12	21	20
	enable	Y	12	36			4	7	26	20	42	32
	enable	$\overline{Y}$	15	45			4	7	15	18	24	30
'153	any select	output	14	43			5	9	19	25	29	38
	any data	output	12	43			4	7	10	17	15	26
	enable	output	11	34			4	7	16	21	24	32
'157	select	output	15	46	6.8	11.5	7	10.5	15	18	23	27
	any data	output	12	38	5.6	9.5	4	6	9	9	14	14
	enable	output	12	38	7.1	12.0	7	10.5	13	14	21	23
'182	any $\overline{Gi}, \overline{Pi}$	C1–3	13	41					4.5	4.5	7	7
	any $\overline{Gi}, \overline{Pi}$	$\overline{G}$	13	41					5	7	7.5	10.5
	any $\overline{Pi}$	$\overline{P}$	11	35					4.5	6.5	6.5	10
	C0	C1–3	17	50					6.5	7	10	10.5
'280	any input	EVEN	18	53			6	10	33	29	50	45
	any input	ODD	19	56			6	10	23	31	35	50
'283	C0	any Si	22	66					16	15	24	24
	any Ai, Bi	any Si	21	61					15	15	24	24
	C0	C4	19	58					11	11	17	22
	any Ai, Bi	C4	20	60					11	12	17	17
'381	CIN	any Fi							18	14	27	21
	any Ai, Bi	$\overline{G}$							20	21	30	33
	any Ai, Bi	$\overline{P}$							21	33	23	33
	any Ai, Bi	any Fi							20	15	30	23
	any select	any Fi							35	34	53	51
	any select	$\overline{G}, \overline{P}$							31	32	47	48
'682	any Pi	$\overline{PEQQ}$	26	69			7	11	13	15	25	25
	any Qi	$\overline{PEQQ}$	26	69			7	11	14	15	25	25
	any Pi	$\overline{PGTQ}$	26	69			9	14	20	15	30	30
	any Qi	$\overline{PGTQ}$	26	69			9	14	21	19	30	30

ESTIMATING MINIMUM DELAYS	If the minimum delay of an IC is not specified, a conservative designer assumes that it has a minimum delay of zero.

Some circuits won't work if the propagation delay actually goes to zero, but the cost of modifying a circuit to handle the zero-delay case may be unreasonable, especially since this case is expected never to occur. To obtain a design that always works under "reasonable" conditions, logic designers often estimate that ICs have minimum delays of one-fourth to one-third of their published *typical* delays. |

All inputs of an SSI gate have the same propagation delay to the output. Note that TTL outputs usually have different delays for LOW-to-HIGH and HIGH-to-LOW transitions (and separate t_{pLH} and t_{pHL} columns in Tables 6-2 and 6-3), but CMOS outputs usually do not. CMOS outputs have a more symmetrical output driving capability, so any difference between the two cases is usually not worth noting, and a combined t_{pLH},t_{pHL} column appears in the tables.

The delay from an input transition to the corresponding output transition depends on the internal path taken by the changing signal, and in larger circuits the path may be different for different input combinations. For example, the 74LS86 2-input XOR gate is constructed from four NAND gates as shown in Figure 6-68 on page 447, and has two different-length paths from either input to the output. If one input is LOW, and the other is changed, the change propagates through two NAND gates, and we observe the first set of delays shown in Table 6-2. If one input is HIGH, and the other is changed, the change propagates through *three* NAND gates internally, and we observe the second set of delays. Similar behavior is exhibited by the 74LS138 and 74LS139 in Table 6-3.

worst-case delay

To permit a simplified "worst-case" analysis, designers often use a single *worst-case delay* specification that is the maximum of t_{pLH} and t_{pHL} specifications. The worst-case delay through a circuit is then computed as the sum of the worst-case delays through the individual components, independent of the transition direction and other circuit conditions. This may give an overly pessimistic view of the overall circuit delay, but it saves design time and it always works.

Most CMOS MSI and larger parts do not show different specifications for t_{pLH} and t_{pHL}; any difference is typically small enough to be ignored. Thus, the HCT, AHCT, and FCT columns in Table 6-3 give one number that applies to both transition directions.

6.2.4 Timing Analysis

To accurately analyze the timing of a circuit containing more than a few gates and other components, a designer may have to study its logical behavior in excruciating detail. For example, when TTL inverting gates (NAND, NOR, etc.) are placed in series, a LOW-to-HIGH change at one gate's output causes a HIGH-to-LOW change at the next one's, and so the differences between t_{pLH} and t_{pHL} tend to average out. On the other hand, when noninverting gates (AND, OR, etc.) are placed in series, a transition causes all outputs to change in the same direction, and so the gap between t_{pLH} and t_{pHL} tends to widen. As a reader, you'll have the privilege of carrying out this sort of analysis in Drills 6.9–6.15.

Even when a single worst-case delay spec can be used for both transition directions, a moderate-size circuit can have many different paths from a set of input signals to a set of output signals. To determine the minimum and maximum delays through the circuit, you must look at every possible path (and you'll get to do this in Drill 6.17). Thus, for large circuits, analysis of all of the different delay paths is practical only with the assistance of automated tools.

6.2.5 Timing Analysis Tools

CAD environments for logic design include component libraries that typically contain not only the logic symbols and functional models for various logic elements, but also their timing models. A simulator allows you to apply input sequences and observe how and when outputs are produced in response. You typically can control whether minimum, typical, maximum, or some combination of delay values are used.

Timing is important enough that it is a fundamental capability of the HDLs Verilog and VHDL. As we showed in Chapter 5, these languages have facilities for specifying expected delay at the component or module level. And simulators for these languages can use these specifications to determine the overall delay from an input change to the circuit's outputs.

Even with a simulator, you're not off the hook, though. It's up to the designer to supply the input sequences for which the simulator should produce outputs, for example, using a test bench. Thus, you'll need to have a good feel for what to look for and how to stimulate your circuit to produce and observe the worst-case delays.

Instead of using a simulator and supplying your own input sequences, you can use a *timing analysis program* (or *timing analyzer*). Based on the topology of a synthesized circuit, such a program can automatically find all possible delay paths and print out a sorted list of them, starting with the slowest. These results may be overly pessimistic, however, as some paths may not actually be used in normal operation of the circuit; the designer must still use some intelligence to interpret the results properly.

timing-analysis
program
timing analyzer

Also, timing may have to be examined during two or more stages of project development, especially if the design will be realized in a CPLD, an FPGA, or an ASIC. This is true whether the design is done using schematics at the gate and block level or using an HDL.

In the early stages of a design, it's easy enough for the timing analyzer to estimate worst-case path delays in a preliminary realization by finding all the signal paths and adding up the known delays of individual logic elements. However, the final circuit realization is not determined until later in the design, when the complete design is fitted into a CPLD or FPGA, or physically laid out in a ASIC. At that time, other elements of delay will appear, due to capacitive loads, larger buffers inserted to handle heavier-than-expected loads, signal propagation on long wires, and other differences between estimates made in the early stages and the actual synthesized circuit.

On the first try, the timing results for the "final" synthesized circuit may not meet the design's requirements—the circuit may be too slow, or parts of it may be too fast, such that flip-flops' hold-time requirements are not met (in which case, the circuit will not work even at slow speeds; see Section 7.2). As a result, the designer must change parts of the circuit, adding or changing buffers and other components, reworking the internal design of individual modules to get better timing performance, changing signaling between modules, or even talking to the boss about relaxing the performance goals for the project (this is a last resort!). Then, the circuit must be resynthesized and the timing results must be checked again, and the process must be repeated until the performance goals

timing closure

are met. This is called *timing closure* and can take several months in large ASIC projects.

6.3 Combinational PLDs

6.3.1 Programmable Logic Arrays

programmable logic array (PLA)

Historically, the first PLDs were *programmable logic arrays (PLAs)*, and they form an important basis for understanding today's PLDs. A PLA is simply a combinational, two-level AND-OR device that can be programmed to realize any sum-of-products logic expression, subject to the size limitations of the device. Limitations are

inputs
outputs

product terms

- the number of inputs (n),
- the number of outputs (m), and
- the number of product terms (p).

We might describe such a device as "an $n \times m$ PLA with p product terms." In general, p is far less than the number of n-variable minterms (2^n). Thus, a PLA cannot perform arbitrary n-input, m-output logic functions; its usefulness is limited to functions that can be expressed in sum-of-products form using p or fewer product terms.

An $n \times m$ PLA with p product terms contains p $2n$-input AND gates and m p-input OR gates. Figure 6-21 shows a small PLA with four inputs, six AND gates, and three OR gates and outputs. Each input connects to a buffer/inverter that produces both a true and a complemented version of the signal for use

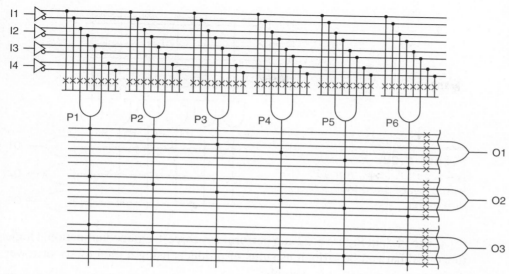

Figure 6-21 A 4 × 3 PLA with six product terms.

within the array. Potential connections in the array are indicated by X's; the device is programmed by keeping only the connections that are actually needed. The selected connections are made by *fuses*, which typically are not actually *PLA fuses* fuses, but are nonvolatile memory cells that can be programmed to make a connection or not, as we'll explain in Section 6.3.5. Thus, each AND gate's inputs can be any subset of the primary input signals and their complements. Similarly, each OR gate's inputs can be any subset of the AND-gate outputs.

As shown in Figure 6-22, a more compact diagram can be used to represent a PLA. Moreover, the layout of this diagram more closely resembles the actual *PLA diagram* internal layout of a PLA chip (e.g., Figure 6-29 on page 380).

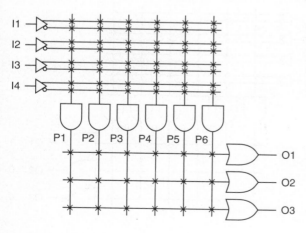

Figure 6-22
Compact representation of a 4 × 3 PLA with six product terms.

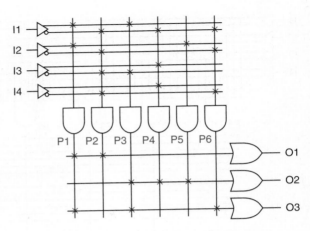

Figure 6-23
A 4 × 3 PLA programmed
with a set of three logic
equations.

The PLA in Figure 6-22 can perform any three 4-input combinational logic functions that can be written as sums of products using a total of six or fewer distinct product terms, for example:

$$O1 = I1 \cdot I2 + I1' \cdot I2' \cdot I3' \cdot I4'$$
$$O2 = I1 \cdot I3' + I1' \cdot I3 \cdot I4 + I2$$
$$O3 = I1 \cdot I2 + I1 \cdot I3' + I1' \cdot I2' \cdot I4'$$

These equations have a total of eight product terms, but the first two terms in the O3 equation are the same as the first terms in the O1 and O2 equations. The programmed connection pattern in Figure 6-23 matches these logic equations.

PLA constant outputs   Sometimes a PLA output must be programmed to be a constant 1 or a constant 0. That's no problem, as shown in Figure 6-24. Product term P1 is always 1 because its product line is connected to no inputs and is therefore always pulled HIGH; this constant-1 term drives the O1 output. No product term

Figure 6-24
A 4 × 3 PLA
programmed to
produce constant
0 and 1 outputs.

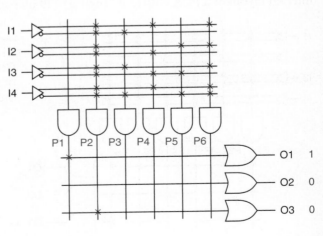

AN UNLIKELY GLITCH	Theoretically, if *all* of the input variables in Figure 6-24 change *simultaneously*, the output of product term P2 could have a brief 0-1-0 glitch. This is highly unlikely in typical applications and is impossible if one input happens to be unused and is connected to a constant logic signal.

drives the O2 output, which is therefore always 0. Another method of obtaining a constant-0 output is shown for O3. Product term P2 is connected to each input variable and its complement; therefore, it's always 0 ($X \cdot X' = 0$).

Our example PLA has too few inputs, outputs, and AND gates (product terms) to be very useful. An *n*-input PLA could conceivably use as many as 2^n product terms, to realize all possible *n*-variable minterms. The actual number of product terms in typical commercial PLAs is far fewer, on the order of 4 to 16 per output, regardless of the value of *n*.

The Signetics 82S100 was a typical example of the PLAs that were introduced in the mid-1970s. It had 16 inputs, 48 AND gates, and 8 outputs. Thus, it had $2 \times 16 \times 48 = 1536$ fuses in the AND array and $8 \times 48 = 384$ in the OR array. Off-the-shelf PLAs like the 82S100 have since been supplanted by GALs, CPLDs, and FPGAs, but custom PLAs are often synthesized to perform complex combinational logic within a larger ASIC.

6.3.2 Programmable Array Logic Devices

A special case of a PLA, and the basis of today's most commonly used PLDs, is the *programmable array logic (PAL) device*. Unlike a PLA, in which both the AND and OR arrays are programmable, a PAL device has a *fixed* OR array.

programmable array logic (PAL) device

The first PAL devices used TTL-compatible bipolar technology and were introduced in the late 1970s. Key innovations in the first PAL devices, besides the introduction of a catchy acronym, were the use of a fixed OR array and bidirectional input/output pins.

FRIENDS AND FOES	PAL is a registered trademark of Advanced Micro Devices, Inc. Like other trademarks, it should be used only as an adjective. Use it as a noun or without a trademark notice at your own peril, as I learned in a letter from AMD's lawyers in February, 1989. Since then, I have suggested that to get around AMD's trademark you should use a descriptive name that is more indicative of the device's internal structure: a *fixed-OR element (FOE)*.

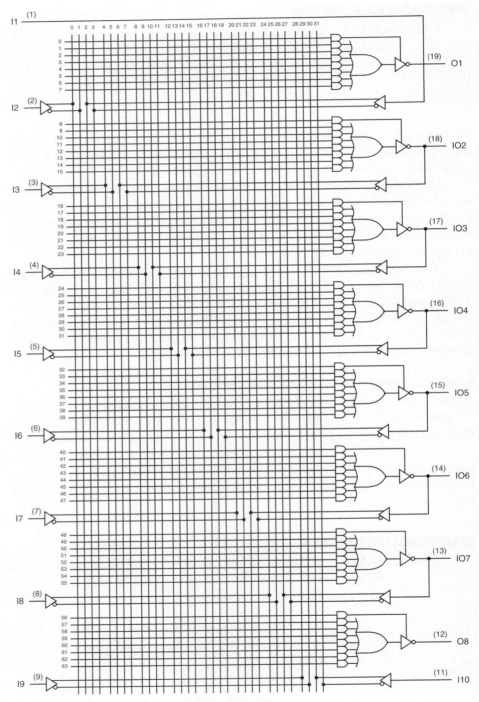

Figure 6-25 Logic diagram of the PAL16L8.

These ideas are well illustrated by the *PAL16L8*, shown in Figures 6-25 and 6-26 and one of today's most commonly used combinational PLD structures. Its programmable AND array has 64 rows and 32 columns, identified for programming purposes by the small numbers in the figure, and $64 \times 32 = 2048$ fuses. Each of the 64 AND gates in the array has 32 inputs, accommodating 16 variables and their complements. The device has up to 16 inputs and 8 outputs; hence the "8" and the "16" in "PAL16L8".

PAL16L8

Eight AND gates are associated with each output pin. Seven of them provide inputs to a fixed 7-input OR gate. The eighth, which we call the *output-enable gate*, is connected to the three-state enable input of the output buffer; the buffer is enabled only when the output-enable gate has a 1 output. Thus, an output of the PAL16L8 can perform only logic functions that can be written as sums of seven or fewer product terms. Each product term can be a function of any or all 16 inputs, but only seven such product terms are available.

output-enable gate

Although the PAL16L8 has up to 16 inputs and up to 8 outputs, it can be housed in a dual in-line package with only 20 pins, including two for power and ground (the corner pins, 10 and 20). This magic is the result of six bidirectional pins (13–18) that may be used as inputs or outputs or both. This and other differences between the PAL16L8 and a PLA structure are summarized below:

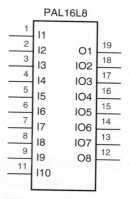

Figure 6-26
Logic symbol for the PAL16L8.

- The PAL16L8 has a fixed OR array, with seven AND gates permanently connected to each OR gate. AND-gate outputs cannot be shared; if a product term is needed by two OR gates, it must be generated twice.

- Each output of the PAL16L8 has an individual three-state output enable signal, controlled by a dedicated AND gate (the output-enable gate). Thus, outputs may be programmed as always enabled, always disabled, or enabled by a product term involving the device inputs.

- There is an inverter between the output of each OR gate and the external pin of the device.

- Six of the output pins, called *I/O pins*, may also be used as inputs. This provides many possibilities for using each I/O pin, depending on how the device is programmed:

  I/O pin

  - If an I/O pin's output-control gate produces a constant 0, then the output is always disabled and the pin is used strictly as an input.

  - If the input signal on an I/O pin is not used by any gates in the AND array, then the pin may be used strictly as an output. Depending on the programming of the output-enable gate, the output may always be enabled, or it may be enabled only for certain input conditions.

  - If an I/O pin's output-control gate produces a constant 1, then the output is always enabled, but the pin may still be used as an input too. In this way, outputs can be used to generate first-pass "helper terms" for logic functions that cannot be performed in a single pass with the

HOW USEFUL ARE SEVEN PRODUCT TERMS?

The worst-case logic function for two-level AND-OR design is an n-input XOR (parity) function, which requires 2^{n-1} product terms. However, less perverse functions with more than seven product terms of a PAL16L8 can often be built by decomposing them into a four-level structure (AND-OR-AND-OR) that can be realized with two passes through the AND-OR array. Unfortunately, besides using up PLD outputs for the first-pass "helper terms," this doubles the delay, since a first-pass input must pass through the PLD twice to propagate to the output.

limited number of AND terms available for a single output. We'll show an example of this case on page 395.

– In another case with an I/O pin always output enabled, the output may be used as an input to AND gates that affect the very same output. That is, we can embed a feedback sequential circuit in a PAL16L8. We'll discuss this case in Section 8.2.6.

PAL20L8

The *PAL20L8* is another combinational PLD similar to the PAL16L8, except that its package has four more input-only pins and each of its AND gates has eight more inputs to accommodate them. Its output structure is the same as the PAL16L8's.

COMBINATIONAL, NOT COMBINATORIAL!

A step *backward* in MMI's introduction of PAL devices was their use and popularization of the word "combinatorial" to describe combinational circuits. *Combinational* circuits have no memory—their output at any time depends on the current input *combination*. For well-rounded computer engineers, the word "combinatorial" should conjure up vivid images of binomial coefficients, problem-solving complexity, and computer-science-great Donald Knuth.

6.3.3 Generic Array Logic Devices

In Section 8.3 we'll introduce sequential PLDs, programmable logic devices that provide flip-flops at some or all OR-gate outputs. These devices can be programmed to perform a variety of useful sequential-circuit functions.

generic array logic
GAL device
GAL16V8

One type of sequential PLD, first introduced by Lattice Semiconductor, is called *generic array logic* or a *GAL device*, and is particularly popular. A single GAL device type, the *GAL16V8*, can be configured (via programming and a corresponding fuse pattern) to emulate the AND-OR, flip-flop, and output structure of any of a variety of combinational and sequential PAL devices, including the PAL16L8 that we described in the preceding subsection. What's more, the GAL device can be erased and reprogrammed. Its "fuses" are actually nonvolatile memory cells.

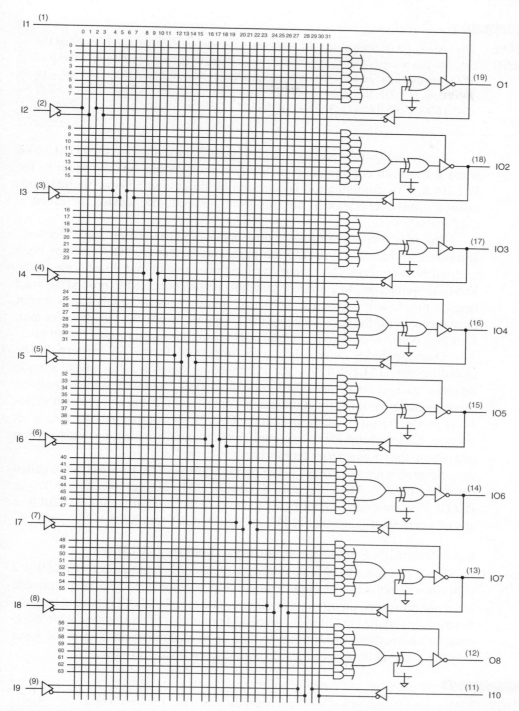

Figure 6-27 Logic diagram of the GAL16V8C.

Figure 6-27 on the previous page shows the logic diagram for a GAL16V8 when it has been configured as a strictly combinational device similar to the PAL16L8. This configuration is achieved by programming two "architecture-control" fuses, not shown. In this configuration, the device is called a *GAL16V8C*.

GAL16V8C

The most important thing to note about the GAL16V8C logic diagram, compared to that of a PAL16L8 on page 374, is that an XOR gate has been inserted between each OR output and the three-state output driver. One of the XOR's is "pulled up" to a logic 1 value but can be connected to ground (0) via a fuse. If this fuse is intact, the XOR gate simply passes the OR-gate's output unchanged, but if the fuse is blown, the XOR gate inverts the OR-gate's output. This fuse is said to control the *output polarity* of the corresponding output pin.

output polarity

Output-polarity control is a very important feature of modern PLDs, including the GAL16V8. As we discussed in Section 5.2.2, given a logic function to minimize, an ABEL compiler finds minimal sum-of-products expressions for both the function and its complement. If the complement yields fewer product terms, it can be used if the GAL16V8's output polarity fuse is set to invert. Unless overridden, the compiler automatically makes the best selection and sets up the fuse patterns appropriately.

PALCE16V8
GAL20V8
PALCE20V8

Several companies make a part that is equivalent to the GAL16V8, called the *PALCE16V8*. There is also a 24-pin GAL device, the *GAL20V8* or *PALCE20V8*, that can be configured to emulate the structure of the PAL20L8 or any of a variety of sequential PLDs, as described in Section 8.3.1.

6.3.4 Complex Programmable Logic Devices (CPLDs)

complex programmable logic device (CPLD)

As shown in Figure 6-28, a *complex programmable logic device (CPLD)* is a collection of individual PLDs on a single chip, accompanied by a programmable interconnection and input/output structure. The individual PLDs have at least the functionality of the GAL devices discussed previously. The programmable interconnect allows these PLDs to be hooked up to each other on-chip in the same way that a clever designer might do with discrete PLDs off-chip.

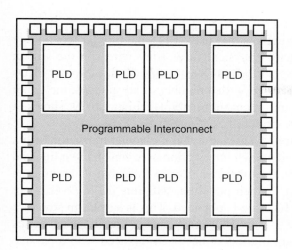

☐ = input/output block

Figure 6-28
General CPLD
architecture.

Different manufacturers have taken many different approaches to the general architecture shown in the figure. Areas in which they differ include features of the individual PLDs (AND array and macrocells), the input/output blocks, and the programmable interconnect, as we'll discuss in Section 9.5.

Before the advent of inexpensive CPLDs, it was common for designers to connect together a number of individual PLDs to realize a complex circuit function. Now, it is usually less expensive and certainly a lot easier to use a single CPLD to realize such functions. Starting with an HDL description of the desired function, a typical synthesis tool can "fit" the function into an available CPLD device, often the smallest possible.

The work of the synthesis tool, often called a *fitter*, includes more than just minimizing the equation for each PLD output, as an ABEL compiler would do when targeting a smaller design to a single PLD. The fitter also partitions the function into the individual PLD blocks, and then tries to find the smallest possible device that has enough PLD blocks, product terms, internal connections, and external input/output pins to realize the specified function.

CPLD fitter

Fitters are better than humans at "turning the crank" and keeping track of details, but they usually can't see "the big picture" for a complex design the way a human designer can. Therefore, fitters typically allow the designer to specify *constraints*, such as "put these outputs together in the same PLD block," to guide the fitter into a better result.

fitter constraints

Field-programmable gate arrays (FPGAs) are very similar to CPLDs in their applications and in the tools that are used to fit designs into them. But their internal structures are quite different—they aren't based on PLAs and PAL devices at all. We discuss FPGAs in detail in Section 9.6. For now, all you need to know is that complex functions can be targeted to either CPLDs and FPGAs, depending on size, performance, cost, and other constraints. The largest FPGAs are bigger than the largest CPLDs but have higher cost and lower performance.

*6.3.5 CMOS PLD Circuits

The earliest PLDs were PAL structures that used TTL-like bipolar technology and were programmed using actual physical fuses (tiny wires on the silicon chip), as described in Section BipolarPLD at DDPPonline. Today, bipolar PLDs have been supplanted by CMOS PLDs with a number of advantages, including reduced power consumption and reprogrammability. Figure 6-29 shows a CMOS design for the 4×3 PLA circuit of Section 6.3.1.

The PLA's programmability is achieved by an n-channel transistor with a programmable connection, placed at each intersection between an input line and a word line. If the input is LOW, then the transistor is "off," but if the input is HIGH, then the transistor is "on," which pulls the AND line LOW. Overall, an inverted-input AND (i.e., NOR) function is obtained. This is similar in structure and function to a normal CMOS k-input NOR gate, except that the usual series connection of k p-channel pull-up transistors has been replaced with a passive pull-up resistor (in practice, the pull-up is a single p-channel transistor with a constant bias).

As shown in color on Figure 6-29, the effects of using an *inverted*-input AND gate are canceled by using the opposite (complemented) input lines for each input, compared with Figure 6-22 on page 371. Also notice that the connection between the AND plane and the OR plane is noninverting, so the AND plane performs a true AND function.

The outputs of the first-level AND functions are combined in the OR plane by another set of NOR functions with programmable connections. The output of each NOR function is followed by an inverter, so a true OR function is realized, and overall the PLA performs an AND-OR function as desired.

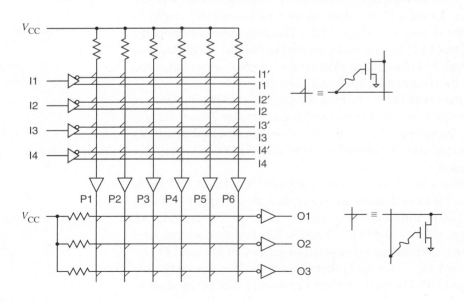

Figure 6-29
A 4×3 PLA built using CMOS logic.

In CMOS PLD and CPLD technologies, the programmable links shown in Figure 6-29 are not normally fuses. In non-field-programmable devices, such as custom VLSI chips, the presence or absence of each link is simply established as part of the metal mask pattern for the manufacture of the device. By far the most common programming technology, however, is electrical and also allows the programming information to be erased, as discussed next.

An *electrically erasable programmable logic device (EEPLD)* can be programmed with any desired link configuration electrically, as well as "erased" to its original state. No, erasing does not cause links to suddenly appear or disappear! Rather, EEPLDs use a different technology, called "floating-gate MOS."

electrically erasable programmable logic device (EEPLD)

As shown in Figure 6-30, an EEPLD uses *floating-gate MOS transistors*. Such a transistor has two gates. The "floating" gate is unconnected and is surrounded by extremely high-impedance insulating material. In the original, manufactured state, the floating gate has no charge on it and has no effect on circuit operation. In this state, all transistors are effectively "connected"; that is, there is a logical link present at every crosspoint in the AND and OR planes.

floating-gate MOS transistor

To program an EEPLD, the programmer applies a high voltage to the non-floating gate at each location where a logical link is not wanted. This causes a temporary breakdown in the insulating material and allows a negative charge to accumulate on the floating gate. When the high voltage is removed, the negative charge remains on the floating gate. During subsequent operations, the negative charge prevents the transistor from turning "on" when a HIGH signal is applied to the nonfloating gate; the transistor effectively gets disconnected from the circuit.

EEPLD manufacturers claim that a properly programmed bit will retain 70% of its charge for at least 10 years, even if the part is stored at 125°C, so for

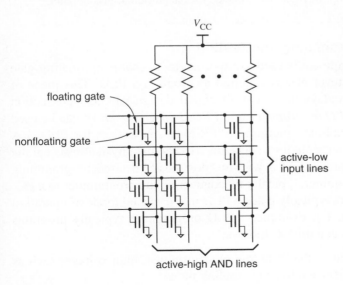

Figure 6-30
AND plane of an EEPLD using floating-gate MOS transistors.

floating gate

nonfloating gate

V_{CC}

active-low input lines

active-high AND lines

most applications the programming can be considered permanent. However, EEPLDs can also be erased.

The floating gates in an EEPLD are surrounded by an extremely thin insulating layer and can be erased by applying a voltage of the opposite polarity as the charging voltage to the nonfloating gate. Thus, the same piece of equipment that is normally used to program a PLD can also be used to erase an EEPLD before programming it.

Most CPLDs also use floating-gate programming and erasing technology. Perhaps they should properly be called "CEEPLDs," but that acronym would be a bit much to swallow.

FPGAs, on the other hand, use read/write memory cells to control the state of each connection. The read/write memory cells are volatile—they do not retain their state when power is removed. Therefore, when power is first applied to the FPGA, all of its read/write memory must be initialized to a state specified by a separate, external nonvolatile memory. This memory typically is either a programmable read-only memory (PROM) chip attached directly to the FPGA or is part of a microprocessor subsystem that initializes the FPGA as part of overall system initialization.

CHANGING HARDWARE ON THE FLY

PROMs are normally used to supply the connection pattern for a read/write-memory-based FPGA, but there are also applications where the pattern actually is read from a microprocessor's boot software. You just downloaded a new software version? Guess what, you just got a new hardware version too!

This concept leads us to the intriguing idea, already being applied in some applications, of "reconfigurable hardware," where a hardware subsystem is redefined, on the fly, to optimize its performance for the particular task at hand.

*6.3.6 Device Programming and Testing

A special piece of equipment is used to vaporize fuses, charge up floating-gate transistors, or do whatever else is required to program a PLD. This piece of equipment, found nowadays in almost all digital design labs and production facilities, is called a *PLD programmer* or a *PROM programmer*. (It can be used with programmable read-only memories, "PROMs," as well as for PLDs.) A typical PLD programmer includes a socket or sockets that physically accept the devices to be programmed, and a way to "download" desired programming patterns into the programmer, typically by connecting the programmer to a PC.

PLD programmer
PROM programmer

PLD programmers typically place a PLD into a special mode of operation in order to program it. For example, a PLD programmer typically programs small PLDs eight fuses at a time as follows:

1. Raise a certain pin of the PLD to a predetermined, high voltage (such as 14 V) to put the device into programming mode.

2. Select a group of eight fuses by applying a binary "address" to certain inputs of the device. (For example, the 82S100 has 1920 fuses, and it would thus require eight inputs to select one of 240 groups of eight fuses.)

3. Apply an 8-bit value to the *outputs* of the device to specify the desired programming for each fuse (the outputs are used as inputs in programming mode).

4. Raise a second predetermined pin to the high voltage for a predetermined length of time (such as 100 microseconds) to program the eight fuses.

5. Lower the second predetermined pin to a low voltage (such as 0 V) to read out and verify the programming of the eight fuses.

6. Repeat steps 1–5 for each group of eight fuses.

Many PLDs, especially larger CPLDs, feature *in-system programmability*. This means that the device can be programmed after it is already soldered into the system. In this case, the fuse patterns are applied to the device serially using four extra signals and pins, called the *JTAG port*, defined by IEEE standard 1149.1. These signals are defined so that multiple devices on the same printed-circuit board can be "daisy chained" and selected and programmed during the board manufacturing process using just one JTAG port on a special connector. No special high-voltage power supply is needed; each device uses a charge-pump circuit internally to generate the high voltage needed for programming.

in-system programmability

JTAG port

As noted in step 5 above, fuse patterns are verified as they are programmed into a device. If a fuse fails to program properly the first time, the operation can be retried; if it fails to program properly after a few tries, the device is discarded (often with great prejudice and malice aforethought).

While verifying the fuse pattern of a programmed device proves that its fuses are programmed properly, it does not prove that the device will perform the logic function specified by those fuses. This is true because the device may have unrelated internal defects such as missing connections between the fuses and elements of the AND-OR array.

The only way to test for all defects is to put the device into its normal operational mode, apply a set of normal logic inputs, and observe the outputs. The required input and output patterns, called test vectors, can be specified by the designer as we showed in Section 5.2.6, or can be generated automatically by a special test-vector-generation program. Regardless of how the test vectors are generated, most PLD programmers have the ability to apply test-vector inputs to a PLD and to check its outputs against the expected results.

Most PLDs have a *security fuse* which, when programmed, disables the ability to read fuse patterns from the device. Manufacturers can program this fuse to prevent others from reading out the PLD fuse patterns in order to copy their product design. Even if the security fuse is programmed, test vectors still work, so the PLD can still be checked.

security fuse

6.4 Decoders

decoder

A *decoder* is a multiple-input, multiple-output logic circuit that converts coded inputs into coded outputs, where the input and output codes are different. The input code generally has fewer bits than the output code, and there is a one-to-one mapping from input code words into output code words. In a *one-to-one mapping*, each input code word produces a different output code word.

one-to-one mapping

The general structure of a decoder circuit is shown in Figure 6-31. The enable inputs, if present, must be asserted for the decoder to perform its normal mapping function. Otherwise, the decoder maps all input code words into a single, "disabled," output code word.

The most commonly used input code is an n-bit binary code, where an n-bit word represents one of 2^n different coded values, normally the integers from 0 through 2^n-1. Sometimes an n-bit binary code is truncated to represent fewer than 2^n values. For example, in the BCD code, the 4-bit combinations 0000 through 1001 represent the decimal digits 0–9, and combinations 1010 through 1111 are not used.

The most commonly used output code is a 1-out-of-m code, which contains m bits, where one bit is asserted at any time. Thus, in a 1-out-of-4 code with active-high outputs, the code words are 0001, 0010, 0100, and 1000. With active-low outputs, the code words are 1110, 1101, 1011, and 0111.

6.4.1 Binary Decoders

binary decoder

The most common decoder circuit is an n-to-2^n decoder or *binary decoder*. Such a decoder has an n-bit binary input code and a 1-out-of-2^n output code. A binary decoder is used when you need to activate exactly one of 2^n outputs based on an n-bit input value.

enable input
decode

For example, Figure 6-32(a) shows the inputs and outputs and Table 6-4 is the truth table of a 2-to-4 decoder. The input code word I1,I0 represents an integer in the range 0–3. The output code word Y3,Y2,Y1,Y0 has Yi equal to 1 if and only if the input code word is the binary representation of i and the *enable input* EN is 1. If EN is 0, then all of the outputs are 0. A gate-level circuit for the 2-to-4 decoder is shown in Figure 6-32(b). Each AND gate *decodes* one combination of the input code word I1,I0.

Figure 6-31
Decoder circuit structure.

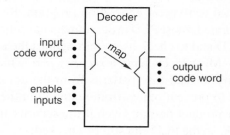

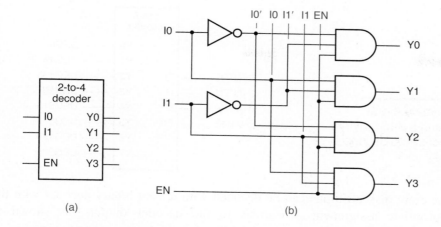

Figure 6-32
A 2-to-4 decoder:
(a) inputs and outputs;
(b) logic diagram.

Inputs			Outputs			
EN	I1	I0	Y3	Y2	Y1	Y0
0	x	x	0	0	0	0
1	0	0	0	0	0	1
1	0	1	0	0	1	0
1	1	0	0	1	0	0
1	1	1	1	0	0	0

Table 6-4
Truth table for a 2-to-4 binary decoder.

The binary decoder's truth table introduces a "don't-care" notation for input combinations. If one or more input values do not affect the output values for some combination of the remaining inputs, they are marked with an "x" for that input combination. This convention can greatly reduce the number of rows in the truth table, as well as make the functions of the inputs more clear.

The input code of an n-bit binary decoder need not represent the integers from 0 through $2^n - 1$. For example, Table 6-5 shows the 3-bit Gray-code output of a mechanical encoding disk with eight positions, as in Figure 2-6 on page 52.

Disk Position	I2	I1	I0	Binary Decoder Output
0°	0	0	0	Y0
45°	0	0	1	Y1
90°	0	1	1	Y3
135°	0	1	0	Y2
180°	1	1	0	Y6
225°	1	1	1	Y7
270°	1	0	1	Y5
315°	1	0	0	Y4

Table 6-5
Position encoding for a 3-bit mechanical encoding disk.

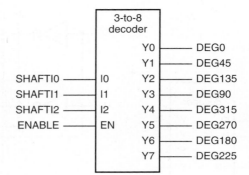

Figure 6-33
Using a 3-to-8 binary
decoder to decode a
Gray code.

The eight disk positions can be decoded with a 3-bit binary decoder with the appropriate assignment of signals to the decoder outputs, as shown in Figure 6-33.

decimal decoder
BCD decoder

Also, it is not necessary to use all of the outputs of a decoder, or even to decode all possible input combinations. For example, a *decimal* or *BCD decoder* decodes only the first ten binary input combinations 0000–1001 to produce outputs Y0–Y9.

6.4.2 Logic Symbols for Larger-Scale Elements

Before describing commercially available 74-series MSI decoders, we need to discuss general guidelines for drawing logic symbols for larger-scale logic elements.

The most basic rule is that logic symbols are drawn with inputs on the left and outputs on the right. The top and bottom edges of a logic symbol are not normally used for signal connections. However, explicit power and ground connections are sometimes shown at the top and bottom.

Like gate symbols, the logic symbols for larger-scale elements associate an active level with each pin. With respect to active levels, it's important to use a consistent convention to naming the internal signals and external pins.

Larger-scale elements almost always have their signal names defined in terms of the functions performed *inside* their symbolic outline, as explained in Section 6.1.4. For example, Figure 6-34(a) shows the logic symbol for a 74x138 3-to-8 decoder, an MSI part that we'll fully describe in the next subsection. When all of the enable inputs G1, G2A, and G2B are asserted, one of the outputs

---

IEEE STANDARD
LOGIC SYMBOLS

Throughout this book, we use "traditional" symbols for larger-scale logic elements. The IEEE standard uses somewhat different symbols for larger-scale logic elements. IEEE standard symbols, as well as pros and cons of IEEE versus traditional symbols, are discussed in <u>Section IEEEsym</u> at <u>DDPPonline</u>.

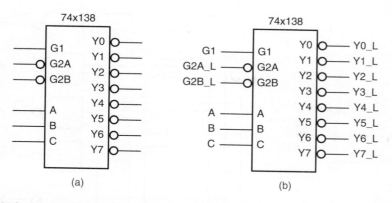

Figure 6-34
Logic symbol for the
74x138 3-to-8 decoder:
(a) conventional symbol;
(b) default signal names
associated with external
pins.

Y0–Y7 is asserted, as selected by a 3-bit code applied to the A, B and C inputs. You can tell from the symbol that the G2A and G2B input pins and all of the output pins are active low.

When the 74x138 symbol appears in the logic diagram for a real application, its inputs and outputs have signals connected to other devices, and each such signal has a name that indicates its function in the application. However, when we describe the 74x138 in isolation, we might still like to have a name for the signal on each external pin. Figure 6-34(b) shows our naming convention in this case. Active-high pins are given the same name as the internal signal, while active-low pins have the internal signal name followed by the suffix "_L".

6.4.3 The 74x138 3-to-8 Decoder

The *74x138* is a commercially available MSI 3-to-8 decoder whose gate-level   *74x138*
circuit diagram is shown in Figure 6-35. Notice that the outputs and the enable
input of the '138 are active low. Most MSI decoders were originally designed

LOGIC FAMILIES   Most logic gates and larger-scale elements are available in a variety of CMOS and TTL families, many of which we described in Sections 3.8 and 3.10.6. For example, the 74LS138, 74S138, 74ALS138, 74AS138, 74F138, 74HC138, 74HCT138, 74ACT138, 74AC138, 74FCT138, 74AHC138, 74AHCT138, 74LC138, 74LVC138, and 74VHC138 are all 3-to-8 decoders with the same logic function, but in electrically different TTL and CMOS families and possibly in different packages. In addition, "macro" logic elements with the same pin names and functions as the '138 and other popular 74-series devices are available as building blocks in most FPGA and ASIC design environments.

Throughout this text, we use "74x" as a generic prefix. And we'll sometimes omit the prefix and write, for example, '138. In a real schematic diagram for a circuit that you are going to build or simulate, you should include the full part number, since timing, loading, and packaging characteristics depend on the family.

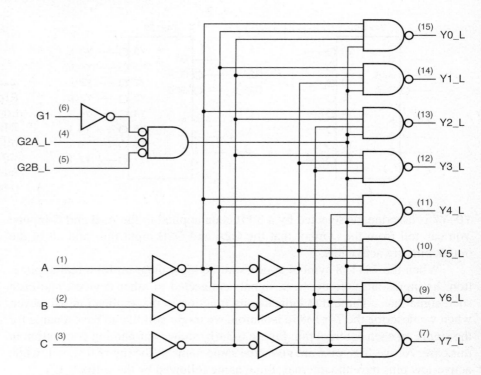

Figure 6-35
Logic diagram for the
74x138 3-to-8
decoder

function table

with active-low outputs, since TTL and CMOS inverting gates are generally faster than noninverting ones. Also notice that the '138 has extra inverters on its select inputs. Without these inverters, each select input would present three AC or DC loads instead of one, consuming much more of the fanout budget of the device that drives it.

The 74x138 has three enable inputs (G1, G2A_L, G2B_L), all of which must be asserted for the selected output to be asserted. The truth table for the '138 is given in Table 6-6. The truth tables in some manufacturers' data books use L and H to denote the input and output signal voltage levels, so there can be no ambiguity about the electrical function of the device; a truth table written this way is sometimes called a *function table*. However, since we use positive logic throughout this book, we can use 0 and 1 without ambiguity. In any case, the truth table gives the logic function in terms of the *external pins* of the device. A truth table for the function performed *inside* the symbol outline would be different (see Drill 6.19).

The logic function of the '138 is straightforward—an output is asserted if and only if the decoder is enabled and the output is selected. Thus, we can easily write logic equations for an internal output signal such as Y5 in terms of the internal input signals:

$$Y5 = \underbrace{G1 \cdot G2A \cdot G2B}_{\text{enable}} \cdot \underbrace{C \cdot B' \cdot A}_{\text{select}}$$

Table 6-6 Truth table for a 74x138 3-to-8 decoder.

Inputs						Outputs							
G1	G2A_L	G2B_L	C	B	A	Y7_L	Y6_L	Y5_L	Y4_L	Y3_L	Y2_L	Y1_L	Y0_L
0	x	x	x	x	x	1	1	1	1	1	1	1	1
x	1	x	x	x	x	1	1	1	1	1	1	1	1
x	x	1	x	x	x	1	1	1	1	1	1	1	1
1	0	0	0	0	0	1	1	1	1	1	1	1	0
1	0	0	0	0	1	1	1	1	1	1	1	0	1
1	0	0	0	1	0	1	1	1	1	1	0	1	1
1	0	0	0	1	1	1	1	1	1	0	1	1	1
1	0	0	1	0	0	1	1	1	0	1	1	1	1
1	0	0	1	0	1	1	1	0	1	1	1	1	1
1	0	0	1	1	0	1	0	1	1	1	1	1	1
1	0	0	1	1	1	0	1	1	1	1	1	1	1

However, because of the inversion bubbles, we have the following relations between internal and external signals:

$$G2A = G2A\_L'$$
$$G2B = G2B\_L'$$
$$Y5 = Y5\_L'$$

Therefore, if we're interested, we can write the following equation for the external output signal Y5_L in terms of external input signals:

$$Y5\_L = Y5' = (G1 \cdot G2A\_L' \cdot G2B\_L' \cdot C \cdot B' \cdot A)'$$
$$= G1' + G2A\_L + G2B\_L + C' + B + A'$$

On the surface, this equation doesn't resemble what you might expect for a decoder, since it is a logical sum rather than a product. However, if you practice bubble-to-bubble logic design, you don't have to worry about this; you just give the output signal an active-low name and remember that it's active low when you connect it to other inputs.

2-TO-4 DECODERS The 74x138 can be used as a 2-to-4 decoder by simply tying the C input to 0 and using the A, B, and enable inputs, and the Y0–Y3 outputs. Information on another popular MSI decoder, the *74x139* dual 2-to-4 decoder, can be found at DDPPonline in Section Dec.

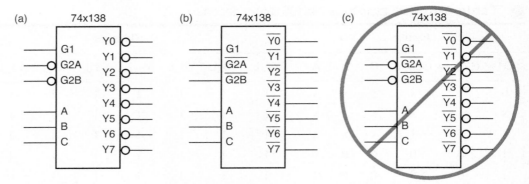

Figure 6-36 Logic symbols for the 74x138: (a) preferred symbol; (b) correct but to be avoided; (c) incorrect because of double negations.

A logic symbol for the 74x138 is shown in Figure 6-36(a). Notice that all of the signal names inside the symbol outline are active high (no "_L"), and that inversion bubbles indicate active-low inputs and outputs.

Some logic designers and schematic drawing programs draw the symbol for 74x138s and other logic functions without inversion bubbles. Instead, they use an overbar on signal names inside the symbol outline to indicate negation, as shown in Figure 6-36(b). This notation is self-consistent, but it is inconsistent with our drawing standards for bubble-to-bubble logic design. The symbol shown in (c) is absolutely *incorrect*: according to this symbol, a logic 1, not 0, must be applied to the G2A and G2B pins to enable the decoder.

6.4.4 Cascading Binary Decoders

Multiple binary decoders can be cascaded hierarchically to decode larger code words. Figure 6-37 shows how to use a 74x138 as a 2-to-4 decoder to decode the two high-order bits of a 5-bit code word, thereby enabling one of four more 74x138s that decode the three low-order bits.

In some cases, it may be possible to combine decoders to make a larger one, without any additional components, especially if the decoders have multiple enable inputs. For example, Figure 6-38 shows how two 3-to-8 decoders can be combined to make a 4-to-16 decoder. The top decoder (U1) is enabled when N3 is 0, and the bottom one (U2) is enabled when N3 is 1.

6.4.5 Decoders in ABEL and PLDs

Nothing in logic design is much easier than writing the PLD equations for a decoder. Since the logic expression for each output is typically just a single product term, decoders are very easily targeted to PLDs and use few product-term resources.

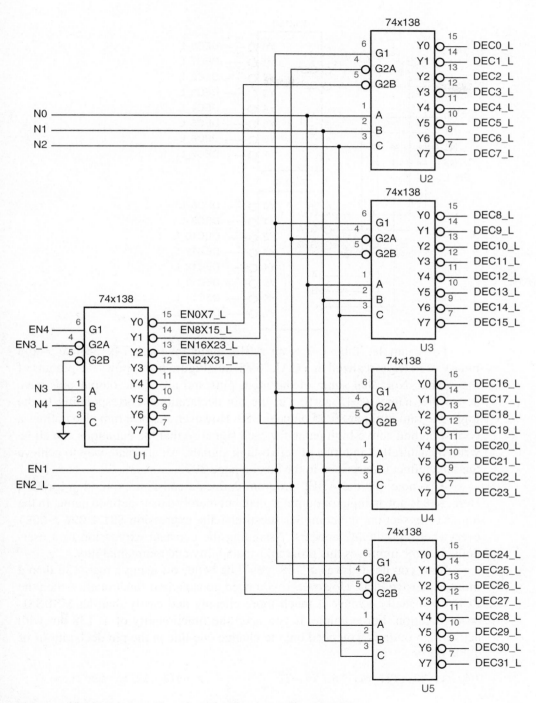

Figure 6-37 Design of a 5-to-32 decoder using 74x138s.

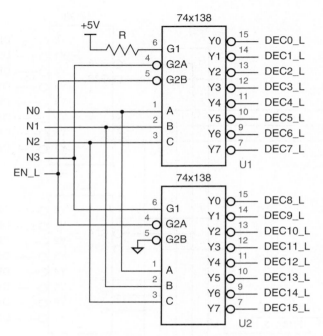

Figure 6-38
Design of a 4-to-16
decoder using
74x138s.

For example, Table 6-7 is an ABEL program for a 74x138-like 3-to-8 binary decoder as realized in a GAL16V8, and Figure 6-39 shows the pinouts of the device. Note that some of the input pins and all of the output pins have active-low names ("_L" suffix) in the pin declarations, corresponding to the logic diagram in Figure 6-35 on page 388. However, the program also defines a corresponding active-high name for each signal so that the equations can all be written "naturally," in terms of active-high signals. An alternate way to achieve the same effect is described in the box on page 397.

Also note that the ABEL program defines a constant expression for ENB. Here, ENB is not an input or output signal, but merely a user-defined name. In the equations section, the compiler substitutes the expression (G1 & G2A & G2B) everywhere that "ENB" appears. Assigning the constant expression to a user-defined name improves this program's readability and maintainability.

If all you needed was a '138, you'd be better off using a real '138 than a more expensive PLD. However, if you need nonstandard functionality, then the PLD can usually achieve it much more cheaply and easily than an MSI/SSI-based solution. For example, if you need the functionality of a '138 but with active-high outputs, you need only to change one line in the pin declarations of Table 6-7:

```
Y0, Y1, Y2, Y3, Y4, Y5, Y6, Y7          pin 19..12 istype 'com';
```

(Also, the original definitions of Y0–Y7 in Table 6-7 must be deleted.) Since each of the equations requires a single product of six variables (including the three in

Table 6-7 An ABEL program for a 74x138-like 3-to-8 binary decoder.

```
module Z74X138
title '74x138 Decoder PLD
J. Wakerly, Stanford University'
Z74X138 device 'P16V8C';

" Input and output pins
A, B, C, G2A_L, G2B_L, G1                    pin 1, 2, 3, 4, 5, 6;
Y0_L, Y1_L, Y2_L, Y3_L, Y4_L, Y5_L, Y6_L, Y7_L    pin 19..12 istype 'com';

" Active-high signal names for readability
G2A = !G2A_L;
G2B = !G2B_L;
Y0 = !Y0_L;
Y1 = !Y1_L;
Y2 = !Y2_L;
Y3 = !Y3_L;
Y4 = !Y4_L;
Y5 = !Y5_L;
Y6 = !Y6_L;
Y7 = !Y7_L;

" Constant expression
ENB = G1 & G2A & G2B;

equations
Y0 = ENB & !C & !B & !A;
Y1 = ENB & !C & !B &  A;
Y2 = ENB & !C &  B & !A;
Y3 = ENB & !C &  B &  A;
Y4 = ENB &  C & !B & !A;
Y5 = ENB &  C & !B &  A;
Y6 = ENB &  C &  B & !A;
Y7 = ENB &  C &  B &  A;

end Z74X138
```

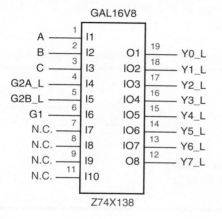

Figure 6-39
Logic diagram for
the GAL16V8C used
as a 74x138 decoder.

the ENB expression), each complemented equation requires a *sum* of six product terms, fewer than the seven available in a GAL16V8C. In addition, the ABEL compiler can select noninverted output polarity to use only one product term per output.

Another easy change is to provide alternate enable inputs that are ORed with the main enable inputs. To do this, you need only define additional pins and modify the definition of ENB:

```
EN1, EN2_L                              pin 7, 8;
...
EN2 = !EN2_L;
...
ENB = G1 & G2A & G2B # EN1 # EN2;
```

This change expands the number of product terms per output to three, each having a form similar to

```
Y0 = G1 & G2A & G2B & !C & !B &!A
   # EN1 & !C & !B & !A
   # EN2 & !C & !B & !A;
```

(Remember that the GAL16V8 has a selectable inverter between the AND-OR array and the output of the PLD, so the actual output can be active low as desired.)

As a final tweak, we can add an input to dynamically control whether the output is active high or active low, and modify all of the equations as follows:

```
POL                     pin 9;
...
Y0 = POL $ (ENB & !C & !B & !A);
Y1 = POL $ (ENB & !C & !B &  A);
...
Y7 = POL $ (ENB &  C &  B &  A);
```

As a result of the XOR operation, the number of product terms needed per output increases to nine, in either output-pin polarity. Thus, a GAL16V8C cannot realize the function as written.

Table 6-8 ABEL program fragment showing two-pass logic.

```
...
" Output pins
Y0_L, Y1_L, Y2_L, Y3_L              pin 19, 18, 17, 16 istype 'com';
Y4_L, Y5_L, ENB, Y6_L               pin 15, 14, 13, 12 istype 'com';

equations
ENB = G1 & G2A & G2B # EN1 # EN2;
Y0 = POL $ (ENB & !C & !B & !A);
...
```

CS_L	RD_L	A2	A1	A0	Output(s) to Assert
1	x	x	x	x	none
x	1	x	x	x	none
0	0	0	0	0	BILL_L, MARY_L
0	0	0	0	1	MARY_L, KATE_L
0	0	0	1	0	JOAN_L
0	0	0	1	1	PAUL_L
0	0	1	0	0	ANNA_L
0	0	1	0	1	FRED_L
0	0	1	1	0	DAVE_L
0	0	1	1	1	KATE_L

Table 6-9
Truth table for a customized decoder function.

The function can still be realized if we create a *helper output* to reduce the product-term explosion. As shown in Table 6-8, we allocate an output pin for the ENB expression (losing the Y7_L output), and move the ENB equation into the equations section of the program. This reduces the product-term requirement to five in either polarity.

helper output

Besides sacrificing a pin for the helper output, this realization has the disadvantage of being slower. Any changes in the inputs to the helper expression must propagate through the PLD twice before reaching the final output. This is called *two-pass logic*. Many PLD and FPGA synthesis tools can automatically generate logic with two or more passes if a required expression cannot be realized in just one pass through the logic array.

two-pass logic

Decoders can be customized in other ways. A common customization is for a single output to decode more than one input combination. For example, suppose you needed to generate a set of enable signals according to Table 6-9. A 74x138 MSI decoder can be augmented as shown in Figure 6-40 to perform the required function. This approach, while possibly slightly less expensive than a PLD, has the disadvantages that it requires extra components and delay to create the required outputs, and it is not easily modified.

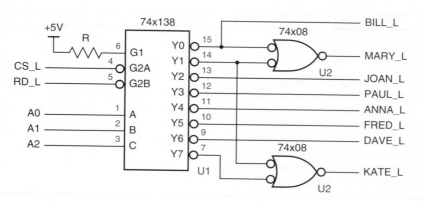

Figure 6-40
Customized decoder circuit.

Table 6-10 ABEL equations for a customized decoder.

```
module CUSTMDEC
title 'Customized Decoder PLD
J. Wakerly, Stanford University'
CUSTMDEC device 'P16V8C';

" Input pins
!CS, !RD, A0, A1, A2          pin 1, 2, 3, 4, 5;
" Output pins
!BILL, !MARY, !JOAN, !PAUL    pin 19, 18, 17, 16 istype 'com';
!ANNA, !FRED, !DAVE, !KATE    pin 15, 14, 13, 12 istype 'com';

equations
BILL = CS & RD & (!A2 & !A1 & !A0);
MARY = CS & RD & (!A2 & !A1 & !A0 # !A2 & !A1 &  A0);
KATE = CS & RD & (!A2 & !A1 &  A0 #  A2 &  A1 &  A0);
JOAN = CS & RD & (!A2 &  A1 & !A0);
PAUL = CS & RD & (!A2 &  A1 &  A0);
ANNA = CS & RD & ( A2 & !A1 & !A0);
FRED = CS & RD & ( A2 & !A1 &  A0);
DAVE = CS & RD & ( A2 &  A1 & !A0);

end CUSTMDEC
```

A PLD solution to the same problem is shown in Table 6-10. Note that this program uses the active-low pin-naming convention described in the box on page 397 (you should be comfortable with either convention). Each of the last six equations uses a single AND gate in the PLD. The ABEL compiler will also minimize the MARY equation to use just one AND gate. Active-high output signals could be obtained just by changing two lines in the declaration section:

```
BILL, MARY, JOAN, PAUL    pin 19, 18, 17, 16 istype 'com';
ANNA, FRED, DAVE, KATE    pin 15, 14, 13, 12 istype 'com';
```

Table 6-11 Equivalent ABEL equations for a customized decoder.

```
ADDR = [A2,A1,A0];

equations
BILL = CS & RD &  (ADDR == 0);
MARY = CS & RD & ((ADDR == 0) # (ADDR == 1));
KATE = CS & RD & ((ADDR == 1) # (ADDR == 7));
JOAN = CS & RD &  (ADDR == 2);
PAUL = CS & RD &  (ADDR == 3);
ANNA = CS & RD &  (ADDR == 4);
FRED = CS & RD &  (ADDR == 5);
DAVE = CS & RD &  (ADDR == 6);
```

Another way of writing the equations is shown in Table 6-11. In most applications, this style is more clear, especially if the select inputs have numeric significance.

ACTIVE-LOW PIN DEFINITIONS

ABEL allows you to use an inversion prefix (!) on signal names in the pin definitions of a program. When a pin name is defined with the inversion prefix, the compiler automatically prepends an inversion prefix to the signal name anywhere it appears elsewhere in the program. If it's already inverted, this results in a double inversion (that is, no inversion at all).

This feature can be used to define a different but consistent convention for defining active-low inputs and outputs—give each active-low signal an active-*high* name, but precede it with the inversion prefix in its pin definition. For the 3-to-8 decoder in Table 6-7, we replace the first part of the program with the code shown in Table 6-12; the equations section of the program stays exactly the same.

Which convention to use may be a matter of personal taste, but it can also depend on the capabilities of the CAD tools that you use to draw schematics. Many tools allow you to automatically create a schematic symbol from a logic block that is defined by an ABEL program. If the tool allows you to place inversion bubbles on selected inputs and outputs of the symbol, then the convention in Table 6-12 yields a symbol with active-high signal names inside the function outline. You can then specify external bubbles on the active-low signals to obtain a symbol that matches the conventions described in Section 6.4.2 and shown in Figure 6-41(a).

On the other hand, you may not be able or want to provide inversion bubbles on CAD-created symbols. In that case, you should use the convention in Table 6-7; this yields a CAD-created symbol in which the active level is indicated by the signal name inside the function outline; no external inversion bubbles are needed. This is shown in Figure 6-41(b). Note that unlike Figure 6-36(b) on page 390, we use a text-based convention (_L) rather than an overbar on the signal name to indicate active level. A properly chosen text-based convention provides portability among different CAD tools.

We'll somewhat arbitrarily select one convention or the other in each of the ABEL examples in the rest of this book, just to help you get comfortable with both approaches.

Table 6-12 Alternate declarations for a 74x138-like 3-to-8 binary decoder.

```
" Input and output pins
A, B, C, !G2A, !G2B, G1              pin 1, 2, 3, 4, 5, 6;
!Y0, !Y1, !Y2, !Y3, !Y4, !Y5, !Y6, !Y7   pin 19..12 istype 'com';

" Constant expression
ENB = G1 & G2A & G2B;
```

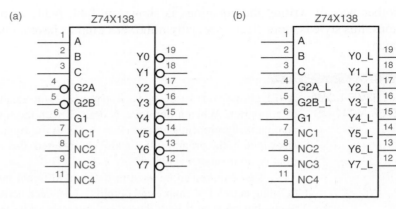

(a)   Z74X138

(b)   Z74X138

Figure 6-41
Possible CAD-created
symbols for the PLD-
based, 74x138-like
decoder: (a) based on
Table 6-12, after
manual insertion of
inversion bubbles;
(b) based on Table 6-7.

6.4.6 Decoders in VHDL

There are several ways to approach the design of decoders in VHDL. The most primitive approach would be to write a structural equivalent of a decoder logic circuit, as Table 6-13 does for the 2-to-4 binary decoder of Figure 6-32 on page 385. The components and3 and inv are assumed to already exist in the target technology. Of course, this mechanical conversion of an existing design into the equivalent of a netlist defeats the purpose of using VHDL in the first place.

Instead, we would like to write a program that uses VHDL to make our decoder design more understandable and maintainable. Table 6-14 shows one

Table 6-13 VHDL structural program for the decoder in Figure 6-32.

```
library IEEE;
use IEEE.std_logic_1164.all;

entity V2to4dec is
  port (I0, I1, EN: in STD_LOGIC;
        Y0, Y1, Y2, Y3: out STD_LOGIC );
end V2to4dec;

architecture V2to4dec_s of V2to4dec is
  signal NOTI0, NOTI1: STD_LOGIC;
  component inv port (I: in STD_LOGIC; O: out STD_LOGIC ); end component;
  component and3 port (I0, I1, I2: in STD_LOGIC; O: out STD_LOGIC ); end component;
begin
  U1: inv port map (I0,NOTI0);
  U2: inv port map (I1,NOTI1);
  U3: and3 port map (NOTI0,NOTI1,EN,Y0);
  U4: and3 port map (   I0,NOTI1,EN,Y1);
  U5: and3 port map (NOTI0,   I1,EN,Y2);
  U6: and3 port map (   I0,   I1,EN,Y3);
end V2to4dec_s;
```

Table 6-14 Dataflow-style VHDL program for a 74x138-like 3-to-8 binary decoder.

```
library IEEE;
use IEEE.std_logic_1164.all;

entity V74x138 is
    port (G1, G2A_L, G2B_L: in STD_LOGIC;      -- enable inputs
          A: in STD_LOGIC_VECTOR (2 downto 0);  -- select inputs
          Y_L: out STD_LOGIC_VECTOR (0 to 7) ); -- decoded outputs
 end V74x138;

architecture V74x138_a of V74x138 is
  signal Y_L_i: STD_LOGIC_VECTOR (0 to 7);
begin
  with A select Y_L_i <=
    "01111111" when "000",
    "10111111" when "001",
    "11011111" when "010",
    "11101111" when "011",
    "11110111" when "100",
    "11111011" when "101",
    "11111101" when "110",
    "11111110" when "111",
    "11111111" when others;
   Y_L <= Y_L_i when (G1 and not G2A_L and not G2B_L)='1' else "11111111";
end V74x138_a;
```

approach to writing code for a 3-to-8 binary decoder equivalent to the 74x138, using the dataflow style of VHDL. The address inputs A(2 downto 0) and the active-low decoded outputs Y_L(0 to 7) are declared using vectors to improve readability. A select statement enumerates the eight decoding cases and assigns the appropriate active-low output pattern to an 8-bit internal signal Y_L_i. This value is assigned to the actual circuit output Y_L only if all of the enable inputs are asserted.

This design is a good start, and it works, but it does have a potential pitfall. Adjustments that handle the fact that two inputs and all the outputs are active low happen to be buried in the final assignment statement. While it's true that most VHDL programs are written almost entirely with active-high signals, if we're defining a device with active-low external pins, we really should handle them in a more systematic and easily maintainable way.

Table 6-15 shows such an approach. No changes are made to the entity declarations. However, active-high versions of the active-low external pins are defined within the V74x138_b architecture, and explicit assignment statements are used to convert between the active-high and active-low signals. The decoder function itself is defined in terms of only the active-high signals, probably the

Table 6-15 VHDL architecture with a maintainable approach to active-level handling.

```
architecture V74x138_b of V74x138 is
  signal G2A, G2B: STD_LOGIC;            -- active-high version of inputs
  signal Y: STD_LOGIC_VECTOR (0 to 7);   -- active-high version of outputs
  signal Y_s: STD_LOGIC_VECTOR (0 to 7); -- internal signal
begin
  G2A <= not G2A_L; -- convert inputs
  G2B <= not G2B_L; -- convert inputs
  Y_L <= not Y;     -- convert outputs
  with A select Y_s <=
    "10000000" when "000",
    "01000000" when "001",
    "00100000" when "010",
    "00010000" when "011",
    "00001000" when "100",
    "00000100" when "101",
    "00000010" when "110",
    "00000001" when "111",
    "00000000" when others;
  Y <= Y_s when (G1 and G2A and G2B)='1' else "00000000";
end V74x138_b;
```

Table 6-16 Hierarchical definition of 74x138-like decoder with active-level handling.

```
architecture V74x138_c of V74x138 is
  signal G2A, G2B: STD_LOGIC;            -- active-high version of inputs
  signal Y: STD_LOGIC_VECTOR (0 to 7);   -- active-high version of outputs
  component V3to8dec port (G1, G2, G3: in STD_LOGIC;
                    A: in STD_LOGIC_VECTOR (2 downto 0);
                    Y: out STD_LOGIC_VECTOR (0 to 7) ); end component;
begin
  G2A <= not G2A_L;    -- convert inputs
  G2B <= not G2B_L;    -- convert inputs
  Y_I <= not Y;        -- convert outputs
  U1: V3to8dec port map (G1, G2A, G2B, A, Y);
end V74x138_c;
```

biggest advantage of this approach. Another advantage is that the design can be easily modified in just a few well-defined places if changes are required in the external active levels.

Active levels can be handled in an even more structured way. As shown in Table 6-16, the V74x138 architecture can be defined hierarchically, using a fully active-high V3to8dec component that has its own dataflow-style definition in Table 6-17. Once again, no changes are required in the top-level definition of the V74x138 entity. Figure 6-42 shows the relationship between the entities.

```
library IEEE;
use IEEE.std_logic_1164.all;

entity V3to8dec is
    port (G1, G2, G3: in STD_LOGIC;
            A: in STD_LOGIC_VECTOR (2 downto 0);
            Y: out STD_LOGIC_VECTOR (0 to 7) );
end V3to8dec;

architecture V3to8dec_a of V3to8dec is
  signal Y_s: STD_LOGIC_VECTOR (0 to 7);
begin
    with A select Y_s <=
      "10000000" when "000",
      "01000000" when "001",
      "00100000" when "010",
      "00010000" when "011",
      "00001000" when "100",
      "00000100" when "101",
      "00000010" when "110",
      "00000001" when "111",
      "00000000" when others;
    Y <= Y_s when (G1 and G2 and G3)='1'
            else "00000000";
end V3to8dec_a;
```

Table 6-17
Dataflow definition of
an active-high 3-to-8
decoder.

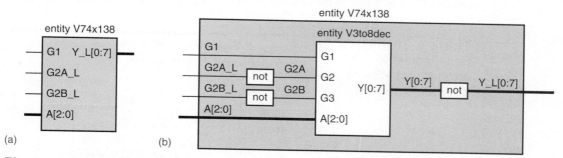

Figure 6-42 VHDL entity V74x138: (a) top level; (b) internal structure using
architecture V74x138_c.

NAME MATCHING   In Figure 6-42, the port names of an entity are drawn inside the corresponding box.
The names of the signals that are connected to the ports when the entity is used are
drawn on the signal lines. Notice that the signal names may match, but they don't
have to. The VHDL compiler keeps everything straight, associating a scope with
each name. The situation is completely analogous to the way variable and parameter
names are handled in structured, procedural programming languages like C.

CONCURRENT EXECUTION   In Table 6-15, we grouped all three of the active-level conversion statements together at the beginning of program, even though a value isn't assigned to Y_L until *after* a value is assigned to Y, later in the program. Remember that this is OK because the assignment statements in the architecture body are executed concurrently. That is, an assignment to any signal causes all the other statements that use that signal to be reevaluated, regardless of their position in the architecture body.

You could put the "Y_L <= not Y" statement at the end of the body if its present position bothers you, but the program is a bit more maintainable in its present form, with all the active-level conversions together.

Still another approach to decoder design is shown in Table 6-18, which can replace the V3to8dec_a architecture of Table 6-17. Instead of concurrent statements, this architecture uses a process and sequential statements to define the decoder's operation in a behavioral style. However, a close comparison of the two architectures shows that they're really not that different except for syntax.

As a final example, a more truly behavioral, process-based architecture for the 3-to-8 decoder is shown in Table 6-19. (Recall that the CONV_INTEGER function was defined in Section 5.3.3.) Of the examples we've given, this is the only one that describes the decoder function without essentially embedding a truth table in the VHDL program. In that respect, it is more flexible because it can be easily adapted to make a binary decoder of any size. In another respect, it

Table 6-18
Behavioral-style architecture definition for a 3-to-8 decoder.

```
architecture V3to8dec_b of V3to8dec is
  signal Y_s: STD_LOGIC_VECTOR (0 to 7);
begin
process(A, G1, G2, G3, Y_s)
  begin
    case A is
      when "000" => Y_s <= "10000000";
      when "001" => Y_s <= "01000000";
      when "010" => Y_s <= "00100000";
      when "011" => Y_s <= "00010000";
      when "100" => Y_s <= "00001000";
      when "101" => Y_s <= "00000100";
      when "110" => Y_s <= "00000010";
      when "111" => Y_s <= "00000001";
      when others => Y_s <= "00000000";
    end case;
    if (G1 and G2 and G3)='1' then Y <= Y_s;
    else Y <= "00000000";
    end if;
  end process;
end V3to8dec_b;
```

```
architecture V3to8dec_c of V3to8dec is
begin
process (G1, G2, G3, A)
  variable i: INTEGER range 0 to 7;
  begin
    Y <= "00000000";
    if (G1 and G2 and G3) = '1' then
      for i in 0 to 7 loop
        if i=CONV_INTEGER(A) then Y(i) <= '1'; end if;
      end loop;
    end if;
  end process;
end V3to8dec_c;
```

Table 6-19
Truly behavioral
architecture definition
for a 3-to-8 decoder.

is less flexible in that it does not have a truth table that can be easily modified to make custom decoders like the one we specified in Table 6-9 on page 395.

6.4.7 Decoders in Verilog

There are several ways to approach the design of decoders in Verilog. The most primitive approach would be to write a structural equivalent of a decoder logic circuit. This is done in Table 6-20 for the 2-to-4 binary decoder of Figure 6-32 on page 385. The design uses gate components AND3 and INV, which are assumed to already exist in the design environment. The port list of each gate-level component in this environment begins with the output and is followed by the gate's one or more inputs.

Of course, the above approach, mechanically converting an existing design into the equivalent of a netlist, defeats the purpose of using Verilog in the first place. Instead, we would like to write a program that uses Verilog to make our decoder design more understandable and maintainable. Table 6-21 shows one approach to writing code for a 3-to-8 binary decoder equivalent to the 74x138,

Table 6-20 Structural-style Verilog module for the decoder in Figure 6-32.

```
module Vr2to4dec(I0, I1, EN, Y0, Y1, Y2, Y3);
  input I0, I1, EN;
  output Y0, Y1, Y2, Y3;
  wire NOTI0, NOTI1;

  INV U1 (NOTI0, I0);
  INV U2 (NOTI1, I1);
  AND3 U3 (Y0, NOTI0, NOTI1, EN);
  AND3 U4 (Y1,    I0, NOTI1, EN);
  AND3 U5 (Y2, NOTI0,    I1, EN);
  AND3 U6 (Y3,    I0,    I1, EN);
endmodule
```

Table 6-21 Functional-style Verilog module for a 74x138-like 3-to-8 binary decoder.

```
module Vr74x138a(G1, G2A_L, G2B_L, A, Y_L);
  input G1, G2A_L, G2B_L;
  input [2:0] A;
  output [0:7] Y_L;
  reg [0:7] Y_L;

  always @ (G1 or G2A_L or G2B_L or A) begin
    if (G1 & ~G2A_L & ~G2B_L)
      case (A)
        0: Y_L = 8'b01111111;
        1: Y_L = 8'b10111111;
        2: Y_L = 8'b11011111;
        3: Y_L = 8'b11101111;
        4: Y_L = 8'b11110111;
        5: Y_L = 8'b11111011;
        6: Y_L = 8'b11111101;
        7: Y_L = 8'b11111110;
        default: Y_L = 8'b11111111;
      endcase
    else Y_L = 8'b11111111;
  end
endmodule
```

using the dataflow style of Verilog. The address inputs A[2:0] and the active-low decoded outputs Y_L[0:7] are declared as vectors to improve readability. An if statement is used to determine if the decoder is enabled. If it is, a case statement enumerates the eight decoding cases and assigns the appropriate active-low output pattern to the output signal Y_L. Otherwise, a value of all 1s is assigned to the output. Note that Y_L is declared as a reg variable as well as an output, so that its value can be set within the always block.

This design is a good start, and it works, but it does have a potential pitfall. The constants and inversions that handle the fact that two inputs and all the outputs are active low are scattered throughout the code. While it's true that most Verilog programs are written almost entirely with active-high signals, if we're defining a device with active-low external pins, we really should handle them in a more systematic and easily maintainable way.

A reg IS NOT A REGISTER   In Table 6-21 and others, Y_L is declared as a reg variable so that its value can be set within the always block. But keep in mind that despite the name, a Verilog reg declaration does *not* create a hardware register (a set of flip-flops for storage). It simply creates an internal variable for the simulator and synthesizer. Mechanisms for creating flip-flops in Verilog modules are discussed in Section 7.13.1.

Table 6-22 Verilog module with a maintainable approach to active-level handling.

```
module Vr74x138b(G1, G2A_L, G2B_L, A, Y_L);
  input G1, G2A_L, G2B_L;
  input [2:0] A;
  output [0:7] Y_L;
  reg G2A,G2B;
  reg [0:7] Y_L, Y;

  always @ (G1 or G2A_L or G2B_L or A or Y) begin
    G2A = ~G2A_L;   // Convert inputs
    G2B = ~G2B_L;
    Y_L = ~Y;         // Convert outputs
    if (G1 & G2A & G2B)
      case (A)
        0: Y = 8'b10000000;
        1: Y = 8'b01000000;
        2: Y = 8'b00100000;
        3: Y = 8'b00010000;
        4: Y = 8'b00001000;
        5: Y = 8'b00000100;
        6: Y = 8'b00000010;
        7: Y = 8'b00000001;
        default: Y = 8'b00000000;
      endcase
    else Y = 8'b00000000;
  end
endmodule
```

Table 6-22 shows such an approach. No changes have been made to the port definitions. However, active-high "reg" variables corresponding to the active-low external pins have been defined within the Vr74x138b module, and explicit assignment statements are used to convert between the active-high and active-low signals. The decoder function itself is defined in terms of only the active-high signals, probably the biggest advantage of this approach. Another advantage is that the design can be easily modified in just a few well-defined places if changes are required in the external active levels.

Active levels can be handled in an even more structured way. As shown in Table 6-23, the Vr74x138c module can be defined hierarchically, using a fully active-high Vr3to8deca component that has its own functional definition in Table 6-24. Here, a structural approach is used to instantiate the single Vr3to8dec component (U1), and assign statements are used to perform the level conversions. Once again, no changes were required in the top-level port definitions of the Vr74x138c module, compared to previous versions of the module. Figure 6-43 shows the relationship between the modules.

Table 6-23 Hierarchical definition of 74x138-like decoder with active-level handling.

```
module Vr74x138c(G1, G2A_L, G2B_L, A, Y_L);
  input G1, G2A_L, G2B_L;
  input [2:0] A;
  output [0:7] Y_L;
  wire G2A,G2B;
  wire [0:7] Y;

  assign G2A = ~G2A_L;  // Convert inputs
  assign G2B = ~G2B_L;
  assign Y_L = ~Y;        // Convert outputs
  Vr3to8deca U1 (G1, G2A, G2B, A, Y);
endmodule
```

Table 6-24
Verilog functional
definition of an active-
high 3-to-8 decoder.

```
module Vr3to8deca(G1, G2, G3, A, Y);
  input G1, G2, G3;
  input [2:0] A;
  output [0:7] Y;
  reg [0:7] Y;

  always @ (G1 or G2 or G3 or A) begin
    if (G1 & G2 & G3)
      case (A)
        0: Y = 8'b10000000;
        1: Y = 8'b01000000;
        2: Y = 8'b00100000;
        3: Y = 8'b00010000;
        4: Y = 8'b00001000;
        5: Y = 8'b00000100;
        6: Y = 8'b00000010;
        7: Y = 8'b00000001;
        default: Y = 8'b00000000;
      endcase
    else Y = 8'b00000000;
  end
endmodule
```

MATCHING UP NAMES   In Figure 6-43, the port names of a module are drawn inside the corresponding box. The names of the signals that are connected to the ports when the module is used are drawn on the signal lines. Notice that the signal names may match, but they don't have to. The Verilog compiler keeps everything straight, associating a scope with each name. The situation is completely analogous to the way variable and parameter names are handled in structured, procedural programming languages like C.

STATEMENT ORDER In Table 6-23, we grouped the active-level conversion statements together at the beginning of module, even though a value isn't assigned to Y_L until "after" a value is assigned to Y, by the instantiation of Vr3to8deca one line later in the module. Remember that this is OK because all statements in the module body are executed concurrently. That is, an assignment to any signal causes all the other statements that use that signal to be reevaluated, regardless of their position in the module's body.

You could put the "assign Y_L = ~Y" statement at the end of the body if its current position bothers you, but the program is a bit more maintainable in its present form, with all the active-level conversions grouped together.

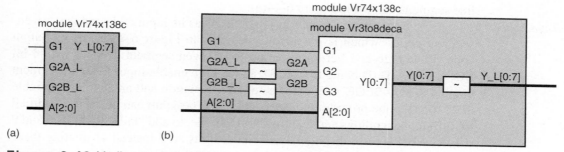

Figure 6-43 Verilog module V74x138c: (a) top level; (b) internal structure using module Vr3to8deca.

As a final example, a behavioral description for the 3-to-8 decoder is shown in Table 6-25. It sets all of the outputs to a default of 0, and then if all of the enable inputs are asserted, a for loop sets to 1 the output bit corresponding to the value of the select input A. Note that even though the for loop looks "sequential," this description generates a combinational circuit. Think of it as the combinational logic equations for the Y[i] outputs being *specified* sequentially.

```
module Vr3to8decb(G1, G2, G3, A, Y);
  input G1, G2, G3;
  input [2:0] A;
  output [0:7] Y;
  reg [0:7] Y;
  integer i;

  always @ (G1 or G2 or G3 or A) begin
    Y = 8'b00000000;
    if (G1 & G2 & G3)
      for (i=0; i<=7; i=i+1)
        if (i == A) Y[i] = 1;
  end
endmodule
```

Table 6-25
Behavioral Verilog definition for a 3-to-8 decoder.

Of the examples we've given, Table 6-25 is the only one that describes the decoder function without implicitly or explicitly embedding a truth table in the Verilog program. In that respect, it is more flexible because it can be easily adapted to make a binary decoder of any size. In another respect, it is less flexible in that it does not have a truth table that can be easily modified to make custom decoders like the one we specified in Table 6-9 on page 395.

*6.4.8 Seven-Segment Decoders

seven-segment display

Look at your wrist and you'll probably see a *seven-segment display*. This type of display, which normally uses light-emitting diodes (LEDs) or liquid-crystal display (LCD) elements, is used in watches, calculators, and instruments to display decimal data. A digit is displayed by illuminating a subset of the seven line segments shown in Figure 6-44(a).

seven-segment decoder

A *seven-segment decoder* has 4-bit BCD as its input code and the "seven-segment code," which is graphically depicted in Figure 6-44(b), as its output code. Table 6-26 is a Verilog program for a seven-segment decoder with 4-bit BCD input A–D (D being the MSB), active-high enable input EN, and segment outputs SEGA–SEGG. Note the use of concatenation and an auxiliary variable SEGS to make the program more readable. The program can be easily modified for different encodings and features, for example, to add "tails" to digits 6 and 9 (Exercise 6.47) or to display hexadecimal digits A–F instead of treating these input combinations as "don't cares" (Exercise 6.48). Comparable programs can be written in ABEL and VHDL.

6.5 Encoders

A decoder's output code normally has more bits than its input code. If the device's output code has *fewer* bits than the input code, the device is usually called an *encoder*. For example, consider a device with eight input bits representing an unsigned binary number, and two output bits indicating whether the number is prime or divisible by 7. We might call such a device a lucky/prime encoder.

encoder

2^n-to-n encoder
binary encoder

Probably the simplest encoder to build is a 2^n-to-n or *binary encoder*. As shown in Figure 6-45(a), it has just the opposite function as a binary *decoder*— its input code is the 1-out-of-2^n code and its output code is n-bit binary. The equations for an 8-to-3 encoder with inputs I0–I7 and outputs Y0–Y2 are given below:

$$Y0 = I1 + I3 + I5 + I7$$
$$Y1 = I2 + I3 + I6 + I7$$
$$Y2 = I4 + I5 + I6 + I7$$

The corresponding logic circuit is shown in (b). In general, a 2^n-to-n encoder can be built from n 2^{n-1}-input OR gates. Bit i of the input code is connected to OR gate j if bit j in the binary representation of i is 1.

Figure 6-44 Seven-segment display: (a) segment identification; (b) decimal digits.

Table 6-26 Verilog program for a seven-segment decoder.

```
module Vr7seg(A, B, C, D, EN,
              SEGA, SEGB, SEGC, SEGD, SEGE, SEGF, SEGG);
  input A, B, C, D, EN;
  output SEGA, SEGB, SEGC, SEGD, SEGE, SEGF, SEGG;
  reg SEGA, SEGB, SEGC, SEGD, SEGE, SEGF, SEGG;
  reg [1:7] SEGS;

  always @ (A or B or C or D or EN or SEGS) begin
    if (EN)
      case ({D,C,B,A})
// Segment patterns    abcdefg
        0:  SEGS = 7'b1111110;  // 0
        1:  SEGS = 7'b0110000;  // 1
        2:  SEGS = 7'b1101101;  // 2
        3:  SEGS = 7'b1111001;  // 3
        4:  SEGS = 7'b0110011;  // 4
        5:  SEGS = 7'b1011011;  // 5
        6:  SEGS = 7'b0011111;  // 6 (no 'tail')
        7:  SEGS = 7'b1110000;  // 7
        8:  SEGS = 7'b1111111;  // 8
        9:  SEGS = 7'b1110011;  // 9 (no 'tail')
        default SEGS = 7'bx;
      endcase
    else SEGS = 7'b0;
    {SEGA, SEGB, SEGC, SEGD, SEGE, SEGF, SEGG} = SEGS;
  end
endmodule
```

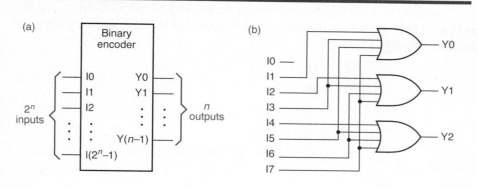

Figure 6-45
Binary encoder:
(a) general structure;
(b) 8-to-3 encoder.

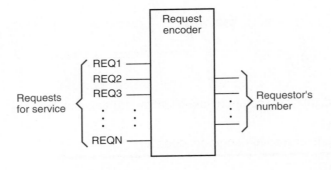

Figure 6-46
A system with 2^n requestors, and a "request encoder" that indicates which request signal is asserted at any time.

6.5.1 Priority Encoders

The 1-out-of-2^n coded outputs of an n-bit binary decoder are generally used to control a set of 2^n devices, where at most one device is supposed to be active at any time. Conversely, consider a system with 2^n *inputs*, each of which indicates a request for service, as in Figure 6-46. This structure is often found in microprocessor input/output subsystems, where the inputs might be interrupt requests.

In this situation, it may seem natural to use a binary encoder of the type shown in Figure 6-45 to observe the inputs and indicate which one is requesting service at any time. However, this encoder works properly only if the inputs are guaranteed to be asserted at most one at a time. If multiple requests can be made simultaneously, the encoder gives undesirable results. For example, suppose that inputs I2 and I4 of the 8-to-3 encoder are both 1; then the output is 110, the binary encoding of 6.

Either 2 or 4, not 6, would be a useful output in the preceding example, but how can the encoding device decide which? The solution is to assign *priority* to the input lines, so that when multiple requests are asserted, the encoding device produces the number of the highest-priority requestor. Such a device is called a *priority encoder*.

priority

priority encoder

The logic symbol for an 8-input priority encoder is shown in Figure 6-47. Input I7 has the highest priority. Outputs A2–A0 contain the number of the highest-priority asserted input, if any. The IDLE output is asserted if no inputs are asserted.

In order to write logic equations for the priority encoder's outputs, we first define eight intermediate variables H0–H7, such that Hi is 1 if and only if Ii is the highest priority 1 input:

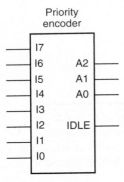

Figure 6-47
Logic symbol for a generic 8-input priority encoder.

$$H7 = I7$$
$$H6 = I6 \cdot I7'$$
$$H5 = I5 \cdot I6' \cdot I7'$$
$$\cdots$$
$$H0 = I0 \cdot I1' \cdot I2' \cdot I3' \cdot I4' \cdot I5' \cdot I6' \cdot I7'$$

Using these signals, the equations for the A2–A0 outputs are similar to the ones for a simple binary encoder:

$$A2 = H4 + H5 + H6 + H7$$
$$A1 = H2 + H3 + H6 + H7$$
$$A0 = H1 + H3 + H5 + H7$$

The IDLE output is 1 if no inputs are 1:

$$IDLE = (I0 + I1 + I2 + I3 + I4 + I5 + I6 + I7)'$$
$$= I0' \cdot I1' \cdot I2' \cdot I3' \cdot I4' \cdot I5' \cdot I6' \cdot I7'$$

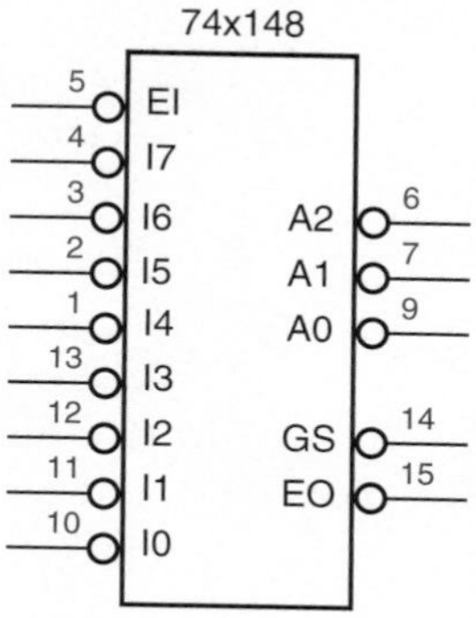

6.5.2 The 74x148 Priority Encoder

The *74x148* is a commercially available, MSI 8-input priority encoder with the logic symbol shown in Figure 6-48. The main difference between this IC and the "generic" priority encoder of Figure 6-47 is that its inputs and outputs are active low.

Instead of an IDLE output, the '148 has a GS_L output that is asserted when the device is enabled and one or more of the request inputs are asserted. The manufacturer calls this "Group Select," but it's easier to remember as "Got Something." Also, the '148 has an enable input, EI_L, that must be asserted for any of its outputs to be asserted. The '148's complete truth table is given in Table 6-27, and its detailed internal schematic can be found at <u>DDPPonline</u> in <u>Section Enc</u>.

Figure 6-48
Logic symbol for the 74x148 8-input priority encoder.

74x148

Table 6-27 Truth table for a 74x148 8-input priority encoder.

Inputs									Outputs				
EI_L	I0_L	I1_L	I2_L	I3_L	I4_L	I5_L	I6_L	I7_L	A2_L	A1_L	A0_L	GS_L	EO_L
1	x	x	x	x	x	x	x	x	1	1	1	1	1
0	x	x	x	x	x	x	x	0	0	0	0	0	1
0	x	x	x	x	x	x	0	1	0	0	1	0	1
0	x	x	x	x	x	0	1	1	0	1	0	0	1
0	x	x	x	x	0	1	1	1	0	1	1	0	1
0	x	x	x	0	1	1	1	1	1	0	0	0	1
0	x	x	0	1	1	1	1	1	1	0	1	0	1
0	x	0	1	1	1	1	1	1	1	1	0	0	1
0	0	1	1	1	1	1	1	1	1	1	1	0	1
0	1	1	1	1	1	1	1	1	1	1	1	1	0

The 148's EO_L signal is an enable *output* that is used for cascading—it is designed to be connected to the EI_L input of another '148 that handles lower-priority requests. EO_L is asserted if EI_L is asserted but no request input is asserted; thus, a lower-priority '148 may be enabled.

Figure 6-49 shows how four 74x148s can be connected in this way to accept 32 request inputs and produce a 5-bit output, RA4–RA0, indicating the highest-priority requestor. Since the A2–A0 outputs of at most one '148 will be enabled at any time, the outputs of the individual '148s can be ORed to produce RA2–RA0. Likewise, the individual GS_L outputs can be combined in a 4-to-2 encoder to produce RA4 and RA3. The RGS output is asserted if any GS output is asserted.

6.5.3 Encoders in ABEL and PLDs

In ABEL, encoders can be designed using equations for intermediate variables to detect the highest-priority asserted input, as we showed in Section 6.5.1. For example, suppose we would like to design a 15-input priority encoder for inputs P0–P14. First, we write equations for 15 variables Hi ($0 \leq Hi \leq 14$) such that Hi is 1 if Pi is the highest-priority asserted input. Then, since at most one Hi variable is 1 at any time, we can combine the Hi's in a binary encoder to obtain a 4-bit number identifying the highest-priority asserted input.

An ABEL program using this approach is shown in Table 6-28, and a logic diagram for the encoder using a single GAL20V8 is given in Figure 6-50. Inputs P0–P14 are asserted to indicate requests, with P14 having the highest priority. If EN_L (Enable) is asserted, then the Y3_L–Y0_L outputs give the number

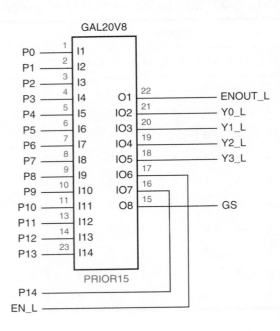

Figure 6-50
Logic diagram for a PLD-based 15-input priority encoder

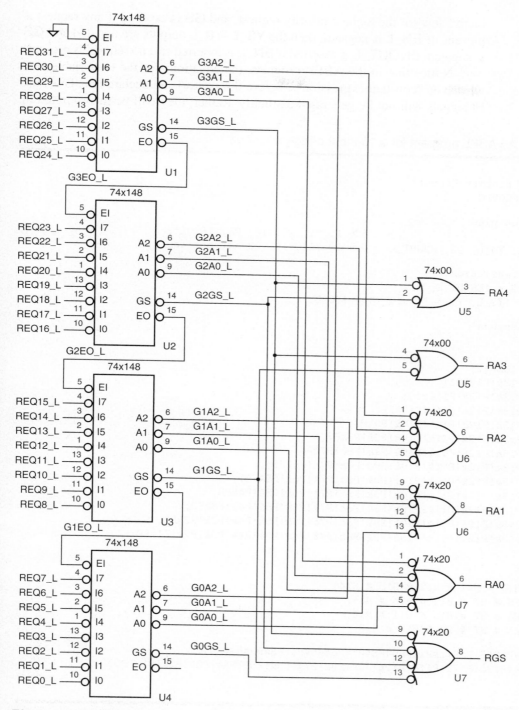

Figure 6-49 Four 74x148s cascaded to handle 32 requests.

(active low) of the highest-priority request, and GS is asserted if any request is present. If EN_L is negated, then the Y3_L–Y0_L outputs are negated and GS is negated. ENOUT_L is asserted if EN_L is asserted and no request is present.

Notice that in the ABEL program, the equations for the Hi variables are written as "constant expressions," before the equations declaration. Thus, the Hi signals will not be generated explicitly. Rather, they will be incorporated in

Table 6-28 An ABEL program for a 15-input priority encoder.

```
module PRIOR15
title '15-Input Priority Encoder '
PRIOR15 device 'P20V8C';

" Input and output pins
P0..P14, EN_L                        pin 1..11, 13, 14, 23, 16, 17;
Y3_L, Y2_L, Y1_L, Y0_L, GS, ENOUT_L  pin 18..21, 15, 22 istype 'com';

" Active-level translation
EN = !EN_L; ENOUT = !ENOUT_L;
Y3 = !Y3_L; Y2 = !Y2_L; Y1 = !Y1_L; Y0 = !Y0_L;

" Constant expressions
H14 = EN&P14;
H13 = EN&!P14&P13;
H12 = EN&!P14&!P13&P12;
H11 = EN&!P14&!P13&!P12&P11;
H10 = EN&!P14&!P13&!P12&!P11&P10;
H9  = EN&!P14&!P13&!P12&!P11&!P10&P9;
H8  = EN&!P14&!P13&!P12&!P11&!P10&!P9&P8;
H7  = EN&!P14&!P13&!P12&!P11&!P10&!P9&!P8&P7;
H6  = EN&!P14&!P13&!P12&!P11&!P10&!P9&!P8&!P7&P6;
H5  = EN&!P14&!P13&!P12&!P11&!P10&!P9&!P8&!P7&!P6&P5;
H4  = EN&!P14&!P13&!P12&!P11&!P10&!P9&!P8&!P7&!P6&!P5&P4;
H3  = EN&!P14&!P13&!P12&!P11&!P10&!P9&!P8&!P7&!P6&!P5&!P4&P3;
H2  = EN&!P14&!P13&!P12&!P11&!P10&!P9&!P8&!P7&!P6&!P5&!P4&!P3&P2;
H1  = EN&!P14&!P13&!P12&!P11&!P10&!P9&!P8&!P7&!P6&!P5&!P4&!P3&!P2&P1;
H0  = EN&!P14&!P13&!P12&!P11&!P10&!P9&!P8&!P7&!P6&!P5&!P4&!P3&!P2&!P1&P0;

equations

Y3 = H8 # H9 # H10 # H11 # H12 # H13 # H14;
Y2 = H4 # H5 # H6 # H7 # H12 # H13 # H14;
Y1 = H2 # H3 # H6 # H7 # H10 # H11 # H14;
Y0 = H1 # H3 # H5 # H7 # H9 # H11 # H13;

GS    = EN&(P14#P13#P12#P11#P10#P9#P8#P7#P6#P5#P4#P3#P2#P1#P0);
ENOUT = EN&!P14&!P13&!P12&!P11&!P10&!P9&!P8&!P7&!P6&!P5&!P4&!P3&!P2&!P1&!P0;

end PRIOR15
```

the subsequent equations for Y0–Y3, which the compiler cranks on to obtain minimal sum-of-products expressions. As it turns out, each Yi output has only seven product terms, as you can see from the structure of the equations.

The priority encoder can be designed even more intuitively using ABEL's when statement. As shown in Table 6-29, a deeply nested series of when statements expresses precisely the logical function of the priority encoder. This program yields exactly the same set of output equations as the previous program.

Table 6-29 Alternate ABEL program for the same 15-input priority encoder.

```
module PRIOR15W
title '15-Input Priority Encoder'
PRIOR15W device 'P20V8C';

" Input and output pins
P0..P14, EN_L                      pin 1..11, 13, 14, 23, 16, 17;
Y3_L, Y2_L, Y1_L, Y0_L, GS, ENOUT_L   pin 18..21, 15, 22 istype 'com';

" Active-level translation
EN = !EN_L; ENOUT = !ENOUT_L;

" Set definition
Y_L = [Y3_L, Y2_L, Y1_L, Y0_L];

equations

when !EN then !Y_L = 0;             " Note: !Y_L === active-high Y
else when P14 then !Y_L = 14;       " Can't define active-high Y set
  else when P13 then !Y_L = 13;     "     due to ABEL set quirks
    else when P12 then !Y_L = 12;
      else when P11 then !Y_L = 11;
        else when P10 then !Y_L = 10;
          else when P9 then !Y_L = 9;
            else when P8 then !Y_L = 8;
              else when P7 then !Y_L = 7;
                else when P6 then !Y_L = 6;
                  else when P5 then !Y_L = 5;
                    else when P4 then !Y_L = 4;
                      else when P3 then !Y_L = 3;
                        else when P2 then !Y_L = 2;
                          else when P1 then !Y_L = 1;
                            else when P0 then !Y_L = 0;
                              else {!Y_L = 0; ENOUT = 1;};

GS = EN&(P14#P13#P12#P11#P10#P9#P8#P7#P6#P5#P4#P3#P2#P1#P0);

end PRIOR15W
```

6.5.4 Encoders in VHDL

The approach to specifying encoders in VHDL is a little different from the ABEL approach. We could embed explicit equations or nested conditionals into the VHDL program, but a behavioral description is far more intuitive. Since VHDL's if-then-else construct best describes prioritization and is available only within a process, we use the process-based behavioral approach.

Table 6-30 is a behavioral VHDL program for a priority encoder whose function is equivalent to the 74x148. It uses a FOR loop to look for an asserted

■ **Table 6-30** Behavioral VHDL program for a 74x148-like 8-input priority encoder.

```
library IEEE;
use IEEE.std_logic_1164.all;

entity V74x148 is
    port (
        EI_L: in STD_LOGIC;
        I_L: in STD_LOGIC_VECTOR (7 downto 0);
        A_L: out STD_LOGIC_VECTOR (2 downto 0);
        EO_L, GS_L: out STD_LOGIC
    );
end V74x148;

architecture V74x148p of V74x148 is
  signal EI: STD_LOGIC;                          -- active-high version of input
  signal I: STD_LOGIC_VECTOR (7 downto 0); -- active-high version of inputs
  signal EO, GS: STD_LOGIC;                      -- active-high version of outputs
  signal A: STD_LOGIC_VECTOR (2 downto 0); -- active-high version of outputs
begin
  process (EI_L, I_L, EI, EO, GS, I, A)
  variable j: INTEGER range 7 downto 0;
  begin
    EI <= not EI_L; -- convert input
    I <= not I_L;   -- convert inputs
    EO <= '1'; GS <= '0'; A <= "000";
    if (EI)='0' then EO <= '0';
    else for j in 7 downto 0 loop
        if I(j)='1' then
          GS <= '1'; EO <= '0'; A <= CONV_STD_LOGIC_VECTOR(j,3);
          exit;
        end if;
      end loop;
    end if;
    EO_L <= not EO; -- convert output
    GS_L <= not GS; -- convert output
    A_L <= not A;   -- convert outputs
  end process;
end V74x148p;
```

input, starting with the highest-priority input. Like some of our previous programs, it performs explicit active-level conversion at the beginning and end. Also recall that the CONV_STD_LOGIC_VECTOR(j,n) function was defined in Section 5.3.3 to convert from an integer j to a STD_LOGIC_VECTOR of a specified length n. This program is easily modified to use a different priority order or a different number of inputs, or to add more functionality such as finding a second-highest-priority input, as explored in Section XCvhd.3 at DDPPonline.

6.5.5 Encoders in Verilog

It is straighforward to write a behavioral description of an encoder in Verilog using a for loop. For example, Table 6-31 is a behavioral Verilog module for a priority encoder function equivalent to the 74x148. Within the always block, it initializes the outputs as if no asserted input will be found. Then it uses a for loop to look for an asserted input, working from the lowest priority to the highest. In the end, A will be set to the number of the last (highest priority) asserted input that was found, if any. Like some of our previous Verilog modules, Table 6-31 performs explicit active-level conversion at the beginning. This module is easily modified to use a different priority order or a different number of inputs, or to add more functionality such as finding a second-highest-priority input, as explored in Section XCver.3 at DDPPonline.

Table 6-31 Behavioral Verilog module for a 74x148-like 8-input priority encoder.

```
module Vr74x148(EI_L, I_L, A_L, EO_L, GS_L);
  input EI_L;
  input [7:0] I_L;
  output [2:0] A_L;
  output EO_L, GS_L;
  reg [7:0] I;
  reg [2:0] A, A_L;
  reg EI, EO_L, EO, GS_L, GS;
  integer j;

  always @ (EI_L or EI or I_L or I or A or EO or GS) begin
    EI = ~EI_L; I  = ~I_L;              // convert inputs
    EO_L = ~EO; GS_L = ~GS; A_L = ~A;  // convert outputs
    EO = 1; GS = 0; A = 0;             // default output values
    begin
      if (EI==0) EO = 0;
      else for (j=0; j<=7; j=j+1) // check low priority first
             if (I[j]==1)
                begin GS = 1; EO = 0; A = j; end
    end
  end
endmodule
```

UPS AND DOWNS   Another possible strategy for the `for` loop in Table 6-31 would be to start with the highest-priority input (`I[7]`) and search down until an asserted input is found. Once one was found, a `disable` statement would be used to exit the `for` loop, so that A would be set to the number of the first (and therefore highest-priority) asserted input. This would be similar to the use of the `exit` statement in the VHDL version in Table 6-30. However, the Verilog `disable` statement is not supported by all synthesis tools, including Xilinx XST, while the version in Table 6-31 always works.

6.6 Three-State Devices

In Section 3.7.3 we described the electrical design of CMOS devices whose outputs may be in one of three states—0, 1, or Hi-Z. In this section we'll show how to use them.

6.6.1 Three-State Buffers

three-state buffer
three-state driver

The most basic three-state device is a *three-state buffer*, often called a *three-state driver*. The logic symbols for four physically different three-state buffers are shown in Figure 6-51. The basic symbol is that of a noninverting buffer [(a), (b)] or an inverter [(c), (d)]. The extra signal at the top of the symbol is a *three-state enable* input, which may be active high [(a), (c)] or active low [(b), (d)]. When the enable input is asserted, the device behaves like an ordinary buffer or inverter. When the enable input is negated, the device output "floats"; that is, it goes to a high-impedance (Hi-Z), disconnected state and functionally behaves as if it weren't even there.

three-state enable

Three-state devices allow multiple sources to share a single "party line," as long as only one device "talks" on the line at a time. Figure 6-52 gives an example of how this can be done. Three input bits, SSRC2–SSRC0, select one of eight sources of data that may drive a single line, SDATA. A 3-to-8 decoder, the 74x138, ensures that only one of the eight SEL lines is asserted at a time, enabling only one three-state buffer to drive SDATA. However, if not all of the EN lines are asserted, then none of the three-state buffers is enabled. The logic value on SDATA is undefined in this case.

Typical three-state devices are designed so that they go into the Hi-Z state faster than they come out of the Hi-Z state. In terms of the specifications in a data

Figure 6-51 Various three-state buffers: (a) noninverting, active-high enable; (b) noninverting, active-low enable; (c) inverting, active-high enable; (d) inverting, active-low enable.

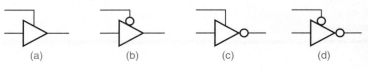

(a)   (b)   (c)   (d)

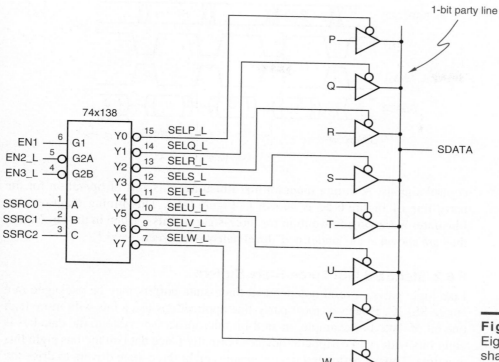

Figure 6-52
Eight sources sharing a three-state party line.

book, t_{pLZ} and t_{pHZ} are both less than t_{pZL} and t_{pZH}; also see Section 3.7.3. This means that if the outputs of two three-state devices are connected to the same party line, and we simultaneously disable one and enable the other, the first device will get off the party line before the second one gets on. This is important because, if both devices were to drive the party line at the same time, and if both were trying to maintain opposite output values (0 and 1), then excessive current would flow and create noise in the system, as discussed in Section 3.7.7. This is often called *fighting*.

fighting

Unfortunately, delays and timing skews in control circuits make it difficult to ensure that the enable inputs of different three-state devices change "simultaneously." Even when this is possible, a problem arises if three-state devices from different-speed logic families (or even different ICs manufactured on different days) are connected to the same party line. The turn-on time (t_{pZL} or t_{pZH}) of a "fast" device may be shorter than the turn-off time (t_{pLZ} or t_{pHZ}) of a "slow" one, and the outputs may still fight.

The only really safe way to use three-state devices is to design control logic that guarantees a *dead time* on the party line during which no one is driving it. The dead time must be long enough to account for the worst-case differences between turn-off and turn-on times of the devices and for skews in the three-state

dead time

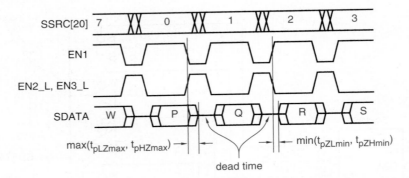

Figure 6-53
Timing diagram for
the three-state
party line.

control signals. A timing diagram that illustrates this sort of operation for the
party line of Figure 6-52 is shown in Figure 6-53. This timing diagram also
illustrates a drawing convention for three-state signals—when in the Hi-Z state,
they are shown at an "undefined" level halfway between 0 and 1.

6.6.2 Standard MSI Three-State Buffers

Like logic gates, several independent three-state buffers may be packaged in a
single SSI IC. However, most party-line applications use a bus with more than
one bit of data. For example, in an 8-bit microprocessor system, the data bus is
eight bits wide, and peripheral devices normally place data on the bus eight bits
at a time. Thus, a peripheral device enables eight three-state drivers to drive the

Figure 6-54
The 74x541 octal three-state
buffer: (a) logic diagram;
(b) traditional logic symbol.

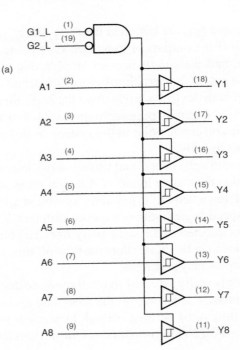

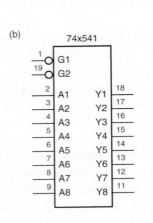

DEFINING "UNDEFINED" The actual voltage level of a floating signal depends on circuit details, such as resistive and capacitive load, and may vary over time. Also, the interpretation of this level by other circuits depends on the input characteristics of those circuits, so it's best not to count on a floating signal as being anything other than "undefined." Sometimes a pull-up resistor is used on three-state party lines to ensure that a floating value is pulled to a HIGH voltage and interpreted as logic 1. This is especially important on party lines that drive CMOS devices, which may consume excessive current when their input voltage is halfway between logic 0 and 1.

bus, all at the same time. Independent enable inputs, as in the application in Figure 6-52, are not necessary.

So, to reduce the package size in wide-bus applications, most commonly used MSI parts contain multiple three-state buffers with common enable inputs. For example, Figure 6-54 shows the logic diagram and symbol for a *74x541* octal noninverting three-state buffer. *Octal* means that the part contains eight individual buffers. Both enable inputs, G1_L and G2_L, must be asserted to enable the device's three-state outputs. The little rectangular symbols inside the buffer symbols indicate *hysteresis*, an electrical characteristic of the inputs that improves noise immunity, as we explained in Section 3.7.2. The 74x541 inputs typically have 0.4 volts of hysteresis.

74x541
octal

hysteresis

Figure 6-55 shows part of a microprocessor system with an 8-bit data bus, DB[0–7], and a 74x541 used as an input port. The microprocessor selects Input Port 1 by asserting INSEL1 and requests a read operation by asserting READ. The selected 74x541 responds by driving the microprocessor data bus with user-supplied input data. Other input ports may be selected when a different INSEL line is asserted along with READ.

Figure 6-55 Using a 74x541 as a microprocessor input port.

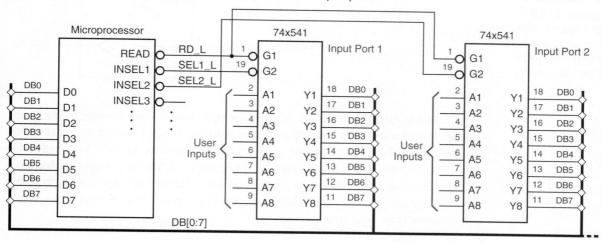

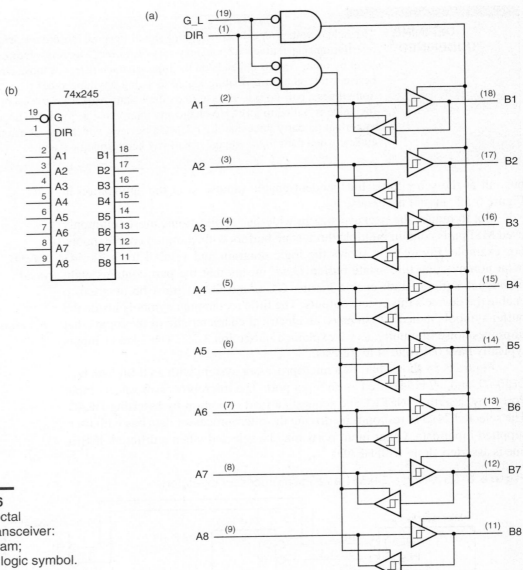

Figure 6-56
The 74x245 octal
three-state transceiver:
(a) logic diagram;
(b) traditional logic symbol.

74x540
74x240
74x241
74x16540
74x32244

Many other varieties of octal three-state buffers are commercially available. For example, the *74x540* is identical to the 74x541 except that it contains inverting buffers. The *74x240* and *74x241* are similar to the '540 and '541, except that they are split into two 4-bit sections, each with a single enable line. There are also 16-bit and even 32-bit versions of three-state buffers, such as the *74x16540* and the *74x32244*, respectively. These parts come in larger packages with more pins, of course.

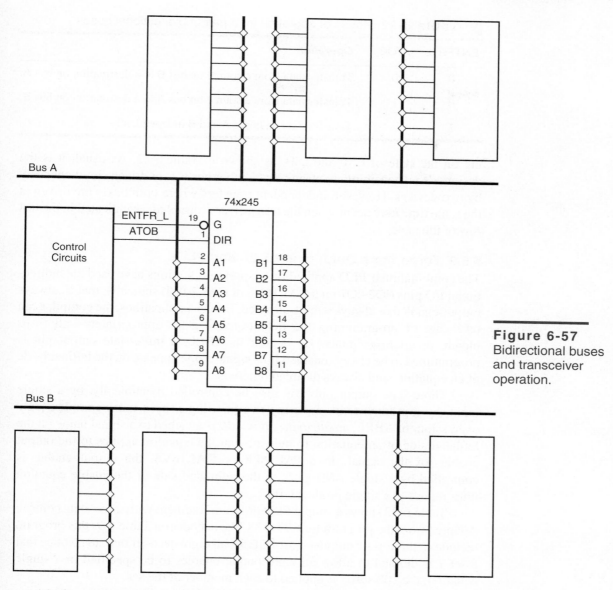

Figure 6-57
Bidirectional buses
and transceiver
operation.

A *bus transceiver* contains pairs of three-state buffers connected in   *bus transceiver*
opposite directions between each pair of pins, so that data can be transferred in
either direction. For example, Figure 6-56 shows the logic diagram and symbol
for a *74x245* octal three-state transceiver. The DIR input determines the direction   *74x245*
of transfer, from A to B (DIR = 1) or from B to A (DIR = 0). The three-state buffer
for the selected direction is enabled only if G_L is asserted.

A bus transceiver is typically used between two *bidirectional buses*, as   *bidirectional bus*
shown in Figure 6-57. Three different modes of operation are possible, depend-

Table 6-32 Modes of operation for a pair of bidirectional buses.

ENTFR_L	ATOB	*Operation*
0	0	Transfer data from a source on bus B to a destination on bus A.
0	1	Transfer data from a source on bus A to a destination on bus B.
1	x	Transfer data on buses A and B independently.

ing on the state of G_L and DIR, as shown in Table 6-32. As usual, it is the designer's responsibility to ensure that neither bus is ever driven simultaneously by two devices. However, independent transfers where both buses are driven at the same time may occur when the transceiver is disabled, as indicated in the last row of the table.

6.6.3 Three-State Outputs in ABEL and PLDs

The combinational-PLD applications in previous sections have used the bidirectional I/O pins (IO2–IO7 on a GAL16V8 or GAL20V8) statically, that is, always output-enabled or always output-disabled. In such applications, the compiler can take care of programming the output-enable gates appropriately—all fuses blown, or all fuses intact. By default in ABEL, a three-state output pin is programmed to be always enabled if its signal name appears on the lefthand side of an equation, and always disabled otherwise.

.OE attribute suffix

Three-state output pins can also be controlled dynamically, by a single input, by a product term, or, using two-pass logic, by a more complex logic expression. In ABEL, an *attribute suffix* .OE is attached to a signal name on the lefthand side of an equation to indicate that the equation applies to the output enable for the signal. In a PAL16L8 or GAL16V8, the output enable is controlled by a single AND gate, so the righthand side of the enable equation must reduce to a single product term.

Table 6-33 shows a simple PLD program fragment with three-state control. Adapted from the program for a 74x138-like decoder on Table 6-7, this program includes a three-state output control OE for all eight decoder outputs. Notice that a set Y is defined to allow all eight output enables to be specified in a single equation; the .OE suffix is applied to each member of the set.

In Table 6-33, the output pins Y0–Y7 are always either enabled or floating, and are used strictly as "output pins." I/O pins (IO2–IO7 in a 16L8 or 16V8) can be used as "bidirectional pins"; that is, they can be used dynamically as inputs or outputs depending on whether the output-enable gate is producing a 0 or a 1. An example application of I/O pins is a four-way, 2-bit bus transceiver with the following specifications:

- The transceiver handles four 2-bit bidirectional buses, A[1:2], B[1:2], C[1:2], and D[1:2].

Table 6-33 ABEL program for a 74x138-like 3-to-8 binary decoder with three-state output control.

```
module Z74X138T
title '74x138 Decoder with Three-State Output Enable'
Z74X138T device 'P16V8C';

" Input pins
A, B, C, !G2A, !G2B, G1, !OE  pin 1, 2, 3, 4, 5, 6, 7;
" Output pins
!Y0, !Y1, !Y2, !Y3            pin 19, 18, 17, 16 istype 'com';
!Y4, !Y5, !Y6, !Y7            pin 15, 14, 13, 12 istype 'com';

" Constant expression
ENB = G1 & G2A & G2B;
Y = [Y0..Y7];

equations
Y.OE = OE;
Y0 = ENB & !C & !B & !A;
...
Y7 = ENB &  C &  B &  A;

end Z74X138T
```

- The source of data to drive the buses is selected by three select inputs, S[2:0], according to Table 6-34. If S2 is 0, the buses are driven with a constant value, otherwise they are driven with one of the other buses. However, when the selected source is a bus, the source bus is driven with 00.

- Each bus has its own output-enable signal, AOE_L, BOE_L, COE_L, or DOE_L. There is also a "master" output-enable signal, MOE_L. The transceiver drives a particular bus if and only if MOE_L and the output-enable signal for that bus are both asserted.

S2	S1	S0	Source selected
0	0	0	00
0	0	1	01
0	1	0	10
0	1	1	11
1	0	0	A bus
1	0	1	B bus
1	1	0	C bus
1	1	1	D bus

Table 6-34
Bus-selection codes for a four-way bus transceiver.

Table 6-35 An ABEL program for a four-way, 2-bit bus transceiver.

```
module XCVR4X2
title 'Four-way 2-bit Bus Transceiver'
XCVR4X2 device 'P16V8C';

" Input pins
A1I, A2I                            pin 1, 11;
!AOE, !BOE, !COE, !DOE, !MOE        pin 2, 3, 4, 5, 6;
S0, S1, S2                          pin 7, 8, 9;
" Output and bidirectional pins
A1O, A2O                            pin 19, 12                    istype 'com';
B1, B2, C1, C2, D1, D2              pin 18, 17, 16, 15, 14, 13 istype 'com';

" Set definitions
ABUSO = [A1O,A2O];
ABUSI = [A1I,A2I];
BBUS  = [B1,B2];
CBUS  = [C1,C2];
DBUS  = [D1,D2];
SEL   = [S2,S1,S0];
CONST = [S1,S0];
" Constants
SELA = [1,0,0];
SELB = [1,0,1];
SELC = [1,1,0];
SELD = [1,1,1];

equations
ABUSO.OE = AOE & MOE;
BBUS.OE = BOE & MOE;
CBUS.OE = COE & MOE;
DBUS.OE = DOE & MOE;
ABUSO = !S2&CONST # (SEL==SELB)&BBUS # (SEL==SELC)&CBUS # (SEL==SELD)&DBUS;
BBUS  = !S2&CONST # (SEL==SELA)&ABUSI # (SEL==SELC)&CBUS # (SEL==SELD)&DBUS;
CBUS  = !S2&CONST # (SEL==SELA)&ABUSI # (SEL==SELB)&BBUS # (SEL==SELD)&DBUS;
DBUS  = !S2&CONST # (SEL==SELA)&ABUSI # (SEL==SELB)&BBUS # (SEL==SELC)&CBUS;

end XCVR4X2
```

Table 6-35 is an ABEL program that performs the transceiver function. According to the enable (.OE) equations, each bus is output enabled if MOE and its own OE are asserted. Each bus is driven with S1 and S0 if S2 is 0, and with the selected bus if a different bus is selected. If the bus itself is selected, the output equation evaluates to 0, and the bus is driven with 00 as required.

Figure 6-58 is a logic diagram for a GAL16V8 with the required inputs and outputs. Since the device has only six bidirectional pins and the specification

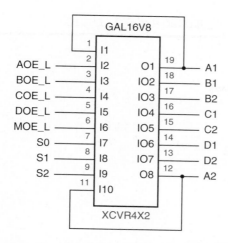

Figure 6-58
PLD inputs and
outputs for a four-way,
2-bit bus transceiver.

requires eight, the A bus uses one pair of pins for input and another for output. This is reflected in the program by the use of separate signals and sets for the A-bus input and output.

*6.6.4 Three-State Outputs in VHDL

VHDL itself does not have built-in types and operators for three-state outputs. However, it does have primitives which can be used to create signals and systems with three-state behavior; the IEEE 1164 package uses these primitives. As a start, the IEEE 1164 STD_LOGIC type defines 'Z' as one of its nine possible signal values; this value is used for the high-impedance state. You can assign this value to any STD_LOGIC signal, and the definitions of the standard logic functions account for the possibility of 'Z' inputs (generally a 'Z' input will cause a 'U' output).

Given the availability of three-state signals, how do we create three-state buses in VHDL? A three-state bus generally has two or more drivers, although the mechanisms we discuss work fine with just one driver. In VHDL, there is no explicit language construct for joining three-state outputs into a bus. Instead, the compiler automatically joins together signals that are driven in two or more different processes, that is, signals that appear on the lefthand side of a signal assignment statement in two or more processes. However, the signals must have the appropriate type, as explained below.

The IEEE 1164 STD_LOGIC type is actually defined as a *resolved type* which is a subtype of an *unresolved type*, STD_ULOGIC. In VHDL, a resolved type is used for any signal that may be driven in two or more processes. The definition of a resolved type includes a *resolution function* that is called every time an assignment is made to a signal having that type. As the name implies, this function resolves the value of the signal when it has multiple drivers. This allows the user to model signal behavior similar to that of real devices.

resolved type
unresolved type
STD_ULOGIC
resolution function

■ **Table 6-36** IEEE 1164 package declarations for STD_ULOGIC and STD_LOGIC.

```
PACKAGE std_logic_1164 IS
-- logic state system (unresolved)
    TYPE std_ulogic IS ( 'U',   -- Uninitialized
                         'X',   -- Forcing  Unknown
                         '0',   -- Forcing  0
                         '1',   -- Forcing  1
                         'Z',   -- High Impedance
                         'W',   -- Weak     Unknown
                         'L',   -- Weak     0
                         'H',   -- Weak     1
                         '-'    -- Don't care
                       );

-- unconstrained array of std_ulogic
    TYPE std_ulogic_vector IS ARRAY ( NATURAL RANGE <> ) OF std_ulogic;

-- resolution function
    FUNCTION resolved ( s : std_ulogic_vector ) RETURN std_ulogic;

-- *** industry standard logic type ***
    SUBTYPE std_logic IS resolved std_ulogic;
...
```

Tables 6-36 and 6-37 show the IEEE 1164 definitions of STD_ULOGIC, STD_LOGIC and the resolution function "resolved". This code uses a two-dimensional array resolution_table to determine the final STD_LOGIC value produced by n processes that drive a signal to n possibly different values passed in the input vector s. If, for example, a signal has four drivers, the VHDL compiler automatically constructs a 4-element vector containing the four driven values, and passes this vector to resolved every time that any one of those values changes. The result is passed back to the simulation.

Notice that the order in which the driven signal values appear in s does not affect the result produced by resolved, due to the strong ordering of "strengths" in the resolution_table: 'U'>'X'>'0','1'>'W'>'L','H'>'-'. That is, once a signal is partially resolved to a particular value, it never further resolves to a "weaker" value; and 0/1 and L/H conflicts always resolve to a stronger undefined value ('X' or 'W').

So, do you need to know all of this in order to use three-state outputs in VHDL? Well, usually not, but it can help if your simulations don't match up with reality. All that's normally required to simulate three-state outputs within VHDL is to declare the corresponding signals as type STD_LOGIC, and let the simulator resolve them during operation.

For example, Table 6-38 on page 430 describes a system that uses four 8-bit three-state drivers (in four processes) to select one of four 8-bit buses, A, B, C,

Table 6-37 IEEE 1164 package body for STD_ULOGIC and STD_LOGIC.

```
PACKAGE BODY std_logic_1164 IS
-- local type
    TYPE stdlogic_table IS ARRAY (std_ulogic, std_ulogic) OF std_ulogic;

-- resolution function
    CONSTANT resolution_table : stdlogic_table := (
    --       ------------------------------------------------------------
    --       |  U    X    0    1    Z    W    L    H    -            |  |
    --       ------------------------------------------------------------
        ( 'U', 'U', 'U', 'U', 'U', 'U', 'U', 'U', 'U' ), -- | U |
        ( 'U', 'X', 'X', 'X', 'X', 'X', 'X', 'X', 'X' ), -- | X |
        ( 'U', 'X', '0', 'X', '0', '0', '0', '0', 'X' ), -- | 0 |
        ( 'U', 'X', 'X', '1', '1', '1', '1', '1', 'X' ), -- | 1 |
        ( 'U', 'X', '0', '1', 'Z', 'W', 'L', 'H', 'X' ), -- | Z |
        ( 'U', 'X', '0', '1', 'W', 'W', 'W', 'W', 'X' ), -- | W |
        ( 'U', 'X', '0', '1', 'L', 'W', 'L', 'W', 'X' ), -- | L |
        ( 'U', 'X', '0', '1', 'H', 'W', 'W', 'H', 'X' ), -- | H |
        ( 'U', 'X', 'X', 'X', 'X', 'X', 'X', 'X', 'X' )  -- | - |
    );

    FUNCTION resolved ( s : std_ulogic_vector ) RETURN std_ulogic IS
        VARIABLE result : std_ulogic := 'Z';   -- weakest state default
    BEGIN
        -- the test for a single driver is essential otherwise the
        -- loop would return 'X' for a single driver of '-' and that
        -- would conflict with the value of a single driver unresolved
        -- signal.
    IF    (s'LENGTH = 1) THEN    RETURN s(s'LOW);
    ELSE
        FOR i IN s'RANGE LOOP
            result := resolution_table(result, s(i));
        END LOOP;
    END IF;
    RETURN result;
    END resolved;
...
```

and D, to drive onto a result bus X. Recall that the construct "(others => 'Z')"
denotes a vector of all Z's, with whatever length is needed to match the lefthand
side of the assignment.

VHDL is flexible enough that you can use it to define other types of bus
operation. For example, you could define a subtype and resolution function for
open-drain outputs such that a wired-**AND** function is obtained. However, you'll
seldom have to use this feature; the definitions for specific output types in PLDs,
FPGAs, and ASICs are usually already done for you in libraries provided by the
component vendors.

Table 6-38 VHDL program with four 8-bit three-state drivers.

```
library IEEE;
use IEEE.std_logic_1164.all;

entity V3statex is
    port (
        G_L: in STD_LOGIC;                        -- Global output enable
        SEL: in STD_LOGIC_VECTOR (1 downto 0);    -- Input select 0,1,2,3 ==> A,B,C,D
        A, B, C, D: in STD_LOGIC_VECTOR (1 to 8); -- Input buses
        X: out STD_LOGIC_VECTOR (1 to 8)          -- Output bus (three-state)
    );
end V3statex;

architecture V3states of V3statex is
begin
  process (G_L, SEL, A)
  begin
    if G_L='0' and SEL = "00" then X <= A;
    else X <= (others => 'Z');
    end if;
  end process;

  process (G_L, SEL, B)
  begin
    if G_L='0' and SEL = "01" then X <= B;
    else X <= (others => 'Z');
    end if;
  end process;

  process (G_L, SEL, C)
  begin
    if G_L='0' and SEL = "10" then X <= C;
    else X <= (others => 'Z');
    end if;
  end process;

  process (G_L, SEL, D)
  begin
    if G_L='0' and SEL = "11" then X <= D;
    else X <= (others => 'Z');
    end if;
  end process;

end V3states;
```

*6.6.5 Three-State Outputs in Verilog

Verilog has built-in bit-data value 'z' for the high-impedance state, so it is very easy to specify three-state outputs. For example, Table 6-39 is a Verilog module

Table 6-39 Verilog module for a 74x540-like 8-bit three-state driver.

```
module Vr74x540(G1_L, G2_L, A, Y);
  input G1_L, G2_L;
  input [1:8] A;
  output [1:8] Y;

  assign Y = (~G1_L & ~G2_L) ? A : 8'bz;
endmodule
```

for an 8-bit three-state buffer similar to the 74x540. Using with the conditional operator (?:), it takes just one continuous-assignment statement to specify the output—a copy of the input if the device is enabled, and eight bits of "z" otherwise.

The preceding example used its three-state port for output only, but output ports can be used as inputs as well if they are declared as type "inout". This capability would be used in a transceiver application with functionality similar to the 74x245 (Figure 6-56 on page 422). A corresponding Verilog module is shown in Table 6-40.

Table 6-40 Verilog module for a 74x245-like 8-bit transceiver.

```
module Vr74x245(G_L, DIR, A, B);
  input G_L, DIR;
  inout [1:8] A, B;

  assign A = (~G_L & ~DIR) ? B : 8'bz;
  assign B = (~G_L &  DIR) ? A : 8'bz;
endmodule
```

Another example application of inout ports is in a four-way, 8-bit bus transceiver with the following specifications:

- The transceiver handles four 8-bit bidirectional buses, A[1:8], B[1:8], C[1:8], and D[1:8].

- Each bus has its own active-low output enable input, AOE_L–DOE_L, and a "master" enable input MOE_L must also be asserted for any bus to be driven.

- The same source of data is driven to all the buses, as selected by three select inputs, S[2:0], according to Table 6-34 on page 425. If S2 is 0, the buses are driven with a constant value, otherwise they are driven with one of the other buses. However, when the selected source is a bus, the selected source bus cannot be driven, even if it is output-enabled.

Table 6-41 Verilog module for four-way, 2-bit bus transceiver.

```verilog
module VrXcvr4x8(A, B, C, D, S, AOE_L, BOE_L, COE_L, DOE_L, MOE_L);
  input [2:0] S;
  input AOE_L, BOE_L, COE_L, DOE_L, MOE_L;
  inout [1:8] A, B, C, D;
  reg [1:8] ibus;

  always @ (A or B or C or D or S) begin
    if (S[2] == 0) ibus = {4{S[1:0]}};
    else case (S[1:0])
      0: ibus = A;
      1: ibus = B;
      2: ibus = C;
      3: ibus = D;
    endcase
  end
  assign A = ((~AOE_L & ~MOE_L) && (S[2:0] != 4)) ? ibus : 8'bz;
  assign B = ((~BOE_L & ~MOE_L) && (S[2:0] != 5)) ? ibus : 8'bz;
  assign C = ((~COE_L & ~MOE_L) && (S[2:0] != 6)) ? ibus : 8'bz;
  assign D = ((~DOE_L & ~MOE_L) && (S[2:0] != 7)) ? ibus : 8'bz;
endmodule
```

A Verilog module that realizes this functionality is shown in Table 6-41. This module contains a mix of procedural and continuous assignments. The procedural assignments appear within an `always` block that sets an internal variable, `ibus`, to the value that should be driven onto any output-enabled port. Notice the use of concatenation to make four copies of the two low-order bits of S[2:0] when a constant source is selected. The continuous assignments at the end of the module drive the output buses when enabled, and include logic to ensure that the selected source bus is not driven even if otherwise output-enabled.

6.7 Multiplexers

multiplexer

A *multiplexer* is a digital switch—it connects data from one of n sources to its output. Figure 6-59(a) shows the inputs and outputs of an n-input, b-bit multiplexer. There are n sources of data, each of which is b bits wide, and there are b output bits. In typical commercially available multiplexers, $n = 1, 2, 4, 8$, or 16, and $b = 1, 2$, or 4. There are s inputs that select among the n sources, so $s = \lceil \log_2 n \rceil$. An enable input EN allows the multiplexer to "do its thing"; when EN = 0, all of the outputs are 0. A multiplexer is often called a *mux* for short.

mux

Figure 6-59(b) shows a switch circuit that is roughly equivalent to the multiplexer. However, unlike a mechanical switch, a multiplexer is a unidirectional device: information flows only from inputs (on the left) to outputs (on the right). Notice that the b bits from a particular input source, say D0, are spread out across b switches, each of which has n inputs to accommodate the n different sources.

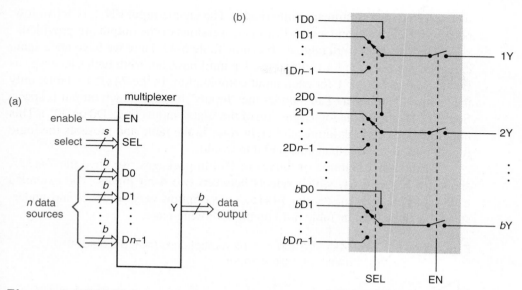

(a)

(b)

Figure 6-59 Multiplexer structure: (a) inputs and outputs; (b) functional equivalent.

We can write a general logic equation for a multiplexer output:

$$Y = \sum_{j=0}^{n-1} EN \cdot M_j \cdot iD$$

Here, the summation symbol represents a logical sum of product terms. Variable iY is a particular output bit ($1 \leq i \leq b$), and variable iDj is input bit i of source j ($0 \leq j \leq n-1$). M_j represents minterm j of the s select inputs. Thus, when the multiplexer is enabled and the value on the select inputs is j, each output iY equals the corresponding bit of the selected input, iDj.

Multiplexers are obviously useful devices in any application in which data must be switched from multiple sources to a destination. One common use in microprocessor systems is in input/output (I/O) devices that have several registers for storing data and control information, where any one of those registers may be selected periodically to be read by software. Suppose there are eight 32-bit registers, and a 3-bit field in the I/O address selects which one to read. This 3-bit field gets connected to the select inputs of an 8-input, 32-bit multiplexer. The multiplexer's data inputs are connected to the eight registers, and its data outputs are connected to the microprocessor's data bus to read the selected register.

6.7.1 Standard MSI Multiplexers

The sizes of commercially available MSI multiplexers are limited by the number of pins available in an inexpensive IC package. Commonly used muxes come in 16-pin packages. At one extreme is the *74x151*, shown in Figure 6-60, which *74x151* selects among eight 1-bit inputs. The select inputs are named S2, S1, and S0, where S2 is most significant numerically. The enable input EN_L is active low; both active-high (Y) and active-low (Y_L) versions of the output are provided.

The 74x151's truth table is shown in Table 6-42. Here we have once again extended our notation for truth tables. Up until now, our truth tables have specified an output of 0 or 1 for each input combination. In the 74x151's table, only the "control" inputs are listed under the "Inputs" heading. Each output is specified as 0, 1, or a simple logic function of the "data" inputs (e.g., D0 or D0′). This notation saves eight columns and eight rows in the table and presents the logic function more clearly than a larger table would.

74x157

At the other extreme of muxes in 16-pin packages, we have the *74x157*, shown in Figure 6-61, which selects between two 4-bit inputs. The extended truth-table notation makes the 74x157's description very compact and understandable, as shown in Table 6-43 on the following page.

Figure 6-60 The 74x151 8-input, 1-bit multiplexer: (a) logic diagram;
(b) traditional logic symbol.

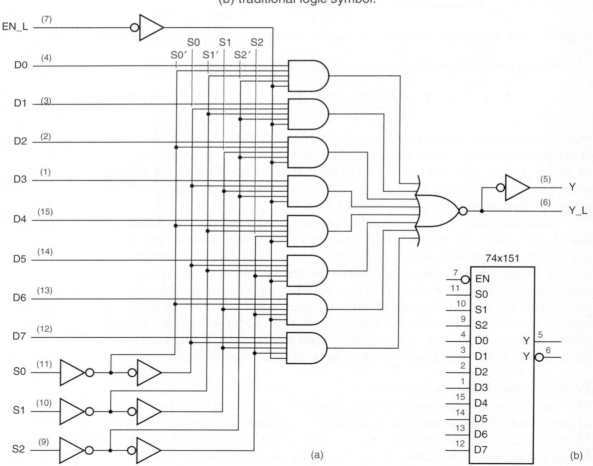

Table 6-42
Truth table for a
74x151 8-input,
1-bit multiplexer.

Inputs				Outputs	
EN_L	S2	S1	S0	Y	Y_L
1	x	x	x	0	1
0	0	0	0	D0	D0'
0	0	0	1	D1	D1'
0	0	1	0	D2	D2'
0	0	1	1	D3	D3'
0	1	0	0	D4	D4'
0	1	0	1	D5	D5'
0	1	1	0	D6	D6'
0	1	1	1	D7	D7'

Figure 6-61 The 74x157 2-input, 4-bit multiplexer: (a) logic diagram;
(b) traditional logic symbol.

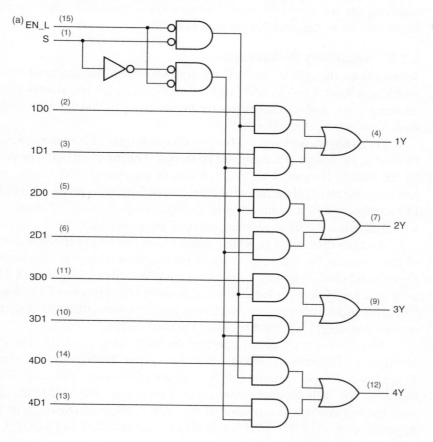
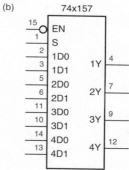

Table 6-43
Truth table for a
74x157 2-input,
4-bit multiplexer.

Inputs		Outputs			
EN_L	S	1Y	2Y	3Y	4Y
1	x	0	0	0	0
0	0	1D0	2D0	3D0	4D0
0	1	1D1	2D1	3D1	4D1

74x153

Intermediate between the 74x151 and 74x157 is the *74x153*, a 4-input, 2-bit multiplexer with separate enable inputs for each output bit. This device's truth table and logic symbol can be found in <u>Section Mux</u> at <u>DDPPonline</u> or in manufacturers' data sheets on the Web.

Some multiplexers have three-state outputs. The enable input of such a multiplexer, instead of forcing the outputs to zero, forces them to the Hi-Z state.

74x251

For example, the *74x251* is identical to the '151 in its pinout and its internal logic design, except that Y and Y_L are three-state outputs. When the EN_L input is negated, instead of forcing the outputs to be negated, it forces the outputs into

74x257

the Hi-Z state. Similarly, the *74x257* is a three-state version of the '157. Three-state outputs are especially useful when *n*-input muxes are combined to form larger muxes, as suggested in the next subsection.

6.7.2 Expanding Multiplexers

Seldom does the size of an MSI multiplexer match the characteristics of the problem at hand. Even in ASIC design, multiplexers are not always available in arbitrary sizes, and it is necessary for the designer to make a large multiplexer from a collection of smaller ones.

For example, we suggested earlier that an 8-input, 32-bit multiplexer might be used in the design of a computer processor. This function could be performed by 32 74x151 8-input, 1-bit multiplexers or equivalent ASIC cells, each one handling one bit of all the inputs and the output. The appropriate 3-bit field of the I/O address would be connected to the S[2:0] inputs of all 32 muxes, so they would all select the same register source at any given time.

Another dimension in which multiplexers can be expanded is the number of data sources. For example, suppose we needed a 32-input, 1-bit multiplexer. Figure 6-62 shows one way to build it. Five select bits are required. A 74x138 is used as a 2-to-4 decoder for the two high-order select bits to enable one of four 74x151 8-input multiplexers. Since only one '151 is enabled at a time, the '151 outputs can simply be ORed to obtain the final output.

The 32-to-1 multiplexer can also be built using 74x251s. The circuit is identical to Figure 6-62, except that the output NAND gate is eliminated. Instead, the Y (and, if desired, Y_L) outputs of the four '251s are simply tied together. The '138 decoder ensures that at most one of the '251s has its three-state outputs enabled at any time. If the '138 is disabled (XEN1_L or XEN2 is negated), then all of the '251s are disabled, and the XOUT and XOUT_L outputs

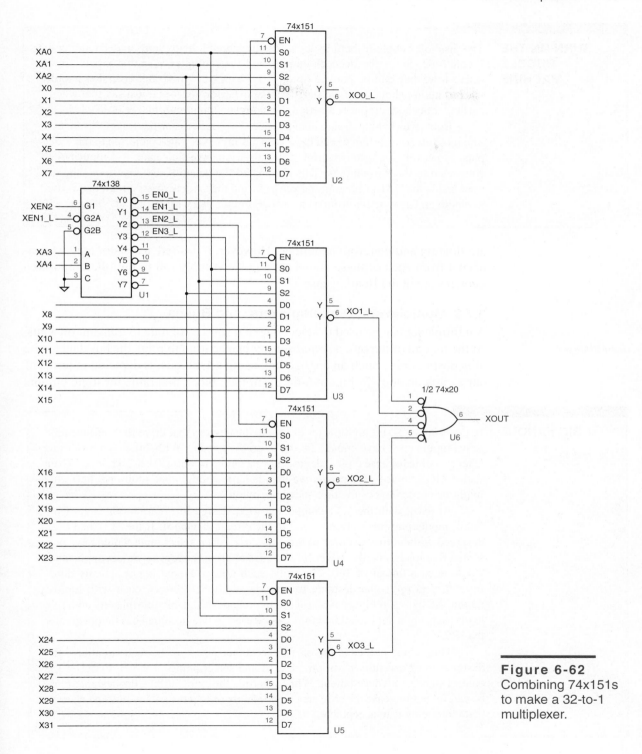

Figure 6-62
Combining 74x151s
to make a 32-to-1
multiplexer.

TURN ON THE
BUBBLE
MACHINE
The use of bubble-to-bubble logic design should help your understanding of Figure 6-62. Since the decoder outputs and the multiplexer enable inputs are all active low, they can be hooked up directly. You can ignore the inversion bubbles when thinking about the logic function that is performed—you just say that when a particular decoder output is asserted, the corresponding multiplexer is enabled.

Bubble-to-bubble design also provides two options for the final OR function. The most obvious design would have used a 4-input OR gate connected to the Y outputs. However, for faster operation, we used an inverting gate, a 4-input NAND connected to the Y_L outputs. This eliminated the delay of two inverters—the one used inside the '151 to generate Y from Y_L, and the extra inverter circuit that is used to obtain an OR function from a basic NOR circuit in a CMOS or TTL OR gate.

are floating and therefore undefined. However, if desired, a resistor may be connected from each of these signals to a power-supply rail to pull the output to a known state in the floating case.

6.7.3 Multiplexers, Demultiplexers, and Buses

demultiplexer

A multiplexer can be used to select one of n sources of data to transmit on a bus. At the far end of the bus, a *demultiplexer* can be used to route the bus data to one of m destinations. Such an application, using a 1-bit bus, is depicted in terms of our switch analogy in Figure 6-64(a). In fact, block diagrams for logic circuits

BIG FANOUT
In the 8-input, 32-bit multiplexer example, the devices that drive the multiplexers' select inputs must have enough fanout to drive 32 loads. With 74LS-series ICs this is not possible because typical devices have a fanout of only 20 LS-TTL loads. Even with CMOS devices, the capacitive load is large enough that additional buffering might be needed to ensure high-speed operation.

At least, with the '151 component logic design in Figure 6-60, each of the S[2:0] inputs presents only one load to the circuit driving it. If the '151 had been designed without the first rank of three inverters, each select input would have presented five loads, and the driver for each select bit in the register-select application would need a fanout of 160. Typically, such a large fanout is not actually done. Instead, it is up to the designer to provide additional buffers, each with limited fanout. As shown in Figure 6-63 for our hypothetical 32 1-bit multiplexers with five loads each, eight additional inverters can be used so that no signal has fanout greater than 20.

This is just one example of a large-fanout problem. In such situations, the designer must carefully partition the load and select points at which to buffer the control signals to reduce fanout. While inserting the extra buffers, the designer must be careful not increase the chip area significantly or to put so many buffers in series that their delay is unacceptable.

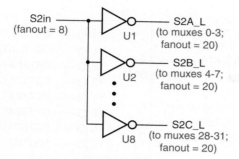

Figure 6-63
Buffers to handle a fanout of 160 in multiplexer control application.

S2in (fanout = 8)

U1 — S2A_L (to muxes 0-3; fanout = 20)

U2 — S2B_L (to muxes 4-7; fanout = 20)

U8 — S2C_L (to muxes 28-31; fanout = 20)

INVERTERS? NO PROBLEM

Notice in Figure 6-63 that we used inverters to buffer the select signal. We did this because inverters are typically smaller and faster than noninverting buffers. This does, however, change the logic values that are driven to the multiplexers, and any given select input S[2:0] will be the complement of what it was without the extra buffering.

But if we need the smaller size and extra speed, this is not much of a problem to overcome. If we invert all of the select inputs of a multiplexer, it still works as a mux. We just have to renumber the data inputs, from 0–7 to 7–0 in this case. That is, we hook up the data inputs in the opposite order.

often depict multiplexers and demultiplexers using the wedge-shaped symbols in (b), to suggest visually how a selected one of multiple data sources gets directed onto a bus and routed to a selected one of multiple destinations.

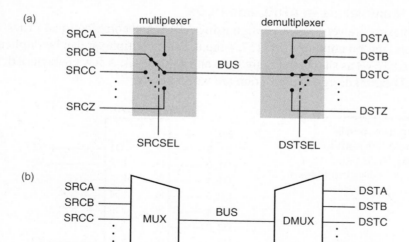

Figure 6-64
A mux driving a bus and a demultiplexer receiving the bus: (a) switch equivalent; (b) block-diagram symbols.

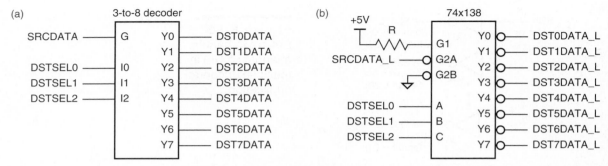

Figure 6-65 Using a 3-to-8 binary decoder as a 1-bit, 8-output demultiplexer: (a) generic decoder; (b) 74x138.

The function of a demultiplexer is just the inverse of a multiplexer's. For example, a 1-bit, n-output demultiplexer has one data input and s inputs to select one of $n = 2^s$ data outputs. In normal operation, all outputs except the selected one are 0; the selected output equals the data input. This definition may be generalized for a b-bit, n-output demultiplexer; such a device has b data inputs, and its s select inputs choose one of $n = 2^s$ sets of b data outputs.

A binary decoder with an enable input can be used as a demultiplexer, as shown in Figure 6-65. The decoder's enable input is connected to the data line, and its select inputs determine which of its output lines is driven with the data bit. The remaining output lines are negated. Thus, the 74x138 can be used as a 1-bit, 8-output demultiplexer. In fact, the manufacturer's catalog typically lists the '138 as a "decoder/demultiplexer."

6.7.4 Multiplexers in ABEL and PLDs

Multiplexers are very easy to design using ABEL and combinational PLDs. For example, the function of a 74x157 4-input, 2-bit multiplexer can be duplicated in a GAL16V8 as shown in Figure 6-66 and Table 6-44. A few characteristics of the PLD-based design and program are worth noting:

Figure 6-66
Logic diagram for the GAL16V8 used as a 74x157-like multiplexer.

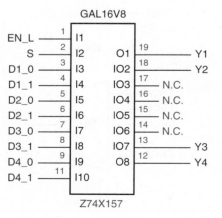

```
module Z74X157
title '74x157-like multiplexer PLD '
Z74X157 device 'P16V8C';

" Input and output pins
EN_L, S                         pin 1, 2;
D1_0, D2_0, D3_0, D4_0          pin 3, 5, 7, 9;
D1_1, D2_1, D3_1, D4_1          pin 4, 6, 8, 11;
Y1, Y2, Y3, Y4                  pin 19, 18, 13, 12 istype 'com';

" Active-level conversion
EN = !EN_L;

equations
Y1 = EN & (!S & D1_0  #  S & D1_1);
Y2 = EN & (!S & D2_0  #  S & D2_1);
Y3 = EN & (!S & D3_0  #  S & D3_1);
Y4 = EN & (!S & D4_0  #  S & D4_1);

end Z74X157
```

Table 6-44
ABEL program for a
74x157-like 2-input,
4-bit multiplexer.

- Signal names in the ABEL program are changed somewhat from the signal names shown for a 74x157 in Figure 6-61 on page 435, since ABEL does not allow a number to be used as the first character of a signal name.

- Two of the outputs (Y1 and Y4) are assigned to pins 19 and 12 on the 16V8, which are usable *only* as outputs. This is preferred over assigning them to I/O pins; given a choice, it's better to leave I/O pins than output-only pins as spares.

Multiplexer functions are even easier to express using ABEL's sets and relations. For example, Table 6-45 on the next page shows the ABEL program for a 4-input, 8-bit multiplexer. No device statement is included, because this function has too many inputs and outputs to fit in any of the PLDs we've described so far. However, it should be clear that a multiplexer of any size can be specified in just a few lines of code in this way.

Likewise, it is easy to customize multiplexer functions using ABEL. For example, suppose that you needed a circuit that selects one of four 18-bit input buses, A, B, C, or D, to drive an 18-bit output bus F, as specified in Table 6-46 by three control bits. There are more control-bit combinations than multiplexer inputs, so a standard 4-input multiplexer doesn't quite fit the bill (but see Exercise 6.66). A 4-input, 3-bit multiplexer with the required behavior can be designed to fit into a single GAL16V8 as shown in Figure 6-67 and Table 6-47, and six copies of this device can be used to make the 18-bit mux. Alternatively, a single, larger PLD could be used. In any case, the ABEL program is very easily modified for different selection criteria.

Table 6-45
ABEL program for
a 4-input, 8-bit
multiplexer.

```
module mux4in8b
title '4-input, 8-bit wide multiplexer PLD'

" Input and output pins
YOE_L               pin;              " Output enable for Y bus
EN_L                pin;              " Enable input (else 0 output)
S1..S0              pin;              " Select inputs, 0-3 ==> A-D
A1..A8, B1..B8, C1..C8, D1..D8 pin;  " 8-bit input buses A, B, C, D
Y1..Y8              pin istype 'com'; " 8-bit three-state output bus

" Sets
SEL = [S1..S0];
A = [A1..A8];
B = [B1..B8];
C = [C1..C8];
D = [D1..D8];
Y = [Y1..Y8];

" Active-level conversions
YOE = !YOE_L;  EN = !EN_L;

equations
Y.OE = YOE;
when (EN == 0) then Y = 0;
else when (SEL == 0) then Y = A;
else when (SEL == 1) then Y = B;
else when (SEL == 2) then Y = C;
else when (SEL == 3) then Y = D;
end mux4in8b
```

Since this function uses all of the available pins on the GAL16V8, we had to make the pin assignment in Figure 6-67 carefully. In particular, we had to assign two output signals to the two output-only pins (O1 and O8), in order to maximize the number of input pins available.

Table 6-46
Function table for
a specialized 4-input,
18-bit multiplexer.

S2	S1	S0	*Input to Select*
0	0	0	A
0	0	1	B
0	1	0	A
0	1	1	C
1	0	0	A
1	0	1	D
1	1	0	A
1	1	1	B

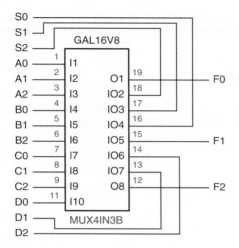

Figure 6-67
Logic diagram for the
GAL16V8 used as a
specialized 4-input,
3-bit multiplexer.

Table 6-47 ABEL program for a specialized 4-input, 3-bit multiplexer.

```
module mux4in3b
title 'Specialized 4-input, 3-bit Multiplexer'
mux4in3b device 'P16V8C';

" Input and output pins
S2..S0                          pin 16..18;              " Select inputs
A0..A2, B0..B2, C0..C2, D0..D2  pin 1..9, 11, 13, 14;    " Bus inputs
F0..F2                          pin 19, 15, 12 istype 'com'; " Bus outputs

" Sets
SEL = [S2..S0];
A = [A0..A2];
B = [B0..B2];
C = [C0..C2];
D = [D0..D2];
F = [F0..F2];

equations
when (SEL== 0) # (SEL== 2) # (SEL== 4) # (SEL== 6) then F = A;
else when (SEL== 1) # (SEL== 7) then F = B;
else when (SEL== 3) then F = C;
else when (SEL== 5) then F = D;

end mux4in3b
```

EASIEST, BUT NOT CHEAPEST   As you've seen, it's very easy to program a PLD to perform decoder and multiplexer functions. Still, if you need the logic function of a standard decoder or multiplexer, it's usually less costly to use a standard MSI chip than it is to use a PLD. The PLD-based approach is best if the multiplexer has some nonstandard functional requirements, or if you think you may have to change its function as a result of debugging.

◾ **Table 6-48** Dataflow VHDL program for a 4-input, 8-bit multiplexer.

```
library IEEE;
use IEEE.std_logic_1164.all;

entity mux4in8b is
    port (
        S: in STD_LOGIC_VECTOR (1 downto 0);       -- Select inputs, 0-3 ==> A-D
        A, B, C, D: in STD_LOGIC_VECTOR (1 to 8); -- Data bus input
        Y: out STD_LOGIC_VECTOR (1 to 8)          -- Data bus output
    );
end mux4in8b;

architecture mux4in8b of mux4in8b is
begin
    with S select Y <=
        A when "00",
        B when "01",
        C when "10",
        D when "11",
        (others => 'U') when others; -- this creates an 8-bit vector of 'U'
end mux4in8b;
```

6.7.5 Multiplexers in VHDL

Multiplexers are very easy to describe in VHDL. In the dataflow style of architecture, the SELECT statement provides the required functionality, as shown in Table 6-48, the VHDL description of 4-input, 8-bit multiplexer.

In a behavioral architecture, a CASE statement is used. For example, Table 6-49 shows a process-based architecture for the same mux4in8b entity.

It is very easy to customize the selection criteria in a VHDL multiplexer program. For example, Table 6-50 is a behavioral-style program for a specialized 4-input, 18-bit multiplexer with the selection criteria of Table 6-46.

◾ **Table 6-49** Behavioral architecture for a 4-input, 8-bit multiplexer.

```
architecture mux4in8p of mux4in8b is
begin
process(S, A, B, C, D)
  begin
    case S is
      when "00" => Y <= A;
      when "01" => Y <= B;
      when "10" => Y <= C;
      when "11" => Y <= D;
      when others => Y <= (others => 'U');  -- 8-bit vector of 'U'
    end case;
  end process;
end mux4in8p;
```

Table 6-50 Behavioral VHDL program for a specialized 4-input, 18-bit multiplexer.

```
library IEEE;
use IEEE.std_logic_1164.all;

entity mux4in18b is
    port (
        S: in STD_LOGIC_VECTOR (2 downto 0);       -- Select inputs, 0-7 ==> ABACADAB
        A, B, C, D: in STD_LOGIC_VECTOR (1 to 18); -- Data bus inputs
        Y: out STD_LOGIC_VECTOR (1 to 18)          -- Data bus output
    );
end mux4in18b;

architecture mux4in3p of mux4in18b is
begin
process(S, A, B, C, D)
variable i: INTEGER;
  begin
    case S is
      when "000" | "010" | "100" | "110" => Y <= A;
      when "001" | "111" => Y <= B;
      when "011" => Y <= C;
      when "101" => Y <= D;
      when others => Y <= (others => 'U'); -- 18-bit vector of 'U'
    end case;
  end process;
end mux4in18p;
```

In each example, if the select inputs are not valid (e.g., contain U's or X's), the output bus is set to "unknown" to help catch errors during simulation.

6.7.6 Multiplexers in Verilog

Multiplexers are very easy to describe in Verilog. In the dataflow style, a series of conditional operators (?:) can provide the required functionality, as shown in Table 6-51, a Verilog module for a 4-input, 8-bit multiplexer.

Table 6-51 Dataflow Verilog program for a 4-input, 8-bit multiplexer.

```
module Vrmux4in8b(YOE_L, EN_L, S, A, B, C, D, Y);
  input YOE_L, EN_L;
  input [1:0] S;
  input [1:8] A, B, C, D;
  output [1:8] Y;

  assign Y = (~YOE_L == 1'b0) ? 8'bz : (
                (~EN_L == 1'b0) ? 8'b0 : (
                  (S == 2'd0) ? A : (
                    (S == 2'd1) ? B : (
                      (S == 2'd2) ? C : (
                        (S == 2'd3) ? D : 8'bx)))));
endmodule
```

Table 6-52 Behavioral Verilog module for a 4-input, 8-bit multiplexer.

```
module Vrmux4in8bc(YOE_L, EN_L, S, A, B, C, D, Y);
  input YOE_L, EN_L;
  input [1:0] S;
  input [1:8] A, B, C, D;
  output [1:8] Y;
  reg [1:8] Y;

  always @ (YOE_L or EN_L or S or A or B or C or D) begin
    if (~YOE_L == 1'b0) Y = 8'bz;
    else if (~EN_L == 1'b0) Y = 8'b0;
    else case (S)
      2'd0: Y = A;
      2'd1: Y = B;
      2'd2: Y = C;
      2'd3: Y = D;
      default: Y = 8'bx;
    endcase
  end
endmodule
```

In a behavioral architecture, a case statement can be used. For example, Table 6-52 is a module using an always block and case statement for the same mux4in8b entity.

It is very easy to customize the selection criteria in a Verilog multiplexer module. For example, Table 6-53 is a behavioral-style program for a specialized 4-input, 18-bit multiplexer with the selection criteria of Table 6-46 on page 442.

In each example, if the select inputs are not valid (e.g., contain z's or x's), the output bus is set to "unknown" to help catch errors during simulation.

Table 6-53 Behavioral Verilog program for a specialized 4-input, 18-bit multiplexer.

```
module Vrmux4in18b(S, A, B, C, D, Y);
  input [2:0] S;
  input [1:18] A, B, C, D;
  output [1:18] Y;
  reg [1:18] Y;

  always @ (S or A or B or C or D)
    case (S)
      3'd0, 3'd2, 3'd4, 3'd6: Y = A;
      3'd1, 3'd7: Y = B;
      3'd3: Y = C;
      3'd5: Y = D;
      default: Y = 8'bx;
    endcase
endmodule
```

6.8 Exclusive-OR Gates and Parity Circuits

6.8.1 Exclusive-OR and Exclusive-NOR Gates

An *Exclusive-OR (XOR)* gate is a 2-input gate whose output is 1 if exactly one of its inputs is 1. Stated another way, an XOR gate produces a 1 output if its inputs are different. An *Exclusive NOR (XNOR)* or *Equivalence* gate is just the opposite—it produces a 1 output if its inputs are the same. A truth table for these functions is shown in Table 6-54. The XOR operation is sometimes denoted by the symbol "⊕", that is,

Exclusive OR (XOR)
Exclusive NOR (XNOR)
Equivalence

$$X \oplus Y = X' \cdot Y + X \cdot Y'$$

⊕

Although EXCLUSIVE OR is not one of the basic functions of switching algebra, discrete XOR gates are fairly commonly used in practice. Most switching technologies cannot perform the XOR function directly; instead, they use multigate designs like the ones shown in Figure 6-68.

The logic symbols for XOR and XNOR functions are shown in Figure 6-69. There are four equivalent symbols for each function. All of these alternatives are a consequence of a simple rule:

- Any two signals (inputs or output) of an XOR or XNOR gate may be complemented without changing the resulting logic function.

X	Y	$X \oplus Y$ (XOR)	$(X \oplus Y)'$ (XNOR)
0	0	0	1
0	1	1	0
1	0	1	0
1	1	0	1

Table 6-54
Truth table for XOR and XNOR functions.

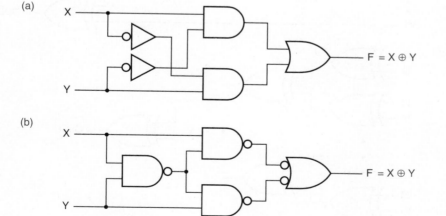

(a)

F = X ⊕ Y

(b)

F = X ⊕ Y

Figure 6-68
Multigate designs for the 2-input XOR function: (a) AND-OR; (b) three-level NAND.

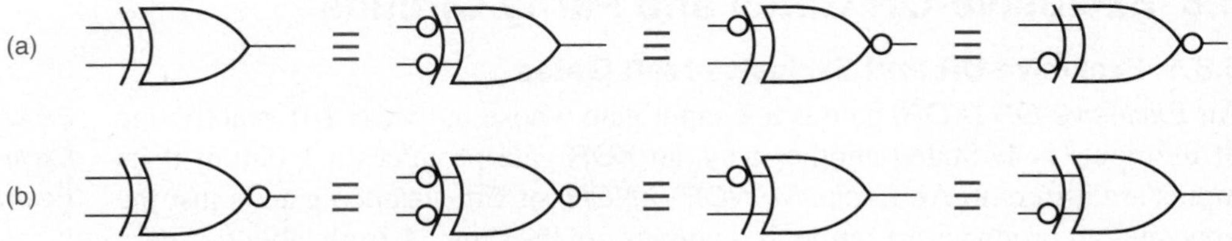

(a)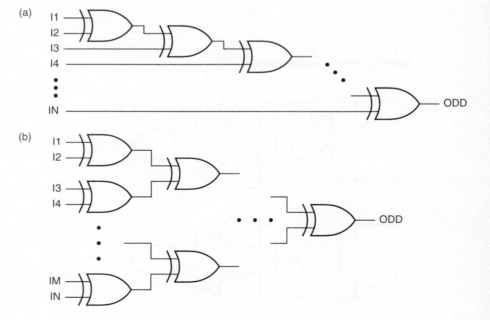

(b)

Figure 6-69 Equivalent symbols for (a) XOR gates; (b) XNOR gates.

In bubble-to-bubble logic design, we choose the symbol that is most expressive of the logic function being performed.

74x86

Four XOR gates are provided in a single 14-pin SSI IC, the *74x86* shown in Figure 6-18 on page 361. Besides providing an XOR gate for output-polarity selection, many PLDs and CPLDs provide an additional XOR gate with product-term inputs as a means of efficiently realizing certain common functions, such as counters. XOR gates are also readily available in FPGA and ASIC libraries and as primitives in HDLs.

6.8.2 Parity Circuits

odd-parity circuit

even-parity circuit

As shown in Figure 6-70(a), *n* XOR gates may be cascaded to form a circuit with $n + 1$ inputs and a single output. This is called an *odd-parity circuit*, because its output is 1 if an odd number of its inputs are 1. The circuit in (b) is also an odd-parity circuit, but it's faster because its gates are arranged in a treelike structure. If the output of either circuit is inverted, we get an *even-parity circuit*, whose output is 1 if an even number of its inputs are 1.

Figure 6-70
Cascading XOR gates:
(a) daisy-chain
connection; (b) tree
structure.

SPEEDING UP THE XOR TREE If each XOR gate in Figure 6-71 were built using discrete NAND gates as in Figure 6-68(b), the 74x280 would be pretty slow, having a propagation delay equivalent to $4 \cdot 3 + 1$, or 13, NAND gates. Instead, a typical implementation of the 74x280 uses a 2-wide AND-OR-INVERT gate to perform the function of each shaded pair of XOR gates in the figure with about the same delay as a single NAND gate. The A–I inputs are buffered through two levels of inverters, so that each input presents just one unit load to the circuit driving it. Thus, the total propagation delay through this realization of the 74x280 is similar to that of five inverting gates, not 13.

6.8.3 The 74x280 9-Bit Parity Generator

Rather than build a multibit parity circuit with discrete XOR gates, it is more economical to put all of the XORs in a single MSI package with just the primary inputs and outputs available at the external pins. The *74x280* 9-bit parity generator, shown in Figure 6-71, is such a device. It has nine inputs and two outputs that indicate whether an even or odd number of inputs are 1.

74x280

6.8.4 Parity-Checking Applications

In Section 2.15 we described error-detecting codes that use an extra bit, called a parity bit, to detect errors in the transmission and storage of data. In an even-parity code, the parity bit is chosen so that the total number of 1 bits in a code word is even. Parity circuits like the 74x280 are used both to generate the correct

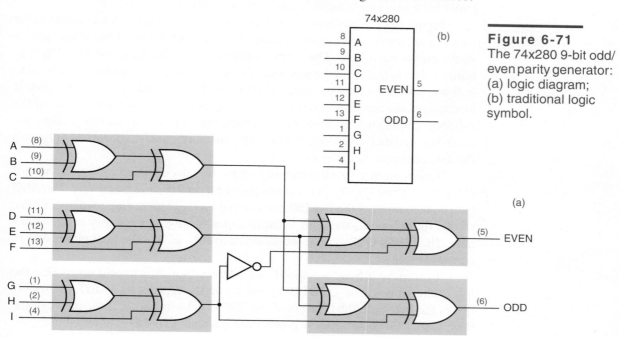

Figure 6-71
The 74x280 9-bit odd/even parity generator:
(a) logic diagram;
(b) traditional logic symbol.

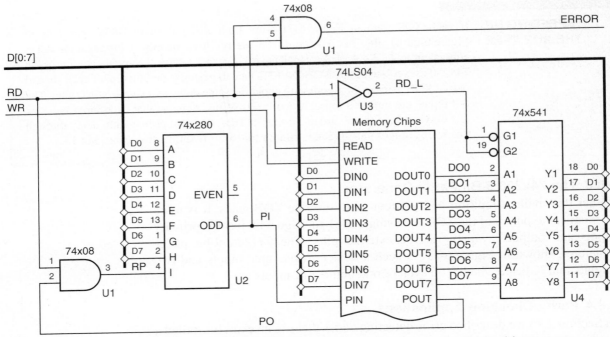

Figure 6-72 Parity generation and checking for an 8-bit-wide memory.

value of the parity bit when a code word is stored or transmitted and to check the
parity bit when a code word is retrieved or received.

Figure 6-72 shows how a parity circuit might be used to detect errors in the
memory of a microprocessor system. The memory stores 8-bit bytes, plus a
parity bit for each byte. The microprocessor uses a bidirectional bus D[0:7] to
transfer data to and from the memory. Two control lines, RD and WR, are used to
indicate whether a read or write operation is desired, and an ERROR signal is
asserted to indicate parity errors during read operations. Complete details of the
memory chips, such as addressing inputs, are not shown; memory chips are
described in detail in Chapter 9. For parity checking, we are concerned only with
the data connections to the memory.

To store a byte into the memory chips, we specify an address (not shown),
place the byte on D[0–7], generate its parity bit on PIN, and assert WR. The AND
gate on the I input of the 74x280 ensures that I is 0 except during read operations,
so that during writes the '280's output depends only on the parity of the D-bus
data. The '280's ODD output is connected to PIN, so that the total number of 1s
stored is even.

To retrieve a byte, we specify an address (not shown) and assert RD; the
byte value appears on DOUT[0–7] and its parity appears on POUT. A 74x541
drives the byte onto the D bus, and the '280 checks its parity. If the parity of the
9-bit word DOUT[0–7],POUT is odd during a read, ERROR is asserted.

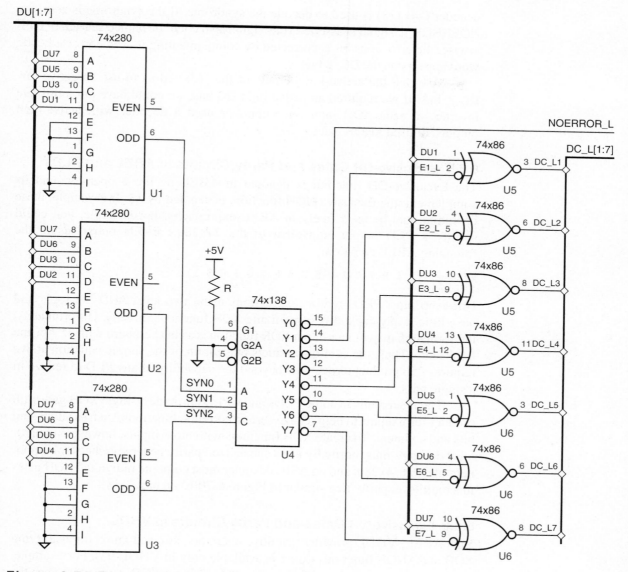

Figure 6-73 Error-correcting circuit for a 7-bit Hamming code.

Parity circuits are also used with error-correcting codes such as the Hamming codes described in Section 2.15.3. We showed the parity-check matrix for a 7-bit Hamming code in Figure 2-13 on page 63. We can correct errors in this code as shown in Figure 6-73. A 7-bit word, possibly containing an error, is presented on DU[1–7]. Three 74x280s compute the parity of the three bit-groups defined by the parity-check matrix. The outputs of the '280s form the syndrome, which is the number of the erroneous input bit, if any. A 3-to-8 decoder (74x138) is used to decode the syndrome. If the syndrome is zero, the NOERROR_L signal is asserted (this signal also could be named ERROR). Otherwise, the erroneous bit is corrected by complementing it. The corrected code word appears on the DC_L bus.

Note that the active-low outputs of the '138 led us to use an active-low DC_L bus. If we required an active-high DC bus, we could have put a discrete inverter on each XOR input or output, or used a decoder with active-high outputs, or used XNOR gates.

6.8.5 Exclusive-OR Gates and Parity Circuits in ABEL and PLDs

The Exclusive-OR function is denoted in ABEL by the $ operator, and its complement, the Exclusive-NOR function, is denoted by !$. In principle, these operators may be used freely in ABEL expressions. For example, you could specify a PLD output equivalent to the 74x280's EVEN output using the following ABEL equation:

```
EVEN = !(A $ B $ C $ D $ E $ F $ G $ H $ I);
```

However, most PLDs realize expressions using two-level AND-OR logic and have little if any capability of realizing XOR functions directly. Unfortunately, the Karnaugh map of an n-input XOR function is a checkerboard with 2^{n-1} prime implicants. Thus, the sum-of-products realization of the simple equation above requires 256 product terms, well beyond the capability of any PLD to realize in a single pass.

The macrocells in some PLDs and CPLDs provide a single XOR gate with product-term inputs to help realize certain common functions, such as adder sum bits and counters. To create XOR functions with more inputs, however, a board-level designer must normally use a specialized parity generator/checker component like the 74x280, and an ASIC designer must combine individual XOR gates in a multilevel parity tree similar to Figure 6-70(b) on page 448.

6.8.6 Exclusive-OR Gates and Parity Circuits in VHDL

Like ABEL, VHDL provides primitive operators, xor and xnor, for specifying XOR and XNOR functions (xnor is available only in VHDL-93). For example, Table 6-55 is a dataflow-style program for a 3-input XOR device that uses the xor primitive. It's also possible to specify XOR or parity functions behaviorally, as Table 6-56 does for a 9-input parity function similar to the 74x280.

When a VHDL program containing large XOR functions is synthesized, the synthesis tool will do the best it can to realize the function in the targeted device technology. There's no magic—if we try to target the VHDL program in Table 6-56 to a 16V8 PLD, it still won't fit!

Typical ASIC and FPGA libraries contain 2- and 3-input XOR and XNOR functions as primitives. In CMOS ASICs, these primitives are usually realized

■ **Table 6-55** Dataflow-style VHDL program for a 3-input XOR device.

```
library IEEE;
use IEEE.std_logic_1164.all;

entity vxor3 is
    port (
        A, B, C: in STD_LOGIC;
        Y: out STD_LOGIC
    );
end vxor3;

architecture vxor3 of vxor3 is
begin
  Y <= A xor B xor C;
end vxor3;
```

■ **Table 6-56** Behavioral VHDL program for a 9-input parity checker.

```
library IEEE;
use IEEE.std_logic_1164.all;

entity parity9 is
    port (
        I: in STD_LOGIC_VECTOR (1 to 9);
        EVEN, ODD: out STD_LOGIC
    );
end parity9;

architecture parity9p of parity9 is
begin
process (I)
  variable p : STD_LOGIC;
  begin
    p := I(1);
    for j in 2 to 9 loop
      if I(j) = '1' then p := not p; end if;
    end loop;
    ODD <= p;
    EVEN <= not p;
  end process;
end parity9p;
```

very efficiently at the transistor level using transmission gates, as shown in Exercises 6.69 and 6.81. Fast and compact XOR trees can be built using these primitives. However, typical VHDL synthesis tools are not smart enough to create an efficient tree structure from a behavioral program like Table 6-56. Instead, we can use a structural program to get exactly what we want.

▓▓ Table 6-57 Structural VHDL program for a 74x280-like parity checker.

```
library IEEE;
use IEEE.std_logic_1164.all;

entity V74x280 is
    port (
        I: in STD_LOGIC_VECTOR (1 to 9);
        EVEN, ODD: out STD_LOGIC
    );
end V74x280;

architecture V74x280s of V74x280 is
component vxor3
 port (A, B, C: in STD_LOGIC; Y: out STD_LOGIC);
end component;
signal Y1, Y2, Y3, Y3N: STD_LOGIC;
begin
  U1: vxor3 port map (I(1), I(2), I(3), Y1);
  U2: vxor3 port map (I(4), I(5), I(6), Y2);
  U3: vxor3 port map (I(7), I(8), I(9), Y3);
  Y3N <= not Y3;
  U4: vxor3 port map (Y1, Y2, Y3, ODD);
  U5: vxor3 port map (Y1, Y2, Y3N, EVEN);
end V74x280s;
```

For example, Table 6-57 is a structural VHDL program for a 9-input XOR function that is equivalent to the 74x280 of Figure 6-71(a) in structure as well as function. In this example, we've used the previously defined vxor3 component as the basic building block of the XOR tree. In an ASIC, we would replace the vxor3 with a 3-input XOR primitive from the ASIC library. Also, if a 3-input XNOR were available, we could eliminate the explicit inversion for Y3N and instead use the XNOR for U5, using the noninverted Y3 signal as its last input.

Our final example is a VHDL version of the Hamming decoder circuit of Figure 6-73 and is shown in Table 6-58. A function syndrome(DU) is defined to return the 3-bit syndrome of a 7-bit uncorrected data input vector DU. In the "main" process, the corrected data output vector DC is initially set equal to DU. The CONV_INTEGER function, which we defined in Section 5.3.3, is used to convert the 3-bit syndrome to an integer. If the syndrome is nonzero, the corresponding bit of DC is complemented to correct the assumed 1-bit error. If the syndrome is zero, either no error or an undetectable error has occurred; the output NOERROR is set accordingly.

6.8.7 Exclusive-OR Gates and Parity Circuits in Verilog

In Verilog, the XOR and XNOR functions are performed by the ^ and ~^ operators, respectively. For example, Table 6-59 is a dataflow-style program for a 3-input XOR device using the XOR operator. It's also possible to specify

Table 6-58 Behavioral VHDL program for Hamming error correction.

```
library IEEE;
use IEEE.std_logic_1164.all;
use IEEE.std_logic_unsigned.all;

entity hamcorr is
  port (
      DU: in STD_LOGIC_VECTOR (1 to 7);
      DC: out STD_LOGIC_VECTOR (1 to 7);
      NOERROR: out STD_LOGIC
  );
end hamcorr;

architecture hamcorr of hamcorr is

function syndrome (D: STD_LOGIC_VECTOR)
    return STD_LOGIC_VECTOR is
variable SYN: STD_LOGIC_VECTOR (2 downto 0);
begin
  SYN(0) := D(1) xor D(3) xor D(5) xor D(7);
  SYN(1) := D(2) xor D(3) xor D(6) xor D(7);
  SYN(2) := D(4) xor D(5) xor D(6) xor D(7);
  return(SYN);
end syndrome;

begin
process (DU)
variable i: INTEGER;
  begin
    DC <= DU;
    i := CONV_INTEGER(syndrome(DU));
    if i = 0 then NOERROR <= '1';
    else NOERROR <= '0'; DC(i) <= not DU(i); end if;
  end process;
end hamcorr;
```

Table 6-59 Dataflow-style Verilog module for a 3-input XOR device.

```
module Vrxor3(A, B, C, Y);
  input A, B, C;
  output Y;

  assign Y = A ^ B ^ C;
endmodule
```

XOR or parity functions behaviorally, as Table 6-60 does for a 9-input parity function similar to the 74x280.

Table 6-60 Behavioral Verilog program for a 9-input parity checker.

```
module Vrparity9(I, EVEN, ODD);
  input [1:9] I;
  output EVEN, ODD;
  reg p, EVEN, ODD;
  integer j;

  always @ (I) begin
    p = 1'b0;
    for (j =1; j <= 9; j = j+1)
      if (I[j]) p = ~p;
    else p = p;
    ODD = p;
    EVEN = ~p;
  end
endmodule
```

When a Verilog program containing large XOR functions is synthesized, the synthesis tool will do the best it can to realize the function in the targeted device technology. There's no magic—if we try to target the Verilog module in Table 6-60 to a 16V8 PLD, it still won't fit!

Typical ASIC and FPGA libraries contain two- and three-input XOR and XNOR functions as primitives. In CMOS ASICs, these primitives are usually realized very efficiently at the transistor level using transmission gates, as shown in Exercises 6.69 and 6.81. Fast and compact XOR trees can be built using these primitives. However, typical Verilog synthesis tools are not smart enough to create an efficient tree structure from a behavioral program like Table 6-56. Instead, we can use a structural program to get exactly what we want.

For example, Table 6-61 is a structural Verilog module for a 9-input XOR function that is equivalent to the 74x280 of Figure 6-71(a) in structure as well as function. In this example, we've used the previously defined Vrxor3 module as the basic building block of the XOR tree. In an ASIC, we would replace the Vrxor3 module with a 3-input XOR primitive from the ASIC library. Also, if a 3-input XNOR were available, we could eliminate the explicit inversion for Y3N and instead use the XNOR for U5, using the noninverted Y3 signal as its last input.

Our final example is a Verilog version of the Hamming decoder circuit of Figure 6-73 and is shown in Table 6-62. A function syndrome is defined to return the 3-bit syndrome of a 7-bit data input vector D. In the main always block, the corrected data output vector DC is initially set equal to the uncorrected data input vector DU. The syndrome function is then called to get the 3-bit syndrome. If the syndrome is zero, either no error or an undetectable error has occurred and the output NOERROR is set to 1. If the syndrome is nonzero, the

Table 6-61 Structural Verilog program for a 74x280-like parity checker.

```
module Vrparity9s(I, EVEN, ODD);
  input [1:9] I;
  output EVEN, ODD;
  wire Y1, Y2, Y3, Y3N;

  Vrxor3 U1 (I[1], I[2], I[3], Y1);
  Vrxor3 U2 (I[4], I[5], I[6], Y2);
  Vrxor3 U3 (I[7], I[8], I[9], Y3);
  assign Y3N = ~Y3;
  Vrxor3 U4 (Y1, Y2, Y3, ODD);
  Vrxor3 U5 (Y1, Y2, Y3N, EVEN);
endmodule
```

Table 6-62 Behavioral Verilog module for Hamming error correction.

```
module Vrhamcorr(DU, DC, NOERROR);
  input [1:7] DU;
  output [1:7] DC;
  output NOERROR;
  reg [1:7] DC;
  reg NOERROR;

  function [2:0] syndrome;
    input [1:7] D;
    begin
      syndrome[0] = D[1] ^ D[3] ^ D[5] ^ D[7];
      syndrome[1] = D[2] ^ D[3] ^ D[6] ^ D[7];
      syndrome[2] = D[4] ^ D[5] ^ D[6] ^ D[7];
    end
  endfunction

  integer i;
  always @ (DU) begin
    DC = DU;
    i = syndrome(DU);
    if (i == 3'b0) NOERROR = 1'b1;
    else begin
      NOERROR = 1'b0; DC[i] = ~DU[i];
    end
  end
endmodule
```

corresponding bit of DC is complemented to correct the assumed 1-bit error, and NOERROR is cleared to 0.

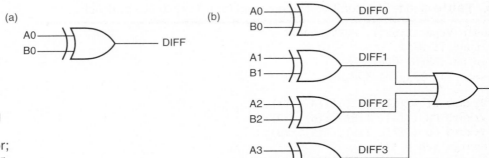

Figure 6-74
Comparators using
XOR gates:
(a) 1-bit comparator;
(b) 4-bit comparator.

6.9 Comparators

Comparing two binary words for equality is a commonly used operation in computer systems and device interfaces. For example, in Figure 2-7(a) on page 56, we showed a system structure in which devices are enabled by comparing a "device select" word with a predetermined "device ID." A circuit that compares two binary words and indicates whether they are equal is called a *comparator*. Some comparators interpret their input words as signed or unsigned numbers and also indicate an arithmetic relationship (greater or less than) between the words. These devices are often called *magnitude comparators*.

comparator

magnitude comparator

6.9.1 Comparator Structure

Exclusive-OR and Exclusive-NOR gates may be viewed as 1-bit comparators. Figure 6-74(a) shows an interpretation of a 2-input XOR gate (such as 74x86) as a 1-bit comparator. The active-high output, DIFF, is asserted if the inputs are different. The outputs of four XOR gates are ORed to create a 4-bit comparator in (b). The DIFF output is asserted if any of the input-bit pairs are different. We can build an n-bit comparator using n XOR gates and an n-input OR gate.

WIDE GATES   There is a practical limit to the width of an individual OR gate in any technology. Wider OR functions can be obtained by cascading individual gates, as we did for wider XOR functions in Figure 6-70 on page 448. As in that example, a faster circuit is obtained by arranging the gates in a tree-like structure rather than a linear cascade.

For a wide OR function, there is an opportunity to make the circuit even faster. Recall that, at the transistor level, inverting gates are typically faster and smaller than noninverting one. For example, an OR-gate circuit is typically designed as a NOR gate followed by an inverter. Figure 6-75 shows two different approaches to building a 16-input OR function. In (a), we use two levels of OR gates, which actually yields four levels of gate delay at the transistor level. In (b), we use one level of NOR gates followed by a NAND gate, resulting in only two levels of gate delay and a smaller circuit at the transistor level, too.

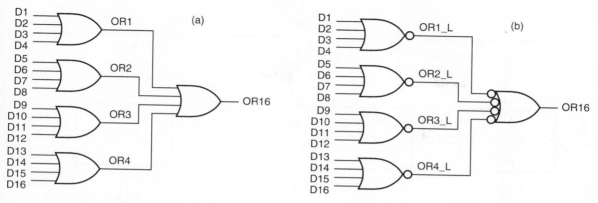

Figure 6-75 16-input OR functions: (a) using OR gates;
(b) using NOR and NAND gates.

Comparators can also be built using Exclusive-NOR (XNOR) gates, some-times called Equivalence gates. A 2-input XNOR gate produces a 1 output if its two inputs are equal. A multibit comparator can be constructed using one XNOR gate per bit, and ANDing all of their outputs together. The output of that AND function is 1 if all of the individual bits are pairwise equal. A wide AND function can be built using the same ideas that we discussed above for wide OR functions.

The n-bit comparators in this subsection are sometimes called *parallel comparators* because they look at each pair of input bits simultaneously and deliver the 1-bit comparison results in parallel to an n-input OR or AND function. It is also possible to design an "iterative comparator" that looks at its bits one at a time using a small, fixed amount of logic per bit. Before looking at an iterative comparator design, you should understand the general class of "iterative circuits" described in the next subsection.

parallel comparator

6.9.2 Iterative Circuits

An *iterative circuit* is a special type of combinational circuit, with the structure shown in Figure 6-76 on the next page. The circuit contains n identical modules, each of which has both *primary inputs and outputs* and *cascading inputs and outputs*. The leftmost cascading inputs are called *boundary inputs* and are con-nected to fixed logic values in most iterative circuits. The rightmost cascading outputs are called *boundary outputs* and usually provide important information.

Iterative circuits are well suited to problems that can be solved by a simple iterative algorithm:

iterative circuit
primary inputs and outputs
cascading inputs and outputs
boundary outputs

1. Set C_0 to its initial value and set i to 0.
2. Use C_i and PI_i to determine the values of PO_i and C_{i+1}.
3. Increment i.
4. If $i < n$, go to step 2.

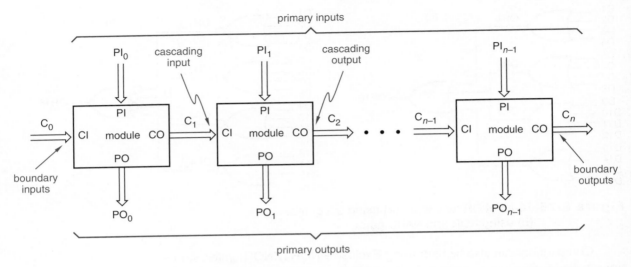

Figure 6-76 General structure of an iterative combinational circuit.

In an iterative circuit, the loop of steps 2–4 is "unwound" by providing a separate combinational circuit that performs step 2 for each value of i.

Examples of iterative circuits are the comparator circuit in the next subsection and the ripple adder in Section 6.10.2. The 74x85 4-bit comparator and the 74x283 4-bit adder are examples of MSI circuits that can be used as the individual modules in a larger iterative circuit. In Section 8.6 we'll explore the relationship between iterative circuits and corresponding sequential circuits that execute the 4-step algorithm above in discrete time steps.

6.9.3 An Iterative Comparator Circuit

Two n-bit values X and Y can be compared one bit at a time using a single bit EQ_i at each step to keep track of whether all of the bit-pairs have been equal so far:

1. Set EQ_0 to 1 and set i to 0.
2. If EQ_i is 1 and X_i and Y_i are equal, set EQ_{i+1} to 1. Else set EQ_{i+1} to 0.
3. Increment i.
4. If $i < n$, go to step 2.

Figure 6-77 shows a corresponding iterative circuit. Note that this circuit has no primary outputs; the boundary output is all that interests us. Other iterative circuits, such as the ripple adder of Section 6.10.2, have primary outputs of interest.

Given a choice between the iterative comparator circuit in this subsection and one of the parallel comparators shown previously, you would probably prefer the parallel comparator. The iterative comparator saves little if any cost,

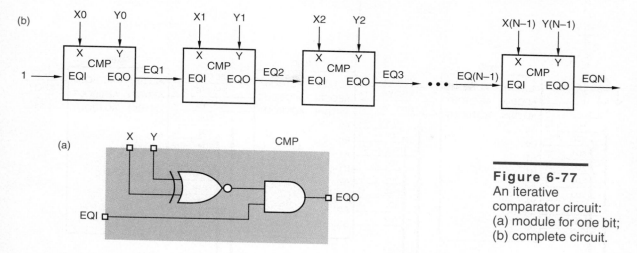

Figure 6-77
An iterative
comparator circuit:
(a) module for one bit;
(b) complete circuit.

and it's very slow because the cascading signals need time to "ripple" from the leftmost to the rightmost module. Iterative circuits that process more than one bit at a time, using modules like the 74x85 4-bit comparator and 74x283 4-bit adder, are much more likely to be used in practical designs.

6.9.4 Standard MSI Magnitude Comparators

Comparator applications are common enough that magnitude comparators have been developed commercially as MSI parts. The *74x85* is a 4-bit comparator with the logic symbol shown in Figure 6-78. It provides a greater-than output (AGTBOUT) and a less-than output (ALTBOUT) as well as an equal output (AEQBOUT). The '85 also has *cascading inputs* (AGTBIN, ALTBIN, AEQBIN) for combining multiple '85s to create comparators for more than four bits. Both the cascading inputs and the outputs are arranged in a 1-out-of-3 code, since in normal operation exactly one input and one output should be asserted.

74x85

cascading inputs

```
            74x85
       ┌──────────────┐
   2 ──┤ ALTBIN  ALTBOUT├── 7
   3 ──┤ AEQBIN  AEQBOUT├── 6
   4 ──┤ AGTBIN  AGTBOUT├── 5
  10 ──┤ A0           │
   9 ──┤ B0           │
  12 ──┤ A1           │
  11 ──┤ B1           │
  13 ──┤ A2           │
  14 ──┤ B2           │
  15 ──┤ A3           │
   1 ──┤ B3           │
       └──────────────┘
```

Figure 6-78
Traditional logic symbol for
the 74x85 4-bit comparator.

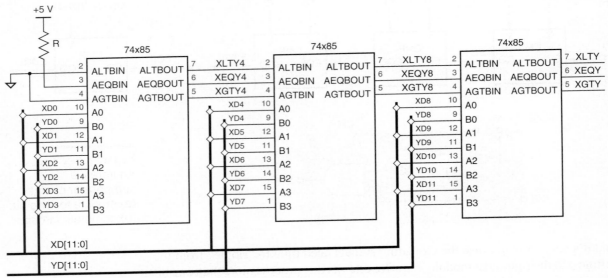

Figure 6-79 A 12-bit comparator using 74x85s.

The cascading inputs are defined so the outputs of an '85 that compares less-significant bits are connected to the inputs of an '85 that compares more-significant bits, as shown in Figure 6-79 for a 12-bit comparator. This is an iterative circuit according to the definition in Section 6.9.2. Each '85 develops its cascading outputs roughly according to the following pseudo-logic equations:

$$\text{AGTBOUT} = (A > B) + (A = B) \cdot \text{AGTBIN}$$

$$\text{AEQBOUT} = (A = B) \cdot \text{AEQBIN}$$

$$\text{ALTBOUT} = (A < B) + (A = B) \cdot \text{ALTBIN}$$

The parenthesized subexpressions above are not logic expressions; rather, they indicate an arithmetic comparison that occurs between the A3–A0 and B3–B0 inputs. In other words, AGTBOUT is asserted if A > B or if A = B and AGTBIN is asserted (if the higher-order bits are equal, we have to look at the lower-order bits for the answer). The arithmetic comparisons can be expressed using normal logic expressions, for example,

$$(A > B) = A3 \cdot B3' +$$
$$(A3 \oplus B3)' \cdot A2 \cdot B2' +$$
$$(A3 \oplus B3)' \cdot (A2 \oplus B2)' \cdot A1 \cdot B1' +$$
$$(A3 \oplus B3)' \cdot (A2 \oplus B2)' \cdot (A1 \oplus B1)' \cdot A0 \cdot B0'$$

Such expressions must be substituted into the pseudo-logic equations above to obtain genuine logic equations for the comparator outputs.

Several 8-bit MSI comparators are also available. The simplest of these is the *74x682*, whose logic symbol is shown in Figure 6-80 and whose internal logic diagram is shown in Figure 6-82 on the next page. The top half of the circuit checks the two 8-bit input words for equality. Each XNOR-gate output is asserted if its inputs are equal, and the PEQQ_L output is asserted if all eight input-bit pairs are equal. The bottom half of the circuit compares the input words arithmetically and asserts PGTQ_L if P[7–0] > Q[7–0].

74x682

Unlike the 74x85, the 74x682 does not have cascading inputs. Also unlike the '85, the '682 does not provide a "less than" output. However, any desired condition, including ≤ and ≥, can be formulated as a function of the PEQQ_L and PGTQ_L outputs, as shown in Figure 6-81.

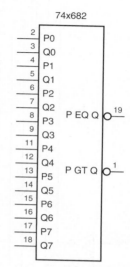

Figure 6-80
Traditional logic symbol for the 74x682 8-bit comparator.

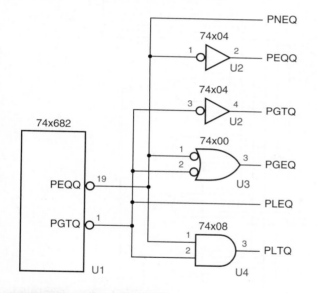

Figure 6-81
Arithmetic conditions derived from 74x682 outputs.

COMPARING COMPARATORS   The individual 1-bit comparators (XNOR gates) in Figure 6-82 are drawn in the opposite sense as the examples of the preceding subsection—outputs are asserted for *equal* inputs and then ANDed, rather than asserted for *different* inputs and then ORed. We can look at a comparator's function either way, as long as we're consistent.

6.9.5 Comparators in HDLs

HDLs such as ABEL, VHDL, and Verilog have built-in operators for equality and magnitude comparison. So, you may think that comparators are easy to design in HDLs, because the compiler does it for you. But, it's better to think of comparators as being easy only to *specify* in your design. With just a few simple relational expressions in your HDL code, you can cause a lot of big, potentially slow comparators to be synthesized. Thus, it's important for you to have a feel

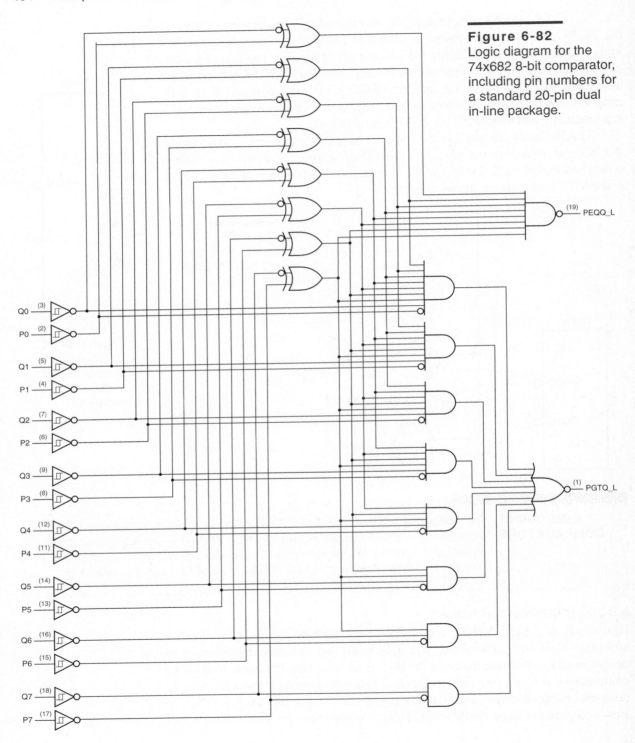

Figure 6-82
Logic diagram for the
74x682 8-bit comparator,
including pin numbers for
a standard 20-pin dual
in-line package.

for what kind of logic will be synthesized when you specify comparison operations in your code.

Comparing two bit-vectors for equality or inequality is very easy to do in an HDL program, in relational expressions using operators such as "==" and "!=" ("=" and "/=" in VHDL). Thus, given the relational expression "(A==B)", where A and B are bit vectors each with n elements, the compiler generates the logic expression,

$$((A1 \oplus B1) + (A2 \oplus B2) + \ldots + (An \oplus Bn))'$$

Recall that "$\oplus$" is the Exclusive OR operator. The logic expression for "A!=B" is just the complement of the one above.

In the preceding logic expression, it takes one 2-input XOR function to compare each bit. Since a 2-input XOR function can be realized as a sum of two product terms, the complete expression can be realized, for example in a PLD, as a relatively modest complemented sum of $2n$ product terms:

$$((A1 \cdot B1' + A1' \cdot B1) + (A2 \cdot B2' + A2' \cdot B2) + \ldots + (An \cdot Bn' + An' \cdot Bn))'$$

Magnitude comparison (checking for greater-than or less-than conditions) is another story. For example, consider the relational expression "(A<B)". To construct the corresponding logic expression, the HDL compiler can first build n equations of the form

$$Li = (Ai' \cdot (Bi + Li\text{-}1)) + (Ai \cdot Bi \cdot Li\text{-}1)$$

for $i = 1$ to n, and L0 = 0 by definition. This is, in effect, an iterative definition of the less-than function, starting with the least significant bit. Each Li variable is asserted if, as of bit i, A is less than B. This is true if Ai is 0 and Bi is 1 or A was less than B as of the previous bit, or if Ai and Bi are both 1 and A was less than B as of the previous bit.

The logic equation for "(A<B)" is simply the equation for Ln. So, after creating the n equations above, the HDL compiler collapses them into a single equation for Ln involving only elements of A and B. It does this by substituting the Ln-1 equation into the righthand side of the Ln equation, then substituting the Ln-2 equation into this result, and so on, until substituting 0 for L0. In the case of a compiler that is targeting a PLD or other sum-of-products realization, the final step is to derive a minimal sum-of-products expression from the Ln equation.

Collapsing an iterative circuit into a two-level sum-of-products realization often creates an exponential expansion of product terms. The "<" comparison function does this, requiring $2^n - 1$ product terms for an n-bit comparator. Thus, comparators larger than a few bits cannot be realized practically in one pass through a PLD.

The results for ">" comparators are identical, of course, and logic expressions for ">=" and "<=" are at least as bad, being the complements of the expressions for "<" and ">". If we use a PLD with output polarity control, the inversion is free and the number of product terms is the same; otherwise, the minimal number of product terms after inverting is $2^n + 2^{n-1} - 1$.

So, a sum-of-products realization for an n-bit magnitude comparator is feasible only for small values of n (typically 4 or less). For larger values of n, and depending on the target technology, the compiler may synthesize a set of smaller comparator modules, along the lines of the 74x85 and 74x682 MSI parts, and then cascade or combine their outputs to create the larger comparison result.

6.9.6 Comparators in ABEL and PLDs

To compare two sets for equality or inequality in ABEL, we use the "==" or "!=" operator in a relational expression. The only restriction is that the two sets must have an equal number of elements. Thus, given the relational expression "A!=B", where A and B are sets each with n elements, the compiler generates the logic expression

```
(A1 $ B1)  # (A2 $ B2)  # ... # (An $ Bn)
```

Recall that "$" is ABEL's Exclusive OR operator. The logic expression for "A==B" is just the complement of the one above. Each XOR operation expands into two product terms, and the entire comparison requires $2n$ product terms.

ABEL also has relational operators for magnitude comparison: >, >=, <, and <=. But the resulting sum-of-products logic expressions are not so small or easy to derive, as shown in the previous subsection. For example, we could write the equation for the PGTQ output of a 74x682 8-bit comparator in one line of ABEL as follows:

```
PGTQ_L = !([P7,P6,P5,P4,P3,P2,P1] > [Q7,Q6,Q5,Q4,Q3,Q2,Q1,Q0]);
```

But the resulting two-level sum-of-products expression has 255 product terms!

6.9.7 Comparators in VHDL

equality, =
inequality, /=

VHDL has comparison operators for all of its built-in types. *Equality (=)* and *inequality (/=)* operators apply to all types; for array and record types, the operands must have equal size and structure, and the operands are compared component by component. We have used the equality operator to compare a signal or signal vector with a constant value in many examples in this chapter. If we compare two signals or variables, the synthesizer generates equations similar to ABEL's in the preceding subsection.

VHDL's other comparison operators, >, <, >=, and <=, apply only to integer types, enumerated types (such as STD_LOGIC), and one-dimensional arrays of enumeration or integer types. Integer order from smallest to largest is the natural ordering, from minus infinity to plus infinity, and enumerated types use the ordering in which the elements of the type were defined, from first to last (unless you explicitly change the enumeration encoding using a command specific to the synthesis tool, in which case the ordering is that of your encoding).

```
library IEEE;
use IEEE.std_logic_1164.all;

entity vcompare is
    port (
        A, B: in STD_LOGIC_VECTOR (7 downto 0);
        EQ, NE, GT, GE, LT, LE: out STD_LOGIC
    );
end vcompare;

architecture vcompare_arch of vcompare is
begin
process (A, B)
  begin
    EQ <= '0'; NE <= '0'; GT <= '0'; GE <= '0'; LT <= '0'; LE <= '0';
    if A = B  then EQ <= '1'; end if;
    if A /= B then NE <= '1'; end if;
    if A > B  then GT <= '1'; end if;
    if A >= B then GE <= '1'; end if;
    if A < B  then LT <= '1'; end if;
    if A <= B then LE <= '1'; end if;
  end process;
end vcompare_arch
```

Table 6-63
Behavioral VHDL program for comparing 8-bit unsigned integers.

The ordering for array types is defined iteratively, starting with the *leftmost* element in each array. Arrays are always compared from left to right, regardless of the order of their index range ("to" or "downto"). The order of the leftmost pair of unequal elements is the order of the array. If the arrays have unequal lengths and all the elements of the shorter array match the corresponding elements of the longer one, then the shorter array is considered to be the smaller.

The result of all this is that the built-in comparison operators compare equal-length arrays of type BIT_VECTOR or STD_LOGIC_VECTOR as if they represented unsigned integers. If the arrays have different lengths, then the operators do *not* yield a valid arithmetic comparison, what you'd get by extending the shorter array with zeroes on the left; more on this in a moment.

Table 6-63 is a VHDL program that produces all of the comparison outputs for comparing two 8-bit unsigned integers. Since the two input vectors A and B have equal lengths, the program produces the desired results.

To allow more flexible comparisons and arithmetic operations, synthesis supplier Synopsys created a package, *std_logic_arith*, which defines two important new types and a host of comparison and arithmetic functions that operate on them. The two new types are SIGNED and UNSIGNED:

std_logic_arith package

```
type SIGNED is array (NATURAL range <>) of STD_LOGIC;
type UNSIGNED is array (NATURAL range <>) of STD_LOGIC;
```

As you can see, both types are defined just as indeterminate-length arrays of STD_LOGIC, no different from STD_LOGIC_VECTOR. The important thing is that the package also defines new comparison functions that are invoked when either or both comparison operands have one of the new types. For example, it defines eight new "less-than" functions with the following combinations of parameters:

```
function "<" (L: UNSIGNED; R: UNSIGNED) return BOOLEAN;
function "<" (L: SIGNED; R: SIGNED) return BOOLEAN;
function "<" (L: UNSIGNED; R: SIGNED) return BOOLEAN;
function "<" (L: SIGNED; R: UNSIGNED) return BOOLEAN;
function "<" (L: UNSIGNED; R: INTEGER) return BOOLEAN;
function "<" (L: INTEGER; R: UNSIGNED) return BOOLEAN;
function "<" (L: SIGNED; R: INTEGER) return BOOLEAN;
function "<" (L: INTEGER; R: SIGNED) return BOOLEAN;
```

Thus, the "<" operator can be used with any combination of SIGNED, UNSIGNED, and INTEGER operands; the compiler selects the function whose parameter types match the actual operands. Each of the functions is defined in the package to do "the right thing," including making the appropriate extensions and conversions when operands of different sizes or types are used. Similar comparison functions are provided for the other five relational operators, =, /=, <=, >, and >=.

The std_logic_arith package is stored in the IEEE library. Using it, you can write programs like the one in Table 6-64. Its 8-bit input vectors, A, B, C, and D, have three different types. In the comparisons involving A, B, and C, the compiler automatically selects the correct version of the comparison function; for example, for "A<B" it selects the first "<" function above, because both operands have type UNSIGNED. The new "<" functions are called *overlaid functions*, because they overlay or take the pace of the built-in function when appropriate.

overlaid functions

In the comparisons involving input D, explicit type conversions are used. The assumption is that the designer wants this particular STD_LOGIC_VECTOR to be interpreted as UNSIGNED in one case and SIGNED in another. The important thing to understand here is that the std_logic_arith package does not make any assumptions about how STD_LOGIC_VECTORs are to be interpreted; the user must specify the conversion.

std_logic_signed package

std_logic_unsigned package

Two other packages, *std_logic_signed* and *std_logic_unsigned*, do make assumptions and are useful if all STD_LOGIC_VECTORs are supposed to be interpreted the same way. Each package contains three versions of each comparison function so that STD_LOGIC_VECTORs are interpreted as SIGNED or UNSIGNED, respectively, when compared with each other or with integers.

When a comparison function is specified in VHDL, realizing the function as a two-level sum of products takes just as many product terms as in ABEL or any other HDL. However, depending on the target technology, the compiler may be able to realize the comparator as an iterative circuit with far fewer gates, albeit more levels of logic. Also, better compilers can detect opportunities to eliminate entire comparator circuits. For example, in the program of Table 6-63 on the preceding page, the NE, GE, and LE outputs could be realized with one inverter each, as the complements of the EQ, LT, and GT outputs, respectively.

Table 6-64 Behavioral VHDL program for comparing 8-bit integers of various types.

```
library IEEE;
use IEEE.std_logic_1164.all;
use IEEE.std_logic_arith.all;

entity vcompa is
    port (
        A, B: in UNSIGNED (7 downto 0);
        C: in SIGNED (7 downto 0);
        D: in STD_LOGIC_VECTOR (7 downto 0);
        A_LT_B, B_GE_C, A_EQ_C, C_NEG, D_BIG, D_NEG: out STD_LOGIC
    );
end vcompa;

architecture vcompa_arch of vcompa is
begin
process (A, B, C, D)
  begin
    A_LT_B <= '0'; B_GE_C <= '0'; A_EQ_C <= '0';
    C_NEG <= '0'; D_BIG <= '0'; D_NEG <= '0';
    if A < B then A_LT_B <= '1'; end if;
    if B >= C then B_GE_C <= '1'; end if;
    if A = C then A_EQ_C <= '1'; end if;
    if C < 0 then C_NEG <= '1'; end if;
    if UNSIGNED(D) > 200 then D_BIG <= '1'; end if;
    if SIGNED(D) < 0 then D_NEG <= '1'; end if;
  end process;
end vcompa_arch;
```

6.9.8 Comparators in Verilog

Like other HDLs, Verilog has built-in comparison operators: >, >=, <, <=, ==, and !=. These operators can be applied to bit vectors, and the bit vectors are interpreted as unsigned numbers with the most significant bit on the left, regardless of how they are numbered. Verilog-2001 also supports signed arithmetic, using the language extensions described in the box on page 301. When a comparison operation is used in a Verilog module, the compiler synthesizes corresponding comparator logic.

Verilog usually does "the right thing" to match up operands of different lengths, by adding zeroes on the left, but in complicated length mismatch situations it is still prudent to consult the Verilog reference manual to be sure that you'll get the desired results, or simply pad out the shorter operand explicitly.

The size and speed of synthesized comparator logic depends on the target technology and the optimization capabilities of the Verilog compiler. Equality and inequality checkers are fairly small and fast. As shown in Section 6.9.1, they they can be built from n XOR or XNOR gates and an n-input AND or OR gate.

Table 6-65 Verilog module with functionality similar to the 74x85 magnitude comparator.

```
module Vr74x85(A, B, AGTBIN, ALTBIN, AEQBIN, AGTBOUT, ALTBOUT, AEQBOUT);
  input [3:0] A, B;
  input AGTBIN, ALTBIN, AEQBIN;
  output AGTBOUT, ALTBOUT, AEQBOUT;
  reg AGTBOUT, ALTBOUT, AEQBOUT;

  always @ (A or B or AGTBIN or ALTBIN or AEQBIN)
    if (A == B)
      begin AGTBOUT = AGTBIN; ALTBOUT = ALTBIN; AEQBOUT = AEQBIN; end
    else if (A > B)
      begin AGTBOUT = 1'b1; ALTBOUT = 1'b0; AEQBOUT = 1'b0; end
    else
      begin AGTBOUT = 1'b0; ALTBOUT = 1'b1; AEQBOUT = 1'b0; end
endmodule
```

The XOR or XNOR gates all operate in parallel, and a reasonably fast AND or OR gate of any size can be built using a tree-like structure.

Checking for greater-than or less-than conditions is another story. As we discussed at the end of Section 6.9.6, the number of product terms needed for an n-bit comparator of this kind grows exponentially, on the order of 2^n, when the comparator is realized as a two-level sum of products. So, a two-level sum-of-products realization is possible only for small values of n (typically 4 or less). For larger values of n, and depending on the target technology, the compiler may synthesize a set of smaller comparator modules, along the lines of the 74x85 and 74x682 MSI parts, whose outputs may be cascaded or combined to create the larger comparison result.

That's basically all you need to know to specify comparators in Verilog modules. However, the comparator examples in the rest of this subsection can give you some practice with Verilog coding and some insight into the synthesis results produced by different coding approaches.

Table 6-65 is a Verilog module with functionality similar to that of the 74x85 magnitude comparator of Section 6.9.4. Like the 74x85, this module is set up for cascading information to flow from less significant to more significant stages. Thus, in the first if statement, if the A and B inputs are equal, then the comparison will depend on less significant stages, and the cascading outputs are set equal to the cascading inputs. If they are unequal, then the next if and the else statements set the cascading outputs solely dependent on the comparison result in the current stage.

Notice that this module does not perform an explicit check for A<B, to avoid synthesizing another comparator. Suppose we missed this optimization and did include the A<B check, as shown in Table 6-66. Then it is necessary also to include a final else statement, to specify the values of the outputs if none of

Table 6-66 Verilog comparator module with three explicit comparisons.

```
module Vr74x85s(A, B, AGTBIN, ALTBIN, AEQBIN, AGTBOUT, ALTBOUT, AEQBOUT);
  input [3:0] A, B;
  input AGTBIN, ALTBIN, AEQBIN;
  output AGTBOUT, ALTBOUT, AEQBOUT;
  reg AGTBOUT, ALTBOUT, AEQBOUT;

  always @ (A or B or AGTBIN or ALTBIN or AEQBIN)
    if (A == B)
      begin AGTBOUT = AGTBIN; ALTBOUT = ALTBIN; AEQBOUT = AEQBIN; end
    else if (A > B)
      begin AGTBOUT = 1'b1; ALTBOUT = 1'b0; AEQBOUT = 1'b0; end
    else if (A < B)
      begin AGTBOUT = 1'b0; ALTBOUT = 1'b1; AEQBOUT = 1'b0; end
    else
      begin AGTBOUT = 1'bx; ALTBOUT = 1'bx; AEQBOUT = 1'bx; end
endmodule
```

the first three comparisons were true. Actually, we know that exactly one of the first three comparisons will always be true, so we really don't care what output values are specified in the final else statement and set them to "x" (don't-care).

You might feel that the final else statement is unnecessary, since exactly one of the first three comparisons will always be true. But the Verilog compiler is not smart enough to figure that out. If you remove the final else clause, you create one of those cases where the compiler "infers a latch" to hold the previous value of each cascading output if none of the logic paths through the always block assigned a value to that output. You may think that no harm is done since this will never occur, but the inferred latches still add size and delay to the final synthesized circuit, even though they're never needed. For example, when this design is targeted to a Xilinx XC9500-series CPLD, the difference is 125 versus 42 product terms and two levels of delay versus one for one of the outputs.

It's also possible to set up a comparator module with cascading in the reverse direction, from more significant to less significant stages, as shown in Table 6-67 on the next page. Here, the first two if statements determine whether the comparison result has already been determined as greater-than or less-than by the more significant stage and, if so, simply pass that result to the cascading outputs. Otherwise, if the comparison has been equal so far, the first else statement sets the cascading outputs according to the comparison in the current stage.

The final else statement sets the cascading outputs to 0 if none of the cascading inputs was asserted. Here again, you might feel that this statement is unnecessary. Since the 74x85 is always supposed to be used with exactly one of its cascading inputs asserted, you really "don't care" what happens if none is asserted. But the Verilog compiler does care. If you remove the final else

Table 6-67 Verilog comparator module with cascading from more to less significant stages.

```verilog
module Vr74x85r(A, B, AGTBIN, ALTBIN, AEQBIN, AGTBOUT, ALTBOUT, AEQBOUT);
  input [3:0] A, B;
  input AGTBIN, ALTBIN, AEQBIN;
  output AGTBOUT, ALTBOUT, AEQBOUT;
  reg AGTBOUT, ALTBOUT, AEQBOUT;

  always @ (A or B or AGTBIN or ALTBIN or AEQBIN)
    if (AGTBIN)
      begin AGTBOUT = 1'b1; ALTBOUT = 1'b0; AEQBOUT = 1'b0; end
    else if (ALTBIN)
      begin AGTBOUT = 1'b0; ALTBOUT = 1'b1; AEQBOUT = 1'b0; end
    else if (AEQBIN)
      begin
        AGTBOUT = (A > B) ? 1'b1 : 1'b0 ;
        AEQBOUT = (A == B) ? 1'b1 : 1'b0;
        ALTBOUT = ~AGTBOUT & ~AEQBOUT;
      end
    else
      begin AGTBOUT = 1'bx; ALTBOUT = 1'bx; AEQBOUT = 1'bx; end
endmodule
```

clause, the compiler "infers a latch" to hold the previous value of each cascading output if none of the logic paths through the `always` block assigned a value to that output.

Since the final `else` statement should never be reached in normal operation, we optimized the design a bit by setting the cascading outputs to "x" in this statement. This allows the compiler to treat the output as a true "don't care" in this case, and may result in a smaller or faster circuit, depending on the target technology and the optimization capabilities of the compiler. Or, for slightly different functionality, you could set the outputs to 0 here, to create a comparator that never asserts any of its cascading outputs during abnormal operation, when none of the cascading inputs is asserted.

Thinking further about this particular design problem, it is apparent that the Verilog code in Table 6-67 is still slightly overspecified. Keep in mind that, with a series of `if-else` statements, the Verilog compiler synthesizes priority logic that checks the first condition, and only then the second, and so on. For example, if both AGTBIN and ALTBIN are asserted, priority is given to AGTBIN and the outputs are set accordingly. Yet, in this design, we never expect AGTBIN and ALTBIN to be asserted simultaneously, and we may not care about the output values in that situation.

To convey a relaxed requirement such as this, we can use a partially enumerated `case` statement, as shown in Table 6-68. Here, the three cascading

Table 6-68 Verilog comparator module using a `case` statement.

```verilog
module Vr74x85rc(A, B, AGTBIN, ALTBIN, AEQBIN, AGTBOUT, ALTBOUT, AEQBOUT);
  input [3:0] A, B;
  input AGTBIN, ALTBIN, AEQBIN;
  output AGTBOUT, ALTBOUT, AEQBOUT;
  reg AGTBOUT, ALTBOUT, AEQBOUT;

  always @ (A or B or AGTBIN or ALTBIN or AEQBIN)
    case ({AGTBIN, ALTBIN, AEQBIN})
      3'b100: begin AGTBOUT = 1'b1; ALTBOUT = 1'b0; AEQBOUT = 1'b0; end
      3'b010: begin AGTBOUT = 1'b0; ALTBOUT = 1'b1; AEQBOUT = 1'b0; end
      3'b001: begin
                AGTBOUT = (A > B) ? 1'b1 : 1'b0 ;
                AEQBOUT = (A == B) ? 1'b1 : 1'b0;
                ALTBOUT = ~AGTBOUT & ~AEQBOUT;
              end
      default: begin AGTBOUT = 1'bx; ALTBOUT = 1'bx; AEQBOUT = 1'bx; end
    endcase
endmodule
```

inputs are concatenated into a 3-bit vector whose value is used as the select variable for the `case` statement. With a 3-bit select variable, there should be eight possible cases. However, only the actions for the three expected cases are individually listed. The remaining cases are covered by the "`default`" case, which sets each of the outputs to "x". This allows the compiler to treat the outputs as don't-cares for these cases.

Yet another approach to coding the comparator is shown in Table 6-69. This module uses a continuous-assignment statement to specify the value of each cascading output. Unlike previous example, this module's output values are fully specified for all situations, including cases where none or more than one of the cascading inputs are asserted, and the functionality for these abnormal cases is slightly different.

Table 6-69 Verilog comparator module using continuous assignments.

```verilog
module Vr74x85re(A, B, AGTBIN, ALTBIN, AEQBIN, AGTBOUT, ALTBOUT, AEQBOUT);
  input [3:0] A, B;
  input AGTBIN, ALTBIN, AEQBIN;
  output AGTBOUT, ALTBOUT, AEQBOUT;

  assign AGTBOUT = AGTBIN | (AEQBIN & ( (A > B) ? 1'b1 : 1'b0 ) );
  assign AEQBOUT = AEQBIN & ((A == B) ? 1'b1 : 1'b0) ;
  assign ALTBOUT = ~AGTBOUT & ~AEQBOUT;
endmodule
```

6.10 Adders, Subtractors, and ALUs

adder

subtractor

Addition is the most commonly performed arithmetic operation in digital systems. An *adder* combines two arithmetic operands using the addition rules described in Chapter 2. As we showed in Section 2.6, the same addition rules and therefore the same adders are used for both unsigned and two's-complement numbers. An adder can perform subtraction as the addition of the minuend and the complemented (negated) subtrahend, but you can also build *subtractor* circuits that perform subtraction directly. MSI devices and ASIC modules called ALUs, described in Section 6.10.6, perform addition, subtraction, or any of several other operations according to an operation code supplied to the device.

*6.10.1 Half Adders and Full Adders

half adder

The simplest adder, called a *half adder*, adds two 1-bit operands X and Y, producing a 2-bit sum. The sum can range from 0 to 2, which requires two bits to express. The low-order bit of the sum may be named HS (half sum), and the high-order bit may be named CO (carry-out). We can write the following equations for HS and CO:

$$HS = X \oplus Y$$
$$= X \cdot Y' + X' \cdot Y$$
$$CO = X \cdot Y$$

full adder

To add operands with more than one bit, we must provide for carries between bit positions. The building block for this operation is called a *full adder*. Besides the addend-bit inputs X and Y, a full adder has a carry-bit input, CIN. The

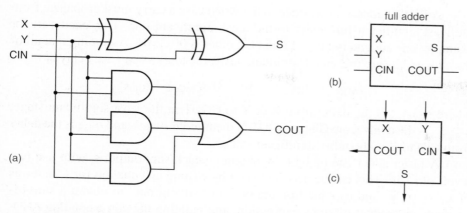

(b)

full adder

(c)

Figure 6-83
Full adder: (a) gate-
level circuit diagram;
(b) logic symbol;
(c) alternate logic
symbol suitable for
cascading.

sum of the three inputs can range from 0 to 3, which can still be expressed with just two output bits, S and COUT, having the following equations:

$$S = X \oplus Y \oplus CIN$$
$$= X \cdot Y' \cdot CIN' + X' \cdot Y \cdot CIN' + X' \cdot Y' \cdot CIN + X \cdot Y \cdot CIN$$
$$COUT = X \cdot Y + X \cdot CIN + Y \cdot CIN$$

Here, S is 1 if an odd number of the inputs are 1, and COUT is 1 if two or more of the inputs are 1. These equations represent the same operation that was specified by the binary addition table in Table 2-3 on page 32.

One possible circuit that realizes the full-adder equations is shown in Figure 6-83(a). The corresponding logic symbol is shown in (b). Sometimes the symbol is drawn as shown in (c), so that cascaded full adders can be drawn more neatly, as in the next subsection.

*6.10.2 Ripple Adders

Two binary words, each with n bits, can be added using a *ripple adder*—a cascade of n full-adder stages, each of which handles one bit. Figure 6-84 shows the circuit for a 4-bit ripple adder. The carry input to the least significant bit (c_0) is normally set to 0, and the carry output of each full adder is connected to the carry input of the next most significant full adder. The ripple adder is a classic example of an iterative circuit as defined in Section 6.9.2.

ripple adder

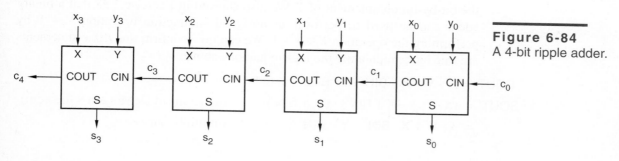

Figure 6-84
A 4-bit ripple adder.

A ripple adder is slow, since in the worst case a carry must propagate from the least significant full adder to the most significant one. This occurs if, for example, one addend is 11 … 11 and the other is 00 … 01. Assuming that all of the addend bits are presented simultaneously, the total worst-case delay is

$$t_{ADD} = t_{XYCout} + (n-2) \cdot t_{CinCout} + t_{CinS}$$

where t_{XYCout} is the delay from X or Y to COUT in the least significant stage, $t_{CinCout}$ is the delay from CIN to COUT in the middle stages, and t_{CinS} is the delay from CIN to S in the most significant stage.

A faster adder can be built by obtaining each sum output s_i with just two levels of logic. This can be accomplished by writing an equation for s_i in terms of x_0–x_i, y_0–y_i, and c_0, "multiplying out" or "adding out" to obtain a sum-of-products or product-of-sums expression, and building the corresponding AND-OR or OR-AND circuit. Unfortunately, beyond s_2 the resulting expressions have too many terms, requiring too many first-level gates and more inputs than typically possible on the second-level gate. For example, even assuming $c_0 = 0$, a two-level AND-OR circuit for s_2 requires 14 4-input ANDs, four 5-input ANDs, and an 18-input OR gate; higher-order sum bits are even worse. Nevertheless, it is possible to build adders with just a few levels of delay using a more reasonable number of gates, as we'll see in Section 6.10.4.

*6.10.3 Subtractors

full subtractor

A binary subtraction operation analogous to binary addition was also specified in Table 2-3 on page 32. A *full subtractor* handles one bit of the binary subtraction algorithm, having input bits X (minuend), Y (subtrahend), and BIN (borrow in), and output bits D (difference) and BOUT (borrow out). We can write logic equations corresponding to the binary subtraction table as follows:

$$D = X \oplus Y \oplus BIN$$
$$BOUT = X' \cdot Y + X' \cdot BIN + Y \cdot BIN$$

These equations are very similar to equations for a full adder, which should not be surprising. We showed in Section 2.6 that a two's-complement subtraction operation, $X - Y$, can be performed by an addition operation, namely, by adding the two's complement of Y to X. The two's complement of Y is $\overline{Y} + 1$, where $\overline{Y}$ is the bit-by-bit complement of Y. We also showed in Exercise 2.28 that a binary adder can be used to perform an unsigned subtraction operation $X - Y$ by performing the operation $X + \overline{Y} + 1$. We can now confirm that these statements are true by manipulating the logic equations above:

$$BOUT = X' \cdot Y + X' \cdot BIN + Y \cdot BIN$$
$$BOUT' = (X + Y') \cdot (X + BIN') \cdot (Y' + BIN') \qquad \text{(generalized DeMorgan's theorem)}$$
$$= X \cdot Y' + X \cdot BIN' + Y' \cdot BIN' \qquad \text{(multiply out)}$$

$$D = X \oplus Y \oplus BIN$$
$$= X \oplus Y' \oplus BIN' \qquad \text{(complementing XOR inputs)}$$

For the last manipulation, recall that we can complement the two inputs of an XOR gate without changing the function performed.

Comparing with the equations for a full adder, the above equations tell us that we can build a full subtractor from a full adder as shown in Figure 6-85. Just to keep things straight, we've given the full-adder circuit in (a) a fictitious name, the "74x999." As shown in (c), we can interpret the function of this same physical circuit to be a full subtractor by giving it a new symbol with active-low borrow in, borrow out, and subtrahend signals.

Thus, to build a ripple subtractor for two n-bit active-high operands, we can use n 74x999s and inverters, as shown in (d). Note that for the subtraction operation, the borrow input of the least significant bit should be negated (no borrow), which for an active-low input means that the physical pin must be 1 or HIGH. This behavior is just the opposite of addition's, where the same input pin is an active-high carry-in that is 0 or LOW.

By going back to the math in Chapter 2, we can show that this sort of manipulation works for all adder and subtractor circuits, not just ripple adders and subtractors. That is, any n-bit adder circuit can be made to function as a

Figure 6-85 Subtractor design using adders: (a) full adder; (b) full subtractor; (c) interpreting 74x999 as a full subtractor; (d) ripple subtractor.

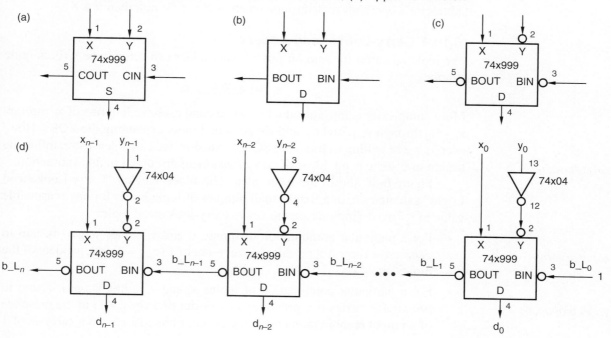

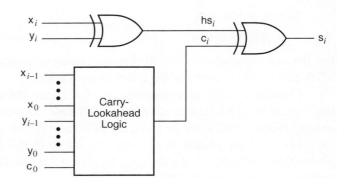

Figure 6-86
Structure of one
stage of a carry-
lookahead adder.

subtractor by complementing the subtrahend and treating the carry-in and carry-out signals as borrows with the opposite active level. The rest of this section discusses addition circuits only, with the understanding that they can easily be made to perform subtraction.

A subtractor can be used as a magnitude comparator. Consider the operation $X - Y$. If this operation produces a borrow, then $Y > X$. One way to build a somewhat smaller magnitude comparator is to start with a subtractor, but eliminate all of the logic that is used only for generating difference bits (typically one XOR gate per bit); only the final borrow is needed for the result. If you wanted to know whether $Y \geq X$, you could keep the difference bits and check them for all zeroes for the "equals" case. But a more efficient design would be to swap the subtractor's operands to determine whether $X > Y$; if not, then $Y \geq X$.

*6.10.4 Carry-Lookahead Adders

The logic equation for sum bit i of a binary adder can actually be written quite simply:

$$s_i = x_i \oplus y_i \oplus c_i$$

More complexity is introduced when we expand c_i above in terms of x_0 through x_{i-1}, y_0 through y_{i-1}, and c_0, and we get a real mess expanding the XORs. However, if we're willing to forgo the XOR expansion, we can at least streamline the design of c_i logic using ideas of *carry lookahead* discussed in this subsection.

carry lookahead

Figure 6-86 shows the basic idea. The block labeled "Carry-Lookahead Logic" calculates c_i in a fixed, small number of logic levels for any reasonable value of i. Two definitions are the key to carry-lookahead logic:

- For a particular combination of inputs x_i and y_i, adder stage i is said to *carry generate*
  generate a carry if it produces a carry-out of 1 ($c_{i+1} = 1$) independent of the inputs on $x_0 - x_{i-1}$, $y_0 - y_{i-1}$, and c_0.

- For a particular combination of inputs x_i and y_i, adder stage i is said to *carry propagate*
  propagate carries if it produces a carry-out of 1 ($c_{i+1} = 1$) in the presence of an input combination on the lower-order bits that causes a carry-in of 1 ($c_i = 1$).

Corresponding to these definitions, we can write logic equations for a carry-generate signal, g_i, and a carry-propagate signal, p_i, for each stage of a carry-lookahead adder:

$$g_i = x_i \cdot y_i$$
$$p_i = x_i + y_i$$

That is, a stage unconditionally generates a carry if both of its addend bits are 1, and it propagates carries if at least one of its addend bits is 1. The carry output of a stage can now be written in terms of the generate and propagate signals:

$$c_{i+1} = g_i + p_i \cdot c_i$$

That is, a stage produces a carry if it generates a carry, or if it propagates a carry and the carry input is 1. To eliminate carry ripple, we recursively expand the c_i term for each stage and multiply out to obtain a two-level AND-OR expression. Using this technique, we can obtain the following carry equations for the first four adder stages:

$$c_1 = g_0 + p_0 \cdot c_0$$
$$c_2 = g_1 + p_1 \cdot c_1$$
$$= g_1 + p_1 \cdot (g_0 + p_0 \cdot c_0)$$
$$= g_1 + p_1 \cdot g_0 + p_1 \cdot p_0 \cdot c_0$$
$$c_3 = g_2 + p_2 \cdot c_2$$
$$= g_2 + p_2 \cdot (g_1 + p_1 \cdot g_0 + p_1 \cdot p_0 \cdot c_0)$$
$$= g_2 + p_2 \cdot g_1 + p_2 \cdot p_1 \cdot g_0 + p_2 \cdot p_1 \cdot p_0 \cdot c_0$$
$$c_4 = g_3 + p_3 \cdot c_3$$
$$= g_3 + p_3 \cdot (g_2 + p_2 \cdot g_1 + p_2 \cdot p_1 \cdot g_0 + p_2 \cdot p_1 \cdot p_0 \cdot c_0)$$
$$= g_3 + p_3 \cdot g_2 + p_3 \cdot p_2 \cdot g_1 + p_3 \cdot p_2 \cdot p_1 \cdot g_0 + p_3 \cdot p_2 \cdot p_1 \cdot p_0 \cdot c_0$$

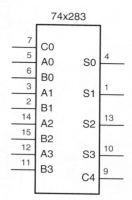

Figure 6-88
Traditional logic symbol for the 74x283 4-bit binary adder.

carry-lookahead adder

Each equation corresponds to a circuit with just three levels of delay—one for the generate and propagate signals, and two for the sum of products shown. A *carry-lookahead adder* uses three-level equations like these in each adder stage for the block labeled "Carry-Lookahead Logic" in Figure 6-86. The sum output for a stage is produced by combining the carry bit with the two addend bits for the stage, as we showed in the figure. In the next subsection we'll study some commercial MSI adders and ALUs that use carry lookahead. Even though you may never use the MSI parts, their internal designs are very interesting to study.

*6.10.5 MSI Adders

The *74x283* is a 4-bit binary adder that forms its sum and carry outputs with just a few levels of logic, using the carry-lookahead technique. Figure 6-88 is a logic symbol for the 74x283. The older *74x83* is identical except for its pinout, which has nonstandard locations for power and ground.

74x283

74x83

Figure 6-87
Logic diagram for
the 74x283 4-bit
binary adder.

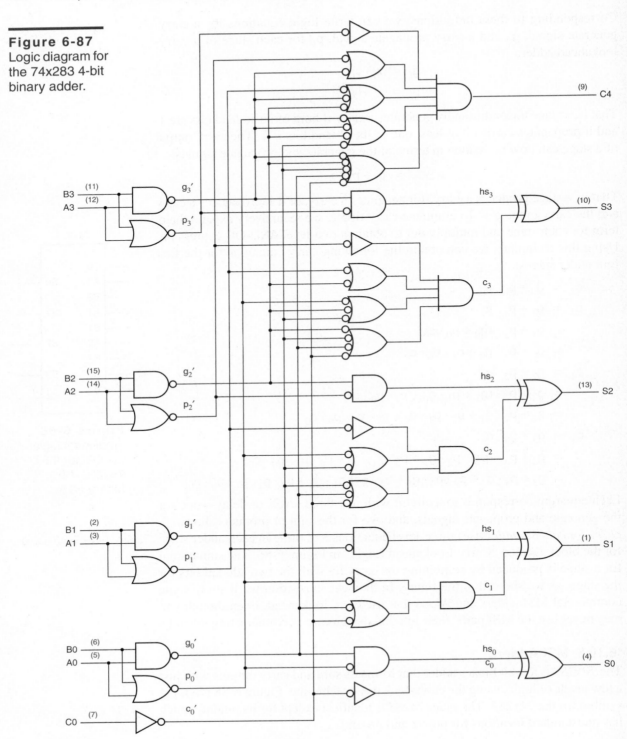

The logic diagram for the '283, shown in Figure 6-87, has just a few differences from the general carry-lookahead design that we described in the preceding subsection. First of all, its addends are named A and B instead of X and Y; no big deal. Second, it produces active-low versions of the carry-generate (g_i') and carry-propagate (p_i') signals, since inverting gates are generally faster than noninverting ones. Third, it takes advantage of the fact that we can algebraically manipulate the half-sum equation as follows:

$$
\begin{aligned}
hs_i &= x_i \oplus y_i \\
&= x_i \cdot y_i' + x_i' \cdot y_i \\
&= x_i \cdot y_i' + x_i \cdot x_i' + x_i' \cdot y_i + y_i \cdot y_i' \\
&= (x_i + y_i) \cdot (x_i' + y_i') \\
&= (x_i + y_i) \cdot (x_i \cdot y_i)' \\
&= p_i \cdot g_i'
\end{aligned}
$$

Thus, an AND gate with an inverted input can be used instead of an XOR gate to create each half-sum bit. That's generally smaller and faster than an XOR gate.

Finally, the '283 creates the carry signals using an INVERT-OR-AND structure (the DeMorgan equivalent of an AND-OR-INVERT), which has about the same delay as a single CMOS or TTL inverting gate. This requires some explaining, since the carry equations that we derived in the preceding subsection are used in a slightly modified form. In particular, the c_{i+1} equation uses the term $p_i \cdot g_i$ instead of g_i. This has no effect on the output, since p_i is always 1 when g_i is 1. However, it allows the equation to be factored as follows:

$$
\begin{aligned}
c_{i+1} &= p_i \cdot g_i + p_i \cdot c_i \\
&= p_i \cdot (g_i + c_i)
\end{aligned}
$$

This leads to the following carry equations, which are used by the circuit :

$$
\begin{aligned}
c_1 &= p_0 \cdot (g_0 + c_0) \\
c_2 &= p_1 \cdot (g_1 + c_1) \\
&= p_1 \cdot (g_1 + p_0 \cdot (g_0 + c_0)) \\
&= p_1 \cdot (g_1 + p_0) \cdot (g_1 + g_0 + c_0) \\
c_3 &= p_2 \cdot (g_2 + c_2) \\
&= p_2 \cdot (g_2 + p_1 \cdot (g_1 + p_0) \cdot (g_1 + g_0 + c_0)) \\
&= p_2 \cdot (g_2 + p_1) \cdot (g_2 + g_1 + p_0) \cdot (g_2 + g_1 + g_0 + c_0) \\
c_4 &= p_3 \cdot (g_3 + c_3) \\
&= p_3 \cdot (g_3 + p_2 \cdot (g_2 + p_1) \cdot (g_2 + g_1 + p_0) \cdot (g_2 + g_1 + g_0 + c_0)) \\
&= p_3 \cdot (g_3 + p_2) \cdot (g_3 + g_2 + p_1) \cdot (g_3 + g_2 + g_1 + p_0) \cdot (g_3 + g_2 + g_1 + g_0 + c_0)
\end{aligned}
$$

If you've followed the derivation of these equations and can obtain the same

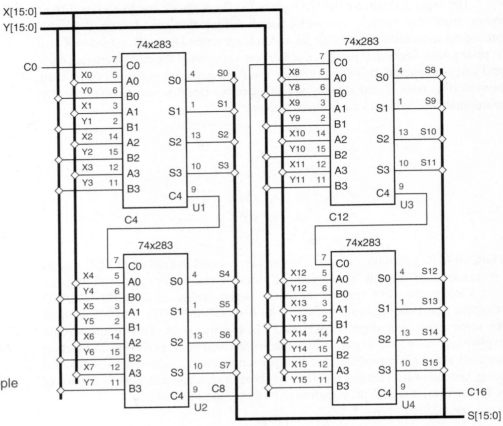

Figure 6-89
A 16-bit group-ripple
adder.

ones by reading the '283 logic diagram, then congratulations, you're up to speed on switching algebra! If not, you may want to review Sections 4.1 and 4.2.

The propagation delay from the C0 input to the C4 output of the '283 is *group-ripple adder* very short, about the same as two inverting gates. As a result, fairly fast *group-ripple adders* with more than four bits can be made simply by cascading the carry outputs and inputs of '283s, as shown in Figure 6-89 for a 16-bit adder. The total propagation delay from C0 to C16 in this circuit is about the same as that of eight inverting gates.

*6.10.6 MSI Arithmetic and Logic Units

arithmetic and logic An *arithmetic and logic unit (ALU)* is a combinational circuit that can perform *unit (ALU)* any of a number of different arithmetic and logical operations on a pair of *b*-bit operands. The operation to be performed is specified by a set of function-select inputs. Typical MSI ALUs have 4-bit operands and three to five function-select inputs, allowing up to 32 different functions to be performed.

74x181 Figure 6-90 is a logic symbol for the *74x181* 4-bit ALU. The operation performed by the '181 is selected by the M and S3–S0 inputs, as detailed in

Table 6-70 Functions performed by the 74x181 4-bit ALU.

Inputs				Function	
S3	S2	S1	S0	$M = 0$ (arithmetic)	$M = 1$ (logic)
0	0	0	0	F = A minus 1 plus CIN	$F = A'$
0	0	0	1	F = A · B minus 1 plus CIN	$F = A' + B'$
0	0	1	0	F = A · B′ minus 1 plus CIN	$F = A' + B$
0	0	1	1	F = 1111 plus CIN	$F = 1111$
0	1	0	0	F = A plus (A + B′) plus CIN	$F = A' \cdot B'$
0	1	0	1	F = A · B plus (A + B′) plus CIN	$F = B'$
0	1	1	0	F = A minus B minus 1 plus CIN	$F = A \oplus B'$
0	1	1	1	F = A + B′ plus CIN	$F = A + B'$
1	0	0	0	F = A plus (A + B) plus CIN	$F = A' \cdot B$
1	0	0	1	F = A plus B plus CIN	$F = A \oplus B$
1	0	1	0	F = A · B′ plus (A + B) plus CIN	$F = B$
1	0	1	1	F = A + B plus CIN	$F = A + B$
1	1	0	0	F = A plus A plus CIN	$F = 0000$
1	1	0	1	F = A · B plus A plus CIN	$F = A \cdot B'$
1	1	1	0	F = A · B′ plus A plus CIN	$F = A \cdot B$
1	1	1	1	F = A plus CIN	$F = A$

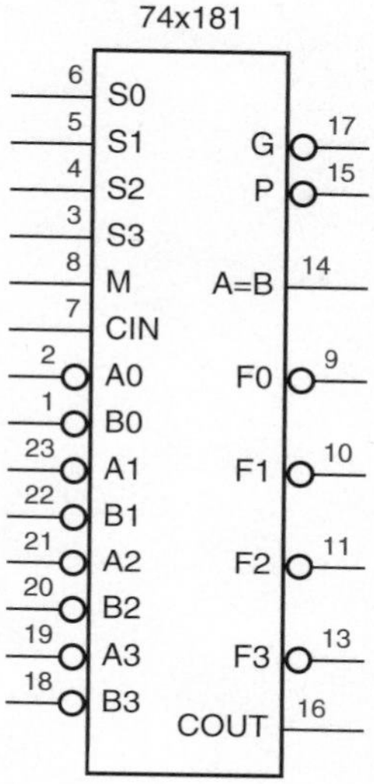

Figure 6-90
Logic symbol for the
74x181 4-bit ALU.

Table 6-70. Note that the identifiers A, B, and F in the table refer to the 4-bit words A3–A0, B3–B0, and F3–F0; and the symbols · and + refer to bit-by-bit logical AND and OR operations.

The 181's M input selects between arithmetic and logical operations. When $M = 1$, logical operations are selected, and each output Fi is a function only of the corresponding data inputs, Ai and Bi. No carries propagate between stages, and the CIN input is ignored. The S3–S0 inputs select a particular logical operation; any of the 16 different combinational logic functions on two variables may be selected.

When $M = 0$, arithmetic operations are selected, carries propagate between the stages, and CIN is used as a carry input to the least significant stage. For operations larger than four bits, multiple '181 ALUs may be cascaded like the group-ripple adder in Figure 6-89, with the carry-out (COUT) of each ALU connected to the carry-in (CIN) of the next most significant stage. The same function-select signals (M, S3–S0) should be applied to all the '181s in the cascade. For faster carry propagation, the group-carry-lookahead outputs G_L and P_L may be used as described in the next subsection.

Figure 6-91
Logic symbols for 4-bit
ALUs: (a) 74x381;
(b) 74x382.

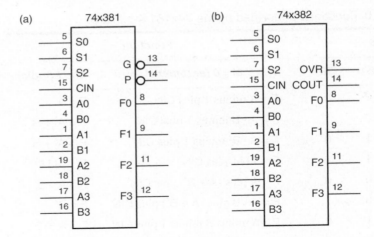

To perform two's-complement addition, we use S3–S0 to select the operation "A plus B plus CIN." The CIN input of the least significant ALU is normally set to 0 during addition operations. To perform two's-complement subtraction, we use S3–S0 to select the operation A minus B minus 1 plus CIN. In this case, the CIN input of the least significant ALU is normally set to 1, since CIN acts as the complement of the borrow during subtraction.

The '181 provides other arithmetic operations, such as "A minus 1 plus CIN," that are useful in some applications (e.g., decrement by 1). It also provides a bunch of weird arithmetic operations, such as "A · B' plus (A + B) plus CIN," that are almost never used in practice, but that "fall out" of the circuit for free.

Notice that the operand inputs A3_L–A0_L and B3_L–B0_L and the function outputs F3_L–F0_L of the '181 are active low. The '181 can also be used with active-high operand inputs and function outputs. In this case, a different version of the function table must be constructed. When M = 1, logical operations are still performed, but for a given input combination on S3–S0, the function obtained is precisely the dual of the one listed in Table 6-70. When M = 0, arithmetic operations are performed, but the function table is once again different. Refer to a '181 data sheet for more details.

74x381
74x382

Two other MSI ALUs, the *74x381* and *74x382* shown in Figure 6-91, encode their select inputs more compactly, and provide only eight different but useful functions, as detailed in Table 6-71. The only difference between the '381 and '382 is that one provides group-carry-lookahead outputs (which we explain next), while the other provides ripple carry and overflow outputs.

*6.10.7 Group-Carry Lookahead

group-carry lookahead

The '181 and '381 provide *group-carry-lookahead* outputs that allow multiple ALUs to be cascaded without rippling carries between 4-bit groups. Like the 74x283, the ALUs use carry lookahead to produce carries internally. However, they also provide G_L and P_L outputs that are carry-lookahead signals for the

Inputs			
S2	S1	S0	*Function*
0	0	0	F = 0000
0	0	1	F = B minus A minus 1 plus CIN
0	1	0	F = A minus B minus 1 plus CIN
0	1	1	F = A plus B plus CIN
1	0	0	F = A $\oplus$ B
1	0	1	F = A + B
1	1	0	F = A $\cdot$ B
1	1	1	F = 1111

Table 6-71
Functions performed by the 74x381 and 74x382 4-bit ALUs.

entire 4-bit group. The G_L output is asserted if the ALU generates a carry—that is, if it will produce a carry-out (COUT = 1) whether or not there is a carry-in (i.e., even if CIN = 0):

$$G\_L = (g_3 + p_3 \cdot g_2 + p_3 \cdot p_2 \cdot g_1 + p_3 \cdot p_2 \cdot p_1 \cdot g_0)'$$

That is, the ALU generates a carry if the most significant stage generates a carry, or if a carry generated by a lower-order stage is guaranteed to be propagated to and through the most significant stage. The P_L output is asserted if the ALU propagates a carry—that is, if it will produce a carry-out if there is a carry-in:

$$P\_L = (p_3 \cdot p_2 \cdot p_1 \cdot p_0)'$$

When ALUs are cascaded, the group-carry-lookahead outputs may be combined in just two levels of logic to produce the carry input to each ALU. A *lookahead carry circuit*, the *74x182* shown in Figure 6-92, performs this operation. The '182 inputs are C0, the carry input to the least significant ALU ("ALU 0"); and G0–G3 and P0–P3, the generate and propagate outputs of ALUs 0–3. Using these inputs, the '182 produces carry inputs C1–C3 for ALUs 1–3. Figure 6-93 shows the connections for a 16-bit ALU using four '381s and a '182.

lookahead carry circuit
74x182

The '182's carry equations are obtained by "adding out" the basic carry-lookahead equation of Section 6.10.4:

$$c_{i+1} = g_i + p_i \cdot c_i$$
$$= (g_i + p_i) \cdot (g_i + c_i)$$

Expanding for the first three values of *i*, we obtain the following equations:

C1 = (G0+P0) $\cdot$ (G0+C0)
C2 = (G1+P1) $\cdot$ (G1+G0+P0) $\cdot$ (G1+G0+C0)
C3 = (G2+P2) $\cdot$ (G2+G1+P1) $\cdot$ (G2+G1+G0+P0) $\cdot$ (G2+G1+G0+C0)

The '182 realizes each of these equations with just one level of delay—an INVERT-OR-AND gate.

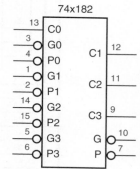

Figure 6-92
Logic symbol for the 74x182 lookahead carry circuit.

Figure 6-93
A 16-bit ALU using
group-carry lookahead.

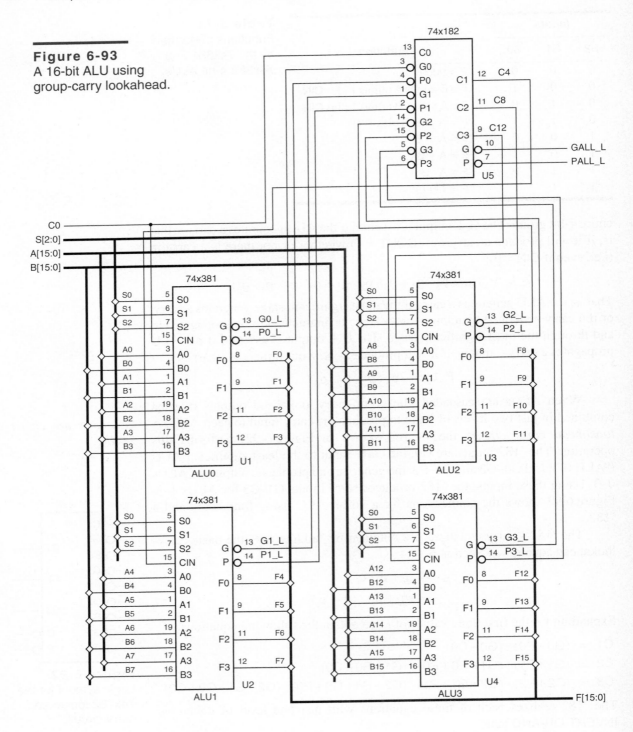

When more than four ALUs are cascaded, they may be partitioned into "supergroups," each with its own '182. For example, a 64-bit adder would have four supergroups, each containing four ALUs and a '182. The G_L and P_L outputs of each '182 can be combined in a next-level '182, since they indicate whether the supergroup generates or propagates carries:

$$G\_L = ((G3+P3) \cdot (G3+G2+P2) \cdot (G3+G2+G1+P1) \cdot (G3+G2+G1+G0))'$$
$$P\_L = (P0 \cdot P1 \cdot P2 \cdot P3)'$$

*6.10.8 Adders in ABEL and PLDs

ABEL supports addition (+) and subtraction (−) operators which can be applied to sets. Sets are interpreted as unsigned integers; for example, a set with n bits represents an integer in the range of 0 to 2^n-1. Subtraction is performed by negating the subtrahend and adding. Negation is performed in two's complement; that is, the operand is complemented bit-by-bit and then 1 is added.

Table 6-72 shows an example of addition in ABEL. The set definition for SUM was made one bit wider than the addends to accommodate the carry out of the MSB; otherwise this carry would be discarded. The set definitions for the addends were extended on the left with a 0 bit to match the size of SUM.

Even though the adder program is extremely small, it takes a long time to compile and it generates a huge number of terms in the minimal two-level sum of products. While SUM0 has only two product terms, subsequent terms SUMi have $5 \cdot 2^i - 4$ terms, or 636 terms for SUM7! And the carry-out (SUM8) has $2^8 - 1 = 255$ product terms. Obviously, adders with more than a few bits cannot be practically realized using two levels of logic.

Table 6-72
ABEL program for an 8-bit adder.

```
module add
title 'Adder Exercise'

" Input and output pins
A7..A0, B7..B0          pin;
SUM8..SUM0              pin istype 'com';

" Set definitions
A = [0, A7..A0];
B = [0, B7..B0];
SUM = [SUM8..SUM0];

equations
SUM = A + B;

end add
```

@CARRY directive

Recognizing that larger adders and comparators are still needed in PLDs from time to time, ABEL provides an *@CARRY directive* which tells the compiler to synthesize a group-ripple adder with *n* bits per group. For example, if the statement "@CARRY 1;" were included in Table 6-72, the compiler would create eight new signals for the carries out of bit positions 0 through 7. The equations for SUM1 through SUM8 would use these internal carries, essentially creating an 8-stage ripple adder with a worst-case delay of eight passes through the PLD.

If the statement "@CARRY 2;" were used, the compiler would compute carries two bits at a time, creating four new signals for carries out of bit positions 1, 3, 5, and 7. In this case, the maximum number of product terms needed for any output is still reasonable, only 7, and the worst-case delay path has just four passes through the PLD. With three bits per group (@CARRY 3;), the maximum number of product terms balloons to 28, which is impractical for most PLDs.

A special case that is often used in ABEL and PLDs is adding or subtracting a constant 1. This operation is used in the definition of counters, where the next state of the counter is just the current state plus 1 for an "up" counter or minus 1 for a "down" counter. The equation for bit *i* of an "up" counter can be stated very simply in words: "Complement bit *i* if counting is enabled and all of the bits lower than *i* are 1." This requires just $i + 2$ product terms for any value of *i*, and can be further reduced to just one product term plus an XOR gate in PLDs and CPLDs that have a product-term controlled (rather than fuse controlled) XOR gate in the output logic.

*6.10.9 Adders in VHDL

addition operator, +
subtraction operator, –

Although VHDL has addition (+) and subtraction (–) operators built in, they work only with the integer, real, and physical types. They specifically do *not* work with BIT_VECTOR types or the IEEE standard type STD_LOGIC_VECTOR. Instead, standard packages define these operators.

As we explained in Section 6.9.7, the std_logic_arith package defines two new array types, SIGNED and UNSIGNED, and a set of comparison functions for operands of type INTEGER, SIGNED, or UNSIGNED. The package also defines addition and subtraction operations for the same kinds of operands as well as STD_LOGIC and STD_ULOGIC for 1-bit operands.

The large number of overlaid addition and subtraction functions may make it less than obvious what type an addition or subtraction result will have. Normally, if any of the operands is type SIGNED, the result is SIGNED, else the

```vhdl
library IEEE;
use IEEE.std_logic_1164.all;
use IEEE.std_logic_arith.all;

entity vadd is
    port (
        A, B: in UNSIGNED (7 downto 0);
        C: in SIGNED (7 downto 0);
        D: in STD_LOGIC_VECTOR (7 downto 0);
        S: out UNSIGNED (8 downto 0);
        T: out SIGNED (8 downto 0);
        U: out SIGNED (7 downto 0);
        V: out STD_LOGIC_VECTOR (8 downto 0)
    );
end vadd;

architecture vadd_arch of vadd is
  begin
    S <= ('0' & A) + ('0' & B);
    T <= A + C;
    U <= C + SIGNED(D);
    V <= C - UNSIGNED(D);
end vadd_arch;
```

Table 6-73
VHDL program for adding and subtracting 8-bit integers of various types.

result is UNSIGNED. However, if the result is assigned to a signal or variable of type STD_LOGIC_VECTOR, then the SIGNED or UNSIGNED result is converted to that type. The length of any result is normally the length of the longest operand. However, when an UNSIGNED operand is combined with a SIGNED or INTEGER operand, its length is increased by 1 to accommodate a sign bit of 0, and then the result's length is determined.

Incorporating these considerations, the VHDL program in Table 6-73 shows 8-bit additions for various operand and result types. The first result, S, is declared to be 9 bits long assuming the designer is interested in the carry from the 8-bit addition of UNSIGNED operands A and B. The concatenation operator & is used to extend A and B so that the addition function will return the carry bit in the MSB of the result.

The next result, T, is also 9 bits long, since the addition function extends the UNSIGNED operand A when combining it with the SIGNED operand C. In the third addition, an 8-bit STD_LOGIC_VECTOR D is type-converted to SIGNED and combined with C to obtain an 8-bit SIGNED result U. In the last statement, D is converted to UNSIGNED, automatically extended by one bit, and subtracted from C to produce a 9-bit result V.

Since addition and subtraction are fairly expensive in terms of the number of gates required, many of the better VHDL synthesis tools will attempt to reuse adder blocks whenever possible. For example, Table 6-74 is a VHDL program

Table 6-74
VHDL program that
allows adder sharing.

```
library IEEE;
use IEEE.std_logic_1164.all;
use IEEE.std_logic_arith.all;

entity vaddshr is
    port (
        A, B, C, D: in SIGNED (7 downto 0);
        SEL: in STD_LOGIC;
        S: out SIGNED (7 downto 0)
    );
end vaddshr;

architecture vaddshr_arch of vaddshr is
begin
    S <= A + B when SEL = '1' else C + D;
end vaddshr_arch;
```

that includes two different additions. Figure 6-94(a) shows a circuit that might be synthesized if the compiler takes the VHDL code literally. However, many VHDL compilers are smart enough to use the approach shown in (b). Rather than selecting the output of one of two separate adders with a multiplexer, the compiler can synthesize just one adder with multiplexed inputs. This creates a smaller circuit realization, since an n-bit 2-input multiplexer requires a lot fewer gates than an n-bit adder.

*6.10.10 Adders in Verilog
Verilog has built-in addition (+) and subtraction (−) operators for bit vectors. The bit vectors are considered to be unsigned or two's-complement signed numbers. As we showed in Section 2.6, the actual addition or subtraction operation is exactly the same for either interpretation of the bit vectors. Since exactly the same logic circuit is synthesized for either interpretation, the Verilog compiler

Figure 6-94 Two ways to synthesize a selectable addition: (a) two adders and a selectable sum; (b) one adder with selectable inputs.

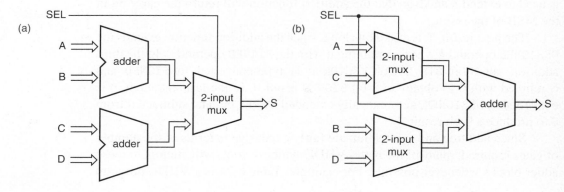

```
module Vradders(A, B, C, D, S, T, OVFL, COUT);
  input [7:0] A, B, C, D;
  output [7:0] S, T;
  output OVFL, COUT;

  // S and OVFL -- signed interpretation
  assign S = A + B;
  assign OVFL = (A[7]==B[7]) && (S[7]!=A[7]);
  // T and COUT -- unsigned interpretation
  assign {COUT, T} = C + D;
endmodule
```

Table 6-75
Verilog program with addition of both signed and unsigned numbers.

doesn't need to know how you're interpreting your bit vectors. Only the handling of carry, borrow, and overflow conditions differs by interpretation, and that's done separately from the addition or subtraction itself.

For example, Table 6-75 is a Verilog module showing both interpretations. In the first addition, 8-bit addends A and B and sum S are considered to be two's-complement numbers. In two's complement addition, any carry out of the high-order bit is discarded, so the sum S is declared to have the same bit width as the addends. Since the carry out of the high-order bit is not used in this module, the Verilog compiler will not synthesize any logic circuits for it. (It would have been S[8] if we had declared S as S[8:0], 9 bits wide.) However, we have declared an additional output bit OVFL to indicate any overflow condition, which by definition occurs if the signs of the addends are the same and the sign of the sum is different.

In the second addition, 8-bit addends C and D are considered to be unsigned numbers. The resulting sum may therefore take up to 9 bits to express, and we could have declared sum T as a 9-bit vector to receive the full sum. Instead, we left T as an 8-bit vector like the others, and declared a separate 1-bit output COUT to receive the high-order bit of the sum.

Addition and subtraction are fairly expensive in terms of the number of gates required, so most Verilog compilers will attempt to reuse adder blocks whenever possible. For example, Table 6-76 is a Verilog module that includes two different additions. Figure 6-94(a) on page 490 shows a circuit that might be

```
module Vraddersh(SEL, A, B, C, D, S);
  input SEL;
  input [7:0] A, B, C, D;
  output [7:0] S;
  reg [7:0] S;

  always @ (SEL, A, B, C, D)
    if (SEL) S = A + B;
    else S = C + D;
endmodule
```

Table 6-76
Verilog module that allows adder sharing.

Table 6-77
Alternate version of
Table 6-76, using a
continuous-assign-
ment statement.

```
module Vraddersc(SEL, A, B, C, D, S);
  input SEL;
  input [7:0] A, B, C, D;
  output [7:0] S;

  assign S = (SEL) ? A + B : C + D;
endmodule
```

synthesized if the compiler takes the Verilog code literally. However, many compilers are smart enough to use the approach shown in (b). Rather than synthesizing two adders and selecting one's output with a multiplexer, the compiler can synthesize just one adder and select its inputs using multiplexers. This creates a smaller circuit realization, since an n-bit 2-input multiplexer is smaller than an n-bit adder.

Just for Verilog practice, Table 6-77 is another module that specifies exactly the same functionality as Table 6-76, this time using a continuous-assignment statement and the conditional operator; a typical compiler should synthesize the same circuit for either module.

For even more practice, a more complicated Verilog module using addition and subtraction is shown in Table 6-78. This module has the same functionality as a 74x381 ALU, except that it has 8-bit inputs and outputs. Its first for loop is used to create the internal carry-generate G[i] and -propagate P[i] signals for each adder stage (i ranges from 0 to 7).

The second for loop combines these signals to create the group carry-generate G_L and -propagate P_L signals for the 8-bit group. These signals are specified iteratively (that is, by a for loop) in a natural way. At iteration i, the variable GG indicates whether ALU will generate a carry as of adder stage i—that is, if the stage generates a carry (G[i]=1) or if it will propagate a previously generated carry (P[i]=1 and GG was 1 in the for-loop's previous iteration). Note that since GG is a variable (declared by reg, not wire), the assignment to it in each iteration takes effect immediately and is propagated to the next iteration. The output signal G_L is just the complement of GG's value after the last iteration.

In a similar way, at iteration i, the variable GP indicates whether ALU will propagate a carry as of adder stage i, that is, if all the P[i] signals through that stage are 1. The final value of GP is just the AND of the P[i] signals for all values of i, and the output signal P_L is the complement of this value.

A case statement is used to select one of eight functions for the output function F. Three of these functions involve addition or subtraction, and the code as written relies on Verilog compiler to synthesize the adder and subtractor blocks.

Alternatively, we could give the compiler some help by writing code to define specify carry bits C[i] for each stage i, based on the already-available GG and GP variables and the CIN signal. That is, the carry C[i] into stage i is 1 if GG

```
module Vr74x381(S, A, B, CIN, F, G_L, P_L);
  input [2:0] S;
  input [7:0] A, B;
  input CIN;
  output [7:0] F;
  output G_L, P_L;
  reg [7:0] F;
  reg G_L, P_L, GG, GP;
  reg [7:0] G, P;
  integer i;

  always @ (S or A or B or CIN or G or P or GG or GP) begin
    for (i = 0; i <= 7; i = i + 1) begin
      G[i] = A[i] & B[i];
      P[i] = A[i] | B[i];
    end
    GG = G[0]; GP = P[0];
    for (i = 1; i <= 7; i = i + 1) begin
      GG = G[i] | (GG & P[i]);
      GP = P[i] & GP;
    end
    G_L = ~GG;  P_L = ~GP;
    case (S)
      3'd0: F = 8'b0;
      3'd1: F = B - A - 1 + CIN;
      3'd2: F = A - B - 1 + CIN;
      3'd3: F = A + B + CIN;
      3'd4: F = A ^ B;
      3'd5: F = A | B;
      3'd6: F = A & B;
      3'd7: F = 8'b11111111;
      default: F = 8'b0;
    endcase
  end
endmodule
```

Table 6-78
Verilog module for an 8-bit 74x381-like ALU.

in the previous stage was 1, or if GP was 1 and CIN is 1. The output function F is then easily specified for the addition and subtraction cases, for example, F = A ^ B ^ C for case 3 (addition), and F = ~A ^ B ^ C for case 1 (subtraction). See Exercise 6.104.

How well a compiler uses our help depends on the target technology and the compiler. For example, when targeted to an XC9500 series CPLD using Xilinx ISE tools, this version was twice as fast (33.5 vs. 67 ns) and used fewer than half as many product terms (280 vs. 635). Still, the synthesized circuit is unlikely to be as small or as fast as the original 74x381 MSI part (about 30 ns and 170 gates for two 4-bit components in "ancient" 74S Schottky TTL). Similarly, a custom-designed ALU in an ASIC "standard-cell" library will usually be much smaller and faster than a synthesized ALU in any CPLD or FPGA.

*6.11 Combinational Multipliers

*6.11.1 Combinational Multiplier Structures

In Section 2.8 we outlined an algorithm that uses n shifts and adds to multiply n-bit binary numbers. Although the shift-and-add algorithm emulates the way that we do paper-and-pencil multiplication of decimal numbers, there is nothing inherently "sequential" or "time dependent" about multiplication. That is, given two n-bit input words X and Y, it is possible to write a truth table that expresses the $2n$-bit product $P = X \cdot Y$ as a *combinational* function of X and Y. A *combinational multiplier* is a logic circuit with such a truth table.

combinational multiplier

Many approaches to combinational multiplication are based on the paper-and-pencil shift-and-add algorithm. Figure 6-95 illustrates the basic idea for an 8×8 multiplier for two unsigned integers, multiplicand $X = x_7 x_6 x_5 x_4 x_3 x_2 x_1 x_0$ and multiplier $Y = y_7 y_6 y_5 y_4 y_3 y_2 y_1 y_0$. We call each row a *product component*, a shifted multiplicand that is multiplied by 0 or 1 depending on the corresponding multiplier bit. Each small box represents one product-component bit $y_i x_j$, the logical AND of multiplier bit y_i and multiplicand bit x_j. The product $P = p_{15} p_{14} \cdots p_2 p_1 p_0$ has 16 bits and is obtained by adding together all the product components.

product component

Figure 6-96 shows one way to add up the product components. Here, the product-component bits have been spread out to make space, and each "+" box is a full adder, equivalent to Figure 6-83(c) on page 475. The carries in each row of full adders are connected to make an 8-bit ripple adder. Thus, the first ripple adder combines the first two product components to produce the first partial product, as defined in Section 2.8. Subsequent adders combine each partial product with the next product component.

It is interesting to study the propagation delay of the circuit in Figure 6-96. In the worst case, the inputs to the least significant adder ($y_0 x_1$ and $y_1 x_0$) can affect the MSB of the product (p_{15}). If we assume for simplicity that the delays from any input to any output of a full adder are equal, say t_{pd}, then the worst-case path goes through 20 adders and its delay is $20 t_{pd}$. If the delays are different, then the answer depends on the relative delays; see Exercise 6.105.

Figure 6-95
Partial products in an 8×8 multiplier.

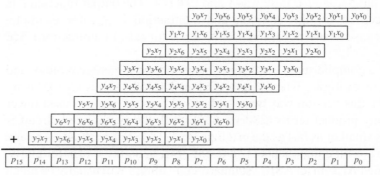

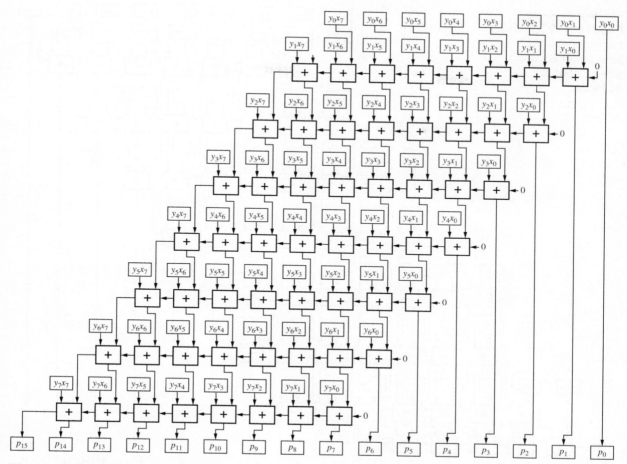

Figure 6-96 Interconnections for an 8×8 combinational multiplier.

Sequential multipliers use a single adder and a register to accumulate the partial products. The partial-product register is initialized to the first product component, and for an $n{\times}n$-bit multiplication, $n-1$ steps are taken and the adder is used $n-1$ times, once for each of the remaining $n-1$ product components to be added to the partial-product register.

sequential multiplier

Some sequential multipliers use a trick called *carry-save addition* to speed up multiplication. The idea is to break the carry chain of the ripple adder to shorten the delay of each addition. This is done by applying the carry output from bit i during step j to the carry input for bit $i+1$ during the *next* step, $j+1$. After the last product component is added, one more step is needed in which the carries are hooked up in the usual way and allowed to ripple from the least to the most significant bit.

carry-save addition

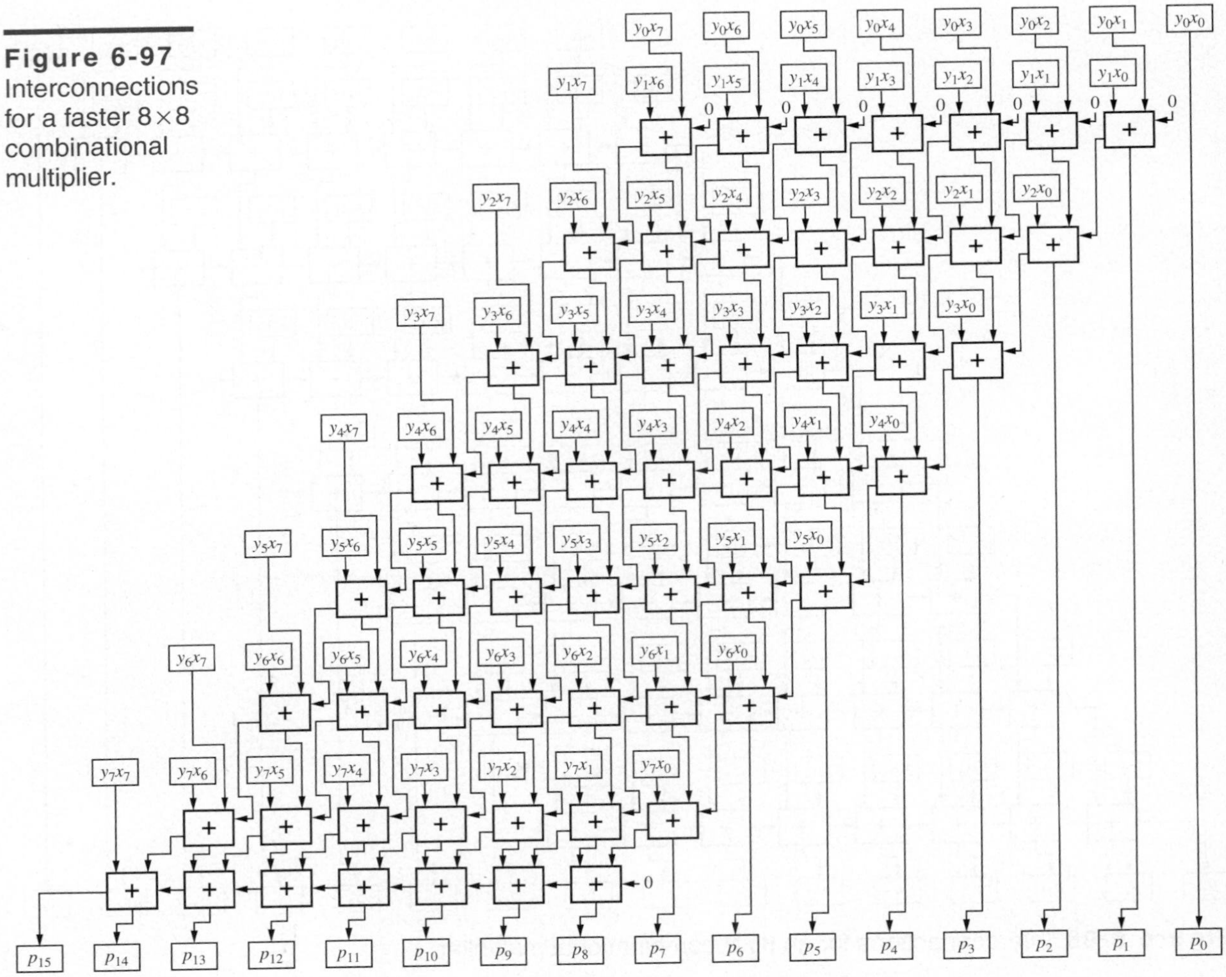

Figure 6-97
Interconnections
for a faster 8×8
combinational
multiplier.

The combinational equivalent of an 8×8 multiplier using carry-save addition is shown in Figure 6-97. Notice that the carry out of each full adder in the first seven rows is connected to an input of an adder *below* it. Carries in the eighth row of full adders are connected to create a conventional ripple adder. Although this adder uses exactly the same amount of logic as the previous one (64 2-input AND gates and 56 full adders), its propagation delay is substantially shorter. Its worst-case delay path goes through only 14 full adders. The delay can be further improved by using a carry-lookahead adder for the last row.

The regular structure of combinational multipliers makes them ideal for VLSI and ASIC realization. The importance of fast multiplication in microprocessors, digital video, and many other applications has led to much study and development of even better structures and circuits for combinational multipliers; see the References.

*6.11.2 Multiplication in ABEL and PLDs

ABEL provides a multiplication operator ∗, but it can be used only with individual signals, numbers, or special constants, not with sets. Thus, ABEL cannot synthesize a multiplier circuit from a single equation like "P = X∗Y."

Still, you can use ABEL to specify a combinational multiplier if you break it down into smaller pieces. For example, Table 6-79 shows the design of a 4×4 unsigned multiplier following the same general structure as Figure 6-95 on page page 494. Expressions are used to define the four product components, PC1, PC2, PC3, and PC4, which are then added in the equations section of the program. This does not generate an array of full adders as in Figure 6-96 or 6-97. Rather, the ABEL compiler will dutifully crunch the addition equation to produce a minimal sum for each of the eight product output bits. Surprisingly, the worst-case output, P4, has only 36 product terms, a little high but certainly realizable in two passes through a PLD.

```
module mul4x4
title '4x4 Combinational Multiplier'

X3..X0, Y3..Y0 pin;    " multiplicand, multiplier
P7..P0          pin istype 'com';    " product

P = [P7..P0];
PC1 = Y0 & [0, 0, 0, 0,X3,X2,X1,X0];
PC2 = Y1 & [0, 0, 0,X3,X2,X1,X0, 0];
PC3 = Y2 & [0, 0,X3,X2,X1,X0, 0, 0];
PC4 = Y3 & [0,X3,X2,X1,X0, 0, 0, 0];

equations
P = PC1 + PC2 + PC3 + PC4;

end mul4x4
```

Table 6-79
ABEL program for a 4×4 combinational multiplier.

*6.11.3 Multiplication in VHDL

VHDL is rich enough to express multiplication in a number of different ways; we'll save the best for last.

Table 6-80 on the next page is a behavioral VHDL program that mimics the multiplier structure of Figure 6-97. In order to represent the internal signals in the figure, the program defines a new data type, array8x8, which is a two-dimensional array of STD_LOGIC (recall that STD_LOGIC_VECTOR is a one-dimensional array of STD_LOGIC). Variable PC is declared as such an array to hold the product-component bits, and variables PCS and PCC are similar arrays to hold the sum and carry outputs of the main array of full adders. One-dimensional arrays RAS and RAC hold the sum and carry outputs of the ripple adder. Figure 6-98 shows the variable naming and numbering scheme. Integer variables i and j are used as loop indices for rows and columns, respectively.

Table 6-80
Behavioral VHDL
program for an 8×8
combinational
multiplier.

```
library IEEE;
use IEEE.std_logic_1164.all;

entity vmul8x8p is
    port ( X: in STD_LOGIC_VECTOR (7 downto 0);
           Y: in STD_LOGIC_VECTOR (7 downto 0);
           P: out STD_LOGIC_VECTOR (15 downto 0) );
end vmul8x8p;

architecture vmul8x8p_arch of vmul8x8p is
function MAJ (I1, I2, I3: STD_LOGIC) return STD_LOGIC is
  begin
    return ((I1 and I2) or (I1 and I3) or (I2 and I3));
  end MAJ;
begin
process (X, Y)
type array8x8 is array (0 to 7) of STD_LOGIC_VECTOR (7 downto 0);
variable PC: array8x8;      -- product component bits
variable PCS: array8x8;     -- full-adder sum bits
variable PCC: array8x8;     -- full-adder carry output bits
variable RAS, RAC: STD_LOGIC_VECTOR (7 downto 0); -- ripple adder sum
                                              --   and carry bits
  begin
    for i in 0 to 7 loop for j in 0 to 7 loop
        PC(i)(j) := Y(i) and X(j); -- compute product component bits
    end loop;  end loop;
    for j in 0 to 7 loop
      PCS(0)(j) := PC(0)(j); -- initialize first-row "virtual"
      PCC(0)(j) := '0';      --    adders (not shown in figure)
    end loop;
    for i in 1 to 7 loop        -- do all full adders except last row
      for j in 0 to 6 loop
        PCS(i)(j) := PC(i)(j) xor PCS(i-1)(j+1) xor PCC(i-1)(j);
        PCC(i)(j) := MAJ(PC(i)(j), PCS(i-1)(j+1), PCC(i-1)(j));
        PCS(i)(7) := PC(i)(7); -- leftmost "virtual" adder sum output
      end loop;
    end loop;
    RAC(0) := '0';
    for i in 0 to 6 loop  -- final ripple adder
      RAS(i)   := PCS(7)(i+1) xor PCC(7)(i) xor RAC(i);
      RAC(i+1) := MAJ(PCS(7)(i+1), PCC(7)(i), RAC(i));
    end loop;
    for i in 0 to 7 loop
      P(i) <= PCS(i)(0);   -- first 8 product bits from full-adder sums
    end loop;
    for i in 8 to 14 loop
      P(i) <= RAS(i-8);    -- next 7 bits from ripple-adder sums
    end loop;
    P(15) <= RAC(7);         -- last bit from ripple-adder carry
  end process;
end vmul8x8p_arch;
```

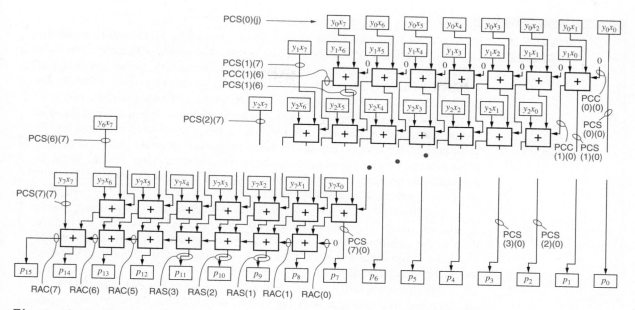

Figure 6-98 VHDL variable names for the 8×8 multiplier.

The program attempts to illustrate the logic gates that would be used in a faithful realization of Figure 6-97, even though a synthesizer could legitimately create quite a different structure from this behavioral program. If you want to control the structure, then you must use structural VHDL, as we'll show later.

In the program, the first, nested `for` statement performs 64 AND operations to obtain the product-component bits. The next `for` loop initializes boundary conditions at the top of the multiplier, using the notion of row-0 "virtual" full adders, not shown in the figure, whose sum outputs equal the first row of PC bits and whose carry outputs are 0. The third, nested `for` loop corresponds to the

---

ON THE THRESHOLD OF A DREAM

A 3-input "majority function," MAJ, is defined at the beginning of Table 6-80 and is subsequently used to compute carry outputs. An n-input *majority function* produces a 1 output if the majority of its inputs are 1, two out of three in the case of a 3-input majority function. (If n is even, $n/2 + 1$ inputs must be 1.)

Over thirty years ago, there was substantial academic interest in a more general class of n-input *threshold functions* which produce a 1 output if k or more of their inputs are 1. Besides providing full employment for logic theoreticians, threshold functions could realize many logic functions with a smaller number of elements than could a conventional AND/OR realization. For example, an adder's carry function requires three AND gates and one OR gate, but just one 3-input threshold gate.

(Un)fortunately, an economical technology never emerged for threshold gates, and they remain, for now, an academic curiosity.

main array of adders in Figure 6-97, all except the last row, which is handled by the fourth `for` loop. The last two `for` loops assign the appropriate adder outputs to the multiplier output signals.

The program in Table 6-80 can be modified to use structural VHDL as shown in Table 6-81. This approach gives the designer complete control over the circuit structure that is synthesized, as might be desired in an ASIC realization. The program assumes that the architectures for AND2, XOR3, and MAJ3 have been defined elsewhere, for example, in an ASIC library.

generate statement

This program makes good use of the *generate statement* to create the arrays of components used in the multiplier. The generate statement must have a label, and similar to a `for-loop` statement, it specifies an iteration scheme to control the repetition of the enclosed statements. Within `for-generate`, the enclosed statements can include any concurrent statements, `if-then-else` statements, and additional levels of looping constructs. Sometimes generate statements are combined with `if-then-else` to produce a kind of conditional compilation capability.

```
architecture vmul8x8s_arch of vmul8x8s is
component AND2
  port( I0, I1: in STD_LOGIC;
        O: out STD_LOGIC );
end component;
component XOR3
  port( I0, I1, I2: in STD_LOGIC;
        O: out STD_LOGIC );
end component;
component MAJ   -- Majority function, O = I0*I1 + I0*I2 + I1*I2
  port( I0, I1, I2: in STD_LOGIC;
        O: out STD_LOGIC );
end component;

type array8x8 is array (0 to 7) of STD_LOGIC_VECTOR (7 downto 0);
signal PC: array8x8;      -- product-component bits
signal PCS: array8x8;     -- full-adder sum bits
signal PCC: array8x8;     -- full-adder carry output bits
signal RAS, RAC: STD_LOGIC_VECTOR (7 downto 0); -- sum, carry
begin
  g1: for i in 0 to 7 generate    -- product-component bits
    g2: for j in 0 to 7 generate
        U1: AND2 port map (Y(i), X(j), PC(i)(j));
    end generate;
  end generate;
  g3: for j in 0 to 7 generate
    PCS(0)(j) <= PC(0)(j);  -- initialize first-row "virtual" adders
    PCC(0)(j) <= '0';
  end generate;
  g4: for i in 1 to 7 generate   -- do full adders except the last row
    g5: for j in 0 to 6 generate
      U2: XOR3 port map (PC(i)(j),PCS(i-1)(j+1),PCC(i-1)(j),PCS(i)(j));
      U3: MAJ  port map (PC(i)(j),PCS(i-1)(j+1),PCC(i-1)(j),PCC(i)(j));
      PCS(i)(7) <= PC(i)(7); -- leftmost "virtual" adder sum output
    end generate;
  end generate;
  RAC(0) <= '0';
  g6: for i in 0 to 6 generate   -- final ripple adder
    U7: XOR3 port map (PCS(7)(i+1), PCC(7)(i), RAC(i), RAS(i));
    U3: MAJ  port map (PCS(7)(i+1), PCC(7)(i), RAC(i), RAC(i+1));
  end generate;
  g7: for i in 0 to 7 generate
    P(i) <= PCS(i)(0); -- get first 8 product bits from full-adder sums
  end generate;
  g8: for i in 8 to 14 generate
    P(i) <= RAS(i-8);  -- get next 7 bits from ripple-adder sums
  end generate;
  P(15) <= RAC(7);     -- get last bit from ripple-adder carry
end vmul8x8s_arch;
```

Table 6-81
Structural VHDL architecture for an 8×8 combinational multiplier.

multiplication, ∗

Well, we said we'd save the best for last, and here it is. The Synopsys `std_logic_arith` package that we introduced in Section 6.9.7 defines *multiplication (∗)* functions for SIGNED and UNSIGNED types, and overlays them onto the "∗" operator. Thus, the program in Table 6-82 can multiply unsigned numbers with a simple one-line assignment statement. The multiplication function in the `std_logic_arith` library is defined behaviorally, using the shift-and-add algorithm. We could have showed this approach at the beginning of this subsection, but then you wouldn't have read the rest of it, would you?

Table 6-82
Truly behavioral VHDL program for an 8×8 combinational multiplier.

```
library IEEE;
use IEEE.std_logic_1164.all;
use IEEE.std_logic_arith.all;

entity vmul8x8i is
    port (
        X: in UNSIGNED (7 downto 0);
        Y: in UNSIGNED (7 downto 0);
        P: out UNSIGNED (15 downto 0)
    );
end vmul8x8i;

architecture vmul8x8i_arch of vmul8x8i is
begin
  P <= X * Y;
end vmul8x8i_arch;
```

Table 6-83
Verilog module for an 8×8 combinational multiplier.

```
module Vrmul8x8i(X, Y, P);
  input [7:0] X, Y;
  output [15:0] P;

  assign P = X * Y;
endmodule
```

SYNTHESIS OF BEHAVIORAL DESIGNS

You've probably heard that compilers for high-level programming languages like C usually generate better code than people do writing in assembly language, even with "hand-tweaking." Most digital designers hope that compilers for behavioral HDLs will also some day produce results superior to a typical hand-tweaked design, be it a schematic or written in structural VHDL or Verilog. Better compilers won't put the designers out of work, they will simply allow them to tackle bigger designs.

We're not quite there yet. However, the more advanced synthesis tools do include some nice optimizations for commonly used behavioral structures. For example, I have to admit that the Xilinx ISE FPGA synthesis tool that I used to test the VHDL programs in this subsection produced just as fast a multiplier from Table 6-82 as it did from any of the more detailed architectures!

*6.11.4 Multiplication in Verilog

Verilog has a built-in multiplication operator, "*", that operates on two bit-vectors that are interpreted as unsigned numbers. The width of the resulting product is the sum of the widths of the two input vectors. Thus, it is very easy to specify an unsigned multiplier in Verilog, as shown in Table 6-83 for two 8-bit inputs, producing a 16-bit product. However, multipliers should not be specified casually. When the small module in Table 6-83 is targeted to a Xilinx XC9500-series CPLD, it uses about 1230 product terms and is very slow (170 ns).

It is possible to specify the design of a multiplier in more detail, using behavioral Verilog code. In Figure 6-97 on page 496 we showed the structure of a reasonably fast 8×8 combinational multiplier, and Table 6-84 on the next page is a behavioral Verilog module corresponding to this structure.

The module begins by declaring its inputs, output, and internal variables. A few two-dimensional arrays are needed for some of the internal variables. Although Verilog-1995 does not have an explicit multidimensional array type, it is possible to declare one-dimensional array variables whose individual elements are bit vectors. These variables are not as convenient as two-dimensional arrays in other languages, because their individual bit elements cannot be accessed directly. To deal with individual bits, you must copy the array element to or from a separate bit vector, and manipulate the bits within that bit vector.

Variables PC, PCS, and PCC are such pseudo-two-dimensional arrays, each of which has eight elements indexed from 0 to 7, where each element is an 8-bit reg[7:0], a bit vector indexed from 7 down to 0. Variable PC holds the product-component bits, and variables PCS and PCC hold the sum and carry outputs of the main array of full adders. Bit vectors RAS and RAC hold the sum and carry outputs of the final ripple adder. Temporary bit-vector variables T, PCS7, and PCC7 are used to manipulate bits within the two-dimensional arrays as needed. The integer variable i is used as a loop index for rows. Figure 6-99 shows the relationship between the signals in the Figure 6-97 multiplier circuit and the corresponding variable names in the Verilog module.

Next, the functions MAJ and MAJ8 are defined to perform the majority function on 1- and 8-bit inputs, respectively. These functions are used to generate full-adder carry outputs later in the module.

In the main body of the module, the first for statement generates the 64 product-component bits as 8 rows of 8 bits each. Each row PC[i] equals either the multiplicand X or 0, depending on the value of the corresponding multiplier bit, Y[i]. The next two assignment statements initialize boundary conditions at the top of the multiplier, using the notion of row-0 "virtual" full adders, not shown in the figure, whose sum outputs equal the first row of PC bits and whose carry outputs are 0. The second for loop corresponds to the main array of 49 adders in Figure 6-97 (but not the final ripple adder).

Notice the use of the right-shift operator ">>" to line up the appropriate bits of PCS[i-1] from the row above into each row of adders. It is critical to the

Table 6-84
Behavioral Verilog
module for an 8×8
combinational
multiplier.

```verilog
module Vrmul8x8p(X, Y, P);
  input [7:0] X, Y;
  output [15:0] P;
  reg [7:0] PC [0:7];          // product-component bits
  reg [7:0] PCS [0:7];         // full-adder sum bits
  reg [7:0] PCC [0:7];         // full-adder carry output bits
  reg [6:0] RAS;               // ripple adder sum
  reg [7:0] RAC;               //    and carry bits
  reg [7:0] T, PCS7, PCC7;     // temporary variables
  reg [15:0] P;                // output variable for assignment
  integer i;

  function MAJ;
    input I1, I2, I3;
      MAJ = (I1 & I2) | (I1 & I3) | (I2 & I3);
  endfunction

  function [7:0] MAJ8;
    input [7:0] I1, I2, I3;
      MAJ8 = (I1 & I2) | (I1 & I3) | (I2 & I3);
  endfunction

  always @ (X or Y) begin
    for (i=0; i<=7; i=i+1)
      PC[i] = Y[i] ? X : 8'b0;   // Compute product-component bits
    PCS[0] = PC[0];             // Set up outputs of first-row "virtual"
    PCC[0] = 8'b0;              //    full adders (not shown in figure).
    for (i=1; i<=7; i=i+1) begin  // Do all "real" full adders.
      PCS[i] = PC[i] ^ (PCS[i-1]>>1) ^ PCC[i-1];
      PCC[i] = MAJ8(PC[i], PCS[i-1]>>1, PCC[i-1]);
    end
    PCS7 = PCS[7];      // Temp needed to access individual bits
    PCC7 = PCC[7];      //    of PCS[7]; ditto for PCC[7].
    RAC[0] = 1'b0;      // No carry into final ripple adder.
    for (i=0; i<=6; i=i+1) begin                 // Final ripple-adder
      RAS[i] = PCS7[i+1] ^ PCC7[i] ^ RAC[i];   //        sum
      RAC[i+1] = MAJ(PCS7[i+1], PCC7[i], RAC[i]); //   and carry bits
    end
    for (i=0; i<=7; i=i+1) begin
      T = PCS[i];
      P[i] = T[0];  // first 8 product bits from full-adder sums
    end
    for (i=8; i<=14; i=i+1)
      P[i] = RAS[i-8];   // next 7 bits from ripple-adder sums
    P[15] = RAC[7];         // last bit from ripple-adder carry-out
  end
endmodule
```

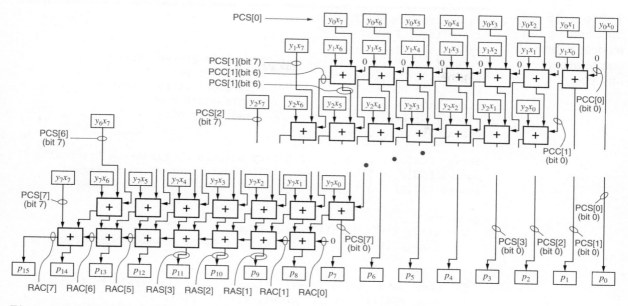

Figure 6-99 Verilog variable names for the 8×8 multiplier.

code's operation that this operator shifts a 0 into the leftmost bit (bit 7) of the shifted bit-vector. This ensures that bit 7 of PCS[i] will equal bit 7 of PC[i], and that bit 7 of PCC[i] will equal 0.

The third for loop corresponds to the final ripple adder in Figure 6-97. Note the use of temporary variables to get at the individual bits of PCS[7] and PCC[7]. The last two for loops and the final statement assign the appropriate adder outputs to the multiplier output signals.

When targeted to a Xilinx XC9500-series CPLD and compared with the multiplier synthesized by Xilinx ISE tools from Verilog's built-in multiplication operator (Table 6-83), the multiplier in Table 6-84 is about 10% smaller (1110 product terms) and 25% faster (125 ns).

Note that the Verilog module in Table 6-84 attempts to illustrate the logic gates that would be used in a faithful realization of Figure 6-97, even though a synthesizer could legitimately create quite a different structure from this behavioral code—and does, if it is targeting a CPLD or an FPGA rather than an ASIC. In an ASIC, the synthesizer *might* follow the structure of your behavioral code, but it doesn't have to. If you want to control the structure, then you must use structural Verilog, as we'll discuss next.

Structural Verilog code for 8×8 multiplication is shown in Table 6-85. This approach gives the designer complete control over the circuit structure that is synthesized, as might be desired in an ASIC realization. This module uses 1-and 8-bit versions of the parameterized majority-function module Maj that we

Table 6-85
Structural Verilog module for an 8×8 combinational multiplier.

```verilog
module Vrmul8x8s(X, Y, P);
  input [7:0] X, Y;
  output [15:0] P;
  wire [7:0] PC [0:7];          // product-component bits
  wire [7:0] PCS [0:7];         // full-adder sum bits
  wire [7:0] PCC [0:7];         // full-adder carry output bits
  wire [6:0] RAS;               // ripple adder sum
  wire [7:0] RAC;               //    and carry bits
  genvar i;

  assign PCS[0] = PC[0];    // Set up outputs of first-row "virtual"
  assign PCC[0] = 8'b0;     //    full adders (not shown in figure).
  assign RAC[0] = 1'b0;     // No carry into final ripple adder.

  generate
    for (i=0; i<=7; i=i+1) begin: PCgen
      assign PC[i] = {8{Y[i]}} & X; // Compute product-component bits
    end

    for (i=1; i<=7; i=i+1) begin: FAgen   // Do all "real" full adders.
      assign PCS[i] = PC[i] ^ PCS[i-1]>>1 ^ PCC[i-1];
      Maj #(8) M_FA ( PCC[i], PC[i], PCS[i-1]>>1, PCC[i-1] );
    end

    for (i=0; i<=6; i=i+1) begin: RAgen     // Final ripple-adder
      xor X_RA ( RAS[i], PCS[7][i+1], PCC[7][i], RAC[i] );    // sum
      Maj M_RA ( RAC[i+1], PCS[7][i+1], PCC[7][i], RAC[i] ); // carry
    end

    for (i=0; i<=7; i=i+1) begin: Pgen0_7
      assign P[i] = PCS[i][0]; // first 8 P bits from full-adder sums
    end

    for (i=8; i<=14; i=i+1) begin: Pgen8_14
      assign P[i] = RAS[i-8]; // next 7 bits from ripple-adder sums
    end
  endgenerate

  assign P[15] = RAC[7];      // last bit from ripple-adder carry out

endmodule
```

defined in Table 5-73 on page 309. This program only works in Verilog-2001, since it uses generate statements to create the arrays of components used in the multiplier (see the box on page 310).

A Verilog test bench that works for all three of the 8×8-multiplier modules is shown in Table 6-86. The module instantiatiation near the beginning of the code determines which version is tested. This test bench uses the "brute-force"

Table 6-86 Verilog test bench for 8×8 combinational multipliers.

```verilog
module Vrmul8x8_tb();
  reg [7:0] X, Y;
  wire [15:0] P;

  Vrmul8x8s UUT ( .X(X), .Y(Y), .P(P) ); // Instantiate the UUT

  task checkP;
    input i, j, P;
    integer i, j, prod;
    reg [15:0] P;
    begin
      prod = i*j;
      if (P !== prod) begin
        $display($time," Error: i=%d, j=%d, expected %d (%16b), got %d (%16b)",
                 i, j, prod, prod, P, P); $stop(1); end;
    end
  endtask

  initial begin : TB    // Start testing at time 0
    integer i, j;
    for ( i=0; i<=255; i=i+1 )
      for ( j=0; j<=255; j=j+1 ) begin
        X = i; Y = j;
        #10;                  // wait 10 ns, then check result
        checkP (i, j, P);
      end
    $stop(1);               // end test
  end
endmodule
```

testing method, checking every possible input combination against the expected result. There are several things to note about this test bench:

- The initial block is named so that local variables i and j can be declared.

- Two nested for loops are used to generate all 2^{16} input combinations.

- A task, checkP, is defined to compare the circuit's output with the expected product, computed by the simulator as the product of i and j.

- The comparison in checkP uses !== rather than !=, so that any x's in the circuit's output are detected. This turned out to be very important when I debugged Vrmul8x8s!

It's impressive how quickly a simulator can simulate the thousand-plus gates of the structural module (Vrmul8x8s) for all 65,536 input combinations—about five seconds on a 2.5-Ghz desktop computer. And, of course, all three multiplier modules pass the test with flying colors!

References

Digital designers who want to improve their writing should start by reading the classic *Elements of Style*, fourth edition, by William Strunk, Jr., E. B. White, and R. Angell (Longman, 2000). Probably the most inexpensive and concise yet very useful guide to technical writing is *The Elements of Technical Writing*, by Gary Blake and Robert W. Bly (Longman, 2000). For a more encyclopedic treatment, see *Handbook of Technical Writing*, fifth edition, by G. J. Alred, C. T. Brusaw, and W. E. Oliu (St. Martin's Press, 2003).

Real logic devices are described in data sheets and data books published by the manufacturers. Updated editions of data books used to be published every few years, but recently the trend has been to minimize or eliminate the hardcopy editions and instead to publish up-to-date information on the Web. Among the better sites for logic-family data sheets and application notes are `www.ti.com` (Texas Instruments), `www.philips.com`, and `www.fairchildsemi.com`.

For a given logic family such as 74AHCT, all manufacturers list generally equivalent specifications, so you can usually get by with just one set of data sheets per family. Some specifications, especially timing, may vary slightly between manufacturers, so when timing is tight it's best to check a couple of different sources and use the worst case. That's a *lot* easier than convincing your manufacturing department to buy a component only from a single supplier.

The first PAL devices were invented at Monolithic Memories, Inc. (MMI) in 1978 by John Birkner and H. T. Chua. The inventors earned U.S. patent number 4,124,899 for their invention, and MMI rewarded them by buying them a brand new Porsche and Mercedes, respectively! Seeing the value in this technology (PAL devices, not fast cars), Advanced Micro Devices (AMD) acquired MMI in the early 1980s and became a leading developer and supplier of new PLDs and CPLDs. In 1997, AMD spun off its PLD operations to a subsidiary, Vantis Corporation, which they sold in 1999 to former competitor Lattice Semiconductor.

Some of the best resources for learning about PLD-based design are provided by the PLD manufacturers. Xilinx Corporation publishes a comprehensive set of FPGA and CPLD data books, user guides, and application notes on their web site (`www.xilinx.com`). Similarly, GAL inventor Lattice Semiconductor has a comprehensive web site (`www.latticesemi.com`).

A much more detailed discussion of the internal operation of LSI and VLSI devices, including PLDs, ROMs, and RAMs, can be found in electronics texts such as *Digital Integrated Circuits* by J. M. Rabaey, A. Chandrakasan, and B. Nikolic (Prentice Hall, 2003, second edition).

Lots of textbooks cover digital design principles, but few cover practices. More useful for the active designer are articles written by other engineers in trade publications like *EDN*, and sometimes collected in anthologies like Clive Maxfield's *Designus Maximus Unleashed!* (Newnes, 1998).

Drill Problems

6.1 Give three examples of combinational logic circuits that require *billions and billions* of rows to describe in a truth table. For each circuit, describe its inputs and output(s) and indicate exactly how many rows the truth table contains; you need not write out the truth table. Do not use circuits found in this chapter.

6.2 Draw the DeMorgan equivalent symbol for a 74x30 8-input NAND gate.

6.3 Draw the DeMorgan equivalent symbol for a 74x27 3-input NOR gate.

6.4 What's wrong with the signal name "READY' "?

6.5 You may find it annoying to have to keep track of the active levels of all the signals in a logic circuit. Why not use only noninverting gates, so all signals are active high?

6.6 In bubble-to-bubble logic design, why would you connect a bubble output to a non-bubble input?

6.7 True or false: either all inputs to a logic gate must have a bubble, or none may have a bubble. Justify your answer.

6.8 A digital communication system is being designed with twelve identical network ports. Which type of schematic structure is probably most appropriate for the design?

6.9 Determine the exact maximum propagation delay from IN to OUT of the circuit in Figure X6.9 for both LOW-to-HIGH and HIGH-to-LOW transitions, using the timing information given in Table 6-2. Repeat, using a single worst-case delay number for each gate, and compare and comment on your results.

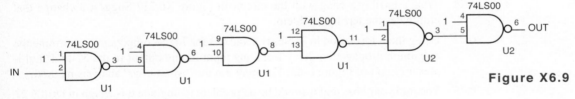

Figure X6.9

6.10 Repeat Drill 6.9, substituting 74AHCT00s for the 74LS00s.

6.11 Repeat Drill 6.9, substituting 74LS21s (with three inputs at constant 1) for the 74LS00s.

6.12 Repeat Drill 6.9, substituting 74AHCT02s for the 74LS00s in U1, using constant 0 instead of constant 1 inputs to U1, and using typical rather than maximum timing for both U1 and U2.

6.13 Estimate the minimum propagation delay from IN to OUT for the circuit shown in Figure X6.13. Justify your answer.

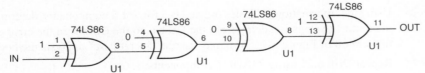

Figure X6.13

6.14   Determine the exact maximum propagation delay from IN to OUT of the circuit in Figure X6.13 for both LOW-to-HIGH and HIGH-to-LOW transitions, using the timing information given in Table 6-2. Repeat, using a single worst-case delay number for each gate, and compare and comment on your results.

6.15   Repeat Drill 6.13, substituting 74HCT86s for the 74LS86s.

6.16   Which CMOS circuit would you expect to be faster, a decoder with active-high outputs or one with active-low outputs?

6.17   Using the information in Table 6-3 for 74LS components, determine the maximum propagation delay from any input to any output in the 5-to-32 decoder circuit of Figure 6-37. Use "worst-case" numbers for propagation delays, independent of transition direction.

6.18   Repeat Drill 6.17, using 74AHCT timing, and performing a detailed analysis for each transition direction.

6.19   In the style of Table 6-6, write the truth table for the logic function performed *inside* the 74x138 symbol outline.

6.20   Show how to build each of the following single- or multiple-output logic functions using one or more 74x138 or 74x139 binary decoders and NAND gates. (*Hint:* Each realization should be equivalent to a sum of minterms.)

   (a) $F = \Sigma_{X,Y,Z}(2,4,7)$ (b) $F = \prod_{A,B,C}(3,4,5,6,7)$

   (c) $F = \Sigma_{A,B,C,D}(0,2,10,12)$ (d) $F = \Sigma_{W,X,Y,Z}(2,3,4,5,8,10,12,14)$

   (e) $F = \Sigma_{W,X,Y}(0,2,4,5)$ (f) $F = \Sigma_{A,B,C}(2,6)$
        $G = \Sigma_{W,X,Y}(1,2,3,6)$ $G = \Sigma_{C,D,E}(0,2,3)$

6.21   What's terribly wrong with the circuit in Figure X6.21? Suggest a change that eliminates the terrible problem.

6.22   Using the information in Tables 6-2 and 6-3 for 74LS components, determine the maximum propagation delay from any input to any output in the 32-to-1 multiplexer circuit of Figure 6-62. You may use the "worst-case" analysis method.

6.23   You told your boss that it would be no problem to upgrade the design in Drill 6.22 to 74AHCT components. But then you discover two problems: 1) there is no 74AHCT20, and 2) there is no room on the board to add another part! Luckily for you, the other half of the '20 is unused, so you can replace the entire part with something else. However, your purchasing department emphatically states that only the parts listed in Table 6-2 are available. Find the fastest solution that uses only the gates in a single package. Then repeat Drill 6.22 using your new design.

6.24   A certain parity circuit in the style of Figure 6-70(a) uses an odd number of XNOR gates. Does it generate odd parity, even parity, or neither? If neither, what function does it generate?

6.25   Using the information in Tables 6-2 and 6-3 for 74LS components, determine the maximum propagation delay from the DU bus to the DC bus in the error-correction circuit of Figure 6-73. You may use the "worst-case" analysis method.

6.26   Repeat Drill 6.25 using 74AHCT components.

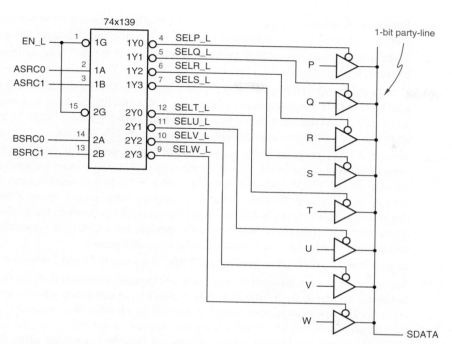

Figure X6.21

6.27   Starting with the equations given in Section 6.9.4, write a complete logic expression for the AEQBOUT output of the 74x85.

6.28   Starting with the logic diagram for the 74x682, write a logic expression for the PEQQ_L output in terms of the inputs.

6.29   Write an algebraic expression for s_3, the forth sum bit of a binary adder, as a function of inputs x_0, x_1, x_2, x_3, y_0, y_1, y_2, and y_3. Assume that $c_0 = 0$, and do not attempt to "multiply out" or minimize the expression.

6.30   Using the information in Table 6-3 for 74LS components, determine the maximum propagation delay from any input to any output of the 16-bit group ripple adder of Figure 6-89. You may use the "worst-case" analysis method.

Exercises

6.31   A possible definition of a BUT gate (Exercise 4.42) is "Y1 is 1 if A1 and B1 are 1 *but* either A2 or B2 is 0; Y2 is defined symmetrically." Write the truth table and find minimal sum-of-products expressions for the BUT-gate outputs. Draw the logic diagram for a NAND-NAND circuit for the expressions, assuming that only uncomplemented inputs are available. You may use gates from 74x00, '04, '10, '20, and '30 packages.

6.32   Find a gate-level design for the BUT gate defined in Exercise 6.31 that uses a minimum number of transistors when realized in CMOS. You may use inverting gates with up to 4 inputs, AOI or OAI gates, transmission gates, or other transistor-level tricks. Write the output expressions (which need not be two-level sums of products), and draw the logic diagram.

butification   6.33   Butify the function $F = \Sigma_{W,X,Y,Z}(5,7,10,11,13,14)$. That is, show how to perform F with a single BUT gate as defined in Exercise 6.31 and a single 2-input OR gate.

6.34   Write a behavioral-style VHDL or Verilog program for the BUT gate defined in Exercise 6.31.

6.35   Write a structural VHDL or Verilog program that instantiates a single 2-input OR gate and the BUT gate component of Exercise 6.34 to realize the logic function in Exercise 6.33. Write a test bench that checks your circuit's output for all 16 possible input combinations and displays a message if there's an error.

6.36   Write a VHDL program for a generic 3-to-8 binary decoder with active-high inputs and outputs, based on Table 6-17 but with only a single enable input. Then write a second VHDL program, based on Table 6-16, that instantiates the first module to emulate a 74x138, including multiple enable inputs. Draw a block diagram similar to Figure 6-42 that shows the relationship between the modules. Synthesize both Table 6-16 and the second module for a CPLD of your choice, and compare the synthesized results. Explain any differences.

6.37   Repeat Exercise 6.36 using Verilog and Tables 6-24 and 6-23 and Figure 6-43.

6.38   Suppose that you are asked to design a new component, a decimal decoder that is optimized for applications in which only decimal input combinations are expected to occur. How can the cost of such a decoder be minimized compared to one that is simply a 4-to-16 decoder with six outputs removed? Write the logic equations for all ten outputs of the minimized decoder, assuming active-high inputs and outputs and no enable inputs.

6.39   How many Karnaugh maps would be required to complete Exercise 6.38 using the formal multiple-output minimization procedure described in <u>Section Min.3</u> at <u>DDPPonline</u>?

6.40   Suppose that a system requires a 5-to-32 binary decoder with a single active-low enable input, similar to Figure 6-37. With the EN1 input pulled HIGH, either the EN2_L or the EN3_L input in the figure could be used as the enable, with the other input grounded. Discuss the pros and cons of using EN2_L versus EN3_L.

6.41   Design a customized decoder with the function table in Table X6.41 using ABEL and a single GAL16V8.

Table X6.41

CS_L	A2	A1	A0	*Output to Assert*
1	x	x	x	none
0	0	0	x	BILL_L
0	0	x	0	MARY_L
0	0	1	x	JOAN_L
0	0	x	1	PAUL_L
0	1	0	x	ANNA_L
0	1	x	0	FRED_L
0	1	1	x	DAVE_L
0	1	x	1	KATE_L

6.42   Repeat Exercise 6.41 using VHDL or Verilog.

6.43 Show how to build all four of the following functions using one SSI package (four 2-input gates) and one 74x138.

$F1 = X' \cdot Y' \cdot Z' + X \cdot Y \cdot Z$ $F2 = X' \cdot Y' \cdot Z + X \cdot Y \cdot Z'$

$F3 = X' \cdot Y \cdot Z' + X \cdot Y' \cdot Z$ $F4 = X \cdot Y' \cdot Z' + X' \cdot Y \cdot Z$

6.44 Twenty years ago, a famous logic designer decided to quit teaching and make a fortune by licensing the circuit design shown in Figure X6.44.

(a) Label the inputs and outputs of the circuit with appropriate signal names, including active-level indications.

(b) What does the circuit do? Be specific and account for all inputs and outputs.

(c) Draw the logic symbol that would go on the data sheet of this circuit.

(d) Write an ABEL or behavioral VHDL or Verilog program for the circuit.

(e) With what standard building blocks did the new circuit compete? Do you think that it was successful as an MSI part?

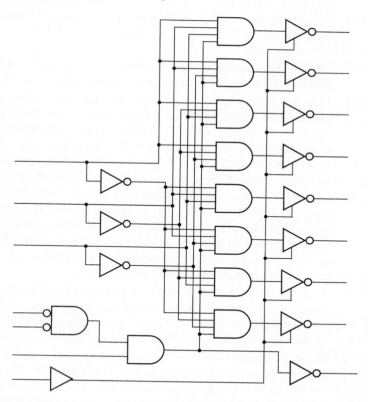

Figure X6.44

6.45 Write VHDL or Verilog code for the lucky/prime encoder described in the first paragraph of Section 6.5.

6.46 Write ABEL or VHDL code for a seven-segment decoder with the specifications described Section 6.4.8 for the Verilog module in Table 6-26.

Figure X6.47

6.47   Redesign the Verilog seven-segment decoder in Table 6-26 so that the digits 6 and 9 have tails as shown in Figure X6.47. In addition, display the character "E" for nondecimal inputs 1010 through 1111.

6.48   Starting with the Verilog module in Table 6-26, write a Verilog module for a seven-segment decoder with the following enhancements:
- The outputs are all active low.
- Two new inputs, ENHEX and ERRDET, control segment-output decoding.
- If ENHEX = 0, the outputs match the behavior of a 74x49.
- If ENHEX = 1, then the outputs for digits 6 and 9 have tails, and the outputs for digits A–F are controlled by ERRDET.
- If ENHEX = 1 and ERRDET = 0, then the outputs for digits A–F look like the letters A–F.
- If ENHEX = 1 and ERRDET = 1, then digits A–F look like the letter U.

6.49   Write ABEL or VHDL code for a seven-segment decoder with the specifications given in Exercise 6.48.

6.50   Design a 10-to-4 encoder with inputs in the 1-out-of-10 code and outputs in a code like normal BCD except that input lines 8 and 9 are encoded into "E" and "F", respectively.

6.51   Draw the logic diagram for a 16-to-4 encoder using just four 8-input NAND gates. What are the active levels of the inputs and outputs in your design?

6.52   Draw the logic diagram for a circuit that uses the 74x148 to resolve priority among eight active-high inputs, I0–I7, where I7 has the highest priority. The circuit should produce active-high address outputs A2–A0 to indicate the number of the highest-priority asserted input. If no input is asserted, then A2–A0 should be 111 and an IDLE output should be asserted. You may use discrete gates in addition to the '148. Be sure to name all signals with the proper active levels.

6.53   Draw the logic diagram for a circuit that resolves priority among eight active-low inputs, I0_L–I7_L, where I0_L has the highest priority. The circuit should produce active-high address outputs A2–A0 to indicate the number of the highest-priority asserted input. If at least one input is asserted, then an AVALID output should be asserted. Be sure to name all signals with the proper active levels. This circuit can be built with a single 74x148 and no other gates.

6.54   A purpose of Exercise 6.53 was to demonstrate that it is not always possible to maintain consistency in active-level notation unless you are willing to define alternate logic symbols for MSI parts that can be used in different ways. Define an alternate 74x148 symbol that provides this consistency in Exercise 6.53.

6.55   Design a combinational circuit with eight active-low request inputs, R0_L–R7_L, and eight outputs, A2–A0, AVALID, B2–B0, and BVALID. The R0_L–R7_L inputs and A2–A0 and AVALID outputs are defined as in Exercise 6.53. The B2–B0 and BVALID outputs identify the second-highest priority request input that is asserted. You should be able to design this circuit using no more than six SSI and MSI packages, but don't use more than 10 in any case.

6.56   Repeat Exercise 6.55 using ABEL. Does the design fit into a single GAL20V8?

6.57   Repeat Exercise 6.55 using VHDL or Verilog.

6.58   Write a version of the VHDL 74x148-like priority-encoder module of Table 6-30 in which the `for` loop starts with the lowest-priority input and searches up. Then synthesize both Table 6-30 and your module for your favorite CPLD and compare the synthesized results.

6.59   Write a version of the Verilog 74x148-like priority-encoder module of Table 6-31 in which the `for` loop starts with the highest-priority input and searches down, using the Verilog `disable` statement to exit the loop when an asserted input is found. Synthesize both Table 6-31 and your module to a CPLD and compare the synthesized results. (*Note:* `disable` is not supported by all Verilog tools.)

6.60   An FCT three-state buffer drives ten FCT inputs and a 3.3-KΩ pull-up resistor to 5.0 V. When the output changes from LOW to Hi-Z, estimate how long it takes for the FCT inputs to see the output as HIGH. State any assumptions that you make.

6.61   On a three-state bus, ten FCT three-state buffers are driving ten FCT inputs and a 3.3-KΩ pull-up resistor to 5.0 V. Assuming that no other devices are driving the bus, estimate how long the bus signal remains at a valid logic level when an active output enters the Hi-Z state. State any assumptions that you make.

6.62   Create a VHDL type, based on IEEE 1164, that models open-collector outputs, where tying outputs together creates a wired-AND function. You should also model a pull-up resistor element such that if there is no pull-up resistor and no device is driving the bus, then an "unknown" signal is produced. Test your definitions by modeling the circuit in Figure X6.62 for all input combinations, both with and without R1 present.

6.63   Design a 3-input, 5-bit multiplexer that fits in a 24-pin IC package. Write the truth table and draw a logic diagram and logic symbol for your multiplexer.

6.64   Write a VHDL or Verilog program for 74x157 multiplexer with the function table shown in Table 6-43.

6.65   Show how to realize the 4-input, 18-bit multiplexer with the functionality described in Table 6-46 using 18 74x151s.

6.66   Show how to realize the 4-input, 18-bit multiplexer with the functionality of Table 6-46 using nine 74x153s and a "code converter" with inputs S2–S0 and outputs C1,C0 such that [C1,C0] = 00–01–10–11 when S2–S0 selects A–B–D–C, respectively.

6.67   Design a 3-input, 2-output combinational circuit that performs the code conversion specified in the previous exercise, using discrete gates.

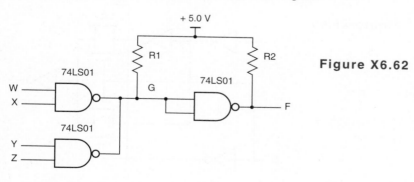

Figure X6.62

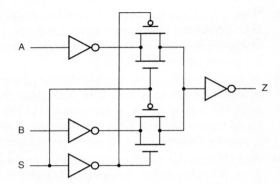

Figure X6.68

6.68   Write the truth table and a logic diagram for the logic function performed by the CMOS circuit in Figure X6.68. (The circuit contains transmission gates, which were introduced in Section 3.7.1.)

6.69   What logic function is performed by the CMOS circuit shown in Figure X6.69?

6.70   A famous logic designer decided to quit teaching again and make a fortune by licensing a circuit design, this time the one shown in Figure X6.70.

(a) Label the inputs and outputs of the circuit with appropriate signal names, including active-level indications.

(b) What does the circuit do? Be specific and account for all inputs and outputs.

(c) Draw the logic symbol that would go on the data sheet of this circuit.

(d) Write an ABEL or behavioral VHDL or Verilog program for the circuit.

(e) With what standard building blocks does the new circuit compete? Do you think it would be successful as an MSI part?

barrel shifter

6.71   A 16-bit *barrel shifter* is a combinational logic circuit with 16 data inputs, 16 data outputs, and 4 control inputs. The output word equals the input word, rotated by a number of bit positions specified by the control inputs. For example, if the input word equals ABCDEFGHIJKLMNOP (each letter represents one bit), and the control inputs are 0101 (5), then the output word is FGHIJKLMNOPABCDE. Design a 16-bit barrel shifter using combinational MSI parts discussed in this chapter. Your design should contain 20 or fewer ICs. Do not draw a complete schematic, but sketch and describe your design in general terms and indicate the types and total number of ICs required.

Figure X6.69

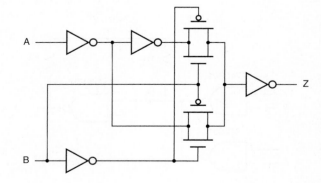

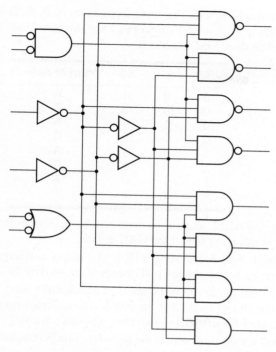

Figure X6.70

6.72 Write an ABEL, VHDL, or Verilog program for the barrel shifter specified in Exercise 6.71.

6.73 Add a three-state-output control input OE to the VHDL multiplexer program in Table 6-49. Your solution should have only one process.

6.74 Using ABEL and a single GAL16V8, design a customized multiplexer with four 3-bit input buses P, Q, R, T, and three select inputs S2–S0 that choose one of the buses to drive a 3-bit output bus Y according to Table X6.74.

Table X6.74

S2	S1	S0	Input to Select
0	0	0	P
0	0	1	P
0	1	0	P
0	1	1	Q
1	0	0	P
1	0	1	P
1	1	0	R
1	1	1	T

6.75 Write a VHDL or Verilog program for a customized multiplexer with four 8-bit input buses P, Q, R, T, and three select inputs S2–S0 that choose one of the buses to drive an 8-bit output bus Y according to Table X6.74.

6.76 Repeat the preceding exercise, adding two control inputs C1 and C0 such that the output bus Y is all 0s, all 1s, the selected input bus, or its complement, depending on whether C1 C0 is 00, 01, 10, or 11 respectively.

6.77 Design a customized multiplexer with five 4-bit input buses A, B, C, D, and E, selecting one of the buses to drive a 4-bit output bus T according to Table X6.77. You may use no more than three MSI and SSI ICs.

Table X6.77

S2	S1	S0	*Input to Select*
0	0	0	A
0	0	1	B
0	1	0	A
0	1	1	C
1	0	0	A
1	0	1	D
1	1	0	A
1	1	1	E

6.78 Repeat Exercise 6.77 using ABEL and one or more PAL/GAL devices from this chapter. Minimize the number and size of the GAL devices.

6.79 Repeat Exercise 6.77 with 8-bit buses using VHDL or Verilog, and targeting a CPLD or FPGA. Determine how many internal resources are used by the design.

6.80 A digital designer who built the circuit in Figure 6-72 accidentally used 74x00s instead of '08s in the circuit and found that the circuit still worked, except for a change in the active level of the ERROR signal. How was this possible?

6.81 Write the truth table and a logic diagram for the logic function performed by the CMOS circuit in Figure X6.81.

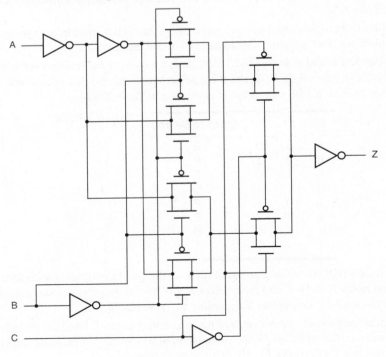

Figure X6.81

6.82 An odd-parity circuit with 2^n inputs can be built with 2^n-1 XOR gates. Describe two different structures for this circuit, one of which gives a minimum worst-case input to output propagation delay and the other of which gives a maximum. For each structure, state the worst-case number of XOR-gate delays, and describe a situation where that structure might be preferred over the other.

6.83 Study the structure of the Xilinx XC9500 CPLD macrocell in Figure 9-41, and determine the largest number of inputs that can be accommodated in an XOR (parity) function that fits in a single macrocell, assuming that "steered" product terms from other macrocells are *not* used (they are slower). Describe which macrocell resources are used to achieve this result and how they are used. *Hint:* Using most HDL tools, you can write and synthesize HDL programs for 2-, 3-, 4-, and 5-input XOR functions and look at the resulting, fitted equations.

6.84 Repeat Exercise 6.83 for the Xilinx XC4000 FPGA macrocell (CLB) shown in Figure 9-45.

6.85 Based on your answer for Exercise 6.83, determine the number of inputs in the largest XOR (parity) function that can be designed in just two levels of XC9500 macrocells, again assuming that "steered" product terms from other macrocells are not used. Draw a block diagram showing how the function is partitioned into macrocells; how many are used?

6.86 Write a structural VHDL or Verilog program for the multibit parity function that you designed in Exercise 6.85, and target it to an XC9500 CPLD. Does the final, fitted circuit have just two levels of delay? If not, why not, and can you discover any tricks or tools that force the synthesis tool to do "the right thing"?

6.87 Write a behavioral VHDL or Verilog program for a multibit parity function with the same number of inputs as your answer to Exercise 6.85. Use a for loop to perform the n-bit XOR operation, and target the design to an XC9500 CPLD. Does the final, fitted circuit have just two levels of delay and use the same number of macrocells as in Exercise 6.85?

6.88 Based on the Hamming code used in the VHDL program in Table 6-58, write a VHDL program for a Hamming encoder entity with 4-bit data inputs and 7-bit encoded data outputs.

6.89 Repeat Exercise 6.88 using Verilog and Table 6-62.

6.90 Write a 4-step iterative algorithm corresponding to the iterative comparator circuit of Figure 6-77.

6.91 Write a VHDL or Verilog program for a 16-bit iterative comparator using the structure of Figure 6-77. Use the language's "generate" capability.

6.92 Design a 64-bit comparator using nine 74x682s, and additional gates as needed, in a treelike structure, such that the maximum delay for a comparison equals twice the delay of one 74x682.

6.93 Write programs in ABEL, VHDL, or Verilog for 8-bit equality and inequality checkers, targeting a PLD or CPLD, and show that both checkers require the same number of product terms. Determine if this would be true even if the device did not have output-polarity control, and explain your answer.

6.94 Write a VHDL program for a device with the functionality of a 74x85.

6.95 Design a comparator similar to the 74x85 that uses the opposite cascading order. That is, to perform a 12-bit comparison, the cascading outputs of the high-order comparator would drive the cascading inputs of the mid-order comparator, and the mid-order outputs would drive the low-order inputs. You needn't do a complete logic design and schematic; a truth table and an application note showing the interconnection for a 12-bit comparison are sufficient.

6.96 Design a 24-bit comparator using three 74x682s and additional gates as required. Your circuit should compare two 24-bit unsigned numbers P and Q and produce two output bits that indicate whether $P = Q$ or $P > Q$.

6.97 Design a 3-bit equality checker with six inputs, SLOT[2–0] and GRANT[2–0], and one active-low output, MATCH_L. The SLOT inputs are connected to fixed values when the circuit is installed in the system, but the GRANT values are changed on a cycle-by-cycle basis during normal operation of the system. Using only SSI and MSI parts that appear in Tables 6-2 and 6-3, design a comparator with the shortest possible maximum propagation delay from GRANT[2–0] to MATCH_L. (*Note:* The author had to solve this problem "in real life" to shave 2 ns off the critical-path delay in a 25-MHz system design.)

6.98 Using the information in Table 6-3, determine the maximum propagation delay from any A or B bus input to any F bus output of the 16-bit carry-lookahead adder of Figure 6-93. You may use the "worst-case" analysis method.

6.99 Using the information in Table 6-3, determine the maximum propagation delay from any A or B bus input to the GALL_L and PALL_L outputs of the 16-bit carry-lookahead adder of Figure 6-93. You may use the "worst-case" analysis method.

6.100 Starting with the logic diagram for the 74x283 in Figure 6-87, write a logic expression for the S3 output in terms of the inputs, and prove that it does indeed equal the fourth sum bit in a binary addition as advertised. You may assume that $c_0 = 0$ (i.e., ignore c_0).

6.101 Estimate the number of product terms in a minimal sum-of-products expression for the c_{32} output of a 32-bit binary adder. Be more specific than "billions and billions," and justify your answer.

6.102 Write a VHDL program for a 74x181-like ALU.

6.103 Augment the Verilog module in Table 6-78 for a 74x381-like ALU by adding COUT (carry-out) and OVFL (overflow) outputs.

6.104 Modify the Verilog module in Table 6-78 for a 74x381-like ALU by including an 8-bit variable C and computing the sum and differences using C, as discussed at the end of Section 6.10.10. Write a test bench that verifies your design for addition and both subtraction operations, for all input combinations.

6.105 Determine the worst-case propagation delay of the multiplier in Figure 6-96, assuming that the propagation delay from any adder input to its sum output is twice as long as the delay to the carry output. Repeat, assuming the opposite relationship. If you were designing the adder cell from scratch, which path would you favor with the shortest delay? Is there an optimal balance?

6.106 Repeat the preceding exercise for the multiplier in Figure 6-97.

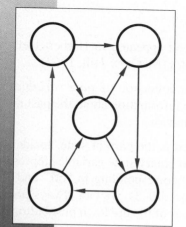

Sequential
Logic Design Principles

L ogic circuits are classified into two types, "combinational" and "sequential." A *combinational* logic circuit is one whose outputs depend only on its current inputs. The heater-fan-speed selection knob in an older car is like a combinational circuit. Its "output" selects a fan speed based only on its current "input"—the position of the knob.

A *sequential* logic circuit is one whose outputs depend not only on its current inputs, but also on the past sequence of inputs, possibly arbitrarily far back in time. The circuit controlled by up and down fan-speed buttons in a newer car is a sequential circuit—the current fan speed depends on an arbitrarily long sequence of up/down pushes, beginning when you first turned on the heater.

So it is inconvenient, and often impossible, to describe the behavior of a sequential circuit using a table that lists outputs as a function of a limited-length input sequence that has been received up until the current time. The circuit may have been operating for a *long* time, so there is no practical bound. With the sequential fan-speed circuit, it's not always possible to determine the current fan speed by looking only at a predetermined number of previous up/down pushes, whether that number is 1, 10, or 1000; the circuit may have received even more up/down pushes.

Instead, we can determine what the output of the fan-speed circuit should be if we know its current "state," and this can be done very concisely.

The best definition of "state" that I've seen appeared in Herbert Hellerman's book on *Digital Computer System Principles* (McGraw-Hill, 1967):

state
state variable

> The *state* of a sequential circuit is a collection of *state variables* whose values at any one time contain all the information about the past necessary to account for the circuit's future behavior.

In the present example, the fan speed is the current state. Inside a three-speed fan, this state might be stored as two binary state variables representing a decimal number between 0 and 3, with 0 corresponding to "off" and 3 to the highest speed. Given the current state (speed 0–3), we can always predict the next state as a function of the inputs (presses of the up/down pushbuttons).

Another example of a sequential circuit is the channel selector on a typical TV using, say, 7 bits to encode 128 channels. Here, one highly visible output of the circuit is an encoding of the state itself—the channel-number display. Other outputs, internal to the TV, may be combinational functions of the state alone (e.g., VHF/UHF/cable tuner selection) or of both state and input (e.g., turning off the TV if the current state is 0 or 1 and the "down" button is pressed).

State variables need not have direct physical significance, and there are often many ways to choose them to describe a particular sequential circuit. For example, in the TV-channel selector, instead of using 7 bits, the state might be stored as three BCD digits (12 bits), with many of the 4096 possible bit combinations going unused.

In a digital logic circuit, state variables are binary values, corresponding to certain logic signals in the circuit, as we'll see in later sections. A circuit with n binary state variables has 2^n possible states. As large as it might be, 2^n is always

finite-state machine

finite, never infinite, so sequential circuits are sometimes called *finite-state machines*.

The state changes of most sequential circuits occur at times specified by a free-running *clock* signal. Figure 7-1 gives timing diagrams and nomenclature for typical clock signals. By convention, a clock signal is active high if state changes occur at the clock's rising edge or when the clock is HIGH, and active

clock

clock period
clock frequency
clock tick
duty cycle

low in the complementary case. The *clock period* is the time between successive transitions in the same direction, and the *clock frequency* is the reciprocal of the period. The first edge or pulse in a clock period or sometimes the period itself is called a *clock tick*. The *duty cycle* is the percentage of time that the clock signal

NON-FINITE-STATE MACHINES   A group of mathematicians recently proposed a non-finite-state machine, but they're still busy listing its states. . . . Sorry, that's just a joke. There *are* mathematical models for infinite-state machines, such as Turing machines. They typically contain a small finite-state-machine control unit, and an infinite amount of auxiliary memory, such as an endless tape.

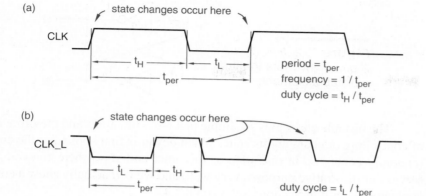

Figure 7-1
Clock signals:
(a) active high;
(b) active low.

is at its asserted level. Typical digital systems, from digital watches to supercomputers, use a quartz-crystal oscillator to generate a free-running clock signal. Clock frequencies might range from 32.768 kHz (for a watch) to 4 GHz (for a CMOS microprocessor with a cycle time of 250 ps); "typical" systems using TTL and CMOS parts have clock frequencies in the 5–500 MHz range.

In this chapter we'll discuss two types of sequential circuits that account for the majority of practical discrete designs. A *feedback sequential circuit* uses ordinary gates and feedback loops to obtain memory in a logic circuit, thereby creating sequential-circuit building blocks such as latches and flip-flops that are used in higher-level designs. A *clocked synchronous state machine* uses these building blocks, in particular edge-triggered D flip-flops, to create circuits whose inputs are examined and whose outputs change in accordance with a controlling clock signal. Other sequential circuit types, such as general fundamental mode, multiple-pulse mode, and multiphase circuits, are sometimes useful in high-performance systems and VLSI and are discussed in advanced texts.

*feedback sequential
  circuit*

*clocked synchronous
  state machine*

7.1 Bistable Elements

The simplest sequential circuit consists of a pair of inverters forming a feedback loop, as shown in Figure 7-2. It has *no* inputs and two outputs, Q and Q_L.

7.1.1 Digital Analysis

The circuit of Figure 7-2 is often called a *bistable*, since a strictly digital analysis shows that it has two stable states. If Q is HIGH, then the bottom inverter has a HIGH input and a LOW output, which forces the top inverter's output HIGH as we assumed in the first place. But if Q is LOW, then the bottom inverter has a LOW input and a HIGH output, which forces Q LOW, another stable situation. We could use a single state variable, the state of signal Q, to describe the state of the circuit; there are two possible states, Q = 0 and Q = 1.

bistable

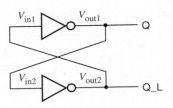

Figure 7-2
A pair of inverters forming
a bistable element.

The bistable element is so simple that it has no inputs and therefore no way of controlling or changing its state. When power is first applied to the circuit, it randomly comes up in one state or the other and stays there forever. Still, it serves our illustrative purposes very well, and we *will* actually show a couple of applications for it in Sections 8.2.3 and 8.2.4.

7.1.2 Analog Analysis

The analysis of the bistable has more to reveal if we consider its operation from an analog point of view. The dark line in Figure 7-3 shows the steady-state (DC) transfer function T for a single inverter; the output voltage is a function of input voltage, $V_{out} = T(V_{in})$. With two inverters connected in a feedback loop as in Figure 7-2, we know that $V_{in1} = V_{out2}$ and $V_{in2} = V_{out1}$; therefore, we can plot the transfer functions for both inverters on the same graph with an appropriate labeling of the axes. Thus, the dark line is the transfer function for the top inverter in Figure 7-2, and the colored line is the transfer function for the bottom one.

Considering only the steady-state behavior of the bistable's feedback loop, and not dynamic effects, the loop is in equilibrium if the input and output voltages of both inverters are constant DC values consistent with the loop connection and the inverters' DC transfer function. That is, we must have

$$
\begin{aligned}
V_{in1} &= V_{out2} \\
&= T(V_{in2}) \\
&= T(V_{out1}) \\
&= T(T(V_{in1}))
\end{aligned}
$$

Figure 7-3
Transfer functions for
inverters in a bistable
feedback loop.

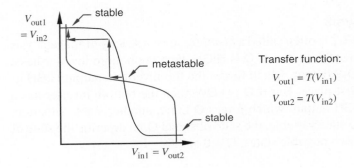

Likewise, we must have

$$V_{in2} = T(T(V_{in2}))$$

We can find these equilibrium points graphically from Figure 7-3; they are the points at which the two transfer curves meet. Surprisingly, we find that there are not two but *three* equilibrium points. Two of them, labeled *stable*, correspond to the two states that our "strictly digital" analysis identified earlier, with Q either 0 (LOW) or 1 (HIGH).

stable

The third equilibrium point, called a *metastable state*, occurs with V_{out1} and V_{out2} about halfway between a valid logic 1 voltage and a valid logic 0 voltage; so Q and Q_L are not valid logic signals at this point. Yet the loop equations are satisfied; if we can get the circuit to operate at the metastable point, it could theoretically stay there indefinitely. This behavior is called *metastability*.

metastable state

metastability

7.1.3 Metastable Behavior

Closer analysis of the situation at the metastable point shows that it is aptly named. It is not truly stable, because random noise will tend to drive a circuit that is operating at the metastable point toward one of the stable operating points, as we'll now demonstrate.

Suppose the bistable is operating precisely at the metastable point in Figure 7-3. Now let us assume that a small amount of circuit noise reduces V_{in1} by a tiny amount. This tiny change causes V_{out1} to *increase* by a small amount. But since V_{out1} produces V_{in2}, we can follow the first horizontal arrow from near the metastable point to the second transfer characteristic, which now demands a lower voltage for V_{out2}, which is V_{in1}. Now we're back where we started, except we have a much larger change in voltage at V_{in1} than the original noise produced, and the operating point is still changing. This "regenerative" process continues until we reach the stable operating point at the upper lefthand corner of Figure 7-3. However, if we perform a "noise" analysis for either of the stable operating points, we find that feedback brings the circuit back toward the stable operating point, rather than away from it.

Metastable behavior of a bistable can be compared to the behavior of a ball dropped onto a hill, as shown in Figure 7-4. If we drop a ball from overhead, it will probably roll down immediately to one side of the hill or the other. But if it lands right at the top, it may precariously sit there for a while before random

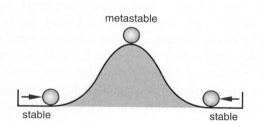

metastable

stable   stable

Figure 7-4
Ball and hill analogy for metastable behavior.

forces (wind, rodents, earthquakes) start it rolling down the hill. Like the ball at the top of the hill, the bistable may stay in the metastable state for an unpredictable length of time before nondeterministically settling into one stable state or the other.

If the *simplest* sequential circuit is susceptible to metastable behavior, you can be sure that *all* sequential circuits are susceptible. And this behavior is not something that only occurs at power-up.

Returning to the ball-and-hill analogy, consider what happens if we try to kick the ball from one side of the hill to the other. Apply a strong force (Superman), and the ball goes right over the top and lands in a stable resting place on the other side. Apply a weak force (Clark Kent), and the ball falls back to its original starting place. But apply a wishy-washy force (Charlie Brown), and the ball goes to the top of the hill, teeters, and eventually falls back to one side or the other.

This behavior is completely analogous to what happens to latches and flip-flops under marginal triggering conditions. For example, we'll soon study S-R latches, where a pulse on the S input forces the latch from the 0 state to the 1 state. A minimum pulse width is specified for the S input. Apply a pulse of this width or longer, and the latch immediately goes to the 1 state. Apply a very short pulse, and the latch stays in the 0 state. Apply a pulse just under the minimum width, and the latch may go into the metastable state. Once the latch is in the metastable state, its operation depends on "the shape of its hill." Latches and flip-flops built from high-gain, fast transistors tend to come out of metastability faster than ones built from low-performance technologies.

We'll say more about metastability in the next section in connection with specific latch and flip-flop types, and in Section 8.9 with respect to synchronous design methodology and synchronizer failure.

7.2 Latches and Flip-Flops

Latches and flip-flops are the basic building blocks of most sequential circuits. Typical digital systems use latches and flip-flops that are prepackaged, functionally specified devices in a standard integrated circuit. In ASIC design environments, latches and flip-flops are typically predefined cells specified by the ASIC vendor. However, within a standard IC or an ASIC, each latch or flip-flop cell is typically designed as a feedback sequential circuit using individual logic gates and feedback loops. We'll study these discrete designs for two reasons—to understand the behavior of the prepackaged elements better, and to gain the capability of building a latch or flip-flop "from scratch," as is required very occasionally in digital-design practice and often in digital-design exams.

flip-flop   All digital designers use the name *flip-flop* for a sequential device that normally samples its inputs and changes its outputs only when a clocking signal is

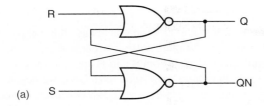

S	R	Q	QN
0	0	last Q	last QN
0	1	0	1
1	0	1	0
1	1	0	0

(a)   (b)

Figure 7-5
S-R latch: (a) circuit design using NOR gates; (b) function table.

changing. On the other hand, most digital designers use the name *latch* for a   *latch*
sequential device that watches its inputs continuously and can change its outputs
at any time (although in some cases requiring an enable signal to be asserted).
We follow this standard convention in this text. However, some textbooks and
digital designers may (incorrectly) use the name "flip-flop" for a device that we
call a "latch."

   In any case, because the functional behaviors of latches and flip-flops are
quite different, it is important for the logic designer to know which type is being
used in a design, either from the device's part number (e.g., 74x373 vs. 74x374)
or from other contextual information. We discuss the most commonly used types
of latches and flip-flops in the following subsections.

7.2.1 S-R Latch

An *S-R (set-reset) latch* based on NOR gates is shown in Figure 7-5(a). The   *S-R latch*
circuit has two inputs, S and R, and two outputs, labeled Q and QN, where QN
is normally the complement of Q. Signal QN is sometimes labeled $\overline{Q}$ or Q_L.

   If S and R are both 0, the circuit behaves like the bistable element—we
have a feedback loop that retains one of two logic states, Q = 0 or Q = 1. As
shown in Figure 7-5(b), either S or R may be asserted to force the feedback loop
to a desired state. S *sets* or *presets* the Q output to 1; R *resets* or *clears* the Q   *set*
output to 0. After the S or R input is negated, the latch remains in the state that it   *preset*
was forced into. Figure 7-6(a) shows the functional behavior of an S-R latch for   *reset*
a typical sequence of inputs. Colored arrows indicate causality, that is, which   *clear*
input transitions cause which output transitions.

Figure 7-6 Typical operation of an S-R latch: (a) "normal" inputs; (b) S and R
                 asserted simultaneously.

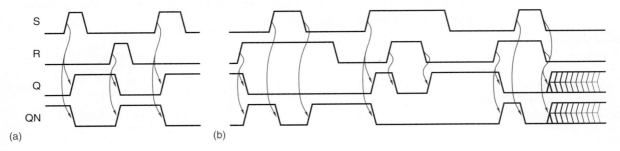

(a)   (b)

$\overline{\text{Q}}$ **VERSUS QN**   In most applications of an S-R latch, the QN (a.k.a. $\overline{\text{Q}}$) output is always the complement of the Q output. However, the $\overline{\text{Q}}$ name is not quite correct, because there is one case where this output is not the complement of Q. If both S and R are 1, as they are in several places in Figure 7-6(b), then both outputs are forced to 0. Once we negate either input, the outputs return to complementary operation as usual. However, if we negate both inputs simultaneously, the latch goes to an unpredictable next state, and it may in fact oscillate or enter the metastable state. Metastability may also occur if a 1 pulse that is too short is applied to S or R.

Three different logic symbols for the same S-R latch circuit are shown in Figure 7-7. The symbols differ in the treatment of the complemented output. Historically, the first symbol was used, showing the active-low or complemented signal name inside the function rectangle. However, in bubble-to-bubble logic design the second form of the symbol is preferred, showing an inversion bubble outside the function rectangle. The last form of the symbol is obviously wrong.

propagation delay   Figure 7-8 defines timing parameters for an S-R latch. The *propagation delay* is the time it takes for a transition on an input signal to produce a transition on an output signal. A given latch or flip-flop may have several different propagation-delay specifications, one for each pair of input and output signals. Also, the propagation delay may be different depending on whether the output makes a LOW-to-HIGH or HIGH-to-LOW transition. With an S-R latch, a LOW-to-HIGH transition on S can cause a LOW-to-HIGH transition on Q, so a propagation delay $t_{\text{pLH(SQ)}}$ occurs, as shown in transition 1 in the figure. Similarly, a LOW-to-HIGH transition on R can cause a HIGH-to-LOW transition on Q, with propagation delay $t_{\text{pHL(RQ)}}$ as shown in transition 2. Not shown in the figure are the corresponding transitions on QN, which would have propagation delays $t_{\text{pHL(SQN)}}$ and $t_{\text{pLH(RQN)}}$.

minimum pulse width   *Minimum-pulse-width* specifications are usually given for the S and R inputs. As shown in Figure 7-8, the latch may go into the metastable state and remain there for a random length of time if a pulse shorter than the minimum width $t_{\text{pw(min)}}$ is applied to S or R. The latch can be deterministically brought out of the metastable state only by applying a pulse to S or R that meets or exceeds the minimum-pulse-width requirement.

Figure 7-7
Symbols for an S-R latch:
(a) without bubble;
(b) preferred for bubble-
to-bubble design;
(c) incorrect because
of double negation.

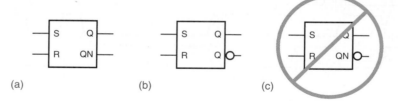

(a)   (b)   (c)

HOW CLOSE IS CLOSE?	As mentioned in the previous boxed note, an S-R latch may go into the metastable state if S and R are negated simultaneously. Often, but not always, a commercial latch's specifications define "simultaneously" (e.g., S and R negated within 10 ns of each other). This parameter is sometimes called the *recovery time*, t_{rec}. It is the minimum delay between negating S and R for them to be considered nonsimultaneous and it is closely related to the minimum-pulse-width specification. Both specifications are measures of how long it takes for the latch's feedback loop to stabilize during a change of state.

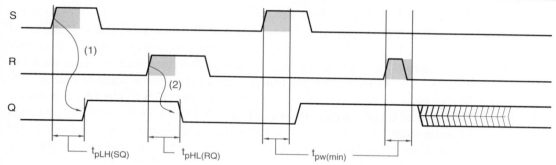

Figure 7-8 Timing parameters for an S-R latch.

7.2.2 $\overline{\text{S}}$-$\overline{\text{R}}$ Latch

An $\overline{\text{S}}$-$\overline{\text{R}}$ *latch* (read "S-bar-R-bar latch") with active-low set and reset inputs may   *S-R latch*
be built from NAND gates as shown in Figure 7-9(a). In CMOS and TTL logic
families, $\overline{\text{S}}$-$\overline{\text{R}}$ latches are used much more often than S-R latches because NAND
gates are preferred over NOR gates.

As shown by the function table, Figure 7-9(b), operation of the $\overline{\text{S}}$-$\overline{\text{R}}$ latch is
similar to that of the S-R, with two major differences. First, $\overline{\text{S}}$ and $\overline{\text{R}}$ are active
low, so the latch remembers its previous state when $\overline{\text{S}} = \overline{\text{R}} = 1$; the active-low
inputs are clearly indicated in the symbols in (c). Second, when both $\overline{\text{S}}$ and $\overline{\text{R}}$ are
asserted simultaneously, both latch outputs go to 1, not 0 as in the S-R latch.
Except for these differences, operation of the $\overline{\text{S}}$-$\overline{\text{R}}$ is the same as the S-R,
including timing and metastability considerations.

Figure 7-9 $\overline{\text{S}}$-$\overline{\text{R}}$ latch: (a) circuit design using NAND gates; (b) function table; (c) logic symbol.

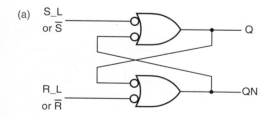

(b)

S_L	R_L	Q	QN
0	0	1	1
0	1	1	0
1	0	0	1
1	1	last Q	last QN

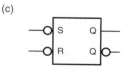

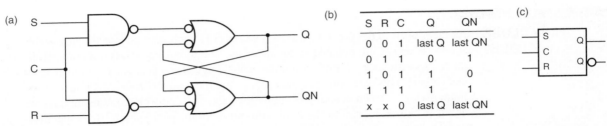

(a)   (b)

S	R	C	Q	QN
0	0	1	last Q	last QN
0	1	1	0	1
1	0	1	1	0
1	1	1	1	1
x	x	0	last Q	last QN

(c)

Figure 7-10 S-R latch with enable: (a) circuit using NAND gates; (b) function table; (c) logic symbol.

7.2.3 S-R Latch with Enable

S-R latch with enable

An S-R or $\overline{S}\text{-}\overline{R}$ latch is sensitive to its S and R inputs at all times. However, it may easily be modified to create a device that is sensitive to these inputs only when an enabling input C is asserted. Such an *S-R latch with enable* is shown in Figure 7-10. As shown by the function table, the circuit behaves like an S-R latch when C is 1, and retains its previous state when C is 0. The latch's behavior for a typical set of inputs is shown in Figure 7-11. If both S and R are 1 when C changes from 1 to 0, the circuit behaves like an S-R latch in which S and R are negated simultaneously—the next state is unpredictable and the output may become metastable.

7.2.4 D Latch

D latch

S-R latches are useful in control applications, where we often think in terms of setting a flag in response to some condition and resetting it when conditions change. So, we control the set and reset inputs somewhat independently. However, we often need latches simply to store bits of information—each bit is presented on a signal line, and we'd like to store it somewhere. A *D latch* may be used in such an application.

Figure 7-12 shows a D latch. Its logic diagram is recognizable as that of an S-R latch with enable, with an inverter added to generate S and R inputs from the

Figure 7-11 Typical operation of an S-R latch with enable.

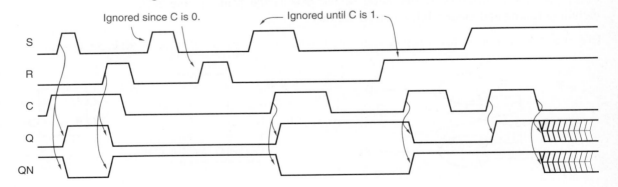

Ignored since C is 0.   Ignored until C is 1.

S

R

C

Q

QN

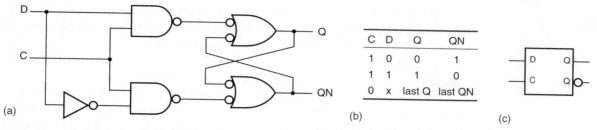

(a)

C	D	Q	QN
1	0	0	1
1	1	1	0
0	x	last Q	last QN

(b)

(c)

Figure 7-12 D latch: (a) circuit design using NAND gates; (b) function table; (c) logic symbol.

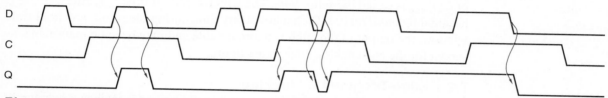

Figure 7-13 Functional behavior of a D latch for various inputs.

single D (data) input. This eliminates the troublesome situation in S-R latches, where S and R may be asserted simultaneously. The control input of a D latch, labeled C in (c), is sometimes named ENABLE, CLK, or G. It is active low in some D-latch designs, and always has a minimum pulse-width requirement.

An example of a D latch's functional behavior is given in Figure 7-13. When the C input is asserted, the Q output follows the D input. In this situation, the latch is said to be "open" and the path from D input to Q output is "transparent"; the circuit is often called a *transparent latch* for this reason. When the C input is negated, the latch "closes"; the Q output retains its last value and no longer changes in response to D, as long as C remains negated.

transparent latch

More detailed timing behavior of the D latch is shown in Figure 7-14. Four different delay parameters are shown for signals that propagate from the C or D input to the Q output. For example, at transitions 1 and 4 the latch is initially

Figure 7-14 Timing parameters for a D latch.

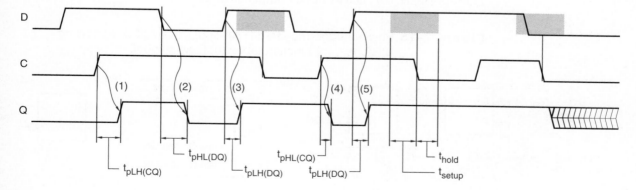

"closed" and the D input is the opposite of Q output, so that when C goes to 1 the latch "opens up" and the Q output changes after delay $t_{pLH(CQ)}$ or $t_{pHL(CQ)}$. At transitions 2 and 3 the C input is already 1 and the latch is already open, so that Q transparently follows the transitions on D with delay $t_{pHL(DQ)}$ and $t_{pLH(DQ)}$. Four more parameters specify the delay to the QN output, not shown.

setup time
hold time

Although the D latch eliminates the S = R = 1 problem of the S-R latch, it does not eliminate the metastability problem. As shown in Figure 7-14, there is a (shaded) window of time around the falling edge of C when the D input must not change. This window begins at time t_{setup} before the falling (latching) edge of C; t_{setup} is called the *setup time*. The window ends at time t_{hold} afterward; t_{hold} is called the *hold time*. If D changes at any time during the setup- and hold-time window, the output of the latch is unpredictable and may become metastable, as shown for the last latching edge in the figure.

7.2.5 Edge-Triggered D Flip-Flop

positive-edge-triggered D flip-flop

A *positive-edge-triggered D flip-flop* combines a pair of D latches, as shown in Figure 7-15, to create a circuit that samples its D input and changes its Q and QN outputs only at the rising edge of a controlling CLK signal. The first latch is called the *master*; it is open and follows the input when CLK is 0. When CLK goes to 1, the master latch is closed and its output is transferred to the second latch, called the *slave*. The slave latch is open all the while that CLK is 1, but changes only at the beginning of this interval, because the master is closed and unchanging during the rest of the interval.

master

slave

dynamic-input indicator

The triangle on the D flip-flop's CLK input indicates edge-triggered behavior and is called a *dynamic-input indicator*. Examples of the flip-flop's functional behavior for several input transitions are presented in Figure 7-16. The QM signal shown is the output of the master latch. Notice that QM changes only when CLK is 0. When CLK goes to 1, the current value of QM is transferred to Q, and QM is prevented from changing until CLK goes to 0 again.

Figure 7-17 shows more detailed timing behavior for the D flip-flop. All propagation delays are measured from the rising edge of CLK, since that's the only event that causes an output change. Different delays may be specified for LOW-to-HIGH and HIGH-to-LOW output changes.

Figure 7-15 Positive-edge-triggered D flip-flop: (a) circuit design using D latches; (b) function table; (c) logic symbol.

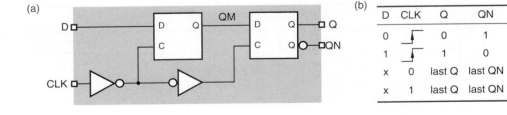

(b)

D	CLK	Q	QN
0	⌐⌐	0	1
1	⌐⌐	1	0
x	0	last Q	last QN
x	1	last Q	last QN

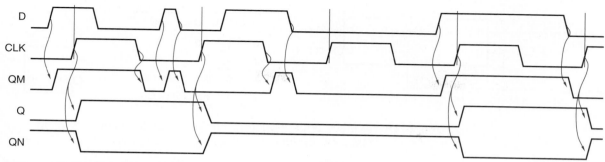

Figure 7-16 Functional behavior of a positive-edge-triggered D flip-flop.

Like a D latch, the edge-triggered D flip-flop has a setup- and hold-time window during which the D inputs must not change. This window occurs around the triggering edge of CLK, and is indicated by shaded color in Figure 7-17. If the setup and hold times are not met, the flip-flop output will usually go to a stable, though unpredictable, 0 or 1 state. In some cases, however, the output will oscillate or go to a metastable state halfway between 0 and 1, as shown at the second-to-last clock tick in the figure. If the flip-flop goes into the metastable state, it will return to a stable state on its own only after a probabilistic delay, as explained in Section 8.9. It can also be forced into a stable state by applying another triggering clock edge with a D input that meets the setup- and hold-time requirements, as shown at the last clock tick in the figure.

A *negative-edge-triggered D flip-flop* simply inverts the clock input, so that all the action takes place on the falling edge of CLK_L; by convention, a falling-edge trigger is considered to be active low. The flip-flop's function table and logic symbol are shown in Figure 7-18.

negative-edge-triggered D flip-flop

Some D flip-flops have *asynchronous inputs* that may be used to force the flip-flop to a particular state independent of the CLK and D inputs. These inputs, typically labeled PR (*preset*) and CLR (*clear*), behave like the set and reset

asynchronous inputs
preset
clear

Figure 7-17 Timing behavior of a positive-edge-triggered D flip-flop.

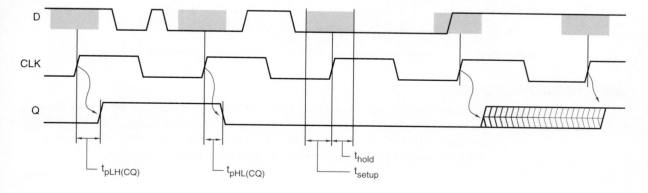

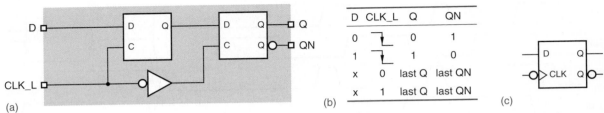

Figure 7-18 Negative-edge triggered D flip-flop: (a) circuit design using D latches; (b) function table; (c) logic symbol.

inputs on an S-R latch. The logic symbol and NAND circuit for an edge-triggered D flip-flop with these inputs is shown in Figure 7-19. Although asynchronous inputs are used by some logic designers to perform tricky sequential functions, they are best reserved for initialization and testing purposes, to force a sequential circuit into a known starting state; more on this when we discuss synchronous design methodology in Section 8.7.

7.2.6 Edge-Triggered D Flip-Flop with Enable

A commonly desired function in D flip-flops is the ability to hold the last value stored, rather than load a new value, at the clock edge. This is accomplished by adding an *enable input*, called EN or CE (*clock enable*). While the name "clock enable" is descriptive, the extra input's function is not obtained by controlling

enable input

clock-enable input

Figure 7-19 Positive-edge-triggered D flip-flop with preset and clear: (a) logic symbol; (b) circuit design using NAND gates.

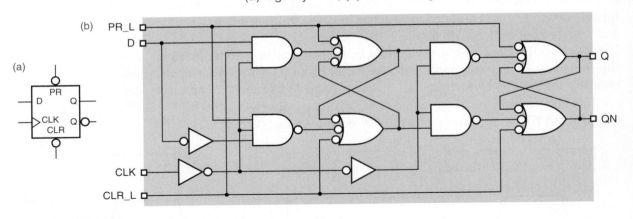

TIME FOR A COMMERCIAL   Commercial TTL positive-edge-triggered D flip-flops do not use the master-slave latch design of Figure 7-15 or Figure 7-19. Instead, flip-flops like the 74LS74 use the six-gate design of Figure 7-20, which is smaller and faster. We'll show how to formally analyze the next-state behavior of both designs in Section 7.9.

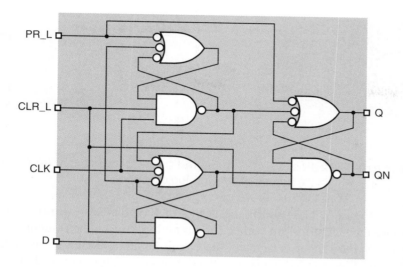

Figure 7-20
Commercial circuit for a positive-edge-triggered D flip-flop such as 74LS74.

the clock in any way whatsoever. Rather, as shown in Figure 7-21(a), a 2-input multiplexer controls the value applied to the internal flip-flop's D input. If EN is asserted, the external D input is selected; if EN is negated, the flip-flop's current output is used. The resulting function table is shown in (b). The flip-flop symbol is shown in (c); in some flip-flops, the enable input is active low, denoted by an inversion bubble on this input.

7.2.7 Scan Flip-Flop

An important flip-flop function for ASIC testing is so-called *scan capability*. *scan capability*
The idea is to be able to drive the flip-flop's D input with an alternate source of data during device testing. When all of the flip-flops are put into testing mode, a test pattern can be "scanned in" to the ASIC using the flip-flops' alternate data inputs. After the test pattern is loaded, the flip-flops are put back into "normal" mode, and all of the flip-flops are clocked normally. After one or more clock ticks, the flip-flops are put back into test mode, and the test results are "scanned out."

Figure 7-21 Positive-edge-triggered D flip-flop with enable: (a) circuit design; (b) function table; (c) logic symbol.

(a)
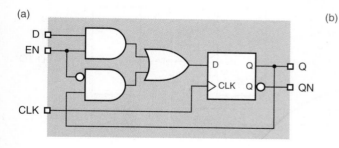

(b)

D	EN	CLK	Q	QN
0	1	⤒	0	1
1	1	⤒	1	0
x	0	⤒	last Q	last QN
x	x	0	last Q	last QN
x	x	1	last Q	last QN

(c)
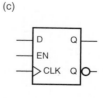

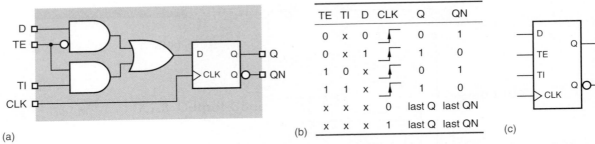

TE	TI	D	CLK	Q	QN
0	x	0	↗	0	1
0	x	1	↗	1	0
1	0	x	↗	0	1
1	1	x	↗	1	0
x	x	x	0	last Q	last QN
x	x	x	1	last Q	last QN

(a)   (b)   (c)

Figure 7-22 Positive-edge-triggered D flip-flop with scan: (a) circuit design; (b) function table; (c) logic symbol.

test-enable input, TE
test input, TI

scan chain

Figure 7-22(a) shows the design of a typical scan flip-flop. It is nothing more than a D flip-flop with a 2-input multiplexer on the D input. When the TE (*test enable*) input is negated, the circuit behaves like an ordinary D flip-flop. When TE is asserted, it takes its data from TI (*test input*) instead of from D. This functional behavior is shown in (b), and a symbol for the device is given in (c).

The extra inputs are used to connect all of an ASIC's flip-flops in a *scan chain* for testing purposes. Figure 7-23 is a simple example with four flip-flops in the scan chain. The TE inputs of all the flip-flops are connected to a global TE input, while each flip-flop's Q output is connected to another's TI input in serial (daisy-chain) fashion. The TI, TE, and TO (test output) connections are strictly for testing purposes; the additional logic connected to the D inputs and Q outputs needed to make the circuit do something useful is not shown.

To test the circuit, including the additional logic, the global TE input is asserted while *n* clock ticks occur and *n* test-vector bits are applied to the global TI input and are thereby scanned (shifted) into the *n* flip-flops; *n* equals 4 in Figure 7-23. Then TE is negated, and the circuit is allowed to run for one or more additional clock ticks. The new state of the circuit, represented by the new values in the *n* flip-flops, can be observed (scanned out) at TO by asserting TE while *n* more clock ticks occur. To make the testing process more efficient, another test vector can be scanned in while the previous result is being scanned out.

Figure 7-23 A scan chain with four flip-flops.

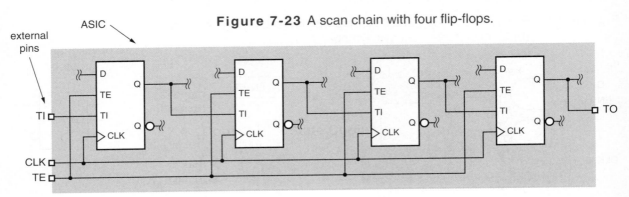

There are many different types of scan flip-flops, corresponding to different types of basic flip-flop functionality. For example, scan capability could be added to the D flip-flop with enable in Figure 7-21 by replacing its internal 2-input multiplexer with a 3-input one. At each clock tick the flip-flop would load D, TI, or its current state, depending on the values of EN and TE. Scan capability can also be added to other flip-flop types, such as J-K and T introduced later in this section.

*7.2.8 Master/Slave S-R Flip-Flop

We indicated earlier that S-R latches are useful in "control" applications, where we may have independent conditions for setting and resetting a control bit. If the control bit is supposed to be changed only at certain times with respect to a clock signal, then we need an S-R flip-flop that, like a D flip-flop, changes its outputs only on a certain edge of the clock signal. This subsection and the next two describe flip-flops that are useful for such applications.

If we substitute S-R latches for the D latches in the negative-edge-triggered D flip-flop of Figure 7-18(a), we get a *master/slave S-R flip-flop*, shown in Figure 7-24. Like a D flip-flop, the S-R flip-flop changes its outputs only at the falling edge of a control signal C. However, the new output value depends on input values not just at the falling edge, but during the entire interval in which C is 1 prior to the falling edge. As shown in Figure 7-25, a short pulse on S any time during this interval can set the master latch; likewise, a pulse on R can reset it. The value transferred to the flip-flop output on the falling edge of C depends on whether the master latch was last set or cleared while C was 1.

master/slave S-R flip-flop

Shown in Figure 7-24(c), the logic symbol for the master/slave S-R flip-flop does not use a dynamic-input indicator, because the flip-flop is not truly edge triggered. It is more like a latch that follows its input during the entire interval that C is 1 but changes its output to reflect the final latched value only when C goes to 0. In the symbol, a *postponed-output indicator* indicates that the output signal does not change until enable input C is negated. Flip-flops with this kind of behavior are sometimes called *pulse-triggered flip-flops*.

postponed-output indicator

pulse-triggered flip-flop

Figure 7-24 Master/slave S-R flip-flop: (a) circuit using S-R latches; (b) function table; (c) logic symbol.

(a)
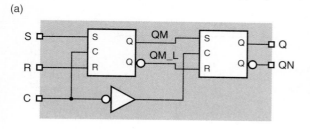

(b)

S	R	C	Q	QN
x	x	0	last Q	last QN
0	0	⎍	last Q	last QN
0	1	⎍	0	1
1	0	⎍	1	0
1	1	⎍	undef.	undef.

(c)
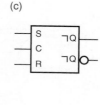

*Throughout this book, optional sections are marked with an asterisk.

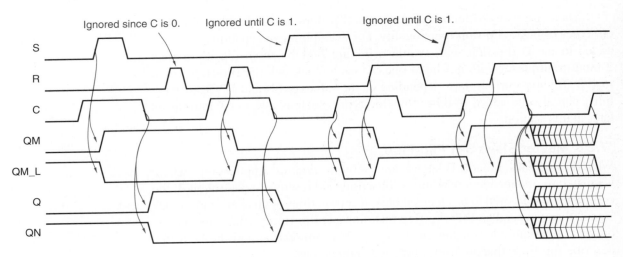

Figure 7-25 Internal and functional behavior of a master/slave S-R flip-flop.

The operation of the master/slave S-R flip-flop is unpredictable if both S and R are asserted at the falling edge of C. In this case, just before the falling edge, both the Q and QN outputs of the master latch are 1. When C goes to 0, the master latch's outputs change unpredictably and may even become metastable. At the same time, the slave latch opens up and propagates this garbage to the flip-flop output.

*7.2.9 Master/Slave J-K Flip-Flop

master/slave J-K flip-flop

The problem of what to do when S and R are asserted simultaneously is solved in a *master/slave J-K flip-flop*. The J and K inputs are analogous to S and R. However, as shown in Figure 7-26, asserting J asserts the master's S input only if the flip-flop's QN output is currently 1 (i.e., Q is 0), and asserting K asserts the master's R input only if Q is currently 1. Thus, if J and K are asserted simultaneously, the flip-flop goes to the opposite of its current state.

Figure 7-26 Master/slave J-K flip-flop: (a) circuit design using S-R latches; (b) function table; (c) logic symbol.

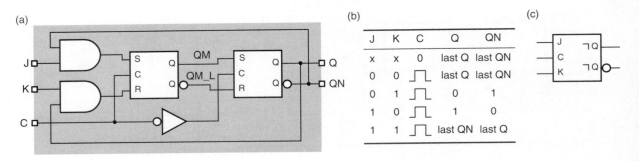

(a)

(b)

J	K	C	Q	QN
x	x	0	last Q	last QN
0	0	⌐⌐	last Q	last QN
0	1	⌐⌐	0	1
1	0	⌐⌐	1	0
1	1	⌐⌐	last QN	last Q

(c)

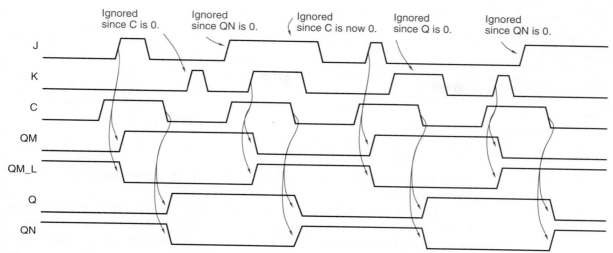

Figure 7-27 Internal and functional behavior of a master/slave J-K flip-flop.

Figure 7-27 shows the functional behavior of a J-K master/slave flip-flop for a typical set of inputs. Note that the J and K inputs need not be asserted at the end of the triggering pulse for the flip-flop output to change at that time. In fact, because of the gating on the master latch's S and R inputs, it is possible for the flip-flop output to change to 1 even though K and not J is asserted at the end of the triggering pulse. This behavior, known as *1s catching*, is illustrated in the second-to-last triggering pulse in the figure. An analogous behavior known as *0s catching* is illustrated in the last triggering pulse. Because of this behavior, the J and K inputs of a J-K master/slave flip-flop must be held valid during the entire interval that C is 1.

1s catching

0s catching

*7.2.10 Edge-Triggered J-K Flip-Flop

The problem of 1s and 0s catching is solved in an *edge-triggered J-K flip-flop*, whose functional equivalent is shown in Figure 7-28. Using an edge-triggered D flip-flop internally, the edge-triggered J-K flip-flop samples its inputs at the

edge-triggered J-K flip-flop

Figure 7-28 Edge-triggered J-K flip-flop: (a) equivalent function using an edge-triggered D flip-flop; (b) function table; (c) logic symbol.

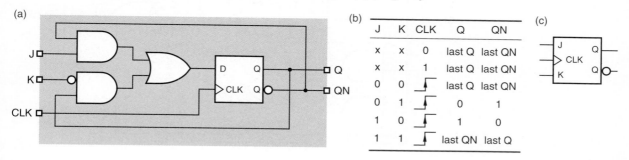

(b)

J	K	CLK	Q	QN
x	x	0	last Q	last QN
x	x	1	last Q	last QN
0	0	⤒	last Q	last QN
0	1	⤒	0	1
1	0	⤒	1	0
1	1	⤒	last QN	last Q

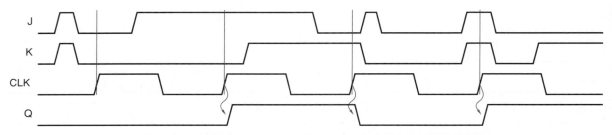

Figure 7-29 Functional behavior of a positive-edge-triggered J-K flip-flop.

rising edge of the clock and produces its next output according to the "characteristic equation" $Q^* = J \cdot Q' + K' \cdot Q$ (see Section 7.3.3).

Typical functional behavior of an edge-triggered J-K flip-flop is shown in Figure 7-29. Like the D input of an edge-triggered D flip-flop, the J and K inputs of a J-K flip-flop must meet published setup- and hold-time specifications with respect to the triggering clock edge for proper operation.

74x109

Because they eliminate the problems of 1s and 0s catching and of simultaneously asserting both control inputs, edge-triggered J-K flip-flops have largely obsoleted the older pulse-triggered types. The *74x109* is a TTL positive-edge-triggered J-$\overline{\text{K}}$ flip-flop with an active-low K input (named $\overline{\text{K}}$ or K_L).

ANOTHER COMMERCIAL (FLIP-FLOP, THAT IS)

The internal design of the 74LS109 is very similar to that of the 74LS74, which we showed in Figure 7-20. As shown in Figure 7-30, the '109 simply replaces the bottom-left gate of the '74, which realizes the characteristic equation $Q^* = D$, with an AND-OR structure that realizes the J-$\overline{\text{K}}$ characteristic equation, $Q^* = J \cdot Q' + K\_L \cdot Q$.

Figure 7-30
Internal logic diagram for the 74LS109 positive-edge-triggered J-$\overline{\text{K}}$ flip-flop.

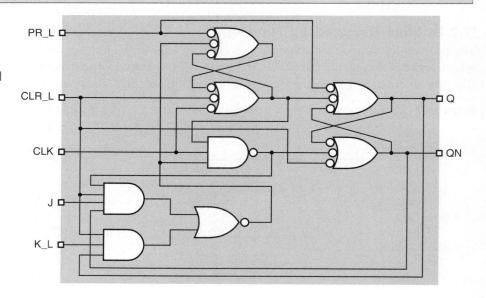

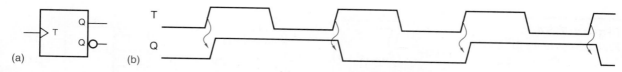

Figure 7-31 Positive-edge-triggered T flip-flop: (a) logic symbol; (b) functional behavior.

J-K flip-flops aren't used much nowadays, but they're sometimes used in clocked synchronous state machines. As we'll explain in Section 7.4.5, the next-state logic for J-K flip-flops is sometimes simpler than for D flip-flops. However, most state machines are still designed using D flip-flops, because the design methodology is a bit simpler and because most sequential programmable logic devices contain D, not J-K, flip-flops. Therefore, we give most of our attention to D flip-flops.

7.2.11 T Flip-Flop

A *T (toggle) flip-flop* changes state on every tick of the clock. Figure 7-31 shows the symbol and illustrates the behavior of a positive-edge-triggered T flip-flop. Notice that the signal on the flip-flop's Q output has precisely half the frequency of the T input. Figure 7-32 shows how to obtain a T flip-flop from a D or J-K flip-flop. T flip-flops are most often used in counters and frequency dividers, as we'll show in Section 8.4.

T flip-flop

In many applications of T flip-flops, the flip-flop need not be toggled on every clock tick. Such applications can use a *T flip-flop with enable*. As shown in Figure 7-33, the flip-flop changes state at the triggering edge of the clock only if the enable signal EN is asserted. Like the D, J, and K inputs on other edge-triggered flip-flops, the EN input must meet specified setup and hold times with respect to the triggering clock edge. The circuits of Figure 7-32 are easily modified to provide an EN input, as shown in Figure 7-34.

T flip-flop with enable

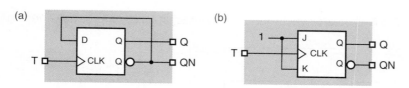

Figure 7-32
Possible circuit designs for a T flip-flop: (a) using a D flip-flop; (b) using a J-K flip-flop.

Figure 7-33 Positive-edge-triggered T flip-flop with enable: (a) logic symbol; (b) functional behavior.

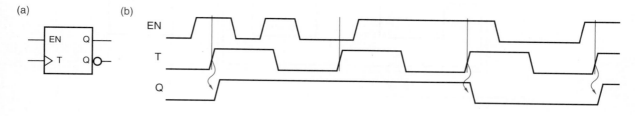

Figure 7-34
Possible circuits for a
T flip-flop with enable:
(a) using a D flip-flop;
(b) using a J-K flip-flop.

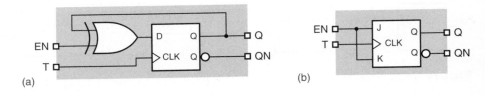

(a)   (b)

7.3 Clocked Synchronous State-Machine Analysis

Although latches and flip-flops, the basic building blocks of sequential circuits, are themselves feedback sequential circuits that can be formally analyzed (and are, in Section 7.9), we'll first study the operation of *clocked synchronous state machines*, since they are the easiest to understand. "State machine" is a generic name given to these sequential circuits; "clocked" refers to the fact that their storage elements (flip-flops) employ a clock input; and "synchronous" means that all of the flip-flops use the same clock signal. Such a state machine changes state only when a triggering edge or "tick" occurs on the clock signal.

clocked synchronous state machine

7.3.1 State-Machine Structure

Figure 7-35 shows the general structure of a clocked synchronous state machine. The *state memory* is a set of n flip-flops that store the current state of the machine, and it has 2^n distinct states. The flip-flops are all connected to a common clock signal that causes them to change state at each *tick* of the clock. What constitutes a tick depends on the flip-flop type (edge triggered, pulse triggered, etc.). For the positive-edge-triggered D flip-flops considered in this section, a tick is the rising edge of the clock signal.

state memory

tick

The next state of the state machine in Figure 7-35 is determined by the *next-state logic F* as a function of the current state and input. The *output logic G*

next-state logic
output logic

Figure 7-35 Clocked synchronous state-machine structure (Mealy machine).

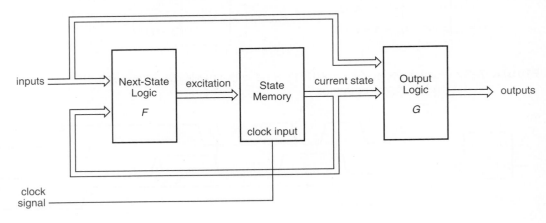

determines the output as a function of the current state and input. Both F and G are strictly combinational logic circuits. We can write

$$\text{Next state} = F(\text{current state, input})$$
$$\text{Output} = G(\text{current state, input})$$

State machines may use positive-edge-triggered D flip-flops for their state memory, in which case a tick occurs at each rising edge of the clock signal. It is also possible for the state memory to use negative-edge-triggered D flip-flops, D latches, or J-K flip-flops. However, inasmuch as most state machines are designed nowadays using PLDs, CPLDs, FPGAs, or ASICs with positive-edge-triggered D flip-flops, that's what we'll concentrate on.

7.3.2 Output Logic

A sequential circuit whose output depends on both state and input as shown in Figure 7-35 is called a *Mealy machine*. In some sequential circuits the output depends on the state alone:

Mealy machine

$$\text{Output} = G(\text{current state})$$

Such a circuit is called a *Moore machine*, and its general structure is shown in Figure 7-36.

Moore machine

Obviously, the only difference between the two state-machine models is in how outputs are generated. In practice, many state machines must be categorized as Mealy machines, because they have one or more *Mealy-type outputs* that depend on input as well as state. However, many of these same machines also have one or more *Moore-type outputs* that depend only on state.

Mealy-type outputs

Moore-type outputs

In the design of high-speed circuits, it is often necessary to ensure that state-machine outputs are available as early as possible and do not change during each clock period. One way to get this behavior is to encode the state so that the state variables themselves serve as outputs. We call this an *output-coded state assignment*; it yields a Moore machine in which the output logic of Figure 7-36 is nothing more than wires.

output-coded state assignment

Figure 7-36 Clocked synchronous state-machine structure (Moore machine).

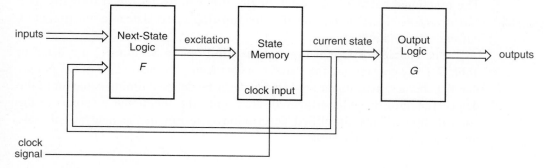

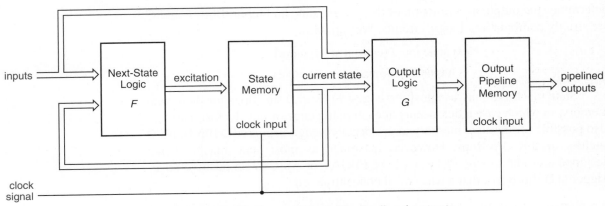

Figure 7-37 Mealy machine with pipelined outputs.

Another approach is to design the state machine so that the outputs during one clock period depend on the state and inputs during the *previous* clock period. We call these *pipelined outputs*, and they are obtained by attaching another stage of memory (flip-flops) to a machine's outputs, as shown for a Mealy machine in Figure 7-37.

With appropriate circuit or drawing manipulations, you can map one state-machine model into another. For example, you could declare the flip-flops that produce pipelined outputs from a Mealy machine to be part of its state memory and thereby obtain a Moore machine with an output-coded state assignment.

The exact classification of a state machine into one style or another is not so important. What's important is how you think about output structure and how it satisfies your overall design objectives, including timing and flexibility. For example, pipelined outputs are great for fast timing, but you can use them only in situations where you can figure out the desired next output value one clock period in advance. In any given application you may use different styles for different output signals. For example, we'll see in Section 7.11.5 that different statements can be used to specify different output styles in ABEL.

7.3.3 Characteristic Equations

The functional behavior of a latch or flip-flop can be described formally by a *characteristic equation* that specifies the flip-flop's next state as a function of its current state and inputs.

The characteristic equations of the flip-flops in Section 7.2 are listed in Table 7-1. By convention, the $*$ suffix in $Q*$ means "the next value of Q." Notice that the characteristic equation does not describe detailed timing behavior of the device (latching vs. edge-triggered, etc.), only the functional response to the control inputs. This simplified description is useful in the analysis of state machines, as we'll soon show.

Table 7-1
Latch and flip-flop
characteristic
equations.

Device Type	Characteristic Equation
S-R latch	$Q* = S + R' \cdot Q$
D latch	$Q* = D$
Edge-triggered D flip-flop	$Q* = D$
D flip-flop with enable	$Q* = EN \cdot D + EN' \cdot Q$
Master/slave S-R flip-flop	$Q* = S + R' \cdot Q$
Master/slave J-K flip-flop	$Q* = J \cdot Q' + K' \cdot Q$
Edge-triggered J-K flip-flop	$Q* = J \cdot Q' + K' \cdot Q$
T flip-flop	$Q* = Q'$
T flip-flop with enable	$Q* = EN \cdot Q' + EN' \cdot Q$

7.3.4 Analysis of State Machines with D Flip-Flops

Consider the formal definition of a state machine that we gave previously:

$$\text{Next state} = F(\text{current state, input})$$

$$\text{Output} = G(\text{current state, input})$$

Recalling our notion that "state" embodies all we need to know about the past history of the circuit, the first equation tells us that what we next need to know can be determined from what we currently know and the current input. The second equation tells us that the current output can be determined from the same information. The goal of sequential circuit analysis is to determine the next-state and output functions so that the behavior of a circuit can be predicted.

The analysis of a clocked synchronous state machine has three basic steps:

1. Determine the next-state and output functions F and G.

2. Use F and G to construct a *state/output table* that completely specifies the next state and output of the circuit for every possible combination of current state and input.

    state/output table

3. (Optional) Draw a *state diagram* that presents the information from the previous step in graphical form.

    state diagram

Figure 7-38 shows a simple state machine with two positive-edge-triggered D flip-flops. To determine the next-state function F, we must first consider the behavior of the state memory. At the rising edge of the clock signal, each D flip-flop samples its D input and transfers this value to its Q output; the characteristic equation of a D flip-flop is $Q* = D$. Therefore, to determine the next value of Q (i.e., Q^*), we must first determine the current value of D.

In Figure 7-38 there are two D flip-flops, and we have named the signals on their outputs Q0 and Q1. These two outputs are the state variables; their value is

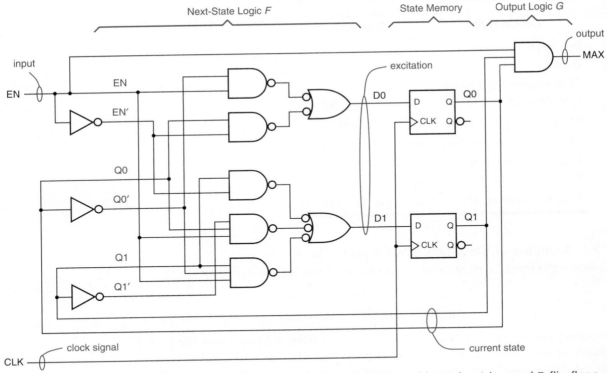

Figure 7-38 Clocked synchronous state machine using positive-edge-triggered D flip-flops.

excitation

excitation equation

the current state of the machine. We have named the signals on the corresponding D inputs D0 and D1. These signals provide the *excitation* for the D flip-flops at each clock tick. Logic equations that express the excitation signals as functions of the current state and input are called *excitation equations* and can be derived from the circuit diagram:

$$D0 = Q0 \cdot EN' + Q0' \cdot EN$$
$$D1 = Q1 \cdot EN' + Q1' \cdot Q0 \cdot EN + Q1 \cdot Q0' \cdot EN$$

As noted previously, the next value of a state variable after a clock tick is denoted by appending a star to the state-variable name, for example, Q0∗ or Q1∗. Using the characteristic equation of D flip-flops, Q∗ = D, we can describe the next-state function of the example machine with equations for the next value of the state variables:

$$Q0∗ = D0$$
$$Q1∗ = D1$$

Substituting the excitation equations for D0 and D1, we can write

$$Q0∗ = Q0 \cdot EN' + Q0' \cdot EN$$
$$Q1∗ = Q1 \cdot EN' + Q1' \cdot Q0 \cdot EN + Q1 \cdot Q0' \cdot EN$$

(a)

Q1 Q0	EN 0	1
00	00	01
01	01	10
10	10	11
11	11	00
	Q1* Q0*	

(b)

S	EN 0	1
A	A	B
B	B	C
C	C	D
D	D	A
	S*	

(c)

S	EN 0	1
A	A, 0	B, 0
B	B, 0	C, 0
C	C, 0	D, 0
D	D, 0	A, 1
	S*, MAX	

Table 7-2
Transition, state, and state/output tables for the state machine in Figure 7-38.

These equations, which express the next value of the state variables as a function of current state and input, are called *transition equations*.

transition equation

For each combination of current state and input value, the transition equations predict the next state. Each state is described by two bits, the current values of Q0 and Q1: (Q1 Q0) = 00, 01, 10, or 11. [The reason for "arbitrarily" picking the order (Q1 Q0) instead of (Q0 Q1) will become apparent shortly.] For each state, our example machine has just two possible input values, EN = 0 or EN = 1, so there are a total of 8 state/input combinations. (In general, a machine with s state bits and i inputs has 2^{s+i} state/input combinations.)

Table 7-2(a) shows a *transition table* that is created by evaluating the transition equations for every possible state/input combination. Traditionally, a transition table lists the states along the left and the input combinations along the top of the table, as shown in the example.

transition table

The function of our example machine is apparent from its transition table—it is a 2-bit binary counter with an enable input EN. When EN = 0, the machine maintains its current count, but when EN = 1, the count advances by 1 at each clock tick, rolling over to 00 when it reaches a maximum value of 11.

If we wish, we may assign alphanumeric *state names* to each state. The simplest naming is 00 = A, 01 = B, 10 = C, and 11 = D. Substituting the state names for combinations of Q1 and Q0 (and Q1* and Q0*) in Table 7-2(a) produces the *state table* in (b). Here "S" denotes the current state and "S*" denotes the next state of the machine. A state table is usually easier to understand than a transition table, because in complex machines we can use state names that have meaning. However, a state table contains less information than a transition table because it does not indicate the binary values assumed by the state variables in each named state.

state names

state table

Once a state table is produced, we have only the output logic of the machine left to analyze. In the example machine there is only a single output signal, and it is a function of both current state and input (this is a Mealy machine). So we can write a single *output equation*:

output equation

$$MAX = Q1 \cdot Q0 \cdot EN$$

The output behavior predicted by this equation can be combined with the next-state information to produce a *state/output table* as shown in Table 7-2(c).

state/output table

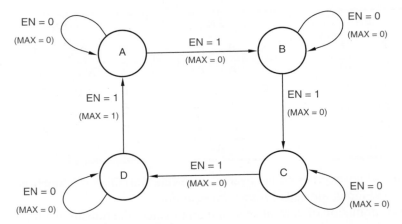

Figure 7-39
State diagram
corresponding to the
state machine of
Table 7-2.

State/output tables for Moore machines are slightly simpler. For example, in the circuit of Figure 7-38 suppose we removed the EN signal from the AND gate that produces the MAX output, producing a Moore-type output MAXS. Then MAXS is a function of the state only, and the state/output table can list MAXS in a single column, independent of the input values. This is shown in Table 7-3.

state diagram
node
directed arc

A *state diagram* presents the information from the state/output table in a graphical format. It has one circle (or *node*) for each state and an arrow (or *directed arc*) for each transition. Figure 7-39 shows the state diagram for our example state machine. The letter inside each circle is a state name. Each arrow leaving a given state points to the next state for a given input combination; it also shows the output value produced in the given state for that input combination.

The state diagram for a Moore machine can be somewhat simpler. In this case, the output values can be shown inside each state circle, since they are

Table 7-3
State/output table for
a Moore machine.

	EN		
S	0	1	MAXS
A	A	B	0
B	B	C	0
C	C	D	0
D	D	A	1
		S*	

A CLARIFICATION   The state-diagram notation for output values in Mealy machines is a little misleading. You should remember that the listed output value is produced continuously when the machine is in the indicated state and has the indicated input, not just during the transition to the next state.

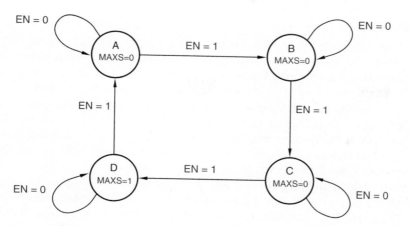

Figure 7-40
State diagram
corresponding to the
state machine of
Table 7-3.

functions of state only. The state diagram for a Moore machine using this convention is shown in Figure 7-40.

The original logic diagram of our example state machine, Figure 7-38, was laid out to match our conceptual model of a Mealy machine. However, nothing requires us to group the next-state logic, state memory, and output logic in this way. Figure 7-41 shows another logic diagram for the same state machine. To analyze this circuit, the designer (or analyzer, in this case) can still extract the required information from the diagram as drawn. The only circuit difference in

Figure 7-41 Redrawn logic diagram for a clocked synchronous state machine.

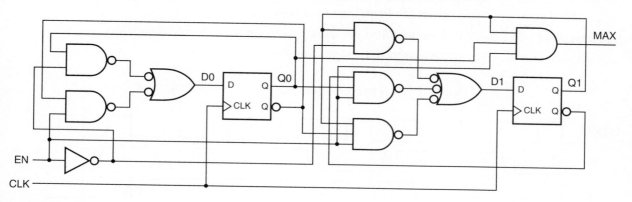

SUGGESTIVE
DRAWINGS

Using the transition, state, and output tables, we can construct a timing diagram that shows the behavior of a state machine for any desired starting state and input sequence. For example, Figure 7-42 shows the behavior of our example machine with a starting state of 00 (A) and a particular pattern on the EN input.

Notice that the value of the EN input affects the next state only at the rising edge of the CLOCK input; that is, the counter counts only if EN = 1 at the rising edge of CLOCK. On the other hand, since MAX is a Mealy-type output, its value is affected by EN at all times. If we also provide a Moore-type output MAXS as suggested in the text, its value depends only on state as shown in the figure.

The timing diagram is drawn in a way that shows changes in the MAX and MAXS outputs occurring slightly later than the state and input changes that cause them, reflecting the combinational-logic delay of the output circuits. Naturally, the drawings are merely suggestive; precise timing is normally indicated by a timing table of the type suggested in Section 6.2.1.

the new diagram is that we have used the flip-flops' QN outputs (which are normally the complement of Q) to save a couple of inverters.

In summary, the detailed steps for analyzing a clocked synchronous state machine are as follows:

excitation equations   1. Determine the excitation equations for the flip-flop control inputs.

transition equations   2. Substitute the excitation equations into the flip-flop characteristic equations to obtain transition equations.

transition table   3. Use the transition equations to construct a transition table.

output equations   4. Determine the output equations.

Figure 7-42 Timing diagram for example state machine.

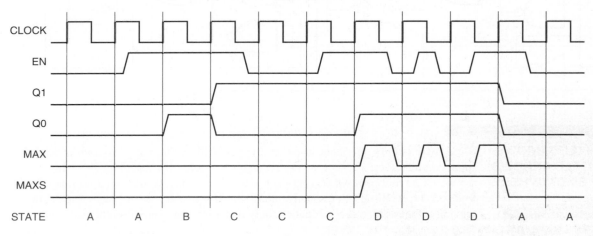

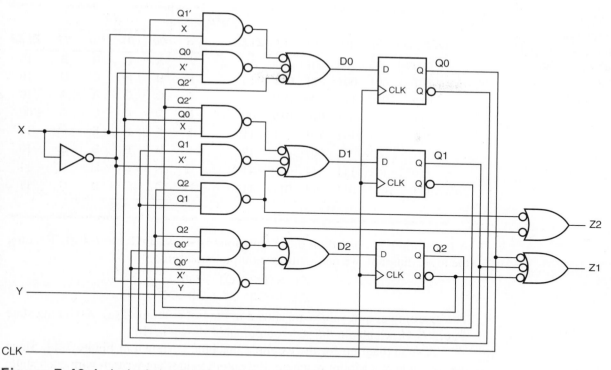

Figure 7-43 A clocked synchronous state machine with three flip-flops and eight states.

5. Add output values to the transition table for each state (Moore) or state/ *transition/output table*
   input combination (Mealy) to create a transition/output table.

6. Name the states and substitute state names for state-variable combinations *state names*
   in the transition/output table to obtain a state/output table. *state/output table*

7. (Optional) Draw a state diagram corresponding to the state/output table. *state diagram*

We'll go through this complete sequence of steps to analyze another clocked synchronous state machine, shown in Figure 7-43. Reading the logic diagram, we find that the excitation equations are as follows:

$$D0 = Q1' \cdot X + Q0 \cdot X' + Q2$$
$$D1 = Q2' \cdot Q0 \cdot X + Q1 \cdot X' + Q2 \cdot Q1$$
$$D2 = Q2 \cdot Q0' + Q0' \cdot X' \cdot Y$$

Substituting into the characteristic equation for D flip-flops, we obtain the transition equations:

$$Q0* = Q1' \cdot X + Q0 \cdot X' + Q2$$
$$Q1* = Q2' \cdot Q0 \cdot X + Q1 \cdot X' + Q2 \cdot Q1$$
$$Q2* = Q2 \cdot Q0' + Q0' \cdot X' \cdot Y$$

Table 7-4
Transition/output
and state/output
tables for the
state machine
in Figure 7-43.

(a)

Q2 Q1 Q0	XY 00	01	10	11	Z1 Z2
000	000	100	001	001	10
001	001	001	011	011	10
010	010	110	000	000	10
011	011	011	010	010	00
100	101	101	101	101	11
101	001	001	001	001	10
110	111	111	111	111	11
111	011	011	011	011	11
	Q2* Q1* Q0*				

(b)

S	XY 00	01	10	11	Z1 Z2
A	A	E	B	B	10
B	B	B	D	D	10
C	C	G	A	A	10
D	D	D	C	C	00
E	F	F	F	F	11
F	B	B	B	B	10
G	H	H	H	H	11
H	D	D	D	D	11
	S*				

A transition table based on these equations is shown in Table 7-4(a). Reading the logic diagram, we can write two output equations:

$$Z1 = Q2 + Q1' + Q0'$$
$$Z2 = Q2 \cdot Q1 + Q2 \cdot Q0'$$

The resulting output values are shown in the last column of (a). Assigning state names A–H, we obtain the state/output table shown in (b).

A state diagram for the example machine is shown in Figure 7-44. Since our example is a Moore machine, the output values are written with each state. Each arc is labeled with a *transition expression*; a transition is taken for input combinations for which the transition expression is 1. Transitions labeled "1" are always taken.

transition expression

Figure 7-44 State diagram corresponding to Table 7-4.

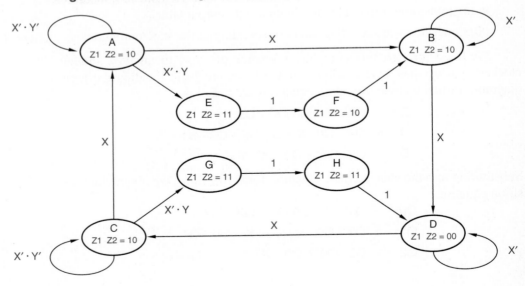

The transition expressions on arcs leaving a particular state must be mutually exclusive and all-inclusive, as explained below:

- No two transition expressions can equal 1 for the same input combination, *mutual exclusion* since a machine can't have two next states for one input combination.

- For every possible input combination, some transition expression must *all inclusion* equal 1, so that all next states are defined.

Starting with the state table, a transition expression for a particular current state and next state can be written as a sum of minterms for the input combinations that cause that transition. If desired, the expression can then be minimized to give the information in a more compact form. Transition expressions are most useful in the *design* of state machines, where the expressions may be developed from the word description of the problem, as we'll show in Section 7.5.

STATE-MACHINE ANALYSIS WITH J-K FLIP-FLOPS
As we mentioned previously, J-K flip-flops are not used much any more in state-machine design. However, you or your parents might have some ancient equipment with J-K flip-flops in your basement or attic. So, we show how to analyze state machines that use J-K flip-flops in Section JKanal at DDPPonline.

7.4 Clocked Synchronous State-Machine Design

The steps for designing a clocked synchronous state machine, starting from a word description or specification, are just about the reverse of the analysis steps that we used in the preceding section:

1. Construct a state/output table corresponding to the word description or *state/output table* specification, using mnemonic names for the states. (It's also possible to start with a state diagram; this method is discussed in Section 7.5.)

2. (Optional) Minimize the number of states in the state/output table. *state minimization*

3. Choose a set of state variables and assign state-variable combinations to *state assignment* the named states.

4. Substitute the state-variable combinations into the state/output table to *transition/output table* create a transition/output table that shows the desired next state-variable combination and output for each state/input combination.

5. Choose a flip-flop type (usually, edge-triggered D) for the state memory. In most cases you'll already have a choice in mind at the outset of the design, but this step is your last chance to change your mind.

6. Construct an excitation table that shows the excitation values required to *excitation table* obtain the desired next state for each state/input combination.

7. Derive excitation equations from the excitation table. *excitation equations*

output equations

logic diagram

8. Derive output equations from the transition/output table.

9. Draw a logic diagram that shows the state-variable storage elements and realizes the required excitation and output equations. (Or realize the equations directly in a programmable logic device.)

design

In this section we'll describe each of these basic steps in state-machine design. Step 1 is the most important, since it is here that the designer really *designs*, going through the creative process of translating a (perhaps ambiguous) English-language description of the state machine into a formal tabular description. Step 2 is hardly ever performed by experienced digital designers, but designers bring much of their experience to bear in step 3.

Once the first three steps are completed, all of the remaining steps can be completed by "turning the crank," that is, by following a well-defined synthesis procedure. Steps 4 and 6–9 are the most tedious, but they are usually automated. You can use an HDL compiler to do the cranking, as we show later for ABEL, VHDL, and Verilog. Still, it's important for you to understand the details of the synthesis procedure, both to give you an appreciation of the compiler's function and to give you a chance of figuring out what's really going on when the compiler produces unexpected results. Therefore, all nine steps of the state-machine design procedure are discussed in the remainder of this section.

7.4.1 State-Table Design Example

There are several different ways to describe a state machine's state table. Later, we'll see how ABEL, VHDL, and Verilog can specify state tables indirectly. In this section, however, we deal only with state tables that are specified directly, in the same tabular format that we used in the previous section for analysis.

We'll present the state-table design process as well as the synthesis procedure in later subsections, using the simple design problem below:

Design a clocked synchronous state machine with two inputs, A and B, and a single output Z that is 1 if:

  – A had the same value at each of the two previous clock ticks, *or*

  – B has been 1 since the last time that the first condition was true.

Otherwise, the output should be 0.

If the meaning of this specification isn't crystal clear to you at this point, don't worry. Part of your job as a designer is to convert such a specification into a state table (or HDL equivalent) that is absolutely unambiguous. Even if the state table doesn't match what was originally intended, it at least forms a basis for further discussion and refinement.

As an additional "hint" or requirement, state-table design problems often include timing diagrams that show the state machine's expected behavior for one or more sequences of inputs. Such a timing diagram is unlikely to specify unambiguously the machine's behavior for all possible sequences of inputs, but,

<table>
<tr><td>

STATE-MACHINE DESIGN AS A KIND OF PROGRAMMING

</td><td>

Designing a state machine (using a state table, a state diagram, or an HDL) is a creative process that is like writing a computer program in many ways:

- You start with a fairly precise description of inputs and outputs, but a possibly ambiguous description of the desired relationship between them, and usually no clue about how to actually obtain the desired outputs from the inputs.

- During the design you may have to identify and choose among different ways of doing things, sometimes using common sense, and sometimes arbitrarily.

- You may have to identify and handle special cases that weren't included in the original description.

- You will probably have to keep track of several ideas in your head during the design process.

- Since the design process is not an algorithm, there's no guarantee that you can complete the state table or program using a finite number of states or lines of code. However, unless you work for the government, you must try to do so.

- When you finally run the state machine or program, it will do exactly what you told it to do—no more, no less.

- There's no guarantee that the thing will work the first time; you may have to debug and iterate on the whole process.

- HDL "programs" that specify state machines actually do look an awful lot like other computer programs!

Although state-machine design is a challenge, there's no need to be intimidated. If you've made it this far in your education, then you've written a few computer programs that worked, and you can become just as good at designing state machines.

</td></tr>
</table>

again, it's a good starting point for discussion and a benchmark against which proposed designs can be checked. Figure 7-45 is such a timing diagram for our example state-table design problem.

The first step in the state-table design is to construct a template. From the word description, we know that our example is a Moore machine—its output depends only on the current state, that is, what happened in previous clock

Figure 7-45 Timing diagram for example state machine.

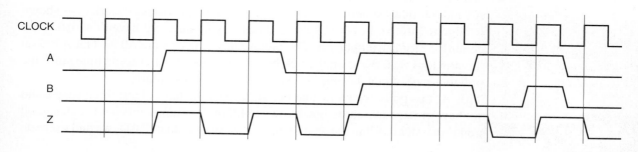

(a)

Meaning	S	A B				Z
		00	01	11	10	
Initial state	INIT					0
		. . .				
		. . .				
		. . .				
			S*			

(b)

Meaning	S	A B				Z
		00	01	11	10	
Initial state	INIT	A0	A0	A1	A1	0
Got a 0 on A	A0					0
Got a 1 on A	A1					0
			S*			

(c)

Meaning	S	A B				Z
		00	01	11	10	
Initial state	INIT	A0	A0	A1	A1	0
Got a 0 on A	A0	OK	OK	A1	A1	0
Got a 1 on A	A1					0
Got two equal A inputs	OK					1
			S*			

(d)

Meaning	S	A B				Z
		00	01	11	10	
Initial state	INIT	A0	A0	A1	A1	0
Got a 0 on A	A0	OK	OK	A1	A1	0
Got a 1 on A	A1	A0	A0	OK	OK	0
Got two equal A inputs	OK					1
			S*			

Figure 7-46 Evolution of a state table.

periods. Thus, as shown in Figure 7-46(a), we provide one next-state column for each possible input combination and a single column for the output values. The order in which the input combinations are written doesn't affect this part of the process, but we've written them in Karnaugh-map order to simplify the derivation of excitation equations later. In a Mealy machine we would omit the output column and write the output values along with the next-state values under each input combination. The leftmost column is simply an English-language reminder of the meaning of each state or the "history" associated with it.

The word description isn't specific about what happens when this machine is first started, so we'll just have to improvise. We'll assume that when power is first applied to the system, the machine enters an *initial state*, called INIT in this example. We write the name of the initial state (INIT) in the first row and leave room for enough rows (states) to complete the design. We can also fill in the value of Z for the INIT state; common sense says it should be 0 because there were *no* inputs beforehand.

initial state

Next, we must fill in the next-state entries for the INIT row. The Z output can't be 1 until we've seen at least two inputs on A, so we'll provide two states, A0 and A1, that "remember" the value of A on the previous clock tick, as shown in Figure 7-46(b). In both of these states Z is 0, since we haven't satisfied the conditions for a 1 output yet. The precise meaning of state A0 is "Got A = 0 on the previous tick, A ≠ 0 on the tick before that, and B ≠ 1 at some time since the previous pair of equal A inputs." State A1 is defined similarly.

At this point we know that our state machine has at least three states, and we have created two more blank rows to fill in. Hmmmm, this isn't such a good trend! In order to fill in the next-state entries for *one* state (INIT), we had to create

(a)

Meaning	S	A B				Z
		00	01	11	10	
Initial state	INIT	A0	A0	A1	A1	0
Got a 0 on A	A0	OK	OK	A1	A1	0
Got a 1 on A	A1	A0	A0	OK	OK	0
Got two equal A inputs	OK	?	OK	OK	?	1
		S*				

(b)

Meaning	S	A B				Z
		00	01	11	10	
Initial state	INIT	A0	A0	A1	A1	0
Got a 0 on A	A0	OK0	OK0	A1	A1	0
Got a 1 on A	A1	A0	A0	OK1	OK1	0
Two equal, A=0 last	OK0					1
Two equal, A=1 last	OK1					1
		S*				

(c)

Meaning	S	A B				Z
		00	01	11	10	
Initial state	INIT	A0	A0	A1	A1	0
Got a 0 on A	A0	OK0	OK0	A1	A1	0
Got a 1 on A	A1	A0	A0	OK1	OK1	0
Two equal, A=0 last	OK0	OK0	OK0	OK1	A1	1
Two equal, A=1 last	OK1					1
		S*				

(d)

Meaning	S	A B				Z
		00	01	11	10	
Initial state	INIT	A0	A0	A1	A1	0
Got a 0 on A	A0	OK0	OK0	A1	A1	0
Got a 1 on A	A1	A0	A0	OK1	OK1	0
Two equal, A=0 last	OK0	OK0	OK0	OK1	A1	1
Two equal, A=1 last	OK1	A0	OK0	OK1	OK1	1
		S*				

Figure 7-47 Continued evolution of a state table.

two new states A0 and A1. If we kept going this way, we could end up with 65,535 states by bedtime! Instead, we should be on the lookout for existing states that have the same meaning as new ones that we might otherwise create. Let's see how it goes.

In state A0, we know that input A was 0 at the previous clock tick. Therefore, if A is 0 again, we go to a new state OK with Z = 1, as shown in Figure 7-46(c). If A is 1, then we don't have two equal inputs in a row, so we go to state A1 to remember that we just got a 1. Likewise in state A1, shown in (d), we go to OK if we get a second 1 input in a row, or to A0 if we get a 0.

Once we get into the OK state, the machine description tells us we can stay there as long as B = 1, irrespective of the A input, as shown in Figure 7-47(a). If B = 0, we have to look for two 1s or two 0s in a row on A again. However, we've got a little problem in this case. The current A input may or may not be the second equal input in a row, so we may still be "OK" or we may have to go back to A0 or A1. We defined the OK state too broadly—it doesn't "remember" enough to tell us which way to go.

The problem is solved in Figure 7-47(b) by splitting OK into two states, OK0 and OK1, that "remember" the previous A input. All of the next states for OK0 and OK1 can be selected from existing states, as shown in (c) and (d). For example, if we get A = 0 in OK0, we can just stay in OK0; we don't have to create a new state that "remembers" three 0s in a row, because the machine's description doesn't require us to distinguish that case. Thus, we have achieved "closure" of the state table, which now describes a *finite*-state machine. As a sanity check, Figure 7-48 repeats the timing diagram of Figure 7-45, listing the states that should be visited according to our final state table.

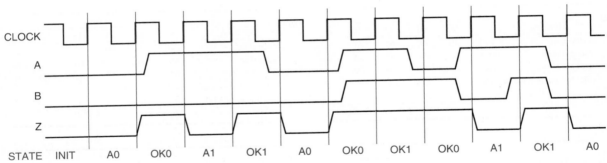

Figure 7-48 Timing diagram and state sequence for example state machine.

REALIZING RELIABLE RESET	For proper system operation, the hardware design of a state machine should ensure that it enters a known initial state on power-up, such as the INIT state in our design example. Most systems have a RESET signal that is asserted during power-up.

The RESET signal is typically generated by an analog circuit. During power-up, such a reset circuit typically detects a voltage (say, 4.5 V) close to the power supply's full voltage, and follows that with a delay (say, 100 ms) to ensure that all components (including oscillators) have had time to stabilize before it "unresets" the system. The Texas Instruments TL7705 is such an analog reset IC; it has an internal 4.5-V reference for the detector and uses an external resistor and capacitor to determine the "unreset" time constant. The TL7705 will also reassert RESET if the power-supply voltage ever falls below the reference voltage.

If a state machine is built using discrete flip-flops with asynchronous preset and clear inputs, the RESET signal can be applied to these inputs to force the machine into the desired initial state. If preset and clear inputs are not available, or if reset must be synchronous (as in systems using high-speed microprocessors), then the RESET signal may be used as another input to the state machine, with all of the next-state entries going to the desired initial state when RESET is asserted.

7.4.2 State Minimization

Figure 7-47(d) is a "minimal" state table for our original word description, in the sense that it contains the fewest possible states. However, Figure 7-49 shows other state tables, with more states, that also do the job. Formal procedures can be used to minimize the number of states in such tables.

equivalent states

The basic idea of formal minimization procedures is to identify *equivalent states*, where two states are equivalent if it is impossible to distinguish them by observing only the current and future *outputs* of the machine (and *not* the internal state variables). A pair of equivalent states can be replaced by a single state.

Two states S1 and S2 are equivalent if two conditions are true. First, S1 and S2 must produce the same values at the state-machine output(s); in a Mealy

(a)

Meaning	S	A B				Z
		00	01	11	10	
Initial state	INIT	A0	A0	A1	A1	0
Got a 0 on A	A0	OK00	OK00	A1	A1	0
Got a 1 on A	A1	A0	A0	OK11	OK11	0
Got 00 on A	OK00	OK00	OK00	OKA1	A1	1
Got 11 on A	OK11	A0	OKA0	OK11	OK11	1
OK, got a 0 on A	OKA0	OK00	OK00	OKA1	A1	1
OK, got a 1 on A	OKA1	A0	OKA0	OK11	OK11	1
			S*			

(b)

Meaning	S	A B				Z
		00	01	11	10	
Initial state	INIT	A0	A0	A1	A1	0
Got a 0 on A	A0	OK00	OK00	A1	A1	0
Got a 1 on A	A1	A0	A0	OK11	OK11	0
Got 00 on A	OK00	OK00	OK00	A001	A1	1
Got 11 on A	OK11	A0	A110	OK11	OK11	1
Got 001 on A, B=1	A001	A0	AE10	OK11	OK11	1
Got 110 on A, B=1	A110	OK00	OK00	AE01	A1	1
Got bb...10 on A, B=1	AE10	OK00	OK00	AE01	A1	1
Got bb...01 on A, B=1	AE01	A0	AE10	OK11	OK11	1
			S*			

Figure 7-49 Nonminimal state tables equivalent to Figure 7-47(d).

machine, this must be true for all input combinations. Second, for each input combination, S1 and S2 must have either the same next state or equivalent next states.

Thus, a formal state-minimization procedure shows that states OK00 and OKA0 in Figure 7-49(a) are equivalent because they produce the same output and their next-state entries are identical. Since the states are equivalent, state OK00 may be eliminated and its occurrences in the table replaced by OKA0, or vice versa. Likewise, states OK11 and OKA1 are equivalent.

To minimize the state table in Figure 7-49(b), a formal procedure must use a bit of circular reasoning. States OK00, A110, and AE10 all produce the same output and have almost identical next-state entries, so they might be equivalent. They are equivalent only if A001 and AE01 are equivalent. Similarly, OK11, A001, and AE01 are equivalent only if A110 and AE10 are equivalent. In other words, the states in the first set are equivalent if the states in the second set are, and vice versa. So, let's just go ahead and say they're equivalent.

IS THIS REALLY ALL NECESSARY?

Details of formal state-minimization procedures are discussed in advanced textbooks, cited in the References. However, these procedures are seldom used by most digital designers.

By carefully matching state meanings to the requirements of the problem, experienced digital designers produce state tables for small problems with a minimal or near-minimal number of states, without ever using a formal minimization procedure. Also, there are situations where *increasing* the number of states may simplify the design or reduce its cost, so even an automated state-minimization procedure doesn't necessarily help. A designer can do more to simplify a state machine during the state-assignment phase of the design, discussed in the next subsection.

INITIAL VERSUS IDLE STATES The example state machine that we've been designing visits its initial state only during reset. Many machines are designed instead with an "idle" state that is entered both at reset and whenever the machine has nothing in particular to do.

7.4.3 State Assignment

coded state
total number of states

The next step in the design process is to determine how many binary variables are required to represent the states in the state table, and to assign a specific combination to each named state. We'll call the binary combination assigned to a particular state a *coded state*. The *total number of states* in a machine with n flip-flops is 2^n, so the number of flip-flops needed to code s states is $\lceil \log_2 s \rceil$, the smallest integer greater than or equal to $\log_2 s$.

unused states

For reference, the state/output table of our example machine is repeated in Table 7-5. It has five states, so it requires three flip-flops. Of course, three flip-flops provide a total of eight states, so there will be $8 - 5 = 3$ *unused states*. We'll discuss alternatives for handling the unused states at the end of this subsection. Right now, we have to deal with lots of choices for the five coded states.

Table 7-5
State and output table for example problem.

	A B				
S	*00*	*01*	*11*	*10*	*Z*
INIT	A0	A0	A1	A1	0
A0	OK0	OK0	A1	A1	0
A1	A0	A0	OK1	OK1	0
OK0	OK0	OK0	OK1	A1	1
OK1	A0	OK0	OK1	OK1	1
			S*		

The simplest assignment of s coded states to 2^n possible states is to use the first s binary integers in binary counting order, as shown in the first assignment column of Table 7-6. However, the simplest state assignment does not always lead to the simplest excitation equations, output equations, and resulting logic circuit. In fact, the state assignment often has a major effect on circuit cost, and it may interact with other factors, such as the choice of storage elements (e.g., D vs. J-K flip-flops) and the realization approach for excitation and output logic (e.g., a sum of products, a product of sums, or an ad hoc design).

So, how do we choose the best state assignment for a given problem? In general, the only formal way to find the *best* assignment is to try *all* the assignments. That's too much work, even for students. Instead, most digital designers

CAUTION: MATH   The number of different ways to choose m coded states out of a set of n possible states is given by a *binomial coefficient*, denoted $\binom{n}{m}$, whose value is $\frac{n!}{m! \cdot (n-m)!}$. (We used binomial coefficients previously in Section 2.10 in the context of decimal coding.) In our example, there are $\binom{8}{5}$ different ways to choose five coded states out of eight possible states, and 5! ways to assign the five named states to each different choice. So there are $\frac{8!}{5! \cdot 3!} \cdot 5!$ or 6720 different ways to assign the five states of our example machine to combinations of three binary state variables. We don't have time to look at all of them.

rely on experience and several practical guidelines for making reasonable state assignments:

- Choose an initial coded state into which the machine can easily be forced at reset (00. . . 00 or 11. . . 11 in typical circuits).

- Minimize the number of state variables that change on each transition.

- Maximize the number of state variables that don't change in a group of related states (i.e., a group of states in which most transitions stay in the group).

- Exploit symmetries in the problem specification and the corresponding symmetries in the state table. That is, suppose that one state or group of states means almost the same thing as another. Once an assignment has been established for the first, a similar assignment, differing only in one bit, should be used for the second.

- If there are unused states (i.e., if $s < 2^n$ where $n = \lceil \log_2 s \rceil$), then choose the "best" of the available state-variable combinations to achieve the foregoing goals. That is, don't limit the choice of coded states to the first s n-bit integers.

- Decompose the set of state variables into individual bits or fields, where each bit or field has a well-defined meaning with respect to the input effects or output behavior of the machine.

- Consider using more than the minimum number of state variables to make a decomposed assignment possible.

Some of these ideas are incorporated in the "decomposed" state assignment in Table 7-6. As before, the initial state is 000, which is easy to force either asynchronously (applying the RESET signal to the flip-flop CLR inputs) or synchronously (by ANDing RESET′ with all of the D flip-flop inputs). After this

Table 7-6
Possible state
assignments for the
state machine in
Table 7-5.

State Name	Assignment			
	Simplest Q1–Q3	Decomposed Q1–Q3	One-Hot Q1–Q5	Almost One-Hot Q1–Q4
INIT	000	000	00001	0000
A0	001	100	00010	0001
A1	010	101	00100	0010
OK0	011	110	01000	0100
OK1	100	111	10000	1000

point, the assignment takes advantage of the fact that there are only four states in addition to INIT, which is a fairly "special" state that is never reentered once the machine gets going. Therefore, Q1 can be used to indicate whether or not the machine is in the INIT state, and when Q1 is 1, Q2 and Q3 can be used to distinguish among the four non-INIT states.

The non-INIT states in the "decomposed" column of Table 7-6 appear to have been assigned in binary counting order, but that's just a coincidence. State bits Q2 and Q3 actually have individual meanings in the context of the state machine's inputs and output. Q3 gives the previous value of A, and Q2 indicates that the conditions for a 1 output are satisfied in the current state. By decomposing the state-bit meanings in this way, we can expect the next-state and output logic to be simpler than in a "random" assignment of Q2,Q3 combinations to the non-INIT states. We'll continue the state-machine design based on this assignment in a later subsection.

one-hot assignment

Another useful state assignment, one that can be adapted to any state machine, is the *one-hot assignment* shown in Table 7-6. This assignment uses more than the minimum number of state variables—it uses one bit per state. In addition to being simple, a one-hot assignment has the advantage of usually leading to small excitation equations, since each flip-flop must be set to 1 for transitions into only one state.

An obvious disadvantage of a one-hot assignment, especially for machines with many states, is that it requires (many) more than the minimum number of flip-flops. However, the one-hot encoding is ideal for a machine with *s* states that is required to have a set of 1-out-of-*s* coded outputs indicating its current state. The one-hot-coded flip-flop outputs can be used directly for this purpose, with no additional combinational output logic.

The last column of Table 7-6 is an "almost one-hot assignment" that uses the "no-hot" combination for the initial state. This makes a lot of sense for two reasons: it's easy to initialize most storage devices to the all-0s state, and the initial state in this machine is never revisited once the machine gets going. Completing the state-machine design using this state assignment is considered in Exercise 7.48.

Now let's consider the disposition of *unused states* when the number of   *unused states*
states available with n flip-flops, 2^n, exceeds the number of states required, s.
There are two reasonable approaches, depending on the design requirements:

- *Minimal risk.* This approach assumes that it is possible for the state machine somehow to get into one of the unused (or "illegal") states, perhaps because of a hardware failure, an unexpected input, or a design error. Therefore, all of the unused state-variable combinations are identified and explicit next-state entries are made so that, for any input combination, the unused states go to the "initial" state, the "idle" state, or some other "safe" state. This is an automatic consequence of some design methodologies if the initial state is coded 00. . . 00.

- *Minimal cost.* This approach assumes that the machine will never enter an unused state. Therefore, in the transition and excitation tables, the next-state entries of the unused states can be marked as "don't-cares." In most cases this simplifies the excitation logic. However, the machine's behavior if it ever does enter an unused state may be pretty weird.

We'll look at both as we complete the design of our example state machine.

7.4.4 Synthesis Using D Flip-Flops

Once we've assigned coded states to the named states of a machine, the rest of
the design process is pretty much "turning the crank." In fact, in later sections
we'll describe software tools that can turn the crank for you when you design a
state machine using an HDL. Just so that you'll appreciate those tools, however,
we'll go through the process by hand in this subsection.

Coded states are substituted for named states in the (possibly minimized)
state table to obtain a *transition table*. The transition table shows the next coded   *transition table*
state for each combination of current coded state and input. Table 7-7 shows the
transition and output table that is obtained from the example state machine of
Table 7-5 on page 560 using the "decomposed" assignment of Table 7-6.

The next step is to write an *excitation table* that shows, for each combina-   *excitation table*
tion of coded state and input, the flip-flop excitation input values needed to make

Table 7-7
Transition and output
table for example
problem.

Q1 Q2 Q3	AB				Z
	00	01	11	10	
000	100	100	101	101	0
100	110	110	101	101	0
101	100	100	111	111	0
110	110	110	111	101	1
111	100	110	111	111	1
	Q1* Q2* Q3*				

the machine go to the desired next coded state. The structure and content of this table depend on the type of flip-flops that are used (D, J-K, T, etc.). We *usually* have a particular flip-flop type in mind at the beginning of a design—and we *certainly* do in this subsection, given its title. In fact, most state-machine designs nowadays use D flip-flops, because of their availability in both discrete packages and programmable logic devices, and because of their ease of use (compare with J-K flip-flops in <u>Section JKSM.2</u> at <u>DDPPonline</u>).

Of all flip-flop types, a D flip-flop has the simplest characteristic equation, $Q* = D$. Each D flip-flop in a state machine has a single excitation input, D, and the excitation table must show the value required at each flip-flop's D input for each coded-state/input combination. Table 7-8 shows the excitation table for our example problem. Since $D = Q*$, the excitation table is identical to the transition table, except for labeling of its entries. Thus, with D flip-flops, you don't really need to write a separate excitation table; you can just call the first table a *transition/excitation table*.

transition/excitation table

The excitation table is like a truth table for three combinational logic functions (D1, D2, D3) of five variables (A, B, Q1, Q2, Q3). Accordingly, we can design circuits to realize these functions using any of the combinational design methods at our disposal. In particular, we can transfer the information in the excitation table to Karnaugh maps, which we may call *excitation maps*, and find a minimal sum-of-products or product-of-sums expression for each function.

excitation maps

Excitation maps for our example state machine are shown in Figure 7-50. Each function, such as D1, has five variables and therefore uses a *5-variable Karnaugh map*. A 5-variable map is drawn as a pair of 4-variable maps, where cells in the same position in the two maps are considered to be adjacent. These maps are a bit unwieldy, but if you want to design by hand any but the most trivial state machines, you're going to get stuck with 5-variable maps and worse. At least we had the foresight to label the input combinations of the original state table in Karnaugh-map order, which makes it easier to transfer information to the maps in this step. However, note that the *states* were not assigned in Karnaugh-map order; in particular, the rows for states 110 and 111 are in the opposite order in the map as in the excitation table.

5-variable Karnaugh map

Table 7-8
Excitation and output table for Table 7-7 using D flip-flops.

	A B				
Q1 Q2 Q3	**00**	**01**	**11**	**10**	**Z**
000	100	100	101	101	0
100	110	110	101	101	0
101	100	100	111	111	0
110	110	110	111	101	1
111	100	110	111	111	1
			D1 D2 D3		

It is in this step, transferring the excitation table to excitation maps, that we discover why the excitation table is not quite a truth table—it does not specify functional values for *all* input combinations. In particular, the next-state information for the unused states, 001, 010, and 011, is not specified. Here we must make a choice, discussed in the preceding subsection, between a minimal-risk and a minimal-cost strategy for handling the unused states. Figure 7-50 has taken the minimal-risk approach: The next state for each unused state and input combination is 000, the INIT state. The three rows of colored 0s in each Karnaugh map are the result of this choice. With the maps completely filled in, we can now obtain minimal sum-of-products expressions for the flip-flop excitation inputs:

$$D1 = Q1 + Q2' \cdot Q3'$$
$$D2 = Q1 \cdot Q3' \cdot A' + Q1 \cdot Q3 \cdot A + Q1 \cdot Q2 \cdot B$$
$$D3 = Q1 \cdot A + Q2' \cdot Q3' \cdot A$$

An output equation can easily be developed directly from the information in Table 7-8. The output equation is simpler than the excitation equations, because the output is a function of state only. We could use a Karnaugh map, but it's easy to find a minimal-risk output function algebraically, by writing it as the sum of the minterms for the two coded states (110 and 111) in which Z is 1:

$$Z = Q1 \cdot Q2 \cdot Q3' + Q1 \cdot Q2 \cdot Q3$$
$$= Q1 \cdot Q2$$

At this point, we're just about done with the state-machine design. If the state machine is going to be built with discrete flip-flops and gates, then the final step is to draw a logic diagram. On the other hand, if we are using a programmable logic device, then we only have to enter the excitation and output equations

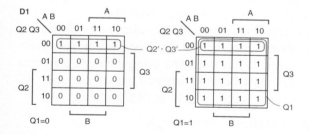

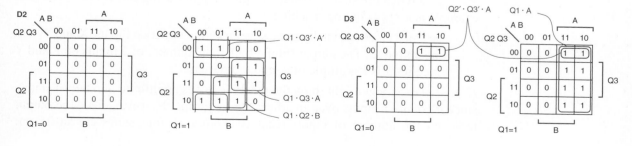

Figure 7-50
Excitation maps for D1, D2, and D3 assuming that unused states go to state 000.

MINIMAL-COST SOLUTION	If we choose in our example to derive minimal-cost excitation equations, we write "don't-cares" in the next-state entries for the unused states. The resulting excitation equations are somewhat simpler than before:

$$D1 = 1$$
$$D2 = Q1 \cdot Q3' \cdot A' + Q3 \cdot A + Q2 \cdot B$$
$$D3 = A$$

For a minimal-cost output function, the value of Z is a "don't-care" for the unused states. This leads to an even simpler output function, $Z = Q2$. (Map minimization with "don't cares" is covered in Section Min.2 at DDPPonline.)

into a computer file that specifies how to program the device, as an example shows in Section 7.11.1. Or, if we were thinking ahead, we specified the machine using an HDL like ABEL, VHDL, or Verilog in the first place, and the computer did all the work in this subsection for us!

*7.4.5 Synthesis Using J-K Flip-Flops

At one time, J-K flip-flops were popular for discrete SSI state-machine designs, since a J-K flip-flop embeds more functionality than a D flip-flop in the same size SSI package. By "more functionality" we mean that the combination of J and K inputs yields more possibilities for controlling the flip-flop than a single D input does. As a result, a state machine's excitation logic may be simpler using J-K flip-flops than using D flip-flops, which reduced package count when SSI gates were used for the excitation logic.

While minimizing excitation logic was a big deal in the days of SSI-based design, the name of the game has changed with PLDs, FPGAs, and ASICs. For example, the need to provide separate AND-OR arrays for the J and K inputs of a J-K flip-flop would be a distinct disadvantage in a sequential PLD.

In ASIC technologies, J-K flip-flops aren't so hot either, since they often use about 25% more chip area than comparable D flip-flops. So, a more cost-effective design can result from using D flip-flops and using the extra chip area for more complex excitation logic in just the cases where it's really needed.

For details of J-K synthesis, see Section JKSM.2 at DDPPonline.

7.4.6 More Design Examples Using D Flip-Flops

We'll give two more state-machine design examples using D flip-flops. The first example is a "1s-counting machine":

Design a clocked synchronous state machine with two inputs, X and Y, and one output, Z. The output should be 1 if the number of 1 inputs on X and Y since reset is a multiple of 4, and 0 otherwise.

At first glance, you might think the machine needs an infinite number of states, since it counts 1 inputs over an arbitrarily long time. However, since the output indicates the number of inputs received *modulo 4*, four states are sufficient.

Meaning	S	X Y				Z
		00	01	11	10	
Got zero 1s (modulo 4)	S0	S0	S1	S2	S1	1
Got one 1 (modulo 4)	S1	S1	S2	S3	S2	0
Got two 1s (modulo 4)	S2	S2	S3	S0	S3	0
Got three 1s (modulo 4)	S3	S3	S0	S1	S0	0
			S*			

Table 7-9
State and output table for 1s-counting machine.

We'll name them S0–S3, where S0 is the initial state and the total number of 1s received in Si is i modulo 4. Table 7-9 is the resulting state and output table.

The 1s-counting machine can use two state variables to code its four states, with no unused states. In this case, there are only 4! possible assignments of coded states to named states. Still, we'll try only one of them. We'll assign coded states to the named states in Karnaugh-map order (00, 01, 11, 10) for two reasons: in this state table, it minimizes the number of state variables that change for most transitions, potentially simplifying the excitation equations; and it simplifies the mechanical transfer of information to excitation maps.

A transition/excitation table based on our chosen state assignment is shown in Table 7-10. Since we're using D flip-flops, the transition and excitation tables are the same. Corresponding Karnaugh maps for D1 and D2 are shown in Figure 7-51. Since there are no unused states, all of the information we need is in the excitation table; no choice is required between minimal-risk and minimal-

Q1 Q2	X Y				Z
	00	01	11	10	
00	00	01	11	01	1
01	01	11	10	11	0
11	11	10	00	10	0
10	10	00	01	00	0
		Q1* Q2* or D1 D2			

Table 7-10
Transition/excitation and output table for 1s-counting machine.

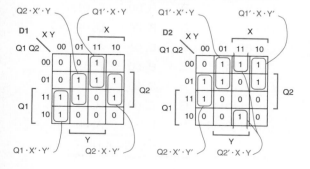

Figure 7-51
Excitation maps for D1 and D2 inputs in 1s-counting machine.

cost approaches. The excitation equations can be read from the maps, and the output equation can be read directly from the transition/excitation table:

$$D1 = Q2 \cdot X' \cdot Y + Q1' \cdot X \cdot Y + Q1 \cdot X' \cdot Y' + Q2 \cdot X \cdot Y'$$
$$D2 = Q1' \cdot X' \cdot Y + Q1' \cdot X \cdot Y' + Q2 \cdot X' \cdot Y' + Q2' \cdot X \cdot Y$$
$$Z = Q1' \cdot Q2'$$

A logic diagram using D flip-flops and AND-OR or NAND-NAND excitation logic can be drawn from these equations.

The second example is a "combination lock" state machine that activates an "unlock" output when a certain binary input sequence is received:

Design a clocked synchronous state machine with one input, X, and two outputs, UNLK and HINT. The UNLK output should be 1 if and only if X is 0 and the sequence of inputs received on X at the preceding seven clock ticks was 0110111. The HINT output should be 1 if and only if the current value of X is the correct one to move the machine closer to being in the "unlocked" state (with UNLK = 1).

It should be apparent from the word description that this is a Mealy machine. The UNLK output depends on both the past history of inputs and X's current value, and HINT depends on both the state and the current X (indeed, if the current X produces HINT = 0, then the clued-in user will want to change X before the clock tick).

A state and output table for the combination lock is presented in Table 7-11. In the initial state, A, we assume that we have received no inputs in the required sequence; we're looking for the first 0 in the sequence. Therefore, as long as we get 1 inputs, we stay in state A, and we move to state B when we receive a 0. In state B, we're looking for a 1. If we get it, we move on to C; if we don't, we can stay in B, since the 0 we just received might still turn out to be the first 0 in the required sequence. In each successive state, we move on to the next

Table 7-11
State and output table for combination-lock machine.

Meaning	S	X 0	X 1
Got zip	A	B, 01	A, 00
Got 0	B	B, 00	C, 01
Got 01	C	B, 00	D, 01
Got 011	D	E, 01	A, 00
Got 0110	E	B, 00	F, 01
Got 01101	F	B, 00	G, 01
Got 011011	G	E, 00	H, 01
Got 0110111	H	B, 11	A, 00
		S∗, UNLK HINT	

Table 7-12
Transition/excitation table for combination-lock machine.

Q1 Q2 Q3	X 0	X 1
000	001, 01	000, 00
001	001, 00	010, 01
010	001, 00	011, 01
011	100, 01	000, 00
100	001, 00	101, 01
101	001, 00	110, 01
110	100, 00	111, 01
111	001, 11	000, 00
	Q1* Q2* Q3*, UNLK HINT	

state if we get the correct input, and we go back to A or B if we get the wrong one. An exception occurs in state G; if we get the wrong input (a 0) there, the previous three inputs might still turn out to be the first three inputs of the required sequence, so we go back to state E instead of B. In state H, we've received the required sequence, so we set UNLK to 1 if X is 0. In each state, we set HINT to 1 for the value of X that moves us closer to state H.

The combination lock's eight states can be coded with three state variables, leaving no unused states. There are 8! state assignments to choose from. To keep things simple, we'll use the simplest, and assign the states in binary counting order, yielding the transition/excitation table in Table 7-12. Corresponding Karnaugh maps for D1, D2, and D3 are shown in Figure 7-52. The excitation equations can be read from the maps:

$$D1 = Q1 \cdot Q2' \cdot X + Q1' \cdot Q2 \cdot Q3 \cdot X' + Q1 \cdot Q2 \cdot Q3'$$
$$D2 = Q2' \cdot Q3 \cdot X + Q2 \cdot Q3' \cdot X$$
$$D3 = Q1 \cdot Q2' \cdot Q3' + Q1 \cdot Q3 \cdot X' + Q2' \cdot X' + Q3' \cdot Q1' \cdot X' + Q2 \cdot Q3' \cdot X$$

Figure 7-52 Excitation maps for D1, D2, and D3 in combination-lock machine.

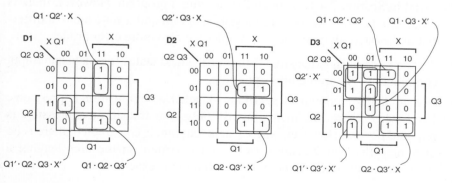

Figure 7-53
Karnaugh maps for output functions UNLK and HINT in combination-lock machine.

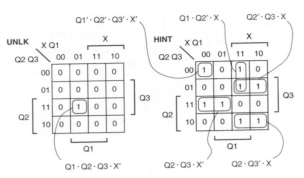

The output values are transferred from the transition/excitation and output table to another set of maps in Figure 7-53. The corresponding output equations are:

$$UNLK = Q1 \cdot Q2 \cdot Q3 \cdot X'$$

$$HINT = Q1' \cdot Q2' \cdot Q3' \cdot X' + Q1 \cdot Q2' \cdot X + Q2' \cdot Q3 \cdot X + Q2 \cdot Q3 \cdot X' + Q2 \cdot Q3' \cdot X$$

Note that some product terms are repeated in the excitation and output equations, yielding a slight savings in the cost of the AND-OR realization. If we went through the trouble of performing a formal multiple-output minimization of all five excitation and output functions, we could save two more gates (see exercise in Section Min.3 at DDPPonline).

7.5 Designing State Machines Using State Diagrams

Aside from planning the overall architecture of a digital system, designing state machines is probably the most creative task of a digital designer. Most people like to take a graphical approach to design, and for that reason, state diagrams are often used to design small- to medium-sized state machines. In this section we'll give examples of state-diagram design and describe a simple procedure for synthesizing circuits from the state diagrams. This procedure is the basis of the method used by CAD tools that can synthesize logic from graphical or HDLbased "state diagrams."

Designing a state diagram is much like designing a state table, which, as we showed in Section 7.4.1, is much like writing a program. However, there is one fundamental difference between a state diagram and a state table, a differ-ence that makes state-diagram design simpler but also more error prone:

- A state table is an exhaustive listing of the next states for each state/input combination. No ambiguity is possible.

- A state diagram contains a set of arcs labeled with transition expressions. Even when there are many inputs, only one transition expression is required per arc. However, when a state diagram is constructed, there is no guarantee that the transition expressions written on the arcs leaving a particular state cover all the input combinations exactly once.

Figure 7-54
T-bird tail lights.

LC   LB   LA   RA   RB   RC

In an improperly constructed (*ambiguous*) state diagram, some state/input combinations may have no next state specified, which is generally undesirable, while
others may have multiple next states, which is just wrong. Thus, considerable
care must be taken in the design of state diagrams; we'll give a few examples.

  Our first example is a state machine that controls the tail lights of a 1965
Ford Thunderbird, shown in Figure 7-54. There are three lights on each side, and
for turns they operate in sequence to show the turning direction, as illustrated in
Figure 7-55. The state machine has two input signals, LEFT and RIGHT, that
carry the driver's request for a left turn or a right turn. It also has an emergency-
flasher input, HAZ, that requests the tail lights to be operated in hazard mode—
all six lights flashing on and off in unison. We also assume the existence of a

*ambiguous state
diagram*

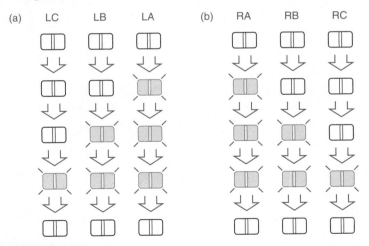

Figure 7-55
Flashing sequence
for T-bird tail lights:
(a) left turn;
(b) right turn.

**WHOSE REAR
END?**   Actually, Figure 7-54 looks more like the rear end of a Mercury Capri, which also
had sequential tail lights.

free-running clock signal whose frequency equals the desired flashing rate for the lights.

Given the foregoing requirements, we can design a clocked synchronous state machine to control the T-bird tail lights. We will design a Moore machine, so that the state alone determines which lights are on and which are off. For a left turn, the machine should cycle through four states in which the righthand lights are off and 0, 1, 2, or 3 of the lefthand lights are on. Likewise, for a right turn, it should cycle through four states in which the lefthand lights are off and 0, 1, 2, or 3 of the righthand lights are on. In hazard mode, only two states are required— all lights on and all lights off.

Figure 7-56 shows our first cut at a state diagram for the machine. A common IDLE state is defined in which all of the lights are off. When a left turn is requested, the machine goes through three states in which 1, 2, and 3 of the lefthand lights are on, and then back to IDLE; right turns work similarly. In the hazard mode, the machine cycles back and forth between the IDLE state and a state in which all six lights are on. Since there are so many outputs, we've included a separate output table rather than writing output values on the state diagram. Even without assigning coded states to the named states, we can write

Figure 7-56
Initial state diagram
and output table for
T-bird tail lights.

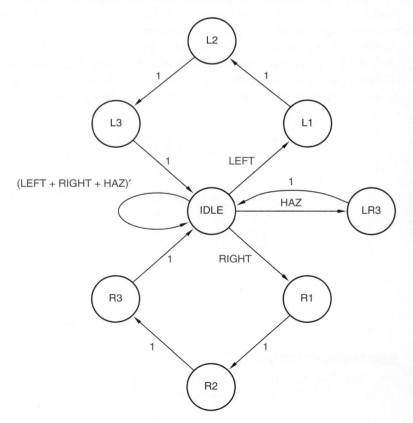

Output Table

State	LC	LB	LA	RA	RB	RC
IDLE	0	0	0	0	0	0
L1	0	0	1	0	0	0
L2	0	1	1	0	0	0
L3	1	1	1	0	0	0
R1	0	0	0	1	0	0
R2	0	0	0	1	1	0
R3	0	0	0	1	1	1
LR3	1	1	1	1	1	1

output equations from the output table, if we let each state name represent a logic expression that is 1 only in that state:

$$LA = L1 + L2 + L3 + LR3 \qquad RA = R1 + R2 + R3 + LR3$$
$$LB = L2 + L3 + LR3 \qquad RB = R2 + R3 + LR3$$
$$LC = L3 + LR3 \qquad RC = R3 + LR3$$

There's one big problem with the state diagram of Figure 7-56—it doesn't properly handle multiple inputs asserted simultaneously. For example, what happens in the IDLE state if both LEFT and HAZ are asserted? According to the state diagram, the machine goes to two states, L1 and LR3, which is impossible. In reality, the machine would have only one next state, which could be L1, LR3, or a totally unrelated (and possibly unused) third state, depending on details of the state machine's realization (e.g., see Exercise 7.66).

The problem is fixed in Figure 7-57, where we have given the HAZ input priority. Also, we treat LEFT and RIGHT asserted simultaneously as a hazard request, since the driver is clearly confused and needs help.

The new state diagram is unambiguous because the transition expressions on the arcs leaving each state are mutually exclusive and all-inclusive. That is,

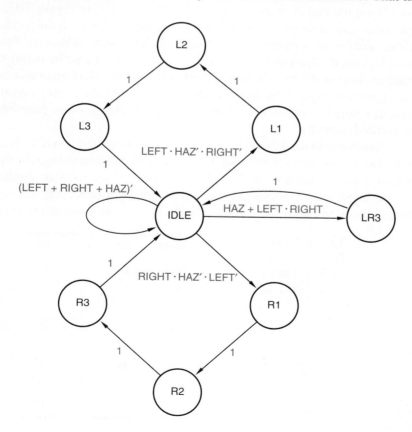

Figure 7-57
Corrected state diagram for T-bird tail lights.

for each state, no two expressions are 1 for the same input combination, and some expression is 1 for every input combination. This can be confirmed algebraically for this or any other state diagram by performing two steps:

mutual exclusion

1. *Mutual exclusion.* For each state, show that the logical product of each possible pair of transition expressions on arcs leaving that state is 0. If there are n arcs, then there are $n(n-1)/2$ logical products to evaluate.

all inclusion

2. *All inclusion.* For each state, show that the logical sum of the transition expressions on all arcs leaving that state is 1.

If there are many transitions leaving each state, these steps, especially the first one, are very difficult to perform by hand. However, typical state machines, even ones with lots of states and inputs, don't have many transitions leaving each state, since most designers can't dream up such complex machines in the first place. This is where the tradeoff between state-table and state-diagram design occurs. In state-table design, the foregoing steps are not required, because the structure of a state table guarantees mutual exclusion and all inclusion. But if there are a lot of inputs, the state table has *lots* of columns.

Verifying that a state diagram is unambiguous may be difficult in principle, but it's not too bad in practice for small state diagrams. In Figure 7-57, most of the states have a single arc with a transition expression of 1, so verification is trivial. Real work is needed only to verify the IDLE state, which has four transitions leaving it. This can be done on a sheet of scratch paper by listing the eight combinations of the three inputs and checking off the combinations covered by each transition expression. Each combination should have exactly one check. As another example, consider the state diagram in Figure 7-44 on page 552; it can be verified mentally.

Returning to the T-bird tail-lights machine, we can now synthesize a circuit from the state diagram if we wish. However, if we want to change the machine's behavior, now is the time to do it, before we do all the work of synthesizing a circuit. In particular, notice that once a left- or right-turn cycle has begun, the state diagram in Figure 7-57 allows the cycle to run to completion, even if HAZ

Table 7-13
State assignment
for T-bird tail-lights
state machine.

State	Q2	Q1	Q0
IDLE	0	0	0
L1	0	0	1
L2	0	1	1
L3	0	1	0
R1	1	0	1
R2	1	1	1
R3	1	1	0
LR3	1	0	0

is asserted. While this may have a certain aesthetic appeal, it would be safer for the car's occupants to have the machine go into hazard mode as soon as possible. The state diagram is modified to provide this behavior in Figure 7-58.

Now we're finally ready to synthesize a circuit for the T-bird machine. The state diagram has eight states, so we'll need a minimum of three flip-flops to code the states. Obviously, many state assignments are possible (8! to be exact); we'll use the one in Table 7-13 for the following reasons:

1. An initial (idle) state of 000 is compatible with most flip-flops and registers, which are easily initialized to the 0 state.

2. Two state variables, Q1 and Q0, are used to "count" in Gray-code sequence for the left-turn cycle (IDLE→L1→L2→L3→IDLE). This minimizes the number of state-variable changes per state transition, which can often simplify the excitation logic.

3. Because of the symmetry in the state diagram, the same sequence on Q1 and Q0 is used to "count" during a right-turn cycle, while Q2 is used to distinguish between left and right.

4. The remaining state-variable combination is used for the LR3 state.

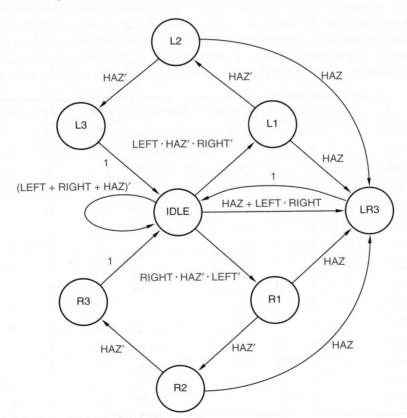

Figure 7-58
Enhanced state diagram for T-bird tail lights.

transition list

The next step is to write a sort of transition table. However, we must use a format different from the transition tables of Section 7.4.4, because the transitions in a state diagram are specified by expressions rather than by an exhaustive tabulation of next states. We'll call the new format a *transition list*, because it has one row for each transition or arc in the state diagram.

Table 7-14 is the transition list for the state diagram of Figure 7-58 and the state assignment of Table 7-13. Each row contains the current state, next state, and transition expression for one arc in the state diagram. Both named and coded versions of the current state and next state are shown. Named states are useful for reference purposes, while coded states are used to develop transition equations.

Once we have a transition list, the rest of the synthesis steps are pretty much just "turning the crank," as described in Section 7.6. Although these steps can be performed manually, they are usually embedded in a CAD tool such as an HDL compiler. Thus, Section 7.6 can help you understand what's going on (or going wrong) in your favorite CAD tool.

We also encountered one "turn-the-crank" step in this section—finding the ambiguities in state diagrams. Even though the procedure we discussed can be easily automated, not all CAD tools perform this step in this way. For example, one company's "state diagram entry" tool silently removes duplicated transitions and goes to the state coded "00...00" for missing transitions, without warning the user. Thus, in most design environments, the designer is responsible for writing a state-machine description that is unambiguous. The HDL-based approaches described at the end of this chapter provide a good way to do this.

Table 7-14
Transition list for
T-bird tail-lights
state machine.

S	Q2	Q1	Q0	Transition Expression	S*	Q2*	Q1*	Q0*
IDLE	0	0	0	(LEFT + RIGHT + HAZ)′	IDLE	0	0	0
IDLE	0	0	0	LEFT · HAZ′ · RIGHT′	L1	0	0	1
IDLE	0	0	0	HAZ + LEFT · RIGHT	LR3	1	0	0
IDLE	0	0	0	RIGHT · HAZ′ · LEFT′	R1	1	0	1
L1	0	0	1	HAZ′	L2	0	1	1
L1	0	0	1	HAZ	LR3	1	0	0
L2	0	1	1	HAZ′	L3	0	1	0
L2	0	1	1	HAZ	LR3	1	0	0
L3	0	1	0	1	IDLE	0	0	0
R1	1	0	1	HAZ′	R2	1	1	1
R1	1	0	1	HAZ	LR3	1	0	0
R2	1	1	1	HAZ′	R3	1	1	0
R2	1	1	1	HAZ	LR3	1	0	0
R3	1	1	0	1	IDLE	0	0	0
LR3	1	0	0	1	IDLE	0	0	0

*7.6 State-Machine Synthesis Using Transition Lists

Once a machine's state diagram has been designed and a state assignment has been made, the creative part of the design process is pretty much over. The rest of the synthesis procedure can be carried out by CAD programs.

As we showed in the preceding section, a transition list can be constructed from a machine's state diagram and state assignment. This section shows how to synthesize a state machine from its transition list. It also delves into some of the options and nuances of state-machine design using transition lists. Although this material is useful for synthesizing machines by hand, its main purpose is to help you understand the internal operation and the external quirks of CAD programs and languages that deal with state machines.

*7.6.1 Transition Equations

The first step in synthesizing a state machine from a transition list is to develop a set of transition equations that define each next-state variable $V*$ in terms of the current state and input. The transition list can be viewed as a sort of hybrid truth table in which the state-variable combinations for the current state are listed explicitly and input combinations are listed algebraically. Reading down a $V*$ column in a transition list, we find a sequence of 0s and 1s, indicating the value of $V*$ for various (if we've done it right, all) state/input combinations.

A transition equation for a next-state variable $V*$ can be written using a sort of hybrid canonical sum:

$$V* = \sum_{\text{transition-list rows where } V* = 1} \text{(transition p-term)}$$

That is, the transition equation has one "transition p-term" for each row of the transition list that contains a 1 in the $V*$ column. A row's *transition p-term* is the product of the current state's minterm and the transition expression.

transition p-term

Based on the transition list in Table 7-14, the transition equation for $Q2*$ in the T-bird machine can be written as the sum of eight p-terms:

$$
\begin{aligned}
Q2* = \ & Q2' \cdot Q1' \cdot Q0' \cdot (\text{HAZ} + \text{LEFT} \cdot \text{RIGHT}) \\
& + Q2' \cdot Q1' \cdot Q0' \cdot (\text{RIGHT} \cdot \text{HAZ}' \cdot \text{LEFT}') \\
& + Q2' \cdot Q1' \cdot Q0 \cdot (\text{HAZ}) \\
& + Q2' \cdot Q1 \cdot Q0 \cdot (\text{HAZ}) \\
& + Q2 \cdot Q1' \cdot Q0 \cdot (\text{HAZ}') \\
& + Q2 \cdot Q1' \cdot Q0 \cdot (\text{HAZ}) \\
& + Q2 \cdot Q1 \cdot Q0 \cdot (\text{HAZ}') \\
& + Q2 \cdot Q1 \cdot Q0 \cdot (\text{HAZ})
\end{aligned}
$$

* This section and all of its subsections are optional.

Some straightforward algebraic manipulations lead to a simplified transition equation that combines the first two, second two, and last four p-terms above:

$$Q2* = Q2' \cdot Q1' \cdot Q0' \cdot (\text{HAZ} + \text{RIGHT})$$
$$+ Q2' \cdot Q0 \cdot (\text{HAZ})$$
$$+ Q2 \cdot Q0$$

Transition equations for Q1∗ and Q0∗ may be obtained in a similar manner:

$$Q1* = Q2' \cdot Q1' \cdot Q0 \cdot (\text{HAZ}')$$
$$+ Q2' \cdot Q1 \cdot Q0 \cdot (\text{HAZ}')$$
$$+ Q2 \cdot Q1' \cdot Q0 \cdot (\text{HAZ}')$$
$$+ Q2 \cdot Q1 \cdot Q0 \cdot (\text{HAZ}')$$
$$= Q0 \cdot \text{HAZ}'$$
$$Q0* = Q2' \cdot Q1' \cdot Q0' \cdot (\text{LEFT} \cdot \text{HAZ}' \cdot \text{RIGHT}')$$
$$+ Q2' \cdot Q1' \cdot Q0' \cdot (\text{RIGHT} \cdot \text{HAZ}' \cdot \text{LEFT}')$$
$$+ Q2' \cdot Q1' \cdot Q0 \cdot (\text{HAZ}')$$
$$+ Q2 \cdot Q1' \cdot Q0 \cdot (\text{HAZ}')$$
$$= Q2' \cdot Q1' \cdot Q0' \cdot \text{HAZ}' \cdot (\text{LEFT} \oplus \text{RIGHT}) + Q1' \cdot Q0 \cdot \text{HAZ}'$$

Except for Q1∗, there's no guarantee that the transition equations above are in any sense minimal—in fact, the expressions for Q2∗ and Q0∗ aren't even in standard sum-of-products or product-of-sums form. The simplified equations, or the original unsimplified ones, merely provide an unambiguous starting point for whatever combinational design method you might choose to synthesize the excitation logic for the state machine—ad hoc, NAND-NAND, MSI-based, or whatever. In a PLD-based design, you could simply plug the equations into an ABEL program and let the compiler calculate the minimal sum-of-products expressions for the PLD's AND-OR array.

*7.6.2 Excitation Equations

While we're on the subject of excitation logic, note that so far we have derived only *transition equations*, not *excitation equations*. However, if we use D flip-flops as the memory elements in our state machines, then the excitation equations are trivial to derive from the transition equations, since the characteristic equation of a D flip-flop is Q∗ = D. Therefore, if the transition equation for a state variable Qi∗ is

$$Qi* = \text{expression}$$

then the excitation equation for the corresponding D flip-flop input is

$$Di = \text{expression}$$

Excitation equations for other flip-flop types, especially J-K, are not so easy to derive by hand (e.g., see <u>Section JKSM.2</u> at <u>DDPPonline</u>). Anyway, the majority of discrete, PLD-based, and ASIC-based state-machine designs use D flip-flops.

*7.6.3 Variations on the Scheme

There are other ways to obtain transition and excitation equations from a transition list. If the column for a particular next-state variable contains fewer 0s than 1s, it may be advantageous to write that variable's transition equation in terms of the 0s in its column. That is, we write

$$V*' = \sum_{\text{transition-list rows where } V* = 0} (\text{transition p-term})$$

That is, $V*'$ is 1 for all of the p-terms for which $V*$ is 0. Thus, a transition equation for $Q2*'$ may be written as the sum of seven p-terms:

$$
\begin{aligned}
Q2*' =\ & Q2' \cdot Q1' \cdot Q0' \cdot ((LEFT + RIGHT + HAZ)') \\
& + Q2' \cdot Q1' \cdot Q0' \cdot (LEFT \cdot HAZ' \cdot RIGHT') \\
& + Q2' \cdot Q1' \cdot Q0 \cdot (HAZ') \\
& + Q2' \cdot Q1 \cdot Q0 \cdot (HAZ') \\
& + Q2' \cdot Q1 \cdot Q0' \cdot (1) \\
& + Q2 \cdot Q1 \cdot Q0' \cdot (1) \\
& + Q2 \cdot Q1' \cdot Q0' \cdot (1) \\
=\ & Q2' \cdot Q1' \cdot Q0' \cdot HAZ' \cdot RIGHT' + Q2' \cdot Q0 \cdot HAZ' + Q1 \cdot Q0' + Q2 \cdot Q0'
\end{aligned}
$$

To obtain an equation for $Q2*$, we simply complement both sides of the reduced equation.

   To obtain an expression for a next-state variable $V*$ directly, using the 0s in the transition list, we can complement the righthand side of the general $V*'$ equation using DeMorgan's theorem, obtaining a sort of hybrid canonical product:

$$V* = \prod_{\text{transition-list rows where } V* = 0} (\text{transition s-term})$$

Here, a row's *transition s-term* is the sum of the maxterm for the current state and the complement of the transition expression. If the transition expression is a simple product term, then its complement is a sum, and the transition equation expresses $V*$ in product-of-sums form.

transition s-term

*7.6.4 Realizing the State Machine

Once you have the excitation equations for a state machine, all you're left with is a multiple-output combinational logic design problem. Of course, there are many ways to realize combinational logic from equations, but the easiest way is just to type them into an ABEL or VHDL program and use the compiler to synthesize a PLD, FPGA, or ASIC realization.

   Combinational PLDs, such as the PAL16L8 and GAL16V8 that we studied in Section 6.3, can be used to realize excitation equations up to a certain number of inputs, outputs, and product terms. Better yet, in Section 8.3 we'll introduce sequential PLDs that include D flip-flops on the same chip with the combinational AND-OR array. For a given number of PLD input and output pins, these sequential PLDs can realize larger state machines than their combinational counterparts, because the excitation signals never have to go off the chip. In Section XSabl.3 at DDPPonline, we show how to realize the T-bird tail-lights machine in a sequential PLD.

7.7 Another State-Machine Design Example

This section gives one more example of state-machine design using a state diagram. The example provides a basis for further discussion of a few topics: unused states, output-coded state assignments, and "don't-care" state codings.

7.7.1 The Guessing Game

Our final state-machine example is a "guessing game" that can be built as an amusing lab project:

Design a clocked synchronous state machine with four inputs, G1–G4, that are connected to pushbuttons. The machine has four outputs, L1–L4, connected to lamps or LEDs located near the like-numbered pushbuttons. There is also an ERR output connected to a red lamp. In normal operation the L1–L4 outputs display a 1-out-of-4 pattern. At each clock tick, the pattern is rotated by one position; the clock frequency is about 4 Hz.

Guesses are made by pressing a pushbutton, which asserts an input Gi. When any Gi input is asserted, the ERR output is asserted if the "wrong" pushbutton was pressed, that is, if the Gi input detected at the clock tick does not have the same number as the lamp output that was asserted before the clock tick. Once a guess has been made, play stops and the ERR output maintains the same value for one or more clock ticks until the Gi input is negated, then play resumes.

Clearly, we will have to provide four states, one for each position of the rotating pattern, and we'll need at least one state to indicate that play has stopped. A possible state diagram is shown in Figure 7-59. The machine cycles through states S1–S4 as long as no Gi input is asserted, and it goes to the STOP state when a guess is made. Each Li output is asserted in the like-numbered state.

The only problem with this state diagram is that it doesn't "remember" in the STOP state whether the guess was correct, so it has no way to control the ERR output. This problem is fixed in Figure 7-60, which has two "stopped" states, SOK and SERR. On an incorrect guess, the machine goes to SERR, where ERR is asserted; otherwise, it goes to SOK. Although the machine's word description doesn't require it, the state diagram is designed to go to SERR even if the user tries to fool it by pressing two or more pushbuttons simultaneously, or by changing guesses while stopped.

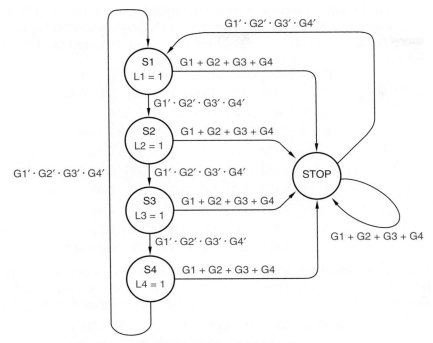

Figure 7-59 First try at a state diagram for the guessing game.

Figure 7-60 Correct state diagram for the guessing game.

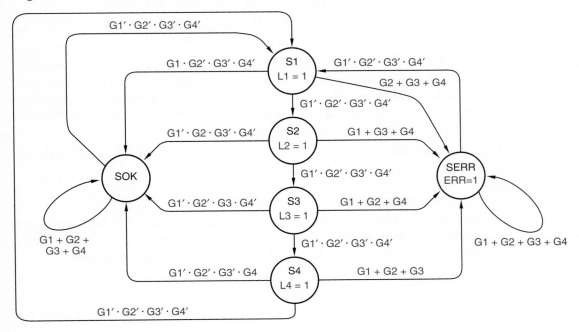

A transition list corresponding to the state diagram is shown in Table 7-15, using a simple 3-bit binary state encoding with Gray-code order for the S1–S4 cycle. Transition equations for Q1* and Q0* can be obtained from the table as follows:

$$
\begin{aligned}
Q1* \ &= \ Q2' \cdot Q1' \cdot Q0 \cdot (G1' \cdot G2' \cdot G3' \cdot G4') \\
&+ Q2' \cdot Q1 \ \cdot Q0 \cdot (G1' \cdot G2' \cdot G3' \cdot G4') \\
&= \ Q2' \ \ \cdot Q0 \cdot G1' \cdot G2' \cdot G3' \cdot G4' \\
Q0* \ &= \ Q2' \cdot Q1' \cdot Q0' \cdot (G1' \cdot G2' \cdot G3' \cdot G4') \\
&+ Q2' \cdot Q1' \cdot Q0' \cdot (G2 + G3 + G4) \\
&+ Q2' \cdot Q1' \cdot Q0 \ \cdot (G1' \cdot G2' \cdot G3' \cdot G4') \\
&+ Q2' \cdot Q1' \cdot Q0 \ \cdot (G1 + G3 + G4) \\
&+ Q2' \cdot Q1 \ \cdot Q0 \ \cdot (G1 + G2 + G4) \\
&+ Q2' \cdot Q1 \ \cdot Q0' \cdot (G1 + G2 + G3) \\
&+ Q2 \ \cdot Q1' \cdot Q0 \ \cdot (G1 + G2 + G3 + G4)
\end{aligned}
$$

Using a logic-minimization program, the Q0* expression can be reduced to 11 product terms in two-level sum-of-products form. An expression for Q2* is best formulated in terms of the 0s in the Q2* column of the transition list:

$$
\begin{aligned}
Q2*' \ &= \ Q2' \cdot Q1' \cdot Q0' \cdot (G1' \cdot G2' \cdot G3' \cdot G4') \\
&+ Q2' \cdot Q1' \cdot Q0 \ \cdot (G1' \cdot G2' \cdot G3' \cdot G4') \\
&+ Q2' \cdot Q1 \ \cdot Q0 \ \cdot (G1' \cdot G2' \cdot G3' \cdot G4') \\
&+ Q2' \cdot Q1 \ \cdot Q0' \cdot (G1' \cdot G2' \cdot G3' \cdot G4') \\
&+ Q2 \ \cdot Q1' \cdot Q0' \cdot (G1' \cdot G2' \cdot G3' \cdot G4') \\
&+ Q2 \ \cdot Q1' \cdot Q0 \ \cdot (G1' \cdot G2' \cdot G3' \cdot G4') \\
&= \ (Q2' + Q1') \cdot (G1' \cdot G2' \cdot G3' \cdot G4')
\end{aligned}
$$

The last five columns of Table 7-15 show output values. Thus, output equations can be developed in much the same way as transition equations. However, since this example is a Moore machine, outputs are independent of the transition expressions; only one row of the transition list must be considered for each current state. The output equations are

$$
\begin{array}{lll}
L1 = Q2' \cdot Q1' \cdot Q0' & L3 = Q2' \cdot Q1 \cdot Q0 & ERR = Q2 \cdot Q1' \cdot Q0 \\
L2 = Q2' \cdot Q1' \cdot Q0 & L4 = Q2' \cdot Q1 \cdot Q0' &
\end{array}
$$

7.7.2 Unused States

Our state diagram for the guessing game has six states, but the actual state machine, built from three flip-flops, has eight. By omitting the unused states from the transition list, we treated them as "don't-cares" in a very limited sense:

- When we wrote equations for Q1* and Q0*, we formed a sum of transition p-terms for state/input combinations that had an explicit 1 in the corresponding columns of the transition list. Although we didn't consider the

Table 7-15 Transition list for guessing-game machine.

S	Q2	Q1	Q0	Transition Expression	S*	Q2*	Q1*	Q0*	L1	L2	L3	L4	ERR
	Current State				Next State				Output				
S1	0	0	0	G1' · G2' · G3' · G4'	S2	0	0	1	1	0	0	0	0
S1	0	0	0	G1 · G2' · G3' · G4'	SOK	1	0	0	1	0	0	0	0
S1	0	0	0	G2 + G3 + G4	SERR	1	0	1	1	0	0	0	0
S2	0	0	1	G1' · G2' · G3' · G4'	S3	0	1	1	0	1	0	0	0
S2	0	0	1	G1' · G2 · G3' · G4'	SOK	1	0	0	0	1	0	0	0
S2	0	0	1	G1 + G3 + G4	SERR	1	0	1	0	1	0	0	0
S3	0	1	1	G1' · G2' · G3' · G4'	S4	0	1	0	0	0	1	0	0
S3	0	1	1	G1' · G2' · G3 · G4'	SOK	1	0	0	0	0	1	0	0
S3	0	1	1	G1 + G2 + G4	SERR	1	0	1	0	0	1	0	0
S4	0	1	0	G1' · G2' · G3' · G4'	S1	0	0	0	0	0	0	1	0
S4	0	1	0	G1' · G2' · G3' · G4	SOK	1	0	0	0	0	0	1	0
S4	0	1	0	G1 + G2 + G3	SERR	1	0	1	0	0	0	1	0
SOK	1	0	0	G1 + G2 + G3 + G4	SOK	1	0	0	0	0	0	0	0
SOK	1	0	0	G1' · G2' · G3' · G4'	S1	0	0	0	0	0	0	0	0
SERR	1	0	1	G1 + G2 + G3 + G4	SERR	1	0	1	0	0	0	0	1
SERR	1	0	1	G1' · G2' · G3' · G4'	S1	0	0	0	0	0	0	0	1

unused states, our procedure implicitly treated them as if they had 0s in the Q1* and Q0* columns.

- Conversely, we wrote the Q2*′ equation as a sum of transition p-terms for state/input combinations that had an explicit 0 in the corresponding columns of the transition list. Unused states were implicitly treated as if they had 1s in the Q2* column.

As a consequence of these choices, all of the unused states in the guessing-game machine have a coded next state of 100 for all input combinations. That's safe, acceptable behavior should the machine stray into an unused state, since 100 is the coding for one of the normal states (SOK).

To treat the unused states as true "don't-cares," we should allow them to go to any next state under any input combination. When developing the excitation equations by hand, this means entering a "d" on the Karnaugh map for each cell corresponding to an unused state and any input combination, and performing "don't-care" minimization (Section Min.2 at DDPPonline). As you know, for all but the smallest problems, Karnaugh maps are unwieldy. Commercially available logic-minimization programs can easily handle larger problems, but many of them don't handle "don't-cares" or they require the designer to insert special code to handle them. However, in ABEL state machines, don't-care next states can be handled fairly easily using the @DCSET directive, as we discuss in Section ABEL.2 at DDPPonline. Likewise, in VHDL and Verilog, the process is straightforward when the right style is used for coding state machines, as discussed in Sections 7.12.2 and 7.13.2, respectively.

7.7.3 Output-Coded State Assignment

output-coded state assignment

Let's look at another realization of the guessing-game machine. The machine's outputs are a function of state only; furthermore, a *different* output combination is produced in each named state. Therefore, we can use the outputs as state variables and assign each named state to the required output combination. This sort of *output-coded state assignment* can sometimes result in excitation equations that are simpler than the set of excitation and output equations obtained with a state assignment using a minimum number of state variables.

Table 7-16 is the guessing-game transition list that results from an output-coded state assignment. Each transition/excitation equation has very few transition p-terms because the transition list has so few 1s in the next-state columns:

$$
\begin{aligned}
L1* \;=\;&\; L1' \cdot L2' \cdot L3' \cdot L4 \cdot ERR' \cdot (G1' \cdot G2' \cdot G3' \cdot G4') \\
&+ L1' \cdot L2' \cdot L3' \cdot L4' \cdot ERR' \cdot (G1' \cdot G2' \cdot G3' \cdot G4') \\
&+ L1' \cdot L2' \cdot L3' \cdot L4' \cdot ERR \cdot (G1' \cdot G2' \cdot G3' \cdot G4') \\
L2* \;=\;&\; L1 \cdot L2' \cdot L3' \cdot L4' \cdot ERR' \cdot (G1' \cdot G2' \cdot G3' \cdot G4') \\
L3* \;=\;&\; L1' \cdot L2 \cdot L3' \cdot L4' \cdot ERR' \cdot (G1' \cdot G2' \cdot G3' \cdot G4') \\
L4* \;=\;&\; L1' \cdot L2' \cdot L3 \cdot L4' \cdot ERR' \cdot (G1' \cdot G2' \cdot G3' \cdot G4') \\
ERR* \;=\;&\; L1 \cdot L2' \cdot L3' \cdot L4' \cdot ERR' \cdot (G2 + G3 + G4) \\
&+ L1' \cdot L2 \cdot L3' \cdot L4' \cdot ERR' \cdot (G1 + G3 + G4) \\
&+ L1' \cdot L2' \cdot L3 \cdot L4' \cdot ERR' \cdot (G1 + G2 + G4) \\
&+ L1' \cdot L2' \cdot L3' \cdot L4 \cdot ERR' \cdot (G1 + G2 + G3) \\
&+ L1' \cdot L2' \cdot L3' \cdot L4' \cdot ERR \cdot (G1 + G2 + G3 + G4)
\end{aligned}
$$

There are no output equations, of course. The ERR* equation above is the worst in the group, requiring 16 terms to express in either minimal sum-of-products or product-of-sums form.

As a group, the equations developed above have just about the same complexity as the transition and output equations that we developed from Table 7-15. Even though the output-coded assignment does not produce a simpler set of equations in this example, it can still save cost in a PLD-based design, since fewer PLD macrocells or outputs are needed overall.

7.7.4 "Don't-Care" State Codings

Out of the 32 possible coded states using five variables, only six are used in Table 7-16. The rest of the states are unused and have a next state of 00000 if the machine is built using the equations in the preceding subsection. Another

Table 7-16 Transition list for guessing-game machine using outputs as state variables.

			Current State						**Next State**				
S	**L1**	**L2**	**L3**	**L4**	**ERR**	**Transition Expression**	**S***	**L1***	**L2***	**L3***	**L4***	**ERR***
S1	1	0	0	0	0	$G1' \cdot G2' \cdot G3' \cdot G4'$	S2	0	1	0	0	0
S1	1	0	0	0	0	$G1 \cdot G2' \cdot G3' \cdot G4'$	SOK	0	0	0	0	0
S1	1	0	0	0	0	$G2 + G3 + G4$	SERR	0	0	0	0	1
S2	0	1	0	0	0	$G1' \cdot G2' \cdot G3' \cdot G4'$	S3	0	0	1	0	0
S2	0	1	0	0	0	$G1' \cdot G2 \cdot G3' \cdot G4'$	SOK	0	0	0	0	0
S2	0	1	0	0	0	$G1 + G3 + G4$	SERR	0	0	0	0	1
S3	0	0	1	0	0	$G1' \cdot G2' \cdot G3' \cdot G4'$	S4	0	0	0	1	0
S3	0	0	1	0	0	$G1' \cdot G2' \cdot G3 \cdot G4'$	SOK	0	0	0	0	0
S3	0	0	1	0	0	$G1 + G2 + G4$	SERR	0	0	0	0	1
S4	0	0	0	1	0	$G1' \cdot G2' \cdot G3' \cdot G4'$	S1	1	0	0	0	0
S4	0	0	0	1	0	$G1' \cdot G2' \cdot G3' \cdot G4$	SOK	0	0	0	0	0
S4	0	0	0	1	0	$G1 + G2 + G3$	SERR	0	0	0	0	1
SOK	0	0	0	0	0	$G1 + G2 + G3 + G4$	SOK	0	0	0	0	0
SOK	0	0	0	0	0	$G1' \cdot G2' \cdot G3' \cdot G4'$	S1	1	0	0	0	0
SERR	0	0	0	0	1	$G1 + G2 + G3 + G4$	SERR	0	0	0	0	1
SERR	0	0	0	0	1	$G1' \cdot G2' \cdot G3' \cdot G4'$	S1	1	0	0	0	0

possible disposition for unused states, one that we haven't discussed before, is obtained by careful use of "don't-cares" in the assignment of coded states to current states.

Table 7-17 shows one such state assignment for the guessing-game machine, derived from the output-coded state assignment of the preceding subsection. In this example, every possible combination of current-state variables corresponds to one of the coded states (e.g., $10111 = S1$, $00101 = S3$). However, *next states* are coded using the same unique combinations as in the preceding subsection. Table 7-18 shows the resulting transition list.

State	**L1**	**L2**	**L3**	**L4**	**ERR**
S1	1	x	x	x	x
S2	0	1	x	x	x
S3	0	0	1	x	x
S4	0	0	0	1	x
SOK	0	0	0	0	0
SERR	0	0	0	0	1

Table 7-17
Current-state assignment for the guessing-game machine using don't-cares.

Table 7-18 Transition list for guessing-game machine using don't-care state codings.

| Current State | | | | | | Transition Expression | Next State | | | | | |
S	L1	L2	L3	L4	ERR		S*	L1*	L2*	L3*	L4*	ERR*
S1	1	x	x	x	x	$G1' \cdot G2' \cdot G3' \cdot G4'$	S2	0	1	0	0	0
S1	1	x	x	x	x	$G1 \cdot G2' \cdot G3' \cdot G4'$	SOK	0	0	0	0	0
S1	1	x	x	x	x	$G2 + G3 + G4$	SERR	0	0	0	0	1
S2	0	1	x	x	x	$G1' \cdot G2' \cdot G3' \cdot G4'$	S3	0	0	1	0	0
S2	0	1	x	x	x	$G1' \cdot G2 \cdot G3' \cdot G4'$	SOK	0	0	0	0	0
S2	0	1	x	x	x	$G1 + G3 + G4$	SERR	0	0	0	0	1
S3	0	0	1	x	x	$G1' \cdot G2' \cdot G3' \cdot G4'$	S4	0	0	0	1	0
S3	0	0	1	x	x	$G1' \cdot G2' \cdot G3 \cdot G4'$	SOK	0	0	0	0	0
S3	0	0	1	x	x	$G1 + G2 + G4$	SERR	0	0	0	0	1
S4	0	0	0	1	x	$G1' \cdot G2' \cdot G3' \cdot G4'$	S1	1	0	0	0	0
S4	0	0	0	1	x	$G1' \cdot G2' \cdot G3' \cdot G4$	SOK	0	0	0	0	0
S4	0	0	0	1	x	$G1 + G2 + G3$	SERR	0	0	0	0	1
SOK	0	0	0	0	0	$G1 + G2 + G3 + G4$	SOK	0	0	0	0	0
SOK	0	0	0	0	0	$G1' \cdot G2' \cdot G3' \cdot G4'$	S1	1	0	0	0	0
SERR	0	0	0	0	1	$G1 + G2 + G3 + G4$	SERR	0	0	0	0	1
SERR	0	0	0	0	1	$G1' \cdot G2' \cdot G3' \cdot G4'$	S1	1	0	0	0	0

In this approach, each unused current state behaves like a nearby "normal" state; Figure 7-61 illustrates the concept. The machine is well behaved and goes to a "normal state" if it inadvertently enters an unused state. Yet the approach still allows some simplification of the excitation and output logic by introducing

Figure 7-61
State assignment using don't-cares for current states.

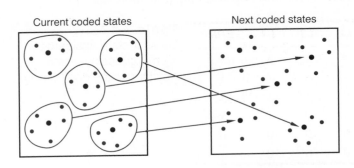

Current coded states   Next coded states

don't-cares in the transition list. When a row's transition p-term is written, current-state variables that are don't-cares in that row are omitted; for example,

$$
\begin{aligned}
\text{ERR*} = \ & \text{L1} \cdot (\text{G2} + \text{G3} + \text{G4}) \\
& + \text{L1}' \cdot \text{L2} \cdot (\text{G1} + \text{G3} + \text{G4}) \\
& + \text{L1}' \cdot \text{L2}' \cdot \text{L3} \cdot (\text{G1} + \text{G2} + \text{G4}) \\
& + \text{L1}' \cdot \text{L2}' \cdot \text{L3}' \cdot \text{L4} \cdot (\text{G1} + \text{G2} + \text{G3}) \\
& + \text{L1}' \cdot \text{L2}' \cdot \text{L3}' \cdot \text{L4}' \cdot \text{ERR} \cdot (\text{G1} + \text{G2} + \text{G3} + \text{G4})
\end{aligned}
$$

Compared with the ERR* equation in the preceding subsection, the one above still requires 16 terms to express as a sum of products. However, it requires only five terms in minimal product-of-sums form, which makes its complement more suitable for realization in a PLD.

7.8 Decomposing State Machines

Just like large procedures or subroutines in a programming language, large state machines are difficult to conceptualize, design, and debug. Therefore, when faced with a large state-machine problem, digital designers often look for opportunities to solve it with a collection of smaller state machines.

There's a well-developed theory of *state-machine decomposition* that you can use to analyze any given, monolithic state machine to determine whether it can be realized as a collection of smaller ones. However, decomposition theory is not too useful for designers who want to avoid designing large state machines in the first place. Rather, a practical designer tries to cast the original design problem into a natural, hierarchical structure, so that the uses and functions of submachines are obvious, making it unnecessary ever to write a state table for the equivalent monolithic machine.

state-machine decomposition

The simplest and most commonly used type of decomposition is illustrated in Figure 7-62. A *main machine* provides the primary inputs and outputs and executes the top-level control algorithm. *Submachines* perform low-level steps under the control of the main machine and may optionally handle some of the primary inputs and outputs.

main machine
submachines

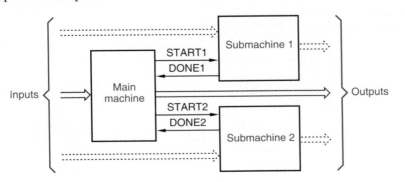

Figure 7-62
A typical, hierarchical state-machine structure.

Perhaps the most commonly used submachine is a counter. The main machine starts the counter when it wishes to stay in a particular main state for n clock ticks, and the counter asserts a DONE signal when n ticks have occurred. The main machine is designed to wait in the same state until DONE is asserted. This adds an extra output and input to the main machine (START and DONE), but it saves $n - 1$ states.

An example decomposed state machine designed along these lines is based on the guessing game of Section 7.7. The original guessing game is easy to win after a minute of practice because the lamps cycle at a very consistent rate of 4 Hz. To make the game more challenging, we can double or triple the clock speed but allow the lamps to stay in each state for a random length of time. Then the user truly must guess whether a given lamp will stay on long enough for the corresponding pushbutton to be pressed.

A block diagram for the enhanced guessing game is shown in Figure 7-63. The main machine is basically the same as before, except that it advances from one lamp state to the next only if the enable input EN is asserted, as shown by the state diagram in Figure 7-64. The enable input is driven by the output of a pseudorandom sequence generator, a linear feedback shift register (LFSR).

Another obvious candidate for decomposition is a state machine that performs binary multiplication using the shift-and-add algorithm, or binary division using the shift-and-subtract algorithm. To perform an n-bit operation, these algorithms require an initialization step, n computation steps, and possible cleanup steps. The main machine for such an algorithm contains states for initialization, step-by-step computation, and cleanup steps, and a modulo-n counter can be used as a submachine to control the number of computation steps executed.

Figure 7-63
Block diagram of guessing game with random delay.

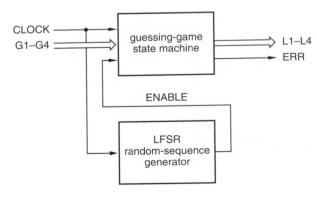

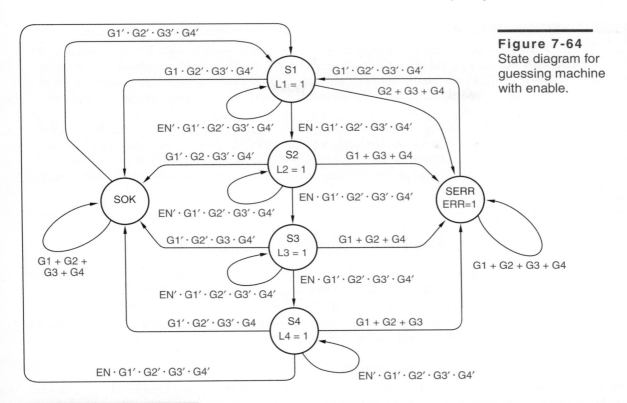

Figure 7-64
State diagram for guessing machine with enable.

A SHIFTY CIRCUIT   LFSR circuits are described in Section 8.5.6. In Figure 7-63, the low-order bit of an n-bit LFSR counter is used as the enable signal. Thus, the length of time that a particular lamp stays on depends on the counting sequence of the LFSR.

In the best case for the user, the LFSR contains 10...00; in this case the lamp is on for $n-1$ clock ticks, because it takes that long for the single 1 to shift into the low-order bit position. In the worst case, the LFSR contains 11...11, and shifting occurs for n consecutive clock ticks. At other times, shifting stops for a time determined by the number of consecutive 0s starting with the low-order bit of the LFSR.

All of these cases are quite unpredictable, unless the user has memorized the shifting cycle ($2^n - 1$ states) or is very fast at Galois-field arithmetic. Obviously, a large value of n (≥ 16) provides the most fun.

WHAT NEXT?   You may or may not be interested in the next two, optional sections on feedback sequential circuits. If not, please skip ahead and read about state-machine design using your favorite HDL—ABEL, VHDL, or Verilog—in Section 7.11.2, 7.12.2, or 7.13.2, respectively. It's a lot easier than what we've covered so far!

*7.9 Feedback Sequential-Circuit Analysis

The simple bistable and the various latches and flip-flops that we studied earlier in this chapter are all feedback sequential circuits. Each has one or more feedback loops that, ignoring their behavior during state transitions, store a 0 or a 1 at all times. The feedback loops are memory elements, and the circuits' behavior depends on both the current inputs and the values stored in the loops.

*7.9.1 Basic Analysis

fundamental-mode circuit

Feedback sequential circuits are the most common example of *fundamental-mode circuits*. In such circuits, inputs are not normally allowed to change simultaneously. The analysis procedure assumes that inputs change one at a time, allowing enough time between successive changes for the circuit to settle into a stable internal state. This differs from clocked circuits, in which multiple inputs can change at almost arbitrary times without affecting the state, and all input values are sampled and state changes occur with respect to a clock signal.

Like clocked synchronous state machines, feedback sequential circuits may be structured as Mealy or Moore circuits, as shown in Figure 7-65. A circuit with n feedback loops has n binary state variables and 2^n states.

To analyze a feedback sequential circuit, we must break the feedback loops in Figure 7-65 so that the next value stored in each loop can be predicted as a function of the circuit inputs and the current value stored in all loops. Figure 7-66 shows how to do this for the NAND circuit for a D latch, which has only one feedback loop. We conceptually break the loop by inserting a fictional buffer in the loop as shown. The output of the buffer, named Y, is the single state variable for this example.

Let us assume that the propagation delay of the fictional buffer is 10 ns (but any nonzero number will do) and that all of the other circuit components have

---

*This section and all of its subsections are optional.

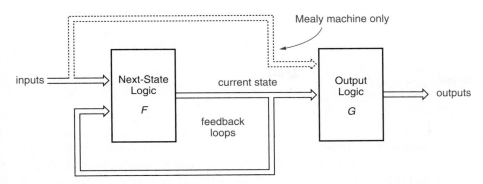

Figure 7-65
Feedback sequential circuit structure for Mealy and Moore machines.

zero delay. If we know the circuit's current state (Y) and inputs (D and C), then we can predict the value Y will have in 10 ns. The next value of Y, denoted Y∗, is a combinational function of the current state and inputs. Thus, reading the circuit diagram, we can write an *excitation equation* for Y∗:

excitation equation

$$Y* = (C \cdot D) + (C \cdot D' + Y')'$$
$$= C \cdot D + C' \cdot Y + D \cdot Y$$

Now the state of the feedback loop (and the circuit) can be written as a function of the current state and input, and enumerated by a *transition table* as shown in Figure 7-67. Each cell in the transition table shows the fictional-buffer output value that will occur 10 ns (or whatever delay you've assumed) after the corresponding state and input combination occurs.

transition table

A transition table has one row for each possible combination of the state variables, so a circuit with n feedback loops has 2^n rows in its transition table. The table has one column for each possible input combination, so a circuit with m inputs has 2^m columns in its transition table.

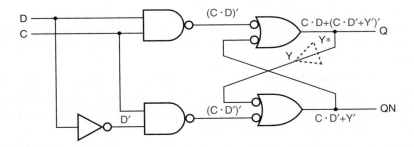

Figure 7-66
Feedback analysis of a D latch.

JUST ONE LOOP   The way the circuit in Figure 7-66 is drawn, it may look like there are two feedback loops. However, once we make one break as shown, there are no more loops. That is, each signal can be written as a combinational function of the other signals, not including itself.

	C D			
Y	00	01	11	10
0	0	0	1	0
1	1	1	1	0
		Y*		

Figure 7-67
Transition table for the
D latch in Figure 7-66.

By definition, a fundamental-mode circuit such as a feedback sequential circuit does not have a clock to tell it when to sample its inputs. Instead, we can imagine that the circuit is evaluating its current state and input *continuously* (or every 10 ns, if you prefer). As the result of each evaluation, it goes to a next state predicted by the transition table. Most of the time, the next state is the same as the current state; this is the essence of fundamental-mode operation. We make some definitions below that will help us study this behavior in more detail.

total state
internal state
input state
stable total state

unstable total state
state table

In a fundamental-mode circuit, a *total state* is a particular combination of *internal state* (the values stored in the feedback loops) and *input state* (the current value of the circuit inputs). A *stable total state* is a combination of internal state and input state such that the next internal state predicted by the transition table is the same as the current internal state. If the next internal state is different, then the combination is an *unstable total state*. We have rewritten the transition table for the D latch in Figure 7-68 as a *state table*, giving the names S0 and S1 to the states and drawing a circle around the stable total states.

To complete the analysis of the circuit, we must also determine how the outputs behave as functions of the internal state and inputs. There are two outputs and hence two *output equations*:

output equation

$$Q = C \cdot D + C' \cdot Y + D \cdot Y$$
$$QN = C \cdot D' + Y'$$

Note that Q and QN are *outputs*, not state variables. Even though the circuit has two outputs, which can theoretically take on four combinations, it has only one state variable Y, and hence only two states.

The output values predicted by the Q and QN equations can be incorporated in a combined state and output table that completely describes the operation of the circuit, as shown in Figure 7-69. Although Q and QN are normally complementary, it is possible for them to have the same value (1) momentarily, during the transition from S0 to S1 under the C D = 11 column of the table.

We can now predict the behavior of the circuit from the transition and output table. First of all, notice that we have written the column labels in our state tables in "Karnaugh map" order, so that only a single input bit changes between adjacent columns of the table. This layout helps our analysis because we assume that only one input changes at a time and that the circuit always reaches a stable total state before another input changes.

	C D			
S	00	01	11	10
S0	(S0)	(S0)	S1	(S0)
S1	(S1)	(S1)	(S1)	S0
		S*		

Figure 7-68
State table for the D latch in Figure 7-66, showing stable total states.

	C D			
S	00	01	11	10
S0	(S0), 01	(S0), 01	S1, 11	(S0), 01
S1	(S1), 10	(S1), 10	(S1), 10	S0, 01
		S*, Q QN		

Figure 7-69
State and output table for the D latch.

At any time, the circuit is in a particular internal state and a particular input is applied to it; we called this combination the total state of the circuit. Let us start at the stable total state "S0/00" (S = S0, C D = 00), as shown in Figure 7-70. Now suppose that we change D to 1. The total state moves to one cell to the right; we have a new stable total state, S0/01. The D input is different, but the internal state and output are the same as before. Next, let us change C to 1. The total state moves one cell to the right to S0/11, which is unstable. The next-state entry in this cell sends the circuit to internal state S1, so the total state moves down one cell, to S1/11. Examining the next-state entry in the new cell, we find that we have reached a stable total state. We can trace the behavior of the circuit for any desired sequence of single input changes in this way.

Now we can revisit the question of simultaneous input changes. Even though "almost simultaneous" input changes may occur in practice, we must assume that nothing happens simultaneously in order to analyze the behavior of sequential circuits. The impossibility of simultaneous events is supported by the varying delays of circuit components themselves, which depend on voltage, temperature, and fabrication parameters. What this tells us is that a set of n

	C D			
S	00	01	11	10
S0	(S0), 01	(S0), 01	S1, 11	(S0), 01
S1	(S1), 10	(S1), 10	(S1), 10	S0, 01
		S*, Q QN		

Figure 7-70
Analysis of the D latch for a few transitions.

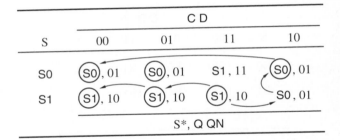

		C D		
S	00	01	11	10
S0	(S0), 01	(S0), 01	S1 , 11	(S0), 01
S1	(S1), 10	(S1), 10	(S1), 10	S0 , 01
		S*, Q QN		

Figure 7-71
Multiple input changes
with the D latch.

inputs that appear to us to change "simultaneously" may actually change in any of $n!$ different orders from the point of view of the circuit operation.

For example, consider the operation of the D latch as shown in Figure 7-71. Let us assume that it starts in stable total state S1/11. Now suppose that C and D are both "simultaneously" set to 0. In reality, the circuit behaves as if one or the other input went to 0 first. Suppose that C changes first. Then the sequence of two left-pointing arrows in the table tells us that the circuit goes to stable total state S1/00. However, if D changes first, then the other sequence of arrows tells us that the circuit goes to stable total state S0/00. So the final state of the circuit is unpredictable, a clue that the feedback loop may actually become metastable if we set C and D to 0 simultaneously. The time span over which this view of simultaneity is relevant is the setup- and hold-time window of the D latch.

Simultaneous input changes don't always cause unpredictable behavior. However, we must analyze the effects of all possible orderings of signal changes to determine this; if all orderings give the same result, then the circuit output is predictable. For example, consider the behavior of the D latch starting in total state S0/00 with C and D simultaneously changing from 0 to 1; it always ends up in total state S1/11.

*7.9.2 Analyzing Circuits with Multiple Feedback Loops

In circuits with multiple feedback loops, we must break all of the loops, creating one fictional buffer and state variable for each loop that we break. There are many possible ways, which mathematicians call *cut sets*, to break the loops in a given circuit, so how do we know which one is best? The answer is that any *minimal cut set*—a cut set with a minimum number of cuts—is fine. Mathematicians can give you an algorithm for finding a minimal cut set, but as a digital designer working on small circuits, you can just eyeball the circuit to find one.

cut set

minimal cut set

Different cut sets for a circuit lead to different excitation equations, transition tables, and state/output tables. However, the stable total states derived from one minimal cut set correspond one-to-one to the stable total states derived from any other minimal cut set for the same circuit. That is, state/output tables derived from different minimal cut sets display the same input/output behavior, with only the names and coding of the states changed.

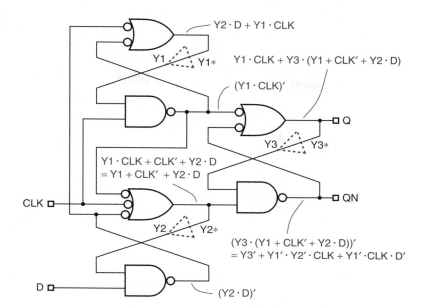

Figure 7-72
Simplified positive
edge-triggered
D flip-flop for analysis.

If you use more than the minimal number of cuts to analyze a feedback sequential circuit, the resulting state/output table will still describe the circuit correctly. However, it will use 2^m times as many states as necessary, where m is the number of extra cuts. Formal state-minimization procedures can be used to reduce this larger table to the proper size, but it's a much better idea to select a minimal cut set in the first place.

A good example of a sequential circuit with multiple feedback loops is the commercial circuit design for a positive edge-triggered TTL D flip-flop that we showed in Figure 7-20. The circuit is redrawn in simplified form in Figure 7-72, assuming that the original circuit's PR_L and CLR_L inputs are never asserted, and also showing fictional buffers to break the three feedback loops. These three loops give rise to eight states, compared with the minimum of four states used by the two-loop design in Figure 7-19. We'll address this curious difference later.

The following excitation and output equations can be derived from the logic diagram in Figure 7-72:

$$Y1* = Y2 \cdot D + Y1 \cdot CLK$$
$$Y2* = Y1 + CLK' + Y2 \cdot D$$
$$Y3* = Y1 \cdot CLK + Y1 \cdot Y3 + Y3 \cdot CLK' + Y2 \cdot Y3 \cdot D$$
$$Q = Y1 \cdot CLK + Y1 \cdot Y3 + Y3 \cdot CLK' + Y2 \cdot Y3 \cdot D$$
$$QN = Y3' + Y1' \cdot Y2' \cdot CLK + Y1' \cdot CLK \cdot D'$$

The corresponding transition table is shown in Figure 7-73, with the stable total states circled. Before going further, we must introduce the concept of "races."

Y1 Y2 Y3	CLK D			
	00	01	11	10
000	010	010	(000)	(000)
001	011	011	000	000
010	(010)	110	110	000
011	(011)	111	111	000
100	010	010	111	111
101	011	011	111	111
110	010	(110)	111	111
111	011	(111)	(111)	(111)
	Y1* Y2* Y3*			

Figure 7-73
Transition table
for the D flip-flop
in Figure 7-72.

*7.9.3 Races

race

In a feedback sequential circuit, a *race* is said to occur when multiple internal variables change state as a result of a single input changing state. In the example of Figure 7-73, a race occurs in stable total state 011/00 when CLK is changed from 0 to 1. The table indicates that the next internal state is 000, a 2-variable change from 011.

As we've discussed previously, logic signals never really change "simultaneously." Thus, the internal state may make the change 011→000 as either 011→001→000 or 011→010→000. Figure 7-74 indicates that the example circuit, starting in total state 011/00, should go to total state 000/10 when CLK changes from 0 to 1. However, it may temporarily visit total state 001/10 or 010/10 along the way. That's OK, because the next internal state for both of these temporary states is 000; therefore, even in the temporary states, the excitation logic continues to drive the feedback loops toward the same stable total

Figure 7-74
Portion of the D flip-flop
transition table showing
a noncritical race.

Y1 Y2 Y3	CLK D			
	00	01	11	10
000	010	010	(000)	(000)
001	011	011	000	000
010	(010)	110	110	000
011	(011)	111	111	000
	Y1* Y2* Y3*			

Y1 Y2 Y3	CLK D			
	00	01	11	10
000	010	010	(000)	(000)
001	011	011	000	000
010	(010)	110	110	110
011	(011)	111	111	000
100	010	010	111	111
101	011	011	111	111
110	010	(110)	111	111
111	011	(111)	(111)	(111)
	Y1* Y2* Y3*			

Figure 7-75
A transition table
containing a critical race.

state, 000/10. Since the final state does not depend on the order in which the state
variables change, this is called a *noncritical race*.   *noncritical race*

Now suppose that the next-state entry for total state 010/10 is changed to
110, as shown in Figure 7-75, and consider the case that we just analyzed.
Starting in stable total state 011/00 and changing CLK to 1, the circuit may end
up in internal state 000 or 111, depending on the order and speed of the internal
variable changes. This is called a *critical race*.   *critical race*

> **WATCH OUT FOR CRITICAL RACES!**   When you design a feedback-based sequential circuit, you must ensure that its
> transition table does not contain any critical races. Otherwise, the circuit may operate
> unpredictably, with the next state for racy transitions depending on factors like
> temperature, voltage, and the phase of the moon.

*7.9.4 State Tables and Flow Tables

Analysis of the real transition table, Figure 7-73, for our example D flip-flop
circuit, shows that it does not have any critical races; in fact, it has no races
except the noncritical one we identified earlier. Once we've determined this fact,
we no longer need to refer to state variables. Instead, we can name the state-
variable combinations and determine the output values for each state/input
combination to obtain a state/output table such as Figure 7-76.

The state table shows that for some single input changes, the circuit takes
multiple "hops" to get to a new stable total state. For example, in state S0/11, an
input change to 01 sends the circuit first to state S2 and then to stable total state
S6/01. A *flow table* eliminates multiple hops and shows only the ultimate desti-   *flow table*

	CLK D			
S	00	01	11	10
S0	S2 , 01	S2 , 01	Ⓢ0 , 01	Ⓢ0 , 01
S1	S3 , 10	S3 , 10	S0 , 01	S0 , 10
S2	Ⓢ2 , 01	S6 , 01	S6 , 01	S0 , 01
S3	Ⓢ3 , 10	S7 , 10	S7 , 10	S0 , 01
S4	S2 , 01	S2 , 01	S7 , 11	S7 , 11
S5	S3 , 10	S3 , 10	S7 , 10	S7 , 10
S6	S2 , 01	Ⓢ6 , 01	S7 , 11	S7 , 11
S7	S3 , 10	Ⓢ7 , 10	Ⓢ7 , 10	Ⓢ7 , 10
		S* , Q QN		

Figure 7-76
State/output table
for the D flip-flop in
Figure 7-72.

nation for each transition. The flow table also eliminates the rows for unused internal states—ones that are stable for no input combination—and eliminates the next-state entries for total states that cannot be reached from a stable total state as the result of a single input change. Using these rules, Figure 7-77 shows the flow table for our D flip-flop example.

The flip-flop's edge-triggered behavior can be observed in the series of state transitions shown in Figure 7-78. Let us assume that the flip-flop starts in internal state S0/10. That is, the flip-flop is storing a 0 (since Q = 0), CLK is 1, and D is 0. Now suppose that D changes to 1; the flow table shows that we move one cell to the left, still a stable total state with the same output value. We can change D between 0 and 1 as much as we want, and just bounce back and

Figure 7-77
Flow and output table
for the D flip-flop in
Figure 7-72.

	CLK D			
S	00	01	11	10
S0	S2 , 01	S6 , 01	Ⓢ0 , 01	Ⓢ0 , 01
S2	Ⓢ2 , 01	S6 , 01	— , –	S0 , 10
S3	Ⓢ3 , 10	S7 , 10	— , –	S0 , 01
S6	S2 , 01	Ⓢ6 , 01	S7 , 11	— , –
S7	S3 , 10	Ⓢ7 , 10	Ⓢ7 , 10	Ⓢ7 , 10
		S* , Q QN		

		CLK D		
S	00	01	11	10
SB	(SB) , 01	S6 , 01	(SB) , 01	(SB) , 01
S3	(S3) , 10	S7 , 10	— , –	SB , 01
S6	SB , 01	(S6) , 01	S7 , 11	— , –
S7	S3 , 10	(S7) , 10	(S7) , 10	(S7) , 10
		S* , Q QN		

Figure 7-79
Reduced flow and output table for a positive edge-triggered D flip-flop.

forth between these two cells. However, once we change CLK to 0, we move to internal state S2 or S6, depending on whether D was 0 or 1 at the time; but still the output is unchanged. Once again, we can change D between 0 and 1 as much as we want, this time bouncing between S2 and S6 without changing the output.

The moment of truth finally comes when CLK changes to 1. Depending on whether we are in S2 or S6, we go back to S0 (leaving Q at 0) or to S7 (setting Q to 1). Similar behavior involving S3 and S7 can be observed on a rising clock edge that causes Q to change from 1 to 0.

In Figure 7-19 we showed a circuit for a positive edge-triggered D flip-flop with only two feedback loops and hence four states. The circuit that we just analyzed has three loops and eight states. Even after eliminating unused states, the flow table has five states. However, a formal state-minimization procedure can be used to show that states S0 and S2 are "compatible," so that they can be merged into a single state SB that handles the transitions for both original states, as shown in Figure 7-79. Thus, the job really could have been done by a four-state circuit. In fact, in Exercise 7.71 you'll show that the circuit in Figure 7-19 does the job specified by the reduced flow table.

		CLK D		
S	00	01	11	10
S0	S2 , 01	S6 , 01	(S0) , 01	(S0) , 01
S2	(S2) , 01	S6 , 01	— , –	S0 , 10
S3	(S3) , 10	S7 , 10	— , –	S0 , 01
S6	S2 , 01	(S6) , 01	S7 , 11	— , –
S7	S3 , 10	(S7) , 10	(S7) , 10	(S7) , 10
		S* , Q QN		

Figure 7-78
Flow and output table showing the D flip-flop's edge-triggered behavior.

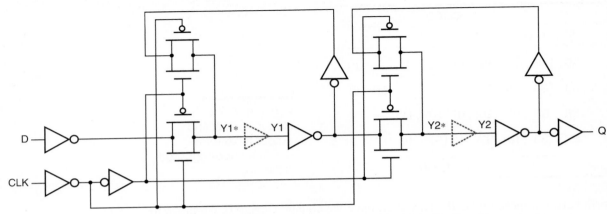

Figure 7-80 Positive edge-triggered CMOS D flip-flop for analysis.

*7.9.5 CMOS D Flip-Flop Analysis

CMOS flip-flops typically use transmission gates in their feedback loops. For example, Figure 7-80 shows the circuit design of the "FD1Q" positive-edge-triggered D flip-flop in LSI Logic's LCA500K series of CMOS gate arrays. Such a flip-flop can be analyzed in the same way as a purely logic-gate-based design, once you recognize the feedback loops. Figure 7-80 has two feedback loops, each of which has a pair of transmission gates in a mux-like configuration controlled by CLK and CLK′, yielding the following loop equations:

$$Y1* = CLK' \cdot D' + CLK \cdot Y1$$
$$Y2* = CLK \cdot Y1' + CLK' \cdot Y2$$

Except for the double inversion of the data as it goes from D to Y2∗ (once in the Y1∗ equation and again in the Y2∗ equation), these equations are very reminiscent of the master/slave-latch structure of the D flip-flop in Figure 7-15. Completing the formal analysis of the circuit is left as an exercise (7.75). Note, however, that since there are just two feedback loops, the resulting state and flow tables will have the minimum of just four states.

FEEDBACK CIRCUIT DESIGN

The feedback sequential circuits that we've analyzed in this section exhibit quite reasonable behavior, since, after all, they are latch and flip-flop circuits that have been used for years. However, if we throw together a "random" collection of gates and feedback loops, we won't necessarily get "reasonable" sequential circuit behavior. In a few rare cases we may not get a sequential circuit at all (see Exercise 7.72), and in many cases the circuit may be unstable for some or all input combinations (see Exercise 7.87). Thus, the design of feedback sequential circuits continues to be something of a black art and is practiced only by a small fraction of digital designers. Still, the next section introduces basic concepts that help you do simple designs.

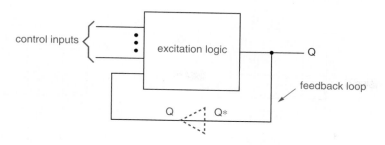

Figure 7-81
General structure
of a latch.

*7.10 Feedback Sequential-Circuit Design

It's sometimes useful to design a small feedback sequential circuit, such as a specialized latch or a pulse catcher; this section will show you how. It's even possible that you might go on to be an IC designer and be responsible for designing high-performance latches and flip-flops from scratch. This section will serve as an introduction to the basic concepts you'll need, but you'll still need considerably more study, experience, and finesse to do it right.

*7.10.1 Latches

Although the design of feedback sequential circuits is generally a hard problem, some circuits can be designed pretty easily. Any circuit with one feedback loop is just a variation of an S-R or D latch. It has the general structure shown in Figure 7-81 and an excitation equation with the following format:

$$Q* = \text{(forcing term)} + \text{(holding term)} \cdot Q$$

For example, the excitation equations for S-R and D latches are

$$Q* = S + R' \cdot Q$$
$$Q* = C \cdot D + C' \cdot Q$$

Corresponding circuits are shown in Figure 7-82(a) and (b).

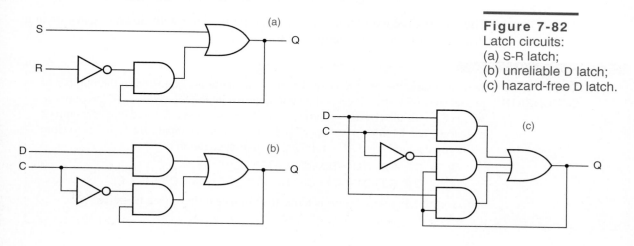

Figure 7-82
Latch circuits:
(a) S-R latch;
(b) unreliable D latch;
(c) hazard-free D latch.

Figure 7-83
Karnaugh maps for
D-latch excitation
functions: (a) original,
containing a static-1
hazard; (b) hazard
eliminated.

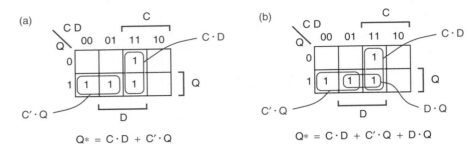

$$Q* = C \cdot D + C' \cdot Q$$

$$Q* = C \cdot D + C' \cdot Q + D \cdot Q$$

hazard-free excitation logic

In general, *the excitation logic in a feedback sequential circuit must be hazard free;* we'll demonstrate this fact by way of an example. Figure 7-83(a) is a Karnaugh map for the D-latch excitation circuit of Figure 7-82(b). The map exhibits a static-1 hazard when D and Q are 1 and C is changing. Unfortunately, the latch's feedback loop may not hold its value if a hazard-induced glitch occurs. For example, consider what happens when D and Q are 1 and C changes from 1 to 0; the circuit should latch a 1. However, unless the inverter is very fast, the output of the top AND gate goes to 0 before the output of the bottom one goes to 1, the OR-gate output goes to 0, and the feedback loop stores a 0.

Hazards can be eliminated using the methods described in Section 4.4. In the D latch, we simply include the consensus term in the excitation equation:

$$Q* = C \cdot D + C' \cdot Q + D \cdot Q$$

Figure 7-82(c) shows the corresponding hazard-free, correct D-latch circuit.

Now, suppose we need a specialized "D" latch with three data inputs, D1–D3, that stores a 1 only if D1–D3 = 010. We can convert this word description into an excitation equation that mimics the equation for a simple D latch:

$$Q* = C \cdot (D1' \cdot D2 \cdot D3') + C' \cdot Q$$

Eliminating hazards, we get

$$Q* = C \cdot D1' \cdot D2 \cdot D3' + C' \cdot Q + D1' \cdot D2 \cdot D3' \cdot Q$$

The hazard-free excitation equation can be realized with discrete gates or in a PLD, as we'll show in Section 8.2.6.

PRODUCT-TERM EXPLOSION

In some cases, the need to cover hazards can cause an explosion in the number of product terms in a two-level realization of the excitation logic. For example, suppose we need a specialized latch with two control inputs, C1 and C2, and three data inputs as before. The latch is to be "open" only if both control inputs are 1, and is to store a 1 if any data input is 1. The minimal excitation equation is

$$Q* = C1 \cdot C2 \cdot (D1 + D2 + D3) + (C1 \cdot C2)' \cdot Q$$
$$= C1 \cdot C2 \cdot D1 + C1 \cdot C2 \cdot D2 + C1 \cdot C2 \cdot D3 + C1' \cdot Q + C2' \cdot Q$$

However, it takes six consensus terms to eliminate hazards (see Exercise 7.82).

*7.10.2 Designing Fundamental-Mode Flow Table

To design feedback sequential circuits more complex than latches, we must first convert the word description into a flow table. Once we have a flow table, we can turn the crank (with some effort) to obtain a circuit.

When we construct the flow table for a feedback sequential circuit, we give each state a meaning in the context of the problem, much as we did in the design of clocked state machines. However, it's easier to get confused when constructing the flow table for a feedback sequential circuit, because not every total state is stable. Therefore, the recommended procedure is to construct a *primitive flow table*—one that has only one stable total state in each row. Since there is only one stable state per row, the output may be shown as a function of state only.

primitive flow table

In a primitive flow table, each state has a more precise "meaning" than it might otherwise have, and the table's structure clearly displays the underlying fundamental-mode assumption: inputs change one at a time, with enough time between changes for the circuit to settle into a new stable state. A primitive flow table usually has extra states, but we can "turn the crank" later to minimize the number of states, once we have a flow table that we believe to be correct.

We'll use the following problem, a "pulse-catching" circuit, to demonstrate flow-table design:

> Design a feedback sequential circuit with two inputs, P (pulse) and R (reset), and a single output Z that is normally 0. The output should be set to 1 whenever a 0-to-1 transition occurs on P, and should be reset to 0 whenever R is 1. Typical functional behavior is shown in Figure 7-84.

Figure 7-85 is a primitive flow table for the pulse catcher. Let's walk through how this table was developed.

We assume that the pulse catcher is initially idle, with P and R both 0; this is the IDLE state, with Z = 0. In this state, if reset occurs (R = 1), we could probably stay in the same state, but since this is supposed to be a *primitive* flow table, we create a new state, RES1, so as not to have two stable total states in the same row. On the other hand, if a pulse occurs (P = 1) in the IDLE state, we definitely want to go to a different state, which we've named PLS1, since we've caught a pulse and we must set the output to 1. Input combination 11 is not considered in the IDLE state, because of the fundamental-mode assumption that only one input changes at a time; we assume the circuit always makes it to another stable state before input combination 11 can occur.

Figure 7-84 Typical functional behavior of a pulse-catching circuit.

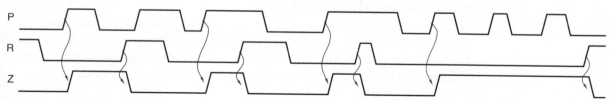

Meaning	S	PR 00	01	11	10	Z
Idle, waiting for pulse	IDLE	(IDLE)	RES1	—	PLS1	0
Reset, no pulse	RES1	IDLE	(RES1)	RES2	—	0
Got pulse, output on	PLS1	PLS2	—	RES2	(PLS1)	1
Reset, got pulse	RES2	—	RES1	(RES2)	PLSN	0
Pulse gone, output on	PLS2	(PLS2)	RES1	—	PLS1	1
Got pulse, output off	PLSN	IDLE	—	RES2	(PLSN)	0

S*

Figure 7-85
Primitive flow table for pulse-catching circuit.

Next, we fill in the next-state entries for the newly created RES1 state. If reset goes away, we can go back to the IDLE state. If a pulse occurs, we must remain in a "reset" state, since, according to the timing diagram, a 0-to-1 transition that occurs while R is 1 is ignored. Again, to keep the flow table in primitive form, we must create a new state for this case, RES2.

Now that we have one stable total state in each column, we may be able to go to existing states for more transitions, instead of always defining new states. Sure enough, starting in stable total state PLS1/10, for R = 1 we can go to RES2, which fits the requirement of producing a 0 output. On the other hand, where should we go for P = 0? IDLE is a stable total state in the 00 column, but it produces the wrong output value. In PLS1, we've gotten a pulse and haven't seen a reset, so if the pulse goes away, we should go to a state that still has Z = 1. Thus, we must create a new state PLS2 for this case.

In RES2, we can safely go to RES1 if the pulse goes away. However, we've got to be careful if reset goes away, as shown in the timing diagram. Since we've already passed the pulse's 0-to-1 transition, we can't go to the PLS1 state, since that would give us a 1 output. Instead, we create a new state PLSN with a 0 output.

Finally, we can complete the next-state entries for PLS2 and PLSN without creating any new states. Notice that, starting in PLS2, we bounce back and forth between PLS2 and PLS1 and maintain a continuous 1 output if we get a series of pulses without an intervening reset input.

*7.10.3 Flow-Table Minimization

As we mentioned earlier, a primitive flow table usually has more states than required. However, there exists a formal procedure, discussed in the References, for minimizing the number of states in a flow table. This procedure is often complicated by the existence of don't-care entries in the flow table.

S	00	01	11	10	Z
		P R			
IDLE	(IDLE)	(IDLE)	RES	PLS	0
PLS	(PLS)	IDLE	RES	(PLS)	1
RES	IDLE	IDLE	(RES)	(RES)	0
		S*			

Figure 7-86
Reduced flow table
for pulse-catching
circuit.

Fortunately, our example flow table is small and simple enough to minimize by inspection. States IDLE and RES1 produce the same output, and they have the same next-state entry for input combinations where they are both specified. Therefore, they are compatible and may be replaced by a single state (IDLE) in a reduced flow table. The same can be said for states PLS1 and PLS2 (replaced by PLS) and for RES2 and PLSN (replaced by RES). The resulting reduced flow table, which has only three states, is shown in Figure 7-86.

*7.10.4 Race-Free State Assignment

The next somewhat creative (read "difficult") step in feedback sequential circuit design is to find a race-free assignment of coded states to the named states in the reduced flow table. Recall from Section 7.9.3 that a race occurs when multiple internal variables change state as a result of a single input change. A feedback-based sequential circuit must not contain any critical races; otherwise, the circuit may operate unpredictably. As we'll see, eliminating races often necessitates *increasing* the number of states in the circuit.

A circuit's potential for having races in its transition table can be analyzed by means of a *state adjacency diagram* for its flow table. The adjacency diagram is a simplified state diagram that omits self-loops and does not show the direction of other transitions (A→B is drawn the same as B→A) or the input combinations that cause them. Figure 7-87 is an example fundamental-mode flow table and Figure 7-88(a) is the corresponding adjacency diagram.

state adjacency diagram

S	00	01	11	10
		X Y		
A	(A)	B	(A)	B
B	(B)	(B)	D	(B)
C	(C)	A	A	(C)
D	(D)	B	(D)	C
		S*		

Figure 7-87
Example flow table for
the state-assignment
problem.

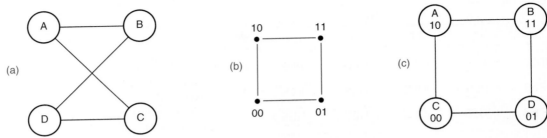

Figure 7-88 State-assignment example: (a) adjacency diagram; (b) a 2-cube; (c) one of eight possible race-free state assignments.

adjacent states

Two states are said to be *adjacent* if there is an arc between them in the state adjacency diagram. For race-free transitions, adjacent coded states must differ in only one bit. If two states A and B are adjacent, it doesn't matter whether the original flow table had transitions from A to B, from B to A, or both. Any one of these transitions is a race if A and B differ in more than one variable. That's why we don't need to show the direction of transitions in an adjacency diagram.

The problem of finding a race-free assignment of states to n state variables is equivalent to the problem of mapping the nodes and arcs of the adjacency diagram onto the nodes and arcs of an n-cube. In Figure 7-88, the problem is to map the adjacency diagram (a) onto a 2-cube (b). You can visually identify eight ways to do this (four rotations times two flips), one of which produces the state assignment shown in (c).

Figure 7-89(a) is an adjacency diagram for our pulse-catching circuit, based on the reduced flow table in Figure 7-86. Clearly, there's no way to map this "triangle" of states onto a 2-cube. At this point, we can only go back and modify the original flow table. In particular, the flow table tells us the destination state that we *eventually* must reach for each transition, but it doesn't prevent us from going through other states on the way. As shown in Figure 7-90, we can create a new state RESA and make the transition from PLS to RES by going through RESA. The modified state table has the new adjacency diagram shown

Figure 7-89 Adjacency diagrams for the pulse catcher: (a) using original flow table; (b) after adding a state; (c) showing one of eight possible race-free state assignments.

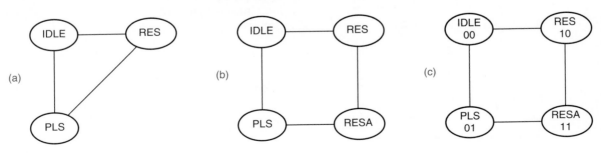

	P R				
S	00	01	11	10	Z
IDLE	(IDLE)	(IDLE)	RES	PLS	0
PLS	(PLS)	IDLE	RESA	(PLS)	1
RESA	—	—	RES	—	–
RES	IDLE	IDLE	(RES)	(RES)	0
			S*		

Figure 7-90
State table allowing a race-free assignment for the pulse-catching circuit.

in Figure 7-89(b), which has many race-free assignments possible. A transition table based on the assignment in (c) is shown in Figure 7-92. Note that the PLS→RESA→RES transition will be slower than the other transitions in the original flow table because it requires two internal state changes, with two propagation delays through the feedback loops.

Even though we added a state in the previous example, we still got by with just two state variables. However, we may sometimes have to add one or more state variables to make a race-free assignment. Figure 7-91(a) shows the worst possible adjacency diagram for four states—every state is adjacent to every other state. Clearly, this adjacency diagram cannot be mapped onto a 2-cube. However, there is a race-free assignment of states to a 3-cube, shown in (b), where each state in the original flow table is represented by two equivalent states in the final state table. Both states in a pair, such as A1 and A2, are equivalent and produce the same output. Each state is adjacent to one of the states in every other pair, so a race-free transition may be selected for each next-state entry.

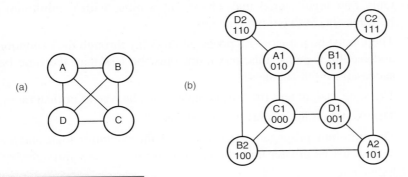

Figure 7-91
A worst-case scenario:
(a) four-state adjacency diagram;
(b) assignment using pairs of equivalent states.

HANDLING THE GENERAL ASSIGNMENT CASE

In the general case of a flow table with 2^n rows, it can be shown that a race-free assignment can be obtained using $2n - 1$ state variables (see References). However, there aren't many applications for fundamental-mode circuits with more than a few states, so the general case is of little more than academic interest.

	P R				
Y1 Y2	00	01	11	10	Z
00	⟨00⟩	⟨00⟩	10	01	0
01	⟨01⟩	00	11	⟨01⟩	1
11	—	—	10	—	–
10	00	00	⟨10⟩	⟨10⟩	0
	Y1∗ Y2∗				

Figure 7-92
Race-free transition
table for the pulse-
catching circuit.

*7.10.5 Excitation Equations

Once we have a race-free transition table for a circuit, we can just "turn the crank" to obtain excitation equations for the feedback loops. Figure 7-92 is the pulse catcher's transition table. Its "don't-care" next-state and output entries can be used in the corresponding Karnaugh maps to simplify the circuit's excitation and output logic. Since the excitation logic in a feedback sequential circuit must be hazard free, it might be necessary to add product terms to eliminate hazards. Detailed derivation of the excitation equations is left as an exercise (7.84), but the resulting circuit will be shown later, in Figure 7-94 on page 610.

*7.10.6 Essential Hazards

After all this effort, you'd think that we'd have a pulse catcher that works reliably all of the time. Unfortunately, we're not quite there yet. A fundamental-mode circuit must generally satisfy five requirements for proper operation:

1. Only one input signal may change at a time, with a minimum bound between successive input changes.

2. There must be a maximum propagation delay through the excitation logic and feedback paths; this maximum must be less than the time between successive input changes.

3. The state assignment (transition table) must be free of critical races.

4. The excitation logic must be hazard free.

5. The minimum propagation delay through the excitation logic and feedback paths must be greater than the maximum timing skew through the "input logic."

Without the first requirement, it would be impossible to satisfy the major premise of fundamental-mode operation—that the circuit has time to settle into a stable total state between successive input changes. The second requirement says that the excitation logic is fast enough to do just that. The third ensures that

	P R				
Y1 Y2	00	01	11	10	Z
00	00	00	10	01	0
01	01	00	11	01	1
11	—	—	10	—	—
10	00	00	10	10	0

Y1* Y2*

Figure 7-93
Transition table for the
pulse-catching circuit,
exhibiting an
essential hazard.

the proper state changes are made, even if the excitation circuits for different state variables have different delays. The fourth ensures that state variables that aren't supposed to change on a particular transition don't.

The last requirement deals with subtle timing-dependent errors that can occur in fundamental-mode circuits, even ones that satisfy the first four requirements. An *essential hazard* is the possibility of a circuit's going to an erroneous next state as the result of a single input change; the error occurs if the input change is not seen by all of the excitation circuits before the resulting state-variable transition(s) propagate back to the inputs of the excitation circuits. In a world where "faster is better" is the usual rule, a designer may sometimes have to *slow down* excitation logic to mask these hazards.

essential hazard

Essential hazards can be found in most but not all fundamental-mode circuits. There's an easy rule for detecting them; in fact, this is the definition of "essential hazard" in some texts:

- A fundamental-mode flow table contains an essential hazard for a stable total state S and an input variable X if, starting in state S, the stable total state reached after three successive transitions in X is different from the stable total state reached after one transition in X.

The pulse catcher's transition table is repeated in Figure 7-93, this time showing arrows for the transitions that prove the existence of the essential hazard, starting in internal state 10 with P R = 10.

The pulse catcher's essential hazard can be seen in its realization, shown in Figure 7-94 on the next page. Suppose we built this circuit on a PCB or a chip, and we (or, more likely, our CAD system) inadvertently connected input signal P through a long, slow path. Let's assume that this delay is longer than the propagation delay of the AND-OR excitation logic.

Now consider what can happen if P R = 10, the circuit is in internal state 10, and P changes from 1 to 0. According to the transition table in Figure 7-93, the circuit should go to internal state 00, and that's that. But let's look at the actual operation of the circuit, as traced in Figure 7-94:

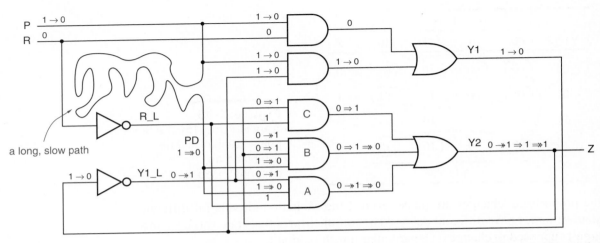

Figure 7-94 Physical conditions in pulse-catching circuit for exhibiting an essential hazard.

- (Changes shown with "→") The first thing that happens after P changes is that Y1 changes from 1 to 0. Now the circuit is in internal state 00.

- (Changes shown with "⟶⟶") Y1_L changes from 0 to 1. The change in Y1_L at AND gate A causes its output to go to 1, which in turn forces Y2 to 1. Whoops, now the circuit is in internal state 01.

- (Changes shown with "⟹") The change in Y2 at AND gates B and C causes their outputs to go to 1, reinforcing the 1 output at Y2. All this time, we've been waiting for the 1-to-0 change in P to appear at point PD.

- (Changes shown with "⟹⟹") Finally, PD changes from 1 to 0, forcing the outputs of AND gates A and B to 0. However, AND gate C still has a 1 output, and the circuit remains in state 01—*the wrong state*.

The only way to avoid this erroneous behavior in general is to ensure that changes in P arrive at the inputs of all the excitation circuits before any changes in state variables do. Thus, the inevitable difference in input arrival times, called *timing skew*, must be less than the propagation delay of the excitation circuits and feedback loops. This timing requirement can generally be satisfied only by careful design *at the electrical circuit level*.

timing skew

In the example circuit, it would appear that the hazard is easily masked, even by non-electrical engineers, since the designer need only ensure that a straight wire has shorter propagation delay than an AND-OR structure—easy in most technologies.

Still, many feedback sequential circuits, such as the TTL edge-triggered D flip-flop in Figure 7-19, have essential hazards in which the input skew paths include inverters. In such cases, the input inverters must be guaranteed to be faster than the excitation logic; that's not so trivial in either board-level or IC design. For example, if the excitation circuit in Figure 7-94 were physically built using AND-OR-INVERT gates, the delay from input changes to Y1_L could be very short indeed, as short as the delay through a single inverter.

A fundamental-mode circuit must have at least three states to have an essential hazard, so latches don't have them. On the other hand, all flip-flops (circuits that sample inputs on a clock edge) do.

THESE HAZARDS ARE, WELL, ESSENTIAL!	Essential hazards are called "essential" because they are inherent in the flow table for a particular sequential function and will appear in any circuit realization of that function. They can be masked only by controlling the delays in the circuit. Compare with static hazards in combinational logic, where we could eliminate hazards by adding consensus terms to a logic expression.

*7.10.7 Summary

In summary, you use the following steps to design a feedback sequential circuit:

1. Construct a primitive flow table from the circuit's word description.   *primitive flow table*

2. Minimize the number of states in the flow table.   *state minimization*

3. Find a race-free assignment of coded states to named states, adding auxiliary states or splitting states as required.   *state assignment*

4. Construct the transition table.   *transition table*

5. Construct excitation maps and find a hazard-free realization of the excitation equations.   *excitation maps and equations*

6. Check for essential hazards. Modify the circuit if necessary to ensure that minimum excitation and feedback delays are greater than maximum inverter or other input-logic delays.   *essential hazards*

7. Draw the logic diagram.   *logic diagram*

Also note that some circuits routinely violate the basic fundamental-mode assumption that inputs change one at a time. For example, in a positive-edge-triggered D flip-flop, the D input may change at the same time that CLK changes from 1 to 0, and the flip-flop still operates properly. The same thing certainly cannot be said at the 0-to-1 transition of CLK. Such situations require analysis of the transition table and circuit on a case-by-case basis if proper operation in "special cases" is to be guaranteed.

A FINAL QUESTION	Given the difficulty of designing fundamental-mode circuits that work properly, let alone ones that are fast or compact, how did anyone ever come up with the 6-gate, 8-state, 74LS74 D flip-flop design in Figure 7-20? Don't ask me, I don't know!

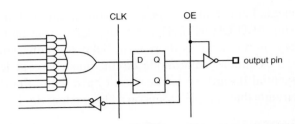

Figure 7-95
PLD registered output.

7.11 ABEL Sequential-Circuit Design Features

7.11.1 Registered Outputs

registered output

ABEL has several features that support the design of sequential circuits. As we'll show in Section 8.3, most PLD outputs can be configured to be *registered outputs* that provide a D flip-flop following the AND-OR logic, as in Figure 7-95. To configure one or more outputs to be registered, an ABEL program's pin declarations normally must contain an `istype` clause using the keyword "reg" (rather than "com") for each registered output. Table 7-19 is an ABEL program for the combination-lock state-machine that we designed in Section 7.4.6 beginning on page 568. This program simply specifies the equations for the machine's three registered and two combinational outputs, as explained next.

reg keyword

.CLK
.OE
.AR
.AP
.SR
.SP

A registered output has at least two other attributes associated with it, both shown in Figure 7-95. The three-state buffer driving the output pin has an output-enable input OE, and the flip-flop itself has a clock input CLK. As shown in Table 7-19, the signals that drive these inputs are specified in the `equations` section of the program. Each input signal is specified as the corresponding main output signal name followed by an attribute suffix, `.CLK` or `.OE`. Some PLDs have flip-flops with additional controllable inputs. For example, asynchronous reset and preset inputs have attribute suffixes `.AR` and `.AP`; synchronous reset and preset inputs use suffixes `.SR` and `.SP`. And some PLDs provide flip-flop types other than D; their inputs are specified with suffixes like `.J` and `.K`.

*clocked assignment
operator, :=*

Within the `equations` section of the ABEL program, the logic values for registered outputs are established using the *clocked assignment operator, :=*. When the PLD is compiled, the expression on the righthand side will be applied to the D input of the output flip-flop. All of the same rules as for combinational outputs apply to output polarity control, on-set generation, don't-cares, and so on. In Table 7-19, the state bits Q1–Q3 are registered outputs, so they use clocked assignment, ":=". The UNLK and HINT signals are Mealy outputs, combinational functions of current state and input, so they use unclocked

---

**IS `istype`
ESSENTIAL?**   Most compilers can deduce from the equations whether a given PLD output should be configured to be registered or not. Still, it's a good idea to include the `istype` information, both as a double check and to enhance design portability.

Table 7-19
ABEL program using
registered outputs.

```
module CombLock
title 'Combination-Lock State Machine'

" Input and Outputs
X, CLOCK        pin;
UNLK, HINT      pin istype 'com';
Q1, Q2, Q3      pin istype 'reg';

Q = [Q1..Q3];

equations
Q.CLK = CLOCK; Q.OE = 1;

" State variables
Q1 := Q1 & !Q2 & X   #  !Q1 & Q2 & Q3 & !X   #   Q1 & Q2 & !Q3;
Q2 := !Q2 & Q3 & X   #   Q2 & !Q3 & X;
Q3 := Q1 & !Q2 & !Q3   #   Q1 & Q3 & !X   #   !Q2 & !X
      #   !Q1 & !Q3 & !X   #   Q2 & !Q3 & X;

" Mealy outputs
UNLK = Q1 & Q2 & Q3 & !X;
HINT = !Q1 & !Q2 & !Q3 & !X   #   Q1 & !Q2 & X   #   !Q2 & Q3 & X
      #   Q2 & Q3 & !X   #   Q2 & !Q3 & X;

end CombLock
```

assignment, "=". A machine with pipelined outputs (Figure 7-37 on page 544) would instead use clocked assignment for such outputs.

ABEL's truth-table syntax (Table 5-6 on page 250) can also be used with registered outputs. The only difference is that the "->" operator between input and output items is changed to ":>".

clocked truth-table operator, :>

You can also design feedback sequential circuits in ABEL without using any of the language's sequential-circuit features. For example, in Section 8.2.6 we show how to specify latches using ABEL.

7.11.2 State Diagrams

The state-machine in Table 7-19 just transcribes the excitation and output equations that we derived by hand in Section 7.4.6, so we didn't save much work by using ABEL. However, most PLD programming languages have a notation for defining, documenting, and synthesizing state machines directly, without ever writing a state, transition, or excitation table or deriving excitation and output equations by hand. Such a notation is called a *state-machine description language*. In ABEL, this notation is called a "state diagram," and the ABEL compiler does all the work of generating excitation and output equations that realize the specified machine.

state-machine description language

In ABEL, the keyword *state_diagram* indicates the beginning of a state-machine definition. Table 7-20 shows the textual structure of an ABEL "state

state_diagram keyword

Table 7-20
Structure of a "state diagram" in ABEL.

```
state_diagram state-vector
state state-value 1 : transition statement ;
state state-value 2 : transition statement ;
    . . .
state state-value 2ⁿ : transition statement ;
```

state-vector

diagram." Here *state-vector* is an ABEL set that lists the state variables of the machine. If there are n variables in the set, then the machine has 2^n possible states corresponding to the 2^n different assignments of constant values to variables in the set. States are usually given symbolic names in an ABEL program; this makes it easy to try different assignments simply by changing the constant definitions.

The on-set for each state variable is created according to the information in the "state diagram." If a state variable also appears on the lefthand side of an equation in the `equations` section, the effects are cumulative (see the box on page 746 for a useful application of this behavior). The keyword `state` indicates that the next states and current outputs for a particular current state are about to be defined; a *state-value* is a constant that defines state-variable values for the current state. A *transition statement* defines the possible next states for the current state.

state keyword

state-value
transition statement

goto statement
if statement

ABEL has two commonly used transition statements. The *goto statement* unconditionally specifies the next state, for example "`goto INIT`". The *if statement* defines the possible next states as a function of an arbitrary logic expression. (There's also a seldom-used `case` statement that we don't cover.)

Table 7-21 shows the syntax of the ABEL `if` statement. Here *TrueState* and *FalseState* are state values that the machine will go to if *LogicExpression* is true or false, respectively. These statements can be nested: *FalseState* can itself be another `if` statement, and *TrueState* can be an `if` statement if it is enclosed in braces. When multiple next states are possible, a nested `if-then-else` structure eliminates the ambiguities that can occur in hand-drawn state diagrams, where the transition conditions leaving a state can overlap (Section 7.5).

Our first example using ABEL's "state diagram" capability is based on our first state-machine design example from Section 7.4.1 on page 554. A state table for this machine was developed in Figure 7-47 on page 557. It is adapted to ABEL in Table 7-22. Several characteristics of this program should be noted:

- The definition of `QSTATE` uses three variables to encode state.
- The definitions of `INIT–XTRA3` determine the individual state encodings.

Table 7-21
Structure of an ABEL `if` statement.

```
if LogicExpression then
    TrueState
else
    FalseState ;
```

Table 7-22
An example of ABEL's
state-diagram
notation.

```
module SMEX1
title 'PLD Version of Example State Machine'

" Input and output pins
CLOCK, RESET_L, A, B            pin;
Q1..Q3                         pin istype 'reg';
Z                              pin istype 'com';

" Definitions
QSTATE = [Q1,Q2,Q3];            " State variables
INIT   = [ 0, 0, 0];
A0     = [ 0, 0, 1];
A1     = [ 0, 1, 0];
OK0    = [ 0, 1, 1];
OK1    = [ 1, 0, 0];
XTRA1  = [ 1, 0, 1];
XTRA2  = [ 1, 1, 0];
XTRA3  = [ 1, 1, 1];
RESET = !RESET_L;

state_diagram QSTATE

state INIT: if RESET then INIT
            else if (A==0) then A0
            else A1;

state A0:   if RESET then INIT
            else if (A==0) then OK0
            else A1;

state A1:   if RESET then INIT
            else if (A==0) then A0
            else OK1;

state OK0:  if RESET then INIT
            else if (B==1)&(A==0) then OK0
            else if (B==1)&(A==1) then OK1
            else if (A==0) then OK0
            else if (A==1) then A1;

state OK1:  if RESET then INIT
            else if (B==1)&(A==0) then OK0
            else if (B==1)&(A==1) then OK1
            else if (A==0) then A0
            else if (A==1) then OK1;

state XTRA1: goto INIT;
state XTRA2: goto INIT;
state XTRA3: goto INIT;

equations

QSTATE.CLK = CLOCK; QSTATE.OE = 1;
Z = (QSTATE == OK0) # (QSTATE == OK1);

end SMEX1
```

- if-then-else statements are nested. A particular next state may appear in multiple places in one set of nested if-then-else clauses (e.g., see states OK0 and OK1).

- Expressions like "(B==1)*(A==0)" were used instead of equivalents like "B*!A" only because the former are a bit more readable.

- The first if statement in each of states INIT–OK1 ensures that the machine goes to the INIT state if RESET is asserted.

- Next-state equations are given for XTRA1–XTRA3 to ensure that the machine goes to a "safe" state if it somehow gets into an unused state.

- The single equation in the "equations" section of the program determines the behavior of the Moore-type output.

Table 7-23 shows the resulting excitation and output equations produced by the ABEL compiler (the reverse-polarity equations are not shown). Notice the use of variable names like "Q1.FB" in the righthand sides of the equations. Here, the ".FB" attribute suffix refers to the "feedback" signal into the AND-OR array

Table 7-23
Reduced equations
for SMEX1 PLD.

```
Q1 := (!Q2.FB & !Q3.FB & RESET_L
      # Q1.FB & RESET_L);
Q1.C = (CLOCK);
Q1.OE = (1);

Q2 := (Q1.FB & !Q3.FB & RESET_L & !A
      # Q1.FB & Q3.FB & RESET_L & A
      # Q1.FB & Q2.FB & RESET_L & B);
Q2.C = (CLOCK);
Q2.OE = (1);

Q3 := (!Q2.FB & !Q3.FB & RESET_L & A
      # Q1.FB & RESET_L & A);
Q3.C = (CLOCK);
Q3.OE = (1);

Z = (Q2 & Q1);
```

USE IT OR ELSE   ABEL's if-then-else structure eliminates the transition ambiguity that can occur in state diagrams. However, the else clause of an if statement is optional. If it is omitted, the next state for some input combinations will be unspecified. Usually this is not the designer's intention.

Nevertheless, if you can guarantee that the unspecified input combinations will never occur, you may be able to reduce the size of the transition logic. If the @DCSET directive is given, the ABEL compiler treats the transition outputs for the unspecified state/input combinations as "don't-cares." In addition, it treats *all* transitions out of unused states as "don't-cares."

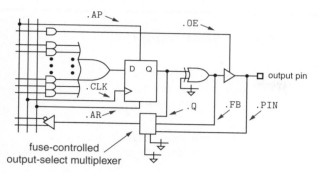

Figure 7-96
Output selection
capability in a
complex PLD.

coming from the flip-flop's Q output. This is done to make it clear that the signal is coming from the flip-flop, not from the corresponding PLD output pin, which can be selected in some complex PLDs. As shown in Figure 7-96, ABEL actually allows you to select among three possible values on the righthand side of an equation using an attribute suffix on the signal name:

.Q   The actual flip-flop output pin before any programmable inversion.   *.Q*

.FB   A value equal to the value that the output pin would have if enabled.   *.FB*

.PIN The actual signal at the PLD output pin. This signal is floating or driven   *.PIN*
      by another device if the three-state driver is not enabled.

Obviously, the .PIN value should not be used in a state-machine excitation equation, since it is not guaranteed always to equal the state variable.

Despite the use of "high-level language," the program's author still had to refer to the original, hand-constructed state table in Figure 7-47 on page 557 to come up with the ABEL version in Table 7-22. A different approach is shown in Table 7-24 on the next page. This program was developed directly from the word description of the state machine, which is repeated below:

Design a clocked synchronous state machine with two inputs, A and B, and a single output Z that is 1 if:

– A had the same value at each of the two previous clock ticks, *or*
– B has been 1 since the last time that the first condition was true.

Otherwise, the output should be 0.

A key idea in the new approach is to remove the last value of A from the state definitions, and instead to have a separate flip-flop that keeps track of it

**PHANTOM
(OF THE)
OPERAND**   Real CPLDs typically have only a 2-input output-select multiplexer and omit the .FB input shown in Figure 7-96. When an equation calls for a signal with the .FB attribute, the ABEL compiler uses the corresponding .Q signal and simply adjusts it with the appropriate inversion (or not).

Table 7-24
A more "natural" ABEL program for the example state machine.

```
module SMEX2
title 'Alternate Version of Example State Machine'

" Input and output pins
CLOCK, RESET_L, A, B           pin;
LASTA, Q1, Q2                  pin istype 'reg';
Z                              pin istype 'com';

" Definitions
QSTATE  = [Q1,Q2];             " State variables
INIT    = [ 0, 0];             " State encodings
LOOKING = [ 0, 1];
OK      = [ 1, 0];
XTRA    = [ 1, 1];
RESET = !RESET_L;

state_diagram QSTATE

state INIT:    if RESET then INIT else LOOKING;

state LOOKING: if RESET then INIT
               else if (A == LASTA) then OK
               else LOOKING;

state OK:      if RESET then INIT
               else if B then OK
               else if (A == LASTA) then OK
               else LOOKING;

state XTRA:    goto INIT;

equations
LASTA.CLK = CLOCK; QSTATE.CLK = CLOCK; QSTATE.OE = 1;

LASTA := A;
Z = (QSTATE == OK);

end SMEX2
```

(LASTA). Then only two non-INIT states must be defined: LOOKING ("still looking for a match") and OK ("got a match or B has been 1 since last match"). The Z output is a simple combinational decode of the OK state.

More ABEL state machines are shown in <u>Section XSabl</u> at <u>DDPPonline</u>.

*7.11.3 External State Memory

In some situations, the state memory of a PLD-based state machine may be kept in flip-flops external to the PLD. ABEL provides a special version of the state_diagram statement to handle this situation:

state_diagram *current-state-variables* -> *next-state variables*

current-state-variables
next-state-variables

Here *current-state-variables* is an ABEL set that lists the input signals which represent the current state of the machine, and *next-state-variables* is a set that

```
state_diagram state-variables
state state-value 1 :
      optional equation;
      optional equation;
      . . .
      transition statement;
state state-value 2 :
      optional equation;
      optional equation;
      . . .
      transition statement;
. . .
state state-value 2ⁿ :
      optional equation;
      optional equation;
      . . .
      transition statement;
```

Table 7-25
Structure of an ABEL state diagram with Moore outputs defined.

lists the corresponding output signals, which are the excitation for external D flip-flops holding the state of the machine, for example,

```
state_diagram [CURQ1, CURQ2] -> [NEXTQ1, NEXTQ2]
```

*7.11.4 Specifying Moore Outputs

The output Z in our example state machine is a Moore output, a function of state only, and we defined this output in Tables 7-22 and 7-24 using an appropriate equation in the equations section of the program. Alternatively, ABEL allows Moore outputs to be specified along with the state definitions themselves. The transition statement in a state definition may be preceded by one or more optional equations, as shown in Table 7-25. To use this capability with the machine in Table 7-24, for example, we would eliminate the Z equation in the equations section and rewrite the state diagram as shown in Table 7-26.

```
state_diagram QSTATE
state INIT:     Z = 0;
                if RESET then INIT else LOOKING;
state LOOKING:  Z = 0;
                if RESET then INIT
                else if (A == LASTA) then OK
                else LOOKING;
state OK:       Z = 1;
                if RESET then INIT
                else if B then OK
                else if (A == LASTA) then OK
                else LOOKING;
state XTRA:     Z = 0;
                goto INIT;
```

Table 7-26
State machine with embedded Moore output definitions.

As in other ABEL equations, when a variable such as Z appears on the left-hand side of multiple equations, the righthand sides are OR'ed together to form the final result (as discussed in Section 5.2.3). Also notice that Z is still specified as a combinational, not a registered, output. If Z were a registered output, the desired output value would occur one clock tick after the machine visited the corresponding state.

*7.11.5 Specifying Mealy and Pipelined Outputs with WITH

with statement

Some state-machine outputs are functions of the inputs as well as state. In Section 7.3.2 we called them Mealy outputs or pipelined outputs, depending on whether they occurred immediately upon an input change or only after a clock edge. ABEL's *with statement* provides a way to specify these outputs side by side with the next states, rather than separately in the equations section of the program.

As shown in Table 7-27, the syntax of the with statement is very simple. Any next-state value which is part of a transition statement can be followed by the keyword with and a bracketed list of equations that are "executed" for the specified transition. Formally, let "E" be an excitation expression that is true only when the specified transition is to be taken. Then for each equation in the with's bracketed list, the righthand side is AND'ed with E and assigned to the lefthand side. The equations can use either unclocked or clocked assignment to create Mealy or pipelined outputs, respectively.

We developed an example "combination lock" state machine with Mealy outputs in Table 7-11 on page 568. The same state machine is specified by the ABEL program in Table 7-28, using with statements for the Mealy outputs. Note that closing brackets take the place of the semicolons that normally end the transition statements for the states.

Based on the combination lock's word description, it is not possible to realize UNLK and HINT as pipelined outputs, since they depend on the current value of X. However, if we redefine UNLK to be asserted for the entire "unlocked" state, and HINT to be the actual recommended next value of X, we can create a new machine with pipelined outputs, as shown in Table 7-29 on page 622. Notice that we used the clocked assignment operator for the outputs. More importantly, notice that the values of UNLK and HINT are different than in the Mealy example, since they have to "look ahead" one clock tick.

Because of "lookahead," pipelined outputs can be more difficult than Mealy outputs to design and understand. In the example above, we even had to

Table 7-27
Structure of ABEL
with statement.

```
next-state with {
    equation;
    equation;
    . . .
}
```

```
module SMEX4
title 'Combination-Lock State Machine'
" Input and output pins
CLOCK, X                      pin;
Q1..Q3                        pin istype 'reg';
UNLK, HINT                    pin istype 'com';
" Definitions
S        = [Q1,Q2,Q3];        " State variables
ZIP      = [ 0, 0, 0];        " State encodings
X0       = [ 0, 0, 1];
X01      = [ 0, 1, 0];
X011     = [ 0, 1, 1];
X0110    = [ 1, 0, 0];
X01101   = [ 1, 0, 1];
X011011  = [ 1, 1, 0];
X0110111 = [ 1, 1, 1];

state_diagram S

state ZIP:      if X==0 then X0     with {UNLK = 0; HINT = 1}
                else ZIP            with {UNLK = 0; HINT = 0}

state X0:       if X==0 then X0     with {UNLK = 0; HINT = 0}
                else X01            with {UNLK = 0; HINT = 1}

state X01:      if X==0 then X0     with {UNLK = 0; HINT = 0}
                else X011           with {UNLK = 0; HINT = 1}

state X011:     if X==0 then X0110 with {UNLK = 0; HINT = 1}
                else ZIP            with {UNLK = 0; HINT = 0}

state X0110:    if X==0 then X0     with {UNLK = 0; HINT = 0}
                else X01101         with {UNLK = 0; HINT = 1}

state X01101:   if X==0 then X0     with {UNLK = 0; HINT = 0}
                else X011011        with {UNLK = 0; HINT = 1}

state X011011:  if X==0 then X0110 with {UNLK = 0; HINT = 0}
                else X0110111       with {UNLK = 0; HINT = 1}

state X0110111: if X==0 then X0     with {UNLK = 1; HINT = 1}
                else ZIP            with {UNLK = 0; HINT = 0}
equations
S.CLK = CLOCK;

end SMEX4
```

Table 7-28
State machine with embedded Mealy output definitions.

modify the problem statement to accommodate them. The advantage of pipelined outputs is that, since they are connected directly to register outputs, they are valid a few gate-delays sooner after a state change than Moore or Mealy outputs, which normally include additional combinational logic. In the combination-lock example, it's probably not that important to open your lock or see your hint a few nanoseconds earlier. However, shaving off a few gate delays can be quite important in high-speed applications.

Table 7-29
State machine with
embedded pipelined
output definitions.

```
module SMEX5
title 'Combination-Lock State Machine'

" Input and output pins
CLOCK, X                        pin;
Q1..Q3, UNLK, HINT              pin istype 'reg';

" Definitions
S        = [Q1,Q2,Q3];          " State variables
ZIP      = [ 0, 0, 0];          " State encodings
X0       = [ 0, 0, 1];
X01      = [ 0, 1, 0];
X011     = [ 0, 1, 1];
X0110    = [ 1, 0, 0];
X01101   = [ 1, 0, 1];
X011011  = [ 1, 1, 0];
X0110111 = [ 1, 1, 1];

state_diagram S

    state ZIP:      if X==0 then X0    with {UNLK := 0; HINT := 1}
                    else ZIP           with {UNLK := 0; HINT := 0}

    state X0:       if X==0 then X0    with {UNLK := 0; HINT := 1}
                    else X01           with {UNLK := 0; HINT := 1}

    state X01:      if X==0 then X0    with {UNLK := 0; HINT := 1}
                    else X011          with {UNLK := 0; HINT := 0}

    state X011:     if X==0 then X0110 with {UNLK := 0; HINT := 1}
                    else ZIP           with {UNLK := 0; HINT := 0}

    state X0110:    if X==0 then X0    with {UNLK := 0; HINT := 1}
                    else X01101        with {UNLK := 0; HINT := 1}

    state X01101:   if X==0 then X0    with {UNLK := 0; HINT := 1}
                    else X011011       with {UNLK := 0; HINT := 1}

    state X011011:  if X==0 then X0110 with {UNLK := 0; HINT := 1}
                    else X0110111      with {UNLK := 1; HINT := 0}

    state X0110111: if X==0 then X0    with {UNLK := 0; HINT := 1}
                    else ZIP           with {UNLK := 0; HINT := 0}

equations
S.CLK = CLOCK; UNLK.CLK = CLOCK; HINT.CLK = CLOCK;

end SMEX5
```

7.11.6 Test Vectors

Test vectors for sequential circuits in ABEL have the same uses and limitations as test vectors for combinational circuits, as described in Section 5.2.6. One important addition to their syntax is the use of the constant ".C." to denote a clock edge, $0 \rightarrow 1 \rightarrow 0$. Thus, Table 7-30 is an ABEL program, with test vectors, for a simple 8-bit register with a clock-enable input. A variety of vectors are used to test loading and holding different input values.

.C., clock edge

```
module REG8EN
title '8-bit register with clock enable'

" Input and output pins
CLK, EN, D1..D8          pin;
Q1..Q8                   pin istype 'reg';

" Sets
D = [D1..D8];
Q = [Q1..Q8];

equations

Q.CLK = CLK;

when EN == 1 then Q := D else Q := Q;

test_vectors ([CLK, EN,  D  ] -> [ Q  ])
             [.C.,  1,  ^h00] -> [^h00]; " 0s in every bit
             [.C.,  0,  ^hFF] -> [^h00]; " Hold capability, EN=0
             [.C.,  1,  ^hFF] -> [^hFF]; " 1s in every bit
             [.C.,  0,  ^h00] -> [^hFF]; " Hold capability
             [.C.,  1,  ^h55] -> [^h55]; " Adjacent bits shorted
             [.C.,  0,  ^hAA] -> [^h55]; " Hold capability
             [.C.,  1,  ^hAA] -> [^hAA]; " Adjacent bits shorted
             [.C.,  1,  ^h55] -> [^h55]; " Load with quick setup
             [.C.,  1,  ^hAA] -> [^hAA]; " Again
end REG8EN
```

Table 7-30
ABEL program with
test vectors for a
simple 8-bit register.

A typical approach to testing state machines is to write vectors that cause the machine not only to visit every state, but also to exercise every transition from every state. A key difference and challenge compared to combinational-circuit test vectors is that the vectors must first drive the machine into the desired state before testing a transition, and then come back again for each different transition from that state.

Thus, Table 7-31 on the next page shows test vectors for the state machine in Table 7-24. It's important to understand that, unlike combinational vectors, these vectors work only if applied in exactly the order they are written. Notice that the vectors were written to be independent of the state encoding. As a result, they don't have to be modified if the state encoding is changed.

We encounter another challenge if we attempt to create test vectors for the combination-lock state machine of Table 7-28 on page 621. This machine has a major problem when it comes to testing—it has no reset input. Its starting state at power-up may be different in PLD devices and technologies—the individual flip-flops may be all set, all reset, or all in random states. In the machine's actual application, we didn't necessarily need a reset input, but for testing purposes we somehow have to get to a known starting state.

Table 7-31 Test vectors for the state machine in Table 7-24.

```
test_vectors
([RESET_L, CLOCK, A, B] -> [QSTATE , LASTA, Z])
 [   0   , .C. , 0, 0] -> [INIT   ,  0  , 0]; " Check -->INIT (RESET)
 [   0   , .C. , 1, 0] -> [INIT   ,  1  , 0]; "  and LASTA flip-flop
 [   1   , .C. , 0, 0] -> [LOOKING,  0  , 0]; " Come out of initialization
 [   0   , .C. , 0, 0] -> [INIT   ,  0  , 0]; " Check LOOKING-->INIT (RESET)
 [   1   , .C. , 0, 0] -> [LOOKING,  0  , 0]; " Come out of initialization
 [   1   , .C. , 1, 0] -> [LOOKING,  1  , 0]; " --> LOOKING since 0!=1
 [   1   , .C. , 1, 0] -> [OK     ,  1  , 1]; " --> OK since 1==1
 [   0   , .C. , 0, 0] -> [INIT   ,  0  , 0]; " Check OK-->INIT (RESET)
 [   1   , .C. , 0, 0] -> [LOOKING,  0  , 0]; " Go back towards OK ...
 [   1   , .C. , 0, 0] -> [OK     ,  0  , 1]; " --> OK since 0==0
 [   1   , .C. , 1, 1] -> [OK     ,  1  , 1]; " --> OK since B, even though 1!=0
 [   1   , .C. , 1, 0] -> [OK     ,  1  , 1]; " --> OK since 1==1
 [   1   , .C. , 0, 0] -> [LOOKING,  0  , 0]; " --> LOOKING since 0!=1
```

synchronizing sequence   Luckily, the combination-lock machine has a *synchronizing sequence*—a fixed sequence of one or more input values that will always drive it to a certain known state. In particular, starting from any state, if we apply X=1 to the machine for four ticks, we will always be in state ZIP by the fourth tick. This is the approach taken by the first four vectors in Table 7-32. Until we get to the known state, we indicate the next state on the righthand side of the vector as being "don't care," so the simulator or the physical device tester will not flag a random state as an error.

Once we get going, we encounter something else that's new—Mealy outputs that must be tested. As shown by the fourth and fifth vectors, we don't have to transition the clock in every test vector. Instead, we can keep the clock fixed at 0, where the last transition left it, and observe the Mealy output values produced by the two input values of X. Then we can test the next state transition.

For the state transitions, we list the expected next state but we show the output values as don't-cares. For a correct test vector, the outputs must show the values attained *after* the transition, a function of the *next* state. Although it's possible to figure them out and include them, the complexity is enough to give you a headache, and they will be tested by the next CLOCK=0 vectors anyway.

Creating test vectors for a state machine by hand is a painstaking process, and no matter how careful you are, there's no guarantee that you've tested all its functions and potential hardware faults. For example, the vectors in Table 7-31

SYNCHRONIZING SEQUENCES AND RESET INPUTS   We lucked out with the combination lock, since not all state machines have synchronizing sequences. This is why most state machines are designed with a reset input, which in effect allows a synchronizing sequence of length one.

Table 7-32 Test vectors for the combination-lock state machine of Table 7-28.

```
test_vectors
([CLOCK, X] -> [   S      , UNLK, HINT])
 [ .C. , 1] -> [.X.      , .X. , .X. ]; " Since no reset input, apply
 [ .C. , 1] -> [.X.      , .X. , .X. ]; "   a 'synchronizing sequence'
 [ .C. , 1] -> [.X.      , .X. , .X. ]; "   to reach a known starting
 [ .C. , 1] -> [ZIP      , .X. , .X. ]; "   state
 [ 0   , 0] -> [ZIP      , 0   , 1   ]; " Test Mealy outputs for both
 [ 0   , 1] -> [ZIP      , 0   , 0   ]; "   values of X
 [ .C. , 1] -> [ZIP      , .X. , .X. ]; " Test ZIP-->ZIP (X==1)
 [ .C. , 0] -> [X0       , .X. , .X. ]; "   and ZIP-->X0 (X==0)
 [ 0   , 0] -> [X0       , 0   , 0   ]; " Test Mealy outputs for both
 [ 0   , 1] -> [X0       , 0   , 1   ]; "   values of X
 [ .C. , 0] -> [X0       , .X. , .X. ]; " Test X0-->X0 (X==0)
 [ .C. , 1] -> [X01      , .X. , .X. ]; "   and X0-->X01 (X==1)
 [ 0   , 0] -> [X01      , 0   , 0   ]; " Test Mealy outputs for both
 [ 0   , 1] -> [X01      , 0   , 1   ]; "   values of X
 [ .C. , 0] -> [X0       , .X. , .X. ]; " Test X01-->X0 (X==0)
 [ .C. , 1] -> [X01      , .X. , .X. ]; " Get back to X01
 [ .C. , 1] -> [X011     , .X. , .X. ]; " Test X01-->X011 (X==1)
```

do not test (A LASTA) = 10 in state LOOKING, or (A B LASTA) = 100 in state OK. Thus, generating a complete set of test vectors for fault-detection purposes is a process best left to an automatic test-pattern-generation program. In Table 7-32 we petered out after writing vectors for the first few states; completing the test vectors is left as an exercise (7.100). Still, on the functional testing side, writing a few vectors to exercise the machine's most basic functions can weed out obvious design errors early in the process. More subtle design errors are best detected by a thorough system-level simulation.

7.12 Sequential-Circuit Design with VHDL

Most of the VHDL features that are needed to support sequential-circuit design, in particular, processes, were already introduced in Section 5.3 and were used in the VHDL sections of Chapter 6. This section introduces just one more feature and then shows how to create sequential circuits in VHDL. More examples appear in the VHDL sections of Chapter 8 and in Section XSvhd at DDPPonline.

7.12.1 Clocked Circuits

In practice, the majority of digital designs that are modeled using VHDL are clocked, synchronous systems using edge-triggered flip-flops. In addition to what we've already learned about VHDL, there's just one more feature needed to describe edge-triggered behavior. The *event attribute* can be attached to a   *event attribute* signal name to yield a value of type boolean that is true if an event on the

Table 7-33
Behavioral VHDL
for a positive-edge-
triggered D flip-flop.

```
library IEEE;
use IEEE.std_logic_1164.all;

entity VposDff is
  port (CLK, CLR, D: in STD_LOGIC;
        Q: out STD_LOGIC );
end VposDff;

architecture VposDff_arch of VposDff is
begin
  process (CLK, CLR)
  begin
    if CLR='1' then Q <= '0';
    elsif CLK'event and CLK='1' then Q <= D;
    end if;
  end process;
end VposDff_arch;
```

signal caused the encompassing process to run in the current simulation cycle, and false otherwise.

Using the event attribute, we can model the behavior of a positive-edge-triggered D flip-flop with asynchronous clear as shown in Table 7-33. Here, the asynchronous clear input CLR overrides any behavior on the clock input CLK and is therefore checked first, in the "if" clause. If CLR is negated, then the "elsif" clause is checked, and its statements are executed on the rising edge of CLK. Note that "CLK'event" is true for any change on CLK, and "CLK='1'" is checked to limit triggering to just the rising edge of CLK. There are many other ways to construct processes or statements with edge-triggered behavior; Table 7-34 shows two more ways to describe a D flip-flop (without a CLR input).

None of the D flip-flops we've shown so far has a QN (complemented Q) output. Table 7-35 shows two different ways of specifying a QN output. The first architecture seems simple enough, initializing and clocking QN in the same way as Q. However, a typical synthesis tool infers two separate D flip-flops from this code—one for Q and the other for QN. The second architecture assigns a value to QN outside of the edge-triggered conditional, and the synthesis tool is forced to generate QN from Q using an inverter.

Table 7-34
Two more ways to
describe a positive-
edge-triggered
D flip-flop.

```
process
  wait until CLK'event and CLK='1';
  Q <= D;
end process;

Q <= D when CLK'event and CLK='1' else Q;
```

SYNTHESIS STUFF   You may be wondering, how does a synthesis tool convert the edge-triggered behavior described in Table 7-33 or 7-34 into an efficient flip-flop realization? Most tools recognize only a few predetermined ways of expressing edge-triggered behavior and map those into predetermined flip-flop components in the target technology.

   The synthesis tool used in the Xilinx ISE version 6.x software can recognize the "CLK'event and CLK='1'" expression that we use in this book to imply an edge-triggered flip-flop. Even with that as a given, VHDL has many different ways of expressing the same functionality, as we showed in Table 7-34. Peter Ashenden, author of *The Designer's Guide to VHDL* (Morgan Kaufmann, 1996), ran these statements and one other, with some modification, through several different synthesis tools. Only one of them was able to synthesize three out of the four forms; most could handle only two. So, you need to follow the method that is prescribed by the tool you use.

Table 7-35
Two architectures for a positive-edge-triggered D flip-flop with a QN output.

```
library IEEE;
use IEEE.std_logic_1164.all;

entity VposDffQN is
  port (CLK, CLR, D: in STD_LOGIC;
        Q, QN: inout STD_LOGIC );
end VposDffQN;

architecture VposDffQN1_arch of VposDffQN is
begin
  process (CLK, CLR)
  begin
    if CLR='1' then Q <= '0'; QN <= '1';
    elsif CLK'event and CLK='1' then Q <= D; QN <= not D;
    end if;
  end process;
end VposDffQN1_arch;

architecture VposDffQN2_arch of VposDffQN is
begin
  process (CLK, CLR, Q)
begin
    if CLR='1' then Q <= '0'; QN <= '1';
    elsif CLK'event and CLK='1' then Q <= D;
    end if;
    QN <= not Q;
  end process;
end VposDffQN2_arch;
```

Table 7-36
Clock process within
a test bench.

```
architecture TB_arch of TB is
signal MCLK: STD_LOGIC;
signal ... -- Declare other input and output signals

process -- Clock generator
begin
  MCLK <= '1';  -- Start at 1 at time 0
  loop
    MCLK <= '0' after 6 ns;
    MCLK <= '1' after 4 ns;
  end loop;
end process;

process -- Generate the rest of the input stimuli, check outputs
begin
  ...
end;
```

In the test bench for a clocked circuit, one of the things you need to do is to generate a system clock signal. This can be done quite easily with a loop inside a process, as shown in Table 7-36 for a 100-MHz clock with a 60% duty cycle.

7.12.2 State-Machine Design with VHDL

There are many possible coding styles for creating state machines in VHDL, including using no consistent style at all. Some styles and especially the last approach are guaranteed to get you in trouble. Without the discipline of a consistent coding style, it is fairly easy to write syntactically correct VHDL code where the simulator's operation, the synthesized hardware's operation, and what you think the machine should be doing are all different!

In this book, we'll use a coding style that has been used by digital-design professionals for more than a decade to give a minimum of errors. This style also has the advantage of separating the major sections of a state machine's operation and structure, making the design easier to understand and maintain.

VHDL state-machine coding style

Our *VHDL state-machine coding style* precisely matches the general structure of Mealy and Moore state machines that we presented in Figures 7-35 and 7-36 on pages 542 and 543. The code is generally divided into three sections:

- *State memory.* This could be specified in behavioral form using a process that is triggered by clock events, as we showed in the preceding subsection for edge-triggered D flip-flops; or it could be done in a structural style with explicit flip-flop instantiations, as we'll show in Section 7.12.8.

- *Next-state (excitation) logic.* This is written as a separate process whose sensitivity list includes the machine's current state and inputs. The bulk of this process is usually a case statement that enumerates all values of the current state. The synthesized logic is combinational.

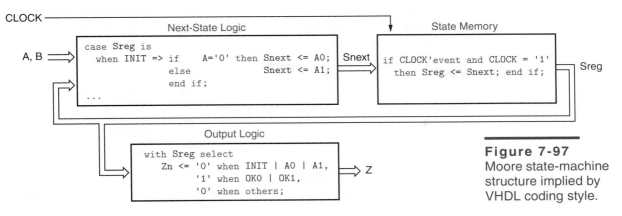

Figure 7-97
Moore state-machine structure implied by VHDL coding style.

- *Output logic.* This is another separate process or dataflow code which also depends on the current state and inputs. It may or may not include a `case` or `select` statement, depending on the complexity of the output function. Again, the synthesized logic is combinational.

As mentioned above, the detailed coding within each section may vary. In cases where there is a tight coupling of next-state and output-logic specifications, it may be desirable to combine the next-state and output logic into a single process, and indeed, into a single `case` statement. When pipelined outputs are used, the output memory could be specified along with the state memory, or a separate process or structural code could be used. Figure 7-97 shows the relationship between our coding style and state-machine structure for the example state-machine code in the next subsection.

TOO MANY CODING STYLES

ABEL has basically just one coding style for designing state machines; VHDL allows many. Why? There is really no significant upside in all the different possibilities offered by VHDL, and there are a lot of ways they can get you into trouble.

The answer is in the history of the two languages. ABEL was designed first and foremost as a hardware description language and was used immediately to target real devices and real digital-design projects. VHDL, on the other hand, was designed as a simulation language, and a very general one at that. Its features were directed primarily at the needs of simulation, including the need to get fast simulation performance in an era when computers were not so fast and cheap. VHDL's use for synthesis came later.

The languages are also different in another dimension. ABEL was designed by two people, David Pellerin and Michael Holley, trying to create a success for their small company. VHDL was a government-inspired and designed-by-committee project. I'll be kind and say that it's debatable whether or not that made a difference.

Table 7-37
State and output table for the example state machine.

S	00	01	11	10	Z
			A B		
INIT	A0	A0	A1	A1	0
A0	OK0	OK0	A1	A1	0
A1	A0	A0	OK1	OK1	0
OK0	OK0	OK0	OK1	A1	1
OK1	A0	OK0	OK1	OK1	1
			S*		

7.12.3 A VHDL State-Machine Example

In Section 7.4.1 we illustrated the state-table design process using the simple design problem below:

> Design a clocked synchronous state machine with two inputs, A and B, and a single output Z that is 1 if:
>
> - A had the same value at each of the two previous clock ticks, *or*
> - B has been 1 since the last time that the first condition was true.
>
> Otherwise, the output should be 0.

In an HDL-based design environment, there are many possible ways of writing a program that meets the stated requirements. We'll look at several.

The first approach is to construct a state and output table by hand and then manually convert it into a corresponding program. This is rarely done in an HDL-based design environment, but since we already developed such a state table in Section 7.4.1, let's use it. We've written it again in Table 7-37, and we've written a corresponding VHDL program in Table 7-38. (We'll show an easier design approach without a state table at the end of this subsection.)

As usual, the VHDL entity declaration specifies only inputs and outputs—CLOCK, A, B, and Z in this example. The architecture definition specifies the state machine's internal operation. The first thing it does is to create an enumerated type, State_type, whose values are identifiers corresponding to the state names. Then it declares signals Sreg and Snext for the machine's current and next states.

The first process in the architecture sets up the state memory. This process is sensitive only to CLOCK and loads the next state Snext into the state register Sreg on the rising edge of CLOCK. During synthesis, positive-edge-triggered D flip-flops will be inferred for Sreg.

The second process specifies the next-state logic using a case statement. This assigns a value to Snext in six cases, corresponding to the five explicitly defined states and a catch-all for other states. For robustness, the "others" case covers undefined states and sends the machine back to the INIT state.

In each case we've used an "if" statement and a final "else" to ensure that a value is always assigned to Snext. If there were any state/input combinations

```vhdl
library IEEE;
use IEEE.std_logic_1164.all;

entity smexamp is
  port ( CLOCK, A, B: in STD_LOGIC;
         Z: out STD_LOGIC );
end;

architecture smexamp_arch of smexamp is
type State_type is (INIT, A0, A1, OK0, OK1);
signal Sreg, Snext: State_type;  -- current state and next state
begin

process (CLOCK) -- state memory
  begin
    if CLOCK'event and CLOCK = '1' then
    Sreg <= Snext; end if;
  end process;

process (A, B, Sreg) -- next-state logic
  begin
    case Sreg is
      when INIT => if    A='0' then Snext <= A0;
                   else            Snext <= A1;
                   end if;
      when A0 =>   if    A='0' then Snext <= OK0;
                   else            Snext <= A1;
                   end if;
      when A1 =>   if    A='0' then Snext <= A0;
                   else            Snext <= OK1;
                   end if;
      when OK0 =>  if    A='0' then Snext <= OK0;
                   elsif A='1' and B='0' then Snext <= A1;
                   else                       Snext <= OK1;
                   end if;
      when OK1 =>  if    A='0' and B='0' then Snext <= A0;
                   elsif A='0' and B='1' then Snext <= OK0;
                   else                       Snext <= OK1;
                   end if;
      when others => Snext <= INIT;
    end case;
  end process;

with Sreg select  -- output logic (based on state only)
    Z <= '0' when INIT | A0 | A1,
         '1' when OK0 | OK1,
         '0' when others;
end smexamp_arch;
```

**RARELY,
BUT NOT NEVER**   Some standards, such as bus communication protocols, are specified using state tables or state diagrams. These lead to the rare situations where you might need to write an HDL program based on an existing state table or state diagram.

NEXT-STATE CODING VARIATIONS

In the next-state process in Table 7-38, some designers would precede the `case` statement with one more line of code, "Snext <= INIT". This establishes a "default" next state for the machine if the `case` statement fails to cover all state/input combinations. This style is also useful for machines where very few transitions go anywhere except to a default state.

Another useful variation occurs in machines where most transitions stay in the current state. Then, the case statement can be preceded by a line of code that maintains the current state as default, "Snext <= Sreg".

Yet another variation is to use the default "Snext <= (others=>'X')". In simulation, this default ensures that if the machine ever encounters an unspecified state/input combination, the state will be undefined (X's), which is easy to detect.

in which no value was assigned `Snext`, the VHDL compiler would infer a latch for `Snext`, something we don't want.

The selected-assignment statement at the end of Table 7-38 handles the machine's single Moore output, Z, which is set to a value as a function of the current state. It would be easy to define Mealy outputs within this statement as well. That is, Z could be a function of the inputs as well as the current state. Since the "`with`" statement is a concurrent statement, any input changes will affect the Z output as soon as they occur.

We really should have included a reset input in Table 7-38 (see box on page 558). A synchronous or asynchronous RESET signal is easily provided by modifying the entity declaration and the state-memory process. For example, Table 7-39 shows how to provide a synchronous reset capability (reset will occur on the rising edge of CLOCK). Table 7-40 shows asynchronous reset capability (reset occurs immediately when RESET is asserted). While there are many ways to code asynchronous and synchronous reset behavior, not all will be recognized and be synthesized by the VHDL compiler. Our examples show coding styles that are recognized by most tools.

Table 7-39
Adding synchronous reset capability to a VHDL state machine.

```
entity smexamprs is
  port ( CLOCK, RESET, A, B: in STD_LOGIC;
         Z: out STD_LOGIC );
end;
...
process (CLOCK) -- state memory with synchronous reset
  begin
    if CLOCK'event and CLOCK = '1' then
      if RESET = '1' then Sreg <= INIT;
      else                Sreg <= Snext; end if;
    end if;
  end process;
```

```
process (CLOCK, RESET) -- state memory with asynchronous reset
  begin
    if RESET = '1' then Sreg <= INIT;
    elsif CLOCK'event and CLOCK = '1' then Sreg <= Snext; end if;
  end process;
```

Table 7-40
Adding asynchronous reset capability to a VHDL state machine.

7.12.4 State Assignment in VHDL

The example in the preceding subsection gave no information on how state-variable combinations were to be assigned to the named states, or even how many binary state variables are needed in the first place. We left it all to the VHDL synthesis tool. But experienced designers know that the choice of state assignments can have a significant effect on the size and speed of a state machine, and is often much too important to be left to chance.

A synthesis tool is free to associate any integer values or binary combinations it likes with the identifiers in an enumerated type, but a typical tool will assign integers in the order the state names are listed, starting with 0. It will then use the smallest possible number of bits to encode those integers, that is, $\lceil \log_2 s \rceil$ bits for s states. Thus, the program in Table 7-38 will typically synthesize with the same, "simplest" state assignment that we chose in the original example in Table 7-6 on page 562. However, VHDL supports a couple of ways that we can force a different assignment.

One way to force an assignment is to use VHDL's *attribute statement* as shown in Table 7-41. Here, *enum_encoding* is a user-defined attribute whose value is a string that specifies the enumeration encoding to be used by the synthesis tool. The VHDL language processor ignores this value, but passes the attribute name and its value to the synthesis tool. The attribute enum_encoding is defined and known by many synthesis tools, including tools from Synopsys, Inc. Notice that a Synopsys attributes package must be "used" by the program; this is needed for the VHDL compiler to recognize enum_encoding as a legitimate user-defined attribute. By the way, the state assignment that we've specified in this program is equivalent to the "almost one-hot" coding in Table 7-6 on page 562.

attribute statement
enum_encoding

```
library IEEE;
use IEEE.std_logic_1164.all;
library SYNOPSYS;
use SYNOPSYS.attributes.all;
...
architecture smexampe_arch of smexamp is
type State_type is (INIT, A0, A1, OK0, OK1);
attribute enum_encoding of State_type: type is
        "0000 0001 0010 0100 1000";
signal Sreg: State_type;
...
```

Table 7-41
Using an attribute to force an enumeration encoding.

Table 7-42
Using standard logic data types and constants to specify a state encoding.

```
library IEEE;
use IEEE.std_logic_1164.all;
...
architecture smexampc_arch of smexamp is
subtype State_type is STD_LOGIC_VECTOR (1 to 4);
constant INIT: State_type := "0000";
constant A0  : State_type := "0001";
constant A1  : State_type := "0010";
constant OK0 : State_type := "0100";
constant OK1 : State_type := "1000";
signal Sreg: State_type;
...
```

Another way to force an assignment, without relying on external packages or synthesis attributes, is to define the state register more explicitly using standard logic data types. This approach is shown in Table 7-42. Here, Sreg is defined as a 4-bit STD_LOGIC_VECTOR, and constants are defined to allow the states to be referenced by name elsewhere in the program. No other changes in the program are required.

7.12.5 Pipelined Outputs in VHDL

Going back to our original VHDL program in Table 7-38 on page 631, one more interesting variation is possible. As written, the program defines a conventional Moore-type state machine with the structure shown in Figure 7-97 on page 629. But we can convert the machine to have pipelined outputs with the structure shown in Figure 7-98. To do this, we need only to declare a "next-output" signal Zn and replace the original VHDL output code with the code shown in Table 7-43. The new machine's behavior is indistinguishable from that of the

Figure 7-98 VHDL state machine with pipelined outputs.

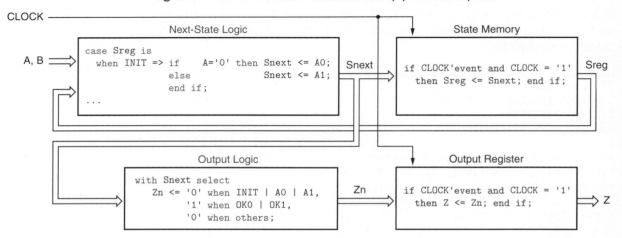

Table 7-43
VHDL pipelined
output code.

```
with Snext select   -- pipelined output logic (based on next state)
  Zn <= '0' when INIT | A0 | A1,
        '1' when OK0 | OK1,
        '0' when others;

process (CLOCK) -- output register
begin
  if CLOCK'event and CLOCK = '1' then
  Z <= Zn; end if;
end process;
```

original machine, except for timing. We've reduced the propagation delay from CLOCK to Z by producing Z directly on a register output, but we've also increased the setup-time requirements of A and B to CLOCK, because of the extra propagation delay through the output logic to the D input of the output register.

7.12.6 Direct VHDL Coding Without a State Table

All of the solutions to the example state-machine design problem that we've shown so far rely on the state table that we originally constructed by hand in Section 7.4.1. However, it is possible to write a VHDL program directly, without writing out a state table by hand.

Based on the original problem statement on page 630, the key simplifying idea is to remove the last value of A from the state definitions, and instead to have a separate register that keeps track of it (LASTA). Then only two non-INIT states must be defined: LOOKING ("still looking for a match") and OK ("got a match or B has been 1 since last match"). A VHDL architecture based on this approach is shown in Table 7-44 on the next page. In the state-memory process, the second assignment statement creates the LASTA register. At the end of the program, the Z output is defined as a simple combinational decode of the OK state.

The next-state logic in Table 7-44 is easier to understand and relate to the word description than the original, and we avoided the work of developing a state table. Clearly, this is what HDL-based state-machine design is all about.

7.12.7 More VHDL State-Machine Examples

The next state-machine example is a "ones-counting machine" with the following specifications:

> Design a clocked synchronous state machine with two inputs, X and Y, and one output, Z. The output should be 1 if the number of 1 inputs on X and Y since reset is a multiple of 4, and 0 otherwise.

We developed a state table for this machine in Table 7-9 on page 567. However, we can use the counting capabilities in the std_logic_arith package to write a VHDL program for this problem directly.

Table 7-44
Simplified VHDL
state-machine
design.

```
architecture smexampa_arch of smexamprs is
type State_type is (INIT, LOOKING, OK);
signal Sreg, Snext: State_type; -- current state and next state
signal lastA: STD_LOGIC; -- remember A from previous tick
begin

  process (CLOCK) -- state memory
  begin
    if CLOCK'event and CLOCK = '1' then
      if RESET = '1' then Sreg <= INIT;  lastA <= '0';
      else                Sreg <= Snext; lastA <= A;  end if;
    end if;
  end process;

  process (A, B, lastA, Sreg) -- next-state logic
  begin
    case Sreg is
      when INIT    =>                         Snext <= LOOKING;
      when LOOKING => if    A=lastA then Snext <= OK;
                      else              Snext <= LOOKING;
                      end if;
      when OK      => if    B='1'    then Snext <= OK;
                      elsif A=lastA then Snext <= OK;
                      else              Snext <= LOOKING;
                      end if;
      when others  =>                         Snext <= INIT;
    end case;
  end process;

  with Sreg select  -- output values based on state
    Z <= '1' when OK,
         '0' when others;

end smexampa_arch;
```

Table 7-45 shows our solution. As always, there are many different ways to solve the problem, and we have picked a way that illustrates several different language features. Within the architecture, we declare a subtype COUNTER which is a 2-bit UNSIGNED value. We then declare signals COUNT and NEXTCNT of this type to hold the current and next ones count, and a constant ZERO of the same type for initializing and checking the value of COUNT.

Within the process, we use the usual method to check for a rising edge on CLOCK, and the second "if" clause performs a synchronous reset when required. The next-state logic is handled by a single concurrent signal-assignment statement that elegantly adds 0, 1, or 2 to COUNT depending on the values of X and Y. Recall that an expression such as "('0', X)" is an array literal; so here we get an array of two STD_LOGIC elements, '0' and the current value of X. The type of this literal is compatible with UNSIGNED, since the number and type of elements

```
library IEEE;
use IEEE.std_logic_1164.all;
use IEEE.std_logic_arith.all;

entity Vonescnt is
  port ( CLOCK, RESET, X, Y: in STD_LOGIC;
          Z: out STD_LOGIC );
end;

architecture Vonescnt_arch of Vonescnt is
subtype COUNTER is UNSIGNED (1 downto 0);
signal COUNT, NEXTCNT: COUNTER;
constant ZERO: COUNTER := "00";
begin

  process (CLOCK) -- state memory
  begin
    if CLOCK'event and CLOCK = '1' then
      if RESET = '1' then COUNT <= ZERO;
      else COUNT <= NEXTCNT;
      end if;
    end if;
  end process;

  NEXTCNT <= COUNT + ('0', X) + ('0', Y);   -- counting logic

  Z <= '1' when COUNT = ZERO else '0'; -- output logic

end Vonescnt_arch;
```

Table 7-45
VHDL program for
a ones-counting
machine.

are the same, so they can be combined using the "+" operation defined in the
std_logic_arith package. The final concurrent signal-assignment statement
sets the Moore output Z to 1 when COUNT is zero.

When synthesized, the counting logic in Table 7-45 doesn't necessarily
yield a compact or speedy circuit. With a simple-minded synthesis tool, it could
yield two 2-bit adders connected in series. Another approach is to replace the
NEXTCNT assignment statement with the process shown in Table 7-46 on the next
page. A good tool may be able to synthesize a more compact incrementer for
each of the two additions. Regardless, formulating the choices in a case
statement makes for a faster circuit, allowing the two adders or incrementers to
operate in parallel, and a multiplexer can be used to select one of their outputs
according to the choices (for example, see Figure 6-94 on page 490).

A final example for this subsection is the combination-lock state machine
from Section 7.4 (below we omit the HINT output in the original specification):

Design a clocked synchronous state machine with one input, X, and one
output, UNLK. The UNLK output should be 1 if and only if X is 0 and the
sequence of inputs received on X at the preceding seven clock ticks was
0110111.

Table 7-46
Alternative VHDL
counting logic for
ones-counting
machine.

```
process (X, Y, COUNT) -- counting logic
  variable ONES: STD_LOGIC_VECTOR (1 to 2);
  begin
    ONES := (X, Y);
    case ONES is
      when "01" | "10" => NEXTCNT <= COUNT + "01";
      when "11"        => NEXTCNT <= COUNT + "10";
      when others      => NEXTCNT <= COUNT;
    end case;
  end process;
```

We developed a state table for this machine in Table 7-11 on page 568. But once again we can take a different approach that is easier to understand. Here, we note that the output of the machine at any time is completely determined by its inputs over the preceding eight clock ticks. Thus, we can a so-called "finite-memory" approach (defined in Exercise 7.59) to design this machine. With this approach, we explicitly keep track of the past seven inputs and then form the output as a combinational function of these inputs.

Table 7-47
VHDL program for
finite-memory design
of combination-lock
state machine.

```
library IEEE;
use IEEE.std_logic_1164.all;

entity Vcomblck is
  port ( CLOCK, RESET, X: in STD_LOGIC;
         UNLK: out STD_LOGIC );
end;

architecture Vcomblck_arch of Vcomblck is
signal XHISTORY: STD_LOGIC_VECTOR (7 downto 1);
constant COMBINATION: STD_LOGIC_VECTOR (7 downto 1) := "0110111";
begin

  process (CLOCK) -- state memory and next-state logic
  begin
    if CLOCK'event and CLOCK = '1' then
      if RESET = '1' then XHISTORY <= "0000000";
      else XHISTORY <= XHISTORY(6 downto 1) & X;
      end if;
    end if;
  end process;

  -- output logic:
  UNLK <= '1' when (XHISTORY=COMBINATION) and (X='0') else '0';

end Vcomblck_arch;
```

The VHDL program in Table 7-47 is a finite-memory design. Within the architecture, the process merely keeps track of the last seven values of X using a "shift register." The bits are shifted left on each clock tick, and bit 7 is the oldest value of X. (The "&" operator is VHDL array concatenation.) We took the liberty of putting the next-state logic into the same process as the state memory. Outside of the process, the concurrent signal-assignment statement sets the Mealy output UNLK to 1 when X is 0 and the 7-bit history matches the combination.

More VHDL examples of state machines, including T-Bird tail lights and the guessing game, appear in <u>Section XSvhd</u> at <u>DDPPonline</u>.

7.12.8 Specifying Flip-Flops in VHDL

Flip-flops are such an important component in any major design that, in practice, it's sometimes risky to let the synthesis tool "infer" a flip-flop from VHDL code such as Table 7-33 or 7-34 on page 626, or any of the state-machine examples in this section. Instead, you can use structural VHDL to select exactly the flip-flop component that you want, as we'll show later in this subsection.

As shown in Table 7-48, flip-flops in typical libraries have different inputs and functions, such as asynchronous resets and presets, clock enabling, and scan inputs. The table shows components from both a Xilinx FPGA/CPLD library and an LSI Logic ASIC library. Most of the basic flip-flop types appear in both

Table 7-48 Some positive-edge-triggered flip-flop types in Xilinx and LSI Logic libraries.

Xilinx Name and Control Inputs		LSI Logic Name and Control Inputs		Description
FD	D	FD1	D	Positive-edge-triggered D
FDC	D, CLR	FD2	D, CD	D with asynchronous clear
		FD2S	D, TI, TE, CD	D with scan and asynchronous clear
FDCP	D, CLR, PRE	FD3	D, CD, SD	D with asynchronous clear and preset
		FD3	D, TI, TE, CD, SD	D with scan and asynchronous clear and preset
FDE	D, CE			D with clock enable
FDCE	D, CLR, CE	FDCE	D, CLR, CE	D with clock enable and asynchronous clear
FDR	D, R	FDS2	D, CR	D with synchronous reset
FDS	D, S			D with synchronous set
FDSRE	D, S, R, CE			D with synchronous set and reset and clock enable
FJKC	J, K, CLR	FJK2	J, K, CD	J-K with asynchronous clear
FJKSRE	J, K, S, R, CE			J-K with synchronous set and reset and clock enable
		FJK2S	J, K, TI, TE, CD	J-K with scan and asynchronous clear
FTC	T, CLR			T with enable and asynchronous clear
		FT2	CD	T with asynchronous clear

libraries, but flip-flops with some combinations of features appear in only one or the other. Also, many of the signal names for the same function vary between libraries (e.g., CLR vs. CD for an asynchronous-clear input).

When your structural VHDL code is targeted to an ASIC, the library component corresponds to a gate- or transistor-level realization that has exactly the specified functionality, and no more. When your code is targeted to a CPLD or FPGA, the specified functionality is synthesized from the flip-flop type(s) that are available in the device; extra combinational logic may be "wrapped" around the device to get all of the required functionality. For example, a multiplexer might be connected to the D input of a simple D flip-flop to get a clock-enable or scan input.

We can modify the example state machine in Table 7-44 on page 636 to use particular flip-flops as shown in Table 7-49. Three changes are needed:

1. The program "uses" the Xilinx component library (Vcomponents), which includes the flip-flop types such as FDR that we listed in the first column of Table 7-48 on the preceding page.

2. The declarations in the architecture are modified to specify a particular state encoding, so we know how many flip-flops we need.

3. The behavioral description of the state memory is replaced with structural code to instantiate the flip-flops.

No changes are required to the next-state logic and output logic in the rest of the VHDL program.

To change the state encoding in Table 7-49, we must change the definitions of the state constants. If the number of bits in the state encoding changes, we must also change the State_type subtype definition and the flip-flop instantiations. For example, Table 7-50 shows the changes for a one-hot state encoding.

Table 7-49
VHDL state machine with explicit flip-flop instantiation.

```
library UNISIM;
use UNISIM.VComponents.all;
...
architecture smexamps_arch of smexamp is
signal lastA: STD_LOGIC;
subtype State_type is STD_LOGIC_VECTOR (1 downto 0);
constant INIT:    State_type := "00";
constant LOOKING: State_type := "01";
constant OK:      State_type := "10";
signal Sreg, Snext: State_type; -- State register and next state

begin
-- Instantiate flip-flops (structural code)
  U1: FDR port map (C=>CLOCK, R=>RESET, D=>Snext(0), Q=>Sreg(0));
  U2: FDR port map (C=>CLOCK, R=>RESET, D=>Snext(1), Q=>Sreg(1));
  U3: FDR port map (C=>CLOCK, R=>RESET, D=>A, Q=>lastA);
...
```

Table 7-50
One-hot state
encoding for state
machine with explicit
flip-flop instantiation.

```
subtype State_type is STD_LOGIC_VECTOR (1 to 3);
constant INIT:    State_type := "100";
constant LOOKING: State_type := "010";
constant OK:      State_type := "001";
signal Sreg, Snext: State_type; -- State register and next state

begin
-- Instantiate flip-flops (structural code)
  U1: FDS port map (C=>CLOCK, S=>RESET, D=>Snext(1), Q=>Sreg(1));
  U2: FDR port map (C=>CLOCK, R=>RESET, D=>Snext(2), Q=>Sreg(2));
  U3: FDR port map (C=>CLOCK, R=>RESET, D=>Snext(3), Q=>Sreg(3));
  U4: FDR port map (C=>CLOCK, R=>RESET, D=>A, Q=>LASTA);
...
```

**PITFALLS
EITHER WAY**   In this subsection, we recommended using structural rather than behavioral VHDL to get exactly the flip-flop that you want. On the other hand, using structural VHDL may tie the flip-flop component name and port names to a particular ASIC or manufacturer's library, hurting your design's portability.

However, experienced designers know about such pitfalls, and use scripts, macros, and other tricks to enhance portability of their designs between different technologies and manufacturers.

7.12.9 VHDL State-Machine Test Benches

We explained the general concept of VHDL test benches in Section 5.3.10. Unlike ABEL test vectors, which are embedded in the ABEL program for a device, a VHDL test bench is a separate VHDL program. The test bench for a state machine has five basic parts:

1. Declaration of the test-bench entity itself. Note that this entity has no inputs and outputs of its own.

2. Component declaration of the state-machine entity to be tested, often called the *unit under test (UUT)*.

   unit under test (UUT)

3. Instantiation of the UUT.

4. A behavioral process to create a free-running clock.

5. A process to initialize the UUT, to apply a sequence of test-vector inputs at each clock tick, and to check for expected output values.

We'll illustrate these ideas with a test bench for our familiar example state machine of Table 7-38 on page 631.

The first thing you should notice about this state machine is that it doesn't have a reset input, so we can't simulate it properly—since its state memory can't be initialized, its starting state is unknown. So, we really need to use a version of the machine that has a reset input. In particular, we'll test the version having a synchronous reset that we showed in Table 7-39 on page 632. With this in mind, we can write the test-bench program shown in Table 7-51.

The declarations in the first two sections of the program are pretty much self-explanatory. The third section instantiates the state machine, giving it the component name "UUT". In the port map statement we happened to use the "explicit" style of associating local signals with ports; notice that the local signal names can be the same as or different from the port names.

Next, we have a process to establish a free-running clock signal with a 10-ns clock period. Since we are running a functional simulation with no embedded timing information, it doesn't matter what clock period we use. However, one subtlety is that, regardless of its period, the clock's transition from undefined to 1 at time 0 may be considered to be a rising edge, and the state flip-flops may respond accordingly. But we won't count on this; we'll keep RST asserted at the beginning of the test.

The rest of the program is devoted to applying inputs and checking the state-machine output. First, we assert RST (reset) and wait 15 ns, to the middle of the second clock period, which should force the machine into the INIT state. Since the state definitions are "hidden" in the smexamprs architecture, the test bench cannot check the state directly, but we know that the output should be 0 in the INIT state, so we use an assert statement to stop the simulation and print a message if Z is not 0 at this point. At the same time (still halfway through the second clock period), we negate RST and apply the next pair of values to A and B to drive the machine to a new state at the next clock tick. At each subsequent step, we check for the expected value on Z, and set up A and B for the next tick. If any of the actual outputs fail to match the expected value, the simulation stops and prints an error message, so we can investigate the problem.

Note that the test bench is checking the machine's *functional* behavior, pretty much at the level of our original word description. Except for a little special knowledge of what happens at initialization, the test bench makes no reference to the actual internal states of the machine. So, the same test bench could be used with different implementations of the same state machine with different states or state assignments, or other subtle differences. For example, we could use it to test any of the architecture versions listed in the caption of Table 7-51.

PEEKING INSIDE   At the smexamprs entity level, VHDL purposely hides the inner workings of the particular implementation (architecture). But for debugging purposes, you'd really like to see what's going on inside the implementation. So, when you run your test bench on an interactive simulator, it gives you the ability to drill down and see signal values within the implementation that has been instantiated by the test bench.

Table 7-51
VHDL test bench for
the state machine of
Table 7-39, 7-40,
7-42, 7-43, 7-44,
7-49, or 7-50.

```
library IEEE;
use IEEE.std_logic_1164.all;

entity smexamp_tb is
end;

architecture smexamp_tb of smexamp_tb is
signal Tclk, RST, A, B, Z: STD_LOGIC;

component smexamprs -- The UUT
  port( CLOCK, RESET, A, B : in STD_LOGIC;
        Z : out STD_LOGIC);
end component;

begin
  UUT: smexamprs port map( CLOCK => Tclk,
                           RESET => RST,
                           A => A,
                           B => B,
                           Z => Z          ); -- instantiate UUT

  process -- create free-running test clock
  begin
    Tclk <= '1';
    wait for 5 ns;       -- clock cycle 10 ns
    Tclk <= '0';
    wait for 5 ns;
  end process;

  process -- create the test vectors and check responses
  begin
    RST <= '1'; -- reset; should get Z=0 in INIT state
    A <= '1'; B <= '1'; wait for 15 ns;
    assert (Z='0') report "Failed test 1" severity error;
    RST <= '0'; -- unreset
    A <= '1'; B <= '1'; wait for 10 ns; -- still Z=0 after INIT
    assert (Z='0') report "Failed test 2" severity error;
    A <= '1'; B <= '0'; wait for 10 ns; -- Two 1s in a row, want Z=1
    assert (Z='1') report "Failed test 3" severity error;
    A <= '0'; B <= '1'; wait for 10 ns; -- B=1 should hold Z=1
    assert (Z='1') report "Failed test 4" severity error;
    A <= '1'; B <= '0'; wait for 10 ns; -- B=0 releases it
    assert (Z='0') report "Failed test 5" severity error;
    A <= '0'; B <= '1'; wait for 10 ns; -- B=1 but nothing to hold
    assert (Z='0') report "Failed test 6" severity error;
    A <= '0'; B <= '0'; wait for 10 ns; -- But now two 0s in a row
    assert (Z='1') report "Failed test 7" severity error;
    A <= '1'; B <= '1'; wait for 10 ns; -- B=1 should hold Z=1
    assert (Z='1') report "Failed test 8" severity error;
    A <= '0'; B <= '0'; wait for 10 ns; -- B=0 releases it
    assert (Z='0') report "Failed test 9" severity error;
    wait;
  end process;

end smexamp_tb;
```

PUNTING ON RESET   If you tried, you might actually get away with simulating a state machine with no reset. Your simulator may initialize flip-flops to a known state, usually 0, instead of unknown. In the example machine with the simplest state assignment, all-0s corresponds to INIT, which is what we wanted anyway.

This behavior may be accurate, but it's dangerous. It may accurately model the physical design, because the flip-flops in many PLDs and FPGAs are guaranteed to come up in the 0 state, as long as power is applied smoothly. It's dangerous for many reasons, some of which are explained below.

At some point during normal circuit operation, the power supply voltage may experience a glitch, enough to change some flip-flop states but not enough to activate the device's automatic power-up reset circuit. This could leave your state machine in an unknown state with no way to bring it back. You might not notice this potential pitfall while debugging in the lab.

During the design process, you might decide to change your machine's state encoding, such that the device's power-on reset state is no longer a good one in all cases. But you might not notice this in simulation.

Late in the game, you (or your production department, or by this point, your successor) might change the PLD or FPGA device containing your state machine to one that has a different or no guaranteed power-on reset state. In the rush to get the revision into production, no one notices.

All of these cases are ones that were never caught in simulation, because the machine always "just worked" with no reset. So, please always provide a reset for your state machines, and use it in simulation.

Creating a comprehensive set of functional-test vectors for a large state machine by hand is a painstaking process. The test vectors should visit all of the states and use all of the transitions out of each state; our example didn't! Using these vectors, you must make sure that the machine's behavior at each step "makes sense." This is more than determining that the machine does what your code said it should—it will in most cases, because you used automated tools to go from the code to the realization. More important is to determine that *what your code says* makes sense in all cases. This is especially important in infrequently used and considered "corner cases." Success in this step comes only with practice and experience.

Creating test vectors for use in manufacturing to detect hardware failures is another matter. Here, the assumption is that your machine's functional definition is correct, and you want to verify that the actual hardware as built matches the specified behavior. Test vectors for this purpose are typically and best left to an automatic test-pattern-generation program. Rather than starting with the VHDL description, such a program typically uses the gate-level description of the circuit to generate tests. In this way, it can create tests that are more likely to catch errors based on the expected physical failure modes of the device.

7.12.10 Feedback Sequential Circuits

The VHDL process and the simulator's event list form VHDL's fundamental mechanism for handling feedback sequential circuits. Feedback sequential circuits may change state in response to input changes, and these state changes are manifested by changes propagating in a feedback loop until the feedback loop stabilizes. In simulation, this is manifested by the simulator putting signal changes on the event list and scheduling processes to rerun in "delta time" and propagate these signal changes until no more signal changes are scheduled.

Table 7-52 is VHDL code for an S-R latch. It has two concurrent assignment statements, each of which creates a process as discussed in Section 5.3.8. These processes interact to create the simple latching behavior of an S-R latch.

The VHDL simulation is faithful enough to handle the case where both S and R are asserted simultaneously. The most interesting result in simulation occurs if you negate S and R simultaneously. Recall from the box on page 528 that a real S-R latch may oscillate or go into a metastable state in this situation. The simulation will potentially loop forever as each execution of one assignment statement triggers another execution of the other. After some number of repetitions, a well-designed simulator will discover the problem—delta time keeps advancing while simulated time does not—and halt the simulation.

```
entity Vsrlatch is
  port (S, R: in STD_LOGIC;
        Q, QN: buffer STD_LOGIC );
end Vsrlatch;

architecture Vsrlatch_arch of Vsrlatch is
begin
  QN <= S nor Q;
  Q  <= R nor QN;
end Vsrlatch_arch;
```

Table 7-52
Dataflow VHDL for an S-R latch.

WHAT DO 'U' WANT?   It would be nice if the S-R-latch model in Table 7-52 produced a 'U' or 'X' output whenever S and R were negated simultaneously, but it's not *that* good. However, the language is powerful enough that experienced VHDL designers can easily write a model with that behavior. Such a model would make use of VHDL's time-modeling facilities, which we haven't discussed, to model the latch's "recovery time" (see box on page 529) and force an 'X' output if a second input change occurred too soon. It's even possible to model a maximum assumed metastability resolution time in this way.

Figure 1: If a circuit has the possibility of entering a metastable state, there's no guarantee that simulation will detect it, especially in larger designs. The best way to avoid metastability problems in a system design is to clearly identify and protect its asynchronous boundaries, as discussed in Section 8.9.

7.13 Sequential-Circuit Design with Verilog

Most of the Verilog features that are needed to support sequential-circuit design, in particular, always blocks, were introduced in Section 5.4 and were used in the Verilog sections of Chapter 6. This section introduces a couple more features and then shows how to create state machines in Verilog. More examples appear in the Verilog sections of Chapter 8 and in <u>Section XSver</u> at <u>DDPPonline</u>.

7.13.1 Clocked Circuits

The majority of Verilog-based digital design is directed to clocked, synchronous systems that use edge-triggered flip-flops. Like combinational behavior, edge-triggered behavior in Verilog is specified using always blocks. The difference between combinational and edge-triggered behavior is in the sensitivity list of the always block. The keyword posedge or negedge is placed in front of the signal name to indicate that the statements in the block should be executed only at the positive (rising) or negative (falling) edge of the named signal.

posedge keyword
negedge keyword

Thus, we can model the behavior of a positive-edge-triggered D flip-flop as shown in Table 7-53. The posedge keyword creates the edge-sensitive behavior. Also note in the declarations that the Q output is declared as a reg variable so that it can appear on the lefthand side of an assignment statement.

It's also possible to create Verilog models for edge-triggered flip-flops that have asynchronous inputs. For example, Table 7-54 models a positive edge-triggered D with active-low preset and clear inputs. It may strike you as unusual that an edge-sensitivity keyword, negedge, would be applied to a level, asynchronous input. But if you think about it, you'll see that it works, and you're

Table 7-53
Behavioral Verilog
for a positive-edge-
triggered D flip-flop.

```
module VrposDff(CLK, D, Q);
  input CLK, D;
  output Q;
  reg Q;

  always @ (posedge CLK)
    Q <= D;
endmodule
```

Table 7-54
Behavioral Verilog
for a positive-edge-
triggered D flip-flop
with preset and clear.

```
module Vrposdffpc(CLK, PR_L, CLR_L, D, Q);
  input CLK, PR_L, CLR_L, D;
  output Q;
  reg Q;

  always @ (posedge CLK or negedge PR_L or negedge CLR_L)
    if (PR_L==0) Q <= 1;
    else if (CLR_L==0) Q <= 0;
    else Q <= D;
endmodule
```

DOMINANCE   The D flip-flop described in Table 7-54 is a *set-dominant* flip-flop. That's because, as written, preset has precedence over clear when both are asserted. If we reversed the order of the tests of PR_L and CLR_L, we would get a *reset-dominant* flip-flop.

Synthesis tools are pretty smart about this sort of thing. When I targeted the code in Table 7-54 to a particular CPLD family, the compiler warned, "Relative priorities of control signals on register Q differ from those commonly found in the selected device family. This will result in additional logic around the register."

unlikely to come up with a more compact expression of the same behavior. More important, Verilog compilers are set up to recognize this particular representation of edge-triggered-plus-asynchronous behavior, and in synthesis they will pick the right flip-flop component to implement it.

Neither of the D flip-flops we've shown so far has a QN (complemented Q) output. Table 7-55 shows two different ways of specifying a QN output. The first module seems simple enough, assigning a value to QN in the same always block as Q. However, a typical synthesis tool infers two separate D flip-flops from this code—one for Q and the other for QN. The second module assigns a value to QN in a second, combinational always block, and the synthesis tool is forced to generate QN from Q using an inverter.

```
module VrposDffQN1(CLK, D, Q, QN);
  input CLK, D;
  output Q, QN;
  reg Q, QN;

  always @ (posedge CLK) begin
    Q <= D; QN <= !D;
  end
endmodule

module VrposDffQN2(CLK, D, Q, QN);
  input CLK, D;
  output Q, QN;
  reg Q, QN;

  always @ (posedge CLK)
    Q <= D;
  always @ (Q)
    QN <= !Q;
endmodule
```

Table 7-55
Two modules for a positive-edge-triggered D flip-flop with a QN output.

ALWAYS USE NONBLOCKING ASSIGNMENTS IN SEQUENTIAL always BLOCKS	In all of our flip-flop examples, we used the nonblocking assignment operator "<=" to assign a value to Q. These modules would have compiled and synthesized correctly even if we had used the blocking assignment operator "=", but there are subtle reasons why nonblocking assignments should *always* be used in sequential always blocks.
	In programs with multiple sequential always blocks using *blocking* assignments, the simulation results can vary depending on the order in which the simulator chooses to execute those blocks. Using *nonblocking* assignments ensures that the righthand sides of all assignments are evaluated before new values are assigned to any of the lefthand sides. This makes the results independent of the order in which the righthand sides are evaluated. More details are given in an excellent paper by Clifford Cummings, cited in this chapter's References section.

Table 7-56
Clock generation within a test bench.

```
`timescale 1 ns / 1 ns
module mclkgen(MCLK);
  output MCLK;
  reg MCLK;

initial begin
  MCLK = 1;  // Start clock at 1 at time 0
end

always begin          // 10 ns clock generation
  #6 MCLK = 0;         // 6 ns HIGH
  #4 MCLK = 1;  end;   // 4 ns LOW

endmodule
```

In the test bench for a clocked circuit, one of things you need to do is to generate a system clock signal. This can be done easily with an always block, as shown in Table 7-56 for a 100-MHz clock with a 60% duty cycle. At time 0, MCLK is set to 1 by the initial block. Then, the always block waits 6 ns, sets MCLK to 0, waits 4 ns, sets MCLK to 1, and repeats forever. This gives a rising edge every 10 ns. Note that the `timescale directive has been used to set up the simulator both a default time unit and a precision of 1 ns.

7.13.2 State-Machine Design with Verilog

There are many possible coding styles for creating state machines in Verilog, including using no consistent style at all. Some styles and especially the last approach are guaranteed to get you in trouble. Without the discipline of a consistent coding style, it is fairly easy to write syntactically correct Verilog code where the simulator's operation, the synthesized hardware's operation, and what you think the machine should be doing are all different!

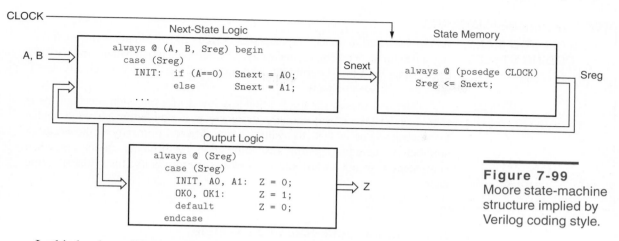

CLOCK

A, B

Next-State Logic

```
always @ (A, B, Sreg) begin
  case (Sreg)
    INIT:  if (A==0)  Snext = A0;
           else       Snext = A1;
    ...
```

Snext

State Memory

```
always @ (posedge CLOCK)
  Sreg <= Snext;
```

Sreg

Output Logic

```
always @ (Sreg)
  case (Sreg)
    INIT, A0, A1:  Z = 0;
    OK0, OK1:      Z = 1;
    default        Z = 0;
  endcase
```

Z

Figure 7-99
Moore state-machine structure implied by Verilog coding style.

In this book, we'll use a coding style that has been used by digital-design professionals for more than a decade to give a minimum of errors. This style also has the advantage of separating the major sections of a state machine's operation and structure, making the design easier to understand and maintain.

Our *Verilog state-machine coding style* precisely matches the general structure of Mealy and Moore state machines that we presented in Figures 7-35 and 7-36 on pages 542 and 543. It also matches the style that we recommended and used in Section 7.12 for VHDL state machines. The code is usually divided into three parts:

Verilog state-machine coding style

- *State memory.* This can be specified in behavioral form using an `always` block that is sensitive to a signal edge, as we showed in the preceding subsection for edge-triggered D flip-flops; or it can use a structural style with explicit flip-flop instantiations, as we'll show in Section 7.13.7.

- *Next-state (excitation) logic.* This is written as a combinational `always` block whose sensitivity list includes the machine's current state and inputs. This block usually contains a `case` statement that enumerates all values of the current state.

- *Output logic.* This is another combinational `always` block that is sensitive to the current state and inputs. It may or may not include a `case` statement, depending on the complexity of the output function.

The detailed coding within each section may vary. In cases where there is a tight coupling of next-state and output-logic specifications, it may be desirable to combine the next-state and output logic into a single combinational `always` block, and indeed, into a single `case` statement. When pipelined outputs are used, the output memory could be specified along with the state memory, or a separate process or structural code could be used. Figure 7-99 shows the relationship between our coding style and state-machine structure for the example state-machine code in the next subsection.

STILL TOO MANY CODING STYLES

As we discussed in the box on page 629, VHDL allows too many different coding styles for state machines, and sadly, Verilog is not much better. And we can't even blame it on the government this time, since Verilog was originally developed by a private company.

The real reason for the Verilog's richness of expression mechanisms is that, like VHDL, it was initially designed as a simulation language, and a fairly general one at that. Its features were directed primarily at the needs of simulation, including getting fast simulation performance in an era when computers were not so fast and inexpensive. Verilog's use for synthesis came later.

7.13.3 A Verilog State-Machine Example

In Section 7.4.1 we illustrated the state-table design process using the simple design problem below:

> Design a clocked synchronous state machine with two inputs, A and B, and a single output Z that is 1 if:
>
> – A had the same value at each of the two previous clock ticks, *or*
>
> – B has been 1 since the last time that the first condition was true.
>
> Otherwise, the output should be 0.

In an HDL-based design environment, there are many possible ways of writing a program that meets the stated requirements. We'll look at several.

The first approach is to construct a state and output table by hand and then manually convert it into a corresponding program. We'll show an easier approach at the end of this subsection, but since we already developed such a state table in Section 7.4.1, let's use it. We've written it again in Table 7-57, and we've written a corresponding Verilog program in Table 7-58.

As usual, the Verilog module declaration specifies its inputs and outputs—`CLOCK`, `A`, `B`, and `Z` in this example. Next, the module declares variables `Sreg` and `Snext` for the machine's current and next states. Finally, using a `parameter` statement, it defines five constants to assign each of the machines's five states to

Table 7-57
State and output table for the example state machine.

	A B				
S	*00*	*01*	*11*	*10*	*Z*
INIT	A0	A0	A1	A1	0
A0	OK0	OK0	A1	A1	0
A1	A0	A0	OK1	OK1	0
OK0	OK0	OK0	OK1	A1	1
OK1	A0	OK0	OK1	OK1	1
	S*				

```verilog
module VrSMex( CLOCK, A, B, Z );
  input CLOCK, A, B;
  output Z;
  reg Z;
  reg [2:0] Sreg, Snext;        // State register and next state
  parameter [2:0] INIT = 3'b000,  // Define the states
                  A0   = 3'b001,
                  A1   = 3'b010,
                  OK0  = 3'b011,
                  OK1  = 3'b100;

  always @ (posedge CLOCK) // Create the state memory
    Sreg <= Snext;

  always @ (A, B, Sreg) begin  // Next-state logic
    case (Sreg)
      INIT:   if (A==0)  Snext = A0;
              else       Snext = A1;
      A0:     if (A==0)  Snext = OK0;
              else       Snext = A1;
      A1:     if (A==0)  Snext = A0;
              else       Snext = OK1;
      OK0:    if (A==0)  Snext = OK0;
              else if ((A==1) && (B==0)) Snext = A1;
              else                       Snext = OK1;
      OK1:    if ((A==0) && (B==0))      Snext = A0;
              else if ((A==0) && (B==1)) Snext = OK0;
              else                       Snext = OK1;
      default Snext = INIT;
    endcase
  end

  always @ (Sreg)          // Output logic
    case (Sreg)
      INIT, A0, A1: Z = 0;
      OK0, OK1:     Z = 1;
      default       Z = 0;
    endcase
endmodule
```

Table 7-58
Verilog program for state-machine example.

a 3-bit value. A different state assignment can be defined here, of course. If it uses more bits, then the definition of Sreg and Snext must be changed too.

The first always block in the module creates the state memory. This block executes on the rising edge of CLOCK and loads the next state Snext into the state register Sreg. During synthesis, positive-edge-triggered D flip-flops will be inferred for Sreg.

The second always block specifies the next-state logic using a case statement. It assigns a value to Snext in six cases, corresponding to the five explicitly defined states and a default for other, undefined states. For robustness, the default case sends the machine back to the INIT state.

NEXT-STATE CODING-STYLE VARIATIONS

In the next-state `always` block in Table 7-58, some designers would precede the `case` statement with one more line of code, "`Snext = INIT`". This establishes a "default" next state for the machine if the `case` statement fails to cover all state/input combinations. (Note that the `default` case at the end handles unused states, but not uncovered input combinations in the other cases.) This style is also useful for machines where very few transitions go anywhere except to a default state.

Another useful variation occurs in machines where most transitions stay in the current state. Then, the case statement can be preceded by a line of code that maintains the current state as default, "`Snext = Sreg`".

Yet another variation is the default "`Snext = 3'bx`". In simulation, this ensures that if the machine ever sees an unspecified state/input combination, the state will be undefined (X's), which is easy to detect in simulation.

Finally, you may have noticed that the `begin-end` block surrounding the `case` statement in the next-state `always` block is not really necessary, syntactically. However, it would still be needed if we added any other statements, such as a default assignment to `Snext`, to the `always` block.

In each case we've used an "`if`" statement and a final "`else`" to ensure that a value is always assigned to `Snext`. If there were any state/input combinations in which no value was assigned `Snext`, the Verilog compiler would infer a latch for `Snext`, something we don't want.

The third and final `always` block in Table 7-58 handles the machine's single Moore output, Z, which is set to a value as a function of the current state. It would be easy to define Mealy outputs here as well, by making Z be a function of the inputs as well as the state in each enumerated case. If this is done, then the inputs should also be added to the sensitivity list of the `always` block.

We really should have included a reset input in Table 7-58 (see box on page 558). A synchronous or asynchronous RESET signal is easily provided by declaring the signal and modifying state-memory `always` block. For example, the first `always` block in Table 7-59 provides synchronous reset capability (reset occurs on the rising edge of CLOCK). The second `always` block provides asynchronous reset capability (reset occurs immediately when RESET is asserted). While there are several valid ways to code asynchronous and synchronous reset behavior, not all will be synthesizable. Our examples show coding styles that are recognized by most tools.

7.13.4 Pipelined Outputs in Verilog

One more interesting variation is possible in our example Verilog state machine. As written, the module defines a conventional Moore-type state machine with the structure shown in Figure 7-99 on page 649. But we can convert the machine to have pipelined outputs with the structure shown in Figure 7-100. To do this,

```
// State memory with active-high synchronous reset
always @ (posedge CLOCK) // Create state memory
    if (RESET==1) Sreg <= INIT; else Sreg <= Snext;

// State memory with active-high asynchronous reset
always @ (posedge CLOCK or posedge RESET) // Create state memory
    if (RESET==1) Sreg <= INIT; else Sreg <= Snext;
```

Table 7-59
Synchronous and asynchronous reset for state machines in Verilog.

we need only to declare a "next-output" variable Zn and replace the original Verilog state-memory and output code with the code shown in Table 7-60. The new machine's behavior is indistinguishable from that of the original machine, except for timing. We've reduced the propagation delay from CLOCK to Z by producing Z directly on a register output, but we've also increased the setup-time requirements of A and B to CLOCK. In addition to their propagation delay through the next-state logic, changes in A and B must also get through the output logic in time to meet the setup time requirement of the output flip-flop's D input.

```
always @ (posedge CLOCK)    // Create output register -- this code
    Z <= Zn; // could be combined with state-memory code if desired

always @ (Snext)            // Output logic
    case (Snext)
        INIT, A0, A1: Zn = 0;
        OK0, OK1:     Zn = 1;
        default       Zn = 0;
    endcase
```

Table 7-60
Verilog pipelined output code.

Figure 7-100 Verilog state machine with pipelined outputs.

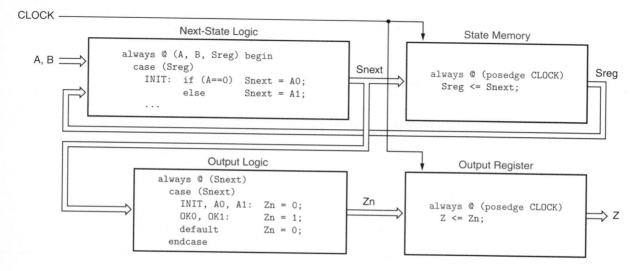

7.13.5 Direct Verilog Coding Without a State Table

All of the variations in the example state-machine design that we've shown so far rely on the state table that we originally constructed by hand in Section 7.4.1. However, it is possible to write a Verilog program directly, without writing out a state table by hand.

Based on the original problem statement on page 630, the key simplifying idea is to remove the last value of A from the state definitions, and instead to have a separate register that keeps track of it (LASTA). Then only two non-INIT states must be defined: LOOKING ("still looking for a match") and OK ("got a match or B has been 1 since last match").

A Verilog module based on this approach is shown in Table 7-61. The first always block creates both the state memory and the LASTA register. The second one creates the next-state logic using our simplified approach. The Z output is a simple combinational decode of the OK state, so we created it using a continuous-assignment statement instead of the more verbose always block and case statement. Note that this required Z to be declared as a wire rather than a reg.

The next-state logic in Table 7-61 is easier to understand and relate to the word description than the original, and we avoided the tedium of developing a state table. Clearly, this is what HDL-based state-machine design is all about.

Table 7-61
Simplified Verilog state-machine design.

```
module VrSMexa( CLOCK, RESET, A, B, Z );
  input CLOCK, RESET, A, B;
  output Z;
  wire Z;                    // declared as wire for continuous assignment
  reg LASTA;                         // LASTA holds last value of A
  reg [1:0] Sreg, Snext;             // State register and next state
  parameter [1:0] INIT    = 2'b00, // Define the states
                  LOOKING = 2'b10,
                  OK      = 2'b11;

  always @ (posedge CLOCK) begin // State memory (with sync. reset)
    if (RESET==1) Sreg <= INIT; else Sreg <= Snext;
    LASTA <= A;
  end

  always @ (A, B, LASTA, Sreg) begin  // Next-state logic
    case (Sreg)
      INIT:    Snext = LOOKING;
      LOOKING: if (A==LASTA)          Snext = OK;
               else                   Snext = LOOKING;
      OK:      if (B==1 || A==LASTA) Snext = OK;
               else                   Snext = LOOKING;
      default                         Snext = INIT;
    endcase
  end

  assign Z = (Sreg==OK) ? 1 : 0;      // Output logic
endmodule
```

7.13.6 More Verilog State-Machine Examples

The next state-machine example is a "ones-counting machine" with the following specifications:

> Design a clocked synchronous state machine with two inputs, X and Y, and one output, Z. The output should be 1 if the number of 1 inputs on X and Y since reset is a multiple of 4, and 0 otherwise.

We developed a state table for this machine in Table 7-9 on page 567. However, we can write a Verilog module for this problem directly, without constructing a state table.

Table 7-62 shows our solution. As always, there are many different ways to solve the problem, and we have picked a way that illustrates several different language features. We declare 2-bit variables COUNT and NEXTCNT to hold the current and next ones count, and a 2-bit constant ZERO for initializing and checking the value of COUNT. The first always block creates a 2-bit register to hold the current state (COUNT), including a synchronous reset capability.

The next-state logic is handled by the second always block. It elegantly adds 0, 1, or 2 to COUNT depending on the values of X and Y. Recall that an expression such as "{1'b0, X}" is a concatenation of bits into a larger bit vector. So here we get a vector of two bits—one bit of 0 and one bit which is the current value of X. So, NEXTCNT is set to the sum of three 2-bit numbers—COUNT, {0,X}, and {0,Y}—which is what we want. The final continuous-assignment statement sets the Moore output Z to 1 when COUNT is zero.

In synthesis, the counting logic in Table 7-62 doesn't necessarily yield a compact or speedy circuit. With a simple-minded synthesis tool, it could yield two 2-bit adders connected in series. Another approach is to replace the NEXTCNT always block with the one shown in Table 7-63 on the next page. A good tool may be able to synthesize a more compact incrementer for each of the two additions. Regardless, formulating the choices in a case statement makes for a

---

```
module Vronescnt( CLOCK, RESET, X, Y, Z );
  input CLOCK, RESET, X, Y;
  output Z;
  wire Z;                   // declared as wire for continuous assignment
  reg [1:0] COUNT, NEXTCNT;      // Current and next count, modulo 4
  parameter [1:0] ZERO = 2'b00;

  always @ (posedge CLOCK)      // State memory (with sync. reset)
    if (RESET==1) COUNT <= ZERO; else COUNT <= NEXTCNT;

  always @ (COUNT, X, Y)        // Counting logic
    NEXTCNT = COUNT + {1'b0, X} + {1'b0, Y};

  assign Z = (COUNT==ZERO) ? 1 : 0;     // Output logic
endmodule
```

Table 7-62
Alternative Verilog module for a ones-counting machine.

Table 7-63
Alternative Verilog counting logic for ones-counting machine.

```
always @ (COUNT, X, Y) case ({X, Y})    // Counting logic
  2'b01, 2'b10: NEXTCNT = COUNT + 2'b01;
  2'b11:        NEXTCNT = COUNT + 2'b10;
  default       NEXTCNT = COUNT;
endcase
```

faster circuit, allowing the two adders or incrementers to operate in parallel, and a multiplexer can be used to select one of their outputs according to the choices (for example, see Figure 6-94 on page 490).

A clever designer can ensure that only one full adder is synthesized in the ones-counting machine by declaring a 2-bit reg variable XY1s and using the counting-logic code shown in Table 7-64. It may not be immediately obvious to you how this works, but if you compare it with effect of the cases in Table 7-63, you should get it; looking at it another way, the two equations in Table 7-64 create a half adder. The best synthesis tools give exactly the same results from the counting logic in Table 7-62 as they do from Table 7-64.

Table 7-64
Fastest and smallest Verilog counting logic for ones-counting machine.

```
always @ (COUNT, X, Y) begin   // Counting logic
  XY1s[0] = X ^ Y;
  XY1s[1] = X & Y;
  NEXTCNT = COUNT + XY1s;
end
```

A final example for this subsection is the combination-lock state machine from Section 7.4 (below we omit the HINT output in the original specification):

Design a clocked synchronous state machine with one input, X, and one output, UNLK. The UNLK output should be 1 if and only if X is 0 and the sequence of inputs received on X at the preceding seven clock ticks was 0110111.

We developed a state table for this machine in Table 7-11 on page 568. But once again we can take a different approach that is easier to understand. Here, we note that the output of the machine at any time is completely determined by its inputs during the current and preceding seven clock ticks. Thus, we can use a "finite-memory" approach (defined in Exercise 7.59) to design this machine. With this approach, we explicitly keep track of the past seven inputs and then form the output as a combinational function of these and the current inputs.

The Verilog module in Table 7-65 is a finite-memory design. This module keeps track of the last seven values of X using what you'll later recognize to be a "shift register." The bits are shifted left on each clock tick, and bit 7 is the oldest

```
module Vrcomblock( CLOCK, RESET, X, UNLK );
  input CLOCK, RESET, X;
  output UNLK;
  wire UNLK;            // declared as wire for continuous assignment
  reg [7:1] XHISTORY; // 7-tick history of X
  parameter [7:1] COMBINATION = 7'b0110111;


  always @ (posedge CLOCK)   // State memory (with sync. reset)
    if (RESET==1) XHISTORY <= 7'b1111111;
    else XHISTORY <= {XHISTORY[6:1], X}; // next-state logic

  // Output logic -- Detect combination
  assign UNLK = (XHISTORY==COMBINATION && X==0) ? 1 : 0;
endmodule
```

Table 7-65
Verilog module for
finite-memory design
of combination-lock
state machine.

value of X. (Recall that the curly brackets in Verilog perform concatenation of bit vectors.) Since the state machine is so simple, we took the liberty of putting the next-state logic into the same always block as the state memory. At the end of the module, the continuous-assignment statement sets the Mealy output UNLK to 1 when X is 0 and the 7-bit history matches the combination. Note that XHISTORY was initialized to all 1s at reset so the user doesn't get the benefit of a "free" 0 right after reset to begin the combination pattern.

More complicated examples of Verilog state machines, including T-Bird tail lights and the guessing game, appear in <u>Section XSver</u> at <u>DDPPonline</u>.

7.13.7 Specifying Flip-Flops in Verilog

Flip-flops are such an important component in any major design that, in practice, it's sometimes risky to let the synthesis tool "infer" a flip-flop from generic Verilog code such as Table 7-53 on page 646 or any of the state-machine examples that we've shown in this section. Instead, you can use structural Verilog to select exactly the flip-flop component that you want, as we'll show later in this subsection.

As shown in Table 7-48 on page 639, flip-flops in typical libraries have different inputs and functions, such as asynchronous resets and presets, clock enabling, and scan inputs. The table shows components from both a Xilinx FPGA/CPLD library and an LSI Logic ASIC library. Most of the basic flip-flop types appear in both libraries, but flip-flops with some combinations of features appear in only one or the other. Also, many of the signal names for the same function vary between libraries (e.g., CLR vs. CD for an asynchronous-clear input).

When your structural Verilog code is targeted to an ASIC, the library component corresponds to a gate- or transistor-level realization that has exactly the specified functionality, and no more. When your code is targeted to a CPLD or FPGA, the specified functionality is synthesized from the flip-flop type(s) available in the device; extra combinational logic may be "wrapped" around the device to obtain all of the required functionality. For example, a multiplexer might be connected to the D input of a simple D flip-flop to get a clock-enable or scan input.

We can modify the example state machine in Table 7-61 on page 654 to use particular flip-flops as shown in Table 7-66. Three changes are needed:

1. The program "includes" the Xilinx component library (`unisim_comp.v`), which includes the flip-flop types such as FD that we listed in the first column of Table 7-48 on page 639. Note that the exact filename for this library may vary in different design environments.

2. The variables Sreg and LASTA are now declared as type `wire` rather than `reg`. This is necessary because their values are assigned within an instantiation of a component, FDR or FD.

3. The behavioral description of the state memory is replaced with structural code to instantiate the flip-flops.

No changes are required to the next-state logic and output logic in the rest of the Verilog module.

To change the state encoding in Table 7-66, we must change the parameter definitions of the states. If the number of bits in the state encoding changes, we must also change the Snext and Sreg definitions and the flip-flop instantiations. For example, Table 7-67 shows the changes for a one-hot state encoding.

Table 7-66
Verilog state machine with explicit flip-flop instantiation.

```
`include "C:/Xilinx/verilog/src/ISE/unisim_comp.v"
module VrSMexs( CLOCK, RESET, A, B, Z );
  input CLOCK, RESET, A, B;
  output Z;
  wire Z;              // declared as wire for continuous assignment
  wire LASTA;          // LASTA holds last value of A
  reg [1:0] Snext;     // Next state
  wire [1:0] Sreg;     // State register
  parameter [1:0] INIT    = 2'b00,  // Define the states
                  LOOKING = 2'b10,
                  OK      = 2'b11;

  FDR U1 (.C(CLOCK), .R(RESET), .D(Snext[0]), .Q(Sreg[0]) );
  FDR U2 (.C(CLOCK), .R(RESET), .D(Snext[1]), .Q(Sreg[1]) );
  FD  U3 (.C(CLOCK), .D(A), .Q(LASTA) );
  . . .
```

YOU DECIDE In this subsection, we showed how to use structural rather than behavioral Verilog code to get exactly the flip-flop that you want. On the other hand, using structural Verilog may tie the flip-flop component name and port names to a particular ASIC or manufacturer's library, compromising your design's portability.

Most Verilog designers use the behavioral code for their flip-flops, and carefully check their synthesis results to make sure that they got what they expected. However, some designers use scripts, macros, and other tricks to enhance portability of their designs to work with different technologies and manufacturers. It's up to you (or your company) to decide which method to use.

```
. . .
    reg [2:0] Snext;      // Next state
    wire [2:0] Sreg;      // State register
    parameter [2:0] INIT    = 3'b100,  // Define the states
                    LOOKING = 3'b010,
                    OK      = 3'b001;

    FDR U1 (.C(CLOCK), .R(RESET), .D(Snext[0]), .Q(Sreg[0]) );
    FDR U2 (.C(CLOCK), .R(RESET), .D(Snext[1]), .Q(Sreg[1]) );
    FDS U3 (.C(CLOCK), .S(RESET), .D(Snext[2]), .Q(Sreg[2]) );
    FD  U4 (.C(CLOCK), .D(A), .Q(LASTA) );
. . .
```

Table 7-67
Verilog code changes for one-hot state encoding in state machine with explicit flip-flop instantiation.

7.13.8 Verilog State-Machine Test Benches

We explained the general concept of Verilog test benches in Section 5.4.13. Unlike ABEL test vectors, which are embedded in the ABEL program for a device, a Verilog test bench is a separate Verilog program. The test bench for a state machine has five basic parts:

1. Declaration of the test-bench entity itself. Note that this entity has no inputs and outputs of its own.

2. Component declaration of the state-machine entity to be tested, often called the *unit under test (UUT)*.

3. Instantiation of the UUT.

4. An `always` statement to create a free-running clock.

5. Statements to initialize the UUT, to apply a sequence of test-vector inputs at each clock tick, and to check for expected output values.

unit under test (UUT)

We'll illustrate these ideas with a test bench for our familiar example state machine of Table 7-58 on page 651.

The first thing you should notice about this state machine is that it doesn't have a reset input, so we can't simulate it properly—since its state memory can't be initialized, its starting state is unknown. So, we really need to use a version of the machine that has a reset input (also see the box on page 644). In particular, we'll test either the version having a synchronous reset that we showed in the first part of Table 7-59 on page 653, or the version in Table 7-61 on page 654. With this in mind, we can write the test-bench module shown in Table 7-68.

The first section of the module declares local variables to apply to the inputs and observe the output of the state machine. The second section instantiates the state machine, giving it the component name "UUT"; notice that the local variable names can be the same as or different from the port names.

Next, we define a task that will be used later to compare the simulated state-machine output Z with an expected value, and print an error message if they are different. This task is called at each step during the actual tests, so we defined it to save typing and clutter in the test code.

The last two blocks create the actual tests. The always block establishes a free-running clock signal with a 10-ns clock period. Since we are running a functional simulation with no embedded timing information, it doesn't matter what clock period we use. However, one subtlety is that, regardless of its period, the clock's transition from undefined to 1 at time 0 may be considered to be a rising edge, and the state flip-flops may respond accordingly. But we won't count on this; we'll keep RST asserted at the beginning of the test.

The initial block is devoted to applying inputs and checking the state-machine output. Since we're new at this, we start with a $monitor task that prints all signals values on the system console any time one of them changes. Then we assert RST (reset) and wait 15 ns, to the middle of the second clock period, which should force the machine into the INIT state. Since the state definitions are "hidden" in the UUT's module definitions, the test bench cannot check the state directly. But we know that the output should be 0 in the INIT state, so we call our checkZ task to print a message and stop the simulation if Z is not 0 at this point. At the same time (still halfway through the second clock period), we negate RST and apply the next pair of values to A and B to drive the machine to a new state at the next clock tick. At each subsequent step, we check for the expected value on Z, and set up A and B for the next tick. If any of the actual outputs fail to match the expected value, the simulation stops and prints an error message, so we can investigate the problem.

LOOKING UNDER THE HOOD   Beyond the port definitions for a particular UUT instantiated by a test bench, Verilog purposely hides the inner workings of the module's implementation. But for debugging purposes, you'd really like to see what's going on inside. So, when you run your test bench on an interactive simulator, you can drill down and see signal values within the UUT module's implementation.

```
module VrSMex_tb ();
reg Tclk, RST, A, B;
wire Z;

VrSMexa UUT ( .CLOCK(Tclk),
              .RESET(RST),
              .A(A),
              .B(B),
              .Z(Z)          ); // instantiate UUT

task checkZ;   // Task to check output values and print if wrong
  input stepnum, expectZ;
  integer stepnum; reg expectZ;
  begin
    if (Z != expectZ) begin
      $display($time," Error, step %d, expected %b, got %b",
               stepnum, expectZ, Z); $stop(1); end;
  end
endtask

always begin     // create free-running test clock with 10 ns period
  #6 Tclk = 0;   // 6 ns high
  #4 Tclk = 1;   // 4 ns low
end

initial begin    // What to do starting at time 0
  $monitor("Time:%d  RST=%b Tclk=%b A=%b B=%b Z=%b",
           $time, RST, Tclk, A, B, Z); // Monitor all signals
  RST = 1;         // Apply reset
  A = 1; B = 1;    // A and B are 1 too
  Tclk = 1;        // Start clock at 1 at time 0
  #15;             // Wait 15 ns
  checkZ(1,0);     // Expect Z=0 initially
  RST = 0;         // unreset
  A = 1; B = 1; #10  checkZ(2,0);  // still Z=0 after INIT
  A = 1; B = 0; #10  checkZ(3,1);  // Two 1s in a row, want Z=1
  A = 0; B = 1; #10  checkZ(4,1);  // B=1 should hold Z=1
  A = 1; B = 0; #10  checkZ(5,0);  // B=0 releases it
  A = 0; B = 1; #10  checkZ(6,0);  // B=1 but nothing to hold
  A = 0; B = 0; #10  checkZ(7,1);  // But now two 0s in a row
  A = 1; B = 1; #10  checkZ(8,1);  // B=1 should hold Z=1
  A = 0; B = 0; #10  checkZ(9,0);  // B=0 releases it
  $stop(1);                        // end test
end
endmodule
```

Table 7-68
Verilog test bench for the state machine of Table 7-58 (with synchronous reset added) or Table 7-60, 7-61, 7-66, or 7-67.

Note that the test bench is checking the machine's *functional* behavior, pretty much at the level of our original word description. Except for a little special knowledge of what happens at initialization, the test bench makes no reference to the actual internal states of the machine. So, the same test bench could be used with different versions of the same state machine with different states or state assignments, or other subtle differences. These other versions are listed in the table caption above.

Creating a comprehensive set of functional-test vectors for a large state machine by hand is a painstaking process. The test vectors should visit all of the states and use all of the transitions out of each state; our example didn't! Using these vectors, you must make sure that the machine's behavior at each step "makes sense." This is more than determining that the machine does what your code said it should—it will in most cases, because you used automated tools to go from the code to the realization. More important is to determine that *what your code says* makes sense in all cases. This is especially important in infrequently used and considered "corner cases." Success in this step comes only with practice and experience.

Creating test vectors for use in manufacturing to detect hardware failures is another matter. Here, the assumption is that your machine's functional definition is correct, and you want to verify that the actual hardware as built matches the specified behavior. Test vectors for this purpose are typically and best left to an automatic test-pattern-generation program. Rather than starting with the Verilog description, such a program typically uses the gate-level description of the circuit to generate tests. In this way, it can create tests that are more likely to catch errors based on the expected physical failure modes of the device.

7.13.9 Feedback Sequential Circuits

The always statement and the simulator's event list are Verilog's fundamental mechanism for handling feedback sequential circuits. Feedback sequential circuits may change state in response to input changes, and these state changes are manifested by changes propagating in a feedback loop until the feedback loop stabilizes. In simulation, this is manifested by the simulator putting signal changes on the event list and scheduling processes to rerun in "delta time" and propagate these signal changes until no more signal changes are scheduled.

Table 7-69 is Verilog code for an S-R latch. Each of its two continuous-assignment statements implies a software process as discussed in Section 5.4.12. These processes interact to emulate the simple latching behavior of an S-R latch.

Table 7-69
Verilog module for an S-R latch.

```
module VrSRlatch( S, R, Q, QN );
   input S, R;
   output Q, QN;

   assign QN = ~(S | Q);
   assign Q  = ~(R | QN);

endmodule
```

The Verilog simulation is faithful enough to handle the case where both S and R are asserted simultaneously. The most interesting result in simulation occurs if you negate S and R simultaneously. Recall from the box on page 528 that a real S-R latch may oscillate or go into a metastable state in this situation. The simulation will potentially loop forever as each execution of one assignment statement triggers another execution of the other. After some number of repetitions, a well-designed simulator will discover the problem—delta time keeps advancing while simulated time does not—and halt the simulation. Other possibilities for modeling metastability are discussed in the box on page 645.

References

The problem of metastability has been around for a long time. Greek philosophers wrote about the problem of indecision thousands of years ago. A group of modern philosophers named Devo sang about metastability in the title song of their *Freedom of Choice* album. The U.S. Congress still can't decide how to "save" Social Security. And I could say that in the previous edition, too!

Scan capability was first deployed in latches, not flip-flops, in IBM IC designs decades ago. Edward J. McCluskey has a very good discussion of this and other scan methods in *Logic Design Principles* (Prentice Hall, 1986).

Most ASICs and MSI-, PLD- and FPGA-based designs use the sequential-circuit types described in this chapter. However, there are other types that are used in both older discrete designs (going all the way back to vacuum-tube logic) and as well as in modern, custom VLSI designs.

For example, clocked synchronous state machines are a special case of a more general class of *pulse-mode circuits*. Such circuits have one or more *pulse inputs* such that (a) only one pulse occurs at a time; (b) nonpulse inputs are stable when a pulse occurs; (c) only pulses can cause state changes; and (d) a pulse causes at most one state change. In clocked synchronous state machines, the clock is the single pulse input, and a "pulse" is the triggering edge of the clock. However, it is also possible to build circuits with multiple pulse inputs, and it is possible to use storage elements other than the familiar edge-triggered flip-flops. These possibilities are discussed very thoroughly in McCluskey's *Logic Design Principles* (Prentice Hall, 1986).

pulse-mode circuit
pulse input

A particularly important type of pulse-mode circuit that is discussed by McCluskey and others is the *two-phase latch machine*. The rationale for a two-phase clocking approach in VLSI circuits is discussed by Carver Mead and Lynn Conway in *Introduction to VLSI Systems* (Addison-Wesley, 1980). These machines essentially eliminate the essential hazards present in edge-triggered flip-flops by using pairs of latches that are enabled by nonoverlapping clocks.

two-phase latch machine

Methods for reducing both completely and incompletely specified state tables are described in advanced logic design texts, including McCluskey's 1986 book. A more mathematical discussion of these methods and other "theoretical" topics in sequential machine design appears in *Switching and Finite Automata Theory*, second edition, by Zvi Kohavi (McGraw-Hill, 1978).

As we showed in this chapter, improperly constructed state diagrams may yield an ambiguous description of next-state behavior. The "if-then-else" structures in ABEL, VHDL, and Verilog can eliminate these ambiguities, but they were not the first to do so. *Algorithmic-state-machine (ASM)* notation, a flowchart-like equivalent of nested if-then-else statements, has been around for over 30 years. So-called *ASM charts* were pioneered at Hewlett-Packard Laboratories by Thomas E. Osborne and were further developed by Osborne's colleague Christopher R. Clare in a book, *Designing Logic Systems Using State Machines* (McGraw-Hill, 1973). Design and synthesis methods using ASM charts subsequently found a home in many digital design texts, including the first two editions of the book you're reading.

algorithmic state machine (ASM)

ASM chart

Many CAD environments for digital design include a graphical state-diagram entry tool. Unfortunately, these typically support only traditional state diagrams, making it very easy for a designer to create an ambiguous description of next-state behavior. As a result, my personal recommendation is that you stay away from state-diagram editors and instead use an HDL to describe your state machines.

Both VHDL and Verilog support many different state-machine coding styles, in fact, too many. Our recommended state-machine coding style in both of these HDLs is based on a 1998 paper by Clifford E. Cummings titled "State-Machine Coding Styles for Synthesis." This and other interesting Cummings papers can be found at his website at www.sunburst-design.com/papers. For example, two of them (coauthored with Don Mills and Steve Golson) describe in great detail the pros and cons of synchronous versus asynchronous reset signals for state machines and clocked systems in general.

We mentioned the importance of synchronizing sequences in connection with state-machine test vectors. There's actually a very well developed but almost forgotten theory and practice of synchronizing sequences and somewhat less powerful "homing experiments," described by Frederick C. Hennie in *Finite-State Models for Logical Machines* (Wiley, 1968). Unless you've got this old classic on your bookshelf and know how to apply its teachings, please just remember to provide a reset input in every state machine that you design!

Drill Problems

7.1 Give two examples of metastability that occur in sports, other than ones discussed in this chapter.

7.2 Find the lyrics for the title song in Devo's *Freedom of Choice* album and write out the lines that refer to metastability.

7.3 In what song do the Lovin' Spoonful sing about metastability?

7.4   Sketch the outputs of an S-R latch of the type shown in Figure 7-5 for the input waveforms shown in Figure X7.4. Assume that input and output rise and fall times are zero, that the propagation delay of a NOR gate is 10 ns, and that each time division below is 10 ns.

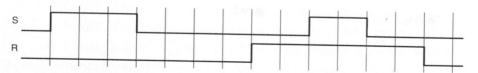

Figure X7.4

7.5   Repeat Drill 7.4 using the input waveforms shown in Figure X7.5. Although you may find the result unbelievable, this behavior can actually occur in real devices whose transition times are short compared to their propagation delay.

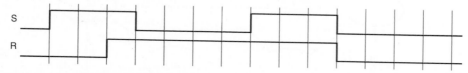

Figure X7.5

7.6   Figure 7-34 showed how to build a T flip-flop with enable using a D flip-flop and combinational logic. Show how to build a D flip-flop using a T flip-flop with enable and combinational logic.

7.7   Show how to build a J-K flip-flop using a T flip-flop with enable and combinational logic.

7.8   Show how to build an S-R latch using a single 74x74 positive-edge-triggered D flip-flop and *no* other components.

7.9   Is it possible to build the equivalent of a master-slave S-R flip-flop using a single 74x74-type edge-triggered D flip-flop and external combinational logic? If so, show the logic. If not, explain why not.

7.10   Is it possible to build the equivalent of a master-slave J-K flip-flop using a single 74x74-type edge-triggered D flip-flop and external combinational logic? If so, show the logic. If not, explain why not.

7.11   Show how to build a flip-flop equivalent to the 74x74 positive-edge-triggered D flip-flop using a 74x109 positive-edge-triggered J-$\overline{\text{K}}$ flip-flop and *no* other components.

7.12   Analyze the clocked synchronous state machine in Figure X7.12. Write excitation equations, excitation/transition table, and state/output table (use state names A–D for Q1 Q2 = 00–11).

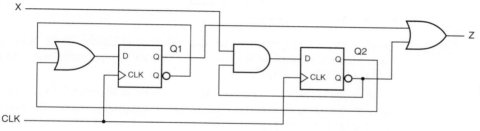

Figure X7.12

7.13   Repeat Drill 7.12, changing AND to NAND gates and OR to NOR gates in the logic diagram, and swapping the true and complemented outputs of each flip-flop. What is the relationship of the new state table vs. the original? What is the relationship of the new observable behavior vs. the original (X, CLK, Z)? .

7.14   Draw a state diagram for the state machine described by Table 7-5.

7.15   Draw a state diagram for the state machine described by Table 7-9.

7.16   Draw a state diagram for the state machine described by Table 7-11.

7.17   Construct a state and output table equivalent to the state diagram in Figure X7.17. Note that the diagram is drawn with the convention that the state does not change except for input conditions that are explicitly shown.

Figure X7.17

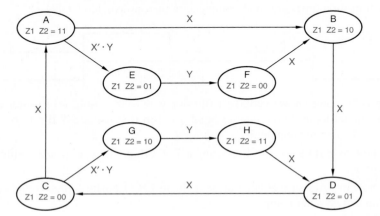

7.18   Analyze the clocked synchronous state machine in Figure X7.18. Write excitation equations, excitation/transition table, and state table (use state names A–H for $Q2\ Q1\ Q0 = 000$–111).

Figure X7.18

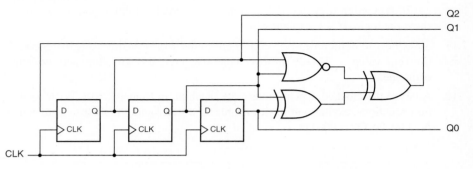

7.19   Analyze the clocked synchronous state machine in Figure X7.19. Write excitation equations, excitation/transition table, and state/output table (use state names A–H for $Q1\ Q2\ Q3 = 000$–111).

7.20   Analyze the clocked synchronous state machine in Figure X7.20. Write excitation equations, excitation/transition table, and state/output table (use state names A–D for $Q1\ Q2 = 00$–11).

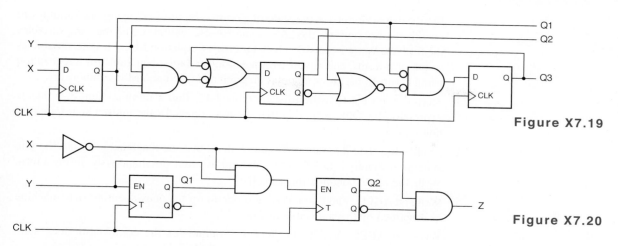

Figure X7.19

Figure X7.20

7.21   All of the state diagrams in Figure X7.21 are ambiguous. List all of the ambigu-
       ities in these state diagrams. (*Hint:* Use Karnaugh maps where necessary to find
       uncovered and double-covered input combinations. *Or*, if you have an HDL
       compiler or other logic minimizer available, you can write and minimize an
       expression for each state that is the OR of the ANDs of all pairs of transition
       expressions leaving that state; the result is 1 for the input values that are double-
       covered. Similarly, write and minimize an expression for each state that is the
       NOR of all the transition expressions leaving that state; the result is 1 for the input
       values that are uncovered.)

(a)
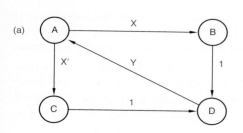

(b)
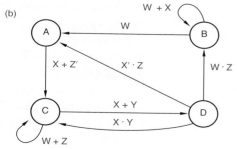

Figure X7.21

(c)
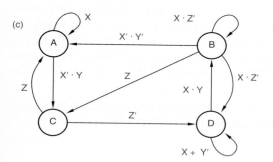

(d)
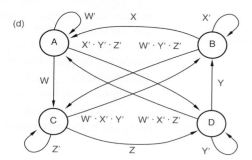

7.22   Synthesize a circuit for the state diagram of Figure 7-58 using six variables to encode the state, where the LA–LC and RA–RC outputs equal the state variables themselves. Write a transition list, a transition equation for each state variable as a sum of p-terms, and simplified transition/excitation equations for a realization using D flip-flops. Draw a circuit diagram using SSI and MSI components.

7.23   Starting with the transition list in Table 7-15, find a minimal sum-of-products expression for Q2*, assuming that the next states for the unused states are true don't-cares.

7.24   Modify the state diagram of Figure 7-58 so that the machine goes into the idle state immediately if LEFT and RIGHT are asserted simultaneously during a turn. Write the corresponding transition list.

7.25   Write an ABEL, VHDL, or Verilog program for the ones-counting state machine as described by the state table in Table 7-9.

7.26   Write an ABEL, VHDL, or Verilog program for the combination-lock state machine as described by the state table in Table 7-11.

7.27   Draw a timing diagram showing the inputs, output, and state of the ABEL state machine in Table 7-24 when the test inputs specified in Table 7-31 are applied to it (13 clock ticks).

7.28   Draw a timing diagram showing the inputs, outputs, and state of the ABEL state machine in Table 7-28 when the test inputs specified in Table 7-32 are applied to it (17 clock ticks).

7.29   Draw a timing diagram showing the inputs, outputs, and state (including lastA) of the VHDL state machine in Table 7-44 when the test bench of Table 7-51 is run. You can try to work this out in your head, or you can just run the test bench!

7.30   Draw a timing diagram showing the inputs, outputs, and state (including lastA) of the Verilog state machine in Table 7-61 when the test bench of Table 7-68 is run. You can try to work this out in your head, or you can just run the test bench!

7.31   Run the VHDL or Verilog test bench in Table 7-51 or 7-68. Instantiate at least one other UUT version mentioned in the table caption, and verify that the test bench still works. Then, introduce a bug in the OK state in the UUT, checking B against 0 instead of 1, and confirm that the test bench catches the bug. Finally, can you come up with a bug in the UUT that the test bench does *not* catch?

7.32   Write an ABEL, VHDL, or Verilog program for a "sticky-counter" state machine with eight states, S0–S7, that are coded into three bits in binary counting order. Besides CLOCK, your machine should have two inputs, RESET and ENABLE, and one output, DONE. The machine should go to state S0 whenever RESET is asserted. When RESET is negated, it should move to next-numbered state only if ENABLE is asserted. However, once it reaches state S7, it should stay there unless RESET is again asserted. The DONE output should be 1 if and only if the machine is in state S7 and ENABLE is asserted.

7.33   Write ABEL test vectors or a VHDL or Verilog test bench to check for proper operation of the sticky counter that you designed in Drill 7.32.

7.34 Write an ABEL, VHDL, or Verilog program for a state machine that is similar to the one specified in Drill 7.32 except that, when enabled, it counts "two steps forward, one step back." The machine should have one additional output, BACK, that is asserted if ENABLE is asserted and the machine is going to count back on the next clock edge. Once the machine gets to state S7, it never counts back. Comment your program to describe your strategy for creating this behavior and how many additional state bits are needed.

7.35 Write ABEL test vectors or a VHDL or Verilog test bench to check for proper operation of the state machine you designed in Drill 7.34.

7.36 Create a VHDL or Verilog test bench for the S-R latch of Table 7-52 or 7-69, respectively. In the test bench, create input waveforms on S and R with timing similar to Figure X7.5. Run the test bench and print or sketch the simulator's input and output waveforms (S, R, Q, and QN). What does the simulator do on the last input transition?

7.37 Modify the VHDL or Verilog S-R latch in Table 7-52 or 7-69 to delay the output transitions on Q and QN by 10 ns, using `after` or `#` delay specifications, respectively, in the assignment statements. Then repeat Drill 7.36.

Exercises

7.38 Explain how metastability occurs in a D latch when the setup and hold times are not met, analyzing the behavior of the feedback loop inside the latch.

7.39 What is the minimum setup time of a pulse-triggered flip-flop such as a master/slave J-K or S-R flip-flop? (*Hint:* It depends on certain characteristics of the clock.)

7.40 Describe a situation, other than the metastable state, in which the Q and QN outputs of a 74x74 edge-triggered D flip-flop may be noncomplementary for an arbitrarily long time.

7.41 Compare the circuit in Figure X7.41 with the D latch in Figure 7-12. Prove that the circuits function identically. In what way is Figure X7.41, which is used in some commercial D latches, better?

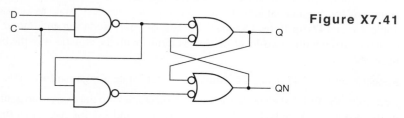

Figure X7.41

7.42 Redesign the state machine in Drill 7.12 using just three inverting gates—NAND or NOR—and no inverters.

7.43 Suppose that a clocked synchronous state machine with the structure of Figure 7-35 is designed using D latches with active-high C inputs as storage elements. For proper next-state operation, what relationships must be satisfied among the following timing parameters?

t_{Fmin}, t_{Fmax} Minimum and maximum propagation delay of the next-state logic.

t_{CQmin}, t_{CQmax} Minimum and maximum clock-to-output delay of a D latch.

t_{DQmin}, t_{DQmax} Minimum and maximum data-to-output delay of a D latch.

t_{setup}, t_{hold} Setup and hold times of a D latch.

t_H, t_L Clock HIGH and LOW times.

7.44 Draw a state diagram for a clocked synchronous state machine with two inputs, INIT and X, and one Moore-type output Z. As long as INIT is asserted, Z is continuously 0. Once INIT is negated, Z should remain 0 until X has been 0 for two successive ticks and 1 for two successive ticks, regardless of the order of occurrence. Then Z should go to 1 and remain 1 until INIT is asserted again. Your state diagram should be neatly drawn and planar (no crossed lines). (*Hint:* No more than ten states are required.)

7.45 Repeat Exercise 7.44, but write the state diagram in ABEL.

7.46 Design a clocked synchronous state machine with the state/output table shown in Table X7.46, using D flip-flops. Use two state variables, Q1 Q2, with the state assignment A = 00, B = 01, C = 11, D = 10.

Table X7.46

	X		
S	0	1	Z
A	B	D	0
B	C	B	0
C	B	A	1
D	B	C	0
	S*		

7.47 Write a new transition table and derive minimal-risk excitation and output equations for the state table in Table 7-5 using the "simplest" state assignment in Table 7-6 and D flip-flops. Compare the cost of your excitation and output logic (when realized with a two-level AND-OR circuit) with the equations in the box on page 566.

7.48 Repeat Exercise 7.47 using the "almost one-hot" state assignment in Table 7-6.

7.49 Determine the full 8-state table for the state machine with the excitation equations in the box on page 566. Use the names U1, U2, and U3 for the states that are unused in the original state table (001, 010, and 011). Draw a state diagram and explain the behavior of the unused states.

7.50   Write a transition table for the nonminimal state table in Figure 7-49(a) that results from assigning the states in binary counting order, INIT–OKA1 = 000–110. Write corresponding excitation equations for D flip-flops, assuming a minimal-cost disposition of the unused state 111. Compare the cost of your equations with the minimal-cost equations for the minimal state table presented in the text.

7.51   In many applications, the outputs produced by a state machine during or shortly after reset are irrelevant, as long as the machine begins to behave correctly a short time after the reset signal is removed. If this idea is applied to Table 7-5, the INIT state can be removed and only two state variables are needed to code the remaining four states. Redesign the state machine using this idea. Write a new state table, transition/excitation table for D flip-flops, and minimal-risk excitation and output equations. Compare the cost of the new design (gates and flip-flops) with the minimal-risk design that was completed in Section 7.4.4.

7.52   Redesign the 1s-counting machine of Table 7-9, assigning the states in binary counting order (S0–S3 = 00, 01, 10, 11). Compare the cost of the resulting sum-of-products excitation equations with the ones derived in the text.

7.53   Redesign the 1s-counting machine of Table 7-9 as an ABEL state diagram. Try to find a state assignment that minimizes the total number of product terms, assuming that you can use either polarity of output equations. How many different state assignments must you examine?

7.54   Redesign the combination-lock machine of Table 7-11, assigning coded states in Gray-code order (A–H = 000, 001, 011, 010, 110, 111, 101, 100). Compare the cost of the resulting sum-of-products excitation equations with the ones derived in the text.

7.55   Find a 3-bit state assignment for the combination-lock machine of Table 7-11 that results in less costly excitation equations than the ones derived in the text. (*Hint:* Use the fact that inputs 1–3 are the same as inputs 4–6 in the required input sequence.)

7.56   You've studied Section 7.3 on state-machine analysis, and your professor has asked you to derive the state/output table for a machine with four edge-triggered D flip-flops, four inputs I1–I4, and one output Z that is a function of the state only. You realize that the state table will have 16 rows and columns, and it is going to be a real pain to derive the 256 next-state entries. However, you have a Verilog or VHDL simulator available to you, and it wouldn't take you very long at all to create a structural model for the circuit. Describe in general terms the structure and operation of a test bench that would derive all of the next-state entries for you, including any modifications that you would make to the state-machine model to simplify the operation of the test bench.

7.57   Modify the VHDL program of Table 7-47 to include the HINT output from the original state-machine specification in Section 7.4.

7.58   Modify the Verilog program of Table 7-65 to include the HINT output from the original state-machine specification in Section 7.4.

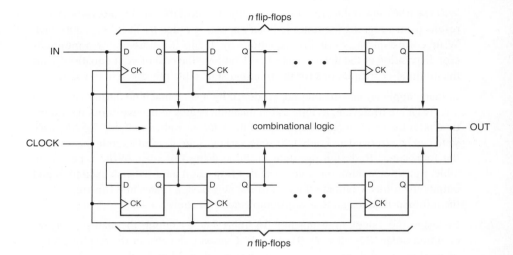

Figure X7.59

7.59   The output of a *finite-memory machine* is completely determined by its current input and its inputs and outputs during the previous *n* clock ticks, where *n* is a finite, bounded integer. For example, Figure X7.59 shows the realization of a finite-memory machine with one input and one output. Note that a finite-*state* machine need not be a finite-*memory* machine; for example, a modulo-*n* counter with an enable input and a "MAX" output has only *n* states, but its output may depend on the value of the enable input at every clock tick since initialization.

Can the state-machine example of Section 7.4.1 be realized as a finite-memory machine? If so, state how many flip-flops are required and show how they are arranged, and if not, describe changes to the machine's description that would allow a finite-memory realization.

7.60   The combination-lock example of Section 7.4.6 can be realized as a finite-memory machine. Draw a logic diagram for the circuit, showing the flip-flops and the combinational output logic.

7.61   Synthesize a circuit for the ambiguous state diagram in Figure 7-56. Use the state assignment in Table 7-13. Write a transition list, a transition equation for each state variable as a sum of p-terms, and simplified transition/excitation equations for a realization using D flip-flops. Determine the actual next state of the circuit, starting from the IDLE state, for each of the following input combinations on (LEFT, RIGHT, HAZ): (1,0,1), (0,1,1), (1,1,0), (1,1,1). Comment on the machine's behavior in these cases.

7.62   Draw a logic diagram for the output logic of the guessing-game machine in Table 7-15 using a single 74x139 dual 2-to-4 decoder. (*Hint:* Use active-low outputs.)

7.63   What does the personalized license plate in Figure 7-54 stand for? (*Hint:* It's the author's old plate, a computer engineer's version of OTTFFSS.)

7.64 A *Fibonacci sequence* is a sequence of integers in which each integer is the sum *Fibonacci sequence* of the previous two integers. When the first two integers in the sequence are defined to be 1, the Fibonacci sequence is 1, 1, 2, 3, 5, 8, 13, ... A *Fibonacci* *Fibonacci number* *number* is an integer that appears in this sequence.

Write a decomposed ABEL, VHDL, or Verilog state machine whose single output bit is asserted in a Fibonacci sequence. Use $n = 8$ for the purposes of this exercise, but write your code so that n can be easily changed if desired. Besides CLOCK, the machine should have two inputs, RESET and an n-bit input bus D for loading the first two defined Fibonacci numbers (usually 1 and 1). It should have two outputs, FIB and DONE.

On the first clock tick after RESET is negated, the machine should load the first defined Fibonacci number (usually 1) from the D bus into an internal n-bit counter A. On the second clock tick, it should load the second defined Fibonacci number (usually 1 also) from the D bus into a second n-bit counter B and assert FIB.

On successive clock ticks, the machine asserts FIB only if it has been j clock ticks since FIB was last asserted, where j is the next Fibonacci number in sequence (starting with the first). You may define another internal n-bit counter C if needed, as well as a top-level state machine to control the overall operation. Some time after the FIB is asserted for the last n-bit Fibonacci number, the machine asserts DONE and waits for RESET to be asserted again.

7.65 Write a VHDL or Verilog test bench that checks for proper operation of the state machine you designed in Exercise 7.64 when the first two Fibonacci numbers are 1 and 1, assuring that it asserts FIB at the proper clock ticks (2, 3, 4, 6, 9, 14, ...) and then asserts DONE within a reasonable period of time.

7.66 Suppose that for a state SA and an input combination I, an ambiguous state diagram indicates that there are two next states, SB and SC. The actual next state SD for this transition depends on the state machine's realization. If the state machine is synthesized using the method ($V* = \Sigma$ p-terms where $V* = 1$) to obtain transition/excitation equations for D flip-flops, what is the relationship between the coded states for SB, SC, and SD? Explain.

7.67 Repeat Exercise 7.66, assuming that the machine is synthesized using the method ($V*' = \Sigma$ p-terms where $V* = 0$).

7.68 Suppose that for a state SA and an input combination I, an ambiguous state diagram does not define a next state. The actual next state SD for this transition depends on the state machine's realization. Suppose that the state machine is synthesized using the method ($V* = \Sigma$ p-terms where $V* = 1$) to obtain transition/ excitation equations for D flip-flops. What coded state is SD? Explain.

7.69 Repeat Exercise 7.68, assuming that the machine is synthesized using the method ($V*' = \Sigma$p-terms where $V* = 0$).

7.70 Given the transition equations for a clocked synchronous state machine that is to be built using master/slave S-R flip-flops, how can the excitation equations for the S and R inputs be derived? (*Hint:* Show that any transition equation, $Qi* = expr$, can be written in the form $Qi* = Qi \cdot expr1 + Qi' \cdot expr2$, and see where that leads.)

7.71   Analyze the feedback sequential circuit in Figure 7-19, assuming that the PR_L and CLR_L inputs are always 1. Derive excitation equations, construct a transition table, and analyze the transition table for critical and noncritical races. Name the states, and write a state/output table and a flow/output table. Show that the flow table performs the same function as Figure 7-79.

7.72   Draw the logic diagram for a circuit that has one feedback loop but is *not* a sequential circuit. That is, the circuit's output should be a function of its current input only. In order to prove your case, break the loop and analyze the circuit as if it were a feedback sequential circuit, and demonstrate that the outputs for each input combination do not depend on the "state."

7.73   Show that a 4-bit ones'-complement adder with end-around carry is a feedback sequential circuit.

7.74   After working the preceding exercise and understanding the solution, show how it is possible to build a purely combinational 16-bit ones'-complement adder using 74x381s, a 74x182, and one 2-input gate. Note: your solution need not have a carry input (C0).

7.75   Complete the analysis of the positive-edge-triggered D flip-flop in Figure 7-80, including transition/output, state/output, and flow/output tables. Show that its behavior is equivalent to that of the D flip-flop in Figure 7-72.

7.76   We claimed in Section 7.10.1 that all single-loop feedback sequential circuits have an excitation equation of the form

$$Q* = (\text{forcing term}) + (\text{holding term}) \cdot Q$$

Why aren't there any practical circuits whose excitation equation substitutes Q' for Q above?

BUT flop

7.77   A *BUT flop* may be constructed from an NBUT gate as shown in Figure X7.77. (An *NBUT gate* is simply a BUT gate with inverted outputs; see Exercise 6.31 for the definition of a BUT gate.) Analyze the BUT flop as a feedback sequential circuit and obtain excitation equations, transition table, and flow table. Is this circuit good for anything, or is it a flop?

Figure X7.77

7.78   Repeat Exercise 7.77 for the asymmetric BUT flop in Figure X7.78.

Figure X7.78

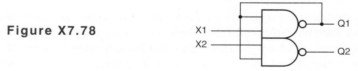

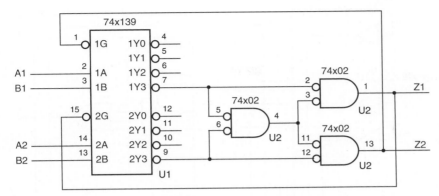

Figure X7.79

7.79 A "clever" student, Sam, designed the circuit in Figure X7.79 to create a BUT gate based on the definition in Exercise 6.31. The circuit appears to have feedback, but Sam analyzed the circuit for all 16 input combinations to make sure it was combinational. He applied each input combination to A1, A2, B1, and B2, assumed that Z1 and Z2 had the correct values, and then checked that the outputs of the '139 and the NOR gates were consistent with that assumption. The circuit seemed to work correctly for all 16 possible input combinations.

But in simulation, when the outputs were simultaneously changed from all 0s to all 1s, the simulator stopped after 5000 simulation cycles, complaining that the outputs hadn't stabilized. And when the circuit was built and the same input transition was tried, the circuit's output sometimes oscillated before settling down. Analyze the circuit as a feedback sequential circuit and explain why this happens.

7.80 Determine and discuss one other situation, besides the one described in the last paragraph of Section 7.2.4, where the output of a D latch may become metastable. To what timing specification of a D latch does this situation relate?

7.81 Simulate the latch circuit of Figure 7-82(b) under the conditions described in the text on page 601. You may write a VHDL or Verilog structural model in which each gate has a delay of 1 ns, or draw the waveforms by hand, again assuming a delay of 1 ns per gate. Does the circuit behave as claimed in the text? Increase the delay of the inverter in the circuit to 3 ns, repeat the simulation, and explain the results. What would you expect to happen in the real circuit?

7.82 Design a latch with two control inputs, C1 and C2, and three data inputs, D1, D2, and D3. The latch is to be "open" only if both control inputs are 1, and it is to store a 1 if any of the data inputs is 1. Use hazard-free two-level sum-of-products circuits for the excitation functions.

7.83 Repeat Exercise 7.82, but minimize the number of gates required; the excitation circuits may have multiple levels of logic.

7.84 Draw Karnaugh maps and derive the excitation equations for the pulse-catching circuit with the transition table shown in Table 7-90.

7.85 Redraw the timing diagram in Figure 7-84, showing the internal state variables of the pulse-catching circuit of Figure 7-94, assuming that it starts in state 00.

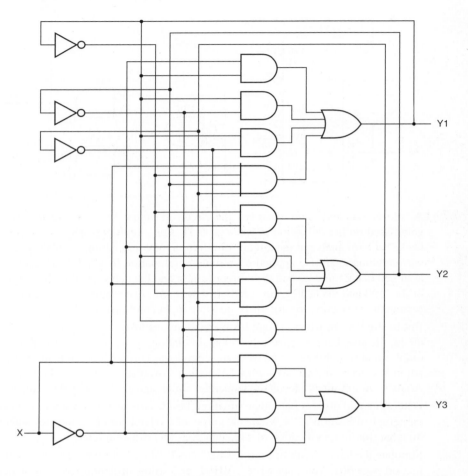

Figure X7.87

7.86   Design a fundamental-mode flow table for a pulse-catching circuit similar to the one described in Section 7.10.2, except that the circuit should detect both 0-to-1 and 1-to-0 transitions on P.

7.87   Analyze the feedback sequential circuit in Figure X7.87. Break the feedback loops, write excitation equations, and construct a transition and output table, showing the stable total states. What application might this circuit have?

7.88   The general solution for obtaining a race-free state assignment of 2^n states using 2^{n-1} state variables yields the adjacency diagram shown in Figure X7.88 for the $n = 2$ case. Compare this diagram with Figure 7-91. Which is better, and why?

7.89   Design a fundamental-mode flow table for a circuit with two inputs, EN and CLKIN, and a single output, CLKOUT, with the following behavior. A clock period is defined to be the interval between successive rising edges of CLKIN. If EN is asserted during an entire given clock period, then CLKOUT should be "on" during the next clock period; that is, it should be identical to CLKIN. If EN is negated during an entire given clock period, then CLKOUT should be "off" (constant 1)

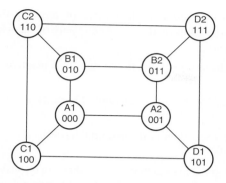

Figure X7.88

during the next clock period. If EN is both asserted and negated during a given clock period, then CLKOUT should be on in the next period if it had been off, and off if it had been on. After writing the fundamental-mode flow table, reduce it by combining "compatible" states if possible.

7.90 Design a circuit that meets the specifications of Exercise 7.89 using edge-triggered D flip-flops (74x74) and NAND and NOR gates without feedback loops. Give a complete circuit diagram and a word description of how your circuit achieves the desired behavior.

7.91 Is the circuit in the preceding exercise subject to metastability, and if so, under what conditions?

7.92 For the flow table in Table X7.92, find an assignment of state variables that avoids all critical races. You may add additional states as necessary, but use as few state variables as possible. Assign the all-0s combination to state A. Draw an adjacency diagram for the original flow table, and write the modified flow table and another adjacency diagram to support your final state-variable assignment.

7.93 Design a fundamental-mode flow table for a double-edge-triggered D flip-flop, one that samples its inputs and changes its outputs on both edges of the clock signal.

Table X7.92

| S | X Y | | | |
	00	01	11	10
A	B	C	—	(A)
B	(B)	E	—	(B)
C	F	(C)	—	E
D	(D)	F	—	B
E	D	(E)	—	(E)
F	(F)	(F)	—	A

S*

7.94   Prove that the fundamental-mode flow table of any flip-flop that samples input(s) and change(s) outputs on the rising edge only of a clock signal CLK contains an essential hazard.

7.95   Locate the essential hazard(s) in the flow table for a positive-edge-triggered D flip-flop, Figure 7-79.

7.96   After doing Exercise 7.89, identify the essential hazards, if any, in the flow table that you developed.

7.97   After doing Exercise 7.93, identify the essential hazards, if any, in the flow table that you developed.

7.98   Build a verbal flip-flop—a logical word puzzle that can be answered correctly in either of two ways depending on state. How might such a device be adapted to the political arena?

7.99   Modify the ABEL program in Table 7-24 to use an output-coded state assignment, thereby reducing the total number of PLD outputs required by one.

7.100   Finish writing the test vectors, started in Table 7-32, for the combination-lock state machine of Table 7-28. The complete set of vectors should test all of the state transitions and all of the output values for every state and input combination.

7.101   Using an available synthesis tool and targeting a CPLD or FPGA, synthesize the two different versions of the example VHDL state-machine in Tables 7-38 and 7-43, corresponding to non-pipelined and pipelined outputs, respectively. Determine whether the actual circuits and timing resulting from these versions differ, and how.

7.102   Using an available synthesis tool and targeting a CPLD or FPGA, synthesize the two different versions of the example Verilog state-machine in Tables 7-58 and 7-60, corresponding to non-pipelined and pipelined outputs, respectively. Determine whether the actual circuits and timing resulting from these versions differ, and how.

74x163

2	CLK	
1	CLR	
9	LD	
7	ENP	
10	ENT	
3	A	QA	14
4	B	QB	13
5	C	QC	12
6	D	QD	11
		RCO	15

Sequential Logic Design Practices

The purpose of this chapter is to familiarize you with the most commonly used and dependable sequential-circuit design methods. Therefore, we will emphasize *synchronous systems*— that is, systems in which all flip-flops are clocked by the same common clock signal. Although all the world does not march to the tick of a common clock, within the confines of a digital system or subsystem we can make it so. When we interconnect digital systems or subsystems that use different clocks, we can usually identify a limited number of asynchronous signals that need special treatment, as we'll show later.

We begin this chapter with a quick summary of sequential-circuit documentation standards. After revisiting the most basic building blocks of sequential-circuit design—latches and flip-flops—we describe some of the most flexible building blocks—sequential PLDs. Next we show how counters and shift registers are realized at the gate and flip-flop level as well as in HDLs, and we show some of their applications. Finally, we show how these elements and state machines come together in synchronous systems and how the inevitable asynchronous inputs are handled.

8.1 Sequential-Circuit Documentation Standards

8.1.1 General Requirements

Basic documentation standards in areas like signal naming, logic symbols, schematic layout, and HDL coding style, which we introduced in previous chapters, apply to digital systems as a whole and therefore to sequential circuits in particular. We highlight the following ideas, however, for system elements that are specifically "sequential":

- *Flip-flops.* The symbols for individual sequential-circuit elements, especially flip-flops, should follow the appropriate drawing standards, so that the type, function, and clocking behavior of the elements are clear.

- *State-machine descriptions.* State machines should be described by state tables, state diagrams, transition lists, or text files in a state-machine description language such as ABEL, VHDL, or Verilog.

- *State-machine layout.* Within an HDL-based design, the flip-flops, next-state logic, and output logic that form each state machine should be specified together in a single module, with no extraneous logic. If you should have occasion to draw a state machine's logic diagram, its flip-flops and combinational logic should be drawn together in a logical format on the same page, so the fact that it is a state machine is obvious.

- *Cascaded elements.* Any registers, counters, and shift registers that use multiple ICs should have the ICs grouped together in the schematic so that the cascading structure is obvious.

- *Timing diagrams.* The documentation package for sequential circuits should include timing diagrams that show the general timing assumptions and timing behavior of the circuit.

- *Timing specifications.* A sequential circuit should be accompanied by a specification of the timing requirements for proper internal operation (e.g., maximum clock frequency), as well as the requirements for any externally supplied inputs (e.g., setup- and hold-time requirements with respect to the system clock, minimum pulse widths, etc.).

8.1.2 Logic Symbols

We introduced traditional symbols for flip-flops in Section 7.2. Flip-flops are always drawn as rectangular-shaped symbols and follow the same general guidelines as other rectangular-shaped symbols—inputs on the left, outputs on the right, bubbles for active levels, and so on. In addition, some specific guidelines apply to the most-used flip-flop symbols:

- A dynamic-input indicator is placed on edge-triggered clock inputs.

- Asynchronous preset and clear inputs may be shown at the top and bottom of a flip-flop symbol—preset at the top and clear at the bottom.

The logic symbols for larger-scale sequential elements, such as the counters and shift register described later in this chapter, are generally drawn with all inputs, including presets and clears, on the left, and all outputs on the right. Bidirectional signals may be drawn on the left or the right, whichever is convenient.

Like individual flip-flops, larger-scale sequential elements use a dynamic indicator to indicate edge-triggered clock inputs. In "traditional" symbols, the names of the inputs and outputs give a clue of their function, but they are sometimes ambiguous. For example, two elements described later in this chapter, the 74x161 and 74x163 4-bit counters, have exactly the same traditional symbol, even though the behavior of their CLR inputs is completely different.

IEEE STANDARD SYMBOLS   IEEE standard symbols have a rich set of notation that can provide an unambiguous definition of every signal's function. A guide to IEEE symbols, including all of the sequential elements in this chapter, appears at <u>DDPPonline</u> in <u>Section IEEEsym</u>.

8.1.3 State-Machine Descriptions

So far we have dealt with seven different representations of state machines:

- Word descriptions
- State tables
- State diagrams
- Transition lists
- ABEL programs
- VHDL programs
- Verilog programs

You might think that having all these different ways to represent state machines is a problem—too much for you to learn! Well, they're not all that difficult to learn, but there *is* a subtle problem here.

Consider a similar problem in programming, where high-level "pseudocode" or perhaps a flowchart might be used to document how a program works. The pseudocode may express the programmer's intentions very well, but errors, misinterpretations, and typos can occur when it is translated into real code. In any creative process, inconsistencies can occur when there are multiple representations of how things work.

The same kind of inconsistencies can occur in state-machine design. A logic designer may document a machine's desired behavior with a 100%-correct hand-drawn state diagram, but you can make mistakes translating the diagram into a program, and there are *lots* of opportunities for error if you have to "turn

inconsistent state-machine representations

the crank" manually to translate the state diagram into a state table, transition table, excitation equations, and logic diagram.

The solution to this problem is similar to the one adopted by programmers who write self-documenting code using a high-level language. The key is to select a representation that is both expressive of the designer's intentions *and* translatable into a physical realization using an error-free, automated process. (You don't hear many programmers screaming "Compiler bug!" when their programs don't work the first time.)

The best solution is to write state-machine "programs" directly in an HDL like ABEL, VHDL, or Verilog, and to avoid alternate representations, other than general, summary word descriptions. When consistent coding styles are followed, HDLs are easily readable and allow automatic conversion of the description into a PLD-, FPGA-, or ASIC-based realization. It's also possible with some CAD tools to specify and synthesize state machines based on state diagrams, or even using sample timing diagrams, but these can often lead to ambiguities and unanticipated results. Therefore, we'll use the HDL approach exclusively for the rest of this book.

8.1.4 Timing Diagrams and Specifications

We showed many examples of timing diagrams in Chapters 6 and 7. In the design of synchronous systems, most timing diagrams show the relationship between the clock and various input, output, and internal signals.

Figure 8-1 shows a fairly typical timing diagram that specifies the requirements and characteristics of input and output signals in a synchronous circuit. The first line shows the system clock and its nominal timing parameters. The remaining lines show a range of delays for other signals.

For example, the second line shows that flip-flops change their outputs at some time between the rising edge of CLOCK and time t_{ffpd} afterward. External

Figure 8-1
A detailed timing diagram showing propagation delays and setup and hold times with respect to the clock.

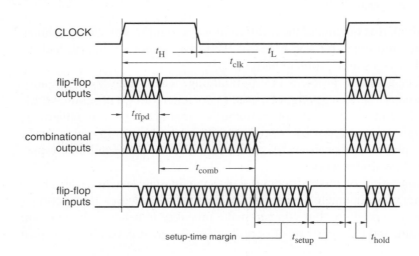

circuits that sample these signals should not do so while they are changing. The timing diagram is drawn as if the minimum value of t_{ffpd} were zero; a complete documentation package would include a timing table indicating the actual minimum, typical, and maximum values of t_{ffpd} and all other timing parameters.

The third line of the timing diagram shows the additional time, t_{comb}, required for the flip-flop output changes to propagate through combinational logic elements, such as flip-flop excitation logic. The excitation inputs of flip-flops and other clocked devices require a setup time of t_{setup}, as shown in the fourth line. For proper circuit operation we must have $t_{clk} - t_{ffpd} - t_{comb} > t_{setup}$.

Timing margins indicate how much "worse than worst-case" the individual components of a circuit can be without causing the circuit to fail. Well-designed systems have positive, nonzero timing margins to allow for unexpected circumstances (marginal components, brownouts, engineering errors, etc.) and clock skew (Section 8.8.1).

timing margin

The value $t_{clk} - t_{ffpd(max)} - t_{comb(max)} - t_{setup}$ is called the *setup-time margin;* if this is negative, the circuit won't work. Note that *maximum* propagation delays are used to calculate setup-time margin. Another timing margin involves the hold-time requirement t_{hold}; the sum of the *minimum* values of t_{ffpd} and t_{comb} must be greater than t_{hold}, and the *hold-time margin* is $t_{ffpd(min)} + t_{comb(min)} - t_{hold}$.

setup-time margin

hold-time margin

The timing diagram in Figure 8-1 does not show the timing differences between different flip-flop inputs or combinational-logic signals, even though such differences exist in most circuits. For example, one flip-flop's Q output may be connected directly to another flip-flop's D input, so that t_{comb} for that path is zero, while another's may go the ripple-carry path of a 32-bit adder before reaching a flip-flop input. When proper synchronous design methodology is used, these relative timings are not critical, since none of these signals affect the state of the circuit until a clock edge occurs. You merely have to find the longest delay path in one clock period to determine whether the circuit will work. However, you may have to analyze several different paths in order to find the worst-case one.

Another, perhaps more common, type of timing diagram shows only functional behavior and is not concerned with actual delay amounts; an example is shown in Figure 8-2. Here, the clock is "perfect." Whether to show signal changes as vertical or slanted lines is strictly a matter of personal taste in this and all other timing diagrams, unless rise and fall times must be explicitly indicated.

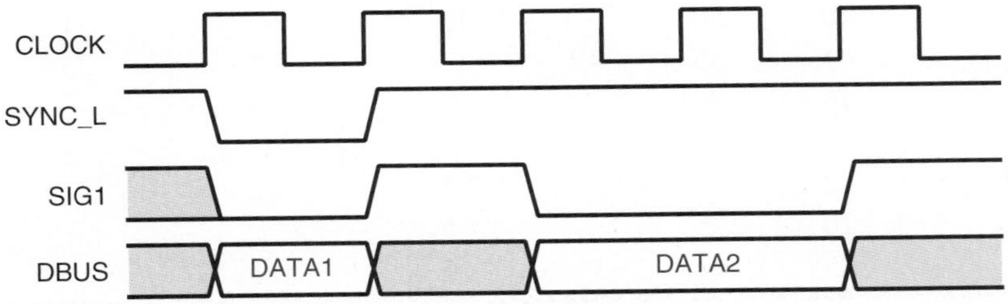

Figure 8-2
Functional timing of a synchronous circuit.

Clock transitions are shown as vertical lines in this and other figures in keeping with the idea that the clock is a "perfect" reference signal.

The other signals in Figure 8-2 may be flip-flop outputs, combinational outputs, or flip-flop inputs. Shading is used to indicate "don't-care" signal values; crosshatching as in Figure 8-1 could be used instead. All of the signals are shown to change immediately after the clock edge. In reality, the outputs change sometime later, and inputs may change just barely before the next clock edge. However, "lining up" everything on the clock edge allows the timing diagram to display more clearly which functions are performed during each clock period. Signals that are lined up with the clock are simply understood to change sometime *after* the clock edge, with timing that meets the setup- and hold-time requirements of the circuit. Many timing diagrams of this type appear in this chapter.

Table 8-1 Timing parameters, in ns, of selected flip-flops, registers, and latches.

Part	Parameter	74HCT Typ.	74HCT Max.	74AHCT Typ.	74AHCT Max.	74FCT Min.	74FCT Max.	74LS Typ.	74LS Max.
'74	t_{pd}, CLK↑ to Q or $\overline{Q}$	35	44	6.3	10			25	40
	t_{pd}, $\overline{PR}$↓ or $\overline{CLR}$↓ to Q or $\overline{Q}$	40	50	8.1	13			25	40
	t_s, D to CLK↑	12	15		5				20
	t_h, D from CLK↑	3	3		0				5
	t_{rec}, CLK↑ from $\overline{PR}$↑ or $\overline{CLR}$↑	6	8		3.5				
	t_w, CLK low or high	18	23		5				25
	t_w, $\overline{PR}$ or $\overline{CLR}$ low	16	20		5				25
'174	t_{pd}, CLK↑ to Q	40	50	6.3	10			21	30
	t_{pd}, $\overline{CLR}$↓ to Q	44	55	8.1	13			23	35
	t_s, D to CLK↑	16	20		5				20
	t_h, D from CLK↑	5	5		0				5
	t_{rec}, CLK↑ from $\overline{CLR}$↑	12	15		3.5				25
	t_w, CLK low or high	20	25		5				20
	t_w, $\overline{CLR}$ low	25	31		5				20

Table 8-1 (continued) Timing parameters, in ns, of selected flip-flops, registers, and latches.

Part	Parameter	74HCT		74AHCT		74FCT		74LS	
		Typ.	Max.	Typ.	Max.	Min.	Max.	Typ.	Max.
'175	t_{pd}, CLK↑ to Q or $\overline{Q}$	33	41					21	30
	t_{pd}, $\overline{CLR}$↓ to Q or $\overline{Q}$	35	44					23	35
	t_s, D to CLK↑	20	25						20
	t_h, D from CLK↑	5	5						5
	t_{rec}, CLK↑ from $\overline{CLR}$↑	5	5						25
	t_w, CLK low or high	20	25						20
	t_w, $\overline{CLR}$ low	20	25						20
'273	t_{pd}, CLK↑ to Q	30	38	6.8	11	2	7.2	18	27
	t_{pd}, $\overline{CLR}$↓ to Q	32	40	8.5	12.6	2	7.2	18	27
	t_s, D to CLK↑	12	15		5	2			20
	t_h, D from CLK↑	3	3		0		1.5		5
	t_{rec}, CLK↑ from $\overline{CLR}$↑	10	13		2.5		2		25
	t_w, CLK low or high	20	25		6.5		4		20
	t_w, $\overline{CLR}$ low	12	15		6		5		20
'373	t_{pd}, C↑ to Q	35	44	8.5	14.5	2	8.5	24	36
	t_{pd}, D to Q	32	40	5.9	10.5	1.5	5.2	18	27
	t_s, D to C↓	10	13		1.5	2			0
	t_h, D from C↓	5	5		3.5		1.5		10
	t_{pHZ}, $\overline{OE}$ to Q	35	44		12	1.5	6.5	12	20
	t_{pLZ}, $\overline{OE}$ to Q	35	44		12	1.5	6.5	16	25
	t_{pZH}, $\overline{OE}$ to Q	35	44		13.5	1.5	5.5	16	28
	t_{pZL}, $\overline{OE}$ to Q	35	44		13.5	1.5	5.5	22	36
	t_w, C low or high	16	20		6.5		5		15
'374	t_{pd}, CLK↑ to Q	33	41	6.4	11.5	2	6.5	22	34
	t_s, D to CLK↑	12	15		2.5	2			20
	t_h, D from CLK↑	5	5		2.5		1.5		0
	t_{pHZ}, $\overline{OE}$ to Q	28	35		12	1.5	6.5		18
	t_{pLZ}, $\overline{OE}$ to Q	28	35		12	1.5	6.5		24
	t_{pZH}, $\overline{OE}$ to Q	30	38		12.5	1.5	5.5		28
	t_{pZL}, $\overline{OE}$ to Q	30	38		12.5	1.5	5.5		36
	t_w, CLK low or high	16	20		6.5		5		15
'377	t_{pd}, CLK↑ to Q	38	48			2	7.2	18	27
	t_s, D to CLK↑	12	15			2			20
	t_h, D from CLK↑	3	3				1.5		5
	t_s, $\overline{EN}$ to CLK↑	12	15			2			25
	t_h, $\overline{EN}$ from CLK↑	5	5				1.5		5
	t_w, CLK low or high	20	25				6		20

Table 8-1 on the preceding pages shows manufacturer's timing parameters for commonly used flip-flops, registers, and latches in CMOS and TTL. "Typical" values are for devices operating at 25°C, but, depending on the logic family, they could be for a typical part and nominal power-supply voltage, or they could be for a worst-case part at worst-case supply voltage. "Maximum" values are generally valid over the commercial operating range of voltage and temperature, except 74LS values, which are specified at 25°C. Also note that the "maximum" values of t_s, t_h, t_{rec}, or t_w are the maximum values of the *minimum* setup time, hold time, recovery time, or pulse width that the specified part will exhibit.

Different manufacturers may use slightly different definitions for the same timing parameters, and they may specify different numbers for the same part. A given manufacturer may even use different definitions for different families or part numbers in the same family. Thus, all of the specifications in Table 8-1 are merely representative; for exact numbers *and* their definitions, you must consult the data sheet for the particular part and manufacturer.

8.2 Latches and Flip-Flops

8.2.1 SSI Latches and Flip-Flops

Several different types of discrete latches and flip-flops are available as SSI parts. These devices are sometimes used in the design of state machines and "unstructured" sequential circuits that don't fall into the categories of shift registers, counters, and other sequential MSI functions presented later in this chapter. However, SSI latches and flip-flops have been eliminated to a large extent in modern designs as their functions are embedded in PLDs and FPGAs. Nevertheless, a few of these discrete building blocks can still appear in many digital systems, as well as in some teaching labs, so it's important to be familiar with them.

74x375

Figure 8-3 shows the pinouts for several SSI sequential devices. The only latch in the figure is the *74x375,* which contains four D latches, similar in function to the "generic" D latches described in Section 7.2.4. Because of pin limitations, the latches are arranged in pairs with a common C control line for each pair.

74x74

Among the devices in Figure 8-3, the most important is the *74x74,* which contains two independent positive-edge-triggered D flip-flops with preset and clear inputs. We described the functional operation, timing, and internal structure of edge-triggered D flip-flops in general, and the 74x74 in particular, in Section 7.2.5. Besides the use of the 74x74 in "random" sequential circuits, fast

74F74
74ACT74
74x109

versions of the part, such as the *74F74* and *74ACT74*, find application in synchronizers for asynchronous input signals, as discussed in Section 8.9.

The *74x109* is a positive-edge-triggered J-$\overline{\text{K}}$ flip-flop with an active-low K input (named $\overline{\text{K}}$ or K_L). We discussed the internal structure of the '109 in Section 7.2.10.

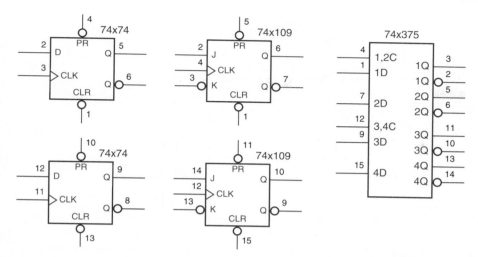

Figure 8-3
Pinouts for SSI
latches and flip-flops.

*8.2.2 Switch Debouncing

A common application of simple bistables and latches is switch debouncing. We're all familiar with electrical switches from experience with lights, garbage disposals, and other appliances. Switches connected to sources of constant logic 0 and 1 are often used in digital systems to supply "user inputs." However, in digital logic applications we must consider another aspect of switch operation, the time dimension. A simple make or break operation, which occurs instantly as far as we slow-moving humans are concerned, actually has several phases that are discernible by high-speed digital logic.

Figure 8-4(a) on the next page shows how a single-pole, single-throw (SPST) switch might be used to generate a single logic input. A pull-up resistor provides a logic-1 value when the switch is opened, and the switch contact is tied to ground to provide a logic-0 value when the switch is pushed.

As shown in (b), it takes a while after a push for the wiper to hit the bottom contact. Once it hits, it doesn't stay there for long; it bounces a few times before finally settling. The result is that several transitions are seen on the SW_L and DSW logic signals for each single switch push. This behavior is called *contact bounce*. Typical switches bounce for 10–20 ms, a very long time compared to the switching speeds of logic gates.

contact bounce

Contact bounce may or may not be a problem, depending on the switch application. For example, some computers have configuration information specified by small switches, called *DIP switches* because they are the same size as a dual in-line package (DIP). Since DIP switches are normally changed only when the computer is inactive, there's no problem. Contact bounce *is* a problem if a switch such as a pushbutton is being used to count or signal some event (e.g.,

DIP switch

---

* Throughout this book, optional sections are marked with an asterisk.

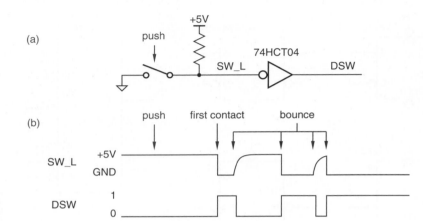

Figure 8-4
Switch input without
debouncing:
(a) logic circuit;
(b) timing diagram.

debounce

laps in a race). Then we must provide a circuit (or, in microprocessor-based systems, software) to *debounce* the switch—to provide just one signal change or pulse for each external event.

*8.2.3 The Simplest Switch Debouncer

Switch debouncing is a good application for the simplest sequential circuit, the bistable element of Section 7.1, which can be used as shown in Figure 8-5. This circuit uses a single-pole, double-throw (SPDT) switch. The switch contacts and wiper have a "break before make" behavior, so the wiper terminal is "floating" at some time halfway through the switch depression.

Figure 8-5
Switch input using
a bistable for
debouncing:
(a) logic circuit;
(b) timing diagram.

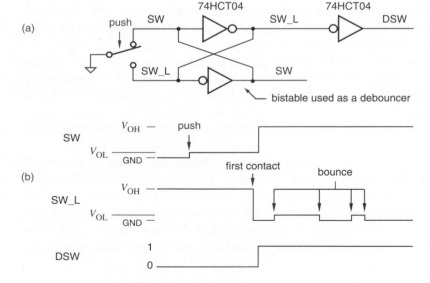

Before the button is pushed, the top contact holds SW at 0 V, a valid logic 0, and the top inverter produces a logic 1 on SW_L and on the bottom contact. When the button is pushed and contact is broken, feedback in the bistable holds SW at V_{OL} (≤ 0.33 V for HCT CMOS driving TTL loads), still a valid logic 0.

Next, when the wiper hits the bottom contact, the circuit operates quite unconventionally for a moment. The top inverter in the bistable is trying to maintain a logic 1 on the SW_L signal; the top transistor in its totem-pole output is "on" and connecting SW_L through a small resistance to +5 V. Suddenly, the switch contact makes a metallic connection of SW_L to ground, 0.0 V. Not surprisingly, the switch contact wins.

A short time later (70 ns for the 74HCT04), the forced logic 0 on SW_L propagates through the two inverters of the bistable, so that the top inverter gives up its vain attempt to drive a 1, and instead drives a logic 0 onto SW_L. At this point, the top inverter output is no longer shorted to ground, and feedback in the bistable maintains the logic 0 on SW_L even if the wiper bounces off the bottom contact, as it does. (It does not bounce far enough to touch the top contact again.)

Advantages of this circuit compared to other debouncing approaches are that it has a low chip count (one-third of a 74HCT04), no pull-up resistors are required, and both polarities of the input signal (active-high and active-low) are produced. In situations where momentarily shorting gate outputs must be avoided, a similar circuit can be designed using an $\overline{S}$-$\overline{R}$ latch and pull-up resistors, as suggested in Figure 8-6.

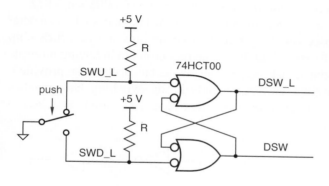

Figure 8-6
Switch input using an $\overline{S}$-$\overline{R}$ latch for debouncing.

*8.2.4 Bus Holder Circuit

In Sections 3.7.3 and 6.6 we described three-state outputs and how they are tied together to create three-state buses. At any time, at most one output can drive the bus; sometimes, no output is driving the bus, and the bus is "floating." When high-speed CMOS inputs are connected to a bus that is left floating for a long time (in the fastest circuits, more than a clock tick or two), bad things can happen. In particular, noise, crosstalk, and other effects can drive the high-impedance floating bus signals to a voltage level near the CMOS devices' input switching threshold, which in turn allows excessive current to flow in the device outputs. For this reason, it is desirable and customary to provide pull-up resistors that quickly pull a floating bus to a valid HIGH logic level.

Pull-up resistors aren't all goodness—they cost money and they occupy valuable printed-circuit-board real estate. A big problem they have in very high-speed circuits is the choice of resistance value. If the resistance is too high, when a bus goes from LOW to floating, the transition from LOW to pulled-up (HIGH) will be slow due to the high *RC* time constant, and input levels may spend too much time near the switching threshold. If the pull-up resistance is too low, devices trying to pull the bus LOW will have to sink too much current.

bus-holder circuit
The solution to this problem is to eliminate pull-up resistors in favor of an active *bus-holder circuit*, shown in Figure 8-7. This is nothing but a bistable with a resistor *R* in one leg of the feedback loop. The bus holder's INOUT signal is connected to the three-state bus line which is to be held. When the three-state output currently driving the line LOW or HIGH changes to floating, the bus holder's righthand inverter holds the line in its current state. When a three-state output tries to change the line from LOW to HIGH or vice versa, it must source or sink a small amount of additional current through *R* to overcome the bus holder. This additional current flow persists only for the short time that it takes for the bistable to flip into its other stable state.

The choice of the value of *R* in the bus holder is a compromise between low override current (high *R*) and good noise immunity on the held bus line (low *R*). In a typical example, bus holder circuits in the 3.3-V CMOS LVC family specify a maximum override current of 500 μA, implying $R \approx 3.3 / 0.0005 = 6.6$ KΩ.

Bus-holder circuits are often built into another MSI device, such as an octal CMOS bus driver or transceiver. They require no extra pins and very little chip area, so they are essentially free. And there's no real problem in having multiple (*n*) bus holders on the same signal line, as long as the bus drivers can provide *n* times the override current for a few nanoseconds during switching. Note that bus holders normally are not effective on buses that have TTL inputs attached to them (see Exercise 8.24).

Figure 8-7
Bus-holder circuit.

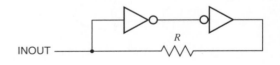

8.2.5 Multibit Registers and Latches

A collection of two or more D flip-flops with a common clock input is called a *register*. Registers are often used to store a collection of related bits, such as a byte of data in a computer. However, a single register can also be used to store unrelated bits of data or control information; the only real constraint is that all of the bits are stored using the same clock signal.

register

Figure 8-8 shows the logic diagram and logic symbol for a commonly used MSI register, the *74x175*. The 74x175 contains four edge-triggered D flip-flops with a common clock and asynchronous clear inputs. It provides both active-high and active-low outputs at the external pins of the device.

74x175

The individual flip-flops in a '175 are negative-edge triggered, as indicated by the inversion bubbles on their CLK inputs. However, the circuit also contains an inverter that makes the flip-flops positive-edge triggered with respect to the device's external CLK input pin. The common, active-low, clear signal (CLR_L) is connected to the asynchronous clear inputs of all four flip-flops. Both CLK and CLR_L are buffered before fanning out to the four flip-flops, so that a device driving one of these inputs sees only one unit load instead of four. This is especially important if a common clock or clear signal must drive many such registers.

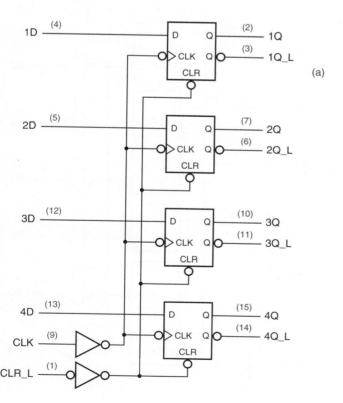

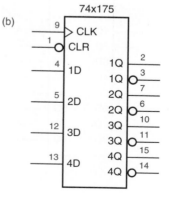

Figure 8-8
The 74x175 4-bit register:
(a) logic diagram, including
pin numbers for a standard
16-pin dual in-line package;
(b) traditional logic symbol.

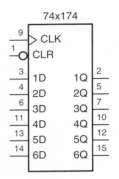

74x174

Figure 8-9
Logic symbol for the
74x174 6-bit register.

The logic symbol for the *74x174*, 6-bit register is shown in Figure 8-9. The internal structure of this device is similar to the 74x175's, except that it eliminates the active-low outputs and provides two more flip-flops instead.

Many digital systems, including computers, telecommunications devices, and stereo equipment, process information 8, 16, or 32 bits at a time; as a result, ICs that handle 8 bits are very popular. One such MSI IC is the *74x374* octal edge-triggered D flip-flop, also known simply as an 8-bit register. (Once again, "octal" means that the device has eight sections.)

As shown in Figure 8-10, the 74x374 contains eight edge-triggered D flip-flops that all sample their inputs and change their outputs on the rising edge of a common CLK input. Each flip-flop output drives a three-state buffer that in turn drives an active-high output. All of the three-state buffers are enabled by a

Figure 8-10
The 74x374 8-bit register:
(a) logic diagram, including pin
numbers for a standard 20-pin
dual in-line package;
(b) traditional logic symbol.

(a)

(b)

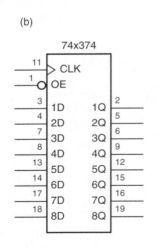

74x374

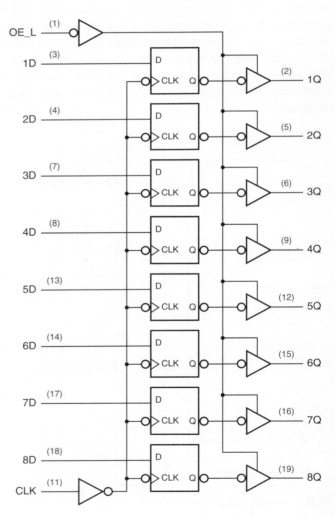

common, active-low OE_L (output enable) input. As in the other registers that we've studied, the control inputs (CLK and OE_L) are buffered so that they present only one unit load to a device that drives them.

One variation of the 74x374 is the *74x373*, whose symbol is shown in Figure 8-11. The '373 uses D latches instead of edge-triggered flip-flops. Therefore, its outputs follow the corresponding inputs whenever C is asserted, and they latch the last input values when C is negated. Another variation is the *74x273*, shown in Figure 8-12. This octal register has non-three-state outputs and no OE_L input; instead it uses pin 1 for an asynchronous clear input CLR_L.

The *74x377*, whose symbol is shown in Figure 8-13(a), is an edge-triggered register like the '374, but it does not have three-state outputs. Instead, pin 1 is used as an active-low clock-enable input EN_L. If EN_L is asserted (LOW) at the rising edge of the clock, then the flip-flops are loaded from the data inputs; otherwise, they retain their present values, as shown logically in (b).

Figure 8-11
Logic symbol for the 74x373 8-bit latch.

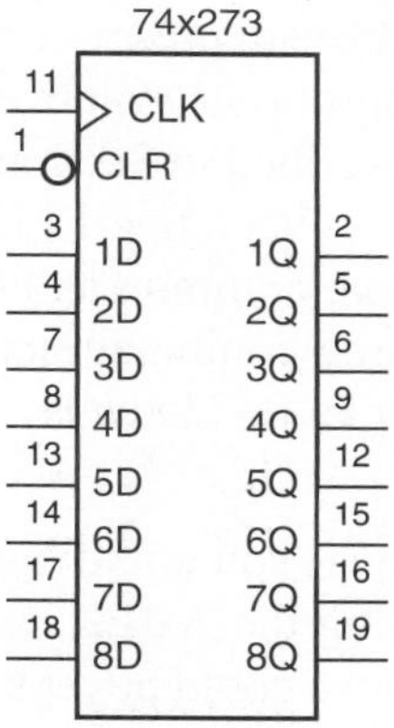

Figure 8-12
Logic symbol for the 74x273 8-bit register.

Figure 8-13 The 74x377 8-bit register with gated clock:
(a) logic symbol; (b) logical behavior of one bit.

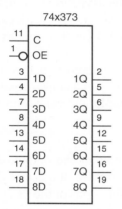

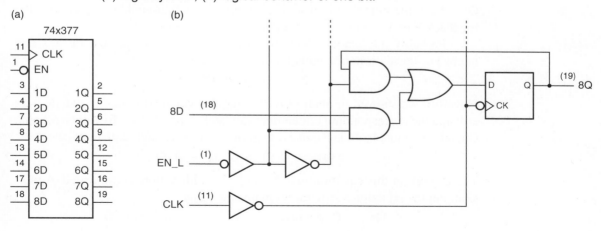

High pin-count surface-mount packaging supports even wider registers, drivers, and transceivers. Most common are 16-bit devices, but there are also devices with 18 bits (for byte parity) and 32 bits. Also, the larger packages can offer more control functions, such as clear, clock enable, multiple output enables, and even a choice of latching vs. registered behavior all in one device.

8.2.6 Registers and Latches in ABEL and PLDs

As we showed in Section 7.11, registers are very easy to specify in ABEL. For example, Table 7-30 on page 623 showed an ABEL program for an 8-bit register with enable. Obviously, ABEL allows the functions performed at the D inputs of register to be customized in almost any way desired, limited only by the number of inputs and product terms in the targeted PLD. We'll describe sequential PLDs soon, in Section 8.3.

With most sequential PLDs, few if any customizations can be applied to a register's clock input (e.g., polarity choice) or to the asynchronous inputs (e.g., different preset conditions for different bits). However, ABEL does provide appropriate syntax to apply these customizations in devices that support them, as described in Section 7.11.1.

Very few PLDs have latches built in; edge-triggered registers are much more common and generally more useful. However, you can also create a latch using combinational logic and feedback. For example, the excitation equation for an S-R latch is

$$Q* = S + R' \cdot Q$$

Thus, you could build an S-R latch using one combinational output of a PLD, using the ABEL equation "Q = S # !R & Q". Furthermore, the S and R signals above could be replaced with more complex logic functions of the PLD's inputs, limited only by the availability of product terms (seven per output in a 16V8C) to realize the final excitation equation. The feedback loop can be created only when Q is assigned to a bidirectional pin (in a 16V8C, pins IO2–IO7, not O1 or O8). Also, the output pin must be continuously output-enabled; otherwise, the feedback loop would be broken and the latch's state lost.

Probably the handiest latch to build out of a combinational PLD is a D latch. The basic excitation equation for a D latch is

$$Q* = C \cdot D + C' \cdot Q$$

However, we showed in Section 7.10.1 that this equation contains a static hazard, and the corresponding circuit does not latch data reliably. To build a reliable D latch, we must include a consensus term in the excitation equation:

$$Q* = C \cdot D + C' \cdot Q + D \cdot Q$$

The D input in this equation may be replaced with a more complicated expression, but the equation's structure remains the same:

$$Q* = C \cdot expression + C' \cdot Q + expression \cdot Q$$

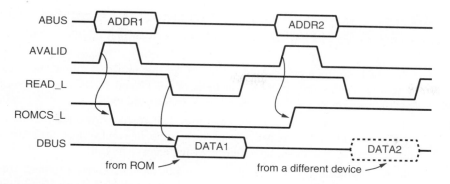

Figure 8-14
Timing diagram for a microprocessor read operation.

It is also possible to use a more complex expression for the C input, as we showed in Section 7.10.1. In any case, it is very important for the consensus term to be included in the PLD realization. The compiler can work against you in this case, since its minimization step will find that the consensus term is redundant and remove it.

Some versions of the ABEL compiler let you prevent elimination of consensus terms by including a keyword "retain" in the property list of the istype declaration for any output which is not to be minimized. In other versions, your only choice is to turn off minimization for the entire design.

retain property

Probably the most common use of a PLD-based latch is to simultaneously decode and latch addresses in order to select memory and I/O devices in micro-processor systems. Figure 8-14 is a timing diagram for this function in a typical system. The microprocessor selects a device and a location within the device by placing an address on its address bus (ABUS) and asserting an "address valid" signal (AVALID). A short time later, it asserts a read signal (READ_L), and the selected device responds by placing data on the data bus (DBUS).

Notice that the address does not stay valid on ABUS for the entire operation. The microprocessor bus protocol expects the address to be latched using AVALID as an enable, then decoded, as shown in Figure 8-15. The decoder selects different devices to be enabled or "chip-selected" according to the high-order bits of the address (the 12 high-order bits in this example). The low-order bits are used to address individual locations of a selected device.

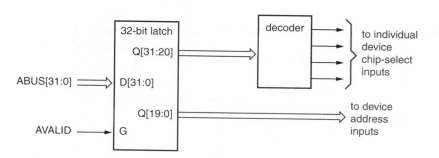

Figure 8-15
Microprocessor address latching and decoding circuit.

WHY A LATCH?   The microprocessor bus protocol in Figure 8-14 raises several questions, and here we give answers:

- Why not keep the address valid on ABUS for the entire operation? In a real system using this protocol, the functions of ABUS and DBUS are combined (multiplexed) onto one three-state bus to save pins and wires.

- Why not use AVALID as the clock input to a positive-edge-triggered register to capture the address? There isn't enough setup time; in a real system, the address may first be valid at or slightly after the rising edge of AVALID.

- OK, so why not use AVALID to clock a negative-edge-triggered register? This works, but the latched outputs are available sooner; valid values on ABUS flow through a latch immediately, without waiting for the falling clock edge. This relaxes the access-time requirements of memories and other devices driven by the latched outputs.

Using a PLD, the latching and decoding functions for the high-order bits can be combined into a single device, yielding the block diagram in Figure 8-16. Compared with Figure 8-15, the "latching decoder" saves devices and pins, and it may produce a valid chip-select output more quickly (see Exercise 8.9).

Table 8-2 is an ABEL program for the latching decoder. Since it operates on only the high-order bits ABUS[31..20], it can decode addresses only in 1-Mbyte or larger chunks ($2^{20} = 1$ M). A read-only memory (ROM) is located in the highest 1-Mbyte chunk, addresses 0xfff00000–0xffffffff, and is selected by ROMCS. Three 16-Mbyte banks of read/write memory (RAM) are located at lower addresses, starting at addresses 0x00000000, 0x01000000, and 0x02000000, respectively. Notice how don't-cares are used in the definitions of the RAM bank address ranges to decode a chunk larger than 1 Mbyte. Other approaches to these definitions are also possible (e.g., see Exercise 8.2).

The equations in Table 8-2 for the chip-select outputs follow the D-latch template that we gave on page 694. The expressions that select a device, such as "ABUS==ROM," each generate a single product term, and each equation generates

Figure 8-16
Using a combined address latching and decoding circuit.

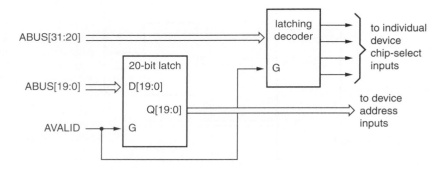

```
module latchdec
title 'Latching Microprocessor Address Decoder'

" Inputs
AVALID, ABUS31..ABUS20              pin;
" Latched and decoded outputs
ROMCS, RAMCS0, RAMCS1, RAMCS2      pin istype 'com,retain';

ABUS = [ABUS31..ABUS20];
ROM = ^hFFF;
RAMBANK0 = [0,0,0,0,0,0,0,0,.X.,.X.,.X.,.X.];
RAMBANK1 = [0,0,0,0,0,0,0,1,.X.,.X.,.X.,.X.];
RAMBANK2 = [0,0,0,0,0,0,1,0,.X.,.X.,.X.,.X.];

equations

ROMCS  = AVALID & (ABUS==ROM) # !AVALID & ROMCS
       # (ABUS==ROM) & ROMCS;
RAMCS0 = AVALID & (ABUS==RAMBANK0) # !AVALID & RAMCS0
       # (ABUS==RAMBANK0) & RAMCS0;
RAMCS1 = AVALID & (ABUS==RAMBANK1) # !AVALID & RAMCS1
       # (ABUS==RAMBANK1) & RAMCS1;
RAMCS2 = AVALID & (ABUS==RAMBANK2) # !AVALID & RAMCS2
       # (ABUS==RAMBANK2) & RAMCS2;

end latchdec
```

Table 8-2
ABEL program
for a latching
address decoder.

three product terms. Notice the use of the "retain" property in the pin declarations to prevent the compiler from optimizing away the consensus terms.

After seeing how easy it is to build S-R and D latches using combinational PLDs, you might be tempted to go further and try to build an edge-triggered D flip-flop. Although this is possible, it is expensive because an edge-triggered flip-flop has four internal states and thus two feedback loops, consuming two PLD outputs. Furthermore, the setup and hold times and propagation delays of such a flip-flop would be quite poor compared to those of a discrete flip-flop in the same technology. Also, as we discussed in Section 7.10.6, the flow tables of all edge-triggered flip-flops contain essential hazards, which can be masked only by controlling path delays, difficult in a PLD-based design. Finally, why bother? Modern PLDs allow you to use a built-in flip-flop on any output.

8.2.7 Registers and Latches in VHDL

Register and latch circuits can be specified using structural VHDL. For example, Table 8-3 on the next page is structural VHDL code corresponding to the D latch circuit of Figure 7-12 on page 531. However, writing structural code is not really our motivation for using VHDL; our goal is to use behavioral code to model the operation of circuits more intuitively.

Table 8-3 VHDL structural program for the D latch in Figure 7-12.

```
entity Vdlatch is
  port (D, C: in STD_LOGIC;
        Q, QN: buffer STD_LOGIC );
end Vdlatch;

architecture Vdlatch_s of Vdlatch is
  signal DN, SN, RN: STD_LOGIC;
  component inv port (I: in STD_LOGIC; O: out STD_LOGIC ); end component;
  component nand2b port (I0, I1: in STD_LOGIC; O: buffer STD_LOGIC ); end component;
begin
  U1: inv port map (D,DN);
  U2: nand2b port map (D,C,SN);
  U3: nand2b port map (C,DN,RN);
  U4: nand2b port map (SN,QN,Q);
  U5: nand2b port map (Q,RN,QN);
end Vdlatch_s;
```

BUFS 'N' STUFF   Note that in Table 8-3 we defined the type of Q and QN to be buffer rather than out, since these signals are used as inputs as well as outputs in the architecture definition. Then we had to define a special 2-input NAND gate nand2b with output type buffer to avoid having a type mismatch (out vs. buffer) in the component instantiations for U4 and U5. Alternatively, we could have used internal signals to get around the problem, as shown in Table 8-4. As you know by now, VHDL has many different ways to express the same thing.

Table 8-5 is a process-based behavioral architecture for the D latch that requires, in effect, just one line of code to describe the latch's behavior. If C is 1, then Q gets D; else Q stays the same.

In order to describe edge-triggered behavior of flip-flops, we need to use one of VHDL's predefined signal attributes, the *event* attribute. If "SIG" is a signal name, then the construction "SIG'event" returns the value true at any delta time when SIG changes from one value to another, and false otherwise.

event attribute

Using the event attribute, we can model a positive-edge-triggered flip-flop as shown in Table 8-6. In the if statement, "CLK'event" returns true on

THE ONE TIME WE REALLY WANT AN INFERRED LATCH   In Table 8-5, we could have omitted the "else Q <= Q" clause and gotten the same results. Such code would not say what to do when C is 0, so the compiler would infer a latch. But in most other VHDL coding, we take great pains to assign a value to each signal in all possible code paths, to avoid inferring latches. So, when we really want a latch, it's better coding style to use an explicit else clause for the "latch closed" case; this also eliminates unneeded compiler warnings about inferred latches.

Table 8-4 Alternative VHDL structural code for the D latch in Figure 7-12.

```
entity Vdlatch is
  port (D, C: in STD_LOGIC;
        Q, QN: out STD_LOGIC );
end Vdlatch;

architecture Vdlatch_s2 of Vdlatch is
  signal DN, SN, RN, IQ, IQN: STD_LOGIC;
  component inv port (I: in STD_LOGIC; O: out STD_LOGIC ); end component;
  component nand2 port (I0, I1: in STD_LOGIC; O: out STD_LOGIC ); end component;
begin
  U1: inv port map (D,DN);
  U2: nand2 port map (D,C,SN);
  U3: nand2 port map (C,DN,RN);
  U4: nand2 port map (SN,IQN,IQ);
  U5: nand2 port map (IQ,RN,IQN);
  Q <= IQ; QN <= IQN;
end Vdlatch_s2;
```

Table 8-5 VHDL behavioral architecture for a D latch.

```
architecture Vdlatch_b of Vdlatch is
begin
process(C, D, Q)
  begin
    if (C='1') then Q <= D; else Q <= Q; end if;
    QN <= not Q;
  end process;
end Vdlatch_b;
```

any clock edge, and "CLK='1'" ensures that D is assigned to Q only on a *rising* edge. Note that the process sensitivity list includes only CLK; changes on D at other times are not relevant in this functional model.

Table 8-6 VHDL behavioral model of an edge-triggered D flip-flop.

```
entity Vdff is
  port (D, CLK: in STD_LOGIC;
        Q: out STD_LOGIC );
end Vdff;

architecture Vdff_b of Vdff is
begin
process(CLK)
  begin
    if (CLK'event and CLK='1') then Q <= D; end if;
  end process;
end Vdff_b;
```

■ **Table 8-7** VHDL model of a 74x74-like D flip-flop with preset and clear.

```
library IEEE;
use IEEE.std_logic_1164.all;

entity Vdff74 is
  port (D, CLK, PR_L, CLR_L: in STD_LOGIC;
        Q, QN: out STD_LOGIC );
end Vdff74;

architecture Vdff74_b of Vdff74 is
signal PR, CLR: STD_LOGIC;
begin
process(CLR_L, CLR, PR_L, PR, CLK)
  begin
    PR <= not PR_L; CLR <= not CLR_L;
    if (CLR and PR) = '1' then Q <= '0'; QN <= '0';
    elsif CLR = '1' then Q <= '0'; QN <= '1';
    elsif PR = '1' then Q <= '1'; QN <= '0';
    elsif (CLK'event and CLK='1') then Q <= D; QN <= not D;
    end if;
  end process;
end Vdff74_b;
```

■ **Table 8-8** VHDL model of a 16-bit register with many features.

```
library IEEE;
use IEEE.std_logic_1164.all;

entity Vreg16 is
  port (CLK, CLKEN, OE_L, CLR_L: in STD_LOGIC;
        D: in STD_LOGIC_VECTOR(1 to 16);        -- Input bus
        Q: out STD_ULOGIC_VECTOR (1 to 16) ); -- Output bus (three-state)
end Vreg16;

architecture Vreg16 of Vreg16 is
signal CLR, OE: STD_LOGIC;  -- active-high versions of signals
signal IQ: STD_LOGIC_VECTOR(1 to 16); -- internal Q signals
begin
process(CLK, CLR_L, CLR, OE_L, OE, IQ)
  begin
    CLR <= not CLR_L;  OE <= not OE_L;
    if (CLR = '1') then IQ <= (others => '0');
    elsif (CLK'event and CLK='1') then
      if (CLKEN='1') then IQ <= D; end if;
    end if;
    if OE = '1' then Q <= To_StdULogicVector(IQ);
    else Q <= (others => 'Z'); end if;
  end process;
end Vreg16;
```

SYNTHESIS RESTRICTIONS   In Table 8-8, the first `elsif` statement theoretically could have included all of the conditions needed to assign D to IQ. That is, it could have read "`elsif (CLK'event) and (CLK='1') and (CLKEN='1') then ...`" instead of using a nested `if` statement to check CLKEN. However, it was written as shown for a very pragmatic reason.

Only a subset of the VHDL language can be synthesized by the VHDL compiler that was used to prepare this chapter; this is true of any VHDL compiler today. In particular, use of the "event" attribute is limited to the form shown in the example, and a few others, for detecting simple edge-triggered behavior. This gets mapped into edge-triggered D flip-flops during synthesis. The nested `if` statement that checks CLKEN in the example leads to the synthesis of multiplexer logic on the D inputs of these flip-flops.

The D-flip-flop model can be augmented to include asynchronous inputs and a complemented output as in the 74x74 discrete flip-flop, as shown in Table 8-7. This more detailed functional model shows the noncomplementary behavior of the Q and QN outputs when preset and clear are asserted simultaneously. However, it does not include timing behavior such as propagation delay and setup and hold times, which are beyond the scope of the VHDL coverage in this book.

Larger registers can be modeled, of course, by defining the data inputs and outputs to be vectors, and additional functions can also be included. For example, Table 8-8 models a 16-bit register with three-state outputs and clock-enable, output-enable, and clear inputs. An internal signal vector IQ is used to hold the flip-flop outputs, and three-state outputs are defined and enabled as in Section 6.6.4.

8.2.8 Registers and Latches in Verilog

Register and latch circuits can be specified using behavioral Verilog code. For example, Table 8-9 uses an `always` block to describe the behavior of a D latch. In effect, just one line of code is needed to describe the basic latch behavior. If C is 1, then Q gets D; else Q stays the same.

Table 8-9 Verilog behavioral module for a D latch.

```
module VrDlatch( C, D, Q, QN );
  input C, D;
  output Q, QN;
  reg Q, QN;

  always @ (C or D or Q) begin
    if (C==1) Q <= D; else Q <= Q;
    QN <= !Q;
  end
endmodule
```

I WANT A LATCH, REALLY In Table 8-9, we could have omitted the "else Q = Q" clause and gotten the same results. Such code would not say what to do when C is 0, so the compiler would infer a latch. But in most other Verilog coding, we take great pains to assign a value to each signal in all possible code paths, to avoid inferring latches. So, when we really want a latch, it's better coding style to use an explicit else clause for the "latch closed" case; this may also eliminate compiler warnings about inferred latches.

Table 8-10
Behavioral Verilog
for a positive-edge-
triggered D flip-flop.

```
module VrDff(CLK, D, Q);
  input CLK, D;
  output Q;
  reg Q;

  always @ (posedge CLK)
    Q <= D;
endmodule
```

In order to describe edge-triggered behavior in a flip-flop, we need to use Verilog's posedge or negedge keyword in the sensitivity list of an always statement. For example, we can model a positive-edge-triggered flip-flop as shown in Table 8-10. The always block is executed only on a rising edge of CLK. We showed Verilog code for a more elaborate D flip-flop, with active-low preset and clear inputs like the 74x74's in Table 7-54 on page 646.

Larger registers can be modeled, of course, by defining the data inputs and outputs to be vectors, and additional functions can also be included. For example, Table 8-11 models a 16-bit register with three-state outputs and clock-enable, output-enable, and clear inputs. An internal signal vector IQ is used to hold the flip-flop outputs, and three-state outputs are defined and enabled as in Section 6.6.5.

Table 8-11 Verilog module for a 16-bit register with many features.

```
module Vrreg16( CLK, CLKEN, OE_L, CLR_L, D, Q );
  input CLK, CLKEN, OE_L, CLR_L;
  input [1:16] D;
  output [1:16] Q;
  reg [1:16] IQ;

  always @ (posedge CLK or negedge CLR_L)
    if (CLR_L==0) IQ <= 16'b0;
    else if (CLKEN==1) IQ <= D;
    else IQ <= IQ;

  assign Q = (OE_L==0) ? IQ : 16'bz;

endmodule
```

8.3 Sequential PLDs

The earliest, bipolar PLD families featured some devices with only combinational outputs, some with only registered outputs, and still others with a certain number of each output type. We described the combinational PAL16L8 in Section 6.3.2, and the older registered types are described at <u>DDPPonline</u> in Section <u>BipolarSeqPLD</u>. All of these have been supplanted by CMOS GAL devices where the type of output, combinational or registered, can be selected when the device is programmed.

8.3.1 Sequential GAL Devices

The GAL16V8 electrically erasable PLD was introduced in Section 6.3.3. Two "architecture-control" fuses are used to select among three basic configurations of this device. Section 6.3.3 described the *16V8C* ("complex") configuration, shown in Figure 6-27 on page 377, a structure similar to that of the PAL16L8. The *16V8S* ("simple") configuration provides a slightly different combinational logic capability (see the box below).

    The third configuration, called the *16V8R*, allows a flip-flop to be provided on any or all of the outputs. Each output has an an *output logic macrocell (OLM)* which can be configured, by fuses, to be either combinational or registered, as shown in Figure 8-17. In the 16V8C configuration, all of the OLMs are programmed to be combinational. In the 16V8R configuration, any or all of the OLMs can be programmed to be registered.

    Figure 8-18 on the next page shows the structure of the device when all of the outputs are programmed to be registered in the 16V8R configuration. All of

16V8C

16V8S

16V8R
output logic macrocell
  (OLM)

Figure 8-17 Output logic macrocells for the 16V8R: (a) combinational; (b) registered.

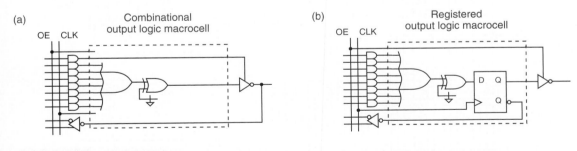

<table>
<tr><td>(a)</td><td>Combinational
output logic macrocell</td><td>(b)</td><td>Registered
output logic macrocell</td></tr>
</table>

THE "SIMPLE"   The "simple" 16V8S configuration of the GAL16V8 is not often used, because its
16V8S   capabilities are mostly a subset of the 16V8C's. This configuration was provided mainly for emulation of certain now-obsolete bipolar PAL devices. See Section <u>BipolarSeqPLD</u> at <u>DDPPonline</u> for more details.

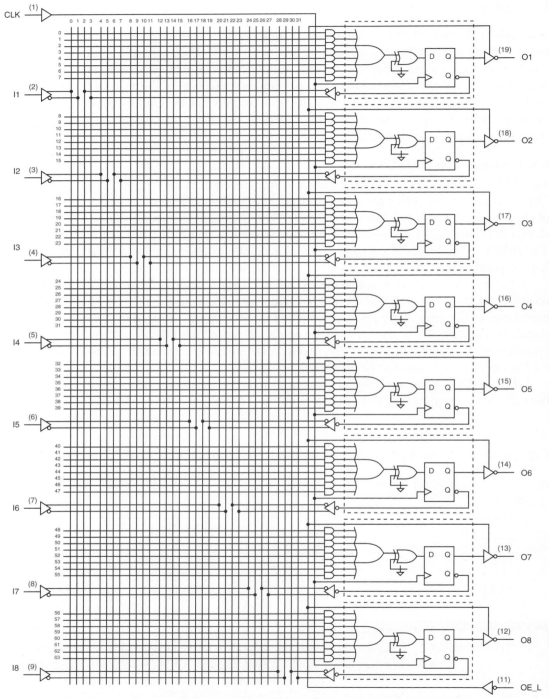

Figure 8-18 Logic diagram for the 16V8 in the "registered" configuration.

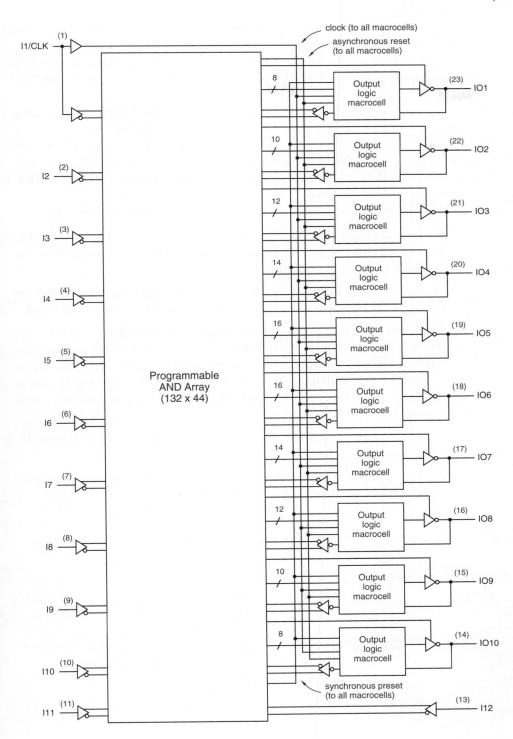

Figure 8-19
Logic diagram
for the 22V10.

20V8

22V10

the flip-flops are controlled by a common clock signal on pin 1. Similarly, all of the output buffers are controlled by a common output-enable signal on pin 11.

The *20V8* is similar to the 16V8 but comes in a 24-pin package with four extra input-only pins. Each AND gate in the 20V8 has 20 inputs, hence the "20" in "20V8."

The *22V10*, whose basic structure is shown in Figure 8-19 on the preceding page, also comes in a 24-pin package but is somewhat more flexible than the 20V8. The 22V10 does not have "architecture control" bits like the 16V8's and 20V8's, but it can realize any function that is realizable with a 20V8, and more. It has more product terms, two more general-purpose inputs, and better output-enable control than the 20V8.

Key differences between the 22V10 and the 20V8 are summarized below:

- Each output logic macrocell is configurable to have a register or not, as in the 20V8R architecture. However, the macrocells are different from the 16V8's and 20V8's, as shown in Figure 8-20.

- A single product term controls the output buffer, regardless of whether the registered or the combinational configuration is selected for a macrocell.

- Every output has at least eight product terms available, regardless of whether the registered or the combinational configuration is selected. Even more product terms are available on the inner pins, with 16 available on each of the two innermost pins. ("Innermost" is with respect to the right-hand side of the Figure 8-19, which also matches the arrangement of these pins on a 24-pin dual-inline package.)

- The clock signal on pin 1 is also available as a combinational input to any product term.

- A single product term is available to generate a global, asynchronous reset signal that resets all internal flip-flops to 0.

Figure 8-20 Output logic macrocells for the 22V10: (a) combinational; (b) registered.

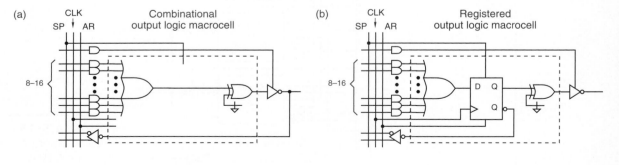

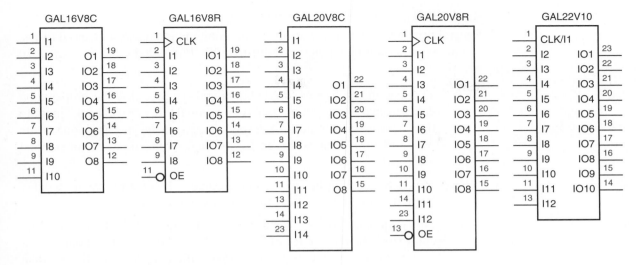

Figure 8-21 Logic symbols for popular GAL devices.

- A single product term is available to generate a global, synchronous preset signal that sets all internal flip-flops to 1 on the rising edge of the clock.

- Like the 16V8 and 20V8, the 22V10 has programmable output polarity. However, in the registered configuration, the polarity change is made at the output, rather than the input, of the D flip-flop. This affects the details of programming when the polarity is changed but does not affect the overall capability of the 22V10 (i.e., whether a given function can be realized). In fact, the difference in polarity-change location is transparent when you use a PLD programming language such as ABEL.

For over a decade, the 16V8, 20V8, and 22V10 have been the most popular and cost-effective PLDs (but see the box on page 710). Figure 8-21 shows generic logic symbols for these three devices. Most of the examples in the rest of this chapter can fit into the smallest of the three devices, the 16V8.

PALS? GALS? Lattice Semiconductor introduced GAL devices including the GAL16V8 and GAL20V8 in the mid-1980s. Advanced Micro Devices later followed up with a pin-compatible device which they call the PALCE16V8 ("C" is for CMOS, "E" is for erasable). Several other manufacturers make differently numbered but compatible devices as well. Rather than get caught up in the details of different manufacturers' names, in this chapter we usually refer to commonly used GAL devices with their generic names, 16V8, 20V8, and 22V10.

8.3.2 PLD Timing Specifications

Several timing parameters are specified for combinational and sequential PLDs. The most important parameters are illustrated in Figure 8-22 and are explained below:

t_{PD} This parameter applies to combinational outputs. It is the propagation delay from a primary input pin, bidirectional pin, or "feedback" input to the combinational output. A *feedback input* is an internal input of the AND-OR array that is driven by the registered output of an internal macrocell.

tPD

feedback input

t_{CO} This parameter applies to registered outputs. It is the propagation delay from the rising edge of CLK to a primary output.

tCO

t_{CF} This parameter also applies to registered outputs. It is the propagation delay from the rising edge of CLK to a macrocell's registered output that connects back to a feedback input. If specified, t_{CF} is normally less than t_{CO}. However, some manufacturers do not specify t_{CF}, in which case you must assume that $t_{CF} = t_{CO}$.

tCF

t_{SU} This parameter applies to primary, bidirectional, and feedback inputs that propagate to the D inputs of flip-flops. It is the setup time during which the input signal must be stable before the rising edge of CLK.

tSU

t_{H} This parameter also applies to signals that propagate to the D inputs of flip-flops. It is the hold time during which the input signal must be stable after the rising edge of CLK.

tH

f_{max} This parameter applies to clocked operation. It is the highest frequency at which the PLD can operate reliably and is the reciprocal of the minimum clock period. Two versions of this parameter can be derived from the previous specifications, depending on whether the device is operating with external feedback or internal feedback.

fmax

external feedback   *External feedback* refers to a circuit in which a registered PLD output is connected to the input of another registered PLD with similar timing; for proper operation, the sum of t_{CO} for the first PLD and t_{SU} for the second must not exceed the clock period.

internal feedback   *Internal feedback* refers to a circuit in which a registered PLD output is fed back to a register in the same PLD; in this case, the sum of t_{CF} and t_{SU} must not exceed the clock period.

Each of the PLDs that we described in previous sections is available in several different speed grades. The speed grade is usually indicated by a suffix on the part number, such as "16V8-10"; the suffix usually refers to the t_{PD}

Table 8-12 Timing specifications, in nanoseconds, of popular CMOS GAL devices in DIPs.

Part numbers	Suffix	t_{PD}	t_{CO}	t_{CF}	t_{SU}	t_H
GAL16V8D, GAL20V8B	-7	7.5	5	3	7	0
GAL16V8D, GAL20V8B	-10	10	7	6	10	0
GAL16V8D, GAL20V8B	-15	15	10	8	12	0
GAL16V8D, GAL20V8B	-25	25	12	10	15	0
GAL22V10D	-7	7.5	4.5	3	4.5	0
GAL22V10D	-10	10	7	2.5	7	0
GAL22V10D	-15	15	8	2.5	10	0
GAL22V10D	-25	25	15	13	15	0

specification, in nanoseconds. Table 8-12 shows the timing of several popular CMOS GAL devices in DIP packages. Note that only the t_{PD} column applies to the combinational outputs of a device, while the last four columns apply to registered outputs. All of these numbers are worst case over the commercial operating range.

When sequential PLDs are used in applications with critical timing, it's important to remember that they normally have longer setup times than discrete edge-triggered registers in the same technology, owing to the delay of the AND-OR array on each D input. Conversely, under typical conditions, a PLD actually has a negative hold-time requirement because of the delay through AND-OR array. However, you can't count on it having a negative hold time—the worst-case specification is normally zero.

Figure 8-22 PLD timing parameters.

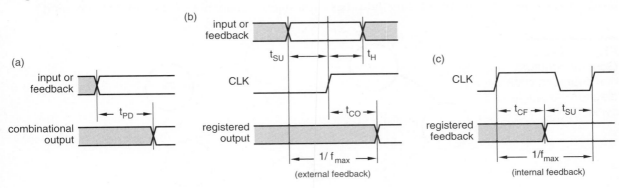

8.4 Counters

counter
modulus

modulo-m counter
divide-by-m counter

The name *counter* is generally used for any clocked sequential circuit whose state diagram contains a single cycle, as in Figure 8-23. The *modulus* of a counter is the number of states in the cycle. A counter with m states is called a *modulo-m counter* or, sometimes, a *divide-by-m counter.* A counter with a non-power-of-2 modulus has extra states that are not used in normal operation.

Figure 8-23
General structure of a counter's state diagram—a single cycle.

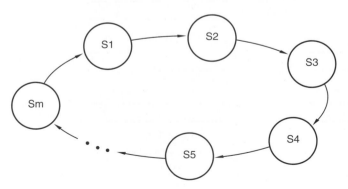

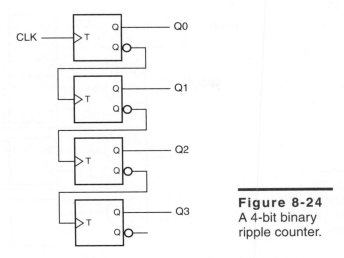

Figure 8-24
A 4-bit binary
ripple counter.

Probably the most commonly used counter type is an *n-bit binary counter.*   *n-bit binary counter*
Such a counter has *n* flip-flops and has 2^n states, which are visited in the
sequence 0, 1, 2, ... , $2^n - 1$, 0, 1, ... Each of these states is encoded as the
corresponding *n*-bit binary integer.

8.4.1 Ripple Counters

An *n*-bit binary counter can be constructed with just *n* flip-flops and no other
components, for any value of *n*. Figure 8-24 shows such a counter for *n* = 4.
Recall that a T flip-flop changes state (toggles) on every rising edge of its clock
input. Thus, each bit of the counter toggles if and only if the immediately
preceding bit changes from 1 to 0. This corresponds to a normal binary counting
sequence—when a particular bit changes from 1 to 0, it generates a carry to the
next most significant bit. The counter is called a *ripple counter* because the carry   *ripple counter*
information ripples from the less significant bits to the more significant bits, one
bit at a time.

8.4.2 Synchronous Counters

Although a ripple counter requires fewer components than any other type of
binary counter, it does so at a price—it is slower than any other type of binary
counter. In the worst case, when the most significant bit must change, the output
is not valid until time $n \cdot t_{TQ}$ after the rising edge of CLK, where t_{TQ} is the
propagation delay from input to output of a T flip-flop.

A *synchronous counter* connects all of its flip-flop clock inputs to the same   *synchronous counter*
common CLK signal, so that all of the flip-flop outputs change at the same time,
after only t_{TQ} ns of delay. As shown in Figure 8-25 on the next page, this requires
the use of T flip-flops with enable inputs; the output toggles on the rising edge of
T if and only if EN is asserted. Combinational logic on the EN inputs determines
which, if any, flip-flops toggle on each rising edge of T.

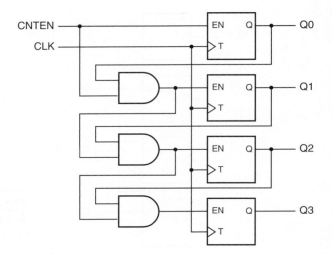

Figure 8-25
A synchronous 4-bit
binary counter with
serial enable logic.

As shown in Figure 8-25, it is also possible to provide a master count-enable signal CNTEN. Each T flip-flop toggles if and only if CNTEN is asserted and all of the lower-order counter bits are 1. Like the binary ripple counter, a synchronous n-bit binary counter can be built with a fixed amount of logic per bit—in this case, a T flip-flop with enable and a 2-input AND gate.

synchronous serial counter

The counter structure in Figure 8-25 is sometimes called a *synchronous serial counter* because the combinational enable signals propagate serially from the least significant to the most significant bits. If the clock period is too short, there may not be enough time for a change in the counter's LSB to propagate to the MSB. This problem is eliminated in Figure 8-26 by driving each EN input

synchronous parallel counter

with a dedicated AND gate, just a single level of logic. Called a *synchronous parallel counter,* this is the fastest binary counter structure.

Figure 8-26
A synchronous 4-bit
binary counter with
parallel enable logic.

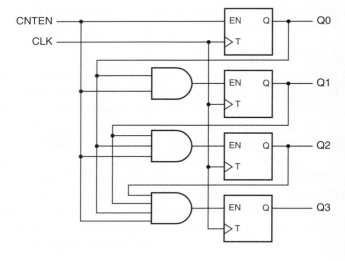

8.4.3 MSI Counters and Applications

The most popular MSI counter is the *74x163*, a synchronous 4-bit binary counter with active-low load and clear inputs. Its logic symbol is shown in Figure 8-27. Its function is summarized by the state table in Table 8-13, and its internal logic diagram is shown in Figure 8-28 on the next page. Most designers nowadays would use an HDL program to create such a counter, but it's still worthwhile to study the 163's internals because it has such a classic and efficient design.

74x163

The '163 uses D flip-flops rather than T flip-flops internally to facilitate the load and clear functions. Each D input is driven by a 2-input multiplexer consisting of an OR gate and two AND gates. The multiplexer output is 0 if the CLR_L input is asserted. Otherwise, the top AND gate passes the data input (A, B, C, or D) to the output if LD_L is asserted. If neither CLR_L nor LD_L is asserted, the bottom AND gate passes the output of an XNOR gate to the multiplexer output.

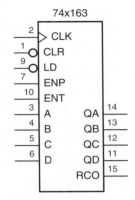

Figure 8-27
Traditional logic symbol for the 74x163.

Table 8-13 State table for a 74x163 4-bit binary counter.

Inputs				Current State				Next State			
CLR_L	LD_L	ENT	ENP	QD	QC	QB	QA	QD*	QC*	QB*	QA*
0	x	x	x	x	x	x	x	0	0	0	0
1	0	x	x	x	x	x	x	D	C	B	A
1	1	0	x	x	x	x	x	QD	QC	QB	QA
1	1	x	0	x	x	x	x	QD	QC	QB	QA
1	1	1	1	0	0	0	0	0	0	0	1
1	1	1	1	0	0	0	1	0	0	1	0
1	1	1	1	0	0	1	0	0	0	1	1
1	1	1	1	0	0	1	1	0	1	0	0
1	1	1	1	0	1	0	0	0	1	0	1
1	1	1	1	0	1	0	1	0	1	1	0
1	1	1	1	0	1	1	0	0	1	1	1
1	1	1	1	0	1	1	1	1	0	0	0
1	1	1	1	1	0	0	0	1	0	0	1
1	1	1	1	1	0	0	1	1	0	1	0
1	1	1	1	1	0	1	0	1	0	1	1
1	1	1	1	1	0	1	1	1	1	0	0
1	1	1	1	1	1	0	0	1	1	0	1
1	1	1	1	1	1	0	1	1	1	1	0
1	1	1	1	1	1	1	0	1	1	1	1
1	1	1	1	1	1	1	1	0	0	0	0

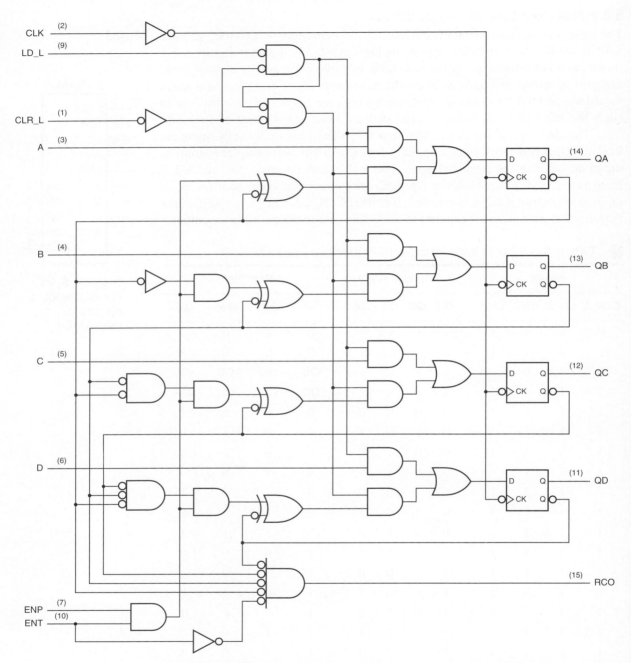

Figure 8-28 Logic diagram for the 74x163 synchronous 4-bit binary counter, including pin numbers for a standard 16-pin DIP package.

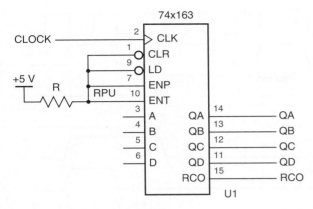

Figure 8-29
Connections for the 74x163 to operate in a free-running mode.

The XNOR gates perform the counting function in the '163. One input of each XNOR is the corresponding count bit (QA, QB, QC, or QD); the other input is 1, which complements the count bit, if and only if both enables ENP and ENT are asserted and all of the lower-order count bits are 1. The RCO ("ripple carry out") signal indicates a carry from the most significant bit position and is 1 when all of the count bits are 1 and ENT is asserted.

Even though most MSI counters have enable inputs, they are often used in a *free-running* mode in which they are enabled continuously. Figure 8-29 shows the connections to make a '163 operate in this way, and Figure 8-30 shows the resulting output waveforms. Notice that, starting with QA, each signal has half the frequency of the preceding one. Thus, a free-running '163 can be used as a divide-by-2, -4, -8, or -16 counter, by ignoring any unnecessary high-order output bits.

free-running counter

Note that the '163 is fully synchronous; that is, its outputs change only on the rising edge of CLK. Some applications need an asynchronous clear function,

Figure 8-30 Clock and output waveforms for a free-running divide-by-16 counter.

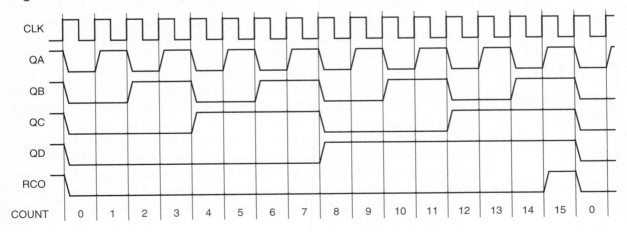

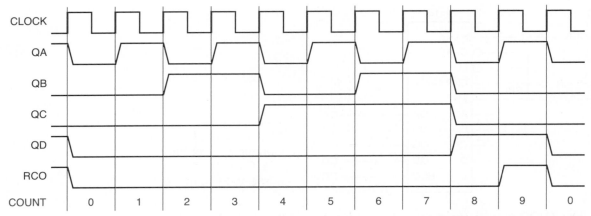

Figure 8-31 Clock and output waveforms for a free-running divide-by-10 counter.

74x161

74x160
74x162
decade counter

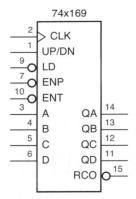

Figure 8-32
Logic symbol for the
74x169 up/down
counter.

74x169

up/down counter

as provided by the *74x161*. The '161 has the same pinout as the '163, but its CLR_L input is connected to the asynchronous clear inputs of its flip-flops.

The *74x160* and *74x162* are more variations with the same pinouts and general functions as the '161 and '163, except that the counting sequence is modified to go to state 0 after state 9. In other words, these are modulo-10 counters, sometimes called *decade counters*. Figure 8-31 shows the output waveforms for a free-running '160 or '162. Notice that although the QD and QC outputs have one-tenth of the CLK frequency, they do not have a 50% duty cycle, and the QB output, with one-fifth of the input frequency, does not have a constant duty cycle. The design of a divide-by-10 counter with a 50% duty-cycle output can be found at <u>DDPPonline</u> in <u>Section Cntr</u>.

Although the '163 is a modulo-16 counter, it can be made to count in a modulus less than 16 by using the CLR_L or LD_L input to shorten the normal counting sequence. For example, to make a modulo-N counter that counts from 0 to $N-1$, we develop an active-low signal that is asserted in state $N-1$ and apply that to the CLR_L input, sending the counter back to state 0 on the next clock tick. This can typically be done with a single NAND gate whose inputs are the state bits that are 1 in the binary encoding of $N-1$. This and other examples using the '163 are described in more detail at <u>DDPPonline</u> in <u>Section Cntr</u>. This section also explains counter cascading and the important difference between the '163's ENP and ENT inputs, which is a mystery even to some experienced digital designers.

Another counter with functions similar to 74x163's is the *74x169,* whose logic symbol is shown in Figure 8-32. One difference in the '169 is that its carry output and enable inputs are active low. More importantly, the '169 is an *up/down counter*; it counts in ascending or descending binary order depending on the value of an input signal, UP/DN. The '169 counts up when UP/DN is 1 and down when UP/DN is 0.

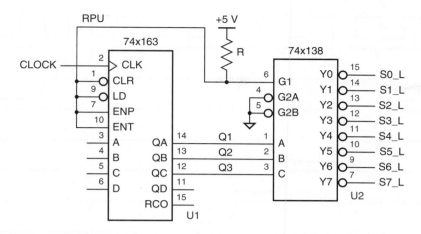

Figure 8-33
A modulo-8 binary
counter and decoder.

8.4.4 Decoding Binary-Counter States

A binary counter may be combined with a decoder to obtain a set of 1-out-of-m-coded signals, where one signal is asserted in each counter state. This is useful when counters are used to control a set of devices, where a different device is enabled in each counter state. In this approach, each output of the decoder enables a different device.

Figure 8-33 shows how a 74x163 wired as a modulo-8 counter can be combined with a 74x138 3-to-8 decoder to provide eight signals, each one representing a counter state. Figure 8-34 on the next page shows typical timing for this circuit. Each decoder output is asserted during a corresponding clock period.

Notice that the decoder outputs may contain "glitches" on state transitions where two or more counter bits change, even though the '163 outputs are glitch free and the '138 does not have any static hazards. In a synchronous counter like the '163, the outputs don't change at exactly the same time. More important, multiple signal paths in a decoder like the '138 have different delays; for example, the path from B to Y1_L is faster than the path from A to Y1_L. Thus, even if the input changes simultaneously from 011 to 100, the decoder may behave as if the input were temporarily 001, and the Y1_L output may have a glitch. In the present example, it can be shown that the glitches can occur in *any* realization of the binary decoder function; this problem is an example of a *function hazard*.

In most applications, the decoder output signals portrayed in Figure 8-34 would be used as control inputs to registers, counters, and other edge-triggered devices (e.g., EN_L in a 74x377, or LD_L or ENP_L in a 74x163). In such a case, the decoding glitches in the figure are not a problem, since they occur *after* the clock tick. The glitches are long gone before the next tick comes along, when the decoder outputs are sampled by other edge-triggered devices. However, the glitches *would* be a problem if they were applied to something like the S_L or R_L inputs of an $\overline{\text{S-R}}$ latch. Likewise, using such potentially glitchy signals as clocks for edge-triggered devices is a definite no-no.

decoding glitches

function hazard

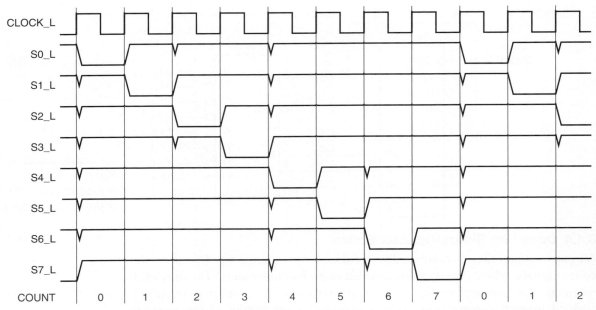

Figure 8-34 Timing diagram for a modulo-8 binary counter and decoder, showing decoding glitches.

If necessary, one way to "clean up" the glitches in Figure 8-34 is to connect the '138 outputs to another register that samples the stable decoded outputs on the next clock tick, as shown in Figure 8-35. Notice that the decoded outputs have been renamed to account for the 1-tick delay through the register. However, once you decide to pay for an 8-bit register, a less costly solution is to use an 8-bit "ring counter," which provides glitch-free decoded outputs directly, as we'll show in Section 8.5.4.

Figure 8-35 A modulo-8 binary counter and decoder with glitch-free outputs.

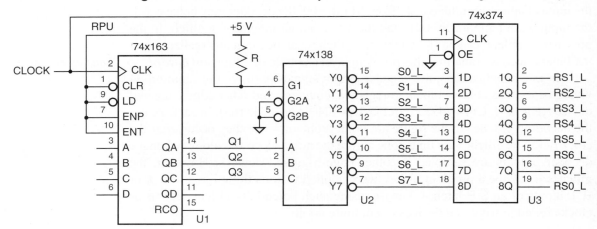

8.4.5 Counters in ABEL and PLDs

Binary counters are good candidates for ABEL- and PLD-based design, for several reasons:

- A large state machine can often be decomposed into two or more smaller state machines, where one of the smaller machines is a binary counter that keeps track of how long the other machine should stay in a particular state. This may simplify both the conceptual design and the circuit design of the machine.

- Many applications require almost-binary-modulus counters with special requirements for initialization, state detection, or state skipping. For example, a counter in an elevator controller may skip state 13. Instead of using an off-the-shelf binary counter and extra logic for the special requirements, a designer can specify exactly the required functions in an ABEL program.

- Most standard MSI counters have only 4 bits, while a single 24-pin PLD can be used to create a binary counter with up to 10 bits. CPLDs and FPGAs can be used for even larger counters.

The most popular MSI counter is the 74x163 4-bit binary counter, shown in Figure 8-28 on page 714. A glance at this figure shows that the excitation logic for this counter isn't exactly simple, especially considering its use of XNOR gates. Nevertheless, ABEL provides a very simple way of defining counter behavior, which we describe next.

ABEL uses the "+" symbol to specify integer addition. When two sets are "added" with this operator, each is interpreted as a binary number; the rightmost set element corresponds to the least significant bit of the number. Thus, the function of a 74x163 can be specified by the ABEL program in Table 8-14 on the next page. When the counter is enabled, 1 is added to the current state.

Table 8-15 shows the minimized logic equations that ABEL generates for the 4-bit counter. Notice that each more significant output bit requires one more product term. As a result, the size of counters that can be realized in a 16V8 or even a 20V8 is generally limited to five or six bits. Other devices, including some CPLDs and FPGAs, contain an XOR structure that can realize larger counters without increasing product-term requirements.

Designing a specialized counting sequence in ABEL is much simpler than adapting an off-the-shelf binary counter. For example, the ABEL program in Table 8-14 can be adapted to count in excess-3 sequence (from 3 to 12, see Section 2.10) by changing the equations as follows:

```
COUNT := !CLR & ( LD & INPUT
      # !LD & (ENT & ENP) &
         ((COUNT==12) & 3) # ((COUNT!=12) & (COUNT + 1))
      # !LD & !(ENT & ENP) & COUNT);

RCO = (COUNT == 12) & ENT;
```

Table 8-14 ABEL program for a 74x163-like 4-bit binary counter.

```
module Z74X163
title '4-bit Binary Counter'

" Input pins
CLK, LD_L, CLR_L, ENP, ENT        pin;
A, B, C, D                        pin;
" Output pins
QA, QB, QC, QD                    pin istype 'reg';
RCO                               pin istype 'com';

" Set definitions
INPUT = [D, C, B, A];
COUNT = [QD, QC, QB, QA];

LD = !LD_L; CLR = !CLR_L;        " Active-level conversions

equations

COUNT.CLK = CLK;

COUNT := !CLR & ( LD & INPUT
                  # !LD & (ENT & ENP) & (COUNT + 1)
                  # !LD & !(ENT & ENP) & COUNT);

RCO = (COUNT == [1,1,1,1]) & ENT;

end Z74X163
```

Table 8-15 Minimized equations for the 4-bit binary counter in Table 8-14.

```
QA := (CLR_L & LD_L & ENT & ENP & !QA
    # CLR_L & LD_L & !ENP & QA
    # CLR_L & LD_L & !ENT & QA
    # CLR_L & !LD_L & A);

QB := (CLR_L & LD_L & ENT & ENP & !QB & QA
    # CLR_L & LD_L & QB & !QA
    # CLR_L & LD_L & !ENP & QB
    # CLR_L & LD_L & !ENT & QB
    # CLR_L & !LD_L & B);

QC := (CLR_L & LD_L & ENT & ENP & !QC & QB & QA
    # CLR_L & LD_L & QC & !QA
    # CLR_L & LD_L & QC & !QB
    # CLR_L & LD_L & !ENP & QC
    # CLR_L & LD_L & !ENT & QC
    # CLR_L & !LD_L & C);
```

```
QD := (CLR_L & LD_L & ENT & ENP
                  & !QD & QC & QB & QA
    # CLR_L & !LD_L & D
    # CLR_L & LD_L & QD & !QB
    # CLR_L & LD_L & QD & !QC
    # CLR_L & LD_L & !ENP & QD
    # CLR_L & LD_L & !ENT & QD
    # CLR_L & LD_L & QD & !QA);

RCO = (ENT & QD & QC & QB & QA);
```

PLDs can be cascaded to obtain wider counters by providing each counter stage with a carry output that indicates when it is about to roll over. There are two basic approaches to generating the carry output:

- *Combinational.* The carry equation indicates that the counter is enabled and is currently in its last state before rollover. For a 5-bit binary up counter, we have

  combinational carry output

  ```
  COUT = CNTEN & Q4 & Q3 & Q2 & Q1 & Q0;
  ```

  Since CNTEN is included, this approach allows carries to be rippled through cascaded counters by connecting each COUT to the next CNTEN.

- *Registered.* The carry equation indicates that the counter is about to enter its last state before rollover. Thus, at the next clock tick, the counter enters this last state and the carry output is asserted. For a 5-bit binary up counter with load and clear inputs, we have

  registered carry output

  ```
  COUT :=  !CLR & !LD & CNTEN
             & Q4 & Q3 & Q2 & Q1 & !Q0
        #  !CLR * !LD * !CNTEN
             & Q4 & Q3 & Q2 & Q1 & Q0
        #  !CLR & LD
             & D4 & D3 & D2 & D1 & D0;
  ```

The second approach has the advantage of producing COUT with less delay than the combinational approach. However, external gates are now required between stages, since the CNTEN signal for each stage should be the logical AND of the master count-enable signal and the COUT outputs of all lower-order counters. These external gates can be avoided if the higher-order counters have multiple enable inputs.

8.4.6 Counters in VHDL

Like ABEL, VHDL allows counters to be specified fairly easily. The biggest challenge in VHDL, with its strong type checking, is to get all of the signal types defined correctly and consistently.

Table 8-16 on the next page is a VHDL program for a 74x163-like binary counter. Notice that the program uses the std_logic_arith package, which includes the UNSIGNED type, described in Section 6.9.7 on page 466. This package includes definitions of "+" and "−" operators that perform unsigned addition and subtraction on UNSIGNED operands. The counter program declares the counter input and output as UNSIGNED vectors and uses "+" to increment the counter value as required.

In the program, we defined an internal signal IQ to hold the counter value. We could have used Q directly, but then we'd have to declare its port type as buffer rather than out. Also, we could have defined the type of ports D and Q to be STD_LOGIC_VECTOR, but then we would have to perform type conversions inside the body of the process (see Exercise 8.51).

Table 8-16 VHDL program for a 74x163-like 4-bit binary counter.

```
library IEEE;
use IEEE.std_logic_1164.all;
use IEEE.std_logic_arith.all;

entity V74x163 is
    port ( CLK, CLR_L, LD_L, ENP, ENT: in STD_LOGIC;
                D: in UNSIGNED (3 downto 0);
                Q: out UNSIGNED (3 downto 0);
                RCO: out STD_LOGIC );
end V74x163;

architecture V74x163_arch of V74x163 is
signal IQ: UNSIGNED (3 downto 0);
begin
process (CLK, ENT, IQ)
  begin
    if (CLK'event and CLK='1') then
      if CLR_L='0' then IQ <= (others => '0');
      elsif LD_L='0' then IQ <= D;
      elsif (ENT and ENP)='1' then IQ <= IQ + 1;
      end if;
    end if;
    if (IQ=15) and (ENT='1') then RCO <= '1';
    else RCO <= '0';
    end if;
    Q <= IQ;
  end process;
end V74x163_arch;
```

Table 8-17 VHDL architecture for counting in the excess-3 sequence.

```
architecture V74xs3_arch of V74x163 is
signal IQ: UNSIGNED (3 downto 0);
begin
process (CLK, ENT, IQ)
  begin
    if CLK'event and CLK='1' then
      if CLR_L='0' then IQ <= (others => '0');
      elsif LD_L='0' then IQ <= D;
      elsif (ENT and ENP)='1' and (IQ=12) then IQ <= ('0','0','1','1');
      elsif (ENT and ENP)='1' then IQ <= IQ + 1;
      end if;
    end if;
    if (IQ=12) and (ENT='1') then RCO <= '1';
    else RCO <= '0';
    end if;
    Q <= IQ;
  end process;
end V74xs3_arch;
```

   As in ABEL, specialized counting sequences can be specified very easily using behavioral VHDL code. For example, Table 8-17 modifies the 74x163-like counter to count in excess-3 sequence (3, ... , 12, 3, ...).

   Unfortunately, some older synthesis tools do not synthesize counters particularly well. In particular, they tend to synthesize the counting step using a binary adder with the counter value and a constant 1 as operands. This approach requires much more combinational logic than what we've shown for discrete counters; it is particularly wasteful in CPLDs and FPGAs containing T flip-flops, XOR gates, or other structures optimized for counters. In this case, a useful alternative is to write structural VHDL that is targeted to the cells available in a particular CPLD, FPGA, or ASIC technology.

   For example, we can construct one bit-cell for a 74x163-like counter using the circuit in Figure 8-36. This circuit is designed to use serial propagation for the carry bits, so the same circuit can be used at any stage of an arbitrarily large counter, subject to fanout constraints on the common signals that drive all of the stages. The signals in the bit-cell have the following definitions:

   CLK   (common) The clock input for all stages.

LDNOCLR   (common) Asserted if the counter's LD input is asserted and CLR is negated.

NOCLRORLD   (common) Asserted if the counter's CLR and LD inputs are both negated.

CNTENP   (common) Asserted if the counter's ENP input is asserted.

   D_i (per cell) Load data input for cell i.

CNTENi   (per cell) Serial count enable input for cell i.

CNTENi+1   (per cell) Serial count enable output for cell i.

   Q_i (per cell) Counter output for cell i.

Figure 8-36 One bit-cell of a synchronous serial, 74x163-like counter.

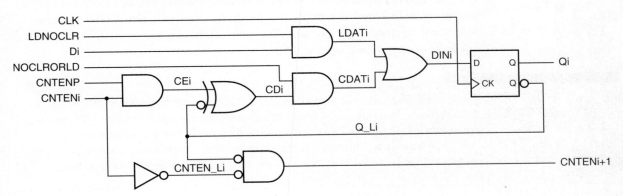

Table 8-18 VHDL program for counter cell of Figure 8-36.

```
library IEEE;
use IEEE.std_logic_1164.all;

entity syncsercell is
  port( CLK, LDNOCLR, NOCLRORLD, CNTENP, D, CNTEN: in STD_LOGIC;
        CNTENO, Q: out STD_LOGIC );
end syncsercell;

architecture syncsercell_arch of syncsercell is
component Vdffqqn
  port( CLK, D: in STD_LOGIC;
        Q, QN: out STD_LOGIC );
end component;
signal LDAT, CDAT, DIN, Q_L: STD_LOGIC;
begin
  LDAT <= LDNOCLR and D;
  CDAT <= NOCLRORLD and ((CNTENP and CNTEN) xor not Q_L);
  DIN  <= LDAT or CDAT;
  CNTENO <= (not Q_L) and CNTEN;
  U1: Vdffqqn port map (CLK, DIN, Q, Q_L);
end syncsercell_arch;
```

Table 8-18 is a VHDL program corresponding to the bit-cell in the figure. In the program, the D flip-flop component Vdffqqn is assumed to be already defined; it is similar to the D flip-flop in Table 8-6 with the addition of a QN (complemented) output. In an FPGA or ASIC design, a flip-flop component type would be chosen from the manufacturer's standard cell library.

Table 8-19 shows how to create an 8-bit synchronous serial counter using the cell defined previously. The first two assignments in the architecture body synthesize the common LDNOCLR and NOCLRORLD signals. The next two statements handle boundary conditions for the serial count-enable chain. Finally, the generate statement (introduced on page 500) instantiates eight 1-bit counter cells and hooks up the count-enable chain as required.

It should be clear that a larger or smaller counter can be created simply by changing a few definitions in the program. You can put VHDL's generic statement to good use here to allow you to change the counter's size with a one-line change (see Exercise 8.53).

A MATTER OF STYLE   Note that Table 8-18 uses a combination of dataflow and structural VHDL styles. It could have been written completely structurally, for example using an ASIC manufacturer's gate component definitions, to guarantee that the synthesized circuit conforms exactly to Figure 8-36. However, most synthesis tools can do a good job of picking the best gate realization for the simple signal assignments used here.

Table 8-19 VHDL program for an 8-bit 74x163-like synchronous serial counter.

```
library IEEE;
use IEEE.std_logic_1164.all;

entity V74x163s is
  port( CLK, CLR_L, LD_L, ENP, ENT: in STD_LOGIC;
        D: in STD_LOGIC_VECTOR (7 downto 0);
        Q: out STD_LOGIC_VECTOR (7 downto 0);
        RCO: out STD_LOGIC );
end V74x163s;

architecture V74x163s_arch of V74x163s is
component syncsercell
  port( CLK, LDNOCLR, NOCLRORLD, CNTENP, D, CNTEN: in STD_LOGIC;
        CNTENO, Q: out STD_LOGIC );
end component;
signal LDNOCLR, NOCLRORLD: STD_LOGIC; -- common signals
signal SCNTEN: STD_LOGIC_VECTOR (8 downto 0); -- serial count-enable inputs
begin
  LDNOCLR <= (not LD_L) and CLR_L; -- create common load and clear controls
  NOCLRORLD <= LD_L and CLR_L;
  SCNTEN(0) <= ENT; -- serial count-enable into the first stage
  RCO <= SCNTEN(8);  -- RCO is equivalent to final count-enable output
  g1: for i in 0 to 7 generate    -- generate the eight syncsercell stages
        U1: syncsercell port map ( CLK, LDNOCLR, NOCLRORLD, ENP, D(i), SCNTEN(i),
                                   SCNTEN(i+1), Q(i));
  end generate;
end V74x163s_arch;
```

8.4.7 Counters in Verilog

Verilog allows counters to be specified very easily. Table 8-20 on the next page is a Verilog module for a 74x163-like binary counter. Although a counter is technically a state machine, we did not use our usual state-machine coding style with separate `always` blocks for state memory and next-state logic. Instead, since the next-state logic is simple and clear enough, we put it in the same `always` block with the edge-triggered flip-flop behavior. Still, a second `always` block was necessarily used to specify the RCO combinational output behavior.

It is very easy to modify the counter program to have other behaviors. For example, Table 8-21 shows how to modify the two `always` blocks for decade (decimal) counting behavior, as in the 74x162 MSI part. Next, Table 8-22 shows modifications for the excess-3 decimal counting sequence (counting from 3 to 12 and repeating). Finally, Table 8-23 models the 74x169 up/down counter. Note the small changes for the '169's active-low enable inputs and carry output, and the use of subtraction for counting down; declaration changes are not shown.

The clear input of any of these counters can be made asynchronous simply by adding "posedge CLR_L" to the first `always` statement's sensitivity list.

Table 8-20 Verilog module for a 74x163-like 4-bit binary counter.

```verilog
module Vr74x163( CLK, CLR_L, LD_L, ENP, ENT, D, Q, RCO );
  input CLK, CLR_L, LD_L, ENP, ENT;
  input [3:0] D;
  output [3:0] Q;
  output RCO;
  reg [3:0] Q;
  reg RCO;

  always @ (posedge CLK)  // Create the counter f-f behavior
    if (CLR_L == 0)                       Q <= 4'b0;
    else if (LD_L == 0)                   Q <= D;
    else if ((ENT == 1) && (ENP == 1))    Q <= Q + 1;
    else                                  Q <= Q;

  always @ (Q or ENT)     // Create RCO combinational output
    if ((ENT == 1) && (Q == 4'd15))       RCO = 1;
    else                                  RCO = 0;
endmodule
```

Table 8-21 Verilog code for a 74x162-like 4-bit decimal counter.

```verilog
always @ (posedge CLK)    // Create the counter f-f behavior
  if (!CLR_L)                           Q <= 4'b0;
  else if (!LD_L)                       Q <= D;
  else if (ENT && ENP && (Q == 4'd9))   Q <= 4'b0;
  else if (ENT && ENP)                  Q <= Q + 1;
  else                                  Q <= Q;

always @ (Q or ENT)       // Create RCO combinational output
  if (ENT && (Q == 4'd9))               RCO = 1;
  else                                  RCO = 0;
```

Table 8-22 Verilog code for the excess-3 decimal counting sequence.

```verilog
always @ (posedge CLK)    // Create the counter f-f behavior
  if (!CLR_L)                            Q <= 4'd3;
  else if (!LD_L)                        Q <= D;
  else if (ENT && ENP && (Q == 4'd12))   Q <= 4'd3;
  else if (ENT && ENP)                   Q <= Q + 1;
  else                                   Q <= Q;

always @ (Q or ENT)       // Create RCO combinational output
  if (ENT && (Q == 4'd12))               RCO = 1;
  else                                   RCO = 0;
```

Table 8-23 Verilog code for a 74x169-like 4-bit up/down counter.

```
always @ (posedge CLK)          // Create the counter f-f behavior
  if (!CLR_L )                          Q <= 4'b0;
  else if (!LD_L)                       Q <= D;
  else if (!ENT_L && !ENP_L &&  UPDN)   Q <= Q + 1;
  else if (!ENT_L && !ENP_L && !UPDN)   Q <= Q - 1;
  else                                  Q <= Q;

always @ (Q or ENT_L or UPDN) // Create RCO_L combinational output
  if       (!ENT_L &&  UPDN && (Q == 4'd15))  RCO_L = 0;
  else if (!ENT_L && !UPDN && (Q == 4'd0 ))  RCO_L = 0;
  else                                        RCO_L = 1;
```

PRETTY GOOD SYNTHESIS   While the Verilog modules Tables 8-20 through 8-23 use addition and subtraction for counting, a good synthesis tool avoids using expensive adders and subtractors for these operations. For example, when targeting a CPLD with T flip-flop emulation, the Xilinx ISE synthesis tool instead creates excitation equations for T flip-flops with enable, using only five product terms per flip-flop for the up/down counter. Even wider counters can be built with only five product terms per T flip-flop.

8.5 Shift Registers

8.5.1 Shift-Register Structure

A *shift register* is an *n*-bit register with a provision for shifting its stored data by one bit position at each tick of the clock. Figure 8-37 shows the structure of a serial-in, serial-out shift register. The *serial input,* SERIN, specifies a new bit to be shifted into one end at each clock tick. This bit appears at the *serial output,*

shift register

serial input

serial output

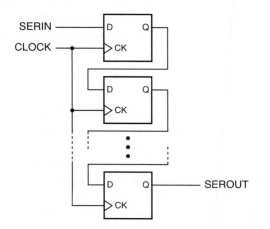

Figure 8-37
Structure of a
serial-in, serial-out
shift register.

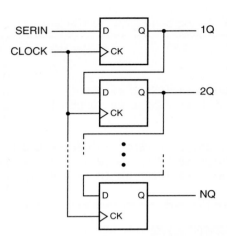

Figure 8-38
Structure of a
serial-in, parallel-out
shift register.

serial-in, parallel-out
shift register

serial-to-parallel
conversion

parallel-in, serial-out
shift register

parallel-to-serial
conversion

parallel-in, parallel-out
shift register

SEROUT, after *n* clock ticks, and is lost one tick later. Thus, an *n*-bit serial-in, serial-out shift register can be used to delay a signal by *n* clock ticks.

A *serial-in, parallel-out shift register,* shown in Figure 8-38, has outputs for all of its stored bits, making them available to other circuits. Such a shift register can be used to perform *serial-to-parallel conversion,* as shown in an example in Section XSbb.2 at DDPPonline.

Conversely, it is possible to build a *parallel-in, serial-out shift register.* Figure 8-39 shows the general structure of such a device. At each clock tick the register either loads new data from inputs 1D–ND or it shifts its current contents, depending on the value of the LOAD/SHIFT control input (which could be named LOAD or SHIFT_L). Internally, the device uses a 2-input multiplexer on each flip-flop's D input to select between the two cases. A parallel-in, serial-out shift register can be used to perform *parallel-to-serial conversion*, as shown in Section XSbb.2 at DDPPonline.

By providing outputs for all of the stored bits in a parallel-in shift register, we obtain the *parallel-in, parallel-out shift register* shown in Figure 8-40. Such a device is general enough to be used in any of the applications of the previous shift registers.

8.5.2 MSI Shift Registers

Traditional MSI logic families provide several different 4-bit and 8-bit shift registers, including the variations described in the previous subsections. Several of these parts are described at DDPPonline in Section Sreg. These MSI parts are seldom used nowadays, because any desired, customized shift-register function can be provided in a PLD or FPGA. However, it will be useful to look at just one MSI part, both to get an idea of a complex shift register's detailed internal design, and to have a component to use in subsequent examples.

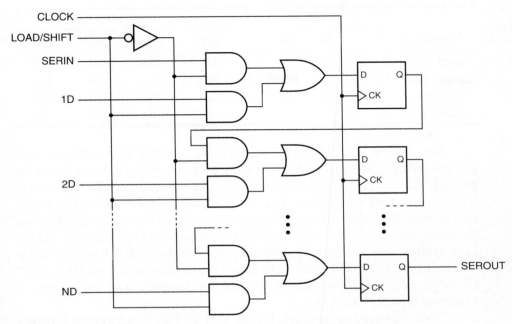

Figure 8-39 Structure of a parallel-in, serial-out shift register.

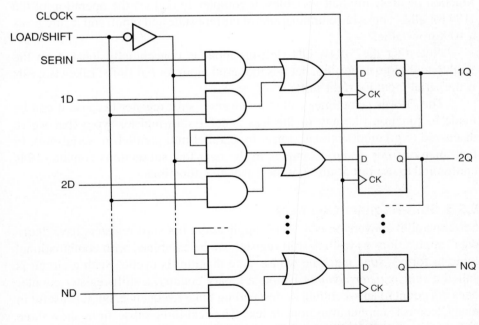

Figure 8-40 Structure of a parallel-in, parallel-out shift register.

Table 8-24
Function table for the
74x194 4-bit universal
shift register.

	Inputs		Next state			
Function	S1	S0	QA*	QB*	QC*	QD*
Hold	0	0	QA	QB	QC	QD
Shift right	0	1	RIN	QA	QB	QC
Shift left	1	0	QB	QC	QD	LIN
Load	1	1	A	B	C	D

74x194

*unidirectional shift
register*

*bidirectional shift
register*

left

right

The *74x194* is an MSI 4-bit bidirectional, parallel-in, parallel-out shift register. Its logic diagram is shown in Figure 8-41. All of the shift registers in the previous subsection are called *unidirectional shift registers* because they shift in only one direction. The '194 is a *bidirectional shift register* because its contents may be shifted in either of two directions, depending on a control input. The two directions are called "left" and "right," even though the logic diagram and the logic symbol aren't necessarily drawn that way. In the '194, *left* means "in the direction from QD to QA," and *right* means "in the direction from QA to QD." Our logic diagram and symbol for the '194 are consistent with these names if you rotate them 90° clockwise.

Table 8-24 is a function table for the 74x194. This function table is highly compressed, since it does not contain columns for most of the inputs (A–D, RIN, LIN) or the current state QA–QD. Still, by expressing each next-state value as a function of these implicit variables, it completely defines the operation of the '194 for all 2^{12} possible combinations of current state and input, and it sure beats a 4096-row table!

Note that the '194's LIN (left-in) input is conceptually located on the "righthand" side of the chip, but it is the serial input for *left* shifts. Likewise, RIN is the serial input for right shifts.

The '194 is sometimes called a *universal* shift register because it can be made to function like any of the less general shift-register types that we've discussed (e.g., unidirectional; serial-in, parallel-out; parallel-in, serial-out). In fact, many of our design examples in the next few subsections contain '194s configured to use just a subset of their available functions.

8.5.3 Shift-Register Counters

shift-register counter

Serial/parallel conversion is a "data" application, but shift registers have "non-data" applications as well. A shift register can be combined with combinational logic to form a state machine whose state diagram is cyclic. Such a circuit is called a *shift-register counter*. Unlike a binary counter, a shift-register counter does not count in an ascending or descending binary sequence, but it is useful in many "control" applications nonetheless. The next three subsections show three different ways to build shift-register counters. Each approach yields a different kind of counting sequence with its own particular advantages.

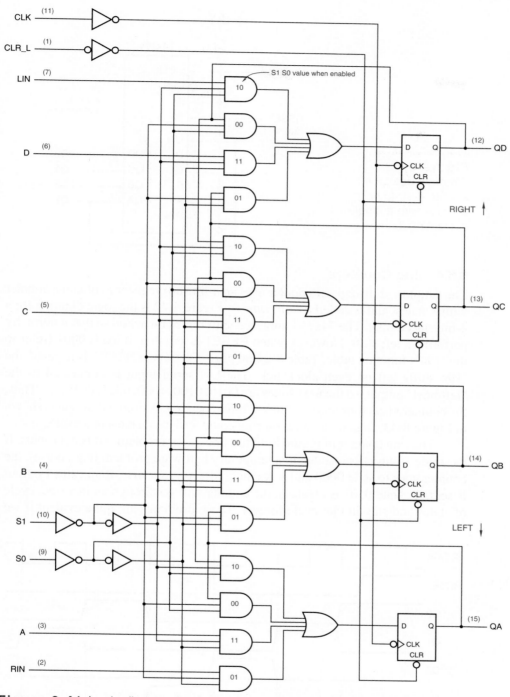

Figure 8-41 Logic diagram for the 74x194 4-bit universal shift register, including pin numbers for a standard 16-pin dual in-line package.

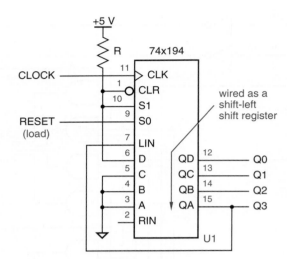

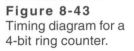

Figure 8-42
Simplest design for a 4-bit, 4-state ring counter with a single circulating 1.

8.5.4 Ring Counters

ring counter

The simplest shift-register counter uses an n-bit shift register to obtain a counter with n states, and is called a *ring counter*. Figure 8-42 is the logic diagram for a 4-bit ring counter. The 74x194 universal shift register is wired so that it normally performs a left shift. However, when RESET is asserted, it loads 0001 (refer to the '194's function table, Table 8-24 on page 730). Once RESET is negated, the '194 shifts left on each clock tick. The LIN serial input is connected to the "leftmost" output, so the next states are 0010, 0100, 1000, 0001, 0010, ... Thus, the counter visits four unique states before repeating. A timing diagram is shown in Figure 8-43. In general, an n-bit ring counter visits n states in a cycle.

The ring counter in Figure 8-42 has one major problem—it is not robust. If its single 1 output is lost due to a temporary hardware problem (e.g., noise), the counter goes to state 0000 and stays there forever. Likewise, if an extra 1 output is set (i.e., state 0101 is created), the counter will go through an incorrect cycle of states and stay in that cycle forever. These problems are quite evident if we

Figure 8-43
Timing diagram for a 4-bit ring counter.

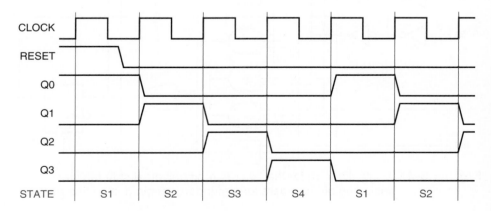

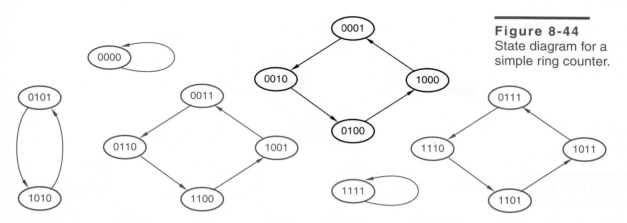

Figure 8-44
State diagram for a
simple ring counter.

draw the *complete* state diagram for the counter circuit, which has 16 states. As shown in Figure 8-44, there are 12 states that are not part of the normal counting cycle. If the counter somehow gets off the normal cycle, it stays off it.

A *self-correcting counter* is designed so that all abnormal states have transitions leading to normal states. Self-correcting counters are desirable for the same reason that we use a minimal-risk approach to state assignment in Section 7.4.3: if something unexpected happens, a counter or state machine should go to a "safe" state.

self-correcting counter

A *self-correcting ring counter* circuit is shown in Figure 8-45. The circuit uses a NOR gate to shift a 1 into LIN only when the three least significant bits are 0. This results in the state diagram in Figure 8-46; all abnormal states lead back into the normal cycle. Notice that, in this circuit, an explicit RESET signal is not necessarily required. Regardless of the initial state of the shift register on power-

self-correcting ring counter

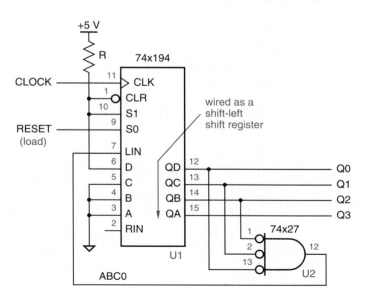

Figure 8-45
Self-correcting 4-bit,
4-state ring counter
with a single
circulating 1.

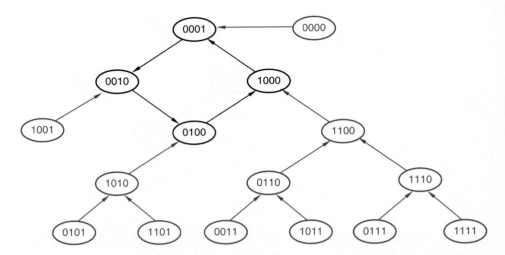

Figure 8-46
State diagram for a
self-correcting ring
counter.

up, it reaches state 0001 within four clock ticks. However, an explicit reset signal
should still normally be provided as shown. This ensures that the counter starts
up at the same clock tick with other devices in the system and also provides a
known starting point in simulation.

In the general case, an n-bit self-correcting ring counter uses an $(n-1)$-
input NOR gate and corrects an abnormal state within $n - 1$ clock ticks.

In CMOS and TTL logic families, wide NAND gates are generally easier to
come by than NORs, so it may be more convenient to design a self-correcting
ring counter as shown in Figure 8-47. States in this counter's normal cycle have
a single circulating 0. This is also useful, of course, if the application requires a
single active-low output signal in each state.

Figure 8-47
Self-correcting
4-bit, 4-state ring
counter with a single
circulating 0.

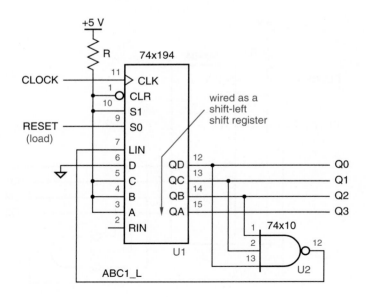

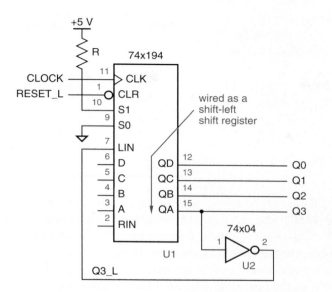

Figure 8-48
Basic 4-bit, 8-state
Johnson counter.

The major appeal of a ring counter for control applications is that its states appear in 1-out-of-*n* decoded form directly on the flip-flop outputs. That is, exactly one flip-flop output is asserted in each state. Furthermore, these outputs are "glitch free"; compare with the binary counter and decoder approach of Figure 8-33 on page 717.

*8.5.5 Johnson Counters

An *n*-bit shift register with the complement of the serial output fed back into the serial input is a counter with *2n* states and is called a *twisted-ring*, *Moebius*, or *Johnson counter*. Figure 8-48 is the basic circuit for a Johnson counter and Figure 8-49 is its timing diagram. The normal states of this counter are listed in Table 8-25. If both the true and complemented outputs of each flip-flop are

twisted-ring counter
Moebius counter
Johnson counter

Figure 8-49 Timing diagram for a 4-bit Johnson counter.

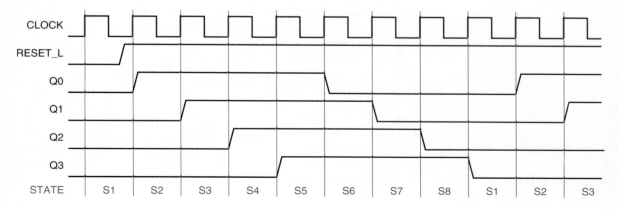

Table 8-25
States of a 4-bit
Johnson counter.

State Name	Q3	Q2	Q1	Q0	Decoding
S1	0	0	0	0	Q3' · Q0'
S2	0	0	0	1	Q1' · Q0
S3	0	0	1	1	Q2' · Q1
S4	0	1	1	1	Q3' · Q2
S5	1	1	1	1	Q3 · Q0
S6	1	1	1	0	Q1 · Q0'
S7	1	1	0	0	Q2 · Q1'
S8	1	0	0	0	Q3 · Q2'

available, each normal state of the counter can be decoded with a 2-input AND or NAND gate, as shown in the table. The decoded outputs are glitch free.

An n-bit Johnson counter has $2^n - 2n$ abnormal states and is therefore *self-correcting Johnson* subject to the same robustness problems as a ring counter. A 4-bit *self-correcting* *counter* *Johnson counter* can be designed as shown in Figure 8-50. This circuit loads 0001 as the next state whenever the current state is 0xx0. A similar circuit using a single 2-input NOR gate can perform correction for a Johnson counter with any number of bits. The correction circuit must load 00...01 as the next state whenever the current state is 0x...x0.

Figure 8-50
Self-correcting
4-bit, 8-state
Johnson counter.

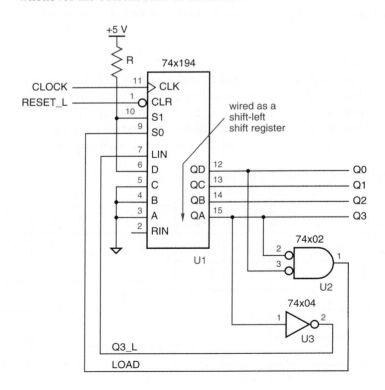

THE SELF-CORRECTION CIRCUIT IS ITSELF CORRECT!	We can prove that the Johnson-counter self-correction circuit corrects any abnormal state as follows. An abnormal state can always be written in the form x...x10x...x, since the only states that can't be written in this form are normal states (00...00, 11...11, 01...1, 0...01...1, and 0...01). Therefore, within $n-2$ clock ticks, the shift register will contain 10x...x. One tick later it will contain 0x...x0, and one tick after that the normal state 00...01 will be loaded.

*8.5.6 Linear Feedback Shift-Register Counters

The n-bit shift register counters that we've shown so far have far less than the maximum of 2^n normal states. An n-bit *linear feedback shift-register (LFSR) counter* can have $2^n - 1$ states, almost the maximum. Such a counter is often called a *maximum-length sequence generator*.

maximum-length sequence generator

The design of LFSR counters is based on the theory of *finite fields,* which was developed by French mathematician Évariste Galois (1811–1832) shortly before he was killed in a duel with a political opponent. The operation of an LFSR counter corresponds to operations in a finite field with 2^n elements.

finite fields

Figure 8-51 shows the structure of an n-bit LFSR counter. The shift register's serial input is connected to the sum modulo 2 of a certain set of output bits. These feedback connections determine the state sequence of the counter. By convention, outputs are always numbered and shifted in the direction shown.

Using finite-field theory, it can be shown that for any value of n, there exists at least one feedback equation that makes the counter go through all $2^n - 1$ nonzero states before repeating. This is called a *maximum-length sequence.*

maximum-length sequence

Figure 8-51 General structure of a linear feedback shift-register counter.

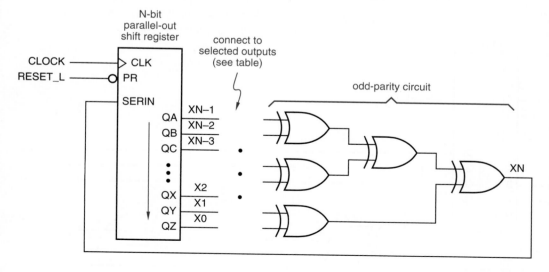

Table 8-26
Feedback equations
for linear feedback
shift-register counters.

n	Feedback Equation
2	$X2 = X1 \oplus X0$
3	$X3 = X1 \oplus X0$
4	$X4 = X1 \oplus X0$
5	$X5 = X2 \oplus X0$
6	$X6 = X1 \oplus X0$
7	$X7 = X3 \oplus X0$
8	$X8 = X4 \oplus X3 \oplus X2 \oplus X0$
12	$X12 = X6 \oplus X4 \oplus X1 \oplus X0$
16	$X16 = X5 \oplus X4 \oplus X3 \oplus X0$
20	$X20 = X3 \oplus X0$
24	$X24 = X7 \oplus X2 \oplus X1 \oplus X0$
28	$X28 = X3 \oplus X0$
32	$X32 = X22 \oplus X2 \oplus X1 \oplus X0$

Table 8-26 lists feedback equations that yield maximum-length sequences for selected values of *n*. For each value of *n* greater than 3, there are many other feedback equations that result in maximum-length sequences, all different.

An LFSR counter designed according to Figure 8-51 can never cycle through all 2^n possible states. Regardless of the connection pattern, the next state for the all-0s state is the same—all 0s.

The logic diagram for a 3-bit LFSR counter is shown in Figure 8-52. The state sequence for this counter is shown in the first three columns of Table 8-27. Starting in any nonzero state, 100 in the table, the counter visits seven states before returning to the starting state.

Figure 8-52 A 3-bit LFSR counter; modifications to include the all-0s state are shown in color.

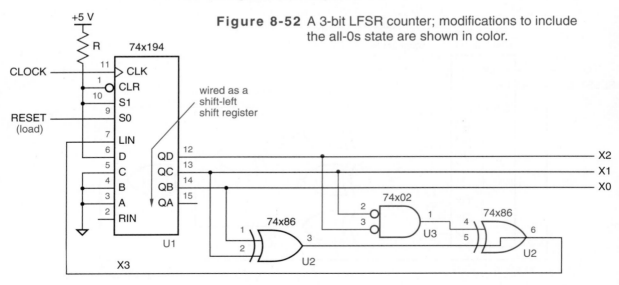

Original Sequence			Modified Sequence		
X2	**X1**	**X0**	**X2**	**X1**	**X0**
1	0	0	1	0	0
0	1	0	0	1	0
1	0	1	1	0	1
1	1	0	1	1	0
1	1	1	1	1	1
0	1	1	0	1	1
0	0	1	0	0	1
1	0	0	0	0	0
.	.	.	1	0	0
.	.	.	.	.	.
.	.	.	.	.	.

Table 8-27
State sequences for the 3-bit LFSR counter in Figure 8-52.

An LFSR counter can be modified to have 2^n states, including the all-0s state, as shown in color for the 3-bit counter in Figure 8-52. The resulting state sequence is given in the last three columns of Table 8-27. In an n-bit LFSR counter, an extra XOR gate and an $n - 1$ input NOR gate connected to all shift-register outputs except X0 accomplishes the same thing.

WORKING IN THE FIELD

A finite field has a finite number of elements and two operators, addition and multiplication, that satisfy certain properties. An example of a finite field with P elements, where P is any prime, is the set of integers modulo P. The operators in this field are addition and multiplication modulo P.

According to finite-field theory, if you start with a nonzero element E and repeatedly multiply by a "primitive" element α, after $P - 2$ steps you will generate the rest of the field's nonzero elements in the field before getting back to E. It turns out that in a field with P elements, any integer in the range 2, ..., $P - 1$ is primitive. You can try this yourself using $P = 7$ and $\alpha = 2$, for example. The elements of the field are 0, 1, ..., 6, and the operations are addition and subtraction modulo 7.

The paragraph above gives the basic idea behind maximum-length sequence generators. However, to apply them to a digital circuit, you need a field with 2^n elements, where n is the number of bits required by the application. On one hand, we're in luck, because Galois proved that there exist finite fields with P^n elements for any integer n, as long as P is prime, including $P = 2$. On the other hand, we're out of luck, because when $n > 1$, the operators in fields with P^n (including 2^n) elements are quite different from ordinary integer addition and multiplication. Also, primitive elements are harder to find.

If you enjoy math, as I do, you'd probably be fascinated by the finite-field theory that leads to the LFSR circuits for maximum-length sequence generators and other applications; see the References. Otherwise, you can confidently follow the "cookbook" approach in this section.

The states of an LFSR counter are not visited in binary counting order. However, LFSR counters are typically used in applications where this characteristic is an advantage. A major application of LFSR counters is in generating test inputs for logic circuits. In most cases, the "pseudorandom" counting sequence of an LFSR counter is more likely than a binary counting sequence to detect errors. LFSRs are also used in the encoding and decoding circuits for certain error-detecting and error-correcting codes, including CRC codes, which we introduced in Section 2.15.4.

In data communications, LFSR counters are often used to "scramble" and "descramble" the data patterns transmitted by high-speed modems and network interfaces, including 100-Mbps Ethernet. This is done by XORing the LFSR's output with the user data stream. Even when the user data stream contains a long run of 0s or 1s, combining it with the LFSR's pseudorandom output improves the DC balance of the transmitted signal and creates a rich set of transitions that allows clocking information to be recovered more easily at the receiver.

8.5.7 Shift Registers in ABEL and PLDs

General-purpose shift registers can be specified quite easily in ABEL and fit nicely into typical sequential PLDs. For example, Figure 8-53 and Table 8-28 show how to realize a function similar to that of a 74x194 universal shift register using a 16V8. Notice that one of the I/O pins of the 16V8, pin 12, is used as an input.

The 16V8 realization of the '194 differs from the real thing in just one way—in the function of the CLR_L input. In the real '194, CLR_L is an asynchronous input, while in the 16V8 it is sampled along with other inputs at the rising edge of CLK.

If you really need to provide an asynchronous clear input, you can use the 22V10, which provides a single product line to control the reset inputs of all

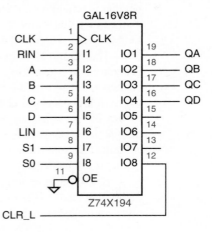

Figure 8-53
PLD realizations of a
74x194-like universal
shift register with
synchronous clear.

Table 8-28 ABEL program for a 4-bit universal shift register.

```
module Z74x194
title '4-bit Universal Shift Register'
Z74X194 device 'P16V8R';

" Input and output pins
CLK, RIN, A, B, C, D, LIN          pin 1, 2, 3, 4, 5, 6, 7;
S1, S0, CLR_L                      pin 8, 9, 12;
QA, QB, QC, QD                     pin 19, 18, 17, 16 istype 'reg';

" Active-level translation
CLR = !CLR_L;

" Set definitions
INPUT   = [ A,  B,   C, D  ];
LEFTIN  = [ QB, QC, QD, LIN];
RIGHTIN = [RIN, QA, QB, QC ];
OUT     = [ QA, QB, QC, QD ];

CTRL  = [S1,S0];
HOLD  = (CTRL == [0,0]);
RIGHT = (CTRL == [0,1]);
LEFT  = (CTRL == [1,0]);
LOAD  = (CTRL == [1,1]);

equations
OUT.CLK = CLK;

OUT := !CLR & (
          HOLD & OUT
        # RIGHT & RIGHTIN
        # LEFT & LEFTIN
        # LOAD & INPUT);

end Z74x194
```

of its flip-flops. This requires only a few changes in the original program (see Exercise 8.70).

The flexibility of ABEL can be used to create shift-register circuits with more or different functionality. For example, Table 8-29 on the next page defines an 8-bit shift register that can be cleared, loaded with a single 1 in any bit position, shifted left, shifted right, or held. The operation to be performed at each clock tick is specified by a 4-bit operation code, OP[3:0]. Despite the large number of "when" cases, the circuit can be synthesized with only five product terms per output.

■   **Table 8-29** ABEL program for a multi-function shift register.

```
module shifty
title '8-bit shift register with decoded load'

" Inputs and Outputs
CLK, OP3..OP0                pin;
Q7..Q0                       pin istype 'reg';

" Definitions
Q = [Q7..Q0];
OP = [OP3..OP0];
HOLD = (OP == 0);
CLEAR = (OP == 1);
LEFT = (OP == 2);
RIGHT = (OP == 3);
NOP = (OP >= 4) & (OP < 8);
LOADQ0 = (OP == 8);
LOADQ1 = (OP == 9);
LOADQ2 = (OP == 10);
LOADQ3 = (OP == 11);
LOADQ4 = (OP == 12);
LOADQ5 = (OP == 13);
LOADQ6 = (OP == 14);
LOADQ7 = (OP == 15);

equations

Q.CLK = CLK;
when HOLD then Q := Q;
else when CLEAR then Q := 0;
else when LEFT then Q := [Q6..Q0, Q7];
else when RIGHT then Q := [Q0, Q7..Q1];
else when LOADQ0 then Q := 1;
else when LOADQ1 then Q := 2;
else when LOADQ2 then Q := 4;
else when LOADQ3 then Q := 8;
else when LOADQ4 then Q := 16;
else when LOADQ5 then Q := 32;
else when LOADQ6 then Q := 64;
else when LOADQ7 then Q := 128;
else Q := Q;

end shifty
```

ABEL can be used readily to specify shift register counters of the various types that we introduced in previous subsections. For example, Table 8-30 is the program for an 8-bit ring counter. We've used the extra capability of the PLD to add two functions not present in our previous MSI designs: counting occurs only if CNTEN is asserted, and the next state is forced to S0 if RESTART is asserted.

Table 8-30 ABEL program for an 8-bit ring counter.

```
module Ring8
title '8-bit Ring Counter'

" Inputs and Outputs
MCLK, CNTEN, RESTART            pin;
S0..S7                         pin istype 'reg';

equations

[S0..S7].CLK = MCLK;

S0 := CNTEN & !S0 & !S1 & !S2 & !S3 & !S4 & !S5 & !S6   " Self-sync
    # !CNTEN & S0                                        " Hold
    # RESTART;                                           " Start with one 1
[S1..S7] := !RESTART & ( !CNTEN & [S1..S7]       " Hold
                        # CNTEN & [S0..S6] );    " Shift
end Ring8
```

Ring counters are often used to generate multiphase clocks or enable signals in digital systems, and the requirements in different systems are many and varied. The ability to reprogram the counter's behavior easily is a distinct advantage of an HDL-based design.

Figure 8-54 shows a set of clock or enable signals that might be required in a digital system with six distinct phases of operation. Each phase lasts for two ticks of a master clock signal, MCLK, during which the corresponding active-low phase-enable signal Pi_L is asserted. We can obtain this sort of timing from a

Figure 8-54 Six-phase timing waveforms required in a certain digital system.

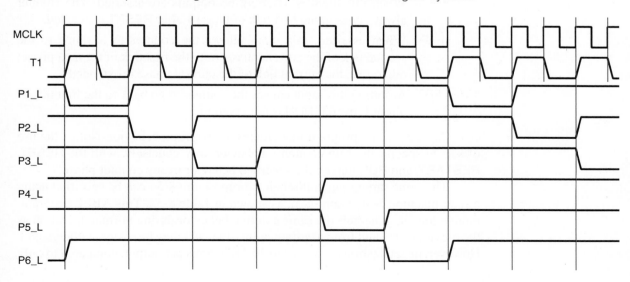

Table 8-31 ABEL program for a six-phase waveform generator.

```
module TIMEGEN6
title 'Six-phase Master Timing Generator'

" Input and Output pins
MCLK, RESET, RUN, RESTART                    pin;
T1, P1_L, P2_L, P3_L, P4_L, P5_L, P6_L      pin istype 'reg';

" State definitions
PHASES = [P1_L, P2_L, P3_L, P4_L, P5_L, P6_L];
NEXTPH = [P6_L, P1_L, P2_L, P3_L, P4_L, P5_L];
SRESET = [1, 1, 1, 1, 1, 1];
P1 =     [0, 1, 1, 1, 1, 1];

equations
T1.CLK = MCLK; PHASES.CLK = MCLK;

when RESET then {T1 := 1; PHASES := SRESET;}
else when (PHASES==SRESET) # RESTART then {T1 := 1; PHASES := P1;}
else when RUN & T1 then {T1 := 0; PHASES := PHASES;}
else when RUN & !T1 then {T1 := 1; PHASES := NEXTPH;}
else {T1 := T1; PHASES := PHASES;}

end TIMEGEN6
```

ring counter if we provide an extra flip-flop to count the two ticks of each phase, so that a shift occurs on the *second* tick of each phase.

The timing generator can be built with a few inputs and outputs of a PLD. Three control inputs are provided, with the following behavior:

RESET When this input is asserted, no outputs are asserted. The counter always goes to the first tick of phase 1 after RESET is negated.

RUN When asserted, this input allows the counter to advance to the second tick of the current phase, or to the first tick of the next phase; otherwise, the current tick of the current phase is extended.

RESTART Asserting this input causes the counter to go back to the first tick of phase 1, even if RUN is not asserted.

Table 8-31 is a program that creates the required behavior. Notice the use of sets to specify the ring counter's behavior very concisely, with the RESET, RESTART, and RUN having the specified behavior in any counter phase.

The same timing-generator behavior in Figure 8-54 can be specified using a state-machine design approach, as shown in Table 8-32. This ABEL program, though longer, generates the same external behavior during normal operation as the previous one, and from a certain point of view it may be easier to understand. However, its realization requires 8 to 20 AND terms per output, compared to only

Table 8-32 Alternate ABEL program for the waveform generator.

```
module TIMEGN6A
title 'Six-phase Master Timing Generator'

" Input and Output pins
MCLK, RESET, RUN, RESTART                     pin;
T1, P1_L, P2_L, P3_L, P4_L, P5_L, P6_L        pin istype 'reg';

" State definitions
TSTATE = [T1, P1_L, P2_L, P3_L, P4_L, P5_L, P6_L];
SRESET = [1, 1, 1, 1, 1, 1, 1];
P1F =    [1, 0, 1, 1, 1, 1, 1];
P1S =    [0, 0, 1, 1, 1, 1, 1];
P2F =    [1, 1, 0, 1, 1, 1, 1];
P2S =    [0, 1, 0, 1, 1, 1, 1];
P3F =    [1, 1, 1, 0, 1, 1, 1];
P3S =    [0, 1, 1, 0, 1, 1, 1];
P4F =    [1, 1, 1, 1, 0, 1, 1];
P4S =    [0, 1, 1, 1, 0, 1, 1];
P5F =    [1, 1, 1, 1, 1, 0, 1];
P5S =    [0, 1, 1, 1, 1, 0, 1];
P6F =    [1, 1, 1, 1, 1, 1, 0];
P6S =    [0, 1, 1, 1, 1, 1, 0];

equations
TSTATE.CLK = MCLK;
when RESET then TSTATE := SRESET;

state_diagram TSTATE

state SRESET: if RESET then SRESET else P1F;

state P1F: if RESET then SRESET else if RESTART then P1F
           else if RUN then P1S else P1F;

state P1S: if RESET then SRESET else if RESTART then P1F
           else if RUN then P2F else P1S;

" States P2F through P5F are defined similarly
" ...

state P6F: if RESET then SRESET else if RESTART then P1F
           else if RUN then P6S else P6F;

state P6S: if RESET then SRESET else if RESTART then P1F
           else if RUN then P1F else P6S;

end TIMEGN6A
```

RELIABLE RESET   Notice in Table 8-32 that TSTATE is assigned a value in the equations section of the program, as well as being used in the state_diagram section. This was done for a very specific purpose, to ensure that the program goes to the SRESET state from any undefined state, as explained below.

ABEL augments the on-set for an output each time the output appears on the lefthand side of an equation, as we explained for combinational outputs on page 248. In the case of registered outputs, ABEL also augments the on-set of each state variable in the state vector for each "state" definition in a state_diagram. For each state-variable output, all of the input combinations that cause that output to be 1 in each state are added to the output's on-set.

The state machine in Table 8-32 has 2^7 or 128 states in total, of which only 13 are explicitly defined and have a transition into SRESET. Nevertheless, the when equation ensures that anytime that RESET is asserted, the machine goes to the SRESET state. This is true regardless of the state definitions in the state_diagram. When RESET is asserted, the all-1s state encoding of SRESET is, in effect, ORed with the next state, if any, specified by the state_diagram. This approach to reliable reset would not be possible if SRESET were encoded as all 0s, for example.

3 to 5 per output for the original ring-counter version. This is a good example of how you can improve circuit efficiency and performance by adapting a standard, simple structure to a "custom" design problem, rather than grinding out a brute-force state machine.

Now let's look at a variation of the previous timing waveforms that might be required in a different system. Figure 8-55 is similar to the previous waveforms, except that each phase output Ri_L is asserted for only one clock tick per phase. This change has a subtle but important effect on the design approach.

In the original design, we used a 6-bit ring counter and one auxiliary state bit T1 to keep track of the two states within each phase. With the new waveforms this is not possible. In the states between active-low pulses (STATE = 0, 2, 4, etc. in Figure 8-55) the phase outputs are all negated, so they can no longer be used to figure out which state should be visited next. Something else is needed to keep track of the state.

There are many different ways to solve this problem. One idea is to start with the original design in Table 8-31 but use the phase outputs P1_L, P2_L, and so on as internal states only. Then, each phase output Ri_L can be defined as a Moore-type combinational output that is asserted when the corresponding Pi_L is asserted *and* we are in the second tick of a phase. The additional ABEL code to support this first approach is shown in Table 8-33.

This first approach is easy, and it works just fine if the Ri_L signals are going to be used only as enables or other control inputs. However, it's a bad idea

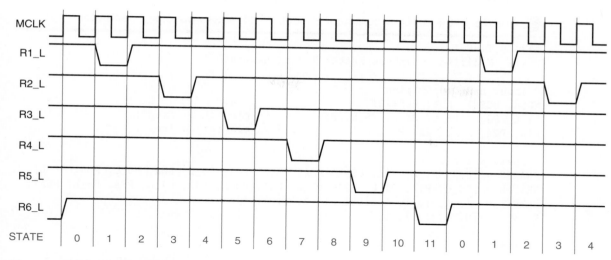

Figure 8-55 Modified timing waveforms for a digital system.

Table 8-33 Additions to Table 8-31 for a modified six-phase waveform generator.

```
module TIMEG12K
...
R1_L, R2_L, R3_L, R4_L, R5_L, R6_L          pin istype 'com';
...
OUTPUTS = [R1_L, R2_L, R3_L, R4_L, R5_L, R6_L];

equations
...
!OUTPUTS = !PHASES & !T1;

end TIMEG12K
```

if these signals are going to be used as clocks, because they may have glitches, as
we'll now explain. The Pi_L and T1 signals are all outputs from flip-flops
clocked by the same master clock MCLK. Although these signals change at
approximately the same time, their timing is never quite exact. One output may
change sooner than another; this is called *output timing skew*. For example,   *output timing skew*
suppose that on the transition from state 1 to 2 in Figure 8-54, P2_L goes LOW
before T1 goes HIGH. In this case, a short glitch could appear on the R2_L
output.

To get glitch-free outputs, we should design the circuit so that each phase
output is a registered output. One way to do this is to build a 12-bit ring counter
and use only alternate outputs to yield the desired waveforms; an ABEL
program using this approach is shown in Table 8-34 on the next page.

■ Table 8-34 ABEL program for a modified six-phase waveform generator.

```
module TIMEG12
title 'Modified six-phase Master Timing Generator'

" Input and Output pins
MCLK, RESET, RUN, RESTART                 pin;
P1_L, P2_L, P3_L, P4_L, P5_L, P6_L        pin istype 'reg';
P1A, P2A, P3A, P4A, P5A, P6A              pin istype 'reg';

" State definitions
PHASES = [P1A, P1_L, P2A, P2_L, P3A, P3_L, P4A, P4_L, P5A, P5_L, P6A, P6_L];
NEXTPH = [P6_L, P1A, P1_L, P2A, P2_L, P3A, P3_L, P4A, P4_L, P5A, P5_L, P6A];
SRESET = [1,  1,  1,  1,  1,  1,  1,  1,  1,  1,  1,  1];
P1 =     [0,  1,  1,  1,  1,  1,  1,  1,  1,  1,  1,  1];

equations

PHASES.CLK = MCLK;

when RESET then PHASES := SRESET;
else when RESTART # (PHASES == SRESET) then PHASES := P1;
else when RUN then PHASES := NEXTPH;
else PHASES := PHASES;

end TIMEG12
```

Still another approach is to recognize that, since the waveforms cycle through 12 states, we can build a modulo-12 binary counter and decode the states of that counter. An ABEL program using this approach is shown in Table 8-35. The states of the counter correspond to the "STATE" values shown in Figure 8-55. Since the phase outputs are registered, they are glitch free. Note that they are decoded one cycle early, to account for the one-tick decoding delay. Also, during reset, the counter is forced to state 15 rather than 0, so that the P1_L output is not asserted during reset.

8.5.8 Shift Registers in VHDL

Shift registers can be specified structurally or behaviorally in VHDL; we'll look at a few behavioral descriptions and applications. Table 8-36 is the function table for an 8-bit shift register with an extended set of functions. In addition to the hold, load, and shift functions of the 74x194, it performs circular and arith-

circular shift
arithmetic shift

metic shift operations. In the *circular shift* operations, the bit that "falls off" one end during a shift is fed back into the other end. In the *arithmetic shift* operations, the edge input is set up for multiplication or division by 2; for a left shift, the right input is 0, and for a right shift, the leftmost (sign) bit is replicated.

Table 8-35 Counter-based program for a six-phase waveform generator.

```
module TIMEG12A
title 'Counter-based six-phase master timing generator'

" Input and Output pins
MCLK, RESET, RUN, RESTART              pin;
P1_L, P2_L, P3_L, P4_L, P5_L, P6_L    pin istype 'reg';
CNT3..CNT0                            pin istype 'reg';

" Definitions
CNT = [CNT3..CNT0];
P_L = [P1_L, P2_L, P3_L, P4_L, P5_L, P6_L];

equations

CNT.CLK = MCLK;  P_L.CLK = MCLK;

when RESET then CNT := 15
else when RESTART then CNT := 0
else when (RUN & (CNT < 11)) then CNT := CNT + 1
else when RUN then CNT := 0
else CNT := CNT;

P1_L := !(CNT == 0);
P2_L := !(CNT == 2);
P3_L := !(CNT == 4);
P4_L := !(CNT == 6);
P5_L := !(CNT == 8);
P6_L := !(CNT == 10);

end TIMEG12A
```

Table 8-36 Function table for an extended-function 8-bit shift register.

Function	Inputs			Next state							
	S2	S1	S0	Q7*	Q6*	Q5*	Q4*	Q3*	Q2*	Q1*	Q0*
Hold	0	0	0	Q7	Q6	Q5	Q4	Q3	Q2	Q1	Q0
Load	0	0	1	D7	D6	D5	D4	D3	D2	D1	D0
Shift right	0	1	0	RIN	Q7	Q6	Q5	Q4	Q3	Q2	Q1
Shift left	0	1	1	Q6	Q5	Q4	Q3	Q2	Q1	Q0	LIN
Shift circular right	1	0	0	Q0	Q7	Q6	Q5	Q4	Q3	Q2	Q1
Shift circular left	1	0	1	Q6	Q5	Q4	Q3	Q2	Q1	Q0	Q7
Shift arithmetic right	1	1	0	Q7	Q7	Q6	Q5	Q4	Q3	Q2	Q1
Shift arithmetic left	1	1	1	Q6	Q5	Q4	Q3	Q2	Q1	Q0	0

Table 8-37 VHDL code for an extended-function 8-bit shift register.

```
entity Vshftreg is
    port (
        CLK, CLR, RIN, LIN: in STD_LOGIC;
        S: in STD_LOGIC_VECTOR (2 downto 0); -- function select
        D: in STD_LOGIC_VECTOR (7 downto 0); -- data in
        Q: out STD_LOGIC_VECTOR (7 downto 0) -- data out
    );
end Vshftreg;

architecture Vshftreg_arch of Vshftreg is
signal IQ: STD_LOGIC_VECTOR (7 downto 0);
begin
process (CLK, CLR, IQ)
  begin
    if (CLR='1') then IQ <= (others=>'0'); -- Asynchronous clear
    elsif (CLK'event and CLK='1') then
      case CONV_INTEGER(S) is
        when 0 => null;                        -- Hold
        when 1 => IQ <= D;                     -- Load
        when 2 => IQ <= RIN & IQ(7 downto 1);  -- Shift right
        when 3 => IQ <= IQ(6 downto 0) & LIN;  -- Shift left
        when 4 => IQ <= IQ(0) & IQ(7 downto 1); -- Shift circular right
        when 5 => IQ <= IQ(6 downto 0) & IQ(7); -- Shift circular left
        when 6 => IQ <= IQ(7) & IQ(7 downto 1); -- Shift arithmetic right
        when 7 => IQ <= IQ(6 downto 0) & '0';  -- Shift arithmetic left
        when others => null;
      end case;
    end if;
    Q <= IQ;
  end process;
end Vshftreg_arch;
```

A behavioral VHDL program for the extended-function shift register is shown in Table 8-37. As usual, we define a process and use the event attribute on CLK to get edge-triggered behavior. Several other features are worth noting:

- An internal signal, IQ, is used for what eventually becomes the Q output, so it can be both read and written by process statements. Alternatively, we could have defined the Q output as type "buffer."

- The CLR input is asynchronous; because it's in the process sensitivity list, it is tested whenever it changes. And the if statement is structured so that CLR takes precedence over any other condition.

- A CASE statement is used to define the operation of the shift register for the eight possible values of the select inputs S(2 downto 0).

- In the CASE statement, the "when others" case is required to prevent the compiler from complaining about approximately 2^{32} uncovered cases!

- The "null" statement indicates that no action is taken in certain cases. In case 1, note that no action is required; the default is for a signal to hold its value unless otherwise stated.

- In most of the cases the concatenation operator "&" is used to construct an 8-bit array from a 7-bit subset of IQ and one other bit.

- Because of VHDL's strong requirements for type matching, we used the CONV_INTEGER function that we defined in Section 5.3.3 to convert the STD_LOGIC_VECTOR select input S to an integer in the CASE statement. Alternatively, we could have written each case label as a STD_LOGIC_VECTOR (e.g., "011" instead of integer 3).

One application of shift registers is in ring counters, as in the six-phase waveform generator that we described starting on page 743 with the waveforms in Figure 8-54. A VHDL program that provides the corresponding behavior is shown in Table 8-38. As in the previous VHDL example, an internal active-high signal vector, IP, is used for reading and writing what eventually becomes the circuit's output; this internal signal is conveniently inverted in the last statement to obtain the required active-low output signal vector. The rest of the program is straightforward, but notice that it has three levels of nested if statements.

Table 8-38 VHDL code for a six-phase waveform generator.

```
entity Vtimegn6 is
    port (
        MCLK, RESET, RUN, RESTART: in STD_LOGIC;  -- clock, control inputs
        P_L: out STD_LOGIC_VECTOR (1 to 6) );     -- active-low phase outputs
end Vtimegn6;

architecture Vtimegn6_arch of Vtimegn6 is
signal IP: STD_LOGIC_VECTOR (1 to 6); -- internal active-high phase signals
signal T1: STD_LOGIC;                 -- first tick within phase
begin
process (MCLK, IP)
  begin
    if (MCLK'event and MCLK='1') then
      if (RESET='1') then
        T1 <= '1'; IP <= ('0','0','0','0','0','0');
      elsif ((IP=('0','0','0','0','0','0')) or (RESTART='1')) then
        T1 <= '1'; IP <= ('1','0','0','0','0','0');
      elsif (RUN='1') then
        T1 <= not T1;
        if (T1='0') then IP <= IP(6) & IP(1 to 5); end if;
      end if;
    end if;
    P_L <= not IP;
  end process;
end Vtimegn6_arch;
```

NEXTP(1 to 6)

IP(1 to 6)
(P_L <= not IP)

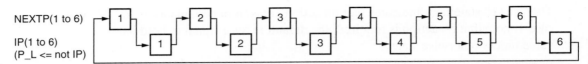

Figure 8-56 Shifting sequence for waveform generator 12-bit ring counter.

A possible modification to the preceding application is to produce output waveforms that are asserted only during the second tick of each two-tick phase; such waveforms were shown in Figure 8-55 on page 747. One way to do this is to create a 12-bit ring counter and use only alternate outputs. In the VHDL realization only the six phase outputs, P_L(1 to 6), would appear in the entity definition. The additional six signals, which we name NEXTP(1 to 6), are local to the architecture definition. Figure 8-56 shows the relationship of these signals for shift-register operation, and Table 8-39 is the VHDL program.

As in the previous program, a 6-bit active-high signal, IP, is declared in the architecture body and is used for reading and writing what eventually becomes the circuit's active-low output, P_L. Another signal, NEXTP, holds the remaining six bits of state. Constants IDLE and FIRSTP improve the program's readability.

MEA CULPA, AND A LESSON   Notice in Table 8-39 that a variable, TEMP, was used to temporarily hold the old value of IP during shifting. The program's author worried that in the assignment to NEXTP, the value of IP would already be different from the previous assignment to IP. But he was wrong. Assignments of new values to NEXTP and IP are scheduled, but they are not executed until the process finishes. See Section 5.3.9. The program's author (I) could have just written "IP <= NEXTP; NEXTP <= IP(6) & IP(1 to 5);". Either way, a synthesis tool creates exactly the same circuit realization.

8.5.9 Shift Registers in Verilog

It's easy to descibe shift registers behaviorally in Verilog; we'll look at a few different shift-register specifications and applications.

Table 8-36 on page 749 is the function table for an 8-bit shift register with an extended set of functions. In addition to the hold, load, and shift functions of the74x194, it performs circular and arithmetic shift operations as defined on page 748. A behavioral Verilog module for the extended-function shift register is shown in Table 8-40. A few other features of this module are worth noting:

- The CLR input is asynchronous and overrides any other condition.

- A case statement is used to define the operation of the shift register for the eight possible values of the select inputs S[2:0].

- In most of the cases, concatenation "{}" and part-select "[]" are used to construct an 8-bit vector from a 7-bit subset of Q and one other bit.

Table 8-39 VHDL code for a modified six-phase waveform generator.

```
entity Vtimeg12 is
    port (
        MCLK, RESET, RUN, RESTART: in STD_LOGIC; -- clock, control inputs
        P_L: out STD_LOGIC_VECTOR (1 to 6) );    -- active-low phase outputs
end Vtimeg12;

architecture Vtimeg12_arch of Vtimeg12 is
signal IP, NEXTP: STD_LOGIC_VECTOR (1 to 6); -- internal active-high phase signals
begin
process (MCLK, IP, NEXTP)
  variable TEMP: STD_LOGIC_VECTOR (1 to 6);  -- temporary for signal shift
  constant IDLE: STD_LOGIC_VECTOR (1 to 6) := ('0','0','0','0','0','0');
  constant FIRSTP: STD_LOGIC_VECTOR (1 to 6) := ('1','0','0','0','0','0');
  begin
    if (MCLK'event and MCLK='1') then
      if (RESET='1') then IP <= IDLE;  NEXTP <= IDLE;
      elsif (RESTART='1') or (IP=IDLE and NEXTP=IDLE) then IP <= IDLE;  NEXTP <= FIRSTP;
      elsif (RUN='1') then
        if (IP=IDLE) and (NEXTP=IDLE) then NEXTP <= FIRSTP;
        else TEMP := IP;  IP <= NEXTP;  NEXTP <= TEMP(6) & TEMP(1 to 5);
        end if;
      end if;
    end if;
    P_L <= not IP;
  end process;
end Vtimeg12_arch;
```

Table 8-40 Verilog module for an extended-function 8-bit shift register.

```
module Vrshftreg ( CLK, CLR, RIN, LIN, S, D, Q );
  input CLK, CLR, RIN, LIN;
  input [2:0] S;
  input [7:0] D;
  output [7:0] Q;
  reg [7:0] Q;

  always @ (posedge CLK or posedge CLR)
    if (CLR == 1) Q <= 0;
    else case (S)
      0: Q <= Q;                 // Hold
      1: Q <= D;                 // Load
      2: Q <= {RIN, Q[7:1]};     // Shift right
      3: Q <= {Q[6:0], LIN};     // Shift left
      4: Q <= {Q[0], Q[7:1]};    // Shift circular right
      5: Q <= {Q[6:0], Q[7]};    // Shift circular left
      6: Q <= {Q[7], Q[7:1]};    // Shift arithmetic right
      7: Q <= {Q[6:0], 1'b0};    // Shift arithmetic left
      default Q <= 8'bx;         // should not occur
    endcase
endmodule
```

Table 8-41 Verilog module for a six-phase waveform generator.

```
module Vrtimegen6 ( MCLK, RESET, RUN, RESTART, P_L );
  input MCLK, RESET, RUN, RESTART;
  output [1:6] P_L;
  reg [1:6] IP;  // internal active-high phase signals
  reg T1;        // first tick within phase

  always @ (posedge MCLK)
    if (RESET == 1) begin T1 <= 1; IP <= 6'b0; end
    else if ( (IP == 6'b0) || (RESTART == 1) )
      begin T1 <= 1; IP <= 6'b100000; end
    else if (RUN == 1)
      begin T1 <= ~T1; if (T1==0) IP <= {IP[6],IP[1:5]}; end
    else IP <= IP;

  assign P_L = ~IP;  // active-low phase outputs
endmodule
```

One application of shift registers is in ring counters, as in the six-phase waveform generator that we described starting on page 743 with the waveforms in Figure 8-54. A Verilog module that provides the corresponding behavior is shown in Table 8-41. A 6-bit active-high variable, IP, is used for what eventually becomes the circuit's output; this internal signal is inverted by a continuous-assignment statement to produce the required 6-bit active-low output P_L. Like the previous example, this one uses concatenation and part-select operators to specify shifting. The rest of the program is straightforward.

A possible modification to the previous application is to produce output waveforms that are asserted only during the second tick of each two-tick phase; such waveforms were shown in Figure 8-55 on page 747. One way to do this is to create a 12-bit ring counter and use only alternate outputs. As in the previous module, a 6-bit active-high variable, IP, is used for what eventually becomes the circuit's output, P_L. The extra six shift-register bits, named NEXTP[1:6], are interleaved with P_L[1:6] as shown in Figure 8-57. The Verilog module for this scheme is shown in Table 8-42. Parameters IDLE and FIRSTP are defined to improve the program's readability.

Figure 8-57 Shifting sequence for waveform generator 12-bit ring counter.

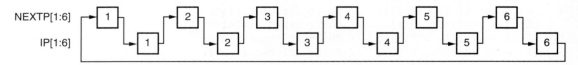

Table 8-42 Verilog module for a modified six-phase waveform generator.

```verilog
module Vrtimegen12 ( MCLK, RESET, RUN, RESTART, P_L );
  input MCLK, RESET, RUN, RESTART;
  output [1:6] P_L;
  reg [1:6] IP;     // internal active-high phase signals
  reg [1:6] NEXTP;  // internal between-phase signals

  parameter IDLE = 6'b0, FIRSTP = 6'b100000;

  always @ (posedge MCLK)
    if (RESET == 1)
      begin IP <= IDLE; NEXTP <= IDLE; end                               // reset case
    else if ( ((IP == IDLE) && (NEXTP == IDLE)) || (RESTART == 1) )
      begin IP <= IDLE; NEXTP <= FIRSTP; end                             // restart case
    else if (RUN == 1)
      begin
        if ({IP,NEXTP} == 12'b0) begin IP <= IDLE; NEXTP <= FIRSTP; end  // error case
        else begin IP <= NEXTP; NEXTP <= {IP[6],IP[1:5]}; end            // normal case
      end
    else begin IP <= IP; NEXTP <= NEXTP; end

  assign P_L = ~IP;  // active-low phase outputs
endmodule
```

! VERSUS ~ (!)   As we explained in the box on page 304, sometimes you can get away with using logical negation (!) when technically bitwise negation (~) should be used. But the continuous-assigment statements in Tables 8-41 and 8-42 are not such places. If you mistakenly used logical negation, the resulting circuit would have all of its output bits except P_L[6] set to a constant 0.

NONBLOCKING VS. BLOCKING ASSIGNMENTS   On page 648 we admonished that you should only use *nonblocking* assignment statements in sequential `always` blocks. Table 8-42 has some code that proves the value of this rule.

   Near the end of the sequential `always` block, this code executes the statement IP <= NEXTP and then NEXTP <= {IP[6],IP[1:5]}. Nonblocking assignments ensure that all of the righthand sides are evaluated before any lefthand sides are changed. Thus, the new value of NEXTP after the clock tick is the shifted value of the *previous* value of IP as desired, not the previous NEXTP, as it would be if this were a C program. The previous NEXTP is assigned to IP at an infinitesimally short delta time *after* the clock tick.

*8.6 Iterative versus Sequential Circuits

We introduced iterative circuits in Section 6.9.2. The function of an n-module iterative circuit can be performed by a sequential circuit that uses just one copy of the module but requires n steps (clock ticks) to obtain the result. This is an excellent example of a space/time trade-off in digital design.

As shown in Figure 8-58, flip-flops are used in the sequential-circuit version to store the cascading outputs at the end of each step; the flip-flop outputs are used as the cascading inputs at the beginning of the next step. The flip-flops must be initialized to the boundary-input values before the first clock tick, and they contain the boundary-output values after the nth tick.

Since an iterative circuit is a combinational circuit, all of its primary and boundary inputs may be applied simultaneously, and its primary and boundary outputs are all available after a combinational delay. In the sequential-circuit version, the primary inputs must be delivered sequentially, one per clock tick, and the primary outputs are produced with similar timing. Therefore, serial-out shift registers are often used to provide the inputs, and serial-in shift registers are used to collect the outputs. For this reason, the sequential-circuit version of an "iterative widget" is often called a "serial widget."

serial comparator

For example, Figure 8-59 shows the basic design for a *serial comparator* circuit. The shaded block is identical to the module used in the iterative comparator of Figure 6-77 on page 461. The circuit is drawn in more detail using SSI chips in Figure 8-60. In addition, we have provided a synchronous reset input that, when asserted, forces the initial value of the cascading flip-flop to 1 at the next clock tick. The initial value of the cascading flip-flop corresponds to the boundary input in the iterative comparator.

An n-bit serial comparison requires $n + 1$ clock ticks. RESET_L is asserted at the first clock tick. RESET_L is negated and data bits are applied at the next n ticks. The EQI output gives the comparison result during the clock period following the last tick. A timing diagram for two successive 4-bit comparisons is shown in Figure 8-61. The spikes in the EQO waveform indicate the time when the combinational outputs are settling in response to new X and Y input values.

Figure 8-58
General structure of the sequential-circuit version of an iterative circuit.

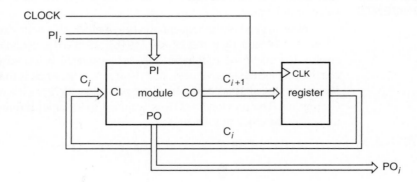

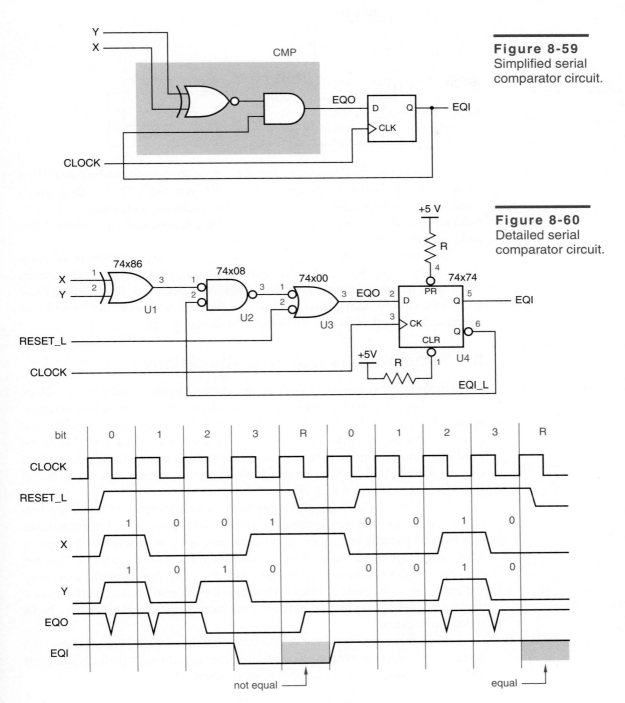

Figure 8-59
Simplified serial comparator circuit.

Figure 8-60
Detailed serial comparator circuit.

Figure 8-61 Timing diagram for serial comparator circuit.

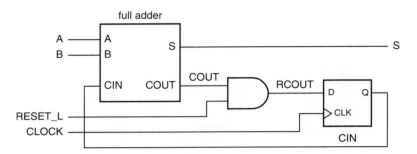

Figure 8-62
Serial binary adder
circuit.

serial binary adder

A *serial binary adder* circuit for addends of any length can be constructed from a full adder and a D flip-flop, as shown in Figure 8-62. The flip-flop, which stores the carry between successive bits of the addition, is cleared to 0 at reset. Addend bits are presented serially on the A and B inputs, starting with the LSB, and sum bits appear on S in the same order.

Because of the large size and high cost of digital logic circuits in the early days, many computers and calculators used serial adders and other serial versions of iterative circuits to perform arithmetic operations. Even though these arithmetic circuits aren't used much today, they are an instructive reminder of the space/time trade-offs that are possible in digital design.

8.7 Synchronous Design Methodology

synchronous system

In a *synchronous system*, all flip-flops are clocked by the same common clock signal, and preset and clear inputs are not used, except for system initialization. Although all the world does not march to the tick of a common clock, within the confines of a digital system or subsystem we can try to make it so. When we must interconnect digital systems or subsystems that use different clocks, we can usually identify a limited number of asynchronous signals that need special treatment, as we'll show in Section 8.8.3.

Races and hazards are not a problem in synchronous systems, for two reasons. First, the only fundamental-mode circuits that might be subject to races or essential hazards are predesigned elements, such as discrete flip-flops or ASIC cells, that are guaranteed by the manufacturer to work properly. Second, even though the combinational circuits that drive flip-flop control inputs may contain static or dynamic or function hazards, these hazards have no effect, since the control inputs are sampled only *after* the hazard-induced glitches have had a chance to settle out.

Aside from designing the functional behavior of each state machine, the designer of a practical synchronous system or subsystem must perform just three well-defined tasks to ensure reliable system operation:

1. Minimize and determine the amount of clock skew in the system, as discussed in Section 8.8.1.

2. Ensure that flip-flops have positive setup- and hold-time margins, including an allowance for clock skew, as described in Section 8.1.4.

3. Identify asynchronous input signals, synchronize them with the clock, and ensure that the synchronizers have an adequately low probability of failure, as described in Sections 8.8.3 and 8.9.

Before we get into these issues, in this section we'll look at a general model for synchronous system structure and an example.

8.7.1 Synchronous System Structure

The sequential-circuit design examples that we gave in Chapter 7 were mostly individual state machines with a small number of states. If a sequential circuit has more than a few flip-flops, then it's not desirable (and often not possible) to treat the circuit as a single, monolithic state machine, because the number of states would be too large to handle.

Fortunately, most digital systems or subsystems can be partitioned into two or more parts. Whether the system processes numbers, digitized voice signals, or a stream of spark-plug pulses, a certain part of the system, which we'll call the *data unit,* can be viewed as storing, routing, combining, and generally processing "data." Another part, which we'll call the *control unit,* can be viewed as starting and stopping actions in the data unit, testing conditions, and deciding what to do next according to circumstances. In general, only the control unit must be designed as a state machine. The data unit and its components are typically handled at a higher level of abstraction, such as:

data unit
control unit

- *Combinational functions.* These include arithmetic and logic units, comparators, and other operations that combine or modify data.

- *Registers.* A collection of flip-flops is loaded in parallel with many bits of "data," which can then be used or retrieved together.

- *Specialized sequential functions.* These include multibit counters and shift registers, which increment or shift their contents on command. They may also include very complex sequential functions, such as data encryption and decryption.

- *Read/write memory.* Individual latches or flip-flops in a collection of the same can be written or read out.

The first topic above was covered in Chapter 6. The next two were discussed earlier in this chapter, and the last is discussed in Chapter 9.

Figure 8-63
Synchronous system
structure.

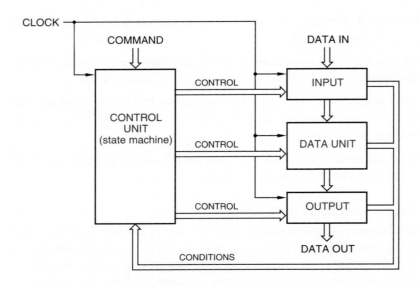

command input
condition input

Figure 8-63 is a general block diagram of a system with a control unit and a data unit. We have also included explicit blocks for input and output, but we could have just as easily absorbed these functions into the data unit itself. The control unit is a state machine whose inputs include *command inputs* that indicate how the machine is to function, and *condition inputs* provided by the data unit. The command inputs may be supplied by another subsystem or by a user to set the general operating mode of the control state machine (RUN/HALT, NORMAL/TURBO, etc.), while the condition inputs allow the control state-machine unit to change its behavior as required by circumstances in the data unit (ZERO_DETECT, MEMORY_FULL, etc.).

A key characteristic of the structure in Figure 8-63 is that the control, data, input, and output units all use the same common clock. Figure 8-64 illustrates the operations of the control and data units during a typical clock cycle:

Figure 8-64 Operations during one clock cycle in a synchronous system.

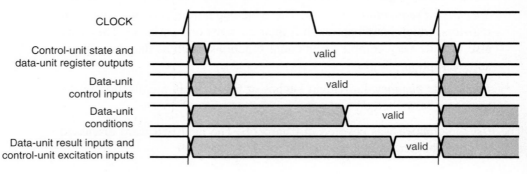

1. Shortly after the beginning of the clock period, the control-unit state and the data-unit register outputs are valid.

2. Next, after a combinational logic delay, Moore-type outputs of the control-unit state machine become valid. These signals are control *inputs* to the data unit. They determine what data-unit functions are performed in the rest of the clock period—for example, selecting memory addresses, multiplexer paths, and arithmetic operations.

3. Near the end of the clock period, data-unit condition outputs such as zero- or overflow-detect are valid and are made available to the control unit.

4. At the end of the clock period, just before the setup-time window begins, the next-state logic of the control-unit state machine has determined the next state based on the current state and command and condition inputs. At about the same time, computational results in the data unit are available to be loaded into data-unit registers.

5. After the clock edge, the whole cycle may repeat.

Data-unit control inputs, which are control-unit state-machine outputs, may be of the Moore, Mealy, or pipelined Mealy type; timing for the Moore type was shown in Figure 8-64. Moore-type and pipelined-Mealy-type outputs control the data unit's actions strictly according to the current state and past inputs, which do not depend on *current* conditions in the data unit. In contrast, Mealy-type outputs may select different actions in the data unit according to *current* conditions in the data unit. This increases flexibility, but typically also increases the minimum clock period for correct system operation, since the delay path may be much longer. Also, Mealy-type outputs must not create feedback loops. For example, a signal that adds 1 to an adder's input if the adder output is nonzero causes an oscillation if the adder output is -1.

One example of a synchronous system with the above structure is an n-bit shift-and-add multiplier. It uses shift registers to hold and shift the operands and result, a combinational adder for each addition step, and a state machine to sequence the operations for n steps. Details of such a multiplier's design using MSI building blocks as well as ABEL, VHDL, and Verilog are given in Sections XSbb.3, XSabl.6, XSvhd.4, and XSver.4, respectively, at DDPPonline.

PIPELINED MEALY OUTPUTS   Some state machines have pipelined Mealy outputs, discussed in Section 7.3.2. In Figure 8-64, pipelined Mealy outputs would typically be valid early in the cycle, at the same time as control-unit state outputs. Early validity of these outputs, compared to Moore outputs that must go through a combinational logic delay, may allow the entire system to operate at a faster clock rate.

8.8 Impediments to Synchronous Design

Although the synchronous approach is the most straightforward and reliable method of digital system design, a few nasty realities can get in the way. We'll discuss them in this section.

8.8.1 Clock Skew

Synchronous systems using edge-triggered flip-flops work properly only if all flip-flops see the triggering clock edge at the same time. Figure 8-65 shows what can happen otherwise. Here, two flip-flops are theoretically clocked by the same signal, but the clock signal seen by FF2 is delayed by a significant amount relative to FF1's clock. This difference between arrival times of the clock at different

clock skew

devices is called *clock skew*.

We've named the delayed clock in Figure 8-65(a) "CLOCKD." If FF1's propagation delay from CLOCK to Q1 is short, and if the physical connection of Q1 to FF2 is short, then the change in Q1 caused by a CLOCK edge may actually reach FF2 *before* the corresponding CLOCKD edge. In this case, FF2 may go to an incorrect next state determined by the *next* state of FF1 instead of the current state, as shown in (b). If the change in Q1 arrives at FF2 only slightly early relative to CLOCKD, then FF2's hold-time specification may be violated, in which case FF2 may become metastable and produce an unpredictable output.

If Figure 8-65 reminds you of the essential hazard shown in Figure 7-94, you're on to something. The clock-skew problem may be viewed simply as a manifestation of the essential hazards that exist in all edge-triggered devices.

We can determine quantitatively whether clock skew is a problem in a given system by defining t_{skew} to be the amount of clock skew and using the other timing parameters defined in Figure 8-1. For proper operation, we need

$$t_{ffpd(min)} + t_{comb(min)} - t_{hold} - t_{skew(max)} > 0$$

In other words, clock skew subtracts from the hold-time margin that we defined in Section 8.1.4.

Figure 8-65
Clock-skew example.

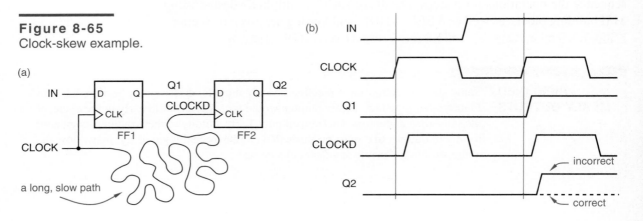

Viewed in isolation, the example in Figure 8-65 may seem a bit extreme. After all, why would a designer provide a short connection path for data and a long one for the clock, when they could just run side by side? There are several ways this can happen; some are mistakes, while others are unavoidable.

In a large system, a single clock signal may not have adequate fanout to drive all of the devices with clock inputs, so it may be necessary to provide two or more copies of the clock signal. The buffering method of Figure 8-66(a) obviously produces excessive clock skew, since CLOCK1 and CLOCK2 are delayed through an extra buffer compared to CLOCK.

A recommended buffering method is shown in Figure 8-66(b). All of the clock signals go through identical buffers and thus have roughly equal delays. Ideally, all the buffers should be part of the same IC package, so that they all have similar delay characteristics and are operating at identical temperature and power-supply voltage. Some manufacturers build special buffers for just this sort of application and specify the worst-case delay variation between buffers in the same package, which can be as low as a few tenths of a nanosecond.

Even the method in Figure 8-66(b) may produce excessive clock skew if one clock signal is loaded much more heavily than the other; transitions on the more heavily loaded clock appear to occur later because of increases in output-transistor switching delay and signal rise and fall times. Therefore, a careful designer tries to balance the loads on multiple clocks, looking at both DC load (fanout) and AC load (wiring and input capacitance).

Another bad situation can occur when signals on a PCB or in an ASIC are routed automatically by a CAD tool. Figure 8-67 on the next page shows a PCB or ASIC with many flip-flops and larger-scale elements, all clocked with a common CLOCK signal. The CAD tool has laid out CLOCK in a serpentine path that winds its way past all the clocked devices. Other signals are routed point-to-point between an output and a few inputs, so their paths are shorter. To make matters worse, in an ASIC some types of "wire" may be slower than others (e.g., polysilicon vs. metal in CMOS technology). As a result, a CLOCK edge may indeed arrive at FF2 quite a bit later than the data change that it produces on Q1.

Figure 8-66 Buffering the clock: (a) excessive clock skew; (b) controllable clock skew.

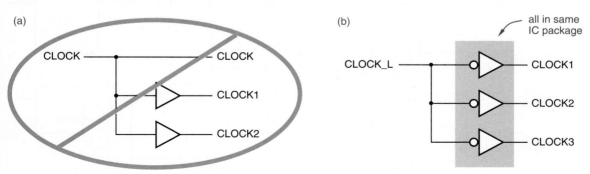

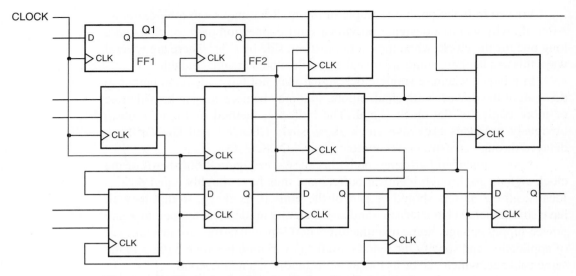

Figure 8-67 A clock-signal path leading to excessive skew.

One way to minimize this sort of problem is to arrange for **CLOCK** to be distributed in a tree-like structure using the fastest type of wire, as illustrated in Figure 8-68. Usually, such a "clock tree" must be laid out by hand or using a specialized CAD tool. Even then, in a complex design it may not be possible to guarantee that clock edges arrive everywhere before the earliest data change. A CAD timing analysis program is typically used to detect these problems, which

Figure 8-68 Clock-signal routing to minimize skew.

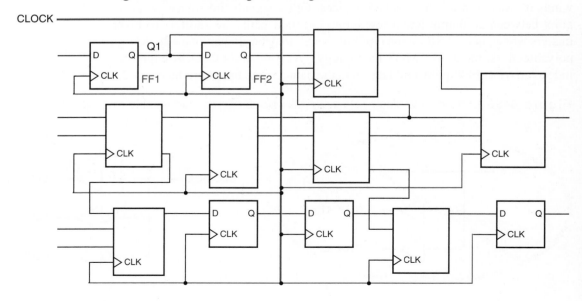

**HOW NOT TO
GET SKEWERED**

Unbalanced wire lengths and loads are the most obvious sources of clock skew, but there are many other subtle sources. For example, *crosstalk*, the coupling of energy from one signal line into another, can cause clock skew. Crosstalk is inevitable when parallel wires are packed together tightly on a printed circuit board or in a chip, and energy is radiated during signal transitions. Depending on whether an adjacent signal is changing in the same or opposite direction as a clock, the clock's transition can be accelerated or retarded, making its transition appear to occur earlier or later.

In a large PCB or ASIC design, it's usually not feasible to track down all the possible sources of clock skew. As a result, most ASIC manufacturers require designers to provide extra setup- and hold-time margin, equivalent to many gate delays, over and above the known simulation timing results to accommodate such unknown factors.

---

generally can be remedied only by inserting extra delay (e.g., pairs of inverters) in the too-fast data paths.

Although synchronous design methodology simplifies the conceptual operation of large systems, we see that clock skew can be a major problem when edge-triggered flip-flops are used as the storage elements. To control this problem, many high-performance systems and VLSI chips use a *two-phase latch design,* discussed in the References. Such designs effectively split each edge-triggered D flip-flop into its two component latches, controlling them with two nonoverlapping clock phases. The nonoverlap between the phases accommodates clock skew.

two-phase latch design

8.8.2 Gating the Clock

Most of the sequential MSI parts that we introduced in this chapter have synchronous function-enable inputs. That is, their enable inputs are sampled on the clock edge, along with the data. The first example that we showed was the 74x377 register with synchronous load-enable input; other parts included the 74x163 counter and 74x194 shift register with synchronous load-enable, count-enable, and shift-enable inputs. Nevertheless, many MSI parts, FPGA macros, and ASIC cells do not have synchronous function-enable inputs; for example, the 74x374 8-bit register has three-state outputs but no load-enable input.

So, what can a designer do if an application requires an 8-bit register with both a load-enable input *and* three-state outputs? One solution is to use a 74x377 to get the load-enable, and follow it with a 74x241 three-state buffer. However, this increases both cost and delay. Another approach is to use a larger, more expensive part, the 74x823, which provides both required functions as well as an asynchronous CLR_L input. A riskier alternative sometimes employed by designers who don't know any better is to use a '374, but to suppress its clock input when it's not supposed to be loaded. This is called *gating the clock.*

gating the clock

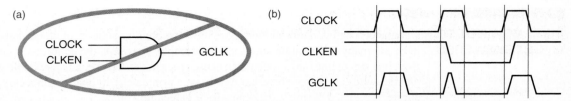

Figure 8-69 Bad clock gating: (a) simple-minded circuit; (b) timing diagram.

Figure 8-69 illustrates an obvious but wrong approach to gating the clock. A signal CLKEN is asserted to enable the clock and is simply ANDed with the clock to produce the gated clock GCLK. This approach has two problems:

1. If CLKEN is a state-machine output or other signal produced by a register clocked by CLOCK, then CLKEN changes some time *after* CLOCK has already gone HIGH. As shown in (b), this produces glitches on GCLK and false clocking of the registers controlled by GCLK.

2. Even if CLKEN is somehow produced well in advance of CLOCK's rising edge (e.g., using a register clocked with the *falling* edge of CLOCK, an especially nasty kludge), the AND-gate delay gives GCLK excessive clock skew, which causes more problems all around.

A method of gating the clock that generates only minimal clock skew is shown in Figure 8-70. Here, both an ungated clock and several gated clocks are generated from the same active-low master clock signal. Gates in the same IC package are used to minimize the possible differences in their delays. The CLKEN signal may change arbitrarily whenever CLOCK_L is LOW, which is when CLOCK is HIGH. That's just fine; a CLKEN signal is typically produced by a state machine whose outputs change right after CLOCK goes HIGH.

The approach of Figure 8-70 is acceptable in a particular application only if the clock skew that it creates is acceptable. Furthermore, note that CLKEN

Figure 8-70 Acceptable clock gating: (a) circuit; (b) timing diagram.

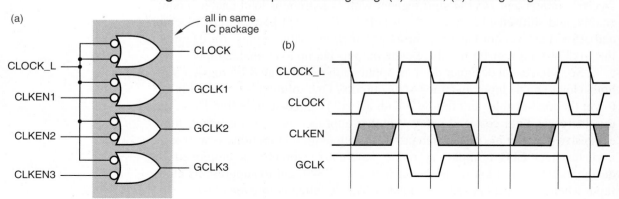

must be stable during the entire time that CLOCK_L is HIGH (CLOCK is LOW). Thus, the timing margins in this approach are sensitive to the clock's duty cycle, especially if CLKEN suffers significant combinational-logic delay (t_{comb}) from the triggering clock edge. A truly synchronous function-enable input, such as the 74x377's load-enable input in Figure 8-13, can be changed at almost any time during the entire clock period, up until a setup time before the triggering edge.

8.8.3 Asynchronous Inputs

Even though it is theoretically possible to build a computer system that is fully synchronous, you couldn't do much with it, unless you could synchronize your keystrokes with a 2-GHz clock. Digital systems of all types inevitably must deal with *asynchronous input signals* that are not synchronized with the system clock.

asynchronous input signal

   Asynchronous inputs are often requests for service (e.g., interrupts in a computer) or status flags (e.g., a resource has become available). Such inputs normally change slowly compared to the system clock frequency, and they need not be recognized at a particular clock tick. If a transition is missed at one clock tick, it can always be detected at the next one. The transition rates of asynchronous signals may range from less than one per second (the keystrokes of a slow typist) to 200 MHz or more (access requests for a 2-GHz multiprocessor system's shared memory).

   Ignoring the problem of metastability for the moment, it is easy to build a *synchronizer,* a circuit that samples an asynchronous input and produces an output that meets the setup and hold times required in a synchronous system. As shown in Figure 8-71, a D flip-flop samples the asynchronous input at each tick of the system clock and produces a synchronous output that is valid during the next clock period.

synchronizer

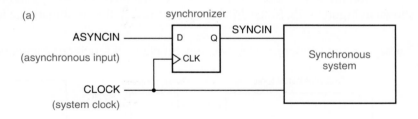 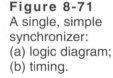
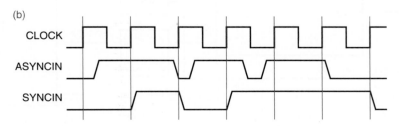

Figure 8-71
A single, simple synchronizer:
(a) logic diagram;
(b) timing.

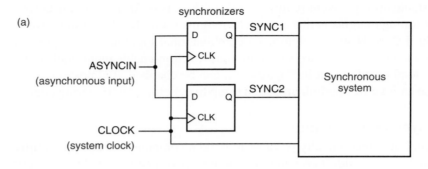

It is essential for asynchronous inputs to be synchronized at only *one place* in a system; Figure 8-72 shows what can happen otherwise. Because of physical delays in the circuit, the two flip-flops will not see the clock and input signals at precisely the same time. Therefore, when asynchronous input transitions occur near the clock edge, there is a small window of time during which one flip-flop may sample the input as 1 and the other may sample it as 0. This inconsistent result may cause improper system operation, as one part of the system responds as if the input were 1, and another part responds as if it were 0.

Combinational logic may hide the fact that there are two synchronizers, as shown in Figure 8-73. Since different paths through the combinational logic will

Figure 8-73 An asynchronous input driving two synchronizers through combinational logic.

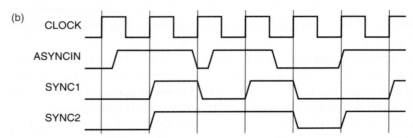

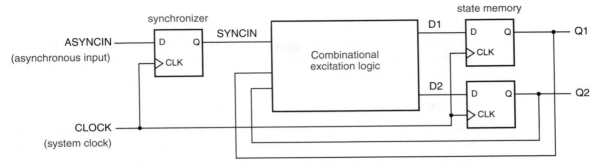

Figure 8-74 An asynchronous state-machine input coupled through a single synchronizer.

inevitably have different delays, the likelihood of an inconsistent result is even greater. This situation is especially common when asynchronous signals are used as inputs to state machines, since the excitation logic for two or more state variables may depend on the asynchronous input. The proper way to use an asynchronous signal as a state-machine input is shown in Figure 8-74. All of the excitation logic sees the same synchronized input signal, SYNCIN.

WHO CARES?   As you probably know, even the synchronizers in Figures 8-71 and 8-74 sometimes fail. The reason is that the setup and hold times of the synchronizing flip-flop are sometimes violated, because the asynchronous input can change at any time. "Well, who cares?" you may say. "If the D input changes near the clock edge, then the flip-flop will either see the change this time or miss it and pick it up next time; either way is good enough for me!" The problem is, there is a third possibility, discussed in the next section.

8.9 Synchronizer Failure and Metastability

We showed in Section 7.1 that when the setup and hold times of a flip-flop are not met, the flip-flop may go into a third, *metastable* state halfway between 0 and 1. Worse, the length of time it may stay in this state before falling back into a legitimate 0 or 1 state is theoretically unbounded. When other gates and flip-flops are presented with a metastable input signal, some may interpret it as a 0 and others as a 1, creating the sort of inconsistent behavior that we showed in Figure 8-72. Or the other gates and flip-flops may produce metastable outputs themselves (after all, they are now operating in the *linear* part of their operating range). Luckily, the probability of a flip-flop output remaining in the metastable state decreases exponentially with time, though never all the way to zero.

8.9.1 Synchronizer Failure

synchronizer failure

Synchronizer failure is said to occur if a system uses a synchronizer output while the output is still in the metastable state. You can avoid synchronizer failure only by ensuring that the system waits "long enough" before using a synchronizer's output—"long enough" that the mean time between synchronizer failures is a few orders of magnitude longer than your expected length of employment.

Metastability is more than an academic problem. More than a few experienced designers of high-speed digital systems have built (and released to production) circuits that suffer from intermittent synchronizer failures. In fact, the initial versions of many commercial ICs have suffered from metastability problems. In previous editions of this book, we cited metastability problems in old microprocessors and peripherals from Zilog, Intel, and AMD. Now, in the "modern" era, it's easy to find metastability admissions on-line, for example, in the errata sheet for Texas Instruments' OMAP5910 processor (2004). It makes you wonder, are the designers of these parts still employed?

There are two ways to get a flip-flop out of the metastable state:

1. Force the flip-flop into a valid logic state using input signals that meet the published specifications for minimum pulse width, setup time, and so on.

2. Wait "long enough," so the flip-flop comes out of metastability on its own.

Inexperienced designers often attempt to get around metastability in other ways, and they are usually unsuccessful. Figure 8-75 shows an attempt by a designer who thinks that since metastability is an "analog" problem, it must have an "analog" solution. After all, Schmitt-trigger inputs and capacitors can normally be used to clean up noisy signals. However, rather than eliminate metastability, this circuit enhances it—with the "right" components, the circuit will oscillate forever, once it is excited by negating S_L and R_L simultaneously. (*Confession:* It was the author who tried this over 25 years ago!) Exercise 8.86 gives an example of a valiant but also failed attempt to eliminate metastability. These examples should give you the sense that synchronizer problems can be very subtle, so you must be careful. The only way to make synchronizers reliable is to wait long enough for metastable outputs to resolve. We answer the question "How long is 'long enough'?" later in this section.

Figure 8-75
A failed attempt to build a metastable-proof $\overline{S}$-$\overline{R}$ flip-flop.

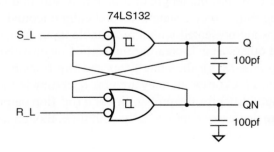

8.9.2 Metastability Resolution Time

If the setup and hold times of a D flip-flop are met, the flip-flop output settles to a new value within time t_{pd} after the clock edge. If they are violated, the flip-flop output may be metastable for an arbitrary length of time. In a particular system design, we use the parameter t_r, called the *metastability resolution time*, to denote the maximum time that the output can remain metastable without causing synchronizer (and system) failure.

> t_r
> *metastability resolution time*

For example, consider the state machine in Figure 8-74 on page 769. The available metastability resolution time is

$$t_r = t_{clk} - t_{comb} - t_{setup}$$

where t_{clk} is the clock period, t_{comb} is the propagation delay of the combinational excitation logic, and t_{setup} is the setup time of the flip-flops used in the state memory.

> t_{clk}
> t_{comb}
> t_{setup}

8.9.3 Reliable Synchronizer Design

The most reliable synchronizer is one that allows the maximum amount of time for metastability resolution. However, in the design of a digital system, we seldom have the luxury of *slowing down* the clock to make the system work more reliably. Instead, we are usually asked to *speed up* the clock to get higher performance from the system. As a result, we often need synchronizers that work reliably with very short clock periods. We'll present several such designs, and show how to predict their reliability.

We showed previously that a state machine with an asynchronous input, built as illustrated in Figure 8-74, has $t_r = t_{clk} - t_{comb} - t_{setup}$. In order to maximize t_r for a given clock period, we should minimize t_{comb} and t_{setup}. The value of t_{setup} depends on the type of flip-flops used in the state memory; in general, faster flip-flops have shorter setup times. The minimum value of t_{comb} is zero and is achieved by the synchronizer design of Figure 8-76, whose operation we explain next.

Inputs to flip-flop FF1 are asynchronous with the clock and may violate the flip-flop's setup and hold times. When this happens, the META output may become metastable and remain in that state for an arbitrary time. However, we

Figure 8-76 Recommended synchronizer design.

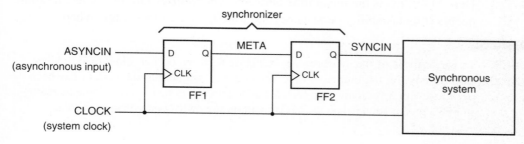

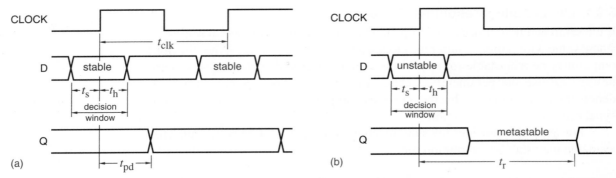

Figure 8-77 Timing parameters for metastability analysis: (a) normal flip-flop operation; (b) metastable behavior.

assume that the maximum duration of metastability after the clock edge is t_r. (We show how to calculate the probability that our assumption is correct in the next subsection.) As long as the clock period is greater than t_r plus the FF2's setup time, SYNCIN becomes a synchronized copy of the asynchronous input on the next clock tick without ever becoming metastable itself. The SYNCIN signal is distributed as required to the rest of the system.

8.9.4 Analysis of Metastable Timing

decision window

Figure 8-77 shows the flip-flop timing parameters that are relevant to our analysis of metastability timing. The published setup and hold times of a flip-flop with respect to its clock edge are denoted by t_s and t_h, and they bracket an interval called the *decision window*, when the flip-flop samples its input and decides to change its output if necessary. As long as the D input changes outside the decision window, as in (a), the manufacturer guarantees that the output will change and settle to a valid logic state before time t_{pd}. If D changes inside the decision window, as in (b), metastability may occur and persist until time t_r.

Theoretical research suggests, and experimental research has confirmed, that when asynchronous inputs change during the decision window, the duration of metastable outputs is governed by an exponential formula:

$$\text{MTBF}(t_r) = \frac{\exp(t_r/\tau)}{T_o \cdot f \cdot a}$$

Here $\text{MTBF}(t_r)$ is the mean time between synchronizer failures, where a failure occurs if metastability persists beyond time t_r after a clock edge, where $t_r \geq t_{pd}$.

DETAILS, DETAILS   In our analysis of the synchronizer in Figure 8-76 we do not allow metastability, even briefly, on the output of FF2, because we assume that the system has been designed with zero timing margins. If the system can in fact tolerate some increase in FF2's propagation delay, the MTBF will be somewhat better than predicted.

This MTBF depends on f, the frequency of the flip-flop clock; a, the number of asynchronous input changes per second applied to the flip-flop; and T_o and τ, constants that depend on the electrical characteristics of the flip-flop. For a typical 74LS74, $T_o \approx 0.4$ s and $\tau \approx 1.5$ ns, according to researcher Thomas Chaney (see Table 8-43 on the next page and the References).

f
a
T_o
τ

Now suppose that we build an embedded microprocessor system with a slow (by today's standards) 10-MHz clock and use the circuit of Figure 8-76 to synchronize an asynchronous input. If ASYNCIN changes during the decision window of FF1, the output META may become metastable until time t_r. If META is still metastable at the beginning of the decision window for FF2, then the synchronizer fails, because FF2 may have a metastable output; system operation is unpredictable in that case.

Let us assume that the D flip-flops in Figure 8-76 are 74LS74s. The setup time t_s of a 74LS74 is 20 ns, and the clock period in our example microprocessor system is 100 ns, so t_r for synchronizer failure is 80 ns. If the asynchronous input changes 100,000 times per second, then the synchronizer MTBF is

$$\text{MTBF(80 ns)} = \frac{\exp(80/1.5)}{0.4 \cdot 10^7 \cdot 10^5} = 3.6 \cdot 10^{11} \text{s}$$

That's not bad, about 115 centuries between failures! Of course, if we're lucky enough to sell 11,500 copies of our system, one of them will fail in this way every year. But, no matter, let us consider a more serious problem.

Suppose we upgrade our system to use a faster microprocessor chip with a clock speed of 16 MHz. We may have to replace some components in our system to operate at the higher speed, but 74LS74s are still perfectly good at 16 MHz. Or are they? With a clock period of 62.5 ns, the new synchronizer MTBF is

$$\text{MTBF(42.5 ns)} = \frac{\exp(42.5/1.5)}{0.4 \cdot 1.6 \cdot 10^7 \cdot 10^5} = 3.1 \text{ s!}$$

UNDERSTANDING A AND F

Although a flip-flop output can go metastable *only* if D changes during the decision window, the MTBF formula does not explicitly specify how many such input changes occur. Instead, it specifies the total number of asynchronous input changes per second, a, and assumes that asynchronous input changes are uniformly distributed over the clock period. Therefore, the fraction of input changes that actually occur during the decision window is "built in" to the clock-frequency parameter f—as f increases, the fraction goes up.

If the system design is such that input changes might be clustered in the decision window rather than being uniformly distributed (as when synchronizing a slow input with a fixed but unknown phase difference from the system clock), then a useful rule of thumb is to use a frequency equal to the reciprocal of the decision window (based on published setup and hold times), times a safety margin of 10.

The only saving grace of this synchronizer at 16 MHz is that it's so lousy, we're likely to discover the problem in the engineering lab before the product ships! Thank goodness the MTBF wasn't one year.

8.9.5 Better Synchronizers

Given the poor performance of the 74LS74 as a synchronizer at moderate clock speeds, we have a couple of alternatives for building more reliable synchronizers. The simplest solution, which works for many design requirements, is simply to use a flip-flop from a faster technology. Nowadays much faster technologies are available for flip-flops, whether discrete or embedded in PLDs, FPGAs, or ASICs. Of course, system clock frequencies tend to increase too with technology improvements, so this isn't always a solution.

Based on published data discussed in the References, Table 8-43 lists the metastability parameters for several common logic families and devices. These numbers were all derived experimentally and vary with a chip's internal circuit design and IC fab process, and with the experimental test setup. Thus, unlike guaranteed logic signal levels and timing parameters, published metastability numbers can vary dramatically among different manufacturers of the same part and must be used conservatively. For example, Drill 8.17 compares the results of the previous example using TI's estimates of 74LSxx parameters in the table.

Table 8-43 Metastability parameters for some common devices.

Reference	Device	τ (ns)	T_o (s)	t_r (ns)
Chaney (1983)	74LS74	1.50	$4.0 \cdot 10^{-1}$	77.7
Chaney (1983)	74S74	1.70	$1.0 \cdot 10^{-6}$	66.1
Chaney (1983)	74F74	0.40	$2.0 \cdot 10^{-4}$	17.7
TI (1997)	74LSxx	1.35	$4.8 \cdot 10^{-3}$	64.0
TI (1997)	74Sxx	2.80	$1.3 \cdot 10^{-9}$	90.3
TI (1997)	74ALSxx	1.00	$8.7 \cdot 10^{-6}$	41.1
TI (1997)	74ASxx	0.25	$1.4 \cdot 10^{3}$	15.0
TI (1997)	74Fxx	0.11	$1.9 \cdot 10^{8}$	7.9
TI (1997)	74HCxx	1.82	$1.5 \cdot 10^{-6}$	71.6
TI (1997)	74ACxx	0.36	$1.1 \cdot 10^{-4}$	15.7
Cypress (1997)	PALC22V10B-20	0.26	$5.6 \cdot 10^{-11}$	7.6*
Cypress (1997)	PALCE22V10-7	0.19	$1.3 \cdot 10^{-13}$	4.4*
Xilinx (1997)	7300-series CPLD	0.29	$1.0 \cdot 10^{-15}$	5.3*
Xilinx (1997)	9500-series CPLD	0.17	$9.6 \cdot 10^{-18}$	2.3*

Note that different authors and manufacturers may specify metastability parameters differently. For example, author Chaney and manufacturer Texas Instruments (TI) measure the metastability resolution time t_r from the triggering clock edge, as in our previous subsection. On the other hand, manufacturers Cypress and Xilinx define t_r as the *additional* delay beyond a normal clock-to-output delay time t_{pd}.

The last column in the table gives a somewhat arbitrarily chosen figure of merit for each device. It is the metastability resolution time t_r required to obtain an MTBF of 1000 years when operating a synchronizer with a clock frequency of 25 MHz and with 100,000 asynchronous input changes per second. For the Cypress and Xilinx devices, their parameter values yield a value of t_r marked with an asterisk, consistent with their own definition as introduced above.

As you can see, the 74LS74 is one of the worst devices in the table. If we replace FF1 in the 16-MHz microprocessor system of the preceding subsection with a 74ALS74, we get

$$\text{MTBF(42.5 ns)} = \frac{\exp(42.5/1.00)}{8.7 \cdot 10^{-6} \cdot 1.6 \cdot 10^7 \cdot 10^5} = 2.06 \cdot 10^{11}\text{s}$$

If you're satisfied with a synchronizer MTBF of about 65 centuries per system shipped, you can stop here. However, if FF2 is also replaced with a 74ALS74, the MTBF gets better, since the 'ALS74 has a shorter setup time than the 'LS74, only 10 ns. With the 'ALS74, the MTBF is over 20,000 times better:

$$\text{MTBF(52.5 ns)} = \frac{\exp(52.5/1.00)}{8.7 \cdot 10^{-6} \cdot 1.6 \cdot 10^7 \cdot 10^5} = 4.54 \cdot 10^{15}\text{s}$$

Even if we ship a million systems containing this circuit, we (or our heirs) will see a synchronizer failure only once in 144 years. Now that's job security!

Actually, the margins above aren't as large as they might seem. (How large does 144 years seem *to you*?) Most of the numbers given in Table 8-43 are *averages* and are seldom specified, let alone guaranteed, by the device manufacturer. Furthermore, calculated MTBFs are extremely sensitive to the value of τ, which in turn may depend on temperature, voltage, and the phase of the moon. So the operation of a given flip-flop in an actual system may be much worse (or much better) than predicted by our table.

For example, consider what happens if we increase the clock in our 16-MHz system by just 25%, to 20 MHz. Your natural inclination might be to think that metastability will get 25% worse, or maybe 250% worse, just to be conservative. But, if you run the numbers, you'll find that the MTBF using 'ALS74s for both FF1 and FF2 goes down from $4.54 \cdot 10^{15}$ s to just $3.7 \cdot 10^9$ s, over a million times worse! The new MTBF of about 429 years is fine for one system, but if you ship a million of them, one will fail every four hours. You've just gone from generations of job security to corporate goat!

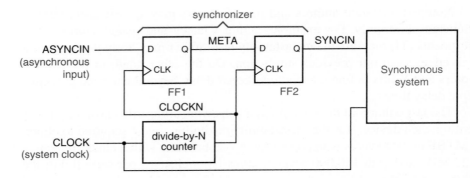

Figure 8-78
Multiple-cycle
synchronizer.

8.9.6 Other Synchronizer Designs

We promised to describe a couple of ways to build more reliable synchronizers. The first way was to use faster flip-flops, that is, to reduce the value of τ in the MTBF equation. Having said that, the second way is obvious—to *increase* the value of t_r in the MTBF equation.

multiple-cycle
synchronizer

For a given system clock, the best value we can obtain for t_r using the circuit of Figure 8-76 is t_{clk}, if FF2 has a setup time of 0. However, we can get values of t_r on the order of $n \cdot t_{clk}$ by using the *multiple-cycle synchronizer* circuit of Figure 8-78. Here we divide the system clock by n to obtain a slower synchronizer clock and longer $t_r = (n \cdot t_{clk}) - t_{setup}$. Usually a value of $n = 2$ or $n = 3$ gives adequate synchronizer reliability.

In the figure, note that the edges of CLOCKN will lag the edges of CLOCK because CLOCKN comes from the Q output of a counter flip-flop that is clocked by CLOCK. This means that SYNCIN, in turn, will be delayed or skewed relative to other signals in the synchronous system that come directly from flip-flops clocked by CLOCK. If SYNCIN goes through additional combinational logic in the synchronous system before reaching its flip-flop inputs, their setup time may be inadequate. If this is the case, the solution in Figure 8-79 can be used. Here, SYNCIN is reclocked by CLOCK using FF3 to produce DSYNCIN, which will have the same timing as other flip-flop outputs in the synchronous system. Of

Figure 8-79 Multiple-cycle synchronizer with deskewing.

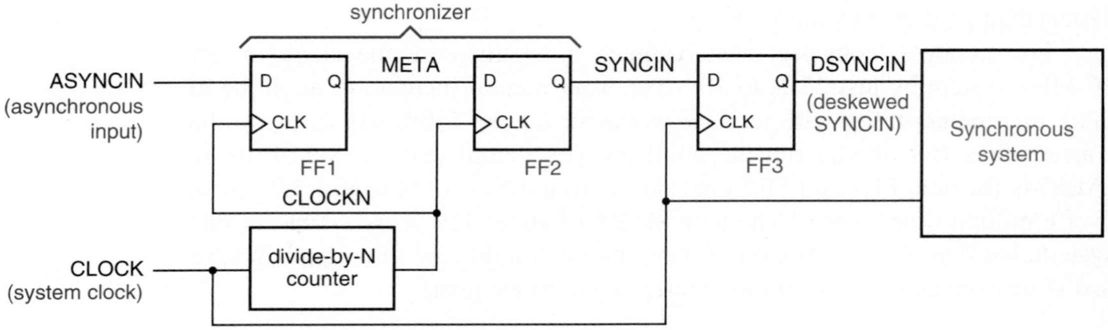

course, the delay from CLOCK to CLOCKN must still be short enough that SYNCIN meets the setup time requirement of FF3.

In an n-cycle synchronizer, the larger the value of n, the longer it takes for an asynchronous input change to be seen by the synchronous system. This is simply a price that must be paid for reliable system operation. In typical microprocessor systems, most asynchronous inputs are for external events—interrupts, DMA requests, and so on—that need not be recognized very quickly, relative to synchronizer delays. In the time-critical area of main memory access, experienced designers use the processor clock to run the memory subsystem too, if possible. This eliminates the need for synchronizers and provides the fastest possible system operation.

At higher frequencies, the feasibility of the multiple-cycle synchronizer design shown in Figure 8-78 tends to be limited by clock skew. For this reason, rather than use a divide-by-n synchronizer clock, some designers use *cascaded synchronizers*. This design approach simply uses a cascade (shift register) of n flip-flops, all clocked with the high-speed system clock. This approach is shown in Figure 8-80.

cascaded synchronizers

With cascaded synchronizers, the idea is that metastability will be resolved with some probability by the first flip-flop, and failing that, with an equal probability by each successive flip-flop in the cascade. So the overall probability of failure is on the order of the nth power of the failure probability of a single-flip-flop synchronizer at the system clock frequency. While this is partially true, the MTBF of the cascade is poorer than that of a multiple-cycle synchronizer with the same delay ($n \cdot t_{clk}$). With the cascade, the flip-flop setup time t_{setup} must be subtracted from t_r, the available metastability resolution time, n times, but in a multiple-cycle design, it is subtracted only once.

PLDs that contain internal flip-flops can be used in synchronizer designs, where the two flip-flops in Figure 8-76 on page 771 are simply included in the PLD. This is very convenient in most applications, because it eliminates the need for external, discrete flip-flops. However, a PLD-based synchronizer typically has a poorer MTBF than a discrete circuit built with the same or similar technology. This happens because each flip-flop in a PLD has a combinational logic array on its D input that increases its setup time and thereby reduces the amount of time t_r available for metastability resolution during a given system

Figure 8-80 Cascaded synchronizer.

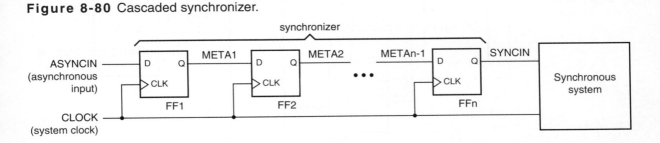

clock period t_{clk}. To maximize t_r without using special components, FF2 in Figure 8-76 should be a short-setup-time discrete flip-flop. Some manufacturers also make devices with two high-speed flip-flops FF1 and FF2 already connected on-chip for synchronizer applications; see <u>Section FFmh</u> at <u>DDPPonline</u>.

8.9.7 Synchronizing High-Speed Data Transfers

A very common problem in computer systems is synchronizing external data transfers with the computer system clock. A simple example is the interface between personal computer's network interface card and a 100-Mbps Ethernet link. The interface card may be connected to a PCI bus, which has a 33.33-MHz clock. Even though the Ethernet speed is an approximate multiple of the bus speed, the signal received on the Ethernet link is generated by another computer whose transmit clock is not synchronized with the receive clock in any way. Yet the interface must still deliver data reliably to the PCI bus.

Figure 8-81 shows the problem. NRZ serial data RDATA is received from the Ethernet at 100 Mbps. The digital phase-locked loop (DPLL) recovers a 100-MHz clock signal RCLK which is centered on the 100-Mbps data stream and allows data to be clocked bit-by-bit into an 8-bit shift register. At the same time, a byte synchronization circuit searches for special patterns in the received data stream that indicate byte boundaries. When it detects one of these, it asserts the SYNC signal and does so on every eighth subsequent RCLK tick, so that SYNC is asserted whenever the shift register contains an aligned 8-bit byte. The rest of the system is clocked by a 33.33 MHz clock SCLK. We need to transfer each aligned byte RBYTE[7:0] into a register SREG in SCLK's domain. How can we do it?

Figure 8-82 shows some of the timing. We immediately see that the byte-aligned signal, SYNC, is asserted for only 10 ns per byte. We have no hope of consistently detecting this signal with the asynchronous SCLK, whose period is a much longer 30 ns.

Figure 8-81 Ethernet synchronization.

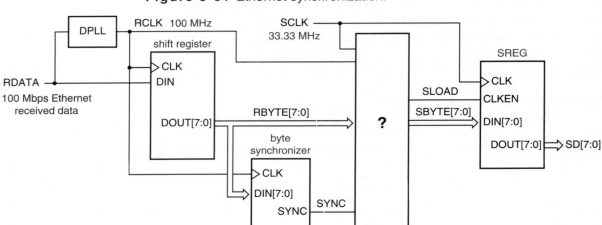

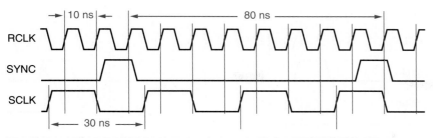

Figure 8-82
Ethernet link and system clock timing.

The strategy almost universally followed in this kind of situation is to transfer the aligned data first into a holding register HREG in the *receive* clock (RCLK) domain. This gives us a lot more time to sort things out—80 ns in this case. Thus, the "?" box in Figure 8-81 can be replaced by Figure 8-83, which shows HREG and a box marked "SCTRL." The job of SCTRL is to assert SLOAD during exactly one 30-ns SCLK period, so that the output of HREG is valid and stable for the setup and hold times of register SREG in the SCLK domain. SLOAD also serves as a "new-data available" signal for the rest of the interface, indicating that a new data byte will appear on SBYTE[7:0] during the next SCLK

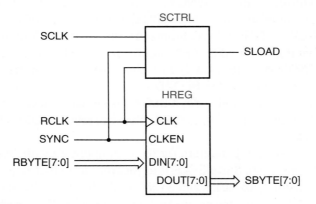

Figure 8-83
Byte holding register and control.

ONE NIBBLE AT A TIME   The explanation of 100-Mbps Ethernet reception above is oversimplified, but sufficient for discussing the synchronization problem. In reality, the received data rate is 125 Mbps, where each 4 bits of user data is encoded as a 5-bit symbol using a so-called 4B5B code. By using only 16 out of 32 possible 5-bit codewords, the 4B5B code guarantees that regardless of the user data pattern, the bit stream on the wire will have a sufficient number of transitions to allow clock recovery. Also, the 4B5B code includes a special code that is transmitted periodically to allow nibble (4-bit) and byte synchronization to be accomplished very easily.

As a result of nibble synchronization, a typical 100-Mbps Ethernet interface does not see an unsynchronized 100-MHz stream of bits. Instead, it sees an unsynchronized 25-MHz stream of nibbles. So, the details of a real 100-Mbps Ethernet synchronizer are different, but the same principles apply.

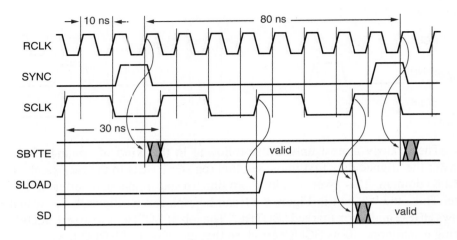

Figure 8-84
Timing for SBYTE
and possible timing
for SLOAD.

period. Figure 8-84 shows possible timing for SLOAD based on this approach and the previous timing diagram.

Figure 8-85 is a circuit that can generate SLOAD with the desired timing. The idea is to use SYNC to set an S-R latch as a new byte becomes available. The output of this latch, NEWBYTE, is sampled by FF1 in the SCLK domain. Since NEWBYTE is not synchronized with SCLK, FF1's output SM may be metastable, but it is not used by FF2 until the next clock tick, 30 ns later. Assuming that the AND gate is reasonably fast, this gives plenty of metastability resolution time. FF2's output is the SLOAD signal. The AND gate ensures that SLOAD is only one SCLK period wide; if SLOAD is already 1, it can't be set to 1 on the next tick. This gives time for the S-R latch to be reset by SLOAD in preparation for the next byte.

A timing diagram for the overall circuit with "typical" timing is shown in Figure 8-86. Since SCLK is asynchronous to RCLK, it can have an arbitrary relationship with RCLK and SYNC. In the figure, we've shown a case where the next SCLK rising edge occurs well after NEWBYTE is set. Although the figure shows a window in which SM and SM1 could be metastable in the general case, metastability doesn't actually happen when the timing is as drawn. Later, we'll show what can happen if the SCLK edge occurs when NEWBYTE is changing.

We should make several notes about the circuit in Figure 8-85. First, the SYNC signal must be glitch free, since it controls the S input of a latch, and it must be wide enough to meet the minimum pulse-width requirement of the latch.

Figure 8-85
SCTRL circuit for
generating SLOAD.

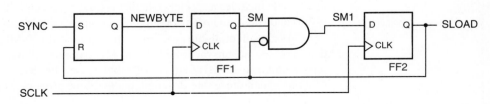

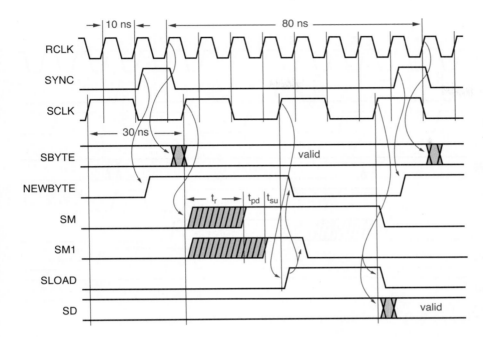

Figure 8-86
Timing for the SCTRL
circuit in Figure 8-85.

Since the latch is set on the leading edge of SYNC, we actually cheated a little; NEWBYTE may be asserted a little *before* a new byte is actually available in HREG. This is OK, because we know that it takes two SCLK periods from when NEWBYTE is sampled until SREG is loaded. In fact, we might have cheated even more if an earlier version of SYNC had been available (see Exercise 8.88).

Assuming that t_{su} is the setup time of a D flip-flop and t_{pd} is the propagation delay of the AND gate in Figure 8-85, the available metastability resolution time t_r is one SCLK period, 30 ns, minus $t_{su} + t_{pd}$, as shown in Figure 8-86. The timing diagram also shows why we can't use SM directly as the reset signal for the S-R latch. Since SM can be metastable, it could wreak havoc. For example, it could be semi-HIGH long enough to reset the latch but then fall back to LOW; in that case, SLOAD would not get set and we would miss a byte. By using instead the output of the synchronizer (SLOAD) both for the latch reset and for the load signal in the SCLK domain, we ensure that the new byte is detected and handled consistently in both clock domains.

The timing that we showed in Figure 8-86 is nominal, but we also have to analyze what happens if SCLK has a different phase relationship with RCLK and SYNC than what is shown. You should be able to convince yourself that if the SCLK edge occurs earlier, so that it samples NEWBYTE just as it's going HIGH, everything still works as before, and the data transfer just finishes a little sooner. The more interesting case is when SCLK occurs even earlier, so that it just misses NEWBYTE as it's going HIGH and catches it one SCLK period later. This timing is shown in Figure 8-87.

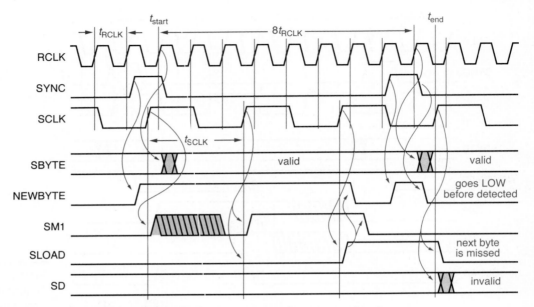

Figure 8-87 Maximum-delay timing for SCTRL circuit.

In the timing diagram, we have shown NEWBYTE going high around the same time as the SCLK edge—less than FF1's t_{su} before the edge. Thus, FF1 may not see NEWBYTE as HIGH or its output may become metastable, and it does not solidly capture NEWBYTE until one SCLK period later. Two SCLK periods after that, we get the SCLK edge that loads SBYTE into SREG.

This timing scenario is bad news, because by the time the load occurs, SBYTE is already changing to the *next* received byte. In addition, SLOAD happens to be asserted during and a little bit after the SYNC pulse for this next received byte. Thus, the latch has both S and R asserted simultaneously. If they are removed simultaneously, the latch output may become metastable. Or, as we've shown in the timing diagram, if NEWBYTE (R) is negated last, then the latch is left in the reset state, and this next received byte is never detected and loaded into the SCLK domain.

Thus, we need to analyze the maximum-delay timing case carefully to determine if a synchronizer will work properly. Figure 8-87 shows a starting reference point t_{start} for the SCTRL circuit, namely the RCLK edge on which a byte is loaded into HREG, at end of SYNC pulse. The ending reference point t_{end} is the SCLK edge on which SBYTE is loaded into SREG. The maximum delay between these two reference points, which we'll call t_{maxd}, is the sum of the following components:

$-t_{RCLK}$ Minus one RCLK period, the delay from t_{start} back to the edge on which SYNC was asserted. This number is negative because SYNC is asserted one clock tick before the tick that actually loads HREG.

t_{CQ} One flip-flop CLK-to-Q maximum delay. Assuming that SYNC is a direct flip-flop output in the RCLK domain, this is delay from the RCLK edge until SYNC is asserted.

t_{SQ} Maximum delay from S to Q in the S-R latch in Figure 8-85. This is the delay for NEWBYTE to be asserted.

t_{su} Setup time of FF1 in Figure 8-85. NEWBYTE must be asserted at or before the setup time to guarantee detection.

t_{SCLK} One SCLK period. Since RCLK and SCLK are asynchronous, there may be a delay of up to one SCLK period before the next SCLK edge comes along to sample NEWBYTE.

t_{SCLK} After NEWBYTE is detected by FF1, SLOAD is asserted on the next SCLK tick.

t_{SCLK} After SLOAD is asserted, SBYTE is loaded into SREG on the next SCLK tick.

Thus, $t_{maxd} = 3t_{SCLK} + t_{CQ} + t_{SQ} + t_{su} - t_{RCLK}$. A few other parameters must be defined to complete the analysis:

t_h The hold time of SREG.

$t_{CQ(min)}$ The minimum CLK-to-Q delay of HREG, conservatively assumed to be 0.

t_{rec} The recovery time of the S-R latch, the minimum time allowed between negating S and negating R (see box on page 529).

To be loaded successfully into SREG, SBYTE must be remain valid until at least time $t_{end} + t_h$. The point at which SBYTE changes and becomes invalid is 8 RCLK periods after t_{start}, plus $t_{CQ(min)}$. Thus, for proper circuit operation we must have

$$t_{end} + t_h \leq t_{start} + 8t_{RCLK}$$

For the maximum-delay case, we substitute $t_{end} = t_{start} + t_{maxd}$ into this relation and subtract t_{start} from both sides to obtain

$$t_{maxd} + t_h \leq 8t_{RCLK}$$

Substituting the value of t_{maxd} and rearranging, we obtain

$$3t_{SCLK} + t_{CQ} + t_{SQ} + t_{su} + t_h \leq 9t_{RCLK} \tag{8-1}$$

as the requirement for correct circuit operation. Too bad. Even if we assume very short component delays (t_{CQ}, t_{SQ}, t_{su}, t_h), we know that $3t_{SCLK}$ (90 ns) plus anything is going to be more than $9t_{RCLK}$ (also 90 ns). So this design will never work properly in the maximum-delay case.

Even if the load-delay analysis gave a good result, we would still have to consider the requirements for proper operation of the SCTRL circuit itself. In particular, we must ensure that when the SYNC pulse for the next byte occurs, it is not negated until time t_{rec} after SLOAD for the previous byte was negated. So, another condition for proper operation is

$$t_{end} + t_{CQ} + t_{rec} \leq t_{start} + 8t_{RCLK} + t_{CQ(min)}$$

Substituting and simplifying as before, we get another requirement that isn't met by our design:

$$3t_{SCLK} + 2t_{CQ} + t_{SQ} + t_{su} + t_{rec} \leq 9t_{RCLK} \tag{8-2}$$

There are several ways that we can modify our design to satisfy the worst-case timing requirements. Early in our discussion, we noted that we "cheated" by asserting SYNC one RCLK period before the data in HREG is valid, and that we actually might get away with asserting SYNC even sooner. Doing this can help us meet the maximum-delay requirement, because it reduces the "$8t_{RCLK}$" term on the righthand side of the relations. For example, if we asserted SYNC two RCLK periods earlier, we would reduce this term to "$6t_{RCLK}$". However, there's no free lunch; we can't assert SYNC arbitrarily early. We must also consider a *minimum-delay* case, to ensure that the new byte is actually available in HREG when SBYTE is loaded into SREG. The minimum delay t_{maxd} between t_{start} and t_{end} is the sum of the following components:

$-nt_{RCLK}$ Minus n RCLK periods, the delay from t_{start} back to the edge on which SYNC was asserted. In the original design, $n = 1$.

$t_{CQ(min)}$ This is the minimum delay from the RCLK edge until SYNC is asserted, conservatively assumed to be 0.

t_{SQ} This is the delay for NEWBYTE to be asserted, again assumed to be 0.

$-t_h$ Minus the hold time of FF1 in Figure 8-85. NEWBYTE might be asserted at the end of the hold time and still be detected.

$0t_{SCLK}$ Zero times the SCLK period. We might get "lucky" and have the SCLK edge come along just as the hold time of FF1 is ending.

t_{SCLK} A one-SCLK-period delay to asserting SLOAD, as before.

t_{SCLK} A one-SCLK-period delay to loading SBYTE into SREG, as before.

In other words, $t_{mind} = 2t_{SCLK} - t_h - nt_{RCLK}$.

For this case, we must ensure that the new byte has propagated to the output of HREG when the setup time window of SREG begins, so we must have

$$t_{end} - t_{su} \geq t_{start} + t_{co},$$

where t_{co} is the maximum clock-to-output delay of HREG. Substituting $t_{end} = t_{start} + t_{mind}$ and subtracting t_{start} from both sides, we get

$$t_{mind} - t_{su} \geq t_{co}.$$

Substituting the value of t_{mind} and rearranging, we get the final requirement,

$$2t_{\text{SCLK}} - t_h - t_{su} - t_{co} \geq nt_{\text{RCLK}} \qquad (8\text{-}3)$$

If, for example, t_h, t_{su}, and t_{co} are 10 ns each, the maximum value of n is 3; we can't generate SYNC more than two clock ticks before its original position in Figure 8-87. This may or may not be enough to solve the maximum-delay problem, depending on other delay values; this is explored for a particular set of components in Exercise 8.88.

Moving the SYNC pulse earlier may not give enough delay improvement or may not be an available option in some systems. An alternative solution that can always be made to work is to increase the time between successive data transfers from one clock domain to the other. We can always do this because we can always transfer more bits per synchronization. In the Ethernet-interface example, we could collect 16 bits at a time in the RCLK domain and transfer 16 bits at a time to the SCLK domain. This changes the previously stated $8t_{\text{RCLK}}$ terms to $16t_{\text{RCLK}}$, providing a lot more margin for the maximum-delay timing requirements. Once 16 bits have been transferred into the SCLK domain, we can still break them into two 8-bit chunks if we need to process the data a byte at a time.

It may also be possible to improve performance by modifying the design of the SCTRL circuit. Figure 8-88 shows a version where SLOAD is generated directly by the flip-flop that samples NEWBYTE. In this way, SLOAD appears one SCLK period sooner than in our original SCTRL circuit. Also, the S-R latch is cleared sooner. This circuit works only if a couple of key assumptions are true:

1. A reduced metastability resolution time for FF1 is acceptable, equal to the time that SCLK is HIGH. Metastability must be resolved before SCLK goes LOW, because that's when the S-R latch gets cleared if SLOAD is HIGH.

2. The setup time of SREG's CLKEN input (Figure 8-81) is less than or equal to the time that SCLK is LOW. Under the previous assumption, the SLOAD signal applied to CLKEN might be metastable until SCLK goes LOW.

3. The time that SCLK is LOW is long enough to generate a reset pulse on RNEW that meets the minimum pulse-width requirement of the S-R latch.

Note that these behaviors makes proper circuit operation dependent on the duty cycle of SCLK. If SCLK is relatively slow and its duty cycle is close to 50%, this

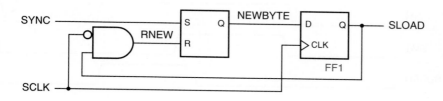

Figure 8-88
Half-clock-period SCTRL circuit for generating SLOAD.

circuit generally works fine. But if SCLK is too fast or has a very small, very large, or unpredictable duty cycle, the original circuit approach must be used.

All of these synchronization schemes require the clock frequencies to be within a certain range of each other for proper circuit operation. This must be considered for testing, where the clocks are usually run slower, and for upgrades, where one or both clocks may run faster. For example, in the Ethernet interface example, we wouldn't change the frequency of standard 100-Mbps Ethernet, but we might upgrade the PCI bus from 33 to 66 MHz.

The problems caused by clock-frequency changes can be subtle. To get a better handle on what can go wrong, it's useful to consider how a synchronizer works (or doesn't work!) if one clock frequency changes by a factor of 10 or more.

For example what happens to the synchronizer timing in Figure 8-86 if we change RCLK from 100 MHz to 10 MHz? At first glance, it would seem that all is well, since a byte now arrives only once every 800 ns, giving much more time for the byte to be transferred into the SCLK domain. Certainly, Eq. (8-1) on page 783 and Eq. (8-2) on page 784 are satisfied with much more margin. However, Eq. (8-3) is no longer satisfied, unless we reduce n to zero! This could be accomplished by generating SYNC one RCLK tick later than is shown in Figure 8-86.

But even with this change, there's *still* a problem. Figure 8-89 shows the new timing, including the later SYNC pulse. The problem is that the SYNC pulse

Figure 8-89 Synchronizer timing with slow (10-MHz) RCLK.

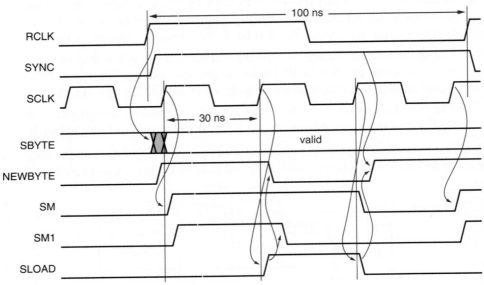

is now 100 ns long. As before, NEWBYTE (the output of the S-R latch in Figure 8-85 on page 780) is set by SYNC and is cleared by SLOAD. The problem is that when SLOAD goes away, SYNC is still asserted, as shown in the new timing diagram. Thus, the new byte will be detected and transferred twice!

The solution to the problem is to detect only the leading edge of SYNC, so that the circuit is not sensitive to the length of the SYNC pulse. A common way of doing this is to replace the S-R latch with an edge-triggered D flip-flop, as shown in Figure 8-90. The leading edge of SYNC sets the flip-flop, while SLOAD is used as an asynchronous clear as before.

The circuit in Figure 8-90 solves the slow-RCLK problem, but it also changes the derivation of Eqns. (8-1) through (8-3) and may make timing more constrained in some areas (see Exercise 8.89). Another disadvantage is that this circuit cannot be realized in a typical PLD, which has all flip-flops controlled by the same clock; instead, a discrete flip-flop must be used to detect SYNC.

After reading almost ten pages to analyze just one "simple" example, you should have a strong appreciation of the difficulty of correct synchronization-circuit design. Several guidelines can help you:

- Minimize the number of different clock domains in a system.

- Clearly identify all clock boundaries and provide clearly identified synchronizers at those boundaries.

- Provide sufficient metastability resolution time for each synchronizer so that synchronizer failure is rare, much more unlikely than other hardware failures.

- Analyze synchronizer behavior over a range of timing scenarios, including faster and slower clocks that might be applied as a result of system testing or upgrades.

- Simulate system behavior over a wide range of timing scenarios as well.

The last guideline above is a catch-all for modern digital designers, who usually rely on sophisticated, high-speed logic simulators to find their bugs. But it's not a substitute for following the first four guidelines. Ignoring them can lead to problems that cannot be detected by a typical, small number of simulation scenarios. Of all digital circuits, synchronizers are the ones for which it's most important to be "correct by design"!

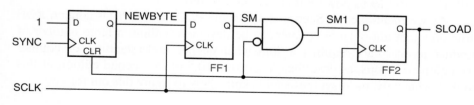

Figure 8-90
Synchronizer with edge-triggered SYNC detection.

References

Historically, probably the first comprehensive set of examples of sequential MSI parts and applications appeared in *The TTL Applications Handbook*, edited by Peter Alfke and Ib Larsen (Fairchild Semiconductor, 1973). This highly practical and informative book was invaluable to this author and to many others who developed digital design curricula in the 1970s.

Moving quickly from the almost forgotten to the yet-to-be discovered, manufacturers' web sites are an excellent source of information on digital design practices. For example, a comprehensive discussion of bus-holder circuits can be found in Texas Instruments' "Implications of Slow or Floating CMOS Inputs" (publ. SCBA004B, December 1997), available on TI's web site at www.ti.com. Another discussion of bus-holder circuits appears in Fairchild Semiconductor's application note, "Designing with Bushold," (*sic*, publ. AN-5006, April 1999), at www.fairchildsemi.com.

Announcements and data sheets for all kinds of new, improved MSI and larger parts can also be found on the Web. For example, chip manufacturers have introduced "wide-bus" registers, drivers, and transceivers that cram 16, 18, or even 32 bits of function into a high-pin-count surface-mount package. Descriptions of many such parts can be found at the Texas Instruments web site (search for "widebus"). Other sites with a variety of data sheets, application notes, and other information include Fairchild (www.fairchildsemi.com) and Philips Semiconductor (www.philipslogic.com).

The field of logic design is fast moving, so much so that sometimes I wish that I wrote fiction, so that I wouldn't have to revise the "practices" discussions in this book every few years. Luckily for me, this book does cover some unchanging theoretical topics (a.k.a. "principles"), and this chapter is no exception. Logic hazards have been known since at least the 1950s, and function hazards were discussed by Edward J. McCluskey in *Logic Design Principles* (Prentice Hall, 1986). Galois fields were invented centuries ago, and their applications to error-correcting codes, as well as to the LFSR counters of this chapter, are described in introductory books on coding theory, including *Error-Control Techniques for Digital Communication* by A. M. Michelson and A. H. Levesque (Wiley-Interscience, 1985). A mathematical theory of state-machine decomposition has been studied for years; Zvi Kohavi devotes a chapter to the topic in his classic book *Switching and Finite Automata Theory*, second edition (McGraw-Hill, 1978). But let us now return to the less esoteric.

As we mentioned in Section 8.4.5, some PLDs and CPLDs contain XOR structures that allow large counters to be designed without a large number of product terms. This requires a somewhat deeper understanding of counter excitation equations, as described in Section 10.5 of the second edition of this book. Fortunately, most synthesis tools know how to figure this out for you.

The general topics of clock skew and multiphase clocking are discussed in McCluskey's *Logic Design Principles*, while an illuminating discussion of these topics as applied to VLSI circuits can be found in *Introduction to VLSI Systems* by Carver Mead and Lynn Conway (Addison-Wesley, 1980). Mead and Conway also provide an introduction to the important topic of *self-timed systems* that eliminate the system clock, allowing each logic element to proceed at its own rate. To give credit where credit is due, we note that all of the Mead and Conway material on system timing, including an outstanding discussion of metastability, appears in their Chapter 7, which was written by Charles L. Seitz.

self-timed systems

Thomas J. Chaney spent decades studying and reporting on the metastability problem. One of his more important works, "Measured Flip-Flop Responses to Marginal Triggering" (*IEEE Trans. Comput.*, Vol. C-32, No. 12, December 1983, pp. 1207–1209), reports some of the results that we showed in Table 8-43.

For the mathematically inclined, Lindsay Kleeman and Antonio Cantoni have written "On the Unavoidability of Metastable Behavior in Digital Systems" (*IEEE Trans. Comput.*, Vol. C-36, No. 1, January 1987, pp. 109–112); the title says it all. The same authors posed the question, "Can Redundancy and Masking Improve the Performance of Synchronizers?" (*IEEE Trans. Comput.*, Vol. C-35, No. 7, July 1986, pp. 643–646). Their answer in that paper was "No," but a response from a reviewer caused them to change their minds to "Maybe." Obviously, they went metastable themselves! Having two authors and a reviewer didn't improve their performance, so the obvious answer to their original question is "No"! In any case, Kleeman and Antonio's papers provide a good set of pointers to mainstream scholarly references on metastability.

The most comprehensive set of early references on metastability (not including Greek philosophers or Devo) is Martin Bolton's "A Guided Tour of 35 Years of Metastability Research" (*Proc. Wescon 1987*, Session 16, "Everything You Might Be Afraid to Know about Metastability," www.wescon.com).

In recent years, as system clock speeds have steadily increased, many IC manufacturers have become much more conscientious about measuring and publishing the metastability characteristics of their devices, often on the Web. Texas Instruments (www.ti.com) provides a very good discussion including test circuits and measured parameters for ten different logic families in "Metastable Response in 5-V Logic Circuits" by Eilhard Haseloff (TI pub. SDYA006, 1997); we used these numbers in Table 8-43.

Cypress Semiconductor (www.cypress.com) publishes an application note, "Are Your PLDs Metastable?" (1997) that is an excellent reference including some history (going back to 1952!), an analog circuit analysis of metastability, test and measurement circuits, and metastability parameters for Cypress PLDs. Another recent note is "Metastability Considerations" from Xilinx Corporation (www.xilinx.com, publ. XAPP077, 1997), which gives measured parameters for their XC7300 and XC9500 families of CPLDs. Of particular interest is the clever circuit and methodology that allows them to count metastable events *inside* the device, even though metastable waveforms are not observable on external pins.

Most digital design textbooks now give good coverage to metastability, prompted by the existence of metastability in real circuits and perhaps also by competition—since 1990, the textbook you're reading has been promoting the topic by introducing metastability in its earliest coverage of sequential circuits. On the analog side of the house, Howard Johnson and Martin Graham provide a nice introduction and a description of how to observe metastable states in their *High-Speed Digital Design: A Handbook of Black Magic* (Prentice Hall, 1993).

Drill Problems

8.1   In Figure 8-5, is the inverter with output DSW really required, or can the SW signal be used directly as the debounced output?

8.2   Suppose that in Table 8-2, the second RAM bank (RAMCS1) is decoded instead using the expression ((ABUS >= 0x010) & (ABUS < 0x020)). Does this yield the same results as the original expression, (ABUS == RAMBANK1)? Explain.

8.3   How many "fuses" are contained in the 16V8 as described in the text? (The commercial device has additional fuses, not described in the text, for user-specific information and security.)

8.4   How many "fuses" are contained in the 22V10 as described in the text? (The commercial device has additional fuses, not described in the text, for user-specific information and security.)

8.5   Determine f_{max} with external feedback for all of the devices in Table 8-12.

8.6   Determine f_{max} with internal feedback for all of the GAL devices in Table 8-12.

8.7   Write an ABEL program for a 16V8 that gives it exactly the same functionality as a 74x374.

8.8   Write an ABEL program for a GAL16V8, GAL20V8, or GAL22V10 that gives it exactly the same functionality as a 74x175. Use the simplest possible device.

8.9   Compare the propagation delays from AVALID to a chip-select output for the two decoding approaches shown in Figures 8-15 and 8-16. Assume that 74FCT373 latches and 10-ns 16V8C devices are used in both designs. Repeat for the delay from ABUS to a chip-select output.

8.10   What would happen if you replaced the edge-triggered D flip-flops in Figure 7-38 with D latches?

8.11   Modify the ABEL program in Table 8-14 to perform the function of a 74X162 decade counter.

8.12   Modify the ABEL program in Table 8-14 to perform the function of a 74X161 counter. Does it still fit in a 16V8?

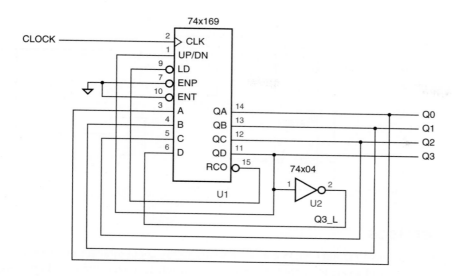

Figure X8.13

8.13   What is the counting sequence of the circuit shown in Figure X8.13?

8.14   A 74x163 counter is hooked up with inputs ENP, ENT, and D always HIGH, inputs A, B, and C always LOW, input LD_L = (QA · QC)′, and input CLR_L = (QB · QD)′. The CLK input is hooked up to a free-running clock signal. Draw a logic diagram for this circuit. Assuming that the counter starts in state 0000, write the output sequence on QD QC QB QA for the next 15 clock ticks.

8.15   Determine the widths of the glitches shown in Figure 8-34 on the Y2_L output of a 74x138 decoder, assuming that the '138 is internally structured as shown in Figure 6-35 on page 388, and that each internal gate has a delay of 10 ns.

8.16   Starting with state 0001, write the sequence of the first ten (10) states for a 5-bit LFSR counter designed according to Figure 8-51 and Table 8-26.

8.17   Redo the two synchronizer MTBF calculations on page 773, but instead of using Chaney's estimates for T_o and τ for the 74LS74, use TI's estimates for the 74LSxx family. What do your results tell you about these sorts of estimates and calculations?

8.18   In some synchronizer applications, the clock frequency f is substituted for the parameter a in metastability MTBF calculations, assuming that an asynchronous input change can occur on *every* clock tick. Redo the two synchronizer MTBF calculations on page 773 under this assumption.

8.19   Calculate the MTBF of a synchronizer built according to Figure 8-76 using 74F74s, assuming a clock frequency of 25 MHz and an asynchronous transition rate of 1 MHz. Assume the setup time of an 'F74 is 5 ns and the hold time is zero.

8.20   Calculate the MTBF of the synchronizer shown in Figure X8.20 on the next page, assuming a clock frequency of 30 MHz and an asynchronous transition rate of 2 MHz. Assume that the setup time t_{setup} and the propagation delay t_{pd} from clock to Q or QN in a 74ALS74 are both 10 ns.

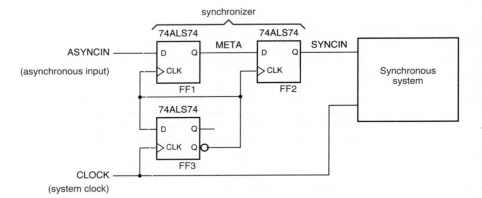

Figure X8.20

Exercises

8.21   What do TTL and CMOS data sheets have to say about momentarily shorting the outputs of a gate to ground as we do in the switch debounce circuit of Figure 8-5? Does the answer vary by family?

8.22   Investigate the behavior of the switch debounce circuit of Figure 8-5 if 74HCT04 inverters are used; repeat for 74AC04 inverters.

8.23   Suppose you are asked to design a circuit that produces a debounced logic input from an SPST (single-pole, *single*-throw) switch. What inherent problem are you faced with?

8.24   Explain why CMOS bus holder circuits don't work well on three-state buses with TTL devices attached. (*Hint:* Consider TTL input characteristics.)

8.25   Write a single VHDL program that combines the address latch and latching decoder of Figure 8-16 and Table 8-2. Use the signal name LA[19:0] for the latched address outputs.

8.26   Design a 4-bit ripple *down* counter using four T flip-flops and no other components.

8.27   Design a 4-bit ripple *down* counter using four D flip-flops and no other components.

8.28   What is the maximum propagation delay from clock to output for the 4-bit ripple counter of Exercise 8.27 using 74HCT74 flip-flops? Repeat, using 74AHCT74 and 74LS74 flip-flops.

8.29   What limits the maximum counting speed of a ripple counter, if you don't insist on being able to read the counter value at all times?

8.30   Based on the design approach in Exercise 8.27 and the answer to Exercise 8.29, what is the maximum counting speed (frequency) for a 4-bit ripple counter using 74HCT74 flip-flops? Repeat, using 74AHCT74 and 74LS74 flip-flops.

8.31   Write a formula for the maximum clock frequency of the synchronous serial binary counter circuit in Figure 8-25. In your formula, let t_{TQ} denote the propagation delay from T to Q in a T flip-flop, t_{setup} the setup time of the EN input to the rising edge of T, and t_{AND} the delay of an AND gate.

8.32 Repeat Exercise 8.31 for the synchronous parallel binary counter circuit shown in Figure 8-26, and compare results.

8.33 Repeat Exercise 8.31 for an n-bit synchronous serial binary counter.

8.34 Repeat Exercise 8.31 for an n-bit synchronous parallel binary counter. Beyond what value of n is your formula no longer valid?

8.35 Using a 74x163 4-bit binary counter, design a modulo-11 counter circuit with the counting sequence 4, 5, 6, …, 13, 14, 4, 5, 6, ….

8.36 Find the datasheet on the Web and look up the internal logic diagram for a 74x162 synchronous decade counter, and write its state table in the style of Table 8-13, including its counting behavior in the normally unused states 10–15.

8.37 Devise a cascading scheme for 74x163s, analogous to the synchronous parallel counter structure of Figure 8-26, such that the maximum counting speed is the same for any counter with up to 36 bits (nine '163s). Determine the maximum counting speed using worst-case delays from a manufacturer's data sheet for the '163s and any SSI components used for cascading.

8.38 Design a modulo-129 counter using only two 74x163s and no additional gates.

8.39 Write an ABEL program for an 8-bit modulo-N counter with clear and load inputs using a PAL22v10, where the value of N is specified by a constant N in the program.

8.40 Write a VHDL or Verilog program for an 8-bit modulo-N counter with clear and load inputs, where the value of N is specified by a constant N in the program.

8.41 Repeat the preceding exercise, but let N be determined by a value that is loaded from the data inputs into a second 8-bit register when a control signal "MLOAD" is asserted. Use comments to document what happens when more than one control input is asserted; your design should exhibit reasonable behavior in these cases.

8.42 Design a clocked synchronous circuit with four inputs, N3, N2, N1, and N0, that represent an integer N in the range 0–15. The circuit has a single output Z that is asserted for exactly N clock ticks during any 16-tick interval (assuming that N is held constant during the interval of observation). (*Hints:* Use combinational logic with a 74x163 set up as a free-running divide-by-16 counter. The ticks in which Z is asserted should be spaced as evenly as possible, that is, every second tick when $N = 8$, every fourth when $N = 4$, and so on.)

8.43 Modify the circuit of Exercise 8.42 so that Z produces N *transitions* in each 16-tick interval. The resulting circuit is called a *binary rate multiplier* and was once sold as a TTL MSI part, the 7497. (*Hint:* Gate the clock with the level output of the previous circuit.)

binary rate multiplier

8.44 Repeat Exercises 8.42 and 8.43 using an 8-bit input N7–N0, and realize the circuit using an ABEL program for a single PAL22V10.

8.45 Repeat Exercises 8.42 and 8.43 using an 8-bit input N7–N0, and describe the design using a behavioral VHDL or Verilog program for an available PLD, CPLD, or FPGA.

8.46 Design a modulo-16 counter, using one 74x169 and at most one SSI package, with the following counting sequence: 7, 6, 5, 4, 3, 2, 1, 0, 8, 9, 10, 11, 12, 13, 14, 15, 7, ….

8.47 Write an ABEL program for an 8-bit counter that realizes a counting sequence similar to the one in Exercise 8.46.

8.48 Write a VHDL or Verilog program for an n-bit counter that realizes a counting sequence similar to the one in Exercise 8.46. Write your code so that the size of the counter can be changed by changing the value of a single constant N.

8.49 Design a binary up/down counter for the elevator controller in a 20-story building, using a single 16V8. The counter should have enable and up/down control inputs. It should stick at state 1 when counting down, stick at state 21 when counting up, and skip state 13 in either mode. Draw a logic diagram and write ABEL equations for your design.

8.50 Repeat the preceding exercise using VHDL or Verilog.

8.51 Modify the VHDL program in Table 8-16 so that the type of ports D and Q is STD_LOGIC_VECTOR, including conversion functions as required.

8.52 Modify the program in Table 8-18 to use structural VHDL, so it conforms exactly to the circuit in Figure 8-36, including the signal names shown in the figure. Define and use any of the following entities that don't already exist in your VHDL library: AND2, INV, NOR2, OR2, XNOR2, Vdffqqn.

8.53 Modify the program in Table 8-19 to use VHDL's generic statement, so that the counter size can be changed using the generic definition.

8.54 Suppose you are asked to design a serial computer, one that moves and processes data one bit at a time. The first decision you must make is which bit to transmit and process first, the LSB or the MSB. Which would you choose, and why?

8.55 Design an 8-bit self-correcting ring counter whose states are 11111110, 11111101, ..., 01111111, using only two SSI/MSI packages.

8.56 Write a VHDL or Verilog program for an 8-bit self-correcting ring counter whose states are 11111110, 11111101, ..., 01111111. Include reset and enable inputs, where the counter goes to the initial state when reset is asserted, and counts only if the enable input is asserted.

8.57 Design two different 2-bit, 4-state counters, where each design uses just a single 74x74 package (two edge-triggered D flip-flops) and no other gates.

8.58 Design a 4-bit Johnson counter and decoding for all eight states using just four flip-flops and eight gates. Your counter need not be self-correcting.

8.59 Write a VHDL or Verilog program for an 8-bit Johnson counter that starts in the all-0s state. Include reset and enable inputs, where the counter goes to the initial state when reset is asserted, and counts only if the enable input is asserted.

8.60 Prove that an even number of shift-register outputs must be connected to the odd-parity circuit in an n-bit LFSR counter if it generates a maximum-length sequence. (Note that this is a necessary but not a sufficient requirement. Also, although Table 8-26 is consistent with what you're supposed to prove, simply quoting the table is not a proof!)

8.61 Prove that X0 must appear on the righthand side of any LFSR feedback equation that generates a maximum-length sequence. (*Note:* Assume the LFSR bit ordering and shift direction are as given in the text; that is, the LFSR counter shifts right, toward the X0 stage.)

8.62   Suppose that an n-bit LFSR counter is designed according to Figure 8-51 and Table 8-26. Prove that if the odd-parity circuit is changed to an even-parity circuit, the resulting circuit is a counter that visits $2^n - 1$ states, including all of the states except $11\ldots11$.

8.63   Find a feedback equation for a 4-bit LFSR counter, other than the one given in Table 8-26, that produces a maximum-length sequence.

8.64   Given an n-bit LFSR counter that generates a maximum-length sequence ($2^n - 1$ states), prove that an extra XOR gate and an $n-1$ input NOR gate connected as suggested in Figure 8-52 produce a counter with 2^n states.

8.65   Prove that a sequence of 2^n states is still obtained if a NAND gate is substituted for a NOR above, but that the state sequence is different.

8.66   Write a VHDL or Verilog program for an 8-bit LFSR counter. Use a constant POLY to define the bit pattern for the polynomial, but use the 8-bit polynomial in Table 8-26. Also write a test bench for your program that proves that your counter visits 255 states before repeating. (*Hint:* In the test bench, use an array of 256 bits to keep track of which states have been visited.)

8.67   After completing Exercise 8.66, try to guess another polynomial that yields a maximum-length sequence. Use your test bench to determine whether each guessed polynomial works.

8.68   After completing Exercise 8.67, modify your test bench to discover and display *all* 8-bit polynomials that yield maximum-length sequences. How many are there?

8.69   Design an iterative circuit for checking the parity of a 16-bit data word with a single even-parity bit. Does the order of bit transmission matter?

8.70   Modify the shift-register program in Table 8-28 to provide an asynchronous clear input using a 22V10.

8.71   Determine the number of product terms required for each output of the RING8 PLD in Table 8-30. Does it fit in a 16V8R?

8.72   In what situations do the ABEL programs in Tables 8-31 and 8-32 give different operational results?

8.73   Modify the ABEL program in Table 8-31 so that the phases are always at least two clock ticks long, even if RESTART is asserted at the beginning of a phase. RESET should still take effect immediately.

8.74   Repeat the preceding exercise for the program in Table 8-32.

8.75   Modify the VHDL program in Table 8-38 or the Verilog program in Table 8-41 so that the phases are always at least two clock ticks long, even if RESTART is asserted at the beginning of a phase. RESET should still take effect immediately. Write a test bench to ensure that your program works as desired.

8.76   Suppose the timing generator of Table 8-31 is used to control a dynamic memory system, such that all six phases must be completed to read or write the memory. If the timing generator is reset during a write operation without completing all six phases, the memory contents may be corrupted. Modify the equations in Table 8-31 to avoid this problem.

8.77   A student proposed to create the timing waveforms of Figure 8-55 by starting with the ABEL program in Table 8-32 and changing the encoding of each of states P1F, P2F, ..., P6F so that the corresponding phase output is 1 instead of 0, so that the phase output is 0 only during the second tick of each phase, as required. Is this a good approach? Comment on the results produced by the ABEL compiler when you try this.

8.78   The output waveforms produced by the ABEL programs in Tables 8-34 and 8-35 are not identical when the RESTART and RUN inputs are changed. Explain the reason for this, and then modify the program in Table 8-35 so that its behavior matches that of Table 8-34.

8.79   The ABEL ring-counter implementation in Table 8-31 is not self-synchronizing. For example, describe what happens if the outputs [P1_L..P6_L] are initially all 0, and the RUN input is asserted without ever asserting RESET or RESTART. What other starting states exhibit this kind of non-self-synchronizing behavior? Modify the program so that it *is* self-synchronizing.

8.80   Repeat the preceding exercise for the VHDL ring-counter in Table 8-38 or the Verilog version in Table 8-41. Write and use a test bench to confirm that your modified code works as desired.

8.81   Design an iterative circuit with one input B_i per stage and two boundary outputs X and Y such that $X = 1$ if at least two B_i inputs are 1 and $Y = 1$ if at least two *consecutive* B_i inputs are 1.

8.82   Suppose that the SYNCIN signal in Drill 8.20 is connected to a combinational circuit in the synchronous system, which in turn drives the D inputs of 74ALS74 flip-flops that are clocked by CLOCK. What is the maximum allowable propagation delay of the combinational logic?

8.83   The circuit in Figure X8.83 includes a deskewing flip-flop so that the synchronized output from the multiple-cycle synchronizer is available as soon as possible after the edge of CLOCK. Ignoring metastability considerations, what is the maximum frequency of CLOCK? For a 74AC74, $t_{setup} = 4.5$ ns and $t_{pd} = 10.5$ ns.

8.84   Using the maximum clock frequency determined in Exercise 8.83, and assuming an asynchronous transition rate of 4 MHz, determine the synchronizer's MTBF.

Figure X8.83

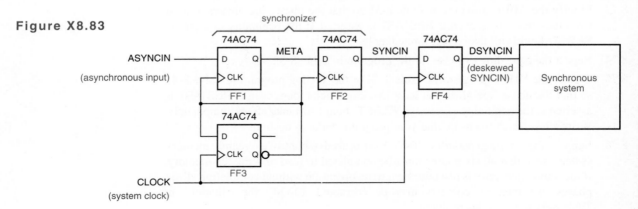

8.85   Determine the MTBF of the synchronizer in Figure X8.83, assuming an asynchronous transition rate of 4 MHz and a clock frequency of 40 MHz, which is less than the maximum determined in Exercise 8.83. In this situation, "synchronizer failure" really occurs only if DSYNCIN is metastable. In other words, SYNCIN may be allowed to be metastable for a short time, as long as it doesn't affect DSYNCIN. This yields a better MTBF.

8.86   A famous digital designer devised the circuit shown in Figure X8.86(a), which is supposed to eliminate metastability within one period of a system clock. Circuit M is a memoryless analog voltage detector whose output is 1 if Q is in the metastable state, 0 otherwise. The circuit designer's idea was that if line Q is detected to be in the metastable state when CLOCK goes low, the NAND gate will clear the D flip-flop, which in turn eliminates the metastable output, causing a 0 output from circuit M and thus negating the CLR input of the flip-flop. The circuits are all fast enough that this all happens well before CLOCK goes high again; the expected waveforms are shown in Figure X8.86(b).

Unfortunately, the synchronizer still failed occasionally, and the famous digital designer is now designing pockets for blue jeans. Explain, in detail, how it failed, including a timing diagram.

8.87   Look up U.S. patent number 5,764,710, "Meta-stable-resistant front-end to a synchronizer with asynchronous clear and asynchronous second-stage clock selector," and look at the first two flip-flops in Fig. 3. Compare their functionality with a conventional multi-stage synchronizer, shown in Fig. 1, and describe any benefits that the additional logic provides. (*Hints:* Patents can be found at www.uspto.gov).

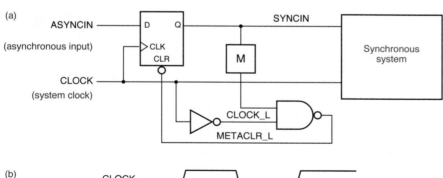

Figure X8.86

8.88   In the synchronization circuit of Figures 8-81, 8-83, and 8-85, you can reduce the delay of the transfer of a byte from the RCLK domain to the SCLK domain if you use an earlier version of the SYNC pulse to start the synchronizer. Assuming that you can generate SYNC during any bit of the received byte, which bit should you use to minimize the delay? Also determine whether your solution satisfies the maximum-delay requirements for the circuit. Assume that all the components have 74AHCT timing and that the S-R latch is built from a pair of cross-coupled NOR gates, and show a detailed timing analysis for your answers.

8.89   Instead of using a latch in the synchronization control circuit of Figure 8-85, some applications use an edge-triggered D flip-flop as shown in Figure 8-90. Derive the maximum-delay and minimum-delay requirements for this circuit, corresponding to Eqs. (8-1) through (8-3), and discuss whether this approach eases or worsens the delay requirements.

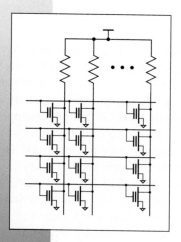

chapter 9

Memory, CPLDs, and FPGAs

A
ny sequential circuit has memory of a sort, since each flip-flop or latch stores one bit of information. However, we usually reserve the word "memory" to refer to bits that are stored in a structured way, usually as a two-dimensional array in which one row of bits is accessed at a time.

This chapter describes several different types of memory organizations and commercially available memory chips. The same kinds of memory may be embedded into larger VLSI chips, where they are combined with other circuits to perform a useful function.

The applications of memory are many and varied. In a microprocessor's central processing unit (CPU), a "read-only memory" may be used to define multiple small steps used to execute each complex instruction in the CPU's instruction set, or to store "seed" constants used in a division algorithm. Alongside the CPU, a fast "static memory" may serve as a cache to hold recently used instructions and data. And a microprocessor's main-memory subsystem may contain billions of bits in "dynamic memory" that store complete operating systems, programs, and data.

Applications of memory are not limited to microprocessors or even to purely digital systems. For example, equipment in the public telephone system uses read-only memories to perform certain transformations on digitized voice signals, and fast "static memories" as a "switching fabric" to route digitized voice between subscribers. Most portable audio compact-

disc players "read ahead" and store several seconds of audio in a "dynamic memory" so that the unit can keep playing even if it is physically jarred (this requires over 1.4 million bits per second of stored audio). And there are many examples of modern audio/visual equipment that use memories to temporarily store digitized signals for enhancement through digital signal processing.

This chapter begins with a discussion of read-only memory and its applications and then describes two different types of read/write memory. Optional subsections discuss the internal structure of the different memory types.

The last two sections in this chapter discuss CPLDs and FPGAs. These devices are akin to memories in that they are large, regular structures that can be used in a variety of applications. By enabling very fast development of customized logic functions, they have become essential building blocks in modern digital design.

9.1 Read-Only Memory

read-only memory (ROM)

address input

data output

A *read-only memory (ROM)* is a combinational circuit with n inputs and b outputs, as shown in Figure 9-1. The inputs are called *address inputs* and are traditionally named A0, A1, ... , An−1. The outputs are called *data outputs* and are typically named D0, D1, ... , Db−1.

A ROM "stores" the truth table of an n-input, b-output combinational logic function. For example, Table 9-1 is the truth table of a 3-input, 4-output combinational function; it could be stored in a $2^3 \times 4$ (8×4) ROM. Neglecting propagation delays, a ROM's data outputs at all times equal the output bits in the truth-table row selected by the address inputs.

Since a ROM is a combinational circuit, you would be correct to say that it's not really a memory at all. In terms of digital circuit operation, you can treat

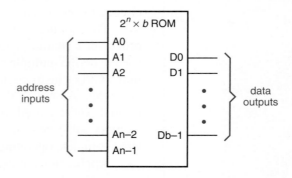

Figure 9-1
Basic structure of a $2^n \times b$ ROM.

MEMORY—NOT!   Most types of read-only memory are not really memory in the strictest sense of the word, because they are combinational, not sequential, circuits. They are called "memory" because of the organizational paradigm that describes their function.

Inputs			Outputs			
A2	A1	A0	D3	D2	D1	D0
0	0	0	1	1	1	0
0	0	1	1	1	0	1
0	1	0	1	0	1	1
0	1	1	0	1	1	1
1	0	0	0	0	0	1
1	0	1	0	0	1	0
1	1	0	0	1	0	0
1	1	1	1	0	0	0

Table 9-1
Truth table for a
3-input, 4-output
combinational logic
function.

a ROM like any other combinational logic element. However, you can also think of information as being "stored" in the ROM when it is manufactured or programmed (we'll say more about how this is done in Section 9.1.4).

Although we think of ROM as being a type of memory, it has an important difference from most other types of integrated-circuit memory. ROM is *non-volatile memory*; that is, its contents are preserved even if no power is applied.

nonvolatile memory

9.1.1 Using ROMs for "Random" Combinational Logic Functions

Table 9-1 is actually the truth table of a 2-to-4 decoder with an output-polarity control, a function that can be built with discrete gates as shown in Figure 9-2. Thus, there are at least two different ways to build the decoder—with discrete gates, or with an 8×4 ROM that contains the truth table, as shown in Figure 9-3.

The assignment pattern of decoder inputs and outputs to ROM inputs and outputs in Figure 9-3 is a consequence of the way that the truth table in Table 9-1 is constructed. Thus, the physical ROM realization of the decoder is not unique.

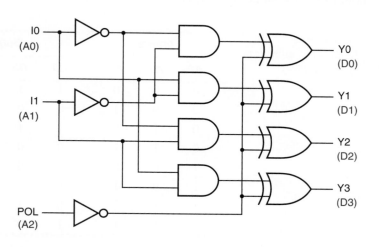

Figure 9-2
A 2-to-4 decoder
with output-polarity
control.

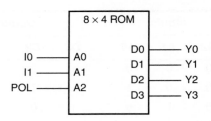

Figure 9-3
Connections to build the
2-to-4 decoder using an 8×4
ROM that stores Table 9-1.

That is, we could write the rows or columns of the truth table in a different order and use a physically different ROM to perform the same logic function, simply by assigning the decoder signals to different ROM inputs and outputs. Another way to look at this is that we can rename the individual address inputs and data outputs of the ROM.

For example, swapping the bits in the D0 and D3 columns of Table 9-1 would give us the truth table for a physically different ROM. However, the new ROM could still be used to build the 2-to-4 decoder simply by swapping the Y0 and Y3 labels in Figure 9-3. Likewise, if we shuffled the data rows of the truth table as shown in Table 9-2, we would get another different ROM, but it could still be used as the 2-to-4 decoder with a rearrangement of the address inputs, A0 = POL, A1 = I0, A2 = I1.

When constructing a ROM to store a given truth table, input and output signals reading from right to left in the truth table are normally assigned to ROM address inputs and data outputs with ascending labels. Each address or data combination may then be read as a corresponding binary integer with the bits numbered in the "natural" way. A data file is typically used to specify the truth table to be stored in the ROM when it is manufactured or programmed. The data file usually gives the address and data values as hexadecimal numbers. For example, a data file may specify Table 9-2 by saying that ROM addresses 0–7 should store the values E, 1, D, 2, B, 4, 7, 8.

Table 9-2
Truth table with data
rows shuffled.

Inputs			Outputs			
A2	A1	A0	D3	D2	D1	D0
0	0	0	1	1	1	0
0	0	1	0	0	0	1
0	1	0	1	1	0	1
0	1	1	0	0	1	0
1	0	0	1	0	1	1
1	0	1	0	1	0	0
1	1	0	0	1	1	1
1	1	1	1	0	0	0

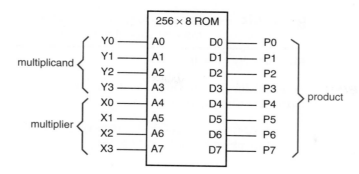

Figure 9-4
Connections to perform a 4 × 4 unsigned binary multiplication using a 256 × 8 ROM.

Another simple example of a function that can be built with ROM is 4×4 unsigned binary multiplication. We showed an ABEL program for this function in Section 6.11.2 and found that the number of product terms required (36) was too high to obtain with just one pass through a conventional PLD's AND-OR array. Alternatively, we can realize the function with one pass through a $2^8 \times 8$ (256×8) ROM with the connections shown in Figure 9-4.

A ROM's contents are normally specified by a file that contains one entry for every address in the ROM. For example, Table 9-3 is a hexadecimal listing of the 4×4 multiplier ROM contents. Each row gives a starting address in the ROM and specifies the 8-bit data values stored at 16 successive addresses.

The nice thing about ROM-based design is that you can usually write a simple program in a high-level language to calculate what should be stored in the ROM. For example, it took only a few minutes to write a C program, shown in Table 9-4, that generated the contents of Table 9-3.

Table 9-3 Hexadecimal text file specifying the contents of a 4 × 4 multiplier ROM.

```
00:  00 00 00 00 00 00 00 00 00 00 00 00 00 00 00 00
10:  00 01 02 03 04 05 06 07 08 09 0A 0B 0C 0D 0E 0F
20:  00 02 04 06 08 0A 0C 0E 10 12 14 16 18 1A 1C 1E
30:  00 03 06 09 0C 0F 12 15 18 1B 1E 21 24 27 2A 2D
40:  00 04 08 0C 10 14 18 1C 20 24 28 2C 30 34 38 3C
50:  00 05 0A 0F 14 19 1E 23 28 2D 32 37 3C 41 46 4B
60:  00 06 0C 12 18 1E 24 2A 30 36 3C 42 48 4E 54 5A
70:  00 07 0E 15 1C 23 2A 31 38 3F 46 4D 54 5B 62 69
80:  00 08 10 18 20 28 30 38 40 48 50 58 60 68 70 78
90:  00 09 12 1B 24 2D 36 3F 48 51 5A 63 6C 75 7E 87
A0:  00 0A 14 1E 28 32 3C 46 50 5A 64 6E 78 82 8C 96
B0:  00 0B 16 21 2C 37 42 4D 58 63 6E 79 84 8F 9A A5
C0:  00 0C 18 24 30 3C 48 54 60 6C 78 84 90 9C A8 B4
D0:  00 0D 1A 27 34 41 4E 5B 68 75 82 8F 9C A9 B6 C3
E0:  00 0E 1C 2A 38 46 54 62 70 7E 8C 9A A8 B6 C4 D2
F0:  00 0F 1E 2D 3C 4B 5A 69 78 87 96 A5 B4 C3 D2 E1
```

Table 9-4 Program to generate the text file specifying the contents of a 4 × 4 multiplier ROM.

```
#include <stdio.h>

/* Procedure to print d as a hex digit. */
void PrintHexDigit(int d)
{
    if (d<10) printf("%c", '0'+d);
    else printf("%c", 'A'+d-10);
}

/* Procedure to print i as two hex digits.  */
void PrintHex2(int i)
{
    PrintHexDigit((i / 16) % 16);
    PrintHexDigit(i % 16);
}

void main()
{
  int x, y;

  for (x=0; x<=15; x++) {
    PrintHex2(x*16); printf(":");
    for (y=0; y<=15; y++) {
      printf(" ");
      PrintHex2(x*y);
    }
    printf("\n");
  }
}
```

*9.1.2 Internal ROM Structure

The mechanism used by ROMs to "store" information varies with different ROM technologies. In most ROMs, the presence or absence of a diode or transistor distinguishes between a 0 and a 1.

Figure 9-5 is the schematic of a primitive 8 × 4 ROM that you could build yourself using an MSI decoder and a handful of diodes. The address inputs select one of the decoder outputs to be asserted. Each decoder output is called a *word line* because it selects one row or word of the table stored in the ROM. The figure shows the situation with A2–A0 = 101 and ROW5_L asserted.

word line

bit line

Each vertical line in Figure 9-5 is called a *bit line* because it corresponds to one output bit of the ROM. An asserted word line pulls a bit line LOW if a diode is connected between the word line and the bit line. There is only one diode in

---

*Throughout this book, optional sections are marked with an asterisk.

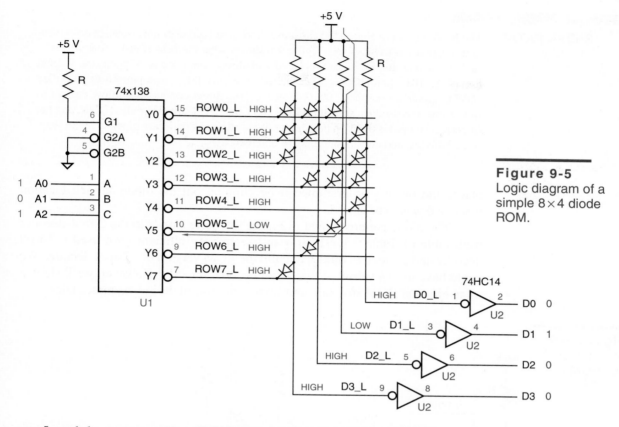

Figure 9-5
Logic diagram of a
simple 8×4 diode
ROM.

row 5, and the corresponding bit line (D1_L) is pulled LOW. The bit lines are buffered through inverters to produce the D3–D0 ROM outputs, 0010 for the case shown.

In the ROM circuit of Figure 9-5, each intersection between a word line and a bit line corresponds to one bit of "memory." If a diode is present at the intersection, a 1 is stored; otherwise, a 0 is stored. If you were to build this circuit in the lab, you would "program" the memory by inserting and removing diodes at each intersection. Primitive though it may seem, owners of the DEC PDP-11 minicomputer (circa 1970) made use of similar technology in the M792 32×16 "bootstrap ROM module." The module was shipped with 512 diodes soldered in

**DETAILS,
DETAILS**   Inverters with CMOS input thresholds are used in Figure 9-5 to improve the circuit's noise margins, because the 0.7-volt drop across the diodes creates a LOW level on the bit lines that is not really so low. Fortunately, with the 74HC04, a LOW level is anything less than 1.35 V. Of course, you'd never build this circuit except in an academic lab—it's easier just to buy and program a commercial ROM chip.

SNEAK PATHS   The ROM circuit of Figure 9-5 must use diodes, not direct connections, at each location where a 1 is to be stored. Figure 9-6 shows what happens if just a few diodes—such as the ones in row 3—are replaced with direct connections. Suppose the address inputs are 101; then ROW5_L is asserted, and only D1_L is supposed to be pulled LOW to create an output of 0010. However, the direct connections allow current to flow along *sneak paths*, so that bit lines D2_L and D0_L are also pulled LOW, and the (incorrect) output is 0111. When diodes are used, sneak paths are blocked by reverse-biased diodes, and correct outputs are obtained.

place, and owners programmed it by clipping out the diode at each location where a 0 was to be stored.

The diode pattern shown in Figure 9-5 corresponds to the 2-to-4-decoder truth table of Table 9-1. This doesn't seem very efficient—we used a 3-to-8 decoder and a bunch of diodes to build the ROM version of a 2-to-4 decoder. We could have used a subset of the 3-to-8 decoder directly! However, we'll show a more efficient ROM structure and some more useful design examples later.

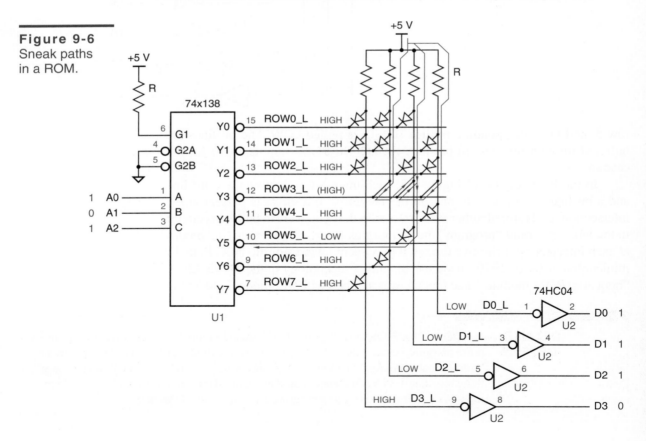

Figure 9-6
Sneak paths
in a ROM.

*9.1.3 Two-Dimensional Decoding

Suppose you wanted to build a 128×1 ROM using the kind of structure described in the preceding subsection. Have you ever thought about what it would take to build a 7-to-128 decoder? Try 128 7-input NAND gates to begin with, and add 14 buffers and inverters with a fanout of 64 each! ROMs with millions of bits or more are available commercially; trust me, they do not contain 20-to-1,048,576 decoders or worse. Instead, a different structure, called *two-dimensional decoding*, is used to reduce the decoder size to something on the order of the square root of the number of addresses.

two-dimensional decoding

The basic idea in two-dimensional decoding is to arrange the ROM cells in an array that is as close as possible to square. For example, Figure 9-7 shows a possible internal structure for a 128×1 ROM. The three high-order address bits, A6–A4, are used to select a row. Each row stores 16 bits starting at address (A6, A5, A4, 0, 0, 0, 0). When an address is applied to the ROM, all 16 bits in the selected row are "read out" in parallel on the bit lines. A 16-input multiplexer selects the desired data bit based on the low-order address bits.

Figure 9-7 Internal structure of a 128×1 ROM using two-dimensional decoding.

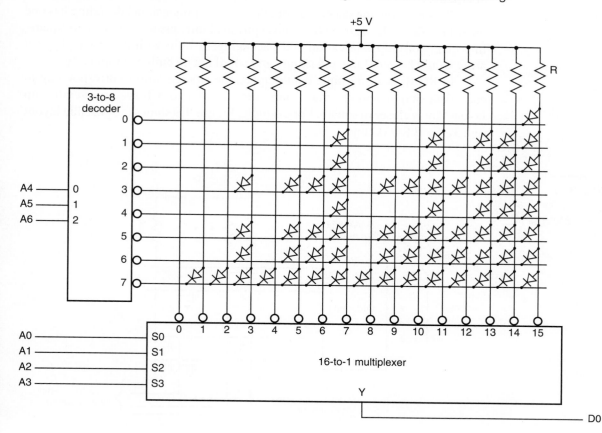

TRANSISTORS AS ROM ELEMENTS

MOS ROMs actually use a transistor instead of a diode at each location where a bit is to be stored; Figure 9-8 shows the basic idea. The row decoder has active-high outputs. When a row line is asserted, the NMOS transistors in that row are turned on, which pulls the corresponding bit lines low. A similar idea can be used in ROMs built with bipolar transistors.

By the way, the diode pattern in Figure 9-7 was not chosen at random. It performs a very useful 7-input combinational logic function that would require 35 4-input AND gates to build as a minimal two-level AND-OR circuit (see Exercise 9.7). The ROM version of this function could actually save a fair amount of engineering effort and space compared to a gate-level design.

Two-dimensional decoding allows a 128×1 ROM to be built with a 3-to-8 decoder and a 16-input multiplexer (whose complexity is comparable to that of a 4-to-16 decoder). A $1M \times 1$ ROM could be built with a 10-to-1024 decoder and a 1024-input multiplexer—not easy, but a lot simpler than the one-dimensional alternative.

Besides reducing decoding complexity, two-dimensional decoding has one other benefit—it leads to a chip whose physical dimensions are close to square, important for chip fabrication and packaging. A chip with a $1M \times 1$ physical array would be *very* long and skinny and could not be built economically.

In ROMs with multiple data outputs, the storage arrays corresponding to each data output may be made narrower in order to achieve an overall chip layout that is closer to square. For example, Figure 9-9 shows the possible layout of a $32K \times 8$ ROM chip.

Figure 9-8
MOS transistors as storage elements in a ROM.

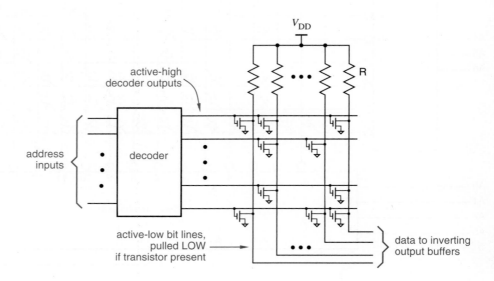

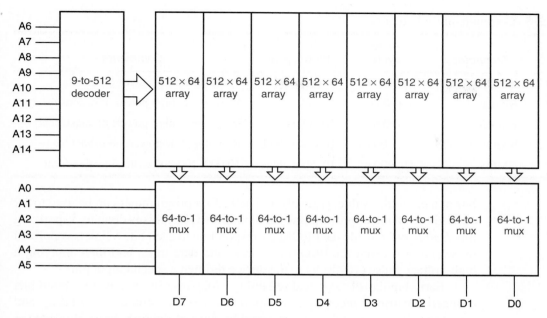

Figure 9-9 Possible layout of a 32K × 8 ROM.

9.1.4 Commercial ROM Types

Unless you visit the Computer History Museum in Mountain View, CA, you won't find any ROM modules built with discrete diodes. A modern ROM is fabricated as a single IC chip; one that stores 16 megabits can be purchased for well under $5. Various methods are used to "program" the information stored in a ROM, as discussed below and summarized in Table 9-5.

Most of the early integrated-circuit ROMs were *mask-programmable ROMs* (or, simply, *mask ROMs*). A mask ROM is programmed by the pattern of connections and no-connections in one of the *masks* used in the IC manufacturing process. To program or write information into the ROM, the customer gives the manufacturer a listing of the desired ROM contents, using a floppy disk or other transfer medium. The manufacturer uses this information to create one or more customized masks to manufacture ROMs with the required pattern. ROM manufacturers impose a *mask charge* of several thousand dollars for the "customized" aspects of mask-ROM production. Because of mask charges and the four-week delay typically required to obtain programmed chips, mask ROMs are normally used today only in very high-volume applications. For low-volume applications there are more cost-effective choices, discussed next.

A *programmable read-only memory (PROM)* is similar to a mask ROM, except that the customer may store data values (i.e., "program the PROM") in just a few minutes using a *PROM programmer*. A PROM chip is manufactured with all of its diodes or transistors "connected." This corresponds to having all

mask-programmable ROM

mask ROM

mask

mask charge

programmable read-only memory (PROM)

PROM programmer

Table 9-5 Commercial ROM types.

Type	Technology	Read cycle	Write cycle	Comments
Mask ROM	NMOS, CMOS	10–200 ns	4 weeks	Write once; low power
Mask ROM	Bipolar	< 100 ns	4 weeks	Write once; high power; low density
PROM	Bipolar	< 100 ns	10–50 μs/byte	Write once; high power; no mask charge
EPROM	NMOS, CMOS	25–200 ns	10–50 μs/byte	Reusable; low power; no mask charge
EEPROM	NMOS	50–200 ns	10–50 μs/byte	10,000–100,000 writes/location limit

fusible link

bits at a particular value, typically 1. The PROM programmer can be used to set desired bits to the opposite value. In bipolar PROMs, this is done by vaporizing tiny *fusible links* inside the PROM corresponding to each bit. A link is vaporized by selecting it using the PROM's address and data lines, and then applying a high-voltage pulse (10–30 V) to the device through a special input pin.

Early bipolar PROMs had reliability problems. Sometimes the stored bits changed because of incompletely vaporized links that would "grow back," and sometimes intermittent failures occurred because of floating shrapnel inside the IC package. However, these problems were worked out, and reliable fusible-link technology was later used not only in bipolar PROMs, but also in the bipolar PLD circuits that we describe in Section BiPLD in DDPPonline.

erasable programmable read-only memory (EPROM)

Introduced later, an *erasable programmable read-only memory (EPROM)* can be programmed like a PROM, but can also be "erased" to the all-1s state by exposing it to ultraviolet light. No, the light does not cause fuses to grow back! Rather, EPROMs use a different technology, called "floating-gate MOS."

floating-gate MOS transistor

As shown in Figure 9-10, an EPROM has a *floating-gate MOS transistor* at every bit location. Each transistor has two gates. The "floating" gate is not connected and is surrounded by extremely high-impedance insulating material. To program an EPROM, the programmer applies a high voltage to the nonfloating gate at each bit location where a 0 is to be stored. This causes a temporary breakdown in the insulating material and allows a negative charge to accumulate on the floating gate. When the high voltage is removed, the negative charge remains. During subsequent read operations, the negative charge prevents the MOS transistor from turning on when it is selected.

EPROM manufacturers "guarantee" that a properly programmed bit will retain 70% of its charge for at least 10 years, even if the part is stored at 125°C, so EPROMs definitely fall into the category of "nonvolatile memory." However, they can also be erased. The insulating material surrounding the floating gate becomes slightly conductive if it is exposed to ultraviolet light with a certain

EPROM erasing

wavelength. Thus, EPROMs can be erased by exposing the chips to ultraviolet light, typically for 5–20 minutes, when the chip is housed in a package with a transparent quartz lid.

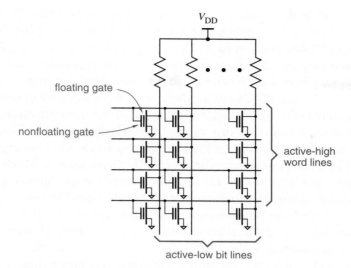

Figure 9-10
Storage matrix in an EPROM using floating-gate MOS transistors.

At one time, the most common application of EPROMs was to store programs in microprocessor systems. EPROMs were typically used during program development, where the program or other information in the EPROM must be repeatedly changed during debugging. However, ROMs and PROMs usually cost less than EPROMs of similar capacity. Therefore, once a program is finalized, a ROM or PROM may be used in production to save cost. Most of today's PROMs are actually EPROMS housed in inexpensive plastic packages without quartz lids for erasing; these are called *one-time programmable (OTP) ROMs.*

An *electrically erasable programmable read-only memory (EEPROM)* is like an EPROM, except that individual stored bits may be erased electrically. The floating gates in an EEPROM are surrounded by a much thinner insulating layer and can be erased by applying a voltage of the opposite polarity as the charging voltage to the nonfloating gate. Large EEPROMs (1 Mbit or larger) allow erasing only in fixed-size blocks, typically 128–1024 Kbits (16–128 Kbytes) at a time. These memories are usually called *flash EPROMs* or *flash memories*, because an entire block can be erased "in a flash."

As noted in Table 9-5 on page 810, writing an EEPROM location takes much longer than reading it, so an EEPROM is no substitute for the read/write memories discussed later in this chapter. Also, because the insulating layer is so thin, it can be worn out by repeated programming operations. As a result, EEPROMs can be reprogrammed only a limited number of times, as few as 10,000 times per location. Therefore, EEPROMs are typically used for storing data that must be preserved when the equipment is not powered, but that doesn't change very often, such as the default configuration data for a computer.

Popular ROMs for microprocessors and other moderate-speed ROM applications include the *28C64*, *28C256*, *28C010*, and *28C040* EEPROMs, whose logic symbols are shown in Figure 9-11. Each of these devices includes a "WE"

one-time programmable (OTP) ROM

electrically erasable programmable read-only memory (EEPROM)

flash EPROM
flash memory

28C64
28C256
28C010
28C040

(write-enable) input for programming operations. Older 27-series EPROMS had a "VPP" pin to apply a high voltage for programming, but the newer 28C-series EEPROMs don't need it. Their programming-voltage requirements are lower, and they are able to generate the needed programming-voltage pulses from the logic power supply using on-chip analog circuits such as "charge pumps."

Larger ROMs are available with more bits and in some cases wider data outputs of 16 or 32 bits. In 2005, one of the most impressive was the Intel P30 family of flash memory, whose largest device actually assembles a stack of four individual 256-Mbit EEPROM dice in a single SMT package to yield a total of 128 Mbytes of memory in 1024 128-Kbyte sectors. Much smaller ROMs are also produced with 3-bit serial interfaces for specialized applications, such as downloading the programming information into FPGAs.

Multiple flash memories are often packaged into a single credit-card-size module for applications requiring large amounts of nonvolatile storage. The most common application of these modules is in digital cameras, where storing a single uncompressed high-resolution image may require 10 Mbytes or more of storage. In 2005, the largest flash card was sold by industry leader SanDisk Corporation and contained 4 Gbytes (32,768 Mbits) of memory.

Figure 9-11
Logic symbols for standard EEPROMs in 28- and 32-pin dual in-line packages.

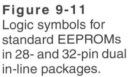

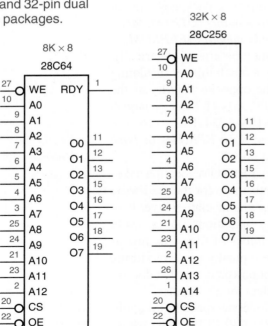

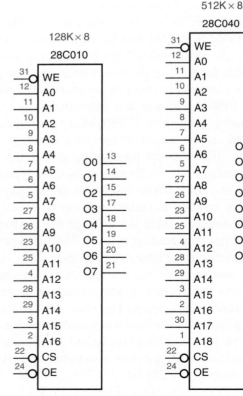

9.1.5 ROM Control Inputs and Timing

The outputs of a ROM must often be connected to a three-state bus, where different devices may drive the bus at different times. Therefore, most commercial ROM chips have three-state data outputs and an *output-enable (OE) input* that must be asserted to enable the outputs.

output-enable (OE) input

Many ROM applications, especially program storage, have multiple ROMs connected to a bus, where only one ROM drives the bus at a time. Most ROMs have a *chip-select (CS) input* to simplify the design of such systems. In addition to OE, a ROM's CS input must be asserted to enable the three-state outputs.

chip-select (CS) input

Figure 9-12 shows how the OE and CS inputs could be used when connecting four 32K × 8 EEPROMs to an 8-bit microprocessor system that requires 128 Kbytes of EEPROM. The microprocessor has an 8-bit data bus and a 20-bit address bus, for a maximum address space of 1 Mbyte (2^{20} bytes). The EEPROM is supposed to be located in the highest 128K of the address space. To obtain this behavior, a NAND gate is used to produce the HIMEM_L signal, which is asserted when the address bus contains an address in the highest 128K (A19–A17 = 111). A 74x139 2-to-4 decoder then selects one of the four 32K × 8

Figure 9-12 Address decoding and EEPROM enabling in a microprocessor system.

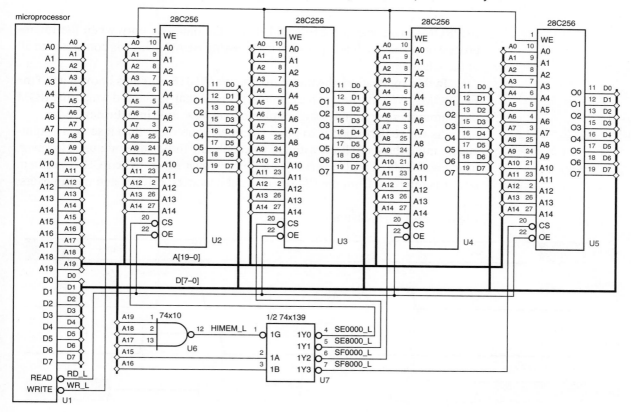

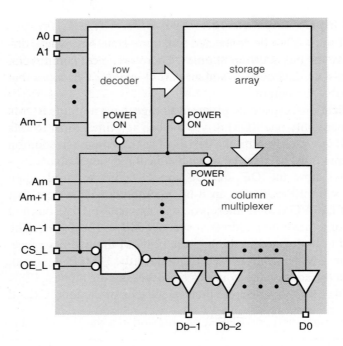

Figure 9-13
Internal ROM
structure, showing
use of control inputs.

EEPROMs. The selected EEPROM drives the data bus only when the microprocessor requests a read operation by asserting READ, which is connected to all of the OE inputs.

In this application, the microprocessor's WRITE output is hooked up to the EEPROMs' WE (write-enable) inputs. This signal is used during EEPROM programming operations, for example, to load new code into the device.

As we've described it so far, a CS input is no more than a second output-enable input that is ANDed with OE to enable the three-state outputs. However, in many ROMs, CS also serves as a *power-down input*. When CS is negated, power is removed from the ROM's internal decoders, drivers, and multiplexers.

power-down input

Figure 9-14 ROM timing.

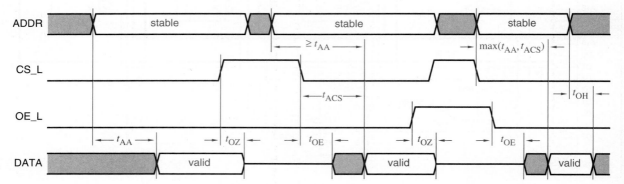

In this *standby mode* of operation, a typical ROM consumes less than 10% of the power it uses in *active mode* with CS asserted. In Figure 9-12, at most one ROM is selected at any time, so the total power consumption of all the ROM chips is much closer to that of one chip than four.

standby mode
active mode

Figure 9-13 shows how CS and OE inputs are used inside a typical ROM. Figure 9-14 shows typical ROM timing, including the following parameters:

t_{AA} *Access time from address.* The access time from address of a ROM is the propagation delay from stable address inputs to valid data outputs. When designers talk about "a 100-ns ROM," they are usually referring to this parameter.

t_{AA}
access time from address

t_{ACS} *Access time from chip select.* The access time from chip select of a ROM is the propagation delay from the time CS is asserted until the data outputs are valid. In some chips, this is longer than the access time from address, because the chip takes a little while to "power up." In others, this time is shorter because CS controls only output enabling.

t_{ACS}
access time from chip select

t_{OE} *Output-enable time.* This parameter is usually much shorter than access time. The output-enable time of a ROM is the propagation delay from OE and CS both asserted until the three-state output drivers have left the Hi-Z state. Depending on whether the address inputs have been stable long enough, the output data may or may not be valid at that point.

t_{OE}
output-enable time

t_{OZ} *Output-disable time.* The output-disable time of a ROM is the propagation delay from the time OE or CS is negated until the three-state output drivers have entered the Hi-Z state.

t_{OZ}
output-disable time

t_{OH} *Output-hold time.* The output-hold time of a ROM is the length of time that the outputs remain valid after a change in the address inputs, or after OE_L or CS_L is negated.

t_{OH}
output-hold time

As with other components, the manufacturer specifies maximum and, sometimes, typical values for all timing parameters. Usually, minimum values are also specified for t_{OE} and t_{OH}. The minimum value of t_{OH} is usually specified to be 0; that is, the minimum combinational-logic delay through the ROM is 0.

NOT ALL INPUTS ARE CREATED EQUAL
Given the decoding and multiplexing structure in Figure 9-13, you might think that the address access time is shorter from some address inputs than it is from others. In a given application, if some address-input signals were delayed relative to the others, you could recover this delay by connecting the slower signals to the "faster" ROM inputs. After all, any input signal can be connected to any ROM address input if you're willing to rearrange the ROM contents accordingly.

However, ROM manufacturers don't specify which, if any, inputs are faster. In fact, the internal electrical characteristics of most ROMs may be such that the difference is not enough to bother with.

UNBELIEVABLY FAST ROMS   The actual delay through a ROM is never 0, of course, but it can easily be just slightly less than what you need to meet a nonzero hold-time requirement elsewhere in a design. So it's best to assume that t_{OH} for a ROM is 0, unless you really know what you're doing.

9.1.6 ROM Applications

As we mentioned earlier, the most common application of ROMs is for program storage in microprocessor systems. However, in many applications a ROM can provide a low-cost realization of a complex or "random" combinational logic function. In this section we'll give a couple of examples of ROM-based circuits that are used in the digital telephone network.

When an analog voice signal enters a typical digital telephone system, it is sampled 8,000 times per second and converted into a sequence of 8-bit bytes representing the analog signal at each sampling point. In this section we'll describe the coding of these 8-bit bytes, which is more complicated than you might expect. Then show how, despite the complexity, ROM-based circuits can easily manipulate this highly encoded information.

The simplest 8-bit encoding of the sign and amplitude of an analog signal would be an 8-bit integer in the two's-complement or signed-magnitude system; this is called a *linear encoding*. However, an 8-bit linear encoding yields a *dynamic range*—the ratio between range of representable numbers and the smallest representable difference—of only 2^8 or 256. For you audiophiles, this corresponds to a dynamic range in signal power of 20 log 256 or about 48 dB. By comparison, compact audio discs use a 16-bit linear encoding with a theoretical dynamic range of 20 log 2^{16} or about 96 dB.

Instead of a linear encoding, the North American telephone network uses an 8-bit *companded encoding* called *μ-law PCM* (pulse-code modulation). (The European network uses a different 8-bit companding formula called *A-law*.) Figure 9-15 shows the format of an 8-bit coded byte, a sort of floating-point representation containing sign (*S*), exponent (*E*), and mantissa (*M*) fields. The analog value *V* represented by a byte in this format is given by the formula

$$V = (1-2S) \cdot [(2^E) \cdot (2M + 33) - 33]$$

An analog signal represented in this format can range from $-8159 \cdot k$ to $+8159 \cdot k$, where k is an arbitrary scale factor. The range of signals is $2 \cdot 8159$ and the smallest difference that can be represented is only 2 (when $E = 0$), so the

linear encoding
dynamic range

companded encoding
μ-law PCM
A-law PCM

Figure 9-15
Format of a μ-law PCM byte.

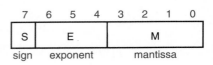

With μ-law PCM you don't get something for nothing, of course. In the companded encoding, the difference between successive coded values is greater at high amplitudes than it is at low amplitudes, so the encodings of large analog signals suffer from more quantizing distortion (caused by the difference between the sampled analog value and the nearest available coded representation). Expressed as a percentage of peak signal amplitude, though, quantizing distortion is roughly constant across the entire range of representable values.

By the way, μ-law PCM is one of several different formats that can be used to encode voice in internet telephony, or voice-over-IP (VoIP) applications, where this coding standard is known as G.701. In VoIP, multiple voice samples, typically 5–10 ms worth (40-80 bytes in G.701), are packed together and transmitted in a single IP packet.

dynamic range is 20 log 8159 or about 78 dB, quite an improvement over an 8-bit linear code.

Now let's look at some ROM applications involving μ-law coded voice signals. Believe it or not, in many types of phone connections your voice is purposely attenuated by a few decibels to make things work better. In an analog phone network, attenuation was performed by a simple, passive analog circuit, but not so in the digital world. Given a μ-law PCM byte, a *digital attenuator* *digital attenuator* must produce a different PCM byte that represents the original analog signal multiplied by a specified attenuation factor.

One way to build a digital attenuator is shown in Figure 9-16. The input byte is applied to a μ-law decoder that expands the byte according to the formula given earlier to produce a 14-bit signed-magnitude integer. This 14-bit linear value is then multiplied by a 14-bit binary fraction corresponding to the desired attenuation amount. The fractional bits of the product are discarded, and the result is reencoded into a new 8-bit μ-law PCM byte. The complete circuit would require dozens of MSI chips or a moderately large CPLD or FPGA.

Figure 9-17 on the next page is the logic diagram for a digital attenuator that uses a single, inexpensive $8K \times 8$ ROM instead. This ROM can apply any of 32 different attenuation factors to a μ-law input byte—it simply stores 32 different attenuation tables. The high-order address bits select a table, and the low-order address bits select an entry. Each entry is a precomputed μ-law byte corre-

Figure 9-16 Block diagram of a digital attenuator using discrete components.

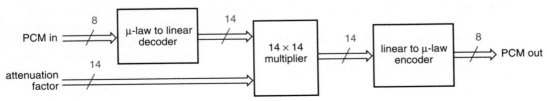

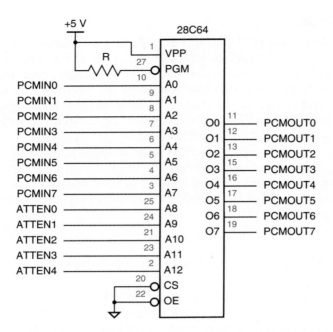

Figure 9-17
A digital attenuator.

sponding to the given attenuation code and input byte. Table 9-6 is a C program that generates the ROM contents. The details of the `UlawToLinear` and `LinearToUlaw` functions are left as an exercise.

Another ROM application in digital telephony is a digital conference circuit. In the analog telephone network, it's fairly easy to make a conference connection between three or more parties. Just connect the analog phone wires together and you get an analog summing junction, so each person hears everyone else (it's not quite that easy to do it right, but you get the idea). In the digital network, of course, chaos would result from just shorting together digital output signals. Instead, a digital conference circuit must include a digital *adder* that produces output samples corresponding to sums of the input samples.

You know how to build a binary adder for two 8-bit operands, but binary adders cannot process μ-law PCM bytes directly. Instead, the 8-bit PCM bytes must be converted into 14-bit linear format, then added, and then reencoded.

. . . AND THE CHECK'S FOR FREE

The digital attenuator is another good example of the many cost-effective space/time trade-offs that became possible when the telephone network "went digital." A single analog voice signal produces an 8-bit μ-law PCM sample once every 125 μs, but the digital attenuator ROM can produce a valid output in a few hundred nanoseconds or less. Thus, in a digital telephone system, a single ROM chip can attenuate hundreds of digital voice streams, where hundreds of analog attenuator networks would have been required in the old days.

Table 9-6 Program to generate the contents of an 8K × 8, 32-position attenuator ROM for μ-law coded bytes.

```c
#include <stdio.h>
#include <math.h>

extern int UlawToLinear(int in);
extern int LinearToUlaw(int x);

void main()
{
  int i, j, position;
  int pcmIN, linearOUT, pcmOUT;
  double atten, attenDB, fpcmOUT;

for (position=0; position<=31; position++) {  /* Make 32 256-byte tables. */
    printf("%i attenuation (dB): ");  /* Get amount in dB from designer,    */
    scanf("%f\n", attenDB);    /*  negative for attenuation, positive for gain. */
    atten = exp(log(10)*attenDB/10); /* Convert to fraction. */
    for (i=0; i<=15; i++) {  /* Construct output file in rows of 16. */
      printf("%04x:", position*256 + i*16);
      for (j=0; j<=15; j++) {
        pcmIN = i*16 + j;
        fpcmOUT = atten * UlawToLinear(pcmIN);
        if (fpcmOUT >=0) linearOUT = floor(fpcmOUT + 0.5);  /* Rounding */
        else linearOUT = ceil(fpcmOUT - 0.5);
        pcmOUT = LinearToUlaw(linearOUT);
        printf(" %2x", pcmOUT);
      }
      printf("\n");
    }
  }
}
```

Like the digital attenuator circuit, a discrete design for this function would be pretty big. Alternatively, the function could be performed by a single 64K × 8 ROM, as shown in Figure 9-18 on the next page. The ROM has 16 address inputs, accommodating two 8-bit μ-law PCM operands. For each pair of operand values, the corresponding ROM address contains the precomputed μ-law PCM sum. Table 9-7 is a C program that can be used to generate the ROM contents.

These examples illustrate the many advantages of building complex combinational functions with ROMs. We usually consider a function to be "complex" if we know that a gate-level circuit for the function will be a real pain to design. However, most "complex" functions, like the examples in this subsection, have fairly straightforward word descriptions. Such a description can generally be translated into a computer program that "figures out" what the function's outputs should be for every possible input combination, so the function can be built simply by dropping its truth table into a ROM.

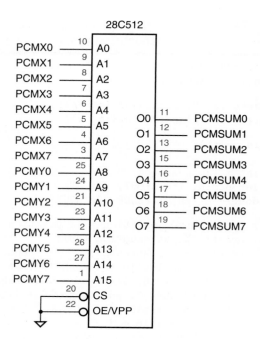

Figure 9-18
An adder circuit for
μ-law coded bytes.

In addition to ease and speed of design, a ROM-based circuit has other important advantages:

- For a moderately complex function, a ROM-based circuit is usually faster than a circuit using multiple SSI/MSI devices and PLDs, and often faster than an FPGA or custom LSI chip in a comparable technology.

- The program that generates the ROM contents can easily be structured to handle unusual or undefined cases that would require additional hardware in any other design. For example, the adder program in Table 9-7 easily handles out-of-range sums. (Also see Exercise 9.22.)

- A ROM's function is easily modified just by changing the stored pattern, usually without changing any external connections. For example, the PCM attenuator and adder ROMs in this subsection can be changed to use 8-bit A-law PCM, the standard digital voice coding in Europe.

- The prices of ROMs and other structured logic devices are always falling, making them more economical, and their densities are always increasing, expanding the scope of problems that can be solved with a single chip.

There are a few disadvantages of ROM-based circuits, too:

- For simple to moderately complex functions, a ROM-based circuit may cost more, consume more power, or run slower than a circuit using a few SSI/MSI devices and PLDs or a small FPGA.

Table 9-7 Program to generate the contents of a 64K × 8 adder ROM
for μ-law coded bytes.

```c
#include <stdio.h>
#include <math.h>
#define MINLINEAR -8159
#define MAXLINEAR 8159

void main()
{
  int i, j, linearSum;
  int pcmINX, pcmINY;

  for (pcmINY=0; pcmINY<=255; pcmINY++) {  /* For all Y samples... */
    for (i=0; i<=15; i++) {  /* Construct output file in rows of 16. */
      printf("%04x:", pcmINY*256 + i*16);
      for (j=0; j<=15; j++) {  /* For all X samples... */
        pcmINX = i*16 + j;
        linearSum = UlawToLinear(pcmINX) + UlawToLinear(pcmINY);
        /* The next two lines perform "clipping" on overflow. */
        if (linearSum < MINLINEAR) linearSum = MINLINEAR;
        if (linearSum > MAXLINEAR) linearSum = MAXLINEAR;
        printf(" %02x", LinearToUlaw(linearSum));
      }
      printf("\n");
    }
  }
}
```

- For functions with more than about 25 inputs, a ROM-based circuit is impractical because of the limit on ROM sizes that are available. For example, you wouldn't want to build a 16-bit adder in ROM—it would require billions and billions of bits.

9.2 Read/Write Memory

The name *read/write memory (RWM)* is given to memory arrays in which we can store and retrieve information at any time. Most of the RWMs used in digital systems nowadays are *random-access memories (RAMs)*, which means that the time it takes to read or write a bit is independent of the bit's location in the RAM. From this point of view, ROMs are also random-access memories, but the name "RAM" is generally used only for read/write random-access memories.

In a *static RAM (SRAM)* ("S-ram"), once a word is written at a location, it remains stored as long as power is applied to the chip, unless the same location is written again. In a *dynamic RAM (DRAM)* ("D-ram"), the data stored at each location must be refreshed periodically by reading it and then writing it back again, or else it disappears. We'll discuss both types in this section.

read/write memory (RWM)

random-access memory (RAM)

static RAM (SRAM)

dynamic RAM (DRAM)

volatile memory
nonvolatile memory

Most RAMs lose their memory when power is removed; they are a form of *volatile memory*. Some RAMs retain their memory even when power is removed; they are called *nonvolatile memory*. Examples of nonvolatile RAMs are old-style magnetic core memories and modern CMOS static memories in an extra-large package that includes a lithium battery with a 10-year lifetime.

SERIAL-ACCESS MEMORY

Random-access memory can be contrasted with *serial-access memory*, where one particular location is immediately accessible at a particular time, but other locations take additional steps to access.

Some early computers used electromechanical serial-access memory devices, such as delay lines and rotating drums. Instructions and data were stored in a rotating medium with only one location under the "read/write head" at any time. To access a random location, the machine would have to wait until the constant rotation brought that location under the head.

In the 1970s, electronic equivalents of serial-access rotating memories were developed, including memories based on charge-coupled devices (CCDs) and others that used magnetic bubbles. Both types of devices were roughly equivalent to very large serial-in, serial-out shift registers with their serial output connected back into the serial input. This connection point was the logical equivalent of a hard disk's "read/write head." To read a particular location, you would clock the shift register until the desired bit appeared at the serial output, and to write the location, you would substitute the desired new value at the serial input.

Although they offered higher density (more bits) than DRAMs at the time they were developed, CCD and magnetic-bubble memories never gained much commercial acceptance. One reason for this was the enormous inconvenience of serial access. Another was that they were never more than a couple years ahead of DRAMs in the densities that they could achieve.

9.3 Static RAM

9.3.1 Static-RAM Inputs and Outputs

Like a ROM, a RAM has address and control inputs and data outputs, but it also has data inputs. The inputs and outputs of a simple $2^n \times b$-bit static RAM are shown in Figure 9-19. The control inputs are comparable to those of a ROM, with the addition of a *write-enable (WE) input*. When WE is asserted, the data inputs are written into the selected memory location.

write-enable (WE) input

The memory locations in a static RAM behave like D latches, rather than edge-triggered D flip-flops. This means that whenever the WE input is asserted, the latches for the selected memory location are "open" (or "transparent"), and input data flows into and through the latch. The actual value stored is whatever is present when the latch closes.

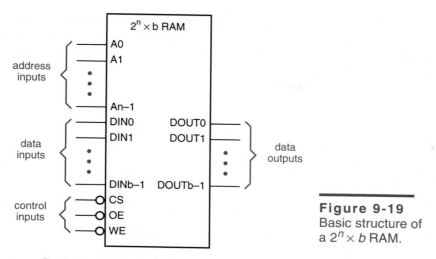

Figure 9-19
Basic structure of
a $2^n \times b$ RAM.

Static RAM normally has just two defined access operations:

Read   An address is placed on the address inputs while CS and OE are
asserted. The latch outputs for the selected memory location are
delivered to DOUT.

Write   An address is placed on the address inputs and a data word is placed on
DIN; then CS and WE are asserted. The latches in the selected memory
location open, and the input word is stored.

A certain amount of care is needed when accessing SRAM, because it is
possible to inadvertently "clobber" one or more other locations while writing to
a selected one, if the SRAM's timing requirements are not met. The following
subsection gives details on SRAM internal structure to show why this is so, and
the next one explains the actual timing behavior and requirements.

9.3.2 Static-RAM Internal Structure

Each bit of memory (or *SRAM cell*) in a static RAM has the same functional   *SRAM cell*
behavior as the circuit in Figure 9-20. The storage device in each cell is a D latch.
When a cell's SEL_L input is asserted, the stored data is placed on the cell's output, which is connected to a bit line. When both SEL_L and WR_L are asserted,
the latch is open and a new data bit is stored.

Figure 9-20 Functional behavior of a static-RAM cell.

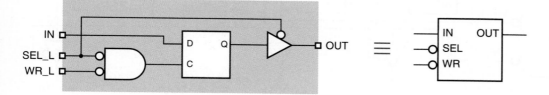

SRAM cells are combined in an array with additional control logic to form a complete static RAM, as shown in Figure 9-21 for an 8×4 SRAM. As in a simple ROM, a decoder on the address lines selects a particular row of the SRAM to be accessed at any time.

Figure 9-21 Internal structure of an 8×4 static RAM.

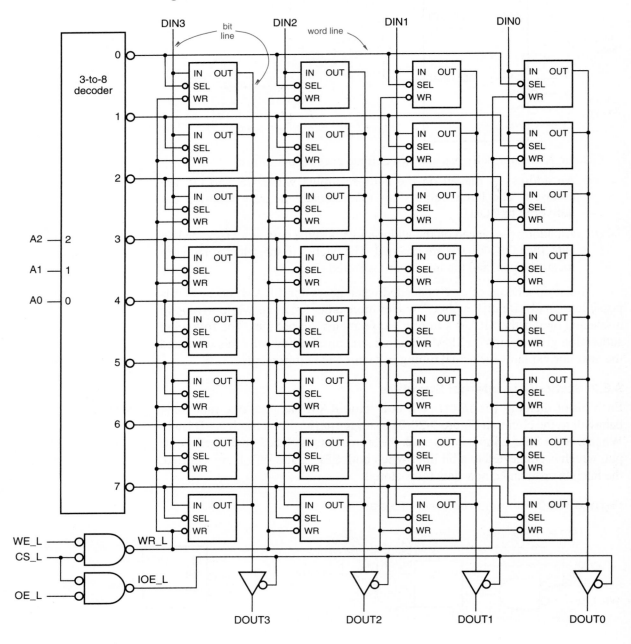

Although Figure 9-21 is a somewhat simplified model of internal SRAM structure, it accurately portrays several important aspects of SRAM behavior:

- During read operations, the output data is a combinational function of the address inputs, as in a ROM. No harm is done by changing the address lines while the output data bus is enabled. The access time for read operations is specified from the time that the last address input becomes stable.

- During write operations, the input data is stored in *latches*. This means that the data must meet certain setup and hold times with respect to the *trailing* edge of the latch enable signal. That is, the input data at a latch's D input need not be stable at the moment WR_L is asserted internally; it must only be stable a certain time before WR_L is negated.

- During write operations, the address inputs *must* be stable for a certain setup time before WR_L is asserted internally and for a hold time after WR_L is negated. Otherwise, data may be "sprayed" all over the array because of the glitches that may appear on the SEL_L lines when the address inputs of the decoder are changing.

- Internally, WR_L is asserted only when both CS_L and WE_L are asserted. Therefore, a *write cycle* begins when both CS_L and WE_L are asserted and ends when either is negated. Setup and hold times for address and data are specified with respect to these events.

write cycle

9.3.3 Static-RAM Timing

Figure 9-22 shows the timing parameters that are typically specified for read operations in a static RAM; they are described below:

t_{AA} *Access time from address.* Assuming that the OE and CS inputs are already asserted, or will be soon enough not to make a difference, this is how long it takes to get stable output data after a change in address. When designers talk about a "70-ns SRAM," they're usually referring to this number.

t_{AA}
access time from address

Figure 9-22 Timing parameters for read operations in a static RAM.

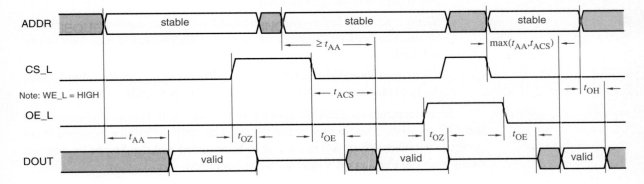

t_{ACS}
access time from chip select

t_{ACS} *Access time from chip select.* Assuming that the address and OE are already stable, or will be soon enough not to make a difference, this is how long it takes to get stable output data after CS is asserted. Often this parameter is identical to t_{AA}, but sometimes it's longer in SRAMs with a "power-down" mode and shorter in SRAMs without one.

t_{OE}
output-enable time

t_{OE} *Output-enable time.* This is how long it takes for the three-state output buffers to leave the high-impedance state when OE and CS are both asserted. This parameter is normally less than t_{ACS}, so it is possible for the RAM to start accessing data internally before OE is asserted; this feature is used to achieve fast access times while avoiding "bus fighting" in many applications.

t_{OZ}
output-disable time

t_{OZ} *Output-disable time.* This is how long it takes for the three-state output buffers to enter the high-impedance state after OE_L or CS_L is negated.

t_{OH}
output-hold time

t_{OH} *Output-hold time.* This parameter specifies how long the output data remains valid after a change in the address inputs.

If you've been paying attention, you may have noticed that the timing diagram and timing parameters for SRAM read operations are identical to what we discussed for ROM read operations in Section 9.1.5. That's the way it is; when they're not being written, SRAMs can be used just like ROMs. The same is not generally true for DRAMs, as we'll see later.

Timing parameters for write operations are shown in Figure 9-23 and are described below:

t_{AS}
address setup time

t_{AS} *Address setup time before write.* All of the address inputs must be stable at this time before both CS and WE are asserted. Otherwise, the data stored at unpredictable locations may be corrupted.

t_{AH}
address hold time

t_{AH} *Address hold time after write.* Analogous to t_{AS}, all address inputs must be held stable until this time after CS or WE is negated.

t_{CSW}
chip-select setup time

t_{CSW} *Chip-select setup before end of write.* CS must be asserted at least this long before the end of the write cycle in order to select a cell.

t_{WP}
write-pulse width

t_{WP} *Write-pulse width.* WE must be asserted at least this long to reliably latch data into the selected cell.

t_{DS}
data setup time

t_{DS} *Data setup time before end of write.* All of the data inputs must be stable at this time before the write cycle ends. Otherwise, the data may not be latched.

t_{DH}
data hold time

t_{DH} *Data hold time after end of write.* Analogous to t_{DS}, all data inputs must be held stable until this time after the write cycle ends.

WE-controlled write
CS-controlled write

Manufacturers of SRAMs specify two write-cycle types, *WE-controlled* and *CS-controlled*, as shown in the figure. The only difference between these cycles is whether WE or CS is the last to be asserted and the first to be negated when enabling the SRAM's internal write operation.

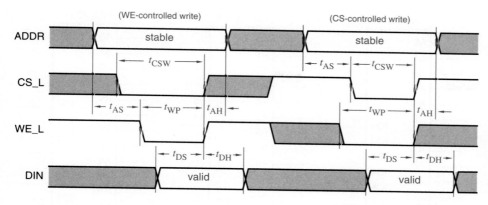

Figure 9-23
Timing parameters for write operations in a static RAM.

The write-timing requirements of SRAMs could be relaxed somewhat if, instead of using latches, the cells contained edge-triggered D flip-flops with a common clock input and enable inputs controlled by SEL and WR. However, this just isn't done, because it would at least double the chip area of each cell, since a D flip-flop is built from two latches. Thus, the logic designer is left to reconcile the SRAM's latch-type timing with the edge-triggered register and state-machine timing used elsewhere in a system.

A large SRAM does not contain a physical array whose dimensions equal the logical dimensions of the memory. As in a ROM, the SRAM cells are laid out in an almost square array, and an entire row is read internally during read operations. For example, the layout of a 32K × 8 SRAM chip might be very similar to that of a 32K × 8 ROM shown in Figure 9-9 on page 809. During read operations, column multiplexers pass the required data bits to the output data bus, as specified by a subset of the address bits (A5–A0 in the ROM example). For write operations, the write-enable circuitry is designed so that only one column in each subarray is enabled, as determined by the same subset of the address bits.

*9.3.4 Standard Static RAMs

Static RAMs are available in many sizes and speeds. In 2005, the largest conventional SRAMs used CMOS technology, were organized as 2M × 16 bits, (32 Mbits), and had access times as fast as 70 ns. Faster access times of 12ns could be obtained from smaller 256K × 16-bit CMOS SRAMs. Even faster synchronous SRAMs were also available, as described in the next subsection.

Part numbers for SRAM components are not standardized among manufacturers, although the components themselves often have identical pinouts and are interchangeable. Figure 9-24 on the next page shows part numbers and pinouts for Renesas (formerly Hitachi) SRAMs, ranging in size from standard 8K × 8 to 512K × 8, that you might use in a digital design lab project; they all use a 5-V power supply and come in DIP packages. These devices are also available in SMT packages, and newer SRAM devices are typically available only in SMT packages and use lower power-supply voltages, such as 3.3 V or 2.5 V.

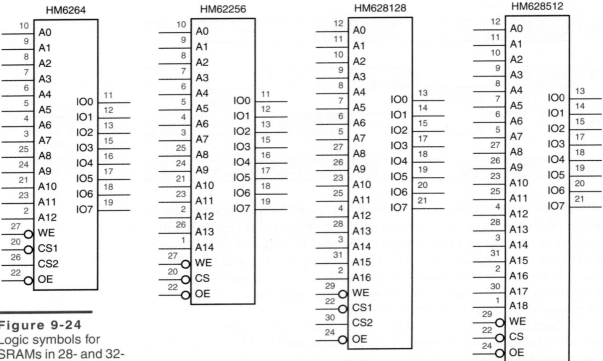

Figure 9-24
Logic symbols for SRAMs in 28- and 32-pin DIP packages.

HM6264

HM62256

HM628128
HM628512

The first two SRAMs in the figure use 28-pin DIP packages with pinouts that are patterned after the like-size EEPROMs in Figure 9-11 on page 812. The *HM6264* 8K × 8 SRAM follows the pinout of a 28C64 EEPROM, except for an extra chip-select input; CS1_L and CS2 both must be asserted to enable the chip. The *HM62256* 32K × 8 SRAM follows the pinout of a 28C256 EEPROM. The last two SRAMs in Figure 9-24 use 32-pin DIP packages with pinouts that follow the two largest EEPROMs in Figure 9-11. The *HM628128* is a 128K × 8 SRAM and the *HM628512* is a 512K × 8 SRAM. All of these chips are available from many manufacturers, often with different part numbers, and have access times in the range of 15–150 ns.

The SRAMs in Figure 9-24 have bidirectional data buses—that is, they use the same data pins for both reading and writing. This necessitates a slight change in their internal control logic, as shown in Figure 9-25. The output buffer is automatically disabled whenever WE_L is asserted, even if OE_L is asserted. However, the timing parameters and requirements for read and write operations are almost identical to what we described in the preceding subsection.

A common use of SRAMs is to store data in small microprocessor systems, often in "embedded" applications (telephones, toasters, electric bumpers, etc.). General-purpose computers more often use DRAMs, discussed in Section 9.4, because their density is greater and their cost per bit lower.

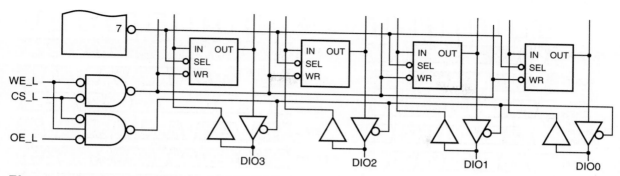

Figure 9-25 Output-buffer control in an SRAM with a bidirectional data bus.

Very fast SRAMs are used in the "cache" memories of microprocessors to store frequently used instructions and data. In the late 1990s, the need for speed in PC and networking applications led to the development of a faster, clocked SRAM interface. The standard SRAMs in this subsection are now called *asynchronous SRAMs* to distinguish them from the new style discussed next.

asynchronous SRAM

*9.3.5 Synchronous SRAM

A new variety of SRAM, called a *synchronous SRAM (SSRAM)* ("S-S-ram"), still uses latches internally but has a clocked interface for control, address, and data. As shown in Figure 9-26, internal edge-triggered registers **AREG** and **CREG** are placed on the signal paths for address and control. As a result, an operation that is set up before the rising edge of the clock is performed internally during a subsequent clock period. Register **INREG** captures the input data for

synchronous SRAM (SSRAM)

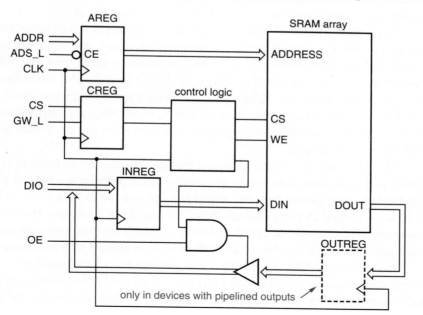

Figure 9-26
Internal structure of a synchronous SRAM.

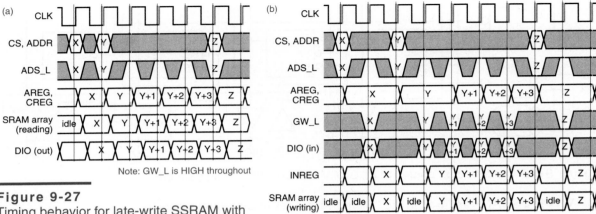

Figure 9-27
Timing behavior for late-write SSRAM with flow-through outputs: (a) read operations; (b) write operations.

write operations and, depending on whether the device has "pipelined" or "flow-through" outputs, register OUTREG is or is not provided to hold read data.

late-write SSRAM with flow-through outputs

The first variety of SSRAM to be introduced was the *late-write SSRAM with flow-through outputs*. For a read operation, shown in Figure 9-27(a), the control and address inputs are sampled at the rising edge of the clock, and the internal address register AREG is loaded only if ADS_L is asserted. During the next clock period, the internal SRAM array is accessed and read data is delivered to the device's DIO data-bus pins. The device also supports a burst mode, in which data at a sequence of addresses is read. In this mode AREG behaves as a counter, eliminating the need to apply a new address at each cycle. (The control signals that support burst mode are not shown in Figures 9-26 or 9-27.)

For a write operation, shown in (b), the write data is stored temporarily in an on-chip register INREG, which is sampled one clock tick *after* the address register is loaded. Therefore, ADS_L must be inhibited for at least one tick after loading the address, so that the address in AREG is still valid when the write takes place. The write takes place during the clock period following the edge on which the "global write" control signal GW_L is asserted. As with reading, the device has a burst mode where a sequence of addresses can be written without supplying a new address.

Note that the "late-write" protocol makes it impossible to write to two different, nonsequential addresses in successive clock periods; the SRAM array is idle for one clock period between writes (except in burst mode). From the point of view of internal chip capabilities, this behavior is not necessary. However, the late-write protocol was designed this way to match the bus protocols of older microprocessors that use these SSRAMs in their external cache subsystems.

late-write SSRAM with pipelined outputs

A *late-write SSRAM with pipelined outputs* is like the previous version, except that a register OUTREG is placed between the SRAM array output and the device output for read operations. As shown in Figure 9-28, this delays the

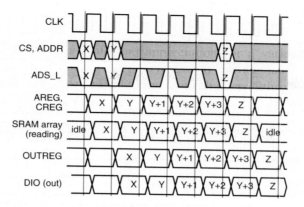

read output data at the device pins until the beginning of the next clock period, but it also provides the benefit that the data is now valid for almost the entire clock period. The write cycle behaves the same as with flow-through outputs. Compared to flow-through outputs, pipelined outputs provide much better setup time for the device receiving the read data, and therefore may allow operation at higher clock frequencies.

As we showed in Figure 9-26, conventional SSRAMs share the same pins for both input data and output data. During a given clock period the data I/O pins can be used for reading or writing but not both. If you study the pattern of data-bus and SRAM-array use in both styles of late-write SSRAM, you'll find cases where it's not possible to initiate a read one clock cycle after initiating a write or vice versa, due to resource conflict (see Exercise 9.32). Thus, late-write SSRAMs suffer a *turn-around penalty*, a clock period in which the internal SRAM array must be idle when a read is followed by a write or vice versa.

turn-around penalty

The turn-around penalty is eliminated in so-called *zero-bus-turn-around (ZBT) SSRAMs*. The timing for a *ZBT SSRAM with flow-through outputs* is shown in Figure 9-29 on the next page. The type of operation (read or write) is selected by a control signal R/$\overline{W}$ that sampled at the same clock edge as the address. Regardless of whether the operation is a read or a write, the DIO bus is used during the next clock period to transfer the read or write data. As a result, there is no data-bus-usage conflict, as long as OE is controlled properly to avoid bus-fighting between successive cycles. However, if a write is followed by a read, both operations would like to use the SRAM array during the same clock period. To avoid this resource conflict, the write operation is deferred until the next available SRAM cycle. This opportunity occurs when either another write operation or no operation is initiated on the address and control lines.

zero-bus-turn-around (ZBT) SSRAM

Although a ZBT SSRAM can access the internal SRAM array on every clock cycle, this performance improvement is not without a price. While a write operation is pending, the write address and related information must be stored in another register, WAREG, since AREG is reused by other operations; this costs chip area. More significantly for some applications, a write operation may be

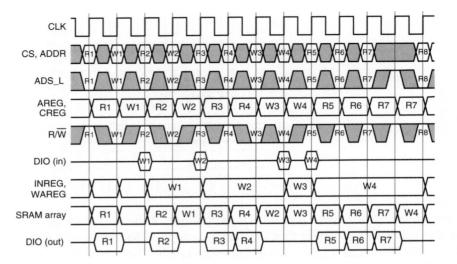

Figure 9-29
Timing behavior for a ZBT SSRAM with flow-through outputs.

deferred indefinitely if it is immediately followed by a continuous series of read operations. This anomaly may require tricky controller design to detect the case where one of these read operations attempts to access the address that was just written, since the value stored in the SRAM array is "stale"!

A *ZBT SSRAM with pipelined outputs* adds OUTREG to the read data path but is otherwise similar to the previous device. In this device, both reads and writes use the DIO bus during the second clock period following the clock edge in which the operation was initiated. As in the previous device, writes to the internal SRAM array are deferred until an available cycle, so that reads can take precedence. Timing is shown in Figure 9-30. As implied by the timing, two levels of internal registers are needed for write address and data, since up to two writes may be deferred while a sequence of reads occurs.

Among the four styles of SSRAM that we described, no single one is the "best." The best SSRAM is the one that best fits the bus protocol and other requirements of the system in which it is used. SSRAM access protocols are very beneficial in high-speed systems. For example, address, control, and write inputs can be applied with more-or-less conventional setup and hold times with respect to the system clock, and read data on pipelined output pins is available for almost a complete clock cycle. Very importantly, the designer does not have to worry about the tricky circuits and timing paths that are otherwise needed to enable conventional SRAM latch-style operation.

quad-data-rate (QDR) SSRAM

The latest *quad-data-rate (QDR) SSRAMs* make timing tricky again, by transferring data on both edges of the clock. But they also simplify operations and eliminate the turn-around penalty by using separate input and output buses (hence the claim that they are "four" times as fast). QDR devices were available in 2005 with sizes up to 36 Mbits and clock frequencies as high as 333 MHz.

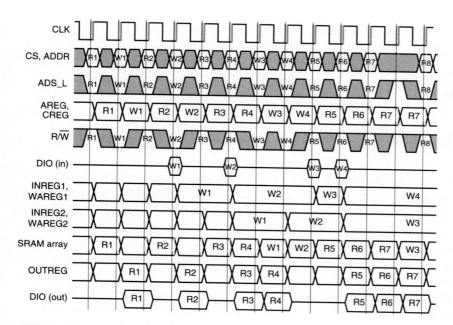

Figure 9-30
Timing behavior for a ZBT SSRAM with pipelined outputs.

9.4 Dynamic RAM

The basic memory cell in an SRAM, a D latch, requires four gates in a discrete design, and four to six transistors in a custom-designed SRAM LSI chip. In order to build RAMs with higher density (more bits per chip), chip designers invented memory cells that use as little as one transistor per bit.

9.4.1 Dynamic-RAM Structure

It is not possible to build a bistable element with just one transistor. Instead, the memory cells in a *dynamic RAM (DRAM)* store information on a tiny capacitor accessed through a MOS transistor. Figure 9-31 shows the storage cell for one bit of a DRAM, which is accessed by setting the word line to a HIGH voltage. To store a 1, the bit is accessed and a HIGH voltage is placed on the bit line, which charges the capacitor through the "on" transistor. To store a 0, a LOW voltage placed on the bit line discharges the capacitor.

dynamic RAM (DRAM)

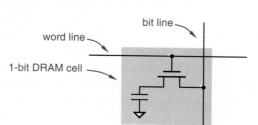

Figure 9-31
Storage cell for one bit in a DRAM.

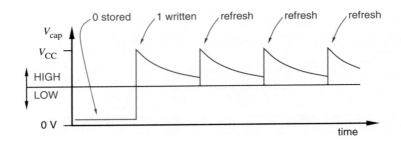

Figure 9-32
Voltage stored in a DRAM cell after writing and refresh operations.

precharge

sense amplifier

To read a DRAM cell, the bit line is first *precharged* to a voltage halfway between HIGH and LOW, and then the word line is set HIGH. Depending on whether the capacitor voltage is HIGH or LOW, the precharged bit line is pulled slightly higher or slightly lower. A *sense amplifier* detects this small change and recovers a 1 or 0 accordingly. Note that reading a cell destroys the original voltage stored on the capacitor, so that the recovered data must be written back into the cell after reading.

The capacitor in a DRAM cell has a very small capacitance, but the MOS transistor that accesses it has a very high impedance. Therefore, it takes a relatively long time (100 milliseconds or more) for a HIGH voltage to discharge to the point that it looks more like a LOW voltage. In the meantime, the capacitor stores one bit of information.

Naturally, using a computer would be no fun if you had to reboot every 100 milliseconds because its memory contents disappeared (the typical behavior of some operating systems notwithstanding). Therefore, DRAM-based memory

refresh cycle

systems use *refresh cycles* to update every memory cell periodically, typically once every 64 milliseconds. This involves sequentially reading the somewhat degraded contents of each cell into a D latch and writing back a nice solid LOW or HIGH value from the latch. Figure 9-32 illustrates the electrical state of a cell after a write and a sequence of refresh operations.

The first DRAMs, introduced in the early 1970s, contained only 1024 bits, but modern DRAMs are available containing 512 *megabits* or more. If you had to refresh every cell, one at a time, in 64 milliseconds, you'd have a problem—that works out to far less than 1 ns per cell, and includes no time for useful read and write operations. Fortunately, as we'll show, DRAMs are organized using two-dimensional arrays, and a single operation refreshes an entire row of the array. Early DRAM arrays had 256 rows, requiring 256 refresh operations every four milliseconds, or one about every 15.6 µsec. Newer arrays have 4096 rows but need to be refreshed only once every 64 ms, which still works out to one row per 15.6 µsec. A refresh operation typically takes less than 100 ns, so the DRAM is available for useful read and write operations over 99% of the time.

For simplicity, we'll describe DRAM operations in terms of a relatively small, generic 4M × 4-bit DRAM. Larger DRAMs typically contain multiple

DRAM bank

arrays (called *banks*) with sizes that may be different from what is shown here.

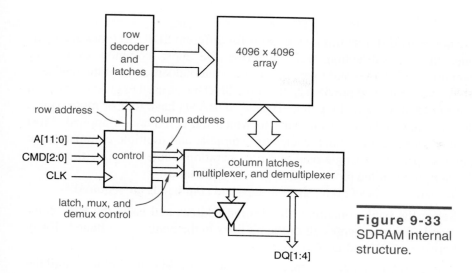

Figure 9-33
SDRAM internal structure.

Figure 9-33 is a block diagram of the internal structure of our example 4M × 4 DRAM. This device is called a *synchronous DRAM (SDRAM)* because its control and data operations are all referenced to a common clock signal, CLK. Older DRAMs had asynchronous control signals; for more information, see the third edition of this book.

synchronous DRAM (SDRAM)

The logical array in Figure 9-33 has 4M × 4 bits, but the physical array is square, containing 4096 × 4096 bits. Many commercial DRAM chips have non-square individual arrays, but multiple nonsquare arrays (banks) are arranged to yield an overall chip that is close to square.

In the earliest SDRAMs, the clock signal CLK runs at 100 MHz; newer SDRAMs run at 200 MHz or more. Various commands, explained shortly, can be applied to the device on the 3-bit CMD bus at each rising edge of CLK.

Although the example SDRAM has 4M (2^{22}) locations, the chip has only 12 *multiplexed address inputs* A[11:0]. A complete 22-bit address is presented to the chip in two steps at two clock ticks, as determined by operation codes on the CMD bus. Multiplexing the address inputs saves pins, important for compact design of memory systems, and also fits quite naturally with the two-step SDRAM access methods that we'll describe shortly.

multiplexed address inputs

One advantage of having multiple banks in larger SDRAMs is to ease the electrical and physical design problems that would occur with a single, very large memory array. But even more important is the parallelism that can occur when there are multiple banks. As we'll see in the next subsection, SDRAM operation is much more complicated than SRAM operation. Taking advantage of the multiple banks in larger, high-speed SDRAMs, a modern SDRAM memory controller can perform several operations in parallel—for example, completing a write operation in one bank while initiating a read operation in another. This increases the effective throughput of the memory.

9.4.2 SDRAM Timing

There are many different timing scenarios for different SDRAM types and operations. In this subsection we'll describe the most common cycles for conventional SDRAMs and relate them to the internal structure of the device.

As we mentioned previously, the 3-bit CMD bus is used to give a command to the SDRAM at each clock tick. Typical SDRAMs have four or more banks; additional input bits select the bank to which the command is applied. Most commands take several clock cycles to complete, and multiple commands are required to perform a single read or write operation. Table 9-8 gives the names and descriptions of the most commonly used commands.

read cycle

To perform a *read cycle*, several steps and commands are required:

1. Select the bank containing the desired address and issue the PRE command. This precharges all of the bit lines in the bank to a voltage halfway between HIGH and LOW.

2. Wait a few clock ticks (as specified by the SDRAM manufacturer) until the precharge operation has completed.

row address
row-address register

3. Once again select the desired bank, apply the high-order bits of the desired address (the *row address*) to the A[11:0] inputs, and issue the ACTV command. The row address is stored in an internal *row-address register* and the word line for the selected row is activated, so the entire row can be read and stored in an internal 4096-bit *row latch*.

row latch

RAS-CAS delay

4. Wait a few clock ticks (the so-called *RAS-CAS delay*) for the 4096-bit word just read to stabilize internally.

column address

column-address register

5. Apply the low-order bits of the desired address (the *column address*) to the A[11:0] inputs, and issue the READ command. The column address is stored in an internal *column-address register* and is applied to the column multiplexer to select four bits out of the 4096-bit row latch to be delivered to the DQ[1:4] output pins. (Only pins A[9:0] are used for the 10-bit column address in this example.)

Table 9-8
Commonly used
SDRAM commands.

Command Name	Description
NOP	No operation
ACTV	Row-address strobe and activate bank
READ	Column address and read command
READA	Read with auto-precharge
WRIT	Column address and read command
WRITA	Write with auto-precharge
REF	Auto refresh
PRE	Precharge

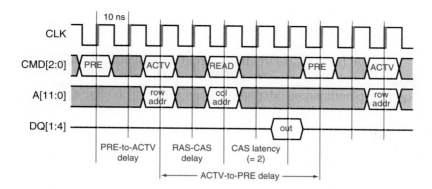

Figure 9-34
SDRAM read-cycle timing.

6. Wait a few more clock ticks (the so-called *CAS latency*) for the addressed four bits to propagate through the column multiplexer and to the DQ[1:4] outputs. During this time, the 4096-bit row latch is also written back into the selected row. (Remember, all the capacitors in the row were discharged by the read operation back in step 3.)

7. Finally, read the data on the DQ[1:4] data input/output pins.

CAS latency

These operations are illustrated in Figure 9-34 assuming a fairly generic SDRAM with a 100-MHz clock and a CAS latency of 2. A memory controller or microprocessor applies commands and addresses on the CMD and A buses in order to be valid at the rising edge of CLK with a few nanoseconds of setup and hold time. The SDRAM eventually places read data on the DQ bus shortly (typically 5 ns) after a rising edge of CLK, so that the memory controller or microprocessor can read it reliably on the next rising edge.

SDRAMs have all sorts of complicated timing requirements that are specified by the manufacturer. For example, once a read cycle has completed, it may or may not be possible to request a new precharge cycle immediately—first, an active-to-precharge delay must elapse, as shown in the figure. The timing requirements also vary depending on whether read and write operations are interleaved, and whether successive operations are going to the same bank or different banks. This makes the design of SDRAM memory controllers very challenging, but ripe with opportunities for increasing efficiency.

WHEN PRE BECOMES POST
The need to precharge a DRAM's bit lines prior to a read or write adds significant delay to these operations. Therefore, most DRAM controllers are designed to precharge the bit lines *after* each operation completes. That way, there's a good chance that the precharge will be completed by the time a new operation to the bank is requested. In SDRAMs, the READA and WRITA commands automatically perform a precharge on the just-used bank as a read or write operation is completed, and no separate PRE command needs to be given.

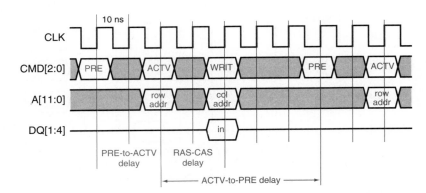

Figure 9-35
SDRAM write-cycle
timing.

write cycle

As shown in Figure 9-35, SDRAM *write cycles* are like read operations, with one main difference. The memory controller or microprocessor drives the write-data onto the DQ bus at the same time that it issues the WRIT command. During the next few clock cyles (step 6 in our previous description of read operations), the SDRAM merges the write-data into the addressed column in the row latch and then writes the entire, updated 4096-bit value back into selected row.

As you can see from the timing diagrams, it takes a lot of time and effort to read or write a single location in an SDRAM—a total of seven clock cycles in our read and write examples just to obtain one clock cycle with an actual data transfer. Compare with SSRAMs (Section 9.3.5), which can perform a data transfer on every clock cycle.

SDRAMs can achieve higher data transfer rates when multiple locations in the same row of the internal memory array are accessed successively. After all, in our example SDRAM, the entire 4096-bit row is stored in the row latch during a read operation, and it is a relatively simple matter to bring out a different 4-bit word to the DQ bus on successive clock ticks.

burst-read cycle

Thus, Figure 9-36 shows the timing for a *burst-read cycle*, assuming a burst length of four. The first 4-bit word is delivered at the same time as in a normal read cycle, and additional words from successive locations are delivered during the next three clock cycles. A typical SDRAM can support burst lengths

page

of 1, 2, 4, or 8 words, or the entire row latch (also called a *page*, 1024 words in this example).

Figure 9-36
SDRAM burst-read-
cycle timing.

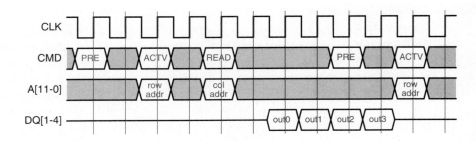

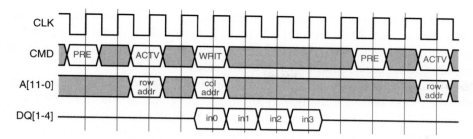

Figure 9-37
SDRAM burst-write-cycle timing.

The burst length is not specified on a per-operation basis; rather, it is specified statically, using a few bits in an internal *configuration register*. The memory controller programs the configuration register when the system begins operation. Other static operating parameters, such as CAS latency (2 or 3) and the method for generating successive burst addresses (sequential or interleaved), are also programmed in the configuration register.

configuration register

As shown in Figure 9-37, operations for a *burst-write cycle* are similar, with the memory controller or microprocessor delivering one word to the DQ bus per cycle, starting in the same clock cycle as the WRIT command. A new precharge command cannot be given until two ticks after the last write-data appears on the DQ bus. This provides time for the updated row latch to be written back into the selected row.

burst-write cycle

Before we forget. we should discuss one other very important SDRAM operation—the *auto-refresh cycle*. In this cycle, initiated by the REF command, the SDRAM reads one row of each bank's internal array into its row latch, and writes it back. No address is applied to the A bus; instead, the SDRAM uses the value of an internal 12-bit *refresh counter* as the row address, and increments it after the refresh operation. A total of 4096 refresh operations must be performed every 64 ms to prevent data loss. All banks must be precharged before a REF command is given, and the command precharges the banks as it completes.

auto-refresh cycle

refresh counter

9.4.3 DDR SDRAMs

Double-data-rate (DDR) SDRAMs do just that—they double the data-transfer rate of an SDRAM by transferring data on both edges of the clock, rising and falling. Note that address and command operations still require one clock cycle, the same as in a conventional SDRAM. So, the actual data-transfer rate is increased only for burst operations.

double-data-rate (DDR) SDRAM

DDR operation is "simple" from a functional point of view. For example, just imagine eight words coming out in the same interval that four are shown in the SDRAM burst cycles in Figures 9-36 and 9-37, with even-numbered words referenced to the rising edge of the clock, and odd-numbered to the falling edge.

But DDR operation is very tricky from a timing and analog implementation point of view. Remember, the whole point of DDR is to go *fast*. To maintain precise timing, DDR SDRAMs use differential clock inputs—complementary *delay-locked loop*

versions of the clock signal with very little timing skew between them. An on-chip analog *delay-locked loop (DLL)* locks onto this clock signal and generates internal and external signals, including output data and input and output latch enables, with precise delays relative to this clock.

Board-level designers must be very careful to balance the delays, minimize the skew, and optimize the quality of all signals going to and from the DDR SDRAM. Even after all this work, DDR operation provides faster data transfers only during burst-mode operations, so the benefit is application dependent.

9.5 Complex Programmable Logic Devices

Since their introduction years ago, programmable logic devices such as the 16V8 and 22V10 have been very flexible workhorses of digital design. As IC technology advanced, there was naturally great interest in creating larger PLD architectures to take advantage of increased chip density. The question is, why didn't manufacturers just scale the existing architectures?

For example, if DRAM densities increased by a factor of 64 over the last 10 years, why couldn't manufacturers scale the 16V8 to create a "128V64"? Such a device would have 64 input pins, 64 I/O pins, and some number of 128-variable product terms (say, 8) for each of its 128 logic macrocells. It could combine the functions of a larger collection of 16V8s and offer terrific performance and flexibility in using any input in any output's logic function.

Or could it? Yes, a 128V64 would be very flexible, but it would not have very good performance. Unlike the 16V8, which has 32 inputs (16 signals and their complements) per AND term, this device would have 256. Due to capacitive effects, leakage currents, and so on, such a large wired-AND structure would be at least eight times slower than the 16V8's AND array.

Figure 9-38
General CPLD architecture.

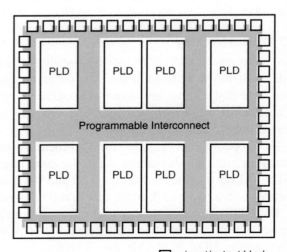

☐ = input/output block

Worse from a manufacturer's point of view, a 128V64 would not make very cost-effective use of chip area. It would use about 64 times the chip area of a 16V8, but provide the same number of inputs and outputs as only eight 16V8s. That is, for n times as much logic (in terms of inputs, outputs and AND terms), a 128V64 would use n^2 as much chip area. In terms of efficiency of silicon use, a clever designer would be better off partitioning a desired function into eight 16V8s, if such a partitioning were possible.

This is where the idea of *complex programmable logic devices (CPLDs)* came from. As shown in Figure 9-38, a CPLD is just a collection of individual PLDs on a single chip, accompanied by a programmable interconnection structure that allows the PLDs to be hooked up to each other on-chip in the same way that a clever designer might do with discrete PLDs off-chip. Here, the chip area for n times as much logic is only n times the area of a single PLD, plus the area of the programmable interconnect structure.

complex programmable logic device (CPLD)

Different manufacturers have taken many different approaches to the general architecture shown in the figure. Architectural elements in which they differ include the individual PLDs (AND array and macrocells), the input/output blocks, and the programmable interconnect. We'll discuss each of these areas in the rest of this section, using the Xilinx 9500-series CPLD architecture as a representative example.

9.5.1 Xilinx XC9500 CPLD Family

The Xilinx XC9500 series is a family of CPLDs with a similar architecture but varying numbers of external input/output (I/O) pins and internal PLDs (which Xilinx calls function blocks—FBs). As we'll see later, each internal PLD has 36 inputs and 18 macrocells and outputs and might be called a "36V18." As shown in Table 9-9 on the next page, devices in the family are named according to the number of macrocells they contain. The smallest has 2 FBs and 36 macrocells, and the largest has 16 FBs and 288 macrocells.

Another important feature of this and most CPLD families is that a given chip, such as the XC95108, is available in several different packages. This is important not only to accommodate different manufacturing practices but also to provide some choice and potential savings in the number of external I/O pins provided. In most applications, it is not necessary for all internal signals of a state machine or subsystem to be visible to and used by the rest of the system.

So, even though the XC95108 has 108 internal macrocells, the outputs of at most 69 of them can be connected externally in the 84-pin-PLCC version of the device. In fact, many of the 69 I/O pins would typically be used for inputs, in which case even fewer outputs would be visible externally. That's OK; the remaining macrocell outputs are still quite usable internally, since they can be hooked up internally through the CPLD's programmable interconnect. Macro-cells whose outputs are usable only internally are sometimes called *buried macrocells*.

buried macrocell

Table 9-9 Function blocks and external I/O pins in Xilinx 9500-series CPLDs.

	Part number					
	XC9536	*XC9572*	*XC95108*	*XC95144*	*XC95216*	*XC95288*
FBs / macrocells	2 / 36	4 / 72	6 / 108	8 / 144	12 / 216	16 / 288
Package	Device I/O Pins					
44-pin VQFP	34					
44-pin PLCC	34	34				
48-pin CSP	34					
84-pin PLCC		69	69			
100-pin TQFP		72	81	81		
100-pin PQFP		72	81	81		
160-pin PQFP			108	133	133	
208-pin HQFP					166	168
352-pin BGA					166	192

Another important dimension of Table 9-9 is the horizontal one. All but two of the packages support at least two different devices in the same package and, as it turns out, with compatible pinouts. This is a life-saver in making last-minute design changes. For example, suppose you were to target a design to an XC9572 in an 84-pin PLCC. You might find that the 69 I/O pins of the device are quite adequate. You would like to use the XC9572 for its low cost, but you might be a little nervous if your initial design used 68 out of the 72 available internal macrocells (I know that I would be!). Based on Table 9-9, you can sleep well knowing that if bug fixes or design-specification changes necessitate a more complex design internally, you can always move up to the XC95108 in the same package and pick up another 36 macrocells.

Figure 9-39 is a block diagram of the internal architecture of a typical XC9500-family CPLD. Each external I/O pin can be used as an input, an output, or a bidirectional pin according to the device's programming, as discussed later. The pins at the bottom of the figure can also be used for special purposes. Any of three pins can be used as "global clocks" (GCK); as we'll see later, each macrocell can be programmed to use a selected clock input. One pin can be used as a "global set/reset" (GSR); again, each macrocell can programmably use this signal as an asynchronous preset or clear. Finally, two or four pins (depending on device) can be used as "global three-state controls" (GTS); one of these signals can be selected in each macrocell to output-enable the corresponding output driver when the macrocell's output is hooked up to an external I/O pin.

Only four FBs are shown in the figure, but the XC9500 architecture scales to accommodate 16 FBs in the XC95288. Regardless of the specific family

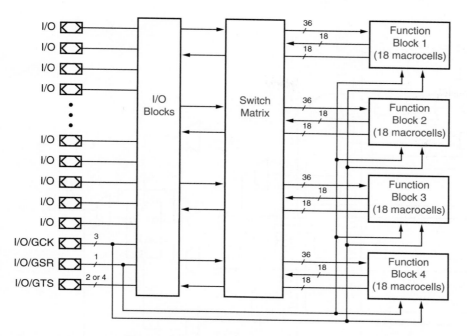

Figure 9-39
Architecture of Xilinx
9500-family CPLDs.

member, each FB programmably receives 36 signals from the switch matrix. The inputs to the switch matrix are the 18 macrocell outputs from each of the FBs and the external inputs from the I/O pins. We'll say more about how the switch matrix hooks things up in Section 9.5.4.

Each FB also has 18 outputs that run "under" the switch matrix as drawn in Figure 9-39 and connect to the I/O blocks. These are merely the output-enable signals for the I/O-block output drivers; they're used when the FB macrocell's output is hooked up to an external I/O pin.

9.5.2 Function-Block Architecture

The basic structure of an XC9500 FB is shown in Figure 9-40. The programmable AND array has just 90 product terms. Compared to 16V8- and 22V10-style PLDs, the XC9500 and most CPLD macrocells have fewer AND terms per macrocell—where the 16V8 has 8 and the 22V10 has 8–16, the XC9500 has only 5. However, this is not all that bad, because of *product-term allocation*. The

product-term allocation

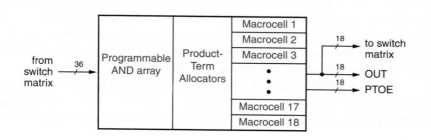

Figure 9-40
Architecture of
function block (FB).

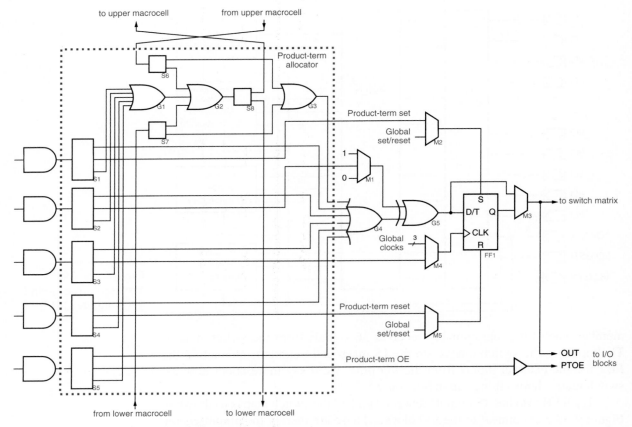

Figure 9-41 XC9500 product-term allocator and macrocell.

product-term allocator   XC9500 and other CPLDs have *product-term allocators* that allow a macrocell's unused product terms to be used by other nearby macrocells in the same FB.

Figure 9-41 is a logic diagram of the XC9500 product-term allocator and macrocell. In this figure, the rectangular boxes labeled S1–S8 are programmable signal-steering elements that connect their input to one of their two or three outputs. The trapezoidal boxes labeled M1–M5 are programmable multiplexers that connect one of their two to four inputs to their output.

The five AND gates associated with the macrocell appear on the lefthand side of the figure. Each one is connected to a signal-steering box whose top output connects the product term to the macrocell's main OR gate G4. Considering just this, only five product terms are available per macrocell. However, the top, sixth input of G4 connects to another OR gate G3 that receives product terms from the macrocells above and below the current one.

Any of the macrocell's product terms that are not otherwise used can be steered through S1–S5 to be combined in an OR gate G1 whose output can eventually be steered to the macrocell above or below by S8. Before steering,

> **ONE WAY**   In a given XC9500 macrocell, you wouldn't normally steer daisy-chained product terms back in the direction from which they came. For example, if product terms are arriving at S6 from above, we can use them locally by having S6 steer them to G3, or S6 can steer them to G2. In the latter case, S8 should steer the output of G2 down to the lower macrocell; there's no point in steering the product terms back up to the upper macrocell. In fact, if S6 and S8 in this macrocell were steering product terms up, and S7 and S8 in the macrocell above were steering product terms down, we would have a nasty loop.

these product terms may be combined with product terms from below or above through S6, S7, and G2. Thus, product terms can be "daisy-chained" through successive macrocells to create larger sums of products. In principle, all 90 product terms in the FB could be combined and steered to one macrocell, although that would leave 17 out of the FB's 18 macrocells with no product terms at all.

Besides depriving other macrocells of product terms, daisy-chaining terms has an additional price. A small additional delay is incurred for each "hop" made by steered product terms. This delay can be minimized by careful allocation of product-term-hungry macrocells so they are adjacent to macrocells with low product-term requirements. For example, a macrocell can make use of 13 product terms with only one extra hop delay if it is positioned between two macrocells that use only one product term each.

The third, middle choice for each of the steering boxes S1–S5 is to use the product term for a "special function." The special functions are flip-flop clock, set, and reset; XOR control; and output enable. Most of these special functions are not normally used.

Getting closer to the heart of the macrocell, OR gate G4 forms a sum-of-products expression using all selected product terms and feeds it into XOR gate G5. The other input of G5 can be 0, 1, or a product term, as selected by multiplexer M1. Setting this input to 1 inverts G4's sum-of-products expression, so the macrocell can be configured to use either polarity of minimized logic equations. Setting this input to a product term is useful in the design of counters. The product term is arranged to be 1 when the lower-order counter bits are 1 and counting is enabled, and the output of G4 is arranged to be the current value of the counter bit; thus, the counter bit is complemented as required.

The macrocell's flip-flop FF1 can be programmed to behave either as a D flip-flop or as a T flip-flop with enable; the latter is also useful in some styles of counter realization. Multiplexer M4 selects the flip-flop's clock input from one of four sources—the CPLD's three global clock inputs or a product term. This last choice is a no-no in synchronous design methodologies, except in well-defined synchronization applications, as in Figure 8-90 on page 787.

The flip-flop also has asynchronous set and reset inputs with input sources controlled by multiplexers M2 and M5. In most applications, set or reset would be connected to the CPLD's global set/reset input and would be used only at system initialization. However, these inputs can also be used to access an S-R latch in which the CLK input is not used, or, if you're very careful, you can use CLK and S or R in synchronization applications as in Figure 8-90.

A final multiplexer M3 selects either the flip-flop output or its data input to be used as the macrocell output, OUT. This signal is sent to the switch matrix, where it can be used by any other macrocell. It is also sent to the I/O blocks, along with a product term selected by S5 that can be used as the output-enable signal PTOE if needed.

9.5.3 Input/Output-Block Architecture

I/O block (IOB)

The structure of the XC9500 *I/O block (IOB)* is shown in Figure 9-42. There are seven, count them, seven choices of output-enable signals for the three-state driver buffer. It can be always on, always off, controlled by the product term PTOE from the corresponding macrocell, or controlled by any of up to four global output enables. The global output enables are selectable as active-high or active-low versions of the external GTS pins.

The XC9500's IOB is a good example of an important trend in CPLD and FPGA I/O architectures—providing many "analog" controls in addition to "logic" ones like output enables. Three different analog controls are provided:

- *Slew-rate control.* The rise and fall time of the output signals can be set to be fast or slow. The fast setting provides the fastest possible propagation delay, while the slow setting helps to control transmission-line ringing and system noise at the expense of a small additional delay.

- *Pull-up resistor.* When enabled, the pull-up resistor prevents output pins from floating as the CPLD is powered up. This is useful if the outputs are used to drive active-low enable inputs of other logic that is not supposed to be enabled during power up.

- *User-programmable ground.* This feature actually reallocates an I/O pin to be a ground pin, not a signal pin at all. This is useful in high-speed, high-slew-rate applications. Extra ground pins are needed to handle the high dynamic currents that flow when multiple outputs switch simultaneously.

In addition to these features, the XC9500 family provides compatibility with both 5-V and 3.3-V external devices. The input buffer and the internal logic run from a 5-V power supply (V_{CCINT}). Depending on the operating voltage of external devices, the output driver uses either a 5-V or a 3.3-V supply (V_{CCIO}). Notice that the pull-up resistor pulls to the I/O supply voltage, V_{CCIO}. Diodes *D1* and *D2* are used to clamp voltages above V_{CCINT} or below ground that can occur due to transmission-line ringing.

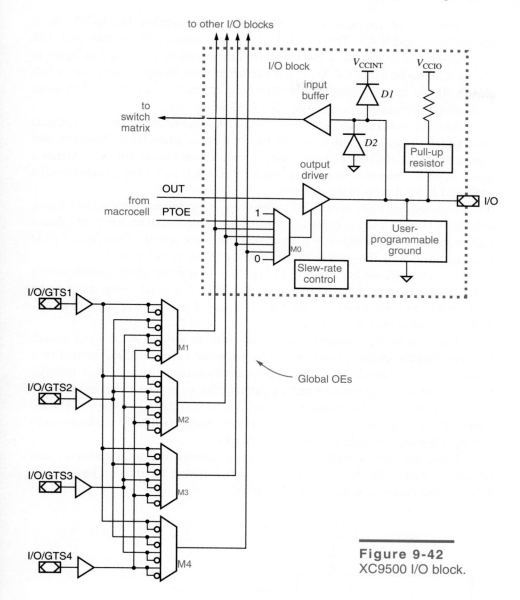

Figure 9-42
XC9500 I/O block.

9.5.4 Switch Matrix

Theoretically, a CPLD's programmable interconnect should allow any internal PLD output or external input pin to be connected to any internal PLD input. Likewise, it should allow any internal PLD output to connect to any external output pin. But if you think about this, you'll see that we're back to the same n^2 problem that we would have in building a 128V64.

The case of a typical Xilinx XC9500 family member, the XC95108, is shown in Figure 9-43. There are 108 internal macrocell outputs and 108 external-pin inputs, a total of 216 signals which should be connected as inputs to the switch matrix. Since the XC95108 has 6 FBs with 36 inputs each, the switch matrix should have (coincidentally) 216 outputs, each of which is a 216-input multiplexer driving one input of an FB's AND array.

A switch matrix such as the one shown in the figure can be built in a chip as a rectangular structure, with a column for each input, a row for each output, and a pass transistor (or transmission gate) at each crosspoint to control whether a given input is connected to a given output. But this is still a big structure—216 rows and 216 columns in the example.

With today's high-density IC technology, the problem is not so much size but speed. Having a large number of transistors connected to each row or column makes for high capacitance, which makes for slow speed. Therefore, CPLD manufacturers look for ways to reduce the size of the switch matrix.

For example, we can observe in Figure 9-43 that not every switch-matrix input must be connectable to every output. We only need every input to be connectable to *some* input of each FB, since any FB input can connect to any AND gate within the FB's AND array.

Then again, the requirement is not quite as simple as we just stated. Suppose that the switch-matrix output for FB input i ($0 \le i \le 35$) is created by a simple 8-input multiplexer whose inputs are switch-matrix inputs $6i$ through $6i + 7$. There are many interconnection patterns that cannot be accommodated by such a switch matrix. For example, connecting switch-matrix inputs 0–35 to the same FB would not be possible. As soon as switch-matrix input 0 is connected to FB input 0, switch-matrix inputs 1–5 are blocked.

Thus, the switch-matrix connectivity requirement must be stated more broadly: For each FB, any combination of switch-matrix inputs must be connectable to some combination of the FB's inputs.

Figure 9-43
XC95108 switch-matrix requirements.

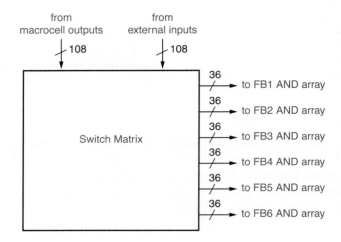

A typical CPLD switch matrix is a compromise between the minimal multiplexer scheme and a full, nonblocking crosspoint array. With anything less than a nonblocking crosspoint array, the problem of allocating input-output connections in the switch matrix is nontrivial. For each different CPLD-based design, a set of switch-matrix connections must be found by "fitter" software provided to the designer by the CPLD's manufacturer.

Finding a complete set of connections through a sparse switch matrix is one of those *NP*-complete problems that you hear about in computer science. In lay terms, that means that for some designs, the fitter software may have to run a lot longer than you care to wait to find out whether there is a solution. If the switch matrix has too few crosspoints, as in our minimal multiplexer example, even the best fitter software running "forever" will not be able to find a complete set of connections for some designs.

Thus, the design of a CPLD's switch matrix is a compromise between chip performance (speed, area, cost) and fitter-software capabilities. The fitter software usually determines not only the final connections through the switch matrix, but also the assignment of CPLD inputs and outputs to FBs, macrocells, and external pins, and of "buried logic" to FBs and macrocells. These assignments interact in turn with both the switch-matrix-connection and product-term allocation problems. The solutions to these problems are the "secret sauce" of CPLD chip and software design, and are not typically disclosed by CPLD manufacturers.

PIN LOCKING   Another important issue in CPLD chip and software design is *pin locking*. In most CPLD applications, it's OK to let the fitter software pick any pins that it likes for the device's external input and output signals. However, once the design is complete and a PCB has been fabricated, the designer would like to "lock down" the pin assignments so they remain the same even if small (or large!) changes are made to the design for bug-fixing purposes. This spares everyone the time, expense, and hassle of reworking or redesigning and refabricating the PCB.

"Locked" pin assignments are typically specified in a file that is read by the fitter software. With early CPLDs and FPGAs, locking down pins before making a small change did not guarantee success—the fitter would throw up its hands and complain that it was too constrained. If you unlocked the pins, the fitter could find a new allocation that worked, but it might be completely scrambled from the original.

These problems were not necessarily the fault of the fitter software; the CPLDs and FPGAs simply did not have rich enough internal connectivity to support frequent design changes under the constraint of pin locking. The device manufacturers have learned from this experience and improved their internal device architectures to accommodate frequent design changes. For example, some devices contain an "output switch matrix" that guarantees that any internal macrocell signal can be connected to any external I/O pin.

9.6 Field-Programmable Gate Arrays

A field-programmable gate array (FPGA) is kind of like a CPLD turned inside-out. As shown in Figure 9-44, the logic is broken into a large number of programmable logic blocks that are individually smaller than a PLD. They are distributed across the entire chip in a sea of programmable interconnections, and the entire array is surrounded by programmable I/O blocks. An FPGA's programmable logic block is less capable than a typical PLD, but an FPGA chip contains a lot more logic blocks than a CPLD of the same die size has PLDs.

Popular FPGA manufacturers include Xilinx, Altera, and Lattice. The internal architectures of FPGAs differ among different manufacturers and even among different families from the same manufacturer. In this section we'll show the XC4000E FPGA family from Xilinx as a representative architecture.

9.6.1 Xilinx XC4000 FPGA Family

The programmable logic blocks in the Xilinx XC4000 family of FPGAs are
configurable logic block (CLB) called *configurable logic blocks (CLBs)*. When the family was introduced, the smallest part, the XC4003E, contained a 10×10 array of CLBs, and the largest, the XC4025E, contained a 32×32 array for a total of 1024 CLBs. Xilinx later created the XC4000XL and XC4000XLA extended families, based on the XC4000E family, with additional resources and features not discussed here. The largest member of the extended families, the XC4085XLA, has 3136 CLBs. Table 9-10 from Xilinx shows members of the original and extended families.

Note that Xilinx now recommends its other, newer FPGA families for new designs. However, the new families are derived from, and in some cases have a subset of, the XC4000 architecture, which is still a good starting point for us.

Like a CPLD family, the XC4000 family spans a range of device sizes and input/output capabilities. The table column labeled "Max. User I/O" refers to the maximum number of input/output blocks that are provided on-chip. However,

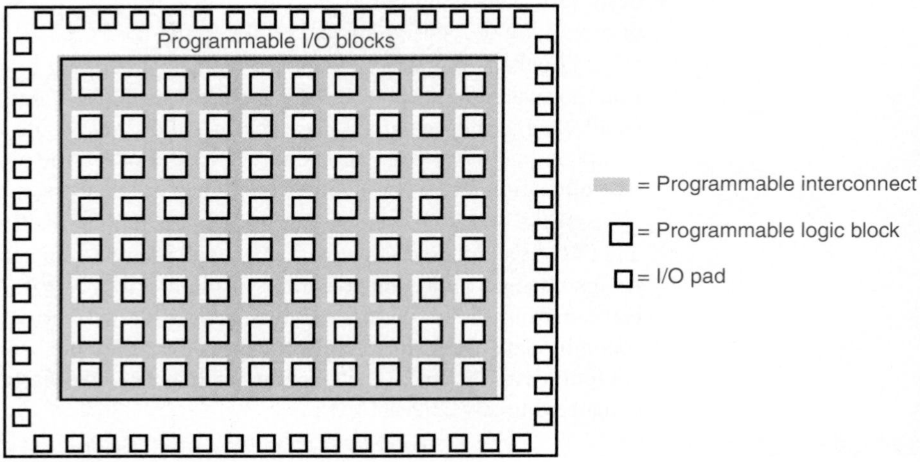

Figure 9-44
General FPGA chip architecture.

= Programmable interconnect

□ = Programmable logic block

□ = I/O pad

Table 9-10 Resources in Xilinx XC4000-series FPGAs.

Device	CLB matrix	Total CLBs	Max. user I/O	Flip-flops	Max. RAM bits (no logic)	Max. gates (no RAM)	Typical gate range (logic and RAM)
XC4002XL	8×8	64	64	256	2,048	1,600	1,000–3,000
XC4003E	10×10	100	80	360	3,200	3,000	2,000–5,000
XC4005E/XL	14×14	196	112	616	6,272	5,000	3,000–9,000
XC4006E	16×16	256	128	768	8,192	6,000	4,000–12,000
XC4008E	18×18	324	144	936	10,368	8,000	7,000–15,000
XC4010E/XL	20×20	400	160	1,120	12,800	10,000	7,000–20,000
XC4013E/XLA	24×24	576	192	1,536	18,432	13,000	10,000–30,000
XC4020E/XLA	28×28	784	224	2,016	25,088	20,000	13,000–40,000
XC4025E	32×32	1,024	256	2,560	32,768	25,000	15,000–45,000
XC4028XLA	32×32	1,024	256	2,560	32,768	28,000	18,000–50,000
XC4036XLA	36×36	1,296	288	3,168	41,472	36,000	22,000–65,000
XC4052XLA	44×44	1,936	352	4,576	61,952	52,000	33,000–100,000
XC4085XLA	56×56	3,136	448	7,168	100,352	85,000	55,000–180,000

XC4000 devices are available in a variety of packages, and not all of the I/Os are brought out to external pins of the smaller packages. As with CPLDs, the FPGA user has the opportunity to migrate a design from smaller to larger devices in the same package, or from a smaller package to a larger one.

The "Flip-flops" column counts all of the flip-flops in the device, two per CLB and two per I/O block, as we'll see later. Only a fraction of the available flip-flops are used in a typical design, but this number is a figure of merit that designers look at when roughly sizing an FPGA for a design. The "Max. RAM bits" column is another such figure of merit. As we'll see, instead of being used for logic, each CLB can be configured as a small SRAM storing up to 32 bits.

The "Max. gates" number is fuzzy. For the XC4002XL, the table claims that each CLB can perform the same function as about 25 gates in a discrete design. The XC4003E is even better, at 30 gates per CLB. Is this reasonable? And just what is a "gate"? Do XORs or wide NAND gates count as one gate? You can decide for yourself later, after you know more about the CLB architecture. At the same time, you can decide whether this column was created by engineering or by marketing people.

The last column of the table must certainly have been written by marketing folks, since the high end of each "typical" gate range is higher than the maximum in the column before it! Actually, there *is* a reasonable explanation for this seeming inconsistency. This column assumes that 20–30% of the CLBs are

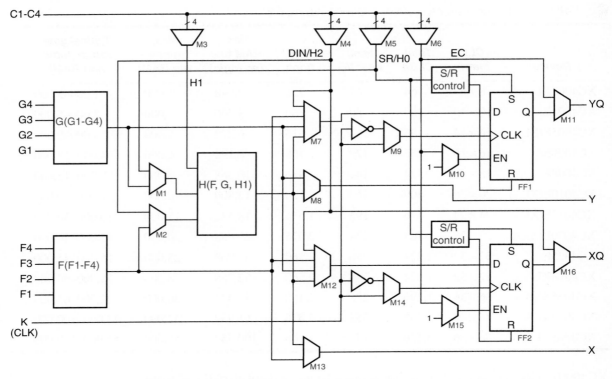

Figure 9-45 XC4000 configurable logic block.

used for memory rather than logic, at 32 bits of SRAM per CLB. The minimum gate-level implementation of an SRAM cell is a D latch using four gates (Figure X7.41 on page 669), so we can count each CLB as 128 gates when it's used as SRAM. The number in the last column, therefore, is the number of gates used for logic *plus* the number of equivalent gates used for SRAM.

9.6.2 Configurable Logic Block

Since an FPGA can have lots and lots of CLBs, it's important that we understand them first! Figure 9-45 shows the internal structure of an XC4000-series CLB.

The CLB's most important programmable elements are the logic-function generators F, G, and H. Both F and G can perform any combinational logic function of their four inputs, and H can perform any combinational logic function of its three inputs.

How do F, G, and H work? Given the task of building a "universal" function generator for 4-input logic functions, what kind of gate-level circuit would you come up with? Think about it, and we'll come back to it later.

As in our CPLD discussion, the trapezoidal boxes in Figure 9-45 represent programmable multiplexers. Notice that the outputs of F and G as well as other

CLB inputs can be directed to inputs of H by multiplexers M1–M3, so it's possible to realize some functions of more than four inputs. A taxonomy of the functions that can be realized by F, G, and H in a single CLB is given below:

- Any function of up to four variables, plus any second function of up to four unrelated variables, plus any third function of up to three unrelated variables.

- Any single function of five variables (see Exercise 9.34).

- Any function of four variables, plus some second functions of six unrelated variables.

- Some functions of up to nine variables, including parity checking and a cascadable equality checker for two 4-bit inputs (see Exercises 9.35 and 9.36).

With appropriate programming of multiplexers M7–M8 and M12–M13, the outputs of the function generators can be directed to CLB outputs X and Y, or they can be captured in edge-triggered D flip-flops FF1 and FF2. The flip-flops can use the rising or falling edge of a common clock input, K, as selected by multiplexers M9 and M14. They can also make use of a clock-enable signal, EC, selected by M10 and M15. The sources of EC and three other internal signals are selected from a set of four miscellaneous inputs C1–C4 by multiplexers M3–M6 at the top of the CLB.

The XQ and YQ outputs of the CLB carry the flip-flop outputs out of the CLB. If a flip-flop is not used in the CLB, multiplexer M11 or M16 can select XQ or YQ to be a "bypass output" that is simply a copy of a CLB input selected by M4 or M6.

The block labeled "S/R control" from each flip-flop determines whether the flip-flop is set or reset at configuration. It also determines whether the flip-flop responds to a global set/reset signal (not shown) or to the CLB's SR signal selected by multiplexer M5.

Wow, that's a lot of programmability! Naturally, the configuration of CLBs within an XC4000 part, whether it has 3136 CLBs or only 64, is not carried out by hand. The manufacturer provides a fitter tool that allocates, configures, and connects CLBs to match a higher-level design description written in ABEL, VHDL, Verilog, or schematic form.

Let's come back to our question of how to build a universal function generator for 4-input logic functions. It's a hard problem if you think about it at the gate level, but pretty easy if you think about it from another point of view. Any 4-input logic function can be described by its truth table, which has 16 rows. Suppose we store the truth table in a 16-word by 1-bit-wide memory. When we apply the function's four input bits to the memory's address lines, its data output is the value of the function for that input combination.

This is exactly the approach that was taken by the FPGA designers at Xilinx. Function generators F and G are actually just very compact and fast 16×1 SRAMs, and H is an 8×1 SRAM. When a CLB is used to perform logic, the truth tables of logic functions F, G, and H are loaded into SRAM at configuration time from an external read-only memory. The programmable multiplexers in Figure 9-45 are also controlled by "SRAM," actually individual D latches that are also loaded at configuration time. This programming is done for all of the CLBs in the FPGA.

Besides convenience, using memory to store the truth tables has another important benefit. Any XC4000 CLB can be configured at start-up to be used as memory rather than logic. Several different modes can be configured:

- *Two 16 ×1 SRAMs.* F and G are used as SRAMs with independent address and write-data inputs. They share a common write-enable input, however.
- *One 32 ×1 SRAM.* The same four address bits are used for F and G, and a fifth address bit is applied to the H function generator and the write-enable circuitry to select between F and G, the upper and lower halves of the memory.
- *Asynchronous or synchronous.* For write operations, the SRAMs above can be configured to have "normal" asynchronous latching behavior, or they can be configured to occur on a designated edge of the K clock signal.
- *One 16 ×1 dual-port SRAM.* The two sets of address inputs are used to independently read and write different locations in the same SRAM. Only synchronous write operations are supported in this mode.

In these modes, function inputs F1–F4 and G1–G4 supply address, other CLB inputs H0–H2 provide data inputs and the write-enable signal, and data outputs are provided on the F and G generator outputs and can be captured in flip-flops FF1 and FF2 or can exit at CLB outputs X and Y.

9.6.3 Input/Output Block

I/O block (IOB)

The structure of the XC4000 *I/O block (IOB)* is shown in Figure 9-46. An I/O pin can be used for input or output or both.

The XC4000 IOB has more "logic" controls than its cousin in the XC9500 CPLD. In particular, its input and output paths contain edge-triggered D flip-flops selectable by multiplexers M5–M7. Placing input and output flip-flops "up close" to the device I/O pins is especially useful in FPGAs. On output, relatively long delays from internal CLB flip-flop outputs to the IOBs can make it difficult to connect to external synchronous systems at very high clock rates. On input,

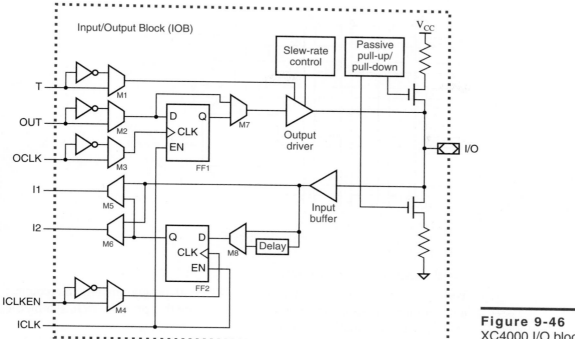

Figure 9-46
XC4000 I/O block.

long delays from the I/O pins to CLB flip-flop inputs can make it difficult to meet external system setup and hold times if external inputs are clocked directly into a CLB flip-flop without being captured first by a flip-flop at the IOB pin. Of course, using IOB flip-flops is possible only if the FPGA's external interface specifications allow "pipelining" of inputs and outputs.

For pipelined inputs, the XC4000 IOB actually goes one step further by providing a delay element, selectable by M8, in series with the D input of input flip-flop FF2. The effect of this element is to delay the D input relative to the FPGA's internal copies of the system clock, guaranteeing that the input will have a zero hold-time requirement with respect to the external system clock. This benefit comes at the expense of increased setup time, of course.

The IOB's other logic controls are selectable polarity, using multiplexers M1–M4, for its four inputs that come from the CLB array via the programmable interconnect. These inputs, OUT, T, OCLK, and ICLKEN, are the output bit, its three-state enable, the output clock, and the input clock enable, respectively.

Like the XC9500 IOB, the XC4000 IOB also has analog controls. The output driver's slew rate is programmable, and a pull-up or pull-down resistor may be connected to the I/O pin.

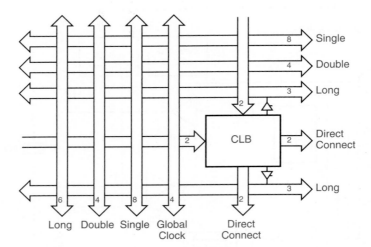

Figure 9-47
XC4000 general
interconnect
structure.

9.6.4 Programmable Interconnect

Well, we saved the best for last. The XC4000 programmable interconnect architecture is a fascinating example of a structure that provides rich, symmetric connectivity in a small silicon area.

As we showed in Figure 9-44 on page 850, each CLB in an FPGA is embedded in the interconnect structure, which is really just wires with programmable connections to them. Figure 9-47 gives a little more detail of the XC4000's connection scheme. Wires are not really "owned" by any one CLB, but an XC4000 CLB array is created by tiling the chip with exactly the structure shown in the figure. For example, 100 copies of this figure make the 10×10 CLB array of an XC4003.

The number in each arrow indicates the number of wires in that signal path. Thus, you can see that a CLB has two wires (outputs) each going to the CLBs immediately below and to the right of it. It also connects to three groups of wires above, one below, and four to its left. Signals on these wires can flow in either direction.

The four wires in the group labeled "Global Clock" are optimized for use as clock inputs to the CLBs, providing short delay and minimal skew. The two "Single" groups are optimized for flexible connectivity between adjacent blocks, without the small number and unidirectional limitation of wires in the "Direct Connect" groups.

It's possible to connect a CLB to another that's more than one hop away using "Single" wires, but they have to go through a programmable switch for each hop, which adds delay. Wires in the "Double" groups travel past two CLBs before hitting a switch, so they provide shorter delays for longer connections.

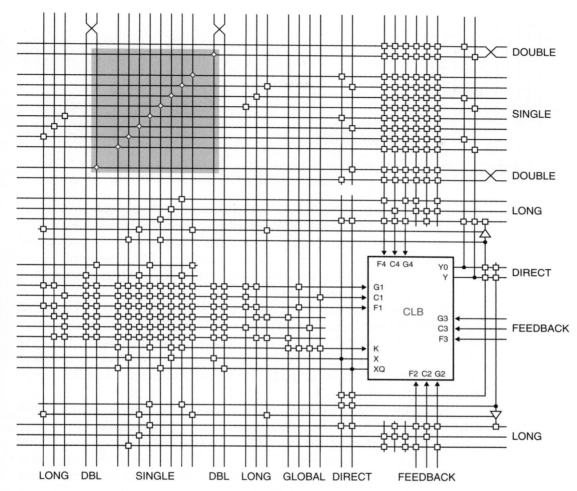

Figure 9-48 XC4000 CLB and wire connection details.

For really long connections, the "Long" groups don't go through any programmable switches at all; instead, they travel all the way across or down a row or column and are driven by three-state drivers near the CLB.

Figure 9-48 shows a CLB and wires in a lot more detail. The small squares are programmable connections—a horizontal wire is connected or not to a vertical one, depending on the state of the programming bit (again, in a latch) for that switch. Additional, specialized programmable interconnect is provided at the edges of the CLB array for connections to the IOBs.

In the figure, the shaded area in color is called a *programmable switch matrix (PSM)*. The PSM is shown in more detail in Figure 9-49. Each of the

programmable switch matrix (PSM)

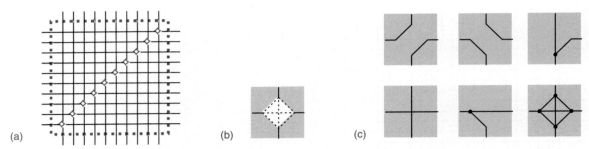

Figure 9-49 XC4000 programmable connections: (a) programmable switch matrix (PSM); (b) programmable switch element (PSE); (c) a few possible connections.

programmable switch element (PSE)

diamonds in (a) is a *programmable switch element (PSE)* that can connect any line to any other, as shown in (b). With four lines, there are six possible pairwise connections as shown in (b), and the PSE has a transmission gate for each one of them. Some, none, or all of the transmission gates in a PSE may be enabled—again, by configuration bits stored in latches. Thus, many different connection patterns are possible, as shown in (c).

The PSM is essential for hooking things up in the wiring structure of Figure 9-48. By enabling and disabling connections, PSEs extend or isolate wire segments in the "Single" and "Double" groups. More importantly, the PSM allows signals to "turn the corner" by connecting a horizontal wire to a vertical one. Without this, CLBs would not be able to connect to others in a different row or column of the array.

While the PSM is essential, using it has a price—signals incur a small delay each time they hop through a PSE. Therefore, high-quality FPGA fitter software searches for not just any CLB placement and wire connections that work. The "placement and routing" tool spends a lot of time trying to optimize device performance by finding a placement that allows short connections, and then routing the connections themselves.

Like CPLDs, FPGAs are judged by the flexibility of their architectures and the consistency of the results obtained from a fitter after small design changes are made. There's nothing more frustrating than making a small change to a large design and finding that it no longer meets timing requirements. Thus, FPGA manufacturers have learned to provide "extra" resources in their architectures to help ensure consistent results.

GOOD PRACTICE   Placement and routing is actually a pretty well understood problem, because it is the major part of the "back end" of any custom chip design. Thus, the same kind of tools and the same tool vendors are involved with placement and routing for both FPGAs and ASICS. So, you might like to consider any FPGA experience that you get to be good practice for ASIC design!

References

Manufacturers of ROMs and RAMs publish data books with their device specifications for their parts, and most publish individual data sheets and application notes on their web sites. The data sheets for most types and sizes of EEPROM can be found at Renesas Technology's site (america.renesas.com). The sites for Advanced Micro Devices (www.amd.com), Intel (www.intel.com), and SanDisk (www.sandisk.com/oem) have information on very large EPROMs and flash-memory chips and modules. Companies whose web sites list various SRAMs and/or DRAMs include Renesas, Integrated Device Technology (www.idt.com), NEC Electronics (www.necel.com), and Micron Technology (www.micron.com).

In addition to the memories discussed in this chapter, several types of "specialty" memory devices have widespread use. Probably the most common are *first-in, first-out (FIFO) memories*; these are typically used to transfer data from one processor or clock domain to another. The web sites of IDT and Texas Instruments (www.ti.com) are good sources of information on FIFOs. Although it might seem that FIFOs magically solve the metastability problems that occur when crossing clock domains, they do not. For example, see "FIFO Memories: Solution to Reduce FIFO Metastability" by Tom Jackson (Texas Instruments publ. SCAA011A, March 1996).

first-in, first-out (FIFO) memories

Another type of specialty memory is the dual-port memory, which has two independent sets of address, data, and control lines and allows independent operations to be performed on both ports simultaneously. Integrated Device Technology is a leading source for these devices; in addition to data sheets, their web site has an excellent set of application notes on the devices.

Several manufacturers introduced different CPLD and FPGA architectures at about the same time. While Xilinx (www.xilinx.com) was and is the leader in FPGAs, the CPLD field is much more crowded. The first two CPLD families were introduced in the early 1990s by Altera Corporation (www.altera.com) and Advanced Micro Devices. AMD's CPLD product line is now owned by former competitor Lattice Semiconductor (www.latticesemi.com), who has greatly enhanced it. Other suppliers include Atmel (www.atmel.com) and Actel (www.actel.com). All of these companies have excellent resources available on their web sites.

Drill Problems

9.1   Determine the ROM size needed to realize the combinational logic functions in Exercise 6.31 and each of the following figures: 6-37, 6-73, 6-93, and X6.44. Which are feasible using at most a handful of today's ROM devices?

9.2   Determine the ROM size needed to realize the combinational logic function performed by each of the following MSI parts: 74x49, 74x139, 74x153, 74x257, 74x381, 74x682.

9.3   Draw a logic symbol for and determine the size of a ROM that realizes a combinational logic function that can perform the function of either a 74x381 or a 74x382 depending on the value of a single MODE input.

9.4   Draw a logic symbol for and determine the size of a ROM that realizes an 8×8 combinational multiplier.

9.5   Show how to design a 2M×8 SRAM using HM628512 SRAMs and a combinational MSI part as building blocks.

Exercises

9.6   Our discussion of ROM sneak paths in connection with Figure 9-6 claimed that with A2–A0 = 101, bit lines D2_L and D0_L are pulled LOW through the direct connections. That's not really correct, unless the 74x138 is replaced with a decoder with open-collector outputs. Explain.

9.7   Describe the logic function of seven variables that is performed by the 128×1 ROM in Figure 9-7. Starting with the ROM pattern, one way to describe the logic function is to write the corresponding truth table and canonical sum. However, since the canonical sum has 64 seven-variable product terms, you might want to look for a simple but precise word description of the function.

9.8   For the two-output BUT-gate logic function defined in Exercise 6.31, compare the number of diodes or transistors needed in the AND-OR, AND, or storage array for PLA, PAL, and ROM realizations.

9.9   Show how to double the number of different attenuation amounts that can be selected in the digital attenuator of Figure 9-17 without increasing the size of the ROM.

9.10   Write the C functions UlawToLinear and LinearToUlaw that are required in Table 9-6. In LinearToUlaw, you should select the μ-law byte whose theoretical value is closest to the linear input. (*Hint:* The most efficient approach builds, at program initialization, a 256-entry table that is used by both functions.) Both functions should report out-of-range inputs.

9.11   Modify the C program in Table 9-6 to perform clipping in any cases where the designer has specified a particular attenuation amount to be a gain, such that multiplying an input value by the attenuation factor produces an out-of-range result.

9.12   Write a C program to generate the contents of a 256×8 ROM that converts from 8-bit binary to 8-bit Gray code. (*Hint:* Your program should embody the second Gray-code construction method in Section 2.11.)

9.13   Write a C program to generate the contents of a 256×8 ROM that converts from 8-bit Gray code to 8-bit binary. (*Hints:* You may use the results of Exercise 9.12. It doesn't matter if your program is slow.)

9.14   A certain communication system has been designed to transmit ASCII characters serially on a medium that requires an average signal level of zero, so a 5-out-of-10 code is used to code the data. Each 7-bit ASCII input character is transmitted as a 10-bit word with five 0s and five 1s. Write a C program to generate the contents of a 128×10 ROM that converts ASCII characters into coded words.

9.15 The receiving end of the system in Exercise 9.14 must convert each 10-bit coded word back into a 7-bit ASCII character. Write a C program to generate the contents of a $1K \times 8$ ROM that converts coded words into ASCII characters. The extra output bit should be an "error" flag that indicates when a noncode word has been received.

9.16 How many ROM bits would be required to build a 16-bit adder/subtracter with mode control, carry input, carry output, and two's-complement overflow output? Be more specific than "billions and billions," and explain your answer.

9.17 Repeat Exercise 9.16 assuming that you may use *two* ROMs, so that the delay for a 16-bit addition or subtraction is twice the delay through one ROM. Assume that the two ROMs must be identical in both size and programming. Try to minimize the total number of ROM bits required, and sketch the resulting adder/subtracter circuit. Can the number of ROM bits be further reduced if the two ROMs are allowed to be different?

9.18 Show how, using additional SSI/MSI parts, a 2764 $8K \times 8$ ROM can be used as a $64K \times 1$ ROM. What is the access time of the $64K \times 1$ ROM?

9.19 Show how, using additional SSI/MSI parts, a 2764 $8K \times 8$ ROM can be used as a $2K \times 32$ ROM. You may assume the existence of a free-running clock signal whose period is slightly longer than the access time of the 2764. What is the access time of the $2K \times 32$ ROM?

9.20 Show how to build the μ-law adder circuit of Figure 9-18 with a $32K \times 8$ ROM and two XOR gates. Also, write a C program to generate the ROM contents.

9.21 Determine the ROM size needed to build the fixed-point to floating-point encoder of Figure XCbb-3 in Section XCbb.2 at DDPPonline. Draw a logic diagram using a commercially available ROM.

9.22 Write a C program to generate the ROM contents for Exercise 9.21. Unlike the original MSI solution, your C program should perform rounding; that is, for each fixed-point number it should generate the nearest possible floating-point number.

9.23 Draw a complete logic diagram for a ROM-based circuit that performs combinational multiplication of a pair of 8-bit unsigned or two's-complement integers. Signed vs. unsigned operation should be selected by a single input, SIGNED. You may use any of the commercial ROMs in Figure 9-11, as well as discrete gates.

9.24 Write and test a C program that generates the contents of the ROM(s) in Exercise 9.23.

9.25 Write a C program that generates a $256K \times 4$ ROM that computes the next move in a Tic-Tac-Toe game, using the input and output encodings of Section XCabl.7 at DDPPonline. Your program must be smart enough to pick a winning move whenever possible.

9.26 Repeat Exercise 9.25 using a $32K \times 4$ ROM. To accomplish this, the board state must be encoded in only 15 bits. Explain your coding algorithm, and write C functions to translate a cell number in either direction between your encoding and the encoding of Section XCabl.7 at DDPPonline.

9.27 For each of the timing parameters defined in Section 9.3.3, determine whether its value for the $128K \times 8$ SRAM you designed in Drill 9.5 is the same as the

HM628512's. If it is different, indicate the new value. Use the worst-case values in the 74FCT column of Table 6-3 to determine the delays for the MSI part.

9.28   Using an HM6264 8K × 8 SRAM, a handful of MSI parts, and a PLD as building blocks, design an 8K × 8 late-write SSRAM with flow-through outputs.

9.29   Using an HM6264 8K × 8 SRAM, a handful of MSI parts, and a PLD as building blocks, design an 8K × 8 ZBT SSRAM with pipelined outputs.

9.30   Define the relevant timing parameters for the synchronous SRAM as defined in Exercise 9.28.

9.31   Calculate the values of the timing parameters you defined in Exercise 9.30 for your solution to Exercise 9.28.

9.32   In the style of Figure 9-27, draw the timing diagram for a late-write SSRAM with flow-through outputs for a series of interleaved reads and writes in the pattern R-R-W-W-R-W-R-W. Run the individual cycles as close together as possible, but be sure to account for resource conflicts that prevent back-to-back cycles. What is the average utilization of the SRAM array if the SSRAM is presented with a continuous streams of R-W-R-W-R-W requests?

9.33   Repeat the preceding exercise for a late-write SSRAM with pipelined outputs.

9.34   Using one of the theorems in Section 4.1, prove that the Xilinx XC4000-series CLB can realize any logic function of five variables.

9.35   Show how to use the function generators in an XC4000-series CLB to realize a 9-bit even parity function.

9.36   Show how to use the function generators in an XC4000-series CLB to realize an equality checker for two 4-bit operands. You should be able to cascade your design to check 4n-bit operands with just n CLBs.

INDEX

A